The Real World

An Introduction to Sociology

SEVENTH HIGH SCHOOL EDITION

Kerry Ferris | Jill Stein

W. W. NORTON
NEW YORK • LONDON

W. W. Norton & Company has been independent since its founding in 1923, when William Warder Norton and Mary D. Herter Norton first published lectures delivered at the People's Institute, the adult education division of New York City's Cooper Union. The firm soon expanded its program beyond the Institute, publishing books by celebrated academics from America and abroad. By mid-century, the two major pillars of Norton's publishing program—trade books and college texts—were firmly established. In the 1950s, the Norton family transferred control of the company to its employees, and today—with a staff of five hundred and hundreds of trade, college, and professional titles published each year—W. W. Norton & Company stands as the largest and oldest publishing house owned wholly by its employees.

Director of High School Publishing: Jenna Bookin Barry
Editor: Sasha Levitt
Project Editor: Laura Dragonette
Assistant Editor: Erika Nakagawa
Editorial Assistant: Anna Goodlett
Managing Editor, College: Marian Johnson
Managing Editor, College Digital Media: Kim Yi
Associate Managing Editor: Melissa Atkin
Production Manager: Eric Pier-Hocking
Media Editor: Eileen Connell
Media Project Editor: Danielle Belfiore
Associate Media Editor: Ariel Eaton

Media Editorial Assistant: Samuel Wen-Cyien Tang
High School Marketing and Market Development Manager: Christina Magoulis
Marketing Manager, Sociology: Julia Hall
Design Director: Rubina Yeh
Photo Editor: Ted Szczepanski
Director of College Permissions: Megan Schindel
College Permissions Manager: Bethany Salminen
Composition: Brad Walrod/Kenoza Type, Inc.
Illustrations: Alex Eben Meyer
Figure Art: Graphic World
Manufacturing: LSC, Kendallville

Permission to use copyrighted material begins on p. C-1.

ISBN: 978-0-393-41936-8
The Library of Congress has cataloged another edition as follows:

Library of Congress Cataloging-in-Publication Data
Names: Ferris, Kerry, author. | Stein, Jill, author.
Title: The real world : an introduction to sociology / Kerry Ferris, Jill Stein.
Description: Seventh Edition. | New York : W. W. Norton & Company, 2020. | Revised edition of
    the authors' The real world, [2018] | Includes bibliographical references and index.
Identifiers: LCCN 2019046947 | ISBN 9780393690743 (paperback)
Subjects: LCSH: Sociology. | United States—Social conditions—21st century. | Popular culture—United States.
Classification: LCC HM586 .F48 2020 | DDC 301.0973—dc23
LC record available at https://lccn.loc.gov/2019046947

W. W. Norton & Company, Inc., 500 Fifth Avenue, New York, NY 10110
wwnorton.com
W. W. Norton & Company Ltd., 15 Carlisle Street, London W1D 3BS

2 3 4 5 6 7 8 9 0

About the Authors

KERRY FERRIS is Associate Professor of Sociology at Northern Illinois University, where she teaches introduction to sociology, qualitative methods, mass media and popular culture, and sociology of food. She uses ethnographic methods and a symbolic interactionist approach to study celebrity as a system of social power. Her past studies have included analyses of fan-celebrity relations, celebrity sightings, celebrity stalking, red-carpet celebrity interviews, the work lives of professional celebrity impersonators, and the experiences of local celebrities. Her current project examines dead celebrities and their fans. Her work has been published in *Symbolic Interaction*, *Journal of Contemporary Ethnography*, *The Journal of Popular Culture*, and *Text & Performance Quarterly*. She is the coauthor, with Scott R. Harris, of *Stargazing: Celebrity, Fame, and Social Interaction*.

JILL STEIN is Professor of Sociology at Santa Barbara City College, which was recently named the top community college in the United States by the Aspen Institute. She teaches introduction to sociology in both face-to-face and online formats every semester. She also teaches classes on social psychology, media, culture and society, and social problems. In addition, she is involved in many student-success initiatives at the local and state levels. Her research has examined narrative processes in twelve-step programs, the role of popular culture in higher learning, and group culture among professional rock musicians. Her work has been published in *Symbolic Interaction*, *Youth & Society*, the *Journal of Culture & Society*, and *TRAILS* (Teaching Resources and Innovations Library).

Contents

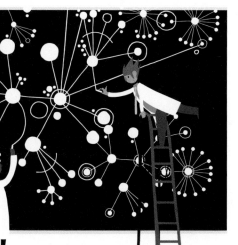

PART II: Framing Social Life 64

CHAPTER 4: Socialization, Interaction, and the Self 90

PART III: Understanding Inequality 168

CHAPTER 7: Social Class: The Structure of Inequality 172

PART IV: Social Institutions and the Micro-Macro Link 266

CHAPTER 10: Social Institutions: Politics, Education, and Religion 270

CHAPTER 12: Life at Home: Families and Relationships 338

PART V: Envisioning the Future and Creating Social Change 416

Preface

Welcome to the Seventh High School Edition of *The Real World: An Introduction to Sociology*. We hope you will appreciate what is new not only in the textbook's fresh look and updated materials, but also in the innovative ways it goes about teaching sociology. That's exactly what we set out to do when we first embarked on the original project of writing this textbook, and it's what we continue to do here in the Seventh High School Edition.

At the beginning, we had had years of experience in classrooms, teaching introductory sociology to thousands of students from all backgrounds and walks of life; we had discovered a lot about what works and what doesn't when it comes to making sociology exciting and effective. As seasoned instructors, we had developed an approach to teaching and learning that reflected our passion for the subject and our concern with best practices in pedagogy. But we were having trouble finding a textbook that encompassed all the elements we had identified and that made such a difference in our own experience. We were tired of seeing the same old formulas found in almost every textbook. And we figured we were not alone. Other students and instructors were probably equally frustrated with repetitive formats, stodgy styles, and seemingly irrelevant or overly predictable materials. That is a great misfortune, for sociology, at its best, is a discipline that holds great value and is both intellectually stimulating and personally resonant. Although the impetus to write this textbook began as a way of answering our own needs, our goal became to create a textbook of even greater benefit to others who might also be looking for something new.

We are gratified by the response *The Real World* has received from instructors and students alike, so we are preserving many of the features that have made the textbook a success. At the same time, we have done more than just simply revise the textbook. In this edition, you will find significant new content and added features that will further enhance the teaching and learning process and keep us as close to the cutting edge as possible. Many of the original elements we developed for students and instructors appear again in these pages. As a foundation, we have maintained a writing style that we hope is accessible and interesting as well as scholarly. One of the core pedagogical strengths of this textbook is its focus on everyday life, the media, technology, and pop culture. We know that the combination of these themes is inherently appealing to students and that it relates to their lives. And because both new generations and more experienced sociology instructors might also be looking for something different, another of this book's strengths is an integrated emphasis on critical thinking and analytic skills. Rather than merely presenting or reviewing major concepts in sociology, which can often seem dry and remote, we seek to make the abstract more concrete through real-world examples and hands-on applications.

In this text we take a fresh and accessible theoretical approach appropriate to our contemporary world. While we emphasize the interactionist perspective, we cover a range of theoretical thought, including postmodernism. We also build innovative methodological exercises into each chapter, giving students the opportunity to put into practice what they are learning. We present material that is familiar and relevant to students in a way that allows them to make profound analytic connections between their individual lives and the structure of their society. We provide instructors with ways to reenergize their teaching, and we give even general education students a reason to be fascinated by and engrossed in their sociology courses. We do this by staying in touch with our students and the rapidly changing real world, and by bringing our insight, experience, and intellectual rigor to bear on a new way of teaching introductory sociology.

Whether you are a student or an instructor, you have probably seen a lot of textbooks. As authors, we have thought very carefully about how to write this textbook to make it more meaningful and effective for you. We think it is important to point out some newly added and unique features of this textbook and to tell you why they are included and what we hope you will get out of them.

Part Introductions

The sixteen chapters in this text are grouped into five parts, and each part opens with its own introductory essay. Each part introduction highlights a piece of original sociological research that encompasses the major themes that group the chapters together. The in-depth discussion of the featured book shows what the real work of academic sociologists consists of and reveals how sociological research frequently unites topics covered in separate chapters in introductory textbooks.

Opening Vignettes

Each chapter begins with an opening vignette that gives students an idea about the topics or themes they will encounter in the chapter. The vignettes are drawn from current events and everyday life, the media, arts, and popular culture. They are designed to grab your attention and stimulate your curiosity to learn more by reading the chapter that follows.

How to Read This Chapter

After the vignette, you will find a section that provides you with some goals and strategies that we believe will be useful in reading that particular chapter. We know from our experience in teaching introductory sociology that it is often worthwhile to let students know what to expect in advance so that they can better make their way through the material. Not all chapters require the same approach; we want to bring to your attention what we think is the best approach to each one, so you can keep that in mind while reading.

Theory in Everyday Life

Although we provide thorough coverage in Chapter 1, we find that students often benefit from additional help with understanding the mechanics of social theory and how to apply it to various real-world phenomena. These boxes in every chapter break down the major theoretical approaches and illustrate how each perspective might be used to analyze a particular real-world case study. This serves as a simple, practical model for students to then make their own applications and analyses.

Bolded In-Text Terms

As a student of sociology, you will be learning many new concepts and terms. Throughout each chapter, you will see a number of words or phrases in bold type. You may already recognize some of these from their more common vernacular use. But it is important to pay special attention to the way that they are used sociologically.

For this reason you will find definitions in the margins of each page, where you can refer to them as you read. You should consider these bolded words and phrases your conceptual "tools" for doing sociology. As you progress through the chapters in this textbook, you will be collecting the contents of a toolkit that you can use to better understand yourself and the world around you. The bolded terms can also be found in the Glossary at the back of the book.

Relevance Boxes

In each chapter you will find Relevance Boxes with three different themes: On the Job, In Relationships, and In the Future. Relevance Boxes allow students to see the practical implications and personal value of sociology in their lives. On the Job explores the ways different people use sociological training or insights in a variety of work settings. In Relationships looks at how sociology can help us to better understand our friendships, intimate partnerships, and family relations. In the Future provides a glimpse into emerging trends in a rapidly changing society, and what students might expect to encounter on the horizon. We include these boxes to show how taking this course could bear fruit in your life (and in the lives of others).

Data Workshops

Data Workshops are designed to give students the opportunity to gain hands-on experience in the practice of sociology while they are learning. We think this is one of the most fun parts of being a sociologist. Each chapter features two Data Workshops, one on "Analyzing Everyday Life" and one on "Analyzing Media and Pop Culture." Students will use one of the research methods covered in Chapter 2 to deal with actual data from the real world—whether it's data they collect themselves or raw data provided from another source. The Data Workshops lead students through the process of analyzing data using the related conceptual tools they have just acquired in the chapter.

Global Perspective Boxes

Although this textbook focuses primarily on contemporary American society, we believe that in this time of increasing globalization, it is also important to look at other societies around the world. Global Perspective boxes throughout the book highlight some of the differences and similarities between the United States and other cultures. This feature will help students develop the ability to see comparative and analogous patterns across cultures, which is one of the key functions of a sociological perspective.

Images and Graphics

We think that it is crucial to include not only written information but also images and graphics in the textbook. This kind of presentation is increasingly common and students are likely to encounter complex information in graphical form in many of their textbooks. We want to help students gain in visual literacy as they are exposed to a variety of materials and learn in different ways. We also know that students share our interest in media, technology, and popular culture, and we want to show the connections between real life and sociological thinking. For these reasons, you will find many kinds of images and graphics in each chapter. These are not just decorations; they are an integral part of the text, so please study these as carefully as you would the rest of the printed page.

Closing Comments

Each chapter ends with closing comments that wrap up the discussion and give some final thoughts about the important themes that have been covered. This gives us a chance not so much to summarize or reiterate but to reflect, in a slightly different way, on what we have discussed, as well as to point to the future. We hope that the closing comments will give you something to think about, or even talk about with others, long after you've finished reading the chapter.

End-of-Chapter Materials

The end of each chapter contains additional materials that will enhance the learning process. The "Applying What You've Learned" review apparatus at the end of each chapter features thoughtful application questions and suggestions for further reading and viewing, including articles from the popular press, journal articles, books, blog posts, and films. These discussion questions and suggested materials are designed both to encourage students to apply what they've learned from the chapter to their own lives and also to provide opportunities for further exploration.

In our experience, the most important thing for students to take away from an introductory sociology class is a sociological perspective—not just a storehouse of facts, which will inevitably fade over time. Sociology promises a new way of looking at and thinking about the social world, which can serve students in good stead no matter what they find themselves doing in the future. We hope that this textbook delivers on that promise, making introductory sociology an intellectually stimulating and personally relevant enterprise for professors and students, in the classroom as well as outside it.

Resources

InQuizitive

digital.wwnorton.com/realworld7hs

InQuizitive is Norton's award-winning, easy-to-use adaptive learning tool that personalizes the learning experience for students and helps them master key sociological concepts and theories. When completed as a pre-lecture assignment, InQuizitive ensures that students come to class better prepared, giving instructors more time for meaningful discussions, activities, and Data Workshops.

Writing Tutorials

These tutorials give students a new way to hone key writing skills such as evaluating sources, developing research questions, choosing a research method, and writing an effective introductory paragraph.

Online Data Workshops

Each of these sixteen workshops has students go out into the real world to get hands-on experience with the methods of sociological research, whether it's participant observation research, survey research, or an interview study.

Streaming Video Clips

Ideal for initiating classroom discussions, the Sociology in Practice: Thinking about Sociology film clip series contains more than ten hours of footage drawn from documentary films. Students and instructors can access these clips at digital.wwnorton .com/realworld7hs while gradable quizzes for select clips can be assigned directly in the instructor's learning management system.

The Real World Ebook

Norton Ebooks give students and instructors an enhanced reading experience. The ebook for *The Real World* can be viewed on—and synced among—all computers and mobile devices and allows students to take notes, bookmark, search, highlight, and even read offline. Instructors can add their own notes for students.

Resources for Your LMS

Easily add high-quality Norton digital resources to your online, hybrid, or lecture course. All materials can be accessed right within an instructor's existing learning management system, and many components are customizable. Resources include:

- Chapter-review quizzes (about twenty questions per chapter)
- Key-term flashcards and quizzes
- *Sociology in Practice* video clips and short-answer exercises

Interactive Instructor's Guide

The easy-to-navigate Interactive Instructor's Guide makes lecture development easy with an array of teaching resources that can be searched and browsed according to a number of criteria. Resources include chapter outlines, lecture ideas, Data Workshop resources, discussion questions, and service learning activities that encourage students to apply their sociological imaginations in their communities.

Everyday Sociology Blog

everydaysociologyblog.com

Designed for a general audience, this exciting and unique online forum encourages visitors to actively explore sociology's relevance to pop culture, media, and everyday life. Moderated by Karen Sternheimer (University of Southern California), the blog features postings on topical subjects, video interviews with well-known sociologists, as well as contributions from special guests during the academic year.

Acknowledgments

The authors would like to thank the many people who helped make this textbook possible. To everyone at W. W. Norton, we believe that you are absolutely the best publisher in the business and that we are fortunate to get to work with you. Thank you, Roby Harrington, for signing us. Our deep appreciation goes out to Steve Dunn for believing in us and playing such a critical role in shaping the original vision of this project. Thank you for showing us we could do this and for your substantial support throughout. We would like to acknowledge Melea Seward for her efforts during the early drafts of the book. Her innovative approach and enthusiasm were much appreciated. We owe much gratitude to Karl Bakeman for his tremendous talent, work, and dedication on our behalf. His vision and leadership have been an inspiration, and a central reason for the success of this book. We feel so lucky to be a part of your team. This edition marks the third with our gifted editor Sasha Levitt, who brought phenomenally great ideas, energy, and enthusiasm to the project as well as a special talent for corralling wayward authors. We appreciate how much you invested in joining us in this work. This edition is all the better because of your exceptional generosity, creativity, and determination.

We have many others to thank as well. We are especially grateful to our project editor, Laura Dragonette; production manager, Eric Pier-Hocking; and assistant editor, Erika Nakagawa, for managing the countless details involved in creating this book. Elyse Rieder and Ted Szczepanski showed wonderful creativity in the photo research that they did for *The Real World*. Media editor Eileen Connell, associate media editor Ariel Eaton, and assistant media editor Samuel Tang developed the best textbook-support materials in sociology. Design director Rubina Yeh, illustrator Alex Eben Meyer, and designer Jillian Burr deserve special thanks for creating the beautiful design and art for the book. And we are very appreciative of the exceptional Norton "travelers"; it is through their efforts that this book has gotten out into the world.

In the course of our creating the Seventh Edition, many instructors offered advice and comments on particular chapters, or in some cases, large sections of the text. We are deeply indebted to them.

Diana Ayers-Darling, Mohawk Valley Community College
Sadia Babar, Three Rivers Community College
Maggie Bohm-Jordan, University of Wisconsin–Stevens Point
Jessica Brown, Houston Community College
Paul E. Calarco Jr., Hudson Valley Community College
LaTasha K. Cooper, Bunker Hill Community College
Rosemary Diaz, Westchester Community College
Dana Fennell, University of Southern Mississippi

Tammie J. Foltz, Des Moines Area Community College
Erin Hatton, University at Buffalo
Ann Marie Kinnell, University of Southern Mississippi
Camelia-Manuela Lataianu, Bergen Community College
Phil S. Lewis, Hudson Valley Community College
Laurie C. Linhart, Des Moines Area Community College
Laszlo Marcus, County College of Morris
Dina Radeljas, Mohawk Valley Community College
Don Rittner, Westchester Community College
Peter R. Sawyer, Hudson Valley Community College
Charles Selengut, County College of Morris
Gerald D. Titchener, Des Moines Area Community College
Jerrol David Weatherly, Coastal Carolina Community College
Arthur Weiner, Westchester Community College
Jessica White-Magellan, San Diego City College and University of San Diego
Amy Wong, San Diego State University

We would also like to thank the research assistants who worked with us on this project: Laurica Brown, Nathaniel Burke, Whitney Bush, Kate Grimaldi, Lauren Gunther, Mary Ingram, Ja'Nean Palacios, and Karl Thulin. Very special thanks to Neil Dryden, and also to Natasha Chen Christiansen, whose thoughtful contributions to multiple editions of the text have proved invaluable.

We wish to especially thank Al Ferris for his wise and generous counsel in helping us to establish our corporate identity and at every juncture along the way. Thanks to Kevin Ebenhoch for his friendly and efficient services. We would like to thank our families and friends whose encouragement and support helped to sustain us through the length of this project and beyond. It is also with great pleasure that we thank our spouses Greg Wennerdahl and David Unger, respectively—you appeared in our lives just as we were completing the first edition, and your continued presence through this process has been a source of strength and joy. We are happy to have shared these many editions with you. To Marissa Unger, an impressive reader, writer, and teacher herself, thanks for being such a positive model of your generation for us. And to our youngest reader, E.J. Ferris-Wennerdahl: May you always approach life's challenges with wonder, hope, and a sense of endless possibility.

We are grateful to colleagues who have served as mentors in our intellectual development and as inspiration to a life of writing. And finally, we offer our thanks to all of the students we have had the privilege to work with over the years. Getting to share the sociological imagination with you makes it all worthwhile.

Kerry Ferris
Jill Stein

Changes in the Seventh Edition

Chapter 1 (Sociology and the Real World): In response to reviewer feedback, the chapter has been streamlined by 10 percent and the number of key terms has been pared. The chapter opener about reality television now begins with a discussion of the Netflix reboot *Queer Eye*. Victoria Leto DeFrancisco's article "The Sounds of Silence: How Men Silence Women in Marital Relations" is presented as an example of research that takes a micro approach. The discussion of gossip blogs in the "Theories of Celebrity Gossip" Data Workshop has been updated. The bio of famous sociology major Kal Penn has been updated in the On the Job box.

Chapter 2 (Studying Social Life: Sociological Research Methods): In the section on the scientific method, the authors now discuss the importance of replicability. In the section on ethnography, David Calvey's research on masculinity and the physical culture of club bouncers is highlighted as a new example of covert research. The controversial New Family Structures Survey is presented as an example of how bias can influence research. A new In the Future feature, titled "Emerging Methods in Sociology," introduces readers to action research, netnography, and mapping methods. *Deductive approach* and *inductive approach* have been added as new key terms.

Chapter 3 (Culture): The chapter opener on bathroom bills has been updated and now highlights a 2018 study that found no connection between transgender bathroom access and bathroom crime. The explanation of the Sapir-Whorf hypothesis has been expanded. In the section on culture wars, the discussion of the alt-right has been updated. The "Analyzing Media and Pop Culture" Data Workshop now references Cardi B's influence on consumer choice. The discussion of cultural imperialism now mentions soaring obesity rates in sub-Saharan Africa due to the proliferation of fast-food restaurants. The In Relationships box on university culture has been updated and now points to Georgetown University and Boston College as examples of private institutions that do not offer the full range of sexual-health care services to their students.

Chapter 4 (Socialization, Interaction, and the Self): A new chapter opener uses the phenomenon of finstagram accounts—or fake Instagram accounts—to get students thinking about where our sense of "self" comes from and about key sociological concepts such as impression management. The section on social isolation references the 2018 case of the Turpin family in California. The discussion of the family as an agent of socialization now highlights the important role of neighborhoods. The section on peer pressure discusses Kreager and Haynie's research on adolescent drinking behavior. The section on the media as an agent of socialization now discusses the controversial Netflix series *13 Reasons Why*, highlighting a 2019 study that found that suicide rates among young people surged in the month after the series came out in 2017.

The "Analyzing Media and Pop Culture" Data Workshop references new shows such as *Killing Eve* and *Succession*. The section on adult socialization uses military recruits as a new example when discussing total institutions. Senator Tammy Duckworth, the first senator to give birth while in office, is now discussed in the section on multiple roles and role conflict. The In the Future feature on "Genetics and Sociology" has been updated with recent research on the important role that social factors play in regulating genetic action.

Chapter 5 (Separate and Together: Life in Groups): The section on social networks now discusses Martha A. Martinez and Howard Aldrich's research on family businesses and weak ties. The discussion of virtual communities references a 2017 study of how the Internet, particularly social media, can increase feelings of loneliness. The Trump administration, specifically the revolving members of his cabinet, is provided as a new example of groupthink. The section on "Power, Authority, and Style" points to Congressional Representative Alexandria Ocasio-Cortez as an example of someone who displays an instrumental leadership style. The discussion of Burning Man has been streamlined.

Chapter 6 (Deviance): The section on functionalism uses the controversial killing of Cecil the lion as an example of the functions of deviance. A new discussion uses the characters from *Black Panther* to explain Merton's typology of deviance. The case of Elizabeth Holmes and the implosion of her blood-testing start-up Theranos is presented as an example of white-collar crime. Data on incarceration rates by race, gender, and age as well as statistics on property crime, violent crime, and hate crime have all been updated. The chapter now discusses Devah Pager's research on the effect of a criminal record on one's chances of getting a job. The "Analyzing Media and Pop Culture" Data Workshop includes an updated list of TV shows. The discussion of capital punishment now highlights Katherine Beckett and Heather Evans's landmark study on racial bias and the death penalty in Washington State. The feature on cyberbullying has been updated with more current research from the Pew Research Center.

Part 3 (Understanding Inequality): A new two-page part opener introduces students to the pathbreaking research of Princeton sociologist Matthew Desmond, whose ethnography of eviction and homelessness earned him a Pulitzer Prize and a MacArthur Genius Grant.

Chapter 7 (Social Class: The Structure of Inequality): A new chapter opener focuses on food and housing insecurity among college students, drawing on the "Hungry and Homeless in College" survey research by Sara Goldrick-Rab and colleagues. Data on human trafficking have been updated. The discussion of post-apartheid South Africa has been updated. The section on symbolic interactionism now

discusses Sarah Kristian's study of linguistic patterns and how they correlated with ambitions for social mobility among youth in a rural Newfoundland town. The section on socioeconomic status and families explores Jessi Streib's study of the unique challenges of cross-class marriages. A new figure shows the relationship between income level and college participation rates. The discussion of the distribution of income and the related figure have been updated based on the most recent report from the Congressional Budget Office. In the section on education, data on the median earnings of young adults by educational attainment and college participation and graduation rates by income level have all been updated. The discussion of work and income has been substantially reworked and now looks at income growth in the aftermath of the Great Recession and increasing wealth inequality. The section on criminal justice now references research by Beckett and Evans as well as research conducted by the Heartland Alliance in Chicago on the connection between socioeconomic status and exposure to violent crime. Forrest Stuart's ethnography of Skid Row is also discussed. An expanded discussion of social mobility highlights recent research by Raj Chetty on how social mobility in the United States varies widely by geographic area. Data on poverty rates by race, gender, and age; federal spending; public opinion on a government safety net; and homelessness have all been updated. In the On the Job box, the discussion of the working poor has been updated. The discussion of the digital divide has been updated based on a 2019 report from the Pew Research Center that found evidence of a "homework gap." The discussion of student loan debt in the "Analyzing Media and Pop Culture" Data Workshop has been updated based on a report on the class of 2017. A reconceived In the Future box looks at how wealth inequality contributes to global warming, highlighting a 2017 study in the journal *Science* that found that, by the end of the twenty-first century, the burden of climate change in the United States will fall disproportionately to the poorer parts of the country.

Chapter 8 (Race and Ethnicity as Lived Experience): The chapter opener on driving while black now references a 2017 report on traffic stops in Missouri and a similar study in Oakland, California. Data on the racial and ethnic breakdown of the U.S. population have been updated. Public opinion of race relations in the United States has been updated. The section on prejudice and discrimination now includes a discussion of implicit bias and related research. *Implicit bias* has been added as a new key term. The discussion of institutional racism draws on Richard Rothstein's new book *The Color of Law*. The section on white nationalism now touches on Arlie Hochschild's study of Tea Party supporters from *Strangers in Their Own Land* as well as recent data from the Southern Poverty Law Center, which show a rise in hate groups since the 2016 election. The discussion of white privilege references the example of black ballet dancers and their difficulty finding pointe shoes. The section on cultural appropriation now includes an example of Ohio University's "We're a culture, not a costume" campaign. The section on embodied and disembodied identities discusses Adam Love and Matthew Hughey's study of racialized conversations in online basketball forums. Public opinion on interracial marriage has been updated in the In Relationships box. The section on health disparities among racial groups includes a new discussion of "weathering" and the impact of racism on one's health. The discussion of the Affordable Care Act references a 2018 study on how disparities in uninsured rates remain. The "Analyzing Media and Pop Culture" Data Workshop includes an updated list of TV shows.

Chapter 9 (Constructing Gender and Sexuality): A brand-new chapter opener focuses on Tarana Burke and the origins of the #MeToo movement. The section on gender identity now includes a discussion of nonbinary identity as a form of gender nonconformity. Statistics pertaining to sexuality and sexual orientation have been updated. The discussion of peer influence on sex, gender, and sexuality highlights Sarah Miller's new study of adolescent bullying. The section dedicated to how media contributes to gender role socialization has been updated to highlight the growing presence of gender nonconformity on TV and now references nonbinary actor Asia Kate Dillon. A reworked section titled "Sexism in Its Many Forms" includes a new explanation of male privilege. A new section examines how sexism operates through prejudice and discrimination. A new section on hegemonic and toxic masculinity, which have also been added as key terms, explores the rise of the incel movement. The discussion of microaggressions now includes more examples, including an incident involving tennis superstar Serena Williams. The section on family includes a discussion of LGBTQ youth and research on the impact of family acceptance on well-being. In the section on work and income, data on the labor force participation of men and women, the gender pay gap, and occupational segregation have all been updated. The In the Future box on human trafficking has been updated based on a recent report by the United Nations Office on Drugs and Crime. Data in the section on criminal justice, including arrest rates by sex, incarceration rates, intimate partner violence, and hate crimes, have all been updated. A reworked On the Job box is dedicated to exploring issues surrounding gender and sexuality in the military.

Chapter 10 (Social Institutions: Politics, Education, and Religion): Paul Kagame of Rwanda and Bashar al-Assad of Syria are now highlighted as examples in the section on authoritarianism. The discussion of voter turnout references the 2018 midterms, which had the highest turnout for a midterm election since 1914. The discussion of registration and voter ID laws has been updated. A new discussion of gerrymandering, including a new figure on the evolution of North Carolina's Twelfth Congressional District, has been added to the section on voting. Data on the incumbent advantage have been updated in the section on the pluralist model. The section on the media and the political process now discusses the role of social media in recent social movements such as Black Lives Matter and #MeToo. The 2016 presidential election's influence on perceptions of the press as a "watchdog" is used as an example of how politics can shape our opinion of the media. The "Analyzing Media and Pop Culture" Data Workshop references a recent study that found that satirical news shows can reinforce a viewer's preexisting attitudes as much as traditional news. The section on social media and politics now examines filter bubbles and Russian interference in the 2016 presidential election. The #NeverAgain social movement is explored in the section on patriotism and protest. Data related to education, including graduation and dropout rates, earnings, unemployment, college accessibility, and pay gaps by gender and class, have all been updated. The discussion of Randall Collins's *The Credential Society* has been expanded and *credential society* has been added as a key term. The discussion of the Common Core has been updated and includes new information on public opinion. America's College Promise Act is now mentioned in the discussion of community colleges. The discussion of religious trends draws on a recent report from the Public Religion Research Institute that found that white Christians now account for less than half of the public. A new In the Future feature introduces readers to the new faces of the 116th Congress, including Alexandria Ocasio-Cortez, Rashida Tlaib, and Ilhan Omar.

Chapter 11 (The Economy and Work): The section on capitalism has been expanded to more fully discuss how capitalism contributes to wealth inequality. The discussion of the Agricultural, Industrial, and Information Revolutions and patterns of work has been streamlined and reworked into a single section titled "The Nature of Work." The section on unions has been reworked and updated with more recent data on membership and on the number of strikes. Highlighted in the text are recent strikes by hotel workers, health-care workers, and, most notably, teachers. The recent Volkswagen emissions scandal is discussed as an example of corporate malfeasance, while the Bill & Melinda Gates Foundation is highlighted as an example of good corporate citizenship. The discussion of transnational corporations has been updated, including Table 11.1, which ranks the world's economies and shows how the largest corporations, such as Walmart, compare in size. The section on global sweatshop labor discusses a 2016 U.S. Department of Labor investigation that discovered widespread violations at a number of garment factories in Los Angeles. A new section discusses medical outsourcing, including the rise of teleradiology. Data on the contingent and alternative workforce as well as the third sector and volunteerism have been updated.

Chapter 12 (Life at Home: Families and Relationships): The definition of *polyamory* now references Elisabeth Sheff's research. Data on household types, cohabitation, living arrangements of children, and childfree living have all been updated. A new figure looks at intermarriage rates by race. The discussion of divorce now highlights 2019 research by Philip Cohen on how marriage is becoming both more stable and rarer. The discussion of divorce among same-sex couples has been updated based on newer data that found that same-sex marriages are about as likely to end in divorce as heterosexual marriages. The section on aging in the family has been updated with more current data, including the size of the older population, life expectancy, the living arrangements of older adults, and poverty among older adults. The list of films in the "Analyzing Media and Pop Culture" Data Workshop has been updated with films such as *Crazy Rich Asians* and *A Star Is Born*.

Chapter 13 (Leisure and Media): The "Trends in Leisure" section has been expanded and now includes a dedicated discussion of the digitization of leisure. A new figure breaks down how the average American spends their leisure time. Data in the section on the commodification of leisure, including spending on entertainment, have been updated. The discussion of the NBA as big business has been updated. The "Analyzing Media and Pop Culture" Data Workshop now highlights Disney's 2019 acquisition of 21st Century Fox. The section on growing concentration discusses the 2017 repeal of net neutrality and its potential consequences. AMC, Live Nation, and Ticketmaster are featured as examples of monopolies and vertical integration. A new discussion uses Amazon to highlight key trends in the media industries. The section on Internet regulation has been expanded and now considers the role Facebook played in the 2016 election and the debate over whether Facebook should regulate content. "Filter bubbles" are mentioned as an example in the section on reinforcement theory. Data related to travel and tourism have been updated. A new In the Future feature explores the growing popularity of "DNA tourism."

Chapter 14 (Health and Illness): The chapter opener on the Flint water crisis has been updated and now cites new research on environmental racism. The recent measles outbreaks across the country, including the outbreak in Brooklyn, New York, among ultra-Orthodox Jews, are presented as an example of how social milieu affects your risk of disease. The top ten causes of death have been updated. A new In the Future box covers the origins and current state of the opioid epidemic. The "Analyzing Everyday Life" Data Workshop has been updated based on the 2018 American College Health Association survey. The data pertaining to HIV/AIDS have been updated. The discussion of the relationship between education and health has been updated. The section on the intersections of race and health has been substantively reworked and now considers disparities in infant and maternal mortality rates as well as diabetes. A discussion of weathering and the impact of racism on health has been added. Life expectancy by race has been updated. The discussion of the intersections of gender and health presents Ambien as an example of how the male body is perceived as the standard in medical research. The section dedicated to exploring doctor–patient relationships now considers how racism and sexism produce disparities in health care, highlighting the differential treatment and management of chronic pain. The "Analyzing Media and Pop Culture" Data Workshop includes an updated list of TV shows. The discussion of the Affordable Care Act now explains the individual mandate. Data on public opinion of the ACA have been updated. The discussion of Autism Spectrum Disorder, including data on prevalence by racial/ethnic groups, has been updated.

Chapter 15 (Population, Cities, and the Environment): Data in the section on demography, including fertility rates, mortality rates, and life expectancy, have been updated. The discussion of population trends now references the graying of the U.S. population. Statistics related to populations in cities have been updated. The discussion of affordable housing has been updated. The discussion of energy sources and consumption has been updated. The section on biodiversity discusses a 2019 UN report that found that humans are speeding extinction and transforming the natural world at a rate "unprecedented in history." The section detailing the problems of waste references the findings of a landmark 2018 report by the United Nations' scientific panel on climate change. Public opinion on global warming and climate change has been updated. The Green New Deal is now highlighted in the discussion of environmental movements. New examples of environmental racism have been added and a new passage is dedicated to the first Environmental Justice Caucus in 2019. New examples of sustainable solutions, including xeriscape gardening and "fishface" software, have been added.

Chapter 16 (Social Change): The ALS Ice Bucket Challenge is provided as an example of emergent norm theory. The examples in the fads and fashion section have been updated. The discussion of resource mobilization explores how the Time's Up movement raised more than $20 million on the crowdfunding website GoFundMe. A new In Relationships box on hashtag activism examines the rise of the #NeverAgain movement.

Correlation with the American Sociological Association (ASA) National Standards for High School Sociology

Domain 1: The Sociological Perspective and Methods of Inquiry

Assessable Competency 1.1: Students will identify sociology as a scientific field of inquiry.

1.1.1) Scientific method 1.1.2) Hypotheses 1.1.3) Independent and dependent variables 1.1.4) Scientific study of society	Chapter 1 ("Sociology and the Real World") introduces readers to sociology as a discipline, defining it as "the systematic or scientific study of human society and social behavior" (p. 9). In Chapter 2 ("Studying Social Life: Sociological Research Methods"), readers learn about the different tools, or methods, sociologists use to study social life, beginning with the scientific method (pp. 39–41). "Scientific method," "hypothesis," "independent variable," and "dependent variable" are bolded key terms.

Assessable Competency 1.2: Students will compare and contrast the sociological perspective and how it differs from other social sciences.

1.2.1) Impact of social context on human behavior 1.2.2) Social construction of reality 1.2.3) Sociological imagination	In Chapter 1 ("Sociology and the Real World"), the authors contrast sociology with other social sciences, including anthropology, psychology, economics, political science, history, geography, and communication studies, in order to demonstrate how sociology takes a uniquely comprehensive and integrative approach to understanding human life (p. 9). The authors then introduce readers to the "sociological perspective," or looking at the world in a unique way and seeing it in a whole new light. The Data Workshop on p. 11 asks students to develop their own sociological imagination by practicing "beginner's mind." In Chapter 4 ("Socialization, Interaction, and the Self"), readers learn how the self is connected to all social phenomena (such as gender, race, and the media) and how interaction constructs them all. "Social construction" is defined as "the process by which a concept or practice is created and maintained by participants who collectively agree that it exists" (p. 101). The Data Workshop on pp. 102–3 ("Impression Management in Action") encourages readers to observe themselves in two different social situations and then complete a comparative analysis of their presentation of self in each setting. Later in Chapter 4, the authors explore the social construction of emotions (pp. 110–12), explaining how our emotions are actually sociological phenomena.

Assessable Competency 1.3: Students will evaluate the strengths and weaknesses of the major methods of sociological research.

1.3.1) Surveys and interviews 1.3.2) Experiments 1.3.3) Observations 1.3.4) Content analysis 1.3.5) Research ethics	Chapter 2 ("Studying Social Life: Sociological Research Methods") provides an overview of the major methods of sociological research, including participant observation, interviews, surveys, existing sources, and experiments (pp. 41–60). For each method, the authors clearly outline the advantages and disadvantages. The chapter concludes with a discussion of research ethics, which includes an in-depth look at the Nuremberg trials (p. 61). "Content Analysis" is a bolded key term on p. 53. After introducing students to sociological research methods, Data Workshops (two in every chapter) ask students to employ these new tools to conduct their own sociological research.

Assessable Competency 1.4: Students will identify, differentiate among, and apply a variety of sociological theories.

1.4.1) Functionalist perspective 1.4.2) Conflict theory 1.4.3) Symbolic interaction	Although the authors provide thorough coverage of the three main theoretical paradigms in Chapter 1 (pp. 19–30), "Theory in Everyday Life" tables in every chapter help students understand the mechanics of social theory and how to apply it to various real-world phenomena. These boxes in every chapter break down the major theoretical approaches and illustrate how each perspective might be used to analyze a particular real-world case study. The authors also explain how the major sociological paradigms can help us better understand deviance (Chapter 6, pp. 149–55), social stratification (Chapter 7, pp. 182–86), race and ethnicity (Chapter 8, pp. 219–24), gender inequality (Chapter 9, pp. 253–54), religion (Chapter 10, pp. 295–97), and family (Chapter 12, pp. 341–44).

Domain 2: Social Structure: Culture, Institutions, and Society

Assessable Competency 2.1: Students will describe the components of culture.

2.1.1) Nonmaterial culture, including norms and values 2.1.2) Material culture 2.1.3) Subcultures	Chapter 3 ("Culture") introduces students to the sociological study of culture, first defining culture and then breaking it down into its constituent parts: material culture and symbolic culture (pp. 71–76). Within the discussion of symbolic culture, the authors consider values, norms, and sanctions (pp. 76–79). In the section on variations in culture, the authors explore subcultures and countercultures (pp. 80–81).

Assessable Competency 2.2: Students will analyze how culture influences individuals, including themselves.

2.2.1) Ethnocentrism 2.2.2) Cultural relativity	Chapter 3 ("Culture") introduces students to the concepts of ethnocentrism and cultural relativity. Both are bolded key terms (pp. 71–73).
2.2.3) Culture shock	Culture shock is introduced in Chapter 1 ("Sociology and the Real World") within a discussion of the sociological perspective. It is a bolded key term (pp. 11–12).
2.2.4) American values	Chapter 3 ("Culture") concludes with a discussion of American culture in perspective (pp. 87–88).

Assessable Competency 2.3: Students will evaluate important social institutions and how they respond to social needs.

2.3.1) Social institutions such as: family, education, religion, economy, and government	Part IV ("Social Institutions and the Macro-Micro Link") explores how the macro-level patterns and structures of major social institutions shape our own micro-level individual experiences: • Chapter 10: "Social Institutions: Politics, Education, and Religion" (pp. 270–305) • Chapter 11: "The Economy and Work" (pp. 306–37) • Chapter 12: "Life at Home: Families and Relationships" (pp. 338–61) • Chapter 13: "Leisure and Media" (pp. 362–89) • Chapter 14: "Health and Illness" (pp. 390–415)
2.3.2) Social statuses and roles	Chapter 4 ("Socialization, Interaction, and the Self") introduces students to social statuses and roles, different kinds of statuses, and the issues that arise when we have to juggle multiple roles: role conflict. "Status," "ascribed status," "master status," "role," "role conflict," "role strain," and "role exit" are all bolded key terms (pp. 109–10).

Assessable Competency 2.4: Students will assess how social institutions and cultures change and evolve.

2.4.1) Shifting historical context such as: industrial revolution, urbanization, globalization, the Internet age	Part V ("Envisioning the Future and Creating Social Change") includes Chapter 15 ("Populations, Cities, and the Environment") and Chapter 16 ("Social Change"). Chapter 11 ("The Economy and Work") includes thorough coverage of the Industrial Revolution (pp. 313–15) and the Information Age, or Internet age (pp. 315–18). The authors again discuss the reality of the digital age in Chapter 16 in the section titled "Living in a Postmodern World" (pp. 471–74). Chapter 15 explores the process of urbanization in depth (pp. 428–37). "Urbanization" is a bolded key term in Chapter 15. The process of globalization is discussed in Chapter 16 and is a bolded key term (pp. 470–71).
2.4.2) Countercultures	Countercultures and subcultures are introduced in Chapter 3 ("Culture"). Both are bolded key terms (pp. 80–81).
2.4.3) Social movements	Chapter 16 ("Social Change") includes substantive coverage of social movements, including an in-depth look at the history of voting rights in the United States. The authors examine the stages in a social movement as well as who takes part. Lastly, the section titled "Promoting and Resisting Change" looks at emerging social movements. A boxed feature titled "Hashtag Activism: #NeverAgain and #EnoughIsEnough" explores gun-control activism as an example of a social movement. "Social movements" is a bolded key term (pp. 459–64).

Domain 3: Social Relationships: Self, Groups, and Socializations

Assessable Competency 3.1: Students will describe the process of socialization across the life course.

3.1.1) Primary agents of socializations: family, peers, media, schools, and religion	The main agents of socialization—including the family, schools, peers, and the media—are examined in Chapter 4 ("Socialization, Interaction, and the Self") (pp. 103–9).
3.1.2) Deviance and conformity	Chapter 6 ("Deviance") (pp. 144–67)

Assessable Competency 3.2: Students will explain the process of the social construction of the self.

3.2.1) I & me	Chapter 4 ("Socialization, Interaction, and the Self") introduces students to the major theories of the self, including psychoanalytic theory and Freud as well as the contributions of Charles Cooley and George Herbert Mead. Within the discussion of Mead, the authors introduce readers to the concept of the dual nature of the self ("I" and "me") (pp. 96–102).
3.2.2) Role taking	Role taking is explored in the section titled "Statuses and Roles" in Chapter 4 ("Socialization, Interaction, and the Self") (pp. 109–10).
3.2.3) Generalized other	Within the discussion of George Herbert Mead in Chapter 4 ("Socialization, Interaction, and the Self"), the authors introduce the perspective of the generalized other, which is a bolded key term (p. 99).
3.2.4) Identity	Identity is explored in-depth throughout Chapter 4 ("Socialization, Interaction, and the Self") (pp. 90–115).

Assessable Competency 3.3: Students will examine the social construction of groups and their impact on the life chances of individuals.

3.3.1) Reference groups	Chapter 5 ("Separate and Together: Life in Groups") includes a section on reference groups. "Reference group" is a bolded key term (p. 127).
3.3.2) Primary and secondary groups	At the start of Chapter 5 ("Separate and Together: Life in Groups"), the authors differentiate between primary groups and secondary groups, providing examples of both. Both are bolded key terms (p. 119).
3.3.3) In-groups and out-groups	Within the section on group dynamics in Chapter 5 ("Separate and Together: Life in Groups") the authors introduce in-groups and out-groups. Both are bolded key terms (pp. 126–27).

Domain 4: Stratification and Inequality

Assessable Competency 4.1: Students will identify common patterns of social inequality.

4.1.1) Privilege	Part III ("Understanding Inequality") explores the different systems used to group, rank, and categorize people:
4.1.2) Power	• Chapter 7: "Social Class: The Structure of Inequality"
4.1.3) Racial and ethnic inequality	• Chapter 8: "Race and Ethnicity as Lived Experience"
4.1.4) Class inequality	• Chapter 9: "Constructing Gender and Sexuality"
4.1.5) Gender inequality	In the section on socioeconomic status and life chances, the authors explore the respective privileges and hardships associated with different levels of the social hierarchy. At the very beginning of Chapter 7, the authors define social inequality as the unequal distribution of wealth, power, and prestige. Racial and ethnic inequality is explored in-depth in Chapter 8. Class inequality is explored in-depth in Chapter 7. Gender inequality is explored in-depth in Chapter 9 (pp. 236–65).

Assessable Competency 4.2: Students will analyze the effects of social inequality on groups and individuals.	
4.2.1) Life chances	In the section titled "Socioeconomic Status and Life Chances" in Chapter 7, the authors explore the relationship between socioeconomic status and life chances. They examine the impact of SES on family, health, education, work and income, and crime (pp. 187–91).
4.2.2) Social problems	Part III ("Understanding Inequality")
4.2.3) Inter- and intra-group conflict	Conflict in groups is explored in the section on group dynamics in Chapter 5 ("Life in Groups") (pp. 126–30).

Assessable Competency 4.3: Students will explain the relationship between social institutions and inequality.	
4.3.1) Distribution of power through social institutions 4.3.2) Potential of institutions to produce, reinforce, or challenge inequality	Part IV ("Social Institutions and the Macro-Micro Link") includes: • Chapter 10: "Social Institutions: Politics, Education, and Religion" • Chapter 11: "The Economy and Work" • Chapter 12: "Life at Home: Families and Relationships" • Chapter 13: "Leisure and Media" • Chapter 14: "Health and Illness" The section titled "Education and Inequality" in Chapter 10 explores how education institutions can replicate systems of inequality (pp. 287–88). The section titled "Who Rules America?" in Chapter 10 explores how power is concentrated in the hands of the richest Americans (pp. 276–78). The section on postindustrial work in Chapter 11 looks at inequalities of power in service work, referencing Barbara Ehrenreich's landmark study *Nickel and Dimed* (pp. 315–18). Chapter 12 on family includes an in-depth discussion of the hierarchies of inequalities that shape family life, including the unequal division of family labor (pp. 352–54). Trouble in families, including domestic abuse, child abuse, and elder abuse, are explored later in the chapter (pp. 356–59).

Assessable Competency 4.4: Students will assess responses to social inequality.	
4.4.1) Individual responses to inequality	Part III ("Understanding Inequality") (Chapter 7, Chapter 8, Chapter 9)
4.4.2) Group responses to inequality such as social movements	In addition to Chapter 16 ("Social Change"), Chapter 9 on gender and sexuality includes substantive coverage of the movement for women's rights, men's movements, and LGBTQ rights movements (pp. 262–64). Chapter 10 includes a discussion of the Black Lives Matter movement (pp. 283–85). Chapter 11 includes a discussion of campus protests and sit-ins against sweatshop labor (pp. 327–29).
4.4.3) Social policy responses to inequality	Part III ("Understanding Inequality") (Chapter 7, Chapter 8, Chapter 9, Chapter 10) Within the discussion of poverty in Chapter 7, the authors include coverage of social welfare and welfare reform (pp. 194–97). Chapter 9 includes a discussion of the repeal of Don't Ask, Don't Tell as well as the military's recent response to gender discrimination and sexual assault in the armed forces (p. 250). The legalization of same-sex marriage is also discussed in this chapter (pp. 263–64). Chapter 10 includes coverage of education policy such as the Common Core. The authors also look at charter schools, school vouchers, early college high schools, and community colleges (pp. 290–95).

PART I
Thinking Sociologically and Doing Sociology

Pepper went to Yale when the school had just begun to admit female students, and some campus buildings didn't even have women's restrooms yet. She was soon documenting the sexual revolution as it took shape on campus. Her academic work spilled over into the popular media, when she began writing a sex advice column for *Glamour* magazine. Since then she has become a go-to authority on everything sex, love, and relationships.

Victor was a gang member who dropped out of school when he was fourteen and learned to steal cars, landing him in juvenile detention. If it had not been for the intervention of one extraordinarily dedicated high school teacher who held on to her high expectations for him, Victor's life story might not have turned out so well. He went on to earn a doctorate in ethnic studies, examining the street life he had once known.

Matthew worked as a wildland firefighter in the rugged backcountry of northern Arizona where he grew up, earning money in this dangerous profession to help put himself through college. Like many of his fellow firefighters, he came from a rural, working-class background where the practical skills he acquired proved useful in the context of this risky, sometimes even deadly, job. He drew upon this experience when writing his first book, *On the Fireline: Living and Dying with Wildland Firefighters*. Matthew was likewise inspired by another event from his past—losing his childhood home to foreclosure. The anger and humiliation he felt at the time later drove him to study issues surrounding housing. When he was a graduate student at the University of Wisconsin, he moved into a trailer park in Milwaukee to better understand how evictions exacerbate poverty.

What do these people have in common? They are all prominent American sociology professors. You may not have heard of them (yet), but they have each made an exceptional impact on their profession.

Pepper Schwartz, a sociology professor at the University of Washington, is a leading researcher on sex and intimate relationships. Her work has resonated widely with the public; she is often cited in the press and makes frequent appearances across a variety of media outlets. Since 2014, she has appeared as a regular cast member on the reality TV show *Married at First Sight*. Victor Rios has become a sought-after author and speaker whose sometimes autobiographical research on race, law enforcement, and social control also led him to found a program for at-risk youth in Santa Barbara, where he is a professor at the University of California. Matthew Desmond is a sociology professor at Princeton University. *Evicted: Poverty and Profit in the American City*, his powerful firsthand account of deep poverty and homelessness in America, earned widespread acclaim, including a Pulitzer Prize. In 2017, he founded the Eviction Lab with the aim of collecting national data on eviction to better understand residential instability in the United States.

Each sociologist has a unique story about how they ended up in sociology and built a career in academia. It was not obvious from the beginning that any of them would be academic superstars; they each faced a different set of obstacles to success but were somehow motivated to keep on. Perhaps

Pepper Schwartz

Victor Rios

Matthew Desmond

it was because they had been deeply touched by something happening in the real world, something that was also relevant to their own lives. It inspired in them a passion for pursuing a question, an issue, or a cause that was meaningful to them. They have each made important connections between their personal lives and their professional careers. In turn, their work extends beyond academia, making a collective contribution to the lives of individuals and even to society as a whole.

Their paths to sociology were very different, and they have each taught and researched different topics. Despite these differences, they share a way of looking at the world. Sociologists have a unique viewpoint called the "sociological perspective." In fact, we hope that you will acquire your own version of the sociological perspective over the course of this term. Then you will share something in common with these and other sociology professors, including your own.

Schwartz, Rios, and Desmond also hold in common their commitment to sociological theories and concepts. This means that their ideas—and the questions they ask and answer—are guided by the established traditions of sociological thought. They may build on those traditions or criticize them, but every sociologist engages in a theoretical dialogue that links centuries and generations. You will become part of this dialogue as you learn more about sociological theory.

Finally, Schwartz, Rios, Desmond, and others like them conduct their research using specific sociological methods. Whether quantitative or qualitative, these means of gathering and analyzing data are distinctive to sociology, and every sociologist develops research projects using the methods best suited to the questions they want to answer.

Each sociologist's personal journey affects their professional legacy, and knowing something about an author's life helps students understand the author's work. A person's values, experiences, and family context all shape their interests and objectives—and this is as true of eminent sociologists as it will be for you.

In this first part, we will introduce you to the discipline of sociology and its theoretical traditions (Chapter 1) and to the work of sociology and its research methodologies (Chapter 2). This section is your opportunity to get to know sociology—its perspectives, theories, and research practices.

Perhaps someday your intellectual autobiography will be added to those of Schwartz, Rios, and Desmond—and your story will start by opening this book.

CHAPTER 1

Sociology and the Real World

A shiny black SUV pulls up in front of your home or workplace and suddenly you are under the spell of the Fab Five: Antoni, Bobby, Jonathan, Karamo, and Tan—a quintet of gay men skilled in culture, fashion, grooming, design, and cuisine. Their mission each week: to save a different sad-sack from himself. The Fab Five are there to get him a much-needed pedicure, tweak his pasta salad recipe, redecorate his living room, take him to trapeze class, get him into a slimming pair of jeans, shave off that stubbly beard, and teach him how to overcome his fears or be a better dad. They have great chemistry and always get their man, toasting his success from their hip ATL loft at the end of each episode.

Each week, two contestants, one man and one woman, total strangers and completely naked, are dropped deep into the wilderness with almost no supplies to see if they can survive together for twenty-one days. In journeys across six continents, in such places as the Australian outback, the jungles of Belize, and the savannah of Namibia, these pairs of contestants are tested both physically and mentally, forced to discover what they're truly made of. Will they "tap out" and ask to leave the competition early, or will they have the fortitude to prevail through whatever hardships their journey delivers? And perhaps most importantly, can these strangers forge a working partnership so essential to the act of survival, or will pride, fear, or some other human weakness undermine their success?

Three sisters, whose names all start with the letter *K*, alternately squabble and cooperate with each other and members of their large blended family, including a brother, mother, stepparent, half sisters, stepbrothers, and assorted significant others. Their privileged lives are on continual display, and they have become famous mainly for being famous. Their family dramas, rife with both glamorous and embarrassing moments, are chronicled in excruciating detail. With her music mogul husband on her arm, Kim attends galas, fashion shows, and awards ceremonies with fellow members of the glitterati. Meanwhile, sisters Khloe and Kourtney jet set around the globe, opening up boutiques in cities like New York and Miami. The sisters shop constantly and take countless selfies while millions of fans follow them on Instagram.

Is any of this real? Yes—kind of. It's "reality television," specifically Netflix's *Queer Eye*, Discovery's *Naked and Afraid,* and E!'s *Keeping Up with the Kardashians.* And there's a lot more where those came from. *Dancing with the Stars, The Voice, Top Chef, The Bachelor,* and *Teen Mom* are just a few of the more popular shows, as well as the show that started it all in 1992, MTV's *The Real World.*

Some of the shows claim to follow real people through their everyday lives or on the job, while others impose bizarre conditions on participants, subject them to stylized competitions and gross-out stunts, or make their dreams come true. Millions tune in every week to see real people eat bugs, get fired, suffer romantic rejection, reveal their poor parenting, get branded as fat or ugly, cry over their misfortunes, or get voted out of the house or off the island—mortifying themselves on camera for the possibility of success, money, or fame.

Why are we so interested in these people? Because people are interesting! Because we are people, too. No matter how different we are from the folks on reality TV, we are part of the same society, and for that reason we are curious about how they live. We compare their lives with ours, wonder how common or unusual they or we are, and marvel that we are all part of the same, real world. We, too, may want to win competitions, date an attractive person, find a high-profile job, feel pretty or handsome, be part of an exclusive group, or have a lovely home and family. We may even want to be on a reality show ourselves.

How to Read This Chapter

You are embarking on a fascinating journey as you learn to see, think, and analyze yourself and the world around you from a sociological perspective. The tools presented here will help you build a foundation for new knowledge and insights into social life.

We will also share the story of the historical and intellectual development of the discipline of sociology. We want to show you how the ideas that shape sociology are linked and introduce you to the interesting men and women who came up with those ideas. Too often, theorists seem to be talking heads, icons of social analysis who experience neither life-altering calamities nor shifting professional fortunes. We want to overcome that perception. We believe that our individual experiences and historical contexts shape our thoughts and the professional worlds we choose to join. This is as true for Karl Marx as it is for Kerry Ferris, as true for Jane Addams as it is for Jill Stein—it's true for all of us; your own experiences and cultural and historical contexts will shape your ideas and work. In fact, someday, someone may write a chapter about you!

As authors and teachers, we encourage you to develop some basic study techniques that will assist you in your success as a new student to sociology (and perhaps beyond). You may want to highlight portions of the text or take notes while you read. Mark passages you don't understand, or keep a list of questions about any aspect of the chapter. Don't hesitate to discuss those questions with your instructor or fellow students; those dialogues can be one of the most gratifying parts of the learning process. Finally, we recommend that you attend class regularly—whether you're in a face-to-face classroom or online—as there is really no substitute for the shared experience of learning sociology with others.

We are excited to join you on this journey of discovery. Though you may know a lot about social life already, we hope to introduce you to even more—about yourself and the world around you—and to provide valuable tools for the future. We wouldn't want you to miss a thing. So here is where we start.

WHAT IS SOCIOLOGY?

Even among those working in the field, there is some debate about defining **sociology**. A look at the term's Latin and Greek roots, *socius* and *logos*, suggests that sociology means the study of **society**, which is a good place to start. A slightly more elaborate definition might be the systematic or scientific study of human society and social behavior. This could include almost any level within the structure of society, from large-scale institutions and mass culture to small groups and relationships between individuals.

Another definition comes from Howard Becker (1986), who suggests that sociology can best be understood as the study of people "doing things together." This version reminds us that neither society nor the individual exists in isolation and that humans are essentially social beings. Not only is our survival contingent on the fact that we live in various groups (families, neighborhoods, dorms), but also our sense of self derives from our membership in society. In turn, the accumulated activities that people do together create the patterns and structures we call society. So sociologists want to understand how humans affect society, as well as how society affects humans.

One way to better understand sociology is to contrast it with other **social sciences**, disciplines that examine the human or social world, much as the natural sciences examine the natural or physical world. These include anthropology, psychology, economics, political science, and sometimes history, geography, and communication studies. Each has its own particular focus on the social world. In some ways, sociology's territory overlaps with other social sciences, even while maintaining its own approach.

Like history, sociology compares the past and the present in order to understand both; unlike history, sociology is more likely to focus on contemporary society. Sociology is interested in societies at all levels of development, while anthropology is more likely to concentrate on traditional or small, indigenous cultures. Sociology looks at a range of social institutions, unlike economics or political science, which each focuses on a single institution. Like geography, sociology considers the relationship of people to places, though geography is more concerned with the places themselves. And like communication studies, sociology examines human communication—at both the social and the interpersonal levels, rather than one or the other. Finally, sociology looks at the individual in relationship to external social forces, whereas psychology specializes in internal states of mind. As you can begin to see, sociology covers a huge intellectual territory, making it exceptional among the social sciences in taking a comprehensive, integrative approach to understanding human life (Figure 1.1).

> **SOCIOLOGY** the systematic or scientific study of human society and social behavior, from large-scale institutions and mass culture to small groups and individual interactions
>
> **SOCIETY** a group of people who shape their lives in aggregated and patterned ways that distinguish their group from others
>
> **SOCIAL SCIENCES** the disciplines that use the scientific method to examine the social world

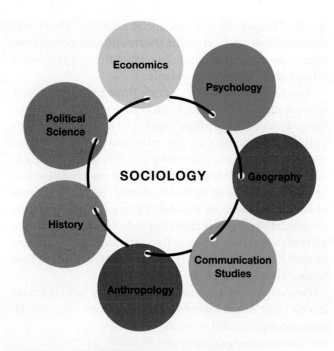

FIGURE 1.1 Sociology and the Social Sciences
Sociology overlaps with other social sciences, but much of the territory it covers is unique.

HOW TO THINK LIKE A SOCIOLOGIST

How do sociologists go about understanding human life in society? The first step is to develop what we call the **sociological perspective**, which is also referred to as taking a sociological approach or thinking sociologically. In any case, it means looking at the world in a unique way and seeing it in a whole new light. You may be naturally inclined to think sociologically, but, for many, the following practices are helpful.

Practical vs. Scientific Knowledge

You already possess many of the skills of an astute analyst of social life, but you take your knowledge for granted because you gained it as an everyday actor. In this course, you will build a new identity: social analyst. These are two very different ways of experiencing the same social world.

The everyday actor approaches his social world with what is referred to as "reciped," or practical, knowledge (Schutz 1962), which allows him to get along in his everyday life. However, practical knowledge is not necessarily as coherent, clear, and consistent as it could be. For example, you are probably very skilled at using a smartphone. It brings you into daily contact

SOCIOLOGICAL PERSPECTIVE a way of looking at the world through a sociological lens

BEGINNER'S MIND approaching the world without preconceptions in order to see things in a new way

with friends and family, puts you in touch with the pizza delivery guy, and allows you to register for classes and find out your grades at the end of the term. But you probably can't explain how it works in a technical way; you know only how it works for you in a practical, everyday way. This is the important feature of the everyday actor's knowledge: It is practical, not scientific.

To acquire knowledge about the social world that is systematic, comprehensive, coherent, clear, and consistent, you'll need to take a different approach. The social analyst has to "place in question everything that seems unquestionable" to the everyday actor (Schutz 1962, p. 96). In other words, the social analyst takes the perspective of a stranger in the social world; she tries to verify what the everyday actor might just accept as truth. For instance, people tend to believe that women are more talkative than men. This might seem so evident, in fact, as not to be worth investigating. The social analyst, however, *would* investigate and deliver a more complex conclusion than you might think.

There are strengths and weaknesses in both approaches: The analyst sees with clarity what the actor glosses over, but the actor understands implicitly what the analyst labors to grasp. Once you've learned more about the theories and methods that come next, you'll be able to combine the virtues of both analyst and actor. The result will be a more profound and comprehensive understanding of the social world in which we all live.

Beginner's Mind

One technique for gaining a sociological perspective comes from Bernard McGrane (1994), who promotes a shift in thinking borrowed from the Zen Buddhist tradition. McGrane suggests that we practice what is called **beginner's mind**—the opposite of expert's mind, which is so filled with facts, projections, assumptions, opinions, and explanations that it can't learn anything new. If we would like to better understand the world around us, we must unlearn what we already know. Beginner's mind approaches the world without knowing in advance what it will find; it is open and receptive to experience.

Perhaps our greatest obstacle to making new discoveries is our habitual ways of thinking. "Discovery," McGrane says, "is not the seeing of a new thing—but rather a new way of seeing things" (1994, p. 3). One way to achieve this kind of awareness is to practice being present in the moment. You might have tried this already if you've done any training in what is called "mindfulness." The problem is we are all too often preoccupied with thoughts and feelings that prevent us from fully participating in reality. If we can find some inner stillness and stop our normal mental chatter, McGrane says, then there is a possibility for true learning to occur. It is in this quiet space that a personal "paradigm shift" (a new model for understanding self and society) can take place.

DATA WORKSHOP

Analyzing Everyday Life

Doing Nothing

Zen sociologist Bernard McGrane suggests that we actually "do" sociology, rather than just study it. His book *The Un-TV and the 10 MPH Car* (1994) features exercises designed to help students experience the mundane, routine, and everyday level of society in a new way. This Data Workshop is an adaptation of one of his experiments. You will be practicing beginner's mind, one of the ways to gain a sociological perspective, or to think like a sociologist.

Step 1: Conducting the Experiment
This exercise requires that you stand in a relatively busy public space (a mall, street corner, park, or campus quad) and literally do nothing for ten minutes. That means just standing there and being unoccupied. Don't wait for someone, take a break, sightsee, or otherwise engage in a normal kind of activity. Also don't daydream or think about the past or the future; don't entertain yourself with plans or internal dialogues. Don't whistle, hum, fidget, look in your bag, play with your phone, take notes, or do anything else that might distract you from just being there and doing nothing. Do, however, observe the reactions of others to you, and pay attention to your own thoughts and feelings during these ten minutes.

Step 2: Taking Notes about the Experience
Immediately after conducting the experiment, write some informal notes about what happened or did not happen. These notes can be loosely structured (with sentence fragments or bullet points, if you wish), and they should be casual and written in the first person. Discuss the experience and its meaning to you in as much detail as possible. Include a description of other people's reactions as well as your own thoughts and feelings before, during, and after the experiment.

This exercise may seem deceptively simple at first, but the subtle change from "doing something" to "doing nothing" makes everything different. It helps turn the ordinary world into a strange place. It makes you more aware of your own sense of self (or lack thereof) and how identity is constructed through interaction. You may find it a challenge to put aside the mental and physical activities that you normally engage in to pass the time. And you may feel uncomfortable standing in a public place when other people can't quite figure out who you

Doing Nothing How does standing in a crowded place and doing nothing change how you experience the ordinary world?

are and what you're doing. Finally, you will no longer be able to take for granted how the meaning of a situation is being defined or interpreted. Divested of your role as an everyday actor, you'll learn how the most mundane activities (like just standing around) can become major objects of sociological inquiry.

There are two options for completing this Data Workshop:

PREP-PAIR-SHARE Complete the exercise and bring your written notes to class. Partner with another student and take turns presenting your findings. Discuss the ways in which your experiences were similar or different. What was it like to "do" sociology? Did you see things in a new way? What was the most interesting part about conducting the experiment?

DO-IT-YOURSELF Complete the exercise and write a two- to three-page essay based on the main concepts and prompts from this Data Workshop. Describe your experience and the results of your research. How did the experiment help you learn to think more like a sociologist? You may want to include snippets of your informal written notes to illustrate your points. Attach the informal notes to your finished essay.

Culture Shock

Peter Berger (1963) describes what kind of person becomes a sociologist: someone with a passionate interest in the world of human affairs, someone who is intense, curious, and daring in

IN RELATIONSHIPS
It's Official: Men Talk More Than Women

The practice of sociology may seem to be about just a bunch of common sense. But this is true only part of the time. Some of what you learn may indeed seem familiar and may confirm some of the conclusions you've made about it. Drawing on the personal knowledge you have accumulated in life will be a valuable asset as a starting place, but it can also be a stumbling block to deeper understanding. There are times that the things that "everyone knows" turn out not to be true, or at least not as simple as we might have thought.

Take, for instance, the widely held belief that women talk more than men. Experience seems to confirm that this is true, obviously! Women are chatty, and a lot of men, if not the strong silent type, definitely have trouble getting a word in edgewise. And women have a hard time getting men to talk when they want them to; sometimes, to get a man to tell you what he's thinking, you have to drag it out of him. While you may recognize this description of the different genders, and may be able to relate with your own anecdote of such an encounter (or perhaps many such encounters), your casual assumptions about who talks more may need some revising.

Numerous sociological studies that analyze conversational dynamics show that, despite stereotypes to the contrary, it's actually men who are slightly more talkative (Leaper and Ayres 2007). How could that be?

Well, it depends on the context. Men are more talkative with their wives and with strangers. Women are more talkative with their children and with college classmates. With close friends and families, men and women are equally talkative. Studies have also shown other, perhaps more easily predictable, gender differences. For example, men use speech that is more assertive (they want to persuade others), while women use speech that is more affiliative (they are more focused on connecting with others). Sociologists have long noted that men are also more dominant in conversations, cutting off and interrupting women more often (Anderson and Leaper 1998; Hancock and Rubin 2015; Kollock, Blumstein, and Schwartz 1985).

"Mansplaining" is another way that men assert their dominance in conversations (Solnit 2008). The word is rather new, but the idea has been around for decades (Rothman 2012). Mansplaining is the tendency, especially for men, to

---

the pursuit of knowledge. "People who like to avoid shocking discoveries . . . should stay away from sociology," he warns (p. 24). The sociologist cares about the issues of ultimate importance to humanity, as well as the most mundane occurrences of everyday existence.

Another way to gain a sociological perspective is to attempt to create in ourselves a sense of **culture shock**. Anthropologists use the term to describe the experience of visiting an "exotic" foreign culture. The first encounters with the local natives and their way of life can seem so strange to us that they produce a kind of disorientation and doubt about our ability to make sense of things. Putting all judgment aside for the moment, this state of mind can be very useful. For it is at this point, when we so completely lack an understanding of our surroundings, that we are truly able to perceive what is right in front of our eyes.

CULTURE SHOCK a sense of disorientation that occurs when entering a radically new social or cultural environment

SOCIOLOGICAL IMAGINATION a quality of the mind that allows us to understand the relationship between our individual circumstances and larger social forces

As sociologists, we try to create this effect without necessarily displacing ourselves geographically: We become curious and eager visitors to our own lives. We often find that what is familiar to us, if viewed from an outsider's perspective, is just as exotic as some foreign culture, only we've forgotten this is true because it's our own and we know it so well. To better understand this state of mind, you might imagine what it would be like to return home after being shipwrecked and living alone on a desert island. Or, if you've traveled abroad or moved away to attend college, perhaps it's something you've already experienced but didn't know what to call.

The Sociological Imagination

One of the classic statements about the sociological perspective comes from C. Wright Mills (1916–1962), who describes a quality of mind that all great social analysts seem to possess: the **sociological imagination**. By this, he means the ability to understand "the intersection between biography and history," or the interplay of the micro world of the self and individual psychology and the macro world of

explain things in a condescending or patronizing way, with the presumption that the one doing the explaining knows more than the listener (even when this is clearly not the case). Men are more likely to "mansplain" in conversations with women, reinforcing gender stereotypes about who has more power and, in these cases, more knowledge. Perhaps because so many people have been on the receiving end of mansplaining, the word has gained acceptance into the current lexicon as well as the *Oxford English Dictionary* (Steinmetz 2014). It has become a useful label for a widely recognized behavior. Of course, it's not only men who engage in mansplaining to women; sometimes men mansplain to other men, and sometimes women do it to men or to each other (McClintock 2016).

These findings seem to defy what has been considered a biological fact, that the female brain is wired to be more verbal and, therefore, that women talk more. But because who talks more varies by situation, the evidence seems to point to language and conversational differences as influenced more by social than biological forces, including power dynamics. So despite how it might feel from your own personal experience, sociology has debunked some common myths about women and men, requiring us to rethink simplistic gender stereotypes.

This is why doing sociology is in some regards a radical undertaking. It requires of us a willingness to suspend our

Kanye West takes the microphone away from Taylor Swift to give an impromptu speech at the MTV Video Music Awards.

own preconceptions, assumptions, and beliefs about the way things are. As sociologists, we need to learn to question everything, especially our own taken-for-granted notions about others and ourselves. Once these notions have been set aside, even temporarily, we gain a fresh perspective with which to uncover and discover aspects of social life we hadn't noticed before. We are then able to reinterpret our previous understanding of the world, perhaps challenging, or possibly confirming, what we thought we already knew.

larger social forces; this is sociology's task and its "promise" (Mills 1959).

We normally think of our own problems as being a private matter of character, chance, or circumstance, and we overlook the fact that these may be caused in part by, or at least occur within, a specific cultural and historical context. For example, if you can't find a job, you may feel that it's because you don't have the right skills, educational background, or experience. But it may also be the result of problems in the larger economy such as outsourcing, downsizing, restrictive policies, changing technologies, or migration patterns. In other words, your individual unemployment may be part of a larger social and historical phenomenon.

Most of the time, we use psychological rather than sociological arguments to explain the way things are. For instance, if someone is carrying a lot of credit card debt, psychological reasoning might focus on the person's lack of self-control or inability to delay gratification. Sociological reasoning, however, might focus on the impact of cultural norms that promote a lifestyle beyond most people's means, or on economic changes that require more Americans to rely

on credit cards because their wages have not kept up with inflation.

The sociological imagination searches for the link between micro and macro levels of analysis. We must look for how larger social forces, such as race, class, gender, religion, economics, or politics, are involved in creating the context of a person's life. Mills's characterization of sociology as the inter-

C. Wright Mills

section between biography and history reminds us that the process works in both directions: While larger social forces influence individual lives, individual lives can affect society as well.

One of the most important benefits of using the sociological imagination is access to a world beyond our own immediate sphere, where we can discover radically different ways of experiencing life and interpreting reality. It can help us appreciate alternative viewpoints and understand how they may have come about. This, in turn, helps us to better understand how we developed our own values, beliefs, and attitudes.

Sociology asks us to see our familiar world in a new way, and doing so means we may need to abandon, or at least reevaluate, our opinions about that world and our place in it. It is tempting to believe that our opinions are widely held, that our worldview is the best or, at least, most common. Taking a sociological perspective forces us to see fallacies in our way of thinking. Because other individuals are different from us— belonging to different social groups, participating in different social institutions, living in different cities or countries, listening to different songs, watching different TV programs, engaging in different religious practices—they may look at the world very differently than we do. But a sociological perspective also allows us to see the other side of this equation: In cases where we assume that others are different from us, we may be surprised to find that their approach to their everyday world is quite similar to ours.

LEVELS OF ANALYSIS: MICRO- AND MACROSOCIOLOGY

Consider a photographer with state-of-the-art equipment. She can view her subject through either a zoom lens or a wide-angle lens. Through the zoom lens, she sees intricate details about the subject's appearance; through the wide-angle lens, she gets the "big picture" and a sense of the broader context in which the subject is located. Both views are valuable in understanding the subject, and both result in photographs of the same thing.

Sociological perspectives are like the photographer's lenses, giving us different ways of looking at a common subject (Newman 2000). Sociologists can take a microsociological (zoom lens) perspective, a macrosociological (wide-angle lens) perspective, or any number of perspectives located on the continuum between the two (Figure 1.2).

Microsociology concentrates on the interactions between individuals and the ways in which those interactions construct the larger patterns, processes, and institutions of society. As the word indicates ("micro" means small), microsociology looks at the smallest building blocks of society in order to understand its large-scale structure. A classic example of research that takes a micro approach is Victoria Leto DeFrancisco's article "The Sounds of Silence: How Men Silence Women in Marital Relations" (1991). Like many scholars who had observed the feminist movements of the 1960s and '70s, DeFrancisco was concerned with issues of

MICROSOCIOLOGY the level of analysis that studies face-to-face and small-group interactions in order to understand how they affect the larger patterns and structures of society

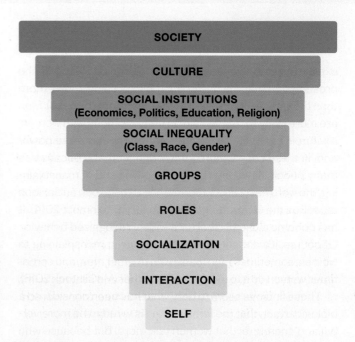

FIGURE 1.2 The Macro-Micro Continuum
Sociology covers a wide range of topics at different levels of analysis.

power and domination in male–female relationships: Are men more powerful than women in our society? If so, how is this power created and maintained in everyday interactions? In her research, DeFrancisco recorded and analyzed heterosexual couples' everyday conversations in their homes. She found some real differences in the conversational strategies of men and women and some surprising results about gender, power, and silence in everyday talk.

One conversation took place in the living room, where a woman was having a difficult time engaging her husband in a discussion about an encounter she had had while shopping. He failed to respond for long stretches of time, sometimes staying quiet for four and even eight seconds at a time and only rarely uttering an "mm-hmm" or an "aahh" to fill the gap. The husband even walked outside twice while the wife was speaking! But she persisted, trying to keep control of the conversation and maintain her right to continue.

DeFrancisco recorded many more conversations between couples and saw this pattern over and over: men using silence to suppress women's talk. DeFrancisco noted that when men withhold what are called "supportive responses" ("mm-hmm," "oh," "a-ha," etc.), they are violating a firmly held rule of conversational structure. Supportive responses help storytellers continue speaking, knowing that they are being heard and understood. Without supportive responses from men, women must work harder to keep a conversation going, which also makes it more likely that they will be silenced by their partner's lack of response. Thus, in her micro-level analysis of conversation, DeFrancisco was able to see how macro-level ("macro" means large) phenomena

IN THE FUTURE
C. Wright Mills and the Sociological Imagination

The "sociological imagination" is a term that seemingly every sociology student encounters. It was first introduced by C. Wright Mills in his 1959 book by the same name, and over time it has become an enduring cornerstone of the discipline. It captures the spirit of inquiry, the quality of mind, and the guiding principles that all sociologists should embrace. Mills was sometimes critical of sociology as a discipline, so he offered himself as a "public intellectual," one who could speak beyond the confines of academia and address some of the most pressing social issues of the time. Mills was convinced that sociology had something to offer everyone, not just academics.

Mills highlighted the distinction between "personal troubles" and "public issues" as "an essential tool of the sociological imagination and a feature of all classic work in social science" (Mills 1959, p. 8). He explained that almost any feature of an individual's daily life can be better understood if this distinction is applied to it. Unemployment, war, marriage, and housing are all experienced as personal troubles, but to be fully understood, they must also be seen as manifestations of long-standing institutions and larger social structures. As Mills pointed out, "In so far as an economy is so arranged that slumps occur, the problem of unemployment becomes incapable of personal solution" (Mills 1959, p. 10). This lesson was driven home again during the Great Recession, which began in 2007. A series of major banks had created securities that bundled a large number of mortgages made to so-called subprime borrowers. When many of these mortgages went into default, it led to an economic chain reaction that culminated in unemployment levels higher than any seen since the Great Depression of the 1930s. For the many millions of people thrown out of work, unemployment was experienced as a personal trouble, but one that could be understood only as a public issue.

In even more fundamental ways, Mills believed that people are shaped by the connections between "the patterns of their own lives and the course of world history" (Mills 1959, p. 4). These connections could influence the most personal features of someone's life, shaping the very kind of people "they are becoming" (p. 4). In her book *Unbearable Weight* (1995), Susan Bordo describes how anorexia came to be recognized as a national mental health problem. In 1973, psychiatrists still considered anorexia quite rare, so why is there so much awareness about eating disorders now? Anorexia and bulimia are experienced in intensely personal ways, and eating disorders are usually explained in purely psychological terms. But Bordo, thinking about them sociologically, argues that cultural factors help create eating disorders. Contemporary culture's obsession with bodies that are "slim, tight, and young" (p. 140) shapes individual psychologies. Eating disorders, then, are symptoms of a troubled culture as well as a troubled individual. This is not to deny that personal and psychological factors are important, but it is a reminder that social and cultural factors create the environment that makes it possible to experience problems like eating disorders in the first place.

Today you may be a student in an introductory sociology class; every year, around 30,000 students will receive bachelor's degrees in sociology (U.S. Department of Education 2017d). Whether or not you end up majoring in sociology, C. Wright Mills wanted everyone to develop and sharpen a sociological imagination. In fact, that is the goal we share in writing this textbook. How might the sociological imagination be useful to you in the future?

Personal Troubles and Public Issues High foreclosure rates in the wake of the recession were both a personal trouble and a public issue.

Levels of Analysis These two views of the New York Public Library represent different levels of analysis in sociology. Microsociology zooms in to focus on individuals, their interactions, and groups in order to understand their contribution to larger social structures. In contrast, macrosociology pulls back to examine large-scale social processes and their effects on individuals and groups.

such as gender and power are manifested in everyday interactions.

Macrosociology approaches the study of society from the opposite direction, by looking at large-scale social structure to determine how it affects the lives of groups and individuals. If we want to stick to the topic of gender inequality, we can find plenty of examples of research projects that take a macro approach; many deal with the workplace. Despite the gains made in recent years, the U.S. labor market is still predominately sex segregated—that is, men and women are concentrated in different occupations. Sociologist Christine Williams found that while women in male-dominated fields experience limits on their advancement, dubbed the "glass ceiling" effect, men in female-dominated occupations experience unusually rapid rates of upward mobility—what she called the "glass escalator" (Williams 1992, 1995, 2013). Here, then, we see a macro approach to the topic of gender and power: Large-scale features of social structure (patterns of occupational sex segregation) create the constraints within which individuals and groups (women and men in the workplace) experience successes or failures in their everyday lives.

As you can see, these two perspectives make different assumptions about how society works: The micro perspective assumes that society's larger structures are shaped through individual interactions, while the macro perspective assumes that society's larger structures shape those individual interactions. It is useful to think of these perspectives as being on a continuum with each other; while some sociologists adhere to radically micro or exclusively macro perspectives, most are somewhere in between. The next part of this chapter explores some specific theoretical traditions within sociology and shows you where each falls along this continuum.

SOCIOLOGY'S FAMILY TREE

Great thinkers have been trying to understand the world and our place in it since the beginning of time. Some have done this by developing **theories**: abstract propositions about how things are as well as how they should be. Sometimes we also refer to theories as "approaches," "schools of thought," "**paradigms**," or "perspectives." Social theories, then, are guiding principles or abstract models that attempt to explain and predict the social world.

As we embark on the discussion of theory, it may be useful to think of sociology as having a "family tree" made up of real people who were living in a particular time and place and who were related along various intertwining lines to other members of the same larger family tree. First, we will examine sociology's early historical roots. Then, as we follow the growth of the discipline, we will identify its major branches and trace the relationships among their offshoots and the other "limbs" that make up the entire family tree. Finally, we will examine some of the newest theoretical approaches and members of the family tree (page 17) and consider the possible future of sociological theory.

Sociology's Roots

The earliest Western social theorists focused on establishing society as an appropriate object of scientific scrutiny, which was itself a revolutionary concept. None of these early theorists were themselves sociologists (since the

---

MACROSOCIOLOGY the level of analysis that studies large-scale social structures in order to determine how they affect the lives of groups and individuals

THEORIES abstract propositions that explain the social world and make predictions about the future

PARADIGM a set of assumptions, theories, and perspectives that makes up a way of understanding social reality

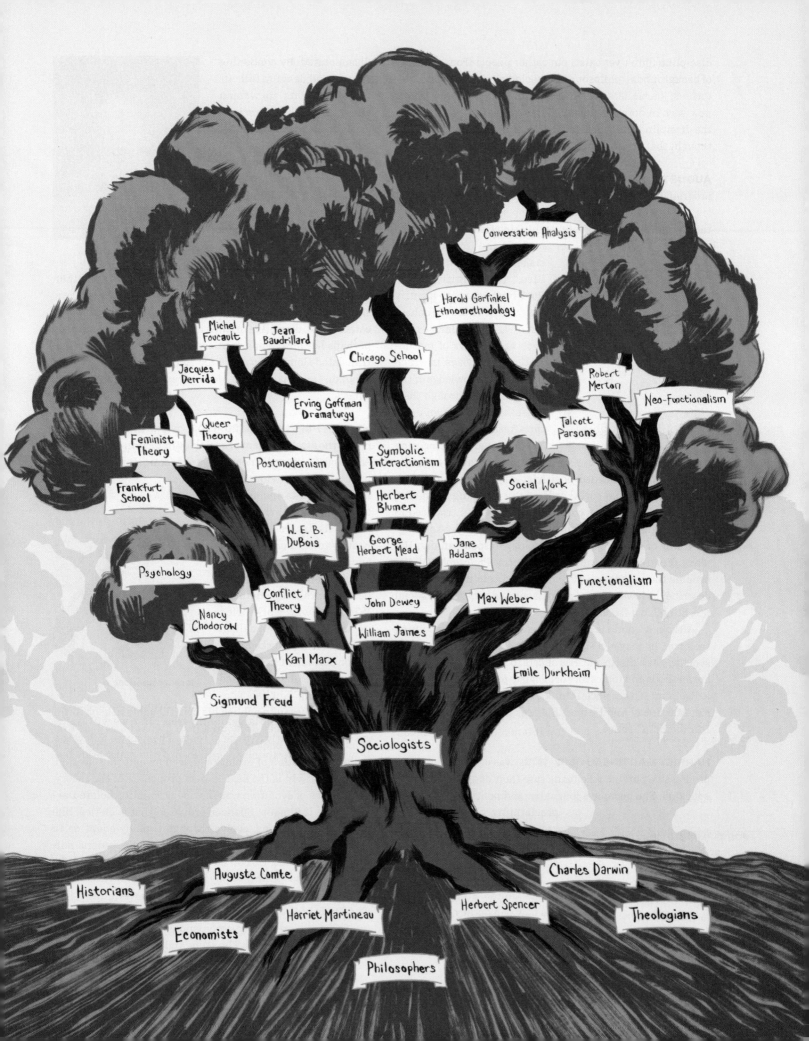

discipline didn't yet exist) but rather people from a variety of backgrounds—philosophers, theologians, economists, historians, journalists—who were trying to look at society in a new way. In doing so, they laid the groundwork not only for the discipline as a whole but also for the different schools of thought that are still shaping sociology today.

AUGUSTE COMTE (1798–1857) was the first to provide a program for the scientific study of society, or a "social physics," as he labeled it. Comte, a French scientist, developed a theory of the progress of human thinking from its early theological and metaphysical stages toward a final "positive," or scientific, stage. **Positivism** seeks to identify laws that describe the behavior of a particular reality, such as the laws of mathematics and physics, in which people gain knowledge of the world directly through their senses. Having grown up in the aftermath of the French Revolution and its lingering political instability, Comte

Auguste Comte

felt that society needed positivist guidance toward both social progress and social order. After studying at an elite science and technology college, where he was introduced to the newly discovered scientific method, he began to imagine a way of applying the methodology to social affairs. His ideas, featured in *Introduction to Positive Philosophy* (1842), became the foundation of a scientific discipline that would describe the laws of social phenomena and help control social life; he called it "sociology."

Although Comte is remembered today mainly for coining the term, he played a significant role in the development of sociology as a discipline. His efforts to distinguish appropriate methods and topics for sociologists provided the kernel of a discipline. Other social thinkers advanced his work: Harriet Martineau and Herbert Spencer in England and Émile Durkheim in France.

HARRIET MARTINEAU (1802–1876) was born in England to progressive parents who made sure their daughter was well educated. She became a journalist and political economist, proclaiming views that were radical for her time: endorsing labor unions, the abolition of slavery, and women's suffrage.

In 1835, Martineau traveled to the United States to judge the new democracy on its own terms rather than by European standards. But she was disappointed: By condoning slavery and denying full citizenship rights to women and blacks, the American experiment was, in her eyes, flawed and hypocritical. She wrote two books describing her observations, *Society in America* (1837) and *Retrospect of Western Travel* (1838), both critical of American leadership and culture. By holding the United States

Harriet Martineau

to its own publicly stated democratic standards, rather than seeing the country from an ethnocentric British perspective, she was a precursor to the naturalistic sociologists who would establish the discipline in America. In 1853, Martineau made perhaps her most important contribution to sociology: She translated Comte's *Introduction to Positive Philosophy* into English, thus making his ideas accessible in England and America.

HERBERT SPENCER (1820–1903) was primarily responsible for the establishment of sociology in Britain and America. Although Spencer did not receive academic training, he grew up in a highly individualistic family and was encouraged to think and learn on his own. His interests leaned heavily toward physical science and, instead of attending college, Spencer chose to become a railway engineer. When railway work dried up, he turned to journalism and eventually worked for a major periodical in London. There he became acquainted with leading English aca-

Herbert Spencer

demics and began to publish his own thoughts in book form.

In 1862, Spencer drew up a list of what he called "first principles" (in a book by that name), and near the top of the list was the notion of evolution driven by natural selection. Charles Darwin is the best-known proponent of the theory, but the idea of evolution was in wide circulation before Darwin made it famous. Spencer proposed that societies, like biological organisms, evolve through time by adapting to changing conditions, with less successful adaptations falling by the wayside. He coined the phrase "survival of the fittest," and his social philosophy is sometimes known as **social Darwinism**. In the late 1800s, Spencer's work, including *The Study of Sociology* (1873) and *The Principles of Sociology* (1897), was virtually synonymous with sociology in the English-speaking world. The scope and volume of his writing

POSITIVISM the theory that sense perceptions are the only valid source of knowledge

SOCIAL DARWINISM the application of the theory of evolution and the notion of "survival of the fittest" to the study of society served to announce sociology as a serious discipline and laid the groundwork for the next generation of theorists, whose observations of large-scale social change would bring a new viewpoint to social theory.

MACROSOCIOLOGICAL THEORY

Theorists in late-nineteenth-century Europe were living during extraordinary times. They were attempting to explain social order, social change, and social inequality while the world around them changed as a result of the Industrial Revolution. At the same time, they were witnessing political upheaval and the birth of democracy brought about by the French and American Revolutions. These were changes on the grandest of scales in the macro order of society. Frequently referred to as classical sociology, the theories that arose during this period reflect the broad subject matter of a sweeping era.

Structural Functionalism

Structural functionalism, or functionalist theory, was the dominant theoretical perspective within sociology well into the mid-twentieth century. New (or neo-) functionalists continue to apply their own vision of the theory to study a wide variety of social phenomena today.

FOUNDER AND KEY CONTRIBUTIONS Émile Durkheim (1858–1917) is the central figure in functionalist theory. He was born into a close-knit and deeply religious Jewish

Émile Durkheim

family who instilled in him a strong sense of morality (not just as an abstract concept but as a concrete influence on social relations) and a strong work ethic. After witnessing the ravages of the Franco-Prussian War (1870–1871), he hoped that applied science could stabilize and revitalize France in the aftermath of its devastating defeat. He did not believe that traditional, abstract moral philosophy was effective in increasing understanding and bringing about social change, so he turned instead to the concrete science of sociology as represented in Comte's work.

In his first major study, *The Division of Labor in Society* (1893), Durkheim stated that **solidarity**, or unity, was present in all types of societies but that different types of societies created different types of social bonds. He suggested that people in a simple agricultural society were bound together by **mechanical solidarity**—that is, on the basis of shared traditions, beliefs, and experiences. In industrial societies, where factory work was becoming increasingly specialized, **organic solidarity** prevailed: People's bonds were based on the tasks they performed, interdependence, and individual rights. Both types of solidarity have interpersonal bonds—just with different qualities.

Durkheim believed that even the most individualistic actions have sociological explanations and set out to establish a scientific methodology for studying these actions. He chose for his case study the most individualistic of actions, suicide, and used statistical data to show that suicides were related to social factors such as religious affiliation, marital status, and employment. Explaining a particular suicide by focusing exclusively on the victim's psychological makeup neglected the impact of social bonds. According to Durkheim in his now-classic study *Suicide* (1897), even the darkest depression has its roots in an individual's connections to the social world, or rather his lack of connection. Durkheim theorized that suicide is one result of **anomie**, a sense of disconnection brought about by the changing conditions of modern life. The more firmly anchored a person is to family, religion, and the workplace, the less anomie he is likely to experience.

In his final major study, *The Elementary Forms of Religious Life* (1912), Durkheim suggested that religion was a powerful source of social solidarity because it reinforced collective bonds and shared moral values. He believed that society could be understood by examining the most basic forms of religion. Durkheim's study of the indigenous peoples of Australia led him to a universal definition of religion: Though religious traditions might differ, any form of religion is unified in its definition of what is considered to be **sacred** and **profane**. Every person who follows a particular set of beliefs and practices will "unite into one single moral community" (Durkheim 1912/1995, p. 44).

Durkheim's attempt to establish sociology as an important, independent academic discipline was enormously successful. He not only made significant contributions to the

STRUCTURAL FUNCTIONALISM a paradigm based on the assumption that society is a unified whole that functions because of the contributions of its separate structures

SOLIDARITY the degree of integration or unity within a particular society; the extent to which individuals feel connected to other members of their group

MECHANICAL SOLIDARITY the type of social bonds present in premodern, agrarian societies, in which shared traditions and beliefs created a sense of social cohesion

ORGANIC SOLIDARITY the type of social bonds present in modern societies, based on difference, interdependence, and individual rights

ANOMIE "normlessness"; term used to describe the alienation and loss of purpose that result from weaker social bonds and an increased pace of change

SACRED the holy, divine, or supernatural

PROFANE the ordinary, mundane, or everyday

existing literature but also demonstrated the effectiveness of using scientific, **empirical** methods to study "social reality," essentially validating Comte's proposal from half a century earlier. Durkheim became the first professor of social science in France, at the University of Bordeaux in 1887, and later won a similar appointment at the Sorbonne in Paris, the very heart of French academic life. Today, Durkheim's eminence in the social sciences is as strong as ever, and his ideas are still applied and extended by contemporary theorists.

ORIGINAL PRINCIPLES The origins of structural functionalism can be traced back to the roots of sociology. Auguste Comte proposed that society itself could and should be studied. Herbert Spencer added the idea that societies are living organisms that grow and evolve, just like other species on the planet. As the discipline of biology might study the physical organism of the human body, the discipline of sociology could study social organisms in the world of human development. Durkheim integrated and advanced these insights into a comprehensive theory for understanding the nature of society.

There are two main principles of functionalism. First, society is conceived as a stable, ordered system made up of interrelated parts, or **structures**. Second, each structure has a function that contributes to the continued stability or equilibrium of the unified whole. Structures are identified as social institutions such as the family, the educational system, politics, the economy, and religion. They meet society's needs by performing different functions, and every function is necessary to maintain social order and stability. Any disorganization or **dysfunction** in a structure leads to change and a new equilibrium; if one structure is transformed, the others must also adjust. For example, if families fail to discipline children, then schools, churches, and the courts must pick up the slack.

It may seem contradictory that a theory concerned with order and stability would emerge in a discipline that arose in a period of rapid social change. But it is important to remember that change had previously occurred much more slowly and that one response to rapid social change is to try to understand what has come before—stability, order, and equilibrium.

OFFSHOOTS Structural functionalism was the dominant theoretical perspective in Europe for much of the early twentieth century. It was exported and updated by American functionalists, who increased its popularity and helped spread its reach well into the 1960s. For example, Talcott Parsons (1902–1979) elaborated on the theory and applied it to modern society, specifying some of the functions that social structures might fulfill in contemporary life. A healthy society must provide a means for people to adapt to their environment; for example, families, schools, and religious institutions work together to socialize children. A functional society includes opportunities

Talcott Parsons

for success—for example, promoting education to help members of society pursue and realize their goals. For society to survive, there must be social cohesion; for example, shared religious and moral values.

Another modern American functionalist, Robert Merton (1910–2003), delineated the theory even further, identifying manifest and latent functions for different social structures. **Manifest functions** are the obvious, intended functions of a social structure, while **latent functions** are the less obvious, perhaps unintended functions. For example, the manifest functions of education are to prepare future members of society by teaching them how to read and write and by instructing them on society's system of norms, values, and laws. However, education has a

Robert Merton

latent function as well, which is to keep kids busy and out of trouble eight hours a day, five days a week, for twelve years (or longer). Do not doubt that this is also an important contribution to social order!

ADVANTAGES AND CRITIQUES One of the great advantages of functionalism is its inclusion of all social institutions. Functionalism attempts to provide a universal social theory, a way of explaining society in one comprehensive model. Part of functionalism's appeal may also lie in its ability to bring order to a potentially disorderly world. Were it not for some of the volcanic social upheavals of recent history—the civil rights, antiwar, and women's liberation movements are not easily explained using this model—functionalist theory might still reign supreme in American sociology. Functionalism, generally preoccupied with stability, takes the position that only dysfunction can create social change. This conservative bias is part of a larger problem with the theory: Functionalism provides little insight into social processes because its model of society is static rather than dynamic. Its focus on the macro level also means that functionalism has less interest in explaining independent human action; there is no apparent approach to the lives of individuals except as part of social institutions.

Functionalism's explanations of social inequality are especially unsatisfying: If poverty, racism, and sexism exist, they must serve a function for society; they must be necessary and inevitable. This view is problematic for many. Sociologist Herbert Gans, in a critical essay (1971), reviewed the functions of poverty for society. The poor, for example, do our "dirty work," filling the menial, low-wage jobs that are necessary to keep society running smoothly but that others refuse to do. The poor provide a market for used and off-price goods and keep thrift stores and social welfare agencies in business. They have symbolic value as well, allowing those higher in the social hierarchy to feel compassion toward the "deserving" poor and to feel threatened by the "undeserving" poor, who are often seen as dangerous social deviants. Ultimately, the circular reasoning that characterizes functionalist thought turns out to be its biggest problem: The mere persistence of an institution should not be seen as an adequate explanation for its existence.

Conflict Theory

Conflict theory is the second major school of thought in sociology. Like structural functionalism, it's a macro-level approach to understanding social life that dates to mid-nineteenth-century Europe. As conflict theory developed, however, its emphasis on **social inequality** as the basic characteristic of society helped answer some of the critiques of structural functionalism.

FOUNDER AND KEY CONTRIBUTIONS The work of Karl Marx (1818–1883), a German political economist, was the inspiration for conflict theory, so the terms "conflict theory" and "Marxism" are sometimes used interchangeably in the social sciences. Marx's ideas have become better known to the world as the basis for communism, a political system some countries claim to have adopted (Cuba and North Korea, for example), though these systems are actually totalitarian dictatorships; they bear no resemblance to Marx's ideal society. This misunderstanding has led many to a narrow

Karl Marx

belief that Marx was nothing more than a misguided agitator who helped cause more than a century of political turmoil. It is important to recognize that Marx would not have supported the ways political leaders used his ideas decades later. Sociologists have found that Marx's theory continues to provide a powerful tool for understanding social phenomena. The idea that conflict between social groups is central to the workings of society and serves as the engine of social change is one of the most vital perspectives in sociology today.

Marx grew up in a modernizing, industrializing, yet politically and religiously conservative monarchy; this, plus the fact that his was a restless, argumentative personality, accounts in great part for his social theory. For most of his life, he led an economically fragile existence. He managed to maintain a tenuous middle-class lifestyle, but only with financial support from his close friend and chief intellectual collaborator Friedrich Engels, who studied the conditions of the English working class. Marx's own circumstances may have sparked his interest in social inequality, or the uneven and often unfair distribution of resources (in this case, wealth) in society, but he never experienced firsthand the particular burdens and difficulties of the working class.

The Industrial Revolution was a time of rapid social change, when large numbers of people were moving from an agricultural life in rural areas to manufacturing jobs in urban areas. Technological advances and a wage-based economy promised an age of prosperity and abundance, but they created new kinds of poverty, crime, and disease. Marx believed that most of those problems were a result of capitalism, the emerging economic system based on the private for-profit operation of industry. He proposed a radical alternative to the inherent inequalities of this system in the *Manifesto of the Communist Party* (1848), perhaps his most famous book.

In industrial society, the forces of capitalism were creating distinct social and economic classes, exacerbating the disparities between the wealthy and the poor. Marx felt that this would inevitably lead to class struggle between those who owned the **means of production** (anything that could create more wealth: money, property, factories, other types of businesses) and those who worked for them. He argued that the most important factor in social life was whether someone was a worker, and thus a member of the **proletariat**, or an

CONFLICT THEORY a paradigm that sees social conflict as the basis of society and social change and that emphasizes a materialist view of society, a critical view of the status quo, and a dynamic model of historical change

SOCIAL INEQUALITY the unequal distribution of wealth, power, or prestige among members of a society

MEANS OF PRODUCTION anything that can create wealth: money, property, factories, and other types of businesses, and the infrastructure necessary to run them

PROLETARIAT workers; those who have no means of production of their own and so are reduced to selling their labor power in order to live

GLOBAL PERSPECTIVE
Eurocentrism and Sociological Theory

You might get the impression from this chapter that the major sociological theorists were all either European or American. In fact, some ideas central to sociological theory were proposed in Asia, Africa, and the Middle East centuries before Marx, Weber, and Durkheim were even born, but we give these Western thinkers all the credit. Why?

Both the social world and social theory are often **Eurocentric**: They tend to privilege Europe and the West over other cultures. This means that hierarchies of global power, in which superpowers such as the United States and former colonial rulers such as Britain and France dominate, are replicated in academic disciplines like sociology. Scholars who work against inequality and exploitation should note this distressing irony.

EUROCENTRIC the tendency to favor European or Western histories, cultures, and values over those of non-Western societies

One influential non-Western thinker was Ibn Khaldun (1332–1406), an Arab Muslim philosopher and politician who lived in fourteenth-century North Africa. His coining of the term *as sabiyah*, or "social cohesion," precedes Durkheim's work on the same subject by more than 500 years, and his argument that larger social and historical forces shape individual lives predates Mills's insight about sociology as "the intersection of biography and history" by almost 600 years! Yet Khaldun is rarely credited for proposing sociology as a discipline—*ilm alumran*, he called it, or "the science of civilization." This honor is reserved for French scholar Auguste Comte, working centuries later in the West.

Also overlooked in conventional histories of sociology are Indian scholar Benoy Sarkar (1887–1949), Filipino activist and poet José Rizal (1861–1896), and Japanese folklorist Kunio Yanagita (1875–1962)—all of whom applied sociological insights to the problems of their nations. Sarkar explored India's religious divisions, Rizal analyzed the Philippines' fight for independence from Spain, and Yanagita used qualitative methods to explore Japan's culture and its long-standing isolationism. They have received virtually no notice for their achievements outside their own countries (Alatas and Sinha 2001).

Ibn Khaldun

Filipino sociologist Clarence Batan (2004) argues that Western theorists like Marx, Weber, and Durkheim may inspire non-Western scholars but that their theories arose in response to specific social problems that were particular to Western societies. Non-Western societies face different issues, including the legacy of colonialism imposed by the Western countries from which those classical sociological theories sprang. Batan calls for sociologists in non-Western countries to respond to the needs of their societies by developing new theoretical frameworks that take postcolonial realities into account. Batan himself, along with other contemporary non-Western sociologists, works toward this goal every day in his research and teaching. Shouldn't your sociology professors do the same?

owner, and thus a member of the **bourgeoisie**. Everything of value in society resulted from human labor, which was the proletariat's most valuable asset. Yet they suffered from what Marx called **alienation** because they were unable to directly benefit from the fruits of their own labor. Workers were paid wages, but it was the factory owners who grew rich as a result of their toil.

The powerful few in the bourgeoisie were not only wealthy but also enjoyed social privilege and power. They were able to protect their interests, preserve their positions, and pass along their advantages to their heirs. The proletariat were often so absorbed in making a living that they were less apt to protest the conditions that led to their oppression. But eventually, Marx believed, the oppression would become unbearable, and the proletariat would rise up against the bourgeoisie, abolishing capitalism for good. He envisioned in capitalism's place a classless society with no private ownership in which each person contributed to and benefited from the public good. Freed from oppressive conditions, individuals would then be able to pursue higher interests such as art and education and eventually live in a more egalitarian, utopian society. But in order to achieve such a state, the oppressed must first recognize how the current system worked against them.

In 1849, Marx withdrew from political activity in order

to concentrate on writing *Das Kapital* (edited by Engels and published in 1890). The multivolume work provided a thorough exposition of his program for social change, which later became the foundation of political systems such as communism and socialism. Because Marx held such radical ideas, his ideas were not immediately embraced by sociologists in general. It was not until the 1960s when conflict theory became a dominant perspective that Marx was truly received as a giant of sociology.

ORIGINAL PRINCIPLES Conflict theory proposes that conflict and tension are basic facts of social life and suggests that people have disagreements over goals and values and are involved in struggles over both resources and power. The theory thus focuses on the processes of dominance, competition, upheaval, and social change.

Conflict theory takes a materialist view of society (focused on labor practices and economic reality) and extends it to other social inequalities. Marx maintained that economic productivity is related to other processes in society, including political and intellectual life. The wealthy and powerful bourgeoisie control major social institutions, reinforcing the class structure so that the state, education, religion, and even the family are organized to represent their interests. Conflict theory takes a critical stance toward existing social arrangements and attempts to expose their inner workings.

Because the ideology, or belief system, that permeates society arises from the values of the ruling class, beliefs that seem to be widely held are actually a kind of justification that helps rationalize and explain the status quo. Most people readily accept the prevailing ideology, despite its failure to represent the reality of their lives. Marx referred to this acceptance as **false consciousness**, a denial of the truth that allows for the perpetuation of the inequalities inherent in the class structure. For example, he is often quoted as saying, "Religion is the opiate of the masses." This is not a criticism of religion so much as a criticism of the use of religion to create false consciousness in the working class. Encouraged in their piety, the proletariat focus on the happiness promised in the afterlife rather than on deprivations suffered in this world. Indeed, heaven is seen as a reward for patiently suffering those deprivations. How does this serve the interests of the ruling class? By keeping the working class from demanding better conditions in this life.

Conflict theory sees the transformation of society over time as inevitable. Marx argued that the only way to change the status quo is for the masses to attain **class consciousness**, or revolutionary consciousness. This can happen only when people recognize how society works and challenge those in power. He believed that social change would occur when there was enough tension and conflict.

OFFSHOOTS Marx's work has been reinterpreted and applied in various ways, and conflict theory has evolved within the greater intellectual community. Despite Marx's single-minded focus on economic exploitation and transformation, his ideas have helped inspire theorists interested in all forms of power and inequality.

One of the most widely adopted forms of modern Marxism is called **critical theory** (also sometimes referred to as the Frankfurt School or neo-Marxism). From the 1930s to the 1960s, critical theory was arguably at the cutting edge of social theory. Critical theorists were among the first to see the importance of mass communications and popular culture as powerful ideological tools in capitalist societies. They coined the term "culture industries" to refer to these increasingly important social institutions, which came to dominate and permeate social life (Adorno and Horkheimer 1979). They also criticized the growing consumerism associated with the spread of capitalism, believing that it could ultimately lead to a decline in personal freedom and the decay of democracy (Marcuse 1964, 1991). Critical theory influenced several generations of radical thinkers throughout Europe and the United States, inspiring the cultural studies movement and the postmodernists, who were considered the cutting edge of social theory in the 1980s and '90s (Habermas 1984, 1987).

Other modern perspectives have taken conflict theory's insights on economic inequality and adapted them to the study of contemporary inequalities of race, gender, and sexuality (Crenshaw et al. 1996; Matsuda et al. 1993). Beginning with the pioneering work of W.E.B. DuBois, sociology started to focus on inequalities of race and ethnicity, inspiring important studies about the causes and consequences of prejudice and discrimination and helping propel momentous social changes resulting from the civil rights movement of the 1960s. **Critical race theory**, which emerged out of legal scholarship in the 1970s and '80s, is concerned with the relationship among race, racism, and power. This controversial theory argues that racism is deeply embedded in American institutions, including our laws. This institutional racism serves to both perpetuate white privilege and marginalize people of color. Adherents of critical race theory are dedicated to not just studying race—and how it intersects with

BOURGEOISIE owners; the class of modern capitalists who own the means of production and employ wage laborers

ALIENATION the sense of dissatisfaction the modern worker feels as a result of producing goods that are owned and controlled by someone else

FALSE CONSCIOUSNESS a denial of the truth on the part of the oppressed when they fail to recognize that the interests of the ruling class are embedded in the dominant ideology

CLASS CONSCIOUSNESS the recognition of social inequality on the part of the oppressed, leading to revolutionary action

CRITICAL THEORY a contemporary form of conflict theory that criticizes many different systems and ideologies of domination and oppression

CRITICAL RACE THEORY the study of the relationship among race, racism, and power

bell hooks Feminist theorists such as bell hooks consider the intersection of gender and race.

other identities such as sex and class—but also actively working to end racial oppression (Bonilla-Silva 2015; Delgado and Stefancic 2012). We will return to critical race theory in more detail in Chapter 8.

Feminist theory developed alongside the twentieth-century women's rights movement. By applying assumptions about gender inequality to various social institutions—the family, education, the economy, or the media—feminist theory allows for a new way of understanding those institutions and the changing role of gender in contemporary society.

Theorists such as Judith Butler (1999), bell hooks (2003), and Catharine MacKinnon (2005) link gender with inequality in other social hierarchies—race and ethnicity, class, and sexual orientation—and argue that gender and power are inextricably intertwined in our society.

The gay and lesbian rights movement that gained momentum in the 1970s and '80s inspired a new set of theoretical and conceptual tools for social scientists: **queer theory**. Queer theory proposes that categories of sexuality—homo, hetero, bi, trans—should be viewed as "social constructs" (Seidman 2003). It asserts that no sexual category is fundamentally deviant or normal; we create such definitions, so we can change them as well. Indeed, some theorists, such as Marjorie Garber (1997), argue that strict categories themselves are no longer relevant and that more fluid notions of identity should replace conventional dichotomies such as gay/straight. We will return to both feminist and queer theories in more detail in Chapter 9.

FEMINIST THEORY a theoretical approach that looks at gender inequities in society and the way that gender structures the social world

QUEER THEORY social theory about gender and sexual identity; emphasizes the importance of difference and rejects ideas of innate identities or restrictive categories

PRAXIS the application of theory to practical action in an effort to improve aspects of society

ADVANTAGES AND CRITIQUES One of Karl Marx's great contributions to the social sciences is the principle of **praxis**, or practical action: Intellectuals should act on what they believe. Marx wished not only to describe the world but also to change it. Indeed, Marxist ideas have been important in achieving change through many twentieth-century social movements, including civil rights, antiwar, women's rights, gay rights, animal rights, environmentalism, and multiculturalism. If these groups had not protested the status quo, we might never have addressed some of the century's social problems. Conflict theory is useful in understanding not only macro-level social issues (such as systematic discrimination against minority groups) but also micro-level personal interactions (such as those between bosses and employees).

Conflict theory stands in sharp contrast to structural functionalism. Conflict theory argues that a social arrangement's existence does not mean that it's beneficial; it may merely represent the interests of those in power. The theory challenges the status quo and emphasizes the need for social upheaval. In focusing on tension and conflict, however, conflict theory can often ignore those parts of society that are truly orderly, stable, and enduring. Although society certainly has its share of disagreements, there are also shared values and common beliefs that hold it together. Conflict theory can be criticized for overlooking these less controversial dimensions of social reality.

Weberian Theory

Max Weber (1864–1920) was another important European macrosociological theorist during the Industrial Revolution. His work forms another large branch of sociology's family tree, and his ideas continue to inspire in their current application, yet he is not always included among the three *major* branches of the discipline. Weberian theory is not a minor branch of sociology, nor is it considered merely an offshoot of one of the other major branches of the tree. It draws from a background shared by the other macro theorists but forms its own independent limb.

Max Weber

Weber grew up in the German city of Berlin. Both his parents were Protestants and descendants of victims of religious persecution. Weber, though not religious himself, exhibited the relentless work ethic held in high regard by devout Protestants. Although he was sickly and withdrawn as a young man, work served as a way for him to rebel against his father and the leisure classes in general. He studied law and history and worked as a lawyer while establishing his credentials for a university teaching position.

Weber rapidly established himself as a prominent member of the German intellectual scene. He might have continued in this manner had it not been for a disastrous visit from his parents in 1897, during which Weber fought bitterly with his father and threw him out of the house. When his father died a month later, Weber suffered a nervous breakdown that left him unable to work for several years. The strain of these events and years of incessant labor had apparently caught up with him. He eventually recovered and resumed his intense scholarship, but the breakdown left Weber disillusioned with the strict academic regimen.

Weber subsequently expressed a pessimistic view of social forces, such as the work ethic, that shaped modern life. Like other social theorists of his time, Weber was interested in the shift from a more traditional society to a modern industrial one. Perhaps his most overriding concern was with the process of **rationalization**, or the application of economic logic to all spheres of human activity. In *Economy and Society* (1921), Weber proposed that modern industrialized societies were characterized by efficient, goal-oriented, rule-governed **bureaucracies**. He believed that individual behavior was increasingly driven by such bureaucratic goals, which had become more important motivational factors than traditions, values, or emotions. Weber's classic sociological discussion of the origins of the capitalist system, *The Protestant Ethic and the Spirit of Capitalism* (1904), concluded with the image of people trapped by their industrious way of life in what he called an **iron cage** of bureaucratic rules. He believed that contemporary life was filled with disenchantment (similar to Durkheim's concept of anomie and Marx's concept of alienation) as the inevitable result of the dehumanizing features of the bureaucracies that dominated the modern social landscape.

Weber's insights into the nature of society continue to inspire sociologists today. For instance, George Ritzer (1996, 2013) has applied Weber's theories of bureaucracy and rationalization to the fast-food industry and has warned about "McDonaldization" creeping into other aspects of contemporary life, such as education and law enforcement. More recently, Ritzer has applied Weberian theory to the forces of globalization, demonstrating how the principles of McDonaldization have been exported and adopted across the globe (Ritzer and Ryan 2007).

The key concepts we have touched on here will be expanded as we apply Weberian theory to a variety of topics in upcoming chapters of the text. In addition to making some of the most important contributions to theory within the discipline, Weber was also influential in improving research methods by suggesting that researchers avoid imposing their own opinions on their scientific analysis; we'll examine these ideas more closely in Chapter 2.

Weber's work served as a bridge between early social theory, which focused primarily on the macro level of society, and subsequent theories that focused more intently on the micro level. He was interested in how individual motivation led to certain social actions and how those actions helped shape society as a whole. Unlike Marx and Durkheim, Weber was cautious about attributing any reality to social institutions or forces independent of individual action and meaningful thought. He invoked the German term **verstehen** ("empathic understanding") to describe how a social scientist should study human action: that is, with a kind of scientific empathy for actors' experiences, intentions, and actions. In this way, Weber helped lay the groundwork for the third grand theory in sociology.

MICROSOCIOLOGICAL THEORY

As the twentieth century dawned and the careers of the macro theorists such as Durkheim, Marx, and Weber matured, political, cultural, and academic power began to shift from Europe. As manifested by the waves of emigrants leaving the Old World for the New World, America was seen as the land of opportunity, both material and intellectual. So it was in the twentieth century, and increasingly in the United States, that the discipline of sociology continued to develop and the ideas of its third major school of thought began to coalesce.

Symbolic Interactionism

Sociology's third grand theory, **symbolic interactionism** (or interactionist theory), proved its greatest influence through much of the 1900s. It is America's unique contribution to the discipline and an answer to many of the criticisms of other paradigms. Symbolic interactionism helps us explain both our individual personalities and the ways in which we are all linked together; it allows us

RATIONALIZATION the application of economic logic to human activity; the use of formal rules and regulations in order to maximize efficiency without consideration of subjective or individual concerns

BUREAUCRACIES secondary groups designed to perform tasks efficiently, characterized by specialization, technical competence, hierarchy, written rules, impersonality, and formal written communication

IRON CAGE Max Weber's pessimistic description of modern life, in which we are caught in bureaucratic structures that control our lives through rigid rules and rationalization

VERSTEHEN "empathic understanding"; Weber's term to describe good social research, which tries to understand the meanings that individuals attach to various aspects of social reality

SYMBOLIC INTERACTIONISM a paradigm that sees interaction and meaning as central to society and assumes that meanings are not inherent but are created through interaction

ON THE JOB
Famous Sociology Majors

Sociology continues to be a popular major at colleges and universities in the United States and in countries such as Canada, the United Kingdom, and Australia. According to the Department of Education (2017d), over a half million bachelor of arts degrees in sociology were awarded in the United States between 1990 and 2015. Clearly, there are many reasons students are enthusiastic about the subject. What may be less clear is how to turn this passion into a paycheck. Students considering majoring in the subject often ask, "What can I do with a degree in sociology?" Their parents may be asking the same question.

Students interested in academic careers can pursue graduate degrees and become professors and researchers—real practicing sociologists. But the vast majority of sociology majors will not necessarily become sociologists with a capital S. Their studies have prepared them to be valuable, accomplished participants in a variety of fields, including law and government, business administration, social welfare, public health, education, counseling and human resources, advertising and marketing, public relations and the media, and the nonprofit sector. A major in sociology, in other words, can lead almost anywhere. And while the roster of former sociology majors contains names both well known and unsung, from President Ronald Reagan and civil rights leader Martin Luther King Jr. to the public defender giving legal aid to low-income clients and the health-care professional bringing wellness programs into large corporations, we will focus here on three important Americans you may not have associated with sociology.

The first individual may be the least likely to be identified as a sociology major, since his career was centered in the arts. Saul Bellow (1915–2005) was one of the most acclaimed

Saul Bellow

Michelle Obama

Kal Penn

American novelists of the twentieth century; his books include *Seize the Day*, *Herzog*, and *Humboldt's Gift*. He won numerous literary awards, including the National Book Award (three times), the Pulitzer Prize, and the Nobel Prize for Literature. He was also a successful playwright and journalist and taught at several universities. Bellow was born in Montreal to Jewish parents, Russian émigrés who later settled in

---

to understand the processes by which social order and social change are constructed. As a theoretical perspective, it is vital, versatile, and still evolving.

FOUNDER AND KEY CONTRIBUTIONS Symbolic interactionism is derived largely from the teachings of George Herbert Mead (1863–1931). But there were many others involved in the development of this particular school of thought, and it is worthwhile to examine the social context in which they lived and worked.

At the start of the twentieth century, sociology was still something of an import from the European intellectual scene, and American practitioners had just begun developing their own ideas regarding the nature and workings of society. The University of Chicago in the 1920s provided a stimulating intellectual setting for a handful of academics who built on each other's work and advanced what became known as the first new major branch within the discipline. Since there were so few social theorists in the country, the head of

George Herbert Mead

the slums of Chicago while he was still a child. He began his undergraduate studies in English at the University of Chicago but left within two years after being told by the department chair that no Jew could really grasp English literature. He then enrolled at Northwestern University, graduating in 1937 with honors in sociology. Literary critics have noted that Bellow's background in sociology, as well as his own personal history, may have influenced both the style and subject of his work. Many of the great themes of American social life appear in his novels: culture, power, wealth and poverty, war, religion, urban life, gender relations, and, above all, the social contract that keeps us together in the face of forces that threaten to tear us apart.

Our next profile is of Michelle Robinson Obama (b. 1964), the first African American First Lady of the United States. Michelle Obama has become one of the most recognizable and widely admired sociology majors in the world, using her role as First Lady to fight childhood obesity, help working mothers and military families, and encourage public service. Born and raised in working-class Chicago, she can trace her ancestry to slaves on both sides of her family tree. Her father worked for the city's water department but saw both of his children graduate from Princeton University and go on to successful professional careers. After obtaining her BA in sociology—her senior thesis dealt with alienation experienced by African American students in an Ivy League institution—she earned her law degree at Harvard, worked at a prestigious law firm in Chicago, and then served in the mayor's office. In addition to law and politics, her choice of majors was a critical stepping-stone on her way to success.

Our last sociology major is Kalpen Modi (b. 1977), who served as an associate director with the White House Office of Public Engagement (OPE) in 2009. In this role, he acted as a liaison to young Americans, the arts, and Asian American and Pacific Islander communities. He also served on the President's Committee on the Arts and Humanities. This may come as a surprise to those who know him as the actor Kal Penn, most famous for his role as the wisecracking, easy-going stoner Kumar in the *Harold and Kumar* film series or as Kevin on *How I Met Your Mother*. As an actor, Penn has been critical of the racial and ethnic stereotypes often associated with playing a person of South Asian descent. At one point, he nearly turned down a recurring role as a terrorist on the TV drama *24* because he didn't want to reinforce the negative "connection between media images and people's thought processes" (Yuan 2007). While it might be easy to make similar claims against *Harold and Kumar Go to White Castle*, one of his co-stars defended the film by arguing that it "approached the level of sociology, albeit scatological, sexually obsessed sociology," as "it probed questions of ethnic identity, conformism and family expectations versus personal satisfaction" (Garvin 2008, p. M1). Penn continues to juggle politics with acting, reflecting a deep commitment to sociological ideals and a desire to use his influence to help build more positive media portrayals of minorities. In addition to playing the White House press secretary in *Designated Survivor*, Penn created and stars in *Sunnyside*, a new TV show that focuses on a motley crew of new immigrants learning what it means to be American.

Regardless of whether you go any further in this discipline—or if you end up working in politics, the arts, or public service—the most important thing to take away from an introductory sociology class is a sociological perspective. Sociology promises a new way of looking at, thinking about, and taking action in the world around us, which will serve you well no matter where you find yourself in the future.

the department, Albion Small, a philosopher by training, recruited professors from various eastern colleges who had often studied other disciplines such as theology and psychology. The fledgling sociology department grew to include such influential members as Robert Park, W. I. Thomas, Charles Horton Cooley, and later George Herbert Mead and Herbert Blumer. This group, the theories they developed together, and the way they went about studying the social world are frequently referred to (either individually or collectively) as the **Chicago School** of sociology.

Chicago was in many ways a frontier city in the early twentieth century. Rapidly transformed by industrialization, immigration, and ethnic diversity, Chicago became a unique laboratory in which to practice a new type of sociology that differed both theoretically and methodologically from the European models. Instead of doing comparative and historical work like the macro theorists before them, the members of the Chicago School went out into the city to conduct interviews and collect observational data. Their studies were particularly inspired by Max Weber's concept of *verstehen* as the proper attitude to adopt in the field. Their focus was on the micro level of everyday interactions (such as race relations in urban neighborhoods) as the

> **CHICAGO SCHOOL** a type of sociology practiced at the University of Chicago in the 1920s and 1930s that centered on urban settings and field research methods

building blocks of larger social phenomena (such as racial inequality).

The new school of thought was strongly influenced by a philosophical perspective called **pragmatism**, developed largely by William James and John Dewey, which was gaining acceptance among American social theorists in the early 1900s. To James, pragmatism meant seeking the truth of an idea by evaluating its usefulness in everyday life; in other words, if it works, it's true! He thought that living in the world involved making practical adaptations to whatever we encountered; if those adaptations made our lives run more smoothly, then the ideas behind them must be both useful and true. James's ideas inspired educational psychologist and philosopher John Dewey, who also grappled with pragmatism's main questions: How do we adapt to our environments? How do we acquire the knowledge that allows us to act in our everyday lives? Unlike the social Darwinists, pragmatists implied that the process of adaptation is essentially immediate and that it involves conscious thought. George Herbert Mead would be the one who eventually pulled these ideas (and others, too) together into a theory meant to address questions about the relationship between thought and action, the individual and society.

> **PRAGMATISM** a perspective that assumes organisms (including humans) make practical adaptations to their environments; humans do this through cognition, interpretation, and interaction

Mead came from a progressive family and grew up in the Midwest and Northeast during the late 1800s. Mead attended college at Oberlin and Harvard and did his graduate studies in psychology at the universities of Leipzig and Berlin in Germany. Before he became a full-time professor of psychology at the University of Michigan and later the University of Chicago, Mead waited tables and did railroad surveying and construction work. He was also a tutor to William James's family in Cambridge, Massachusetts; since his later theories were influenced by James, we can only wonder exactly who was tutoring whom in this arrangement! Mead's background and training uniquely positioned him to bridge the gap between sociology and psychology and to address the links between the individual and society.

Mead proposed that both human development and the meanings we assign to everyday objects and events are fundamentally social processes; they require the interaction of multiple individuals. And what is crucial to the development of self and society is language, the means by which we communicate with one another. For Mead, there is no mind without language, and language itself is a product of social interactions (1934, pp. 191–192). According to Mead, the most important human behaviors consist of linguistic "gestures," such as words and facial expressions. People develop the ability to engage in conversation using these gestures; further, both society and individual selves are constructed through this kind of symbolic communication. Mead argued that we use language to "name ourselves, think about ourselves, talk to ourselves, and feel proud or ashamed of ourselves" and that "we can act toward ourselves in all the ways we can act toward others" (Hewitt 2000, p. 10). He was curious about how the mind develops but did not believe that it develops separately from its social environment. For Mead, then, society and self are created through communicative acts such as speech and gestures; the individual personality is shaped by society, and vice versa.

Herbert Blumer (1900–1987), a graduate student and later a professor at the University of Chicago, was closely associated with Mead and was largely credited with continuing Mead's life's work. Blumer appealed for researchers to get "down and dirty" with the dynamics of social life. He also published a clear and compelling series of works based on Mead's fundamental ideas. After Mead's death in 1931, Blumer gave Mead's theory the name it now goes by: symbolic interactionism. Thus, Mead and Blumer became the somewhat unwitting founders of a much larger theoretical perspective. Blumer's long career at the University

Herbert Blumer

of Chicago and later at the University of California, Berkeley, ensured the training of many future scholars and secured the inclusion of symbolic interactionism as one of the major schools of thought within the discipline.

Despite its geographical location in a city full of real-world inequality (or perhaps because of it), the Chicago School of sociology had very few women or people of color among its membership. Take W.E.B. DuBois and Jane Addams, for example: These two scholars were neither students nor faculty members at the University of Chicago, although both are often associated with Chicago School perspectives, values, and methods. Both led the way for other minorities and women to become influential scholars in the discipline of sociology.

William Edward Burghardt (W.E.B.) DuBois (1868–1963) was a notable pioneer in the study of race relations as a professor of sociology at Atlanta University and one of the most influential African American leaders of his time. After becoming the first African American to earn a PhD from Harvard University, DuBois did groundbreaking research on the history of the slave trade, post–Civil War Reconstruction, the problems of urban ghetto life, and the nature of

W.E.B. DuBois

black American society. DuBois was so brilliant and prolific that it is often said that all subsequent studies of race and racial inequality in America depend to some degree on his work. Throughout his life, DuBois was involved in various forms of social activism. He was an indispensable forerunner in the civil rights movement; among his many civic and political achievements, DuBois was a founding member, in 1909, of the National Association for the Advancement of Colored People (NAACP), an organization committed to the cause of ending racism and racial injustice. Because of his antiracist, antipoverty, and antiwar activism, DuBois was targeted by FBI Director J. Edgar Hoover and Senator Joseph McCarthy as a communist. However, he did not become a member of the Communist Party until he was ninety-three years old, and then only did so as a form of political protest against the persecution of its members by the U.S. government. Eventually, DuBois became disillusioned by the persistent injustices of American society and emigrated to Ghana, where he died at ninety-five, one year before the historic Civil Rights Act of 1964 was signed into law.

Jane Addams (1860–1935) was another pioneer in the field of sociology whose numerous accomplishments range from the halls of academia to the forefront of social activism. Though she never officially joined the faculty because she feared it would curtail her political activism, Addams did teach extension courses at the University of Chicago and was among a handful of women teaching in American universities at the time. Though not a mother herself, Addams believed that women have a special kind of responsibility for solving social problems because they are trained to care for others. She was one of the first proponents of applied sociology—addressing the most pressing problems of her day through hands-on work with the people and places that were the subject of her research. This practical approach is perhaps best demonstrated by Hull House, the Chicago community center she established in 1889 to offer shelter, medical care, legal advice, training, and education to new immigrants, single mothers, and the poor. As a result of her commitment to delivering support and services where they were most needed, Addams is often considered the founder of what is now a separate field outside the discipline: social work. Addams also helped found two important organizations that continue to fight for freedom and equality today: the American Civil Liberties Union (ACLU) and, along with W.E.B. DuBois, the NAACP. She served as the president of the Women's International League for Peace and Freedom and in 1931 became the first American woman to receive the Nobel Peace Prize.

Jane Addams

ORIGINAL PRINCIPLES For symbolic interactionists, society is produced and reproduced through our interactions with each other by means of language and our interpretations of that language. Symbolic interactionism sees face-to-face interaction as the building block of everything else in society, because it is through interaction that we create a meaningful social reality.

Here are the three basic tenets of symbolic interactionism, as laid out by Blumer (1969, p. 2). First, *we act toward things on the basis of their meanings*. For example, a tree can provide a shady place to rest, or it can be an obstacle to building a road or home; each of these meanings suggests a different set of actions. This is as true for physical objects like trees as it is for people (like mothers or cops), institutions (church or school), beliefs (honesty or equality), or any social activity. Second, *meanings are not inherent; rather, they are negotiated through interaction with others*. That is, whether the tree is an obstacle or an oasis is not an intrinsic quality of the tree itself but rather something that people must figure out among themselves. The same tree can mean one thing to one person and something else to another. And third, *meanings can change or be modified through interaction*. For example, the contractor who sees the tree as an obstacle might be persuaded to spare it by the neighbor who appreciates its shade. Now the tree means the same thing to both of them: It is something to protect and build around rather than to condemn and bulldoze.

Symbolic interactionism proposes that social facts exist only because we create and re-create them through our interactions; this gives the theory wide explanatory power and a versatility that allows it to address any sociological issue. Although symbolic interactionism is focused on how self and society develop through interaction with others, it is useful in explaining and analyzing a wide variety of specific social issues, from inequalities of race and gender to the group dynamics of families or co-workers.

OFFSHOOTS Symbolic interactionism opened the door for innovative sociologists who focused on social acts (such as face-to-face interaction) rather than social facts (such as vast bureaucratic institutions). They were able to extend the field in a variety of ways, allowing new perspectives to come under the umbrella of symbolic interactionism.

Erving Goffman (1922–1982) furthered symbolic interactionist conceptions of the self in a seemingly radical way, indicating that the self is essentially "on loan" to us from society; it is created through interaction with others and hence ever changing within various social contexts. For example,

Erving Goffman

you may want to make a different kind of impression on a first date than you do on a job interview or when you face an opponent in a game of poker. Goffman used the theatrical metaphor of **dramaturgy** to describe the ways in which we engage in a strategic presentation of ourselves to others. In this way, he elaborated on Mead's ideas in a specific fashion, utilizing a wide range of data to help support his arguments.

Harold Garfinkel, the founder of **ethnomethodology** (the study of "folk methods," or everyday analysis of interaction), maintains that as members of society we must acquire the necessary knowledge and skills to act practically in our everyday lives (Garfinkel 1967). He argues that much of this knowledge remains in the background, "seen but unnoticed," and that we assume that others have the same knowledge we do when we interact with them. These assumptions allow us to make meaning out of even seemingly troublesome or ambiguous events; but such shared understandings can also be quite precarious, and there is a good deal of work required to sustain them, even as we are unaware that we are doing so.

Conversation analysis, pioneered by sociologists at the University of California, Los Angeles, is also related to symbolic interactionism. It is based on the ethnomethodological idea that as everyday actors we are constantly analyzing and giving meaning to our social world (Clayman 2002; Heritage and Clayman 2010; Schegloff 1986, 1999, 2007). Conversation analysts are convinced that the best place to look for the social processes of meaning production is in naturally occurring conversation and that the best way to get at the meanings an everyday actor gives to the things others say and do is to look closely at how they respond. Conversation analysts therefore use highly technical methods to scrutinize each conversational turn closely, operating on the assumption that any larger social phenomenon is constructed step-by-step through interaction.

ADVANTAGES AND CRITIQUES As society changes, so must the discipline that studies it, and symbolic interactionism has invigorated sociology in ways that are linked to the past and looking toward the future. The founding of symbolic interactionism provided a new and different way of looking at the world. It is "the only perspective that assumes an active, expressive model of the human actor and that treats the individual and the social at the same level of analysis" (O'Brien and Kollock 1997, p. 39). Therein lies much of its power and its appeal.

As a new school of thought focusing on the micro level of

DRAMATURGY an approach pioneered by Erving Goffman in which social life is analyzed in terms of its similarities to theatrical performance

ETHNOMETHODOLOGY the study of "folk methods" and background knowledge that sustain a shared sense of reality in everyday interactions

CONVERSATION ANALYSIS a sociological approach that looks at how we create meaning in naturally occurring conversation, often by taping conversations and examining their transcripts

---

society, symbolic interactionism was not always met with immediate approval by the academy. Over time, symbolic interactionism has been integrated relatively seamlessly into sociology, and its fundamental precepts have become widely accepted. During the second half of the twentieth century, the scope of symbolic interactionism widened, its topics multiplied, and its theoretical linkages became more varied. In fact, there was some concern that symbolic interactionism was expanding so much that it risked erupting into something else entirely (Fine 1993). One of symbolic interactionism's most enduring contributions is in the area of research methods. Practices such as ethnography and conversation analysis are data rich, technically complex, and empirically well grounded (Katz 1997; Schegloff 1999), giving us new insights into perennial questions about social life.

As a relative newcomer to the field of social theory, symbolic interactionism was dubbed "the loyal opposition" (Mullins 1973) by those who saw it solely as a reaction or as merely a supplement to the more dominant macrosociological theories that preceded it. Gary Fine sums up the critiques in this way: Symbolic interactionism is "apolitical (and hence, supportive of the status quo), unscientific (hence, little more than tenured journalism), hostile to the classical questions of macrosociology (hence, limited to social psychology), and astructural (hence, fundamentally nonsociological)" (1993, p. 65). Critics argue that the scope of symbolic interactionism is limited, that it cannot address the most important sociological issues, and that its authority is restricted to the study of face-to-face interaction.

Each of these critiques has been answered over the years. Ultimately, some critics have seen the usefulness of an interactionist perspective and have even begun incorporating it into more macro work. Even in the hotly contested micro-versus-macro debate, a kind of détente has been established, recognizing that all levels of analysis are necessary for sociological understanding and that interactionist theories and methods are critical for a full picture of social life.

DATA WORKSHOP

Analyzing Media and Pop Culture

Theories of Celebrity Gossip

TMZ, which debuted in 2005, has become one of the most popular celebrity gossip websites in the world. It is consistently among the top 100 sites (of any kind) in the United States, with upward of 25 million unique visitors a month. TMZ provides users with up-to-the-minute

---

pop culture news, publishing hundreds of posts each day that expose the real and rumored doings of celebrities. It has become the go-to site anytime a celebrity gets arrested, dies, goes to rehab, cheats, or behaves badly in some other way.

TMZ is part of a new breed of celebrity gossip outlets, including PerezHilton, ONTD, Radar Online, Dlisted, and PopSugar, that have radically transformed the way that celebrities and other public figures are covered in the media. These sites are providing more coverage than ever and at greater speed. Stories that used to take at least a week to appear in pre-digital-era print magazines such as *People* or *Us* can now be posted online nearly instantaneously. That sometimes puts gossip sites on the forefront of breaking news. For instance, TMZ was the first outlet to report the news of Prince's death in 2016.

It's not just the volume or speed of delivery that's different; celebrity gossip sites are changing the substance of the coverage as well. Print magazines or mainstream television programs such as *Entertainment Tonight* or *E! News* used to provide mostly flattering coverage of celebrities. They were unwilling to report too many negative stories because they relied on the goodwill of celebrities to gain access into their lives. This tends to remain the rule in entertainment news, where there is still no shortage of promotional puff pieces and lightweight fare without much bite.

But more recently, gossip sites such as TMZ and others have been taking a harsher, more critical stance toward their subjects. They've also started engaging in investigative journalism practices, something that was formerly reserved for the mainstream news media. And they're covering a wider range of "celebrities" that regularly includes professional athletes as well as business executives and even political figures.

Whatever your opinion of tabloid news, and many people regard it as just mean, stupid, or shallow, you don't have to enjoy celebrity gossip to see its sociological relevance. For this Data Workshop, we'd like you to immerse yourself in the celebrity gossip site of your choice. Pick three stories to work with. Scrutinize the pictures, read the headlines and text carefully, and review the reader comments. Then consider how you might answer the following questions according to each of sociology's three major schools of thought:

1. Structural Functionalism

What is the function (or functions) of celebrity gossip for society? What purpose(s) does it serve, and how does it help society maintain stability and order? Discuss how notions of the sacred and profane are characterized. Are

Celebrity Gossip and Society Founded in 2005, TMZ is a leading purveyor of celebrity and entertainment news.

there manifest and latent functions of celebrity gossip? And are there any dysfunctions in it?

2. Conflict Theory

What forms of inequality are revealed in celebrity gossip? In particular, what does it have to say about class, race, gender, sexuality, or other inequalities? Whose interests are being served and who gets exploited? Who suffers and who benefits from celebrity gossip?

3. Symbolic Interactionism

What does celebrity gossip mean to society as a whole? What does it mean to individual members of society? Can gossip have different meanings for different individuals or groups of individuals? How do those meanings get constructed in interaction? And how does celebrity gossip shape and influence our everyday lives?

There are two options for completing this Data Workshop:

PREP-PAIR-SHARE Print out your three stories and bring them to class. Consider how each of the three sets of questions might be applied. Jot down your thoughts and make note of particular images and text. Get together in groups of two or three, and talk about your findings. How does each sociological theory fit with your examples? What new insights were provided by each perspective?

DO-IT-YOURSELF Select the material you will analyze, and answer each of the three sets of questions in a three-page essay. Discuss the main principles of the three theoretical perspectives and explain how each can be applied. You will want to include specific examples from your chosen stories to illustrate your points. Did the theories overlap at all, or did they contradict each other? Was there any one theory you felt did a better or worse job of explaining celebrity gossip? Attach the stories to your paper.

NEW THEORETICAL APPROACHES

Because the three major schools of thought and their off-shoots all have weaknesses as well as strengths, they will probably never fully explain the totality of social phenomena, even when taken together. And because society itself is always changing, there are always new phenomena to explain. So new perspectives will, and indeed must, continue to arise. In this section, we will consider two more contemporary approaches: postmodernism and midrange theory. Both grew out of the deep groundwork established by the other major schools of thought within sociology, as well as by looking beyond the confines of the discipline for inspiration. Each is a response to conditions both in the fast-changing social world around us and within the ongoing intellectual dialogues taking place among those continuing to study our times and ourselves.

POSTMODERNISM a paradigm that suggests that social reality is diverse, pluralistic, and constantly in flux

MODERNISM a paradigm that places trust in the power of science and technology to create progress, solve problems, and improve life

Postmodern Theory

In the late twentieth century, some social thinkers looked at the proliferation of theories and data and began to question whether we could ever know society or ourselves with any certainty. What is truth, and who has the right to claim it? Or, for that matter, what is reality, and how can it be known? In an era of increasing doubt and cynicism, has meaning become meaningless? **Postmodernism**, a theory that encompasses a wide range of areas—from art and architecture, to music and film, to communications and technology—addresses these and other questions.

The postmodern perspective developed primarily out of the French intellectual scene in the second half of the twentieth century and is still associated with three of its most important proponents. It's probably worth noting that postmodernists themselves don't really like that label, but nonetheless Jacques Derrida (1930–2004), Jean Baudrillard (1929–2007), and Michel Foucault (1926–1984) are the major figures most often included in the group.

In order to understand postmodernism, we first need to juxtapose it with **modernism**, the movement against which it reacted. Modernism is both a historical period and an ideological stance that began with the eighteenth-century Enlightenment, or Age of Reason. Modernist thought values scientific knowledge, a linear (or timeline-like) view of history, and a belief in the universality of human nature. In postmodernism, on the other hand, there are no absolutes—no claims to truth, reason, right, order, or stability. Everything is therefore relative—fragmented, temporary, and contingent. Postmodernists believe that certainty is illusory and prefer to play with the possibilities created by fluidity, complexity, multidimensionality, and even nonsense. They propose that there are no universal human truths from which we can interpret the meaning of existence. On one hand, postmodernism can be celebrated as a liberating influence that rescues us from the stifling effects of rationality and tradition. On the other hand, it can be condemned as a detrimental influence that imprisons us in a world of relativity, nihilism, and chaos.

Postmodernists are also critical of what they call "grand narratives," overarching stories and theories that justify dominant beliefs and give a (false) sense of order and coherence to the world. Postmodernists are interested in deconstruction, or taking apart and examining these stories and theories. For example, they claim that "factual" accounts of history are no more accurate than those that might be found in fiction. They prefer the notion of mini-narratives, or small-scale stories, that describe individual or group practices rather than narratives that attempt to be universal or global. These mini-narratives can then be combined in a variety of ways, creating a collage of meaning.

One way of understanding what postmodernism looks like is to examine how it has crept into our popular culture. Hip-hop is an example of a postmodern art form. It is a hybrid that borrows from other established genres, from rhythm-and-blues to rock and reggae. Hip-hop also takes samples from existing songs, mixes these with new musical tracks, and overlays it all with rap lyrics, resulting in a

Jacques Derrida, Michel Foucault, and Jean Baudrillard

TABLE 1.1 **Theory in Everyday Life**

Perspective	Approach to Society	Case Study: College Admissions in the United States
Structural Functionalism	Assumes that society is a unified whole that functions because of the contributions of its separate structures.	Those who are admitted are worthy and well qualified, while those who are not admitted do not deserve to be. There are other places in society for them besides the university.
Conflict Theory	Sees social conflict as the basis of society and social change and emphasizes a materialist view of society, a critical view of the status quo, and a dynamic model of historical change.	Admissions decisions may be made on the basis of criteria other than grades and scores. For example, some applicants may get in because their parents are major university donors, while others may get in because of their talents in sports or music. Some may be denied admission based on criteria like race, gender, or sexuality.
Symbolic Interactionism	Asserts that interaction and meaning are central to society and assumes that meanings are not inherent but are created through interaction.	University admissions processes are all about self-presentation and meaning-making in interaction. How does an applicant present themself to impress the admissions committee? How does the admissions committee develop an understanding of the kind of applicant it's looking for? How do applicants interpret their acceptances and rejections?
Postmodernism	Suggests that social reality is diverse, pluralistic, and constantly in flux.	An acceptance doesn't mean you're smart, and a rejection doesn't mean you're stupid; be careful of any "facts" you may be presented with, as they are illusory and contingent.

unique new sound. Mash-ups are another postmodern twist in music. Take, for instance, the *Grey Album* by DJ Danger Mouse, which uses tracks from the Beatles' classic *White Album* and combines them with Jay-Z's *Black Album* to create something wholly new yet borrowed.

Sociologists are quick to criticize postmodernism for discarding the scientific method and the knowledge they believe it has generated. Social leaders with a conservative agenda have been suspicious of the postmodern impulse to dismiss moral standards. While it is clear that many people criticize postmodernism, a much larger number are probably oblivious to it, which in itself may be more damning than any other response.

Although it is not a widely practiced perspective, postmodernism *has* nevertheless gained supporters. Those who challenge the status quo, whether in the arts, politics, or the academy, find attractive postmodernism's ability to embrace a multiplicity of powerful and promising alternatives. At the very least, postmodernism allows us to question scientific ideals of clarity and coherence, revealing inherent shortcomings and weaknesses in our current arguments and providing a way toward a deeper, more nuanced understanding of social life. As one of the most contemporary of the theoretical perspectives, postmodernism corresponds to the Information Age and feels natural and intuitive for many students whose lives are immersed in this world. By focusing on individuals and small-scale activities in which change happens on a local, limited basis, postmodernism offers an alternative to such cultural trends as consumerism and globalization. However

unwelcome the theory might be to some critics, it is likely that the postmodern shifts we have seen in society (in music and films, for example) will continue.

Midrange Theory

The second new theoretical approach is **midrange theory**. It shares some views with postmodernism, especially in its preference for mini-narratives over sweeping statements or "grand theories" made by the classical social theorists—a period dominated by what Robert Merton calls "total sociological systems" (1996, p. 46), which provided an overarching, comprehensive explanation of society as a whole.

Merton feared that an uncritical reverence for classical theory and an excessive attachment to tradition could impede the flow of new ideas and was just as likely to hold sociology back as to advance it. Because classical theories sought to develop large-scale theoretical systems that applied to the most macro level of society, they were often extremely difficult to test or research in any practical way. As one critic lamented, too "many sociological products can—effectively and unfortunately—be considered both bad science and bad literature" (Boudon 1991, p. 522).

> **MIDRANGE THEORY**
> an approach that integrates empiricism and grand theory

To counter this tendency, Merton proposed that sociologists focus more on "theories of the middle range." Midrange (or middle range) theory is not a theory of something in particular, but rather a *style* of theorizing. It is an attempt not so much to make the elusive micro-macro link, but to strike a balance somewhere between those polarities, shifting both the sights and the process of doing sociology. Work in this vein concentrates on incorporating research questions and empirical data into smaller-scale theories that eventually build into a more comprehensive body of sociological theory. Midrange theories are those "that lie between the minor but necessary working hypotheses that evolve in abundance during day-to-day research and the all-inclusive systematic efforts to develop a unified theory that will explain" the whole social world (Merton 1996, p. 41).

Since the 1990s and 2000s, a host of sociologists have taken up the call to midrange theory, from Sharon Hays's study of the contradictions within modern motherhood (1996), to Dalton Conley's work on racial identity (2000) and his examination of what constitutes leisure in the digital age (2009), to Peter Bearman's work on public health issues such as the rise of "vaccine refusers" (2010). Midrange theory connects specific research projects that generate empirical data with larger-scale theories about social structure. It aims to build knowledge cumulatively while offering a way to make sociology more effective as a science rather than just a way of thinking. With more sociologists appreciating such a stance, midrange theory is helping to push the discipline forward into the sociology of the future.

Closing Comments

Many of you will have already started a sociological journey, although likely a casual or personal one … until now. The popularity of reality TV speaks to our fascination with the everyday lives of other people, whether *RuPaul's Drag Race* or *Shark Tank* or *The Real Housewives of* _____ (fill in the blank). As students of sociology, we are interested in everyday life because we are excited to understand more about how its patterns and processes create our larger social reality. As we become better social analysts, using strategies to set aside any blinding preconceptions or distracting conclusions, we can become better acquainted with some of the fundamental tools that can turn our natural curiosity into scientific inquiry. A sociological perspective allows us to grasp the connection between our individual experiences and the forces and structures of society. As Bernard McGrane says, "Sociology is both dangerous and liberating" (1994, p. 10), as much because of what we can learn about ourselves as because of what we can learn about the world around us.

As a discipline, sociology possesses some of the qualities of the society it seeks to understand: It is broad, complex, and ever changing. This can make mastering sociology a rather unwieldy business, as much for the students and teachers who grapple with it in the classroom as for the experts out working in the field. We want you to become familiar with the members of sociology's family tree from its varied historical roots to the tips of its offshoots that might one day become important future branches. Because we have no single acknowledged universal sociological theory that satisfactorily explains all social phenomena (despite claims otherwise by some theorists), new theories can be developed all the time. Social theory tries to explain what is happening in, to, and around us. For any and every possible new, different, or important phenomenon—from the most mundane personal experience to questions of ultimate global significance—sociologists will attempt to explain it, understand it, analyze it, and predict its future. By looking at the development of the discipline, we are reminded that the contemporary grows out of the classical, and that older theories inspire and provoke newer ones. Theorists past and present remain engaged in a continual and evolving dialogue through their ideas and their work, and until such time as society is completely explained, the branches of sociology's family tree will continue to grow in remarkable ways.

We know this chapter covered a lot of ground. It's okay if it didn't all sink in. We will revisit many of these concepts and theories in later chapters. We hope you will treat this chapter as a first introduction to key sociological concepts, figures, and theories and that you will return to it for reference as you delve further into the text.

Let's Talk More

1. The sociological theorists in this chapter are almost all white males from Europe or the United States, evidence of Eurocentric, racist, and sexist bias in sociology. Do your classes in other disciplines have these same deficiencies?

2. Think about the last time you returned home from a long trip. Did ordinary, everyday things seem strange or unfamiliar? How could culture shock help you be a better sociologist?

3. What does it mean to possess a sociological imagination? Think of your favorite food. What historical events had to happen and what social institutions have to function in order for this food to be available?

Let's Explore More

1. **Film** Zemeckis, Robert, dir. *Cast Away*. 2000.

2. **Article** Irwin, Neil. "What If Sociologists Had as Much Influence as Economists?" *The New York Times*. March 17, 2017.

3. **Blog Post** Raskoff, Sally. "Fiction with a Sociological Attitude." *Everyday Sociology* (blog). November 16, 2015. *https://WWNorton.com/rd/b7BEr.*

CHAPTER 2

Studying Social Life: Sociological Research Methods

Humorist Dave Barry, the Pulitzer Prize–winning columnist and author, has written many entertaining articles as a reporter and social commentator. Some of his thoughts on college, however, seem particularly appropriate for this chapter. In one of his most popular essays, Barry advises students not to choose a major that involves "known facts" and "right answers" but rather a subject in which "nobody really understands what anybody else is talking about, and which involves virtually no actual facts" (Barry 1987, p. 203). For example, sociology:

For sheer lack of intelligibility, sociology is far and away the number-one subject. I sat through hundreds of hours of sociology courses, and read gobs of sociology writing, and I never once heard or read a coherent statement. This is because sociologists want to be considered scientists, so they spend most of their time translating simple, obvious observations into scientific-sounding code. If you plan to major in sociology, you'll have to learn to do the same thing. For example, suppose you have observed that children cry when they fall down. You should write: "Methodological observation of the sociometrical behavior tendencies of prematurated isolates indicates that a causal relationship exists between groundward tropism and lachrimatory, or 'crying' behavior forms." If you can keep this up for fifty or sixty pages, you will get a large government grant.

Although Barry exaggerates a bit, if there weren't some truth to what he is saying, his joke would be meaningless. While sociologists draw much of their inspiration from the natural (or "hard") sciences (such as chemistry and biology) and try to study society in a scientific way, many people still think of sociology as "unscientific" or a "soft" science. In response, some sociologists may try too hard to sound scientific and incorporate complicated terminology in their writing.

It is possible, of course, to conduct research and write about it in a clear, straightforward, and even elegant way, as the best sociologists have demonstrated. Contrary to Barry's humorous claims, sociology can be both scientific and comprehensible. So let's turn now to a discussion of how sociologists conduct their research, which includes the methods of gathering information and conveying that information to others. For the record, Dave Barry went to Haverford College near Philadelphia, where he majored in English.

How to Read This Chapter

In Chapter 1 we introduced you to a set of tools that will help you develop a sociological imagination and apply particular theoretical perspectives to the social world. In this chapter, you will acquire methodological tools that will help you to further understand social life. The tools will also help you in the Data Workshops throughout the book, which are designed to give you the experience of conducting the same type of research that professional sociologists do. For this reason, we recommend that you look at this chapter as a sort of "how-to" guide: Read through all the "directions" first, recognizing that you will soon be putting these methods into practice. Then remember that you have this chapter as a resource for future reference. These methods are your tools for real-world research—it's important that you understand them, but even more important that you get a chance to use them.

AN OVERVIEW OF RESEARCH METHODS

While theories make hypothetical claims, methods produce data that will support, disprove, or modify those claims. Sociologists who do **quantitative research** work with numerical data; that is, they translate the social world into numbers that can then be manipulated mathematically. Any type of social statistic is an example of quantitative data: You may have read in the newspaper, for instance, that in 2017 some 32 percent of male drivers involved in fatal motor vehicle crashes had a blood alcohol content at or above 0.08 percent, compared with 20 percent of female drivers (Insurance Institute for Highway Safety 2018). Quantitative methodologies distill large amounts of information into numbers that are more easily communicated to others, often in the form of rates and percentages or charts and graphs.

Sociologists who do **qualitative research** work with non-numerical data such as texts, written field notes, interview transcripts, videos, or photographs. Rather than condensing lived experience into numbers, qualitative researchers try to describe the cases they study in great detail. They may engage in participant observation, in which they enter the social world they wish to study, or they may do in-depth interviews; analyze transcripts of conversations; glean data from historical books, letters, or diaries; and even use social networking sites or text messages as sources of data for their investigations. Sociologist Gary Fine, for example, has observed a variety of different social worlds, including those of professional restaurant chefs (1996), members of high school debate teams (2001), and meteorologists who predict the weather (2010). Fine was able to discover important sociological insights

Social Research Sociologists use both quantitative methods, such as surveys, and qualitative methods, such as participant observation, to study the social world. The U.S. Census, which is conducted every ten years, is an example of a survey.

through immersion in each of the social worlds he studied. Qualitative researchers like Fine find patterns in their data by using interpretive rather than statistical analysis.

The Scientific Approach

The **scientific method** is the standard procedure for acquiring and verifying empirical (concrete, scientific) knowledge. The scientific method provides researchers with a series of basic steps to follow; over the years, sociologists have updated and modified this model so that it better fits the study of human behaviors. While not every sociologist adheres to each of the steps in order, the scientific method provides a general plan for conducting research in a systematic way (see Figure 2.1).

QUANTITATIVE RESEARCH research that translates the social world into numbers that can be treated mathematically; this type of research often tries to find cause-and-effect relationships

QUALITATIVE RESEARCH research that works with nonnumerical data such as texts, field notes, interview transcripts, photographs, and tape recordings; this type of research more often tries to understand how people make sense of their world

SCIENTIFIC METHOD a procedure for acquiring knowledge that emphasizes collecting concrete data through observation and experimentation

LITERATURE REVIEW a thorough search through previously published studies relevant to a particular topic

1. In the first step, the researcher identifies a problem or asks a general question, like "Does violent TV lead to violent behavior?" and begins to think about a specific research plan designed to answer that question.

2. Before proceeding, however, a researcher usually does a **literature review** to become thoroughly familiar with all other research done previously on a given topic. Doing so will prevent a researcher from duplicating

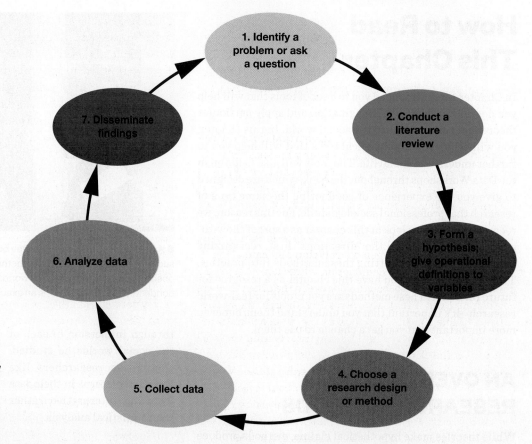

FIGURE 2.1 Steps of the Scientific Method
While not all sociologists follow these seven steps in lock-step order, the scientific method provides a general overview of the research process.

The circular diagram shows:
1. Identify a problem or ask a question
2. Conduct a literature review
3. Form a hypothesis; give operational definitions to variables
4. Choose a research design or method
5. Collect data
6. Analyze data
7. Disseminate findings

work that has already been done and may also provide the background upon which to conduct new research.

3. Next, the researcher forms a **hypothesis**, a theoretical statement that she thinks will explain the relationship between two phenomena, which are known as **variables**. In the hypothesis "Watching violence on TV causes children to act violently in real life," the two variables are "watching violence on TV" and "acting violently." In short, the researcher is saying one variable has a causal connection to the other. The researcher can use the hypothesis to predict possible outcomes: "If watching violence on TV causes children to act violently in real life, then exposing five-year-olds to violent TV shows will make them more likely to hit the inflatable clown doll placed in the room with them." The researcher must give a precise **operational definition** to the variables so that they can observe and measure them accurately and ensure that their readers have a clear understanding of just what is being measured.

HYPOTHESIS a theoretical statement explaining the relationship between two or more phenomena

VARIABLES two or more phenomena that a researcher believes are related; these will be examined in the experiment

OPERATIONAL DEFINITION a clear and precise definition of a variable that facilitates its measurement

For example, there is a wide range of violence on television and in real life. Does "violence" include words as well as actions, a slap as well as murder? The operational definition will specify.

4. In this step, the researcher chooses a research design or method to use to conduct their study. A classic example is to perform an experiment meant to isolate variables in order to best examine their relationship to one another. Sociologists use a range of methods and sometimes combine one or more methods. These will be discussed in greater depth later in the chapter.

5. The researcher then collects the data. In this case, the researcher would conduct the experiment by first exposing kids to TV violence, then observing their behavior toward the clown doll. Data might be collected by using video equipment as well as by taking notes.

6. Next, the researcher must analyze the data, evaluating the accuracy or inaccuracy of the hypothesis in predicting the outcome. In the real-life experiment on which this example is based, the children were more likely to hit the clown doll themselves if they saw the TV actors being rewarded for their violent behavior; if the actors were punished for their behavior, the children were less likely to hit the doll (Bandura 1965).

7. The researcher then disseminates the findings of the experiment in the scientific community (often through presentations at professional meetings, through publications, or in the classroom) as well as among the general public, thus completing the next-to-last step in the research process.

Finally, all of this is repeated. An important feature of scientific results is **replicability**, the ability to repeat or replicate the research, either by the same researcher or by others who are interested in the same topic. While not all methods are equally replicable, this is still an important step for much scientific work.

One limitation of the scientific method is that it can't always distinguish between **correlation** and **causation**. If two variables change in conjunction with each other, or if a change in one seems to lead to a change in the other, they are correlated. Even if they are correlated, though, the change in one variable may not be caused by the change in the other variable. Instead, there may be some **intervening variable** that causes the changes in both. The classic example is the correlation between ice cream sales and rates of violent crime. As ice cream sales increase, so do rates of violent crime like murder and rape. Does ice cream consumption cause people to act violently? Or do violent actions cause people to buy ice cream? Turns out, it's neither—this is what is known as a **spurious correlation**. Both ice cream sales and violent crime rates are influenced by a third variable: weather. As the temperature climbs, so do people's rates of ice cream purchase and the likelihood that they'll be involved in a violent crime (probably because they are outside for more hours of the day

and hence available to each other in a way that makes violent crime possible). Knowing that correlation does not equal causation is important, as it can help us all be more critical consumers of scientific findings.

We are constantly gathering data in order to understand what is true. Philosopher of science Thomas Kuhn, in fact, argued that truth is relative and dependent on the paradigm through which one sees the world (1962/1970). Paradigms are broad theoretical models about how things work in the social and natural worlds. For example, humans believed for centuries that the universe revolved around the earth. It's easy to understand why. The available data, after all, seemed to support such a theory: We don't feel the earth moving beneath us, and it appears from our vantage point that the stars, sun, and moon rise and set on our horizon. This earth-centered, or geocentric, view of the universe was the basis for all scientific theory until 1543, when the Polish astronomer Nicolaus Copernicus proposed that the earth revolved around the sun (Armitage 1951). Using mathematical methods, Copernicus arrived at a new theory, heliocentrism, in which the earth rotates around the sun and on its own axis—thereby accounting for the twenty-four-hour days as well as the four seasons of the year. This caused what Kuhn called a paradigm shift, a major break from the assumptions made by the previous model. Paradigm shifts occur when new data force new ways of looking at the world. And methods are what generate data.

> **REPLICABILITY** the ability of research to be repeated and, thus, later verified by other researchers
>
> **CORRELATION** a relationship between variables in which they change together and may or may not be causal
>
> **CAUSATION** a relationship between variables in which a change in one directly produces a change in the other
>
> **INTERVENING VARIABLE** a third variable, sometimes overlooked, that explains the relationship between two other variables
>
> **SPURIOUS CORRELATION** the appearance of causation produced by an intervening variable

Which Method to Use?

Since each sociological method has specific benefits and limitations, each is more appropriate for certain types of research. Thus, when a researcher begins a project, one of her most important decisions is which methods to use. Suppose, for example, a sociologist is interested in studying Woodstock, one of the major musical and cultural milestones of the 1960s. Although there are many ways to approach this event, our sociologist wants to study the attendees' experiences. What was it really like to be at Woodstock? What did it mean to those who were there? What are their interpretations of this iconic moment in hippie culture?

During the event itself, the ideal method for studying the festivalgoers at Woodstock might have been to assemble a

Violence on Television In his famous 1965 study, Albert Bandura supported his hypothesis that watching violence on TV causes children to act violently in real life by observing children who, after watching a video of an adult beating a doll, then behaved similarly toward the doll.

What Was It Really Like at Woodstock? You could use many different methodologies to investigate this question, including interviews, surveys, existing sources, or experiments.

team of researchers trained in participant observation; that is, they would actually be in the thick of things, observing and participating at the same time. They could gather firsthand data on the music, clothes, dancing, drugs, "free love," and so forth. However, the opportunity to be a participant observer of that particular cultural phenomenon has long since passed. What are some other options?

Interviews are a possibility. The researcher could ask Woodstock attendees to recount their experiences. But how would she recruit them? Woodstock-goers live all over the world now, and it might be difficult (and expensive) to track down enough of them to make an interview study feasible. Another problem with interviewing this group: The three-day event happened more than forty years ago. How would the passage of time affect their memories? How much detail could they actually remember about the experience after so long?

How about a survey? The researcher could certainly send a questionnaire through the mail or administer it online, and this method would be much less expensive than face-to-face interviews. But here she runs into the same problem as with an interview study: How does she find all these folks? A standard tactic for recruiting survey participants involves placing an ad in a local newspaper. But an ad

in the *New York Times*, for example, or even on a community website like Craigslist, would draw only a limited number of Woodstock alumni. Also, some attendees might want to put that part of their lives behind them; others who receive the questionnaire in the mail might send it straight into the trash. Finally, the researcher might encounter the problem of impostors—people who say they were at Woodstock but were really nowhere near it.

What about using existing sources? Plenty has been written about Woodstock over the years. Many firsthand accounts have been published, and there is an abundance of film and photography as well. Our researcher could use these materials to analyze the concert from the perspectives of the participants. These accounts would necessarily be selective, focusing only on particular aspects of the Woodstock experience.

Is it possible to conduct an experiment that replicates the original Woodstock? Some would say that Woodstock 1999 was such an experiment and that it failed miserably, with fires, violence, arrests, and acres of mud. However, systematic scientific experiments are different from blatant attempts to cash in on the Woodstock mystique. While the unique conditions of the 1969 gathering cannot be re-created in a lab setting, it is possible to identify some of the defining features of the Woodstock experience and to explore those experimentally. Over a three-day period, tens of thousands of strangers came together in a mass gathering, mostly devoid of any official presence (no cops, fences, roads, ticket booths, or porta-potties) and had an almost entirely peaceful experience. How did this happen? Altruism, cooperation, and trust between strangers are some of the measurable group qualities that seem to have been present. An experimenter might be able to create laboratory environments in which subjects participate in activities that highlight one or more of these qualities—even without the mud, music, and drugs that were part of the original Woodstock experience.

No matter what methodological choice our researcher makes, she will sacrifice some types of information in order to acquire others, and she will trade in one set of advantages and disadvantages for another. Her choices will be guided not only by what she wants to accomplish sociologically but also by the methods she is a competent practitioner of, the time in which she wants to complete the project, the resources available from any funding agencies, and her access to cooperative, qualified people, both as respondents and as research assistants.

The rest of this chapter will discuss six methods in detail: ethnography/participant observation, interviews, surveys, existing sources, experimental methods, and social network analysis. We will see how various sociologists have used these methods to conduct research on the general topic of "family dynamics."

ETHNOGRAPHY/ PARTICIPANT OBSERVATION

Ethnography is one of the most commonly used research methods in the social sciences. Also referred to as ethnographic research, it is a qualitative method that allows for the study of a wide variety of people and places. A key feature of this method is fieldwork; research takes place in naturally occurring social environments out in the real world, where the researcher can study firsthand the day-to-day lives of the people there. Ethnographic research is conducted through **participant observation**, so the terms are often used interchangeably. With this method the researcher must become a participant in the group or setting being studied as well as an observer of it. This method often entails deep immersion into a field site, sometimes lasting over a period of months or even years, so that the researcher can develop a member's eye view and come to know the social world from the inside out. Ethnography, which literally means "writing [from the Greek *graphos*] culture [*ethnos*]," is also the term used for the product of participant observation research; it is a written report of the results of the study, often presented in book form.

The first order of business in participant observation research is to gain entry or access to the chosen field site or setting. Certain groups may be more or less difficult to approach, as you can imagine, and there may be some places where no outsider is allowed to go. Still, sociologists have been able to study an astounding number of different and varied social worlds. Once access has been negotiated, it is also important for researchers to establish good **rapport** with their subjects. Researchers may differ in their levels of involvement with a group or in their closeness to certain members. But it is often the case that trust and acceptance are necessary before research can begin in earnest.

Data are collected primarily through writing detailed **field notes** every day to document what happened. Some researchers may also take photos or videos in the course of their fieldwork, but honing their own observational skills is most critical. Field notes describe the scene or setting, as well as the activities and interactions of the researcher and the group members, in as much detail as possible; they become the basis of the data analysis the researcher does later on.

Some researchers do a form of participant observation called **autoethnography**, where they produce richly detailed accounts of their own thoughts, feelings, and experiences in the field as a focal point of their study (Ellis 1997). Autoethnographers theorize a link between personal and cultural experiences, and their writings are meant to evoke responses in the readers. Both personal and analytical, autoethnography is one of the newer qualitative methods employed by sociologists (Ellis, Adams, and Bochner 2010).

Researchers sometimes take brief, sketchy notes in the field, writing key words or short quotations in small notebooks, on cocktail napkins, or in text messages. These jottings can help jog their memories when they sit down to write at the end of the day and elaborate on the details. Sometimes, however, it is not possible to write while in the field and researchers must rely on "head notes," that is, on memory alone.

Anthropologist Clifford Geertz (1973), well known for his work on Indonesian culture and society, coined the term **thick description** to convey the qualities of well-written field

ETHNOGRAPHY a naturalistic method based on studying people in their own environment in order to understand the meanings they attribute to their activities; also, the written work that results from the study

PARTICIPANT OBSERVATION a methodology associated with ethnography whereby the researcher both observes and becomes a member in a social setting

RAPPORT a positive relationship often characterized by mutual trust or sympathy

FIELD NOTES detailed notes taken by an ethnographer describing their activities and interactions, which later become the basis of the analysis

AUTOETHNOGRAPHY a form of participant observation where the feelings and actions of the researcher become a focal point of the ethnographic study

THICK DESCRIPTION the presentation of detailed data on interactions and meaning within a cultural context, from the perspective of its members

REFLEXIVITY how the identity and activities of the researcher influence what is going on in the field setting

DEDUCTIVE APPROACH an approach whereby the researcher formulates a hypothesis first and then gathers data to test that hypothesis

INDUCTIVE APPROACH an approach whereby the researcher gathers data first, then formulates a theory to fit the data

GROUNDED THEORY an inductive method of generating theory from data by creating categories in which to place data and then looking for relationships among categories

VALIDITY the accuracy of a question or measurement tool; the degree to which a researcher is measuring what they think they are measuring

REPRESENTATIVENESS the degree to which a particular studied group is similar to, or represents, any part of the larger society

BIAS an opinion held by the researcher that might affect the research or analysis

notes. It takes more than mere photographic detail to make field notes "thick"; sensitivity to the context and to interactional details such as facial expression and tone of voice enriches what might otherwise be just a list of events. Thick description involves exploring all the possible meanings of a phenomenon (for example, a blinking eye) within a particular cultural setting. A good ethnography is not only systematic and holistic, but it should also allow the reader to understand what the world is like from another's perspective.

One example of participant observation research is Kathryn Edin and Maria Kefalas's study of poor moms, in their ethnography *Promises I Can Keep: Why Poor Women Put Motherhood before Marriage* (2005). Edin and Kefalas wanted to examine a group that faces harsh judgments from the mainstream: urban single moms. For years, policymakers and mainstream Americans have focused on single motherhood as the source of a variety of social problems. Edin and Kefalas wanted to see the issue from the perspective and lives of the women being stigmatized in order to uncover the realities of single motherhood. Their goal was to give poor single mothers the ability to personally answer the question that wealthier Americans ask of them: Why don't they get married? And why have babies if they have to struggle so hard to support them? Edin moved her entire family to East Camden, New Jersey, where they lived for two and a half years while she did her research. In order to become more integrated into the community, she joined the local church, volunteered at after-school and summer programs, ate at local restaurants, shopped at local stores, taught Sunday school, and went to community events. Kefalas volunteered at the local GED tutoring program for teen mothers.

Edin and Kefalas were able to study 162 black, white, and Puerto Rican mothers with an average age of twenty-five. All of the women were single parents who earned less than $16,000 a year. What Edin and Kefalas discovered was that motherhood, from the perspective of many of the women they met, was a stabilizing agent in their lives. Rather than disrupting their path to success, many of the moms viewed their babies as the only positive factor in their lives. Numerous stories detailed the troubled directions in which the women's lives were heading before they had their children. The conclusions Edin and Kefalas were able to draw from their ethnographic research were contrary to widespread opinion about the consequences of single motherhood for many women in poverty: The (perceived) low cost of early child-rearing and the high value and worth of mothering are enough to combat the difficulties of single motherhood.

Ethnographic researchers must pay attention to how their own social statuses—including gender, age, race, and parenthood—shape the kind of access they can have and, hence, the kind of knowledge they can obtain as part of their research. The fact that Edin and Kefalas were women and mothers themselves played a role in their ability to create rapport and gain access as they lived and worked in East Camden. Participant observers must also consider that their own presence probably affects the interactions and relationships in the group they are observing, an idea known as **reflexivity**. A researcher's personal feelings about the members of a group also come into play. Ethnographers may feel respect, contempt, curiosity, boredom, and other emotions during their time in the field, and these feelings may influence their observations. It is true that other kinds of researchers also have to take their feelings into account. But because ethnographers have such close personal ties to the people they study, the issue of reflexivity is especially important to them.

Like Edin and Kefalas, most ethnographers are "overt" about their research roles; that is, they are open about their sociological intentions. Overt research is generally preferred, because it eliminates the potential ethical problems of deception. Sometimes, however, circumstances dictate that researchers take a "covert" role and observe members without letting them know that they are doing research. For example, sociologist David Calvey kept his identity secret for many years while conducting research for a study of masculinity and the physical culture of bouncers in British clubs (2018). In order to be a participant observer in such groups, Calvey worked as a bouncer himself, taking advantage of his large physique, martial arts expertise, and clubbing experiences to present himself as an "ordinary lad" who worked the doors. Often this meant witnessing violence and criminality without intervening. Calvey had to deceive the other bouncers in order to gain their trust; also, living in the neighborhood of the clubs he worked at meant he was always at risk of being revealed as a fraud. However, he felt that the value of the research was worth the risk because it provided insight into an interesting group that would otherwise go unstudied.

Ethnographers look for patterns and themes that are revealed in their field notes. While the scientific method generally uses a **deductive approach**—forming a hypothesis first and then testing to see whether it is accurate—ethnographers use an **inductive approach**, beginning with

Covert Research Studying bar bouncers meant that Calvey sometimes had to witness conflict, criminal behavior, and even violence without intervening, for fear of revealing his identity as a researcher.

specific observations and then forming broad generalizations from them. They start by immersing themselves in their field notes and fitting the data into categories, such as "episodes of conflict" or "common vocabulary shared by members." Identifying relationships among these categories then allows ethnographers to build theoretical propositions, a form of analysis known as **grounded theory** (Glaser and Strauss 1967).

Advantages and Disadvantages

ADVANTAGES

1. Ethnographic research excels at telling richly detailed stories that contribute to our understanding of social life. It offers a means of studying groups whose stories might not otherwise be told (Katz 1997). These include deviant groups such as fight clubs (Jackson-Jacobs 2004) as well as exceptional groups such as elite college athletes (Adler and Adler 1991).

2. Ethnographic research can challenge our taken-for-granted notions about groups we thought we knew. For instance, from Edin and Kefalas's work on single mothers, we learn that these women are not the irresponsible, unstable individuals we may have thought they were. They desire and seek out the best for their children, just like mothers in other groups and communities.

3. The detailed nature of ethnographic research can help reshape the stereotypes we hold about others and on which social policy is often based. A study like that of Edin and Kefalas can have policy consequences

because it sheds light on the motivations and needs of single urban mothers, as well as giving us a clear picture of the resources available to them.

4. Much of the pioneering methodological innovation of the last half-century has come from ethnography, especially on the issue of reflexivity and researcher roles in the field.

DISADVANTAGES

1. Ethnographic research suffers from a lack of replicability, the ability of another researcher to repeat or replicate the study. Repeating a study in order to test the **validity** of its results is an important element of the scientific method, but because of the unique combinations of people, timing, setting, and researcher role, no one can ever undertake the same study twice.

2. A major critique has to do with an ethnographic study's degree of **representativeness**—whether a particular study can apply to anything larger. What is the value of studying relatively small groups of people if one cannot then say that these groups represent parts of the society at large? Though Edin and Kefalas's work focused on East Camden, their conclusions are supposed to apply to single mothers in any number of other cities as well.

3. Participant observers must also be wary of personal **bias**. There is always a possibility that prejudice or favor can slip into the research process. Not all researchers are transparent about their own agendas. We need to keep in mind how a researcher's own values and opinions might affect their research and analysis.

DATA WORKSHOP

Analyzing Everyday Life

Watching People Talk

Participant observation research requires a keen eye and ear, and field notes must faithfully capture the details of what is seen and heard. While writing field notes may sound fairly easy (don't we all know how to describe the things we've observed?), it's actually one of the most grueling forms of data collection in the social sciences. Why? Because thick description is a much more demanding task than the casual description you're used to providing in everyday conversation. It requires a rigorous consciousness of what is going on around you while it is happening and a strenuous effort to recall those goings-on after leaving the field and returning to your computer to type them up.

This Data Workshop gives you an opportunity to practice doing ethnographic research (make sure you have read and reviewed that section of the chapter). Specifically, it is an exercise in writing field notes using what Clifford Geertz calls thick description. To make things a little easier, you'll focus on listening first and then on watching. The verbal and the visual are separated so that you can concentrate on one kind of description at a time. In your future ethnographic work, you'll be writing field notes that describe both verbal and nonverbal behavior at once.

- *Field Observations:* First, for five to ten minutes, listen to (eavesdrop on) a conversation whose participants you can't see. They might be sitting behind you on a bus or at a nearby table in a restaurant—you're close enough to hear them but positioned so that you can't see them. Then, for five to ten minutes, observe a conversation you can't hear—one taking place, for example, on the other side of the campus quad. Even though you can't hear what's being said, you can see the interaction as it takes place.

- *Written Descriptions:* Write an extremely detailed description of each conversation. Describe the participants and the setting, and include your ideas about what you think is going on and what you think you know about the participants. Try to describe everything you heard or saw to support any conclusions you draw. For each of the five- to ten-minute observation periods, you should aim to take two or more double-spaced pages of field notes.

There are two options for completing this Data Workshop:

PREP-PAIR-SHARE Choose a partner and exchange your field notes. As you read through your partner's descriptions, mark with an asterisk (*) the passages where you can see and hear clearly the things your partner describes. Circle the passages that contain evaluative words (like "angry" or "sweet") or summaries of action or conversation rather than detailed description (like "They argued about who would pay the bill"). And place a question mark next to the passages where you are left feeling like you would like to know more. Your partner will do this with your descriptions as well, and you can discuss your responses to each other's work. Finally, as a class, use your discussions to develop a group consensus about what constitutes good descriptive detail. This is the kind of detail ethnographers strive to produce in their field notes every day.

DO-IT-YOURSELF Write a two- to three-page essay discussing your fieldwork experience. What was it like to do participant observation research? Did you find listening or watching more or less difficult, and why? How did your data differ with each of the observations? Provide examples of thick description from your field notes, and make sure to attach your field notes to your paper.

INTERVIEWS

You've probably seen countless interviewers, microphone in hand, clamoring to ask their questions at the crime scene, after the big game, or on the red carpet. Sociologists also use **interviews**—face-to-face, information-seeking conversations—to gather qualitative data directly from research subjects, or **respondents**. When sociologists conduct interviews, they try to do so systematically and with a more scientific approach than is used for the kind of interviews you might typically see on TV or read in the news. Sometimes, interviews are the only method used in a research project, but sociologists may also combine interviews with other methods, such as participant observation or analysis of existing sources. Closely related to interviews are surveys, which we will consider in the next section. Both methods are concerned with asking people questions, usually very specific groups of people as well as particular kinds of questions. Interviews, however, are always conducted by the researcher, whereas surveys may be taken independently by the respondent.

When using interviews to collect data about a particular question or project, sociologists must first identify a **target population**, or group that is the focus of their study. If it is a large group, for instance, all parents with children under eighteen years of age, it might be impossible to study each and every one of them. Researchers, then, must select a **sample**, or a smaller group that is representative of the larger group. The sample will be used to make generalizations that can apply to the larger target population. The number of possible respondents in a sample depends on the type of study, the nature of the questions, and the amount of time and staff available. In most research studies, interviews can be administered to only a limited number of people, so the scope of such projects is usually smaller than for other methods, such as surveys. While most interviews are conducted one-on-one, some researchers will organize a **focus group**, in which a number of participants (perhaps five to ten) will be interviewed at the same time, also allowing for group members to interact with one another. This may be one means of increasing the sample size of a study. Researchers must get **informed consent** from those who will be participating in the study; in other words, respondents must know what they are getting into and

Turning Play into Work
Tamara Mose conducted interviews with parents of young children in New York City for her study of playdates and how these organized meetings reproduce inequalities based on race and class.

explicitly agree to participate. This is particularly important because most interviews are audio or video recorded.

Sociologist Tamara Mose used interviews in her recent study of how parents and children benefit from playdates. Her curiosity about the ritual of the playdate arose as she raised her own children in a diverse and gentrifying neighborhood in Brooklyn, New York. In her 2016 book, *The Playdate: Parents, Children and the New Expectations of Play,* Mose looks at how parents arrange private play opportunities, ostensibly for their children, but also for their own professional and personal benefit. As she conducted and analyzed her interviews, Mose noticed that playdates often ensure that both parents and children socialize with people much like themselves. Even the type of snacks provided at playdates makes a difference. One health-conscious mom grumbled that another child's parents had served Domino's pizza and was contemplating switching schools so that he would no longer be exposed to such undesirable refreshments—or the families who serve them (Mose 2016, pp. 133–134). By excluding others who are different, less affluent, or even just "out of zone" (New York City slang for kids from a different school district), playdates reproduce inequalities of class and race as well as enhance family privilege.

Arlie Hochschild used interviews to conduct her landmark study on parents in two-career families, *The Second Shift* (Hochschild and Machung 1989). In this book, Hochschild looks at how couples handle the pressures of working at a job and then coming home to what she calls "the second shift"— doing housework and taking care of children. Hochschild, who was herself in a two-career family, wanted to find out how couples were dealing with changing family roles in light of the fact that more women had entered the workforce. Were women able to juggle all their responsibilities, and to what extent were men helping their wives in running the household? Hochschild and her assistants interviewed fifty couples in two-career marriages and forty-five other people who were also a part of the respondents' domestic arrangements, such as babysitters, day-care providers, and teachers. From this sample of households that Hochschild studied, we can now extrapolate to a much larger population; her findings should also be applicable to similar couples elsewhere.

When conducting an interview, how do you know what to ask? Composing good questions is one of the most difficult parts of interviewing. Most interviewers use many different questions, covering a range of issues related to the project. Questions may be closed- or open-ended. A **closed-ended question** imposes a limit on the possible response: for example, "Are you for or against couples living together before they are married?" An

INTERVIEWS person-to-person conversations for the purpose of gathering information by means of questions posed to respondents

RESPONDENT a participant in a study from whom the researcher seeks to gather information

TARGET POPULATION the entire group about which a researcher would like to be able to generalize

SAMPLE the members of the target population who will actually be studied

FOCUS GROUP a process for interviewing a number of participants together that also allows for interaction among group members

INFORMED CONSENT a safeguard through which the researcher makes sure that respondents are freely participating and understand the nature of the research

CLOSED-ENDED QUESTION a question asked of a respondent that imposes a limit on the possible responses

IN THE FUTURE
Emerging Methods in Sociology

Other methods are being developed and used by sociologists. These emerging methods may not yet rival the major social science methods in popularity, but each has its own novel merits.

Action Research: Combining Research and Social Change

A growing trend in social science methodology, action research combines social science research with community problem solving and social change, in a way that calls into question some of sociology's closely held beliefs about ethics, bias, and the role of the researcher. Action researchers see their research skills as problem-solving tools, and they view those whom others might call "research subjects" as active, collaborative, equal participants in the project. In other words, action researchers do research *with* people, not *on* people, and see their work as part of a "scholarship of engagement" (Rajaram 2007, p. 139), rather than one of erudite distance. While action research is not exactly new, it has been gaining popularity recently, across the social sciences as well as in practice-oriented disciplines such as nursing, public health, education, urban planning, and management.

An award-winning example of action research is the work of Chicago's Community Organizing and Family Issues

group (COFI). Its project "Why Isn't Johnny in Preschool?" sought to answer this question, particularly among families in low-income, racially diverse neighborhoods, where kids are less likely to be enrolled in early childhood education programs. They sent community members, trained in sociological interview methods, out into their neighborhoods to talk with more than 5,000 other parents about the barriers to preschool enrollment. These findings were then used to design outreach and public awareness campaigns that promoted the importance of preschool attendance and provided information packets that helped families find solutions to some of the problems identified in the research. Preschool attendance increased in the targeted neighborhoods as a result (COFI 2009).

"Netnography"

Netnography, or cyberethnography, involves the use of participant observation methods to study online communities. We interact with others and engage in group activities online more and more, and so it makes sense that sociologists would begin working to understand online social worlds using the discipline's distinctive methods. While it's true that our online communications are not exactly the same as our communications in real life (IRL), rather than invent new

---

OPEN-ENDED QUESTION a question asked of a respondent that allows the answer to take whatever form the respondent chooses

LEADING QUESTIONS questions that predispose a respondent to answer in a certain way

DOUBLE-BARRELED QUESTIONS questions that attempt to get at multiple issues at once, and so tend to receive incomplete or confusing answers

LIFE HISTORY an approach to interviewing that asks for a chronological account of the respondent's entire life or some portion of it

open-ended question, on the other hand, allows for a wide variety of responses: "What do you think about couples living together before they are married?"

Researchers must be careful to avoid biased or **leading questions**, those that predispose a respondent to answer in a certain way. Overly complex questions are a problem, as are **double-barreled questions**, those that involve too many issues at one time. It is also important to be aware of any ambiguous or inflammatory language that might confuse or

spark an emotional reaction on the part of the respondent. Asking a single parent how difficult her life is will elicit data about the difficulties, but not about the joys, of parenthood. More neutral language, such as "Tell me about the pluses and minuses of single parenthood," is preferable. In some studies, researchers will solicit the entire **life history** of a respondent, a chronological account of the story of his life from childhood to the present or of some portion of it.

Once the interviews have been conducted, they are usually transcribed so that researchers can analyze them in textual form; they can sort through the material looking for patterns of similarities and differences among the answers. Some researchers may use computer applications designed to help analyze such data; others do it "by hand." For her analysis, Hochschild categorized the types of household chores done by men and women and quantified the amount of time spent daily and weekly on those chores. She then categorized couples as "traditional," "transitional," or

methods with which to study Internet life it seems appropriate to use adapted versions of real-life ethnography to study online social worlds and social interactions.

Online ethnographers study (mostly) written communication as it occurs in online locations—gaming environments, social media platforms, and other web-based locations. They collect observational data as they participate in the activities of these online settings, and they code and analyze that data interpretively, just as traditional ethnographers do. In doing so, cyberethnographers can draw conclusions about the culture of online life and can use those findings to expand our knowledge of human interaction in all sorts of settings, from cosmetic surgery (Langer and Beckman 2005) to prescription drug use (Del Fresno and Peláez 2014) and beyond. For example, Dutch ethnographer Brigitte Borm (2017) studied the online discussions of Airbnb hosts, focusing on changes in their definition of "home" after they had rented their places to strangers using the house-sharing app. Netnography can open fascinating windows onto online social worlds and interactions we might not otherwise see.

Mapping Methods

Another emerging method in sociology is GIS, or Geographic Information Systems, a type of computer software that attaches social science data (like population demographics) to geographic locations. This allows sociologists to know not just that 13 percent of a city's population lives below the poverty line, but also to know exactly where they live in the city. Maps of instances of illness, for example, can be overlaid on maps of pollutant exposure to examine the correlation between the two. Maps of job locations can be overlaid with maps of those looking for work, to see where matches or mismatches can be found. The ability to include spatial and geographic data in sociological analysis makes GIS especially useful for studying diseases, matching populations with services, and answering questions around migration (Sianko and Small 2017).

In a real-world example of the use of GIS in research, sociologists Deirdre Oakley and Keri Burchfield (2009) looked at what happened to residents of Chicago's notorious public housing projects when the buildings were demolished and the residents relocated in the early 2000s. These relocations were ostensibly meant to improve the situations of the former public housing residents—to move them out of neighborhoods of concentrated poverty, crime, racial segregation, and general disadvantage. Residents were given vouchers to assist with their moves. Oakley and Burchfield used sophisticated GIS techniques to map the residents' original locations with where they ended up after relocation, mapping each neighborhood's characteristics, such as poverty and crime rates. What they found was that while the residents may have moved to different neighborhoods, those locations weren't necessarily "better" neighborhoods. In fact, Oakley and Burchfield write, "The prospects of escaping high-poverty neighborhoods through relocation are very slim" (2009, p. 606), and it is through the use of GIS that their research shows this unfortunate outcome.

"egalitarian," depending on how they divided up household labor.

Advantages and Disadvantages

ADVANTAGES

1. Interviews allow respondents to speak in their own words; they can reveal their own thoughts, feelings, and beliefs, internal states that would not necessarily be accessible by any other means. In many other instances, it is the researcher who tells the story. A book like *The Second Shift*, which features direct quotations from interview transcripts, provides the reader with an authentic and intimate portrait of the lives of married couples. Hochschild was able to get at the different subjective experiences of the women and men in her study and to see how each of them perceived the reality of their situation.

2. Interviews may help the researcher dispel certain preconceptions and discover issues that might have otherwise been overlooked. For example, before Hochschild began her project, many other studies had already been conducted on families with two working parents, but few seemed to examine in depth the real-life dilemma of the two-career family that Hochschild herself was experiencing.

DISADVANTAGES

1. Interview respondents are not always forthcoming or truthful. They may be selective about what they say in order to present themselves in the most favorable light. Sometimes they are difficult to talk to, and at other times they may try too hard to be helpful. Although an adept interviewer will be able to encourage meaningful responses, she can never take at face value what any respondent might say. To counteract

this problem, Hochschild observed a few of the families she had interviewed. She saw that what these couples said about themselves in interviews was sometimes at odds with how they acted at home.

2. Another problem is representativeness: whether the conclusions of interview research can be applied to larger groups. Because face-to-face interviewing is time-consuming, interviews are rarely used with large numbers of people. Can findings from a small sample be generalized to a larger population? In regard to Hochschild's research, can we say that interviews with fifty couples, although carefully selected by the researcher, give a true picture of the lives of all two-career families? Hochschild answered this question by comparing selected information about her couples with data from a huge national survey.

SURVEYS

How many times have you filled out a survey? Probably more times than you realize. If you responded to the last U.S. government census, if you have ever been solicited by a polling agency to give your opinion about a public issue, or if you have ever been asked to evaluate your college classes and instructors at the end of a semester, you were part of somebody's survey research.

Surveys are questionnaires that are administered to a sample of respondents selected from a target population. One of the earliest sociologists to use informal surveys was Karl Marx. In the 1880s, Marx sent questionnaires to more than 25,000 French workers in an effort to determine the extent to which they were exploited by employers. Although we don't know how many surveys were returned to him or what the individual responses were, the project clearly influenced his writing, which focused heavily on workers' rights.

Today, many universities have research centers devoted to conducting survey research. One such center is the National Marriage Project at Rutgers University in New Jersey, where

sociologists have been engaged in ongoing studies of the health of marriage and family in America, issuing a series of reports on what they call "The State of Our Unions" over the past several years. Researchers have surveyed young adults in their twenties about a range of topics, including their attitudes toward dating, cohabitation, marriage, and parenthood.

Survey research tends to be macro and quantitative in nature: It looks at large-scale social patterns and employs statistics and other mathematical means of analysis. Social scientists who use surveys must follow specific procedures in order to produce valid results. They need a good questionnaire and wise sample selection. Most surveys are composed of closed-ended questions, or those for which all possible answers are provided. Answers may be as simple as a "yes" or "no" or more complex. A common type of questionnaire is based on the **Likert scale**, a format in which respondents can choose along a continuum—from "strongly agree" to "strongly disagree," for example. Some questionnaires also offer such options as "don't know" or "doesn't apply." Surveys may include open-ended questions, or those to which the respondents provide their own answers. These are often formatted as write-in questions and can provide researchers with more qualitative data.

Both questions and possible (given) answers on a survey must be written in such a way as to avoid confusion or ambiguity. While this is also true for interviews, it is even more important for surveys because the researcher is not generally present to clarify any misunderstandings. Common pitfalls are leading questions; **negative questions**, which ask respondents what they don't think instead of what they do; and double-barreled questions. Bias can also be a problem if questions or answers are worded in a slanted fashion.

The format of a questionnaire is also important. Something as simple as the order in which the items are presented can influence responses. Mentioning an issue like divorce or infidelity in earlier questions can mean that respondents are thinking about it when they answer later questions, and as a result, their answers might be different than they would otherwise have been. Questionnaires should be clear and easy to follow. Once a questionnaire is constructed, it is a good idea to have a small group pretest it to ensure it is clear and comprehensible. A preliminary small-scale **pilot study** can help to work out any issues with the survey design before administering it to a larger group.

Another important element in survey research is sampling techniques. As with interviews, the researcher must identify the specific target population she wishes to study: for example, "all married couples with children living at home" or "all young adults between the ages of twenty and twenty-nine." By using correct sampling techniques, researchers can survey a smaller number of respondents and then make accurate inferences about the larger population. In quantitative research, social scientists use **probability sampling**, in which random number generation is used to select participants. By

---

SURVEYS research method based on questionnaires that are administered to a sample of respondents selected from a target population

LIKERT SCALE a way of formatting a survey questionnaire so that the respondent can choose an answer along a continuum

NEGATIVE QUESTIONS survey questions that ask respondents what they don't think instead of what they do think

PILOT STUDY a small-scale study carried out to test the feasibility of conducting a study on a larger scale

PROBABILITY SAMPLING any sampling procedure that uses randomization

SIMPLE RANDOM SAMPLE a particular type of probability sample in which every member of the population has an equal chance of being selected

RESPONSE RATE the number or percentage of surveys completed by respondents and returned to researchers

RELIABILITY the consistency of a question or measurement tool; the degree to which the same questions will produce similar answers

randomly choosing participants, researchers ensure that the sample is unbiased and therefore representative of the target population. The most basic type of probability sample is a **simple random sample**, where each member of the larger target population has an equal chance of being included in the sample based on random number generation. A simple random sample is equivalent to randomly drawing names from a hat.

In order for a survey to be considered valid, there must be a sufficiently high **response rate**. It is sometimes difficult to get enough individuals to participate in a survey. Even if only half of a sample group actually returned the completed surveys, that would be considered a very good result. General claims can be made about a larger population from a survey with a response rate of only 20 to 30 percent as long as proper sampling techniques were used. Once the surveys are returned, the researchers begin the process of tabulating and analyzing the data. Responses are usually coded or turned into numerical figures so that they can be more easily analyzed on a computer. Researchers often want to understand the relationship between certain variables; for instance, what is the effect of infidelity on divorce? There are many computer applications, such as SPSS (Statistical Package for the Social Sciences) and Stata, that can help researchers perform complicated calculations and reach conclusions about relationships. This is where advanced statistical skills become an important part of social analysis.

An increasing number of researchers use the Internet rather than conduct survey research in person or by mail (Best and Krueger 2004; Sue and Ritter 2007). The Internet has opened up new possibilities for reaching respondents as more and more people have Internet access. While online surveys promise a certain amount of ease and cost-effectiveness, they also present researchers with significant challenges, especially in terms of scientific sampling. For example, Survey Monkey provides free online survey capabilities to just about anyone. While the software does offer some assistance in writing good questions, calculating randomness, and doing representative sampling, users who are not trained social scientists will likely not make use of these features. This creates a conundrum: Survey Monkey and other online survey tools can make survey methods more accessible to users, but it is still the users themselves—not the software—who have to make sure the survey is reliable, valid, and representative. As more researchers use online methods, the perception of them as unconventional or out of the mainstream is fading (Roberts et al. 2016).

Advantages and Disadvantages

ADVANTAGES

1. Survey research is one of the best methods for gathering original data on a population that is too large to study by other means, such as by direct observation or interviews. Surveys can be widely distributed, reaching a large number of people. Researchers can then generalize their findings to an even larger population.

2. Survey research is also relatively quick and economical and can provide a vast amount of data. Online surveys now promise a way to gain access to even greater numbers of people at even lower cost.

3. In general, survey research is comparatively strong on **reliability**. This means that we can be sure that the same kind of data are collected each time the same question is asked.

4. In survey research, there is less concern about interviewer or observer bias entering into the research process. Respondents may feel more comfortable giving candid answers to sensitive questions because they answer the questions in private and are usually assured of the anonymity of their responses.

DISADVANTAGES

1. Survey research generally lacks qualitative data that might better capture the social reality the researcher wishes to examine. Because most survey questions don't allow the respondent to qualify his answer, they don't allow for a full range of expression and may not accurately reflect the true meaning of the respondent's thoughts. For example, asking a respondent to choose one reason from a list of reasons for divorce might not provide a full explanation for the failure of that person's marriage. The reasons may have been both financial and emotional, but the survey may not provide the respondent with the ability to convey this answer. Adding write-in questions is one way to minimize this disadvantage.

2. In general, since not all respondents are honest in self-reports, survey research is comparatively weak on validity. For example, a respondent may be ashamed about his divorce and may not want to reveal the true reasons behind it to a stranger on a questionnaire.

3. Often there are problems with the sampling process, especially when respondents self-select to participate, that make generalizability more difficult. Gathering data online only exacerbates this problem. For instance, if a survey seeking to know the incidence of domestic violence in the population is administered only to the members of a domestic violence support group, then the incidence of domestic violence will be 100 percent—misrepresenting the true rate of incidence in the larger population.

4. It's possible that survey research will be used to make a claim or support a point of view rather than for pure scientific discovery; for example, a manufacturer of SUVs

may report that 90 percent of all American families surveyed wish they had a larger car. We will consider this limitation later, in the section on nonacademic uses of research methods.

DATA WORKSHOP

Analyzing Media and Pop Culture

Media Usage Patterns

The average American spends around eleven hours a day using some type of electronic media—computers, tablets, TV, radio, smartphones, and so on (Nielsen 2018). That's almost half a day, or nearly two-thirds of our waking hours. For many people this means that they rarely unplug. But there is more to the picture than just the total number of hours Americans spend using media. What other kinds of questions might we be interested in asking about this increasingly important aspect of our lives?

For example, we might ask people what kind of media they are using. How much time is spent with each of these, as well as when and where? How much money do individuals spend on media-related equipment or activities? How much do people multitask, using more than one device at a time? Do different groups prefer different types of media? How do factors like age, education, gender, or income influence media usage? What else do people do while using media—do they work, eat, clean, talk, drive, exercise, study, or even sleep? Now come up with more of your own questions!

In this Data Workshop, you will be conducting your own survey research about media usage in everyday life. Consult the relevant section of this chapter for a review of this method. Your task is twofold. First, you will get some practice designing a study and constructing and administering a survey questionnaire. Second, you will get the chance to do a preliminary analysis of the data you collect and possibly discover something for yourself about the patterns of media usage among those who participate in your pilot study.

Because of the variety of ways of doing such a project, you should choose how you would like to customize your research. Since this is only a preliminary effort at survey research, the project will have to be somewhat limited. Nonetheless, try to follow these basic steps in order to make your research process as scientific as possible:

1. Decide what aspects of media usage you want to study.

2. Select a sample from the target population you wish to study (student athletes, seniors, people with a college degree, and so on).

3. Write and format your survey questionnaire.

4. Administer the questionnaire to the individuals in your sample.

5. Analyze the data collected in the survey, and present your findings.

There are two options for completing this Data Workshop:

PREP-PAIR-SHARE Working in small groups of three to four students, begin designing a survey project by discussing Steps 1 and 2. Then collaborate on Step 3. If time allows, play the role of a pilot group and test the questionnaire by filling out the survey as outlined in Step 4. Then consider Step 5, looking for any patterns that may have emerged from the data. Finally, discuss as a group what needs to be changed or what else needs to be accomplished to complete an actual survey.

DO-IT-YOURSELF Design your own survey research project, completing all of the preceding steps. Choose at least five to eight people to be included in your sample. After administering the questionnaire, write a three- to four-page essay discussing the research process and your preliminary findings. What was the most challenging part of doing survey research? What insights did you gain about media usage from the participants in your study? What would you change if you intended to do a larger study in the future? Remember to attach the survey questionnaire to your paper.

EXISTING SOURCES

Nearly all sociologists use **existing sources** when they approach a particular research question. As the term implies, an almost unlimited amount of data already exists out there in the world that can be useful to sociologists for their studies. With other methods, researchers have to generate their own data firsthand from field notes, interviews, or surveys. With existing (or secondary) sources, researchers may discover a treasure trove of data in unexpected places or hidden in plain view, ready for the taking. This material can include everything from archival or historical records such as marriage licenses or building permits to various forms of media such as books, magazines, TV shows, or websites. While all these materials may have been created for another purpose, they can constitute valuable data to be used in social research. Existing sources are considered **unobtrusive measures** because they don't require that the researcher intrude upon or disturb the people in a social context or setting they are studying.

Sociologists take different approaches to working with existing sources. For instance, social demographers study the size, composition, growth, and distribution of human populations. The statistical information used in such research is generally produced by other social scientists or by government agencies such as public health departments. In fact, the U.S. Census Bureau makes a massive amount of its data freely available to the public on its website, Census.gov. Other sociologists do what could be called "social archaeology." They dig through and examine the social environment in order to understand the people in it. For instance, the average American throws away over two pounds of garbage a day. What might we learn by looking through someone's trash?

Some sociologists do **comparative historical research**, which seeks to understand relationships between elements of society in various regions and time periods. These researchers go back in time and analyze cultural artifacts such as literature, paintings, newspapers, and photographs (Bauer and Gaskell 2000). As an example, social historian Peter Stearns (2004) consulted various existing sources for his book *Anxious Parents: A History of Modern Childrearing in America* to investigate the changing meanings of childhood during the nineteenth and twentieth centuries and how these changing views influenced the way Americans parent their children. He examined child-rearing manuals that were popular at the time, as well as newspapers and journals.

These documents showed that, while children were once viewed as self-sufficient mini-adults whose labor both within and outside the home was necessary to keep families afloat, prevailing social norms began to change in the late 1800s. The world was changing rapidly: Industrial expansion, rapid population growth, urbanization, and technological advances in sanitation, transportation, and communication bewildered parents and led to a wave of advice-giving from "experts." In the face of unsettling social change, children were seen as particularly vulnerable. Parents felt an urgent obligation to protect them from strong emotions like fear, loneliness, or grief; from afflictions like polio, tooth decay, poor posture, and "crib death" (SIDS); from kidnappers, murderers, sexual predators, and schoolyard bullies; from poisoned Halloween candy, boredom, loss of innocence, and errant dodgeballs. Being held responsible for their children's protection from these endless sources of harm, many parents experienced a sense of guilt and anxiety that increased steadily over the course of the twentieth century. Stearns charted these changes using existing sources and found them ominous. Indeed, his work may have predicted the advent of today's "helicopter parent."

Content analysis is another widely used approach to

"Your mom is a little overprotective, isn't she?"

Helicopter Parents Peter Stearns used existing sources such as child-rearing manuals for his study of the changing meanings of childhood.

working with existing sources. Researchers look for recurrent themes or count the number of times that specific variables—such as particular words or visual elements—appear in a text, image, or media message. They then analyze the variables and relationships among them. For example, content analysis has repeatedly shown that the roles women play on television are typically of lower status than are the roles of men and continue to reinforce traditional gender stereotypes. Women are more likely than men to be portrayed as nonprofessionals—housewives and mothers—and are more likely to be sexualized and shown in provocative clothing, whereas men usually hold professional statuses in addition to being portrayed as husbands and fathers (Collins 2011). Despite some recent improvements in the depiction of women in the media, this pattern has persisted.

> **EXISTING SOURCES** materials that have been produced for some other reason but that can be used as data for social research
>
> **UNOBTRUSIVE MEASURES** research methods that rely on existing sources and where the researcher does not intrude upon or disturb the social setting or its subjects
>
> **COMPARATIVE HISTORICAL RESEARCH** research that uses existing sources to study relationships among elements of society in various regions and time periods
>
> **CONTENT ANALYSIS** a method in which researchers identify and study specific variables or themes that appear in a text, image, or media message

Advantages and Disadvantages

ADVANTAGES

1. Researchers are able to work with information they could not possibly obtain on their own. The U.S. Census Bureau, for example, collects information about

the entire national population (family size, education, income, occupational status, and residential patterns), something an individual researcher has neither the time nor funds to do. In addition, the analysis of existing data can be a convenient way for sociologists to pool their resources; one researcher can take data collected by another and use it for his own project, thereby increasing what can be learned from the same set of data.

2. Using sources such as newspapers, political speeches, and cultural artifacts, sociologists are able to learn about many social worlds, in different time periods, that they would never be able to enter themselves; for example, preserved letters and diaries from the early 1800s have allowed researchers to analyze the experiences of wives and mothers on the American frontier (Peavy and Smith 1998).

3. Researchers can use the same data to replicate projects that have been conducted before, which is a good way to test findings for reliability or to see changes across time.

DISADVANTAGES

1. Researchers drawing on existing sources often seek to answer questions that the original authors did not have in mind. If you were interested in the sex lives of those frontier women in the early 1800s, for example, you would be unlikely to find any clear references in their letters or diaries.

2. Similarly, content analysis, although it can describe the messages inherent in the media, does not illuminate how such messages are interpreted. So we can say that women's roles on television have lower status than men's, but additional research would be required to identify the effects of these images on viewers.

EXPERIMENTAL METHODS

Unlike participant observation, interviews, surveys, or existing sources, **experiments** actually closely resemble the scientific method with which we began this chapter. You might

EXPERIMENTS formal tests of specific variables and effects, performed in a setting where all aspects of the situation can be controlled

EXPERIMENTAL GROUP the members of a test group who receive the experimental treatment

CONTROL GROUP the members of a test group who are allowed to continue without intervention so that they can be compared with the experimental group

INDEPENDENT VARIABLE the factor that is predicted to cause change

DEPENDENT VARIABLE the factor that is changed (or not) by the independent variable

associate experiments with laboratory scientists in white coats, but experimental research methods are also used by social scientists, some of whom are interested in such issues as group power dynamics, racial discrimination, and gender socialization. Experiments take place not only in laboratory settings but also in corporate boardrooms and even on street corners.

When sociologists conduct experiments, they start with two basic goals. First, they strive to develop precise tools with which to observe, record, and measure their data. Second, they attempt to control for all possible variables except the one under investigation: They regulate everything except the variable they're interested in so that they can draw clearer conclusions about what caused that variable to change (if it did).

For instance, a classic social experiment might be set up like this: A researcher who is interested in divorce wants to investigate whether marriage counseling actually helps couples stay together. He would recruit couples for the experiment and then randomly assign them to two different groups, making sure that members of each group were similar in terms of age, income, education, and religion as well as length of time married. One group, the **experimental group**, would receive marriage counseling, while the other, the **control group**, would not. In this experiment, marriage counseling is the **independent variable**; it is the factor that is predicted to cause change in the experimental group. The **dependent variable** (or factor that is changed by the independent variable) is the likelihood of staying married or getting divorced. In such an experiment, the researcher could compare the two groups and then make conclusions about whether receiving marriage counseling leads to more couples staying married, leads to more couples getting divorced, or has no impact at all.

Another area in which sociological experiments have been conducted is gender-role socialization in families. Research has shown that a child's earliest exposure to what it means to be a boy or girl comes from parents and other caregivers. Boy and girl infants are treated differently by adults—from the way they're dressed to the toys they're given to play with—and are expected to act differently (Thorne 1993). In one experiment, adult subjects were asked to play with a small baby, who was dressed in either pink or blue. The subjects assumed the gender of the infant by the color of its clothes and acted accordingly. When they thought it was a boy (in blue), they handled the baby less gently and talked in a louder voice, saying things like, "Aren't you a big, strong boy?" When they thought it was a girl (in pink), they held the baby closer to themselves and spoke more softly: "What a sweet little girl!" In both cases, it was actually the same baby; only the color of the clothing (independent variable) was changed. The study subjects' reactions (dependent variable), however, changed as a result. From this experiment, we can see how gender

Gender-Role Socialization Starts in Infancy In Barrie Thorne's experiment, she asked adults to play with babies dressed in either blue or pink. Thorne found that people treated the baby differently depending on whether they thought it was a girl or a boy.

influences the way that we perceive and interact with others from a very early age.

Sociologists may also use quasi-experimental methods when they study ethnic and gender discrimination in housing, employment, or policing (Brief et al. 1995; Charles 2001; Correll, Benard, and Paik 2007; Pager 2007). In these studies, individuals who were similar in all respects except for ethnicity or gender were asked to interview for the same jobs, apply for the same mortgage loans, or engage in some other activity. As in the pink-and-blue baby experiment, people who had exactly the same qualifications were treated differently based on their race and gender, with whites and men given better jobs or mortgage rates, and women and minorities given inferior jobs or rates or none at all. Through such studies, researchers are able to observe behaviors that may indicate discrimination or unequal treatment.

On the whole, data analysis for experimental sociology tends to be quantitative rather than qualitative, because the main goal of an experiment is to isolate a variable and explore the degree to which that variable affects a particular social situation (Smith 1990). The quantitative techniques for analyzing data range from straightforward statistical analyses to complex mathematical modeling.

Advantages and Disadvantages

ADVANTAGES

1. Experiments give sociologists a way to manipulate and control the social environment they seek to understand. Experiments can be designed so that there is a minimal amount of outside interference. A researcher can construct a model of the social situation she is interested in and watch as it unfolds before her, without any of the unpredictable intrusions of the real world. Researchers can also select participants who have exactly the

characteristics they want to explore, such as the babies and adults in the gender-role socialization experiment.

2. Experimental methods are the best methods for establishing causality—whether a change in the independent variable *causes* a change in the dependent variable. This ability to assess causality makes experiments particularly effective at detecting bias and discrimination, such as discrimination against mothers in the workplace, known as the "motherhood penalty" (Correll, Benard, and Paik 2007).

3. Much like physics experiments, highly controlled sociological experiments can theoretically be repeated—they have replicability—so that findings can be tested more than once. An experiment such as the pink-and-blue baby study could easily be performed again and again to gauge historical and cultural changes in gender socialization.

DISADVANTAGES

1. Experiments are applicable only to certain types of research that can be constructed and measured in a controlled setting. Laboratories are by design artificial environments. We take a leap in claiming that the same results found in the lab will also occur in the real world.

2. Achieving distance from the messy realities of the social world is also the major weakness with sociological experiments. Although experiments can be useful for the development of theory and for explaining the impact of isolated variables, they are generally not very effective for describing more complex processes and interactions. By definition, experiments seek to eliminate elements that will have an unforeseen effect, and that's just not the way the real world works.

SOCIAL NETWORK ANALYSIS

Starting in the early twentieth century, social scientists began to explore how people are connected to one another and how these connections influence their behavior, put them at risk for disease, and even predict mental health. Social network analysis (SNA) is a tool for measuring and visualizing the structure of social relationships between two or more people. Using a questionnaire, researchers ask respondents to name who within a given community they look to for information, advice, support, and so on. These data are then used to study disease transmission, information diffusion, adolescent risk behaviors, corporate behavior, and many other topics (Kadushin 2012).

For example, Figure 2.2 is a network diagram of friendships among twelve-year-old students in one sixth-grade class. Each colored dot is a girl (red) or boy (blue) in the class, and the arrows represent social ties. As you can see, the girls are almost exclusively friends with other girls, as are boys with other boys. Looking at the cluster of girls, you see a few girls with a lot of arrows pointing to them. This means that many other students identified these girls as their friends. The more arrows pointing *in*, the more popular—or "central"—that person is within the network.

Another important position within this network is those students who link the boys and girls to one another. These "bridges" enable information to flow between the groups (also called "cliques"). It is worth noting that only girls identified boys as friends; no boys identified girls as friends (as shown by the directionality of the arrows). Thus, we can say that these ties lack *reciprocity*, meaning the arrows, or connections, flow in only one direction. Finally, every member of this network is connected in about three steps or has an average of three degrees of separation from every other member. Researchers use these types of data to understand how social networks influence substance abuse, bullying and victimization, and delinquency and to design interventions to address adolescent issues.

With the advent of social media, especially Facebook in the early 2000s, "social network" became a household phrase. While many people today mistakenly think that SNA began with the study of online social networks, it well predates the Internet. Some of the earliest work in the area of SNA began with sociologist Georg Simmel, who studied social ties among members of a community and how the size of a group affects the relationships among its members, or *actors*. In the late 1960s, Stanley Milgram's work on the "small world" phenomenon brought publicity to the field with his studies showing that everyone is connected by an average of five and a half to six steps to everyone else in the world (Travers and Milgram 1969). This phenomenon was later termed the "six degrees of separation." The advent of computer programs for analyzing networks helped create a large, diverse field that incorporates scientists from varying fields, including sociology, anthropology, political science, medicine, physics, and computer science.

Social network programs have now been created to study large-scale networks such as Instagram, Facebook, Twitter, Snapchat, and LinkedIn. Today, social network researchers can study Twitter feeds and other social media sites to discover patterns of communication between and within terrorist groups in order to disrupt their activities (Everton 2012). Studies of social media are also being conducted to better understand the flow of information, the nature of political discourse, and types of civic engagement. One such study looked at how organizers of the Occupy Wall Street movement used Twitter to organize and spread the movement (Tremayne 2014).

Advantages and Disadvantages

ADVANTAGES

1. Social network analysis can trace the route of just about anything—an idea, disease, rumor, or trend—as it moves through a social group, community, or society. This makes SNA a useful method for epidemiologists (scientists who study diseases within populations), political sociologists, and market researchers.

2. Social network analysis contributes to the production of "big data"—data sets so large that typical computer and storage programs cannot handle them—which has become increasingly popular in both the academic and the business worlds. Big data enables corporations to identify major trends quickly, target audiences effectively, and make predictions. Big data also creates new fields of research for social scientists (Lazar et al. 2009).

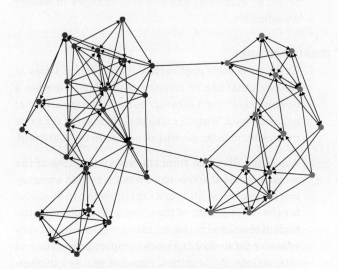

FIGURE 2.2 Network Diagram of Friendships among Students in One Sixth-Grade Class

SOURCE: Valente 2015.

DISADVANTAGES

1. Social network analysis, because it is fundamentally quantitative, can gloss over important details and diversity in the experiences of social actors.

2. Big data is expensive to collect and analyze, and large social network data sets often come from sources that have been assembled for other purposes (such as advertising) or that pose a threat to privacy. Big data is often criticized as nontheoretical "data dumps." If you look at a network with thousands or millions of links, you're likely to discover *some* sort of finding. The question becomes one of asking whether such a finding would hold up in a smaller, more connected, interpersonal network.

ISSUES IN SOCIOLOGICAL RESEARCH

As sociologists, we don't conduct our research in a cultural vacuum. In our professional as well as personal lives, all our actions have consequences, and we must be aware of how the things we do affect others. For this reason, any introduction to sociological methods is incomplete without a discussion of three topics: the nonacademic uses of sociological research; values, objectivity, and reactivity in the research process; and the importance of ethics in conducting social research.

Nonacademic Uses of Research Methods

The research methods discussed in this chapter are frequently applied outside the field of sociology. The U.S. Census Bureau, for example, has been taking a survey of the total population once every ten years since 1790. The census attempts to reach every person residing in the country and makes reports available on a wide range of social, demographic, and economic features. Many government decisions, from where to build a new school or hospital to where to install a new stoplight, are made using demographic data from the census and other major surveys.

Sociological research methods are also used by private organizations, such as political campaign offices and news agencies. You are probably familiar with polls (another form of survey research) conducted by organizations like Gallup, Zogby, and Roper. And you have certainly seen the results of election polls, which indicate the candidates or issues voters are likely to support. Polls, however, do not just reflect public opinion; they can also be used to shape it. Not all of them are conducted under strict scientific protocols. Whenever you hear poll results, try to learn who commissioned the poll and determine whether they are promoting (or opposing) any particular agenda.

Businesses and corporations have turned to sociological research in order to better understand the human dynamics within their companies. Some ethnographers, for instance, have studied organizational culture and reported their findings to executives. Edgar Schein (1997, 2010) is often referred to as an industrial ethnographer because he conducts fieldwork in business settings in order to help management identify and deal with dilemmas in the workplace, such as how to motivate workers. Many of the experimental "games" developed by sociological researchers can be put to use in the business world to build teams, train employees, or even conduct job interviews. During a corporate retreat, for example, employees might be asked to participate in an obstacle or ropes course, in which they have to work together in order to succeed. By observing the strategies participants use, an employer might learn how task-oriented networks are formed, how leaders are chosen, or how cooperation emerges under pressure. Similarly, experimental games that require subjects to budget imaginary money or communicate an idea in a round of charades may offer insight into how social groups operate or may identify the most effective communicators from a pool of applicants.

Market research is perhaps the most common of all nonacademic uses of sociological methods. In order to be successful, most companies will engage in some sort of study of the marketplace, either through their own internal sales and marketing departments or by hiring an outside consultant. The efforts of all these companies to understand the buying public have created a multibillion-dollar marketing and advertising industry. If you've ever clicked "yes" on a pop-up dialog box from a website, allowed "cookies" onto your browser, or cast a vote for your favorite contestants on *Dancing with the Stars*, then someone has gathered data about your tastes and habits. It is important to note, however, that not all market studies, in fact probably very few, meet the rigorous standards that are otherwise applied to "scientific" research. Remember, too, that the bottom line for any company that uses market research is the desire to sell you their products or services. Just how well do these marketers know you already?

Values, Objectivity, and Reactivity

It's important to recognize that scientific research is done by human beings, not robots. Humans have flaws, prejudices, and blind spots, and all these things can affect the way they conduct research.

VALUES Like biological or physical scientists, most sociologists believe that they should not allow their personal beliefs to influence their research. The classic sociological statement on neutrality comes from Max Weber (1925/1946), who, in his essay "Science as a Vocation," coined the phrase "value-free" sociology to convey the idea that in doing

ON THE JOB
Sociology, Market Research, and Design Strategy

After college graduation, Whitney Bush moved to Chicago because some of her best friends already lived there. It was a personal decision—she didn't have a job waiting for her, and she hadn't thought much about where to look for one. She had double-majored in sociology and math because she enjoyed both and did well in them. She headed for the Windy City, married her college sweetheart, and set about looking for a way to pay the rent. After submitting applications for a number of entry-level positions, she was called for an interview at the Nielsen Company, a leader in the commercial study of consumer behavior (what is often called "market research"). She got the job: "Working in market research was a way for me to combine my favorite part of math (statistics—the discipline of looking for meaningful patterns) with my sociology-informed curiosity about what people think, feel, and do in their everyday lives. I began learning to tell stories from data." And those stories were used by Nielsen's clients to get consumers to watch and buy products, from television shows to floor wax.

Bush quickly moved from her data-analyst role into positions that involved mentoring, managing, and training personnel at Nielsen offices all over the world. As she traveled and sometimes stayed for extended periods of time in places like Mumbai, India, she found her sociology education helpful in other ways, too, and enjoyed learning about and adapting to new cultures as part of her work. But then Bush's personal life took an unexpected turn. Getting divorced while still in her twenties was a source of uncertainty and anxiety, but it was also an opportunity to think deliberately about what she wanted to do with her future.

Bush decided to go back to school, moving across the country to enter a San Francisco–based MBA program in a field of study that hadn't even existed when she was in college. Design strategy is a discipline that combines qualitative research, design-driven innovation, and entrepreneurial

business skills to help firms make novel and profitable decisions. Despite being an emergent field and, as such, a bit of a risk, "it was a no-brainer for me," Bush said. She has since earned her MBA and returned to the world of market research, this time with a new angle: "It feels like a big lean [back] into sociology, both from the perspective of designing research as social interactions (e.g., group activities, in-context observation, etc.), as well as using sociological lenses to understand what people say and do (e.g., real vs. projected self—thanks, Erving Goffman!) and then to take strategic action."

As Bush carves out her new niche in an emergent area of work, she recognizes the ways in which her sociology degree prepared her for this unique career trajectory: "[It] cultivated in me an ability to observe, to ask why things are the way that they are, and to generate alternatives to the status quo—in my personal life as well as in my career."

Leaning into Sociology Whitney Bush's sociology degree—and well-developed sociological imagination—set her up to succeed in market research.

research, sociologists need to separate facts from their own individual values. Although most sociologists agree with this ideal, some challenge the notion of value-free sociology. For instance, some Marxist researchers believe it is appropriate to combine social research and social action, or praxis. For them, the study of society is intimately linked to a commitment to actively solve social problems. Likewise, action

research seeks not only to understand but also to change the social world. On the other hand, some symbolic interactionists, like David Matza (1969), believe that the very intention of changing the world prohibits a researcher from truly understanding that world. The question of whether sociologists should engage only in **basic research**, which is justified as the search for knowledge for its own sake, or rather engage in applied research, which requires putting into action what is learned, continues to be debated within the discipline.

Despite the safeguards built into research methods, there are still opportunities for bias, or personal preferences, to subtly influence how the work is done. Bias can infiltrate every part of the research process—from identifying a project to selecting a sample, from the wording of questions to the analysis and write-up of the data. And if bias is present in research, it can then influence any public policy decisions for which that research is used. An example is the fallout from the 2012 New Family Structures Survey (NFSS). Conducted by conservative Catholic sociologist Mark Regnerus, the NFSS found "suboptimal" outcomes for children with a gay or lesbian parent compared to children in intact, biological, mother-father families (Regnerus 2012). In other words, Regnerus claimed that kids whose parents had gay or lesbian relationships in their past or present were more likely to encounter difficulties like unemployment or marijuana use as young adults. The study was published in a reputable journal at a moment in time when the controversy surrounding same-sex marriage and LGBT parenting was especially intense.

Responses from inside and outside the sociological community were immediate. A letter signed by hundreds of researchers was published, citing a number of red flags: The research was funded by conservative and religious foundations; the article was reviewed by unqualified reviewers with obvious ties to the author; the researchers grouped all types of same-sex relations together—both long-term partnerships and brief or one-time affairs; the researchers also included in the category "children of gay parents" those children who had never or only briefly lived with a gay or lesbian parent; the researchers used analytic categories that did not distinguish between family structure and family stability, important variables for a study of youth outcomes; and the article came out just in time to be included in "friend of the court" briefs against marriage equality in significant Supreme Court cases (Oppenheimer 2012; Sherkat 2012). Even now that same-sex marriage is the law of the land, Regnerus's case raises the question of whether and how religious values and convictions can shape research questions, methods, and outcomes—and how those outcomes can influence public policy.

OBJECTIVITY The notion of **objectivity**, or impartiality, plays a fundamental role in scientific practice. As far back as Auguste Comte, sociologists have maintained that they could study society rationally and objectively. If a researcher is rational and objective, then he should be able to observe reality, distinguish actual facts from mental concepts, and separate truth from feeling or opinion. This ideal may be desirable and reasonable, but can "facts" really speak for themselves? And if so, can we discover those facts without somehow involving ourselves in them?

Some "facts" that sociologists once took to be objective

Biased Research? Many critics within and outside the discipline of sociology weighed in on Mark Regnerus's arguably biased research on gay and lesbian parents.

reality have since been invalidated. Racist, sexist, and ethnocentric perspectives long dominated the field and passed for "truth." For many years, scientific reality consisted only of the experience of white European males, and the realities of women, ethnic minorities, and other marginalized groups were categorically ignored or dismissed.

For example, until recently, heart problems in women were likely to go undiagnosed, which meant that women were more likely than men to die from heart attacks. Why? Because medical research on heart attacks used mostly male subjects and so had not discovered that women's symptoms are different from men's (Rabin 2008). It is easy now, through hindsight, to see that our "knowledge" was severely distorted. We must, therefore, be willing to recognize that what currently passes for fact may someday be challenged.

Another obstacle to achieving objectivity is our subjective nature as human beings. Our own experience of the world and, therefore, our sense of reality are inevitably personal and idiosyncratic. Although we recognize our innate subjectivity, we still long for and actively pursue what we call absolute truth. But some social scientists question this ideal; they propose that subjectivity is not only unavoidable but also may be preferable when it comes to the study of human beings. This is especially true of sociologists who do autoethnography, in which they themselves—and their own thoughts, feelings, and experiences—are the focus

BASIC RESEARCH the search for knowledge without an agenda or practical goal in mind

APPLIED RESEARCH the search for knowledge that can be used to create social change

OBJECTIVITY impartiality; the ability to allow the facts to speak for themselves

of their study (Ellis 1997). Furthermore, some postmodern thinkers have gone so far as to reject the notion that there is any objective reality out there in the first place. Their arguments parallel certain trends in the physical sciences as well, where developments such as chaos theory and fuzzy logic suggest the need to reconsider the assumption of an orderly universe.

REACTIVITY In addition to maintaining their objectivity, social scientists must be concerned with **reactivity**, the ways that people and events respond to being studied. One classic example of reactivity comes from studies that were conducted from 1927 to 1932 at the Hawthorne plant of Western Electric in Chicago. Elton Mayo (1949), a Harvard business school professor, sought to examine the effect of varying work conditions on motivation and productivity in the factory. When he changed certain conditions—such as lighting levels, rest breaks, and even rates of pay—he found that each change resulted in a rise in productivity both in the individual worker and in the group. What was more surprising, however, was that returning to the original conditions also resulted in a rise in productivity. Mayo concluded, then, that the variables he had manipulated were not the causes of productivity; rather, *it was the effect of being studied*, or what is now referred to as the **Hawthorne effect**. In other words, the workers had responded to the researchers' interest in their performance, and it was this attention that had caused the improvement.

> **REACTIVITY** the tendency of people and events to react to the process of being studied
>
> **HAWTHORNE EFFECT** a specific example of reactivity, in which the desired effect is the result not of the independent variable but of the research itself
>
> **DECEPTION** the extent to which the participants in a research project are unaware of the project or its goals
>
> **CONFIDENTIALITY** the assurance that no one other than the researcher will know the identity of a respondent

Researchers must always be aware that their subjects, whether in an experiment or in a natural observation, are active and intelligent participants. The subjects may be able to sense what the researchers are trying to understand or prove and in effect "give them what they want" by responding to even the unspoken goals of the research. Our presence as researchers always has some effect on those we study, whether noticeable to us or not.

Research Ethics

Doing research that involves other human beings means that we must address moral issues (questions about right and wrong conduct) as we make decisions that will affect them. For this reason, various academic disciplines have developed ethical guidelines—professional standards for honest and honorable dealings with others—meant to help direct the decision making of such researchers. When we use other people as means to an end, we must protect them as ends in themselves.

It's easy to understand the risks of participating in, say, a pharmaceutical drug trial or a study of the effects of radiation treatment on certain types of cancers. The risks of participating in social research are different and more subtle. It is often the case, for example, that social researchers don't fully explain the details of their research project to the participating subjects. Sometimes this is necessary; survey respondents, for example, must be able to answer questions without interference from the researcher. Also, ethnographic fieldworkers operate on various levels of secrecy, or **deception**; even when an ethnographer has openly declared herself a researcher, it is often impossible for her to remind every person she speaks with that she is a scientific observer as well as a participant. And if she engages in covert research and deliberately presents an inauthentic self to the group, that makes all her interactions inauthentic as well. This can affect the fieldworker's ability to discover the members' real, grounded meanings. What, then, has she really been able to learn about the setting and its members?

Codes of ethics in the social sciences do not provide strict rules for researchers to abide by in these cases; rather, they set out principles to guide the researcher's decision making. Secrecy and deceit are thus never strictly prohibited; instead, researchers are cautioned to acquire the informed consent of their subjects and to conduct themselves in a way that protects the subjects from harm.

What other kinds of harm can come to participants? They're not likely to get diseases, and there is usually little physical risk in sitting down to complete a survey questionnaire! But harm *can* result, mostly as a result of the breaching of **confidentiality**. Research subjects are entitled to "rights of biographical anonymity": Researchers are required to protect their privacy. This protection is essential to gathering valid data, especially when dealing with controversial topics or vulnerable populations. Respondents must be guaranteed that no one will be able to identify them from reading the research findings. But while most researchers take steps to disguise the identities of individuals and locations, it is sometimes difficult to keep others from uncovering them. For example, in two classic sociological studies the pseudonym "Middletown" was used to evoke the notion of an "average" American city and to conceal that city's real name and location (Lynd and Lynd 1929/1959, 1937). In spite of this intention, it was long ago revealed to be Muncie, Indiana—and since the town featured in the Middletown studies was widely viewed as an example of the shallowness and triviality of modern American culture, this was not such a good thing for Muncie's reputation!

Sometimes, worse than having others recognize a place or person is having subjects themselves find out what was written about them. Carolyn Ellis (1995, 2007) had an unsettling

GLOBAL PERSPECTIVE
The Nuremberg Code and Research Ethics

The origins of contemporary research ethics can be traced back to the Nuremberg military tribunals of the late 1940s, in which a group of Nazi doctors were tried for the horrific "experiments" they had performed during World War II. These experiments involved the torture and death of thousands of concentration camp inmates. Of the twenty-three Nazi doctors tried at Nuremberg, sixteen were convicted of war crimes. Besides a kind of justice for the deaths of so many, the other enduring result of the trials was the Nuremberg Code, a set of moral and ethical guidelines for performing research on human beings. According to these guidelines, developed by two doctors, Andrew Ivy and Leo Alexander, scientists must accept certain responsibilities: to perform only research that can "yield fruitful results for the good of society, unprocurable by other methods"; to protect their human subjects from "all unnecessary physical and mental suffering and injury"; and to perform research only on subjects who give their informed, noncoerced consent.

In the United States, there was strong support for the Nuremberg Code. But at the same time that the code was being developed, the U.S. government was involved in its own medical atrocity, though it would not be revealed to the public until decades later: the Tuskegee Syphilis Study. In 1932, the U.S. Public Health Service began a forty-year-long study of "untreated syphilis in the male negro": 399 African American men from Tuskegee, an impoverished region of Alabama, who were infected with syphilis were left untreated

so that doctors could observe the natural progression of the disease. The symptoms include painful sores, hair loss, sterility, blindness, paralysis, and insanity—and almost always led to death. The disease can be transmitted by men to their sexual partners, and infected women can pass it on to their infants. By 1947, penicillin was widely accepted as the preferred treatment for syphilis, but government doctors decided to leave the Tuskegee men untreated to avoid interfering with the study's results. Black lives were seen as dispensable. These doctors may not have intentionally inflicted the disease on the subjects, but they did not offer a cure when it became available.

The full story of the Tuskegee experiment was not revealed until 1972, and it was not until 1997 that President Bill Clinton issued an official apology from the U.S. government to the victims and their families. Clearly, Americans were as guilty of violating moral and ethical codes as Germans had been at a similar time in history.

What is important to take away from this lesson is the need for all scientific research to adhere to ethical standards—this includes the social as well as medical sciences. In either case, researchers must consider the potential harm that they can cause to human subjects. You may not think of sociologists as dealing with life-and-death issues; yet, as researchers, we often find ourselves in positions where certain kinds of studies cannot be undertaken because of concerns for the well-being of the potential subjects.

The Nuremberg Code In the wake of the Nuremberg military tribunals after World War II, science organizations adopted a set of guidelines to regulate researchers' ethical conduct. Whether in biology, psychiatry, or sociology, researchers must consider the potential harm they can cause to research participants.

"Middletown" Although Robert S. Lynd and Helen Merrell Lynd used the pseudonym "Middletown" in their classic studies of stagnation and change in modern American culture, it was long ago revealed that Middletown is actually Muncie, Indiana.

experience when she returned to the small mid-Atlantic fishing village in which she had spent years living and doing fieldwork. In the time she had been gone, she had published a book about the village, and excerpts had made their way back to the villagers, who were upset with the way that Ellis had depicted them. These villagers, who had considered Ellis to be their friend, felt deeply betrayed; they felt that she had abused their hospitality and misrepresented them as uncouth, uneducated hicks. Despite her protests that she was simply doing her job as a sociologist, many villagers refused to speak with her again, and she was shut out of a social world of which she had once been an integral part.

More recently, Alice Goffman (yes, daughter of Erving) incited a heated debate on research ethics with her controversial ethnography on the troubled lives of a group of young black men in Philadelphia, whom she spent six years getting to know. *On the Run: Fugitive Life in an American City* was published to great acclaim, catapulting the young scholar into the spotlight—and inciting a serious backlash. The book reignited important, age-old questions about the politics of representation, or who can speak for whom. Can a privileged white woman with expensive degrees really

CODE OF ETHICS ethical guidelines for researchers to consult as they design a project

INSTITUTIONAL REVIEW BOARD a group of scholars within a university who meet regularly to review and approve the research proposals of their colleagues and make recommendations for how to protect human subjects

speak for these marginalized minority men? But it was an anonymous sixty-page critique that really put Goffman in the hot seat. The unsigned letter included a long list of alleged inconsistencies that called into question the truthfulness of Goffman's account of events. Goffman explained that many of the inconsistencies were the result of her efforts to protect the anonymity of her sources, as required by the American Sociological Association (ASA) Code of Ethics.

One particularly problematic passage, according to her critics, constitutes not only an ethical violation but also a prosecutable felony. In the wake of a friend's murder, "Mike" searches for the shooter in order to kill him, and Goffman often served as his chauffeur. Not only were some of her fellow social scientists disturbed by this admission, legal experts were too. Northwestern University law professor Steven Lubet wrote in a review article: "Taking Goffman's narrative at face value, one would have to conclude that her actions—driving around with an armed man, looking for somebody to kill—constituted conspiracy to commit murder under Pennsylvania law" (Lubet 2015).

As we noted earlier, ethical violations are not the same as criminal violations, and in this case, the alleged criminal violation is a serious one. Goffman has not been and likely will not be charged with any crime, at least in part because the statute of limitations has expired. But her case reminds us that even sociologists can sometimes find themselves on the wrong side of the law.

In order to encourage the protection of research subjects, each academic discipline has adopted its own **code of ethics** to provide guidelines for researchers. The ASA Code of Ethics, for example, sets out recommendations for how to avoid bias, adhere to professional standards, and protect respondents from harm. In addition, universities where research is conducted have a body known as an **institutional review board**, or IRB, a group of scholars who meet regularly to review the research proposals of their colleagues. If an IRB has reservations about the safety of the participants in a given research project, it may require changes to the protocol or may even stop the project from going forward. In extreme cases, funding may be revoked if the participants are being put at undue risk; entire university power structures have been undermined as a result of pervasive research ethics problems.

The power invested in IRBs is seen as controversial by some. The boards are often made up entirely of scholars in medicine, biology, chemistry, and physics; social scientists have questioned these scholars' ability to make judgments about social research. Because IRBs have the power to shut down research projects, perhaps they should be discipline-specific, with biologists judging biologists, psychologists judging psychologists, and sociologists judging sociologists.

Closing Comments

In this chapter, you have learned the different methods used by sociologists to investigate the social world. Each method has its strengths and limitations, and each can be fruitfully applied to a variety of research questions. In fact, this is exactly what you will be doing.

Each chapter from this point on will feature two Data Workshops in which you will be asked to apply one of the methods from this chapter to an actual sociological research project. You will get a chance to practice doing the work of sociological research by actually gathering and analyzing your own data. You may find yourself referring back to this chapter to remind yourself of the specific mechanics of one or another of the research methods. This is exactly what you should be doing; it's okay if two months from now you don't remember all the details. Just because you're moving on to Chapter 3, don't forget that Chapter 2 can continue to be useful to you throughout the term—and maybe even beyond that.

APPLYING WHAT YOU'VE LEARNED

Let's Talk More

1. Quantitative and qualitative methods make different assumptions and use different types of data and analysis. Compare and contrast these differences.

2. Try to write a survey or interview question that asks about a respondent's political affiliation without being biased or using language that might spark an emotional response.

3. The ASA Code of Ethics guides sociologists' treatment of people who participate in their research. As a student of sociology, what are your ethical obligations?

Let's Explore More

1. **Film** Condon, Bill, dir. *Kinsey*. 2004.

2. **Article** Oppenheimer, Mark. "Sociologist's Paper Raises Questions on Role of Faith in Scholarship." *The New York Times*. October 12, 2012.

3. **Blog Post** Sternheimer, Karen. "What Is Sociological Research?" *Everyday Sociology* (blog). June 3, 2019. *https://WWNorton.com/rd/Gt64F.*

PART II
Framing Social Life

How does culture shape our social worlds? How are our personal identities produced by our cultural contexts and social interactions? How does participation in group life shape both individual experience and social structure? How are what is normal and what is deviant defined, and what are the consequences for people who are labeled accordingly? Part II of this text addresses these questions in the next four chapters on culture (Chapter 3), the self and interaction (Chapter 4), groups (Chapter 5), and deviance (Chapter 6). The ability to examine, describe, analyze, and explain the points of intersection between the individual world and the social world is sociology's special contribution to the larger scholarly endeavor. Within the next four chapters, you will encounter many works by sociologists that illustrate the links between the individual and society. Leila Rupp and Verta Taylor's book *Drag Queens at the 801 Cabaret* (2003) is perfect for highlighting these themes.

Drag Queens at the 801 Cabaret is an ethnographic portrait of a Key West, Florida, drag club, where gay male performers don sexy dresses, lavish wigs, and theatrical makeup and sing and dance for a diverse audience: tourists and locals, men and women, gays and straights. Rupp and Taylor spend time getting to know the "801 girls" as well as their friends, family, and audience members.

Rupp and Taylor recognize that the particular culture of the 801 Cabaret is nestled within multiple contemporary American subcultures. For example, Key West is an island subculture that offers a year-round touristy, carnivalesque atmosphere as part of its charm. It "remains a flamboyant mix of cultures.... [I]t shelters not only vibrant Cuban and Bahamian enclaves, but also artistic, hippie, and gay communities.... The city [says journalist Charles Kuralt] is 'full of dreamers, drifters, and dropouts, spongers and idlers and barflies, writers and fishermen, islanders from the Caribbean and gays from the big cities, painters and pensioners, treasure hunters, real estate speculators, smugglers, runaways, old Conchs and young lovers...all elaborately tolerant of one another'" (Rupp and Taylor 2003, pp. 50–51). For the 801 girls, this means that the subcultures associated with both gay masculinity and drag performance are supported and sustained on the island in ways they might not be on the mainland. Because of the island's unique mix of subcultures, one of the performers asserts that "Key West is the true home of accepted diversity" (p. 55).

In Key West's culture, many kinds of people feel free to be themselves. But what does that really mean? For the drag queens at the 801 Cabaret, their performances are about putting on a different identity than the one they present in their everyday lives. These are men with flashy female alter egos: Kevin becomes "Kylie"; Roger becomes "Inga"; Dean becomes "Milla." And their process of becoming is elaborate and grueling:

> Some of the girls shave all over their bodies, some their faces, chests, legs, and arms, some just their faces.... They powder their faces, necks, and chests, using a thick base to hide their beards.... Eyeliner, eye shadow, mascara, false eyelashes, lip liner, and lipstick are painstakingly applied. (pp. 12–13)

So far, this doesn't sound all that different from the rituals many women perform every morning in front of the mirror. After the makeup, however, things get a little more intricate, as the "girls"

Performing Gender Drag queens and "real" women perform femininity in similar ways.

Drag Queens on Stage How do drag queens use entertainment and performance to undermine gender stereotypes?

tuck their penises and testicles between their legs, using a gaff [a special panty], or several, to make sure everything stays out of sight…panty hose, sometimes several layers…corsets and waist cinchers…they all, of course, wear bras…[filled with] water balloons (the tied end makes an amazingly realistic nipple), half a Nerf football, lentil beans in a pair of nylons, foam or silicone prostheses. (pp. 20–21)

All this work to look like women—and that's not taking into account the exhausting work of acting the part, onstage and off. While drag queens do not seek to convince their audiences that they are "real" women, they do move, speak, sing, and dance in stereotypically feminine style as part of their performances. And that's the insight that drag queens provide about our own identities: It's *all* performance! Our male and female selves are the products of interactional accomplishments, and "real" women do many of the same things that drag queens do in order to express femininity.

Because the drag queens perform different identities onstage and off, the 801 Cabaret calls into question some of our most important and taken-for-granted boundaries between social groups: males and females, and gays and straights. In fact, drag queens are living examples of the intersections between these groups. One of the performers says:

> Last night—though this happens almost every night— [this woman] goes, "I'm straight, I'm a woman, I'm not a lesbian, but you're so beautiful, I find you so attractive" …[and] a straight guy, has been straight for like fifty years or something like that…goes, "You know, I've been straight all my life, and I know you're a man, but you're so beautiful.…I can't keep my eyes off you." (p. 201)

Drag queens and drag shows allow others to cross between groups, to see what life might be like in a world in which gender boundaries are fluid and homosexuality is normal:

> As one of the few ways that straight people encounter gay culture—where, in fact, straight people live for an hour or two in an environment where gay is normal and straight is other—drag shows…play an important role for the gay/lesbian movement. Precisely because drag shows are entertaining, they attract people who might never otherwise be exposed to gay politics. As one female audience member put it, they "take something difficult and make it light." (pp. 207–208)

Finally, drag shows also challenge our notions about what is normal and what is deviant; performers embrace what would otherwise be considered a stigmatized identity and turn it into something to be proud of. Drag queens can be seen as voluntary outsiders, unconcerned about fitting into mainstream society. Rupp and Taylor make the argument that drag is a form of social protest—against a society in which gender and sexual orientation are crammed into limiting, two-category systems; in which identities are seen as immutable; and in which certain forms of cultural expression are marginalized. Their analysis of the social world of one Key West drag club offers sociological insights into the lives of the individual performers who work against social stigma and limitations to provide new ways of looking at culture, self, and society.

CHAPTER 3

Culture

For most of us, deciding which public bathroom to use is something we do without much deliberation. In fact, the norm of sex-segregated bathrooms is so pervasive it appears natural or logical. But we can actually learn a great deal about culture from restrooms. For example, the fact that women's restrooms often have baby-changing stations while men's restrooms do not demonstrates cultural values about who is expected to be responsible for child care.

Similarly, anxieties over who can use which bathroom tell us something else about our culture. For example, many mothers may allow their young sons to use the women's public restroom. Other women using the restroom don't usually see this as a problem. We're less comfortable, however, with fathers bringing their young daughters into men's public restrooms. And once children are old enough to use the restroom on their own, there is an expectation that their sex will dictate the one they should use. Thus, if an adult man were

found using the women's restroom, he would likely face some social, and possibly legal, sanctions for violating that protocol. What does our reaction to such scenarios reveal about our beliefs and assumptions?

The United States is currently embroiled in cultural and legal debates over transgender persons and whether they should be allowed to use the bathroom aligned with their gender identity. A number of states, including North Carolina, have recently considered legislation that would require residents to use the restroom that matches their sex assigned at birth or face legal sanctions. Such "bathroom bills" are described by proponents as "common-sense" legislation that protects people who feel their privacy or safety may be violated if a person of the opposite sex uses their restroom. Opponents, by contrast, claim these bills are anti-LGBTQ—essentially discrimination condoned and reinforced by law. Opponents believe these bathroom bills have the potential to inspire future laws that permit other types of discrimination based on one's gender identity.

These battles over bathroom bills are an example of a "culture war," a term used to describe the clashes that occur as a result of conflicting viewpoints (Bloom 1987; Garber 1998). Trans activists have been on the front line of this culture war, using social media to protest what they perceive as discriminatory laws with hashtags such as #Occupotty and #WeJustNeedToPee. There have also been responses at the level of government, including a recent change to the White House floor plan: the designation of its first gender-neutral restroom. Under the Obama administration, the Education Department and the Justice Department issued guidelines to public schools, saying they must permit trans students to use the bathrooms aligned with their gender identity. The letter also urged schools to allow students to dress for prom and graduation in the way they feel most comfortable. The administration based these guidelines on Title IX, a federal law that prohibits discrimination based on a student's sex, arguing that this includes a person's gender identity. Soon after President Trump took office in 2017, however, he revoked the guidelines, allowing schools to create their own policies for transgender students.

Restroom restriction laws are based on the essentialist premise that gender emerges naturally from one's sex assigned at birth—either male or female. This binary approach to sex and gender has long been used to organize social life. It goes along with another assumption about gender—the perception that men represent more of a threat to others, with women often the target of such threats. This assumption provides a key insight into why lawmakers have attempted to ban trans people from using the restroom aligned with their gender identity. They argue that trans people using the "wrong" bathroom present a risk to vulnerable people: namely, women and children. As sociologists, we must ask what these arguments communicate about the values and norms of a society and investigate the veracity of these claims. Recent research has shown no link between transgender bathroom access and bathroom crime (Hasenbush, Flores, and Herman 2018). Despite the lack of evidence for the main argument of bathroom restriction laws, many people still support them, demonstrating our culture's deeply held ideas about sex and gender. For the moment, the gender-neutral restroom in the White House remains. But the culture wars are far from over.

How to Read This Chapter

Culture is one of the fundamental elements of social life and thus a very important topic in sociology. Many of the concepts presented here will come up again in almost every subsequent chapter. You will need to keep these concepts in mind as you learn about other substantive areas. You will also want to think about how culture is relevant to the things you already know from your own life experience. Try to come up with some of your own examples as you read along. The subject of culture is inherently interesting to most people. But although culture is familiar to all of us, you should be seeing it in a new and different way by the time you finish this chapter.

WHAT IS CULTURE?

Culture encompasses practically all of human civilization and touches on almost every aspect of social life. It is so much a part of the world around us that we may not recognize the extent to which it shapes and defines who we are. In the broadest sense, we can say that **culture** is the entire way of life of a group of people. It can include everything from language and gestures to style of dress and standards of beauty, from customs and rituals to tools and artifacts, from music and child-rearing practices to the proper way for customers to line up in a grocery store. It forms basic beliefs and assumptions about the world and the way things work, and it defines the moral parameters of what is right and wrong, good and bad.

Although culture varies from group to group, all societies develop some form of culture. It is the human equivalent of instinct in animals: Although we humans do have some basic instincts, culture actually accounts for our great success as a species. We are totally dependent on it to deal with the demands of life in society. As culture develops, it is shared among members of a group, handed down from generation to generation, and passed along from one group or individual to another.

Although culture may seem to us to be "second nature," it is actually learned rather than innate. Because we learn it so slowly and incrementally, we are often unaware of the process. For instance, few of us would be conscious of having *learned* all the slang words we currently use or the distance we typically maintain from others while talking with them. We may not remember exactly when we first felt patriotic or how we formed our opinions about people in the upper class. We all carry culture inside ourselves; it becomes ingrained and internalized into our way of thinking and acting. Culture guides the way we make sense of the world around us and the way we make decisions about what to do and how to do it. We can talk about the culture of a given country, state, or community, of people belonging to an ethnic or religious group, or of those working in the same profession. We can even say that sports enthusiasts, schoolmates, or a clique of friends all share in a common culture. We'll discuss some of these cultural variations later in the chapter.

How Has Culture Been Studied?

People study culture in a variety of ways. Theologians and philosophers, for example, might debate the morals and values of an ideal culture. Art, literature, and film scholars focus on certain aspects of culture—novels, films, paintings, plays—as expressive, symbolic activities. Cultural anthropologists often investigate societies outside the United States, traveling around the world engaging in empirical fieldwork, while archaeologists study the cultures of the past, digging for artifacts that document the historical realities of peoples long dead.

In contrast, sociologists usually focus on culture closer to home, often in the same societies to which they belong. At the same time, however, sociologists may also engage in the process of "othering" by studying the unusual, extraordinary, or deviant in cultural groups. In so doing, they may fail to consider some aspects of the culture that is right in front of them. This is where the sociology of everyday life offers certain benefits. By studying the mundane as well as the exceptional, we can learn about culture in all of its interesting permutations. We can learn not only about the differences between cultural groups—"us" and "them"—but also about the similarities.

> **CULTURE** the entire way of life of a group of people (including both material and symbolic elements) that acts as a lens through which one views the world and that is passed from one generation to the next

Ethnocentrism and Cultural Relativism

Culture acts as a lens through which we view the world. That lens, however, can either elucidate or obscure what we are looking at. Often, we can't clearly see our own culture, precisely because we are so familiar with it. Yet, when exposed to another culture, through travel, television, or other means, we can readily see what is different or seemingly "exotic." Rarely does our perspective allow us to recognize the strangeness in our own culture.

One of the best examples of the challenges in observing culture is presented in a famous article by Horace Miner titled "Body Ritual among the Nacirema" (1956). The article focuses on the beliefs and practices of this North American people concerning the care of their bodies. Miner observes that their fundamental belief appears to be that the human body is ugly and is susceptible to decay and disease and that the only way to counter these conditions is to engage in elaborate ceremonies and rituals. All members of the Nacirema culture conform to a greater or lesser degree to these practices and then pass them along to their children. One passage describes the household shrine where many of the body rituals take place:

> While each family has at least one shrine, the rituals associated with it are not family ceremonies but are private and secret.... The focal point of the shrine is a box or chest which is built into a wall. In this chest are kept the many charms and magical potions without which no native believes he could live.... Beneath the charm-box is a small font. Each day every member of the family, in succession, enters the shrine room, bows his head before the charm-box, mingles different sorts of holy water in the font, and proceeds with a brief rite of ablution. (p. 504)

The Nacirema regularly visit medicine men, "holy-mouth men," and other specialized practitioners from whom they procure magical potions:

> The Nacirema have an almost pathological horror of and fascination with the mouth, the condition of which is believed to have a supernatural influence on all social relationships. Were it not for the rituals of the mouth, they believe that their teeth would fall out, their gums bleed, their jaws shrink, their friends desert them, and their lovers reject them. The daily body ritual performed by everyone includes a mouth-rite. It was reported to me that the ritual consists of inserting a small bundle of hog hairs into the mouth, along with certain magical powders, and then moving the bundle in a highly formalized series of gestures.

Do the Nacirema seem like a strange group of people, or are they somehow familiar? Miner writes as though he were an anthropologist studying some exotic tribe of primitive people. In actuality, the passages above describe the bathroom and personal health-care habits of the average American. (Note that "Nacirema" is "American" spelled backward.) He doesn't embellish or make up anything; he merely approaches the topic as if he knows nothing about its meaning. So the "charm-box" is a medicine cabinet, the "holy water" font is a sink, the medicine men and "holy-mouth men" are doctors and dentists, and the exotic "mouth-rite" is the practice of brushing teeth.

"Body Ritual among the Nacirema" Horace Miner reminds us how easy it is to overlook aspects of our own culture, precisely because they seem so normal to us.

One of the reasons that Miner's article has become so popular is that it demonstrates how easy it is to fail to see our own culture, precisely because we take it for granted. The article reminds students who are becoming social analysts how useful **culture shock** is in helping to see even what is most familiar as bizarre or strange. Throughout this chapter, keep in mind that your powers of observation must be applied to looking at both "them" and "us."

Another, related problem arises when trying to understand cultures other than our own. Generally, we think of our own culture as being the "normal" one, a belief known as **ethnocentrism**. We don't realize that culture is something learned and that there is nothing inherently better about ours. Ethnocentrism means that we use our own culture as a kind of measuring stick with which to judge other individuals or societies; anyone outside our group seems "off-center" or abnormal. While ethnocentrism may give us a sense of pride in our own group, it can also prevent us from seeing and understanding others. In some cases, ethnocentrism can be a source of prejudice and hostility.

As sociologists, we want to have as clear a view of any society as possible; this requires that we suspend, at least temporarily, our ethnocentrism. There are several ways to do this. In Chapter 1, we learned about the beginner's mind, culture shock, and the sociological imagination—all ways to see the world anew. We can add to that list **cultural relativism**,

CULTURE SHOCK a sense of disorientation that occurs when entering a radically new social or cultural environment

ETHNOCENTRISM the principle of using one's own culture as a means or standard by which to evaluate another group or individual, leading to the view that cultures other than one's own are abnormal or inferior

CULTURAL RELATIVISM the principle of understanding other cultures on their own terms, rather than judging or evaluating according to one's own culture which means seeing each different culture as simply that—different. Not better or worse, not right or wrong, but on its own terms. Doing so helps us place different values, beliefs, norms, and practices within their own cultural context. By practicing cultural relativism, or being culturally sensitive, we begin to see other people more clearly and without judgment and, therefore, to appreciate their way of life. We can discover viewpoints and interpretations of reality different from our own. Cultural relativism becomes all the more important in our increasingly diverse society.

COMPONENTS OF CULTURE

Since culture is such a broad concept, it is more easily grasped if we break it down into its constituent parts. Sociologists conceive of culture as consisting of two major categories: material culture and nonmaterial or symbolic culture.

Material Culture

Material culture is any physical object to which we give social meaning: art and artifacts, tools and utensils, machines and weapons, clothing and furniture, buildings and toys—the list is immense. Any physical thing that people create, use, or appreciate might be considered material culture.

Examining material culture can tell us a great deal about a particular group or society. Just look around you, whether in your dorm room, a library, a coffeehouse, or a park—there should be many items that you can identify as belonging to material culture. Start with your own clothes and accessories and then extend your observations to your surroundings—the room, building, landscaping, street, neighborhood, community, and farther outward. For instance, the designer label on a woman's purse might convey that she follows the current fashion trends, or the athletic logo on a man's T-shirt might tell us that he is into skateboarding. Likewise, the carpeting, light fixtures, furniture, and artwork in a building can tell us something about the people who live or work there. And the sports arenas, modes of transportation, historical monuments, and city dumps reveal the characteristics of a community. Perhaps the proliferation of drive-thru fast-food restaurants in practically every corner of the United States says something about American tastes and lifestyle: We spend more time on the road, cook fewer meals at home, and prefer the ease and predictability of knowing what we'll get each time we pull up to our favorite chain. If you were visiting another country, you might see some very different items of material culture.

Studying the significance of material culture is like going on an archaeological dig, but learning about the present rather than the distant past. Let's take as an example a sociological "dig" in Santa Barbara, California, where one of the authors of this book lives. Local leaders there have been active in preserving the image of the city, particularly in its

Material Culture and the Architecture of Santa Barbara Local leaders have preserved the city's history and resisted the pressures of encroaching urban development by insisting on maintaining the look of "old California."

downtown historical area. The original mission, *presidio* (military post), courthouse, and other landmarks built by early Spanish settlers are all still intact. Although the town has grown up around these buildings, zoning regulations require that new construction fit with the distinctive Mediterranean architecture of the "red tile roof" district. The size and design are restricted, as are the use of signs, lighting, paint, and landscaping. Thus, the newly built grocery store with its textured stucco walls, tile murals, and arched porticos may be difficult to distinguish from the century-old post office a few blocks away. By studying its material culture, we can see how Santa Barbara manages to preserve its history and heritage and successfully resist the pressures of encroaching urban development. The distinctive "old California" look and feel of the city is perhaps its greatest charm, something that appeals to locals and a steady flock of tourists alike.

> **MATERIAL CULTURE** the objects associated with a cultural group, such as tools, machines, utensils, buildings, and artwork; any physical object to which we give social meaning
>
> **SYMBOLIC CULTURE** the ideas associated with a cultural group, including ways of thinking (beliefs, values, and assumptions) and ways of behaving (norms, interactions, and communication)

Nonmaterial or Symbolic Culture

Nonmaterial or **symbolic culture** reflects the ideas and beliefs of a group of people. It can be something as specific as a certain rule or custom, such as driving on the right side of the road in the United States and on the left side in the

United Kingdom. It can also be a broad social system, such as democracy, or a large-scale social pattern, such as marriage. Because symbolic culture is so important to social life, let's look further at some of its main components.

COMMUNICATION: SIGNS, GESTURES, AND LANGUAGE

One of the most important functions of symbolic culture is to allow us to communicate—through signs, gestures, and language. These form the basis of social interaction and are the foundation of culture.

Signs (or symbols) such as traffic signals, price tags, notes on sheet music, or product logos have all been designed to meaningfully represent something else. They all convey information. Numbers and letters are the most common signs, but you are probably familiar with lots of other graphic symbols indicating, for instance, which is the men's or women's restroom or whether it's unisex, where the elevator is going, how to pause the video you're watching, or in which lane you should be driving.

While we can easily take for granted the meaning of most

SIGNS symbols that stand for or convey an idea

GESTURES the ways in which people use their bodies to communicate without words; actions that have symbolic meaning

symbols, others we may have to learn when we first encounter them. Some symbols may be nearly universal, while others may be particular to a given culture. It may take some interpretive work to understand what a sign means if you are unfamiliar with the context in which it is displayed.

Take emojis, for instance, those cute (or devious) little expressions that we can add to our text messages and social media posts. Originally developed in Japan, where the word *emoji* means "pictograph," these symbols have become ubiquitous around the world. Over one thousand emojis are now recognized as part of the Unicode Standard for computing, and more are being added every year. Recently, the human emojis (or emoticons) were modified so that you could choose among a range of skin tones and hair colors in an attempt to better represent our diversity. Although widely used, not every emoji is understood in the same way by all people. The sleepy face emoji is one of the most confusing; because it has a water drop between the eyes and mouth, most people think it's crying, but in fact that's not a tear but rather a droplet of drool, which is supposed to indicate sleeping.

Gestures are signs made with the body—clapping, nodding, smiling, or any number of facial expressions. Sometimes, these acts are referred to as "body language" or "nonverbal communication," since they don't require any

Gestures and Body Language If you travel to a foreign country, pay special attention to how others interpret your body language. Common friendly gestures in one culture can be offensive or confusing in another.

words. Gestures can be as subtle as a knowing glance or as obvious as a raised fist. Most of the time, we can assume that other people will get what we are trying to say with our gestures. But, while gestures might seem natural and universal, just a matter of common sense, few of them besides those that represent basic emotions are innate; most have to be learned. For instance, the "thumbs up" sign, which is associated with praise or approval in the United States, might be interpreted as an obscene or insulting gesture in parts of Asia or South America. Every culture has its own way of expressing praise and insulting others. So before leaving for a country whose culture is unfamiliar, it might be worth finding out whether shaking hands and waving goodbye are appropriate ways to communicate.

Language, probably the most significant component of culture, is what has allowed us to fully develop and express ourselves as human beings. Although language varies from culture to culture, it is a human universal and present in all societies. It is one of the most complex, fluid, and creative symbol systems: Letters or pictograms are combined to form words, and words combined to form sentences, in an almost infinite number of possible ways.

Language is the basis of symbolic culture and the primary means through which we communicate with one another. It allows us to convey complicated abstract concepts and to pass along a culture from one generation to the next. Language helps us to conceive of the past and to plan for the future; to categorize the people, places, and things around us; and to share our perspectives on reality. In this way, the cumulative experience of a group of people—their culture—can be contained in and presented through language.

Language is so important that many have argued that it shapes not only our communication but our perception—the way that we see things—as well. In the 1930s, anthropologists Edward Sapir and Benjamin Lee Whorf conducted research on the impact of language on the mind. In working with the Hopi tribe in the American Southwest, the anthropologists claimed to have discovered that the Hopi had no words to distinguish the past, present, or future and that, therefore, they did not "see" or experience time in the same way as those whose language provided such words. The result of this research was the development of what is known as the **Sapir-Whorf hypothesis** (sometimes referred to as the *principle of linguistic relativity*). Their hypothesis broke from traditional understandings about language by asserting that language actually structures thought. We can understand how perceiving things in the world suggests the need for words with which to express what is perceived; but the Sapir-Whorf hypothesis goes further in suggesting that the words themselves help create those same perceptions (Sapir 1949; Whorf 1956). In this case, the Hopi's use of words that did not distinguish among the past, present, and future helped inform their perception of time.

The studies by Sapir and Whorf were not published until

the 1950s, when they were met with competing linguistic theories. In particular, the idea that Eskimos (or Inuits, as they are now called) had many more words for snow than people of Western cultures was sharply challenged, as was the notion that the Hopi had no words for future or past tense (Martin 1986; Pullum 1991). Although there is still some disagreement about how strongly language influences thought (Edgerton 1992), the ideas behind the Sapir-Whorf hypothesis continue to influence numerous social thinkers. Language does play a significant role in how people construct a sense of reality and how they categorize the people, places, and things around them. In a country like the United States, where there are more than 43 million foreign-born people, who speak well over 100 different languages, there are bound to be differences in perceptual realities as a result (Lopez, Bialik, and Radford 2018).

Does the Sapir-Whorf hypothesis hold true for your world? Let's take an example closer to home. Perhaps you have seen the 2004 movie *Mean Girls*, loosely based on a pop sociology book by Rosalind Wiseman, *Queen Bees and Wannabes*, about the culture of high school girls (2002). Both book and film present a social map of the cafeteria and school grounds, identifying where different groups of students—the "jocks," "cheerleaders," "goths," "preppies," "skaters," "nerds," "hacky-sack kids," "easy girls," and "partiers"—hang out. The book also includes the "populars" (referred to in the movie as the "plastics") and the popular "wannabes."

You were probably aware of similar categories for

The Cafeteria Classification System A scene from *Mean Girls* illustrates the different classification schemes that are used to identify and categorize the world around us.

distinguishing groups at your school. Do such classification systems influence the way you see other people? Do they lead you to identify people by type and place them into those categories? If no such labels existed (or if your school had different labels), would you still perceive your former classmates the same way? Probably not. These kinds of questions highlight how important language is to the meanings we give to our everyday world.

Values, Norms, and Sanctions

Values and norms are symbolic culture in thought and action. When we know the values of a particular group and see how individuals are controlled by its social norms, then we can appreciate a group's beliefs and ideals and find the evidence of these throughout members' everyday lives.

VALUES Values are the set of shared beliefs that a group of people considers to be worthwhile or desirable in life—what is good or bad, right or wrong, beautiful or ugly. They articulate the essence of everything that a cultural group cherishes in its society. For instance, most Americans value the equality and individual freedoms of democracy. Structural functionalists, such as Durkheim, stress the strength of shared values and their role in regulating the behavior of society's members. However, there is not always widespread agreement about which values should represent a society, and values may change or new values may emerge over time. For example, workers' loyalty to their company was once much more important than it is now. In today's economy, workers realize that they may be "downsized" in times of financial trouble or that they may change careers over the course of their lifetime, and hence they feel less obligation to an employer.

NORMS Norms are the rules and guidelines regarding what kinds of behavior are acceptable; they develop directly out of a culture's value system. Whether legal regulations or just social expectations, norms are largely agreed upon by most members of a group. Some norms are formal, which means they are officially codified and explicitly stated. These include **laws** such as those making it illegal to speed in a school zone or drink before you turn twenty-one. Other formal norms include the rules for playing basketball or the requirements for membership in your college's honor society, the rights secured by the Amendments to the U.S. Constitution, and the behavioral prescriptions conveyed in the Ten Commandments. Despite the relative authority of formal norms, they are not always followed.

Other norms are informal, meaning that they are implicit and unspoken. For instance, when we wait in line to buy tickets for a movie, we expect that no one will cut in front of us. Informal norms are so much a part of our assumptions about life that they are embedded in our consciousness; they cover almost every aspect of our social lives, from what we say and do to even how we think and feel. Though we might have difficulty listing all the norms that are a part of everyday life, most of us have learned them quite well. They are simply "the way things are done." Often, it is only when norms are violated (as when someone cuts in line) that we recognize they exist.

VALUES ideas about what is right or wrong, good or bad, desirable or worthy in a particular group; they express what the group cherishes and honors

NORMS rules or guidelines regarding what kinds of behavior are acceptable and appropriate within a particular culture; these typically emanate from the group's values

LAWS types of norms that are formally codified to provide an explicit statement about what is permissible or forbidden, legal or illegal in a given society

FOLKWAYS loosely enforced norms involving common customs, practices, or procedures that ensure smooth social interaction and acceptance

TABLE 3.1 Theory in Everyday Life

Perspective	Approach to Culture	Case Study: Religion
Structural Functionalism	Values and norms are widely shared and agreed upon; they contribute to social stability by reinforcing common bonds and constraining individual behavior.	Religion is an important social institution that functions as the basis for the morals and ethics that followers embrace and that are applied to both society and the individual, thus promoting social order.
Conflict Theory	Values and norms are part of the dominant culture and tend to represent and protect the interests of the most powerful groups in society.	Religion serves to control the masses by creating rules for behavior; sanctions against violators may not be equally or fairly applied. Culture wars reflect tensions among groups over which values and norms will dominate.
Symbolic Interactionism	Values and norms are social constructions that may vary over time and in different contexts; meaning is created, maintained, and changed through ongoing social interaction.	Religion consists of beliefs and rituals that are part of the interaction among followers. Reciting the Lord's Prayer, bowing toward Mecca, and keeping a kosher home are meaningful displays of different religious values and norms. Leaders may play a role in creating social change.

IN RELATIONSHIPS
Individual Values vs. University Culture

Let's talk about sex on campus.

At many public, state-funded colleges and universities, like the ones where both Dr. Ferris and Dr. Stein work, the norm is to provide on-campus sexual health services for students, including a wide range of contraceptive choices, STI (sexually transmitted infection) testing and treatment, and pregnancy testing. Does your college health services center offer these services, too?

In fact, many private colleges and universities do not offer students the full range of sexual health-care services, and some offer none at all. For example, Gonzaga University in Spokane, Washington, offers no contraceptive benefits to students but does cover STIs. At Georgetown University, the student health center will prescribe contraceptives if medically indicated but not directly for contraception. While only a small percentage of Catholic universities in the United States offer any kind of contraception to students, there has been some pushback at campuses such as Fordham and Boston College, especially since the passage of the Affordable Care Act, which mandates coverage (Catholics for a Free Choice 2002; Edwards-Levy 2012).

It's harder to generalize about non-Catholic religious schools: Brigham Young University in Salt Lake City and Texas Christian University in Fort Worth, for example, do offer contraception to students, while Liberty University in Virginia and Eastern Nazarene College in Massachusetts don't appear to offer any birth control services. Schools without religious affiliations are more likely to offer contraceptive services if they have a student health center, but these are not found on all campuses.

Universities have their own cultures that include traditions, customs, beliefs, and values, just like any other cultural group. This means that some of your most personal, private, individual choices may have already been made for you (or at least made more complicated for you) by your school. Some universities borrow their cultural values from the larger organizations (such as religious groups) that sponsor them; even unaffiliated schools have statements of their

institutional values on their websites. These institutional values may conflict with student culture. For example, at Boston College, Students for Sexual Health is prohibited from operating on campus despite a 2018 referendum in which 94 percent of students voted in favor of allowing the group to distribute contraception (Hunt 2018).

If your university's institutional values and your individual values are different, you may find yourself in a situation where the university has some unanticipated control over your everyday life and personal relationships. Schools can mandate who your dorm roommate can be (and whether you can room with someone you know, or someone of the same or opposite sex); they can make and enforce rules about your academic and athletic activities; they can decide what kind of health-care services you can get on campus. They can even influence your sex life.

University Culture Like other cultural groups, universities have traditions, customs, beliefs, and values that can affect students' everyday lives.

Norms can be broken down further into three types. **Folkways** are the ordinary conventions of everyday life about what is acceptable or proper and are not always strictly enforced. Folkways are the customary ways that people do

things, and they ensure smooth and orderly social interactions. Examples are standards of dress and rules of etiquette: In most places, wearing flip-flops with a business suit and eating with your fingers from the buffet line is just not done!

Norms Are Specific to a Situation, Culture, and Time Period For example, Mardi Gras and spring break are often considered "moral holidays," times when mild norm violations are tolerated.

When people do not conform to folkways, they are thought of as peculiar or eccentric but not necessarily dangerous.

Mores are norms that carry a greater moral significance and are more closely related to the core values of a cultural group. Unlike folkways, mores are norms to which practically everyone is expected to conform. Breaches are treated seriously and in some cases can bring severe repercussions. Such mores as the prohibition of theft, rape, and murder are also formalized so that there is not only public condemnation for such acts but also strict laws against them. **Taboos**, actually a type of mores, are the most powerful of all norms. We sometimes use the word in a casual way to indicate, say, a forbidden subject. But as a sociological term it holds even greater meaning. Taboos are extremely serious. Sociologists say that our sense of what is taboo is so deeply ingrained that the very thought of committing a taboo act, such as cannibalism or incest, evokes strong feelings of disgust or horror.

Norms are specific to a culture, time period, and situation. What are folkways to one group might be mores to another. For instance, public nudity is acceptable in many cultures, whereas it is not only frowned upon in American culture but also illegal in most instances. At the same time, Americans do permit nudity in such situations as strip clubs and nudist resorts, allowing for a kind of **moral holiday** from the strictures of imposed norms. At certain times, such as Mardi Gras and spring break, mild norm violations are tolerated. Certain places may also lend themselves to the suspension of norms—think Las Vegas (and the slogan "What happens in Vegas, stays in Vegas").

Similarly, what would be considered murder on the city streets might be regarded as valor on the battlefield. And we are probably all aware of how the folkways around proper etiquette and attire can vary greatly from one generation to the next; fifty years ago, girls were just starting to wear jeans to school, for example. Now they come to school in all sorts of casual attire, including pajama bottoms and slippers.

SANCTIONS **Sanctions** are a means of enforcing norms. They include rewards for conformity and punishments for violations. *Positive sanctions* express approval and may come in the form of a handshake, a smile, praise, or perhaps an award. *Negative sanctions* express disapproval and may come in the form of a frown, harsh words, or perhaps a fine or incarceration.

From a functionalist perspective, we can see how sanctions help to establish **social control**, ensuring that people behave to some degree in acceptable ways and thus promoting social cohesion. There are many forms of authority in our culture—from the government and police to school administrators, work supervisors, and even parents. Each has a certain amount of power that they can exercise to get others to follow their rules. So when someone is caught violating a norm, there is usually some prescribed sanction that will then be administered, serving as a deterrent to that behavior.

But equally important in maintaining social order is the process of socialization by which people internalize norms. For instance, in 1983, the U.S. Department of Transportation pioneered the slogan "Friends don't let friends drive drunk"; a few years later, the term "designated driver" was introduced into the popular lexicon. Over the years, these slogans have

MORES norms that carry great moral significance, are closely related to the core values of a cultural group, and often involve severe repercussions for violators

TABOO a norm ingrained so deeply that even thinking about violating it evokes strong feelings of disgust, horror, or revulsion

MORAL HOLIDAY a specified time period during which some norm violations are allowed

SANCTIONS positive or negative reactions to the ways that people follow or disobey norms, including rewards for conformity and punishments for violations

SOCIAL CONTROL the formal and informal mechanisms used to elicit conformity to values and norms and thus promote social cohesion

helped change the way we think about our personal responsibility for others, with nearly 80 percent of Americans now claiming that they have taken action to prevent someone from driving while intoxicated. What began as an external statement of social mores quickly became our own personal sense of morality. We are often unaware of the extent to which our own conscience keeps us from violating social norms in the first place. If we have internalized norms, then outside sanctions are no longer needed to make us do the right thing. Social control, then, frequently looks like self-control and is taught through the socialization process by family, peers, the media, and religious organizations, among others.

DATA WORKSHOP

Analyzing Everyday Life

Seeing Culture in a Subculture

When it comes to culture, we are like fish in water. Because we're so deeply immersed in it, we may not really see it. When culture becomes something we take for granted, we lose sight of what's distinctive or different about it. One of the best ways to "see" culture is to approach it as an outsider, or as someone who is learning about it for the first time. Even if it's a culture to which you've belonged your entire life, you can always act as if you are a new member trying to understand your group. In any event, to better appreciate culture you'll need to suspend your ethnocentrism and practice cultural relativism.

In this Data Workshop, you will be examining a

Culture on Campus College campuses are home to myriad subcultures, including members of the Muslim Students Association.

subcultural group to which you belong. As someone living in a diverse, modern society, you are likely to belong to many subcultural groups. You'll be doing some participant observation research in a social setting (and taking field notes), focusing on various components of material and symbolic culture that help to define your group. At the same time, you'll be reflecting on your own membership in the group and writing a short ethnography about it. Refer to the section in Chapter 2 on participant observation/ethnographic research methods for a review before conducting your study.

Step 1: Choosing Your Cultural Group
Begin by choosing a subculture to which you belong. There are numerous possibilities. You could choose your ethnic group (such as Latino or African American), your nationality (such as Mexican or Swedish), your religion (such as Catholic or Mormon), your occupation (such as server or parking valet), a sports team or club you belong to (such as intramural Ultimate Frisbee or student government), or an interest or hobby (such as video gaming or crafting). With so many from which to choose, the most important thing is to select one that gives you plenty of material to work with and is easy to observe. Provide a brief description of the subcultural group and its members.

Step 2: Observing Group Culture
Find a place where you can observe members of your subculture in some naturally occurring social setting. Depending on which subculture you choose, you might visit a church, park, or gym; a retail store or restaurant; the student center on campus; or a large family gathering. Spend at least 30 minutes in the setting, considering both the material and symbolic culture embodied in your field site. Jot down notes with some specific details about what you see, both in the physical environment and in social interactions among members of the group.

Step 3: Identifying Cultural Components
Read through your field notes and reflect on your experience. Then consider the following questions:

- What aspects of material culture did you notice in the setting? This can include the physical surroundings, architecture, furniture, equipment, clothing, artwork, food, or other objects. Can you explain the meaning, function, or purpose of particular items of material culture?

- What did you notice about language in the setting? Are there any particular words, terms, mottos, or sayings that are commonly used among members? What are their meanings? What else did you notice about talk and interaction in the setting? Were there any signs or other written materials associated with the setting?

- What aspects of symbolic culture are part of this subculture? Describe values that members of the group uphold, listing at least three values that are key to the group's culture. What are the group's ideas, beliefs, or attitudes? Does the group have a mission or goal?

- What kinds of social norms guide the behavior of individuals, and how are these norms related to group values? What are the folkways of the group? How do these folkways shape what members do or say? What are some of the rules governing members? Why are they important?

- What did you observe in the setting that seemed especially familiar or unfamiliar to you? Was there anything that surprised you? What insights were you able to gain by suspending ethnocentrism and practicing cultural relativism? What did you learn about yourself as a member of the subculture after conducting this study?

There are two options for completing this Data Workshop:

PREP-PAIR-SHARE Do the fieldwork outlined in Steps 1 and 2, and bring your field notes with you to class for reference. In groups of two or three, discuss your experiences and exchange answers to the questions in Step 3. Take this opportunity to learn more about different subcultural groups.

DO-IT-YOURSELF Write a three- to four-page essay analyzing your field experiences and taking into consideration the questions in Step 3. Make sure to refer to your field notes in the essay and include them as an attachment to your paper.

VARIATIONS IN CULTURE

We know there are differences between cultures, but there can also be variations within cultures. For instance, sociologists who have tried to identify the core values that make up American society (Bellah, Sullivan, and Tipton 1985; Williams 1965) have found that while there do seem to be certain beliefs that most Americans share, such as freedom and democracy, there are also inconsistencies between such beliefs as individualism (in which we do what is best for ourselves) and humanitarianism (in which we do what is best for others), and between equality and group superiority. New values such as self-fulfillment and environmentalism

could also be added to the list, having gained popularity in recent years.

It is even difficult to speak of an "American culture." "Cultural diversity" and "multiculturalism" have both become buzzwords in the past few decades, precisely because people are aware of the increasing variety of cultural groups within American society. **Multiculturalism** generally describes a policy that involves honoring the diverse racial, ethnic, national, and linguistic backgrounds of various individuals and groups. In the following chapters, we will explore some of these differences in greater depth.

Dominant Culture

Although "culture" is a term we usually apply to an entire group of people, what we find in reality is that there are often many subgroups within a larger culture, each with its own particular makeup. These subgroups, however, are not all equal. Some, by virtue of size, wealth, or historical happenstance, are able to lay claim to greater power and influence in society than others. The values, norms, and practices of the most powerful groups are referred to as the mainstream or **dominant culture**, while others are seen as "alternative" or minority views. The power of the dominant culture may mean that other ways of seeing and doing things are relegated to second-class status—in this way, dominant culture can produce cultural **hegemony**, or dominance (Gramsci 1985, 1988).

Let's take popular music as an example. Commercial radio stations often have very limited playlists. No matter what the genre (country, pop, hip-hop, metal), the songs played are determined by station and record company business interests, not your artistic preferences. Truly new artists and alternative sounds are more likely to be heard on public, college, or satellite radio stations or online. Even music streaming services like Pandora or Spotify must deliver audiences to advertisers, which may make it harder to resist the pressure to "mainstream." The dominant status of commercial radio (even online) and the corporate interests of the music industry dictate that musicians outside the mainstream will never be as big as Ed Sheeran or Taylor Swift.

Subcultures and Countercultures

If sociologists focus only on the dominant culture in American society, we risk overlooking the inequalities that structure our society—as well as the influences that even small cultural groups outside the mainstream can exert. The United States is filled with thousands of different cultural groups, any of which could be called a **subculture**—a culture within a culture. A subculture is a particular social group that has a distinctive way of life, including its own set of values and norms, practices, and beliefs, but that exists harmoniously within the larger mainstream culture. A subculture can be based on ethnicity, age, interests, or anything else that draws individuals together. Any of the following groups could be considered subcultures within American society: Korean Americans, senior citizens, snowboarders, White Sox fans, greyhound owners, firefighters, Trekkers.

A **counterculture**, another kind of subgroup, differs from a subculture in that its norms and values are often incompatible with or in direct opposition to the mainstream (Zellner 1995). Some countercultures are political or activist groups attempting to bring about social change; others resist mainstream values by living outside society or practicing an alternative lifestyle. In the 1960s, hippies, antiwar protesters, feminists, and others on the so-called political left were collectively known as "the counterculture." But radicals come in many stripes. Any group that opposes the dominant culture—whether its members are eco-terrorists, computer hackers, or modern-day polygamists—can be considered a counterculture.

In the mid-1990s, American countercultures of the far right gained prominence in the wake of two high-profile events. The FBI's 1993 siege of the Branch Davidian compound in Waco, Texas, which resulted in eighty-two deaths, became a source of inspiration for other groups that promote armed resistance to government forces. Two years later, in April 1995, a man with ties to "militia" or "patriot" groups, Timothy McVeigh, detonated a bomb in the Alfred R. Murrah Federal Building in Oklahoma City, killing 168 people. Members of the "militia movement," who trace their heritage to the Minutemen of the American Revolution (an elite fighting force, the first to arrive at a battle), and other "sovereign citizen" groups, see themselves as the last line of defense for the liberties outlined in the U.S. Constitution. Moreover, they believe that the federal government has become the enemy of those liberties. They hold that gun control, environmental protection laws, and other legislation violate individual and states' rights.

Anonymous, an international group of cyber activists—or "hacktivists"—who carry out their attacks online, is another example of a countercultural group. While loosely organized, members of Anonymous are united in their opposition to censorship or governmental or institutional control of the Internet. As such, their targets have included large corporations and major financial institutions such as Nissan, Visa, PayPal, Bank of America, and the New York Stock Exchange. Members of Anonymous have also sought to undermine the operations of terrorist organizations such as ISIS. Their tactics often involve disrupting or disabling the computer networks or social media accounts of their adversaries or leaking damaging classified or sensitive information. At the same time, Anonymous has also lent its computer skills to social movements such as Black Lives Matter to help advance their cause.

MULTICULTURALISM a policy that values diverse racial, ethnic, national, and linguistic backgrounds and so encourages the retention of cultural differences within the larger society

DOMINANT CULTURE the values, norms, and practices of the group within society that is most powerful (in terms of wealth, prestige, status, influence, etc.)

HEGEMONY term developed by Antonio Gramsci to describe the cultural aspects of social control, whereby the ideas of the dominant group are accepted by all

SUBCULTURE a group within society that is differentiated by its distinctive values, norms, and lifestyle

COUNTERCULTURE a group within society that openly rejects or actively opposes society's values and norms

Culture Wars

Although a countercultural group can pose a threat to the larger society, conflict does not always come from the extreme margins of society; it can also emerge from within the mainstream. Culture in any diverse society is characterized by points of tension and division. There is not

Culture Wars Today a culture war is waging over abortion. Alabama recently passed legislation that bans nearly all abortions. As a 49ers player, Colin Kaepernick protested racial inequality and oppression by kneeling during the National Anthem, inspiring others to do the same.

GLOBAL PERSPECTIVE
Otaku Culture and the Globalization of Niche Interests

If you are not an *otaku*, you probably don't know what *otaku* is. If you are an *otaku*, you may not want others to know what *otaku* is, since *otaku* culture has often been misunderstood by those on the outside. So, what is *otaku*?

Otaku is a Japanese word used to describe devoted fans, usually of manga, anime, or video games. *Otaku* are extremely knowledgeable about whatever it is they are fans of—and while that kind of obsessive interest is sometimes looked down upon by others, *otaku* themselves see this intense knowledge as a badge of honor. They view themselves as dedicated rather than obsessed, connoisseurs rather than fanatics, and superior to other hobbyists who aren't as erudite about the object of their enthusiasm. In fact, *otaku* may now be certified as experts in Japan by taking a rigorous, nationally recognized exam (McNicol 2006).

Organizing and displaying their belongings is a central part of *otaku* culture—many *otaku* have special rooms in their homes for their museum-like collections of action figures, paintings, or comic books. Photographs of *otaku* in their "*otaku* spaces" (Galbraith 2012) illuminate the connection among fantasy worlds, material commodities, and virtual communities that *otaku* culture uniquely embodies.

Once confined entirely to Japan (and to small neighborhood clubs even there), the Internet has made *otaku* culture accessible to people all over the world. Indeed, fans of just about everything now depend on social media to connect them with one another and to allow them to share their fascinations with others who appreciate what it means to be truly dedicated. *Otaku* who in the past might have been viewed with suspicion because of their intense involvement in what others considered a fringe pastime can now validate their commitments by interacting with others who share their interests, whether they are down the street or a world away.

Closely related to its reliance on social media, *otaku* culture is also characterized by its global reach. Indeed, what is distinctive about *otaku* culture is the uncommon direction in which it has diffused. Instead of the United States

or another Western culture spreading eastward, *otaku* culture is an example of the East influencing the West: *Otaku* represents the globalization and transnationalization of what had previously been Japan specific. As science fiction writer William Gibson (2001) says, "There is something post-national about it, extra-geographic," meaning that in *otaku* culture, citizenship matters less than shared interests, nationality less than knowledge, and location less than expertise. Your identity is defined by what you're into, by where your passions lie, and by what "geeks you out."

Whether or not your passion is for manga, anime, or video games, if you're an obsessive fan of some other genre of entertainment, and you're deeply involved in its culture of fandom, then perhaps you can also appreciate what it means to be an *otaku*.

East to West The Internet helped spread *otaku* culture from Japan to the rest of the world.

CULTURE WARS clashes within mainstream society over the values and norms that should be upheld

always uniform agreement about which values and norms ought to be upheld, leading to **culture wars** like the one

currently unfolding over transgender rights. These clashes are frequently played out in the media and online, where social commentators, political pundits, and bloggers debate the issues. Culture wars are mainly waged over values and morality and the solutions to social problems, with liberals and conservatives fighting to define culture in the United States (Hunter 1991, 2006).

Culture wars often play out on the political stage. To some degree, the rise of the ultraconservative Tea Party movement in the last decade was a response to a host of contentious social issues such as abortion and same-sex marriage. Republican-based Tea Partyers favor small government and have called for drastic cuts in taxes and social welfare funding, among other things. More recently, the alt-right, a more extreme conservative spin-off, has gained power and visibility. The alt-right movement—which lives mainly online—embraces white nationalism and eschews multiculturalism, feminism, and political correctness. This far-right ideology stands in opposition to mainstream American culture and its values of diversity and equality, highlighting deep political and cultural divisions among Americans.

Popular culture is another site of frequent debate in the culture wars. One area of concern is the content of entertainment media and its potential to influence audiences, especially when it contains graphic material such as violence, drug use, or sexuality. Celebrities and sports figures who serve as role models may also stir controversy. During the 2016–2017 NFL season, Colin Kaepernick, then quarterback for the San Francisco 49ers, caused an uproar when he protested racial oppression and police brutality in the United States by kneeling during the National Anthem. A wave of other NFL players followed suit. Many saw it as a deeply unpatriotic gesture, while others saw it as a fundamental expression of the right to free speech. In 2018, Nike made Kaepernick—a free agent after no NFL team signed him in the wake of the controversy—the new face of their "Just Do It" ad campaign. The tagline read, "Believe in something. Even if it means sacrificing everything."

We could add many more examples to the list of battleground issues, including gun violence, family values, LGBTQ rights, immigration, biomedical ethics, and school prayer. Culture wars are bound to continue as we confront the difficult realities that are a part of living in a multicultural, democratic society.

Ideal vs. Real Culture

Some norms and values are more aspired to than actually practiced. It is useful to draw a distinction between **ideal culture**, the norms and values that members of a society believe should be observed in principle, and **real culture**, the patterns of behavior that actually exist. Whether it is an organization that falls short of its own mission statement or a person who says one thing and does another (a self-described vegetarian, for example, who sometimes enjoys a Big Mac), what people believe in and what they do may be two different things.

An enduring example of the difference between ideal and real cultures is the United States itself. For a nation that has enshrined in its founding documents the notion that "all men are created equal," it continues to have trouble realizing full equality for all its citizens. From slavery to Western expansion, from the oppression of women and discrimination against ethnic minorities to the battle for LGBTQ rights, we are still a nation that believes in equality but doesn't always deliver it.

> **IDEAL CULTURE** the norms, values, and patterns of behavior that members of a society believe should be observed in principle
>
> **REAL CULTURE** the norms, values, and patterns of behavior that actually exist within a society (which may or may not correspond to the society's ideals)

DATA WORKSHOP
Analyzing Media and Pop Culture
How the Image Shapes the Need

Yet another glamorous photo of rapper Cardi B is splashed across social media. There's the one of her at a party during New York Fashion Week, wearing a red Dolce & Gabbana gown and dripping with thick gold chains. There's another of her in sky-high Aquazzura powder puff sandals leaning up against the hood of her custom orange Bentley Bentayga. Most of us cannot afford such status symbols, but it doesn't stop us from wondering what it would be like to wear designer clothes or drive a luxury car worth a quarter of a million dollars. In fact, advertisers want to sell us just those kinds of fantasies, effectively cashing in on two of our most basic human needs in contemporary society—clothing and transportation. For most people, clothes and cars have become something of a necessity of modern life, even if we don't actually need these things to survive. For many reasons we need to get dressed and we need to get around somehow, but our desire for clothing and transportation is not determined by instinct alone. So how does culture, in particular through the media, influence the ways in which we satisfy those needs?

For this Data Workshop, you will be using existing sources—specifically, popular magazines in print or online—to discover how culture gives meaning to items considered necessary for modern living. You will be doing content analysis to arrive at your conclusions. Refer back to Chapter 2 for a review of this research method.

Popular Magazines What kinds of lifestyles are these magazines trying to sell to consumers?

Pick your necessity—clothes or cars. Now go to your local bookstore or newsstand, or go online, and identify a magazine dedicated to that necessity. For example, you could choose a magazine such as *InStyle*, *Essence*, or *Vogue* for women's clothing, or *GQ*, *Details*, or *Esquire* for men's clothing. For cars, you could choose *Car and Driver*, *Road and Track*, or *Motor Trend*. Immerse yourself in the content of the magazine, looking over the headlines, articles, photo spreads, and advertisements. Then consider the following questions. Support your answers with data in the form of clippings, photocopies, or screenshots of images and text taken from the print magazines or their websites.

- How is the modern necessity of [clothing or cars] presented in the magazine? Can you find any themes, patterns, or topics that seem predominant in the magazine?

- Describe one example of material culture (physical objects) and one example of symbolic culture (language, norms) that best represent the magazine's approach to [clothing or cars].

- What values or beliefs about [clothing or cars] are reflected in the magazine? What kinds of messages are embedded in the images and text in articles and advertisements?

- How does the magazine suggest that we satisfy our needs for [clothing or cars]? How much of the magazine's content is about satisfying just the bare minimum of our need for [clothing or cars]?

- Who is the magazine's intended audience? How are you addressed as the reader? How does the magazine affect you and your desires for [clothing or cars]?

- Do you find yourself wanting the [clothing or cars] pictured?

- Who benefits when you act on your desires by purchasing the products featured in the magazine?

- Finally, which force is more important in shaping human behavior when it comes to modern necessities—instinct or culture?

There are two options for completing this Data Workshop:

PREP-PAIR-SHARE Collect your data from the magazine and jot down some preliminary notes based on your answers to the questions provided. Bring your examples to class and present them to a partner who has chosen the same topic (cars or clothing). Compare and contrast your answers and develop them further together.

DO-IT-YOURSELF Write a three- to four-page essay based on your answers to the questions provided. In addition, discuss your experience of doing content analysis of existing sources for research. Provide your examples of data (in print or digital format) as an attachment to the paper.

CULTURAL CHANGE

Cultures usually change slowly and incrementally, although change can also happen in rapid and dramatic ways. We saw rapid change as a result of the social movements of the 1960s, and we may be seeing it again, albeit for different reasons, as we move through the early decades of the 2000s. Change is usually thought of as "progress"—we move from what seem to be outmoded ways of doing things to more innovative practices. Earlier in the chapter, we saw how variations in culture, whether they resulted from multiculturalism, countercultures, or culture wars, could all lead to growth and change in the larger society. Now we look at several other important processes that can also contribute to cultural change.

Technological Change

One of the most significant influences on any society is its material culture. And most changes in material culture tend to be technological. We usually equate **technology** with "hi-tech" electronic or digital devices. But technology can be anything from a hammer to the space shuttle, from graffiti to a search engine algorithm to hypertext markup language (HTML), as well as the "know how" it takes to use it.

New technology often provides the basis and structure through which culture is disseminated to members of a social group. For instance, we are currently living in the Digital Age or Information Age, a revolutionary time in history spurred by the invention of the computer microchip. This technology has already produced radical changes in society, much as the steam engine did during the Industrial Revolution of the eighteenth and nineteenth centuries.

One of the most prominent features of this Information Age is the spread of mass and social media. It was not until the 1950s that television became a regular part of daily life in the United States and only in the 1990s that the Internet became commonplace. Cell phones morphed into smartphones in the 2000s, while tablet devices and cloud computing allowed for storing and streaming content in the 2010s. Even those of us who were alive before these technological advancements may have trouble remembering life before them; that's how much we rely on them and take them for granted. This digital revolution is shaping our culture—and the rest of the world—at an increasingly rapid pace.

Cultural Diffusion, Imperialism, and Leveling

Cultural change can also occur when different groups share their material and nonmaterial culture with each other, a process called **cultural diffusion**. Since each culture has its own tools, beliefs, and practices, exposure to another culture may mean that certain aspects of it will then be appropriated. For example, as McDonald's-style restaurants set up shop in cultures where fast food had previously been unknown, it wasn't only hamburgers that got relocated—other aspects of fast-food culture came along as well.

Eric Schlosser (2002) began seeing the effects of a Western diet on the Japanese during the 1980s, when they doubled their consumption of fast-food meals—and their rates of obesity. Their risks of heart disease and stroke also increased. Although Japan has some of the lowest obesity rates in the world, there was enough concern about it that a law was passed in 2008 requiring people between the ages of forty-five and seventy-four to have their waistlines measured once a year. Those falling outside the acceptable range are encouraged to seek medical attention (Marsh 2016). The "Metabo Law" addresses other diet-related problems, such as high blood pressure and high cholesterol levels, and has been widely promoted in the country. While it is difficult to prove how much fast food is to blame for worsening health conditions in Japan, it is clear that a single cultural product cannot be exported without carrying a raft of cultural consequences with it. More recently, obesity rates in sub-Saharan African countries like Ghana have surged as Western fast food companies such as Yum! Brands, which owns KFC and Pizza Hut, have increased their presence in the region.

Cultural diffusion usually occurs in the direction from more developed to less developed nations. In particular, "Western" culture has spread rapidly to the rest of the world—driven by capitalism and globalization and aided by new forms of transportation and communication that allow for

TECHNOLOGY material artifacts and the knowledge and techniques required to use them

CULTURAL DIFFUSION the dissemination of material and symbolic culture (tools and technology, beliefs and behavior) from one group to another

A Taste of Kentucky in Ghana
Obesity rates have surged in the African nation as the country has embraced Western imports like fried chicken, pizza, and french fries.

IN THE FUTURE
Online Radicalization: Spreading Extremism

Online recruitment: Colleges use it to attract students. Employers use it to attract applicants. The armed services use it to attract trainees. Nonprofits use it to attract volunteers. Charities use it to attract donors. And extremist groups use it to attract followers.

Terrorist organizations, such as ISIS, or the Islamic State, have found a powerful new tool in the Internet to spread their ideological message and recruit new members to their cause. Social media in particular has allowed such groups to reach people in Western nations, including the United States. Until very recently, a new recruit would have to actually travel to a hotbed of terrorist activity such as Afghanistan, Iraq, or Syria in order to join in with militants using extreme violence in pursuit of their goals. Now, that same person can become radicalized more quickly than ever before, and all without leaving the country.

Terrorist organizations take advantage of computer whizzes in their ranks and English-speaking militants who are familiar with Western culture to produce and distribute materials that appeal to vulnerable young men cruising the Internet. Twitter and YouTube have proved to be active platforms for American ISIS sympathizers to pick up terrorist propaganda. This has inspired some to become lone wolf, homegrown, or self-radicalized terrorists such as those who carried out the 2013 bombing in Boston, the 2015 mass shooting in San Bernardino, and the 2016 massacre in Orlando.

Of course, social media user policies explicitly prohibit content that supports or promotes violent or illegal activities, but it still gets through. Twitter has suspended more than 635,000 accounts linked to the Islamic State since 2015, and Facebook and YouTube regularly take down material linked to militant groups. More recently, these social media companies (along with Microsoft) teamed up to develop and share a new program that can more quickly identify and remove the most egregious content, such as recruitment videos and beheadings (Hennigan 2017). But they haven't been able to prevent foreign operatives from finding new recruits online, who then move their conversations to encrypted messaging apps such as WhatsApp and Telegram, where they can avoid detection.

State intelligence agencies and law enforcement around the world have been largely ineffective in curtailing this communication pipeline. They struggle to identify, understand, and intervene in a process that is difficult to trace and that often happens anonymously over the Internet. While military actions in Afghanistan and elsewhere have substantially reduced the territory that ISIS can claim as its Islamic caliphate (or base), the group has been able to survive, and expand, online.

While Islamic extremist groups have been the focus of much attention regarding their online recruitment tactics, they are not the only ones who use them. Domestic extremist groups such as white nationalist and neo-Nazi groups also use the same strategies and tools. In August 2017, members of far-right groups descended on Charlottesville, Virginia, for a Unite the Right rally that erupted in violence when James Alex Fields Jr. drove his car through a group of counterprotesters, killing one woman and injuring nineteen others. He was said to be inspired by reading the notorious neo-Nazi website the Daily Stormer, the same one Dylann Roof visited before his murderous rampage on a black church in Charleston, South Carolina, in 2015.

The web-hosting company Go Daddy moved swiftly after Charlottesville to take down the Daily Stormer, and it has been rejected by every other domain registrar in the United States and abroad. This shutout has likely sent the site to relocate on the dark web, which can be accessed only by heavily encrypted software that protects a user's identity (Gaffey 2017). But this doesn't mean that its extremist ideas—or those espoused by other hate groups—have completely disappeared. It would seem certain that we are going to grapple with issues of free speech and online terrorist recruitment for some time to come.

Far-Right Radicalization Far-right groups use Facebook, Twitter, and YouTube, among other tools, to radicalize young people who feel alienated by the mainstream culture. The Internet has made these young people—who refer to themselves as "NEETS," or "not in education, employment, or training"—more reachable than ever.

ever faster exchanges. You can watch MTV in India and *Game of Thrones* in Uzbekistan or listen to Rihanna in Morocco. Many view this increased access to information and entertainment as good news for the spread of freedom and democracy. But the media are necessarily a reflection of the culture in which they are produced. So not only are we selling entertainment, but also we are implicitly promoting certain Western ideas. And it can become a problem when the images and ideas found in the media conflict with the traditional norms and values of other countries.

The proliferation of Western media amounts to what some social critics call **cultural imperialism** (Schiller 1995). These critics conceive of media as a kind of invading force that enters a country and takes it over—much like an army, but with film, television, music, soft drinks, and running shoes instead of guns. Historically, imperialism involved the conquering of other nations by monarchies for their own glory and enrichment. The British Empire, for example, was once able to use its military might to occupy and control a third of the world's total land area. But now it is possible to cross a border and to occupy a territory culturally, without setting foot on foreign soil. Because they command so many economic resources, Western media companies are powerful enough to create a form of cultural domination wherever their products go.

Of the countries that consider the messages in Western media dangerous, some forbid or restrict the flow of information, others impose various kinds of censorship, and still others try to promote their own cultural productions. Iran, for example, officially censors all non-Islamic media content on television, radio, film, and the Internet (though many Iranians use hidden satellite dishes to plug into illegal Western programming). In the long run, it may be very difficult to prevent cultural imperialism from spreading.

Cultural leveling occurs when cultures that were once distinct become increasingly similar to one another. If you travel, you may have already seen this phenomenon in towns across the United States and countries around the world. The Walmarts on the interstates, for instance, have driven independent mom-and-pop stores from Main Streets all over the country. Many people bemoan this development and the consequent loss of uniqueness and diversity it represents. As cultures begin to blend, new mixes emerge. This can result in an interesting hybrid—for example, of East and West—but it can also mean a blander, more diluted culture of sameness.

While Western culture is a dominant force in this process, cultural diffusion and cultural leveling do not have to occur in a one-way direction. Other societies have also had an influence on culture in the United States. For instance, Japanese anime was for many years a fringe interest in the United States, usually associated with computer geeks and other outsiders; now Disney has teamed up with Hayao Miyazaki, Japan's leading anime filmmaker, to sell his movies (such as *Spirited Away*, *Howl's Moving Castle*, and *Ponyo*)

Welcome Back to Japan Some social critics maintain that the spread of Western media, such as pop music by Ariana Grande, amounts to cultural imperialism.

to a mainstream American audience. Still, the United States, the dominant producer of global media, remains the primary exporter of cultural content throughout the world.

AMERICAN CULTURE IN PERSPECTIVE

Because American culture is highly visible worldwide, the country's moral and political values have equally high visibility. That means when reruns of *Friends* or *Grey's Anatomy* air in places like Egypt or Malaysia or Lebanon, American values on the topics of sex, gender, work, and family are being transmitted as well. When such military ventures as Operation Enduring Freedom (in Afghanistan) or Operation Iraqi Freedom are undertaken, part of their mission involves exporting the political values associated with democracy, capitalism, and even Christianity. Well, you may say, *Friends* is funny, and *Grey's* is a great way to kill time, and democracy is a good thing—so what's the problem here?

In some parts of the world, the premise of these shows would be unthinkable in real life: In many traditional cultures, both women and men live with their parents until they marry, sometimes to partners chosen for them by their families. A show in which young men and women live on their own,

> **CULTURAL IMPERIALISM** the imposition of one culture's beliefs and practices on another culture through media and consumer products rather than by military force
>
> **CULTURAL LEVELING** the process by which cultures that were once unique and distinct become increasingly similar

with almost no family involvement, dating and sleeping with people to whom they are not married, presents values that are distasteful in these cultures. American values, or at least the perceptions of them shaped by Hollywood and pop-culture exports, can breed negative feelings toward the United States. The value placed on individualism, sexual freedom, and material satisfaction in American life can antagonize cultures that place a higher value on familial involvement and moral and social restraint and may result in anti-American sentiment.

Politics can generate the same anti-American feelings. For example, the United States has recently been involved in attempts to stem the development of nuclear weapons in developing countries like North Korea, Iran, and Pakistan while still maintaining its own nuclear arsenal at home. Other nations may question why American politicians think they should be able to withhold from other countries privileges the United States itself enjoys, such as developing a nuclear weapons program. Much of the resentment against the United States abroad emerges as a result of this type of phenomenon—America's perceived failure to live up to its own political values and ideals or to apply them fairly to others.

Putting American culture in perspective means recognizing that because it is pervasive, it may also be viewed with suspicion and even contempt when the values it expresses clash with those of other cultures. But the nature of anti-Americanism is complex—it's not merely a failure by other nations to understand "good" television shows or accept "superior" political systems. There are meaningful cultural differences between Americans and others, and we should keep those differences in mind as we read about or travel to other cultures. Indeed, there are cultural differences of similar magnitude within the United States as well. The question of the meaning of American culture in a larger global context is a complicated one.

Closing Comments

In this chapter, we have seen how seemingly simple elements of material culture (cars and comic books) and symbolic culture (norms and values) create complex links between the individual and society, as well as between different societies around the globe. American culture in particular, sociologists often argue, is hegemonic (dominant), in that certain interests (such as creating a global market for American products) prevail, while others (such as encouraging local development and self-determination) are subordinated. Within the United States, this can mean that the cultural norms, values, beliefs, and practices of certain subcultures—such as minority ethnic or religious groups—are devalued. Elsewhere, it can mean that the United States is accused of cultural imperialism by nations whose values and practices are different from its own.

Whose cultural values and practices are "better" or "right"? The sociological perspective avoids these evaluative terms when examining culture, choosing instead to take a relativistic approach. In other words, different cultures should (in most cases) be evaluated not according to outside standards but according to their own sets of values and norms. But we should always recognize that this commitment to cultural relativism is a value in itself—which makes cultural relativism neither right nor wrong but rather a proper subject for intellectual examination.

Let's Talk More

1. List five pieces of material culture you have with you right now, and explain what these pieces indicate about the tastes, habits, and lifestyles supported by your cultural group.

2. When was the last time you violated a norm? How were you sanctioned? What sorts of sanctions do we impose on those who go against our accepted cultural rules?

3. Make a list of ways in which the media—including advertisements—reach you each day. How many of these media messages represent mainstream Western ideals? What kinds of media messages do not conform to these norms?

Let's Explore More

1. **TV show** David, Larry, creator. *Curb Your Enthusiasm.*

2. **Book** Joy, Melanie. 2010. *Why We Love Dogs, Eat Pigs, and Wear Cows: An Introduction to Carnism.* Berkeley, CA: Conari.

3. **Blog Post** Sternheimer, Karen. "Subcultures among Us: The Amish." *Everyday Sociology* (blog). March 8, 2012. *https://WWNorton.com/rd/Xf5a9.*

CHAPTER 4

Socialization, Interaction, and the Self

Take a picture of this. For many young people, and some older ones as well, Instagram has become a primary means for presenting themselves to the world. An Instagram account is more than just a scrapbook of images and words; nowadays, it's a way of establishing one's identity, of making a claim about who you are. There is an implicit demand to document and display all the right moments of our lives, so a smartphone camera must always be at the ready.

Everyone is a photographer now, clambering to find the perfect shot that's going to convey what we want to say about our lives and ourselves. Accounts are built and meticulously curated to create just the right impression. The best photos must first be selected.

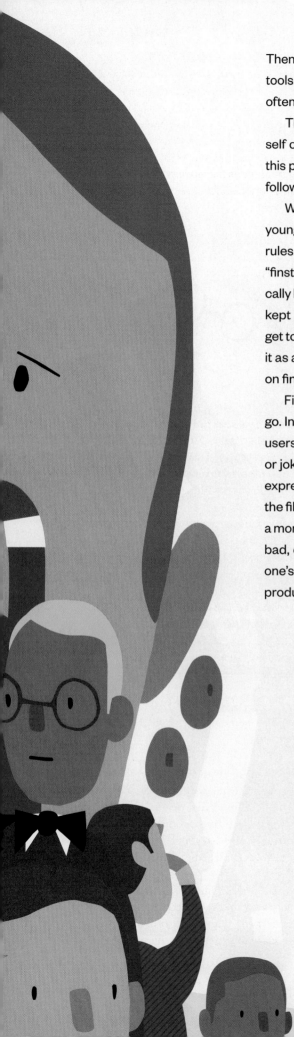

Then they are cropped, filtered, and further enhanced using an expansive array of editing tools. Clever captions are thought up and hashtags applied to every post. We must post often but not too much, lest we spoil the effect.

The point of this is not only to create our own sense of self but also to project that self out into the world for approval. So we must always keep up appearances. And it's this part—about having to manipulate how we look to others, about seeking and getting followers, likes, and comments—that has some Instagram users thinking twice.

While many are still content with the platform as is, a small but growing number of young people are setting up secondary accounts on Instagram that upend the normal rules. Contrary to "rinsta" (or real Instagram), these "finstagram" (fake Instagram), or "finsta," accounts are closely guarded from public view. These private accounts are typically locked so that followers can be carefully screened for admission and their numbers kept purposely low. This means that only one's closest friends, and sometimes family, get to see what's posted. Because finsta is so intimate (relative to Instagram), users see it as a safe place where they can act naturally and be more themselves. Paradoxically, on finstagram people may be less fake and more authentic than they are on rinsta.

Finsta offers more control at the same time that it's a way for some people to just let go. Instead of worrying about being overexposed, misunderstood, or degraded, finsta users don't hesitate to post as often as they'd like and to include unflattering selfies or joke pictures and references that only insiders will get. Users feel more freedom to express themselves and less self-conscious about their image. Whereas rinsta features the filtered version of who you are and how you want to be perceived, finsta represents a more genuine picture of your true self across a multitude of moments—whether good, bad, or ugly—that make up a real life. But what is your "true self"? And where does one's sense of self come from? As you'll learn in this chapter, the self is largely a social product—one that is created and modified through social interaction.

How to Read this Chapter

In this chapter, you will learn how the self is connected to all social phenomena (such as gender, race, and the media) and how interaction constructs them all. You will be acquiring some new analytic tools, including the concepts of socialization and impression management, which will be referenced again in the chapters to come. In addition, you will be introduced to a new way of looking at the self—indeed, a new way of looking at *your* self—that emphasizes the role of the social in creating the individual. And you will be reminded of the reverse: As your society makes you who you are, you have a role (in fact, many roles) to play in shaping your society.

WHAT IS HUMAN NATURE?

"That's just human nature" is a phrase often used to explain everything from violence and jealousy to love and altruism. But what is human nature, really? What is the thing about us that is unique and irreducible, that we all have in common and that separates us from other creatures? From a sociologist's perspective, culture and society are what make us human. These things that we have created also make us who we are. We have to learn the meanings we give to food, housing, sex, and everything else, and society is the teacher.

You would be a very different person if you had been born in fourteenth-century Japan, in an Aztec peasant family, or in the Norwegian royal court. You would have learned a different language, a different set of everyday skills, and a different set of meanings about how the world works. Also, your sense of who you are would be radically different in each case because of the particular social structures and interactions you would encounter. If you were a member of an Aztec peasant family, for example, you would expect to be married to someone of your parents' choosing in your early teens (McCaa 1994). Girls were considered old maids if they were still single at age fifteen and might have ended up as prostitutes or concubines if they had not found a husband by this tender age.

The Nature vs. Nurture Debate

If it is culture and society that make us human, what role does our genetic makeup play? Aren't we *born* with certain instincts? These are questions posed in what is often called the **nature vs. nurture debate**. Those taking the nature side—often sociobiologists, some psychologists, and others in the natural sciences—argue that behavioral traits can be explained by genetics. Those taking the nurture side—sociologists and others in the social sciences—argue that human behavior is learned and shaped through social interaction. Which of these arguments is right?

Both are right. You don't have to look far to see that genetics, or nature, plays a role in who we are. For example, research shows that high levels of testosterone contribute to stereotypically masculine traits such as aggressiveness and competitiveness. However, it is also true that facing a competitive challenge (such as a baseball game) causes testosterone levels to rise. So is it the hormone that makes us competitive, or is it competition that stimulates hormone production? An additional example involves a study of moral and social development in people with brain injuries. Steven W. Anderson and colleagues (1999) studied patients whose prefrontal cortex had been damaged. Those who had received the injury as infants struggled with moral and social reasoning, finding it difficult or impossible to puzzle out questions like "Is it acceptable for a man to steal the drug needed to save his wife's life if he can't afford to pay for it?" People who received the same injury as adults, however, were able to deal with such issues. Anderson and his research team hypothesized that there is a crucial period in brain development when people acquire the capacity for moral reasoning. In other words, nature provides a biological window through which social and moral development occurs.

The point is, there is a complex relationship between nature and nurture. Neither one alone is sufficient to explain what makes us human. Certainly, heredity gives us a basic potential, but it is primarily our social environment that determines whether we will realize or fall short of that potential. We are subject to social influences from the moment we are born (and even before), and these influences only increase over the years. In part because the influence of social contact happens so gradually and to some extent unconsciously, we don't really notice what or how we are learning.

THE PROCESS OF SOCIALIZATION

We often speak of "socializing" with our friends, yet the idea of "socializing" is only part of what sociologists mean by **socialization**. Socialization is a twofold process. It includes the process by which a society, culture, or group teaches individuals to become functioning members, and the process by which individuals learn and internalize the values and norms of the group.

Socialization thus works on both an individual and a social level: We learn our society's way of life and make it our own. Socialization accomplishes two main goals. First, it teaches members the skills necessary to satisfy basic human needs

> **NATURE VS. NURTURE DEBATE** the ongoing discussion of the respective roles of genetics and socialization in determining individual behaviors and traits
>
> **SOCIALIZATION** the process of learning and internalizing the values, beliefs, and norms of our social group, by which we become functioning members of society

IN THE FUTURE
Genetics and Sociology

Sociologists have long been interested in resolving the nature vs. nurture debate and just how much each side contributes to human behavior, or even determines it. In the 1990s, dramatic new possibilities for gathering scientific data were made available as a result of discoveries in the emerging field of genetics. In 2003, the Human Genome Project was completed, which identified all the genes constituting human DNA. At the same time that geneticists had hoped that knowledge of the genes would reveal all the answers to human behavior, they were finding that the social environment could actually change genes. Thus geneticists became interested in some of the same questions that a small but influential offshoot of sociologists had also been studying.

SOCIOBIOLOGY a branch of science that uses biological and evolutionary explanations for social behavior

Sociobiology became a controversial topic within sociology in 1975 with the publication of Edward O. Wilson's *Sociobiology: The New Synthesis*. Many sociologists criticized the book, seeing it as an example of genetic determinism, as Wilson came down squarely on the nature side of the debate when he proposed that genes play a far greater role in human behavior than social or cultural factors. Wilson continued to develop these ideas in his 1978 work *On Human Nature*, in which he argued "that the evidence is strong that

a substantial fraction of human behavioral variation is based on genetic difference" (p. 43).

Other sociologists who followed Wilson's argument that genes play a larger role in human behavior caused further controversy as they stood in opposition to long-held and widely embraced sociological models of the self. Books such as *The Bell Curve: Intelligence and Class Structure in American Life* (Herrnstein and Murray 1994), which proposed a genetic basis for IQ that differed by race, incited new rounds of heated argument and criticism (Pinker 2005). Matters were further complicated as the media rushed to report, often in misleading or oversimplified ways, any new research on the relationship between genetics and behavior. These debates made discussion of genes and behavior frustrating, and challenges from a variety of different critics eventually led to sociobiology falling out of favor.

Since Wilson's time, explosive advances have been made in the area of gene research. And with these advancements has emerged a new generation of sociologists who are trying to unite genetics and sociology in more interesting and nuanced ways, beyond a simple opposition between nature and nurture or one-dimensional assertions of cause and effect. There is now a growing appreciation of how our social and environmental context can significantly alter the way a gene expresses itself. Researchers have taken to calling

---

and to defend themselves against danger, thus ensuring that society itself will continue to exist. Second, socialization teaches individuals the norms, values, and beliefs associated with their culture and provides ways to ensure that members adhere to their shared way of life.

Social Isolation

We can appreciate how important socialization is when we see what happens to people who are deprived of social contact. For twenty-seven years, Christopher Knight—better known as the North Pond hermit—lived undetected in the woods of rural Maine. Sometime in the mid-1980s, at the age of twenty, Knight left civilization and eventually established a campsite on private land some distance from the cabins ringing North Pond. And there he stayed, in complete isolation. During that time, he spoke to only one person (an

accidental encounter) and made no purchases of any kind. It is estimated that Knight committed more than 1,000 burglaries over the years, and although local authorities conducted numerous searches, he managed to elude capture until he was finally arrested, at the age of forty-seven, in the spring of 2013.

In an interview with a journalist, Knight reflected on the power of social isolation on one's identity:

> I did examine myself. Solitude did increase my perception. But here's the tricky thing—when I applied my increased perception to myself, I lost my identity. With no audience, no one to perform for, I was just there. There was no need to define myself; I became irrelevant. The moon was the minute hand, the seasons the hour hand. I didn't even have a name. I never felt lonely. To put it romantically: I was completely free." (Finkel 2014)

their work "genetically informed sociology" (Guo, Tong, and Cai 2008) or, more commonly, "social genomics" or sociogenomics (Conley and Fletcher 2017; Bliss 2018).

This next generation of trailblazers has helped to establish that genetics are conditioned by social experience and that genes do not work independently of social or cultural factors; rather, they work with them. There is increasing evidence "pointing to the importance of social factors in regulating genetic action" (Shanahan, Bauldry, and Freeman 2010, p. 37). Genomic analysis is allowing researchers to examine key issues in sociology using a different lens. Recent studies have examined how outcomes such as educational attainment, risk-taking behaviors, alcoholism, and obesity are the result of a complex interplay between genetics and social factors (Perry et al. 2013; Guo et al. 2009). For example, using data from twins, siblings, and half siblings, sociologist Molly Martin (2008) was able to show that the link between parents' and children's weight is due not only to shared genes but also to shared lifestyle. In fact, social factors like how often a family misses meals or how much time is spent watching TV or playing video games are just as influential as parental obesity in determining a teen's weight.

With an arsenal of new scientific tools at our disposal, and an increasingly sophisticated understanding of the intersection of biology and social environment, we can reframe the nature vs. nurture debate and put an end to that war. Instead of choosing sides, researchers must consider both nature and nurture and, more importantly, the interaction between the two (Conley 2016). There is much shared excitement about the possibilities for research now and in the future. According to Conley and Fletcher, "The genetics revolution may be well underway, but the social genomics revolution is just getting started" (2017, p. 11). Indeed, in the next decade or two we may look back at this time and see it as "the start of a golden age for the field" (Freese 2018).

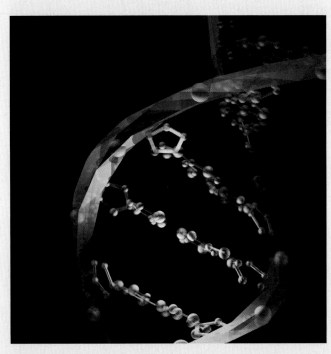

Nature vs. Nurture What parts of your life are affected by your genes? By your society?

Perhaps even more demonstrative of the importance of socialization are cases of **feral children**. When infants are born, they exhibit almost none of the learned behaviors that characterize human beings. Even their instincts for food or shelter or self-preservation are barely recognizable and almost impossible for them to act on alone. Babies do have innate capacities but can fully develop as human beings only through contact with others. There are several startling cases that demonstrate this (Newton 2004). Though rare, these cases give social scientists the chance to study the effects of social isolation and to better understand the relationship between human development and socialization (Davis 1940; Davis and Moore 1947).

One well-known modern case involves a child named Genie (a pseudonym), who was discovered by child welfare services in 1970 (Rymer 1994). At the time, she was thirteen years old and had been living with her family in Arcadia, California, where she had been severely neglected and abused. The authorities were shocked to find that the young girl had not developed like a normal child. Since infancy, Genie's father had kept her locked in a small room, where she was often tied to a potty chair or crib, and she was deprived of practically all human interaction. She had not been exposed to language much and therefore had not learned to speak. Because her movements had been restricted and she was also malnourished, Genie lacked in physical development. She was afraid of strangers and devoid of any social skills. She exhibited some animal-like qualities; she clawed and sniffed and spat frequently.

Genie was taken into custody and placed in the care of a team of scientists who were given an unprecedented

FERAL CHILDREN in myths and rare real-world cases, children who have had little human contact and may have lived in social isolation from a young age

Mowgli, the "Man Cub" Fictional accounts of feral children, such as Mowgli, the hero of the animated Disney film *The Jungle Book*, are quite different from real socially isolated children, who struggle to learn language and interact with others.

opportunity to both study and treat her case. Would it be possible to reverse the effects of extreme social isolation? Could Genie learn language? Could she be socialized and learn to interact with others? Or would it be too late for her to develop normally? The team commenced at once to study the process of socialization and language acquisition, exposing Genie to caring people and a whole new world. At first she made rapid progress with both sign language and nonverbal communication. She was also learning to vocalize, quickly adding new words to her vocabulary. She was gaining some social skills and forming relationships with the researchers, all of which made them optimistic about Genie's prognosis for recovery.

The team began to splinter as they disagreed about Genie's care. Funding to support further research was ultimately withdrawn, and all testing and scientific observation ended. Genie was placed in a series of foster homes, where she suffered further abuse and lost much of her capacity for speech. Genie's case was effectively closed in 1978, and we know little about her current status. There is still debate over the ethics of such research on humans.

Unfortunately, Genie was not the last child to be raised in social isolation. Cases occasionally emerge, such as the 2018 case of the Turpin family in California. David and Louise Turpin allegedly held their thirteen children captive for years, possibly decades, until one of them escaped and contacted the police. The children were kept in their rooms, shackled to their beds, for about twenty hours a day and were regularly beaten and tortured. When authorities arrived at the Turpin home, the

SELF the individual's conscious, reflexive experience of a personal identity separate and distinct from others

children appeared not only physically stunted as a result of their appalling living conditions, but they also seemed to lack cognitive skills and even basic knowledge about the outside world. Such cases confirm that the effects of extreme social isolation are devastating and tragic. It is only through contact with others that people develop the qualities we consider natural and normal in a human being.

The socialization process begins in infancy and is especially productive once a child begins to understand and use language (Ochs 1986). But socialization is not complete at that point. It is a lifelong process that continues to shape us through experiences such as school, work, marriage, and parenthood, as we will see in the next few sections.

THEORIES OF THE SELF

Having a sense of one's self is perhaps the most fundamental of all human experiences. When seventeenth-century philosopher René Descartes exclaimed, "I think, therefore I am," he was expressing this basic fact—that we possess a consciousness about ourselves. More recently, some have examined whether primates and other higher mammals might also have this same self-consciousness; while that has yet to be determined, we do know that consciousness is at the core of humanness.

The **self** is our experience of a distinct, real, personal identity that is separate and different from all other people. We can be "proud of ourselves," "lose control of ourselves," or want to "change ourselves," suggesting that we have the ability to think about ourselves as if we were more than one being and to see ourselves from the vantage point of an observer. Our thoughts and feelings emanate both *from* and *toward* ourselves; this is, in effect, how we come to "know" ourselves.

But just where does this sense of a self come from? How do we arrive at self-knowledge? When sociologists address these questions, they look at both the individual and society to find the answer. They believe that the self is created and modified through social interaction over the course of a lifetime. But while sociologists agree that the self is largely a social product, there are still a number of theories about how the self develops, as we will see.

Psychoanalytic Theory: Sigmund Freud

The psychoanalytic perspective on the self, which is usually associated with Sigmund Freud, emphasizes childhood and sexual development as indelible influences on an individual's identity, and in turn how society is upheld through the transformation of human instincts. While Freud's ideas have generated a great deal of controversy, they remain compelling for sociologists.

Perhaps Freud's greatest contribution to understanding the self is his idea of the unconscious mind, as featured in

The Interpretation of Dreams (1900/1955). Freud believed that the conscious level of awareness is but the tip of the iceberg and that just below the surface is a far greater area of the mind, the subconscious and the unconscious. He proposed that this unconscious energy is the source of conscious thoughts and behavior. For example, the unconscious urge to slay one's rivals may manifest itself in a conscious decision to work harder at the office in order to outshine a competitive co-worker.

According to Freud, the mind consists of three interrelated systems: the id, the ego, and the superego. The **id**, which is composed of biological drives, is the source of instinctive, psychic energy. Its main goal is to achieve pleasure and to avoid pain in all situations, which makes the id a selfish and unrealistic part of the mind. For example, although you know that hard work and dedication are necessary for your advancement, the id may urge you to slack off instead, maybe have a few (or even many) drinks to help you deal with all that workplace stress. The **ego**, by contrast, is the part that deals with the real world. It operates on the basis of reason and helps to mediate and integrate the demands of both the id and the superego. So the ego is the part of the self that says, "Okay, this time the other guy got the job, but if I keep trying, I'm bound to get that promotion eventually."

The **superego** is composed of two components: the conscience and the ego-ideal. The conscience serves to keep us from engaging in socially undesirable behavior, and the ego-ideal upholds our vision of who we believe we should ideally be. The superego develops as a result of parental guidance, particularly in the form of the rewards and punishments we receive as children. It inhibits the urges of the id and encourages the ego to find morally acceptable forms of behavior. So the superego helps suppress the urge to kill your competitor and keeps you working toward getting that raise in socially acceptable ways. Each of these systems serves a different mental or emotional function, yet they all work together to keep the individual in a more or less healthy state of balance.

Freud (1905) also proposed that between infancy and adulthood, the personality passes through four distinct **psychosexual stages of development**. Each stage is associated with a different erogenous zone. Freud's theory emerged from his therapy work with adult patients who were asked to try to recall earlier periods from their lives. According to the theory, a child passes through the first three stages of development between the ages of one and five. Most people have little or no memory whatsoever of this period. Yet, according to psychoanalytic theory, it sets the stage for the rest of one's adult life. The last stage of development begins around the age of twelve, but few people successfully complete this final transition to maturity. In some cases, the transitions through the first three stages are not completely successful either, so that people may find themselves stuck, or "fixated," at an earlier stage. Perhaps you've known someone who is considered to have an "oral fixation"—this person, thought to be partially stuck in the first stage of development, might smoke, overeat, or be verbally aggressive. Someone who is "anal retentive"—a neatnik, tightwad, or control freak—is thought to be partially stuck in the second stage. These kinds of personality traits, rooted in early childhood (according to Freud), appear as "hang-ups" in the adult.

Another of Freud's important contributions to sociology is found in his later work *Civilization and Its Discontents*

Dreams and the Subconscious In his book *The Interpretation of Dreams*, psychoanalyst Sigmund Freud outlined three psychological systems—the id, the ego, and the superego—that regulate subconscious drives and help keep an individual mentally balanced.

ID, EGO, AND SUPEREGO according to Freud, the three interrelated parts that make up the mind: the id consists of basic inborn drives that are the source of instinctive psychic energy; the ego is the realistic aspect of the mind that balances the forces of the id and the superego; the superego has two components (the conscience and the ego-ideal) and represents the internalized demands of society

PSYCHOSEXUAL STAGES OF DEVELOPMENT four distinct stages of the development of the self between birth and adulthood, according to Freud; personality quirks are a result of being fixated, or stuck, at any stage

(1930/2010). In it he extended his thesis to show how the psychological makeup of the individual helps to create social order, or civilization, while at the same time being constrained by society's structures and demands, causing the person to become discontent. Again Freud focused on the subconscious drives or instincts of the individual. He referred to two main impulses: "Eros," the libido or life instinct, and "Thanatos," which is aggression or the death instinct. To live successfully in human community, we must find socially acceptable ways of channeling these instincts. We cannot simply act out on our sexual or aggressive impulses without harming ourselves and others and threatening the larger collective. The raw and primitive drives of the individual must be managed somehow. When instincts are repressed or turned inward, they become the conscience and a source of guilt and neuroses. When instincts are sublimated or turned outward, they are positively transformed. There are many constructive ways of expressing sexual energy, redirecting it toward creative pursuits that produce the great works of culture, commerce, or science. Likewise, aggressive instincts can find appropriate outlets in competitive sports, politics, and other competitions, or can be felt vicariously through forms of entertainment like video games or amusement park rides. To live in a civilized society means agreeing to norms and sanctions that infringe on personal freedom but serve to protect the well-being of the group. Civilization demands that we give up some satisfaction of acting on instinct to gain the lesser happiness but greater security of living within the bounds of society.

Other sociologists have extended Freud's work, focusing especially on gender identity—seeing oneself as feminine or masculine. Nancy Chodorow, a feminist and psychoanalytic sociologist, has written widely on human behavior and internal psychic structures and how patterns of gendered parenting and early childhood development can lead to the reproduction of traditional gender roles in society (1978, 1994).

LOOKING-GLASS SELF
the notion that the self develops through our perception of others' evaluations and appraisals of us

PREPARATORY STAGE
the first stage in Mead's theory of the development of self wherein children mimic or imitate others

PLAY STAGE the second stage in Mead's theory of the development of self wherein children pretend to play the role of the particular or significant other

PARTICULAR OR SIGNIFICANT OTHER the perspectives and expectations of a particular role that a child learns and internalizes

GAME STAGE the third stage in Mead's theory of the development of self wherein children play organized games and take on the perspective of the generalized other

GENERALIZED OTHER the perspectives and expectations of a network of others (or of society in general) that a child learns and then takes into account when shaping his or her own behavior

DUAL NATURE OF THE SELF the idea that we experience the self as both subject and object, the "I" and the "me"

The Looking-Glass Self: Charles Cooley

Around the same time Freud was developing his theories (early 1900s), other social theorists interested in the self were working on the other side of the Atlantic. Charles Cooley, an early member of the Chicago School of sociology, devised a simple but elegant way to conceptualize how individuals gain a sense of self. His idea is captured in the following short poem, which summarizes a profound and complex process.

> *Each to each a looking-glass,*
> *Reflects the other that doth pass.*

Cooley (1909) referred to this concept as the **looking-glass self**. He believed that we all act like mirrors to each other, reflecting back to one another an image of ourselves. We do this in three steps (Yeung and Martin 2003).

1. *We imagine how we look to others*—not just in a physical sense, but in how we present ourselves. For example, we may imagine that others find us friendly, funny, or hardworking. The idea we have of ourselves is particularly important in regard to significant others. Whether they are parents, bosses, friends, or partners, we care about how we look to these people.

2. *We imagine other people's judgment of us.* We try to picture others' reactions and to interpret what they must be feeling. What is their opinion of me? Do they think I am smart enough? Lazy? Boring? Too tall?

3. *We experience some kind of feeling about ourselves based on our perception of other people's judgments.* If we imagine, for instance, that they think of us as competent, we may feel pride; conversely, if we think they consider us inadequate, we may feel shame or embarrassment. The important point here is that we respond to the judgments that we *believe* others make about us, without really knowing for sure what they think. And we're not always right. We may draw wildly unrealistic conclusions. But according to Cooley, it is these perceptions, not reality, that determine the feelings we ultimately have about ourselves.

The social looking glass—the way we see ourselves reflected back from others—together with the feelings we develop as a result of what we imagine they see in us, forms our concept of self. For Cooley, there could be no sense of self without society, for there is no individual self without a corresponding "other" to provide us with our looking-glass self-image.

The suggestion that we are dependent on what others think of us—or rather what we think they think—for our own self-concept might seem appalling: Are we really that hung up on what other people think? But while some of us may be influenced to a greater or lesser degree, *all* of us come to know ourselves through relationships, either real or imagined, with others.

Mind, Self, and Society: George Herbert Mead

Another member of the Chicago School, George Herbert Mead, expanded on Cooley's ideas about the development of the self and laid the essential groundwork that became the theory of symbolic interactionism. Mead also believed that the self is created through social interaction. He believed that this process starts in childhood—that children begin to develop a sense of self at about the same time that they begin to learn language. The acquisition of language skills coincides with the growth of mental capacities, including the ability to think of ourselves as separate and distinct and to see ourselves in relationship to others (Mead 1934).

According to Mead, the development of the self unfolds in several stages as we move through childhood. First is the **preparatory stage**. Children under the age of three lack a completely developed sense of self, and so they have difficulty distinguishing themselves from others. Such children begin the development process by simply imitating or mimicking others around them (making faces, playing patty-cake) without fully understanding the meaning of their behavior. After age three, children enter the **play stage** of development when they start to pretend or play at being "mommy," "firefighter," "princess," or "doctor." This is referred to as taking the role of the **particular or significant other**. As children learn the behavior associated with being a mother or doctor, they internalize the expectations of those particular others and begin to gain new perspectives in addition to their own. Such play also serves the purpose of anticipatory socialization for the real-life roles a child might play in the future.

In the final or **game stage** of development, children's self-awareness increases through a process Mead described using the example of games. By the early school years, children begin to take part in organized games. Each child must follow the rules of the game, which means that he or she must simultaneously take into account the roles of all the other players. Mead called this overview the perspective of the **generalized other**. Thus, children begin to understand the set of standards common to a social group—their playmates—and to see themselves from others' viewpoints. By taking the perspective of the generalized other, children are able to see themselves as objects. They gradually learn to internalize the expectations of the generalized other for themselves and to evaluate their own behavior. This is the beginning of understanding the attitudes and expectations of society as a whole.

The Particular Other According to Mead, children begin to develop a sense of self by imitating others and playing roles.

Mead also recognized the dialectical or **dual nature of the self**—that is, the self as both subject and object. What we refer to as "I" is the subject component—the experience of a spontaneous, active, and creative part of ourselves, somewhat less socialized. What we refer to as "me" is the object component—the experience of a norm-abiding, conforming part of ourselves, more socialized and therefore reliant on others. The two components are inseparable and are united to form a single self in each of us. It is this process of recognizing the dual nature of the self, taking the role of the particular other, and seeing the perspective of the generalized other that Mead suggested leads to the development of the self.

Dramaturgy: Erving Goffman

Erving Goffman is another among the group of symbolic interactionists who saw micro-level, face-to-face interaction as the building block of every other aspect of society. Goffman believed that all meaning, as well as our individual selves, is constructed through interaction. Many of his key ideas are expressed in *The Presentation of Self in Everyday Life* (1956).

THOMAS THEOREM classic formulation of the way individuals determine reality, whereby "if people define situations as real, they are real in their consequences"

DEFINITION OF THE SITUATION an agreement with others about "what is going on" in a given circumstance; this consensus allows us to coordinate our actions with others and realize goals

EXPRESSIONS OF BEHAVIOR small actions such as an eye roll or head nod that serve as an interactional tool to help project our definition of the situation to others

EXPRESSIONS GIVEN expressions that are intentional and usually verbal, such as utterances

EXPRESSIONS GIVEN OFF observable expressions that can be either intended or unintended and are usually nonverbal

To understand Goffman's work, we first need to briefly consider another of the early Chicago School sociologists, W. I. Thomas. What is now called the **Thomas theorem** states that "if people define situations as real, they are real in their consequences" (Thomas and Thomas 1928, p. 572). In other words, because we encounter ambiguous situations every day, many meanings are possible. The way we define each situation, then, becomes its reality.

For example, suppose you're walking down the street and you witness a woman slapping a man in public. What are the possible meanings of that situation? It could be a fight; it could be a joke or a friendly greeting, depending on how hard the slap is; it could be that he has just passed out and she is hoping to revive him; or the participants could be actors shooting a scene from a film. Each of these definitions leads to a different set of potential consequences—you might intervene, call the police, stand by and laugh, ignore them, summon paramedics, or ask for an autograph, depending on which meaning you act

upon. Each **definition of the situation** lends itself to a different approach, and the consequences are real.

Goffman looked at how we define situations interactionally—not just cognitively within our own heads but also in interaction with others. Think about it: How do you get your definition of the situation across to others? If you think a classroom lecture is boring, you may look over at your best friend and roll your eyes . . . they nod, indicating that they know what you mean. The eye roll and the nod are **expressions of behavior**, tools we use to project our definitions of the situation to others.

What Goffman called **expressions given** are typically verbal and intended—most of our speech falls into this category. Almost all of what we say, we *mean* to say, at least at that moment. Only in situations of extreme emotional response—such as fear, pain, or ecstasy—might we make unintended utterances. **Expressions given off**, like the eye roll and the nod, are typically nonverbal but observable in various ways and may be intended or unintended. Things like facial expressions, mannerisms, body language, and styles of dress are important indicators to others about the definition of the situation.

IMPRESSION MANAGEMENT Reading meaning in others' expressions of behavior requires a bit of caution. We know that people may deliberately say things to hide what they really feel, so we tend to think we get more real insight from expressions given off because we believe them to be unintended. But expressions given off can be manipulated as well. In a sense, Goffman was saying that it's not just what you say

TABLE 4.1   Theory in Everyday Life

Perspective	Approach to Self and Interaction	Case Study: Identity in Childhood
Psychoanalysis	Freud's theory of the unconscious mind as composed of an interrelated system (id, ego, superego) that underlies human behavior; personality develops through psychosexual stages.	Parents instill a conscience (superego) in children through rules that govern their instinctual behavior (id) until children mature and are self-governing (ego).
Looking-Glass Self	Cooley's theory of the self-concept; our sense of self is derived from how we imagine others see us, and the feelings about our selves based on the perceived judgments of others.	Parents and significant others serve as a reflection to children, who develop a sense of self based on their appraisals, real or imagined.
Mind, Self, and Society	Mead's theory of the self that develops through three stages (preparatory, play, and game); in role taking the particular or generalized other, we learn to see ourselves as others do.	Children gain a sense of self through imitation, play, and games, in which they learn various roles and take on the perspectives of others.
Dramaturgy	Goffman's theory of the presentation of self; we are like actors on a stage, whose performance strategies aid in impression management.	Children learn the arts of impression management and may present a different self to their parents than to other children or to teachers.

but also how you say it that creates meaning. And he was a cynic, although he believed that everyday actors can be sincere. Goffman saw social life as a sort of con game, in which we work at controlling the impressions others have of us. He called this process **impression management**. Like actors on a stage, we play our parts and use all our communicative resources (verbal and nonverbal) to present a particular impression to others. We say and do what we think is necessary to communicate who we are and what we think, and we refrain from saying and doing things that might damage the impression we want others to have of us.

It is this focus on the performance strategies of impression management that has led scholars to refer to Goffman's central ideas as **dramaturgy**—and the theatrical allusion is entirely intended. As in the theater, we use certain tools to aid in our impression management. The **front**, for example, is the setting that helps establish a particular meaning (like a classroom for teaching or a bar for drinking). The specific social setting, or **region** (which includes the location, scenery, décor, and props), provides more elements that help establish the boundaries of the interactional context. You might carry a briefcase into a bar, but it's probably not a good idea to carry a bottle of beer into the classroom.

The front makes a big difference in how we perceive and interact with the people we encounter there. Students and professors recognize one another and know how to interact when on campus or in the classroom. But in other venues, we are out of context, and this can confuse us. We seldom think of our professors as people who have off-campus lives—it's hard to see them as people who dine out, see movies, or buy underwear (for that matter, professors rarely think of their students this way either!). So when we encounter one another in unfamiliar regions, we often don't know how to behave because the old classroom scripts don't work.

Our **personal front**—appearance, manner, and style of dress (or "costume"), as well as gender, race, and age—helps establish the definition of the situation as well. For example, Dr. Ferris is told quite often that she "doesn't look like a professor." This illustrates how we use elements of personal front to make judgments about people: If our images of professors involve gruff, grizzled, older men in unfashionable clothes, then someone who is younger, friendlier, and female must work harder at convincing others that she is in fact a professor. Similarly, when a student happens to see Dr. Ferris at a restaurant, movie theater, or department store, the student's response is almost always the same: "What are you doing here?"

In addition, there are places known as back regions, or **backstage**, where we prepare (or rehearse) for our performances. And then there are front regions, or **frontstage**, where we play a particular role and perform for an "audience" of others. We behave differently—and present different selves—frontstage than we do backstage; your professor behaved differently this morning while he showered, shaved, dressed, and made breakfast for his kids than he is behaving now, lecturing and answering questions in his sociology class. For Goffman, the key to understanding these nuances in impression management is recognizing that we present different selves in different situations, and the responses of others to those selves continually shape and mold our definitions of situation *and* self. Thus we can say that the self is a **social construction** (Berger and Luckmann 1966). The self is something that is created or invented in interaction with others who also participate in agreeing to the reality or meaning of that self as it is being presented in the situation.

We also make claims about who we are in our interactions. These claims can be either accepted or contradicted by others, which can make things either easier or harder for our self-image. Most of the time, others support the selves we project. For example, when your professor starts lecturing and you begin to take notes, you are supporting the version of self that he is presenting: He is "doing professor," and in response, you are "doing student." Another way that we support the selves that people present is to allow them to save face—to prevent them from realizing that they've done something embarrassing. Goffman called this **cooling the mark out**, a phrase borrowed from con games, but it can be used as a tool of civility and tact as well. When the professor mixes up two related concepts in a lecture, for example, you let it pass because you know what she really meant to say. Or, even worse, you overlook the spinach between your professor's teeth until it can be called to his attention privately!

There are also situations in which the selves we project are contested or even destroyed. For example, if you raised your hand in a 200-person lecture hall and told the professor that he had spinach between his teeth, you would be undermining the self he is trying to present. His identity as an expert,

IMPRESSION MANAGEMENT the effort to control the impressions we make on others so that they form a desired view of us and the situation; the use of self-presentation and performance tactics

DRAMATURGY an approach pioneered by Erving Goffman in which social life is analyzed in terms of its similarities to theatrical performance

FRONT in the dramaturgical perspective, the setting or scene of performances that helps establish the definition of the situation

REGION the context in which the performance takes place, including location, décor, and props

PERSONAL FRONT the performance tactics we use to present ourselves to others, including appearance, costume, and manner

BACKSTAGE the places where we rehearse and prepare for our performances

FRONTSTAGE the places where we deliver our performances to an audience of others

SOCIAL CONSTRUCTION the process by which a concept or practice is created and maintained by participants who collectively agree that it exists

COOLING THE MARK OUT behaviors that help others to save face or avoid embarrassment, often referred to as civility or tact

an authority figure, and a senior mentor would be publicly damaged once you called attention to his dental gaffe (unless he was able to deflect the situation gracefully). In Goffman's view, then, the presentation of self and impression management are about power as well as about self. If you embarrass your professor in front of an auditorium full of students, he no longer possesses quite as much power as he did a few moments before.

Goffman's view of our interactions can be disturbing to some people, for it suggests that we are always acting, that we are never being honest about who we really are. But Goffman would challenge this interpretation of his work. Yes, some people deliberately deceive others in their presentation of self, but we must all present *some* type of self in social situations. Why wouldn't those selves be presented sincerely? As Goffman-inspired sociologist Josh Meyrowitz said, "While a dishonest judge may pretend to be an honest judge, even an honest judge must play the role of 'honest judge'" (1985, p. 30).

DATA WORKSHOP

Analyzing Everyday Life

Impression Management in Action

They say that you never get to make a first impression twice, that people can size us up in a matter of seconds and quickly jump to conclusions about who we are. How well do you know yourself and the impressions you make on others? This exercise is designed to help make your own impression-management work visible—and to help you see how integral it is to your everyday life. For this Data Workshop you will be doing participant observation research with yourself as the subject. Research that involves observing one's own behavior is known as autoethnography. Refer to Chapter 2 for a review of this method.

Your task will be to observe yourself as you participate in two different social situations. Afterward, you will do a comparative analysis of your presentation of self in each setting. As you examine the most minute details of yourself in interactions, you will probably discover that you perform somewhat different versions of yourself in the two situations. "Doing student," for instance, might be very different from "doing partner." Let's see.

Step 1: Observation
Choose two different situations that you will encounter this week in your everyday life and commit to observing yourself for thirty minutes as you participate in each. For example, you may observe yourself at work, at a family birthday celebration, at lunch with friends, in your math class, riding on the bus or train, or watching an athletic match. The two situations you choose don't need to be extraordinary in any way; in fact, the more mundane, the better. But they should be markedly different from each other.

Step 2: Field notes
In an autoethnography, your own actions, thoughts, and feelings are the focus of study. Write some informal field notes about your experience so that you can refer to them when you discuss your findings. Your notes can be casual in tone and loose in format, but, as always, it's a good idea to write them as soon as possible after your time in the field. That way, you capture more of the details you'll want to remember. Aim for at least one (or more!) full page of notes for each of the two situations.

Step 3: Analysis
After observing yourself in the two situations, read through your field notes and consider the following questions:

- What type of "front" do you encounter when you enter each situation? What role do you play and who is your "audience"?

- How does the "region" or setting (location, scenery, and props) affect your presentation of self there?

- Can you identify "backstage" and "frontstage" regions for each situation? Which of your activities are preparation and which are performance?

- What type of "personal front" (appearance, manner, dress) do you bring to each situation?

- How are your facial expressions, body language, and so forth ("expressions given off") different in each situation?

- What kinds of things do you say ("expressions given") in each situation?

- How convincing are you at managing the impression you want to make on others in each of the two situations?

- Who are you in each situation? Do you present a slightly different version of yourself in each? Why?

A final Goffman-inspired question to ask is this: Does engaging in impression management mean that we have no basic, unchanging self? If we bring different selves to different situations, what does that say about the idea of a "true self"? This issue is an important one, and we hope you use your Data Workshop findings to pursue it in greater depth.

There are two options for completing the Data Workshop:

PREP-PAIR-SHARE Carry out your observations and bring your field notes to class with you. Partner with another student and discuss your experiences. Work together on developing your analysis by responding to the Data Workshop questions. Use this as a way to learn more about yourself and others.

DO-IT-YOURSELF For Step 1, use ethnographic methods of data gathering. Create written field notes to record your actions, interactions, and thoughts during each thirty-minute observation period. Be as detailed as possible. Then write a three- to four-page essay applying Goffman's dramaturgical analysis to your own experiences, in response to the questions in Step 3. Refer to your field notes in the essay, and include them with your paper.

AGENTS OF SOCIALIZATION

Since our sense of self is shaped by social interaction, we should now turn our attention to the socializing forces that have the most significant impact on our lives. These forces, called **agents of socialization**, provide structured situations in which socialization takes place. While there are a variety of such influences in American society, notably religion, as well as our political and economic systems, we will focus here on what may be the four most predominant agents of socialization: the family, schools, peers, and the media.

The Family

The family is the single most significant agent of socialization in all societies. It's easy to see why. The family is the original group to which we belong. It is where early emotional and social bonds are created, where language is learned, and where we first begin to internalize the norms and values of our society. Most of our primary socialization, which teaches us to become mature, responsible members of society, takes place within the family. For example, one of the most important lessons we learn in families is about gender roles: We see what moms and dads, sisters and brothers are expected to do (like mow the lawn or fold the laundry) and convert

these observations into general rules about gender in society (Chodorow 1978).

Socialization differs from family to family because each family has its own particular set of values and beliefs. The family's own ethnic, class, religious, educational, and political background can all influence a child. A single family can also change over time. As years pass, children may not be raised in the same way as their older siblings, for the simple reason that parents have no experience with babies when their first child is born but plenty of experience by the time the youngest comes along. Nor are all aspects of socialization deliberate; some in fact are quite unintentional (as when a father's violent temper or a mother's depression is passed down to the next generation).

AGENTS OF SOCIALIZATION social groups, institutions, and individuals (especially the family, schools, peers, and the mass media) that provide structured situations in which socialization takes place

The family has such a powerful impact on us partly because as young children we have limited outside contact (until we start day care or school) and therefore few if any other influences. The family is our world. But the family is also *in* the world. Where a family is located, both geographically and socially, will affect family members (Lareau 2003). Childhood socialization takes place in the particular neighborhoods and communities in which we live (Handel, Cahill, and Elkin 2007). Location matters, and different neighborhoods provide very different resources, conditions, and problems for those living there (Sharkey 2018). Where a person grows up may affect his or her educational outcomes, chances for social mobility, and even health (Brooks-Gunn et al. 1993).

The Power of Family The family is the original group to which each person belongs, and it is the most important agent of socialization.

Schools

Public elementary and secondary schools were first established in the United States in the 1800s. While attendance was uneven at first, education advocates believed that schooling played a critical role in maintaining a democracy (though blacks and women still lacked the right to vote) and in shaping future generations of citizens. Over the years, schools have gradually taken on greater responsibilities than merely teaching a prescribed curriculum. Schools now provide physical education, meals, discipline, and child care, all formerly the provinces of other social institutions.

When children begin attending school (including preschool and day care), it may be their first significant experience away from home. School helps them to become less dependent on the family, providing a bridge to other social groups. In school, children learn that they will be judged on their behavior and on academic performance. They learn not only formal subjects but also a **hidden curriculum** (Jackson 1968), a set of behavioral traits such as punctuality, neatness, discipline, hard work, competition, and obedience, and even ideologies like racial and gender hegemony (Jay 2003). The socialization children receive from teachers, staff members, and other students occurs simultaneously and overlaps with what they learn in the family.

HIDDEN CURRICULUM values or behaviors that students learn indirectly over the course of their schooling

Recently, there has been increasing scrutiny regarding the role of teachers, especially in public schools. Because teachers are such potent role models for students, parents are concerned about the moral standing of those who are in charge of teaching their children, as well as their training and competence (Goldstein 2014). There is increasing pressure for schools to take on even more responsibilities, including dealing with issues that used to be taught at home or in church—such as sex, violence, drugs and alcohol, and general morality and citizenship.

Peers

Peer groups are groups of people who are about the same age and have similar social characteristics. Peers may be friends at school or from the neighborhood, members of a sports team, or cabin mates at summer camp. As children get older, peers often become more important than parents as agents of socialization. As the influence of peers increases, the influence of parents decreases. While the family still has the most long-lasting influence on an individual, it is peers who have the most intense and immediate effect on one another.

By adolescence, young people spend more time with their peers than with their parents or anyone else (Larson and Richards 1991). Membership in a peer group provides young people with a way of exercising independence from, and possibly reacting against, adult control. Young people tend to form peer subcultures that are almost entirely centered on their own interests, such as gaming or disc golf or garage bands, with distinct values and norms related to those interests. But peer groups, while providing important and enjoyable social bonds, can also be the source of painful self-doubt, ridicule, or rejection.

The need to "fit in" with a peer group may seem overwhelming to some young people. Some will do almost anything to belong—even betray their own values: Bradley and

13 Reasons Why **and Teen Suicide** Within a month of the show's premiere, suicide rates among young people ages ten to seventeen surged. To what extent do the media act as an agent of socialization?

Wildman (2002) found that peer pressure was a predictor of adolescent participation in risky behaviors such as dangerous driving, unsafe sex, and drug and alcohol use. Interestingly, Kreager and Haynie (2011) found that adolescent drinking behavior is more powerfully influenced by the friends of a teen's partner than by the teen's own friends or partner; in other words, dating someone whose friends drink heavily is more likely to lead a teen to engage in dangerous drinking behaviors, such as binge drinking, than are the habits of the teen's own friends. But peer pressure can also produce beneficial outcomes, such as increased engagement and success with academic work (McCabe 2016) and a positive sense of ethnic identity (Shin, Daly, and Vera 2007).

The Media

The media's role as one of the most significant sources of socialization is a somewhat recent phenomenon. Television began infiltrating American homes in the 1950s, and Internet usage has become widespread only in the past two decades. Yet, for many of us, it would be almost impossible to imagine life without the media—whether print, broadcast, or digital. American adults spend an average of more than 11 hours per day interacting with media (Nielsen 2018). This huge explosion, the dawning of the Information Age, is something we already take for granted, but we don't always see the ways in which it is changing our lives.

Many sociologists question whether the media may have even usurped some of the functions of the family in teaching basic norms and values and giving advice on common problems. A classic example comes from the people of Fiji, a South Pacific island that lacked widespread access to television until 1995. A team of researchers took this unique opportunity to study the effects of television on the local population. Specifically, they were interested in the ways in which Western programs influenced eating habits and body image among adolescent girls in a culture that "traditionally supported robust appetites and body shapes" (A. Becker et al. 2002).

Research began in 1995, just months after TV was introduced, and was carried out again in 1998. The team was able to conclude that Western television was in fact affecting the Fijian girls. In just three years the percentage with an eating disorder jumped from 12 to 29, and the percentage who reported self-induced vomiting as a form of weight control rose from zero to 11. Dieting and dissatisfaction with weight were prevalent—and 83 percent of the girls who were interviewed reported that they felt television "had specifically influenced their friends and/or themselves to feel differently about or change their body shape or weight" (A. Becker et al. 2002).

The media have often been scrutinized for their alleged role in glamorizing or promoting risky behaviors (for instance, smoking, drinking, drug use, and violence), especially among impressionable adolescents and teens. Recently, the popular Netflix series *13 Reasons Why*, which centers on

Fashion for Whom? Most women do not look like this model, yet her body type is held up as the ideal in magazines and other forms of media.

a high school student who takes her own life, incited a great deal of concern because of its graphic depiction of teen suicide. Critics feared that it might have a "contagion" effect among youth, a phenomenon that had already been well documented in other cases, resulting in a spate of copycat attempts (Fu and Yip 2009). Some initial research seemed to find evidence of this contagion effect. One new study showed that suicide rates among young people ages ten to seventeen surged in the month after the series came out in 2017. While the show's main character is a teenage girl, the increase was primarily driven by boys, whose suicide rate rose nearly 30 percent during that time. Using data from the Centers for Disease Control and Prevention, the researchers found that in the nine months after the premiere, there were an additional 195 suicide deaths in this age group than would otherwise have been expected (Bridge et al. 2019). Another study looked at reactions to *13 Reasons Why* in a high-risk sample of young viewers who had been admitted to psychiatric emergency rooms. Over half of the viewers believed that the series had increased their own risk of committing suicide. Those teens who had previously reported symptoms of depression or suicidal ideation, or who identified closely with the lead character, were the most vulnerable to the show's themes (Hong et al. 2018).

It is clear that we internalize many of the values, beliefs, and norms presented in the media and that their powerful influence in our lives only stands to increase as we proceed deeper into the Information Age. It's important to ask: Whose messages are we listening to, and what are we being told about ourselves and one another?

DATA WORKSHOP

Analyzing Media and Pop Culture

TV as an Agent of Socialization

Television is a powerful and surreptitious agent of socialization. It is everywhere, and we devour thousands of hours of it—so it seems important to ask what kinds of messages we are getting about ourselves and our society from all that viewing. How does TV socialize us? You're going to help answer that question.

For this Data Workshop you will be using existing sources and doing a content analysis of a particular TV program. See the section on existing sources in Chapter 2 for a review of this research method. Choose one of the most popular TV series currently on the air—at the time of this writing, your choices might include *NCIS*, *The Good Doctor*, or *This Is Us*. Choose a regular drama or comedy series rather than a news program, talk show, game show, or reality show. Make sure that the show takes place in contemporary times (rather than in the past or in some fantasy world), since your aim will be to analyze how the show depicts modern society and affects today's viewer.

Now choose some aspect of social status and individual identity that you want to focus on, such as gender (how women or men are portrayed), sexuality (heterosexuals, gay men, or lesbians), disability (people who are deaf or blind or in wheelchairs), or class (poor people, wealthy people, or the middle class). For instance, you might look at the depiction of women in *Killing Eve* or men in *Succession*, the representation of people with disabilities in *Speechless* or *Switched at Birth*, or the wealthy in *Empire* or *Billions*.

Watch an episode of your chosen program in its entirety. You will want to record the program or look for an episode on Netflix, Hulu, or another online source so that you can review certain scenes or bits of dialogue

several times. It is important to take some notes as you watch, paying attention to the program's content with reference to your particular topic choice.

To give you an example of how to do this workshop, we use depictions of women (in brackets) as our topic and the program *Modern Family*. You should substitute your own TV program and choice of topic for each of the following questions:

- In this episode of the program, how many [women] characters are there? How does the number of [women] characters compare with the number of other characters? Are the [women's] roles major characters or minor characters? How can you tell?

- What types of roles do the [women] characters have? What are their activities, attitudes, and interactions like on the show? What kinds of things do they do and say that tell you who they are and what they are like?

- Are the portrayals of [women] positive or negative? Humorous or serious? One-dimensional or multidimensional? How can you tell?

- What image(s) of [women] does this program portray? In other words, what messages do the words, pictures, plot lines, and characters convey to viewers about [women] in general?

In the case of *Modern Family*, there are some interesting portrayals of women to analyze. There are two adult women as part of the main cast: Claire Dunphy and Gloria Pritchett. The women are related to each other through Jay Pritchett, who is Claire's father and Gloria's husband (it's a second marriage for both). Claire and Gloria are both stay-at-home moms. Gloria appears to be just a sexy, gold-digging "trophy wife" but is also portrayed as having a depth of wisdom and strength that results from her experiences in a tough neighborhood of her Colombian hometown. Claire is a "daddy's girl" who is initially jealous of Gloria and who searches for meaningful work as her children grow older (she eventually gets a job at her father's company). These women relate to each other, as well as to the men in their lives, in ways that provide powerful messages about gender roles and femininity.

Now that you have examined the roles and portrayals, let's consider the effects on society:

- How does the content of this program contribute to our socialization process? What do we learn about [women] in society from watching the program? After finishing your analysis, what do you think about TV's powers of socialization?

Adult Socialization

Being an "adult" somehow signifies that we've learned well enough how to conduct ourselves as autonomous members of society. But adults are by no means completely socialized. Life is continually presenting us with new situations and new roles with unfamiliar norms and values. We are constantly learning and adjusting to new conditions over the life course and thereby participating in secondary socialization.

For example, your college training will teach you a great deal about the behaviors that will be expected of you in your chosen profession, such as responsibility and punctuality. But after graduating and obtaining a job, you will likely find further, unanticipated expectations. At the very least, you will be socialized to the local culture of a specific workplace, where new rules and customs (like "Always be closing!" in a real estate office) are observed. As your career unfolds, such episodes of socialization will recur as you take on different responsibilities or switch jobs.

Other examples of altered life circumstances include marrying, becoming divorced or widowed, raising a family, moving to a new community, losing a job, or retiring—all of which require modifying attitudes and behaviors. For example, being divorced or widowed after many years of marriage means jumping into a dating pool that may look quite different from the last time you were in it—"safe sex," "splitting the check," and other new norms may be hard for older daters to assimilate. Adult socialization often requires the replacement of previously learned norms and values with different ones, what is known as **resocialization**. Facing a serious illness or growing old also often involves intensive resocialization. In order to cope with a new view of what their aging body will permit them to do,

> **RESOCIALIZATION** the process of replacing previously learned norms and values with new ones as part of a transition in life

Resocialization Total institutions such as the military and cults put new members through a process of resocialization by controlling most aspects of their lives and stripping them of old identities to create new ones. On the left, instructors lead new recruits through drills at boot camp; on the right, followers of Sun Myung Moon's Unification Church, "Moonies," get married en masse.

IN RELATIONSHIPS
Sister Pauline Quinn and Training Dogs in Prison

Can adopting a puppy change your fundamental sense of self for the better? According to Sister Pauline Quinn, a Dominican nun, it can when the puppies are adopted by prison inmates who train them to become service or therapy dogs. Sister Pauline knew something firsthand about life in a total institution, and not just the convent. Born Kathy Quinn, she was once a chronic runaway because of a dysfunctional family life and was eventually institutionalized for lack of another place for her to go. For several years afterward, she was homeless, staying in abandoned buildings and trying to avoid getting picked up by the police as a vagrant. Kathy Quinn could well have died on the streets of Los Angeles, but instead her life was turned around when she found Joni, a German shepherd.

Quinn felt that the dog was the beginning of the process of resocialization that helped her reestablish herself as a functioning member of society. It was the first time she had a true friend, one whose unconditional love was restoring her badly damaged self-esteem. Her time in institutions had left her "depersonalized," stripped of any positive identity with which to tackle the demands of life on the "outside." The bond that forms between a human and a dog provides positive feedback and a loving relationship that can influence one's sense of self. The work that Quinn did in training Joni transformed not only the dog but the person as well, eventually leading her to a happier and more productive life devoted to helping others.

Quinn was particularly drawn to the plight of women prisoners and believed that they, too, could find similar benefits through contact with dogs. She knew that life in prison could be extremely depersonalizing, especially for women, and that rehabilitation, if it was offered at all, was too often unsuccessful, returning convicts to the streets without having rebuilt their identities and their lives. In 1981, with the assistance of Dr. Leo Bustad, a professor of veterinary science at the University of Washington, she approached the Washington State Correctional Center for Women and proposed that inmates volunteer to train puppies adopted from local shelters and rescue organizations to become service and therapy dogs. The result was the Prison Pet Partnership Program.

The women selected to participate in the program get more than just dogs to train; they get the opportunity for substantial resocialization, which helps them to develop new, positive identities and learn valuable social skills that can translate to the outside world. The labor-intensive process of training a dog is perfectly suited to the needs and abilities of inmates, who have a great surplus of time and a desperate need to find constructive ways to occupy it. The rigors of dog training, which places an emphasis on achieving discipline and obedience through repetition and positive reinforcement, is a lesson not lost on the trainers. During the months of training, the animals even sleep with the inmates, providing added psychological benefits. Prisons report significant improvements in morale and behavior once dog-training programs are in place. Allowing prisoners access to the dogs' unconditional love and giving the prisoners a chance to contribute to society in a meaningful way increase the likelihood that the prisoners will reenter mainstream society successfully.

More than half of state prisons have now established similar dog-training programs, and military prisons have begun comparable programs to train service dogs for disabled veterans. A service animal can cost as much as $10,000 to train, so these prison programs make a difference in placing more dogs with the people who need them. Just as important here, each relationship with a dog transforms the life of the inmate, who gets another chance at developing a more positive sense of self in the process.

Rehabilitation through Dog Training Inmates reap many benefits when they train service and therapy dogs, including learning new skills that can help them find jobs once they leave prison.

people must discard previous behaviors in favor of others (not working out every day, for example).

Another dramatic example of resocialization is found in **total institutions** (Goffman 1961) such as prisons, cults, and mental hospitals, and, in some cases, even boarding schools, nursing homes, monasteries, and the military. In total institutions, residents are severed from their previous relations with society, and their former identities are systematically stripped away and reformed. Take new military recruits, for instance. One of the first things that happens is they are given a uniform and new name—cadet. If they're men, they also get their heads shaved. Very quickly they have lost signs of their individuality, only to begin building a new identity: soldier. There may be different ends toward which total institutions are geared, such as creating good monks, punishing criminals, or managing mental illness, but the process of resocialization is similar: All previous identities are suppressed, and an entirely new, disciplined self is created.

Relatively few adults experience resocialization to the degree of the total institution. All, however, continue to learn and synthesize norms and values throughout their lives as they move into different roles and social settings.

STATUSES AND ROLES

While agents of socialization play an important role in developing our individual identities, so does the larger scaffolding of society. This happens as we take on (or have imposed upon us) different statuses and roles.

A **status** is a position in a social hierarchy that comes with a set of expectations. Sometimes these positions are formalized: "professor," "president," or even "parent." Parental obligations, for example, are written into laws that prohibit the neglect and abuse of children. Other statuses are more informal: You may be the "class clown," for instance, or the "conscience" of your group of friends. The contours of these informal statuses are less explicit but still widely recognizable. We all occupy a number of statuses, as we hold positions in multiple social hierarchies at once. Some statuses change over the course of a lifetime (e.g., marital or parental status), while others usually do not (e.g., race, ethnicity, or gender).

There are different kinds of statuses. An **ascribed status** is one we are born with that is unlikely to change (such as our gender or race). An **embodied status** is located in our physical selves (such as beauty or disability). Finally, an **achieved status** is one that we have earned through our own efforts (such as an occupation, hobby, or skill) or that has been acquired in some other way (such as a criminal identity, mental illness, or drug addiction). All statuses influence how others see and respond to us. However, some ascribed, embodied, or achieved statuses take on the power of what sociologists call a **master status**—a status that seems to override all others in our identities.

Master statuses carry with them expectations that may blind people to other facets of our personalities. People quickly make assumptions about what women, Asians, doctors, or alcoholics are like and may judge us according to those expectations rather than our actual attributes. This kind of judgment, often referred to as **stereotyping**, is looked upon as negative or destructive. However, it is important to realize that we all use these expectations in our everyday lives; stereotyping, as problematic as it is, is all but unavoidable.

A **role** is the set of behaviors expected from a particular status position. Sociologists such as Erving Goffman (1956) and Ralph Turner (1978) deliberately used the theatrical analogy to describe how roles provide a kind of script, outlining what we are expected to say and do as a result of our position in the social structure. Professors, then, are expected to be responsible teachers and researchers. Employment contracts and faculty handbooks may specify the role even further: Professors must hold a certain number of office hours per week, for example, and must obtain permission from the university in order to skip classes or take a leave of absence. Class clowns don't sign a contract, nor are they issued a handbook, but they have role expectations nonetheless: They are expected to turn a classroom event into a joke whenever possible and to sacrifice their own success in order to provide laughs for others.

TOTAL INSTITUTIONS institutions in which individuals are cut off from the rest of society so that they can be controlled and regulated for the purpose of systematically stripping away previous roles and identities in order to create new ones

STATUS a position in a social hierarchy that carries a particular set of expectations

ASCRIBED STATUS a status that is inborn; usually difficult or impossible to change

EMBODIED STATUS a status generated by physical characteristics

ACHIEVED STATUS a status earned through individual effort or imposed by others

MASTER STATUS a status that is always relevant and affects all other statuses we possess

STEREOTYPING judging others based on preconceived generalizations about groups or categories of people

ROLE the set of behaviors expected of someone because of their status

Multiple Roles and Role Conflict

In setting out general expectations for behavior, roles help shape our actions in ways that may come to define us to ourselves and others. For example, we often describe ourselves according to personality traits: "I am a responsible person," "a nurturer," "competitive," or "always cheerful." These traits are often the same as the role expectations attached to our various statuses as professionals, parents, athletes, or friends. We all play a number of roles in life, and when a person can play many different roles well, it can enhance his or her sense of self. At the same time, it is not always easy to juggle the varying demands and expectations associated with multiple roles. Sometimes problems arise in our everyday lives because of our roles.

The story of Tammy Duckworth is a case in point. Duckworth has played many roles, including doctoral student, Army helicopter pilot, double-amputee, and the first disabled woman elected to Congress. She was also the first U.S. senator to give birth while in office. Senate rules at the time prohibited members from bringing children under the age of one onto the Senate floor during votes, preventing Duckworth from fulfilling her constitutional responsibilities. This highlights what is known as **role conflict**, a situation in which two or more roles have contradictory expectations. Duckworth's occupational role as a senator was seemingly incompatible with her familial role as a mother. Duckworth may have also experienced **role strain**, which occurs when there are contradictory expectations within one single role a person plays. As a parent, Duckworth had to balance societal expectations to be present and involved with the competing expectation to help support her growing family financially, which requires her to be away in Washington.

Because of Duckworth's efforts, the Senate passed a rare rule change—the first since 1977, when it voted to accommodate service dogs—and now allows senators to bring babies onto the floor. Hopefully, this historic rule change will ensure that other future senators won't have to experience **role exit**, when a person leaves behind a role they once occupied. While Duckworth's situation is unique, you will certainly find yourself in situations where there are competing demands among multiple roles or within a single role you play. How will you resolve those tensions?

Statuses and roles help shape our identities by providing guidelines (sometimes formal, sometimes informal) for our own behavior and by providing the patterns that others use to interact with us. They are part of the construction of our social selves.

EMOTIONS AND PERSONALITY

As Duckworth's experience demonstrates, role conflicts can be very emotional events. Our emotions are intensely personal responses to the unique situations of our lives. We react with happiness, anger, fear, or sorrow to our own experiences, as well as to things that happen to others, even fictionalized events in books, movies, or video games. Individuals sometimes react very differently—what makes one person laugh may make another cry. It would seem, then, that our emotions are the one thing about our lives that aren't dictated by society, that can't be explained with reference to sociological concepts or theories.

Well, our emotions aren't fully determined by society, but they are indeed social. We respond individually, but there are also social patterns in our emotional responses. For example, some emotional responses differ according to the culture—even an emotion as personal as grief, as noted in the Global Perspective box that follows.

The Social Construction of Emotions

Sometimes our interaction with others affects our emotional responses: We may yell angrily at a political rally along with everyone else, realizing only later that we don't really feel that strongly about the issue at all; we may stifle our tears in front of the coach but shed them freely after the game. **Role-taking emotions**, such as sympathy, embarrassment, and shame, require that we be able to see things from someone else's point of view. When a friend is injured in an accident, you know she is feeling pain, so you feel sympathy for her. **Feeling rules** (Hochschild 1975) are socially constructed norms regarding appropriate feelings and displays of emotion. We

ROLE CONFLICT experienced when we occupy two or more roles with contradictory expectations

ROLE STRAIN experienced when there are contradictory expectations within one role

ROLE EXIT the process of leaving a role that we will no longer occupy

ROLE-TAKING EMOTIONS emotions such as sympathy, embarrassment, or shame that require that we assume the perspective of another person or group and respond accordingly

FEELING RULES norms regarding the expression and display of emotions; expectations about the acceptable or desirable feelings in a given situation

Senator Tammy Duckworth's Multiple Roles As a senator and new mother, Tammy Duckworth experienced both role conflict and role strain. She also helped change long-standing Senate rules to better accommodate working parents.

GLOBAL PERSPECTIVE
Cross-Cultural Responses to Grief

When it comes to emotions, grief seems to be one of the strongest. No matter what we believe about the afterlife (or lack thereof), we mourn the passing of our loved ones. In many different societies, the cultural practices surrounding grief and mourning are directed toward giving the deceased a proper send-off and comforting those left behind. But you might be surprised at what other cultures consider comforting in times of grief!

For example, Maoris (the native people of New Zealand) believe that death is not final until all funeral rites are complete—which takes an entire year. Though the body is buried after three days, the relatives and friends of the deceased speak of and to the deceased as if this person were alive until the year of mourning is complete.

The Roma (often incorrectly referred to as "Gypsies") mourn in particularly intense and public ways: Both men and women refuse to wash, shave, or comb their hair; neglect to eat for three days; and absorb themselves totally in the process of mourning, sometimes to the point of harming themselves. In addition to this passionate grieving, Roma mourners provide the dead with clothes, money, and other useful objects for their journey to the afterlife. In contrast to Western societies, where black is the prevailing color of grief, Roma mourners traditionally wear white clothes, and the favored color for funeral decorations is red.

Red is also the color of grief for the Ashanti of Ghana, who wear red clothing, smear red clay on their arms and foreheads, and wear headbands festooned with red peppers. Proper Ashanti expressions of grief are distinguished by gender: Women must wail, and men must fire guns into the air. In fact, the amount of gunpowder used in a funeral is considered a mark of the grieving family's status in the community.

When mourning their dead, many cultures, including the Irish, hold "wakes": long-lasting, heavily attended parties honoring and celebrating the lives of the dead. At a wake, while tears may fall, there is also likely to be singing, dancing, drinking, laughing, and all manner of seemingly celebratory emotional outbursts. So despite the fact that all cultures mourn and all individuals feel grief, we express those emotions in different ways depending on the society of which we are a part.

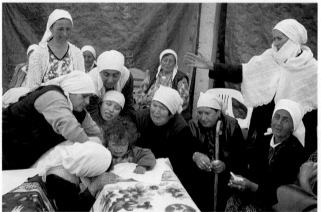

How Different Cultures Grieve Maori warriors row a coffin to their burial ground (top), mourning Roma women weep over a coffin (center), and Ashanti women practice a traditional funeral dance (bottom).

are aware of the pressure to conform to feeling rules even when they are unspoken or we don't agree with them (for example, "Boys don't cry," "No laughing at funerals"). Emotions are thus sociological phenomena, and our individual reactions are influenced (if not determined) by our social and cultural surroundings.

Finally, emotions can also be influenced by social institutions, such as workplaces or religious groups. Arlie Hochschild's (1983) study of flight attendants revealed that when airlines required their employees to be cheerful on the job, the employees' authentic emotions were displaced (they weren't necessarily always cheerful). Flight attendants had to manage their own feelings as a requirement of their job—what Hochschild calls **emotion work**—maintaining a bright, perky, happy demeanor in-flight, no matter what they actually felt. Because of the structural pressures of emotion work, they became alienated from their own real feelings.

INTERACTING ONLINE

As we learned in earlier chapters, sociological theories and approaches can change over time—indeed, they must. As the society around them changes, sociologists can't always hold on to their tried-and-true ways of looking at the world. New and innovative approaches take the place of traditional paradigms.

Most sociological perspectives on interaction, for example, focus on interactions that occur in **copresence**—that is, when individuals are in one another's face-to-face, physical company. More and more, however, we find ourselves in situations outside physical copresence, aided by rapidly developing technologies.

Businesspeople can hold video conferences with colleagues in other cities. The lovelorn can seek relationship advice and find prospective mates online. Students can text their friends at faraway colleges and carry on real-time conversations using Skype or FaceTime. Doctors on the mainland can perform remote robotic surgery on shipboard patients in the middle of the ocean. Do conventional theories have the explanatory power to encompass these new ways of interacting? And since interaction is vital to the development of the self, how do these new ways of interacting create new types of social identities?

Researchers like Josh Meyrowitz (1985), Marc Smith and Peter Kollock (1998), Steve Jones (1997), Philip Howard (Jones and Howard 2003), and Barry Wellman (2004) were among the pioneers in the sociology of technologically mediated interaction. They looked at how we began interacting

EMOTION WORK (EMOTIONAL LABOR) the process of evoking, suppressing, or otherwise managing feelings to create a publicly observable display of emotion

COPRESENCE face-to-face interaction or being in the presence of others

Mediating Interaction With technologies like FaceTime, we can interact with each other outside of physical copresence. How will these new technologies affect our interactions and identities?

with one another in virtual space and via electronic media—and how we interacted with the machines themselves. Today, people like Sherry Turkle, who directs the Initiative on Technology and Self at the Massachusetts Institute of Technology (MIT), study different ways that technology and identity intersect—through our use of computers, robots, technologically sophisticated toys, and so on (1997, 2005). In *Alone Together* (2011), Turkle focuses on the problems of the social media age. Online interactions allow us to contain and reduce risks—not risk to life and limb, necessarily, but risk to self. When we interact online, we can control when, where, and how we communicate. This means that, if we want, we can keep others at arm's length, which further allows us to perform a self that may or may not correspond to who we are in real life. We have become less willing to take risks in terms of forging intimate bonds online, and while we may have lots of connections (friends, fans, followers), we experience less depth in our relationships with them. Turkle believes that we all lose something in a world of mediated relationships, and her latest work, *Reclaiming Conversation* (2015), contains a call to put down our devices, pull up a chair, and talk to one another in real, old-fashioned copresence. Turkle is concerned that when we replace face-to-face communication with tweets, texts, and snaps, our ability to conduct meaningful face-to-face communication atrophies and with it our capacity for empathy.

danah boyd is slightly less gloomy about technology. She finds that Internet users—especially teens—seek private spaces in which to conduct their personal relationships and view online environments like Facebook, Instagram, and Twitter as places that can offer such privacy. They invite only their close friends into their electronic circles and then use those virtual spaces as getaways from the pressures of parents, teachers, and other adults. This is contrary to the ways that adults use social media—grownups tweet and post to expand their social circles and spread the word

ON THE JOB
The Wages of Emotion Work

In her groundbreaking work *The Managed Heart*, sociologist Arlie Hochschild (1983) introduced the concept of emotion work, or the ways in which workers are expected to manage—and sell—their feelings in the name of good service. Conducted in the 1980s, Hochschild's research focused on flight attendants. The almost entirely female corps of flight attendants were required to present a cheerful and calm front regardless of how they felt on the inside or how badly they were treated by passengers. The airlines promised pretty, perky, and perfectly obliging stewardesses as part of their ad campaigns, raising clients' gendered and sexualized expectations for their onboard experiences.

In the years since this landmark book, other researchers have explored the role of gender, sex, and emotional labor in many different types of service work. But flight attendants remain the archetypal emotion workers—stuck at 30,000 feet with demanding, irate, and/or sexually aggressive clients, in an industry where smiling subservience is a job requirement. Louwanda Evans's book *Cabin Pressure: African American Pilots, Flight Attendants and Emotional Labor* (2011), adds a new dimension—race—to Hochschild's concept of emotional labor. Black pilots work in a setting dominated by white men (fewer than 1 percent of commercial airline pilots are black), and black flight attendants work in a setting dominated by white women (about 14 percent of flight attendants are black) (2011, p. 6). This means that in addition to the emotional labor expected of all crew members, black crew members must manage their own and their passengers' emotions around race, racialized stereotypes, and other types of race-based expectations.

For example, black pilots describe over and over again the assumptions made about them by passengers: that they are incompetent and unqualified compared to their white counterparts. This is a tough emotional burden to bear while on the job. "The black pilot has to prove that he's not a jackass. You are assumed to be inept," said one of the pilots Evans interviewed (2011, p. 17). Another pilot overheard a passenger in the boarding area complain to the gate agent: "That [N-word] better not be flying my plane" (p. 1).

Flight attendants, who have the most intensive in-flight contact with passengers, bear the burden of racialized emotion work as well. One senior black flight attendant describes what happened when she offered a white male passenger a drink:

"Would you mind getting someone else to bring me my drink? I would prefer you not touch my cup." Initially, I thought that maybe it was something religious and based on my gender because we get that sometimes. But then a white female flight attendant served him his Coke with no problems. I was shocked and upset, and as a matter of fact, I did not want him to have a drink at all! (2011, p. 1)

The problem for emotional laborers, of course, is that it doesn't matter what they want, or how they feel, or how they might like to respond to a rude or racist customer. It is a requirement of their job that they keep smiling, get the passenger what he or she wants (in this case, a drink served by white hands), and force themselves not to show how they really feel.

The rise of the service economy has led to what Hochschild refers to as the "commercialization of feeling" (1983). Emotion work is a requirement of many different types of work, including retail sales workers, front desk receptionists, restaurant wait staff, even your Uber driver eager for that five-star rating (Stark, 2016). In fact, you probably have a job that requires at least some emotional labor. Are there gendered, racialized, or sexualized aspects to that work? Are you expected to keep your mouth shut when clients, customers, patients, or passengers say or do something you don't like? Are you required to do it while trapped in an airtight, enclosed space five miles above the earth? Will this change how you see and treat the flight crew the next time you board an airplane?

Emotion Work at 30,000 Feet Black pilots and flight attendants must manage their emotions when they confront racism on the job.

about their accomplishments, while teens do so only for the chosen few. The differences in generational cohorts' perspectives on online interaction are conveyed by the title of boyd's book: *It's Complicated* (2014).

These and other researchers seek answers to the following question: Who will we become as we increasingly interact with and through digital technologies? Their work is helping sociology enter the age of interactive media and giving us new ways of looking at interactions and identities.

Postmodern theorists claim that the role of technology in interaction is one of the primary features of postmodern life. They believe that in the Information Age, social thinkers must arrive at new ways to explain the development of the self in light of the digital media that inundate our social world (Holstein and Gubrium 2000). We are now exposed to more sources and multiple points of view that may shape our sense of self and socialize us in different ways than ever before (Gottschalk 1993). Kenneth Gergen (1991) coined the term the **saturated self** to refer to this phenomenon and claims that the postmodern individual tends to have a "pastiche personality," one that "borrow[s] bits and pieces of identity from whatever sources are available" (p. 150). What this means is that the self is being constructed in new ways that were unforeseen by early symbolic interactionists, who could not have imagined that interaction would one day include so

SATURATED SELF a postmodern idea that the self is now developed by multiple influences chosen from a wide range of media sources

AGENCY the ability of the individual to act freely and independently

many possible influences from both the real world and the world of virtual reality.

Closing Comments

By now you may be wondering, are we all just prisoners of socialization? How much freedom do we really have if we are all shaped and influenced to such an extent by others and by society? Are our ideas of ourselves as individuals—unique and independent—just a sorry illusion?

It is true that the process of socialization can be rather homogenizing. And it tends to be conservative, pushing people toward some sort of lowest common denominator, toward the mainstream. But still, not everybody ends up the same. In fact, no two people are ever really alike. Despite all the social forces at play in creating the individual, the process by which we gain a sense of self, or become socialized members of society, is never wholly finished.

We are not just passive recipients of all the influences around us. We are active participants. We possess what is called **agency**, meaning that we are spontaneous, intelligent, and creative. We exercise free will. Symbolic interactionism tells us that we are always doing the work of interpreting, defining, making sense of, and responding to our social environment. That gives us a great deal of personal power in every social situation. The process is not unilateral; rather, it is reciprocal and multidirectional. Remember that you are shaping society as much as it is shaping you.

Let's Talk More

1. According to Erving Goffman, we all engage in impression management to control what others think of us. Choose one interaction you participated in today and list every aspect of the personal front you used to manage the impression you intended to create.

2. Sometimes the messages we get from different agents of socialization (family, peers, school, religion, media, etc.) challenge or conflict with one another. Has this happened to you? If so, how did you resolve the conflict?

3. Describe yourself in terms of your statuses and roles. Which are master statuses? Which roles are less important? Which statuses have changed over the course of your lifetime? Which roles do you anticipate occupying in the future?

Let's Explore More

1. **Film** Moselle, Crystal, dir. *Skate Kitchen*. 2018.

2. **Article** Homayoun, Ana. "The Secret Social Media Lives of Teenagers." *The New York Times*. June 7, 2017.

3. **Blog Post** Raskoff, Sally. "Managing Hearts in the Happiest Place on Earth." *Everyday Sociology* (blog). November 1, 2010. *https://WWNorton.com/rd/t7LJn.*

CHAPTER 5

Separate and Together: Life in Groups

f you're a college student and a musician, we hope you're *not* familiar with these terms and their definitions: "hot seat" (being beaten with drum sticks, mallets, and straps while covered with a blanket in the back of the band bus) and "crossing over" (being kicked and hit by your bandmates as you run down the aisle of the bus). It might seem like being subjected to these brutal attacks would mean that it is time to quit the band. In reality, this ritual is how your bandmates might let you know that they want you to stay—and even advance in the band leadership hierarchy. But on November 19, 2011, this ritual went horribly wrong on the Florida A&M University (FAMU) "Marching 100" band bus. Drum major Robert Champion suffered such severe injuries at the hands of his bandmates that he died at a hospital later

that night. His family, friends, fellow musicians, and university community were grief-stricken, of course. But his death also touched off a national controversy over "hazing" that has yet to subside.

The hazing process is meant to test newcomers and transform them into group members; if you can endure the abuse, you can be part of the group. Although hazing is usually associated with college fraternities, it has been known to occur in high school and college clubs, athletic teams, sororities, marching bands, and even church groups, as well as in police and fire departments and the military. Although hazing is against the law in almost every state and is usually prohibited by group charters, it is still a popular—though risky—way of initiating new members. Every year, it results in at least one death and countless injuries. All told, there have been over 150 hazing deaths among U.S. college students since 1970. Experts estimate that alcohol plays a major role in around 80 percent of these incidents (Nuwer 2018, 2019).

The FAMU hazing has left a tragic legacy. Twelve of Champion's bandmates were charged with manslaughter in his death and four were ultimately convicted and sentenced to prison. The band itself was suspended for nearly two years, the band director was fired, and the FAMU president resigned in the wake of the incident. In addition, Champion's parents filed a wrongful death lawsuit against the university and were ultimately awarded $1.1 million and an apology. They later established the Robert D. Champion Drum Major for Change Foundation to help fight hazing in schools, bands, and athletics nationwide (Hudak 2015).

Despite all of these devastating consequences, some of Champion's bandmates have protested that he and other students volunteered to be hazed that night because they wanted to be able to move into leadership roles in the band. This fact highlights a key question in all hazing cases: Who is responsible when the consequences of hazing include illegality, injury, or even death—the host group or the individual who submits to hazing?

The relationship between the individual and the group is a complex one. We sometimes do things in groups, both good and bad, that we might never do as individuals. Exploring group dynamics from a sociological perspective can help us understand and even eliminate problems like hazing and maximize the benefits of group life as well.

How to Read This Chapter

This chapter explores some of the different ways we organize our lives in groups. Here you will gain some of the analytic tools you can use to understand the specific groups we'll be investigating in later chapters. Concepts such as peer pressure, teamwork, bureaucratization, and anomie can be fruitfully applied to analyses of families, work and volunteer organizations, political groups, and religious communities. Consider this chapter an introduction to group dynamics in general—a springboard from which to begin our sociological analysis of particular types of groups. As you read, think about the groups you belong to and how they affect your values and behavior. What is your influence on such groups? Have you ever "gone along" with group rules but later wished you hadn't?

WHAT IS A GROUP?

We often use the term *"group"* to refer to any collection of two or more people who have something in common, whether it's their appearance, culture, occupation, or just a physical proximity. When sociologists speak of a **group** or social group, however, they mean a collection of at least two people who not only share some attribute but also identify with one another and have ongoing social relations—like a family, a *Star Trek* fan club, a soccer team, a sorority, or the guys you play poker with every month.

A **crowd**, such as the throngs of sightseers at a tourist attraction or people who gather to watch a fire, would not usually be considered a group in the sociological sense. While crowd members do interact (Goffman 1971), they don't necessarily have a sense of common identity, and they rarely assemble again once they disperse. Collections of people such as crowds, audiences, and queues are known as **aggregates**—people who happen to find themselves together in a particular physical location. People in aggregates don't form lasting social relations, but people in groups do. Similarly, people belonging in the same **category**—everyone eighteen years of age, all Korean American men, or all owners of Chevy trucks, for example—don't regularly interact with one another or have any common sense of connection other than their status in the category.

Primary and Secondary Groups

Groups in which we are intimately associated with the other members, such as families and close friends, are known as **primary groups**. Primary groups typically involve more face-to-face interaction, greater cooperation, and deeper feelings of belonging. Members often associate with each other for no other reason than to spend time together.

Charles Horton Cooley (1909) introduced the term *"primary"* for this type of group because such groups have the most profound effects on us as individuals. Primary groups provide most of our emotional satisfaction through interaction with other members, are responsible for much of our socialization, and remain central to our identities throughout our lives. We measure who we are, and perhaps how we've changed, by the way we interact with primary group members. To Cooley (as we saw in Chapter 4), primary groups represent the most important "looking glasses" in the formation of our social selves—they constitute our "significant others."

Larger, less intimate groups are known as **secondary groups**: These include co-workers, college classes, athletic organizations, labor unions, and political parties. Interaction here is more formal and impersonal. Secondary groups are usually organized around a specific activity or the accomplishment of a task. Membership is often temporary and does not usually carry the same potential for emotional satisfaction that primary group membership does. Nonetheless, a great deal of what we do involves secondary groups.

Because secondary groups can include larger numbers of people and be geographically diffuse, membership can be almost completely anonymous. At the same time, however, secondary group membership often generates primary group ties as well. Close personal relationships can begin with the more impersonal ties of secondary groups (the friends you make at work, for example) and are sometimes a direct outgrowth of our attempts to counteract the depersonalizing nature of secondary groups. For this reason, it is sometimes difficult to classify a particular group. Your soccer team may indeed be goal oriented, but you've probably also developed personal ties to at least some of your teammates. So, is your team a primary or secondary group? It features elements of both, proving that real life can be even more complex than the models sociologists devise to explain it.

GROUP a collection of people who share some attribute, identify with one another, and interact with each other

CROWD a temporary gathering of people in a public place; members might interact but do not identify with each other and will not remain in contact

AGGREGATES collections of people who share a physical location but do not have lasting social relations

CATEGORY people who share one or more attributes but who lack a sense of common identity or belonging

PRIMARY GROUPS groups composed of the people who are most important to our sense of self; members' relationships are typically characterized by face-to-face interaction, high levels of cooperation, and intense feelings of belonging

SECONDARY GROUPS groups that are larger and less intimate than primary groups; members' relationships are usually organized around a specific goal and are often temporary

Primary Groups Families are an example of what Cooley referred to as primary groups. Deborah Daniels (front left, in pink) opened her home to four generations of her family after Hurricane Katrina destroyed their New Orleans homes in 2005.

There are other ways that seemingly insignificant relationships with near strangers can have a powerful and positive impact on our own lives. Many social researchers are interested in examining the ways in which people make up for the loss of intimate contact that is commonly shared among those who belong to primary groups. Melinda Blau and Karen Fingerman (2009) have identified what they call "consequential strangers"—people we might not think of as mattering much to our sense of happiness or well-being but who nonetheless play an important role in our otherwise fragmented postmodern lives. These people are not total strangers but are more likely to be acquaintances from the places where we work, shop, play, or conduct business—from the local barista at the coffeehouse or our favorite manicurist to the checkout clerk at the grocery store or that guy at the gym. These are people who become familiar and essential parts of our everyday lives. These people serve as social anchors, just as our close friends or family members do. Blau and Fingerman suggest that we need a new framework or perspective with which to look at the people in our world and perhaps to expand their number and range, as well as the value we ascribe to them. It seems that we need both primary and secondary relationships, as well as those along the continuum between the two, in order to function optimally in our environments.

SOCIAL NETWORK the web of direct and indirect ties connecting an individual to other people who may also affect the individual

SOCIAL TIES connections between individuals

Social Networks

You and your family, your friends, peers, colleagues, teachers, and co-workers constitute a **social network**. Sociologists who study networks call the connections between individuals **social ties**. Social ties can be direct, such as the tie between you and your friend, or indirect, such as the tie between you and your friend's cousin whom you've never met.

To understand how a social network works, think of yourself at the center with lines connecting you to all your friends, family, peers, and so on. These lines represent direct ties. Now think about all the family, friends, and peers who belong to each of *these* people. The lines connecting you to this second group must pass through the people in your first network; this second set of lines represents indirect ties. Indirect ties can include business transactions—flows of goods, services, materials, or monies—between organizations or nations. They can even represent the flow of ideas. For instance, when you read ancient Greek philosophy, you become part of a network that spans centuries of writing, thinking, and educating.

In Chapter 2 you learned about the principle of "six degrees of separation," which suggests that everyone in the world is connected to everyone else within six steps: "If you know 100 people, and each of them knows 100 more, then you have 10,000 friends of friends. Take that a step further to three degrees and you are connected to 1 million people. At six degrees, the number increases to 9 billion" (Schofield 2004). This means, theoretically, that you're connected to every human on the planet. It might be the case that somebody you know knows someone who knows somebody else who knows the president of the United States or a yak herdsman in the Himalayas; in other words, you might be separated from either of these others by just four degrees.

Sociologists who study networks are concerned not only with how networks are constructed but also with how influence moves along a network and, thus, which persons or organizations have more influence than others within the network. In his book *Six Degrees: The Science of a Connected Age* (2003), sociologist Duncan Watts examined not only the connections individuals have to one another but also how those connections shape our actions. He found, for example, that we may change our minds about whom to vote for if enough of our friends are voting for the other candidate. The study of social networks can help us understand everything from the spread of fads and fashions to the way people hear about job openings to how sexually transmitted diseases are spread among various segments of the population.

WINNERS, LOSERS, AND INFLUENCE How does the flow of influence work at the level of an international organization? We could take the World Trade Organization (WTO) as an example. Comprising 161 member nations, the WTO monitors the trade rules among countries and resolves international disputes over trade. While all member nations are part of the network, they hold different positions of power within it. We might hypothesize that nations that win the most disputes have the most influence within the network. But Joseph Conti (2003, 2005, 2010) finds that while the United States, one of the most powerful members of the WTO, is involved in the vast majority of disputes, it usually loses. The question that remains for the network theorist is whether "winning" or "losing" is an effective way to measure influence. What Conti concludes is that America's *centrality*, a network analysis term that means an actor with the most ties in a given network, is what gives it powerful influence and not the actual outcomes of the disputes.

JOBS, GENDER, AND NETWORKS How does the flow of influence work at the level of interactions between individuals? Sociologists look at how personal ties, both direct and indirect, can influence a person's life.

In the pathbreaking work "The Strength of Weak Ties" (1973), Mark Granovetter measured how a person's distant relatives and acquaintances, attached to different social networks, pass along information about job opportunities. People tend to form homogeneous social networks—to have direct ties to those who are like themselves, whether through race, class background, national origin, or religion. An individual with high socioeconomic status, or SES (taking into account income, education, and occupation), for example, usually has relatives and acquaintances with similarly high SES. Because those relatives and acquaintances belong to different social networks, all with high SES, the job seeker now has indirect connections with a vast array of high-SES contacts who can provide job leads. Granovetter's findings show the importance of weak ties for things like job hunting,

because the types of weak ties we have (high SES or low SES) can determine the types of jobs we can get.

More recently, Matt Hoffman and Lisa Torres (2002) found that women who are part of networks that include more men than women are more likely to hear about good job leads. But if their networks include more women than men, then those same women are less likely to hear about quality jobs. The number of men or women within a man's network doesn't seem to matter; men are just as likely to get quality information about job opportunities from both men and women in their social networks. Hoffman and Torres offer two rationales to explain their findings. First, women are simply less likely than men to hear about job leads. Second, women who do hear about job leads are more likely to pass along that information to men; they may feel threatened by the idea of more women in their places of employment and fear loss of their own jobs. So our networks work for us, but they may also work against us.

Networks are important not just for individuals but for businesses as well. Martha A. Martinez and Howard Aldrich (2014) study family businesses, which do not benefit as much from weak ties as other types of businesses do. Family ties are strong ties, and while there are also benefits to strong ties—cohesion, solidarity, commitment to the enterprise—family businesses may enjoy the benefits of strong ties while forgoing the benefits of weak ties. Family businesses, according to Martinez and Aldrich, may be less innovative and may devalue diverse points of view because they do not include nonfamily members in the company (or in company decision making). They may have limited sources of information because their networks are smaller and less diverse. With fewer weak ties in a business, there will also be fewer points of intersection with external market connections. So weak ties do important work for all kinds of organizations, even

TABLE 5.1 Theory in Everyday Life

Perspective	Approach to Groups	Case Study: Fraternities
Structural Functionalism	Life in groups helps to regulate and give meaning to individual experience, contributing to social cohesion and stability.	Affiliation groups like fraternities help create social cohesion in the context of a larger, possibly alienating, university system by bringing young men with shared values together.
Conflict Theory	Group membership is often the basis for the distribution of rewards, privileges, and opportunities in our society. An individual may be treated preferentially or prejudicially based on their group membership.	In-group and out-group dynamics can contribute to stereotyping and conflict as fraternity brothers develop an "us vs. them" perspective regarding other frats and non-Greeks.
Symbolic Interactionism	Group norms, values, and dynamics are generated situationally, in interaction with other members.	The pressure to conform to group culture (as in the cases of peer pressure and groupthink) can lead individuals to do things they might never do alone, and can have negative consequences, as in the case of fraternity hazing and binge drinking. It can also lead to positive actions, such as when fraternity members volunteer or raise money for charity.

those built on the strongest and closest of ties—family businesses (Martinez and Aldrich 2014).

SEXUAL HEALTH AND NETWORKS Nicholas Christakis and James Fowler (2009, 2013) provide another example of how transmission happens between individuals belonging to similar social networks. They explain two principles: First, all social networks have a *connection*, and second, there is *contagion*, which refers to what flows through social ties. While we may have complete control over whom we are connected to directly, we exert little control over our indirect connections. Contagion not only influences an individual's health but also can spread everything from obesity to smoking and substance abuse. For example, sexually transmitted diseases are more likely among people who have had four or more partners in the past year. In particular, Christakis and Fowler's research, which focused almost exclusively on whites, found that those who have many partners tend to have sex with others who have many partners, and those who have few partners tend to have sex with others who have few partners. STDs, then, are kept in "core" groups of active white partners and are found less often in less active groups. This spread of STDs can be seen as a literal consequence of the *contagion* principle of social networks.

When we think of someone as being "well connected," we imagine that they not only have lots of close friends but also might have relationships and acquaintances in a large and diverse social circle. As the old adage goes, it's not *what* you know, it's *who* you know. And who they know, and who *they* know—and now you have a social network.

> **ANOMIE** "normlessness"; term used to describe the alienation and loss of purpose that result from weaker social bonds and an increased pace of change

SEPARATE FROM GROUPS: ANOMIE OR VIRTUAL MEMBERSHIP?

According to Durkheim, all the social groups with which we are connected (families, peers, co-workers, and so on) have this particular feature: The norms of the group place certain limits on our individual actions. For example, you may have wanted to backpack through Europe with your friends after you graduated from high school, but your parents demanded that you stay home, work, and save money for college. You may want to go barefoot and shirtless into the restaurant, but the sign says "No Shirt, No Shoes, No Service." You may want that new guitar, but you don't have the money, and you know you can't just take it. Durkheim argues that we need these limits—otherwise, we would want many things we could never have, and the lengths to which we would go in search of our unattainable desires would be boundless. Think about it: If you were always searching for but never getting the things you wanted, you would be very unhappy and over time might even become suicidal. Durkheim (1893/1964) called such a state of normlessness **anomie**—a feeling of being disconnected from group life. Durkheim believed that group membership not only anchors us to the social world, it's what keeps us alive.

Durkheim was worried that in our increasingly fragmented modern society, anomie would become more and more common. Other scholars share Durkheim's position, noting that Americans today are less likely than ever to belong to the types of civic organizations and community groups that can combat anomie and keep us connected to one another. Harvard professor Robert Putnam, in his book *Bowling Alone: The Collapse and Revival of American Community* (2000), argues

The Good Old Days? In *Bowling Alone*, Robert Putnam argues that the decline of group activities, such as bingo nights or league bowling, represents a decline in civic engagement. However, technologies such as the Internet and social networking sites have allowed large numbers of people to gather, connect, and avoid anomie.

IN THE FUTURE
What Happens to Group Ties in a Virtual World?

Virtual reality (VR) is no longer the stuff of science fiction. In fact, VR has recently gone from being a technology that most of us simply imagined or read about to one that has begun to appear in peoples' homes, with Facebook, Google, Sony, and Microsoft all bringing new products to market. For example, Oculus Rift is a virtual reality headset that creates an immersive 3D vision and sound experience (Urstadt and Frier 2016). When Mark Zuckerberg bought the company behind Oculus Rift for $2 billion, he said in his announcement, "Imagine enjoying a courtside seat at a game, studying in a classroom of students and teachers all over the world or consulting with a doctor face-to-face just by putting on goggles in your home."

As Zuckerberg highlighted, virtual reality not only offers the potential for enhanced games but also may increase access to the arts, medicine, education, and even travel for all members of society. If a musician performs a concert in virtual reality, will all concertgoers be able to access front-row seats, indicating a leveling of class-based access to consumer products, or will industries replicate real-world inequalities in the services and products offered in virtual reality?

VR also has the potential to create greater empathy and understanding across cultures; filmmakers and journalists have a new tool to bring us closer to the lives of others (Berman 2017). As part of a campaign to highlight the plight of refugees, the United Nations released the first-ever VR film, *Clouds over Sidra*, which drops viewers inside Jordan's Zaatari refugee camp.

And virtual reality doesn't simply end at visual and mental stimulation. Japanese developer Tenga has created a full-body virtual interface that includes not only a headset but also a bodysuit with sensors that send impulses all over the wearer's body to make it feel like the wearer is being touched by another human being. It might not be a surprise to learn that companies like Tenga are using VR to simulate sexual contact and thereby capitalize on the lucrative market for adult toys.

If we no longer have to meet up in physical places to engage in such activities, how will this shape our relationships with family, friends, and even strangers? In the future, with virtual reality and full-body sensors, you might be able to experience giving a hug to a loved one in another part of the country, or doctors might be able to virtually guide mechanized surgical equipment to provide medical services to those in geographically remote locations.

Virtual realities might alter nearly everything we do in the future, which can raise some real anxieties. How far will such technologies reach into our lives and in what ways? Is doing something in virtual reality the same as doing it in "meatspace" (the physical world)? How do the experiences compare? For example, for years, researchers and educators have been concerned with the effectiveness of online courses as compared to face-to-face instruction. How will virtual reality factor into that debate? Will VR eliminate the need for physical classrooms?

Virtual reality has seemingly unlimited potential. You and your friends might all be able to watch a movie in a VR theater, each in your own home, but experience it together. You could join them to tour museums across the globe, attend lectures at Harvard University, walk the streets through one of Rio de Janeiro's favelas, or climb Mount Everest together. But just because you're capable of doing something with other people in virtual reality doesn't necessarily mean you won't opt to do it alone. Will technologies such as this bring us closer together or drive us further apart?

Virtual Reality Will VR facilitate relationships and civic engagement? Or will this new technology undermine our "real world" connections?

VIRTUAL COMMUNITIES social groups whose interactions are mediated through information technologies, particularly the Internet

that we no longer practice the type of "civic engagement" that builds democratic community and keeps anomie at bay: Fewer people bowl in leagues than ever before, and people are less likely to participate in organizations like the League of Women Voters, PTA, or Kiwanis or engage in regular activities like monthly bridge games or Sunday picnics. He even offers statistics on how many angry drivers "flip the bird" at other drivers every year—all part of his argument about our disintegrating collective bonds. Putnam's critics argue that he longs for the "good ol' days" that will never be again (and perhaps never were). It may be true that we don't belong to bridge clubs anymore, but we have a new set of resources to help us connect with others and avoid anomie.

In the years since Putnam's influential work first appeared, there has been an explosion of new technologies and, with it, some similar debates about the potential effects on social life. Some social thinkers are concerned that the Internet will serve only to exacerbate our condition of isolation and separation from one another. They argue that the Internet makes us more lonely, replacing our face-to-face bonds with a set of "broader but shallower" online connections that don't really do the trick (Marche 2012). This argument also includes the criticism that we are more disconnected from our communities as a result of our immersion in online worlds: We are not as committed to civic life, local politics, or public service as we should be or once were. Even scholars who once saw promise in the rise of the Internet, such as MIT's Sherry Turkle (2011, 2015), now worry that we have come to prioritize technologies over relationships and that, furthermore, we may need to unplug from our devices in order to reclaim the most basic person-to-person connections.

Findings from the Pew Research Center's Internet and American Life Project (Greenwood, Perrin, and Duggan 2016; Hampton et al. 2011; Lenhart 2015) contradict many of these tech-induced anxieties. According to Pew, users of social media may actually be more connected with others than nonusers. Facebook users were found to have more close relationships and higher levels of social support and to be more trusting of others and more politically engaged than users of other social media and nonusers. In addition, sociologists Eric Klinenberg (2012a) and Claude Fischer (2011) make the case that, despite a rise in social media use and an increase in single-person households, Americans are no more or less lonely or detached from one another than they have ever been.

The Internet has made it possible for people who might not otherwise have met to come together—albeit in cyberspace—and to belong to a variety of online groups. From participants involved in massively multiplayer online role-playing games (MMORPGs), such as *World of Warcraft* or *Fortnite*,

to support groups that "meet" regularly to deal with personal issues or medical conditions, to fans of different authors, bands, artists, or filmmakers swapping comments, technology offers us new opportunities to connect by making us members of **virtual communities**. However, while the Internet may indeed help many people feel more connected, there are studies that show that in vulnerable times of life, such as adolescence, or during a period of personal difficulty, the Internet and especially social media may lead to more loneliness, not less. According to researchers at the University of Chicago, when social media is used as an escape mechanism to avoid the social world and the "social pain of interaction," it can increase feelings of loneliness (Nowland, Necka, and Cacioppo 2017).

So what will the future hold with regard to technology and our relationships with one another? To answer that, we might actually want to look to the past. Remember Émile Durkheim's concerns about anomie and modern life? Durkheim was worried that the technological and cultural changes that accompanied the Industrial Revolution would cause people to become more disconnected from one another and that this disconnection would be detrimental both to individuals (who might be more likely to commit suicide as a result) and for society (which would lack necessary cohesion and solidarity). Over a hundred years later, critics have similar concerns about the changes being ushered in by the Digital Age. It seems that rapid changes in technology and society, no matter what they look like or when they occur, induce anxiety.

DATA WORKSHOP

Analyzing Media and Pop Culture

"Who's in Your Feed?"

Did you know that almost 70 percent of all adults—and 88 percent of young adults between the ages of eighteen and twenty-nine—use social media (Pew Research Center 2018b)? That Facebook has nearly 1.5 billion active daily users, that 500 million tweets are sent on Twitter every day, or that 1.1 billion people use Instagram every month? And then there's also the tens (or hundreds) of millions of things that are happening right now on LinkedIn, Pinterest, and Snapchat. The statistics for social media usage are astounding. And there's a good chance you're adding to those numbers with each status update, selfie, or pin.

The skyrocketing popularity of social media has social scientists scrambling to keep up with studying what this rapidly evolving technology means not only for our personal identity and everyday lives but also for our relationships with others and the nature of social interaction in groups. The very idea of what constitutes a group has changed, and sociologists have had to broaden their definition of the term to include what people are doing in online or virtual communities. If people gather together to share interests, offer advice, provide support, or exchange ideas but never meet in person, are they still a group?

In sociological terms, we can see how social media can help us make the most of our primary and secondary group connections. It is easier than ever to stay in touch with the important people in our lives (even if they are not in close physical proximity) and reconnect with old acquaintances. Social media has brought people together who might not have been able to find each other in the past, when it was not possible to search for others based on their common interests, backgrounds, and demographic details. Now you can find that long-lost friend from fifth grade, meet new people who are into the same things as you, or keep tabs on someone you already see on a daily basis. So, who's in your feed?

For this Data Workshop you will be conducting interviews to find out how people use social media in their everyday lives and to discover its role in shaping individual and group identity online. You'll begin to see how group life is created, maintained, and changed online by group members who might share many things in common—especially other people. Your task will be to construct a set of interview questions and to gather responses from subjects you recruit to take part in your pilot study. Then you can make some preliminary analyses based on your findings. Refer to the section on interviews in Chapter 2 for a review of this research method.

There are several choices to make in the way you structure your research project. Because this is such a small-scale study, you do not need to take a scientific sample, but you should include members of the target population you want to study—for example, college students or poker players. Because there are many social networking sites that people use, you will also need to choose whether to focus on just one, such as Facebook, or to make your questions apply more broadly to multiple sites. You'll need to customize your interview questions accordingly. Here are some questions to get you started. You may choose some or all of these, modify them as needed, put them in a different order, or add some questions of your own.

- What social networking sites do you use? When, where, and how often?
- How do you decide to whom to send friend/connection/follower requests?
- How do you decide from whom to accept friend/connection/follower requests?
- How many people do you feel comfortable having on your friends/connections/followers list?
- How many of the people in your social network do you know in real life?
- Are there people in your life with whom you refuse to interact on social media?
- Are your networks public or for approved friends/connections/followers only?
- When you look at your list of friends/connections/followers, how much diversity is there in terms of race, ethnicity, gender, class, age, sexuality, geographic location, or other factors?
- What do you like to do most on social media?
- How often do you post to social media?
- Does your friends/connections/followers list affect what you decide to post online?
- What kinds of groups have you joined online? Why?
- Does social media help you feel more connected to others? Why or why not?
- What other functions does social media play in your life?

There are two options for completing this Data Workshop:

PREP-PAIR-SHARE Construct your interview questions and obtain some initial responses from yourself and one or two others. Jot down some notes about your preliminary findings. Bring your questionnaire to class and interview a partner. Discuss your answers and what else you might like to know about social networking. Listen for any differences in others' insights.

DO-IT-YOURSELF Conduct a small pilot study on social networking. Prepare a questionnaire and interview three to five respondents. Ask permission if you would like to record their answers. Write a three- to four-page essay discussing your experience and preliminary findings. What more would you like to know about social networking?

GROUP DYNAMICS

Sociologists have always been interested in how groups form, change, disintegrate, achieve great goals, or commit horrendous wrongs. Add all these phenomena together and they constitute **group dynamics**. How do groups affect an individual's sense of self? What forces bind members to a group? How do groups influence their members? When do groups excel at the tasks they undertake? What are the qualities of group leaders? When are groups destructive to the individual? How can relations between groups be improved? We will attempt to answer some of these questions in the next sections.

Dyads, Triads, and More

The size of a group affects how it operates and the types of individual relationships that can occur within it (Figure 5.1). A **dyad**, the smallest possible social group, consists of only two members—a romantic couple, two best friends, or two siblings, for example (Simmel 1950). Although relationships in a dyad are usually intense, dyads are also fundamentally unstable, because if one person wants out of the group, it's over. A **triad** is slightly more stable because the addition of a third person means that conflicts between two members can be refereed by the third. As additional people are added to a group, it may no longer be possible for everyone to know or interact with everyone else personally (think of all the residents of a large apartment building), and so policies may have to be established to enable communication and resolve conflicts. The features of dyads and triads point out an important axiom of group dynamics in general: The smaller a group is, the more likely it is to be based on personal ties; larger groups are more likely to be based on rules and regulations (as we'll see later when we examine bureaucracies).

GROUP DYNAMICS the patterns of interaction between groups and individuals

DYAD a two-person social group

TRIAD a three-person social group

IN-GROUP a group that one identifies with and feels loyalty toward

OUT-GROUP a group toward which an individual feels opposition, rivalry, or hostility

REFERENCE GROUP a group that provides a standard of comparison against which we evaluate ourselves

In-Groups and Out-Groups

An **in-group** is a group a member identifies with and feels loyalty toward. Members usually feel a certain distinctness from or even hostility toward other groups, known as **out-groups**. Most of us are associated with a number of in- and out-groups, stemming from our ethnic, familial, professional, athletic, and educational backgrounds, for example.

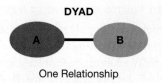

DYAD

One Relationship

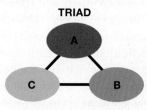

TRIAD

Three Relationships

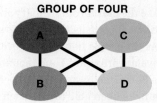

GROUP OF FOUR

Six Relationships

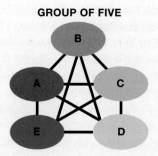

GROUP OF FIVE

Ten Relationships

FIGURE 5.1 The Effects of Group Size on Relationships
Smaller groups feature fewer and more intimate personal ties; larger groups feature more relationships, but they are also likely to be more impersonal.

Group loyalty and cohesion intensify when differences are strongly defined between the "us" of an in-group and the "them" of an out-group; we may also feel a sense of superiority toward those who are excluded from our in-group. School sports rivalries make clear in-group and out-group distinctions, as evident in this popular slogan seen on T-shirts and bumper stickers all over Los Angeles: "My favorite teams are UCLA and whoever's playing USC!"

As we might expect, in-group membership can be a source of prejudice and discrimination based on class, race, gender, sexual orientation, religion, or political opinion. The differences attributed to an out-group often become exaggerated, if not entirely fabricated to begin with: "All Irishmen are drunks" or "All Mexicans are lazy," for example. Robert Merton (1968) noted how the same qualities or behaviors that are viewed positively when they are "ours" are viewed negatively when they are "theirs": The out-group is "lazy," whereas the in-group is "laid-back"; they are "snobbish," we are "classy"; they are "zealots," we are "devout." At their worst, in-group/out-group dynamics create the backdrop for such social tragedies as slavery and genocide.

Reference Groups

Our perception of a group and what it takes to be a *bona fide* member can be crucial to our sense of self. When a group provides standards by which a person evaluates his own personal attributes, it is known as a **reference group**. A common reference group is one's peers. We might ask ourselves: Am I maintaining a higher or lower grade point average than other students in my class? Am I faster or slower than other runners on the track team? We often try to live up to the standards of our peers and compare ourselves to them. If we don't see ourselves as having the same desirable qualities, we may adopt a negative self-image. We make such comparisons often, evaluating whether and how we measure up to those who provide a model or benchmark for us.

A reference group may also be one to which we aspire to belong but of which we are not yet a member. Take a professional group, for example. If someday we plan on becoming a nurse or lawyer, we may look to those groups and wonder if we, too, have what it takes to join their ranks. We can base our comparisons on real people we know or on fictional characters we see in film and TV or online. We may even compare ourselves to celebrities or sports stars; while it's unlikely we'll join their ranks, the glitterati can still serve as a powerful reference group, influencing our actions and our own sense of self.

DATA WORKSHOP

Analyzing Everyday Life

The Twenty Statements Test: Who Am I?

The Twenty Statements Test (TST) is a well-known instrument that is widely used to measure self-concept. The TST was originally developed in the 1950s by social psychologist Manfred Kuhn as a way of determining the degree to which we base our self-concepts on our membership in different groups (Kuhn and McPartland 1954). Group affiliation proved to be a significant and prevalent quality that defined Americans of the 1950s and 1960s. In the following decades, the TST was adopted by other researchers for its ease of use and ability to provide direct, firsthand data from respondents. Despite some methodological critiques, the TST has been used to examine the self-concept of members of various ethnic, gender, and generational groups, as well as to make cross-cultural comparisons (Carpenter and Meade-Pruitt 2008).

In some of the earliest and most influential work using the TST, Louis Zurcher (1977) studied the changing self-images of Americans in the 1970s and 1980s. Zurcher found that respondents in this later group were more likely to base their self-concept on individual traits and independent action rather than on group membership. These results represented a major shift in how people defined themselves and, perhaps, in society as a whole. Zurcher and his colleague Ralph Turner (1976) became concerned about this shift away from group identification and toward a more radically individualistic sense of self. Why were they so concerned? We might also ask, what are people like now? Have things continued to change since the 1980s? What can the TST tell us about contemporary society and ourselves today?

For this Data Workshop, you will be using the Twenty Statements Test to examine how self-concept is defined within a particular group of respondents. The TST is a questionnaire that elicits open-ended responses; it can be treated as a quasi-survey research method. Return to the section in Chapter 2 for a review of survey research. We have provided a format for the questionnaire. Start by completing Steps 1 and 2 and taking this simple test yourself. Then we will find out more about what your responses mean—for you and for society, in Step 3.

Step 1: The Twenty Statements Test (TST)
In the spaces provided below, write down twenty different responses to the question "Who am I?" Don't worry about evaluating the logic or importance of your responses—just write the statements quickly and in whatever order they occur to you. Leave the "Response Mode" spaces blank for the moment; they will be used for scoring after you have completed the statements. Give yourself five minutes to complete this task.

Statements   **Response Mode**

1. I am _____ . _____
2. I am _____ . _____
3. I am _____ . _____
4. I am _____ . _____
5. I am _____ . _____
6. I am _____ . _____
7. I am _____ . _____
8. I am _____ . _____
9. I am _____ . _____
10. I am _____ . _____
11. I am _____ . _____
12. I am _____ . _____
13. I am _____ . _____
14. I am _____ . _____
15. I am _____ . _____
16. I am _____ . _____
17. I am _____ . _____
18. I am _____ . _____
19. I am _____ . _____
20. I am _____ . _____

TOTALS: A-Mode: _____ **B-Mode:** _____

C-Mode: _____ **D-Mode:** _____

Step 2: Scoring

Now it's time to score your responses according to the following four categories. Evaluate, to the best of your ability, which responses fall into the A-mode, B-mode, C-mode, and D-mode categories.

A-mode responses are physical characteristics of the type that might be found on your driver's license: "I am a blonde"; "I am short"; "I am a Wisconsin resident"; "I am strong"; "I am tired."

B-mode responses describe socially defined roles and statuses usually associated with group membership of some sort: "I am a college student"; "I am a Catholic"; "I am an African American"; "I am a quarterback"; "I am a daughter"; "I am a sales clerk."

C-mode responses reflect personal traits, styles of behavior, or emotional states: "I am a happy person"; "I am a country music fan"; "I am competitive"; "I am laid-back"; "I am a fashionable dresser."

D-mode responses are more general than specific; they may express an abstract or existential quality:

"I am me"; "I am part of the universe"; "I am a human being"; "I am alive."

You may have some difficulty deciding how to categorize certain responses—for example, where does "I am an American" go? Is it an A-mode, because it is where I live as a physical location, or is it a B-mode, because it is my nationality and the country with which I identify? Or where does "I am lazy" go? Is it an A-mode, because it describes my current physical state, or is it a C-mode, because it is one of my habitual character traits? Use your best judgment. Now count the number of each type of response and provide the totals for each mode at the bottom.

So, which category got the most responses?

We predict that although some of you may have given more B-mode responses, the predominant mode among those taking the test will be C-mode. Often, respondents have a combination of these two modes. People with more B-mode responses base their self-concept on group membership and institutional roles, whereas people with more C-mode responses see themselves as more independent and define themselves according to their individual actions and emotions rather than their connections to others. It is likely that there are few (if any) people whose responses fall predominantly in the A or D mode. Those with more A-mode responses may feel that they have a "skin deep" self-concept, based more on their appearance to others than on their internal qualities. Those with more D-mode responses are harder to categorize and may feel uncertain about the source of their sense of self.

Step 3: Analysis

Does the shift from a predominantly B-mode society to a predominantly C-mode society still hold today? And if so, what are we to make of it? The primary characteristics of the B-mode, or "institutional," self are a willingness to adhere to group standards and accept group obligations as well as an orientation toward the future and a sense that the individual is linked to others (Turner 1976). The primary characteristics of the C-mode, or "impulsive," self are the pursuit of individual satisfaction, an orientation toward the present, and a sense that the individual should not be linked to others and that group obligations inhibit individual expression. Zurcher and Turner worried that a society full of self-interested (and even selfish), impulsive individuals might no longer care about the common good and would work only to satisfy their own needs.

What do you think are the consequences for a society overwhelmingly populated by one type of mode or the other? How would schools, families, workplaces, sports teams, governments, and charitable organizations and other groups function if almost everyone fell into the B-mode or C-mode category? Are these two orientations mutually exclusive, or can you combine the best parts of both? What can you do to optimize the qualities of each mode for yourself and for the groups you belong to?

There are two options for completing this Data Workshop:

PREP-PAIR-SHARE Take the TST yourself (Step 1), and score it (Step 2). Get ready to discuss the results with others by jotting down some initial thoughts about your results. Bring your completed questionnaire and notes to class, and discuss them with two or more students in small groups. How many "institutional" or "impulsive" selves are part of your discussion group? Compare your responses and work together on analyzing the group's findings (Step 3).

DO-IT-YOURSELF Conduct a pilot study using the TST. Find a small sample population of three to five other people and administer the test to each of them. Collect, compare, and analyze the responses from your group. Present and analyze your findings in a three-page essay. Make sure to refer to your TST data in the essay; as long as you've preserved the confidentiality of respondents, include the completed questionnaires with your paper.

Group Cohesion

A basic concept in the study of group dynamics is **group cohesion**, the sense of solidarity or team spirit that members feel toward their group. Put another way, group cohesion is the force that binds members together. A group is said to be more cohesive when individuals feel strongly tied to membership, so it is likely that a group of fraternity brothers is more cohesive than a random group of classmates. The life of a group depends on at least a minimum level of cohesion. If members begin to lose their strong sense of commitment, the group will gradually disintegrate (Friedkin 2004; Friedkin, Jia, and Bullo 2016).

Cohesion is enhanced in a number of ways. It tends to rely heavily on interpersonal factors such as shared values and shared demographic traits like race, age, gender, or class (Cota et al. 1995). We can see this kind of cohesion, for example, in a clique of junior high school girls or members of a church congregation. Cohesion also tends to rely on an attraction to the group as a whole or to certain individuals as exemplars of the group. Cohesion may be enhanced when members are able to cooperate and work together in achieving goals (Thye and Lawler 2002). This might help explain cohesion among fans of the Green Bay Packers or members of a local Elks lodge.

Group Cohesion Why might fraternity brothers feel more group cohesion than a large group of students attending a lecture?

GROUPTHINK Whereas a high degree of cohesion might seem desirable, it can also lead to the kind of poor decision making seen in hazing cases. In a process Irving Janus (1971, 1982) called **groupthink**, highly cohesive groups may demand absolute conformity and punish those who threaten to undermine the consensus. Although groupthink does help maintain solidarity, it can also short-circuit the decision-making process, letting a desire for unanimity prevail over critical reasoning. When this happens, groups may begin to feel invulnerable and morally superior (White 1989). Members who would otherwise wish to dissent may instead cave in to peer pressure and go along with the group.

> **GROUP COHESION** the sense of solidarity or loyalty that individuals feel toward a group to which they belong
>
> **GROUPTHINK** in very cohesive groups, the tendency to enforce a high degree of conformity among members, creating a demand for unanimous agreement

IN RELATIONSHIPS
Social Networking: You're Not the Customer—You're the Product

Social networking sites have come a long way since the early days of the Internet. Today Facebook, Twitter, LinkedIn, and Instagram are all in the top twenty-five sites most visited by Internet users in the United States. Facebook alone boasts nearly 1.5 billion active daily users.

The rise of social networking has been so rapid that social scientists can barely keep pace with studying what this new technology means, but it has become clear that when social networks become *online* social networks, they also become big business. "When something online is free, you're not the customer, you're the product." This aphorism seems to have been independently coined by a number of different people, and it expresses one of the most significant features of social networking websites. Online, social networks exist because businesses like Facebook facilitate them. For everyone who participates, the rewards and benefits are obvious—staying in touch with faraway friends and family, sharing photos of cute babies and kittens, organizing for political change. But are there risks as well?

In 2014 researchers at Facebook and Cornell University published a paper arguing that "emotional states can be transferred to others via emotional contagion, leading people to experience the same emotions without their awareness," and this can happen through exposure to emotionally charged posts on Facebook (Kramer, Guillory, and Hancock 2014). The researchers wondered if "exposure to emotional content led people to post content that was consistent with the exposure." Does seeing happy posts lead to more happy posts, and seeing sad posts lead to more downbeat ones?

To test this hypothesis, Facebook performed an experiment on almost 700,000 users. Every time someone logs into Facebook, the site displays a newsfeed of posts by people in their network; however, rather than simply displaying every post, Facebook uses an algorithm to pick a smaller subset of material. For one week Facebook tweaked this algorithm so hundreds of thousands of unwitting users saw posts that were either slightly more positive, or slightly more negative, than usual. Researchers then analyzed the emotional content of the posts created by their test subjects and determined that the users who saw happier content wrote posts with more positive words, while users who saw more depressing content created posts with more negative words.

An uproar followed the publication of these findings. Not

The problem of groupthink can be found in insular groups such as fraternities or private clubs and even reach into the highest level of industry or government, sometimes with disastrous results. For instance, there are those who believe that the explosion of the space shuttle *Challenger* in 1986 may have been a result of NASA scientists' failing to take seriously those who suspected weaknesses in the shuttle's launch design (Vaughan 1996). In the instance of the U.S. military, groupthink may have been to blame for the failure of the CIA and the White House to accurately assess the state of Saddam Hussein's programs for weapons of mass destruction; the perceived existence of such weapons was a primary rationale for waging the Iraq War in 2003. A report by the Senate Intelligence Committee claimed that a groupthink dynamic caused those involved to lose objectivity and to embellish or exaggerate findings that justified the U.S. invasion (Ehrenreich 2004; Isikoff 2004).

The 2016 U.S. presidential election points to another

SOCIAL INFLUENCE group impact on others' decisions

possible instance of groupthink, this time on the part of the media. In the months and weeks leading up to the election, news outlets and polling organizations were nearly unanimous in predicting a win for Democratic presidential candidate Hillary Clinton. As such, Trump's victory on November 8 produced widespread shock and disbelief among many Americans. Trump then fostered groupthink in his administration by firing an unusually high number of staffers and Cabinet-level appointees and replacing them with others who agreed more closely with his opinions (Lu and Yourish 2019).

SOCIAL INFLUENCE (PEER PRESSURE)

While you may not have any personal experience with groupthink, you are certain to find the next set of sociological concepts all too familiar. When individuals are part of groups, they are necessarily influenced by other members. Sociologists refer to this as **social influence**, or peer pressure.

only did Facebook experiment on people without their knowledge or permission, but it did so in a way that caused emotional harm. Facebook was almost universally condemned, and the lead investigator of the study issued a public apology. However, not everyone thought Facebook was in the wrong. Its most prominent defender was Christian Rudder, the co-founder of dating/social networking website OkCupid. In the aftermath of Facebook's experiment he posted a blog entry on OkCupid titled "We Experiment on Human Beings!" Rudder is unapologetic about OkCupid's practices and doesn't think anyone should be upset at Facebook either: "We noticed recently that people didn't like it when Facebook 'experimented' with their newsfeed.... Guess what, everybody: If you use the Internet, you're the subject of hundreds of experiments at any given time, on every site. That's how websites work."

Although he detailed a number of "experiments," the one that got the most attention was based on OkCupid's "match percentage." OkCupid asks users a number of questions and then matches people who answered in complementary ways. For this experiment it took people who were only a 30 percent match and told them they were a 90 percent match. It found that when people were told they were a better match, the odds of them carrying on a conversation online did in fact increase, but some were shocked that a site dedicated to helping people find love would resort to this kind of deception.

Facebook apologized for the way it handled the publication of the experiment, while OkCupid seemed positively proud of its practices, but neither organization said anything to indicate that it would stop doing such experiments. Online social networks are an increasingly important part of people's lives, but the consequences of giving so much power over our personal lives to a for-profit business are still not well understood. What does it mean to live in a world where a corporation has a profit motive to meddle in our social networks?

Social Networks Are Big Business Facebook conducted an experiment on users of the social networking site to determine whether emotional states can be transferred via contagion.

Knowing how social influence works can help you when you need to convince others to act in a certain way (like agreeing on a specific restaurant or movie). In turn, it can also help you recognize when others are trying to influence you (to drink too much or drive too fast, for example).

The idea of social influence is not new: The Greek philosopher Aristotle considered persuasion in his *Rhetoric*. But the more modern studies on social influence date back to World War II, when social scientists were trying to help in the war effort by using motivational films to boost morale among servicemen. Since then, the study of social influence has become an expanding part of the field devoted to discovering the principles that determine our beliefs, create our attitudes, and move us to action (Cialdini and Trost 1998; Friedkin and Cook 1990; Friedkin and Granovetter 1998). Recent research on social influence has revealed that everything from our performance in school (Altermatt and Pomerantz 2005), to our brand loyalty as consumers (Laroche, Habibi, and Richard 2013), to the likelihood that we will commit rape (Bohner, Siebler, and Schmelcher 2006) can be subject to the influence of others. We will focus here on how social influence functions in everyday situations.

Almost all members of society are susceptible to what is either real or imagined social pressure to conform. In general, we conform because we want to gain acceptance and approval (positive sanctions) and avoid rejection and disapproval (negative sanctions). We follow *prescriptions,* doing the things we're supposed to do, as well as *proscriptions,* avoiding the things we're not supposed to do.

Social psychologists have determined that social influence produces one of three kinds of conformity: compliance, identification, or internalization (Kelman 1958). *Compliance,* the mildest kind of conformity, means going along with something because you expect to gain rewards or avoid punishments. When people comply, however, they don't actually change their own ideas or beliefs. Take, for example, someone who is court ordered to attend Alcoholics Anonymous meetings because of a drunk driving offense. This person might comply in order to avoid a jail sentence or hefty fine, but they might not be persuaded to join AA once the required visits are done.

Identification, a somewhat stronger kind of conformity, is induced by a person's desire to establish or maintain a relationship with a person or group. It's possible that the person required to attend AA might actually begin to identify with other members. A person who identifies with a group conforms to the members' wishes and follows their behavior. This is especially true when there is a strong attraction to the group. So perhaps the person who was first ordered to attend AA decides to keep going to meetings, stay sober, and become a member of the group.

Internalization, the strongest kind of conformity and most long-lasting, occurs when individuals adopt the beliefs of a leader or group as their own. When internalization occurs, there is no separation between beliefs and behavior; people believe in what they are doing and feel that it is morally right. Members of Alcoholics Anonymous practice the principles of the twelve-step program, making it an integral part of their identity and way of life.

Experiments in Conformity

Three rather famous social-psychological studies were conducted in the 1950s, 1960s, and 1970s with the related goal of trying to understand more about the dynamics of social pressure and, in particular, about group conformity and obedience to authority.

THE ASCH EXPERIMENT The first of these experiments was a study on compliance conducted in 1951 by Solomon Asch (1958), who gathered groups of seven or eight students to participate in what he called an experiment on visual perception. In fact, only one of the students in each group was a real research subject; the others knew ahead of time how they were supposed to act. During the experiment, the participants were asked to look at a set of three straight lines and to match the length of a fourth line to one of the other three (see Figure 5.2). In each case, the real research subject would be the last to give an answer. At first, all participants

gave the same correct answer. After a few rounds, however, the experimenter's confederates began to give the same consistently wrong answer. They were completely unanimous in perceiving the line lengths incorrectly. How would the real subject react when it came to their turn?

Most subjects felt considerable pressure to comply with the rest of the group. A third (33 percent) were "yielders" who gave in at least half the time to what they knew were the wrong answers. Another 40 percent yielded less frequently but still gave some wrong answers. Only 25 percent were "independents," refusing to give in to the majority. In a debriefing period after the experiment, some subjects reported that they had assumed the rest of the participants were right and they were wrong. Other subjects knew they were not wrong but did not want to appear different from the rest of the group. Almost all of them were greatly distressed by the discrepancy between their own perceptions and those of the other participants. Clearly, it can be difficult to resist peer pressure and to maintain independence in a group situation. What would you have done?

THE MILGRAM EXPERIMENT Stanley Milgram's experience as a graduate student of Solomon Asch's led him to work further on conformity. His first experiments were conducted in 1961, just after the trial of Nazi war criminal Adolf Eichmann had begun in Israel. Many of those who were prosecuted in the years after World War II offered the defense that they were "only following orders." But it was not just soldiers who sent millions of innocents to concentration camps—ordinary citizens turned in their neighbors. Milgram wanted to know whether something particular about the German national psyche had led so many to act as accomplices to the mass executions, why they had complied with authority figures even when orders conflicted with their own consciences.

The Milgram experiment (1963, 1974) used a laboratory setting to test the lengths to which ordinary people would follow orders from a legitimate authority figure. The experiment included three roles: the "experimenter" (a scientist in a white lab coat), a "teacher," and a "learner." In reality, the learners were confederates of the experimenters; the teachers were the only real research subjects in the experiment. When roles were assigned at the outset of the experiment, the research subjects were always picked to play the teacher, despite a seemingly random assignment of roles.

The stated goal of the experiment was to measure the effect of punishment on memory and learning. The teacher was instructed to read aloud a set of random word pairings for the learner to memorize. The teacher would then repeat the first word in the pair, and the learner was to repeat the second. The teacher was told to administer a shock of increasing voltage to the learner for each incorrect answer the learner gave. The teacher watched while the experimenter strapped the learner to a chair and applied electrodes to his arms. The teacher was then directed to an adjoining room where he

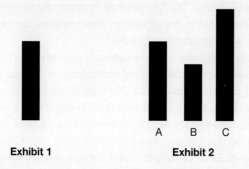

A   B   C
Exhibit 1   Exhibit 2

FIGURE 5.2 Which Line in Exhibit 2 Matches Exhibit 1?
Solomon Asch's studies showed that some people will go against the evidence of their own senses if others around them seem to have different perceptions.

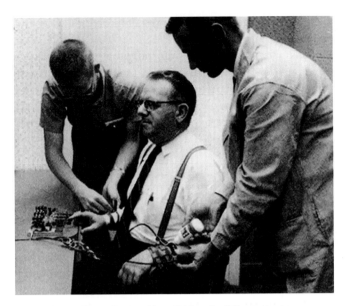

The Milgram Experiment How did Stanley Milgram test participants' obedience to authority? Do you think he would get the same results today?

THE STANFORD PRISON EXPERIMENT The Stanford Prison Experiment, conducted by Milgram's high school classmate Philip Zimbardo (1971), also examined the power of authority. Twenty-four undergraduates deemed psychologically healthy and stable were recruited to participate in a two-week mock prison simulation. Role assignment as prisoner or guard was based on a coin toss. Guards were given batons, khaki clothing, and mirrored sunglasses and were told they could not physically harm the prisoners but could otherwise create feelings of boredom, fear, or powerlessness. Prisoners were "arrested" and taken to a mock "jail" set up in the basement of a university building, where they were strip-searched, dressed in smocks and stocking caps (to simulate shaven heads), and assigned identity numbers. A research assistant played the role of warden, while Zimbardo himself was the superintendent.

The students quickly inhabited their roles, but soon exceeded the experimenters' expectations, resulting in an abusive and potentially dangerous situation. Rioting began by the second day; the guards quelled it harshly, harassing the prisoners and depriving them of food, sleep, and basic

could communicate with, but not see, the learner. This room contained a machine with a series of levers indicating the increasing levels of voltage that would be administered for each successive incorrect answer. (In actuality, the machine was not connected to the learner, and he received no shocks.)

The experiment began. As the teacher amplified the voltage for each incorrect answer, the learner responded in increasingly vocal ways. In reality, the teacher was hearing a prerecorded tape that included exclamations, banging on the wall, complaints by the learner about a heart condition, and finally, silence. Many subjects grew uncomfortable at around 135 volts, often pausing and expressing a desire to check on the learner or discontinue the experiment. At that point, the experimenter would give a succession of orders, prodding the teacher to continue. After being assured that they would not be held responsible, most subjects continued, many reaching the maximum of 450 volts. In the first set of experiments, 65 percent of the participants administered the maximum voltage, though many were very uncomfortable doing so and all paused at some point. Only one participant refused outright to administer even low-voltage shocks.

Milgram and his colleagues were stunned by the results. They had predicted that only a few of the subjects would be willing to inflict the maximum voltage. Milgram's results highlight the dynamics of conformity revealed in the Asch experiment. A subject will often rely on the expertise of an individual or group, in this case the experimenter, when faced with a difficult decision. We also see how thoroughly socialized most people are to obey authority and carry out orders, especially when they no longer consider themselves responsible for their actions. Clearly, few people have the personal resources to resist authority, even when it goes against their consciences.

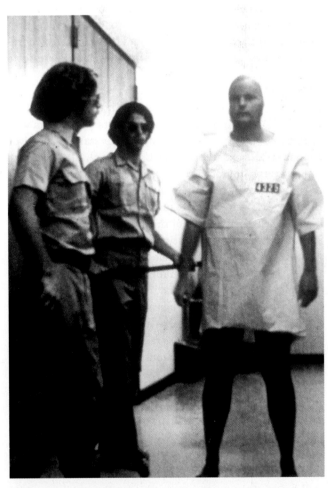

The Stanford Prison Experiment Why do you think the students in Zimbardo's experiment inhabited their roles so completely? What does it reveal about group behavior?

sanitation. Several guards became increasingly sadistic as the experiment went on, degrading and punishing any prisoner who challenged their authority, and several prisoners showed signs of psychological trauma. After only six days, Zimbardo was compelled to shut down the experiment after a graduate student researcher (whom he later married) became appalled by the conditions.

The Stanford Prison Experiment provided another example of the way situational dynamics, rather than individuals' personal attributes, can determine behavior.

MILGRAM REVISITED Some researchers have claimed that the Asch experiment was a "child of its time"—that students in the 1950s were more obedient in their roles and that the culture placed greater emphasis on the value of conformity (Perrin and Spencer 1980, 1981). Researchers in recent decades who have replicated the Asch experiment have in fact seen significantly lower rates of compliance, suggesting that the historical and cultural context in which the experiment was conducted had an effect on how subjects performed (Bond and Sussex 1996). This conclusion echoes some of Ralph Turner's findings about the institutional or impulsive self, discussed in an earlier Data Workshop; namely, he found that patterns of behavior can change over time and that separate generations may respond differently to social pressures.

> **SOCIAL LOAFING**
> the phenomenon in which each individual contributes a little less as more individuals are added to a task; a source of inefficiency when working in teams

The power of the group continues to interest sociologists, psychologists, and others who want to understand what drives our powerful impulse to comply (Gaither et al. 2018). Both the Milgram and Stanford Prison experiments would be considered unethical by today's professional standards. Although each of the experiments revealed important truths about obedience to authority, some of the participants suffered real, and in some cases long-lasting, psychological pain beyond what is considered an acceptable threshold of minimal harm.

Yet the experiments remain relevant because real-life examples of crimes of obedience continue to occur—whether in the case of the abusive guards at the American military prison at Abu Ghraib, Iraq, or in a serial telephone hoax perpetrated on fast-food workers in which a caller posing as a police officer instructed assistant managers to abuse fellow workers (Wolfson 2005).

Nearly half a century elapsed before researchers at Santa Clara University found a means of replicating the Milgram experiment that would pass the institutional review board process for research on human subjects. After a careful screening process, Jerry Burger (2009) conducted a modified version of the famous experiment that protected the well-being of the participants while still providing a valid comparison to the original. Contrary to expectations, obedience rates were only slightly lower in Burger's replication than they had been in Milgram's lab more than forty-five years earlier.

Looking at the forces of conformity that caused research participants to cave in to social pressure, we might like to imagine ourselves as being more able to resist. However, it's likely that if we found ourselves in situations similar to those created in the laboratory, we'd go along and obey authority, too.

WORKING TOGETHER: TEAMS AND LEADERSHIP

What does it mean to make a "group effort"? Sometimes we can accomplish things together that we could not do alone. But such outcomes are far from guaranteed. Whether group efforts result in synergy or inefficiency may depend on a number of factors, including the makeup of the group's members and the relationship between leaders and followers.

Teamwork

Are two heads better than one? Or do too many cooks spoil the broth? Early research on groups (Homans 1951) typically assumed that it was always more productive to work in a team than alone. However, researchers soon recognized that both the nature of the task and the characteristics of the group have a lot to do with the comparative advantage or disadvantage of working in a group (Goodacre 1953). When we measure productivity, groups almost always outperform single individuals. Things get a bit more complicated, however, when groups are compared with the same number of people working by themselves.

In one of the earliest attempts to systematically study group productivity, experimental social psychologist Ivan Steiner (1972) compared the potential productivity of a group (what it should be able to do) with the group's actual productivity (what it in fact got done). According to Steiner, actual group productivity can never equal potential productivity because there will always be losses in the team process. Two major sources of inefficiency in particular come with the group process, and both get worse as group size increases. One source is organization: coordinating activities and delegating tasks. For example, if four friends are going to help you move to a new apartment, some time will be lost while you figure out who should pack what, how the furniture will be arranged in the truck, where the boxes should go in the new apartment, and so forth.

Another source of inefficiency is the phenomenon known as **social loafing**, which means that as more individuals are added to a task, each one takes it a little easier (Karau and Williams 1993). Furthermore, as more people become involved, the harder it is to discern individual effort. If it is impossible for any single person to receive credit or blame, motivation

ON THE JOB
Teamwork and the Tour de France

The Tour de France is the world's premiere competitive cycling event. It is a race that lasts more than three weeks, covers more than 2,000 miles, and traverses the European Alps. Each summer, it draws a television audience of millions worldwide, many of whom never ride their own bikes and do not pay attention to any other bicycle racing events at any other time of year. It has also seen more than its share of controversy: Seven-time Tour winner Lance Armstrong was stripped of his medals and banned from competitive cycling for life after admitting to "doping," or using banned substances to improve his athletic performance. Other recent winners, including American Floyd Landis and Spain's Alberto Contador, have also been stripped of their wins and been banned for doping; in fact, in the more than 110-year history of the Tour de France, the race has been fraught with doping scandals. Early riders used alcohol, ether, and strychnine to improve their stamina and speed.

Since 2010, the winners of the Tour have been verifiably drug free. But they still cannot say that their victories were achieved without assistance. In fact, no one wins the Tour de France on his own. Winning riders are supported by teams of eight other premier athletes who must coordinate complex teamwork relations to prevail over the other twenty or so teams in competition. As with so many other areas of social life, individual success is buoyed by the work of many. No one can become president of the United States, win an Oscar, reach the summit of Mount Everest, open a restaurant, meet a sales quota, or earn a bachelor's degree without relying on others—groups as well as individuals—to support his or her efforts. So, although the winner of the Tour is listed individually, he didn't do it alone.

Each team member has a particular specialty, and each stage of the race requires a different strategy. Sprinters may be needed to make a "breakaway" early in the race; "super-climbers" are necessary in the mountainous regions; and sometimes the entire team has to protect the team leader, "blocking" and "drafting" in order to save energy. Teamwork is required to organize bathroom and food breaks, as the race stops for no man. Extremely consistent riders (*rouleurs*) are prized, as are those who ride with aggressiveness and bravery (*combativité*). When the individual winner crosses the finish line on the Champs-Elysées in Paris, it is the sacrifices of his altruistic teammates that have made his win possible.

Which position will you find yourself in when you enter the workplace? Will you be the team leader whose individual successes depend on the contributions of others? Or will you be the team member whose special skills support the achievements of the group? It is likely that you will find yourself in both situations over the course of your working life. So remember, when you don the *maillot jaune* (the yellow jersey worn by the Tour de France leader), in most cases it takes a team effort to get you to the winner's circle.

Group Effort Bernal Egan, in the yellow jersey, won the Tour de France with the support of his teammates.

usually suffers. Have you ever asked too many people to help you move to a new apartment? If so, chances are that a few did most of the work, some showed up late and helped out a bit, and others did very little but had a good time talking and eating pizza. Having too many "helpers" may contribute to social loafing. Amazon founder Jeff Bezos has taken this quite seriously, instituting something referred to as the two pizza rule. If a team of Amazon workers cannot be fed by two pizzas, then that team is too large. Too many people means too much miscommunication, chaos, and bureaucracy, which leads to social loafing, reduces efficiency, and slows progress (Morgan 2014).

Solutions to the problem of social loafing include recognizing individual effort and finding ways to make a task more interesting or personally rewarding. But such solutions are

SOCIAL IDENTITY THEORY a theory of group formation and maintenance that stresses the need of individual members to feel a sense of belonging

POWER the ability to control the actions of others

COERCIVE POWER power that is backed by the threat of force

INFLUENTIAL POWER power that is supported by persuasion

AUTHORITY the legitimate right to wield power

not always possible. It might be difficult, for instance, to make "moving day" more rewarding. Another solution, however, is suggested by **social identity theory**. Having a social identity, as opposed to a personal one, involves thinking and feeling like a representative of a group (Turner and Killian 1987); you have a real desire to belong to, not simply keep company with, the group. According to this model, the most efficient teams are characterized by the greatest shared social identity among their members; such social identity increases motivation and places the needs of the group above purely personal concerns (Turner and Reynolds 2010).

Power, Authority, and Style

Effective group leaders possess a variety of qualities, some of which are particular to the kind of group they lead. The leader of a therapeutic support group, for example, needs the proper credentials as well as experience and compassion for his patients. The captain of a sports team must display expertise at her game as well as the ability to inspire her teammates. An office manager must be well organized and good at dealing with different kinds of people. A police commander must be in

good physical shape, skilled in law enforcement tactics, and quick-thinking in a crisis.

One thing almost all leaders have in common, though, is **power**—the ability to control the actions of others. Whether it is **coercive power** (backed by the threat of force) or merely **influential power** (supported by persuasion), leadership involves getting people to do things they may or may not want to do. For example, a football coach might wield both coercive and influential power over his players. Although the athletes want to win games, they might not want to run their training drills every day. During a workout, team members might respond to either the threat of being kicked off the team or encouragement from the coach. Power, in whatever form it takes, is both a privilege and a requirement of leadership.

Because leadership requires the exercise of power, most formal organizations have institutionalized it in some officially recognized form of **authority**. Max Weber (1913/1962) identified three types of authority that may be found in social organizations. **Traditional authority**, based in custom, birthright, or divine right, is usually associated with monarchies and dynasties. Kings and queens inherit the throne, not only through lineage but also by divine appointment, meaning by higher authority. Their personal qualities don't really matter, and they can't be replaced by legal proceedings. **Legal-rational authority**, on the other hand, is based in laws and rules, not in the lineage of any individual leader. Modern presidencies and parliaments are built on this kind of authority. The third type, **charismatic authority**, is based in the remarkable personal qualities of the leader. Neither rules nor traditions are necessary for the establishment of a charismatic leader—indeed, the leader can be a revolutionary,

Qualities of Leadership
Nelson Mandela, pictured here with the South African rugby team, the Springboks, is an example of a leader with both legal-rational and charismatic authority. Mandela used his charismatic leadership to unite post-apartheid South Africa through rugby.

AOC Congressional representative Alexandria Ocasio-Cortez displays an instrumental leadership style. She has quickly become one of the most highly visible and engaged political leaders, while also stirring controversy.

an expressive leader conveys interest in group members' emotions as well as their achievements. We often consider leadership styles through the lens of gender, expecting men to be more instrumental and women to be more expressive. In fact, we sometimes feel surprised or upset when these gendered expectations aren't met: A male leader with a more expressive style like former vice president Joe Biden, who has been known to cry in public, is sometimes seen as weak. By contrast, a female leader with a more instrumental style such as New York congressperson Alexandria Ocasio-Cortez, whose ambition and drive have earned her criticism throughout her political career, is sometimes seen as pushy.

Such gender stereotypes can keep women out of boardrooms. Some women may hesitate to take on leadership roles for fear of being called "bossy," "pushy," or even a "ball buster" when they assert themselves in the workplace and elsewhere. In her best-selling book *Lean In: Women, Work, and the Will to Lead,* Facebook COO Sheryl Sandberg encourages girls and women to aspire to leadership roles. Sandberg's own style has been characterized as a blend of expressive and instrumental leadership. In an effort to reach a larger and younger audience, Sandberg partnered with the Girl Scouts and other powerful women in politics, business, and the arts, including Beyoncé, Jennifer Garner, and Condoleeza Rice, to launch the "ban bossy" campaign. Perhaps by example, more girls and women will embrace being leaders, and more people will feel comfortable following them.

> **TRADITIONAL AUTHORITY** authority based in custom, birthright, or divine right
>
> **LEGAL-RATIONAL AUTHORITY** authority based in laws, rules, and procedures, not in the heredity or personality of any individual leader
>
> **CHARISMATIC AUTHORITY** authority based in the perception of remarkable personal qualities in a leader
>
> **INSTRUMENTAL LEADERSHIP** leadership that is task or goal oriented
>
> **EXPRESSIVE LEADERSHIP** leadership concerned with maintaining emotional and relational harmony within the group
>
> **BUREAUCRACY** a type of secondary group designed to perform tasks efficiently, characterized by specialization, technical competence, hierarchy, written rules, impersonality, and formal written communication

breaking rules and defying traditions. This is perhaps the only place we will ever find Jesus Christ and Adolf Hitler in the same category—by all accounts both were extremely charismatic leaders.

The three types of authority are not necessarily mutually exclusive; they can coexist within the same leader. Bill Clinton and Ronald Reagan were appealing and charismatic leaders within the context of the legal-rational authority of the presidency; the Kardashian family is considered an American entertainment dynasty of sorts, while also using their charisma as pop culture influencers. The late King Hussein of Jordan was revered for his extraordinary charisma and statesmanship despite his traumatic ascent to the throne: As a teenager, he witnessed his grandfather's assassination and, as his heir, was crowned less than a year later. For people like King Hussein (a traditional ruler) and Barack Obama (a legal-rational ruler), their charisma was not necessarily the root of their authority, but it did play a part in their ability to rule.

In addition to different types of power and authority, group leaders may exhibit different personal leadership styles as well. Some are more **instrumental**—that is, they are task or goal oriented—while others are more **expressive**, or concerned with maintaining harmony within the group (Parsons and Bales 1955). An instrumental leader is less concerned with people's feelings than with getting the job done, whereas

BUREAUCRACY

Examples of **bureaucracy**, a specific type of secondary group, are everywhere in your life—your university, employer, Internet service provider, fast-food restaurant, and even church are likely to be organized bureaucratically. Bureaucracies are designed to perform tasks efficiently, and they approach their tasks, whatever they are, with calculations designed deliberately to meet their goals. As groups grow bigger, they also necessarily become more structured, hierarchical, and bureaucratic.

Bureaucracies Are Everywhere Bureaucratic regulations are supposed to make organizations run smoothly; however, bureaucracy can also be impersonal, inflexible, and hyperrational.

Bureaucracies have certain organizational traits that help them operate efficiently. Max Weber (1921/1968) identified these characteristics as follows:

1. Specialization: All members of a bureaucracy are assigned specialized roles and tasks.

2. Technical competence: All members are expressly trained and qualified for their specific roles within the organization.

3. Hierarchy: Bureaucracies always feature the supervision of subordinates by higher-ranking managers and bosses.

4. Rules and regulations: These are meant to make all operations as predictable as possible.

5. Impersonality: In a bureaucracy, rules come before people; no individual receives special treatment.

6. Formal written communication: Documents such as memos (or e-mails) are the heart of the organization and the most effective way to communicate.

You can see these traits in action at your own college or university. Take specialization and technical competence, for instance. Virtually none of your professors could teach another's classes: Your sociology professor would likely be completely useless in a chemistry lab, a math classroom, or even an English seminar. The groundskeepers, campus police officers, soccer coaches, and librarians are all specially qualified to do their own jobs and no one else's. In addition, there are layers of hierarchy at a university, from the trustees and president to the vice chancellors, provosts, deans, and department chairs. Professors are, in some ways, at the bottom of the academic hierarchy (except for you, the students)! And every other campus unit (athletics, residence life, food service, facilities maintenance) has its own hierarchy as well.

Regulations keep a university running smoothly—or at least that's what they are meant to do. Undoubtedly, though, you have run up against a regulation that kept you from doing something you really wanted to do—for example, add a class after a deadline or move into a campus apartment. This is where the feature of impersonality also comes into play: The rules of the bureaucracy trumped your individual needs, no matter how deserving you thought you were. This is especially true at larger universities; at small schools, special treatment is still sometimes possible. But big bureaucracies often treat you "like a number"—and in fact, you *are* a number to your college; your student ID number is the first thing you are issued on arrival.

The McDonaldization of Society

Weber's model of bureaucracy seems cold and heartless, alienating and impersonal, rule-bound, inflexible, and undemocratic. Indeed, many bureaucracies *are* like this. They are highly efficient secondary groups that operate on the principle of **rationalization**, where logical procedures are the focus, rules and regulations are paramount, and an individual's unique personal qualities are unimportant. Worse yet, some of the hyperrationalized features of successful bureaucracies are trickling down into other areas of our everyday lives.

Sociologist George Ritzer (1993) called this trickle-down rationalization process **McDonaldization**. We touch-tone our way through telephone calls at work, never speaking to a real person; at lunch, we construct our own salads at the salad bar and bus our own tables afterward; at the bank, we no longer interact with human tellers but rather drive through the ATM on the way home, where we microwave our dinners and watch increasingly predictable sitcoms or movie sequels on TV. Ritzer is critical of the dehumanizing aspects of McDonaldization and hopes that increased awareness of the process will help us avoid the "iron cage" of bureaucracy—a term coined by Weber to illustrate the way bureaucracies can trap individuals.

Sociologist Robin Leidner delved further into the McDonaldization phenomenon in her book *Fast Food, Fast Talk* (1993). Through fieldwork in actual McDonald's franchises, Leidner developed a model for understanding the increasing routinization of service industries, in this case the ubiquitous fast-food restaurant. In particular, she looked at how standardized "scripts" for interaction help shape customers' experiences. The physical atmosphere of a McDonald's is not conducive to hanging out (unlike, say, a café); customers don't expect to sit down and be waited on. Rather, they respond to expectations that they will enter, order food from a predetermined menu and pay for it, eat quickly, deposit trash in the receptacles, and then leave. Leidner exposed these processes of routinization by looking at what happens when breakdowns occur in these expectations.

For example, Leidner noted that McDonald's trains workers to refer to customers as "guests," reinforcing the obligation to serve them respectfully even if that respect is not reciprocated. Leidner observed that if customers were angry or uncooperative, workers tried even harder to serve them swiftly so that they would leave faster and have less time to make trouble in the restaurant. Workers developed a mind-set that allowed them to handle problem customers in a way that minimized trouble and facilitated the workers' routinized job.

Responding to Bureaucratic Constraints

Not everything about bureaucracies is bad. In fact, in contemporary, postindustrial society, just about everything you need or want is created, produced, distributed, and serviced by a bureaucracy. The water in the tap, the lights, the streets, the car and its insurance, the food on the table, the table itself, the clothes on your back, and the movies, songs, and books you

McDonaldization in Action According to Ritzer, there are four main principles of McDonaldization: predictability, calculability, efficiency, and control. What other industries are adopting these principles?

enjoy—all are the products of bureaucratic organizations. As problematic as they are, we can't live without them. So how can we benefit from our contact with bureaucracies without being controlled by them?

For one thing, even the most overrationalized, McDonaldized bureaucracy is populated by people who are capable of forming primary group relationships as well, who might celebrate birthdays, throw parties, and go out for drinks after work. Indeed, interpersonal interactions help humanize bureaucracies. Further, in forward-thinking organizations, new management strategies meant to address alienation and disenchantment are being implemented. Yes, bureaucracies still seek to be as efficient and predictable as possible in their daily operations. But some, such as Apple, Toyota, and Google, are trying to play up their human side as well—becoming "enlightened" bureaucracies by being inclusive, sharing responsibility, and providing opportunities for all to advance.

In fact, businesses like Google have come to believe that corporate success and employee well-being are complementary. Larry Page and Sergey Brin founded Google with the idea that analyzing information could lead

> **RATIONALIZATION**
> the application of economic logic to human activity; the use of formal rules and regulations in order to maximize efficiency without consideration of subjective or individual concerns
>
> **MCDONALDIZATION** George Ritzer's term describing the spread of bureaucratic rationalization and the accompanying increases in efficiency and dehumanization

GLOBAL PERSPECTIVE
Group vs. Individual Norms: Honor Killings

In American culture, when reports emerge of family members murdering each other, the reasons generally include abuse, crimes of passion, or monetary gain. The murder of Kathleen Savio by her ex-husband Drew Peterson in 2004 is among the most notorious cases of murder within a family. Her death was ruled an accident until 2007, when the case grabbed headlines as Peterson's fourth wife, Stacy, vanished without a trace. What made matters all the more fishy was that Stacy had also been Peterson's alibi on the night that Savio went missing. This led law enforcement to reopen the case into Savio's death and eventually led to Peterson being convicted of her murder and sentenced to thirty-eight years in prison. Despite his conviction in the Savio case, many believe Drew Peterson still got away with murder: The Stacy Peterson case remains unsolved.

While "murders involving family members killing other family members are not terribly rare," the reaction to such tragedies is especially harsh, judging murderers like Peterson as dishonorable traitors to their families, men who were more concerned with their own personal gain than their loyalty to family (Berman 2014). But what if the reason for a murder of a family member is to uphold the reputation of the family as a whole? **Honor killing** is the murder of a family member based on the belief that the victim is bringing dishonor to the family or the community. In honor killings, which are primarily seen in Middle Eastern and South Asian cultures, the victims are usually women who have not lived up to the moral codes set by the religion or community. Reasons for honor killings may include refusing to enter into an arranged marriage, being a rape victim, dressing or acting immodestly, or having sex outside marriage.

HONOR KILLING the murder of a family member—usually female—who is believed to have brought dishonor to the family

The United Nations has estimated that as many as 5,000 women a year are murdered in honor killings worldwide, though there is no reliable or definitive accounting, and these crimes are rarely classified or prosecuted as such (United Nations 2000). Researchers believe the numbers may be far greater, and they point to an increase in the last two decades (Chesler 2010; McCoy 2014). In Pakistan alone, there were more than 1,000 honor killings in 2015 (British Broadcasting Corporation 2016). The methods of killing range from shooting the victim to setting her on fire or stoning her to death. In each case, the person who commits the murder is seen as the norm enforcer and not the norm violator, as he is doing it to seek vindication and to right a wrong. In this cultural context, the murdered woman is viewed as someone who deserved to die for betraying and dishonoring her family.

Some who study honor killings maintain that in countries with less access to basic resources, health care, and human capital, there is a correlating lack of social power and equality for women. Gender inequality is exacerbated in places where there are fewer social resources, making honor killings more likely (Wilkinson 2005). Clashes occur when the cultural practice of honor killing is brought to Western countries like France, Canada, and the United States, where a woman's sexual freedom may face informal sanctions but is widely accepted as the norm. In some cases it is the adoption of Western values by women in traditional societies, such as India, Iraq, or Yemen, that is invoked as the grounds for honor killings.

One such case made global headlines in 2016. It involved the murder of Qandeel Baloch, a twenty-six-year-old model and social media star who some called the Kim Kardashian of Pakistan (Zraick 2016). Baloch was celebrated by many as a new feminist hero, a strong, independent woman unafraid to express herself or stir controversy. But Baloch also drew harsh criticism by many who disapproved of her provocative online pictures and videos. While sleeping at her parents' home, Baloch was drugged and strangled to death by her brother, who then proudly proclaimed to the press that he had killed his sister for the "shameful" pictures she had posted to Facebook. "She was bringing dishonor to our family," he said (Iftikhar 2016). Baloch's murder incited a massive public outcry, with many petitioning authorities to prosecute and convict Waseem Azeem for murder, a rare outcome in a case of honor killing. Pakistani law permits honor killings to be resolved by the families themselves.

The cultural norm promoting strong family values that causes disgust toward murderers such as Drew Peterson is the same norm behind honor killings. However, in honor killings, the family is seen as more important than any one family member; therefore, an individual member should suffer severe punishment for bringing shame to the family. While Waseem Azeem's actions appear to most Americans' individualist notions of justice as a betrayal of the family, in countries such as Pakistan these same actions are viewed as justified within the larger cultural understandings of family honor.

to a better search engine, and as their company grew, they also embraced the idea that data analysis could create a better, happier workplace. For example, they found that they weren't hiring enough women, and those they hired were quitting significantly faster than men. When they crunched the numbers, Google's human resources department—or, as they call it, People Operations—found that women who turned down job offers had disproportionately been interviewed by men, a problem that was easily solved (Miller 2012). When they looked at who exactly was quitting, they found that "women who had recently given birth were leaving at twice Google's average departure rate," a problem they addressed by increasing maternity leave (Manjoo 2013).

For the past few decades, businesses have spent an increasing amount of time and money on employee training and development, with over $46 billion devoted to just team-building games and exercises alone (Browning 2014). Many large businesses are also involved in organizing employee retreats to teach managers how to understand individual strengths and weaknesses, support individual skills and talents, and encourage cooperation, trust, and leadership. Some, such as Fidelity Financial, have adopted the Japanese management technique called *kaizen*, in which lower-level workers are encouraged to suggest innovative ways to improve the organization, and upper-level managers are required to actually put these ideas into practice, rewarding individual creativity and benefiting the company at the same time (Hakim 2001; Pollack 1999). Make no mistake—corporations are not sacrificing the bottom line for the good of the individual. They're still looking for ways to improve productivity and cut costs. But often they are finding that the needs of the individual and those of the organization are not mutually exclusive.

BURNING MAN In the barren Black Rock Desert of Nevada, some people actively seek out an escape from their bureaucratically regimented life, at least for one week every summer, at a festival called Burning Man (Chen 2004; Sonner 2002). The festival, begun in 1990 on a beach near San Francisco with just twenty participants, drew around 90,000 people in 2016. Burning Man is hard to describe for those who have never attended. It is a freewheeling experiment in temporary community, where there are no rules except to protect the well-being of participants ("burners") and where everyone gathers together to celebrate various forms of self-expression and self-reliance not normally encountered in everyday life.

Much of what is appealing about Burning Man is that it challenges many of the norms and values of mainstream society, especially those associated with conformity, bureaucracy, and capitalism. Black Rock resembles a city when the thousands of participants converge, but one composed of tents and RVs gathered into neighborhoods with names like

Burning Man Finale Each year thousands of "burners" gather in the Black Rock Desert to celebrate the rejection of such values as conformity, bureaucracy, and capitalism.

"Tic Toc Town" and "Capitalist Pig Camp" (Doherty 2000, 2004). The city has its own informal economy as well. Once an admission fee is paid, money is no longer used. Participants must bring enough supplies to support themselves or use alternate forms of currency, such as barter, trade, gifts, or services. Corporate sponsorship is strictly avoided, and logos of any kind are banned.

On the last night of the festival, the giant wooden structure known as the Burning Man is lit on fire, and the celebrants discover their own personal epiphanies as they watch it burn. When the festival is over, participants are committed to leaving no trace behind. One burner called the festival "authentic life," with the other days of the year "a tasteless mirage, a pacific struggle against the backwardness of Middle America—consumer culture, bad politics, *Fear Factor,* and fear thy neighbor" (Babiak 2004). So while Burning Man participants don't abandon permanently the web of contemporary bureaucracies that shapes their lives, they gain some relief by ditching it all once a year, if just for a few days.

Closing Comments

Groups make our lives possible by providing the necessities of our existence—food, clothes, cars, homes, and all the other things we use on a daily basis. Groups make our lives enjoyable by providing us with companionship and recreation—from our friends and families to the entertainment conglomerates that produce our favorite music and films. Groups also make our lives problematic. Bureaucracies can squelch our individuality, major manufacturers can create social and environmental problems, and some organizations can engender conflict and prejudice among groups. We are at our best in groups, and our worst. We can do great things together, and horrible things. Sociology helps us understand group life at both extremes and everywhere in between.

Let's Talk More

1. Which groups serve as your in-groups? Which groups serve as your out-groups?

2. Which groups serve as your reference groups? Are you a member of all your reference groups? How do these reference groups affect your self-image?

3. When people say "it's a small world," what are they talking about? Is it really a small world, or just a crowded social network?

4. Theorist George Ritzer believes that McDonaldization, the spread of the organizational principles of bureaucracies to all areas of life, is a growing concern. Thinking about Weber's six characteristics of bureaucracies, can you identify areas of your life that have been McDonaldized?

Let's Explore More

1. **Film** Schepisi, Fred, dir. *Six Degrees of Separation*. 1993.

2. **Book** Mahlendorf, Ursula R. 2009. *The Shame of Survival: Working Through a Nazi Childhood*. University Park: Pennsylvania State University Press.

3. **Blog Post** Inniss, Janice Prince. "Victimization and Conformity: Just Following Orders." *Everyday Sociology* (blog). November 10, 2011.
   http://WWNorton.com/rd/s5Y7B.

CHAPTER 6

Deviance

Would it surprise you to learn that both George Washington and Thomas Jefferson were cannabis farmers? They called it "hemp" and used the fibrous stalks to make fabric, rope, and paper, including the paper on which Jefferson drafted the Declaration of Independence. There is no evidence that the Founding Fathers used their crop to get high: The fact that they harvested hemp for its stalks may have meant that its flowers (in which the intoxicating resin THC is located) had not had a chance to bloom.

Over time, hemp as an industrial crop began to have more and more competition—from other agricultural products, such as cotton and timber, and from other chemical and industrial processes that had the backing of powerful industries and individuals. In the 1920s and

1930s, William Randolph Hearst, along with others in hemp-competitive industries, exerted pressure on government officials to make hemp's intoxicating by-product, marijuana, illegal. A propaganda campaign against marijuana was led by Hearst's media outlets, promoting it as a dangerous threat to America's youth, public health, and national security. A film called *Reefer Madness* was shown in schools as an anti-marijuana propaganda piece, using images of insanity, rape, and murder to paint a picture of pot as a catastrophic scourge on society. Marijuana was associated with criminals, reprobates, jazz musicians, and (gasp!) ethnic minorities and was presented to schoolchildren as the cause of immediate social and moral chaos. By 1937, every state had outlawed the use of marijuana as an intoxicant, and cannabis farming had been effectively eliminated by the passage of the prohibitively high Marijuana Tax Act.

Fast-forward to the present, in which the current surge in environmentalism is part of the change in views about *Cannabis sativa*: Restoring legal hemp farming nation-wide would allow the production of tree-free paper and other fiber and textile products, which would please many people who are worried about the depletion of environmental resources. Today, a majority of U.S. states have legalized marijuana in some form or another. This is good news for patients whose conditions may be helped by medical marijuana use, for recreational users who think pot should be treated like alcohol in the eyes of the law, and for businesspeople eager to capitalize on new opportunities for profit. Many hope that other states will legalize marijuana as well, and that the "dominoes" will continue to fall.

How is it possible that there could be such different reactions to the users of this plant? Changing values lead to changing laws and changing practices in everyday life. Along with cultural values, definitions of deviance change over time, and we can some-times observe them as they swing back and forth, from one extreme to the other, over the course of history. What was once mainstream becomes defined as deviant; what is now seen as deviant may soon become normal and acceptable. Shouldn't we be able to agree on whether marijuana production and use are deviant? As we shall see, nothing is inherently deviant—rather, it is the cultural, historical, and situational context that makes it so.

How to Read This Chapter

Have you ever driven faster than the posted speed limit? Have you ever gotten caught picking your nose in public? Did you have your first taste of beer, wine, or hard liquor before you reached the legal drinking age? Did you pierce something (your lip, eyebrow, or belly button) that your grandmother wouldn't have wanted you to pierce? If you work in an office, did you ever take home a pen, pencil, or packet of Post-it notes?

If you answered yes to any of these questions, you are the embodiment of what we seek to understand in this chapter: You are deviant. Remember this as you read the chapter.

DEFINING DEVIANCE

Deviance is a behavior, trait, or belief that departs from a norm and generates a negative reaction in a particular group. The norms and the group reactions are necessary for a behavior or characteristic to be defined as deviant (Goode 1997). The importance of norms becomes clear when we remember that what is deviant in one culture might be normal in another (see Chapter 3); even within the same culture, what was deviant a century ago—like marijuana use—might be perfectly acceptable now (and vice versa). The importance of group reactions is clear when we look at the varied reactions that norm violations generate: Some violations are seen as only mildly deviant (like chewing with your mouth open), while others are so strongly taboo that they are almost unthinkable (like cannibalism).

Deviant behavior must be sufficiently serious or unusual to spark a negative sanction or punishment. For example, if you were having dinner at a fancy restaurant with friends and used the wrong fork for your salad, you would be violating a minor norm but your friends probably wouldn't react in a negative fashion; they might not even notice. On the other hand, if you ate an entire steak dinner—meat, mashed potatoes, and salad—with your hands, your friends probably *would* react. They might criticize your behavior strongly ("That's totally disgusting!") and even refuse to eat with you again. This latter example, then, would be considered deviant behavior among your group of friends—and among most groups in American society. But it wouldn't be deviant at all in India or Ethiopia, where eating with your hands is commonplace. Just make sure to use your right hand; eating with the left hand is considered not only bad luck but bad manners too.

Because definitions of deviance are constructed from cultural, historical, and situational norms, sociologists are interested in a number of topics under the rubric of deviance. First, how are norms and rules created, and how do certain norms and rules become especially important? Second, who is subject to the rules, and how is rule breaking identified?

Challenging Norms As a pregnant transgender man, Trystan Reese faced criticism for challenging society's norms about gender and parenting and was labeled deviant by some.

Third, what types of sanctions (punishments or rewards) are dispensed to society's violators? Fourth, how do people who break the rules see themselves, and how do others see them? And finally, how have sociologists attempted to explain rule making, rule breaking, and responses to rule breaking?

DEVIANCE ACROSS CULTURES

It is important to remember that when sociologists use the term "deviant," they are making a social judgment, never a moral one. If a particular behavior is considered deviant, this means that it violates the values and norms of a *particular* group, not that it is inherently wrong or that other groups will make the same judgment.

Much of the literature on deviance focuses on crime. Not only do different cultures define strikingly different behaviors as criminal, but they also differ in how those crimes are punished. Most serious crime in the United States today is punished by imprisonment. This method of punishment was rare until the nineteenth century, however, as maintaining a prison requires considerable resources. Buildings must be constructed and maintained,

> **DEVIANCE** a behavior, trait, belief, or other characteristic that violates a norm and causes a negative reaction

GLOBAL PERSPECTIVE
Body Modification

Branding has long since died out as a method of punishment, but in a perfect illustration of the mutability of deviance, it has made something of a comeback as a form of body decoration (Parker 1998). What used to be an involuntary mark of shame has been reclaimed as a voluntary mark of pride. Small branding irons of stainless steel are heated with a blowtorch until white hot and are held on the skin for a second or two. Some who undergo the procedure burn incense to cover the smell of their own flesh burning. Many African American fraternities have a long tradition of branding, usually in the shape of one of the fraternity's Greek letters. The practice has received a public boost as several popular athletes have prominently displayed their fraternity brands. Basketball legend Michael Jordan sports such a brand, as does the NFL's Malcolm Jenkins. Branding is spreading to other subcultures, where it is just another extension of tattoos, Mohawks, and body piercings as an outward manifestation of youthful rebellion or an expression of personal aesthetic or group identification.

When it comes to body modification, what Americans might label deviant might be identified as desirable or normal in other cultures and vice versa. Among the Suri of southwestern Ethiopia, progressively larger plates are inserted into the lower lip so that it gradually becomes enlarged. The Padaung women of Burma stretch their necks with brass rings. Young girls begin by encircling their necks with just a few rings, then add more as they grow; by the time of maturity, their necks are considerably elongated. Breast augmentation surgery is commonplace in the United States, while butt augmentation is popular in Brazil.

Body modification does not always need to be dramatic. In reality, there are a great number of subtle methods of body modification practiced by most Americans that may not seem so obvious if we concentrate on eyebrow rings and neck tattoos. First of all, there have always been body modifications for the middle and upper classes. Corsets, worn by women through the ages until the early twentieth century, are an obvious example. Stomachs were flattened with "stays," long strips of some rigid material like whalebone. A tightly laced corset could achieve a dramatically narrow waistline but often at a serious cost to the wearer's health. Women sometimes even had ribs removed in order to accommodate them. The hair salon is another great unacknowledged center for body modification. If you get a perm, you are breaking the disulfide bonds in your hair and reshaping them to straighten them or make them curly. Even a simple haircut is a type of body modification—luckily for those of us who have gotten bad haircuts, they're temporary!

Some body modifications seem so "normal" that we practice them as routines without considering how they may seem deviant elsewhere. Other cultures may view Americans' obsession with hair removal—shaving, tweezing, and waxing—as bizarre. As you can see, whether it's wearing a corset, branding yourself, or shaving your legs, the boundaries between beauty and deviance are fluid across time and place.

guards and other staff must be paid, and prisoners must be fed and clothed. For groups without these resources, incarceration is not a possibility, even assuming it would be a desirable option. Instead, there are a whole host of other techniques of punishment.

For example, the Amish, a religious community whose members do without modern devices like electricity, cars, and telephones, practice *meidung*, which means shunning those who violate the strict norms of the group (Kephart 2000). A biblical rule instructs them "not to associate with any one who bears the name of brother if he is guilty of immorality or greed, or is an idolater, reviler, drunkard, or robber—not even to eat with such a one" (1 Corinthians 5:11). In other words, the Amish believe they should not associate with rule breakers even when they come from within their own family. No one does business with, eats with, or even talks to the guilty party. The shunning is temporary, however: After a short period, the violator is expected to publicly apologize and make amends and is then welcomed back into the community.

A much more permanent method of punishment is total banishment from the community. For many Native American people, the social group was so important that banishment was considered a fate worse than death (Champagne 1994). It was one of a variety of practices used to maintain social control (along with shaming songs, contests, and challenges of strength) and something of a rarity because it completely severed ties between the group and the individual. Banishment has a long history of use in all parts of the world, from British prisoners being "transported" to Australia to Russian dissidents being exiled to Siberia, and has been one of the most cost-effective methods of punishment ever discovered.

Just as methods of punishment vary between societies and groups, they also change over time. In Colonial America, for example, corporal punishment was the rule for the majority of crimes (Walker 1997). These days, the phrase "corporal punishment" may conjure up images of elementary school teachers spanking students, probably because spanking was the last vestige of what was once a vast repertoire of techniques. Thieves, pickpockets, and others who would today be considered petty criminals were flogged, had their ears cropped, had their noses slit, had their fingers or hands cut off, or were branded. These punishments were designed not only to deliver pain but also to mark the offender. As such, the particular punishment was often designed to fit the crime. A pickpocket might have a hand cut off; a forger might have an "F" branded on his forehead. Brands were also used to mark African American slaves as property during the 1800s.

THEORIES OF DEVIANCE

In this section, we will learn how three sociological paradigms discussed in Chapter 1—functionalism, conflict theory, and symbolic interactionism—can be applied to deviance. We will also learn about other related theories that have been developed specifically to explain particular aspects of deviance.

Functionalism

As you may recall, adherents of functionalism argue that each element of social structure helps maintain the stability of society. What, then, is the function of deviance for society? Émile Durkheim came up with a couple of functions. First, deviance can help a society clarify its moral boundaries. We are reminded about our shared notions of what is right when we have to address wrongdoings of various sorts. Take the case of Cecil the lion, a well-known and well-loved black-maned lion who was killed in Zimbabwe by an American trophy hunter in 2015. The 13-year-old lion had protected status within the borders of the Hwange National Park but was allegedly lured outside the park confines by a fresh elephant carcass, making it possible for Walter Palmer, a dentist from Minnesota, to track and eventually kill the lion on a neighboring farm. Cecil was then skinned and his head removed, his body left behind with his GPS collar missing. Palmer reportedly paid more than $50,000 to participate in the hunt, which was organized by a professional hunter. In his defense, Palmer claimed that everything about the trip was legal and properly conducted. But many felt that the killing of such a rare and magnificent lion was immoral, even if it was legal.

Another function of deviance is to promote social cohesion (one of functionalism's valued ideals); people can be brought together as a community in the face of crime or other violations. For example, when photos of a grinning Palmer astride his "kill" surfaced in the news, the outrage was swift and global in its reach. The story became a viral sensation,

Can Deviance Be Functional? After a beloved lion was killed by an American dentist during an organized hunt in Zimbabwe, activists came together in protest, igniting a debate over trophy hunting.

uniting people in a worldwide outcry against big-game hunting in general and Palmer in particular. Millions of people spoke out on social media and some even demonstrated outside his office in Bloomington, forcing him into hiding. His Facebook page and Yelp account were inundated with vitriolic posts. He was condemned by primatologist Jane Goodall and PETA (People for the Ethical Treatment of Animals) and excoriated in the press and late-night talk shows.

Social cohesion is central to other theories of deviance as well. Travis Hirschi's **social control theory** hypothesizes that the stronger one's social bonds—to family and religious, civic, and other groups—the less likely one is to commit crime. Such bonds tend to increase one's investment in the community and also increase one's commitment to that community's shared values and norms. With both internal and external forces regulating behavior, Hirschi argued that social bonds promote conformity (Hirschi 1969).

STRUCTURAL STRAIN THEORY Sociologist Robert Merton (1938) provides a bridge between functionalist and conflict theories of deviance. Like Durkheim, Merton acknowledged that some deviance is inevitable in society. But like conflict theorists, he argued that an individual's position in the social structure will affect his experience of deviance and conformity. Social inequality can create situations in which people experience tension (or strain) between the goals society says they should be working toward (like financial success) and the means they have available to meet those goals (not everyone is able to work hard at a legitimate job).

Our society's intense emphasis on financial success and materialism—through the mythology of the "American Dream"—can be stressful for those whose chances of realizing that dream are limited (Messner and Rosenfeld 2012). The rewards of conformity are available only to those who can pursue approved goals through approved means. Any other combination of means and goals is deviant in one way or another (see Figure 6.1). **Innovators**, for example, might seek financial success via unconventional means (such as drug dealing or embezzlement). **Ritualists** go through the conventional motions while abandoning all hope of success, and **retreatists** (like dropouts or hermits) renounce the culture's goals and means entirely and live outside conventional norms altogether. At the far end of the continuum, **rebels** reject the cultural definitions of success and the normative means of

SOCIAL CONTROL THEORY a theory of crime, proposed by Travis Hirschi, that posits that strong social bonds increase conformity and decrease deviance

INNOVATORS individuals who accept society's approved goals but not society's approved means to achieve them

RITUALISTS individuals who have given up hope of achieving society's approved goals but still operate according to society's approved means

RETREATISTS individuals who renounce society's approved goals and means entirely and live outside conventional norms altogether

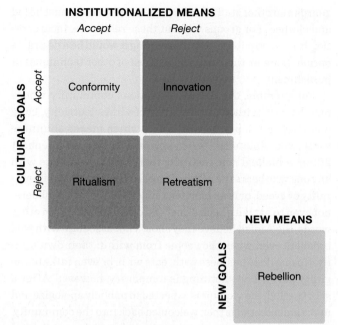

FIGURE 6.1 Merton's Typology of Deviance
Different orientations toward society's goals and differential access to the means to achieve those goals combine to create different categories of deviance.

achieving it and advocate radical alternatives to the existing social order.

For example, consider the characters in *Black Panther*, a superhero film set in Wakanda, a highly developed African country that possesses vibranium, a substance from a meteorite that fuels its technology, as well as a heart-shaped herb that gives its king superpowers. Wakanda has kept these marvels a secret by isolating itself from the rest of the world and posing as an impoverished nation. The initial cultural goal in the film is to preserve Wakanda's futuristic achievements and protect the country from outsiders. T'Challa, who assumes the throne upon the death of his father, is a conformist. He feels a great responsibility as the new leader of Wakanda, and so upholds its traditional separatist policies. M'Baku is a retreatist and ruler of the Jabari, a tribe that lives in the mountains of Wakanda. The Jabari denounce control by the central government and reject any dependence upon vibranium. M'Baku challenges T'Challa for the throne but is thwarted in combat. Nakia is a highly trained spy who works undercover to stop human trafficking in Africa; she is also a confidant to the king, and his ex-girlfriend. Nakia is an innovator who believes that sharing Wakanda's culture and technology would be good for the country and help uplift black communities around the world. She gently tries to persuade T'Challa to open up Wakanda.

Erik "Killmonger" Stevens is a rebel who was born and raised in Oakland, California, to a Wakandan prince and an African American mother; he is also the cousin of T'Challa.

Deviance in Wakanda (From left) Nakia, the innovator; T'Challa, the conformist, and Okoye, the ritualist. Each of these *Black Panther* characters fits into different Mertonian categories of deviance and conformity.

An officer in the special forces, Killmonger witnesses the oppression of African Americans up close and seeks to avenge them. He returns to Wakanda and wins the throne in battle. As the new king, he launches a mission to destroy the rest of the world using Wakanda's weapons and technology. Okoye is the top general in the royal guard, and its strongest warrior. She is fiercely loyal to king and country. Finally, Okoye is a ritualist who continues to protect Wakanda from outsiders even after Killmonger takes the throne. But Okoye loses faith in the king's new cultural goal of worldwide annihilation, and eventually leads the battle (alongside M'Baku and the Jabari down from the mountain) to overthrow him. In this analysis of *Black Panther*, it's interesting to note the critical role the innovator plays in eventually changing the other characters and the culture of Wakanda itself.

Conflict Theory

Conflict theorists, who study inequalities of wealth and power, note that inequalities are present in our definitions of deviance as well. In other words, conflict theorists believe that rules are applied unequally and that punishments for rule violators are unequally distributed: Those at the top are subject to different rules and sanctions than those nearer the bottom, and the behaviors of less powerful groups and individuals are more likely to be criminalized than the behaviors of the powerful. American criminologist Richard Quinney theorized that capitalism—and the exploitation and oppression of the working class—make deviant and even criminal behavior nearly inescapable for workers. The ruling class can make laws that target the poor. When the poor act out against repression, they become targets for law enforcement, while the rich and powerful remain free to do what they like.

Norms, rules, and laws are used to regulate the behavior of individuals and groups. This process, known as **social control**, can be either informal, as in the exercise of control through customs, norms, and expectations, or formal, as in the exercise of control through laws or other official regulations. Both formal social control and informal social control can be exercised unequally in a hierarchical society, and this is what conflict theory is concerned with when it comes to the topic of deviance.

As recently as 2003, more than a dozen U.S. states still imposed heterosexuality on their citizens through anti-sodomy laws, which prohibited any sexual acts that did not lead to procreation. While in theory anti-sodomy laws could include acts like masturbation and heterosexual oral sex, in practice these laws were generally imposed against same-sex partners. Before a Supreme Court ruling invalidated all state anti-sodomy laws in *Lawrence v. Texas* (2003), sexual acts done in the privacy of your own home could be penalized with fines and jail time in states such as Florida, Idaho, and Michigan. From a conflict theorist perspective, anti-sodomy laws were a way for the heterosexual majority to exercise control over same-sex minorities.

As another example, the Great Recession of 2008 was in large part caused by banks engaging in risky and often predatory mortgage lending. Millions of ordinary people lost not only their homes but also their jobs and life savings during

> **REBELS** individuals who reject society's approved goals and means and instead create and work toward their own (sometimes revolutionary) goals using new means
>
> **SOCIAL CONTROL** the formal and informal mechanisms used to elicit conformity to values and norms and thus promote social cohesion

IN RELATIONSHIPS
Cyberbullying, Trolls, and Online Deviance

With the advent of the Internet came new ways of interacting with one another ... and new ways of being deviant. Or maybe they're just old ways of being deviant in a new relational context. Because bullies and trolls go way, way back.

Although parents and schools have always worried about bullying, their concerns have multiplied since children and teenagers started using the Internet. The phenomenon of **cyberbullying**—the use of electronic and social media to tease, threaten, or humiliate someone—catapulted to the forefront of national consciousness after the suicide of thirteen-year-old Megan Meier in October 2006. Megan had received an online message from a boy named Josh, who said that he lived nearby but that his family didn't have a phone. During the next several weeks, they sent messages back and forth and seemed to have become close very quickly. Then, without warning, Josh started taunting and abusing her. Megan was devastated and hanged herself in her closet. Several weeks later, the Meiers learned that "Josh" was not a real person and that the online account had been created by neighborhood mom Lori Drew, in order to get back at Megan for snubbing her daughter.

Unfortunately, Megan's is not an isolated case. A recent survey by the Pew Research Center found that a majority of U.S. teens—fully 59 percent—have been victims of cyberbullying at some point in their lives (Anderson 2018). In several ways, cyberbullying is more frightening than its off-line equivalent. Like every phenomenon created by the Information Revolution, cyberbullying is faster and connects more people than off-line activity. On Instagram, for example, hurtful comments and images can go viral in hours and it's easy to set up new, anonymous accounts—known as hate pages—for the express purpose of bullying (Lorenz 2018). Traditional bullying usually happens at school, while cyberbullying can happen anytime and in the privacy of your own home. Likewise, the effects are longer lasting. One of the most common forms of cyberbullying is spreading rumors about someone. Traditional bullying relied on word of mouth or the proverbial graffiti on the bathroom wall to do this. But word of mouth is limited, and only so many people can read a nasty comment scrawled on the stall in the bathroom before the janitor washes it off. Online, there is almost no limit to how many people might see a nasty comment, even if it is later taken down.

CYBERBULLYING the use of electronic media (web pages, social networking sites, e-mail, Twitter, cell phones) to tease, harass, threaten, or humiliate someone

DIFFERENTIAL ASSOCIATION THEORY Edwin Sutherland's hypothesis that we learn to be deviant through our associations with deviant peers

the ensuing economic crisis, and both the national economy and global economy were on the verge of collapse. But the banks and corporations were bailed out with taxpayer money, and only a single Wall Street executive was ever prosecuted in relation to the crash (Lewis 2011). This unhappy episode in American history is just one illustration of the ways that wealth and privilege protect the powerful from being defined as deviant or being punished for their violations.

Symbolic Interactionism

While conflict theorists and functionalists focus on inequalities and the social functions of deviance, interactionists consider the ways that interpersonal relationships and everyday interactions shape definitions of deviance.

DIFFERENTIAL ASSOCIATION THEORY One such approach is Edwin Sutherland's **differential association theory** (Sutherland 1939; Sutherland, Cressey, and Luckenbill 1992), which asserts that we learn to be deviant through our interactions with others who break the rules. This is the theory of deviance that your parents subscribed to when you were a teenager: Don't hang out with the bad kids! Simple peer pressure by those you associate with can lead to deviant behavior. For instance, an athlete who uses steroids to help build strength might also influence his teammates to start "doping" even though this practice is banned in most sports. Have you ever been influenced by others to do something deviant that you would have never tried on your own?

This theory of deviance seems at first glance to be pretty sensible—interacting often with those who break the rules would seem to socialize an individual into their rule-breaking culture. But, as it turns out, not all who hang out with deviants become deviant themselves, and plenty of people who engage in deviant acts have never consorted with other rule

So far, most research has focused on cyberbullying that is perpetrated by someone who knows the victim in real life, but there have always been Internet bullies (or "trolls") who seek to abuse people they've never met or have encountered only online. For example, after Megan Meier's suicide, a blog was created by someone with no connection to her case, called "Megan Had It Coming," that contained posts from a cast of characters who purported to know Megan, all expressing a distinct lack of remorse. The blogger, a thirty-two-year-old computer programmer from Seattle, had a history of humiliating others online and expressed pride in his achievements. Indeed, "trolls" seem to enjoy their abusive activities and often continue under different usernames even after they have been blocked by service providers or website administrators. Trolls make a game of harrassing, bullying, and stalking others online: Threats of violence are common, as is "doxxing," or the practice of publishing private, humiliating information (photos, financial data, etc.) online for all to see (Stein 2016).

As more and more of people's lives play out online, cyberbullying will only become more common. Will we treat it the way we treat other related forms of deviance? In "real" life, abuses like slander, harassment, and stalking can be prosecuted as crimes. But it is harder to apply such penalties to Internet trolls and cyberbullies, given the questions about identity and jurisdiction that arise in online settings. Perhaps the only way to respond to this type of deviance is to troll the trolls?

Cyberbullying Tina Meier holds pictures of her daughter Megan, who committed suicide after receiving cruel online messages.

breakers. Also, in cases where deviance is not the result of a willful act (mental illness, for example), a learning theory such as this one is not a useful explanation. While differential association theory seeks to explain "why they do it," it cannot fully explain every case of deviant behavior—nor can any theory of deviance.

LABELING THEORY Howard Becker's **labeling theory** (1963) proposes that deviance is not inherent in any act, belief, or condition; instead, it is determined by the social context. A man who kills an intruder who is attacking his child may be labeled a hero, while a man who kills a cashier in the process of robbing a store may be labeled a villain. Even though the act of homicide is the same, the way the person who did it is treated differs greatly depending on the label.

Labeling theory recognizes that labels will vary depending on the culture, time period, and situation. David Rosenhan's study "On Being Sane in Insane Places" (1973) provides a striking demonstration of the power of labeling and the importance of context. Rosenhan and seven other researchers gained admission to psychiatric hospitals as patients. Other than falsifying their names and occupations, the eight subjects gave honest answers to all but one of the questions in the entrance examination. They all complained of hearing voices, a symptom often linked to schizophrenia. Nevertheless, the subjects felt certain that once they were hospitalized, they would be quickly exposed as "pseudo-patients," not really mentally ill.

In fact, the opposite turned out to be true. Once admitted, the pseudo-patients turned immediately to the task of getting themselves discharged—and failed miserably. Although they behaved as normally and pleasantly as possible, doctors and nurses continued to treat them as mentally ill patients in need of treatment. No amount of explanation on the part of the

LABELING THEORY Howard Becker's idea that deviance is a consequence of external judgments, or labels, that modify the individual's self-concept and change the way others respond to the labeled person

Labeling Theory Deviant labels such as "teen mom" vary based on culture, time period, and context.

pseudo-patients could convince the hospital staff of their sanity (though, in an interesting twist, it was usually obvious to the other patients). When they were finally discharged (after one to seven weeks!), it was not because the staff had finally seen through the deception; they were all released with their schizophrenia "in remission." Rosenhan concluded, "Once labeled schizophrenic, the pseudo-patient was stuck with that label" (1973, p. 253). The effects of this "sticky" deviant label on actual patients can follow them through their lives, even after they leave the hospital. Rosenhan's famous study has recently come under scrutiny for inconsistencies between the data he collected and the findings he published (Cahalan 2019). Critics suspect that Rosenhan, who died in 2012, may have even made up the identities of some of the pseudo-patients. Though questions remain, Rosenhan's central argument about the power of labels has been documented by others many times (Rios 2017).

Labeling theory is also concerned with how individuals think of themselves once a deviant label has been applied. Recall Cooley's concept of the "looking-glass self": How we perceive ourselves depends in part on how others see us, so if others react to us as deviant,

we are likely to internalize that label (even if we object to it). Applying deviant labels can also lead to further deviance, as a person moves from **primary deviance** (the thing that gets them labeled in the first place) to **secondary deviance** (a deviant identity or career) (Lemert 1951).

If you've watched NBC's *The Biggest Loser*, you've seen examples of both types of deviance. On the show, overweight and obese contestants sign up for an intensive weight-loss boot camp, and viewers follow the ups and downs of their progress over the course of each season. Their excess body weight, which is seen as deviant in contemporary U.S. culture, is an example of primary deviance, and contestants' recognition that they are "fatties" who need to slim down is an example of secondary deviance.

Although deviant labels are sticky and hard to shake, it is sometimes possible for an individual to turn what could have been a negative identity into a positive one. John Kitsuse (1980) calls this **tertiary deviance**, which occurs when the person labeled deviant rejects the notion of deviance entirely and attempts to redefine their "deviant" attributes or behavior as normal. Some members of *The Biggest Loser* cast demonstrated this level of deviance as well. Many contestants gain the weight back after the show, their bodies fighting to return to their original weights; for some, this leads them to a newfound acceptance of their body shape and size (Huddleston 2016; Kolata 2016). This argument—"Sure, I'm fat, but there shouldn't be anything wrong with that"—is an attempt to recast that identity as acceptable difference rather than deviance.

Some of the most exciting, but also disturbing, research on labeling theory has focused on **self-fulfilling prophecy**, a term coined by Robert Merton. Merton's concept was derived from the so-called Thomas theorem, formulated by sociologist W. I. Thomas in 1928, which held that "if men define situations as real, they are real in their consequences." From this theorem, Merton developed his notion of the self-fulfilling prophecy, which is basically a prediction that causes itself to come true merely by being stated. He offered the example of a bank in the Depression-era 1930s that collapsed through "a rumor of insolvency," when enough investors became convinced that the bank was out of money (1948, p. 194).

Merton argued that the self-fulfilling prophecy can be used to explain some racial issues in the United States, and subsequent research has borne him out. For example, Elijah Anderson's classic *Streetwise* (1990) details how the police and community perceive black male inner-city teenagers as a criminal element, with the result that they are more likely to be arrested than other teenagers, and citizens are also more likely to report black males for crimes. This cloud of suspicion requires black urban teens to defend their innocence in situations that other teens can negotiate with little or no difficulty. Young black males are also more likely to be incarcerated, which only feeds the public image of criminality. The racial discrimination and profiling by police and the community thus lead to a negative cycle that is difficult to break.

PRIMARY DEVIANCE in labeling theory, the initial act or attitude that causes one to be labeled deviant

SECONDARY DEVIANCE in labeling theory, the subsequent deviant identity or career that develops as a result of being labeled deviant

TERTIARY DEVIANCE redefining the stigma associated with a deviant label as a positive phenomenon

SELF-FULFILLING PROPHECY an inaccurate statement or belief that, by altering the situation, becomes accurate; a prediction that causes itself to come true

STEREOTYPE THREAT a kind of self-fulfilling prophecy in which the fear of performing poorly—and confirming stereotypes about their social groups—causes students to perform poorly

TABLE 6.1 Theory in Everyday Life

Perspective	Approach to Deviance	Case Study: Plagiarism
Structural Functionalism	Deviance clarifies moral boundaries and promotes social cohesion.	Punishing those who plagiarize separates those who should be in college from those who aren't responsible enough.
Control Theory	Strong social bonds increase conformity and decrease deviance.	Requiring incoming college students to sign an honor code on the first day of orientation pledging that they will not cheat while they are a member of their college community.
Structural Strain Theory	An individual's position in society determines whether they have the means to achieve their goals or must otherwise turn to deviance.	A student's attitude about plagiarizing depends on whether they have the means to write the paper.
Conflict Theory	Definitions and rules of deviance are applied unequally based on power.	Students with fewer resources are punished harshly and have fewer options afterward; students with more money or connections can either transfer to another school or rely on their parents for help.
Symbolic Interactionism	The definition of deviance is relative and depends on the culture, time period, and situation.	Plagiarism may be labeled as deviant in the United States but not in Russia or India.
Differential Association Theory	Deviance is learned through interactions with others who break the rules.	Students learn to cheat because they hang out with other students who plagiarize.
Labeling Theory	Deviance is determined by the reactions of others; applying deviant labels to an individual may lead them to further deviance.	A student who is caught plagiarizing may come to believe they are unable to write without cheating.

Stereotypes are often part of self-fulfilling prophecies. Claude Steele's research (1997, 2010) on **stereotype threat** shows that when students worry that their own poor academic performance could unintentionally confirm a negative stereotype about their social group, they actually perform poorly. In Steele's studies, students were asked to identify their race, gender, or other group membership associated with negative stereotypes before beginning an exam. When primed in this way, students performed more poorly than when they weren't asked any background questions. Stereotype threat has been measured in high-achieving African American students as well as highly ranked female math students (Spencer, Steele, and Quinn 1999).

Stereotypes and self-fulfilling prophecies are not always negative. Jennifer Lee and Min Zhou (2014) found that Asian American students can actually benefit from both. In the case of **stereotype promise**, Asian American students are more likely to be placed in Advanced Placement (AP) classes, receive high grades, and be treated well by teachers because others assume that they are high achievers. In both cases, the stereotypes become real as people (teachers, students, others) act based on them—even in cases where students are trying to avoid this very problem.

Labels alone are not 100 percent deterministic, and prophecies are not always self-fulfilling. But in our society, deviant labels can override other aspects of individual identity and exert a powerful influence on self-image, treatment by others, and even social and institutional policies.

THE STIGMA OF DEVIANCE

In ancient Greece, criminals and slaves were branded with hot irons, making a mark called a **stigma**, from the Greek word for tattoo. The stigma was meant to serve as an outward indication that there was something shameful about the bearer, and to this day we continue to use the term to signify some disgrace or failing. Although we no longer live in a society where we are forced to wear our rule violations branded onto our bodies, stigmatized identities still carry serious social consequences.

Stigma, a central concept in the sociology of deviance, was analyzed and elaborated by Erving Goffman (1962) in his book of the same name. Once an individual has been labeled as deviant, he is stigmatized and acquires what Goffman calls a "spoiled identity." There

STEREOTYPE PROMISE a kind of self-fulfilling prophecy in which positive stereotypes, such as the "model minority" label applied to Asian Americans, lead to positive performance outcomes

STIGMA Erving Goffman's term for any physical or social attribute that devalues a person or group's identity and that may exclude those who are devalued from normal social interaction

ON THE JOB
Is "Cash Register Honesty" Good Enough?

While we might like to think that most employees wouldn't take money from the cash register or merchandise from the showroom floor, walk away with a laptop computer, drive away with the company car, or filter sales receipts to their own bank account, employee theft is still a major problem. According to the Association of Certified Fraud Examiners (2012), the typical business is estimated to lose about 5 percent of its annual revenues to employee fraud. This translates to a median loss of $140,000 per year per organization. Others estimate that employee theft is involved in up to one-third of all U.S. corporate bankruptcies (Russakoff and Goodman 2011). The U.S. Chamber of Commerce reports that 75 percent of all employees steal once, and that half of those individuals will steal repeatedly (Jones 2012). Michael Cunningham (Cunningham and Jones 2010), a professor of psychology at the University of Louisville and a consultant to the security industry, warns that only one in every three potential employees will be completely trustworthy. Of the other two, one may be tempted to steal given the opportunity, while the other will be more or less constantly looking for a chance to get away with taking company property.

Although we may consider ourselves the trustworthy ones, we may not recognize that our own behavior could still be contributing to the tens of billions of dollars lost each year. How? Well, have you ever taken home paper clips, Post-it notes, a pen, or a pad of paper from the office? Made personal copies on the office copier? Used your work computer to surf the web, download music or movies, play video games, or send an e-mail to a friend? Eaten or drunk company products? How about taking a little more time than you're supposed to on your lunch break or leaving work a little early?

It's called "pilfering," and it happens on the job tens of thousands of times a day. And it all adds up. Most companies consider these kinds of losses as just another factor in the cost of doing business. But how is it that so many people think nothing of these small infractions in spite of prevailing social norms that discourage stealing and while otherwise being upstanding or even exemplary employees?

You could say that these people are practicing "cash register honesty." That is, they draw the line at actually stealing money (or its equivalent) out of the till but don't hesitate to make off with other odds and ends that might have a less easily calculable value. Employees may be deterred by informal social control or by more formal surveillance measures such as videotaping, keystroke logging, or other kinds of scanning and searching practiced by employers. But even when they do get away with taking home a pen or snacking on the merchandise, they might be appalled at the suggestion that they are deviant, especially since everyone else seems to take something now and then.

---

are three main types of stigma: physical (including physical or mental impairments), moral (signs of a flawed character), and tribal (membership in a discredited or oppressed group). Almost any departure from the norm can have a stigmatizing effect, including a physical disability, a past battle with alcohol or mental illness, time served in jail, or sexual transgressions. Goffman recognized that what may once have been a stigmatized identity may change over time or may vary according to culture or social context. Being black or Jewish is a stigma only if one lives in a racist or anti-Semitic society. In a community entirely populated by African Americans, it is white people who may be stigmatized; an all-Jewish enclave may see non-Jews as outside the norm. Goffman was careful to note that not all stigmatized identities are just or deserved—only that they are specific to the norms and prejudices of a particular group, time period, or context.

Managing Deviant Identities

Goffman was particularly interested in the effects of stigmatization on individual identity and interactions with others. At the macro level, society does not treat the stigmatized very well; if you suffer from serious depression, for example, you may find that your health insurance does not cover your treatment. At the micro level, you may also find that your friends don't fully understand your depression-related problems. In fact, you may find yourself working to keep others from finding out that you are depressed or receiving treatment for depression, precisely in order to avoid such situations. Having a stigmatized identity—of any sort—makes navigating the social world difficult.

PASSING How can stigmatized individuals negotiate the perils of everyday interaction? One strategy analyzed by Goffman is called **passing**, or concealing stigmatizing information. The allusion to racial passing is entirely intended—Goffman meant to call to mind the experiences of light-skinned African Americans who, for more than 300 years and particularly in the decades before the civil rights movement of the 1960s, sought access to the privileges of whiteness (and relief from discrimination) by concealing their racial heritage and passing as white. The case of racial passing is instructive in developing an understanding of all types of passing—such as the passing engaged in by employees who dress to conceal their tattoos when at work, or people with illnesses like diabetes or depression or with disabilities such as hearing impairments who try to keep their conditions a secret.

IN-GROUP ORIENTATION Not everyone can pass, though, because not all stigma is concealable. While it may be possible to conceal your status as an ex-convict or survivor of rape, it is more difficult to conceal extreme shortness or obesity. And while some people cannot pass, others refuse to do so as a matter of principle. These people don't believe that their identities should be seen as deviant, and they certainly don't believe that they should have to change or conceal those identities just to make "normals" feel more comfortable. They have what Goffman called an **in-group orientation**—they reject the standards that mark them as deviant and may even actively propose new standards in which their special identities are well within the normal range. For example, such groups as PFLAG (Parents, Families, and Friends of Lesbians and Gays), NAD (National Association of the Deaf), and NAAFA (National Association to Advance Fat Acceptance) have allowed members of stigmatized groups to feel greater self-esteem and to unite in fighting against prejudice and discrimination. Activism might also take the more individual form of merely being "out," open, and unapologetic about one's identity. This in itself can be difficult and exhausting (as passing is); however, those with an in-group orientation see it as a powerful way to address society's changing definitions of deviance.

DEVIANCE AVOWAL AND VOLUNTARY OUTSIDERS Under most circumstances, people reject the deviant label and what it seems to imply about their personal identity. However, there are some who *choose* to be called a deviant. Those who belong to a particular subculture, for example—whether outlaw biker, rock musician, or eco-warrior—may celebrate their membership in a deviant group. Howard Becker (1963) referred to such individuals as **outsiders**, people living in one way or another outside mainstream society. They may pass among "normals," continuing to work and participate in everyday life. Or their deviant identity may have become a master status, thus preventing them from interacting along conventional lines; when this happens, a person's deviance may be thought to reveal his underlying nature. For instance,

Body Positivity In *Shrill*, Aidy Bryant's character, Annie, attends a body-positive event—the Fat Babe Pool Party—and develops an in-group orientation as a result.

members of the punk subculture, easily identified by their distinctive look, are generally assumed to be loud troublemakers, whatever their individual personality traits may be.

Some potential deviants may actually initiate the labeling process against themselves or provoke others to do so, a condition Ralph Turner (1972) called **deviance avowal**. Turner suggested that it may be useful to conceive of deviance as a role rather than as an isolated behavior that violates a single norm. And in some cases, it may be beneficial for an individual to identify with the deviant role. In the Alcoholics Anonymous program, for example, the first step in recovery is for a member to admit that she is an alcoholic. Since total abstinence from drinking is the goal, only those who believe they have a drinking problem and who willingly accept the label of alcoholic can take the suggested steps toward recovery.

Deviance avowal can also help a person avoid the pressures of having to adopt certain conventional norms, or what Turner called the "neutralization of commitment." For instance, a recovering alcoholic might resist taking a typical nine-to-five job, claiming that the stress of corporate work had always made them drink before. Another recovering

PASSING presenting yourself as a member of a different group than the stigmatized group to which you belong

IN-GROUP ORIENTATION among stigmatized individuals, the rejection of prevailing judgments or prejudice and the development of new standards that value their group identity

OUTSIDERS according to Howard Becker, those labeled deviant and subsequently segregated from "normal" society

DEVIANCE AVOWAL process by which an individual self-identifies as deviant and initiates their own labeling process alcoholic who refuses to attend family gatherings might offer as an excuse that they can't be around family because they drink at every occasion. In such ways, people become voluntary outsiders, finding it preferable to be a deviant in spite of the prevailing norms of mainstream society.

Alcoholics Anonymous offers an interesting case where members choose to embrace a deviant identity as a positive aspect of themselves, one that is critical to their success in the program. Research by Melvin Pollner and Jill Stein (1996, 2001) has focused on the role of narrative storytelling as a key feature of reconstructing the alcoholic's sense of self and turning a stigmatized identity into a valued asset in the process of recovery. The basic text of the twelve-step program is laid out in the book *Alcoholics Anonymous* (1939/2001), often referred to by members as the "Big Book." Its first 164 pages have remained virtually the same since it was first published in 1939; it is now in its fourth edition. The book also includes dozens of personal stories written by AA members themselves. These chapters always begin with the "Pioneers of AA," but in each subsequent edition some new (and more modern) stories are added, while others are dropped. That such a large part of the Big Book is devoted to the personal stories of members shows their importance. They are intended to help newcomers to the program identify with and relate to the lives of other recovering alcoholics and to follow their examples.

In this Data Workshop, you will examine the story of "Marty M."—one of AA's pioneers and one of the first women to join the program, way back in 1939, when the book was just being written. Her story is the fourth that appears (but not until the second and subsequent editions) and is called "Women Suffer Too." The title refers to a widely held notion at the time that only men could be alcoholics. The idea of a woman alcoholic was almost unthinkable. Marty M. defied the conventions of her day in many ways. She was a divorcee, entrepreneur, world traveler, and later, philanthropist. But first and foremost, she was a sober drunk. Marty M.'s story follows the classic narrative structure of all AA stories: what

we used to be like, what happened, and what we are like now. It is told from the perspective of a sober alcoholic looking back on her life and understanding that through the process of deviance avowal (by accepting her alcoholism) she was able to transform a negative past into a positive life.

For this Data Workshop you will be examining an existing source and doing a content analysis of the story "Women Suffer Too." Refer to Chapter 2 for a review of this research method. The text of the story can be found in the Big Book and accessed online at various websites, including http://www.aa.org/assets/en_US/en_bigbook_personalstories_partI.pdf.

Read the story in its entirety, keeping in mind how the study of life histories or oral histories can reveal important features of societal norms and everyday life. Remember that Marty M. lived in a particular time period and social context. Pay close attention to how the story describes both deviant behavior and the process of deviance avowal, and consider the following questions:

- Identify the instances of deviance described in the author's story. Why were these behaviors considered deviant?

- In what ways was she in denial about her condition early on? How did she actively try to disavow the deviant label?

- At what point did she begin the process of deviance avowal? How did admitting that she was an alcoholic affect her self-concept?

- In what ways did deviance avowal allow her to see her past in a different light? How did her deviant identity finally become a positive part of her life?

- How have our perceptions about alcoholics and alcoholism changed since the pioneer days of AA?

There are two options for completing this Data Workshop:

PREP-PAIR-SHARE Based on your answers to the questions, prepare some written notes that you can refer to during in-class discussions. Share your reactions and conclusions with other students in small groups. Listen for any differences in one another's insights.

DO-IT-YOURSELF Write a three- to four-page essay answering the questions. Include your own reactions to the story. Make sure to refer to specific passages from the story that help to support your analysis.

STUDYING DEVIANCE

When studying deviance, sociologists have often focused on the most obvious forms of deviant behavior—crime, mental illness, and sexual deviance. This "nuts and sluts" approach (Liazos 1972) usually focuses on the deviance of the poor and powerless, while accepting the values and norms of the powerful in an unacknowledged way. Social scientists tended to apply definitions of deviance uncritically in their research and failed to question the ways in which the definitions themselves may have perpetuated inequalities and untruths.

David Matza (1969), a sociologist at the University of California, Berkeley, set out to remedy this situation. He urged social scientists to set aside their preconceived notions in order to understand deviant phenomena on their own terms—a perspective he called "naturalism." Leila Rupp and Verta Taylor, for example, spent three years with a dozen drag queens in order to gain perspective for their research in *Drag Queens at the 801 Cabaret* (2003); see Part II's introduction to read more. Matza's fundamental admonition to those studying deviance is that they must appreciate the diversity and complexity of a particular social world—the world of street gangs, drug addicts, strippers, fight clubs, outlaw bikers, homeless people, or the severely disfigured. If such a world is approached as a simple social pathology that needs correcting, the researcher will never fully understand it. A sociological perspective requires that we seek insight without applying judgment—a difficult task indeed.

The Emotional Attraction of Deviance

Most sociological perspectives on deviance focus on aspects of a person's background that would influence him to act in deviant ways. This is the case with both functionalist and conflict perspectives. For example, many sociological studies of crime make the case that youth with limited access to education may be more likely to turn to drug dealing or theft. Labeling theory also suggests that a person's social location is a crucial determinant: It shapes how others see the person, as well as his or her own self-view, and these perceptions can lead a person from primary to secondary deviance and into a deviant career. One of the main problems with such theories, however, is that they can't explain why some people with backgrounds that should incline them to deviance never actually violate any rules, while others with no defining background factors do become deviant.

Approaches that focus exclusively on background factors neglect one very important element: the deviant's own in-the-moment experience of committing a deviant act, what sociologist Jack Katz refers to as the "foreground" of deviance. In *The Seductions of Crime* (1988), Katz looks at how emotionally seductive crime can be, how shoplifting or even committing murder might produce a particular kind of rush that becomes the very reason for carrying out the act. For example, what shoplifters often seek is not the DVD or perfume itself as much as the "sneaky thrill" of stealing it. Initially drawn to stealing by the thought of just how easy it might be, the shoplifter tests her ability to be secretly deviant—in public—while appearing to be perfectly normal. This perspective explains why the vast majority of shoplifters are not from underprivileged backgrounds but are people who could easily afford the stolen items. How else might we explain why a wealthy and famous actress such as Lindsay Lohan would try to steal a necklace from a jewelry store?

Similarly, muggers' and robbers' actions reveal that they get more satisfaction from their crimes than from the things they steal. They are excited by the sense of superiority they gain by setting up and playing tricks on their victims. In fact, they can come to feel morally superior, thinking that their victims deserve their fate because they are less observant and savvy. Even murderous rages can be seen as seductive ways to overcome an overwhelming sense of humiliation. A victim of adultery, for example, may kill instead of simply ending the relationship because murder, or "righteous slaughter," feels like the most appropriate response.

Katz's foreground model of deviance deepens our appreciation for the complexity of deviant behavior and reminds us that social actors are not mere products of their environment but are active participants in creating meaningful experiences for themselves, even if harmful to others.

THE STUDY OF CRIME

Crime is a particular type of deviance: It is the violation of a norm that has been codified into law, for which you could be arrested and imprisoned. Official state-backed sanctions, such as laws, exert more power over the individual than do nonlegal norms. For example, if you risked arrest for gossiping about your roommate, you might think twice about doing it. "Might," however, is the key word here; the risk of arrest and jail time does not always deter people from breaking laws. In fact, ordinary people break laws every day without really thinking about it (speeding, underage drinking, stealing those pens and pencils from the office).

These are among the many reasons that sociologists study crime—in fact, there's a word for the study of crime, criminals, and the criminal justice system: **criminology**. Criminologists ask and attempt to answer questions like the following: Who makes the laws? Who breaks them? Who benefits from defining and enforcing them? How do individuals

> **CRIME** a violation of a norm that has been codified into law
>
> **CRIMINOLOGY** the systematic scientific study of crime, criminals, and criminal justice

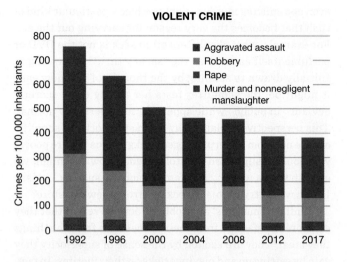

VIOLENT CRIME

Legend:
- Aggravated assault
- Robbery
- Rape
- Murder and nonnegligent manslaughter

Y-axis: Crimes per 100,000 inhabitants
X-axis: 1992, 1996, 2000, 2004, 2008, 2012, 2017

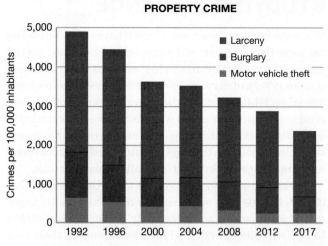

PROPERTY CRIME

Legend:
- Larceny
- Burglary
- Motor vehicle theft

Y-axis: Crimes per 100,000 inhabitants
X-axis: 1992, 1996, 2000, 2004, 2008, 2012, 2017

FIGURE 6.2 Crime in the United States, 1992–2017

SOURCE: Federal Bureau of Investigation 2018a.

begin committing crime, and how do they desist? What are the intentions and outcomes of law enforcement institutions? Using systematic data and social scientific theory, the work of criminologists contributes to our understanding of this type of deviance in our society.

In the United States, crime is officially measured by the **Uniform Crime Report (UCR)**, the FBI's tabulation of every crime reported by more than 18,000 law enforcement agencies around the country. In particular, the UCR is used to track the "crime index," or the eight offenses considered especially reprehensible in our society (see Figure 6.2). Murder, rape, aggravated assault, and robbery are categorized as **violent crime**. Burglary (theft inside the home), larceny (of personal property), motor vehicle theft, and arson are considered **property crime**. Even though the UCR has been shown to be a flawed system (participation by agencies is voluntary, and the FBI rarely audits it for accuracy), it is useful in helping to track trends in overall crime as well as particular patterns; it also records the number of arrests made compared with the number of crimes committed, which is the most traditional measure of police effectiveness.

One notable finding from UCR data is that rates of violent crime declined significantly in the last decade of the

twentieth century. The year 1991 saw the highest homicide rates in U.S. history, at 9.8 per 100,000 persons, or 24,700 murders. Between 1991 and 2000, there was a dramatic drop in homicide rates, and the rate has stayed low ever since (Federal Bureau of Investigation 2018a). Other findings from the UCR include the observation that murder rates peak in the months of July and August. Perhaps related to summer heat and humidity, murder rates are also higher in the southern states. Financial hardship may influence murder rates, as southern states also have the lowest median family incomes.

Other patterns identifiable in UCR data: Murder is committed most frequently by a friend or relative of the victim and seldom by a stranger. Robbery occurs most frequently in urban areas among youth. Property crimes occur more frequently than violent crimes. The most common crime is larceny, with burglary and motor vehicle theft trailing far behind. Although there has also been a decline in rates of property crime in the last decade, it is not as extreme as the drop in violent crime. And with the arrival of the Information Age, the category of **cybercrime** has emerged, covering a wide variety of illegal violations committed via the Internet.

Crime and Demographics

When criminologists look at quantitative crime data, which provide information on who is more likely to commit or be a victim of crime, they may learn more about the cause of crime. We should, however, question the assumptions and biases of the data. For example, Robert Merton's theory of the self-fulfilling prophecy prompts us to ask, if society has a tendency to cast certain categories of people as criminal types, will this assumption ensure that they will indeed be labeled and treated like criminals? This certainly seems to be true in

UNIFORM CRIME REPORT (UCR) an official measure of crime in the United States, produced by the FBI's official tabulation of every crime reported by more than 18,000 law enforcement agencies

VIOLENT CRIME crime in which violence is either the objective or the means to an end, including murder, rape, aggravated assault, and robbery

PROPERTY CRIME crime that does not involve violence, including burglary, larceny-theft, motor vehicle theft, and arson

CYBERCRIME crime committed via the Internet, including identity theft, embezzlement, fraud, sexual predation, and financial scams

the many cases of unarmed black men being killed by police. And, as David Matza warned, will our preconceived notions about a category of people influence our interpretations of numerical data? In this section, we look at the relationship between crime and demographics such as class, age, gender, and race and examine alternate explanations for what may seem like clear numerical fact.

CLASS Statistics consistently tell us that crime rates are higher in poor urban areas than in wealthier suburbs, but these higher crime rates may not actually be the result of increased criminal behavior. Rather, police tend to concentrate their efforts in urban areas, which they assume are more prone to crime, and thus make more arrests there. It appears that social class is more directly related to how citizens are officially treated by the police, courts, and prisons than to which individuals are likely to commit crime. And even if we do accept these statistics as an accurate representation of crime rates, such theorists as Robert Sampson and William Julius Wilson (2005) argue that the same factors that cause an area to become economically and socially disadvantaged also encourage criminal activity. Lack of jobs, lack of after-school child care, and lack of good schools, for example, are all factors that can lead to economic strain and criminal activity.

On the other end of the social class spectrum, **white collar crime** has been defined by sociologist Edwin Sutherland as "a crime committed by a person of respectability and high social status in the course of his occupation." White collar crime can include fraud, embezzlement, or insider trading. Most white collar criminals come from a relatively privileged background (Shover and Wright 2001), and it is no coincidence that white collar crime is policed and punished less strenuously than street crime.

Take the case of Elizabeth Holmes, founder and CEO of the now-defunct health technology company Theranos. Holmes launched the Silicon Valley blood-testing start-up in 2003 at the age of nineteen after dropping out of Stanford University. She was touted as the next tech visionary, in the mold of Steve Jobs or even Thomas Edison. She was poised to revolutionize the health-care industry with her blood-testing machine—nicknamed the Edison—that she claimed could run hundreds of tests with just a single drop of blood. Coming from a privileged background, Holmes was able to court big-money investors, including Rupert Murdoch, Betsy DeVos, Henry Kissinger, and the Walmart family heirs. By 2015, the company was valued at a staggering $9 billion. But there were growing concerns about the viability of the Edison machines and the company's testing methods, particularly after Theranos entered into a high-profile partnership with Walgreens pharmacies. Behind the scenes, things had been unraveling because the machines simply didn't work the way she said they did—a fact that Holmes had fought to keep secret. But the subterfuge caught up to her, leading to the spectacular implosion of Theranos after Holmes's deceptions were uncovered.

Blood on Her Hands? In 2018, Elizabeth Holmes, founder of the now-defunct blood-testing company Theranos, was charged by the Securities and Exchange Commission with "massive fraud" for deceiving both investors and patients. Fraud is a form of white collar crime.

In 2018, Holmes was charged by the Justice Department with defrauding her investors and forced to step down as CEO.

AGE The younger the population, the more likely its members are to commit crimes. Criminologists have shown that this relationship between age and crime has remained stable since 1935, with the peak age for arrests being nineteen. In the United States, fifteen- to nineteen-year-olds make up less than 7 percent of the population yet account for 12 percent of criminal arrests (Federal Bureau of Investigation 2018a). In addition, there is a specific set of laws, courts, and correctional facilities for juveniles.

> **WHITE COLLAR CRIME**
> crime committed by a high-status individual in the course of their occupation

Some acts are crimes only when they are committed by people under eighteen—curfew violations, for example. Juvenile courts usually involve bench trials (no jury), and some sentences (such as moving the offender into a foster home) are applied only in juvenile cases.

On the other end of the spectrum, people sixty-five and older make up about 15 percent of the population and account for only 1 percent of arrests (Federal Bureau of Investigation 2018a). We call this trend *aging out of crime*. Here, too, however, we must be careful about what we read into official

The Who, What, Where, and When of Crime The HBO series *The Wire* was set in Baltimore and focused on topics such as drug dealing, government corruption, and failed school systems. How would a criminologist explain this scene?

statistics. Since our stereotypical image of a criminal is youthful, it may be that the public and police are more likely to accuse and arrest young people and less likely to target seniors. In addition, youth may commit more visible crimes (like robbery or assault), while older people may commit crimes that are more difficult to detect, like embezzlement or fraud.

GENDER Males are more likely than females to commit crime. In fact, males accounted for 88 percent of arrests for murder and 73 percent of all arrests in 2017 (Federal Bureau of Investigation 2018a). Earlier researchers hypothesized that the gender difference in crime rates was based on physical, emotional, and psychological differences between men and women. The logic was that women were too weak, passive, or unintelligent to commit crime. This argument has been replaced by a focus on the social and economic roles of women. Starting in the 1970s, criminologists found that lower crime rates among women could be explained by their lower status in the power hierarchy. Conflict theorists such as James Messerschmidt (1993) argued that once women start gaining power in the labor market through education and income, crime rates among women will rise to more closely match those among men. This hypothesis has been largely supported by recent trends. Between 2008 and 2017, the number of males arrested decreased by a quarter (25 percent), while the number of females arrested decreased by only 14 percent (Federal Bureau of Investigation 2018a). So while at first glance it may seem logical to argue that women's crime rates are lower because of genetics, on closer examination, we see that social structure plays an important role.

RACE The relationship between race and crime is a controversial one. According to the UCR, African Americans make up 13 percent of the U.S. population but account for 27 percent of all arrests and 33 percent of all prisoners (Bronson and Carson 2019; Federal Bureau of Investigation 2018a). But sociologists caution against making a link between race and criminality. Instead, they highlight the role of institutional racism, where blacks have been disproportionately targeted by police and subjected to differential treatment in other parts of the judicial process. Sociologists also point to the role of class variables in explaining the relationship between race and crime. For example, we could hypothesize that African Americans are exposed to higher rates of crime because they are more likely to live in lower-income communities with more police presence and fewer opportunities and resources—and that here, it is class that matters more than race.

Race shapes life experiences even after criminal offenders have paid their debt to society: Legal scholar Michelle Alexander makes the argument that once African Americans (and in particular, African American men) come into contact with the criminal justice system, they are permanently stigmatized and stripped of their civil rights. As she explains in *The New Jim Crow: Mass Incarceration in the Age of Colorblindness*, "They are legally denied the ability to obtain employment, housing, and public benefits—much as African Americans were once forced into a segregated, second-class citizenship in the Jim Crow era" (2011, p. 4). For example, sociologist Devah Pager (2003) found that the stigma of a criminal record is much more damaging for black men than white men when it comes to finding a job. As part of her study, Pager sent out equally matched pairs of job applicants—one black and one white—and had them apply for actual entry-level jobs. The men took turns presenting themselves as having a criminal record. The results of Pager's study were eye-opening: While a criminal record closes many doors for both blacks and whites, it had a more deleterious effect on the black applicants. Perhaps even more shocking was the fact the study showed that a white man with a criminal record is more likely to receive a job call-back than a black man with no criminal record.

HATE CRIMES When criminals deliberately target victims because of their demographic characteristics (race, national origin, religion, gender, sexual orientation, or disability status) it's classified as a hate crime. Hate crime charges are usually added to other criminal charges, such as assault, arson, or vandalism, when it is suspected that the original crime was motivated by bias. Such crimes are investigated and prosecuted at both the local and federal levels. National hate crime statistics are collected by the FBI, although not all local jurisdictions participate in the counts. Given this information, we should recognize the likelihood that official statistics underreport hate crimes. In 2017, the FBI reported

IN THE FUTURE
American vs. Scandinavian Prisons

Because of the way we think about punishment in the United States, American prisons are usually imposing, windowless buildings, walled off with high fences, barbed wire, and armed guards. They are infamously overcrowded and often violent, and prisoners are in need of medical, rehabilitative, and mental health care of which they receive little. American prisons are placed either in the middle of nowhere (rural and less inhabited areas) or in the middle of impoverished and depopulated urban areas (so as to remain largely invisible to those who live in more privileged circumstances). Visiting a prison is something we consider doing only if we have an incarcerated relative to see or we want to rack up some volunteer hours. We certainly wouldn't consider touring prisons as vacation spots, nor would we want to stay long at any vacation spot that was itself too near a prison. We react to prisons and prisoners with fear and revulsion and institutionalize those emotions in the way we situate, construct, operate, and populate our penitentiaries.

This is not always the case in other parts of the world. In Scandinavia (Sweden, Denmark, and Norway) and neighboring Nordic countries like Finland and Iceland in particular, many of the penal complexes are what criminologists call "open" prisons. Organized more like boarding schools than detention centers, open prisons operate on a model very different from that used in the United States. Instead of focusing on retribution and incapacitation, Scandinavia's open prisons provide prisoners with an opportunity to rehabilitate themselves and reenter society as reformed, contributing members.

For example, Helsinki's Suomenlinna Island prison is not walled off from the surrounding town, which is located in a scenic archipelago that caters to tourists, arts patrons, and picnickers. Prisoners live in dormitory-like accommodations and hold jobs in the town's maintenance and tourism departments, doing upkeep on the facilities for wages that run from $6 to $10 per hour. They wear their own clothes, cook their own meals, and have televisions and sound systems in their rooms. They can visit with their families in Helsinki, and they have supportive rather than adversarial relationships with the guards.

Places like Sweden, Denmark, Finland, and Norway are, of course, smaller than the United States and somewhat more demographically homogeneous. However, Scandinavian prison populations are *proportionally* much smaller than U.S. prison populations (U.S. rates are ten times those of Scandinavian countries) and much more representative of the larger society in terms of racial and ethnic diversity. And after serving their debt to society, Scandinavian ex-cons are far less likely to reoffend: They have a recidivism rate that is less than half that of U.S. prisoners.

How do these countries do it?

Pundits will, of course, argue about which Scandinavian strategy is the key to such successful prisoner rehabilitation. But throughout the Nordic countries, criminal justice policy is governed by research rather than politics. Legislators do not make decisions about how to house, treat, or control prison populations; instead, social scientists do. Criminological research on what does and doesn't work forms the basis for decision making, and professionals in the criminal justice field are the ones who make those decisions. This is in stark contrast to the United States, in which "tough on crime" politics, fear-mongering media, and private corporate interests have created an overcrowded, violent, expensive, and ineffective prison system. If we were to approach criminal offenders with compassion rather than fear, would the results be different? Is this something we are willing to try?

Open Prisons Norway's Halden Prison uses education, job training, and therapy to help rehabilitate inmates. The Norwegian Correctional Service makes all inmates a "reintegration guarantee," helping them find homes and jobs once they are released.

7,175 hate crimes, of which close to 60 percent were racially motivated (Federal Bureau of Investigation 2018b). This represents an increase of 30 percent in just three years. The Southern Poverty Law Center (2019) has also documented a 30 percent increase in the number of hate groups in the United States since 2014, roughly coinciding with the Trump campaign and presidency.

CRIME AND INTERSECTIONALITY Finally, it is important to recognize that none of these variables—class, age, gender, race—affects crime rates in isolation; they work together to shape the experiences of individuals as well as the larger society. Nikki Jones's (2012) ethnographic study of inner-city African American girls in Philadelphia shows how all of these variables contribute to young women's experiences with violence in their everyday lives. For example, the girls in Jones's study find themselves caught in a bind as they attempt to navigate community standards of both respectability and practicality. In order to be perceived as "respectable," they must adhere to expectations, be "good girls," and avoid violence, while also meeting feminine and race-based appearance norms (such as slender bodies and light complexions). On the other hand, the practical realities of life in what are often risky neighborhoods mean these girls must be ready at any time to look and act tough and be willing to fight to defend themselves and others in direct violation of the "good girl" expectations. Thus, their race, class, gender, and age put them in a situation where they must navigate the competing demands of respectability and toughness, balancing their good girl image while always being prepared for the realities of crime and violence.

Deviance on TV Barry's hit man and RuPaul's drag queens are all norm violators.

DATA WORKSHOP

Analyzing Media and Pop Culture

Norm Breaking on Television

It's clear that deviance is a fascinating subject not only for sociologists but for millions of television viewers as well. That's why we've seen a proliferation of shows in recent years that feature people breaking almost every kind of social norm imaginable, from folkways to taboos. We might expect to see deviance covered in a talk show or newsmagazine program, but it's a staple of many other genres. We see it in reality TV shows like *Teen Mom*, which focuses on how high schoolers deal with pregnancy and parenthood, and *RuPaul's Drag Race,* which is a competition for the next drag queen superstar. But

it's not just reality TV shows that feature deviance. Dramas such as *Succession, Ozark,* or *The Handmaid's Tale*, comedies such as *The Good Place* or *Veep*, hybrids such as *Barry* or *Orange Is the New Black*, and even animated shows such as *The Simpsons* or *BoJack Horseman* all deal with various elements of the pathological or dysfunctional. And there are many more such shows that we could add to the list.

Why is there so much deviance on television? Are these shows merely entertainment, or is something more going on here? When we watch them, do we feel morally superior or get some kind of vicarious thrill? Does exposure to so much deviance help reinforce our social norms or serve to erode them?

For this Data Workshop you will be using existing sources and doing a content analysis of an episode from a particular TV show. Return to Chapter 2 for a review of this research method. Choose a contemporary TV show that is available for multiple viewings, either by recording it or accessing it online or on DVD. As you watch the episode, take some notes about the content and try to document all the ways in which deviant behavior is portrayed on the show. Then consider the following questions:

- Who is the intended audience for this program? Why did you choose it?

- What kind of deviance is featured? Give specific examples of situations, scenes, dialogue, or characters, and explain why they are examples of deviance.

- What kinds of deviance are missing from media portrayals?

- Is the deviance celebrated or condemned?

- How does it make you feel to watch the program?

- What effect do you think the show has on other viewers?

- Do you think the program supports or challenges prevailing social norms?

There are two options for completing this Data Workshop:

PREP-PAIR-SHARE Watch your chosen episode and bring some written notes to class that you can refer to in small-group discussions. Compare and contrast the analyses of the different programs in your group. What are the similarities and differences among programs?

DO-IT-YOURSELF View your chosen TV program, taking some informal notes about the episode. Write a three- to four-page essay answering the questions and reflecting on your own experience conducting this content analysis. What do you think these shows tell us about contemporary American society and our attitudes toward deviance? Attach your notes to the paper, and include a citation for the episode you viewed.

The Criminal Justice System

The question of **deterrence** is part of an ongoing debate about our criminal laws. Theorists who maintain that offenders carefully calculate the cost and benefits of each crime argue that punishment has a deterrent effect—that if the punishment seems too severe, people won't commit the crime. That's the logic behind California's controversial "three strikes" law: The punishment for three felonies is an automatic life sentence. While deterrence theory seems practical enough, it is important to note that in matters of sociology, seldom is there such a direct and causal link between two factors—in this case, the cost of punishment versus the benefit of the crime.

Other justifications for punishment include **retribution**—the notion that society has the right to "get even"—and **incapacitation**, the notion that criminals should be confined or even executed to protect society from further injury.

Some argue, though, that society should focus not on punishment but on **rehabilitation**: The prison system should try to reform the criminal so that once released, they will not return to a life of crime. Each approach to punishment invokes different ideas about who the criminal is and what their relationship is to the larger society: Are they someone who can plan ahead and curb their illegal behavior so as not to face a possible negative outcome? Are they someone who can work toward personal transformation? Are they someone who must be punished quid pro quo? Or should they just be removed from society permanently?

In the United States, the local, state, and federal government bureaucracies responsible for making laws, together with the police, courts, and prison systems, make up the **criminal justice system**—a system that, like any other social institution, reflects the society in which it operates. This means that while the American criminal justice system provides important benefits, such as social control and even employment for its workers, it also replicates some of the inequalities of power in our society. The research of Victor Rios, whom we introduced in the Part I opener, focuses on this issue.

Rios, a professor of sociology at the University of California, Santa Barbara, went from gang member to PhD partly because a teacher intervened and put him in touch with a mentoring program at a local university. Otherwise, Rios believes, he would have become another victim of the "youth control complex," his term for the way a variety of institutions, including law enforcement, the judicial system, and public schools, work together to "criminalize, stigmatize, and punish" working-class youth, particularly youth of color. Rios believes that the educational system has embraced a self-defeating strategy by adopting the attitudes and tactics of law enforcement, even as law enforcement and the judicial system have turned to more draconian measures. Increasingly, our society attempts to control gang violence and drug use with brute force, but this sort of indiscriminate policing often creates the very crime it is designed to eliminate as "enhanced policing, surveillance, and punitive treatment of youth of color" help to create a "school-to-prison pipeline" (Rios 2009, p. 151).

The death penalty is another case in point of the dysfunctions of the criminal justice system. Sociologists Katherine Beckett and Heather Evans's landmark study of capital murder cases in Washington State revealed that

DETERRENCE an approach to punishment that relies on the threat of harsh penalties to discourage people from committing crimes

RETRIBUTION an approach to punishment that emphasizes retaliation or revenge for the crime as the appropriate goal

INCAPACITATION an approach to punishment that seeks to protect society from criminals by imprisoning or executing them

REHABILITATION an approach to punishment that attempts to reform criminals as part of their penalty

CRIMINAL JUSTICE SYSTEM a collection of social institutions, such as legislatures, police, courts, and prisons, that creates and enforces laws

CAPITAL PUNISHMENT the death penalty

POSITIVE DEVIANCE actions considered deviant within a given context but later reinterpreted as appropriate or even heroic

black defendants were more than four times more likely to be sentenced to death than defendants of other races (Beckett and Evans 2014, 2016). In 2018, the Washington State Supreme Court ruled that the death penalty was unconstitutional. The justices cited Beckett and Evans's research, writing that the death penalty was "imposed in an arbitrary and racially biased manner." State governors in Illinois and California have placed a moratorium on **capital punishment** or have sought to abolish it altogether. When inequities and errors such as these exist in the criminal justice system, we must question the true meaning of the word "justice" in our society.

THE PRISON-INDUSTRIAL COMPLEX One trend in corrections in the United States is the switch from government-run prison systems to privately run penitentiaries. Once prisons are privately contracted, they become for-profit businesses that push for increased state subsidies while adopting cost-saving measures such as requiring unpaid labor from inmates and reducing spending on education, health care, and food for inmates. When prisons become businesses, they become more focused on their bottom line and pleasing shareholders than rehabilitating their prisoners. Critics of private prisons question the benefit of this trend, especially given the growth in the prison population that has coincided with prison privatization over the last twenty years.

RECONSIDERING DEVIANCE?

Because definitions of deviance are historically, culturally, and situationally specific, they are often in flux and can be contested in a variety of ways. If you think about it, most of our interpersonal arguments, legislative battles, and movements for social change are about the question of what is deviant. Remember the case of marijuana use and cultivation from the opening pages of this chapter? It's a perfect example of how the question of defining deviance is one that we will constantly wrestle with as a society.

Even in Durkheim's hypothetical "society of saints" (1895), deviance is unavoidable. But are there instances in which a rule violation is actually a principled act that should generate a positive rather than negative reaction? Sociologists use the term **positive deviance** to describe situations in which norms are broken in the name of the good. Next we provide two examples of positive deviance: In both cases, individuals broke laws and were initially seen as criminals. In hindsight, they are now considered heroes.

The first example is the simple act of civil disobedience performed by Rosa Parks on December 1, 1955, in Montgomery, Alabama, an act often considered pivotal in launching the civil rights movement. In those days, a Montgomery city ordinance required buses to be segregated: Whites sat in front and blacks in the back. Rosa Parks defied the law by refusing to give up her front seat to a white man and move to the back. Her arrest galvanized the black community and triggered a bus boycott and subsequent protests that eventually ended segregation in the South.

It is worth recognizing that Parks was not an accidental symbol; she was an experienced activist. In her one small, courageous act of defiance, she served as a catalyst that eventually helped to advance the fight against racial discrimination all across America. More than forty years after the day she took her seat on the bus, Parks was awarded the Presidential Medal of Freedom in 1996. When she died in 2005, it was front-page news. Her funeral was attended by luminaries of all types and races: mayors, members of Congress, presidents, CEOs, clergy, celebrities, and as many others as could fit into the packed church and spill outside its doors.

The second example is the story of three soldiers who put a stop to a massacre during the Vietnam War. On March 16, 1968, the men of Charlie Company, a U.S. battalion under the command of Lieutenant William Calley, stormed into the village of My Lai in South Vietnam on a "search and destroy" mission and opened fire on its civilian inhabitants. The boys and men of the village had gone to tend the fields, leaving only unarmed women, children, and the elderly. Hundreds were killed on that terrible day, in direct violation of military law. Although the soldiers should have ceased fire when they saw that the enemy (members of the Viet Cong) was not present, they obeyed the commands of their leaders and continued ravaging the village. Calley was later convicted in a court martial; his men, claiming that they were only "following orders," were not held responsible.

The massacre would have continued unchecked had it not been for three other American soldiers—Hugh Thompson, Lawrence Colburn, and Glenn Andreotta—who flew their helicopter into the middle of the carnage at My Lai, against the orders of their superiors, and called for backup help to airlift dozens of survivors to safety. They then turned their guns on their fellow Americans, threatening to shoot if they tried to harm any more villagers. For years, the army tried to cover up the three men's heroism in order to keep the whole ugly truth of My Lai a secret. But finally, in 1998, the men were recognized for their bravery and heroism with medals and citations—for having had the courage and skill to perform a perilous rescue and the moral conviction necessary to defy authority.

Can you think of a time when someone in your community exhibited positive deviance?

Closing Comments

The sociological study of crime and deviance raises complicated issues of morality and ethics. When we study sensitive topics like rape and alcoholism or vulnerable populations like juvenile delinquents and the mentally ill, we have a responsibility as scholars to recognize the effects our attention may have on the people we study. As David Matza noted, we must try to eschew moral judgments in our work, no matter how difficult that may be. And as our professional code of ethics demonstrates, we must protect the people we study from any negative outcomes. Groups lodged under the rubric of deviance can be disempowered by this label, and policy decisions made on the basis of social science research may further injure an already marginalized group. On the other hand, a sociological perspective on deviance and crime provides for the possibility that groups previously labeled and marginalized may someday receive assistance and legitimacy from the larger society as well. The sociological perspective is a powerful tool.

APPLYING WHAT YOU'VE LEARNED

Let's Talk More

1. There are many ways to be mildly deviant without breaking any laws. How do we sanction minor deviant acts?

2. Have you ever known someone to reject the "deviant" label and turn his or her negative identity into a positive one? What was the deviant identity? What term describes this sort of deviance? Do you know anyone who has embraced a stigmatized role through deviance avowal? How might these strategies be useful to individuals?

3. The United States has the dubious distinction of leading the world in both the largest total number and the largest percentage of incarcerated citizens. Why do you think America has more prisoners than any other country?

4. Provide a real-life example of positive deviance. What norms were violated? What was the outcome? Does your belief system affect whether you perceive this deviance as positive? (How might someone else have viewed it as negative?)

Let's Explore More

1. **Film** DuVernay, Ava, dir. *13th.* 2016.

2. **Article** Young, Molly. "Pet Walruses, Hidden Bacon and Other Violations of Actual U.S. Law." *The New York Times.* May 23, 2019.

3. **Blog Post** Kaufman, Peter. "Understanding Violence Sociologically." *Everyday Sociology* (blog). October 14, 2014.
   http://WWNorton.com/rd/f2RJb.

PART III
Understanding Inequality

All societies have systems for grouping, ranking, and categorizing people, and within any social structure some people occupy superior positions and others hold inferior positions. While such distinctions may appear to be natural, emanating from real differences among people, they are actually social constructions. Society has created and given meaning to such concepts as class, race, and gender, and consequently, those concepts have taken on great social significance. The social analyst's job is to understand how these categories are established in the first place, how they are maintained or changed, and how they affect society and the lives of individuals.

Sociologist Matthew Desmond's book *Evicted: Poverty and Profit in the American City* (2016) tells the story of eight families struggling to keep a roof over their heads. Desmond embedded himself in two communities in Milwaukee to conduct his ethnographic study, living alongside and closely following these families as they contended with eviction and its fallout. He weaves together several story lines: One is about impoverished residents and their troubles finding stable, affordable places to live, and the landlords who profit from this arrangement; one about black and white tenants living in separate parts of a segregated city; and another about the different life experiences and social outcomes for men, women, and children. The book considers the intersections among class (Chapter 7), race (Chapter 8), and gender (Chapter 9) in the social structure of the city and in the inhabitants' lived experiences. In many ways, *Evicted* brings together the themes of these next three chapters.

Arleen and her two sons—Jori and Jafaris—are evicted from their home when a man kicks down their front door after Jori throws a snowball at the man's car. Arleen is forced to take her boys to a local shelter, where they stay for a few months before moving to an apartment without regular running water on Milwaukee's largely black North Side. Just a few weeks after they move in, the city deems the place uninhabitable and Arleen is forced to move again, this time to an apartment deeper in the inner city that she soon finds is a haven for drug dealers. After four months, she's able to find her and her boys an apartment in one of the three dozen buildings owned by Sherrena, a busy and successful landlord who specializes in renting to poor and disadvantaged tenants. Her other tenants include Lamar, a Vietnam veteran who lost his legs in an accident, and his two sons; Doreen and her four children; Patrice, Doreen's daughter, who has three children of her own; and Crystal, a teenager dealing with mental illness. All of them, including Arleen and her sons, will eventually be evicted.

College Mobile Home Park is located on the far South Side of Milwaukee, a largely white area of town. Among the residents are Scott, a drug addict who lost his nursing license for stealing opioids from patients; Pam and Ned, who are also addicts and expecting a baby, to add to Pam's other two children; and Larraine, a woman suffering from numerous health problems. The run-down trailer park is owned by Tobin, who lives some seventy miles away, and is managed by Lenny and Susie. All of them will be evicted, too, or lose their jobs, when Tobin brings in a new property manager after receiving multiple code violations and hundreds of police calls related to the trailer park.

Every year, millions of Americans are evicted from their homes. While we might assume most poor families receive federal assistance or live in public housing, the reality is much more complicated. The wait for public housing can last for decades. In fact, nationwide, three out of four families who qualify for assistance receive nothing. Pushed into the private housing market, poor families are often forced to spend 70 to 80 percent of their income on rent, leaving them with very little to live on.

Part of the problem is that the market rate for private housing in poorer neighborhoods is rarely much cheaper than rents in better-off parts of town. As Sherrena tells Desmond, "The 'hood is good" (p. 152). The high demand for affordable housing keeps vacancy rates low, creating a situation ripe for exploitation. Without a clean record, a decent credit rating, or a paycheck stub to show for themselves, marginalized families are often compelled to accept whatever they can get. Much of the time the housing is substandard: Clogged sinks and toilets, broken doors and windows, and filthy carpets infested with vermin are just some of the conditions tenants are forced to live with. For landlords keen to make a profit, it may be less expensive to evict a tenant who complains about their housing than to maintain or repair a rental property. And it's not hard to find a reason to evict someone; just being

a day late on rent or making a 911 call may be cause enough in places like Milwaukee. Of the landlords Desmond followed, Sherrena cleared $10,000 a month on rentals that were filled with people at or below the poverty line, while Tobin hauled in over $400,000 a year from the trailer park.

Eviction court is another of the places where class, race, and gender intersect to create vast disparities among different groups of people. Only about 30 percent of renters show up to fight an eviction, and they are often outmatched. Most landlords can afford a lawyer to appear with them in court, while the low-income defendants are not provided with public defenders as they would be in a criminal proceeding. Some 90 percent of landlords have attorneys representing them, while 90 percent of tenants do not. In a typical housing court in Milwaukee, three in four people are black. Of those, three in four are women—many with children living at home. As Desmond notes, "If incarceration had come to define the lives of men from impoverished black neighborhoods, eviction was shaping the lives of women. Poor black men were locked up. Poor black women were locked out" (p. 98).

You might assume that poverty leads to eviction, but it also works the other way around. Desmond is emphatic on this point: "Eviction is a cause, not just a condition, of poverty" (p. 299). It is hard to overstate how traumatic and all-consuming eviction is; it upends people's lives and has far-reaching consequences. As Desmond explains, "Losing a home sends families to shelters, abandoned houses, and the street. It invites depression and illness, compels families to move into degrading housing in dangerous neighborhoods, uproots communities, and harms children" (p. 5). Social change may be difficult, but Desmond believes it is possible: "Solutions depend on a single question: do we believe that the right to a decent home is part of what it means to be American?" (p. 300). *Evicted*, which was awarded the Pulitzer Prize in 2017, addresses many of the same issues around social inequality and the intersections of class, race, and gender that we will consider in the next set of chapters.

CHAPTER 7

Social Class: The Structure of Inequality

College is supposed to enhance your future career choices and increase your future earning power, right? But the thing about these future benefits is just that—they are awarded in the future, not in the now. While you're still in school, the cliché of the "broke college student" may not be a cliché at all: Students make many sacrifices in order to attend school, and among those sacrifices may be their own immediate financial security. Statistics show that almost half of students struggle to find a stable living situation while in college, and almost as many experience what is called food insecurity: limited or uncertain access to the food they need to survive while in school.

Sociologist Sara Goldrick-Rab and her colleagues at the Wisconsin HOPE Center have conducted the largest-ever studies of the experiences of college students with food and housing insecurity. Their "Hungry and Homeless" surveys focus on the ability—and inability—of students at two- and four-year institutions to meet their basic needs for food and housing. Many struggle to do so: 36 percent of university students and 42 percent of community college students were food insecure in the 30 days preceding the 2017 survey (Goldrick-Rab et al. 2018). Nearly one in three community college students and one in four university students indicated that they skipped meals or reduced the size of their meals because they didn't have enough money.

Goldrick-Rab and her colleagues also found that 36 percent of university students and 51 percent of community college students were housing insecure, meaning that they had difficulty paying rent or utilities or faced other housing-related challenges. Finally, 9 percent of university students and 12 percent of community college students were home-less in the last year. The proportions of students struggling to meet these basic needs were higher for women than for men, and for LGBTQ students compared to heterosexual students. And as you might imagine, this kind of basic needs insecurity is not good for academic outcomes—students who struggle with food and housing issues have worse grades and lower graduation rates (Broton 2017).

As a result, many colleges and universities have begun trying to help in various ways, such as stocking and staffing on-campus food pantries for students in need. At Northern Illinois University, for instance, the pantry started off campus at a local church, and then moved on campus into unused space in the old field house; it now serves students one evening a week. Other campuses, like Chicago's DePaul University, operate emergency home-placement services so that homeless students can find shelter with local families who are willing to help. Kennesaw State University in Georgia provides year-round housing so that students have somewhere to live over winter and summer breaks. And Amarillo College in Texas has an on-campus emergency aid center that consolidates information and services for students in need.

How shocking is it for you to realize that in the world's wealthiest country, students struggle like this as they try to better themselves? Unfortunately, given the scope of the problem, it may not be a surprise to you at all. Inequalities on college campuses are real, and they reflect the inequalities of the larger society as well.

How to Read This Chapter

In this chapter, we will examine the phenomenon of stratification that occurs in all human societies, our own included. Despite rhetorical claims about equality of opportunity for all, America is a profoundly hierarchical society, with the benefits and rewards of living here unequally distributed among its people. A sociological perspective on stratification will increase your understanding in several important ways. First, it will help you recognize inequities in places you may have overlooked, such as your own town, neighborhood, or school, and in the media. Second, it will help you consider how social divisions and hierarchies of privilege and disadvantage appear across many of our institutions; access to health care, the justice system, employment, and housing are all governed by structures of inequality. Third, it should enable you to identify your own place in these social arrangements and to see how some of your own life chances have been shaped by your position (or your family's position) in certain hierarchies. Finally, a knowledge of stratification may help you play a role in changing systems of inequality. Look for ways that you can alleviate some of the problems that social inequality causes—if you can have an impact, even a small one, then this chapter will not have been in vain!

SOCIAL STRATIFICATION AND SOCIAL INEQUALITY

Social stratification in one form or another is present in all societies. This means that members of a given society are categorized and divided into groups, which are then placed in a social hierarchy. Members may be grouped according to their gender, race, class, age, or other characteristics, depending on whatever criteria are important to that society. Some groups will be ranked higher in the social strata (levels), while others will fall into the lower ranks. The higher-level groups enjoy more access to the rewards and resources within that society, leaving lower-level groups with less.

This unequal distribution of wealth, power, and prestige results in what is called **social inequality**. We find several different systems of stratification operating in the United States, where it is not hard to demonstrate that being wealthy, white, heterosexual, or male typically confers a higher status (and all that goes along with it) on a person than does being poor, nonwhite, queer, or female. Because social inequality affects a person's life experience so profoundly, it is worthwhile to examine how stratification works.

There are four basic principles of social stratification. First, it is a characteristic of a society, rather than a reflection of individual differences. For instance, if we say that in

Japan men rank higher in the social hierarchy than women, this doesn't mean that a particular woman, such as actress/singer Ryoko Hirosue, couldn't attain a higher status than a particular man; it means only that in Japan as a whole, men rank higher. Second, social stratification persists over generations. In Great Britain, a child inherits not only physical characteristics such as race but also other indicators of class standing, such as regional accent. It is because of this principle of stratification that wealthy families remain wealthy from one generation to the next.

Third, while all societies stratify their members, different societies use different criteria for ranking them. For instance, the criterion in industrialized nations is material wealth (social class), but in hunter-gatherer societies, such as the Khoisan Bushmen of southern Africa, it is gender. Fourth, social stratification is maintained through beliefs that are widely shared by members of society. In the United States, it is still common to think that people are poor not only because of the existing class structure but also because they have somehow failed to "pull themselves up by their bootstraps."

> **SOCIAL STRATIFICATION** the division of society into groups arranged in a social hierarchy
>
> **SOCIAL INEQUALITY** the unequal distribution of wealth, power, or prestige among members of a society
>
> **SLAVERY** the most extreme form of social stratification, based on the ownership of people

SYSTEMS OF STRATIFICATION

In order to better understand social stratification, it is useful to examine various historical periods and to make global comparisons across cultures. So here we look at three major systems of stratification: slavery, caste, and social class.

Slavery

Slavery, the most extreme system of social stratification, relegates people to the status of property, mainly for the purpose of providing labor for the slave owner. Slaves can thus be bought and sold like any other commodity. They aren't paid for their labor and in fact are forced to work under mental or physical threat. Occupying the lowest rank in the social hierarchy, slaves have none of the rights common to free members of the same societies in which they live.

Slavery has been practiced since the earliest times (the Bible features stories of the Israelites as slaves in Egypt) and has continued for millennia in South America, Europe, and the United States. Sometimes the race, nationality, or religion of the slave owners was the same as that of the slaves, as was the case in ancient Greece and Rome. Historically, a person could become enslaved in one of several ways. One way was through debt: A person who couldn't repay what he

CASTE SYSTEM a form of social stratification in which status is determined by one's family history and background and cannot be changed

APARTHEID the system of segregation of racial and ethnic groups that was legal in South Africa between 1948 and 1991

owed might be taken into slavery by his creditor. Another way was through warfare: Groups of vanquished soldiers might become slaves to the victors, and the women and children of the losing side could also be taken into slavery. A person who was caught committing a crime could become a slave as a kind of punishment and as a means of compensating the victim. And some slaves were captured and kidnapped, as in the case of the transatlantic slave trade from Africa to the Americas.

Slavery as an economic system was profitable for the slave owner. In most systems of slavery, people were slaves for life, doing work in agriculture, construction, mining, or domestic service, and sometimes in the military, industry, or commerce. Their children would also become slaves, thus making the owner a greater profit. In some systems, however, slavery was temporary, and some slaves could buy their own freedom.

Slavery is now prohibited by every nation in the world, as stated in the Universal Declaration of Human Rights. Not only is it illegal, but it is considered immoral as well. Nevertheless, the shocking fact is that slavery continues to exist today in such places as India, South Asia, West Africa, and many other places around the world in the form of child soldiers, serfdom, forced and bonded laborers, human trafficking, and sex slaves.

Modern-Day Slavery Women and children work in a brickyard in Pakistan. Bonded labor is one form of modern slavery.

America and the Western world are not exempt from these same shocking practices either, where people are held as agricultural, domestic, and sex slaves. The National Human Trafficking Hotline reported over 8,500 cases of slavery in the United States in 2017 alone; more than 70 percent of those cases involved sexual slavery, and more than 30 percent occurred in just three states (California, Texas, and Florida). Americans also play an indirect role in supporting slavery elsewhere in the world by purchasing and using products made with slave labor (Bales and Soodalter 2009). Using a somewhat broader definition of slavery that includes all of the above plus other conditions such as forced marriage, debt bondage, and the sale or exploitation of children, researchers at the International Labour Organization and the Walk Free Foundation (2017) believe there are more than 40 million people trapped in some form of modern slavery.

Caste

Caste represents another type of social stratification found in various parts of the world. The traditional **caste system** is based on heredity, whereby whole groups of people are born into a certain stratum. Castes may be differentiated along religious, economic, or political lines, as well as by skin color or other physical characteristics. The caste system creates a highly stratified society where there is little or no chance of a person changing her position within the hierarchy, no matter what she may achieve individually. Members must marry within their own group, and their caste ranking is passed on to their children. In general, members of higher-ranking castes tend to be more prosperous, whereas members of lower-ranking castes tend to have fewer material resources, live in abject poverty, and suffer discrimination.

India is the country most closely associated with the caste system, based there in the Hindu (majority) religion. The caste system ranks individuals into one of five categories: *Brahman* (scholars and priests), *ksatriya* or *chhetri* (rulers and warriors), *vaisya* (merchants and traders), *sudra* (farmers, artisans, and laborers), and *the untouchables* (social outcasts). The caste system is a reflection of what Hindus call *karma*, the complex moral law of cause and effect that governs the universe (Cohen 2001). According to this belief, membership in a particular caste is seen as a well-deserved reward or punishment for virtuous or sinful behavior in a past life. Caste is thus considered a spiritual rather than material status, but it still results in real-world inequalities. Caste-related segregation and discrimination were prohibited in 1949 by India's constitution, but they are still prevalent. Resistance to social change remains, and thus far the social ramifications of the caste system have not been completely dismantled.

THE CASE OF SOUTH AFRICA An important example of the caste system was **apartheid**, a legal separation of racial and ethnic groups that was enforced between 1948 and 1991 in

South Africa. The term itself literally means "apartness" in Afrikaans and Dutch. The consequence of apartheid was to create great disparity among those in the different strata of society.

South Africans were legally classified into four main racial groups: white (English and Dutch heritage), Indian (from India), "colored" (mixed race), and black. Blacks formed a large majority, at 60 percent of the population. These groups were geographically and socially separated from one another. Blacks were forcibly removed from almost 80 percent of the country, which was reserved for the three minority groups, and were relocated to independent "homelands" similar to the Indian reservations in the United States. They could not enter other parts of the country without a pass—usually in order to work as "guest laborers" in white areas. Ironically, African Americans visiting South Africa were given "honorary white" status and could move freely within the country. Social services for whites and nonwhites were separate as well: Schools, hospitals, buses, parks, beaches, libraries, theaters, public restrooms, and even graveyards were segregated. Indians and "coloreds" were also discriminated against, though they usually led slightly more privileged lives than blacks. Despite claims of "separate but equal," the standard of living among whites far exceeded that of any other group.

In South Africa under the apartheid system, whites held all the political, economic, and social power, despite being a numerical minority. It was not long before civil unrest and resistance to the system began developing within both South Africa and the international community. Blacks and even some whites began to organize wage strikes and demonstrations, and sanctions were imposed by Western nations. The plights of high-profile anti-apartheid leaders such as Steve Biko and Nelson Mandela became known worldwide. Pressure on the white government continued to grow, until the country was in an almost constant state of emergency. In 1991, apartheid as a legal institution was finally abolished. Its legacy, however, has been much more difficult to dismantle.

It has been over twenty-five years since democratic elections in which all South African citizens could participate were first held in 1994. And still change is happening very slowly. Although nonwhites now share the same rights and privileges as whites, social inequality and discrimination have decreased little (Nattras and Seekings 2001; Seekings and Nattras 2005). South Africa remains a country with one of the most unequal distributions of income in the world. The wealthiest 10 percent of the population own more than 90 percent of national wealth and earn more than 55 percent of total income; this upper economic stratum is almost exclusively composed of whites, a group that makes up just 8 percent of South Africa's population (Orthofer 2016). Though black incomes and employment rates have improved, a large income gap remains, with the rich, and especially the already rich whites, getting richer (Boyle 2009). On average, whites are still paid three times more than blacks (World Bank 2018).

Multiracial Comedian *Daily Show* host Trevor Noah was born in South Africa to a black mother and a white father during the apartheid era. His memoir is titled *Born a Crime*.

There are other measures of wealth inequality that persist as well. Whites still own around 72 percent of the individually held land in South Africa, despite promises to redistribute land to blacks (Mbatha 2018; Atauhene 2011). The restoration of land seized during apartheid is only slowly being accomplished and at a price to those making claims. Similar inequalities between whites and other races in South Africa are present in education, health care, and the criminal justice system. In some ways, new patterns of class stratification are replacing rather than erasing old patterns of racial stratification.

THE NEW JIM CROW Law professor and civil rights attorney Michelle Alexander (2011) argues that there is a similar caste system in the United States but that it operates through the criminal justice system. While it is no longer legal or socially acceptable to discriminate against people based on race, Americans still allow discrimination based on criminal convictions; in other words, felons are denied many of their citizenship rights, including voting, in many states, even after they have been released from prison. And since black men are disproportionately represented in the prison population, they are also disproportionately affected by felon disenfranchisement and the lifelong stigmatization associated with the identity of the ex-con. "An extraordinary percentage of black men in the United States are legally barred from voting today, just as they have been throughout most of American history,"

Although stratification systems in other countries may appear different from those in the United States, they all result in patterns of inequality. Brazil, for example, has a system of stratification based on skin color rather than (but closely related to) race. In Iran the most important distinction is religious: Muslim versus non-Muslim. Finally, Sweden tries to minimize economic inequality (but doesn't entirely succeed) with government support programs for all.

Brazil

Race is a powerful influence on social stratification in Brazil, where the situation is even more complex than in the United States. By any standards, Brazil is a remarkably diverse nation. The early settlers to the area were mainly European, and with their arrival the number of native inhabitants declined sharply as a result of violence and disease. Through the mid-1800s, slaves from Africa were imported, and in the twentieth century, a new wave of immigrants arrived from Asia and the Middle East.

For much of Brazilian history, the European whites enjoyed a privileged status. However, as people from different races married and raised children, new racial categories emerged. Sociologist Gilberto Freyre claimed in 1970 that this new mixture of races and cultures was a unique strength that led to

Polite Racism While intermarriage has eliminated distinct racial groups, Brazil remains stratified by race.

SOCIAL CLASS a system of stratification based on access to such resources as wealth, property, power, and prestige

SOCIOECONOMIC STATUS (SES) a measure of an individual's place within a social class system; often used interchangeably with "class"

argues Alexander. "They are also subject to legalized discrimination in employment, housing, education, public benefits, and jury service, just as their parents, grandparents, and great-grandparents were." Instead of slavery or the segregation laws of the Jim Crow era, Alexander writes, discriminatory criminal laws and an unfair justice system enforce racial inequality in the United States today.

Social Class

Social class, a system of stratification practiced primarily in capitalist societies, ranks groups of people according to their wealth, property, power, and prestige. It is also referred to by sociologists as **socioeconomic status (SES)** to keep in mind the social as well as economic basis of this system of

stratification. The social class system is much less rigid than the caste system. Although children tend to "inherit" the social class of their parents, during the course of a lifetime they can move up or down levels in the strata. Strictly speaking, social class is not based on race, ethnicity, gender, or age, although, as we will see, there is often an overlap between class and other variables.

INTERSECTIONALITY It is important to recognize that while social statistics often address issues of inequality one variable at a time, social actors do not. In other words, we experience our lives not just as "middle-class" or "working-class" or "upper-class" people, but as women and men; blacks, whites, Latinos, and Asians; college or high school graduates; Christians, Jews, or Muslims; spouses or singles; and so on. Our lived experience is one of **intersectionality**, a concept that acknowledges that multiple dimensions of status and inequality intersect to shape who we are and how we live (Crenshaw 1991). Our life chances are influenced by our class *and* our race *and* our gender *and* our religion *and* our age (*and* multiple other categories) all together, not one at a time.

something like a "racial democracy." Although the idea was appealing, it was subsequently challenged by other social scientists, who argued that Brazil was still highly stratified by race, if only in a less obvious way (Telles 2004). Intermarriage may have eliminated clearly defined racial groups, but skin color still largely defines an individual's place in society, with light-skinned Brazilians enjoying privileges of wealth and power denied to their dark-skinned counterparts. Contemporary critics have referred to this inequality as *racismo cordial*, or "polite racism."

Iran

The basis for social stratification in Iran has undergone radical changes since the Islamic Revolution in 1979, which transformed the country from a constitutional monarchy to a theocracy. Before the revolution, political and economic power was concentrated in the upper class, made up of landowners, industrialists, and business executives; the middle class consisted of entrepreneurs, small-business owners, merchants, and members of the civil service. Economic mobility was an option largely for those with secular values and a Western education—that is, those who had gone to college in the United States or Europe and who believed in the separation of church and state. After the revolution, however, religion became a primary influence on stratification. Many members of the civil service who were not Muslim or who held Western university degrees were forced into exile; those who remained were required to attend special classes on Islamic law in order to keep their positions. Strict observance of Islamic law and custom has become a prerequisite for maintaining one's social position, and many of the new political elites are religious leaders.

Sweden

Sweden has deliberately attempted to craft a system that lessens social inequality, a policy made somewhat easier, perhaps, by the country's relative homogeneity of race, ethnicity, and religion. Sweden provides its citizens with a far greater number of social services than the United States does: The government guarantees its citizens a high level of access to health care, education, child and elderly care, unemployment benefits, and public facilities like libraries and parks. In order to furnish such programs, taxes are high, with a top taxation rate of 60 percent for the wealthiest Swedes. Although the Swedish system certainly has its problems (high taxation rates among them), there are demonstrated benefits, including increased life expectancy and literacy, and decreased infant mortality, homelessness, poverty, and crime.

An example of this can be seen in the ethnographic research of sociologist Karyn R. Lacy (2007), who studied black middle-class suburbanites in the Washington, DC, region. As Lacy's findings show, social status is more complex than just a "middle-class" salary might indicate: Her respondents' identities were shaped by their income, occupation (in mostly white-dominated professions), residential status (as suburban homeowners), and race. In fact, many reported being frustrated as they tried to convince others (such as store employees, real-estate agents, and bankers) that they were among the middle class in the first place; their race obscured their class in the eyes of whites and made it difficult for whites to see them as "belonging" in certain neighborhoods or business establishments at all. This is an example of how, in the reality of everyday life, race and class are experienced as inseparable; their effects on our experiences are intertwined, even as we attempt to unravel them in different chapters in sociology textbooks. Keep this concept of intersectionality in mind as you read on about class and then again in subsequent chapters when we address other forms of social inequality.

Sociologists are not always in agreement about what determines class standing or where the boundaries are between different social classes. We will consider some of these disagreements after first taking a look at the United States and its class system.

SOCIAL CLASSES IN THE UNITED STATES

It is difficult to draw exact lines between the social classes in the United States; in fact, it may be useful to imagine them as occurring along a continuum rather than being strictly divided. The most commonly identified categories are upper class, middle class, and lower class. If we want to make even finer distinctions, the middle class can be divided into the upper-middle, middle, and working (or lower-middle) class (Gilbert 2014; Wright et al. 1982). You probably have some idea of which class you belong to,

> **INTERSECTIONALITY** a concept that identifies how different categories of inequality (race, class, gender, etc.) intersect to shape the lives of individuals and groups

UPPER CLASS an elite and largely self-sustaining group who possess most of the country's wealth

UPPER-MIDDLE CLASS social class consisting of mostly highly educated professionals and managers who have considerable financial stability

even if you don't know the exact definition of each category. Interestingly, most Americans claim that they belong somewhere in the middle class even when their life experiences and backgrounds would suggest otherwise. While keeping in mind that the borders between the classes can be blurry, let's examine a typical model of the different social classes (Figure 7.1).

The Upper Class

The **upper class** makes up just 1 percent of the U.S. population, but its total net worth is greater than that of the bottom 90 percent combined (Wolff 2017). The upper class consists of elites who have gained membership in various ways. Some, like the Rockefellers and Carnegies, come into "old money" through family fortunes; others, like Elon Musk or Cardi B, generate "new money" through individual achievements. Many in the upper class maintain that status by investing enormous sums of money and taking advantage of whopping tax deductions offered to those with investment-based fortunes. Members of this class make more than $1.5 million per year (and sometimes far more than that), mostly through investments rather than income from working, and are often highly educated and influential. They tend to attend private schools and prestigious universities and display a distinctive lifestyle; some seek positions of power in government or philanthropy. The upper class is largely self-sustaining, with most members remaining stable and few new ones able to gain membership in its ranks.

The Upper-Middle Class

The **upper-middle class** comprises about 14 percent of the population. This group tends to be well educated (with college or postgraduate degrees) and highly skilled. Members work primarily in executive, managerial, and professional jobs. They may enjoy modest support from investments but generally depend on income from salaried work, making around $150,000 per year. As a result, the upper-middle class is most likely to feel some financial stability. They usually own their homes and may especially value activities like travel and higher education.

CLASS	Percentage of Population	Typical Household Incomes	Typical Occupations	Typical Education
UPPER CLASS	1%	$2 million	Investors, heirs, executives, media/sports personalities	Some prestigious university degrees
UPPER-MIDDLE CLASS	14%	$150,000	Professionals and managers	College and university degrees, some graduate degrees
MIDDLE CLASS	30%	$70,000	Semi-professionals, lower-level managers, white collar and highly skilled blue collar jobs	Two- and four-year college degrees
WORKING (LOWER-MIDDLE) CLASS	30%	$40,000	Semiskilled labor, service, manual, and clerical jobs	High school degrees
WORKING POOR	13%	$25,000	Low and unskilled workers, lower-paid manual and service jobs, seasonal work	Some high school
UNDERCLASS	12%	$15,000	Seldom employed or unemployed, part-time labor, many rely on public or private assistance	Some high school

FIGURE 7.1 The U.S. Social Class Ladder

SOURCE: Gilbert 2014.

The Middle Class

The **middle class** makes up about 30 percent of the population, a number that has recently stabilized after shrinking for several years as a result of a variety of phenomena, including economic recession, along with high unemployment, corporate downsizing, and outsourcing of work to foreign countries. Many people who would have once been considered middle class may have moved down to the lower-middle class, while some others have moved up to the upper-middle class. The middle class comprises primarily **white collar** workers, skilled laborers in technical and lower-management jobs, small entrepreneurs, and others earning around $70,000 per year. Most members have a high school education and a two- or four-year college degree. While members of the middle class have traditionally been homeowners (a sign of having achieved the American Dream), this trend changed during the recent recession and the associated banking and mortgage crises. Along with issues like the cost of housing, and given other debts carried by many Americans, not all middle-class people can afford their own homes anymore.

The Working (Lower-Middle) Class

The **working class**, or **lower-middle class**, makes up about 30 percent of the population. Members typically have a high school education and generally work in manual labor, or **blue collar**, jobs, as well as in the service industry (retail, restaurant, tourism, etc.)—jobs that are often more routine, where employees have little control in the workplace. Members of the working class typically earn around $40,000 per year. A small portion, especially those who belong to a union, may earn above-average incomes for this class. Working-class people typically have a low net worth and live in rental housing or in a modest home they have inherited or long saved for.

The Working Poor and Underclass

The **working poor** constitute approximately 13 percent of the population. Members are generally not well educated; most have not completed high school and experience lower levels of literacy than the other classes. They may also lack other work skills valuable in the job market. Typical occupations include unskilled, temporary, and seasonal jobs—including minimum-wage jobs, housekeeping, day labor, and migrant agricultural work. The average income is around $25,000. This group suffers from higher rates of unemployment and underemployment, with some members receiving social welfare subsidies.

Another 12 percent of the population, the **underclass**, could be categorized as truly disadvantaged. These Americans live in poverty conditions and typically earn $15,000 or less per year. As such, they may have chronic difficulty getting enough money to support their basic needs. They may hold a few steady jobs and depend on public benefits or charity to survive. They are often found in inner cities, where they live in substandard housing or are homeless; their numbers are increasing in the suburbs as well. They are part of a group that is considered officially impoverished by federal government standards. A separate section later in this chapter will be devoted to discussing poverty.

Problematic Categories

Because SES is based on a collection of complex variables (including income, wealth, and education, as well as power or prestige), it is difficult to say exactly where, for example, middle class ends and upper class begins. In addition, individuals may embody a variety of characteristics that make precise SES classification difficult. Someone may be highly educated, for example, but make money cleaning houses while working on her novel.

So how would we categorize a person such as the late Sam Walton, founder of Walmart? He was the product of a struggling "Okie" family, a farm boy and state college graduate who became a billionaire businessman. Walton did not come from a background of privilege; he neither attended an elite university nor worked in a prestigious occupation. He was called "America's shopkeeper," and despite amassing a huge fortune, Walton remained close to his rural roots. What sociologists would say is that Walton is an example of **status inconsistency**, or stark contrasts between the levels of the various statuses he occupied. Another example is Mother Teresa, a Catholic nun who ministered to the poor, sick, and dying in Calcutta, India. As a member of the clergy, she held some occupational prestige, but her religious order took vows of poverty, and she had virtually no personal wealth. Yet Mother Teresa was regularly ranked as among the most admired people of the twentieth century. She garnered numerous

MIDDLE CLASS social class composed primarily of white collar workers with a broad range of education and incomes

WHITE COLLAR a description characterizing lower-level professional and management workers and some highly skilled laborers in technical jobs

WORKING CLASS or **LOWER-MIDDLE CLASS** social class consisting of mostly blue collar or service industry workers who are less likely to have a college degree

BLUE COLLAR a description characterizing skilled and semiskilled workers who perform manual labor or work in service or clerical jobs

WORKING POOR poorly educated manual and service workers who may work full-time but remain near or below the poverty line

UNDERCLASS the poorest group, comprising the homeless and chronically unemployed who may depend on public or private assistance

STATUS INCONSISTENCY a situation in which an individual holds differing and contradictory levels of status in terms of wealth, power, prestige, or other elements of socioeconomic status

Status Inconsistencies
Sam Walton, the "Okie" billionaire, and Mother Teresa, the Catholic nun who was revered around the world but had no personal wealth, are two examples that complicate SES classifications.

FEUDAL SYSTEM a system of social stratification based on a hereditary nobility who were responsible for and served by a lower stratum of forced laborers called serfs

WEALTH a measure of net worth that includes income, property, and other assets

PRESTIGE the social honor people are given because of their membership in well-regarded social groups

honors, including the Nobel Peace Prize, but she was most concerned with how to parlay whatever power she gained into helping the world's most needy.

Of course, not all examples are quite this dramatic, but status inconsistencies are especially prevalent in the United States because of our "open" class system. Class mobility (which will be discussed in more detail later) is less easily attainable here than in many other countries (Chetty et al. 2014b), though Americans tend to strongly believe otherwise. While we seem to be able to recognize class distinctions implicitly, there are no systematic ways of delineating each category. Still, sociologists have made an effort to understand and define class, and we turn now to the theories that result from those efforts.

THEORIES OF SOCIAL CLASS

In this section, we will look at social stratification from the perspectives of each of the major schools of thought within sociology. We start with classical conflict and Weberian theories and structural functionalism, and then consider postmodern and symbolic interactionist theories. Each

perspective offers different ideas about what determines social class, with the macro theorists focusing on larger-scale social structures and the postmodern and micro theorists focusing more on meaning, interpretation, and interactions in everyday life.

Conflict Theory

Karl Marx formed his social theories at a time when monumental changes were occurring in the stratification systems that characterized nineteenth-century Europe. The **feudal system**, which consisted of a hierarchy of privileged nobles who were responsible for and served by a lower stratum of serfs (forced laborers), was breaking down. Cities were growing larger as more people moved from rural areas to take part in the new forms of industry that were emerging there. With these changes, what had traditionally determined a person's social standing (whether one was born a noble or a serf) was no longer as relevant. Marx was concerned about a new kind of social inequality that he saw emerging—between the capitalists (bourgeoisie), who owned the means of production, and the workers (proletariat), who owned only their own labor.

Marx argued that economic relationships were quickly becoming the only social relationships that mattered: The impersonal forces of the market were creating a new, rigid system of social stratification in which capitalists had every economic advantage and workers had none. He believed that the classes would remain divided and social inequality would grow; that wealth and privilege would be concentrated among a small group of capitalists and that workers would continue to be exploited. Contemporary conflict theorists continue to understand social class in a similar way. Erik Olin Wright (1997), for example, describes an animated film he made as a student in which the pawns on a chessboard attempt to overthrow the aristocracy (kings, queens, knights, and bishops) but realize that the "rules of the game" doom them to relive the same unequal roles—a metaphor for the way social structure shapes and sustains inequality.

Weberian Theory

Max Weber noted that owning the means of production was not the only way of achieving upper-class status; a person could also accumulate **wealth** consisting of income and property. As a contemporary example, Microsoft and Facebook are both publicly traded companies on the stock market, which means that they are owned by thousands of individual shareholders who benefit when the company turns a profit. But the people who started those companies have amassed far greater fortunes. In 2018, Amazon founder Jeff Bezos (worth $160 billion) was the richest person in the world, while Facebook co-founder Mark Zuckerberg (worth $71 billion) was #5 (Kroll and Dolan 2018). Weber suggested that power (the ability to impose one's will on others) should be considered as part of the equation when measuring a person's class standing. Although they may not own their corporations, executives can exert influence over the marketplace, consumers, and the work lives of their employees. And they can use their wealth to support various causes and campaigns.

Weber believed that another important element in social class has to do with **prestige**, the social honor granted to people because of their membership in certain groups. A person's occupation is a common source of prestige: In a typical ranking, you might find physicians near the top and janitors near the bottom. Take note that athletes rank higher than sociologists in Table 7.1. People's relative prestige can affect not only their wealth or power but also how they are perceived in social situations. Wealth by itself can also be a source of prestige, though not always. In some social circles, especially those that are more traditional or have a history of aristocracy, a distinction is made between "old money" and "new money." In the United States it is more prestigious to come from a family heritage of wealth than to have recently made a fortune.

For Weber, wealth, power, and prestige are interrelated because they often come together, but it is also possible to convert one to the other. The Kardashian sisters, for example, whose father Robert was a wealthy attorney (most memorably in the O.J. Simpson case) and a businessman who inherited his parents' meat-packing fortune, turned that aspect of their status into a certain type of contemporary prestige—celebrity. They did little themselves to gain their prestige besides being born into wealth and being willing to participate in the reality

TABLE 7.1 The Relative Social Prestige of Selected Occupations in the United States

White-Collar Occupations	Prestige Score	Blue-Collar Occupations
Physician	86	
Lawyer	75	
Professor	74	
Architect	73	
Dentist	72	
Member of the Clergy	69	
Pharmacist	68	
Registered Nurse	66	
	65	Athlete
Electrical Engineer	64	
Veterinarian	62	
Airplane Pilot	61	
Sociologist	61	
	60	Police Officer
Actor	58	
	53	Firefighter
Social Worker	52	
	51	Electrician
	46	Secretary
	40	Farmer
	36	Child-Care Worker
	36	Hairdresser
	31	Auto-Body Repairperson
Cashier	29	
	28	Waiter/Waitress
	22	Janitor

SOURCE: National Opinion Research Center 2015.

shows that now bear their names. Still, it is important to distinguish these three elements: Property and wealth can be inherited or earned, power usually comes from occupying certain roles within organizations, and prestige is based on a person's social identity and is bestowed by others.

Structural Functionalism

Functionalism emphasizes social order and solidarity based on commonly shared values about what is good and worthwhile. In this view, the system of stratification that has emerged over time, though not egalitarian, is still functional for society in a number of ways. Because there are a variety of roles to perform for the maintenance and good of the whole, there must be incentives to ensure that individuals will occupy those roles that are most necessary or important. Kingsley Davis and Wilbert Moore (1945) discussed some of the principles of stratification that result in a system of rewards that are unequally distributed among various roles. The assumption is that some roles are more desirable than others and may require greater talent or training. In addition, certain roles may be more critical than others to the functioning of society, as well as difficult to fill, so there must be a mechanism for attracting and securing the best individuals to those positions. This would mean that there is widespread consensus about which positions are most important—either in terms of their special qualifications or the potential scarcity of qualified individuals to occupy those positions—and that society accepts the need to bestow rewards upon people who are considered of greater importance.

SOCIAL REPRODUCTION the tendency of social classes to remain relatively stable as class status is passed down from one generation to the next

CULTURAL CAPITAL the tastes, habits, expectations, skills, knowledge, and other cultural assets that help us gain advantages in society

Take, for instance, the role of a physician, which has the highest ranking of occupational prestige in American society (National Opinion Research Center 2015). Doctors play an important role in providing highly prized services to other members of society. Think of the steps it takes to become a doctor. A person must have an extensive education and graduate training and must complete a long and intensive internship before being certified to practice medicine. This individual also devotes a great deal of personal resources of time and money to this process. It is further assumed that there are only so many people who might have the talent and determination to become doctors, and so it follows that there must be incentives or rewards for them to enter the field of medicine.

The functionalist perspective helps explain the existing system of social stratification and its persistence, but it still leaves us with questions about the structured inequalities that it continues to reproduce. Is it really functional for social rewards (such as wealth, power, and prestige) to be so

unequally divided among members of society? And while we might agree that doctors are very important to society, are they more so than teachers and carpenters? Our heroes of pop culture (famous actors, athletes, musicians) can rise to the highest ranks while our everyday heroes (day-care providers, firefighters, mechanics) may struggle to make a living. Whose values are structuring the system and, after closer scrutiny, is it clear that compensating stockbrokers more than bricklayers is really functional to society as a whole? We will revisit some of these questions in later sections of the chapter.

Postmodernism

Sociologist Pierre Bourdieu (1973, 1984) studied French schools to examine a phenomenon referred to as **social reproduction**, which means that social class is passed down from one generation to the next and thus remains relatively stable. According to Bourdieu, this happens as a result of each generation's acquisition of what he called **cultural capital**: Children inherit tastes, habits, and expectations from their parents, and this cultural capital either helps or hinders them as they become adults. For example, having highly educated parents who can help with homework and enforce useful study habits makes it more likely a child will succeed in school. Just the parents' expectation that their children will earn similar credentials can be a powerful incentive. Since better-educated parents tend to come from the middle and upper classes, their children will also have better chances to attain that same status.

According to Bourdieu, cultural capital also shapes the perceptions that others form about a person. For instance, in job interviews, the candidates who can best impress a potential

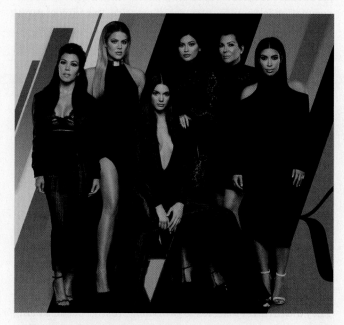

Social Reproduction The Kardashian sisters are famous for being famous. How did their inherited wealth influence their career paths?

employer with their social skills may be chosen over other workers who may be equally qualified but less adept socially. Since cultural capital has such profound effects, people often try to acquire it—to "better" themselves. They may take adult education classes, attend lectures and concerts, join a tennis club, or travel to Europe—all in an attempt to increase their cultural capital. Often, however, the effects of early childhood are too powerful to overcome. It can be difficult for someone who grew up in a less privileged environment to project a different class background; accent, for example, may be a giveaway ("He talks like a hillbilly," "She just sounds too 'street'").

Symbolic Interactionism

Macrosociologists, who study social systems on a large scale, believe that there is little an individual can do to change systems of structured inequality. Interactionists, on the other hand, believe that all social structures—including systems of inequality—are constructed from the building blocks of everyday interaction. For instance, sociologist David Sudnow (1972) argues that we make split-second judgments about who people are and which social status they occupy based on appearance. We take action based on what we observe "at a glance." Along the same lines, Aaron Cicourel (1972) suggests that we make inferences about the status of others when we encounter them in different social situations. For example, you may assume that the passengers sitting in the first-class cabin of an airplane are wealthier than those in coach. But perhaps one of those first-class passengers is a "starving student" whose seat was upgraded because coach was overbooked—by thrifty millionaires. "Wealthy," "poor," and "middle class" are statuses that, rather than existing in and of themselves, are continuously being negotiated in interaction.

Erving Goffman (1956) noted that we "read" different aspects of identity by interpreting the behavior of others and that we become accustomed to others "reading" our behavior in the same way. This means that our clothing, our speech, our gestures, the cars we drive, the homes we live in, the people we hang out with, and the things we do on vacation are all part of our presentation of self and provide information that others use to make judgments about our SES. In turn, we look for these same clues in the behavior of others. This type of **everyday class consciousness**, or awareness of our own and others' social status, is important for us to understand but difficult to identify empirically.

As a humorous answer to this dilemma, University of Pennsylvania English professor Paul Fussell (1983) created the "living room scale," which lists items that we may find in someone's living room and attaches point values to them. For example, if you have a copy of the *New York Review of Books* on your coffee table, add five points. A copy of *Popular Mechanics*? Subtract five. A working fireplace? Add four. A wall unit with built-in television and stereo? Subtract four. Add three points for each black-and-white family photograph

Everyday Class Consciousness Clothes, cars, homes, and vacation plans are all indicators of socioeconomic status. What impression does this living room give of who might live here?

in a sterling silver frame; subtract three points for any work of art depicting cowboys. When we total the final score, higher numbers indicate higher SES, and vice versa.

While Fussell's living room scale may seem like a joke, we really do make snap judgments about the status of others based on just this sort of information. (Here it should be noted that in Dr. Stein's living room, the fireplace and TV wall unit are side by side, while Dr. Ferris's living room features a silver-framed black-and-white photograph of her father as a child—dressed like a cowboy, on horseback! As we've said before, real life sometimes defies easy categorization.) The Data Workshop that follows will help you see how swiftly and automatically you employ class categories in your interactions with others.

> **EVERYDAY CLASS CONSCIOUSNESS** awareness of one's own social status and that of others

While we have considered the theories of macrosociologists and symbolic interactionists separately here, there are actually some intersections between interaction and structure. Our identities as "working class" or "privileged" individuals may be structured by preexisting categories, yet those identities are also performed every day in our interactions with others. Contemporary scholars have conducted studies that make this connection clear. For example, Sarah Kristian (2018), who studied young people in an isolated, rural Newfoundland town, found that the way the young people spoke correlated with their ambitions for social mobility. The youths who aspired to get out of their remote location in order to seek socioeconomic opportunities elsewhere tended to speak more standard English, while the youths without such aspirations spoke in more nonstandard, rural-identified ways (such as dropping the "g" in "-ing" words). These linguistic patterns suggest that who one wants to be, including one's socioeconomic aspirations, shapes one's interactional style.

All the information we gather at a glance is used to make evaluations of others' wealth, income, occupation, education, and other categories that indicate status and prestige. In some ways, it doesn't matter whether we're right—especially in anonymous public places like airports. You should be aware, however, that you do use these cues to evaluate the status of others in split seconds and that you act on those evaluations every day. Maybe you chose to stand on the bus or on the subway rather than sit next to someone who didn't look quite "right"—whatever that means to you. Often, we end up falling back on stereotypes that may lead us to false conclusions about a person's status or character. When it comes to everyday class consciousness, appearances are sometimes deceiving, but they are always consequential.

DATA WORKSHOP

Analyzing Everyday Life

Everyday Class Consciousness

When we are out in public places, we can quickly gather bits of information about other people in the social environment. These "data" are useful in forming judgments and evaluations about them. Even the smallest presentational details can tell us something about who they are. So, how do you know which social class other people belong to? How do you feel about the fact that others will also be trying to figure out *your* class status? Do the assessments we make about others (and that they make about us) influence our thoughts, attitudes, and behavior? What are the consequences of everyday class consciousness?

In this Data Workshop, you will be conducting participant observation research to understand more about how we size up other people in terms of their socioeconomic status. Return to the section in Chapter 2 for a refresher on ethnography/participant observation research methods. First, choose a location to be the field site for your study; it should be a busy public place with a variety of passersby. You will want to be both a participant and an observer in the setting. So, for example, you could pretend to be waiting for someone at the airport, sitting in the food court at the mall, or standing in line at the post office. Next, you'll want to make some discreet but in-depth observations about a small number of people in the setting. One way to take a simple sample of the population is to select every seventh or tenth person who walks by you. Spend several long moments looking closely at him or her. Ask yourself quickly: What class status do you think this person holds? Don't think too long at this point; just register your guess. Continue this process as you observe another three or four people. Now it is time to write some ethnographic field notes, preferably while you're still in the field or as soon as possible afterward. You'll want your notes to include as many details as possible about the people you selected.

Consider the following questions as you analyze your data. What kinds of things did you observe about others that helped inform your evaluation of their class status—height, weight, race, age, gender, hairstyle, tattoos, piercings, watch or other jewelry, or makeup? Perhaps their style of dress, the colors, fabrics, or logos on a T-shirt, hat, purse, sunglasses, or shoes caught your attention. Did you notice anything else, such as the person's posture, voice, or mannerisms? If you observed someone on the street, did you see the car they were driving? What was its make, year, and condition? Did you notice other status clues in any accessories the person had—a laptop or smartphone, a baby stroller or shopping bags? How did the setting itself (mall, post office, airport) influence your assumptions about their social class standing?

There are two options for completing this Data Workshop:

PREP-PAIR-SHARE Conduct your participant observation research according to the instructions. Prepare some ethnographic field notes that you can refer to in class. Get together with one or more of your fellow students and share your experiences. Note similarities and differences in the criteria used by each group member to determine the social class of the people they observed.

DO-IT-YOURSELF Conduct your research in a public place and write a three- to four-page essay describing your observations of four to five people from the field site. Answer the questions in the preceding section, and make specific reference to your field notes as the data to support your analysis (remember to attach the field notes to your paper). What are the consequences of everyday class consciousness? How does it affect your perceptions, attitudes, and behavior?

SOCIOECONOMIC STATUS AND LIFE CHANCES

Belonging to a certain social class brings such profound consequences that it's possible to make general predictions about a person's life chances in regard to education, work, crime, family, and health just by knowing his or her SES. The following discussion may help you appreciate the respective privileges and hardships associated with different levels of the social hierarchy.

Family

Sociologists know that people are likely to marry or have long-term relationships with persons whose social and cultural backgrounds are similar to their own—not because they are looking for such similarities, but simply because they have more access to people like themselves. When you develop ties to classmates, fellow workers, neighbors, and members of clubs, these people may share your cultural background as well as your social class. It is from such groups that marriage and domestic partners most often come.

Of course, people do marry across class lines, and when they do, these class differences can pose problems for the couples. Sociologist Jessi Streib found that many unanticipated conflicts can crop up in cross-class marriages, such as differing approaches to career advancement or child-rearing practices (Streib 2015): Partners with higher socioeconomic status are often more deliberate and organized about such things, while partners with lower socioeconomic status are more likely to be open to various possibilities and willing to "go with the flow." But she also found that cross-class partners often found each other attractive specifically because of some of these differences, and that lasting unions were possible across socioeconomic lines.

Social class also plays a role in the age at which people marry: While men and women across all social classes are delaying marriage, people with college degrees get married later on average than their less educated peers (Wang 2018). People with higher levels of education are also less likely to get divorced (Lewis and Kreider 2015; Wang 2015). The age at which people start a family and the number of children they have are also related to educational attainment. The average age at which women with a master's degree or more have their first child is thirty, while the average age for women with a high school diploma is just twenty-four. Less educated women also have a higher average number of births throughout their lifetime than more educated women. On average, women without a high school diploma have 2.9 children, whereas women with a bachelor's degree or higher have about 2.2 children (Livingston 2015).

Health

Those at the bottom of the social class ladder are the least likely to obtain adequate nutrition, shelter, clothing, and health care and are thus more prone to illness. Often they cannot afford to see a doctor, fill a prescription, or go to a hospital. Instead of preventing an illness from becoming worse, they must wait until a health crisis occurs, and then they have no option but expensive emergency room care. Health-care reforms, such as those provided by the Affordable Care Act, are meant to help change that pattern.

A recent study out of Stanford University found that for men, the richest 1 percent live, on average, nearly fifteen years longer than the poorest 1 percent. For women, the gap in life expectancy was just over ten years (Chetty et al. 2016b). One factor that contributes to these disparities in health is exercise. As income increases, so does the likelihood of a person engaging in some physical activity. For instance, only 14 percent of respondents living below the poverty level meet federal guidelines for physical activity, compared with 31 percent of those living at the higher income level (National Center for Health Statistics 2018). Education may have something to do with these disparities, as more knowledge about the health benefits of exercise may lead to more active participation. But we can also see exercise as a luxury for those in higher social classes, who are not struggling with the day-to-day efforts to survive that characterize the lives of the poor.

Education

How children perform in school determines whether and where they go to college, what professions they enter, and how much they are paid. And generally, those with more education make more money. The median annual earnings for young adults with bachelor's degrees is $51,800; with high school diplomas it's $32,000; and without a high school diploma it's $26,000 (National Center for Education Statistics 2019a). On the surface, these earnings may seem fair. After all, shouldn't people with more education make more money? However, as sociologists, we must probe further and ask some fundamental questions; for example, who has access to education, and how good is that education?

One of the main goals of education is to make sure students get a chance to succeed both in school and in life. But to meet this goal, schools would have to serve all students equally, and they aren't always able to do so. Because schools are financed with local property taxes, and school district borders are usually drawn along lines that reflect residential segregation by both class and race, schools themselves are still often racially segregated and unequally funded (Lombardo 2019). Schools with low-income students often receive fewer resources, have greater difficulty in attracting qualified teachers, and experience less support from parents (Fischer and Kmec 2004).

A student's social class background will also influence their attitude toward education. The higher the family's SES, the higher the student's expectations for educational achievement. Students from higher social classes are expected to complete more years of school and are more likely to attend—and graduate from—college than those from lower social classes (Bozick et al. 2010; Reardon 2012). It's not surprising to find that 78 percent of high school students from the highest family income quartile enroll in college, compared to just 48 percent of those in the lowest quartile (Figure 7.2). Even larger than the gap in college enrollment between the rich and poor is the gap in graduation rates: Young adults from families in the top income group are nearly five times more likely to earn a bachelor's degree or higher by age twenty-four than young adults from families in the bottom income group (62 percent versus 13 percent) (Cahalan et al. 2019).

Although educational attainment is at an all-time high in the United States, a high school education doesn't mean what it once did. College and advanced degrees are becoming more important. If the trends continue, fewer and fewer jobs will be available to those without college degrees, and of those jobs, fewer will support middle-class lifestyles. Yet not all students are equally prepared for or able to afford a college education, which creates a risk that children from lower socioeconomic backgrounds will slip farther down the social class ladder.

Work and Income

Income is the product of work, and members of different social classes, with unequal educational opportunities, tend to work in different types of jobs—jobs that produce unequal levels of income. In the past couple of decades, we have seen a widening income gap between those at the top, middle, and bottom of the scale (Figure 7.3). And in the past few years those at the top of the income scale have seen much greater recovery from the Great Recession than those in the middle or at the bottom. In fact, when comparing 2007 income with 2017 income, those in the middle have barely recovered to their pre-recession incomes, while some at the bottom have yet to do so. Those in the top income groups, on the other hand, have exceeded the income growth rates of the others by hundreds of percentage points (Gould and Wolfe 2018).

At the bottom of the scale, members of the lower class generally experience difficulties in the job market and may endure periods of unemployment or underemployment (working in a job that doesn't pay enough to support a person's needs, is seasonal or temporary, or doesn't make full use of the person's skills). This includes the working poor, people whose incomes keep them in poverty despite the fact that they spend at least half of the year in the labor force. The working poor often hold jobs in service occupations such as food service, housekeeping, and maintenance (U.S. Bureau of Labor Statistics 2018a). Also included in the lower class are people receiving various forms of government aid.

Members of the working (lower-middle) class work for wages in a variety of blue collar jobs. They can generally earn a dependable income through skilled or semiskilled occupations, but they may also experience periods of unemployment tied to fluctuations in the economy, layoffs, and plant closings. While factory work and other types of skilled labor were once enough to support a middle-class lifestyle, most middle-class jobs today are found in the service, information,

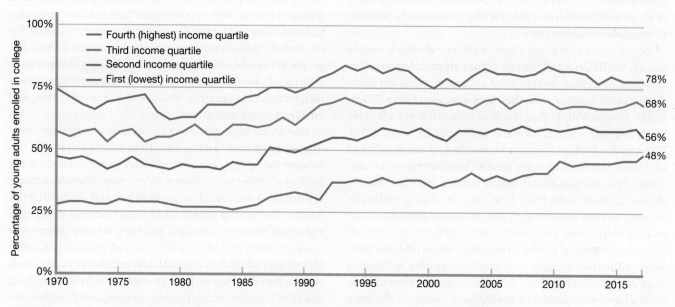

FIGURE 7.2 Two- or Four-Year College Participation Rates, by Income Level, 1970–2017

SOURCE: Cahalan et al. 2019.

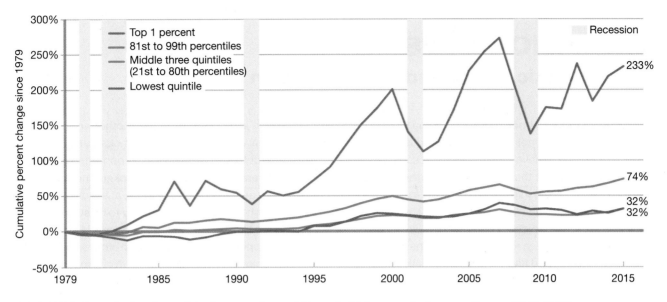

FIGURE 7.3 Cumulative Growth in Average Annual Household Income, by Income Group, 1979–2015

SOURCE: Congressional Budget Office 2018.

and technology sectors. Most households here require two incomes to maintain a comfortable lifestyle, and many middle-class jobs require some sort of college degree. Those in the upper-middle class tend to work in executive and professional fields. Some members are business owners; a small portion own large farms or ranches. Others, known as the "creative class" (Florida 2002)—architects, writers, scientists, artists, professors, and engineers—tend to cluster in "creative" cities, such as Austin, San Francisco, and Seattle.

Through exceptional success in any profession or art, or through inheritance, one can join the upper class. In the United States, the upper class is influential in politics, business, and culture, largely because of its economic privilege: In our highly stratified society, the top 1 percent consistently captures around 20 percent of all income, through jobs in finance, management, medicine, and law, for example. The incomes of the top 10 percent hover at around 50 percent of all income, while the other 50 percent of all income is distributed among the remaining 90 percent of the population (Saez 2019).

As a result of the recent recession, workers—most often in lower-middle and lower-class occupations—increasingly find themselves engaging in what is termed "precarious labor" (Kalleberg 2009). Precarious labor is work that is uncertain, unpredictable, and unprotected, such as contract labor, temporary work, or part-time work. Economic fluctuations often affect these workers first, placing them at greater risk of layoffs because of downsizing and outsourcing. Corporations seeking to cut costs have resorted to a variety of strategies. Some have restructured their workforce and made do with leaner payrolls, while others have relocated their operations overseas in countries where labor costs are lower. Both

manufacturing and service jobs are subject to downsizing and outsourcing, meaning that blue collar and white collar workers—and even some higher-ranking executives—are now vulnerable. Their jobs, and class status, may be more precarious than ever before.

Criminal Justice

In general, people of lower SES are more likely to encounter the criminal justice system, whether as a perpetrator or victim of a crime, than those of higher SES. But the statistics are not as straightforward as they might seem. People in lower classes are often more visible, less powerful, and thus more likely to be apprehended and labeled as criminals than those from higher social classes. There are also differences in how crimes are prosecuted. White collar criminals are less likely to be arrested, prosecuted, or convicted than ordinary "street" criminals (Schwellenbach 2008). White collar criminals (such as Enron heads Jeffrey Skilling and the late Kenneth Lay, and Bernie Madoff, whose Ponzi scheme bilked wealthy clients out of billions of dollars) can also afford the best legal representation and hence enjoy distinct advantages in the courtroom. If white collar criminals are convicted, their sentences are likely to be lighter.

Studies have found that 90 percent of inmates on death row could not afford to hire a lawyer when they were tried (Lane and Tabak 1991) and that the quality of representation, rather than the actual facts presented in a trial, determines whether someone is sentenced to death (ACLU 2003). Studies have also shown that race and SES influence whether the death penalty is sought. Prosecutors are more likely to seek the death penalty in counties with larger black

IN RELATIONSHIPS
Socioeconomic Status and Mate Selection

You say you don't judge a book by its cover? You say it's the person who matters, and not the social categories he or she belongs to? We may believe these things, but sociological studies strongly suggest that we don't act on them. When it comes to dating, courtship, and marriage ("mate selection" activities, as defined by social scientists), we tend to make homogamous choices. **Homogamy** ("like marries like") means that we choose romantic partners based on our similarities in background and group membership. Despite the old adage that "opposites attract," decades of sociological research show that we make choices based on similarities in race, ethnicity, religion, class, education, age—even height and levels of physical attractiveness (Kalmijn 1998). Homogamy based on socioeconomic status is especially clear: We tend to marry those who share the same economic and educational backgrounds. This holds true even if we practice **heterogamy** (marrying someone who is different from us) in other areas, such as race or religion. Why is class-based homogamy so prevalent?

As it turns out, we have relatively few opportunities to meet people of different socioeconomic backgrounds during the course of our everyday lives. At home, at school, on the job, at the coffee shop or gym, we are likely to be surrounded by those who are like us, classwise. Homogamy is more strictly enforced in upper-class families than in other social classes. Those who enjoy the privileges of wealth often want to make sure those privileges continue into the next generation and may monitor their children's activities by sending them to prestigious schools and posh summer camps so that they don't get the opportunity to meet anyone but other privileged kids. This helps ensure that wealth and power remain consolidated within a relatively small community. If you spend all your free time at the country club pool instead of getting a summer job at Starbucks or McDonald's, your opportunities to meet the hoi polloi are limited.

If we focus only on those in the public eye, it is easy to see how limits on opportunity result in marriages between affluent and powerful families. This happens in political families. For example, Julie Nixon, daughter of a former U.S. president, married David Eisenhower, grandson of another former president. Kerry Kennedy, daughter of

HOMOGAMY the tendency to choose romantic partners who are similar to us in terms of class, race, education, religion, and other social group membership

HETEROGAMY the tendency to choose romantic partners who are dissimilar to us in terms of class, race, education, religion, and other social group membership

HYPERGAMY marrying "up" in the social class hierarchy

HYPOGAMY marrying "down" in the social class hierarchy

populations, and juries are more likely to sentence black defendants to death (Beckett and Evans 2014). Meanwhile, those who are able to hire legal counsel are less likely to be sentenced to death. Therefore, the intersection of race and SES can dramatically affect the outcome of criminal sentencing (Phillips 2009).

Lower-class people are also more likely to be the victims of violent crime. In fact, people living in poor households are more than twice as likely to be victims of violent crime than those in high-income households (Harrell et al. 2014). The work of researchers with the Heartland Alliance in Chicago suggests that this is in part because poverty and violence can stem from the same causes, including cycles of unaddressed trauma and historical discrimination in poor neighborhoods and rural areas (Buitrago, Rynell, and Tuttle 2017).

At the same time, people with lower SES are also more likely to feel at risk of harassment by police. As both education and income decreased, respondents reported

feeling more threatened by police; as education and income increased, they felt less threatened (Levinson 2002). Those at the very bottom of the socioeconomic hierarchy—such as the homeless people living on Los Angeles's Skid Row—often feel hassled by the police no matter what kind of contact they have (Stuart 2016). According to sociologist Forrest Stuart, who conducted an in-depth ethnography of Skid Row, some police officers consider it their job to help homeless people (what Stuart refers to as "therapeutic policing") but have only certain types of tools available with which to do so. They use arrests and ticketing for minor offenses like jaywalking and loitering as leverage to push homeless individuals into shelters or rehabilitation programs, something the individuals themselves see as harassment. And in one case, when homeless men started their own weight-lifting program to keep themselves healthy and occupied, the police shut it down, claiming it was an unacceptable distraction from the programs offered by the formally operated shelters. Skid

former attorney general Robert Kennedy, married (and later divorced) Andrew Cuomo, son of former New York governor Mario Cuomo. After the divorce, Andrew ascended to the New York governor's mansion as well and found love again with Food Network star Sandra Lee. And it happens among celebrities, whether movie stars Ryan Reynolds and Blake Lively, singers Beyoncé and Jay-Z, or NFL quarterback Tom Brady and supermodel Gisele Bündchen. All practiced a form of status homogamy by partnering with people from the same social circles—other famous and wealthy celebrities. Whether they met on set, at the yacht club, or at an awards show, they met in a status-restricted setting to which not everyone is eligible for entry.

Questions have arisen recently about how Internet technologies may facilitate—or impede—our tendency toward homogamy. Dating apps allow people who occupy vastly different social circles to meet online—and perhaps fall in love. In this way, it would seem that Internet dating has the potential to inhibit our off-line predilection for people who belong to the same social groups as we do. On the other hand, Internet dating can also assist us in choosing people who are like us, in that certain sites cater to particular social groups: J Date (for Jewish singles), The League (for Ivy Leaguers), BlackPeopleMeet (for black singles), and even TrekDating.com (for *Star Trek* fans). As these and other such sites specifically select for social group membership, they may actually strengthen homogamous effects in online mate selection processes.

Jay-Z and Beyoncé Knowles "Like marries like."

Vast differences in class standing between marital partners are usually the stuff of fairy tales and fantasy. The "Cinderella story," in which a low-status woman is romantically "rescued" by a high-status man, is familiar to us all—yet we likely have seen it happen only in storybooks and movie theaters. Classics like *Sabrina* and *Pretty Woman* feature low-status women being wooed by wealthy men. The only touch of sociological reality in these tales is the portrayal of women's **hypergamy** and men's **hypogamy**; that is, when class boundaries are crossed, women usually marry up while men marry down. Take a look at the role of SES in your own mate selection activities: Are you homogamous or heterogamous?

Row residents are, in a sense, unable to protect themselves from the efforts of police to compel them into rehab or shelter life. Even if police are doing it "for their own good," it is also disempowering, and for a group with so little power already, this is a big deal.

Social class affects more than just our financial or material state—it is intricately woven into the fabric of our lives. You may once have concluded that differences in people's education, work, family, or health were simply a matter of individual preference or effort, or that each individual is responsible for her own circumstances. While this may be true to some extent, research shows that social class background has a profound impact on one's life chances, leading those with different statuses into very different life courses. This means that we can't take for granted whatever advantages or disadvantages we might experience but should acknowledge how hierarchies of inequality have helped create our particular social realities.

SOCIAL MOBILITY

How do people move from one social class to another? In other words, how do they achieve social mobility? Sociologists use the concept of **social mobility** to measure movement within the stratification system of a particular society, whether it's a small town, a state, or a nation. In some societies, social mobility is highly restricted by formal or informal rules. India's caste system is an example of what sociologists refer to as a **closed system**: There is very little opportunity for social mobility among classes. The United States, where social mobility is possible, is perceived to be an **open system**. But that wasn't

> **SOCIAL MOBILITY** the movement of individuals or groups within the hierarchical system of social classes
>
> **CLOSED SYSTEM** a social system with very little opportunity to move from one class to another
>
> **OPEN SYSTEM** a social system with ample opportunities to move from one class to another

College Admissions Scandal People at the top of the social class ladder, like Lori Loughlin, can use their money and power to ensure their children remain at the top.

INTERGENERATIONAL MOBILITY movement between social classes that occurs from one generation to the next

INTRAGENERATIONAL MOBILITY movement between social classes that occurs during the course of an individual's lifetime

HORIZONTAL SOCIAL MOBILITY the movement of individuals or groups within a particular social class, most often a result of changing occupations

VERTICAL SOCIAL MOBILITY the movement between different class statuses, often called either upward mobility or downward mobility

STRUCTURAL MOBILITY changes in the social status of large numbers of people as a result of structural changes in society

always the case. In the period before the Civil War, slavery was widespread, keeping African Americans from climbing the social class ladder, and there are still vestiges of this problem with us today.

The movement of people among social classes can happen in three ways: through intergenerational mobility, intragenerational mobility, or structural mobility. **Intergenerational mobility** refers to the movement that occurs from one generation to the next, when a child eventually moves into a different social class from that of her parents. Americans have always placed great faith in the idea of economic mobility. Research shows that Baby Boomers (the generation of children born immediately after World War II) have, for the most part, achieved upward intergenerational mobility: On the whole, they amassed more wealth during the course of their lives and consequently moved up the social class ladder.

Since then, however, mobility seems to have stalled and in the last fifty years it has not gotten any easier to climb the social class ladder, despite progressive social policy changes that were intended to help more people. A recent study of trends in intergenerational mobility found that a child born into the bottom fifth of the income distribution has just a 9 percent chance of moving into the top fifth (Chetty et al. 2014b). Conversely, there are many mechanisms in place, such as tax laws and social policies, that allow those at the top of the ladder to protect their assets and pass them down to the next generation, making it more difficult for the middle and lower classes to improve their positions. This phenomenon can be amplified when members of elite groups use their wealth and power to sidestep the rules that apply to the rest of us. For example, in 2019 news broke of a college admissions scandal in which a number of already privileged families bribed college admissions officials and consultants in order to get their kids into selective schools like Yale, Stanford, Georgetown, and the University of Southern California.

Interestingly, social mobility in the United States varies widely by geographic area: In San Jose, California, for example, a child born into the bottom fifth has a 13 percent chance of moving into the top fifth; for a child born in Charlotte, North Carolina, it's only 4 percent (Chetty et al. 2014a). What contributes to these vast disparities in social mobility? This study identified five characteristics of high-mobility areas: less residential segregation, less income inequality, better schools, greater social capital, and greater family stability.

Intragenerational mobility refers to the movement that occurs during the course of an individual's lifetime. In other words, it is the measure between the social class a person is born into and the social class status they achieve during their lifetime. Intragenerational mobility can be measured in two directions. **Horizontal social mobility**, which is fairly common, refers to the changing of jobs within a social class: A therapist who shifts careers so that they can teach college experiences horizontal mobility. **Vertical social mobility** is movement up or down the social ladder and thus is often called upward or downward mobility. If this same therapist marries a president of a large corporation, they might experience upward mobility. On the other hand, if they or their partner become unemployed, they might experience downward mobility. People are far more likely to experience horizontal than vertical social mobility.

Although we usually think of social mobility as the result of individual effort (or lack thereof), other factors can contribute to a change in one's social class. **Structural mobility** occurs when large numbers of people move up or down the social ladder because of structural changes in society as a whole, particularly when the economy is affected by large-scale events. For instance, during the Great Depression of the early 1930s, precipitated by the stock market crash of 1929, huge numbers of upper- and middle-class people suddenly found themselves among the poor. Conversely, during the dot-com boom of the late 1990s, developing and investing in new technologies made many people into overnight millionaires. Both of these extreme periods eventually leveled out. Still, many people in the Depression era remained in their new class, never able to climb up the social ladder again.

POVERTY

Social mobility is most difficult—and most essential—for those who live at the bottom of the socioeconomic ladder. In this section, we look at what it means to experience poverty in the United States.

Poverty can be defined in relative or absolute terms. **Relative deprivation** is a comparative measure, whereby people are considered impoverished if their standard of living is lower than that of other members of society—for example, a retail clerk who works part-time for minimum wage might be considered among the working poor compared with a neurosurgeon whose salary places them comfortably in the upper-middle class. Many communities are characterized by such dual realities. **Absolute deprivation**, on the other hand, is a measure whereby people are unable to meet minimal standards for food, shelter, clothing, and health care. In the African country of Eswatini (also known as Swaziland), for example, more than a quarter of adults are living with HIV/AIDS. Many lack access to health care, exacerbating the HIV epidemic and making this country among the lowest in terms of life expectancy, averaging less than fifty-eight years (Central Intelligence Agency 2019). Hunger, malnutrition, and the inability to afford medications are some of the basic indicators of absolute poverty.

In the United States, the **federal poverty line**—an absolute measure, calculated annually—indicates the total annual income below which a family would be considered impoverished. These figures are derived from either the poverty thresholds established by the Census Bureau or the guidelines determined by the Department of Health and Human Services. In 2019, the poverty threshold was $25,750 for a family of four, $21,330 for a family of three, $16,910 for a family of two, and $12,490 for an individual (U.S. Department of Health and Human Services 2019). It is important to highlight that families making much more than these amounts, although not officially qualifying as below the poverty line, might still be unable to afford some basic necessities.

How many people fall below the poverty line? The numbers are startling, given that we usually think of the United States as a wealthy nation. In 2017, 12.3 percent of the population, or 39.7 million people, were considered to be living in poverty (Fontenot, Semega, and Kollar 2018). During the past forty years, the percentage of people living in poverty has fluctuated in the low teens, but it has never dipped below 10 percent. In fact, the number has occasionally risen to more than 15 percent, as it did in 2009 and 2011, while in the late 1950s it rose to as high as 22 percent (see Figure 7.4).

Contrary to popular myth, most people living in poverty are not unemployed; this is why they are often categorized as among the working poor. The annual earnings of a full-time worker making $7.25 an hour (the prevailing federal

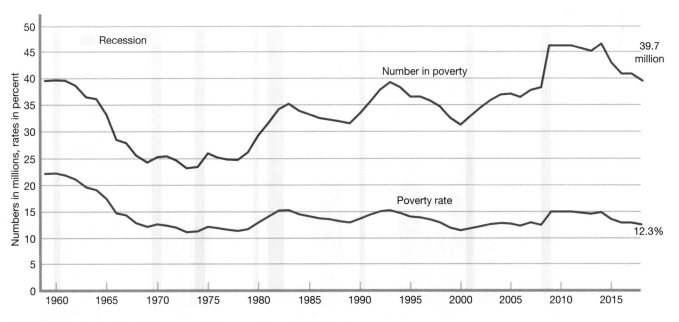

FIGURE 7.4 Number in Poverty and Poverty Rate, 1959–2017

SOURCE: Fontenot, Semega, and Kollar 2018.

minimum wage since 2009) still put them below the poverty line if they are trying to support a family. In fact, at no time in its nearly eighty-year history has the federal minimum wage been sufficient for a worker to exist above the poverty line with a dependent, such as a child, unemployed spouse, or other family member. According to researchers, more than 80 percent of low-income minimum-wage workers, even if they are working full-time, are not earning enough to guarantee a decent standard of living, and many cannot afford some of the basic necessities (Wicks-Lim and Thompson 2010).

The poverty line has often been criticized because of the way it is uniformly applied without regard to regional or other differences. For instance, a family living in Washington, DC, might need two or three times as much income as a family in Des Moines, Iowa, for expenses like rent, transportation, health insurance, and child care (exceptions are made for Alaska and Hawaii, both states with extremely high costs of living). In addition, since the poverty line is based solely on cash income, it doesn't take into consideration government assistance, such as the Supplemental Nutrition Assistance Program (SNAP) or the earned income tax credit (EITC). Finally, the poverty line has been criticized for placing too much emphasis on food costs, which have become a much smaller portion of a family's budget compared to things like housing costs, which have risen considerably since the poverty measure was developed in 1963. Thus, many working families live close to the edge and struggle to make ends meet but are not included as part of the official poverty statistics (Gould, Cooke, and Kimball 2015; Sherman 2012; Waldron, Roberts, and Reamer 2004).

Poverty is also more prominent among certain population groups (Figure 7.5). For instance, poverty rates are higher among blacks (21 percent) and Hispanics (18 percent) than Asians (10 percent) or whites (9 percent) (Fontenot, Semega, and Kollar 2018). They are higher for the disabled and those who are foreign born, as well as for women, children, and single-parent households. By geographic region, poverty is highest in the South, though there are concentrations of people living in poverty in every region of the country, in inner cities, in rural areas, and also in suburbs (Plumer 2013).

Social Welfare and Welfare Reform

Some of the most heated debates about the nature of poverty involve how or even whether society should help those who are impoverished. Some argue that government assistance lifts people out of poverty and helps them become self-supporting; others say that it fosters a dependence on aid and causes further problems.

The idea behind the current American welfare state, which consists of such programs as Social Security, unemployment insurance, and Temporary Assistance for Needy Families (TANF), was first proposed by President Franklin D. Roosevelt during the Great Depression. These programs, among others, collectively called the New Deal, were a response to a national crisis and were meant to serve as a safety net for citizens, helping them in times of adversity or old age, poverty, or joblessness. The 1960s ushered in a new war on poverty. A second wave of programs, such as Medicaid and Head Start,

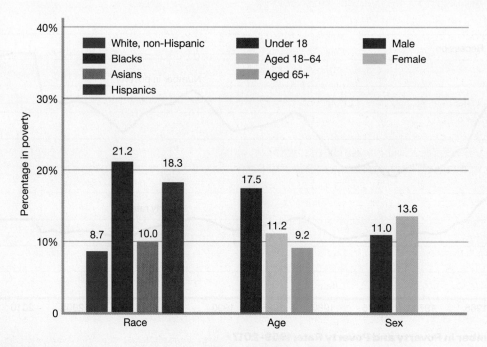

FIGURE 7.5 Poverty in the United States by Selected Characteristics, 2017

SOURCE: Fontenot, Semega, and Kollar 2018.

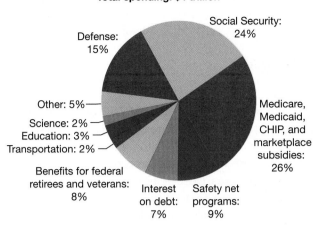

Total spending: $4 trillion

Social Security: 24%
Defense: 15%
Other: 5%
Science: 2%
Education: 3%
Transportation: 2%
Benefits for federal retirees and veterans: 8%
Medicare, Medicaid, CHIP, and marketplace subsidies: 26%
Interest on debt: 7%
Safety net programs: 9%

FIGURE 7.6 Federal Spending, 2017

SOURCE: Center on Budget and Policy Priorities 2019.

intended to solve a variety of social and economic problems, was proposed by President John F. Kennedy and instituted by President Lyndon B. Johnson as part of his Great Society program in 1964.

The welfare system attempted to be fair by providing uniform, standard benefits to all the nation's needy without regard to their personal circumstances and with no time limit. Social Security and Medicaid lifted aging retirees and others with medical issues out of poverty, and programs like Head Start and Upward Bound offered educational support for poor children. Food stamps, now called SNAP, improved nutrition for those with limited incomes, and job-training programs helped the poor gain marketable skills. By 1970, the poverty rate had declined from 22.2 percent to 12.6 percent (Califano 1999), the fastest it has ever dropped.

In the 1980s, political opinion turned against social welfare programs despite their successes. Critics claimed that these programs were responsible for creating a permanent underclass of people living off government checks—some receiving benefits they didn't deserve—and essentially discouraging them from seeking work. Much of the rhetoric surrounding welfare programs stems from concerns about federal spending. People commonly assume that welfare constitutes a large portion of the federal budget, when in fact only 9 percent of the federal budget in 2017 ($357 billion) was spent on safety net programs such as the earned income tax credit, Supplemental Security Income for the elderly and disabled poor, low-income housing assistance, and unemployment insurance (Center on Budget and Policy Priorities 2019). Compare that with Social Security (about 24 percent of spending, or $945 billion) or defense and the war on terror (about 15 percent of spending, or $611 billion) (Figure 7.6).

In response to criticism of welfare programs, reforms arrived in the 1990s. Under President Bill Clinton, the Personal Responsibility and Work Opportunity Reconciliation Act was passed into law. Often referred to as the Welfare

Reform Act, it ended the concept of "entitlements" by requiring recipients to find work within two years of receiving assistance and imposing a limit of five years as the total amount of time in which families could receive assistance. The act also decentralized the federal system of public assistance, allowing individual states to design their own programs, some of which would deny or reduce certain benefits and impose their own criteria for eligibility. The rationale was to encourage people on welfare to take responsibility for working themselves out of poverty. In 2003, Congress approved changes to the act, requiring an even larger percentage of recipients to take jobs and work longer hours.

While welfare reform has been an economic "success" in terms of reducing the number of people on welfare, there is still a great deal to be learned about its impact on the lives of the poor. Evidence suggests that moving from welfare to work does not increase income levels—in other words, federal assistance is merely replaced with an equally low-paying job, which has the effect of keeping families beneath the poverty line once they're off welfare. The reasons for this—the increased costs of child care, health insurance, and transportation—make it difficult for former welfare recipients to succeed outside the system (Hao and Cherlin 2004; Hays 2003; Slack et al. 2006).

As the twentieth anniversary of Clinton's welfare reform approached, sociologists Kathryn Edin and H. Luke Shaefer began investigating what had happened to families and individuals affected by welfare reform—in other words, those who had "maxed out" their state's benefit caps and who were on their own, without the social safety net that social welfare programs had once provided (their research centered on Cleveland, Ohio, and environs). In their book, *$2 a Day: Living*

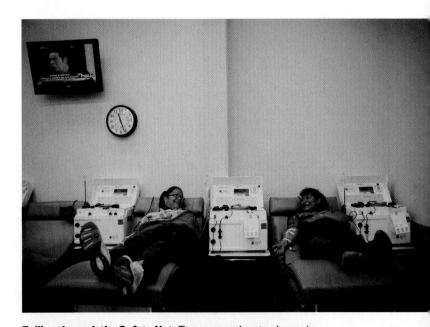

Falling through the Safety Net Two women donate plasma in Eagle Pass, Texas. Without cash assistance from welfare programs, many Americans struggle to get by.

ON THE JOB
Get a Job! Minimum Wage or Living Wage?

There are many misconceptions about people living in poverty, and one is that they're in such conditions because they're unwilling to work. What many fail to realize is that working, even full-time at forty or more hours per week, may not be enough to lift workers and their families out of poverty. So telling someone to just go get a job (assuming work is available) may be shortsighted. While unemployment and underemployment are both issues in themselves, full-time employment in a minimum-wage job can also be problematic.

Who are minimum-wage workers? While the common perception is that they are predominately teenagers or other young people working part-time, the average minimum-wage worker is thirty-six years old, female, and working full-time. Fully 89 percent of minimum-wage workers are at least twenty, and 37 percent are over forty (Cooper and Essrow 2015). They work largely in service industries such as hospitality and retail and are particularly concentrated in the fast-food sector.

First passed into law as part of the New Deal in the years following the Great Depression, the federal minimum wage—the lowest hourly amount an employer is permitted to pay workers—is considered a fundamental measure to protect workers from exploitation. Since 2009, the federal minimum wage has been set at $7.25 per hour (though individual states may mandate higher minimum wages, as many states currently do). At the federal rate, a full-time minimum-wage worker earns approximately $1,256 per month before taxes. Despite increases over the years, the minimum wage has not kept pace with inflation. There are other problems as well. When adjusted for real dollars, the hourly minimum wage is worth $4 less today than in the late 1960s, making it increasingly difficult to survive on minimum wage. In 2016, 7.6 million workers were among the working poor, people who spent at least twenty-seven weeks in the labor force but who still didn't make enough to escape poverty, including 11 percent of service workers (U.S. Bureau of Labor Statistics 2018a).

In response, there is a growing movement to establish a "living wage" instead of a minimum wage. Whereas the minimum wage is defined as pay sufficient for basic survival, a living wage is defined as the minimum income necessary for a decent standard of living. Most consider it the minimum income necessary to obtain not only food, clothing, and shelter, but also utilities, transportation, health care, education, and savings for retirement. A living wage, then, might vary depending on the community and its cost of living, but it can

on *Almost Nothing in America* (2016a), Edin and Shaefer report that while welfare rolls have declined over 75 percent since 1996, the number of Americans living in absolute poverty has skyrocketed to approximately 1.5 million families (including 3 million children). Full-time, well-paid jobs are hard to find, and with neither cash assistance from welfare programs nor sufficient earnings from stable work, poor people are unable to meet even the most basic needs of their families: "[The] biggest problem—by far—has been the lack of access to a cash safety net—money—when failing to find or keep a job. In 21st-century America, a family needs at least some cash to have any chance at stability. Only money can pay the rent (though a minority of families get subsidies via a housing voucher). Only money buys socks, underwear, and school supplies. Money is what's needed to keep the utilities on" (Edin and Shaefer 2016b).

Without this cash safety net, how are the truly disadvantaged getting by? People in need may be driven to extreme measures; in 2014, for example, plasma "donations" (sales, really, of a vital bodily fluid) hit an all-time high of 32.5 million, tripling since 2004 (Edin and Shaefer 2016b). Food pantry usage almost doubled in the same time period, to a high of close to 7 million families (Barrocio and Shaefer 2016). The disadvantaged may live with friends or in their cars or on the streets. In other words, without a robust social safety net, the poorest of our citizens are *not* getting by.

Support for a government social safety net to help the poor has long been split, often along political lines. A majority of 55 percent say that helping people escape poverty is a major role of the government, jumping as high as 72 percent for Democrats compared to just 36 percent of Republicans (Pew Research Center 2015b). Americans are similarly divided when it comes to perceptions of the impact of government aid to the poor: While nearly half (49 percent) of all people say government aid to the poor "does more good than harm because people are unable to escape poverty until basic needs are met," nearly the same proportion (44 percent) feel it "does

run from 50 to 150 percent higher than a minimum wage (or from about $11 to about $18 if we use the federal minimum as a starting point). More than 125 U.S. municipalities have already passed some form of living wage ordinance since the first one was instated in Baltimore in 1994 (National Employment Law Project 2011; Neumark 2004), including such major cities as Seattle, St. Louis, Philadelphia, Chicago, and Miami. Activists in dozens more cities across the country, both large and small, have launched living wage campaigns, the largest of which is "Fight for $15," a movement that seeks to turn the minimum wage into a living wage by raising it to at least $15 per hour everywhere. Among some of the most high profile are living wage movements in Los Angeles and New York City, both places with millions of low-wage workers and high costs of living (Kirkham and Hsu 2014).

In the wake of more cities passing local minimum wage ordinances, some of America's biggest retail firms have also followed suit. Walmart, the nation's largest private employer, raised wages for its lowest-paid workers to $10 per hour in 2016. This was seen as something of a victory, although activists were pushing for a starting rate of $15 per hour, a figure that is closer to a living wage. Other retailers soon did likewise, including McDonald's, Target, and Gap, Inc. Costco and IKEA went even higher, to $12 per hour (Gustafson 2015). Amazon recently raised its minimum wage to $15 per hour, though it also started phasing out other benefit programs, including stock options for hourly workers.

The Fight for $15 Low-wage workers in Los Angeles protest for a $15 per hour nationwide minimum wage.

Debates about raising the federal minimum wage have persisted over many decades. It is a complex issue that brings up many questions about whether higher wages will also lead businesses to increase consumer prices, lay off workers, or relocate to where labor is less expensive. More important, will raising the minimum wage or establishing a living wage help reduce poverty in America and provide millions more working people with a decent standard of living? Your future, or that of someone you know, is likely at stake.

more harm than good by making people dependent on the government" (Pew Research Center 2015e).

Americans remain conflicted in their opinions about people living in poverty. Overall, 52 percent say that circumstances beyond one's control are more often to blame if a person is impoverished, while about a third (31 percent) say that an individual's lack of effort is more often to blame (Dunn 2018). Still, 37 percent of registered voters acknowledge that hard work in itself is no guarantee of success (Pew Research Center 2016c).

The "Culture of Poverty" and Its Critics

Some argue that what keeps people impoverished is not public policy but rather entrenched cultural attitudes. Oscar Lewis (1959) first promoted the idea of a **culture of poverty** after he studied poor Hispanics in Mexico and the United States. Lewis suggested that the poor, because they were excluded from the mainstream, developed a way of life that was qualitatively different from that of middle-class groups to allow them to cope with the dire circumstance of poverty. This way of life includes attitudes of resignation and fatalism, which lead them to accept their fate rather than trying to improve their lot. It also emphasizes immediate gratification, making it difficult for impoverished people to plan or save for the future or to join trade unions or community groups that might help them improve their situation. Once such a culture is formed, Lewis argued, it takes on a life of its own and is passed on from parents to children, leaving them ill-equipped to change.

The culture of poverty theory was later adopted by other social scientists (Banfield 1970) and applied to Americans living in poverty, particularly those in inner cities. Not surprisingly, though, the theory has been met with considerable

CULTURE OF POVERTY entrenched attitudes that can develop among poor communities and lead the poor to accept their fate rather than attempt to improve their lot

controversy, in part because it suggests that there is little point in trying to eradicate poverty because it's more a problem of culture (attitudes, lifestyle, and behavior) than of economics. By focusing on individual character and personality, the theory tends to blame the victims of poverty for their own misfortunes while overlooking the force of their social conditions.

The tendency to see victims of social injustice as deserving of their fates is explained by what social psychologists call the **just-world hypothesis**. According to this argument, we have a strong need to believe that the world is orderly, predictable, and fair in order to achieve our goals in life. When we encounter situations that contradict this belief, we either act quickly to restore justice and order or persuade ourselves that no injustice has occurred. This can result in assuming that victims have "asked for it" or deserve whatever has befallen them. This attitude is continually reinforced through the morality tales that are a ubiquitous part of our news and entertainment, which tell us that good is rewarded and evil punished.

The just-world hypothesis, developed by Melvin Lerner (1965, 1980), was tested through a series of experiments that documented how people can convince themselves that others deserve what they get. In these experiments, cash prizes were randomly distributed to students completing the exact same tasks in the exact same way. Observers, however, judged the cash recipients as the more deserving, harder workers. Other researchers (Rubin and Peplau 1975) have found that people with strong beliefs in a just world tend to "feel less of a need to engage in activities to change society or to alleviate the plight of social victims." In the face of poverty, many simply become apathetic. It is important to be aware of our own tendencies to follow such thinking, so that we might avoid becoming blind to others' misfortunes.

Another problem with the culture of poverty theory is that it lacks a certain sociological imagination. It fails to take into account the structural factors that shape culture and contribute to the situation in which impoverished individuals find themselves. Dalton Conley (2002) argues that to solve the problem of poverty, we must examine wealth as well. A social system that allows extremes of both wealth and poverty (as ours does) reveals structural reasons why poverty persists, such as laws that protect the inheritances of the wealthy but provide few breaks for working families. Research like Conley's helps us understand that there are alternative explanations for why people are poor and even suggests that extreme wealth ought to be conceptualized as a social problem similar to that of extreme poverty.

The Invisibility of Poverty

Although we are used to seeing televised images of abject poverty from overseas—crying children with bloated bellies and spindly limbs in Asia, Africa, or Latin America—we rarely see similar images from the United States. While it may be true that few Americans are as impoverished as people living in Yemen, Haiti, or Honduras, nearly 40 million Americans lived below the poverty line in 2017 (Fontenot, Semega, and Kollar 2018). That's more than 12 percent of the population of the wealthiest nation in the world. How can such large numbers of people remain all but hidden to their fellow Americans? What makes poverty invisible? Consider some of these factors.

RESIDENTIAL SEGREGATION One factor is **residential segregation**—the geographical isolation of the impoverished from the rest of the city (or in the case of rural areas, from any neighbors at all). Such segregation often occurs along racial as well as socioeconomic lines, further exacerbating class divisions (Massey and Denton 1993). In the phrase "wrong side of the tracks," used to describe poverty-stricken neighborhoods, there is usually a racial connotation as well, since railroad tracks traditionally served as boundaries that kept black neighborhoods separated from white ones in the nineteenth century (Ananat 2005).

Residential segregation is accomplished most notably through public housing projects, which are typically high-density, low-income apartment complexes in urban areas, funded and managed by the Department of Housing and Urban Development (HUD). Living in these apartment complexes, many of which are in high-crime neighborhoods and are poorly maintained, can be dangerous as well as unpleasant. But when housing authorities attempt to reintegrate low-income tenants into other parts of town, neighbors often complain, vociferously, that they do not want "those" people in their neighborhood.

Residential segregation is also exacerbated by the practice of "redlining," in which banks and mortgage lenders identify high-risk areas (usually low-income or minority neighborhoods) and either refuse mortgages to applicants from those neighborhoods or offer loans at prohibitively high rates. Redlining keeps low-income people from acquiring assets (such as real estate) that might allow them to rise out of poverty and move to a more affluent neighborhood. Though redlining is technically illegal, there is evidence that it is still practiced today in banking, insurance, and other industries, disproportionately affecting the poor and minorities (Wilson 2009). In one instance, a major mortgage company, MidAmerica Bank, settled a redlining case in Chicago by agreeing to open more branches in low-income and minority neighborhoods and to include consumers from those communities in

---

JUST-WORLD HYPOTHESIS argument that people have a deep need to see the world as orderly, predictable, and fair, which creates a tendency to view victims of social injustice as deserving of their fates

RESIDENTIAL SEGREGATION the geographical separation of the poor from the rest of an area's population

DISENFRANCHISEMENT the removal of the rights of citizenship through economic, political, or legal means

TABLE 7.2   Theory in Everyday Life

Perspective	Approach to Social Inequality	Case Study: Poverty
Structural Functionalism	Social inequality is a necessary part of society. Different reward structures are necessary as an incentive for the best qualified people to occupy the most important positions. Even poverty has functions that help maintain social order.	Poverty is functional for society: The poor take otherwise undesirable jobs and housing, purchase discount and secondhand goods, and provide work for thousands, including social service caseworkers and others who work with the poor.
Conflict Theory	Social inequality creates intergroup conflict—poor and rich groups have different interests and may find themselves at odds as they attempt to secure and protect these interests.	Social welfare programs that assist the poor are funded by tax dollars, which some wealthy citizens may be reluctant to provide because taxes reduce their net income. This can create conflict between rich and poor groups in society.
Symbolic Interactionism	Social inequality is part of our presentation of self. We develop everyday class consciousness as a way to distinguish the status of others.	Poor and wealthy persons have differential access to the "props" used to project particular versions of self. In particular, professional clothing such as business suits can be too expensive for poor individuals to purchase, which can put them at a disadvantage in job interviews for which a professional image is necessary. Organizations like Dress for Success provide professional clothing for those who can't afford it, leveling the playing field a bit in terms of impression management.

the bank's advertising campaigns, which had previously targeted only buyers at higher income levels.

POLITICAL DISENFRANCHISEMENT People living in poverty may also remain invisible to the larger society because of their lack of political power. **Disenfranchisement** is a correlate of poverty: The impoverished are less likely to vote or otherwise participate in political life (Michener 2016). When everyday life is a struggle, it is difficult to muster the extra energy necessary to work for political change. The impoverished may also feel that the system has not served them; if the government ignores their interests, why bother to become involved? Because of their lack of involvement, the impoverished lack political clout and the resources to make their plight a high-profile political priority. Politicians at the local and national levels have little motivation to address their needs, because as a constituency the impoverished wield less power than such groups as senior citizens, "soccer moms," and small-business owners.

When the impoverished do organize politically, even their successes may not be well known. One group, Mothers of East Los Angeles (whose motto includes the phrase "not economically rich, but culturally wealthy"), has been successfully protecting its neighborhood from environmental degradation and exploitation for decades. The group has rebuffed plans to build a prison, toxic waste plants, and an oil pipeline near homes and schools in its community. But have you ever heard of it?

High-profile occasions, such as political conventions and major sporting events, put a media spotlight on city streets. In the run-up to the 2016 Olympics in Rio de Janeiro, Brazil, city officials and representatives of the International Olympic Committee promised that construction and infrastructure projects would benefit not just wealthy international tourists coming to the Games but also the impoverished favela (or slum) dwellers who make up almost 25 percent of Rio's population. In reality, though, the "improvements" either took place in already affluent areas or demolished favela housing without plans for replacement or relocation. So favela residents became activists themselves, marching in the streets to demand inclusion in government decision making. Favela advocacy groups helped craft a plan for improved services and human rights protections for poor residents and neighborhoods (Waldron 2016). Activism like this can turn previously invisible communities into forces to be reckoned with politically.

THE DIGITAL DIVIDE In a postindustrial economy, most people will have to demonstrate a certain level of computer proficiency in order to secure a job. One way or another, the majority of jobs in contemporary society involve computers, so it's likely you'll have to know how to use certain programs to do your work, whatever it may be. Because you are attending college, you'll probably be lucky enough to acquire some of these skills in the course of your education. But not everyone has the same opportunities, and many Americans lack the basic computer literacy, experience, and access necessary to compete in a job market that increasingly demands such skills. This inequality in access to and use of digital technology is known as the **digital divide**.

The hierarchies of inequality in the larger society—such as socioeconomic status, race,

DIGITAL DIVIDE the unequal access to computer and Internet technology, both globally and within the United States

IN THE FUTURE
Inequality and Global Warming

The very rich are getting richer, and everyone else, no matter how hard they work, is either getting poorer or struggling to stay even. This is a problem not only for those who are at the bottom of the economic hierarchy—it is a problem for the entire planet. This is the argument of Professor Andrew Sayer, who makes a case for extreme wealth as a serious social problem in his book *Why We Can't Afford the Rich* (2016). For Sayer, the **wealth gap** is about social justice (and injustice) in more ways than one. Not only does inequality mean that some individuals and groups suffer more than others in our society, but the uber-wealthy are also a threat to the entire planet through their disproportionate contributions to global warming.

WEALTH GAP the unequal distribution of assets across a population

The link between inequality and global sustainability is becoming clearer with each passing year. A 2017 study in the journal *Science* found that, by the end of the twenty-first century, the burden of climate change in the United States will fall disproportionately on the poorer parts of the country (Hsiang et al. 2017). For example, hotter days will have more negative effects in the poorer-than-average South, in the form of decreasing crop yields and labor productivity and increasing mortality and crime, than in wealthier-than-average New England or the Pacific Northwest (*The Economist* 2017). This means that global warming will intensify preexisting regional economic inequality in the United States (and likely the world). And the horrible irony here is that the rich (wealthier individuals, regions, and nations) make bigger contributions to the problem of global warming—even though it will have less effect on their everyday lives over the next 80 to 100 years.

How do the wealthy contribute to global warming? For one thing, the super-rich are super-consumers (Sayer 2016). This seems fairly obvious—the more money they have, the more they probably spend. But think about what this means if you take it to its logical end point: Excessive consumption means excessive use of scarce resources such as energy, water, and raw materials such as lumber, metals, and rubber. Not only does excessive consumption deplete these resources, but it leads to waste and pollution as well. Think of the many celebrities who have multiple homes in various locales. Each of those homes needs electricity to turn on the lights, irrigation systems to water the lawn, and other resource-guzzling functions to maintain the property, even when no one is living

there. Oprah Winfrey (who owns five houses from Chicago to Hawaii), we're talking to you!

In addition, wealth depends on continued use of fossil fuels—to create and maintain it and to live the lifestyle of the "rich and famous" (Sayer 2016). With this comes disproportionate environmental impact. We all use fossil fuels, but most of us drive just one car to work and probably fly in airplanes once or twice a year, if at all. Former late night host Jay Leno owns 150 cars. Actor Patrick Dempsey competes in prestigious "24 hour" races all over the world where he drives high-performance race cars really fast for twenty-four hours straight with no destination at all. Those weekly trips in the corporate jet also make the carbon footprints of the rich much bigger than those of ordinary folk.

To paraphrase F. Scott Fitzgerald, the very rich live differently than you and I. And as their wealth grows, it translates into a more insecure global environment for the rest of the population. The wealthy can use their greater resources to shield themselves from the outcomes of global warming, famine, disease, and uprising for a while—but not forever. And some of the truly wealthy are trying to help solve the problems associated with global warming as well (take billionaire Elon Musk and his electric vehicle company, Tesla, for example). Looking toward the future, a more sustainable society must be based on a fairer distribution of economic resources. We must pioneer different ways of living in order to reduce inequalities of wealth, power, consumption, and waste, and keep our planet alive.

Conspicuous Consumption One reason we can't afford the rich, according to Sayer, is because the wealthy are super-consumers.

age, and educational attainment—all shape one's access to technology (Glaser 2007). For example, while 88 percent of all adults in the United States use the Internet regularly, there are differences in access among various demographic groups. In 2018 there were lower Internet usage rates among households with incomes under $30,000 (81 percent), those with a high school education or less (65 percent), and seniors (66 percent) (Pew Research Center 2018a). Similarly, while nearly all adults (97 percent) with an income over $100,000 own a desktop or laptop computer, only 56 percent of those with an income of less than $30,000 do (Anderson 2017).

With the rise in popularity and availability of smartphones, more underrepresented groups are gaining Internet access. Still, even thirty years after the birth of the Internet, there remains a digital divide between lower- and higher-income Americans, including what's referred to as the "homework gap." More than a third of lower-income households with school-age children do not have high-speed Internet at home (Anderson and Kumar 2019). These disparities mirror the contours of other sorts of social inequality because technology requires resources—funds to purchase devices and the means to get online. The digital divide is really about the benefits of having technological competence and access, especially in terms of the additional opportunities and advantages these bring. Most important, the digital divide matters in the areas of education and the job market. Internet access and proficiency are quickly becoming a requirement for both finding and keeping a job, meaning that those without such access or proficiency are at a disadvantage (Smith 2015).

HOMELESSNESS In certain situations, the people who are most impoverished are deliberately removed from public view. Police are sometimes ordered to scour the streets, rousting the homeless and herding them out of sight, as they did in 1988 in New York City's Tompkins Square Park (an infamous riot ensued).

Mostly, though, the homeless remain invisible. We don't know exactly how many homeless live in the United States. The Census Bureau focuses its population counts on households, so the homeless living in long-term shelters may get counted, but not those on the streets. One recent estimate is that at least 2.5 to 3.5 million people (approximately 1 percent of the U.S. population) will experience homelessness at least once during a given year, with an additional 7.4 million people living doubled up with others out of economic necessity (National Law Center on Homelessness and Poverty 2015). The recent recession left many people unemployed and with their finances drained, creating a surge in homelessness that included many who were formerly among the middle classes. "We have this emergence of a very visible and very large homeless population in the shadow of tremendous affluence," said Jennifer Friedenbach, executive director of the Coalition on Homelessness in San Francisco (Gee et al. 2017). The U.S. Department of Housing and Urban Development (2018)

Counting the Homeless Volunteers participate in the all-night Homeless Outreach Population Estimate (HOPE). The goal is to obtain an estimate of individuals living on the street in New York City in order to help the government provide better services for the homeless population.

estimates that on any given night, roughly 553,000 people are homeless.

The homeless also remain invisible to most of us because of our own feelings of discomfort and guilt. John Coleman, a former college president and business executive, discovered this when he lived in poverty, if only temporarily, on the streets of Manhattan. Coleman went "undercover" as a homeless man for ten days and found that the minute he shed his privileged identity, people looked at him differently—or not at all. During his days on the streets, Coleman passed by and made eye contact with his accountant, his landlord, and a co-worker—each looked right through him, without recognition. But he was not invisible to everyone. Police officers often shook him awake to get him moving from whatever meager shelter he had found for the night. A waiter at a diner took one look at him and forced him to pay up front for his 99-cent breakfast special. Other homeless men, though, showed him kindness and generosity (Coleman 1983).

To whom are the homeless (and others living in poverty) most visible? Those who work with them: caseworkers, social service providers, government bureaucrats, volunteers and charity workers, clergy, cops, business owners (including those who may not want to deal with them, as well as those who may exploit them). And now, they are more visible to you.

With a sociological perspective, you can now see the effects of social stratification everywhere you turn. And when you recognize the multiple, complex causes of poverty—such as limited educational and job opportunities, stagnating wages, economic downturns, racism, mental illness, and substance abuse—it will no longer be as simple to consider each individual responsible for his or her own plight. Finally, the sociological perspective will give you the ability to imagine possible solutions to the problems associated with poverty—solutions that focus on large-scale social changes as well as individual actions, including your own. Don't let poverty remain invisible.

INEQUALITY AND THE IDEOLOGY OF THE AMERICAN DREAM

Ask almost anyone about the American Dream and they are likely to mention some of the following: owning your own home; having a good marriage and great kids; finding a good job that you enjoy; being able to afford nice vacations; having a big-screen TV, nice clothes, or season tickets to your team's home games. For most Americans, the dream also means that all people, no matter how humble their beginnings, can succeed in whatever they set out to do if they work hard enough. In other words, a poor boy or girl could grow up to become president of the United States, an astronaut, a professional basketball player, a captain of industry, or a movie star.

One problem with the American Dream, however, is that it doesn't usually match reality. It's more of an ideology: a belief system that explains and justifies some sort of social arrangement, in this case America's social class hierarchy.

The American Dream Oprah Winfrey's meteoric rise from a childhood of poverty to her position as one of the most powerful celebrities in America is often cited as a prime example of the American Dream. How does Oprah's success represent the exception rather than the rule?

MERITOCRACY a system in which rewards are distributed based on merit

SIMPLICITY MOVEMENT a loosely knit movement that opposes consumerism and encourages people to work less, earn less, and spend less, in accordance with nonmaterialistic values

The ideology of the American Dream legitimizes stratification by reinforcing the idea that everyone has the same chance to get ahead and that success or failure depends on the person (Hochschild 1996). Inequality is presented as a system of incentives and rewards for achievement. If we can credit anyone who does succeed, then logically we must also blame anyone who fails. The well-socialized American buys into this belief system, without recognizing its structural flaws. We are caught in what Marx would call "false consciousness," the inability to see the ways in which we may be oppressed.

Nevertheless, it's not easy to dismiss the idea of the American Dream, especially when there are so many high-profile examples. Take, for instance, Oprah Winfrey. Born in Mississippi in 1954, Winfrey endured a childhood of abject poverty. In 2018, *Forbes* magazine listed her as #298 of the 400 richest Americans, with an impressive personal wealth of $2.8 billion. In 2010, *Forbes* honored her as the world's most powerful celebrity (of 100), based on a composite that included earnings ($165 million that year) and dominance across various media. In that same year, Winfrey launched her own independent cable network—the Oprah Winfrey Network, or OWN. The accolades and awards span many categories. Not only is she extremely successful as a media mogul and personality, but she is also widely praised for her philanthropic efforts and is admired as a symbol of what can be achieved in pursuit of the American Dream. The problem is, we tend to think of her as representing the rule rather than the exception. For most Americans, the rags-to-riches upward mobility she has achieved is very unrealistic.

Though popular opinion and rhetoric espouse the American Dream ideology or that the United States is a **meritocracy** (a system in which rewards are distributed based on merit), sociologists find contrary evidence. In fact, no matter how hard they work, most people will make little movement at all. And the degree of mobility they do achieve can depend on their ethnicity, class status, or gender rather than merit. For example, whites are more likely to experience upward mobility than persons of color (Chetty et al. 2018), and married women are more likely to experience upward mobility than nonmarried women (Thompson 2013). New immigrants are likely to experience downward social mobility in the first generation but upward mobility in the second (Papademetriou et al. 2009).

A recent Harvard poll showed college-age millennials evenly split on the issue of the American Dream: About half said it still exists, while half declared it dead (Harvard IOP 2015). The numbers shift when broken down by such factors as education, gender, and race of the respondent. More college graduates (58 percent) believe in the American Dream than those with just a high school education (42 percent). While 52 percent of Hispanics believe in the American Dream, the same is true of 49 percent of whites and just 44 percent of blacks.

Although the American Dream tends to promote consumerism as a way to achieve "the good life," the fact is that chasing after it has left us feeling less secure and satisfied—not to mention less wealthy—than previous generations (De Graaf, Waan, and Naylor 2002). Some pundits suggest that we have lost focus on the original meaning of the American Dream, that our increasing obsession with the idea of "more (or newer or bigger) is better" is leading to more debt, less free time, and greater discontent. A recent Gallup poll reported that about half of Americans feel that they do not have enough time to do all of the things they need to do in their everyday lives (Newport 2015).

A countervailing trend in American life, sometimes referred to as the **simplicity movement**, rejects rampant consumerism and seeks to reverse some of its consequences for the individual, for society, and for the planet. This movement, a backlash against the traditional American Dream, encourages people to "downshift" by working less, earning less, and spending less in order to put their lifestyles in sync with their (nonmaterialistic) values (Grigsby 2004; Schor 1999). What does this mean in practice? Growing your own vegetables, perhaps, or riding your bike to work, wearing secondhand clothes, and spending more time with friends and family and less time commuting, shopping, or watching TV.

One of the most radical extensions of this philosophy is embraced by "freegans" (Barnard 2016)—a term that merges "free" with "vegan" (a person who eats no animal products). Freegans are people who avoid consumerism and who engage in strategies to support themselves without participating in a conventional economic system. This can mean scavenging for usable food, clothing, and other goods, sometimes called "urban foraging" or "dumpster diving," along with sharing housing and transportation with others in order to work less and minimize their impact on the planet.

DATA WORKSHOP

Analyzing Media and Pop Culture

Advertising and the American Dream

We are surrounded by advertising, which aims not only to give us information about products but also to create and stimulate a buying public with demands for an ever-increasing array of goods and services. Advertising shapes our consciousness and tells us what to dream and how to pursue those dreams. Advertising equates shopping and acquisition with emotional fulfillment, freedom, fun, happiness, security, and self-satisfaction.

And the sales pitch seems to be working. Like no other generation, today's eighteen- to thirty-four-year-olds have grown up in a consumer culture with all its varied enticements, but they are having a harder time reaching financial stability in adulthood than did their parents. Many young people are finding themselves caught in a difficult job market, with too few positions and too little pay, at the same time they are carrying larger student loans and mounting credit card debt.

In 2017, about two in three college graduates left school with student loan debt; the average amount owed was $28,650 (TICAS 2018). On top of that, more than half of all college students use credit cards (Sallie Mae 2016). Many young people embrace easy credit only to discover that late-payment fees and high interest rates can keep them from paying down their balances. And the appeal to spend more is always there, urging you to buy your way into the American Dream, and perhaps leading you further into debt. So let's examine where some of this pressure to spend comes from—advertising.

In this Data Workshop, you will analyze some advertisements in terms of the ideology of the American Dream. This entails the use of existing sources and doing a content analysis to look for patterns of meaning within and across the ads. See the section on existing sources in Chapter 2 for a review of this research method.

To start your research, find three or four ads from magazines, newspapers, websites, or television sources. Look for ads that are of interest to your particular age, gender, or other demographic group. In particular, try to identify ads that are selling the idea of the American Dream of wealth, success, or living the "good life." Examine both the visual (images and layout) and textual (words) elements of the advertisements.

For each of the ads, consider the following questions:

- What product or service is being advertised?

- For whom is the advertisement intended?

- Does the ad "work"? Would you like to buy the product or service? Why or why not?

- In addition to a product or service, what else are the advertisers trying to "sell"?

- What are the explicit (obvious) and implicit (subtle) messages conveyed in the ad?

- How do these messages make you feel? Do they play on your emotions, desires, or sense of self-worth? If so, in what ways?

Once you have examined all the ads, consider these more general questions:

- What were the similarities or differences among the ads you chose with regard to their underlying ideology?

- How do the ads represent a particular lifestyle that you should aspire to? How does that influence your buying habits?

- What types of ads have a strong effect on you? Why?

- What kinds of pressures do you feel to keep up with the material possessions of your friends, neighbors, or co-workers?

- Why do you think we are lured into shopping and acquiring material possessions?

There are two options for completing this Data Workshop:

PREP-PAIR-SHARE Select three ads and bring them with you to class (either the physical ads from a magazine or newspaper, photocopies, web links, or screen shots of ads). Reflect on the questions as they apply to one or more of your ads, and be ready to discuss your answers with other students, in pairs or small groups. Compare and contrast one another's contributions.

DO-IT-YOURSELF Write a three- to four-page essay discussing your general thoughts on advertising, consumption, and the American Dream. Include an analysis of the specific ads you chose, answering the sets of questions. Make sure to attach the ads to your paper.

Closing Comments

Social stratification is all about power. Stratification systems, like SES, allocate different types of social power, such as wealth, political influence, and occupational prestige, and do so in fundamentally unequal ways. These inequalities are part of both the larger social structure and our everyday interactions. In the following chapters, we will examine other systems of stratification—namely, race and ethnicity, and gender and sexuality. While we separate these topics for organizational purposes, they are not experienced as separate in our everyday lives. We are women or men, working class or upper class, black or white, gay or straight simultaneously. Our experiences of these social categories are intertwined. We will continue to examine intersectionality and the complex relationship between our positions in the social structure and the varying social forces that shape our lives.

Let's Talk More

1. Think about your own class status. Is it consistent across the criteria that make up socioeconomic status (income, wealth, education, occupation, and power)? Or are you an example of status inconsistency?

2. According to Pierre Bourdieu, the cultural tools we inherit from our parents can be very important in trying to gain economic assets. What sort of cultural capital did you inherit? Has it ever helped you materially? Have you ever done something to acquire more cultural capital?

3. Erving Goffman said we "read" other people through social interaction to get a sense of their class status. What sort of clues can tell you about a person's social class within thirty seconds of meeting that person?

Let's Explore More

1. **Film** Johnson, Jamie, dir. *Born Rich*. 2003.

2. **Book** Edin, Kathryn; and Shaefer, H. Luke. 2015. *$2.00 a Day: Living on Almost Nothing in America*. New York: Houghton Mifflin Harcourt.

3. **Blog Post** Sternheimer, Karen. "Cleaning and Class." *Everyday Sociology* (blog). May 10, 2012. *http://WWNorton.com/rd/Fz4t8*.

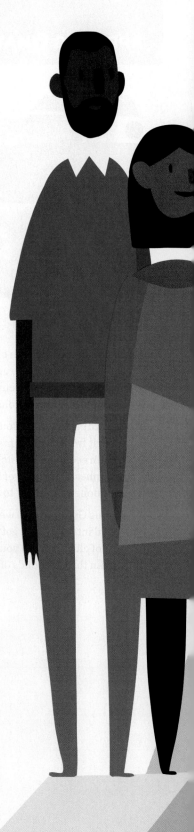

CHAPTER 8

Race and Ethnicity as Lived Experience

ike a lot of celebrities, comedian and actor Chris Rock has a verified Twitter account. Unlike many of his peers, he isn't a big fan of tweeting selfies. But in 2015 he posted three of them in less than two months, each taken immediately after he had been pulled over by the police.

Social media posts such as Chris Rock's selfies have put real faces on the issue of racial profiling by police. Racial profiling is the practice of suspecting that someone has committed a crime based on his or her race. Racial profiling of black drivers even has a name: "driving while black." Racial profiling is pervasive on America's roads and highways. And this is nothing new: Civil rights groups in the 1950s and 1960s were already voicing bitter

complaints about "the stopping of Negroes on foot or in cars without obvious basis" (Harris 1999). It would be nice to think that half a century would be enough time to solve such a serious social problem, but today both the political and legal situation make driving while black a fundamentally different experience.

Politically, the war on drugs has made driving while black (or brown) even riskier than before. In the 1980s the federal government dramatically increased its efforts to catch drug smugglers. Nationally this meant an increasingly militarized border and airport security. At the state and local levels, however, it meant law enforcement wanted to search a lot more cars. Despite overwhelming evidence that rates of illegal drug use are similar across racial lines, police and highway patrol officers have often disproportionately targeted nonwhite motorists when searching for drug couriers. Of course, it's not legal to stop drivers just because of their race; however, the current legal situation allows the police to stop more or less anyone, at any time, because "traffic codes are so minutely drawn that virtually every driver will break some rule within a few blocks" (LaFraniere and Lehren 2015). This led to massive increases in "pretext stops," where the violation cited as justifying the traffic stop is just a pretext to investigate the people in the car. In 1996, the Supreme Court found that pretext searches did not violate the Fourth Amendment protection against unreasonable search and seizure.

The phrase "driving while black" is an explicit claim about racial injustice. Are we all afforded the same rights, or are black and white drivers treated differently? For a long time this question was hard to answer empirically due to a lack of data on race and traffic stops. Even now there is no comprehensive nationwide database on who gets stopped, but the data that do exist make it clear that race matters. For example, a 2017 report on traffic stops in Missouri found that black drivers were 85 percent more likely than whites to be pulled over. And when pulled over, black drivers were 51 percent more likely to be searched, despite the report's finding that white drivers were more often found with contraband (Hawley 2018). Similarly, a study in Oakland, California, found that while blacks made up 28 percent of the city's population, they accounted for 60 percent of police stops; black men were also four times more likely than their white counterparts to be searched during those stops (Hetey et al. 2016).

We don't just see racial disparities in traffic stops. Countless studies have found "evidence of racial disparities at many levels of law enforcement, from traffic stops to drug-related arrests to use of force" (Weir 2016). In the African American community, having "the talk" with your kids isn't just about sex; it often involves talking to them about how to interact with the police. As Ta-Nehisi Coates (2015) warns his own son in *Between the World and Me*, "The police departments of your country have been endowed with the authority to destroy your body. It does not matter if the destruction is the result of an unfortunate overreaction. It does not matter if it originates in a misunderstanding. It does not matter if the destruction springs from a foolish policy."

Driving while intoxicated is a crime, and the only thing that parents need to tell their children is not to do it. Driving while black is not a crime, but black parents are forced to tell their children that sometimes it will be treated like it is.

How to Read
This Chapter

Our goal in this chapter is for you to acquire a fundamental understanding of race and ethnicity as socially constructed categories. While each is based on traits such as skin color or facial features, the meanings attached to race and ethnicity are created, maintained, and modified over time through social processes in which we all take part.

When a society categorizes people based on their race and ethnicity (and all societies do), it creates a system of stratification that leads to inequality. Society's resources—wealth, power, privilege, opportunity—are distributed according to these categories, thereby perpetuating inequalities that are all too familiar here in the United States. We also hope you will come to understand the importance of race and ethnicity in forming individual identity. Our racial and ethnic identities have profound effects on our sense of self, and our bonds to other people may be based on shared identities—or may transcend those categories entirely.

DEFINING RACE
AND ETHNICITY

"Race" and "ethnicity" are words we use so often in everyday speech that we might not think we need a definition of either. But people tend to use the words interchangeably, as if they mean essentially the same thing. There is, however, a significant difference between commonsense notions of race and ethnicity and what social scientists have to say about them.

The idea of different races as belonging to distinguishable categories has existed for hundreds of years. In the nineteenth century, biologists came up with a schema that grouped humans into three races: Negroid, Mongoloid, and Caucasoid (corresponding roughly to black, Asian, and white). It was believed that each race was characterized by its own biological makeup, separate and distinct from the others. Modern scientists, however, possess advanced tools for examining race in a much more sophisticated way. What they have found, ironically, is that there are no "pure" races—that the lines among races are blurry rather than fixed. A person who looks white will inevitably have biological material from other races, as will someone who looks black. There is also no such thing as a "superior" race, as race itself is not the reason that different groups might display positive or negative characteristics (such as intelligence, athleticism, or artistic ability). Furthermore, there is greater genetic diversity *within* racial populations than between them. So within the Asian population, members differ more from each other (Koreans from Chinese, for example) than they do from whites. From a biological standpoint, the difference between someone with type O blood and someone with type A blood is much more significant than the differences between a dark-skinned and a light-skinned person. And yet blood types are not used in our society as a way of distinguishing groups for any reason other than medical treatment.

The physical differences we see between groups, such as skin color or hair texture, are due to geographic adaptations. People living in places closer to the equator have more melanin (and darker skin) to protect them from too

What Is Race? Rashida Jones (left) is the daughter of black producer Quincy Jones and white actress and model Peggy Lipton. Twins Kian and Remee, with their parents Remi Horder and Kylee Hodgson, were born within a minute of each other with different skin colors.

much sunlight, while people living closer to the poles have less melanin (and lighter skin), which allows them to absorb enough sunlight to produce vitamin D (a compound necessary for human health). We have attributed great significance to quite superficial differences. Such conclusions overlook the fact that all humans, whatever racial categories they seem to inhabit, are 99.9 percent genetically identical. And of that remaining 0.1 percent of our genetic material, only 15 percent of its variation occurs between geographically distinct groups. In other words, there's not enough "wiggle room" in the human genome for race to be a genetic trait (*Harvard Magazine* 2008). There is no race chromosome in our DNA. Sociologists, then, have come to understand **race** as a social category, based on real or perceived biological differences between groups of people. Race is more meaningful to us on a social level than it is on a biological level (Montagu 1998).

RACE a socially defined category based on real or perceived biological differences between groups of people

ETHNICITY a socially defined category based on a common language, religion, nationality, history, or some other cultural factor

Ethnicity is another social category that is applied to a group with a shared ancestry or cultural heritage. The Scotch-Irish (or Scots-Irish), for instance, are a distinct ethnic group in American society, linked by a common cultural heritage that includes language, religion, and history. In the eighteenth century they migrated to frontier territories in the United States and settled into parts of Virginia, North Carolina, South Carolina, Georgia, Kentucky, and Tennessee. Many Scotch-Irish are clustered in rural Appalachia. J. D. Vance (2016) wrote about this group in his best-selling memoir, *Hillbilly Elegy: A Memoir of a Family and Culture in Crisis*. He characterized the Scotch-Irish as a tight-knit and fiercely loyal group that clings to traditional family values, evangelical Christianity, and conservative politics. The Jewish people are another example; contrary to what the Nazis and other white supremacists may believe, Jews are an ethnic group but not a race. They share a religious and cultural background but are dispersed in many parts of the world. The stereotypical image is challenged when we see a blond, blue-eyed Jew from Scandinavia or a black Ethiopian Jew.

As an example of the social construction of race and ethnicity, let's look at the evidence documenting the historical changes in the boundaries of the category "white." In the early 1900s, native-born Americans, who were frequently Protestant, did not consider recent Irish, Italian, or Jewish immigrants to be white and restricted where these groups could live and work (Brodkin 1999; Ignatiev 1996, 2008). Such housing discrimination forced new immigrants to cluster in urban neighborhoods or "ghettos." After World War II, however, as the second generation of Irish, Italian, and Jewish immigrants reached adulthood, the importance of ethnic identity declined and skin color became the main way to differentiate

Mulberry Street at the Turn of the Century In the early 1900s, Irish, Italian, and Jewish immigrants were not considered "whites." Because of residential segregation, new immigrants poured into densely populated neighborhoods like this one on New York's Lower East Side, where they had little choice but to live in squalid tenements and work in sweatshops.

Symbolic Ethnicity Irish and Mexican Americans often embrace ethnic identity on holidays like St. Patrick's Day and Cinco de Mayo.

between who was white and who was not. Today, the question is whether people of Middle Eastern descent are white. In the post–9/11 war on terrorism climate, Arabs and Muslims have been identified as racially and ethnically distinct in significant and even harmful ways. While these groups possess a range of skin colors and facial features, it may be their symbolic labeling in these difficult times that makes them "nonwhite."

"Ethnic Options": Symbolic and Situational Ethnicity

How do we display our racial and ethnic group membership? We may do so in a number of ways: through dress, language, food, and religious practices; through preferences in music, art, or literature; even through the projects we find interesting and the topics we pursue at school. Sometimes these practices make our group membership obvious to others; sometimes they don't. White ethnics like Irish Americans and Italian Americans, for example, can actually choose when and how they display their ethnic group membership to others.

One way group membership is displayed is through **symbolic ethnicity**, enactments of ethnic identity that occur only on special occasions. For example, most Irish Americans have been so fully assimilated for multiple generations that their Irish ancestry may not matter much to them on a daily basis. But on St. Patrick's Day (especially in cities like Boston and New York), displays of Irish identity can be pretty overwhelming! Parades, hats, "Kiss me, I'm Irish" buttons, green clothing, green beer (and in Chicago, a green river!), corned beef and cabbage—all are elements of symbolic ethnicity. Similar ethnic displays occur on such holidays as Passover, Cinco de Mayo, and Nouruz.

Another way we can show group membership is through **situational ethnicity**, when we deliberately assert our ethnicity in some situations while downplaying it in others. Situational ethnicity involves a kind of cost-benefit analysis that symbolic ethnicity does not: We need to appraise each situation to determine whether or not it favors our ethnicity. For example, Dr. Ferris's Lebanese ancestry never mattered much, outside her own family, when she lived in Southern California. In fact, it was often something she felt she should downplay, given a political climate in which people of Arabic background were sometimes viewed with suspicion. But when she moved to Peoria, Illinois, she discovered that this small city had a relatively large population of Lebanese descent and that the mayor, a city councilman, the state senator, the congressman, local business, arts, and religious leaders, and prominent families were all Lebanese. This suddenly made Dr. Ferris's ethnicity a valuable asset in a way that it had never been before. She received a good deal of social support and made new friends based on shared revelations of ethnic group membership. In the case of situational ethnicity, we see how larger social forces can govern the identities we choose—if we have a choice.

Neither situational nor symbolic ethnicity is available to those who are visibly nonmainstream, whatever that may look like in a given society. In the United States, this generally means that nonwhites do not have a choice about whether to display their group membership. Most nonwhites don't have "ethnic options" that they can take or leave. As sociologist Mary Waters explains, "The social and political consequences of being Asian or Hispanic or black are not, for the most part, symbolic, nor are they voluntary. They are real, unavoidable, and sometimes hurtful" (1990, p. 156).

> **SYMBOLIC ETHNICITY** an ethnic identity that is relevant only on specific occasions and does not significantly affect everyday life
>
> **SITUATIONAL ETHNICITY** an ethnic identity that can be either displayed or concealed depending on its usefulness in a given situation

Analyzing Everyday Life

Displaying Ethnicity

Choose a setting where you can watch people "doing" ethnicity, either situational or symbolic. You should be able to find multiple places, occasions, or other opportunities to conduct this kind of research. For instance, you can go to a St. Patrick's Day parade, if your city hosts one, or attend an ethnic festival of some sort (such as St. Anthony's Feast Day in Boston's Italian North End or Los Angeles's annual African Marketplace). Or just visit one of your city's ethnic neighborhoods: Stroll through an Italian market in South Philadelphia, or shop the streets of Chicago's Ukrainian Village, Greektown, or Pilsen (a Mexican American neighborhood). You could check out the windmills and eat pastry in Solvang, a small city in central California founded by Danish teachers. If you think your town is too tiny to have any ethnic diversity, think again: Even minuscule Postville, Iowa (population 2,200), includes a large Hasidic Jewish population, with significant clusters of Mexican, Guatemalan, Ukrainian, Nigerian, Bosnian, and Czech immigrants. You may even find an appropriate setting on your college campus or at one of your own family gatherings.

For this Data Workshop you will be doing participant observation in order to produce a short ethnographic study. Return to Chapter 2 for a review of this research method. Once you have chosen a setting, notice your surroundings. Join in the activities around you while at the same time carefully observing how the other participants display their ethnic membership. As part of your observation, you will be writing field notes. Consider the following:

- What are participants wearing: traditional ethnic costumes, contemporary T-shirts, other symbols displaying their ethnic identity?

- What kind of music is being played, and what types of foods or crafts are available?

- Are different languages being spoken? If so, by whom and in what situations?

- What are the differences in the activities of adults and children, men and women, members and visitors?

- Listen for snatches of conversation in which members explain such traditions as buying a goldfish on the first day of spring (Iranian), wrapping and tying a tamale (Mexican), or wearing the claddagh ring (Irish).

- Can you identify any other elements relating to ethnicity in the setting, such as architecture, decor, art, or other items of material culture?

Finally, ask yourself these questions about your own ethnic identity:

- Do you have the option to display your ethnicity in some situations and withhold it in others? Why or why not?

- How do you decide whether, when, and how to display your ethnicity? What kind of cost-benefit analysis do you use?

- What role do ethnic and racial stereotypes, or stereotypes based on nationality, play in the process of displaying ethnicity?

- How do you think ethnic displays are received by others?

There are two options for completing this Data Workshop:

PREP-PAIR-SHARE Prepare written notes about your fieldwork that you can refer to in class. Discuss your experience with two or more students in a small group. Compare and contrast your fieldwork findings with those of your fellow group members. Listen as each person describes his or her own ethnic displays. As a group, can you come up with an overarching statement (or set of statements) about situational and/or symbolic ethnicity that helps explain what you learned?

DO-IT-YOURSELF Prepare written notes about your fieldwork. Consider all the questions and prompts provided and write a three-page paper describing your observations and experience, applying the concepts of situational and symbolic ethnicity in your analysis. Remember to attach your field notes to the paper.

THE U.S. POPULATION BY RACE

With each new generation, the United States is becoming a more diverse nation. Figure 8.1 shows the breakdown of various racial and ethnic groups and their percentage of the U.S. population. In 2018, whites made up approximately 60 percent of the population, Hispanics/Latinos 18 percent, blacks 13 percent, Asians 6 percent, and Native Americans about

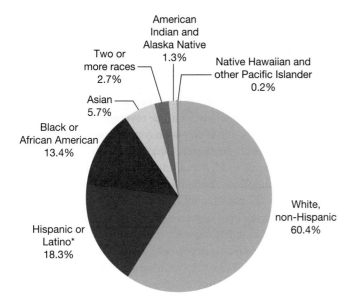

FIGURE 8.1 Racial and Ethnic Populations in the United States, 2018

*Hispanic origin is considered an ethnicity, not a race. Hispanics may be of any race. As a result, the total exceeds 100 percent.

SOURCE: U.S. Census Bureau 2019d.

1 percent (U.S. Census Bureau 2019d). The picture is actually more complicated than these categories suggest. Many Americans identify themselves as belonging to two or more races.

The U.S. Census Bureau conducts a comprehensive nationwide survey of the American people every ten years, with smaller-scale surveys in the intervening years. In the 2000 Census, Americans were given the opportunity for the first time to identify with more than one race, thus creating fifty-seven possible racial combinations. Of course, there have always been multiracial people in the United States, beginning with the European settlers who mixed with Native Americans and black slaves alike (Brooks 2002; Clinton and Gillespie 1997). Immigrant populations coming to the United States have added to its multicultural makeup. It is only logical that the separate lineages of the American people would eventually meld to a greater degree. We might, therefore, wonder: Will race and ethnicity continue to be as important in the future as they have been in the past?

What Is a Minority?

A *minority* is commonly thought of as a group that's smaller in number than the majority group. Thus, we could say that in the United States, whites are a majority while African Americans, Asians, Hispanics/Latinos, and Native Americans are minorities, because whites outnumber each of these other groups. But numbers don't tell the whole story. Sociologists define a **minority group** as people who are recognized as belonging to a social category (here either a racial or ethnic

group) and who suffer from unequal treatment as a result of that status. A minority group is denied the access to power and resources generally accorded to others in the dominant groups. Therefore, it is possible to be in the numerical majority and still have minority status with regard to power and opportunity. Take South Africa, for example: Blacks there dramatically outnumber whites by a ratio of seven to one, yet before the 1994 election of President Nelson Mandela, a small white minority controlled the country while blacks occupied the lowest status in that society.

California provides us with another example. In 2018, whites made up less than 40 percent of the state's population, whereas other ethnic groups (Hispanics/Latinos, blacks, Asian Americans, Native Americans) when added together constituted a majority of over 60 percent (U.S. Census Bureau 2019f). California, then, is a majority-minority state. Whites represent less than half the population; however, this doesn't make whites a minority group. Notably, whites remain the dominant group in terms of power, resources, and representation in social institutions. For instance, Hispanics/Latinos continue to be underrepresented in the University of California system (as both students and faculty) as well as in state government and as business owners but overrepresented in prisons, in poverty counts, and as victims of violent crimes. Similar disparities can be found in Hawaii, Texas, and New Mexico, all of which are majority-minority states, as is the District of Columbia.

Historically, whites have constituted a considerable majority of the American population, but this proportion is shrinking. In 1965, whites made up 85 percent of the population, compared to just over 60 percent now. The proportion of the U.S. population that is black has remained constant over the last few decades, while the proportions of Asians and Hispanics/Latinos have grown. Demographers predict that these trends will continue, and that by 2045, whites will make up just 49.7 percent of the U.S. population. This means that no single racial or ethnic group will represent the majority of the U.S. population, making the United States a majority-minority country (Frey 2018). Should we change the language of racial relations? Are the words "majority" and "minority" too confusing now that racial demographics have changed?

Membership in a minority group may serve as a kind of "master status," overriding any other status, such as gender or age. Members may be subjected to racist beliefs about the group as a whole and thus suffer from a range of social disadvantages. Unequal and unfair treatment, as well as lack of access to power and resources, typically generates a strong sense of common identity and solidarity among members of minority groups.

> **MINORITY GROUP** a social group that is systematically denied the same access to power and resources available to society's dominant groups though its members are not necessarily fewer in number than the dominant groups

RACISM IN ITS MANY FORMS

In order for social inequality to persist, the unequal treatment that minority groups suffer must be supported by the dominant groups. **Racism**, an ideology or set of beliefs about the claimed superiority of one racial or ethnic group over another, provides this support; it is used to justify unequal social arrangements between the dominant and nondominant groups (Kendi 2016). Racist beliefs are often rooted in the assumption that differences among groups are innate, or biologically based. They can also arise from a negative view of a group's cultural characteristics. In both cases, racism presumes that one group is better than another.

Some students have difficulty recognizing just how persistent and pervasive racism is in contemporary American society, while others experience it on a daily basis. We hear claims that it has been erased, but while we've made tremendous strides, especially in the wake of the civil rights movement, and again with renewed calls for social justice from the Black Lives Matter movement, racism is not yet a thing of the past. Racism is woven into the fabric of American society, from its historical roots to the present day. It is part of our national legacy and still persists within our social institutions.

There is still deep skepticism about whether negative racial attitudes are changing in America (Bobo et al. 2012). Many were hopeful that the election of the first black president, Barack Obama, in 2008 and again in 2012 was a sign of racial healing. But during his terms in office, racial strife continued and some would say worsened. Numerous high-profile incidents of police brutality and the killing of unarmed black men, including Freddie Gray, Michael Brown Jr., Eric Garner, and Philando Castile, contributed to social unrest. By 2016, polls showed that 69 percent of Americans thought that race relations were generally bad—the same level of racial discontent reported in 1992 after the Rodney King riots (Russonello 2016). Concerns about race relations deepened in the wake of Trump's election, fueled by his arguably racist references in speeches and tweets. In 2019, polls revealed that 40 percent of Americans said they personally worried "a great deal" about race relations in the United States, up from just 17 percent in 2014 (Gallup 2019).

RACISM a set of beliefs about the claimed superiority of one racial or ethnic group; used to justify inequality and often rooted in the assumption that differences among groups are genetic

PREJUDICE an idea about the characteristics of a group that is applied to all members of that group and is unlikely to change regardless of the evidence against it

DISCRIMINATION unequal treatment of individuals based on their membership in a social group; usually motivated by prejudice

IMPLICIT BIAS attitudes or stereotypes that are embedded at an unconscious level and may influence our perceptions, decisions, and actions

Prejudice and Discrimination

Racism can express itself through both prejudice and discrimination, and though the terms are often used interchangeably, there are important distinctions between them. **Prejudice**, literally a "prejudgment," is an inflexible attitude (usually negative, although it can work in the reverse) about a particular group of people that is rooted in generalizations or stereotypes. Examples of prejudice include opinions like "All Asians are good at math" or "All Mexicans are lazy." Prejudiced ideas don't always flow from the dominant group toward minorities. For instance, it's possible for members of a nondominant or minority group to hold negative stereotypes about the dominant group. It is also possible for minority group members to be prejudiced against themselves or their own group—what is sometimes referred to as "internalized racism" (Pyke 2010). Prejudiced ideas circulate through culture, making them hard to avoid, even for those who would wish not to have them. As we are socialized into the values and norms of society, we may unknowingly pick up some prejudice as well.

Prejudice often, but not always, leads to **discrimination**: an action or behavior that results in the unequal treatment of individuals because of their membership in a certain racial or ethnic group. A person might be said to suffer discrimination if they are turned down for a job promotion or a home loan because they're black or Hispanic. It is possible, though unlikely, that a person can be prejudiced and still not discriminate against others—sociologist Robert Merton called people in this category "timid bigots" (Merton 1949). For example, a teacher can believe that Asian American students are better at math yet know they should not let this belief influence their behavior as they grade Asian American students' work. Conversely, a person may not be prejudiced at all (or may not think they are prejudiced) but still unknowingly participate in discrimination by carrying out institutional policies, in schools or workplaces, that have discriminatory outcomes. An example would be promoting workers based on seniority, which almost always privileges dominant group members since minorities will usually be newer employees due to the history of discrimination in hiring.

Members of the dominant group, which is still whites in America, may thus enjoy certain benefits and advantages denied to minority group members without knowing that discrimination is the reason. Whites may believe in equality but still not act in such a way as to challenge the injustices perpetuated by our systems of stratification. This may be attributable to a phenomenon called **implicit bias**, meaning unrecognized or unconscious prejudices and stereotypes that shape our interactions with others. Studies have found, for example, that implicit bias affects how pediatricians treat pain management in children: White patients get more pain management help while black patients get less (Sabin and Greenwald 2012). School discipline is another example: Students of color are disciplined more often and

Ferguson, Missouri Protests erupted after the killing of unarmed black teenager Michael Brown by police in 2014. The Department of Justice confirmed that the Ferguson Police Department had violated the civil rights of black residents.

more harshly than white students (Lhamon and Samuels 2014).

Racial discrimination can take different forms. **Individual discrimination** (sometimes referred to as individual or interpersonal racism) occurs when one person treats others unfairly because of their race or ethnicity. A racist teacher might discriminate against a Hispanic student by assigning them a lower grade than they deserve. **Institutional discrimination** (sometimes referred to as systemic discrimination or systemic or institutional racism), in contrast, is more systematic and widespread and occurs when institutions (such as government agencies, schools, or banks) practice discriminatory policies that affect whole groups.

A powerful example of institutional discrimination involves the city of Ferguson, Missouri. Protests broke out in 2014 after a police officer shot and killed unarmed black teenager Michael Brown. Unrest over the issue escalated when a grand jury failed to charge the officer with murder. This led to an investigation by the U.S. Department of Justice (2015), which found that the Ferguson Police Department had been routinely violating the constitutional rights of its black residents. The DOJ issued a scathing report that documented widespread racial bias that pervaded practically every aspect of the local criminal justice process. In a city where blacks comprised 67 percent of the population, they accounted for 85 percent of vehicle stops, 88 percent of cases involving use of force, and 93 percent of arrests.

But institutional racism is not limited to the criminal justice system. Other major social institutions in our society also have policies with discriminatory outcomes. Richard Rothstein (2017) studied a century of housing policy in the United States and found that the Federal Housing Authority systematically and explicitly enacted policies that excluded African Americans while benefiting whites. In his book *The Color of Law*, Rothstein shows how, in the 1930s, the federal agency refused to insure mortgages for black borrowers—in both black and white neighborhoods—severely restricting the ability of blacks to own homes at all, much less in desirable, middle-class (read "white") subdivisions. Though it is now illegal, this policy, known as "redlining" (referring to the way African American neighborhoods were designated on federal maps), continues to this day and so does the segregation it produced. This is what systemic, institutional racism and discrimination looks like.

White Nationalism

Groups such as the Ku Klux Klan (KKK), Aryan Brotherhood, and Neo-Nazis espouse overtly racist and anti-Semitic ideas about white supremacy and racial separation. They believe that whites are innately superior to all other races and should thus hold power and control over all social institutions and resources. They want an all-white nation. Images of men in white robes and hoods burning crosses, lynch mobs, and skinheads with swastika tattoos are meant to strike terror and intimidate. While the KKK may be an extreme example, some of the ideas embraced by white supremacist groups are also part of the more populist alt-right movement. They share a common commitment

INDIVIDUAL DISCRIMINATION discrimination carried out by one person against another

INSTITUTIONAL DISCRIMINATION discrimination carried out systematically by institutions (political, economic, educational, and others) that affects all members of a group who come into contact with it

to **white nationalism**, or the belief that the nation should be built around a white identity that is reflected in religion, politics, economics, and culture.

White nationalism has gained traction in recent years, becoming much more visible during the presidential campaign and election of Donald Trump. Trump's anti-immigrant ideas (for example, his desire to limit the number of immigrants from Latin America) dovetail with white nationalist sentiment, and his administration has sought to bring those ideas into the political mainstream. Many of us watched in horror in August 2017 as white nationalists descended upon Charlottesville, Virginia, for a Unite the Right rally that erupted in violence. However, writing in the aftermath of the violence, sociologist Joe Feagin urges us to remember that white supremacy and white nationalism are nothing new, but rather have been with us since our country's founding. This history, he writes, is key to understanding why "racism today remains extensive, foundational, and systemic" (Feagin 2017, 2000). And while it may be tempting to write off white nationalism as deviant from American values and as the views of a fringe minority, research shows these same racist views are in fact held by many whites across the United States (Picca and Feagin 2007).

For much of American history, white dominance has been a reality. But with changing demographics, advances in civil rights, and greater emphasis on multiculturalism, some whites feel that the country no longer represents their identity or interests. Sociologist Arlie Hochschild spent years conducting interviews and focus groups and doing participant observation research for her study of Tea Party supporters in rural Louisiana. In her book *Strangers in Their Own Land* (2018), Hochschild explains how these blue-collar whites see themselves as "waiting in line" for the benefits of American life, and hence view immigrants and other nonwhite groups as "line-cutters"—people who don't deserve those benefits and who are snatching them out from under those who do deserve them. Those who feel this kind of anxiety about the direction of social change may be attracted to white nationalist ideas.

Of course, many whites and nonwhites alike welcome the nation's growing diversity and inclusivity. As the United States becomes an increasingly nonwhite nation, however, we are likely to see more pushback from the more extreme factions of the far right. The Southern Poverty Law Center (2019) charted a disturbing trend that worsened in 2018, fueled in part by the Trump administration and its anti-immigrant rhetoric and proposals to ban Muslims from entering the country. The number of hate groups in the United States rose to 1,020, up from 892 in 2015. The most dramatic growth was the near tripling of anti-Muslim hate groups from 35 in 2015 to 100 in 2018.

White Privilege and Color-Blind Racism

The concept of **privilege** is gaining greater currency while still garnering much debate. There are various mechanisms of privilege. In a stratified society, one may have privilege based on class, race, gender, sexuality, or other factors. The

WHITE NATIONALISM the belief that the nation should be built around a white identity that is reflected in religion, politics, economics, and culture

PRIVILEGE unearned advantage accorded to members of dominant social groups (males, whites, heterosexuals, the physically able, etc.)

White Privilege Onstage
Ingrid Silva of the Dance Theater of Harlem is changing the ballerina stereotype. In 2018 she still needed to paint her own pointe shoes with makeup to match her skin tone. It wasn't until very recently that pointe shoes for dancers of color were made commercially available. This is another example of how pervasive whiteness and white privilege are in contemporary society.

idea of the privileges of race dates back to early sociology and the work of W. E. B. DuBois (1903). More recently, Peggy McIntosh (1988) reintroduced the idea in a well-known article about "unpacking the invisible knapsack" of white privilege. In the past few decades, the idea has made its way into the various branches of academia and more widely into the national conversation.

"White privilege" is the idea that one group (whites) in a society enjoys certain unearned advantages not available to others (nonwhites) and that group members (whites) are largely unaware of the unequal benefits they possess. Privilege can include a wide range of advantages experienced in our large social institutions as well as in our small everyday interactions (Wise 2011, 2012). For example, whites can more easily assume that their interactions with authority figures (including but not limited to police officers, judges, bosses, and the like) will be with other whites, and this significantly reduces fear of unjust treatment or undeserved outcomes. On a much more microsociological level, whites are able to assume that they can find makeup, underclothes, and other products that match their skin color, whereas people with darker skin often struggle to find products that are truly "nude" when compared to their skin color. For example, for centuries, nonwhite ballerinas had to buy "white" pointe shoes (which were really a very, very light pink) and dye them themselves in order to match the color of their legs. Only in 2018 did brown pointe shoes become commercially available for dancers of color (Marshall 2018).

Because privilege is often invisible to the privileged, it can blind them to the challenges faced by members of nonprivileged groups. Whites may claim, for example, that race no longer matters and that we live in a "color-blind" society. After all, we elected a black president, so racism must be a thing of the past, right? The notion of color blindness sounds good (judging people by the "content of their character" rather than by the color of their skin), but it is also problematic because it implies that race should be both invisible and inconsequential. And that just isn't true.

We don't live in a "postracial" world, at least not yet. Race does matter, and racism does still exist. Racism today is neither as blatant as it once was—blacks and whites don't use separate bathrooms or drinking fountains—nor is it only a black-and-white issue. But it has taken other more subtle forms, such as the high concentration of corner liquor stores in predominantly black urban areas (where bigger supermarkets will not go) or the high concentration of Latino immigrants in low-wage jobs (that native-born Americans will presumably not take). When we claim to not see race, we are actually just engaging in a new, more "civilized" form of racism that sociologist Eduardo Bonilla-Silva calls "color-blind racism" (2003/2017). **Color-blind racism** is a set of beliefs, usually held by but not limited to whites, that we live in a society where racial prejudice and discrimination no longer exists, even though in reality it still does.

Color-blind racism is hard to combat, especially when so many people think it is a good thing to try to overlook race, to say that they don't see it. But there is an alternative: **race consciousness**, or an awareness of the importance of race in our everyday lives and in our dealings with social institutions. A race-conscious approach recognizes that despite the civil rights gains of the last hundred years, race is still a powerful factor in shaping our everyday lives and the world we live in. If we are to have a truly egalitarian society, we must recognize the historical record of racism and the social conditions that perpetuate contemporary inequalities. Whites and others might find that their own racial privilege plays a part in the social structure of racial inequality.

COLOR-BLIND RACISM
an ideology that removes race as an explanation for any form of unequal treatment

RACE CONSCIOUSNESS
an ideology that acknowledges race as a powerful social construct that shapes our individual and social experiences

MICROAGGRESSIONS everyday uses of subtle verbal and nonverbal communications that convey denigrating or dismissive messages to members of certain social groups

Microaggressions

Racism is not always as obvious as a swastika or the "N-word." Sometimes it's much more subtle. Racial **microaggressions** are the small-scale racial slights, insults, and misperceptions that play out in everyday interactions between people (Sue 2010; Sue et al. 2007). These exchanges typically occur between a person from the dominant (white) group and a member of a racial or ethnic minority. While microaggressions are typically subtle, casual, and often unintentional, they still deliver a powerful message that serves to denigrate

Get Out Jordan Peele's horror film *Get Out* dramatizes the microaggressions that black people face in their everyday lives.

or marginalize others because of their group membership. Sometimes these take the form of questions like "What are you?" or "Where are you really from?" that are demands to know a person's racial, ethnic, or national identity and reveal the underlying assumptions of the questioner as well as the persistence of racial stereotypes in shaping how we see and perceive each other.

Microaggressions can also be seen in body language, such as when a white woman clutches her handbag more closely when she passes by a group of Latino men, or when a white person asks to touch a black person's hair to see what it feels like. Microaggressions can include instances when persons of color are treated as second-class citizens, such as when they are mistaken for a service worker in a retail store or when they are passed over by a taxi cab driver who picks up a white person instead. Sometimes a microaggression might look like a compliment on the surface, such as when Asians are praised for how smart they are or mixed-race persons are told that they look exotic, but these statements further affirm stereotypes and may be taken as demeaning as well.

Cultural Appropriation

Cultural appropriation is another, often subtle form of racism. **Cultural appropriation** occurs when members of the dominant group adopt, co-opt, or otherwise take cultural elements from a marginalized group and use them for their own advantage. Cultural elements can include art, music, dance, dress, language, religious rituals, and other forms of expression that originate in a particular group. We see this borrowing (or some would say stealing) of cultural elements in a range of contexts, including costumes for Halloween or for college theme parties. Sometimes cultural appropriation is just insensitive. It can hurt the members of an aggrieved group, who may feel wronged, insulted, and offended. At the same time, it can have broader effects and serve to perpetuate negative stereotypes, exacerbate interracial relations, and further entrench social inequalities.

Let's look at some of the many instances of using the cultural symbols of various Native American peoples. Recent fashion runway trends have included suede and fringe, moccasins, and turquoise jewelry. Add to that some championship sports teams like MLB's Cleveland Indians or the NFL's Washington Redskins, both of which continue to use their derogatory names (and mascots) despite widespread objections. Critics contend that it is a problem when specific items or practices with sacred value (such as a headdress or a sweat lodge) are used without awareness of their significance or in a disrespectful way. Furthermore, cultural appropriation most often benefits the dominant group, which takes

CULTURAL APPROPRIATION the adoption of cultural elements belonging to an oppressed group by members of the dominant group, without permission and often for the dominant group's gain

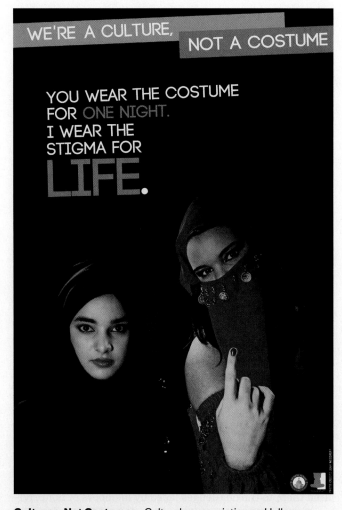

WE'RE A CULTURE, NOT A COSTUME

YOU WEAR THE COSTUME FOR ONE NIGHT. I WEAR THE STIGMA FOR LIFE.

Cultures, Not Costumes Cultural appropriation on Halloween is not just insensitive to another's culture; it's often offensive, too, especially when whites wear costumes associated with ethnic stereotypes or marginalized groups.

an oppressed group's cultural symbols and turns them into a commodity for profit. This kind of pillaging is postmodern cultural imperialism.

Hollywood has a long track record of cultural appropriation and commodification intended to enrich its owners and shareholders. In the early decades of the film industry, white actors often played minority characters, and there is a long list of disgraceful portrayals to name. Yet such practices have continued, despite considerable backlash both past and present. Recently we have seen A-list white actors cast in roles that are distinctly nonwhite, including Matt Damon, who played a Chinese warlord in *The Great Wall*; Scarlett Johansson, who played a Japanese anime character in *Ghost in the Shell*; and Emma Stone, who played a mixed-race Asian character in *Aloha*. These portrayals sparked controversy and were widely criticized as "white-washing" (Burr 2017; Martinelli 2015; Wong 2016). Perhaps this backlash will persuade studios and filmmakers to rethink their casting in the future and instead draw from the pool of talented and culturally appropriate actors waiting to fill such roles. These changes may happen more often as more minorities move into positions of power in the film industry.

Reverse Racism

Reverse racism is the claim that whites can also suffer discrimination based on their race and thus can experience the same kinds of disadvantages that minority groups have regularly encountered. This belief is persistent in the face of much data to refute it. A recent survey found that 49 percent of all Americans agree that discrimination against whites has become as big a problem as discrimination against blacks and other minorities, while another 49 percent disagree (Jones et al. 2016). These responses diverge when broken down by race: Only 29 percent of blacks and 38 percent of Hispanics agreed, compared with 57 percent of whites. Some of this difference of opinion among groups may derive from a fundamental misperception about what racism is and how it works.

Let's break it down. While whites may confront some forms of temporary, occasional, or situational discrimination, they don't suffer from the widespread cumulative disadvantages in almost every sphere of social life that are perpetuated within a historically and pervasively racist society. Even if all people of color espoused a hatred of whites, they would not be in the position to affect white people's ability to get an education or well-paying job or find a home, or increase the odds that whites would be racially profiled and disproportionately imprisoned. Racism against whites is not supported by the social structure or its major social institutions. According to sociologist Robin DiAngelo (2012), racism requires the ongoing use of institutional power and authority to perpetuate prejudiced and discriminatory actions in systemic ways with far-reaching effects. People of color may hold prejudices and discriminate against some whites, but they don't have the collective power to transform our society into one that is systematically biased against whites. Whites have the position and the power to influence the laws, practices, customs, and norms that define American society in ways not widely available to people of color.

AFFIRMATIVE ACTION Affirmative action is a particularly contentious area, and one about which claims of reverse racism have been made. Affirmative action policies, programs, and practices were established to help create opportunities for underrepresented minorities in housing, education, and employment. Some of the goals of affirmative action are to promote diversity and inclusion, provide equal access, and reduce the effects of historical discrimination. In the past few decades, critics have become more vocal in their opposition to affirmative action in the college admissions process. Several high-profile cases of white students suing universities on the grounds of reverse racism (because minority students were admitted when they were denied) have reached the Supreme Court and been struck down. Nevertheless, several states have passed laws banning the practice of affirmative action in higher education. California, which has the largest system of higher education in the nation, has sought to use other means to ensure a more equitable representation of students in its campus populations. While some opponents see affirmative action as giving one group of people unfair preferential treatment over others, proponents of social justice argue that these kinds of programs are necessary for creating a more level playing field in the United States.

> **REVERSE RACISM** the claim by whites that they suffer discrimination based upon their race and, therefore, experience social disadvantages
>
> **ANTIRACIST ALLIES** whites and others working toward the goal of ending racial injustice

Antiracist Allies

In the struggle for racial justice, people of color have necessarily led the way. Whites also have a role to play, and they can work in solidarity toward the same goals by becoming **antiracist allies**. One of the most effective ways that whites can challenge racism is by working with other whites to help them gain a greater awareness of how racism works and what they can do about it. This means more than just lending sympathy or support to organizations such as the Black Lives Matter movement or the Anti-Defamation League. It also means confronting racism in their own everyday lives, when and where they see it. Many whites have begun to think critically about white supremacy and white privilege, and they are in a unique position to recruit other whites to do likewise.

For many, it starts with getting educated about matters of race and racism and by listening to, rather than speaking for, people of color. It may also entail following the work of white antiracist authors and activists. In a growing number of social settings, such as schools, churches, and workplaces, whites are initiating peer group meetings to help support each other in their efforts to become better allies. New and existing organizations, such as the Unitarian Universalist Association (UUA) or Stepping Up for Racial Justice (SURJ), are now organizing around the goal of eradicating racism and can offer a framework for whites who want to be part of the solution. More whites are realizing that if they want a more inclusive, fair, and just society, they can no longer afford to stand on the sidelines.

THEORETICAL APPROACHES TO UNDERSTANDING RACE

Sociologists reject the notion that race has an objective or scientific meaning and instead seek to understand why race continues to play such a critical role in society. They have produced a number of theories about the connections among race, discrimination, and social inequality.

IN THE FUTURE
Whose Lives Matter?

The Black Lives Matter (BLM) movement arose in response to the extrajudicial killings of black men in cities across the United States, starting with the shooting of Trayvon Martin. Its mission is, most urgently, to make the United States a safer place for black people, a mission that challenges our country to acknowledge the continued existence of systemic racism. Systemic racism (sometimes called structural or institutional racism) is found in the policies and practices of social institutions (like education, the economy, the military, etc.) that result in discrimination against and exclusion of members of racial minority groups.

Neither individual intent nor explicitly racist policy is necessary for systemic racism to occur. In fact, most institutional settings (schools, businesses, government agencies) have diversity policies and are populated by individuals who really do want an inclusive environment and equitable outcomes. Plus, it's almost always against the law to craft policies that openly favor one racial group over another, and any institution that tries to do so will likely find itself in court. Systemic racism is built into all of our country's structures and institutions because it was part of our founding principles: The Constitution supported slavery by legally dehumanizing people of African descent, and the racism of our early republic still shapes us centuries later. Many people want to believe that we live in a "postracial" world, that racism isn't a problem anymore, and that those who claim it is—like BLM activists—are themselves racist for suggesting that there is still a racial divide. But if you have been paying attention while reading this chapter, you cannot deny that our country is still riven by racism.

One of the main claims made by BLM is that law enforcement, as one of our most powerful social institutions, discriminates against black people in myriad ways, including shooting to kill in cases where there is little or no actual threat to anyone's safety or when shots would likely not be fired at a white person. In addition, officers are less likely to be charged or convicted when they shoot black people. While cell phone videos and police dashboard and body cameras have finally made this problem visible to all, it is still difficult for many Americans to see these incidents as examples of systemic racism. The temptation is to find some way to blame the victim ("He must have looked at the cop wrong") or to make it about individual "bad apples" in an otherwise upstanding police force. BLM asks that we look at the system in addition to the individuals involved.

As sociologists, we must ask: Why do we resist the idea of systemic racism? In order to dismantle a discriminatory

Structural Functionalism

For example, functionalist theory has provided a useful lens for analyzing how certain ethnic groups, mainly European immigrants (such as the Irish and Italians) arriving in the early 1900s, eventually became assimilated into the larger society. Functionalism, however, has proved less successful in explaining the persistence of racial divisions and why other races and ethnicities, such as African Americans and Hispanics, have continued to maintain their distinct identities alongside the white majority culture today. This is because functionalism sees any kind of persistent social phenomenon through the lens of its contributions to social stability: If it exists/persists, it must be necessary and functional for social order, and that goes for racial inequality as well.

Perhaps what functionalism can best offer is an explanation of how prejudice and discrimination develop, by focusing on social solidarity and group cohesion. Groups have a tendency toward ethnocentrism, or the belief that one's own culture and way of life are right and normal. Functionalists contend that positive feelings about one's group are strong ties that bind people together. At the same time, this cohesiveness can lead members to see others, especially those of other races or ethnicities, in an unfavorable light. According to functionalists, these cultural differences and the lack of integration into the larger society on the part of minorities tend to feed fear and hostility.

Conflict Theory

Conflict theory focuses on the struggle for power and control. Classic Marxist analyses of race, developed by sociologists in the 1960s, looked for the source of racism in capitalist hierarchies. Edna Bonacich (1980), for instance, argued that racism is partly driven by economic competition and the struggle over scarce resources. A "split labor market," in which one

system, mustn't we see and understand it first? How can we plot a future in which Americans of all races acknowledge systemic racism, understand how it works, and commit to breaking it down for the good of all? How long will it take for black lives to matter to all of us? The more we know about the history of race and racism in the United States, the better we will be able to understand that racism did not disappear with the abolition of slavery (or the ratification of the Fifteenth Amendment, or the *Brown v. Board of Education* decision, or the Civil Rights Act, or the election of a black president), and the sooner we will understand that racism is more complicated than just black and white.

What can you contribute to the acknowledgment, apprehension, and obliteration of systemic racism in the United States? First, *learn* about our nation's history—not the sanitized version of it that you may have gotten in elementary or high school, but the real, messy, and complicated version you have access to now as an adult. Maybe start with Howard Zinn's *A People's History of the United States* and Ibram Kendi's *Stamped from the Beginning: The Definitive History of Racist Ideas in America* (2016). You'll also want to *listen*—to people whose experiences are different from yours. This can happen just about anywhere—in the classroom, at the bus stop, in church, at work, or even in your own family.

Then *act*—in whatever way you have the ability to act. That may mean you join a movement like BLM and participate in marches, lobbying, or other political tactics. But it

The Faces of a Movement Meet the co-founders of Black Lives Matter: Opal Tometi, Alicia Garza, and Patrisse Cullors.

can also mean refusing to laugh at racist jokes. It can mean spending money at businesses owned by people of color. It can mean writing a letter to the editor of your local newspaper. It can mean having difficult conversations with your friends or even your kids about race, difference, and inequality. It can mean volunteering in your community. It can mean traveling to other cities, states, or countries. None of these actions alone will solve the problem of systemic racism. But the more people are aware, interested, and active, the better are our chances for a future with less systemic racism.

group of workers (usually defined by race, ethnicity, or gender) is routinely paid less than those in other groups, keeps wages low for racial and ethnic minorities, compounding the effects of racism with those of poverty. William Julius Wilson (1980) posited that openly racist government policies and individual racist attitudes were the driving forces behind the creation of a black underclass but that the underclass is now perpetuated by economic factors, not racial ones. While this link between race and class is useful and important, it doesn't provide a satisfactory explanation for all forms of racial and ethnic stratification.

In recent years, conflict theorists have developed new approaches to understanding race. In his book *Racial Fault Lines: The Historical Origins of White Supremacy in California* (2008), for example, Tomas Almaguer looks at the history of race relations in California during the late nineteenth century. He describes a racial hierarchy that placed whites at the top, followed by Mexicans, blacks, Asians, and Native

Americans at the bottom. Rather than focusing exclusively on class, he examines how white supremacist ideology became institutionalized. Racist beliefs became a part of political and economic life during that period. Ideas like "manifest destiny" (the belief that the United States had a mission to expand its territories) helped justify the taking of lands, and the notion that Native Americans were "uncivilized heathens" helped justify killing them. Sociologists also argue that race isn't just a secondary phenomenon that results from the class system: It permeates both lived experience and larger-scale activity, such as the economy and the government (Omi and Winant 1994, 2015).

Still others have sought to understand the meaning of race from the individual's point of view and have begun to analyze the ways that race, class, and gender inequalities intersect. For instance, writers like Patricia Hill Collins (2006), bell hooks (1990), and Gloria Anzaldúa (1987) argue that race must be explained in the terms in which it is experienced, not as overarching general theories. Though some of these writers have been sharply critical of the symbolic interactionist tradition, which they believe does not take into account macro social forces that shape the realities of stratification, they share with interactionism a conviction that race, like all other aspects of social life, is created symbolically in everyday interactions. We will explore that idea further in the next section.

Critical race theory is an important, though still somewhat controversial, outgrowth of conflict theory (Bell 1980; Delgado and Stefancic 2012; Williams 1991). It was developed in the 1980s by legal scholars who drew upon writings in the social sciences to form a school of thought around the issues of race, politics, and power. They believe that racism permeates our social institutions, especially our judicial system, and must be recognized and addressed as such. One feature of critical race theory is a focus on intersectionality, or taking into account how race is also modified by class, gender, sexuality, and other social statuses. To understand the experiences of racism, one must consider the differing experiences of a woman of color, or a middle-class black man, or a gay Latino. Critical race theory encourages the inclusion of narratives from a multitude of intersecting voices and viewpoints. Another feature of critical race theory is its commitment to challenging racist laws and policies and promoting social justice. Some of the most visible figures in critical race theory engage in what is sometimes called public sociology—bridging legal and scholarly works with frontline involvement in solutions to the real-world problems of racial and gender oppression.

> **CRITICAL RACE THEORY** the study of the relationships among race, racism, and power
>
> **PASSING** presenting yourself as a member of a different group than the stigmatized group to which you belong

Symbolic Interactionism

Symbolic interactionists focus on how we perceive and interpret race in everyday life, looking at the meanings and ideas we hold and how this helps to produce and perpetuate real-world consequences. Meanings can and do change over time, and so has our understanding of race.

THE SOCIAL CONSTRUCTION OF RACE Sociologists understand race as a social rather than a biological category. Many people find this idea confusing, because the everyday understanding of race in the United States is that it is based on skin color, which is an inherited physical trait. Sociologists who study race, however, point out that there is no physical trait that will always accurately identify what race someone belongs to. As Michael Omi and Howard Winant point out in *Racial Formation in the United States* (1994, 2015), "although the concept of race invokes biologically based human characteristics," which particular features are chosen to make racial distinctions "is always and necessarily a social and historical process" (1994, p. 55). Even though they are expressed in terms of physical traits, the definitions of different racial groups are "at best imprecise and at worst completely arbitrary" (Omi and Winant 1994, 2015, p. 55). The definition of race is not stable but rather changes over time as racial categories are contested and developed.

This is not to say that race is unimportant. Omi and Winant show how racial groups are created socially and historically by arguing that "race can be understood as a fundamental dimension of social organization and cultural meaning in the U.S." (1994, p. viii). Real, physical bodies still matter to this process, but it is the meaning attributed to these bodies that determines what racial categories will exist, who will belong in them, and what they will mean.

For example, sociologist Stuart Hall was born in Jamaica but immigrated to England as a young man, where he became one of the founding figures in the development of cultural studies. He explained the social construction of race by recounting a conversation he'd had with his young son, who was the product of a mixed marriage. Hall describes a moment when his "son, who was two and a half, was learning the colors." Hall explained to him, "'You're Black.' And he said, 'No. I'm brown'" (2006, p. 222). Hall's son was thinking in purely physical terms. If race really were biological, he would have been correct, but as Hall explains, it is not skin color that created racial categories. If that were true, his son would belong to a different race than he. Race is not a preexisting biological category; it is a social one that is framed in terms of biological features.

Another aspect of the social construction of race is that we "read" others through myriad cues, and we in turn make ourselves readable to others by our own self-presentations. Our identity is constructed in the negotiation between what we project and what others recognize. Even master statuses such as race, gender, and age are negotiated in this way. So how *do* we project our racial or ethnic identities and read the racial or ethnic identities of others? We might think immediately of stereotypes like surfer dudes, sorority girls, "welfare moms," and so on. But in fact there are more subtle ways in which we project and receive our racial and ethnic identities. The interactional accomplishment of race is often easiest to see in the most unusual situations.

PASSING Racial **passing**, or living as if one is a member of a different racial category, has a long history in the United States. Both during and after slavery, some light-skinned African Americans attempted to live as whites in order to avoid the dire consequences of being black in a racist society. And people of different racial and ethnic backgrounds still pass, intentionally or unintentionally, every day in the United

TABLE 8.1 Theory in Everyday Life

Perspective	Approach to Race and Ethnicity	Case Study: Racial Inequality
Structural Functionalism	Racial and ethnic differences are a necessary part of society. Even racial inequality has functions that help maintain social order.	The functions of racial inequality and conflict for society could include the creation of social cohesion within both the dominant and minority groups.
Conflict Theory	Racial and ethnic differences create intergroup conflict; minority and majority groups have different interests and may find themselves at odds as they attempt to secure and protect their interests.	Some members of majority groups (whites and men in particular) object to affirmative action programs that assist underrepresented groups. This can create conflict among racial groups in society.
Symbolic Interactionism	Race and ethnicity are part of our identity as displayed through our presentation of self.	Some individuals (white ethnics and light-skinned nonwhites in particular) have the option to conceal their race or ethnicity in situations where it might be advantageous to do so. This may allow them as individuals to escape the effects of racial inequality but does not erase it from society at large.

States. Passing involves manufacturing or maintaining a new identity that is more beneficial than one's real identity. W. E. B. DuBois, a pioneer in the study of race, devised the concept of **double-consciousness**, which seems relevant to a discussion of passing. DuBois asked whether one could be black and at the same time claim one's rights as an American. Given the history of oppression and enslavement of African Americans, DuBois was not the only person to wonder whether this was possible. There are many social forces that disenfranchise and exclude minorities, and the phenomenon of passing suggests that in some places and times, it has been more advantageous to appear white if at all possible.

One hundred years later, a different kind of passing is gaining attention in the black community. Black masculinity makes demands on black men that include a public persona of heterosexuality. For black men who have sex with other men, this often creates a pressure to "pass," or live an apparently hetero lifestyle in which sexual relations with men happen only "on the down low" or "DL." Jeffrey McCune's (2014) ethnographic study of a Chicago nightclub catering to gay black men reveals the ways in which race shapes the performance of both gender and sexuality for men on the DL. "The Gate" played hip-hop music, infamous for its hypermasculine, heteronormative, and sometimes homophobic lyrics, but that didn't stop the clientele from turning the Gate into a space where their same-sex desires could be comfortably expressed. In their everyday lives, these men did the interactional work necessary to keep their sexuality private and their conventionally masculine and heterosexual images intact. But on Friday nights at the Gate, McCune observed that they could enjoy the coexistence of their multiple identities. Dancing to hip-hop music with other black men allowed them to both reinforce and accept dominant definitions of race, gender, and sexuality while also resisting and subverting them.

EMBODIED (AND DISEMBODIED) IDENTITIES Are we heading toward a future when race will matter less and less? In a digital age does race disappear when more and more interactions take place exclusively online? When we're interacting online, we may not always be able to see what others look like. In many online spaces, such as in e-mail, chat functions, or text messaging, we may not have any of the kind of physical cues that can tell us something about the other person. We may have only their written words to decipher and maybe just a small, inscrutable thumbnail photo of them in a corner of the posts, which makes it all the more difficult to ascertain their racial or ethnic background. This has been touted as one of the more democratizing traits of the Internet—that it can transcend, even obliterate, the real-world physical traits associated with categories like race, gender, or age that normally define us. It is such aspects of **embodied identity** (the way we are perceived in the physical world) that have historically been used as the basis for discrimination. These same ways of knowing about others through embodied characteristics are not necessarily available to those interacting online.

While the Internet has the potential to minimize race and other visible traits, that's not always what happens. It depends on the context. Adam Love and Matthew Hughey (2015) studied conversations on online men's college basketball forums, arguing that these conversations were implicitly racialized in conventional ways despite the fact that they took place in a disembodied setting. Love and Hughey found that the online conversations they studied largely involved older, affluent

> **DOUBLE-CONSCIOUSNESS**
> W. E. B. DuBois's term for the divided identity experienced by blacks in the United States
>
> **EMBODIED IDENTITY** those elements of identity that are generated through others' perceptions of our physical traits

IN RELATIONSHIPS
From the Lovings to Kimye: Interracial Dating and Marriage

Though it is now rather commonplace, at one point in history forty-one out of the fifty American states prohibited **miscegenation**—the romantic, sexual, or marital relationships between people of different races. In 1958, for example, Mildred and Richard Loving, an African American woman and a white man, married and settled in their native state of Virginia. In July of that year, they were arrested for violating the state's "Act to Preserve Racial Purity" and convicted. The judge sentenced them to a year in prison but suspended the sentence on the condition that the couple leave the state. The Lovings moved to Washington, DC, where in 1967 the Supreme Court overturned all such laws, ruling that the state of Virginia had denied the Lovings their constitutional rights. While the *Loving* decision technically cleared the way for interracial marriages nationwide, states were slow to change their laws. It took until 2000 for the state of Alabama to finally overturn the last antimiscegenation statute left in the nation.

> **MISCEGENATION** romantic, sexual, or marital relationships between people of different races

Just because it's legal doesn't always make it easy. People who date interracially may still face stigma and discrimination at a social and personal level. They may have to deal with in-group pressures from family, peers, and others to date (and especially marry) someone of their own race. Partnering with someone outside of one's group may be perceived as being disloyal and can elicit strong sanctions from other members. Stereotypes about members of different racial and ethnic groups are also slow to disappear.

Mildred and Richard Loving Their marriage was illegal in 1958.

People may hold on to racist and sexist notions about the attributes (or deficits) of men and women from different ethnic backgrounds and their suitability as romantic partners. We see these tensions played out in popular culture, in films, on TV shows, and in our own everyday lives. But real change is happening.

As diversity has rapidly increased in the United States, so has the number of interracial marriages. Young adults have more relationships with more people from diverse

white men talking about younger, less affluent black college students, and doing so in ways that initially appeared to be color-blind—in other words, race was almost never explicitly mentioned. However, racial meanings were still part of these conversations. Specifically, the online interactants were more likely to assign negative characteristics to black players than to white players, assuming, for example, that a player suspended for "breaking team rules" had engaged in criminal behavior if he was black, but attributing more innocent explanations for white players in the same situation. The interactants still engaged in conventional, prejudiced racial talk, as their assumptions were racialized even if their

language was not. The Internet is thus not a place where all the problematic distinctions disappear—they just manifest themselves in different ways.

RACE, ETHNICITY, AND LIFE CHANCES

A law professor decides that it is time to buy a house. After careful research into neighborhoods and land values, she picks one. With her excellent credit history and prestigious job, she easily obtains a mortgage over the phone. When the

backgrounds, and they are more favorable to forming a romantic partnership with someone from another racial or ethnic group. Spurred in part by a rise in immigration to the United States, interracial marriage has increased steadily, from just 0.4 percent of all married people in 1960 to 10 percent in 2015; the share climbs to 17 percent among newlyweds, who have had perhaps the most diverse dating pool of any generation (Livingston and Brown 2017). These figures do not yet reflect same-sex partners or unmarried cohabiters, groups that would certainly add to the trend.

The prevalence of intermarriage varies by demographic group and at the intersections of race, gender, age, and education. While the data point to a marked rise in intermarriage across all the major ethnic and racial groups in the United States, intermarriage is most common among Asians (29 percent of newlyweds) and Hispanics (27 percent), followed by blacks (18 percent) and whites (11 percent). The data are somewhat complex. For instance, if we also consider the variable of gender, Asian women marry outside their race far more often than Asian men do, while African American women marry far less often outside their race than African American men do. Finally, interracial marriage is somewhat more common among those who are college educated (Livingston and Brown 2017).

Since the time of the *Loving* case, society's attitudes about mixed-race relationships have radically changed, becoming much more positive. In 2017, 39 percent of Americans said that marrying someone of a different race was good for society. More Millennials say this is a good trend than do Gen Xers or Baby Boomers (Livingston and Brown 2017). The decline in disapproval rates over time is even more dramatic: The number of nonblack adults who said they would be opposed to a close relative marrying a black person declined from a

The Royal Couple Prince Harry and Meghan Markle's interracial marriage made history. The palace and the public alike have delighted in the couple, hailing their union as a welcome sign of change.

high of 63 percent in 1990 to a low of 14 percent in 2017. Disapproval for interracial marriage to Hispanics or Asians is just 9 percent, and for whites it is 4 percent.

Stigma, prejudice, and restrictive racial stereotypes, as well as entrenched negative beliefs on the part of some people, all remain persistent challenges to creating a more widely accepting, multicultural, and multiracial society. Nonetheless, the rise in interracial marriage is an indication of significant social change. One researcher said that this trend "reflects an important shift toward blurring a long-held color line in the United States" (Frey 2014a).

mortgage forms arrive in the mail, she sees to her surprise that the phone representative has identified her race as "white." Smiling, she checks another box, "African American," and mails back the form. Suddenly, everything changes. The lending bank wants a bigger down payment and a higher interest rate. When she threatens to sue, the bank backs down. She learns that the bank's motivation is falling property values in the proposed neighborhood. She doesn't understand this; those property values were completely stable when she was researching the area. Then she realizes that *she* is the reason for the plummeting values.

Patricia Williams's (1997) experience is not an isolated case. Sociological studies have found that membership in socially constructed categories of race and ethnicity often carries a high price. We now look at other ways this price might be paid in the areas of family, health, education, work, and criminal justice.

Family

Race, ethnicity, and their correlates (such as SES) shape family life in a variety of ways. Data from the U.S. Census Bureau (2018e) show that African Americans are more likely than whites and Hispanics to never marry. While 51 percent of white households and 48 percent of Hispanic households include a married couple, the same is true of just 28 percent of black households (U.S. Census Bureau 2018a). This means that black and Hispanic children are significantly more likely to live in single-parent homes. In 2018, for example, 75 percent of white children lived with two parents compared to 67 percent of Hispanic children and just 40 percent of black children; nearly half of all black children live with their mother only (U.S. Census Bureau 2018d).

Kathryn Edin (Edin and Kefalas 2005) has argued that low-income women of all ethnicities see marriage as having few benefits. They feel that the men they are likely to encounter as possible husbands will not offer the advantages (financial stability, respectability, trust) that make the rewards of marriage worth the risks. This doesn't mean, of course, that most low-income women don't love their male companions; it only means that they believe a legal bond would not substantially improve their lot in life.

In 2015, the birth rates for American teenage mothers (ages fifteen to nineteen) varied significantly by race. The birth rate for white teenage moms was 16 per 1,000 births, while the birth rate for African Americans was 32 per 1,000; for Hispanics it was 35 per 1,000 (Martin et al. 2017). Social thinkers such as Angela Y. Davis argue that African American teenage girls in particular see fewer opportunities for education and work and choose motherhood instead (2001). Davis believes that social policies aimed at punishing teenage mothers of color will be ineffective; only by our attacking the racism inherent in the educational system and the workforce will these teens be at less risk of becoming mothers.

Health

Health is an area in which we find widespread disparity among racial and ethnic groups. Whites have typically fared better in health matters than minorities, although this is not always the case. Recent findings reveal a complicated picture of the nation's health when intersections among race, class, and gender are taken into account.

One way of measuring health is to look at life expectancy and mortality rates. White male children born in 2015 can expect to live to be around 76 years old, while white females can expect to live to 81. African American males' life expectancy is 71 years, and African American females' is 78. Notably, Hispanics have the highest life expectancy, higher even than whites: 79 years for Hispanic men and 84 for Hispanic women (Centers for Disease Control and Prevention 2018a). Other important indicators of health are infant and maternal mortality: Black mothers die from pregnancy complications at a rate of over three times that of other mothers (Creanga et al. 2012), and infant mortality for black babies is more than double that of whites (Villarosa 2018).

These variables are part of a robust case that can be made for the negative effects of racism on the health of racial and ethnic minorities in the United States. Researchers use the term "weathering" (Geronimus et al. 2006) to describe the ways that exposure to racism erodes one's health: High levels of racially differentiated stressors affect black individuals more intensely than whites and lead to higher levels of chronic disease and lower life expectancies. Racial and ethnic minorities are also often disproportionately exposed to other factors that affect life span, such as dangers in the workplace, toxins in the environment, and violence.

Another ongoing issue for Americans is access to health-care insurance and medical services. Many health-care consumers rely on insurance benefits provided through their employer if they have a job with such benefits; if not, they must buy individual insurance policies in order to meet their medical needs, and many Americans cannot afford even basic health-care coverage. While the passage of the Affordable Care Act reduced uninsured rates, particularly among racial and ethnic minorities, disparities remain: In 2017, 16 percent of Hispanics and 11 percent of blacks lacked health insurance, compared to just 6 percent of whites and 7 percent of Asians (Berchick, Hood, and Barnett 2018).

Education

One of America's cultural myths is that everyone has equal access to education, the key to a secure, well-paying job. However, by looking at those who actually receive degrees, we can see that the playing field is not that level. The high school graduation rate in 2017 was 91 percent for Asians, 89 percent for whites, 80 percent for Hispanics, and just 78 percent for blacks (National Center for Education Statistics 2019b). The reasons for dropping out of high school are complex, but the highest rates are associated with those from economically disadvantaged and non-English-speaking backgrounds. In 2015, Hispanics had the highest high school dropout rate of all racial groups, at 9 percent.

Victor Rios (2017) spent five years in schools and community centers documenting what happens to Latino youth in what has been called the school-to-prison pipeline. Rios traces a pattern in which some Latino youth encounter negative experiences with teachers and other school authorities who misunderstand the students' cultural cues and background. This can result in those students being labeled as "bad," "deviant," or "at risk," further stigmatizing them within the school system. There may be greater scrutiny and punishment of Latino youth, sometimes leading to suspension or expulsion from school. This process serves to criminalize Latino youth, sending them on a path away from education and mainstream society. At the same time, these youths are also surveilled by police in their communities, where they may experience similarly negative interactions and consequences.

In higher education, there are similar disparities of achievement. In 2018, 57 percent of Asian Americans over age twenty-five, 39 percent of whites, 25 percent of blacks, and 18

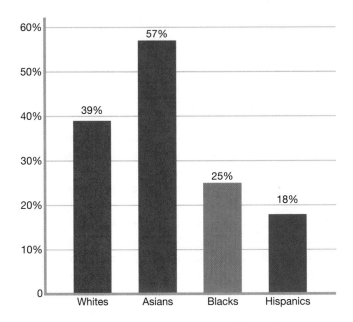

FIGURE 8.2 Americans over Age Twenty-Five with Bachelor's Degrees by Race/Ethnicity, 2018

SOURCE: U.S. Census Bureau 2019a.

percent of Hispanics had a bachelor's degree or higher (Figure 8.2). Thus, Asian Americans and whites enjoy more success overall in the U.S. educational system than African Americans and Hispanics do. The reasons for the disparity are again complex, involving both economic and cultural factors. As noted in Chapter 7, students from lower-income families are less likely to go on to college, and ethnic minority families tend to have lower household incomes than white households.

Claude Steele (2010) has identified something called "stereotype threat," a social-psychological mechanism at play among minority college students that hinders their academic performance. Steele discovered that negative racial stereotypes may adversely affect African American students when they are in highly demanding situations in which they might risk confirming those stereotypes. In competitive, high-stakes academic conditions (such as test-taking), stereotype threat can cause sufficient anxiety in those students to effectively harm their abilities. In less stressful situations, when no negative stereotypes are invoked, these students perform as well as peers of other races. Steele suggests that stereotype threat may help explain some of the achievement gap between racial groups. Jennifer Lee and Min Zhou (2015) have identified an inverse phenomenon that they call "stereotype promise." Because there are positive stereotypes associated with the academic performance of Asian Americans, those students may reap benefits in similarly stressful situations when they might confirm such stereotypes.

Earning an education is extremely important in American society. Not only does it translate to greater success in the workforce, but it also confers social status and cultural capital that can prove valuable in other arenas.

Work and Income

Persons of color carry the burden of some of society's most difficult jobs. In 2018, 36 percent of all nursing, psychiatric, and home health aides and 41 percent of all postal clerks were black, while Hispanics were more likely to be employed in farming (46 percent of all farmworkers) and as maids and housecleaners (49 percent of total) (U.S. Bureau of Labor Statistics 2019c). Except for nursing, these jobs are more likely to be semiskilled or unskilled. Thus, people of color, who are less likely to achieve high levels of education, are more likely to swell the bottom rungs of the job market. Interestingly, some lower-level jobs have shifted from African Americans to Hispanics over time. For instance, in 1983, African Americans accounted for 42 percent and Hispanics for 12 percent of all private household cleaners; by 2018, blacks accounted for only 16 percent. A similar shift may be seen with other low-wage jobs. This means that persons of color increasingly compete with each other for such jobs.

In part due to the segregation of people of color in low-wage occupations, we see enduring income gaps between white workers and black and Hispanic workers. In 2017, the median household income was $68,145 for whites, $50,486 for Hispanics, and $40,258 for African Americans. Asian Americans had the highest median income, at $81,331 (Fontenot, Semega, and Kollar 2018). In other words, in 2017, the median incomes of black and Hispanic households were just 59 percent and 74 percent, respectively, of that of white households. The median incomes of whites and Asian Americans thus place them firmly in the middle and upper-middle class, respectively, while those of blacks and Hispanics place them in the lower-middle class. Blacks and Hispanics are also more likely to live in poverty: In 2017, 9 percent of whites lived below the poverty line, compared with 21 percent of African Americans and 18 percent of Hispanics (Fontenot, Semega, and Kollar 2018). These numbers make it easy to see how race and class intersect to influence life outcomes.

Racial discrimination contributes to the problems minorities face in the U.S. labor market. One study looked at the impact of racially identifiable names on one's chances of receiving job callbacks from employers (Bertrand and Mullainathan 2004). Researchers submitted résumés in response to help-wanted ads in Boston and Chicago. To manipulate the perception of race, each résumé was assigned either a stereotypically white name such as Emily or Greg or a black-sounding name such as Lakisha or Jamal. The study results showed marked discrimination. Résumés with white-sounding names garnered a 50 percent higher callback rate than identical résumés with black-sounding names. When the researchers listed additional qualifications, the higher-quality résumé elicited 30 percent

ON THE JOB
Diversity Programs: Do They Work?

Many workplaces—academic, government, and corporate—are experimenting with different programs in an effort to increase the diversity of their workforces. A quick look at the numbers and it is clear why these programs are necessary: In 2016, there were five African American CEOs of *Fortune* 500 companies and twenty-one female CEOs, representing 1 percent and 4.2 percent of *Fortune* 500 CEOs, respectively. With companies like Bank of America settling huge race-discrimination lawsuits in recent years, the stakes are high, but what do we know about these different diversity initiatives and their ability to truly increase diversity?

Sociologists Frank Dobbin and Alexandra Kalev (2016) analyzed three decades of data from more than 800 U.S. firms, and interviewed hundreds of managers and executives, to learn what works—and what doesn't—when it comes to diversity programs. First, Dobbin and Kalev found that top-down approaches to diversity, including diversity training programs as well as tools like hiring tests and performance ratings, are generally not effective. They found that the positive effects of diversity training typically faded after just a few days and that some companies experienced adverse effects. Part of the problem, they found, is that companies often make these training programs mandatory, evoking anger and resistance from participants. Companies saw much better results when they made the training voluntary. Companies that instituted voluntary diversity training programs saw increases of 9 to 13 percent in women and in black, Hispanic, and Asian men in management positions after five years (Dobbin and Kalev 2016).

But the most effective diversity programs, Dobbin and Kalev found, are not the ones that come from above but rather those that engage managers in solving the problem, increase managers' contact with female and minority workers, and promote social accountability. These programs include mentoring and college recruitment programs. For example, five years after implementing a college recruitment program targeting women, companies saw their share of white, black, Hispanic, and Asian women in management increase by an average of 10 percent. Diversity task forces and diversity managers were also found to be successful, namely by increasing social accountability. When managers knew their hiring decisions were going to be reviewed by a diversity manager, they were more likely to consider all qualified applicants (Dobbin and Kalev 2016). A growing number of organizations, from the Veterans Administration to *Fortune* 500 companies and community colleges, have established new internal offices or centers whose sole directive is infusing diversity, equity, and cultural competency into the workplace culture, policies, and environment.

Of course, there may be some backlash to such organizational changes. A recent study found that high-status groups such as white men interpret pro-diversity messages as unfair and as threatening to their status position. The experiment found that when an organization mentioned being pro-diversity, white male applicants were more likely to express concerns over discrimination and overall performed less well than white men applying to a company that didn't mention diversity (Dover, Major, and Kaiser 2016). There may be those individuals who argue that promoting workplace diversity through training and employee-support programs is neither necessary nor a worthwhile use of organizational resources. Everyone has an equal chance of making it to the top, they say, and women, blacks, Latinos, gays and lesbians, the disabled, and other workers should all just "pull themselves up by their own bootstraps." The debate over whether historically disadvantaged groups should receive any kind of special attention has been with us for decades and will continue to rumble for as long as inequality persists in our society.

But think about it this way: If you were the head of an organization, wouldn't you want to make sure you were doing everything you could to create a diverse, inclusive, and equitable workplace that benefits from the contributions of everyone working for you? And that you weren't overlooking the skills and talents of potential employees for baseless reasons like their gender, race, or sexual orientation?

Diversity Training After a Philadelphia Starbucks employee called the police on two black men merely for sitting in the coffee shop, the company closed all U.S. stores for a day of diversity training.

more callbacks for the white applicants but a far smaller increase for blacks. Discrimination occurred regardless of the job occupation or industry.

Criminal Justice

Although the majority of the U.S. population is white—about 60 percent, as opposed to about 13 percent black and 18 percent Hispanic—we don't find these same proportions in the prison population. Of all state and federal prisoners in 2016, 33 percent were African American, while 30 percent were white and 23 percent Hispanic (Carson 2018). Why are larger proportions of African Americans and Hispanics in prison?

One explanation is the practice of racial profiling in policing, which we discussed in the chapter opener. Data on pedestrian and motor vehicle stops demonstrate that blacks and Hispanics are 127 percent more likely than whites to be stopped and 43 percent more likely to be frisked. Despite this unequal policing, blacks and Hispanics are 42 percent and 32 percent less likely to be in possession of a weapon or drugs than are whites (American Civil Liberties Union 2008). While not justified statistically, these higher stop and search rates increase the likelihood that black and Hispanic drivers and pedestrians will be placed into contact with the criminal justice system and experience unequal treatment in the application of laws. Other factors to consider are higher unemployment rates among minority groups, as well as higher dropout rates; in other words, a lack of both education and job opportunities may contribute to higher incarceration rates.

Some laws that don't seem race based still create racially differentiated outcomes. For example, federal law until 2010 handed out far tougher sentences to crack cocaine users (who were more likely to be black) than to users of powdered cocaine (who were more likely to be white or Hispanic). If you possessed a small amount of crack cocaine, say 5 grams (for personal use), you'd get the same mandatory ten-year sentence that you would receive if you possessed a huge amount of powder cocaine, like 500 grams (enough for hundreds of uses). This disparity was rooted in the misperception of crack as a far more dangerous or damaging substance, when in fact it is actually quite similar to powder cocaine.

During the 1980s and 1990s crack cocaine use soared, in part because of its lower price point. Black communities suffered disproportionately from what was called the "crack epidemic." In 2010, 79 percent of the federally sentenced crack offenders were black, despite research indicating that two-thirds of crack users were white or Hispanic. The Fair Sentencing Act of 2010 reduced the sentencing disparity from a ratio of 100:1 to 18:1. While this judicial reform was a step toward greater fairness, it still means that sentencing for crack cocaine is eighteen times harsher than for powder cocaine. Many social justice advocates call for the complete elimination of the disparity (a 1:1 ratio). Another issue is that the law does not apply retroactively to those offenders who were already sentenced before its passage. Furthermore, the Fair Sentencing Act applies only to federal offenders, leaving a much larger number of nonviolent drug offenders to face far stiffer penalties at the state and local levels.

African Americans are also more likely to be victims of homicide: In 2017, blacks accounted for approximately 52 percent of murder victims nationwide despite representing only 13 percent of the population; whites represented 61 percent of the U.S. population but 43 percent of murder victims (Federal Bureau of Investigation 2018a). Finally, over half of the reported hate crimes in 2017 were attributed to race, ethnicity, or ancestry bias, with 49 percent targeting blacks, 18 percent targeting whites, and 11 percent targeting Hispanics (Federal Bureau of Investigation 2018b).

Intersectionality

As you might have already concluded, race and ethnicity do not shape our life chances in isolation from other social statuses and aspects of identity. Instead, race and ethnicity are frequently enmeshed with social class, gender, sexuality, and more. Sociologist France Winddance Twine (2011b) demonstrates this in her ethnographic study of white women who have families with black men. As the intimate partners of black men, these women effectively lose some of their whiteness—especially in the eyes of their white working-class friends and family—and become "honorary blacks." This loss of whiteness is a form of punishment exacted by their ethnicity- and class-based communities, but it is not meted out equally to white men who marry black women. Twine's work identifies the intersection of class, race, and gender by showing the ways in which "interracial intimacy and the racism that accompanies it is a gendered experience" (p. 30).

An additional social status, motherhood, is also part of the intersectionality in Twine's study. White mothers of interracial children may not possess the racial literacy to raise those children in a world that will almost certainly see and treat them as black. From cooking and hair care to preparation for experiencing racism, these mothers—because they are women and because they are white—must calibrate their

TABLE 8.2 Federal Cocaine Offenders by Race/Ethnicity, 2012

| | Powder | Crack | All Drug Types |
Race/Ethnicity	Percent	Percent	Percent
White	12.6	4.2	21.8
Black	32.3	88.1	38.8
Hispanic	54.2	7.1	37.2
Asian	0.5	0.3	1.5

SOURCE: Bureau of Justice Statistics 2015a.

parenting practices in order to address race and racism in ways that their own mothers did not. In Twine's work, race, class, gender, and parenthood combine to shape the lived experiences of individuals and families.

DATA WORKSHOP

Analyzing Media and Pop Culture

Does TV Reflect the Realities of Race?

Maybe you've noticed a change recently in the TV landscape. In the past several years, we've seen an increase in the number of TV shows that include diverse casts from a range of different racial and ethnic backgrounds. Shows like *Black-ish* and *Atlanta, Fresh Off the Boat,* and *Jane the Virgin* revolve around main characters who are black, Asian, and Latina. And they're not alone. There are many other shows with predominantly nonwhite casts. It wasn't so long ago that TV was largely populated by white characters, with only the occasional minority sidekick thrown in. Today it is much easier to find shows that feature multicultural casts and in which race is a central theme.

While such gains are encouraging, we are still far from reaching something that looks like racial parity onscreen. Nearly 40 percent of the U.S. population is composed of minorities, and yet they remain woefully underrepresented both in front of and behind the camera as actors, writers, and directors (Hunt et al. 2017). During the 2014–2015 season, minorities represented just 11 percent of lead roles in broadcast scripted TV shows, though this does represent a sizable increase from just 5 percent in the 2011–2012 season. According to UCLA media researchers Darnell Hunt and Ana-Christina Ramon, "from the earliest days of the industry, white males have dominated the plum positions in front of and behind the camera, thereby marginalizing women and minorities in the creative process by which a nation circulates popular stories about itself" (2015, p. 53).

One reason we may be seeing more minorities on TV is simply a matter of the bottom line: America's increasingly diverse audiences prefer more diverse TV content. Additionally, as more minorities move into positions of power in the creative process, more TV shows are now taking on race in incisive, courageous, and nuanced ways. Audiences are seeing a broader range of character portrayals and situations and settings that more closely reflect the lived experiences of minorities. Seeing oneself represented in the media is critically important to feeling included in a multicultural society. Greater representation can also serve to challenge racial and ethnic stereotypes and break down preconceived ideas about the members of minority groups. But that's not to say that TV is completely realistic when it comes to race. We are only getting a selective slice of the real world when we watch TV, and often that content can still be narrow, superficial, exaggerated, or just plain unrealistic.

For this Data Workshop, you'll be watching TV and analyzing how it reflects the realities of race and ethnicity in contemporary society. Choose a TV series (drama, comedy, or reality show) that takes place in current times and includes minority characters. You might consider those already mentioned earlier or one of the following:

Ballers	*Insecure*
Being Mary Jane	*The Last O.G.*
Brooklyn Nine-Nine	*Master of None*
The Chi	*One Day at a Time*
Empire	*On My Block*
The Good Place	*Orange Is the New Black*
Greenleaf	*Power*
Grey's Anatomy	*Queen Sugar*
Grown-ish	*Sunnyside*
How to Get Away with	*The Shahs of Sunset*
Murder	*This Is Us*

You will be using existing sources as a research method and doing a content analysis of one episode of the TV series you chose. Refer to Chapter 2 for a review of this research method. Watch a recent episode of your chosen series in its entirety. You will want to record the program or look for an episode on DVD or that you can stream from Netflix, Hulu, or another online source so that you can review certain scenes, interactions, or bits of dialogue several times. Take notes as you watch, paying special attention to the episode's content as it relates to race and ethnicity. Your notes can be informal but should be specific and detailed. Your notes will serve as the data set you'll be analyzing.

Consider your response to the following prompts or add your own questions for analysis:

- Look up your series on IMDb or Wikipedia to learn more about its creators. Who is in control of production, direction, or writing, and how might that affect the show's content?

- Is race an explicit theme of the show, and if so, how is it addressed? Or are matters of race more implicit or in the background?

Diversity on TV *Jane the Virgin* and *Atlanta* are two shows with predominantly nonwhite casts. Despite the success of these shows, minorities still remain highly underrepresented as actors, writers, and directors.

- How many minority characters are featured in the episode? What proportion of the total cast do they represent?

- In what ways are minority characters portrayed? (You may choose to focus on one or two characters or more.) Do the characters uphold certain racial or ethnic stereotypes or challenge them?

- Describe instances in which characters display aspects of situational or symbolic ethnicity.

- How does the race or ethnicity of characters intersect with other social statuses or identities such as class, gender, or sexuality?

- To what extent do you think the show reflects the "real world"? Use the information in the "Race, Ethnicity, and Life Chances" section of this chapter for reference.

- In what ways might the show help to maintain or perpetuate prejudice and discrimination? In what ways might the show help to counteract prejudice and discrimination?

- What kind of an impact did the episode have on you as a viewer? How might it shape the perceptions of other audience members with regard to race or ethnicity?

There are two options for completing this Data Workshop:

PREP-PAIR-SHARE Bring your informal notes to class and be ready to discuss your preliminary analysis of the show. Form a small group with one or more classmates, and take turns talking about your responses to the prompts. Discuss your own findings, and listen to how others in the group analyzed their shows. What kinds of similarities or differences did you find in your respective analyses? Were there any common themes that emerged across everyone's chosen shows?

DO-IT-YOURSELF Take notes while you watch an episode of your chosen TV show. Write a three- to four-page paper discussing your content analysis and responses to the prompts above. Make sure to incorporate and explain the relevant sociological concepts about race and ethnicity in your discussion. Attach your informal notes as an appendix to your paper.

INTERGROUP RELATIONS: CONFLICT OR COOPERATION

The relationships among racial and ethnic groups in a society can take different forms. In some instances, groups may be tolerant and respectful of one another, while in other cases there is unending hostility. In this section, we will examine five basic patterns of intergroup relationships, from the most violent to the most tolerant. Keep in mind that some ethnic groups, such as Native Americans, may suffer several different patterns of hardship over a period of time.

Genocide

The first pattern represents the worst possible outcome between dominant and subordinate groups. Not only has **genocide**—the deliberate and systematic extermination of a racial, ethnic, national, or cultural group—taken place in the past, but it continues today in certain parts of the globe.

The twentieth century witnessed numerous incidents of genocide. From 1915 to 1923, during and after World War I, the Turkish government massacred

> **GENOCIDE** the deliberate and systematic extermination of a racial, ethnic, national, or cultural group

1.5 million Armenians in what is often referred to as the "forgotten genocide." Nazi Germany under Adolf Hitler's rule killed two-thirds of the Jews of Europe. Few paid attention to the Armenian tragedy, and many refused to believe the initial reports of Hitler's death camps as well (Hitler himself recognized this, and is alleged to have asked, "Who remembers the Armenians?" when he embarked on his own genocidal project). In the latter half of the century, such events became all too common. From the atrocities of Darfur to Slobodan Milošević's ethnic cleansing in the Balkans and the Hutu slaughter of Tutsi in Rwanda, genocide has become a familiar feature of the modern landscape.

It is also possible to consider the violence perpetrated by the early Americans against the Native American tribes who occupied North America as a form of genocide. While Native Americans died from diseases introduced by the settlers, they were also systematically killed by the European colonists. In the few hundred years that it took for the United States to be settled from coast to coast, the Native American population was almost completely wiped out. Estimates for the total number killed range anywhere from 15 million up to 100 million (Cook 1998; Stannard 1993).

Population Transfer

The treatment of Native Americans leads us to the next pattern of group relations—**population transfer**, or the forcible removal of a group of people from the territory they have occupied. In the early nineteenth century, Native Americans who had not perished in battles with U.S. soldiers were forced by the U.S. government to move onto Indian reservations (also referred to as tribal lands or American Indian nations) west of the Mississippi River. They were often moved far away from the lands where they had lived for generations (mostly southern states), as these were desirable territories that the whites wished to acquire for themselves. Between 1838 and 1839, in one of the most well-known examples, the state of Georgia and the federal government forcibly marched 17,000 Cherokees westward over 800 miles, a grueling journey known as the Trail of Tears. Along the way, more than 4,000 people died of hunger, exposure, or disease.

The separate territories established for the Native Americans are an example of a kind of partitioning that we can see happening today in Israel between the Israelis and Palestinians in the West Bank and Gaza Strip. There the Israeli government restricts the movement of Palestinians and has even built miles of barriers designed to wall them in and keep them separate from the Israeli population. Sometimes population transfer takes a more indirect form. For instance, it is possible to make life so miserable in a region that a group of people will choose to leave "voluntarily." This was the case with early Mormons, whose religious persecution in the East and Midwest between 1846 and 1869 drove 70,000 to cross the country (taking what is called the Mormon Pioneer Trail) and settle in the Great Salt Lake Valley region of Utah.

Internal Colonialism and Segregation

The term "colonialism" refers to a policy whereby a stronger nation takes control of a weaker nation (the "colony") in order to extend the stronger nation's territory or to exploit the colony's resources for the stronger nation's own enrichment. The British Empire, which once included such distant countries as India, Burma (now Myanmar), the West Indies, South Africa, and Australia, as well as America before its independence, is an example of colonialism.

Internal colonialism describes the exploitation of a minority group within the dominant group's own borders. Internal colonialism often takes the form of economic exploitation and includes some sort of physical **segregation** of groups by race or ethnicity. For example, in the U.S. South up to the 1960s, not only did blacks live in separate neighborhoods, but they also were restricted to "coloreds"-only sections of buses, parks, and restaurants, and even separate drinking fountains. If members of the minority group live close by yet in their own part of town (for instance, on the "other side of the tracks"), they are separate and hence unequal but still near enough to serve as workers for the dominant group. Segregation was not just confined to the South; it permeated other areas of society. Separation by races could be found in divisions serving in the U.S. military and among teams playing in professional sports like baseball, football, and basketball. Efforts to desegregate American society were accelerated through the civil rights movement.

Assimilation

With **assimilation**, a minority group is absorbed into the dominant group; this process is the central idea behind America's "melting pot." On the surface, assimilation seems like a reasonable solution to the potential conflicts among different groups. If everyone belongs to the same group, if the society is largely homogeneous, then conflict will decrease.

During much of the twentieth century, immigrants to the United States were eager to adopt an American way of life, become citizens, learn English, and lose any trace of their "foreign-ness." The Irish, Italians, and Eastern Europeans

POPULATION TRANSFER the forcible removal of a group of people from the territory they have occupied

INTERNAL COLONIALISM the economic and political subjugation of the minority group by the dominant group within a nation

SEGREGATION the physical and legal separation of groups by race or ethnicity

ASSIMILATION a pattern of relations between ethnic or racial groups in which the minority group is absorbed into the mainstream or dominant group, making society more homogeneous

GLOBAL PERSPECTIVE
"The Biggest Humanitarian and Refugee Crisis of Our Time"

It was just a small act of defiance that helped launch a revolution and left 11 million refugees without a place to call home. The roots of the Syrian civil war can be traced back to several different inciting forces. One such spark was a piece of anti-government graffiti, spray-painted on the wall of a school by a teenage boy in the southern city of Daraa in March 2011. The details surrounding who actually wrote the graffiti—or even exactly what it said—are disputed, but soon after the graffiti was discovered, the Syrian *mukhabarat* (intelligence agency) showed up at the school and eventually arrested as many as twenty-two teenage boys. The boys were held in isolation and tortured while their families grew desperate. After weeks of local street protests, the regime finally released the boys. But the protests in Daraa continued, spreading to other parts of Syria, inspired by the Arab Spring protests that had swept the region the previous year. By April the Syrian army was dispatched to Daraa, and the Syrian civil war commenced.

What began as a confrontation between angry pro-democracy protesters and a repressive regime quickly became fantastically complicated. The Assad regime, dominated by Alawite Muslims, is supported by many of Syria's religious minorities, but it is also opposed by at least three distinct groups: the largely Sunni opposition forces, the Islamic State (also known as ISIS or *Daesh*), and Kurdish militias. Each of the four factions has vastly different goals and support from different international sources (including the United States and Russia). This complexity has birthed the bloodiest conflict of the twenty-first century.

Filippo Grandi, head of the United Nations High Commission on Refugees (2016), believes that "Syria is the biggest humanitarian and refugee crisis of our time." Before the war began, Syria had a population of about 22 million. Between 2011 and 2017, almost half the population became refugees, and another 500,000 are estimated to have died in the fighting. More than 6 million of the refugees have fled to other parts of Syria and are officially considered internally displaced people. Another 5 million have left Syria altogether. This level of population transfer has fundamentally transformed Syria and radically altered the lives of the millions of people driven into exile.

The vast majority of the international refugees have gone to countries that share a border with Syria: Turkey, Jordan, Lebanon, and Iraq. A much smaller number have been resettled in Europe and North America. During the first five years of the Syrian civil war, about 12,000 refugees were admitted to the United States, with most of those entering in 2016.

Although efforts are made to resettle refugees in communities with existing Syrian immigrant populations, there are only so many of those places. Of the 231 cities and towns now home to Syrian refugees, San Diego has taken more than any other city, but there has been a real push to place refugees in more affordable medium-sized cities like Boise, Idaho, which has accepted more refugees than New York and Los Angeles combined (Park and Omri 2016).

These refugees face a unique set of challenges linked to ethnic and religious differences, in many cases being among the first Syrians to settle in their communities, without an immigrant or refugee community to turn to for help. The challenge is even greater for refugees coming to a country where their religion, language, and even the way they dress can provoke negative reactions. Asmaa Albukaie, along with her two sons, was the first Syrian refugee to be resettled in Idaho. She says that when she first arrived, Boise was a "very welcoming community," but that the warmth dimmed somewhat over time and that on occasion "people have screamed at her and called her a 'terrorist'" (Margolis 2016). For refugee families, there is constant tension between the importance of assimilation and the need to hold on to some of their own culture. Members of the host country may make assumptions and hold resentments about the newcomers because of their ethnic and religious differences and may engage in discriminatory behavior as well. "None of this is easy," said Ahmad Alabood, one of the new arrivals. It's like "learning American culture in 90 days" (Robertson 2016). If you have a Syrian refugee population in your town (and you might), what can you do to help make their adjustments easier?

Syrian Refugees The resettling of Syrian refugees poses a humanitarian crisis on a global level.

were all once considered "ethnics" but were eventually assimilated into the larger category of white Americans. Today, they are practically unrecognizable as distinct ethnic groups unless they choose to emphasize characteristics that would so distinguish them. It is likely that this process will continue with the newer wave of immigrants; for instance, some census-type forms no longer distinguish Hispanic or Middle Eastern as separate categories from white.

But although there is something to be gained by assimilation—namely, membership in the dominant population—there is also something to be sacrificed. Minority group members may lose their previous ethnic or racial identity, either through **racial assimilation**, having children with the dominant group until the different races are completely mixed, or through **cultural assimilation**, in which members learn the cultural practices of the dominant group. In some cases, both types of assimilation take place at the same time.

In addition, the process of assimilation is not always entered into voluntarily. Sometimes members of immigrant and minority groups may be forced to acquire new behaviors and are forbidden to practice their own religion or speak their own language, until these are all but forgotten. For some, assimilation results in the tragic loss of a distinctive racial or ethnic identity. This is true for many Native Americans, for instance, who in just a few generations have lost the ability to speak their tribal languages or have forgotten cultural practices of their not-so-distant ancestors.

Pluralism

Pluralism not only permits racial and ethnic variation within one society, it actually encourages people to embrace diversity as a positive feature of a society. The traditional image of the melting pot is exchanged with a "salad bowl" in which all the different ingredients maintain their distinct qualities, even as they are tossed together. In the last few decades, the United States has seen more and more groups celebrating their racial or ethnic roots, developing a strong common consciousness, and expressing pride in their unique identity.

At the core of pluralism, also referred to as *multiculturalism,* is tolerance of racial and ethnic differences. An example of successful multiculturalism is seen in Canada. This country's population is diverse, composed of not only two official linguistic groups (English and French) but also ethnic and racial minorities that include European, Chinese, and Indian immigrants as well as members

Jackie Robinson is most often cited as the first athlete to break the "color barrier" in professional sports when he made his Major League Baseball debut in 1947.

of "First Nations," or Canadian native peoples. The Canadian government is committed to the ideals of multiculturalism, with a great deal of funding directed to programs aimed at improving race relations and encouraging multicultural harmony. As a sign of that commitment, the 1988 Canadian Multiculturalism Act declared that the role of government is to bring about "equal access for all Canadians in the economic, social, cultural, and political realms" (Mitchell 1993).

The United States is still moving toward becoming a more multicultural and egalitarian society, although in recent years there has been a backlash against the idea of pluralism. Some critics blame the educational system for allowing what they consider marginal academic areas, such as ethnic studies, women's studies, gay and lesbian studies, and the like, to be featured alongside the classic curriculum. Others question the need for bilingual education and English as a second language (ESL) programs, despite research showing benefits to nonnative speakers (Krashen 1996). And groups such as U.S. English and English First advocate for legislation making English the national language and setting limits on the use of other languages. Nevertheless, since the future seems sure to bring an ever greater racial and ethnic mix to the country, Americans may yet be able to incorporate multiculturalism into our sense of national identity.

RACIAL ASSIMILATION the process by which racial minority groups are absorbed into the dominant group through intermarriage

CULTURAL ASSIMILATION the process by which racial or ethnic groups are absorbed into the dominant group by adopting the dominant group's culture

PLURALISM a cultural pattern of intergroup relations that encourages racial and ethnic variation and acceptance within a society

Closing Comments

Constructing categories of race and ethnicity seems inevitably to lead to stratification and inequality and to such destructive social processes as stereotyping, segregation, prejudice, and discrimination. Are there any positive consequences, either for society or for individuals? As it turns out, there are.

Racial and ethnic categories help to create a sense of identity for members of these groups, which can lead to feelings of unity and solidarity—a sense of belonging to something that is larger than oneself, of cultural connection, and of shared history. We see this in action during ethnic festivals and holidays. When we share our own group unity with others in this way, we contribute to the diversity of our community and society. The more we understand and appreciate the diverse population of our nation, the less likely we may be to contribute to the destructive consequences of racial and ethnic categorization.

The important sociological insight here is that since categories of race and ethnicity are socially constructed, their meanings are socially constructed as well. Historically, we have constructed meanings that favor some and exploit and oppress others. Is it possible to construct meanings for racial and ethnic categories that value and celebrate them all? Over time, and with your newly acquired sociological insights, we hope you will be part of that transformation.

APPLYING WHAT YOU'VE LEARNED

Let's Talk More

1. How do you identify yourself in terms of race or ethnicity? Are there special occasions or situations in which you are more likely to display your ethnicity or race? Do you identify with more than one racial or ethnic group or know anyone who does? What does this tell you about the origin of these categories?

2. Affirmative action in college admissions is one of the most controversial topics in America today. Why would a college want to consider race or ethnicity when making admissions decisions? What factors do you think admissions boards should consider?

3. What is a microaggression, and have you ever experienced or witnessed one?

Let's Explore More

1. **Film** Peele, Jordan, dir. *Get Out*. 2017.

2. **Article** Waldman, Katy. "A Sociologist Examines the 'White Fragility' That Prevents White Americans from Confronting Racism." *The New Yorker*. July 23, 2018.

3. **Blog Post** Gonzales, Teresa Irene. "Popular Culture, Race, and Representation." *Everyday Sociology* (blog). February 26, 2016.

   http://WWNorton.com/rd/q6T9A.

CHAPTER 9

Constructing Gender and Sexuality

If you were anywhere on social media on October 15, 2017, or in the days that followed, you likely saw the avalanche of posts coming from women everywhere claiming #MeToo. When civil rights activist Tarana Burke wrote down those two simple words back in 2006, she could not have foreseen the massive viral sensation they would eventually create; she was just working on a plan of action to better help survivors of sexual violence feel like they could heal. She hoped it could raise awareness about the pervasiveness of the problem. But as it turns out, Burke was laying the foundation for a powerful new social movement.

Earlier in October 2017, *The New York Times* and *The New Yorker* published breaking news that Harvey Weinstein, one of the most powerful men in Hollywood, had been accused by multiple actresses of sexual harassment and assault in the workplace. Like many who were reading those reports, actress Alyssa Milano recognized something familiar in the stories. At the urging of a friend, Milano took to Twitter and wrote: "If all the women and men who have been sexually harassed, assaulted or abused wrote 'me too' as a status, we might give people a sense of the magnitude of the problem. #metoo." The tweet went viral almost instantly. The next day, Milano made a point to publicly credit Tarana Burke after she learned about the term's origination.

Virtually overnight the hashtag exploded across social media, igniting an unprecedented reckoning about sexual misconduct and violence. Within 24 hours, #MeToo was tweeted 825,000 times and featured in more than 12 million Facebook posts. Suddenly people were talking openly about their experiences. MeToo had given a voice to many who had previously felt too scared, isolated, or powerless to address what had happened to them. As Tarana Burke explained, "On one side, it's a bold declarative statement that 'I'm not ashamed' and 'I'm not alone.' On the other side, it's a statement from survivor to survivor that says 'I see you, I hear you, I understand you and I'm here for you'" (Santiago and Criss 2017).

As the larger story of the movement played out in the following weeks and months, MeToo became a national, and even global, phenomenon. Many more high-profile figures in the entertainment industry were accused of sexual misconduct and subsequently ousted from their positions, but it went much further than that. MeToo continued to reverberate and spread, exposing the practice of sexual harassment and assault in the realms of politics and academia, in Silicon Valley, and in places beyond. Importantly, it trickled down to everyday women and men who were finding the courage to speak out and challenge business as usual in their professional and personal lives.

All these conversations served as dramatic evidence of the alarming frequency of such experiences, and of how deeply ingrained sexual harassment and abuse are in our culture. Maybe you recall reading some of those messages in your own newsfeed. Maybe you even posted #MeToo yourself. This moment also speaks to larger issues of sexism and gender inequality and the persistence of social movements fighting on those fronts. It's about the possibility of changing the way we see women—and men—and making a new future in which no one will have to say those two simple words.

How to Read This Chapter

We often think of gender and sexuality as part of our biological inheritance, unchanging and unchangeable. We hope that after reading this chapter you will understand the ways in which our gender and sexual identities are about *what we do* in addition to being about *who we are*. As you read, pay attention to the processes involved in constructing the meanings of genders and sexualities, as well as to the real consequences of gender and sexual inequality. As you become aware of these problems, perhaps you'll begin to think about solutions as well.

SEX AND GENDER

Although people often use the terms "sex" and "gender" interchangeably, sociologists differentiate between the two: Most view "sex" as biological but "gender" as social or cultural. Even though people often identify with the gender that is associated with their sex, this is not always the case, as we will see. Our gender identity and gender expression may differ from the sex we were assigned at birth. This raises the question of which set of attributes—those associated with our sex or those associated with our gender—is most consequential to our everyday lives.

Sex

Sex refers to an individual's membership in one of two biological categories—male or female. The biological factors that distinguish between male and female include chromosomes, hormones, and reproductive organs, all of which make up the **primary sex characteristics**. Males and females also possess different **secondary sex characteristics**, such as facial and body hair, musculature, and other features that are unrelated to reproduction (Table 9.1). Many of these physical differences become evident in puberty.

Most people assume that everyone is either male or female. However, about 17 babies in 1,000 are born **intersex**, having a variant chromosomal makeup and mixed or indeterminate male and female sex characteristics (Fausto-Sterling 2000). While most cases of intersex are detected at birth, some do not appear until puberty or adulthood. When a baby is born intersex, nature hasn't clearly indicated whether the infant is biologically male or female. In modern Western society, the prospect of an ambiguously sexed person seems so threatening and unacceptable that most parents seek out surgical and other procedures to quickly remedy the situation (in most cases, female is the most viable and expedient choice). More recently, the rights of intersex people have come into focus; many adults maintain they should have the freedom to choose for themselves whether to take medical measures or remain as they are. Sociologist Georgiann Davis (2015) has

SEX an individual's membership in one of two categories—male or female—based on biological factors

PRIMARY SEX CHARACTERISTICS biological factors, such as chromosomes, hormones, and reproductive organs, that distinguish males from females

SECONDARY SEX CHARACTERISTICS physical differences between males and females, including facial and body hair, musculature, and bone structure, that are unrelated to reproduction

INTERSEX used to describe a person whose chromosomes or sex characteristics are neither exclusively male nor exclusively female

TABLE 9.1 Human Sex Characteristics

	Females	Males
Chromosomes	XX	XY
Dominant Hormone	Estrogen	Testosterone
Primary Sex Characteristics	Reproductive organs: vagina, cervix, uterus, ovaries, fallopian tubes, other glands	Reproductive organs: penis, testicles, scrotum, prostate, other glands
Secondary Sex Characteristics	Shorter than males; larger breasts; wider hips than shoulders; less facial hair; more subcutaneous fat; fat deposits around buttocks, thighs, and hips; smoother skin texture	Abdominal, chest, body, and facial hair; larger hands and feet; broader shoulders and chest; heavier skull and bone structure; greater muscle mass and strength; Adam's apple and deeper voice; fat deposits around abdominals and waist; coarser skin texture

GLOBAL PERSPECTIVE
Different Societies, Different Genders

In modern Western societies, we are assigned a gender. Someone looks us over at birth (or even before) and declares, "It's a boy!" or "It's a girl!" Even though some infants are born with indeterminate genitals, they are almost always assigned to one gender or the other as soon as possible, even if surgery is required. We are now hearing terms like "genderqueer" and "genderfluid" used to refer to people who don't strictly identify as either male or female. But many Americans still find the idea of such an identity unacceptable. Let's consider three societies that do acknowledge a "third gender."

Berdaches or "Two-Spirit" People

When nineteenth-century explorers and missionaries wrote about the native tribes they encountered in America, they also described individuals within those tribes who were neither male nor female but somehow both. These people—called "berdaches" by nonnatives and "two-spirits" by natives—were usually biological males who dressed as women and took on types of work we think of as feminine, such as cooking and domestic labor. They could also be biological females who took on traditionally male pursuits, such as hunting, trapping, and warfare. Male two-spirits have been documented in nearly 150 Native American cultures and female two-spirits in almost half that number. Some researchers believe that people who became two-spirits were assigned to such a role from a very young age, if not from birth, for reasons of "demographic necessity" (Trexler 2002). In the northern reaches of what is now Canada, for example, couples who had given birth to all girls may have decided that their next child would be raised as a boy (and therefore a hunter who could provide food for the

family)—no matter what. In more southern regions, a family who needed a female child may have deliberately raised a boy as a girl; male two-spirits were valued for their height and strength.

Research on two-spirits seems contradictory. Some believe that, based on the records of the early Europeans, they were looked down on by their own tribes. Others point out that some two-spirits were respected and played important roles in the religious life of their communities. What we do know is that two-spirits were acknowledged as a third gender. Native creation myths include such references as "When the spirit people made men and women, they also made berdaches" (Roscoe 2000, p. 4)—allowing this group a recognized place in the order of things.

Hijras

The *hijras* of South Asia are a modern example of third-gender individuals. Like berdaches, hijras are recognized by their society as an acceptable variation on gender—neither male nor female but something else entirely. They are usually biological males who have all or part of their genitals removed, and most become hijras voluntarily in their teens or twenties. They dress and live as females and are referred to as daughter, sister, grandmother, or aunt.

Like berdaches, hijras take part in the religious life of their people; they are specifically mentioned (and thus validated) in the epic Hindu texts as having been recognized by the deity Rama. Today, the presence of hijras at weddings and at the births of male children is thought to be auspicious. In 2012, the third-gender option was officially added to Pakistan's national identity cards (Frayer 2012).

---

critiqued the practice of classifying intersex as a medical disorder rather than simply as a biological variation; calling it an abnormality is often harmful to intersex people and can have profound life consequences.

Gender

GENDER the physical, behavioral, and personality traits that a group considers normal for its male and female members

Gender refers to the physical, behavioral, and personality traits that a group considers to

be normal, natural, right, and good for its male and female members. In other words, gender reflects our notions about what is appropriately "masculine" or "feminine." Some societies, for example, expect men to be more aggressive and competitive and women to be more emotional and nurturing. We often think of such characteristics as biologically determined or "natural," but no society leaves it completely up to nature to dictate the behavior of its male and female members. While we tend to feel that our gender is a deeply personal part of who we are, we have also all learned to interpret and enact gender

Life Outside the Binary Hijras of South Asia (left) are recognized by society as neither female nor male but a third gender. It is considered good luck to have a hijra at a wedding or at the birth of a male child. In Afghanistan, families with no male children may opt to turn one of their girls into a bacha posh (right). A bacha posh can leave the house without an escort and drive—activities off limits to girls.

Bacha Posh

The *bacha posh* of Afghanistan were largely unknown to the outside world prior to 2010. The term means "a girl who is dressed up and disguised as a boy" and refers to a common practice that's been kept secret for centuries and continues today (Nordberg 2014). In a patriarchal and gender-segregated society, men hold all the power. As such, boy children are strongly preferred over girls. When a wife fails to produce a male baby, it brings shame on the family, undermining the family's ability to gain respect and maintain their position within the community. Consequently, when a family has two, three, four, or more girls but no boys, they may choose to turn one of the girls into a bacha posh.

In the process of becoming a bacha posh, a girl does more than just dress the part. She is raised as a boy, acts like one, and is viewed and accepted as one by society. For Afghan girls, becoming a bacha posh opens up a whole new world

for them. Bacha posh can leave the house without an escort, go to school, drive a car, and even get a job, bringing much needed support to the family. While most bacha posh comply with being turned back into a girl when they hit puberty, some opt to remain a bacha posh into adulthood.

The two-spirit, hijra, and bacha posh may sound similar to transgender persons in Western society, but the analogy isn't entirely appropriate. A two-spirit or hijra is always referred to by that term, not "he" or "she," whereas the bacha posh are not called "son" or "daughter" but always bacha posh. In the United States we still struggle with terminology and fret over how to fit trans people into existing male or female pigeon-holes. Keep in mind the possibility that gender is malleable. The characteristics we think of as definitive, such as sex, gender, and sexuality, may be viewed differently in other cultures and time periods, which means that it should be possible to view them differently here and now.

in ways that are specific to the cultural and historical time in which we were raised.

There are different ways of conceptualizing gender. **Essentialists** see gender as immutable and biological and as an unambiguous, two-category system. Also called the **gender binary**, this system classifies gender into two distinct, opposite, and separate categories. According to this view, you're either male or female from birth to death, and there are no other options. Chromosomes, hormones, and genitalia determine your identity—the way you see yourself, the

way you interact with others, and the activities you engage in every day. Culture, according to essentialists, plays little to no role.

The essentialist perspective is often found in such fields as medicine, theology, and biology. Within the discipline of sociology, essentialism may be found in the subfield

ESSENTIALISTS those who believe gender roles have a genetic or biological origin and therefore cannot be changed

GENDER BINARY a system of classification with only two distinct and opposite gender categories

CONSTRUCTIONISTS those who believe that notions of gender are socially determined, such that a binary system is just one possibility among many

GENDER IDENTITY an individual's self-definition or sense of gender

CISGENDER term used when gender identity and/or expression aligns with the sex assigned at birth

TRANSGENDER term used when gender identity and/or expression is different from the sex assigned at birth

GENDER EXPRESSION an individual's behavioral manifestations of gender

GENDER NONCONFORMING term used when gender identity and/or expression differs from societal expectations about gender roles

SEXUALITY the character or quality of being sexual

SEXUAL ORIENTATION or IDENTITY the inclination to feel sexual desire toward people of a particular gender

of sociobiology, which looks at the biological roots of social behavior. Most mainstream sociologists, however, use a **constructionist** approach to gender: They see gender as a social construction—a concept that has been shaped socially by the culture and the historical time period. Constructionists acknowledge the possibility that binary male-female categories, being socially constructed, aren't the only way to classify an individual's gender. Constructionists believe that the meaning of masculinity and femininity may differ drastically in different societies and historical periods.

GENDER IDENTITY Our deeply held sense of ourselves as male, female, or some other gender is called our **gender identity**. Our gender identity may or may not correspond with the sex we have been assigned at birth. When our sex and gender identity match up (e.g., female sex, female gender identity), we are cisgender—the prefix *cis* means "same," indicating that our sex and gender correspond. We use the term **transgender** (or noncisgender) to describe those whose gender identity does not align with their sex assigned at birth. Former Olympic athlete Caitlyn Jenner, actor Laverne Cox, and activist Chelsea Manning are among well-known transgender women; actor and activist Chaz Bono is a transgender man.

Separate from our gender identity is our **gender expression**, or our external manifestations of gender, which include "masculine" or "feminine" clothing, grooming, behavior, body language, gestures, and even names. There are a wide variety of ways in which people can express their gender identity. Transgender persons ("trans" persons for short) may or may not undergo medical or surgical procedures as part of a transition during which they change their gender expression to align with their gender identity rather than with the sex they were assigned at birth. It is important to remember that transgender identity is not dependent on medical procedures.

Trans individuals are just one group of **gender-nonconforming** persons in contemporary society. Another are those who identify as nonbinary. Nonbinary individuals

Laverne Cox Transgender actor Laverne Cox speaks at the third annual Women's March in Los Angeles. Transgender individuals such as Cox are one group of gender-nonconforming persons.

do not fit neatly into binary classifications of gender; this means that they may not identify as a man or a woman. Other gender-nonconforming individuals include those who identify as genderqueer or genderfluid. Recognizing that this type of gender nonconformity exists is sometimes difficult for people who are used to thinking of sex and gender as binary classifications and assume that there are two, and only two, categories for sex (male/female) and for gender (masculine/feminine) and that our membership in one or the other category is permanent and unchanging. However, it has become clear to sociologists that not everyone experiences sex, gender, or sexuality in unambiguous ways. It can be useful to think of each of these classifications, rather than being binary, as existing on a spectrum. An individual may lie anywhere on, or even outside of, the masculine/feminine gender identity spectrum, for example, and the same is true for sexuality and sexual orientation, which we will turn to next.

SEXUALITY AND SEXUAL ORIENTATION

What is **sexuality**? And what is it doing in a sociology textbook? The term "sexuality" is used in a variety of ways; for example, it is used to describe sexual behavior, desires, and fantasies (the things people actually do as well as the things they think or dream about doing). It is also used to describe **sexual orientation** or **identity**, which is the inclination to feel sexual desire toward and engage in sexual behavior with persons of a particular sex or gender.

Our society recognizes a number of sexual orientations, and they are each related to our two-category, or binary, gender system. **Heterosexuality**, or sexual desire for the other gender, is the normative and dominant category, which may be why the slang term for it is "straight." Most people identify themselves as heterosexual, and there are privileges attached to membership in this category. **Homosexuality**, or sexual desire for the same gender, is a minority category; the National Survey of Sexual Health and Behavior found that about 4 percent of adults self-identify as gay or lesbian (Reece et al. 2010). As with other minority statuses, there are a variety of difficulties and disadvantages attached to membership in this category. **Bisexuality**—sexual attraction to both genders—is also a minority category, with about 3 percent of men and 4 percent of women identifying as bisexual (Reece et al. 2010). **Asexuality** involves the lack of sexual attraction of any kind. Asexual people are basically nonsexual and are a very small minority group, with only about 1 percent of adults identifying as asexual (Bogaert 2004). There have been various claims about and controversy surrounding the exact percentage of adults who identify with each category of sexual orientation. A more recent study found somewhat different numbers: 97.6 percent identified as heterosexual, 1.6 percent gay or lesbian, and 0.8 percent bisexual (Centers for Disease Control and Prevention 2015).

Still, even these categories are limiting. As early as the 1940s, the pioneering sex researcher Alfred Kinsey suggested that human sexuality is far more diverse than commonly assumed. His own studies led him to believe that people are not exclusively heterosexual or homosexual but can fall along a wide spectrum (Kinsey et al. 1948/1998; Kinsey and Gebhard 1953/1998). Kinsey and others who have followed him have suggested that we can best understand sexual orientation not through binary categories (gay versus straight) but rather as a fluid continuum that can change over the course of a person's lifetime (Figure 9.1).

"Queering the Binary"

For most of the twentieth century, "queer" was a pejorative term applied mainly to gay men (before that, it was used to mean "odd" or "peculiar" in a nonsexual way). But in the 1990s, with the emergence of "queer theory," the term underwent a remarkable transformation as both activists and academics began using it in a very different way. In academia, **queer theory** rejects the idea of a single gay, lesbian, bisexual, heterosexual, or transgender identity, emphasizing instead the importance of difference (Butler 1993). It asserts that being queer is about "possibilities, gaps, overlaps, dissonances, and resonances" (Sedgwick 1993, p. 8) and suggests that any kind of categorization is outmoded and limiting.

Queer is now used to describe anything that challenges prevailing binary notions of sex, gender, and sexuality (and is sometimes used to describe nonconformity in other areas as well). "Queer" encompasses a wider range of gender and sexual diversity than terms like "gay" and "trans" and implies a questioning of society's traditional gender and sexual arrangements. It has come to be represented by a "Q" appended to the acronym "LGBT" to make it more inclusive, as in **LGBTQ**. That acronym, and what it stands for, is also contested. Many activists and organizations believe it should be even more inclusive, proposing a longer version—LGBTQIA—that encompasses "intersex" and "asexual" people under the community umbrella. "A" is not for "allies," as some assume, because allies are not oppressed in the same way. Sometimes "+" is added to the end to represent allies as well as people with other sexual identities.

> **HETEROSEXUALITY** sexual attraction toward members of the other gender
>
> **HOMOSEXUALITY** sexual attraction toward members of one's own gender
>
> **BISEXUALITY** sexual attraction toward members of both genders
>
> **ASEXUALITY** the lack of sexual attraction of any kind; no interest in or desire for sex
>
> **QUEER THEORY** social theory about gender and sexual identity; emphasizes the importance of difference and rejects ideas of innate identities or restrictive categories
>
> **LGBTQ** lesbian, gay, bisexual, transgender, and queer

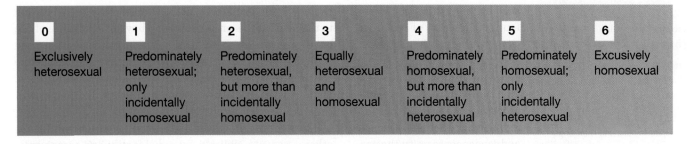

0	1	2	3	4	5	6
Exclusively heterosexual	Predominately heterosexual; only incidentally homosexual	Predominately heterosexual, but more than incidentally homosexual	Equally heterosexual and homosexual	Predominately homosexual, but more than incidentally heterosexual	Predominately homosexual; only incidentally heterosexual	Excusively homosexual

FIGURE 9.1 The Kinsey Scale of Sexuality

IN RELATIONSHIPS
Rape Culture and Campus Social Life

It happened in early 2015, behind a dumpster, just outside a Stanford University fraternity house. Two students saw what they thought was a crime in progress. A man was sexually assaulting a woman who was passed out and half naked on the ground. When they confronted him, he fled, but they chased after him and pinned him down until police arrived. The case against Brock Turner, a Stanford freshman on the swim team, made national headlines. A criminal court convicted Turner on three counts of felony sexual assault. Prosecutors asked for six years in prison, consistent with sentencing guidelines. Instead, the judge handed down a sentence of six months in county jail, feeling a prison sentence might have adverse "collateral consequences" on Turner. He was released after serving just three months.

The problem of sexual assault on campus has become so serious and so widespread that it is now characterized as an epidemic. According to researchers, at least one in five women in college (and one in sixteen men) will be the victim of sexual assault. In a recent college survey, 10 percent of women reported having been physically forced to have intercourse, 15 percent said someone tried to force them but failed, and 11 percent said they had been victimized while passed out, asleep, drugged, or otherwise incapacitated (Ford and England 2015).

Campus sexual assaults have gotten a lot of press lately, as has the concept of **rape culture**, or an environment in which sexual violence against women is normalized and perpetuated through cultural norms and values. While rape culture is not unique to college campuses, there are some features of campus life that make distinctive contributions to rape culture (Armstrong, Hamilton, and Sweeney 2006). For example, a widely held notion about college life is that students are supposed to party. So before first-year students even set foot on campus, they may feel a certain amount of pressure to participate in the party scene. Many campuses have policies that restrict alcohol use. This pushes the party scene off campus, often into privately owned fraternity houses, giving frat brothers more control over how parties are organized, who attends, how alcohol is served, and what happens if something goes wrong. This can be a recipe for disaster, including alcohol poisoning, injury, and death, as well as sexual assault. In fact, most campus assaults happen at or after a party.

> **RAPE CULTURE** a set of beliefs, norms, and values that normalizes sexual violence against women

SOCIALIZATION: SEX, GENDER, AND SEXUALITY

Gender role socialization—the subtle, pervasive process of learning what constitutes masculinity and femininity—begins early and continues throughout our lives. It is accomplished primarily by the four major agents of socialization: families, schools, peers, and the media, though other social institutions, such as religion, may also play a part in the process. In addition to perpetuating binary notions of gender and gender conformity, the process of socialization also tends to support **heteronormativity** (the assumption that heterosexuality is the only acceptable orientation).

> **GENDER ROLE SOCIALIZATION** the lifelong process of learning to be masculine or feminine, primarily through agents of socialization
>
> **HETERONORMATIVITY** the belief that heterosexuality is and should be the norm
>
> **SOCIAL LEARNING** the process of learning behaviors and meanings through social interaction

Families

Families are usually the primary source of socialization. Indeed, Kara Smith (2005) argues that gender role socialization begins even before birth. Because the sex of the fetus can now be determined in utero, families may begin relating to the new baby as either a girl or a boy far in advance of the baby's arrival. Smith's research demonstrates how knowing the baby's sex affects how the mother talks to her fetus—the choice of words as well as tone of voice. Once babies are born, female and male clothes, rooms, and toys will differ, as will the stories the children are told.

Most telling, however, is the way in which significant others—parents, siblings, extended family, and caregivers—interact with the baby. Through **social learning**, the process

The hookup culture that dominates today's college campuses also contributes to rape culture (Wade 2017a). Hookups are all about quick, easy, casual sexual encounters. Both women and men participate in hookup culture, and many genuinely enjoy the freedom, excitement, and pleasure that come with it. But that's not to say that these interactions are always reciprocal, egalitarian, or even agreed upon. Some of the behaviors that are celebrated in hookup culture make it difficult to distinguish between a hookup and sexual assault. Men are encouraged to be on the prowl for women and to do whatever it takes to hook up. This often means getting women drunk (alcohol is the most commonly used date rape drug on campuses), groping them in public, and sometimes being forceful in order to get what they want.

Many universities have notoriously bad records when it comes to investigating and responding to campus sexual assault. When an incident occurs, colleges often seem more concerned about public relations and their own reputations than about the safety of their students. Colleges may be especially keen to protect student athletes and fraternity brothers, men who are disproportionately valuable to the institution. Knowing that little may be done to bring a campus rapist to justice can mean that survivors don't feel comfortable reporting assaults to campus authorities. Even when sexual assault cases are reported, the response is often underwhelming. Fewer than one-third of all campus sexual assault cases result in an expulsion (Kingkade 2014).

Those in charge of student services and campus life often participate in "victim blaming" in their attempts to prevent sexual assault. Women are advised repeatedly on how to avoid being raped (don't go to parties alone, don't get intoxicated, don't accept drinks or rides home from people you don't know, etc.), implying that if a woman is assaulted, it is because she failed to follow these instructions. Meanwhile, there has been far less focus on educating men in rape prevention—skills that can help them challenge other men who engage in risky or violent behaviors and intervene in situations to protect the health and safety of women.

Survivors and their supporters have recently turned to federal civil rights legislation referred to as "Title IX" to exert pressure on colleges to better prevent and respond to reports of sexual violence. Under the U.S. Department of Education's Office for Civil Rights (OCR), Title IX protects people from discrimination based on sex in education programs that receive federal funding. The law recognizes that sexual violence perpetuates inequality and thus violates students' civil rights. In 2011, the OCR issued guidelines to academic institutions about improving how they handle sexual assault allegations. Title IX is backed by the threat of withdrawing federal funding from institutions that are not in compliance. While awareness about the power of Title IX has grown, so has the backlash from those who believe it has overreached.

of learning behaviors and meanings through social interaction, babies respond to and internalize the expectations of others around them. Sometimes there is a conscious effort to instill certain behaviors in children—such as by reprimanding a young boy for crying. At other times, social learning happens in a more subtle way, as the baby learns through observation, imitation, and play. Children rather quickly begin to exhibit gender-stereotyped behaviors. By the age of two, they are aware of their own and others' gender, and by age three, they begin to identify specific traits associated with each gender.

Gender pervades every aspect of family life. It may be implicit in the chores or privileges girls and boys are given (washing the dishes versus mowing the lawn), the way they are disciplined or punished, where they go or don't go, or what they are encouraged or forbidden to do. Lessons such as "that's not very ladylike" and "big boys don't cry" are echoed in children's literature, in toys made specifically for girls or

boys, and in the games they play. And as we grow up, we are always watching our other family members, using them as role models for our own beliefs and behaviors. In adulthood, our families may still influence what kind of career or mate we choose, how we run our household, and how we raise our own children.

How families are formed matters for the socialization process as well. To the extent that laws have historically ratified only heterosexual marriages, we have learned that heterosexuality and biological parenting are the "normal" or "natural" ways to form a family. Of course, these assumptions overlook the many other ways real families are formed.

Schools

Differences in the educational experiences of girls and boys also begin to appear early, both in the classroom and on the playground. Early on, girls and boys are frequently put in same-sex groups and assigned gender-stereotyped tasks, such as playing with dolls or playing with trucks. Same-sex groups also form on the playground, with girls and boys engaging in different kinds of social and athletic activities (Thorne 1993). By the fifth grade, gender norms are firmly established, as can be seen in the segregation that takes place even in co-ed schools.

One of the key areas of difference is in the way that teachers, both women and men, typically interact with students. Whether or not they realize it, teachers tend to favor boys in several ways. Boys receive more attention and instructional time and are more likely to be called on in class. And boys are posed with more challenging questions and tasks and are given more praise for the quality of their work. Boys are also, however, more likely to make teachers angry by misbehaving and therefore to receive some form of punishment (Smith 1999).

Despite boys' favorable treatment, girls in elementary school tend to earn higher grades. But their academic achievements are often discounted. In fact, the media often paint this gender discrepancy as a crisis for boys. When girls do perform well, they are typically credited for hard work rather than intellectual ability. They are encouraged to focus on social skills or appearance rather than brain power. By the time they reach middle or junior high school, girls begin to slip behind and to lose their sense of academic self-esteem. These troubles are compounded in adolescent girls, who begin to feel uneasy about competing with boys, embarrassed by their own success, or uncomfortable engaging in male-dominated subjects like math or science.

Gender role socialization in schools can take other forms as well. Textbooks often still contain sexist language and gender stereotypes. Women and minorities are underrepresented, both as subjects and as authors (Robson 2001). In the social structure of the school itself, women tend to be concentrated at the lower levels, as teachers and aides, while men tend to occupy upper-management and administrative positions. In such ways, schooling as a whole reinforces gender stereotypes.

For LGBTQ students, school is often a place where they learn (or relearn) the lesson that they will be accepted only if they hide their true identities. Heteronormativity pervades school life, from canonical textbooks with images of traditional families, to an emphasis on heterosexual dating (prom and homecoming queens and their kings). The binary division of restrooms in school buildings can also be problematic for transgender students.

Peers

In Western societies, peer groups are an increasingly important agent of socialization. By the age of three, children develop a preference for same-sex playmates, a tendency that increases markedly as childhood progresses. Children in preschool are three times more likely to play with same-sex playmates—eleven times more likely in kindergarten—and it is not until well after puberty that this pattern changes even a little (Maccoby and Jacklin 1987). While some have argued that such gender segregation is the *result* of inherent differences between men and women, there is evidence to support the notion that same-sex peer groups instead help *create* gendered behavior. Researchers have found, for example, that when children play with same-sex peers, their activities are more likely to be gender typed (girls have pretend tea parties, for example) than when boys and girls play together (Fabes, Martin, and Hanish 2003). In addition, children (especially boys) are punished (mocked) by their peers for crossing over these gendered borders (Thorne 1993).

C. J. Pascoe's ethnography of high school boys, *Dude, You're a Fag*, shows just how powerful peer groups can be in enforcing gender roles and the assumptions about sexuality that underlie them. Not only do boys police each other's performance of masculinity by criticizing nonnormative (and, in their minds, effeminate) behavior, dress, and other practices, but also they "lay claim to masculine identities by lobbing homophobic epithets at one another" (Pascoe 2007, p. 5). Calling someone a "fag" inflates the offender's own sense of masculinity, while demonstrating to others the consequences of deviating from masculine norms. Such bullying occurs among adolescent girls as well. Sarah Miller (2016) found that bullying in the form of homophobic labeling and the spreading of sexual rumors (along with "slut shaming") helped reinforce traditional gender and sexuality norms in young women.

The need to impress others and to feel popular with peers increases in the teenage years. Boys tend to gain prestige through athletic ability, a well-developed sense of humor, or taking risks and defying norms (Kimmel 2009). Girls tend to gain prestige through social position and physical attractiveness. It's easy to imagine what kinds of behaviors result from such peer pressure and the consequences of falling short in any way. In the extreme, it can lead to bullying, rebellious behavior, or eating disorders. Similar pressures in regard to dating and mating continue through the early adult years as well, enforcing heteronormativity and privileging cisgender identities by ostracizing transgressors.

The Media

From a variety of media sources, such as movies, comic books, and popular music, we learn "how to behave, how to be accepted, what to value, and what is normal" as well as "how gender fits into society" (Barner 1999). Across the media landscape gender roles are represented in highly stereotypical ways. Boys and girls learn that certain activities and attitudes are more appropriate for one gender than for the other. Girls

Gender-Nonconforming Characters and Actors on TV Asia Kate Dillon (left) is a nonbinary actor who uses singular they pronouns and stars as nonbinary character Taylor Mason on the series *Billions*. Elliot Fletcher (in the right-hand image, on the left) is a trans actor who plays a recurring role as Trevor, a trans man who befriends gay character Ian Gallagher on the series *Shameless*. They are among a growing number of gender-nonconforming actors gaining greater recognition and visibility in the media.

should be beautiful, caring, sensitive, and reserved, while boys should be assertive, strong, and analytic. This starts at a particularly young age: "By the time a child reaches kindergarten, she will 'know' more television characters than real people" (Barner 1999).

In addition to TV, magazines like *Seventeen* and *Teen Vogue* are aimed mostly at adolescents. Some have even speculated that increases in anorexia and bulimia among teenage girls can be linked to the images of women they see in the media (Kilbourne 1999). Teenage girls may consider actresses and models the standard of beauty to aspire to, even though such women "often are far below the normal weight recommendations" (Schiller et al. 1998).

Before the 1960s, sexual diversity was altogether absent from television. When it did appear, it was usually treated in a negative manner: In the 1967 CBS documentary *The Homosexuals*, one psychiatrist claims that "the fact that somebody's homosexual... automatically rules out the possibility that he will remain happy for long." In recent years, however, increasing levels of tolerance and acceptance of LGBTQ people have been reflected in increasingly positive representations of gays, lesbians, and trans persons on television, although these gains have not been without controversy. In 1997, the ABC sitcom *Ellen* introduced the first lesbian lead character in a prime-time series; two years later, the NBC sitcom *Will & Grace* featured two gay male characters. Other shows followed, while cable networks also developed LGBTQ-themed shows such as *Queer as Folk, The L Word,* and *Queer Eye for the Straight Guy* (and its 2018 reboot *Queer Eye*).

The past decade has seen a number of shows featuring gender-nonconforming actors. In 2013, Laverne Cox was cast as a transgender inmate at a women's prison in *Orange Is the New Black*. In 2015, Caitlyn Jenner starred in the documentary series *I Am Cait* about her transition, while the reality series *I Am Jazz* introduced viewers to trans teenager Jazz Jennings. More recently, nonbinary actor Asia Kate Dillon made history with their breakout role as the nonbinary character Taylor Mason on Showtime's *Billions*.

Just because LGBTQ persons are included on television, however, doesn't mean that they have achieved equal status. Clearly, there is not the same kind of acceptance of same-sex relations as of heterosexual relations, as evidenced by how romantic couples are treated on TV. Until 2000, there had never been a gay male kiss on a network program (although there had been two lesbian kisses). As recently as 2014, the sports world was scandalized when Michael Sam, the first openly gay player drafted by the NFL, celebrated joining the St. Louis Rams by kissing his boyfriend on camera. Trans characters are still often presented as villains, victims, or sex workers rather than in more ordinary and more positive roles. Some social scientists argue that more personal contact between members of different social groups reduces prejudice and discrimination (Pettigrew and Tropp 2011). If the media provide people with their only exposure to LGBTQ people, then it is all the more important that these portrayals represent those communities in realistic ways.

For many centuries of human history, children have learned how to act appropriately from family, peers, and school. As the influence of the media becomes more pervasive in our society, we can see how it may compete with or even contradict the influence of other agents of socialization. At the same time, the media also serve to socialize families, peers, and educators, giving the media an even more overarching power in society.

DATA WORKSHOP

Analyzing Media and Pop Culture

The Fashion Police: Gender and the Rules of Beauty

A newborn baby is wrapped in pink or blue. Gender role socialization starts early and continues to permeate every stage in our lives from there. Messages about what it means to be a girl or a boy are everywhere. We are told over and over, and in a million subtle ways, what is appropriate or desirable for each sex. Ideas about masculinity and femininity are played out innumerable times across an expanding media landscape. Gender norms reflect our ideals about beauty, style, fitness, and physical or sexual attractiveness, and examples of these ideals are on constant display—on our TVs and touch screens, in the grocery store, and at the bus stop. We can't avoid them.

This Data Workshop asks you to closely examine the covers of men's and women's magazines to discover what they have to say about gender and the rules of beauty. You will be using existing sources and doing a content analysis of the magazine covers. Refer to the section on existing sources in Chapter 2 for a review of this research method.

Choose one magazine that focuses on either women's fashion or fitness and one that focuses on either men's fashion or fitness. Here are some suggestions:

- For women's fashion: *Vogue, Elle, Essence, Glamour, Latina, InStyle*

- For women's fitness: *Health, Shape,* or *Women's Health,* or a sports-related magazine such as *Outside, Yoga, Golf Digest,* or *Runner's World* that features a female cover model

- For men's fashion: *Details, Esquire, GQ,* or *Maxim*

- For men's fitness: *Men's Health, Men's Fitness,* or *Men's Journal,* or a sports-related magazine such as *Outside, Yoga, Golf Digest,* or *Runner's World* that features a male cover model

Locate a recent issue of each of the two magazines you've chosen; you can find hard copies at a bookstore, library, or newsstand, or you can access a digital issue online. Keep in mind that you'll need a physical copy (or digital file) of the cover to work with, so make a tearsheet or photocopy of it, or take a screen shot or digital photo that you can refer to and share. Once you have your two magazine covers, you're ready to do a content analysis.

Immerse yourself in all the visual elements and text on each cover. Look at the general display and layout, the specific photos, and any other kinds of graphics. Scrutinize the headlines and which words were used. All of this becomes your data. As you examine the covers more closely, consider this set of questions:

- How are the cover models presented? Describe their body type. Does it reflect the ideals for masculine and feminine beauty? How are they posing? What does their posture, facial expressions, gestures, or other physical attributes convey?

- How are the cover models styled? Describe their clothing, hair, makeup, and accessories. Are the cover models engaged in any activities? What do their actions (or inaction) tell us about who they are?

- What is the background or scene of the magazine cover? Does it appear to be taken in a studio, or is it a location shot of some kind? What does the background convey?

- What colors are used for the magazine cover? Look at the background, the title or masthead, and any kind of text or added graphics. What, if any, are the other visual aspects of the cover?

- What words and phrases appear on the cover? Which words are bold, italicized, in capital letters, in larger or smaller font sizes, and why? What is the overall tone? What are the explicit and implicit messages embedded in the words?

- As a whole, what are the major themes and patterns that emerge from the cover? Do these themes support or challenge gender norms and the rules of beauty? Besides gender, do other factors of intersectionality—race, class, age, or sexual orientation—seem to affect the message?

- Compare and contrast the women's and the men's magazines. What are the similarities and differences between the two covers, and how do you explain them? How do you think such magazines influence how we see ourselves and others?

There are two options for completing this Data Workshop:

PREP-PAIR-SHARE Examine the content of the two magazine covers and take some preliminary notes based on your answers to the Data Workshop questions. Bring copies of the magazine covers to class and pair with a partner to discuss them. What kinds of similarities and

SEXISM IN ITS MANY FORMS

As with other aspects of our identities, such as race or ethnicity, gender and sexuality have been used as a basis for establishing and maintaining hierarchies of inequality that benefit the dominant group in a society. What is important to remember is that privileges, opportunities, and resources in an unequal society are distributed based on category membership. Gender inequality can be found in all past and present societies. It invariably takes the form of **patriarchy**, or male domination. There is little evidence that a matriarchal (female-dominated) society has ever existed, although some societies have been more pro-feminine than others. The Vanatinai, for example, are a small society in New Guinea in which women share equal access to positions of prestige, power, and control over the means of production (Lepowsky 1993).

Males in a patriarchal society enjoy certain unearned advantages not available to females. Male **privilege** can include a wide range of advantages experienced in our large social institutions as well as in our small everyday interactions. For instance, men are allowed to take up more physical space wherever they go, are not expected to smile at all times, and are less likely to be interrupted while speaking.

From the patriarchal point of view, gender inequality can be traced back to biological differences in early societies, when activities like hunting and warfare were more essential to the livelihood of human groups. Women could not participate as effectively as men in these activities because of their lesser physical strength and because of the demands of bearing and nursing children. Therefore, a division of labor arose, with women handling activities within the secured "home" territory. Men delivered the scarcest and most prized resources to the group, such as game from hunting or territory from warfare, and became powerful by controlling the distribution of these resources.

This account of the origins of gender inequality does not explain its persistence in contemporary societies. Physical strength is no longer required in the vast majority of jobs. Nor are large numbers of children required for the continuation of society, and women are not necessarily restricted in their activities because of the demands of caring for them. Still, **sexism**—the belief that one sex, usually male, is superior to the other—persists to some degree in all contemporary cultures. As a belief system or ideology, sexism is used to justify gender inequality and reinforce the status quo. Sometimes sexism comes in the form of **misogyny**, which can be expressed as contempt for or dislike or hatred of women.

It may be difficult to recognize how persistent and pervasive sexism is in today's society. It is easy to point to the great strides women have made over the past several decades, and to the many rights that the women's movement has secured. Yet women continue to occupy what could be called a minority position in society, even though they are actually a numerical majority of the population. As members of a minority group, women suffer unequal treatment as a result of their lower status in society. For instance, a woman may earn less money for working the same job as a man or may be passed over for promotion in favor of a less qualified man. New calls for social justice, as demonstrated in the #MeToo movement and elsewhere, point to the need for more work toward greater gender equity.

Prejudice and Discrimination

Sexism is closely associated with prejudice and discrimination. **Prejudice** is an entrenched set of ideas or attitudes (literally pre-judgments) about the presumed characteristics of a group (for instance women, gays, or trans persons) that is applied to all members and that is unlikely to change even in the face of evidence to challenge those ideas. Prejudice is often rooted in stereotypes and generalizations. Take, for example, the stereotype of the dumb blonde or the promiscuous gay man. Prejudiced ideas permeate our shared culture and social institutions, making them hard to avoid.

Prejudice often leads to **discrimination**: a behavior or action that results in the unequal treatment of individual members or an entire group because they belong to a certain social category. We might say that a woman suffers discrimination if she is charged more than her male counterpart when buying a new car or applying for a home loan. Sometimes discrimination happens on an individual level, as when a corporate recruiter consistently favors the men candidates he interviews over women who are

PATRIARCHY literally meaning "rule of the father"; a male-dominated society

PRIVILEGE unearned advantage accorded to members of dominant social groups (males, whites, the physically able, heterosexuals, etc.)

SEXISM the belief that one sex, usually male, is superior to the other

MISOGYNY an ingrained prejudice against women; dislike, contempt, or hatred of women

PREJUDICE an idea about the characteristics of a group that is applied to all members of that group and is unlikely to change regardless of the evidence against it

DISCRIMINATION unequal treatment of individuals based on their membership in a social group; usually motivated by prejudice

ON THE JOB
Gender and Sexuality in the Military

The military provides a particular case study when it comes to issues of work, gender, and sexuality. The huge institution that is the military is composed mostly of men. In fact, women only became eligible for combat roles in every branch of the armed forces in 2016. Currently, only 16 percent of enlisted personnel and 18 percent of officers are female. The number of women in the ranks varies by service branch, with women comprising 19 percent of the U.S. Air Force and Navy and 14 percent of the U.S. Army but only 8 percent of U.S. Marines (Reynolds and Shendruk 2018). In 2008, Lieutenant General Ann E. Dunwoody became the first woman promoted to the highest rank of four-star general in the U.S. armed forces.

The LGBTQ rights movement won a large victory in 2010 with the repeal of Don't Ask, Don't Tell (DADT). Signed into law in 1993, DADT arose amid existing military policies that required the discharge of gay, lesbian, and bisexual military service members. DADT was an attempt to curb those discharges by requiring that military administration not "ask" about a service member's sexual orientation and that service members not "tell" about it, either. Initially offering promise that gay service members would be allowed to serve, DADT brought about an environment of secrecy in which gay, lesbian, and bisexual service members had to keep silent—or lie—about their personal lives, as well as accept or even engage in anti-LGBTQ activities and discourse or face discharge. This environment spurred "witch hunts" that brought about the involuntary discharge of more than 14,000 service members. The repeal of DADT did not come quickly or easily, but President Obama signed the bill into law in 2010, allowing gay, lesbian, and bisexual service members to serve openly without recrimination or threat of discharge.

Transgender people have long been prohibited from serving in the military, with an official ban dating back to the 1960s. Despite this, studies estimate that in 2014 some 134,300 transgender persons were retired veterans, and another 15,500 were currently on active duty (Gates and Herman 2014). But none of them could serve openly until 2016, when the ban was lifted. For the first time, the Defense Department also allowed service members to seek transition-related medical care. Not long after taking office, however, the Trump administration began fighting to keep trans people out of the military.

Rape and sexual assault are increasingly acknowledged as a serious problem in the military, and women are far more likely than men to report gender harassment. Groundbreaking research by Laura Miller (1997) made the distinction that gender harassment, rather than being sexual in nature, instead was used to enforce traditional gender norms, such as aggression in males and nurturing in females, as well as to punish violations of these norms. Interestingly, the men in Miller's study were more likely to report being harassed by their drill sergeants, while the women were more likely to be harassed by their fellow trainees.

The Sexual Assault Prevention and Response Office was formed in 2004 by the Department of Defense to coordinate the military's response to sexual assault. In 2017, the military received 6,769 reports of sexual assault, up from 2,846 reports in 2007 (U.S. Department of Defense 2018). The Pentagon has long acknowledged that the number of officially reported cases of sexual harassment in the military may represent only a fraction of the total number of victims. Counterintuitively, military leaders argue that the recent dramatic increase in reports of sexual assault is good news. Because sexual assault and sexual harassment so often went unreported in the past, "increased reporting signals not only growing trust of command and confidence in the response system, but serves as the gateway to provide more victims with support and to hold a greater number of offenders appropriately accountable" (U.S. Department of Defense 2014). Despite the progress made, the military can still be an inhospitable place for female and LGBTQ service members.

Women in the Military Women now serve in every branch of the military and in all positions, including combat roles.

equally or even better qualified. When such individual actions are cumulative or reproduced across many workplaces and industries, we can say that the impact is felt on an institutional level. Despite many laws in place banning workplace gender discrimination and protecting individual and group rights, corporate culture is still fraught with prejudice and discriminatory practices.

In Silicon Valley, for example, sexism is alive and well, as evidenced by a 3,300-word manifesto circulated by a male engineer at Google in August 2017. Written in response to Google's recent efforts to increase diversity among its heavily white and heavily male workforce, the internal memo argued that the unequal representation of women in tech roles is due to supposed biological differences between men and women. The memo went on to list such gender stereotypes as women's "higher anxiety" and "lower stress tolerance" and "men's higher drive for status" as if these could explain the different outcomes for men and women in tech, when in fact there is no evidence to back such a claim (Swisher 2017).

Prejudice and discrimination can also be based on sexual orientation, gender expression, and gender identity. **Homophobia** (fear of those who are not heterosexual) and **transphobia** (fear of those who don't conform to society's gender expectations) form the basis for discrimination against gays, lesbians, and bisexuals, as well as trans and gender-nonconforming persons. Some have pointed out that homophobia and transphobia are not true "phobias," like agoraphobia or claustrophobia, which are psychological phenomena. Rather, they are prejudices, like racism or sexism, which are cultural norms that are learned and transmitted socially. Some find the terms *"homophobia"* and *"transphobia"* problematic because they suggest that the problems faced by LGBTQ persons are the result of a few maladjusted individuals rather than the product of deeply institutionalized cultural values and norms (Frank 2012; Kitzinger 1987). Indeed, some have suggested that **heterosexism** or **cisgenderism** would be more useful terms in that they are analogous to sexism and racism and describe an ideological system that stigmatizes any nonheterosexual or noncisgender identities or behaviors (Herek 1990; Rothblum 1996).

The discrimination faced by LGBTQ persons ranges from subtle social exclusion to violent assaults and is one of the reasons that gays, lesbians, and trans persons sometimes hide their true identities from family, friends, or co-workers. **Coming out**, or revealing one's gender identity or sexuality, can feel unsafe in an anti-gay, anti-trans society. Some fear not only the social and emotional repercussions they might experience but also becoming the victim of a hate crime. Fully 18 percent of all hate crimes are motivated by anti–sexual orientation or anti–gender identity biases; advocates believe these numbers are underreported (Federal Bureau of Investigation 2018b).

Hegemonic and Toxic Masculinity

Hegemonic masculinity promotes a particular kind of masculine ideal that is held out as superior to any other kind of masculinity, as well as to any form of femininity (Connell and Messerschmidt 2005). It extols the expression of stereotypically masculine characteristics such as independence, aggression, competitiveness, and toughness, and rejects any characteristics that are associated with the feminine, along with homosexuality and any alternate gender expression. Hegemonic masculinity defines a specific standard of manhood to which men must then measure up and prove themselves. But not all men are equally served by its narrow definition. The intersections of a man's class background, race, or sexuality will also figure into a hierarchy where upper-middle-class white, cisgender, heterosexual men are at the top.

The term **toxic masculinity** has recently gained currency, as critics have highlighted the dysfunctional aspects of hegemonic masculinity and the risks associated with trying to achieve its masculine ideal. We usually think of sexism and gender norms as oppressive to women, but men also suffer as a result of the dominant gender ideology. The masculine ideal imposes requirements on men to compete with each other, to be breadwinners and leaders, to suppress any emotions except for anger, and to reject any "feminine" qualities they may feel, such as empathy or nurturance, lest they show weakness and lose status. The narrow definitions of the masculine ideal limit men's options for careers or hobbies and constrict their relationships with friends, colleagues, and family. Toxic masculinity takes a toll on men in a number of ways; it has been cited as a negative factor in men's mental and physical health (Iwamoto et al. 2018).

One of the most extreme and troubling expressions of toxic masculinity appears in the incel movement. Incel is short for "involuntary celibate," a man who feels aggrieved because he

HOMOPHOBIA fear of or discrimination toward gay, lesbian, and bisexual people

TRANSPHOBIA fear of or discrimination toward transgender or other gender-nonconforming people

HETEROSEXISM belief in the superiority of heterosexuality and heterosexuals

CISGENDERISM belief in the superiority of cisgender persons and identities

COMING OUT openly declaring one's true identity to those who might not be aware of it; short for "coming out of the closet," a phrase used to describe how LGBTQ persons have felt compelled to keep their sexual orientation or gender identity secret

HEGEMONIC MASCULINITY a masculine ideal that promotes characteristics such as independence, aggression, and toughness, and rejects any alternate qualities in men

TOXIC MASCULINITY a masculine ideal that espouses extreme and harmful attitudes and behaviors and may lead to various negative effects for women and men

has not been able to find a willing sex partner. These men—who are largely young, white, and heterosexual—feel a sense of entitlement to have sex and believe they are suffering an injustice by being deprived. When they are denied opportunities for sex, their frustration and humiliation turn into rage against women and other sexually active men.

The incel movement has grown over the last several years in online forums where men gather to discuss their resentment, self-pity, and hatred toward women. They revel in a kind of misogyny that objectifies and denigrates women and that in some cases has led to violent outcomes. In 2014, Elliot Rodger wrote a 140-page manifesto linking himself to the incel movement, before killing six people and injuring fourteen more in Isla Vista, California (near the University of California, Santa Barbara), and then killing himself. Tragically, other mass murders by incel-affiliated men have occurred with some regularity. While not all incels become radicalized to this extent, online forums such as a now-banned subreddit with more than 40,000 subscribers espouse hateful and violence-filled rhetoric. The incel movement has migrated to other online platforms, where it continues to attract new members.

MICROAGGRESSIONS everyday uses of subtle verbal and nonverbal communications that convey denigrating or dismissive messages to members of certain social groups

The incel movement has been called a terrorist organization and labeled a hate group; it is included in a listing of other radical men's groups promoting a male supremacist worldview. Male supremacy is a misogynist ideology that proclaims the fundamental inferiority of women, while reducing them to their basic functions as subservient sex partners and caregivers. Inherent in these ideas is the assertion that men are oppressed by changes brought about by modern feminism; proponents blame women for the current crisis to masculinity and so seek to dominate them as before.

Gendered Language and Microaggressions

Some sociologists argue that language shapes culture, while others say the opposite. In any case, by looking at our language, we can see how certain words reflect cultural values and norms, particularly sexism, heterosexism, and cisgenderism. For instance, the English language has long assumed that the default category for all human experience is male. We have traditionally used the generic "he," referred to humanity as "mankind," and noted that "all men are created equal." If something is man-made, it is made by humans, not just male humans. But clearly, not everyone experiences the world from a male perspective, and using this kind of language can make some women feel excluded and demeaned.

Not everyone experiences the world from a heterosexual perspective either, but in most societies heterosexuality is assumed and is part of the structure of society in ways that we may not even notice. For example, some people use the terms "gay" or "queer" to describe things they don't like, implying that being gay or queer is a bad thing. Even less obvious: assumptions of heterosexuality on the part of others, such as the new acquaintance who asks a woman what her husband does, or the well-meaning auntie who buys her cute nephew a T-shirt that says "Ladies' Man." Small acts such as these reinforce heterosexist assumptions and can make gays, lesbians, and bisexuals feel invisible and invalidated.

These small acts are examples of **microaggressions**—subtle verbal and nonverbal communications that convey denigrating or dismissive messages to members of a certain social group (Sue 2010). Whether intentional or not, microaggressions are experienced as insulting and demeaning. For instance, it is not uncommon for women to be told to smile, especially in public. The roots of this unsolicited directive are in the expectation that a woman should conform to a narrow stereotype or ideal of femininity; the implication is that it's not okay for a woman to express herself in a serious way. This happened recently to tennis star Serena Williams, when a male journalist asked her why she was not smiling after winning a hard-fought evening match against her sister. She did not take kindly to his comment, firing back, "It's 11:30. To be perfectly honest with you, I don't want to be here."

Other examples of microaggressions against women include being interrupted in conversations, being labeled as shrill or bossy, or being the target of catcalls and other suggestive remarks by strangers. Trans persons also experience microaggressions when, intentionally or unintentionally, they are "misgendered" by others. While it can be accidental (calling a trans woman "sir" on the phone, or a trans man "ma'am," for example), it is sometimes deliberate, as when an unsupportive family member refuses to use the trans person's preferred name or gender pronoun.

The vocabulary associated with sex, gender, and sexuality may seem to be a confusing minefield for those who are unfamiliar with it. Preferred terms may change faster within LGBTQ communities than outside of them, leaving open the possibility for individuals to give and take offense. Various LGBTQ organizations post glossaries online to help guide speakers, writers, and others. Check out the websites of GLAAD (a media advocacy organization) or HRC (Human Rights Campaign) for examples of such glossaries. It is important to respect LGBTQ people's preferred language, which may vary by person. As tempting as it might be to slap a label on people when we first encounter them, the right thing to do is to allow others to self-identify and to then affirm that self-identification by using a person's chosen name and preferred pronoun—he or she, or a neutral pronoun like they.

SOCIOLOGICAL THEORIES OF GENDER INEQUALITY

Each of the three main sociological paradigms has explained gender inequality in different ways; in addition, there is a theoretical perspective devoted entirely to the questions surrounding gender and gender inequality in society. We will take a brief look at each in this section.

Structural Functionalism

Functionalists generally believe that there are still social roles better suited to one gender than the other, and that societies are more stable when norms are fulfilled by the appropriate sex. In particular, functionalists emphasize how "female" roles may work in tandem with "male" roles within the family. Talcott Parsons, for example, identified two complementary roles (Parsons and Bales 1955). One is an **instrumental role**: being task oriented, a "breadwinner," and an authority figure.

The Function of Gender Inequality In the 1950s, Talcott Parsons argued that gender role expectations upheld the traditional family. Male "breadwinners" fulfilled an instrumental role by being task oriented and authoritative, while female "homemakers" embodied an expressive role by providing emotional support. *The Adventures of Ozzie and Harriet* featured the era's prototypical family.

The other is an **expressive role**: providing emotional support and nurturing. The expressive role is crucial not only for the care of children but also for stabilizing the personality of the instrumental partner against the stresses of the competitive world. In this view, since women are considered better suited to the expressive role and men to the instrumental role, gender segregation serves to uphold the traditional family and its social functions.

Expressive and instrumental roles may be complementary, but the social rewards for filling them are far from equal. The functionalist view does not explain very well why gender relations are characterized by such inequality. While the work of raising children and maintaining a household is intensive and difficult, there is a tendency to dismiss it as being unskilled and instinctive, which results in the devaluation of traditionally feminine work. Those who support a patriarchal society argue that this is again because resources provided by men in their instrumental roles are ultimately more valuable. This value, however, is being questioned in light of evidence indicating that juvenile delinquency and crime rates are higher when there is no adult supervision in the home and that expressive roles are thus important. The functionalist view also fails to acknowledge that families are often sources of social instability, with violence and abuse in families all too common. For these and other reasons, the functionalist perspective is problematic and has fallen out of favor within sociology.

> **INSTRUMENTAL ROLE** the position of the family member who provides material support, often an authority figure
>
> **EXPRESSIVE ROLE** the position of the family member who provides emotional support and nurturing

Conflict Theory

Conflict theorists take a different approach. According to this perspective, men have historically had access to most of society's material resources and privileges, and consequently they generally seek to maintain their dominant status. Thus, conflict theorists see gender inequality in much the same way as they see race and class inequality—as manifestations of exploitation.

Some conflict theorists argue that gender inequality is just a derivative of class inequality and that it therefore originates with private property. This theory was introduced by Friedrich Engels in 1884. Engels noted that capitalists (the owners of property) benefited from maintaining patriarchal families, with women in the private sphere and men in the public workplace, in at least two ways. Women do the work of reproducing the labor force (on which the capitalists depend) without receiving any direct compensation, and they serve as an inexpensive "reserve army" of labor when the need arises. Engels suggested that if private property were abolished, the material inequalities producing social classes would disappear, and there would no longer be powerful interests forcing women into domestic roles.

Conflict theorists point out that whether or not gender inequality is a product of class conflict, all men benefit from it in the short term. Zillah Eisenstein (1979) noted that men stand to lose a good deal if gender segregation disappears: They would have to do more unpaid work, or pay to have their homes kept up and children cared for; they would have to find jobs in a larger and more competitive market; and they would lose some power and prestige if they were no longer the more viable breadwinners.

Symbolic Interactionism

While conflict theorists and functionalists focus on gender from a macrosociological perspective, interactionists emphasize how gender is socially constructed and maintained in our everyday lives. According to interactionists, gender is so important to our social selves that we can barely interact with anyone without first determining that person's gender identity. We need to categorize, and we need to be categorizable as well. For some people, this is no easy matter. For example, gender-nonconforming people such as transgender or nonbinary individuals may not fit easily into society's preexisting categories and may experience difficulty in their interactions with others who expect them to do so.

UCLA's Harold Garfinkel (1967/1984) was one of the first sociologists to focus on the interactional work involved in expressing gender identity in a world of binary categories. He conducted intensive interviews with "Agnes," a trans woman born with male genitalia and raised as a boy, who was undergoing sex-reassignment treatment at the UCLA medical center. While Agnes had always known that she was a "120 percent natural normal woman," it was only when she was seventeen that she began to learn how to "do being female"—to look, behave, and talk like a woman. Agnes got a job and a roommate—even a boyfriend—and set about learning what would be expected of her as a woman. She carefully adopted her female roommate's style of dress, makeup, and body language; she listened to what her female friends said and how they spoke. She learned how to maintain "proper" deference (it was a different era) to her male boss at work, and she listened to her boyfriend and his female family members as they expressed their expectations for her as a future wife and mother. Unlike other women, though, Agnes had to take extra precautions, such as avoiding sexual intercourse with her boyfriend (not too unusual in the early 1960s), wearing skirts and other clothing that would disguise her male anatomy, and avoiding activities (such as swimming at the beach) that would make her differences obvious until after she had completed her surgical transition.

"Passing" as a female was a good deal of work for Agnes, and she constantly dealt with the fear that her secret would be discovered. But even Garfinkel, who knew her secret already, found her enactment of femininity quite convincing. Indeed, he was utterly charmed by her. Agnes's case emphasizes the interactionist's view of gender as something that we "do" in our interactions with others. Even though you may think you have nothing in common with Agnes or other transgender people, you actually enact gender in much the same way Agnes did.

Feminist Theory

Feminist theory has developed in the last thirty years in a way that has revolutionized society and the social sciences. Related to both conflict theory (in its focus on inequality) and interactionist theory (in its focus on people's lived experiences), feminist theory flourished alongside the women's movement, which is dedicated to securing the same rights and freedoms for both women and men in society. Feminist theory developed into a way of looking at the world that focuses on enhancing scholarly understanding of gender inequities in society. By applying assumptions about gender inequality to various social institutions—the family, education, the economy, or the media—feminist theory allows for a new way of understanding those institutions and the changing role of gender in contemporary society. Feminist theory and methods contribute to "writing women back in" to scholarship in history, literature, art, and the social and natural sciences, areas in which the lives and contributions of women have traditionally been minimized or overlooked entirely. Theorists such as Judith Butler (1999), bell hooks (2003), and Catharine MacKinnon (2005) link gender inequality with inequality in other social hierarchies—race and ethnicity, class, and sexual orientation—and argue that gender and power are inextricably intertwined in our society.

GENDER, SEXUALITY, AND LIFE CHANCES

If two infants, one girl and one boy, are born at the same time in the same location from parents of similar racial and socioeconomic backgrounds, sociologists can predict answers to questions like the following: Who is more likely to live longer, attend college, or go to prison? Who might make a good living or live in poverty? Who is more likely to be married, divorced, or widowed, be a single parent or the victim of a violent crime, or join the military?

In this section, we will analyze how our gender and sexuality affect our lives. We will look specifically at how expectations regarding gender and sexuality shape our experiences with family, health, education, work and income, and criminal justice. For instance, women traditionally are caretakers of their families and more likely than men to go to college. Men make more money than women and are more likely to head

TABLE 9.2 Theory in Everyday Life

Perspective	Approach to Gender Inequality	Case Study: Male- and Female-Dominated Occupations
Structural Functionalism	Sex determines which roles men and women are best suited to; it is more appropriate for men to play instrumental roles and for women to play expressive roles.	Women are naturally more nurturing and thus make better nurses and teachers of young children; men are naturally more logical and thus make better lawyers and computer programmers.
Conflict Theory	Because of the traditional division of labor in families, males have had more access to resources and privileges and have sought to maintain their dominance.	Male-dominated occupations generally hold more prestige and are better paid; women may encounter difficulties entering male-dominated occupations, whereas men may more easily succeed in female-dominated occupations.
Symbolic Interactionism	Gender is learned through the process of socialization; gender inequalities are reproduced through interactions with family, peers, schools, and the media.	Girls and boys are socialized differently and may be encouraged to seek out gender-appropriate training, college majors, and career goals, leading them to enter male- and female-dominated occupations.

religious institutions. Members of the LGBTQ community are more likely to suffer from depression and mental illness. These conditions are the result of values and norms that encourage certain behaviors in women and men.

It is important to remember the concept of intersectionality—that gender and sexuality are intertwined with other factors, such as race and class. Therefore, it is difficult to separate out the effects of gender on categories like marriage, education, and work. Single women with children are probably more likely to live in poverty, less likely to have a college education, and more likely to work in service-sector jobs. However, a person is not automatically poor or destined to be divorced because she is female. The categories all work together to construct the complexity of a person's life.

Families

When it comes to family, men are more likely than women to report never having been married (35 percent of men compared to 29 percent of women), perhaps reflecting the stronger societal pressure for women to marry at some point in their lives. Women are also more likely to be widowed (9 percent versus less than 3 percent of men), which is due in part to women's longer life spans (U.S. Census Bureau 2018e).

Divorce has a greater impact on women because they are more likely to retain the primary caregiving role after divorce and to suffer financially because of it. About four of every five custodial parents—parents who live with children while the other parent lives elsewhere—are mothers. Less than half (44 percent) of custodial parents receive the full amount of child support due, and nearly a third receive none. Consequently, about 27 percent of all custodial-parent families live below the poverty level, compared to 16 percent of all families with children (Grall 2018).

And while women are contributing to household income by working outside the home, they are finding that they are still responsible for being the family's primary caregiver. In the workplace, this creates problems. Time taken out of work in order to care for sick children is seen as nonproductive time, and women who do take such time off may face discrimination (Wharton and Blair-Loy 2002). And most women, when they leave work, still face household chores at home—the **second shift**.

Coming out to family members is not always easy for LGBTQ youth, and it may have negative consequences for their mental and physical health. Studies have shown that parental rejection is associated with higher levels of depression and rates of attempted suicide, along with increases in risk-taking behaviors such as unsafe sex and illegal drug use (Ryan et al. 2009; Substance Abuse and Mental Health Services Administration 2015). In contrast, youth with supportive families (and "families of choice") have better self-esteem and are generally healthier (Ryan et al. 2010).

SECOND SHIFT the unpaid housework and child care often expected of women after they complete their day's paid labor

Until fairly recently the right to legally marry was denied to almost all LGBTQ individuals. In June 2015, the Supreme Court ruled in *Obergefell v. Hodges* that same-sex couples have a constitutional right to marry, legalizing gay marriage nationwide. According to Gallup, a majority of same-sex couples (61 percent) are now married, up from 38 percent before the ruling. Just over 10 percent of all LGBTQ adults are currently married to a same-sex spouse (Jones 2017).

Health

Of the more than 325 million Americans, more than half are female. Why are there more women? One reason is that women live longer; females born in 2016 are expected to live for an average of 81.1 years, whereas males are expected to live 76.1 years (Centers for Disease Control and Prevention 2018a). The longer men live, the closer their life expectancy comes to that of women, but the overall average is depressed

IN THE FUTURE
Human Trafficking

We usually think of slavery as something that happened in the past, a deplorable historical artifact that is not only wholly unconscionable by contemporary standards but also outlawed everywhere in the world. The truth is that modern-day slavery not only exists but also is perhaps a problem of greater proportion than we might expect.

In 2017, United States law enforcement uncovered a "modern-day sex slave ring" they described as one of the most elaborate and extensive sex-trafficking operations they had ever seen (Davey 2017). The multimillion-dollar operation had gone on for more than eight years and involved hundreds of women who were shuttled among various cities, including Chicago, Dallas, and Los Angeles. These young women, most of them from impoverished communities in Thailand, had been promised a better life in the United States and that they would be able to help support their families back home. Once they arrived, the women found those promises came at an appallingly high price: They were required to work as prostitutes until they could pay off exorbitant "bondage debts" of up to $60,000 each. The authorities said that the women were kept sequestered in prostitution houses and prevented from leaving; their work hours often ran all day,

every day. While this is a particularly high-profile case, it is not an isolated one. More than 3,500 sex-trafficking cases were reported to the National Human Trafficking Resource Center in 2016 alone.

The United Nations has defined human trafficking as "the recruitment, transportation, transfer, harboring or receipt of persons, by means of the threat or use of force or other forms of coercion, of abduction, of fraud, of deception, of the abuse of power or of a position of vulnerability . . . for the purpose of exploitation." As this definition conveys, human trafficking takes many forms. As with all illegal activities, it is difficult to get accurate numbers on human trafficking. Estimates range from 600,000 to more than 2.5 million people being trafficked worldwide each year. According to a recent report by the United Nations Office of Drugs and Crime (2019), human trafficking has taken on "horrific dimensions," with sexual exploitation accounting for the majority of cases. The report found that armed groups are increasingly using human trafficking as a tool of war to both pay for their operations and boost their workforce. The report also documented an increase in the trafficking of young girls. Fully 70 percent of victims worldwide are female, and 23 percent are girls under

because young men are at greater risk of accidental death. Research by the Centers for Disease Control and Prevention (CDC) shows that men ages twenty to twenty-four are almost three times as likely as women to die as a result of accidents, more than four times as likely to commit suicide, and almost seven times more likely to be murdered (Heron 2018).

These days, however, more women are engaged in stress-related behavior—such as working outside the home, smoking, and drinking—so the gap may be closing, and in fact it's the smallest it's been in fifty years. Some of the change can be attributed to men taking more care with their health, but at the same time women have increased their risk factors for disease. For example, lung cancer used to be thought of as a man's disease, but as more women began lighting up over the past decades, their relative risk of death from lung cancer rose and is now nearly identical to that of men (Thun 2013). Such trends have led researchers to call smoking "the great equalizer" (National Institutes of Health 2014; Perls and Fretts 1998).

While both women and men suffer from heart disease and

cancer in fairly equal numbers, other health disorders are gender related. One example is depression, which women are almost twice as likely to suffer from as men (Burton 2012; Kessler 2003). Historically, the medical profession has diagnosed women far more often than men with depression, "hysteria," and other mental conditions. Thus, women have been denied equal rights and equitable working conditions and pay if they were thought, as a category, to be mentally unfit. This issue, however, is controversial. Some maintain that women may be more likely to report such symptoms, whereas men may ignore them or may feel a greater sense of stigma in reporting them (Byrne 1981; Martin, Neighbors, and Griffith 2013).

Systematic data about the life expectancy of LGBTQ individuals are not available yet, but early research suggests that being gay might have implications for health as well, but only for those who live in less tolerant areas. One study found that "living in communities with high levels of anti-gay prejudice" was associated with a "life expectancy difference of roughly 12 years" (Hatzenbuehler et al. 2014). Some of this decrease

eighteen. Michelle Bachelet, former president of Chile and former head of the UN agency on women's rights and gender equality, called human trafficking "one of the fastest growing" and most lucrative crimes in the world. And according to the United Nations, only 1 in 100 victims is ever rescued (Lederer 2012).

The policy in the United States is to aggressively pursue human-trafficking crimes and to bring their perpetrators to justice. Multiple federal agencies are involved in the effort, including the Department of State (DOS), the Department of Homeland Security (DHS), and the Department of Justice (DOJ). In 2016 these agencies investigated more than 3,800 cases of suspected human trafficking, ultimately securing convictions against 439 traffickers, whose sentences ranged from twelve months to life imprisonment (U.S. Department of State 2017). Advocates have called upon federal prosecutors and courts to award mandatory restitution to victims of human trafficking.

The trafficking of girls and women as sex slaves remains an emotional issue, regardless of the arguments about the accuracy of the numbers. It is still something that is hard to imagine existing in modern-day form, in the United States or elsewhere. Because it is a crime that is so difficult to combat, future efforts to stop trafficking must involve raising awareness of the issue; it is most often community members who first tip off law enforcement when they suspect

Modern-Day Slavery Nadia Murad was kidnapped and held captive by the Islamic State. She now works as a human rights activist seeking to end the trafficking of women and children. Murad was awarded the Nobel Peace Prize in 2018.

this kind of illegal activity. Equally important are identifying and resolving the larger social and economic problems that make people vulnerable to trafficking (such as extreme poverty and sexism) and coordinating international law enforcement efforts and interdiction. Sociological insight is necessary for any and all of these things to occur. A future in which slavery *really* no longer exists is something worth fighting for.

in life expectancy can be connected to issues like suicide and homicide that may also result from prejudice. But researchers also report that "psychosocial stressors are strongly linked to cardiovascular risk, and this kind of stress may represent an indirect pathway through which prejudice contributes to mortality" (Hatzenbuehler et al. 2014). Perhaps relatedly, sexual minorities are more likely to smoke, drink, and use illicit drugs, and they suffer from higher rates of mental illness (Substance Abuse and Mental Health Services Administration 2016). Additionally, LGBTQ adults are less likely to have health insurance and also less likely to have a personal doctor (Gates 2014).

Education

In fall 2018, nearly 20 million students headed off to colleges in the United States, and about 11.2 million of them were female (National Center for Education Statistics 2018a). In fact, since the 1990s, women have increasingly outnumbered men in college, especially in the traditional

eighteen-to-twenty-four age group. Starting in the mid-1990s women have made up the majority of college graduates, and in 2017 they earned 57 percent of bachelor's degrees. By 2000 more women than men were earning master's degrees, and by 2005 more women were earning doctorates as well (National Center for Education Statistics 2018c). However, men earn more than women at every level of education, from those not completing high school to those obtaining advanced degrees. In fact, in order to make as much money as a man with a bachelor's degree, a woman has to have a PhD (Carnevale, Rose, and Cheah 2011). These wage discrepancies make gender inequality very difficult to ignore.

For many queer youth, the most difficult period in dealing with their sexual and gender identities in a transphobic and homophobic culture occurs during their adolescent years. The 2015 National School Climate Survey (Kosciw et al. 2016) showed that nearly nine out of ten LGBTQ students experienced harassment in school. Almost 85 percent of LGBTQ students reported being verbally harassed, while 35 percent reported being physically harassed, and 16 percent reported physical assault in the past year because of their sexual orientation. Not surprisingly, LGBTQ youth are much more likely to attempt suicide: In 2015, 6 percent of heterosexual students compared to 29 percent of gay, lesbian, and bisexual students had attempted suicide (Kann et al. 2016). In response, many schools have enacted anti-bullying policies that can help lower instances of harassment and raise the rates of staff intervention. School programs that heighten all students' awareness of stigma and its consequences can help change campus climate (Rabow, Stein, and Conley 1999).

Work and Income

In whatever aspect of work we analyze—the rates of participation in the labor force, the kinds of jobs, the levels of pay, the balance between work and family—gender inequality is highly visible. For example, in 2017, 69 percent of men were in the labor force compared to 57 percent of women. Because traditional family dynamics still endure, women are more likely than men to be found outside the labor force altogether (U.S. Bureau of Labor Statistics 2018e). Nonetheless, since 1975, the number of mothers in the labor force has been on the rise. Only 47 percent of mothers participated in the labor force in 1975 compared to 71 percent in 2017.

Marriage seems to have opposite effects on women's and men's participation rates. Never-married women are more likely to work than married women, while married men are more likely to work than single men. This discrepancy could possibly be explained by the assumption that men are heads of households, and single women are considered responsible for their own finances.

Many jobs are gendered; they traditionally have been and continue to be performed by women or men. As Table 9.3 shows, nurses, kindergarten teachers, dental hygienists, secretaries, paralegals, and housekeepers are female-dominated professions, whereas airplane pilots, auto mechanics, firefighters, carpenters, and the clergy are male-dominated professions. In 2018, nearly 98 percent of all teachers of young children and 94 percent of secretaries were women. Just 2 percent of all automotive mechanics and just 5 percent of all firefighters were women.

Why are some jobs considered best performed by women and others by men? Why are women vastly underrepresented as pilots and auto mechanics and men nearly absent as secretaries and child-care workers? Socially constructed categories of occupations are extremely resilient. Despite advances in workplace technologies that would enable both women and men to perform similarly in jobs, men still vastly outnumber women in certain professions, especially those with high salaries and prestige.

FEMINIZATION OF POVERTY the economic trend showing that women are more likely than men to live in poverty, caused in part by the gendered gap in wages, the higher proportion of single mothers compared to single fathers, and the increasing costs of child care

TABLE 9.3   Selected Occupations by Gender, 2018

Occupation	Percent Women
Preschool and kindergarten teachers	97.6
Dental hygienists	97.1
Secretaries and administrative assistants	94.0
Maids and housekeepers	90.1
Registered nurses	88.6
Paralegals and legal assistants	86.4
Librarians	78.5
Psychologists	75.9
Physician assistants	72.1
Waiters and waitresses	69.9
Customer service representatives	63.7
News analysts, reporters, and correspondents	51.7
Retail salespersons	48.7
Physicians and surgeons	40.3
Lawyers	37.4
Chief executives	26.9
Clergy	22.4
Computer programmers	21.2
Aircraft pilots and flight engineers	9.0
Firefighters	5.1
Carpenters	2.2
Automotive service technicians and mechanics	2.1

SOURCE: U.S. Bureau of Labor Statistics 2019c.

Currently, women in the United States earn about 81 cents for every dollar a man earns (Figure 9.2). This difference in women's average earnings and men's average earnings is referred to as the gender pay gap. The sex segregation of occupations is one cause of this gap in pay. Female-dominated occupations such as education and health services are consistently undervalued and underpaid compared to male-dominated occupations, reflecting cultural ideas about the value of "women's work" (Chodorow 2009). Motherhood and women's disproportionate responsibility for housework

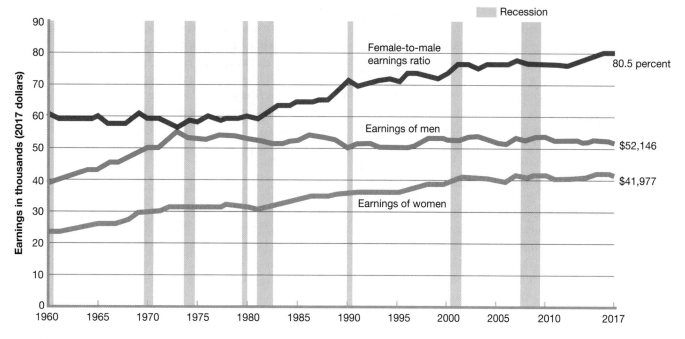

FIGURE 9.2 Female-to-Male Earnings Ratio, 1960–2017

SOURCE: Fontenot, Semega, and Kollar 2018.

and child care, which often limit the amount of time women can spend engaging in paid work, also contribute to the gender pay gap. The gender pay gap also reflects ongoing discrimination against women and inequalities in the job market, and these inequalities are compounded by the effects of race. The gender pay gap is largest for women of color. Black and Hispanic women suffer the greatest losses, earning only 65 cents and 62 cents, respectively, for each dollar that a white man earns (Hegewisch and Hartmann 2019).

Finally, women are more likely to live in poverty than men. This situation, often referred to as the **feminization of poverty**, results from a combination of social forces, including the gender pay gap, the higher proportion of single women taking on the financial responsibility of children, and the increasing costs of child care.

In states that do not have laws prohibiting it, employers can still discriminate against LGBTQ persons in hiring and pay. In a recent survey, between 11 and 28 percent of lesbian, gay, and bisexual workers reported losing a promotion simply because of their sexual orientation, and 27 percent of transgender workers reported being fired, not hired, or denied a promotion (Singh and Durso 2017). Given the number of LGBTQ workers compared to, say, the number of women workers, this means that the rate of LGBTQ discrimination is several times higher—a concerning statistic. The Employment Non-Discrimination Act (ENDA) is proposed legislation that places both sexual orientation and gender identity in a protected class along with race and gender, but it has consistently failed to pass both houses of Congress to make it to the president's desk.

DATA WORKSHOP

Analyzing Everyday Life

The Second Shift: Gender Norms and Household Labor

Gender roles have changed a great deal in recent decades, giving men and women a much larger range of options than before. Still, we continue to conform to many traditional gender norms, both in the workplace and at home. When it comes to couples and families, it is easy to see the extent to which expectations for men and women differ. Sociologist Arlie Hochschild has conducted extensive studies of two-parent households and the division of labor for the many tasks of domestic life (Hochschild and Machung 1989). She coined the term the second shift to refer to the unpaid work—cooking, cleaning, laundry, child care, home repair, yard work—that must be done at home after the day's paid labor, the first shift, is complete.

With the typical couple today, both men and women work outside the home, and for most households it takes two incomes to pay the bills and raise a family. If both people are already working a first shift, then whose responsibility is it to take on all the other tasks waiting at home? It's probably not surprising that Hochschild found that women do most of the second shift—but not always. Perhaps you have noticed this second shift work in your own home or family.

You'll notice that some tasks must be done every day, or even several times each day—like cooking meals, for example. Other tasks, like laundry, are done less often but on a regular basis. Still others are irregular or seasonal, like raking leaves or unstopping a clogged drain. Some tasks are focused on people, like helping kids with homework, whereas others, like cleaning out the gutters, are focused on objects. Studies show that men tend to participate in more instrumental tasks, such as car repair and yard work, while women tend to engage in more expressive tasks, such as mediating arguments and calming upset children. And then there are all the seemingly endless tasks that revolve around the family's daily needs, and who is doing that? Most often, it's women; this is how they rack up an extra month of housework a year (that's a month of twenty-four-hour days)!

For this Data Workshop, you will investigate the second shift by interviewing one working parent in a two-person couple who share a household with one or more children. Return to the section on interviews in Chapter 2 for a review of Hochschild and this research method.

Construct a set of interview questions to ask a working parent about how he or she juggles family and work. These can include some closed-ended as well as open-ended questions. One of the easiest ways to start an interview like this is to just ask the person to describe everything she or he does in a typical day, perhaps using the previous day as an example. This can be done in chronological order. Try to identify all the types of work that your respondent does in a typical day, including paid work, unpaid work, interaction work, emotion work, and so on. Be aware you may need to prompt your respondent if you suspect the person has overlooked some part of his or her day or if you need more details.

You'll also want to ask some other questions about how tasks are divided among members of the household (spouse/partner, children, others). Who does what and why? Ask your interviewee to describe both his or her own tasks and also what his or her partner does. You might also try to determine how completing these tasks (or not completing them) affects the respondent's relationships with other members of the household. Feel free to develop some additional questions of your own.

Once your questionnaire is ready, identify an interviewee who is a member of the target population, and ask for the person's consent to participate in your pilot study. Ask your respondent to be candid and to answer your questions as fully as possible. Be prepared to take detailed notes and/or record your interview. Either way you'll need to produce a rough transcription of the responses to review and analyze.

After completing the interview, refer to your written notes or transcripts and do some further analysis. Reflect on the data and ask yourself the following questions:

- Does there appear to be a gendered division of labor in the home? How are the tasks divided? Who does most of the daily work and why?

- Did your interview confirm that women do more of the second shift, or was your respondent an exception to the rule?

- Is it inevitable that one person in a couple always does more work than the other? What effects might these inequities have on marriages and live-in relationships? Can you think of a better solution to sharing household labor?

- What might you have learned if you could have interviewed the other partner as well?

- Although a single interview is not a scientific sample, do you think your findings could still apply to a larger population?

There are two options for completing this Data Workshop:

PREP-PAIR-SHARE Conduct the interview and bring your questionnaire and notes and/or transcripts to class. Pair up with a partner, present your preliminary findings, and compare and contrast what you learned from the experience. Try to further develop your analyses together.

DO-IT-YOURSELF Conduct the interview and make some preliminary notes and/or transcripts. Write a three-page essay analyzing your data. Make sure to use specific quotations from your respondent to support your analysis. Include a copy of your interview questionnaire and your notes/transcripts as attachments to your paper.

Criminal Justice

The experience of men and women differs with regard to almost every social institution, and the criminal justice system is no exception. The social construction of masculinity as aggressive, dominant, and physical corresponds to statistics on gender and crime. Men are more likely to die violent deaths and to be victims of assault. Women are slightly more likely to be victims of personal theft and much more likely to be victims of rape. Also women are far more likely to be victimized by their intimate partners (spouses or current or former boyfriends). In fact, about half of female homicide victims are killed by current or former intimate partners (Petrosky et al. 2017).

In analyzing arrest rates for 2017, we find that men are overwhelmingly represented in nearly all categories, including murder, rape, sex offenses, theft, assault, and drug charges. There is only one category of crimes where women outnumber men: prostitution (Federal Bureau of Investigation 2018a). It is important for us as sociologists to recognize this discrepancy as an example of how crime is influenced by the social construction of gender. Because males are perceived as being more likely to be involved in violent crime and property crime, they are generally kept under more scrutiny by the police than females are. Of the more than 1.5 million people in state and federal prisons, the vast majority (around 93 percent) are men (Carson 2018).

The experiences of LGBTQ persons are distinctive both as victims and as offenders. Bias-motivated attacks on the basis of sexual orientation are the third-highest category of hate crimes tracked by the federal government (after race and religion). More than 18 percent of all hate crimes are motivated by sexual-orientation or gender or gender-identity bias. In 2017 federal records showed 1,303 anti–sexual orientation hate crimes and 131 anti-transgender or anti–gender-nonconforming attacks (Federal Bureau of Investigation 2018b). Given their proportions within the larger population, LGBTQ people are the most likely targets of hate crimes in America. While it is difficult to find crime statistics that record the sexual orientation and/or gender identity of criminal offenders, it is important to recognize that LGBTQ persons do experience arrest, trial, conviction, and imprisonment. Once in prison, LGBTQ inmates are vulnerable to sexual victimization at up to thirteen times the level of risk for the average inmate (Sexton, Jenness, and Sumner 2009).

Intersectionality

Once again, the issue of intersectionality is important to keep in mind when we discuss gender and life chances: Gender rarely shapes individual experience in isolation but is instead linked to other social statuses in the effects it has on our lives. The intersection of gender with class, race, ethnicity, and immigration status is visible in Miliann Kang's (2010) study of the work of Asian immigrant women (mostly from Korea) in nail salons. Kang argued that the femininity that is central to the beauty rituals performed in salons is also racialized. For example, the expectations our society has for *Asian* women are different from the expectations for their *non-Asian* female clientele. Because the quality of "subservience," for instance, is often seen as "natural" in Asian women, customers may feel that they can make more demands on their manicurists than they would with other service providers. Indeed,

Salons and Status Class, race, and gender intersect at the salon. For some women, manicures represent a hard-won indulgence; for the female salon workers, their immigrant status is often linked to an expectation of subservience.

Kang observed manicurists providing "massage, elder-care, counseling for teens, community outreach [and] therapy for stressed-out clients" (p. 240) in addition to the salon services for which they were ostensibly being paid.

When customers and workers meet over the manicure table, they are not just coming together as women who share gendered experiences. Indeed, they may not share experiences at all, given their different class, race, ethnic, and sexual identities. For example, you might think of manicures as a kind of girly indulgence—an activity that, while not strictly a necessity, may be an important part of a woman's beauty regimen. But not all participants see their manicures the same way. One of Kang's respondents, an African American customer, talked about the meaning of her manicure by referencing race rather than gender: "Black people on a whole have not been the ones who get pampered. There was a time when only white people could do this" (p. 165). For her, manicures are a symbol of progress (for black people, at least) in the arena of racial justice. In addition, male clients were often viewed with suspicion because, as one manicurist said, they came "just to hold a woman's hand" (Kang, 2010, p. 88). Kang's work shows us how race and gender, along with other social statuses like class and sexual orientation, intersect at the nail salon (and in other settings as well).

By analyzing such visible indicators as labor participation rates, income levels, arrest rates, and experiences related to the family, work, education, and the military, we can easily see the real consequences of gender inequality: Women and men experience life differently. So what can we say about the life outcomes of our two infants? The female is likely to live longer. Though they both likely to marry, she is more likely to get divorced or become widowed. If she doesn't drop out in response to anti-LGBTQ harassment or exclusion, she is more likely to graduate from high school and to attend college. However, if the male also attends college, he is more likely to graduate. If they earn the same degree, he will probably earn more money. Each has a good chance of ending up in certain professions over others (the military for him, nursing for her). He is more likely to die a violent death, while she is more likely to experience rape or some other crime perpetrated by someone with whom she is intimate. If either is LGBTQ, that person is at higher risk of bias-motivated attacks as well. While their gender and sexual categories surely do not guarantee these experiences, we as sociologists can safely make such predictions in the aggregate.

SOCIAL MOVEMENTS

Because most societies, throughout most of human history, have been patriarchal and heteronormative, women and LGBTQ people have often struggled to attain and preserve their most basic human and civil rights. In the recent history of the United States, there have been several important political and social movements intended to improve the status of these groups.

Women's Movements

Feminism is the belief in the social, political, and economic equality of the sexes *and* the social movements organized around that belief. Thus, feminism is both a theoretical perspective (as discussed earlier in this chapter) and a social movement. It is important to keep in mind that feminist

The Problem That Had No Name In *The Feminine Mystique*, Betty Friedan (center) articulated a sense of limitation and dissatisfaction that many women felt with their lives.

concepts and goals are not static but are always focused on bringing about greater gender equality in a particular time and place. Rebecca West, an early-twentieth-century feminist, put it this way in 1913: "I myself have never been able to find out precisely what feminism is. I only know that people call me a feminist whenever I express sentiments that differentiate me from a doormat or a prostitute" (Shiach 1999).

FIRST WAVE In the United States, the history of the women's movement can be divided into three historical waves. The **first wave** began with a convention held in Seneca Falls, New York, in 1848, organized by Elizabeth Cady Stanton and Lucretia Mott. The convention, numbering about 300 people, issued a Declaration of Sentiments stating generally that "all men and women are created equal" and demanded specifically that women be given the right to vote. Stanton believed that in a democracy the right to vote is the fundamental right on which all others depend. Not surprisingly, then, the campaign to win the vote, known as the **suffrage movement**, became the cause most identified with the first wave of the women's movement, even though that goal would not be achieved until 1920. Neither Stanton nor Mott nor the well-known suffragist Susan B. Anthony would live to see victory. Of the 100 women and men who signed the Declaration of Sentiments, only one, a young worker named Charlotte Woodward, lived to cast a ballot.

SECOND WAVE Just as the first wave of feminism is most closely associated with the right to vote, the **second wave**, which took place during the 1960s and 1970s, is associated with equal access to education and employment. The publication of Betty Friedan's *The Feminine Mystique* in 1963, the establishment of the National Organization for Women (NOW) in 1966, and the emergence of women's consciousness-raising groups were key events in second-wave feminism. In those decades, young activists felt that the women's movement had lost its momentum after the vote was won and that other issues needed to be addressed. In the opening pages of *The Feminine Mystique*, Friedan spoke of "the problem that had no name," a problem that "lay buried, unspoken, for many years in the minds of American women" (1963, p. 55): the sense of limitation and dissatisfaction that many women felt with their lives.

During one of the most prosperous periods in American history, Friedan was discovering that countless women were unhappy with the traditional roles they had been assigned, that the "mystique of feminine fulfillment" was no longer so fulfilling (1963, p. 18). Women were restricted from pursuing activities outside these traditional roles, whether by cultural norms or by actual laws that barred them from schools, workplaces, and professional organizations. Women who tried to breach these barriers were seen as "unfeminine." Some were even told, as former North Carolina senator Elizabeth Dole was when she entered Harvard

Law School in 1962, that they were taking an opportunity away from a more deserving man.

The second wave of the women's movement pushed for and achieved such reforms as equal opportunity laws, legislation against sexual harassment and marital rape, and a general increase in public awareness about gender discrimination in our society. Some of the public, however, reacted with hostility to women's demands for legal and cultural "liberation," and there continues to be a certain amount of backlash against feminist causes as a result.

THIRD WAVE Beginning in the 1980s and 1990s, the **third wave** of feminism focused primarily on diversity. These feminists criticize the first two waves for concentrating on "women" as one category (mainly white and middle class) and marginalizing the concerns of women of color, lesbians, and working-class women. Third-wave feminists are more focused on intersectionality. And they have become more concerned with ideas about personal identity and freedom from limiting categories. Third-wave feminism is also concerned with globalization and the rights of women in all countries along with environmental and animal rights. The movement includes many if not most college students—even if you don't call yourself a feminist, you likely believe in feminist values, such as equality, diversity, and global interconnectedness. You are the third wave, and you will help make a difference.

Men's Movements

The women's movement, especially the second and third waves, has asked us to rethink gender roles and the place of women in society, and men have responded in a variety of ways. Some have countered feminists' arguments, some have agreed with and supported feminism, and others have taken positions somewhere in between. And just as feminism called existing definitions of womanhood into question, so too did it ask us to reexamine what it means to be a man.

In the mid-1970s, the notion of **men's liberation** (or the need to free men from oppressive gender roles) became more widespread. Influential studies pointed to evidence that men suffer from greater stress, poorer health, and a shorter life expectancy and argued that these resulted from pressures to achieve success combined with men's inability to express themselves and their emotions (Farrell 1975; Goldberg 1976). American men had become confused about what it means to be a "real man" (Kimmel 1987). They were facing new discomfort and anxiety about their masculinity. These ideas became fairly popular, largely among middle-class, white, heterosexual men, and some sought counseling or formed discussion groups about "the male role" (Segal 1990). Men were coming together and organizing in an attempt to address their own concerns and what was called a "crisis of masculinity" (Bly 1990; Connell 1995; Faludi 1999).

As the men's movement grew, it also splintered into two primary factions. The **men's rights movement** (which also includes the fathers' rights movement) argues that because of feminism, men are actually discriminated against and even oppressed both in the legal arena and in everyday life. These men (and some women as well) suggest that feminism has created a new kind of sexism by privileging women, or by attempting to erase differences altogether. The incel movement shares a similar ideology, though it is largely focused on men's "right" to sex.

The **pro-feminist men's movement**, on the other hand, is based in the belief that men should support feminism in the interest of fairness to women and because men's lives are also constrained by gender and sexism and are enriched by feminist social change. Pro-feminist men suggest that the idea that men are superior is a burden and that, in the long term, men will be happier if society becomes less sexist. They argue that men need to share more of the responsibilities of child care, contest economic disparities and violence against women, and generally respect and value women's lives. However much society has changed because of these movements, serious questions remain about men's and women's roles and the future of their relations with each other.

LGBTQ Movements

In 1968, police raided a gay bar in New York City called the Stonewall Inn. At the time, patrons of gay bars were frequently singled out for harassment from the police, and the pent-up resentment and frustration this caused erupted into a week of violence following the raid. Although this was neither the first time gay citizens had been harassed by law enforcement nor the first time gay citizens had protested the harassment, Stonewall was a watershed moment, jump-starting a larger, more visible LGBTQ liberation movement. The Stonewall riots ushered in a new era of campaigning for civil rights for LGBTQ individuals.

Dana Rosenfeld (2003), who studies LGBTQ identity,

FIRST WAVE the earliest period of feminist activism, from the mid-nineteenth century until American women won the right to vote in 1920

SUFFRAGE MOVEMENT the movement organized around gaining voting rights for women

SECOND WAVE the period of feminist activism during the 1960s and 1970s, often associated with the issues of women's equal access to employment and education

THIRD WAVE the most recent period of feminist activism, focusing on issues of diversity, globalization, and the variety of identities women can possess

MEN'S LIBERATION a movement that originated in the 1970s to discuss the challenges of masculinity

MEN'S RIGHTS MOVEMENT an offshoot of male liberation whose members believe that feminism promotes discrimination against men

PRO-FEMINIST MEN'S MOVEMENT an offshoot of male liberation whose members support feminism and believe that sexism harms both men and women

Marriage Equality In June 2015, the Supreme Court legalized gay marriage in *Obergefell v. Hodges*, guaranteeing married same-sex couples the same rights as married opposite-sex couples.

asserts that there are two distinct cohorts among members: those who lived before the gay liberation movement of the 1960s and 1970s and those who lived during and after it. The earlier generation would have felt discredited if their sexual orientation had become public knowledge, whereas the later generation believed that making their identity public was celebrating an essential aspect of the self that should not be denied. This was both a personal and political struggle to advance acceptance and equal rights. There have been many LGBTQ rights groups that emerged after Stonewall, and they continue to fight for progressive change on many fronts, from AIDS research to anti–hate crime legislation. When successful, such social movements can change society and make a difference in the individual lives of many.

For the last several decades, the battle for marriage equality has grown into one of the most visible—and controversial—issues for the LGBTQ rights movements and for the nation as a whole. Some of the first victories for LGBTQ families came from the passage of legal statutes in some parts of the country that granted same-sex couples certain rights as "domestic partners" and greater privileges and protections through civil unions. In 2004, the first states in the nation began legalizing same-sex marriage; at the same time, other states began banning it.

Opponents of same-sex marriage have used the rhetoric of "protecting marriage" or "protecting family," implying that same-sex marriage would harm or destroy those institutions, while others oppose same-sex marriage on religious grounds. Proponents of same-sex marriage emphasize that marriage is a state-sanctioned right, and that denying this right is discriminatory and creates a group of second-class citizens.

Additionally, there are many benefits that legal marriages convey upon spouses that do not apply to those in domestic partnerships and civil unions, including Social Security, veterans' and disability benefits, and the ability to inherit after a partner's passing.

It's important to note that not all people within the LGBTQ community have supported same-sex marriage, some viewing it as assimilationist and as an acceptance of heteronormative structures, such as binary gender roles and monogamy, rather than a critique of them. Lisa Duggan (2003) and Cathy Cohen (2005) contend that arguing for same-sex marriage creates "hierarchies of worthiness," in that benefits are afforded to the most "socially acceptable" within the LGBTQ community—those who most closely mimic heterosexual unions. Some critics argue that instead of trying to fit in, LGBTQ people ought to be challenging marriage as a flawed and failing institution that cannot ultimately serve their advancement or liberation (Sycamore 2008).

In 2015, the Supreme Court made a landmark decision in *Obergefell v. Hodges* that legalized same-sex marriage across the United States. The Court upheld the notion that the right to marry is guaranteed by the Fourteenth Amendment and that same-sex couples should be accorded equal protection under the Constitution. Before that ruling, same-sex marriage was legal in thirty-seven states and the District of Columbia and banned in thirteen states. The United States joined twenty-one other national governments in legally recognizing same-sex marriages.

Public opinion has changed rapidly. In 2001, 57 percent of Americans opposed same-sex marriage and 35 percent were in favor. In a dramatic switch, in 2017, 62 percent of Americans were in favor and 32 percent opposed. Attitudes differed among demographic groups, with young Americans showing the highest approval rates, and white evangelicals and black Protestants showing the lowest levels of support (Pew Research Center 2017b).

LGBTQ rights issues are still plentiful in other areas: Sexual minorities and gender-nonconforming persons face discrimination in housing, education, employment, the military, and health care, as well as everyday microaggressions, harassment, and violence, but awareness of these problems is increasing. Hate crimes based on sexual or gender identity are punishable under federal law, and a growing minority of states and territories (including Puerto Rico and Washington, DC) outlaw discrimination based on sexual orientation, gender identity, or gender expression.

Closing Comments

Sex, gender, sexual orientation, and trans identities are status categories that structure social inequality and shape individual identities. They are different but interrelated, and we all experience their overlap in our everyday lives: We categorize ourselves and others and make assumptions about one another based on these perceived categories. A sociological perspective allows us to see the cultural and environmental influences on what may be considered biologically based identities and lets us identify and critique the stratification systems that have resulted from these influences. Most important, a sociological perspective allows us to see how destructive sexism is for men and women and how crippling homophobia and transphobia can be for the straight, cisgender majority as well as the queer minority. Stereotypes are socially constructed; therefore, they can be socially deconstructed and socially reconstructed as well.

APPLYING WHAT YOU'VE LEARNED

Let's Talk More

1. From an interactionist perspective, gender is not about inner essence but something that is achieved through interaction. This implies that throughout everyday life we are "doing gender." Picture the different ways common behaviors like sitting, walking, or having a conversation are enacted, based on one's gender identity and expression. Can you think of a time when you did gender "wrong" and other people reacted negatively? Why did they react this way?

2. Consider the way you were socialized by your family. In what ways did your socialization conform to traditional gender roles? What toys did you play with? What activities were you encouraged to pursue? What household chores did you perform?

3. The media have played an important role in perpetuating stereotypes about LGBTQ persons. For a long time, such persons were absent from the media landscape, or depicted in a negative way. More recently this has started to change, with many more positive representations appearing in the media. How have such changes affected social attitudes about LGBTQ persons?

Let's Explore More

1. **Film** Jenkins, Barry, dir. *Moonlight.* 2017.

2. **Book** Wade, Lisa. 2017. *American Hookup: The New Culture of Sex on Campus.* New York: W. W. Norton.

3. **Blog Post** Sternheimer, Karen. "Applying Verstehen: Understanding the Transgender Experience." *Everyday Sociology* (blog). January 14, 2019. *http://WWNorton.com/rd/e4PNx.*

PART IV
Social Institutions and the Micro-Macro Link

Our everyday lives take place within the contexts of many overlapping and interdependent social institutions. A social institution is a collection of patterned social practices that are repeated continuously and regularly over time and supported by social norms. Politics, education, religion, the economy, the family, the media, and health care are all social institutions, and you have contact with many of these (and others) on a daily basis. The macro-level patterns and structures of social institutions shape your own micro-level individual experiences; at the same time, it's important to remember that social institutions are created, maintained, and changed by individual actions and interaction.

In the next five chapters, we will look at specific institutions, including politics, education, and religion (Chapter 10), the economy (Chapter 11), the family (Chapter 12), the media (Chapter 13), and the health-care system (Chapter 14), and their role in structuring your everyday life. You will be introduced to a variety of sociological research that focuses on how these social institutions and others work; here, we highlight a sociological researcher whose work integrates many of them. In his book *Heat Wave: A Social Autopsy of Disaster in Chicago* (2002), Eric Klinenberg examines the circumstances surrounding Chicago's catastrophic heat wave in 1995 that killed more than 700 people. Klinenberg analyzes the week-long heat wave as more than a meteorological phenomenon. People died, he argues, because of a combination of disturbing demographic trends and dangerous institutional policies present at all times in all major urban areas.

For one week in mid-July of 1995, the city of Chicago suffered the worst heat wave in its history: Temperatures exceeded 100 degrees for four days in a row, and heat indices (the "real feel" air temperature) hit a high of 126 degrees. Historic buildings baked like ovens, but fear of crime left many people feeling trapped inside their apartments. Children passed out in overheated school buses. City residents blasted their air conditioning (if they had it), mobbed the tiny beaches of Lake Michigan, and broke open fire hydrants to stay cool. As a result, power outages peppered the area and water pressure dropped dangerously. Roads buckled, train tracks warped, and people suffered from heat-related illnesses in large numbers. The city's 911 emergency system overloaded, and some callers waited two hours for ambulances to arrive; more than twenty hospitals closed their emergency rooms, overwhelmed with patients. The death toll mounted, with the elderly and the poor especially vulnerable. In this single week, 739 Chicagoans died as a result of the heat. According to Klinenberg, the individual "isolation, deprivation, and vulnerability" that led to these deaths resulted from a variety of institutional structures, including poverty, racial segregation, family dislocation, and city politics. These institutional arrangements must be examined and changed in order to avoid future tragedies.

Many of those who died during the heat wave were elderly people who lived alone: sick or fragile, their mobility compromised, their neighborhoods changing around them, their families far away or neglectful, and their social networks dissolving. In many cases, the elderly victims of the heat wave were so isolated that no one ever claimed their bodies

(Klinenberg 2002, p. 15). The story of Pauline Jankowitz, eighty-five, who (happily) survived the heat wave, illustrates these demographic trends (pp. 50–54). Pauline lived alone on the third floor of an apartment building with no elevator. She suffered from incontinence and walked with a crutch. She recognized her vulnerability and left her apartment only once every two months. Her two children lived in other states and rarely visited, so a volunteer from a charitable organization did Pauline's weekly grocery shopping. Pauline no longer had any connections with her immigrant neighbors and spent most of her time in her apartment listening to radio talk shows. Pauline's isolation is hardly unique. Her circumstances illustrate the ways that the geographic mobility of the contemporary family, the changing populations of urban neighborhoods, the financial limitations of retirement incomes, and the lack of supportive social services all contribute to situations in which elderly individuals may live, face crises, and die alone.

Klinenberg argues that race and class inequality also contributed to the death toll in the Chicago heat wave. He shows that the death tolls were highest in the city's "black belt," a group of predominantly African American neighborhoods on the south and west sides of the city. (These neighborhoods also have relatively high levels of poverty and crime and relatively large populations of elderly residents.) Social ties in these neighborhoods are hard to maintain: Poverty contributes to residential transiency, so neighbors may not get to know one another before they must move to housing elsewhere. Gang activity and crime make residents afraid to walk down the street or sit on their own front porches. And although some of the neighborhoods in question have powerful religious organizations in their midst, even the most proactive church needs significant financial resources to reach out to its members—and such resources may be hard to come

by in poor neighborhoods. So a person's risk of heat-related death during July 1995 was partly based on place. In Chicago, as in most major cities, place, race, and class are closely connected.

In July 1995, Chicago's government services also failed in a number of ways when the city's residents needed them most. However, Klinenberg argues that the city's bureaucracies were no more ill-prepared to deal with catastrophe during that week than during any other. Long-term, macro-level changes in city politics meant that both the political will and the material resources to provide assistance to the poor were fatally absent. For example, overextended paramedics and firefighters had no centralized office to contact to register their observations or complaints. As a result, many problems went unheeded by the city until emergency services were too swamped to provide timely assistance. There was little coordination among the local, state, and federal agencies that dealt with social welfare and emergency services. Finally, Klinenberg indicts city officials for "governing by public relations" (p. 143)—that is, for using the media to deflect attention from the city's problems, including minimizing both the scope of the heat wave and the city's accountability.

Klinenberg's "social autopsy" reveals the failure of social institutions on a massive scale—and the disturbing prospect that this disaster could happen again, anywhere, if we do not take steps to change flawed social systems. Structural and institutional arrangements—including city government, health-care providers, families, schools, religious organizations, and the media—must change in order to avoid individual tragedies. But individual actions help bring about institutional change, and *Heat Wave* reveals important ways in which all our fates intertwine, as they are shaped by the social institutions we encounter every day. How can we better manage this interdependence, for the good of all?

CHAPTER 10

Social Institutions: Politics, Education, and Religion

You probably know the Pledge of Allegiance by heart and said it countless times in elementary and high school, but you may not have thought much about its words or why you were required to say them.

*I pledge allegiance to the Flag
of the United States of America,
and to the Republic for which it stands:
one Nation, under God, indivisible,
with Liberty and Justice for all.*

For decades, reciting the pledge was just a routine part of being a student in the United States. How could it possibly be controversial? A lot of people think it is. As you will see, the Pledge of Allegiance brings together questions about three important social institutions in American life: politics, education, and religion.

The Pledge of Allegiance was originally written in 1892 and did not contain the phrase "under God"; that was added in 1954, when President Eisenhower signed a bill making the change official. The added words generated no controversy at the time. The president declared that their addition would affirm "the dedication of our nation and our people to the Almighty," and Senator Joseph McCarthy said "it was a clear indication that the United States was committed to ending the threat of 'godless' Communism" (Brinkley-Rogers 2002).

Since as early as 1943, the Supreme Court has ruled that children cannot be forced to recite the pledge. In 1943, the issue revolved around the patriotic nature of the pledge. However, in 2002 the issue became its religious nature. Judge Alfred Goodwin of the Ninth Circuit Court of Appeals ruled that reciting the pledge in public schools "places students in the untenable position of choosing between participating in an exercise with religious content or protesting," an especially damaging scenario because "the coercive effect of the policy here is particularly pronounced in the school setting, given the age and impressionability of schoolchildren" (Weinstein 2003). After all, how many second-graders would be willing to stand out from their peers in so dramatic a fashion?

California physician Dr. Michael Newdow is a longtime activist committed to preserving the separation of church and state. When his daughter's second-grade class began reciting the Pledge of Allegiance, Newdow became disturbed because it contained the phrase "one Nation, *under God*." Newdow filed a lawsuit, and in February 2003 the Ninth Circuit Court held the pledge to be in violation of the Constitution because the reference to God violated the separation of church and state.

Many civic and political leaders—liberals as well as conservatives—denounced the decision. The Senate passed a resolution condemning it, and the attorney general announced that the Justice Department would "spare no effort to preserve the rights of all our citizens to pledge allegiance to the American flag" (Weinstein 2003). Almost universally, lawmakers came out in defense of the pledge, agreeing with Judge Ferdinand Fernandez, who in his dissenting opinion argued that the phrase "under God" had "no tendency to establish a religion in this country or to suppress anyone's exercise, or non-exercise, of religion, except in the fevered eye of persons who most fervently would like to drive all tincture of religion out of the public life of our polity" (Egelko 2002). Ultimately, the case went all the way to the Supreme Court, which overturned the lower court's ruling on a technicality but did not address whether the language in the pledge violates the First Amendment.

Although there is a great deal of disagreement over what should be done in this case, all the participants agree, even if only implicitly, that social institutions play an important role in the lives of Americans. For example, if school starts at 8:00 a.m. and ends at 3:00 p.m., this schedule structures the life of an entire household.

It dictates what time children should go to bed at night and get up in the morning; when breakfast and dinner are prepared, served, and eaten; and what types of arrangements must be made for transportation, after-school activities, and child care. In turn, a school exists only because of the actions of the teachers, students, parents, and administrators who are part of the surrounding community.

Social institutions represent a bit of a sociological paradox. They function at the macro level to shape our everyday interactions, but at the micro level those same everyday interactions construct social institutions. Because they are at the center of both micro- and macrosociology, social institutions give us the opportunity to examine the connection between interaction and structure, between the individual and society. In this chapter, we will focus on the social institutions of politics, education, and religion as places where the micro and the macro come together, and we will show how the intersections among social institutions shape everyday life.

How to Read This Chapter

We have devoted entire chapters to other **social institutions** such as health care, work, and family, but here we have grouped politics, education, and religion together for a reason. These institutions intersect in distinctive and often unexamined ways in our everyday lives—the daily recitation of the Pledge of Allegiance is just one example. Local and national controversies over school vouchers and sex education are other examples of the ways in which political, educational, and religious concerns overlap. Every day we make decisions or engage in debates that address moral values, political practicalities, and educational expectations all bundled together.

When you read this chapter, we want you to be able to see the relationships among these three social institutions as well as make the connection between micro- and macrosociology. This is a key opportunity to use the sociological theories and methods you have learned in previous chapters to find the intersections between individual experience and social structure, and the overlaps among various social institutions in everyday life. After reading this chapter, you should have a deeper understanding of how social institutions shape your individual experience and how you as an individual contribute to shaping those institutions.

WHAT IS POLITICS?

Politics has concerned social thinkers since at least the time of the philosophers in ancient Greece. The word "politics" comes from the Greek *politikos*, meaning "of or relating to citizens." As a sociological term, **politics** pertains especially to the methods and tactics of managing a political entity, such as a nation or state, as well as the administration and control of its internal and external affairs. But it can also mean the attitudes and activities of groups and individuals. To understand the relationship between citizens and their particular political environment, we must first look at the variety of political systems and study the American system of democracy. Then we will examine elections and voting, lobbies and special interest groups, and the role of the media in the political process.

Political Systems: Government

Government is the formal, organized agency that exercises power and control in modern society. Governments are vested with the power and authority to make laws and enforce them. Max Weber defined **power** as the ability to get others to do one's bidding. When sociologists talk about **authority**, they are referring to the legitimate, noncoercive exercise of power (see the discussion of Weber's subtypes of authority in Chapter 5). Throughout the world and throughout history, governments have taken a variety of forms. When evaluating types of governance as sociologists, we ask certain questions about the relationship between leaders and followers: Who has power and who does not, what kind of power is exerted, and how far does that power extend?

TOTAL POWER AND AUTHORITY **Authoritarianism** is a political system that denies ordinary citizens representation by and control over their own government. Thus, citizens have no say in who rules them, what laws are made, or how those laws are enforced. Generally, political power is concentrated in the hands of a few elites who control military and economic resources. A *dictatorship* is one form of authoritarianism. In some instances, a dictator gains power by being elected or through family succession, while in other cases a dictator seizes power through a military coup. Sometimes these tactics are combined. Such is the case of Paul Kagame of Rwanda, who gained de facto control of the country when he served as its minister of defense from 1994 to 2000. He has since been elected president for three consecutive terms, most recently in 2017 when he won 99 percent of the vote in an election that was

SOCIAL INSTITUTIONS systems and structures within society that shape the activities of groups and individuals

POLITICS methods and tactics intended to influence government policy, policy-related attitudes, and activities

GOVERNMENT the formal, organized agency that exercises power and control in modern society, especially through the creation and enforcement of laws

POWER the ability to control the actions of others

AUTHORITY the legitimate right to wield power

AUTHORITARIANISM a system of government by and for a small number of elites that does not include representation of ordinary citizens

Dictators Try to Control All Aspects of Citizens' Lives
Leaders such as Kim Jong Un of North Korea, Paul Kagame of Rwanda, and Bashar al-Assad of Syria are among the world's most notorious dictators.

highly criticized for its irregularities. Another example is Bashar al-Assad, who succeeded his father as president of Syria in 2000. He, too, has served as commander in chief and has been elected to multiple terms in office. In 2014, he faced a political opponent for the first time (previous elections were uncontested) but still won with over 88 percent of the vote. Dictators are most often individuals but can also be associated with political parties or groups, such as the Taliban in Afghanistan.

Totalitarianism is the most extreme and modern version of authoritarianism. The government seeks to control every aspect, public and private, of citizens' lives. Unlike older forms of authoritarianism, a totalitarian government can utilize all the contrivances of surveillance technology, systems of mass communication, and modern weapons to control its citizens (Arendt 1958). Totalitarian governments are usually headed by a dictator, whether a ruler or a single political party. Through propaganda, totalitarian regimes can further control the population by disseminating ideology aimed at shaping their thoughts, values, and attitudes. An example of a modern totalitarian ruler is Kim Jong Un of North Korea, who succeeded his father, the notorious Kim Jong Il, in 2011. Under the Kims, North Korea has maintained one of the worst human rights records in the world, restricting the basic freedoms of its people. The country also has a stagnant, internationally isolated economy, which is further drained by its nuclear arms program.

MONARCHIES AND THE STATE Monarchies are governments ruled by a king or queen. In a **monarchy**, sovereignty is vested in a successive line of rulers, usually within a family, such as the Tudors of England, the Ming Dynasty of China, or the Romanovs of Russia. Nobility is handed down through

MONARCHY a government ruled by a king or queen, with succession of rulers kept within the family

DEMOCRACY a political system in which all citizens have the right to participate

family lines and can include numerous family members who hold royal titles. Monarchs are not popularly elected and are not usually accountable to the general citizenry, and some may rule by "divine right," the claim that they are leaders chosen by God.

Monarchies can be divided into two categories: absolute and constitutional. Absolute monarchs typically have complete authority over their subjects, much like dictators. Constitutional monarchs are royal figures whose powers are defined by a political charter and limited by a parliament or other governing body. Most monarchies were weakened, overthrown, or otherwise made obsolete during the many social revolutions of the eighteenth, nineteenth, and twentieth centuries, such as the French Revolution (1789) and the Russian Revolution (1917). In contemporary times, some Asian and European nations, such as Japan, Thailand, Great Britain, and Sweden, still enjoy their royal families as national figureheads and celebrities, though their kings, queens, princes, and princesses don't have any real power in these constitutional monarchies. There are, however, a few remaining modern examples of more absolute monarchies in the world, among them Saudi Arabia and Brunei.

CITIZENS AND DEMOCRACY Democracy originated in ancient Greece and represented a radical new political system. In a **democracy**, citizens share in directing the activities of their government rather than being ruled by an autocratic individual or authoritarian group. The idea is that educated citizens should participate in the election of officials who then represent their interests in lawmaking, law enforcement, resource allocation, and international affairs. Democracy is not only a political system but also a philosophy that emphasizes the right and capacity of individuals, acting either directly or through representatives, to control through majority rule the institutions that govern them. Democracy is associated with the values of basic human rights, civil liberties, freedom, and equality.

Democracy may seem like the ideal system of government, but remember that not all citizens are equally represented even by a democratic government. In many democratic nations, women, ethnic or racial minorities, members of certain religions, and immigrants have been excluded from citizenship or from equal participation in the political process. In the United States, women did not have the right to vote until 1920. And while the Fifteenth Amendment to the U.S. Constitution technically gave adult males of all races voting rights in 1870, barriers such as poll taxes, literacy tests, and "grandfather clauses" kept African Americans from exercising those rights for almost 100 years, until the 1965 Voting Rights Act was passed. Native Americans were legally excluded from voting in federal elections until 1924, and residents of the District of Columbia were not allowed to vote in presidential elections until 1961. To this day, convicted felons in some states lose their right to vote, even after they have served their sentence and completed their parole, and can regain this right only by bringing a suit against the state. As you can see, even the world's leading democracy has not always seen all citizens as equal.

The American Political System

When American colonists rebelled against British authority in 1776, they created the first modern democracy. American democracy, however, is much more complicated than "rule by the people." In the following sections, we focus on voting, theories about who governs, the power of interest groups, and the influence of the media on the political system.

VOTING IN THE UNITED STATES The American political system prides itself on being a democracy, a government that confers power to the people. In this form of government, power is formally exercised through the election process, which provides each person with a vote. Sociologists have long been interested in the social factors—such as age, education, religion, and ethnic background—that influence whether and how individuals vote.

In the presidential election of 2008, in which Barack Obama, the first African American president, was elected, an estimated 62 percent of eligible voters cast their ballots—the highest turnout in forty years. Notably, 52 to 53 percent of voters between the ages of eighteen and twenty-nine went to the polls—the highest youth turnout since eighteen-year-olds gained the right to vote in 1972. Turnout in the 2012 and 2016 presidential elections held steady at 59 percent and 60 percent of all eligible voters, respectively (McDonald 2019). Voter turnout in midterm elections is typically lower than in presidential elections, especially among younger voters (DeSilver 2014b). In the 2014 midterms, voter participation in the United States hit its lowest mark in seventy years, with just 36 percent of eligible voters turning up at the polls; it jumped up to 50 percent, however, in 2018—the highest turnout for a midterm election since 1914 (Nonprofit Vote 2019).

Even with these fluctuations, voter participation rates are much lower in the United States than in some comparable democratic nations. Why? A number of social factors affect the likelihood that someone will vote. Age, race, gender, sexual orientation, religion, geographic location, social class, and education are all demographic variables that influence voter participation as well as how people vote. Turnout may be affected by factors ranging from the number of items on the ballot to the weather. Older adults are much more likely to vote than young adults—compare a 66 percent reported turnout for those over age thirty with a 50 percent reported turnout among eighteen- to twenty-nine-year-olds in 2016 (Nonprofit Vote 2017). The top reasons people gave for not voting that year were that they "did not like candidates or campaign issues" (25 percent), were "not interested" (15 percent), or were "too busy/scheduling conflict" (14 percent) (U.S. Census Bureau 2017p).

In some instances, however, people do not vote because they are **disenfranchised**—barred from voting. All states except Maine and Vermont disenfranchise convicted felons while they are incarcerated. Thirty-four states disenfranchise felons on parole, thirty do so for felons on probation, and twelve others permanently disenfranchise some or all felons who have completed their sentences. In all, more than 6 million Americans, including one in thirteen African Americans of voting age, are barred from voting due to felon disenfranchisement (Uggen, Larson, and Shannon 2016). Human rights groups have long protested this policy, arguing that it is not a legitimate function of the penal system. In addition, individuals may be mistakenly identified as former felons and improperly stricken from the rolls, which occurred in Florida in the 2000 presidential election (Hull 2002; Uggen and Manza 2002). Consequently, many eligible voters were turned away from the polls.

Another obstacle to potential voters lies with registration. In the United States, even individuals with the legal right to vote cannot do so unless they are registered. Only seventeen states offer same-day registration, in which citizens may register and vote on election day. In most states, registration must be done well in advance of an election, in some cases up to thirty days beforehand. Another problem for many working Americans is that elections are held on a Tuesday rather than a weekend or a national holiday (something done in other democratic countries). In addition, thirty-five states have passed voter identification laws and either request or require voters to present some form of identification in order to vote in federal, state, and local elections. Supporters claim that requiring ID is necessary to combat voter fraud, though studies show that it's an extremely rare occurrence and not

DISENFRANCHISED stripped of voting rights, either temporarily or permanently

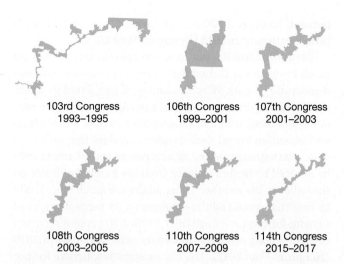

103rd Congress
1993–1995

106th Congress
1999–2001

107th Congress
2001–2003

108th Congress
2003–2005

110th Congress
2007–2009

114th Congress
2015–2017

FIGURE 10.1 Gerrymandering in Action: North Carolina's 12th Congressional District

on a scale that would influence elections (Brennan Center for Justice 2017). Minorities, the elderly, and low-income Americans are disproportionately affected by voter ID laws (Henninger et al. 2018; Fraga and Miller 2018; Hopkins et al. 2017; ACLU 2017). Many Democrats charge that voter ID laws are intended to suppress turnout for these groups, particularly minority and low-income Americans, who tend to vote for the Democratic Party (Newkirk 2017).

The practice of **gerrymandering** is another factor that can impact the outcome of elections. Every state receives a certain number of seats in the House of Representatives based on the Census population count. The state is then divided up into congressional districts of roughly equal size that each elect a representative to the House. Gerrymandering is the redrawing of boundary lines for voting districts within states in a way that gives an advantage to one political party over another; for example, by packing your opponent's supporters into as few districts as possible while ensuring your own party's supporters are spread out over many districts.

Typically, the party in control at the state level can take charge of redistricting, reconfiguring the voting map to further strengthen their position. This practice is done by Democrats and Republicans alike, though some states have independent commissions that set district lines. Gerrymandering has become more common

GERRYMANDERING redrawing the boundary lines of state voting districts in order to advantage one political party over another

POWER ELITE a relatively small group of people in the top ranks of economic, political, and military institutions who make many of the important decisions in American society

PLURALIST MODEL a system of political power in which a wide variety of individuals and groups have equal access to resources and the mechanisms of power

SPECIAL INTEREST GROUPS organizations that raise and spend money to influence elected officials and/or public opinion

and is facilitated by new technologies that can more precisely draw districts. Gerrymandering can effectively sway the direction of elections so that their outcomes no longer represent the actual party makeup of state residents. In some cases when districts are drawn solely for political purposes, the boundaries may look completely absurd (see Figure 10.1). These decisions, however, have serious implications for the composition of Congress and control of the House of Representatives. Challenges to the practice of gerrymandering have gone all the way to the Supreme Court. While it is illegal to draw district lines based on race, for instance, the practice along party lines continues.

Who Rules America?

Ideally, in a democracy, elected officials represent the interests of the people in doing the business of government. But how much do we really know about what legislators do or how government business is conducted? What about the interests of other groups besides "the people"? To what extent do other groups influence how government is run? Who has the most power in directing the course of the nation? The president and Congress? Judges? Big business and the military? What happens behind the scenes? Who really rules America? Sociologists have devised two answers to the question of who rules America—the idea of a *power elite* and the *pluralist* theory of power.

THE POWER ELITE Conflict theorists argue that power is held by a small but extremely influential group of individuals who form an elite social class. C. Wright Mills (1956/1970) was one of the first to propose a theory of the **power elite**, a relatively small number of influential individuals occupying the top positions within the major economic, political, and military institutions of the country. This insular and self-perpetuating group controls many of the key decision-making processes in the United States. Members of the power elite have the full power and weight of their respective institutions at their disposal. Their close association allows them to collaborate in ways that best serve their particular interests, which may not coincide with those of the people. Thus, their actions have tremendous implications for the rest of the population. For instance, military leaders may persuade the president to declare war, senators may pass legislation that cuts billions of dollars from social welfare programs, and corporate executives may post record gains for stockholders or downsize companies and lay off thousands of workers.

G. William Domhoff has studied the power elite extensively, looking at how the economic, political, and military institutions overlap and form a network of influence (1983, 1987, 1990, 2002, 2013). The power elite not only know each other personally and professionally, but they also recognize their status as part of the ultimate "members only" club. Many of them were born into powerful families who still control

TABLE 10.1   Theory in Everyday Life

Perspective	Approach to Social Institutions	Case Study: Understanding Political Power in America
Structural Functionalism	Social institutions such as politics, education, and religion provide critical functions for the needs of society and help maintain order and unity.	The theory of pluralism suggests that in a democracy, power is held in a variety of hands; each group is assumed to have equal access to power and can thus serve as a system of checks and balances.
Conflict Theory	Social institutions such as politics, education, and religion represent the interests of those in power and thus create and maintain inequalities in society.	The theory of the power elite suggests that power in the United States is concentrated in the hands of a small group of decision makers and that the masses have little power in the democratic process.
Symbolic Interactionism	Social institutions such as politics, education, and religion are created through individual participation; they give meaning to and are part of the everyday experience of members.	The theory of the social construction of presidential candidates suggests that the messages we receive from the media help shape our perceptions and influence public opinion and voting behavior.

huge U.S. corporations. Many of the power elite attended the same prep schools and Ivy League colleges. They may live in the same neighborhoods or belong to the same country clubs. They may go to the same churches or give to the same charities. More important, they often serve on each other's boards of directors and do business directly with other members. One related study identified only 5,778 individuals in these elite positions, meaning that less than 0.0026 percent of the entire U.S. population are among the power elite (Dye 2002). These individuals are overwhelmingly white males.

What are the implications of this class dominance theory of power? For one, it debunks the original American rags-to-riches mythology that says anyone who works hard can get to the top. If power is concentrated in such a small fraction of a percentage of the population, chances are that the average person will never wield any real power, regardless of his or her work ethic or life choices. Furthermore, the United States continues to be controlled by white upper-class men. Finally, those who have the power to create social change by economic, political, or military reforms may choose to do so only when it is to their own advantage.

PLURALISM According to the **pluralist model**, power is held by a variety of organizations and institutions (such as corporations, political parties, professional organizations, and ethnic and religious groups), each with its own resources and interests. Each organization is assumed to have equal access to the power structure, and a system of checks and balances in the form of laws, policies, and the courts keeps any one group from having too much power over the others (Dahl 1961).

The American political system is organized so that individuals, groups, and organizations can contribute to candidates' campaigns. **Special interest groups** (sometimes called advocacy groups) play an important role in the political process. These are organizations formed expressly to raise and spend money in order to influence elected officials and public opinion. Special interest groups can include corporate organizations, lobbies, political action committees (PACs), and 527 groups (named after the corresponding IRS code). Many 527s run by special interest groups raise unlimited amounts of "soft money," which can be used for various types of advocacy, if not directly by candidates. Special interest groups' contributions to candidates and causes can reach into the hundreds of millions, and even billions, of dollars (Table 10.2).

TABLE 10.2   Top 10 Spenders on Lobbying, 1998–2018

Lobbying Client	Total
U.S. Chamber of Commerce	$1,506,125,680
National Association of Realtors	$546,116,083
American Medical Association	$393,194,500
American Hospital Association	$372,475,855
Pharmaceutical Research & Manufacturers of America	$364,374,550
General Electric	$358,232,000
Blue Cross/Blue Shield	$347,634,491
Business Roundtable	$284,120,000
AARP	$282,621,064
Boeing	$274,803,310
Northrop Grumman	$272,212,213

SOURCE: Center for Responsive Politics 2019.

The average citizen may have little idea of the influence of wealthy donor organizations in the political process. There is almost always a positive correlation between a candidate's campaign spending and his or her success: Money wins elections. Incumbents (those already occupying the electoral seat) are usually in the best position to raise money because of their high-profile position; incumbency, therefore, is one of the most important advantages a candidate can have. In 2018, 91 percent of incumbent representatives and 84 percent of incumbent senators won reelection (Center for Responsive Politics 2018). It is also an advantage to have your campaign backed by a billionaire (like the Koch brothers or George Soros).

A **political action committee (PAC)** is a type of tax-exempt group that was designed to raise money to campaign for or against candidates or legislation such as ballot measures. A PAC typically supports the interests or agenda of a select group or organization. For instance, BAMPAC, or the Black America Political Action Committee, represents the special interests of African Americans, while AAPAC, the Arab American PAC, lobbies for political interests of Arab Americans. NOW PAC, the National Organization for Women PAC, advocates feminist issues. Some of the biggest PACs are connected to trades, such as the National Education Association or the Carpenters & Joiners Union. The National Football League is represented by the Gridiron PAC, and Major League Baseball has its own PAC as well. Even the interests of extraterrestrials are represented, through X-PPAC, the Extraterrestrial Phenomena PAC.

POLITICAL ACTION COMMITTEES (PACS) organizations that raise money to support the interests of a select group or organization

As a result of a 2010 Supreme Court ruling, corporate funding of independent, campaign-related expenditures is no longer prohibited. In fact, the *Citizens United v. Federal Election Committee* decision allowed unlimited spending by corporations, unions, and other noncampaign entities, calling it a First Amendment right. This opened the door to a new kind of PAC—the "Super PAC," which can accept these unlimited contributions and use the monies to do things like produce and air issue-based ads, as long as they do not coordinate with the candidate or the candidate's political party. What this has meant in practice is that political candidates can benefit from the unlimited spending of a Super PAC without being in violation of the campaign finance laws that still apply to their own party organizations. Following the inception of *Citizens United,* research has shown that Super PACs are being funded primarily by a small group of ultrawealthy contributors.

In the 2016 presidential election cycle, Super PACs spent more than $1 billion in support of all candidates and causes, with conservative organizations outspending liberal organizations by about three to two (Center for Responsive Politics 2016a). These amounts are astronomically higher than they might have been had *Citizens United* not removed the limits on corporate donations by calling them "free speech." Though it has been difficult to make definitive conclusions about the relationships between special interest groups and legislators, the staggering amounts of money these groups generate cannot be ignored. As sociologists, we seek to uncover the mechanisms of influence in our political system. Monitoring the actions of top donors, PACs, Super PACs, and other special interest groups provides insight into how our political system works.

The Media and the Political Process

In addition to the executive, legislative, and judicial branches of government, the media play a key role in the political process. This has been true since the founding of the country, and the media have only taken on even more significant proportions in the Information Age. The media render checks and balances on power by informing and educating the populace and serving as a watchdog on government. As such, the media have been referred to as the "Fourth Estate," or fourth branch of government. In fact, the framers of the U.S. Constitution probably envisioned the watchdog role as the media's primary function. After all, they believed that a free press was essential to the health of the new democracy. Thus, the First Amendment guarantees freedom of expression and freedom of the press (along with other rights).

Still, it's hard to imagine that the country's founders could have envisioned what "the press" would become. To them, it literally meant printing presses. There were no broadcast media or digital media back then—no mass media or social media as we know them. So contemporary lawmakers have had to interpret the Constitution in light of modern concerns and developments. They must try to balance the rights of a free press while protecting the country from abuses of power by the media or by the individuals who own the media. And we must all consider the media's tremendous potential to sway and manipulate our thoughts and feelings and to influence the political process.

The media have always played a role in American politics, informing the public about the important issues of the day. But their role increased dramatically with the spread of television in the 1950s and 1960s and the Internet in the 1990s and 2000s. Many social movements and landmark political events have unfolded on the TV or computer screen. It's unlikely that the civil rights movement, the Vietnam War, Watergate, the attacks of 9/11, or the tragedy of Hurricane Katrina would have emerged, developed, and resolved in quite the way they did without the media bringing the issues and images into our living rooms. More recently, social media such as Facebook and Twitter have added to the immediacy and shared nature of the conversation. The success of the Black Lives Matter and #MeToo movements owes much to social media's ability to spread information quickly and broadly and to engage so many participants. The media have tremendous power; they can make momentous events a part of the national dialogue and involve voters, citizens, and even global attention, influencing public opinion and promoting political activism and change.

And as much as the power of the media has transformed politics, the reverse is also true: Politics shapes our perspective on the media. For example, the 2016 presidential election year started with most Americans—about three-quarters of both Republicans and Democrats alike—believing in the media's role as a "watchdog" for political leaders. But the divisive Trump vs. Clinton campaign season left an enormous partisan gap in that attitude. By the end of 2018, 82 percent of Democrats, compared to just 38 percent

The Media's Role in the Political Process The power of media to bring political news from across the nation has transformed the political process. For example, the Boston Marathon bombings (top left), the attacks on September 11, 2001 (top right), and Hurricane Katrina (bottom) would not have had such widespread impact without the media.

of Republicans, supported the idea of the media as political watchdog, with Trump supporters in particular distrusting the "mainstream media" and turning to Trump-approved fringe outlets such as Breitbart in order to get their news (Gottfried, Stocking, and Grieco 2018).

CAMPAIGNS AND ELECTIONS Some of the most significant changes in the political process have occurred in the realm of campaigns and elections. Political actors have adapted to a media-saturated society, and their strategies for success must include great media savvy (Dutta and Fraser 2008; Skarzynska 2004). Any group or individual wishing to influence voters must court the media, either by attempting to gain coverage of a particular issue or candidate or by directly buying space or time through advertisements.

At one time, the voting public was informed of the issues through local political party representatives, town hall meetings, church groups, speeches made by politicians or activists out on the stump, or exhaustive coverage in newspapers or on radio. Nowadays, media coverage of politics is more likely to emphasize human interest stories, personalities, high-profile spectacles, and planned events—and less likely to explain the background and implications of issues and policy debates (Kellner 2005; J. Thompson 2012). And not all news programs offer strictly objective reporting. We hear a lot about politics through pundits, media personalities who offer political commentary (and their own opinions) along with the news. Sean Hannity, Rachel Maddow, Bill Maher, Glenn Beck, Chris Hayes, Fareed Zakaria, Jon Favreau, Daniel Pfeiffer, Jon Lovett, Tommy Vietor, and Matt Drudge are just a few of the many pundits found on either side of the aisle and across media platforms.

The public is also influenced by **opinion leaders**, high-profile people who interpret political information for us (Katz and Lazarsfeld 1955). Instead of getting information about the issues directly, we allow our views to be shaped by these opinion leaders, whom we trust to tell us what to believe. Someone like Dan Rather and his website "News and Guts," for instance, can influence not only what we read but also our political values. Even within your group of friends, there may be someone who, while not as famous as Rather, is more politically savvy than the rest of the group and can communicate information to you in ways that may influence your opinions.

STYLE OVER SUBSTANCE? One of the first and most dramatic examples of the media's impact on politics occurred during the presidential campaign of 1960. The debates between John F. Kennedy, the Democrat, and Richard Nixon, the Republican, were the first to be broadcast live on television. Kennedy, the younger candidate, recognized the power of television and understood the importance of presenting a "telegenic" image. He allowed media handlers to advise him on makeup, hairstyle, clothes, and the appropriate demeanor for the TV cameras. Conversely, Nixon refused to make any special preparation for the event. As a seasoned politician, he planned to rely on his command of the issues and his considerable debating skills.

Those who watched the debates on television saw dramatic differences between the two candidates. Kennedy looked fresh, young, and energetic; Nixon looked sweaty, old, and tired. Those who listened to the debates on the radio, as previous generations had for years, judged the two candidates not by looks or mannerisms but by the content of their speech. When polled after the debates, TV audiences thought that Kennedy won the debate; radio audiences thought Nixon was the winner. Although Kennedy's performance during the debate was only one factor in the election, it was significant. Now, political candidates are constantly in the spotlight, visible to us across a range of visual media platforms, and looking fresh, energetic, and put-together is a must 24/7.

Another feature of modern politics is "sound bites"—those short audio or visual snippets taken from press releases, press conferences, photo opportunities, or sometimes protests. In our postmodern era, the news has been condensed into just a few seconds' worth of information; many people form their views of candidates from these processed bits of information. It is no wonder that celebrity politicians are becoming more common and popular. After all, who knows better how to use the media, how to stand before the cameras and speak in interviews, than those who have been professionally trained as actors? President Ronald Reagan, for example, formerly a Hollywood actor and commercial spokesperson, knew how to hit his marks and deliver his lines. He was even called "The Great Communicator" despite his inability to speak extemporaneously. Others have followed in Reagan's path, including basketball star Bill Bradley, astronaut John Glenn, and comedian Al Franken, who became senators; wrestler Jesse Ventura and actor Arnold Schwarzenegger, who both became governors; singer Sonny Bono, who became a congressman; and actor Clint Eastwood, who became a mayor.

Donald Trump—a businessman and reality television celebrity—provides another example. As a maverick Republican presidential candidate in the 2016 election, Trump gained notoriety with his impulsive manner and bare-knuckle political combativeness. Critics claimed that he was a case in point of "style over substance." His image as a Washington outsider and "man of the people" was carefully promoted; he resisted being coached and groomed like other candidates, which prompted many voters to see him as authentic. While critics cited his lack of knowledge and experience in governance, supporters saw him as a successful entrepreneur not afraid to speak his mind. During the campaign, Trump made some outlandish and untrue claims—that President Obama was the

OPINION LEADERS high-profile individuals whose interpretation of events influences the public

SIMULACRUM an image or media representation that does not reflect reality in any meaningful way but is treated as real

founder of ISIS, for example—as well as comments that many felt were offensive to women and minority groups. At first the mainstream media presented Trump as harmless entertainment, not a serious presidential contender—all the while giving him considerable free airtime to reach his supporters; later his controversial claims were fodder for headlines and clickbait. Meanwhile, conservative and previously marginal "alt-right" media sources slavered over Trump and promoted his candidacy with disaffected white working-class voters who did take him seriously.

Does the increased focus on a politician's style and personality, rather than platform and policies, mean that we are getting less substance in what we consume? This Data Workshop may help you answer this question.

DATA WORKSHOP

Analyzing Media and Pop Culture

Satirical News Shows

A free press is meant to inform the public about important matters facing the nation. As the formats for media continue to change, so has the delivery of news. Postmodern sociologist Jean Baudrillard claimed that "the image has come to replace the real" (1981/1994). By this, he meant that we have lost the ability to distinguish between what is real and what is unreal, especially where media representations are involved, and that we have also come to accept the unreal as sufficient—thereby no longer needing the real. He called this new artificially constructed "reality" the **simulacrum**, or a simulation that becomes as good as the original.

A key example of Baudrillard's simulacrum can be found in the growing popularity of satirical news shows. Journalism and political satire share a long history, and the number of outlets for this kind of mix has recently exploded. The list includes TV shows like *The Daily Show with Trevor Noah, Last Week Tonight with John Oliver, Full Frontal with Samantha Bee*, and *Saturday Night Live*'s "Weekend Update" segment, as well as online sites like the *Onion News Network*.

Satirical news TV shows so closely resemble real news TV shows that it is often hard to tell which is which. Satirical news TV shows get their humor from parodying real news, so they often mirror the mainstream press in covering certain topics and events. But satirical news, of course, is not held to the same journalistic standards that apply to reporting the real news. Although Trevor Noah, Samantha Bee, and John Oliver only play at being journalists on air, they often look like—and even function like—the real thing, and their shows are made with the same production values viewers have come to expect on the broadcast dial. All of this is making it more and more difficult to tell the difference between the simulation and the real thing.

Although the primary intent of satirical news shows is to be funny and entertaining, that goal doesn't preclude taking on serious subjects and disseminating messages with a viewpoint and the potential to influence audiences. Studies indicate that satirical news programs are not just entertaining but can actually reinforce a viewer's preexisting liberal or conservative attitudes as much as watching serious news (Knobloch-Westerwick and Lavis 2017). As satirical news shows have become more popular and more widespread, what does that mean for real news and its role in educating and informing the people? It seems that satirical news has become an important and enduring voice in humor and in American political culture.

Political Satire on TV *Last Week Tonight with John Oliver* and *Full Frontal with Samantha Bee* mine news headlines for comedy. Should we take them seriously?

This Data Workshop asks you to analyze the phenomenon of satirical news, its real popularity, and its possible influence on young people and politics. Choose your show—*The Daily Show with Trevor Noah, Last Week Tonight with John Oliver*, or *Full Frontal with Samantha Bee*. Select a recent episode of the show, and make sure it is available for multiple viewings. You will be gathering data from an existing source and doing a content analysis of the episode. Refer to the section in Chapter 2 for a review of this research method.

As you watch the episode, consider the following points (you may want to take informal notes while viewing and add more of your own comments and observations afterward):

- In what ways does the show resemble a traditional network news program? Examine the format of the show, the cast and correspondents, the regular program segments (news reporting, interviews), the structure of the stage set, the design of the graphics, and other aspects of the production.

- Make a list of the topics that are covered on the show. Compare the stories presented on the satirical news show with stories presented in the real news during the same time period. How much of the news is completely made up, and how much is actually about real-world events?

- A comedic news show, even when it covers real issues, is not held to the same journalistic standards as traditional news outlets. How does an audience member know what to believe about the truth of any particular statement or story?

- Despite being satirical, these shows also provide serious commentary about important issues in American life. What are some of the underlying messages of the humorous material on the show?

- Are you among the audience members who get political news from comedy shows? To what extent do you believe these shows might influence people's political ideas? Do you think that they increase young people's awareness of issues, or are they a confounding distraction?

- If we consider what postmodernists say about the increasing power of the image or simulacrum in our everyday lives, how can we tell the difference between what is real and what is not real?

There are two options for completing this Data Workshop:

PREP-PAIR-SHARE Choose a recent episode of *The Daily Show with Trevor Noah, Last Week Tonight with*

John Oliver, or *Full Frontal with Samantha Bee* and take notes while watching. Be ready with some preliminary answers to the Data Workshop questions. Pair up with one or more classmates and discuss your findings in small groups. Were your thoughts about satirical news shared by others?

DO-IT-YOURSELF Choose a recent episode of *The Daily Show with Trevor Noah, Last Week Tonight with John Oliver*, or *Full Frontal with Samantha Bee* and take notes while watching. Write a three-page paper answering the Data Workshop questions and analyzing the role of journalism—real and satirical—in the American political process.

SOCIAL MEDIA AND POLITICS As much as the media changed the political process in the twentieth century, it seems likely that new forms of media will transform it all the more. The power of social media goes beyond simply providing information; it also allows users to interact with one another, form networks, and create their own content.

An increasing number of Americans get their political and campaign news online, including on social networking sites. In the 2016 presidential election, Facebook and Twitter took center stage. While all three major-party candidates (Hillary Clinton, Bernie Sanders, and Donald Trump) used Facebook and Twitter extensively in their campaigns, one candidate stood out in the ways that he utilized these social media platforms. Trump offered his Facebook and Twitter feeds as sources of news for his followers by providing links to other news outlets so that users could read content that praised Trump or his policy proposals (Pew Research Center 2016b). Often the links were to Fox News, a recognized conservative-slanting outlet, or even CNN, a more centrist mainstream news source. But Trump's posts also featured links to more marginal news outlets, including the alt-right Breitbart News and conspiracy-theory-rich InfoWars, and his high-profile candidacy shined light on what had previously been dark and ugly corners of the Internet.

The Internet and social media have also created what are called filter bubbles, a phenomenon that was first identified by Internet activist Eli Pariser (2011). A filter bubble is created by search engine algorithms that deliver customized findings based on a user's online history and social media circles. A website such as Google or YouTube may guess what kind of information a user prefers and then selectively produce results based on that assumption. On a larger scale this kind of filtering of information leads to the fragmentation and segregation of users, who become increasingly entrenched in separate and enclosed intellectual streams. Users then lack access to certain kinds of news

"Thanks. Great political discussion."

Echo Point Partisan "news" outlets—especially those found online—contribute to an increase in what pundits have called the political "echo chamber," a phenomenon in which readers seek out and consume only those sources that confirm beliefs they already hold.

and information that might otherwise broaden their knowledge; they get stuck in a political "echo chamber" where they access only sources they already agree with. This can further sow division between groups as well as create opportunities for abuse, as demonstrated by Russian meddling in the 2016 presidential election. Russian agents created false accounts and posted inflammatory messages on Facebook, Twitter, and YouTube in a coordinated effort to swing the election for Donald Trump. For example, Russian trolls and hackers tried to suppress voter turnout among Hillary supporters with targeted ads encouraging voters to text or tweet rather than show up to the polls. Other social media posts used religious memes to drum up support for Trump among churchgoers (Jamieson 2018).

"Fake news" also played an important role in the 2016 election. Because it is relatively easy to design websites with the look and feel of legitimate news outlets, fraudulent news stories can spread quickly online; shares and retweets on Facebook and Twitter keep this kind of fake news alive. One example from the 2016 election included the claim that anti-Trump protesters were paid by the Democratic Party (Maheshwari 2016), a claim that Trump himself took up and continued to level at the resistance movement months after it had been debunked by legitimate news outlets. Other types of fake news proliferated during this election cycle as well. One conspiracy theory—that Democratic candidate Hillary

Clinton was running a child-trafficking ring out of the basement of a DC pizza parlor—seems beyond outlandish. And yet it inspired many believers to threaten and harass the owner and employees, and one man showed up with multiple weapons and fired into the restaurant (Syrluga and Siddiqui 2016).

Further, Trump picked up on the phrase "fake news" and began using it in an attempt to delegitimize recognized and respected mainstream news outlets when they reported something he didn't like. This insistence that mainstream news outlets were lying about him helped widen an already gaping chasm between Trump voters (a numerical minority) and the rest of the country. Fomenting distrust of reliable mainstream news outlets imperils their function as a check and balance on power that the framers of the Constitution had in mind.

Clearly, the media play an important role in informing and educating the voting public. Despite our "free press," however, we must also be aware of how the media can be used to further the purposes of powerful interest groups and individuals—and even foreign governments. The democratic system stands to suffer if only those with the most money or celebrity can influence public opinion, by buying (or hacking) their way into the hearts and minds of Americans.

Patriotism and Protest

Even though freedom of speech is a legal right in the United States, when we criticize some policy or some action of the government, we may, ironically, be called unpatriotic by those who support it. After the terrorist attacks of September 11, 2001, for example, those who questioned the competence of U.S. intelligence agencies (such as journalists, elected representatives, and survivors of those killed in the attacks) were effectively silenced until more than a year later, when Congress impaneled a commission to investigate intelligence agencies' preparation for and response to the attacks. The commission's report confirmed problems within the intelligence community that contributed to the inability to foresee and forestall the attacks—corroborating the criticisms of "unpatriotic" protesters. National protests erupted in 2002 in opposition to the Iraq War, and continued over the course of the war.

More recently, in 2013, the Black Lives Matter movement emerged after George Zimmerman, a neighborhood watch volunteer, was acquitted in the case of the shooting death of black teenager Trayvon Martin. Protests grew in 2014 in the wake of several incidents where unarmed black men, including Michael Brown in Ferguson, Missouri, and Eric Garner in New York City, were killed by police officers. In each case, a grand jury decided not to indict the officers involved. Since then, widely reported incidents of the use of excessive force by police against African Americans across the country have continued to spark large protests. Protesters claim that these are not isolated incidents but rather point to a long and

IN THE FUTURE
New Representatives Change the Face of Politics

If the idea of democracy is a government of the people, by the people, and for the people, then our elected representatives should look pretty much like the American people they serve. That would mean that we'd see similar proportions of men and women, whites, blacks, Latinxs, and other ethnic groups in our government to those found in the population as a whole. Though this has never been the case, as white men have largely been in control, things have started to change. The 116th U.S. Congress, which took office in 2019, presented some historic firsts and a cause for some restrained celebration.

Many were calling 2018 the "year of the woman," and indeed the midterm elections led to a record number of women winning seats in the House of Representatives. This amounted to a new high of 127 women serving in the 116th Congress, an increase of 15 percent from the previous Congress. While this was qualified good news for gender diversity in the House, it brought the share of women Congress members up only from 20.6 percent to 23.7 percent. This modest gain still leaves women heavily underrepresented in Congress, since they make up more than 50 percent of all voters.

Among this group of women, there were many other firsts. The 116th Congress set a record for its number of women of color. Of the 127 women serving, 47 of them, or 37 percent, were women of color. This included Sharice Davids of Kansas and Deb Haaland of New Mexico, the first Native American women elected to Congress. Texas sent its first two Latina members to Congress, Veronica Escobar and Sylvia Garcia, while Massachusetts and Connecticut elected their first two black women representatives, Ayanna Pressley and Jahana Hayes. Rashida Tlaib of Michigan and Ilhan Omar of Minnesota became the first Muslim women elected to serve in Congress; in addition, Tlaib was the first Palestinian American woman, and Omar was the first Somali American. Some other firsts included 29-year-old Alexandria Ocasio-Cortez of New York, the youngest woman ever elected to Congress, who was joined by another of the youngest, 30-year-old Abby Finkenauer of Iowa. Capitol Hill itself had already been undergoing change in order to meet the needs of congressional members. Because there were more women with young children serving in the House of Representatives, a new child-care facility was opened.

So we've got a greater number of women in Congress, more women of color, and more young women, but a bigger question is whether and how they might be different as leaders and lawmakers. We do know a few things about how women govern differently from men. Women lawmakers are more committed to what some would call "women's issues," including families, health, education, and civil rights and liberties. They are more likely to designate spending for specific projects such as for promoting equal pay or combating violence against women. Studies have shown that women legislators bring more spending back to their districts and are better than men at keeping their bills alive longer (Kurtzleben 2018). And it might be worth noting that women in Congress participate in organized social activities more often than men do.

As the 116th Congress confirms, the House of Representatives continues to get more diverse with each successive electoral cycle. What might Congress look like in the next decade or two, and will it be even more representative of the changing demographic makeup of Americans themselves? Just as importantly, will a change in faces among our elected leaders create meaningful change to the political process itself, and help build a better, more effective government for future generations?

The Year of the Woman? More women, women of color, and young women now serve in Congress, but they still make up less than one-quarter of all elected representatives. Will future elections continue to add more women political leaders?

March for Our Lives Millions of young people showed up to protest gun violence and advocate for changes to U.S. gun laws in the wake of the mass shooting at Marjory Stoneman Douglas High School in Parkland, Florida.

ongoing history of inequities in policing in minority communities, racial profiling, and police brutality.

The election of Donald Trump in 2016 also energized activists, who immediately began organizing protest marches and other initiatives aimed at countering Trump's campaign promises, which included banning Muslims from entering the United States; building a border wall; repealing the Affordable Care Act; and eliminating business regulation, environmental protection, and social welfare programs from the federal agenda. The first major demonstration—the Women's March on Washington—occurred on January 21, 2017, the day after Trump was inaugurated. While more than half a million protesters stormed the nation's capital, satellite marches in cities all over the United States drew millions more protesting Trump's promises to restrict women's reproductive rights, defund child-care and health-care programs, and roll back environmental restrictions. One report estimated that about 1 percent of the U.S. population was out in the streets marching against the new president and his agenda, with millions more joining sister marches on every continent—even Antarctica (Darrow 2017).

In February 2018, young people were thrust into the forefront of another protest movement. After a gunman killed seventeen students and staff members at Marjory Stoneman Douglas High School, survivors joined together to create #NeverAgain. Within days of the mass shooting in Parkland, Florida, student leaders started organizing on Facebook and Twitter, using the hashtag and intense media spotlight to rally supporters to the cause of gun control. In the following days, they spoke out at many events and were featured in numerous media outlets criticizing lawmakers and politicians and asking for more aggressive measures against gun violence. The "March for Our Lives" demonstrations, which took place on March 24, 2018, were among the largest youth-led protests since the Vietnam War; more than 880 demonstrations were held nationwide, with an estimated turnout of between 1.2 and 2 million people.

Is it unpatriotic to criticize your government in times of national crisis or to call for change to an unfair legal system? Those who do so argue that such criticism is the most patriotic act of all: that blind acceptance of government is not the same as patriotism and that citizens should make every effort to correct society's flaws. Those on the opposite side may say, "My country, right or wrong" and believe that the decisions of our elected leaders and the actions of those who carry out our laws are beyond reproach. Regardless of your views, keep in mind that those who criticize government policies are doing exactly what our democratic system calls for and protects. Dissent and its tolerance are crucial elements of an open society, and you have a constitutionally protected right to oppose, criticize, and protest.

Politics: The Micro-Macro Link

Political institutions and their products (such as laws or bureaucratic systems) shape our everyday lives. A law such as Title VII of the Civil Rights Act of 1964 ensures your right to apply for and hold a job without being discriminated against because of race, gender, or religion. No matter who you are or what kind of work you do, you are protected by this law.

And even if you have never experienced discrimination in the workplace, this law is probably one of the reasons why.

Huge government bureaucracies like the Department of Education shape your everyday life as well. Even if you attend a private university, you had to submit a FAFSA (Free Application for Federal Student Aid) in order to determine your eligibility for any type of financial aid—federal and state grants and loans and aid programs administered by your campus. All these student aid sources require the FAFSA, and your ability to attend the college of your choice may therefore depend on the decisions made by this government bureaucracy.

In addition to seeing how political institutions shape our everyday lives, it is important to remember that we have built these institutions ourselves, through our participation in the democratic process. When we vote, sign petitions, or participate in demonstrations, we bring our individual influence to bear on the larger social structure—even if, ultimately, the cause or candidate we support doesn't prevail. So remember, micro-macro connections are made every day as you participate with others in political processes and live in a culture shaped by its political institutions.

Democratic processes require a free press and an educated polity; to make decisions and cast votes, you must have the tools to gather information and comprehend the issues your vote will influence. This is only one of the many links between political and educational institutions in our society. As we move into the segment of this chapter that deals with education, try to think of all the ways that politics and education are connected—and remember to look for micro-macro connections as you learn about educational institutions as well.

> **EDUCATION** the process by which a society transmits its knowledge, values, and expectations to its members so they can function effectively

WHAT IS EDUCATION?

Most modern political systems recognize the importance of universal education. The framers of the U.S. Constitution realized that an informed public was essential to the survival of democracy. Education, therefore, was seen as critical to the founding of the new republic. In the United States, public education has traditionally been under state and local control, although the federal government began playing a larger role in the latter half of the twentieth century. However, private schools and religious schools are also involved in education. About 9 percent of K–12 students attend private schools (either religious or secular), 88 percent attend public schools, and 3 percent are homeschooled (U.S. Department of Education 2013).

Education is the central means by which a society transmits its knowledge, values, and expectations to its members. The general goal of education is to give students the necessary understanding for effective social functioning. Education often includes the transmission of information, principles, and values; the regulation of personal character; and discipline of the mind. Education can be either formal or informal and can occur in a variety of settings, although we commonly think of it as tied to school systems.

A Brief History of Modern Education

Formal, institutionalized, secular education in Western civilization began in ancient Greece around the eighth century B.C.E., when students studied philosophy, mathematics, music, and gymnastics. Higher education was carried out by philosophers before the rise of schools as an institution. In the Middle Ages, the church was the main educator, with schools in monasteries and cathedrals, and until about 1200 C.E., the schools focused mainly on training students to be priests. During the thirteenth century, lay education emerged. It consisted of apprentice training for a small group of the common people or education in chivalry for the more privileged. During the Middle Ages, universities offered courses in three subjects—law, theology, and medicine—and these courses were available only to the most privileged members of society: royals, aristocrats, and those from families with ties to the monarchy and the church.

While systems of education have evolved a great deal since the Middle Ages, the roots of what we would recognize as modern mass education can be traced back to the idealism of the European Enlightenment of the eighteenth and nineteenth centuries. During this period, the value of education greatly increased. The leading thinkers of the day, such as Voltaire, Locke, and Franklin, emphasized knowledge—reason, logic, and science—over religious tradition. They were convinced that the well-being and future of modern society depended on enlightened self-knowledge, which could be achieved only through learning.

Education in the United States grew rapidly during this same period. The founders' belief that it is the government's responsibility to provide basic education to all its citizens—and that fulfilling this obligation is beneficial for both society and the individual—helped create the U.S. public education system. Schooling came to be seen as a necessity rather than a luxury and became legally mandatory for all children age sixteen and younger; Massachusetts was the first state to enact such a law, in 1852. As larger proportions of the population began attending schools, curricula became more varied and included both academic and vocational education to prepare students for a diversifying set of future occupations (not just farming or housewifery). By 1929, elementary, junior high, and high schools had spread to every state and territory in the nation, including Alaska, and opportunities for higher education had also expanded, especially in the land-grant colleges of the western United States.

The Rise of Mass Education
Beginning in the nineteenth century, schooling began to be considered a necessity for preparing children to enter modern industrial occupations.

Higher education is now available to everyone in the United States. Before 1900, less than 2 percent of Americans finished high school, and even fewer went on to college. In 2017, the high school graduation rate was 85 percent. High school dropout rates have decreased markedly, particularly among black and Hispanic students. In 2017, just 5 percent of students dropped out of high school, down from more than 10 percent in 2000 (National Center for Education Statistics 2019b).

Education and the Reproduction of Society

Schooling serves a number of important functions in our society. The transmission of knowledge is a clear function of education. In addition, we learn to follow society's rules and to respect authority, and we are socialized to develop other qualities that will eventually make us efficient and obedient workers. In school, we also learn our places in the larger society—practices such as **tracking**, in which students are identified as "gifted" or are placed into remedial or vocational education, teach us about success and achievement and our chances for both. When placed in a lower-ability or remedial track, for instance, students lose access to courses such as calculus and Advanced Placement (AP) classes (Useem 1990), which effectively locks them out of certain colleges, certain majors, and even certain future careers, all by the time they're sixteen years old.

EDUCATION AND INEQUALITY While we firmly believe, as a society, that education is the key to achievement and success, it is also true that educational institutions can replicate systems of inequality. Educational achievements do improve our life chances; U.S. Census data consistently indicate that those with higher educational attainment also have higher median incomes: In 2017, young adults with a high school diploma had median yearly earnings of $32,000 compared to $38,900 for those with an associate's degree, $51,800 for those with a bachelor's degree, and $65,000 for those with a master's degree or higher (National Center for Education Statistics 2019a). Moreover, unemployment rates are directly correlated with educational attainment: In 2018, the unemployment rate was 4.1 percent for people with a high school diploma, 2.2 percent for people with a bachelor's degree, and just 2.0 percent for people with a master's degree (U.S. Bureau of Labor Statistics 2019c).

TRACKING the placement of students in educational "tracks," or programs of study (e.g., college prep, remedial), that determine the types of classes they take

College accessibility remains unequal: Young adults from high-income families are five times more likely to receive a bachelor's degree than young adults from low-income families (Cahalan et al. 2018). We also see disparities among different racial and ethnic groups. In 2018, for example, 39 percent of whites over twenty-five years of age had earned a bachelor's degree, compared to 25 percent of blacks and 18 percent of Hispanics; Asians had the highest rates, with 56 percent earning bachelor's degrees (U.S. Census Bureau 2019a). It is also worth noting some of the complexity of gender inequality in higher education, as we find that among young adults ages twenty-five to twenty-nine, there is a growing gap between the percentage of women (39 percent) and men (32 percent) with bachelor's degrees or higher (National

Center for Education Statistics 2019b). So education benefits everyone, but it does not benefit everyone equally, and inequality in educational benefits mirrors inequality in the larger society.

How do these patterns manifest themselves? What do these educational inequalities look and feel like for students in the classroom? Female students may notice, for instance, that their teachers pay more attention to male students, and they may learn to think that boys are smarter than girls. Caucasian or Asian students may notice that there are fewer African American and Hispanic students in the gifted classroom than in the remedial classroom, and they may learn to think that whites and Asians are smarter than blacks and Hispanics. Children without disabilities may see disabled kids left out of activities or sent to the special-education center and learn to think that these students are less worthy than nondisabled kids. These micro-inequities are common in American classrooms.

> **HIDDEN CURRICULUM** values or behaviors that students learn indirectly over the course of their schooling

They are experienced by individuals but are the result of structural forces external to those individuals. In other words, micro-inequities result from macro-level inequalities in the larger educational and social systems. And these micro-inequities teach us as much as our more explicit lessons in math, literature, or history. Acquiring a sociological perspective on educational institutions and processes will help you "unlearn" these lessons and understand that educational attainment is often as much about social stratification as it is about individual ability.

THE HIDDEN CURRICULUM Sociologists have long been interested in the **hidden curriculum**, the lessons that students learn indirectly but that are an implicit part of their socialization in the school environment (Jackson 1968).

Many sociologists have analyzed the hidden curriculum to explain the nonacademic roles filled by mass education.

One such role is the training of future workers, which was examined by Bowles and Gintis (1977) in their study *Schooling in Capitalist America*. They argue that schools train a labor force with the appropriate skills, personalities, and attitudes for a corporate economy. Although the official curriculum is supposed to promote personal improvement and social mobility, the hidden curriculum of "rules, routines, and regulations" actually produces a submissive and obedient workforce that is prepared to take orders and perform repetitive tasks. According to this analysis, schools look a lot like factories. Students have no control over their curriculum, must obey instructions, and gain little intrinsic satisfaction from their schoolwork. Because students learn these norms and values in school, they are willing to accept similar conditions when they become workers.

A similar analysis can explain how the hidden curriculum reinforces and reproduces conditions of social inequality by presenting and reinforcing an image of what is considered "normal," "right," or "good." While the official curriculum has come a long way toward recognizing the racial, ethnic, and gender diversity of the nation, there are still major gaps and exclusions (FitzGerald 1980; Thornton 2003). Schools cannot always rectify these oversights because the hidden curriculum can work through much more subtle mechanisms as well. How the curriculum is presented and the way the school is organized can be powerful messengers of the hidden curriculum. For instance, even schools that attempt to implement multicultural education may undermine their own efforts if the staff and administration do not mirror the lessons they teach. If teachers and administrators are mostly white, mostly heterosexual, or mostly male (or mostly female, as is the case in lower grades), they may belie the very lessons they try to teach—what students hear and what they see just don't add up. When schools attempt to alter only what is taught and

Hidden Curriculum Sociologists argue that schools train students to be ideal workers by promoting a curriculum of "rules, routines, and regulations."

not the way it is taught, they may change the curriculum, but they won't affect what students are learning (Christakis 1995; Falconer and Byrnes 2003).

Classic Studies of Education

Sociologists and other researchers have studied education from a variety of perspectives. In this section, we review three classic studies of education, each offering a different approach and distinctive insights into its significance, both as a social institution and in the lives of individuals.

A SYMBOLIC INTERACTIONIST STUDY The first study looks at education from the symbolic interactionist perspective, which maintains that the social world is constructed through the interactions of individuals. Robert Rosenthal, a Harvard psychologist, and Leonore Jacobson, an elementary school principal, worked together on *Pygmalion in the Classroom: Teacher Expectation and Pupils' Intellectual Development* (1968). The researchers began the experiment by administering a basic IQ test to students in the first through sixth grades, although they told teachers the test was designed to predict which students would "bloom" academically in the next year. They then randomly selected an experimental group of students and falsely told their teachers that these students were predicted to develop rapidly in the coming school year. At the end of the year, the researchers administered the same IQ test and found that students in the experimental group had increased their IQ scores by a significantly greater margin than their peers in the control group. The researchers concluded that the teachers' attitudes about their students unintentionally influenced the students' academic performance. In other words, when teachers expected students to succeed, the students indeed tended to improve (and it was assumed that the opposite would be true as well).

The results of *Pygmalion in the Classroom* have been critiqued by other researchers, on both theoretical and methodological grounds, especially because the researchers used standardized IQ tests and small subject samples (Baker and Crist 1971). Nonetheless, this study and others support the proposition that teacher expectations affect students' behavior and achievement in measurable ways. Some studies indicate that student labeling is often arbitrary and biased, with the result that teachers—whether consciously or unconsciously—may be reinforcing existing class, ethnic, ability, and gender inequalities (Fairbanks 1992; Sadker and Sadker 1995). This also means that changes in classroom interaction could lead to an improvement in academic performance among students from underprivileged backgrounds.

A CONFLICT STUDY The next study, which also looks at inequalities in schools, is consistent with a conflict perspective, which sees society as a system characterized by inequality and competition. Jonathan Kozol's *Savage Inequalities*

(1991) is an ethnographic study of public schools in cities across the country, including Washington, DC; Chicago; and San Antonio. Kozol, a former teacher, contends that because schools are funded by local property taxes, children in poor neighborhoods are trapped in poor schools, which reinforces inequality. He documents the significant differences among America's schools: "The highest spending districts have twice as many art, music, and foreign language teachers… 75 percent more physical education teachers… 50 percent more nurses, school librarians, guidance counselors, and psychologists… and 60 percent more personnel in school administration than the low-spending districts" (Kozol 1991, p. 167).

When Kozol interviewed the parents and students in wealthy school districts, he discovered that many of them believed educational inequalities were a thing of the past, "something dating maybe back to slavery or maybe to the era of official segregation" but not to anything "recent or contemporary or ongoing" (Kozol 1991, p. 179). In stark contrast to this view, Kozol describes underfunded schools he visited— the hundreds of classrooms without teachers in Chicago, the thousands of children without classrooms in schools throughout New Jersey. His overall impression was that these urban schools were, by and large, extraordinarily unhappy places, lacking in some of the most basic resources necessary for student success. This situation disproportionately hurts low-income and minority students. How, he asks, could the children in such schools have an equal chance at success? A structural functionalist might respond that schools are not intended to provide equal chances.

A STRUCTURAL FUNCTIONALIST STUDY According to the structural functionalist perspective, educational inequality is merely preparation for occupational inequalities later in life. (Remember, functionalists believe that every social phenomenon has a role to play in keeping society at equilibrium.) In the third study, *The Credential Society*, sociologist Randall Collins (1979) argues that class inequalities are reproduced in educational settings and that there is very little schools can do to combat this. In a **credential society** a great deal of emphasis is placed on degrees and certificates as determinants of social status and proof of readiness for the job market. As the demand for these credentials grows, they are subsequently worth less, leading to a process of inflation where students must attain ever-higher levels of achievement to keep up and move ahead. Collins argues that the promise of higher education as a mechanism for social mobility has been stymied by this process, leaving behind those it should serve. Although many people assume that better teachers, better facilities, and better funding can increase student success, Collins points out that

> **CREDENTIAL SOCIETY** a society that emphasizes the attainment of degrees and certificates as necessary requirements for the job market and social mobility

when class background factors are held constant, none of these other factors seems to have any effect.

Collins believes that reproducing the existing class structure is the true function of education. Schools, for example, provide the credentials to ensure that the children of the middle class will continue to receive middle-class jobs. To protect their own job security, members of lucrative occupations, such as accountants, lawyers, and financial analysts, have set up a complicated credential system (education) to keep the number of job applicants down and to ensure that there is a large population forced to work at unpleasant jobs for low wages. Collins makes the radical recommendation that we consider "abolishing compulsory school requirements and making formal credential requirements for employment illegal" (Collins 1979, p. 198). This would make it illegal for employers to ask how much education a job applicant has, much as it is currently illegal to ask about race or gender.

The Present and Future of Education

During the past several decades, many educators, parents, and legislators have come to believe that America's educational system is in crisis, that public schools are failing to provide adequate training for students. Critics list a variety of problems, including low rates of literacy and poor standardized test scores, lack of sufficient funding and crumbling infrastructure, low pay for teachers, overcrowded classrooms, and high rates of crime on campus.

In 1983, the National Commission on Excellence in Education released a report on the state of American public schools. *A Nation at Risk* concluded, in apocalyptic terms, that the American educational system was in a crisis so serious that "if an unfriendly foreign power" had created it, "we might well have viewed it as an act of war." Largely on the basis of declining standardized test scores, the report argued that the United States was "committing an act of unthinking, unilateral educational disarmament." Not all the commission's conclusions have been affirmed, but almost four decades later, numerous studies point to ongoing problems in education and the persistence of an "achievement gap" between students from different demographic groups.

CHARTER SCHOOLS public schools run by private entities to give parents greater control over their children's education

Much of the research surrounding America's failing public education system points toward a connection between poverty and academic underachievement. A recent study showed that more than half of all public school students within the United States live in poverty, marking an increase in the growing rates of poverty within the public education system (Southern Education Foundation 2015). Not surprisingly, much higher proportions of minority students attend high-poverty schools: 44 percent of black and 45 percent of Hispanic students compared to just 8 percent of white students (National Center for Education Statistics 2019b). With only about half of students from high-poverty high schools going on to attend college, poverty remains one of the biggest predictors of academic achievement and educational attainment (Sparks and Adams 2013). Concerns about the decline in American educational standards and competitiveness have elicited a variety of responses on the part of parents, communities, the government, and other agencies. A number of educational trends are already in place and may play an important role in shaping the future of American education.

THE COMMON CORE Some efforts have been aimed at trying to address problems at the K–12 level. One such tactic is the Common Core State Standards, developed in 2010 with the intention to remedy America's stagnant academic achievement levels. The Common Core is a state-led rather than federal initiative, and state adoption of standards is voluntary, although President Obama did create a grant incentive program, Race to the Top, for states that adopt the standards (Common Core State Standards Initiative 2015). At its peak, forty-five states had adopted the Common Core as a way to standardize and improve test scores while better preparing students for college.

While the program initially met with widespread public support, by 2016 only about 50 percent of parents and educators still approved of it (Kerstetter 2016). One of the main controversies about the program involves the use of standardized tests to measure both student and teacher success. The tests have been criticized for being too long, too challenging, or too divergent from the way that subjects like math and English are actually taught. Another point of contention is the perception that the Common Core is a federal mandate; in fact, it has always been voluntary. Many concerns remain, however, regarding the ability of any one-size-fits-all attempt to reform America's education system. President Trump called for decentralization in education, and his secretary of education, Betsy DeVos, has disavowed the program; yet the Common Core persists in one form or another in about forty states. Although some states have changed some standards or adopted different names for their programs, the core of the Common Core still stands (Sawchuk 2017). It remains unclear how the program will affect the trajectory of public education, or what might replace it. Whether states retain or opt out of the Common Core, debates about course content, standards, testing, and accountability continue.

CHARTER SCHOOLS **Charter schools** are public schools that are run by private entities, such as a parents' group or an educational corporation. They operate with relative freedom from many of the bureaucratic regulations that apply to traditional public schools. Charter schools represent a compromise position between public and private schools and provide a way for parents to exercise control over their students' educational experiences without completely abandoning the public school system. State laws regarding charter schools govern sponsorship, number of schools, regulatory waivers, degree of fiscal or legal autonomy, and performance expectations.

The "charter" establishing such schools is a contract detailing the school's mission, program, goals, students served, methods of assessment, and ways to measure success. Charter schools are designed to support educational innovation; some have special emphases like arts or science; others offer special services like health clinics or community-based internships for students. The IDEA charter high school in Washington, DC, instructs students in the skills needed to work in the architecture and construction trades while also teaching the traditional high school curriculum. In Madison, Wisconsin, educators started Nuestro Mundo Community School, a Spanish immersion program. By fifth grade, all students are equally fluent in Spanish and English. The Madison school district created the school to help close the gap between the test scores of Hispanic students and those of their non-Hispanic peers.

Ideally, charter schools can make changes and implement decisions faster than ordinary public schools because of their freedom from district governance. They can monitor their successes (and failures) more closely and be more responsive to the needs of students, parents, and communities. In reality, charter schools face many challenges. Because charter schools are free from certain regulations, they have the freedom to operate independently and on private sponsorship. Still, many of them struggle to raise funds. This can potentially create disparities in public education and exclude certain student populations (National Center for the Study of Privatization in Education 2015).

SCHOOL VOUCHERS First proposed in the 1990s, **school vouchers** allow parents in neighborhoods where the public schools are inadequate to send their children to the private school of their choice. In other words, taxpayers receive a voucher for some of the money that a public school would have received to educate their child, and they apply that money to private school tuition. Most school-voucher programs fund 75 percent to 90 percent of the cost of a private school, with parents making up the rest.

Despite the growing use of school vouchers, there has been little evidence to indicate that vouchers increase academic achievement (Usher and Kober 2011). Proponents of school vouchers argue that they give parents more choice and control over their children's education and pressure public schools to improve or risk the loss of their voucher-eligible student body. Opponents argue that vouchers do not improve public education but do the opposite: They drain funds from vulnerable public schools and cause them to deteriorate further. Opponents also say that if parents use vouchers for parochial schools, public monies are funding religious education, thus threatening the separation of church and state. While the Supreme Court has ruled the voucher system to be constitutional and numerous experimental voucher programs are already in place, the privatization of public education remains controversial in any form.

SCHOOL VOUCHERS payments from the government to parents whose children attend failing public schools; the money helps parents pay private school tuition

HOMESCHOOLING the education of children by their parents, at home

HOMESCHOOLING AND UNSCHOOLING Homeschooling, or home-based education, is the education of school-aged children under their parents' supervision outside a regular

Homeschooling The Wilson family in Myrtle Point, Oregon, study together at the kitchen table as part of their homeschooling program.

ON THE JOB
A College Degree: What's It Worth?

Young Americans are told that a college degree is the best way to prepare for the job market. However, since as far back as the 1970s, sociologists like Randall Collins have wondered whether college is always a sound investment. The usual argument in favor of higher education, even as it has become increasingly expensive, is that students are "investing in themselves." But this "investment" theory makes sense only if education is producing graduates who have skills and knowledge they can turn into higher wages. In *The Credential Society*, Collins argued that "job skills of all sorts are actually acquired in the work situation rather than in a formal training institution," while college provides only a credential (1979, p. 193). That credential can be enormously valuable, of course, but it's subject to inflation. As more and more people attend college, jobs that used to require high school diplomas start wanting bachelor's degrees, and so on. If Collins is correct, or even partially correct, sooner or later school will become a bad investment. Are we there yet? Experts disagree.

Many experts stand by higher education as a sound investment from which graduates reap good returns. Mary Daly, a senior vice president and researcher at the Federal Reserve Bank, says there is strong evidence that a college degree still gives people an "earnings advantage" (Bengali and Daly 2014). Research shows that the benefits of college in terms of higher earnings far outweigh the costs of obtaining a degree. And according to the Pew Research Center, a college degree is worth more than ever as the earnings gap between those with a college education and those without continues to widen (Pew Research Center 2014b). Today workers with a doctoral degree bring in average lifetime earnings of $3.3 million, compared to $2.3 million for workers with a bachelor's degree, $1.3 million for those with only a high school diploma, and just $973,000 for those without a high school diploma (Carnevale, Rose, and Cheah 2011). This means that workers with a college degree earn an average of 75 percent more—or about $1 million—over their lifetime than workers with just a high school diploma.

While supporters see these figures as zingers, there are some cracks in the consensus. The most obvious disclaimer when "investing" in a four-year college is the one attached to any investment: Past returns are no guarantee of future returns. College was a terrific investment in the past, but will that still be true for those applying for admission today? Of course, a lot depends on just how much a particular college costs. For many students, it makes sense to attend a more affordable college, where it still takes about nine years after graduation to get to the break-even point. For those students

---

school campus. Many parents homeschool their children not only to control their academic education but also to limit their exposure to the socializing effects of peer culture in public schools. Some homeschooled children enroll in regular schools part-time or share instruction with other families, but most of their education takes place at home. Currently, an estimated 1.7 million students in the United States are homeschooled, accounting for a little over 3 percent of the school-age population (Grady 2017).

Clearly, homeschooling is a significant phenomenon in education, but how is it working? One of the largest studies of homeschooling arrived at rather startling results. The academic achievement of homeschooled students, on average, was significantly above that of public school students, even if parents were not certified teachers and the state did not highly regulate homeschooling (Ray 1997, 2008, 2013). One advantage of homeschooling seems to be the flexibility in customizing curriculum and pedagogy to the needs of each child. Yet questions remain about the possible academic and social disadvantages to students removed from typical school environments.

More recently, the **unschooling** movement has gained popularity. Although it is similar to homeschooling in that parents oversee their child's learning, unschooling is an alternative to traditional education and homeschooling alike. As its name suggests, unschooling rejects the standard curriculum that is typically taught to students, as well as conventional teaching methods and classroom environments. Unschooling, as a philosophy, advocates student-centered learning by encouraging students to learn through their own freely chosen activities, interests, and real-world experiences. Parents offer support, guidance, and resources, but children initiate their own direction and exploration of

UNSCHOOLING a homeschooling alternative that rejects the standard curriculum in favor of student-driven types of learning

paying higher tuition costs (say, at a private college), it may take closer to seventeen years to break even. Those figures presume that a student finishes a BA in four years.

There's also the question of college major. The annual wages of recent college graduates vary quite widely—from $27,000 to $50,000—based on major (Carnevale, Cheah, and Hanson 2015). Students graduating in some fields, such as engineering or architecture, earn significantly more than those majoring in education, the arts, or psychology. Workers with STEM majors have the highest annual median earnings. For example, the median annual earnings of workers with a major in petroleum engineering is $136,000; compare that to $39,000 for workers with a major in early childhood education or $42,000 for social work majors. This adds up over a worker's lifetime: Workers with the top-paying college majors earn $3.4 million more over a lifetime than those with the lowest-earning majors (Carnevale, Cheah, and Hanson 2015).

Still, there are some pretty high-profile dissenters. Nobel Prize–winning economist James Heckman believes the value of college depends on the student: "Even with these high prices, you're still finding a high return for individuals who are bright and motivated," but for those who aren't "college ready, then the answer is no, it's not worth it" (McArdle 2012). Another skeptic is Peter Cappelli (2015), a professor of management at the University of Pennsylvania's Wharton School. He notes that many college graduates end up in jobs for which they don't need a degree and that some

New College Graduates Is a college degree still a smart investment?

students would be better off financially by not going to college at all.

One of the most visible challenges to the idea that everyone should go to college comes from PayPal co-founder Peter Thiel. In 2011 he created the Thiel Fellowship, which pays twenty young people $100,000 for two years to pursue their ideas and business plans outside of school. With such notable college dropouts as Bill Gates and Mark Zuckerberg to point to, college might actually stand in the way of success for some people. Undoubtedly, though, such cases are the rare exception, making a college degree a pretty safe bet.

subject matter. This approach makes lessons more meaningful to the students and honors their particular aptitudes and learning styles.

Although their numbers are still relatively small, adults who were unschooled report high levels of satisfaction in their later careers. Many proponents of unschooling denounce the traditional model of formal education, which they say is not conducive to learning or future success. Some critics believe that unschooling is too radical an approach and worry about isolation and children who lack social skills and self-motivation. Homeschooling and unschooling are educational trends that continue to grow, as they offer an attractive alternative to the shortcomings of traditional education.

EARLY COLLEGE HIGH SCHOOLS AND DUAL ENROLL-MENT PROGRAMS **Early college high schools** are new institutions that blend high school and college into a coherent educational program in which students earn both a high school diploma and two years of college credit toward a bachelor's degree. The goal of such a program is to serve students who might otherwise face greater obstacles making the transition from high school to higher education. In an effort to address the achievement gap in public education, early college high schools aim to serve low-income students and minorities.

EARLY COLLEGE HIGH SCHOOLS institutions in which students earn a high school diploma and two years of credit toward a bachelor's degree

Each early college high school is a collaborative endeavor between a public school district and an accredited higher education partner. In Oregon, for example, Portland Community College partners with the Native American Youth and Family Center to offer an early college high school program for Native American youth, who have the highest college dropout rate and the lowest graduation rate of any ethnic group in the United States. This type of high school aims to engage students by offering them challenging academic work while simultaneously providing the necessary guidance and support structures. Early college high schools are small (with no more than 75–100 students per grade) and thus can provide the benefits of a close community, an intimate learning environment, and personalized academic attention. A 2013 evaluation research study of the effect of early college high schools found that students enrolled in these schools were significantly more likely to both attend and graduate from college; minority students saw the greatest impact (Berger et al. 2014).

Dual enrollment programs allow high school students to gain college credit for the courses they take through a concurrent enrollment agreement with a local college. Through this exchange, dual enrollment students take classes, often at a local community college, and simultaneously earn high school and college credit for their work. While AP classes provide high-achieving students the opportunity to earn college credits, dual enrollment allows many more high school students the opportunity to take college-level courses. By providing high school students with the opportunity to get a head start on college work, dual enrollment programs can help ease the transition to college and allow students to "try on" or rehearse college attendance (Karp 2012). It has also been shown that dual enrollment programs can increase postsecondary academic achievement while also decreasing the amount of time students take to obtain their degree (Allen and Dadgar 2012).

For many students, the path to postsecondary education is difficult. Large, impersonal middle and high school programs, limited financial resources, and the daunting processes of applying to and entering higher education may hinder academic achievement. By changing the structure of the high school and compressing the number of years required for an undergraduate degree, early college high schools and dual enrollment programs are having a significant impact on high school students, who are demonstrating high levels of attendance, improved promotion rates, and success in college-level courses.

COMMUNITY COLLEGES You know what a community college is—you may even attend one right now. A **community college** is a two-year school that provides general education classes for students who want to save money while preparing to transfer to a four-year university, right? While this definition of a community college is technically true, community colleges have become much more than just a springboard to

DUAL ENROLLMENT programs that allow high school students to simultaneously enroll in college classes, earning credit for both high school and college degrees

COMMUNITY COLLEGE two-year institution that provides students with general education and facilitates transfer to a four-year university

a four-year degree. They provide vocational and technical training for people planning practical careers, retrain "downsized" workers seeking new career paths, and offer enrichment classes for retirees. In 2017, nearly 6 million students were enrolled in two-year community colleges, making up about 35 percent of all undergraduate students enrolled in college in the United States (National Center for Education Statistics 2019b).

The contemporary community college typically offers more than just basic general education and college preparatory courses. In fact, the California Community College system, the largest in the nation, offers classes in more than 175 fields (California Community Colleges Chancellor's Office 2015). Honors programs, study abroad options, intercollegiate sports, music programs, on-campus residence halls, and internships can now be part of the two-year experience. Community colleges help students prepare for careers that give back to the community. Two of the most in-demand programs of study are administration of justice and health sciences. Fully 80 percent of firefighters, police officers, and EMTs and more than half of all new nurses and health-care workers trained at community colleges (American Association of Community Colleges 2011).

Community colleges have gained recognition for playing a critical role in preparing the country's workforce. In an effort to serve more people in need of training, many states are now offering programs in which students enrolled in community college can earn a bachelor's degree on campus, rather than transferring to a four-year university. Community college baccalaureate programs allow students to still earn a bachelor's degree while avoiding the high costs and barriers to access that surround four-year university admission.

In 2015, President Obama launched the American College Promise program, a federal initiative to make community college attendance free for many students. Inspired by the success of Tennessee and Chicago's tuition-free community college programs, the initiative was aimed at helping millions of students by increasing community college accessibility (Parsons 2015). A new bill, America's College Promise Act, or ACPA, was introduced in the United States Senate in 2018. In the meantime, sixteen states have initiated their own college promise programs, and dozens of others have been started at local or regional levels (Mishory 2018). With increasing tuition costs at four-year universities, more-affordable community colleges could help propel many students who would not otherwise be able to afford tuition to pursue higher education.

ONLINE LEARNING Online education (also called distance learning) is not really a new concept—"correspondence courses" have been available for hundreds of years and served as a way for people in remote locations (like farmers or military members and their families) or people who were homebound or physically disabled to benefit from the same educational opportunities available to others. In previous eras, distance learning courses relied on the postal service and more recently on audiotapes and videos to help students learn independently. With the advent of the Internet and real-time electronic communication, distance learning was transformed forever. Universities and private businesses use these technologies to offer courses to anyone with an Internet connection. Certificates and degrees of all kinds are within the reach of students who, because of time, geography, or other constraints, cannot come to campus.

In 2016 more than 66 million, or 31 percent of all college students, were taking at least one class online. Online enrollments have been growing steadily even while overall higher education enrollment has remained flat (Lederman 2018). As with any application of technology to education, there are both pros and cons to online learning. Like the old-fashioned correspondence courses, online technologies provide educational access for those who might otherwise not be able to pursue a degree. However, distance learning is not a good fit for all students, and attrition rates from online courses are notoriously high. Online classes often lack the personal touch and dynamic interaction of standard classroom instruction. For this reason, students may feel that there is something important (if intangible) missing from their educational experience.

Education: The Micro-Macro Link

As societies change, so do educational institutions, and so does the individual's experience of education. For example, a big part of being a student today is knowing how to use digital technology. The typical student today does a good amount of work online, whether it's reading an e-book, accessing course materials online, or watching videos as homework. Digital technology is so integrated into the teaching and learning process that many students now take it for granted. This is one of the many ways that macro-level change (in this case, the development of technology) affects your everyday life through your participation in the social institution of education. What you learn about the world in school on an everyday basis—as well as how you learn it—is shaped by larger social forces.

Education is not the only social institution concerned with teaching members of society important information, values, and norms. Religion is another social institution from which we learn a great deal about being members of society. Even if we rebel against our religious upbringing or have no religious affiliation, our lives are touched in important ways by religion because it is a dominant social institution in the United States. As you read the following section, think about the intersection of the micro and the macro in the study of religion and about the intersection of religion with other social institutions, including politics and education.

WHAT IS RELIGION?

No doubt we each have our own definition of religion based on personal experience. But a sociological definition must be broad enough to encompass all kinds of religious experiences. For sociologists, **religion** includes any institutionalized system of shared beliefs (propositions and ideas held on the basis of faith) and rituals (practices based on those beliefs) that identify a relationship between the **sacred** (holy, divine, or supernatural) and the **profane** (ordinary, mundane, or everyday). Those who study religion recognize that there are different types of religious groups: denominations (major subgroups of larger religions, such as Protestantism within Christianity or Shia within Islam), sects (smaller subgroups, such as the Amish or Mennonites), and cults (usually very small, intense, close-knit groups focused on individual leaders—like David Koresh and the Branch Davidians—or specific issues like the UFO cult Heaven's Gate). Sociologists do not evaluate the truth of any system of beliefs; they study the ways that religions shape and are shaped by cultural institutions and processes, as well as the ways that religions influence and are influenced by the behavior of individuals.

> **RELIGION** any institutionalized system of shared beliefs and rituals that identify a relationship between the sacred and the profane
>
> **SACRED** the holy, divine, or supernatural
>
> **PROFANE** the ordinary, mundane, or everyday

Theoretical Approaches to Religion

Sociological theorists have tried to explain the rise, attraction, and effects of religion, as well as its relationship to the larger society and its role in the lives of individuals. One of the most discussed sociological takes on religion is Max Weber's (1905) theory about the link between Protestant Christian values and the rise of capitalism in the West. According to Weber, Protestants' emphasis on hard work and frugality facilitated the accumulation of property and wealth, contributing to the triumph of capitalism in Europe and the United States. Other sociological theories have focused on the function of religion in society, the ways in which religion promotes inequality and conflict, and how religious meaning is constructed through interaction.

STRUCTURAL FUNCTIONALISM From a structural functionalist perspective, religious beliefs and rituals serve a number of functions for adherents. First, religion shapes everyday behavior by providing morals, values, rules, and norms for its participants. From the Judeo-Christian commandment "Thou shalt not kill" to the Buddhist commitment to reconcile strife to the Qur'anic requirement to eschew

Religion and Social Justice Óscar Romero, the late archbishop of El Salvador, who was beatified by Pope Francis in 2015 (left), and Lech Walesa (right, speaking into a bullhorn) of Poland both led movements against repressive political regimes.

alcohol and impure foods, religious rules govern both the largest and smallest events and actions of followers' daily lives. Religious practices usually include some type of penance or rehabilitation for those who break the rules: Catholics can confess their sins to a priest and be assigned prayer or good works to redeem themselves; Muslims spend the month of Ramadan fasting during daylight hours to purify their bodies and souls; Yom Kippur is the Jewish Day of Atonement and also involves fasting, as well as appeals for wrongs to be forgiven.

Another function of religion is to give meaning to our lives. Religious beliefs can help us understand just about everything we encounter because every religion has a system of beliefs that explains such fundamental questions as: How did we get here? What is our purpose in life? Why do bad things happen to good people? All religious traditions address these questions, helping their followers explain the inexplicable, making the terrible more tolerable, and assuring believers that there is a larger plan. Finally, religion provides the opportunity to come together with others—to share in group activity and identity, form cohesive social organizations, and be part of a congregation of like-minded others.

CONFLICT THEORY These are the (mostly unifying) functions of religion for individuals and for society, but there are also ways in which religion can promote inequality, conflict, and change. From a conflict perspective, the doctrines of the three major **monotheistic** religions—religions that worship one divine figure (Judaism, Christianity, and Islam)—are quite sexist. Orthodox Judaism mandates the separation of men and women in worship and in everyday life; Catholicism and many Protestant sects prohibit women from becoming priests or pastors; traditional, observant Muslim women must keep their bodies completely covered in public. There are very few nonsexist religions, and those with strongly nonsexist values and practices (such as Wicca) are usually marginalized. Some religions have anti-LGBTQ or racist doctrines as well: Some Protestant sects refuse to ordain gay clergy, and until 1978 the Church of Jesus Christ of Latter Day Saints (LDS, or Mormons) believed that people with dark skin were cursed by God and forbade African Americans from marrying in the temple.

Religious organizations have also been agents of social justice and political change. For example, religion has been closely linked to movements for African American rights. The movement for the abolition of slavery was entwined with Christian reformers like the Methodists and Baptists. The civil rights movement in the twentieth century began in Southern Protestant churches and was led by a team of Christian ministers, including the Reverend Martin Luther King Jr. In Africa and Latin America, **liberation theology** has been instrumental in fighting exploitation, oppression, and poverty. Archbishop Óscar Romero of El Salvador used this distinctive combination of Marxism and Christianity to argue against the country's repressive military dictatorship. Though Romero was assassinated while saying Mass in 1980, his legacy lives on in human rights movements all over the world. The Polish labor movement Solidarność, led by Catholic shipyard workers in Gdańsk and supported by the late Pope John Paul II, was the crucible for democratic change in the Eastern bloc in the 1980s. Communist regimes throughout Eastern Europe had restricted religious freedom

MONOTHEISTIC a term describing religions that worship a single divine figure

LIBERATION THEOLOGY a movement within the Catholic Church to understand Christianity from the perspective of the poor and oppressed, with a focus on fighting injustice and labor union organizing for decades; Solidarność helped break down both of those barriers.

From a conflict perspective, then, religion is complex: It can subjugate and oppress at the same time it can liberate. This may help explain Americans' seemingly contradictory approach to religion. While quasi-religious principles are at the core of many of our closely held national ideologies, many Americans also believe that religion should be kept separate from our collective political life.

SYMBOLIC INTERACTIONISM Symbolic interactionist approaches to religion focus on how religious meaning is constructed in interaction and how religion is incorporated into the everyday life of individuals and groups. With its focus on interaction and interpretation, this approach is appropriate for examining religious symbolism, religious communication, and religious practices. For example, one might think that being female in a conservative religion would be oppressive. But interactionist studies show that it is possible to refashion the meaning of religious proclamations about gender in ways that benefit religious women's sense of value and personal power. Orit Avishai's 2008 study of Orthodox Jewish women, for example, shows that they are anything but "doormats"—rather, they are able to construct meaningful ways of "doing religion" that preserve their sense of personal agency and self-determination within the value system of their faith. Similar studies of religious women (Bartkowski and Read 2003; Gallagher 2004; Mahmood 2004) have identified related trends among Muslims and Christians: Despite religious doctrines that appear to prescribe docility, women are able to construct agency, empowerment, and resistance in their everyday interactions by framing their roles as individual choices, their work as central to family and community, and their obedience as a way of triumphing over social and personal problems.

Religion in America

How religious is the American public? That depends on the measures used (Hill and Wood 1999; Theodorou 2015). Sociologists usually define **religiosity** as the consistent and regular practice of religious beliefs, and they gauge religiosity in terms of frequency of attendance at worship services and the importance of religious beliefs to an individual. Researchers have identified two broad categories of religiosity: extrinsic and intrinsic (Allport and Ross 1967). **Extrinsic religiosity** refers to a person's public display of commitment, such as attendance at religious services or other related functions. **Intrinsic religiosity** refers to a person's inner religious life or personal relationship to the divine.

Recent studies have found that 89 percent of Americans believe in God, more than half (53 percent) of Americans say religion is very important to them, and more than a third (36 percent) of Americans say they go to religious services at least once a week (Pew Research Center 2015h; Theodorou 2015). These numbers are somewhat misleading, however, because there are big differences in religious affiliation and participation across demographic groups. Gender, age, race, geographic region, political party, and education are all variables that influence religiosity. For example, nearly one in four American adults and more than a third of Americans under the age of thirty are religiously unaffiliated, the highest percentages ever reported. Whites are more likely to identify as religiously unaffiliated than both blacks and Hispanics, and men are more likely to identify as religiously unaffiliated than women (Public Religion Research Institute 2017). In other words, younger people, whites, and men are less likely to identify as religious than other groups in society. In addition, many Americans switch religions over the course of their lives. Fully a third of American adults identify with a different religion than the one in which they were raised (Pew Research Center 2015a).

There is a moderate level of religious diversity in the United States compared to other countries in the world (Pew Research Center 2015a). The largest group in the United States is composed of Christians (divided into different sects), accounting for about 70 percent of the population. Buddhism, Hinduism, Islam, Judaism, and other religions are also practiced by a portion of the population (see Figure 10.2).

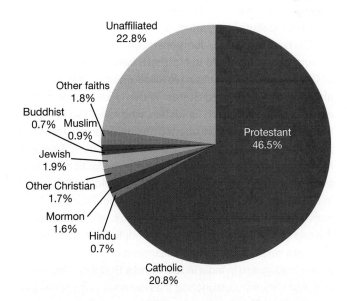

FIGURE 10.2 Religious Composition of the United States

SOURCE: Pew Research Center 2015a.

NOTE: Figures may not add up to 100 percent due to rounding.

GLOBAL PERSPECTIVE
Thou Shalt Not Kill: Religion, Violence, and Terrorism

The history of religious conflict is extensive and convoluted, having been around for as long as humans have worshipped gods. No faith is exempt, and religion has played a significant role in conflicts, from the ancient Israelites and Canaanites around 1200 B.C.E. to al-Qaeda's destruction of New York City's World Trade Center in 2001 to Sri Lanka's civil war between the Hindu Tamil Tigers and the Buddhist Sinhalese, which lasted more than twenty-five years before finally ending in 2009.

Mark Juergensmeyer's book *Terror in the Mind of God* (2003) analyzes the history and meaning of religious violence in general and terrorism in particular. He notes that groups using terror have historically had diverse agendas and motivations, but only within the past thirty years has religion come to play a prominent role in terrorist violence. A more recent study confirms this trend. The number of countries with high or very high levels of social hostilities involving religion reached a peak in 2016. Of the 198 countries studied, some 28 percent had high or very high levels of religion-related social hostility, including violence and harassment. Christians and Muslims, who combined make up more than half of the world's population, faced harassment in the largest number of countries. The harassment of Jews also remained at a ten-year high in 2017 (Pew Research Center 2019).

Juergensmeyer's work uses many examples to illustrate the cross-cultural similarities of religious violence. Within the Christian tradition, Juergensmeyer discusses the Irish Republican Army (IRA) in Northern Ireland and the Army of God, whose adherents have killed doctors who perform abortions, in the United States. Within Judaism, he examines the case of Baruch Goldstein, who killed twenty-eight Muslims in 1994 when he opened fire in the Ibrahim Mosque in the Cave of the Patriarchs, a shrine holy to both Jews and Muslims. Juergensmeyer also investigated Islamic terrorism, such as the first attempt to bomb the World Trade Center in 1993 (done by al-Qaeda–affiliated perpetrators) and the activities of the Palestinian group Hamas, which pioneered the use of suicide bombings in the Middle East. Sikh terrorists were responsible for the assassination of Indira Gandhi by her bodyguard in India in 1984, and a Buddhist Japanese cult, Aum Shinrikyo, launched the notorious sarin nerve gas attack on the Tokyo subway in 1995.

More recently, ISIS or ISIL (Islamic State in Iraq and Syria/Levant), a terrorist group that controls parts of Syria and Iraq and is present in other territories in the Middle East, has asserted its authority to establish an Islamic state and to expand its reach through armed warfare. The group has gained notoriety for using social media as a means of recruitment and to spread its propaganda. The release of videos showing mass executions and beheadings of "infidels," foreign soldiers, aid workers, and journalists has been widely condemned by Muslims and by governments and international organizations worldwide. Sadly, terror in the name of religion persists, and we suspect that you will be able to add new incidents to the list of recent religious violence.

Juergensmeyer argues that the common thread linking religious violence in such disparate traditions and far-flung corners of the world is a reliance on a particular kind of religious perspective. "The social tensions of this moment of history ... cry out for absolute solutions," he says, and in a world that seems increasingly beyond individual control, religious violence offers a way to reassert some kind of power.

The list of wars, conflicts, and terrorist acts inspired or justified by religion is tragically long, extending throughout history and reaching across continents. Religious conflict is not a thing of the past, nor is your country (or your religion, whatever it may be) untouched by it.

Religiously Motivated Violence People comfort one another during a vigil to honor the 22 killed and more than 115 injured during a terrorist attack at an Ariana Grande concert in Manchester, England, in May 2017.

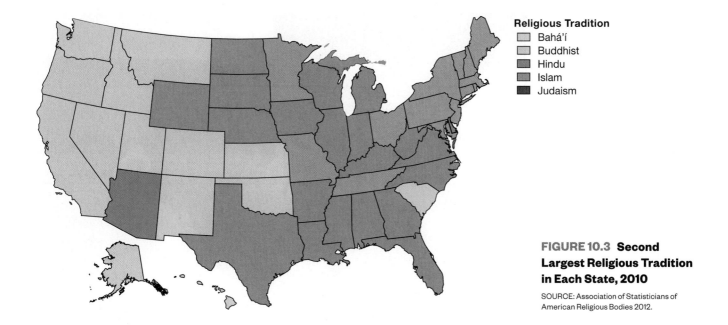

FIGURE 10.3 Second Largest Religious Tradition in Each State, 2010

SOURCE: Association of Statisticians of American Religious Bodies 2012.

While these groups are growing in size, they currently represent less than 10 percent of the U.S. population. Religious diversity varies greatly by state. For instance, New York, New Jersey, Massachusetts, and California are among the most diverse, while Mississippi, Alabama, Arkansas, and South Carolina are among the least.

Religious Trends

Religious identity in the United States has experienced profound shifts in the past few decades. One of those trends is the shrinking white Christian population. Today, less than half of the U.S. population identifies as white and Christian, down from more than eight in ten Americans in 1976. While the Protestant and Catholic populations are both decreasing in size, they are simultaneously experiencing an increase in racial and ethnic diversity. Today, more than a third of the U.S. Catholic population is Hispanic (Public Religion Research Institute 2017). Another trend is toward Fundamentalism, which is not a religion itself but a traditionalist approach that can be applied to any religion. A final trend is away from organized religion toward an "unchurched" spirituality that borrows elements from many traditions but is affiliated with none.

FUNDAMENTALISM Fundamentalist approaches to religious belief and practice have a strong presence both worldwide and in the United States. **Fundamentalism** is a way of understanding and interpreting sacred texts that can be part of any denomination or sect. Fundamentalist Christianity, for example, centers on a strict, sometimes literal, interpretation of the Bible and advocates a return to the historic founding principles of Christianity, arguing that modern approaches to Christianity are corrupt and inauthentic. Other religions have fundamentalist strains as well. Orthodox Judaism, for example, promotes a literal reading of the Torah and other Jewish spiritual and legal tracts. Fundamentalist Islam parallels Jewish and Christian fundamentalisms in that it also requires strict, literal, and traditional interpretations of the Qur'an and other sacred texts. Fundamentalist approaches to all three of these major religions gained popularity in response to the complex social changes of the 1960s and 1970s in the United States and around the world (Patterson 2004) because fundamentalism provides a return to tradition and to simple, unambiguous values and ideologies. Declaring one's loyalty to a traditional religious group that promises certainty in the face of change may be comforting to individuals—but it has broader social and political consequences as well.

Between 1990 and 2001, the number of Americans who described themselves as "fundamentalist Christians" tripled, and the number describing themselves as "evangelical Christians" (a variant of fundamentalist groups) more than quadrupled (Kosmin, Mayer, and Keysar 2001). Fundamentalists who take an **evangelical** approach attempt to convert individuals to their way of worshipping. Currently, about one-quarter of U.S. adults identify as evangelical (Pew Research Center 2015a). Evangelicals see their conversion work as a service to others—an attempt to save souls—and have adopted many media technologies in order to further their cause. Evangelical beliefs can also spill over into other areas of social life, including politics. Evangelical Protestants are less likely to see the separation of church and state

FUNDAMENTALISM the practice of emphasizing literal interpretation of texts and a "return" to a time of greater religious purity; represented by the most conservative group within any religion

EVANGELICAL a term describing conservative Christians who emphasize converting others to their faith

The Changing Christian Population The Protestant and Catholic populations are becoming increasingly diverse. Today, Hispanics make up more than a third of all Catholics in the United States.

as a good thing; they may believe religion plays too little a role in politics rather than too much of one (Pew Research Center 2012).

UNCHURCHED SPIRITUALITY Nearly one-quarter of Americans claim no religious affiliation. This group has roughly tripled in size since the 1990s. Interestingly, the religiously unaffiliated are more likely to be young, male, white, and to live in western and northeastern states (Public Religion Research Institute 2017). Having no religious affiliation, however, does not necessarily mean that a person is an "unbeliever." In fact, only one-quarter of the religiously unaffiliated identify as atheist or agnostic. Conversely, about 16 percent of the unaffiliated identify as religious people. As yet another indicator of our paradoxical attitudes about religion, Americans are increasingly seeking guidance and fulfillment through nontraditional means, with many labeling themselves "spiritual but not religious." This trend involves new definitions of belief and practice, often expressed privately and individually rather than in organized group settings.

UNCHURCHED a term describing those who consider themselves spiritual but not religious and who often adopt aspects of various religious traditions

As noted earlier, some organized religions still include elements of sexism, racial prejudice, homophobia, anti-Semitism, and conformity that turn people off, and so spiritual seekers may utilize a kind of "cafeteria" strategy, choosing elements from various traditions and weaving them together into something unique. This type of **unchurched** spirituality (Fuller 2002), frowned upon by some religious organizations, is becoming increasingly popular, as spiritual seekers mix bits of astrology, alternative healing, twelve-step programs, and even witchcraft with elements of more traditional doctrines.

DATA WORKSHOP

Analyzing Everyday Life

Measures of Religiosity

The term "religiosity" refers to the extent of a person's commitment to a religion. Fully 53 percent of Americans say that religion is very important in their lives, while just 26 percent of Italians, 21 percent of Germans and Spaniards, and 14 percent of the French say the same (Theodorou 2015). Are Americans really that much more religious? Some researchers suspect that these varying results may be caused by the discrepancy between what people say and what they actually do (Holifield 2015; Vedantam 2010). Sociologists debate about how studies are conducted and whether respondents give accurate accounts. Now it is your turn to ask the questions and learn more about the role of religion in everyday life by conducting your own small-scale study.

This Data Workshop asks you to examine the religiosity of a sample group of research participants. You will be designing a questionnaire, conducting interviews, and then analyzing the responses you get. Review the section on interviews in Chapter 2 to help you prepare.

Begin by choosing a population you wish to study. This could be other college students, family members, co-workers, or some other group; remember to ask for their consent to participate. You'll want to gather some basic demographic background from each respondent. Consider such variables as race and ethnicity, class, national background, gender, and/or age of your sample. Because this is a pilot study, the number of people you can interview will necessarily be small. You'll probably have to draw from what is referred to as a "convenience sample" of respondents, rather than using a more scientific random sample.

For this study you will be conducting one-on-one interviews. You will need to record your interviewees' answers, either by taking notes or by digital means. Your questionnaire is likely to have both closed- and open-ended questions. Closed-ended questions typically have yes or no answers, which can be quickly noted, but you can also ask your respondents to elaborate. Open-ended questions, on the other hand, allow respondents to answer in a variety of ways. Whatever kinds of questions you include, you'll need to consider the total length of the interview and just how much talk you can easily transcribe.

To help you with the design of your questionnaire, you can start by choosing from the following list of questions (adapted from Lewis et al. 2001). You may want to modify the order or wording of the questions, or delete some. And definitely try adding some questions of your own. You can create questions that measure people's concrete practice of religion and their abstract sense of what religion means to them. Once you've finalized the questions, you're ready to conduct the interviews.

- Are you affiliated with any religion?

- Are you affiliated with any particular sect or denomination?

- Do you belong to a church, synagogue, temple, or other place of worship?

- How often do you attend religious services?

- Do you participate in other church-related activities?

- How often do you read or study sacred texts or scripture?

- How often do you pray or meditate or engage in some other religious practice?

- How important is your relationship with God [or another religious figure]?

- To what extent is your religious faith important to you?

- To what extent do you consider your religious faith to be an important part of who you are as a person?

- Do you look to your faith as a source of comfort?

- Do you look to your faith as a source of inspiration?

- Do you look to your faith as providing meaning, direction, or purpose in your life?

- Does your faith affect your relationships with other people?

- Does your faith influence your decisions in regard to family, friends, work, school, or other aspects of your life?

- How has your commitment to your religion changed over time?

After gathering data through interviews, you'll want to begin to analyze your findings. Sift through your notes or transcripts and compile the answers to various questions. See what kinds of patterns you can find—similarities, differences, comparisons, and contradictions. What do you think these data reveal about the role of religion in your subjects' lives?

There are two options for completing this Data Workshop:

PREP-PAIR-SHARE Design a questionnaire and conduct interviews with a small sample from your population (perhaps three or four people). Look over their answers, make notes about any preliminary results, and bring them with you to class. Get together with one or two other students and discuss your findings. Look for similarities and differences in both your own findings and those of your fellow discussion group members. See if you can identify any patterns that emerge from the data gathered by the entire group.

DO-IT-YOURSELF Design a questionnaire and conduct interviews with a small group of respondents from your sample (perhaps six or seven people). Write a two- to three-page essay describing the interview research process and analyzing your findings, attaching any notes or transcripts to your paper. How do your findings confirm or refute any hypotheses you might have had before beginning the study? What do your data suggest about the role of religion in society?

IN RELATIONSHIPS
Can a Relationship with God Improve Your GPA?

Sociologists don't usually address questions like "Is there a God?" as these are not questions to which empirical, scientific methods can be applied. It is impossible to prove that God exists (at least by the rules of science)—and it is equally impossible to prove that God doesn't exist. Social scientists can't prove or deny God's existence, but they are interested in studying the important role that religion and spirituality play in our everyday lives. In fact, sociologists have been addressing that question since the discipline first began.

From a sociological perspective, religion serves many functions. It is the basis for community and it permeates many of our social institutions. It is woven into the social fabric and our personal lives. In many cultures, religious participation is a requirement of group membership (Caughey 1984, 1999). On an individual level, members may be expected to demonstrate their belief by engaging in a personal relationship with God (or gods, saints, or spirits). Members are encouraged to work on that relationship through a variety of practices. Prayer and meditation are central to many faiths, and an important means of communicating with a higher power. In many ways a relationship with God resembles our face-to-face interactions in the real world. Many believe that they can talk with and listen to God and that a close relationship brings many of the same kinds of comfort and support that we get from family and friends (Sharp 2010).

Much contemporary research examines religiosity, or the rates at which people engage in religious and spiritual beliefs and practices. Recently, there has been growing concern about the declining rates of religiosity among young people attending college. It raises many questions about what happens over the course of a student's academic life. Does college pose a threat to one's religious or spiritual beliefs, or can it serve to deepen them? Does higher education interfere with a relationship to a higher power or actually make it stronger?

While young Americans as a group are becoming increasingly secular, some researchers have found that there is a renewed engagement with religion and spirituality among undergraduate college students across the United States. College students today can be almost evenly divided into three groups according to their worldviews, with 32 percent identifying as religious, 32 percent identifying as spiritual, and another 28 percent identifying as secular (Kosmin and Keysar 2013). Although some religious behavior (such as attendance at religious services) declines during college, overall spirituality among students increases significantly. According to the 2016 American Freshman survey, 43 percent of first-year college students say that integrating spirituality into their lives is "essential" or "very important" (Eagan et al. 2017).

A major nationwide longitudinal study on spirituality in higher education was recently completed by researchers at UCLA (Astin, Astin, and Lindholm 2010). They collected data from more than 14,500 undergraduates attending 136 colleges and universities. Among the measures they developed were five qualities of spirituality: equanimity (the capacity to maintain a sense of calm centeredness), spiritual quest (the active search for answers to life's big questions), an ethic of caring (a sense of care or compassion for others), charitable involvement (a lifestyle that includes service to others), and an ecumenical worldview (a global perspective that transcends egocentrism and ethnocentrism).

The researchers found that spirituality has a positive effect on traditional college outcomes such as academic performance, psychological well-being, leadership skills, and satisfaction with college. Study-abroad programs, interdisciplinary coursework, service learning, and other forms of civic engagement contribute to spiritual growth by exposing students to new and diverse people, cultures, and ideas. Students also grow in global awareness and caring and are more committed to social justice. Students who are also actively engaged in some form of "inner work," such as self-reflection, contemplation, prayer, or meditation, show the greatest growth in spirituality. Inner work helps facilitate intellectual self-confidence and psychological well-being, and it is even shown to have a positive effect on students' grade point averages.

Spirituality is an important part of many students' lives, and it can also enhance their college experience in many ways. So yes, a relationship with God—if it leads you to spiritual growth—really can improve your GPA.

A Secular Society?

The separation of church and state is a time-honored (and controversial) American principle, established by the founders to preserve freedom of religion—one of the main reasons Europeans came to North America. As important and central as this principle is to American politics, we haven't always been able to maintain it in practice. Consider the dollar bill with the motto "In God We Trust." Witness the 2015 controversy over displaying the Ten Commandments in front of the Oklahoma state capitol building, or President George W. Bush's allocation of federal monies to "faith-based" charitable organizations. Even the school-voucher debate centers on this issue: Should public education funds be used to send children to private schools, many of which are religious? And, of course, specifically Christian values and practices shape the everyday life of all Americans—Christian or not. Whether we are a **secular** society, one that separates church and state, is a complicated issue.

For example, given the Constitution's "establishment clause," it seems we shouldn't be concerned about a president's religious affiliation (or lack thereof). The only official

Separation of Church and State? This six-foot granite monument of the Ten Commandments was removed overnight from the Oklahoma state capitol in 2015 after the Oklahoma Supreme Court ruled that the statue violated the constitution.

eligibility requirements for the job of U.S. president are that the person be at least thirty-five years old, a natural-born U.S. citizen, and a resident in the United States for at least fourteen years. There is no requirement that the president be a man, though all of them have been, or a Christian, but all of them have been. It seems that an unspoken requirement for the presidency includes being a man of Christian faith, with Protestant Christianity being preferred. The only Catholic to hold the office, John F. Kennedy, endured a storm of controversy during his 1960 campaign, when critics feared that America would be ruled by the Pope if Kennedy was elected. Rumors that Barack Obama was Muslim dogged both terms of his presidency.

In both government and private industry, schedules are organized around Christian holidays, with little or no attention paid to religious holidays of other groups. Schools, banks, and government agencies are all closed on Christmas Day, even though this holiday is not observed by more than 15 percent of Americans. Your university's system of vacation periods is likely organized around both Christmas and Easter—important Christian holidays. Universities rarely give days off for Yom Kippur or Passover, two very important Jewish holidays, Eid al-Fitr, the last day of the Muslim holy month of Ramadan, which calls for a variety of special celebrations. This means that Jewish and Muslim students and staff who observe these holidays must go through the hassle of making special arrangements to compensate for classes or meetings missed. They may have to use valuable vacation or sick time or even forfeit credit for exams given on those days. We may take for granted these aspects of our "official" calendars, but they do beg the question: Is every person equally free to practice his or her faith in American society?

Religion: The Micro-Macro Link

Religion is a source of conflict and misunderstanding but also a wellspring of comfort and meaning for many. Whether you are Catholic, Methodist, Jewish, Muslim, or Buddhist, a Mormon or Wiccan or Scientologist, you share common experiences with others in the practice of your religion, no matter how different your belief systems and rituals may be. A sense of meaning, a set of rules and guidelines by which to live your life, a way of explaining the world around you, a feeling of belonging and group identity—sociologists recognize these patterns across religious traditions.

Religion is yet another social institution that helps us see the link between macro-level social structure and micro-level everyday experience. Religious beliefs, practices, and prejudices can inflame global conflicts and resolve them and can shape national political life in observable and unexamined ways. At the same time, religion is integral in the everyday

SECULAR nonreligious; a secular society separates church and state and does not endorse any religion

lives of many Americans who find comfort and kinship in their religious beliefs and practices. "In God We Trust" is the motto for both our nation and many of its people, no matter what their faith.

Closing Comments

All three of the social institutions examined in this chapter—politics, education, and religion—are part of the structure of our society, and they are linked in a variety of ways. For example, state and federal policy decisions about school vouchers affect individual students and neighborhood public schools, and they benefit parochial schools and the religious institutions that run them. Politics, education, religion, and other social institutions influence your everyday life in ways you may not have realized. We hope you have gained greater awareness of how these social institutions shape your life as a member of society—and how you can influence them as well. Your vote changes the political landscape; your role as a student influences the culture of your college and university; your membership in a religious congregation affects the lives of fellow worshippers. Institutions affect individuals, but individuals can influence institutions as well—this is the essence of the sociological imagination and the micro-macro link.

Let's Talk More

1. Were you eligible to vote in the last election? If so, did you? If you didn't vote, why not? The rates for voting-eligible Americans ages eighteen to twenty-four are much lower than for adults over fifty. Why do you think that is?

2. Much of the discussion of the "hidden curriculum" focuses on elementary, middle, and high school education. Do you think this concept also applies to college? Describe the hidden curriculum you've experienced as a college student.

3. There is some debate over how to measure religiosity. Should it be based on how spiritual you feel or on how often you attend religious services? Which way do you think is more valid? Can you think of a better way to understand religiosity?

Let's Explore More

1. **Film** Wilde, Olivia, dir. *Booksmart*. 2019.

2. **Article** Vargas, Nicholas; and Loveland, Matthew. 2011. "Befriending the 'Other': Patterns of Social Ties between the Religious and Non-religious." *Sociological Perspectives*, vol. 54, no. 4: 713–731.

3. **Blog Post** Poling, Jessica. "Culture, Conflict, and Politics." *Everyday Sociology* (blog). April 1, 2019. *http://WWNorton.com/rd/g5Z9A.*

CHAPTER 11

The Economy and Work

The history of one family's jobs and occupations can provide some sociological insight into the development of work and the economy over time. For example, Dr. Ferris's great-grandfathers included a military man in Missouri, a tailor in Texas, and a stonemason and a butcher, both in a tiny mountain village in Lebanon. Despite their geographical and cultural distance from one another, they all were involved in occupations that have existed since ancient times and were still common in the late nineteenth century. Their various jobs represent much of the range of possible jobs in agricultural societies. Some people were skilled craftsmen, some were soldiers, and most others farmed. While

women sometimes helped with the farming or other types of work, their primary tasks were homemaking and child-rearing.

Moving up a generation in the family tree, you can see that in the first half of the twentieth century, Ferris's grandparents were involved in military and service work, with some industrial labor experience as well. One grandfather emigrated from Lebanon to Massachusetts, where he worked in the local brass foundry. This kind of hard physical labor in a stiflingly hot factory was the norm during the industrial era. While he worked at the foundry, his wife secretly worked at a local laundry, hiding her earnings from him. These secret earnings later helped them afford to take a step up in the occupational hierarchy: They bought a restaurant and ran it successfully. Ferris's other grandfather was an army doctor who was stationed all over the United States and the world. His wife followed, making a home with the children wherever they were stationed. She served as a hostess and provided crucial support for her husband's career, which was customary in the early twentieth century.

By the time Ferris's parents started working, in the second half of the twentieth century, her mother was part of a new generation of women who were far more likely than their own mothers to pursue a college education and a career outside the home, even while raising children. Both of Ferris's parents earned advanced degrees (mom an MA and dad a JD); as a writer and an attorney, respectively, they both engaged in service- and knowledge-based work. These areas experienced tremendous growth as the country moved into a postindustrial Information Age economy. Dr. Ferris, as a professor with a PhD, is also a knowledge worker—still just three generations away from great-grandparents without formal educations. Because of historical changes in gendered career expectations, she has enjoyed opportunities her grandmothers and great-grandmothers could never have imagined.

As we move further into the twenty-first century, jobs that were once commonplace in previous time periods may now be disappearing because of automation, outsourcing, or other market changes. Instead, developments in the economic and occupational landscape are likely to create a world in which Dr. Ferris's son, E. J., may hold a job that has not even been invented yet—perhaps in an entirely new, currently unimagined field.

Your own occupational family tree probably holds similar insights into the development of both world and U.S. economic systems over time. And this is no accident—as different as our families and their experiences may be, the patterns and trends in the kinds of work our relatives did can be a rich topic for sociological analysis. Our individual occupational choices are always made within the context of larger economic and social structures, both local and global. In this chapter, we will examine those structures and the experiences of individuals within them.

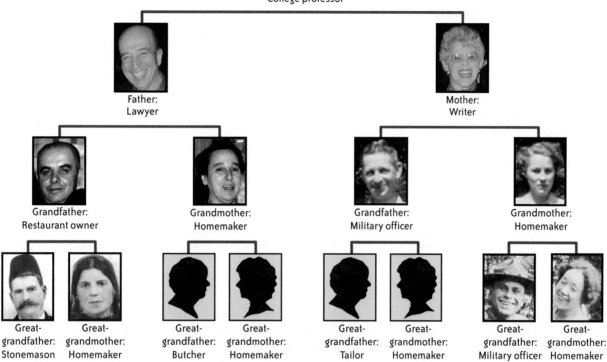

Kerry Ferris:
College professor

Father:
Lawyer

Mother:
Writer

Grandfather:
Restaurant owner

Grandmother:
Homemaker

Grandfather:
Military officer

Grandmother:
Homemaker

Great-
grandfather:
Stonemason

Great-
grandmother:
Homemaker

Great-
grandfather:
Butcher

Great-
grandmother:
Homemaker

Great-
grandfather:
Tailor

Great-
grandmother:
Homemaker

Great-
grandfather:
Military officer

Great-
grandmother:
Homemaker

How to Read This Chapter

After reading this chapter, you should understand why work is a classic topic of sociological inquiry: It is a fulcrum point between the micro and the macro and a link between the individual and the social. You will see the connection between the everyday conditions of your life on the job and the larger structural changes related to history, technology, and the economic system in which you work. We want you to become familiar with the classic and more recent sociological studies in this area and how they have shaped our ways of thinking about the social world of economy and work. You will know something about the past and perhaps have more insight about the future and your place in it.

An economy deals not only with money but also with the production, distribution, and consumption of goods and services within a society. In this chapter, we look at issues regarding the economy, focusing specifically on work, because the economy shapes the types of work available as well as our patterns of working.

WORLD ECONOMIC SYSTEMS

Capitalism, socialism, and communism are political-economic systems found around the world, often in overlapping forms. Each system can be conceived of in an idealized form, but in the real world most nations feature a mix of elements drawn from different systems.

Capitalism

Capitalism is an economic system based on the laws of free market competition, privatization of the means of production, and production for profit. In capitalism's purest form, values for goods and services are derived solely by the market relationship between supply and demand, and the resources necessary for production of goods and services are all privately owned. Owners, or capitalists, must employ workers to make products and perform

CAPITALISM an economic system based on the laws of free market competition, privatization of the means of production, and production for profit

services to generate a profit. Workers sell their labor to owners for a wage. The difference between the cost of production of a product or service and its price is profit, to which the owner is entitled. While capitalism can spur innovation through competition in the marketplace and holds the promise of economic growth, in reality, this economic system also produces some serious social problems.

Capitalism tends to encourage class stratification and increase social inequality. Because owners make profits, they can accumulate wealth. In the United States, an enormous portion of this wealth is concentrated in the hands of the very few. In fact, it is estimated that the top 0.1 percent, which comprises about 160,000 families, currently holds 22 percent of all wealth in the United States (Saez and Zucman 2016). The gap between the ultrarich and the rest of society has widened in the past few decades, in part due to a surge in top incomes. In 2017, the top 10 percent earned more than half of all income (Saez 2019). This unequal distribution of income, coupled with favorable tax laws, has compounded the wealthy's position, helping them to gain not only financially but also in social influence and power.

SOCIALISM an economic system based on the collective ownership of the means of production, collective distribution of goods and services, and government regulation

COMMUNISM a system of government that eliminates private poverty; it is the most extreme form of socialism, because all citizens work for the government and there are no class distinctions

The ideologies of the free market, private property, and profit-seeking motives that define capitalism also shape institutions other than the economy. In capitalist nations, we see increasing privatization of such basic human services as water and transportation systems, health care, housing, and education. Thus, hospitals, public schools, prisons, and even government health and welfare agencies are increasingly taken over by private for-profit firms, whose focus may be more on protecting the bottom line than on serving the public good. Capitalism can also shape our political institutions. Corporations have formed powerful political interest groups with tremendous wealth and clout to fund campaigns and influence lawmakers.

Under capitalism, workers must sell their labor to capitalists for a wage. This sets up a power dynamic ripe for exploitation and puts workers in a structural position that makes it hard for them to ever get ahead financially. Workers also often lack job security. They are constantly pushed to be productive and efficient or else suffer reduced wages, decreased social welfare services such as health insurance and retirement, downsizing, and layoffs. Until recently, under the capitalist system in the United States, disgruntled workers could withhold their labor by striking. Over the last several decades the size and influence of labor unions have drastically declined, leaving many workers more vulnerable and less secure in their jobs. Now, under a transnational capitalist system, firms experiencing strikes may decide to move their operations overseas to countries where few workers have the right to strike.

A capitalist economy encourages efficiency through technological innovation, expansion of markets, and reduction of production costs. Thus, owners, in their efforts to seek efficiency, often seek to replace workers with new technologies, reduce social welfare spending, and cut labor costs. Therefore, workers are responsible for maintaining their own competitiveness. They must seek an education and/or skills to compete for jobs and maintain their competency over their working lifetimes. However, firms must also increase their competitiveness. They may move production operations to overseas sites where they can take advantage of deregulated environments and cheap labor costs.

Socialism

Socialism is an economic system based on collective ownership of the means of production, collective distribution of goods and services, and government regulation of the economy. Under socialism, there are no private for-profit transactions. In its purest form, socialism seeks to meet the basic needs of all citizens rather than encouraging profits for some individuals over others.

In a socialist system, the government rather than individuals owns—or at least regulates the ownership of—all businesses, farms, and factories, and profits are redistributed to the collective citizenry. This system encourages a collectivist work ethic, with individuals theoretically working for the common good of all citizens. Citizens have access to such resources as health care, food, housing, and other social services to meet their basic needs. Unlike with capitalism, these services are an entitlement of all people, not just those who can afford them.

In socialism, a central and usually highly bureaucratic government regulates all aspects of the economy—ownership of resources and means of production, regulation of lending policies, interest rates, and currency values—as well as setting labor policies regarding such issues as parental leave, retirement, and the right to strike. Such intense regulation of the economy should reduce class inequalities and extreme poverty. In **communism**, the most extreme form of socialism, the government owns everything and all citizens work for the government and are considered equal, with no class distinctions. Socialism and communism, like capitalism, are theoretical or ideal types. Thus, no nations are purely socialist or communist. Even communist countries like Cuba and China are increasingly incorporating capitalist ideologies into their regimes.

Under socialism, workers are not at risk of extreme poverty and class division as they might be within a capitalist society. They are not as vulnerable as capitalist workers to being replaced by new technological innovations or the

ON THE JOB
Internships: Free Menial Labor or a Leg Up?

Someone mentions an internship, and you think...what? Bored college students making coffee for the boss? Beleaguered production assistants on a film set? Monica Lewinsky in the White House? Whatever your impression, the fact is internships are an increasingly important part of the college experience. According to the National Association of Colleges and Employers (2017), more than 60 percent of the class of 2017 interned during their undergraduate careers. At worst, the hapless intern may get really good at adding toner to the copier and not much else or, conversely, the employer may engage in exploitative practices in which student interns are overworked and quite often unpaid. At best, however, an internship can benefit both the intern and the company and may be useful in the long run for everyone involved.

Depending on where you're enrolled, you may be able to arrange an internship through your college or university and receive academic credit, or you may have to set up a non-academic internship that leaves out the school altogether. Organizations of all kinds—corporate, public, nonprofit, and others—look for college students to fill some of their employment needs. Of course, there's always the possibility that the work you're assigned as an intern will be mind-numbing or pointless, or that you'll have to work long hours, and oftentimes forgo a paycheck! There is a difference, however, in who gets what kinds of positions. Typically men and students from higher-income backgrounds are more likely to obtain paid internships than are women and lower-income students (Gardner 2011).

Many might ask, why bother with an internship? For starters, an internship may help you decide what you want to be—or don't want to be—when you graduate. After interning in a state's attorney's office, you may decide that being a lawyer isn't everything you thought it would be and you'd like to work with crime victims in a social service capacity instead. Even if you are sure about your future career path, you may want to consider branching out in the internships you apply for. You'll gain diverse skills and experience and be exposed to careers you might like just as much. Most Americans don't remain in the same job for their entire working lives, so keeping your options open during college isn't such a bad idea. Even if you decide you'd prefer not to work for that corporation or in that field, the contacts you develop may help you find another position. These are people who are already established in the profession, and a good reference is always valuable when you're in the job market.

An internship on your résumé is also likely to make you a more attractive job candidate. Many organizations turn first to their own interns when hiring. The entire internship can, in some respects, be viewed as an extended job interview. Even if your experience doesn't deal directly with the job you're applying for, having completed an internship demonstrates to potential employers your ability to work hard and manage your time. Here, too, the benefits of a paid internship go beyond just receiving a paycheck. According to the results of a survey on the graduating class of 2019 by the National Association of Colleges and Employers (2019), students who worked in paid internships were more likely to receive full-time job offers than students who completed unpaid internships. More than 66 percent of students who had a paid internship were offered jobs, compared to just 44 percent of students who had unpaid internships. Students who worked in paid internships were also offered a higher median starting salary than their peers with unpaid internships.

Internships work out well for employers, too—some say too well. At the very least, they're getting cheap (and often free) labor. Critics have raised questions about the value of unpaid internships, further intensifying debates regarding the exploitation of student workers (Perlin 2011, 2012). Recently, unpaid internships made headlines after unpaid interns sued several high-profile companies, including NBC Universal, Fox Searchlight, Sony, and Condé Nast. The lawsuits claimed that the companies violated the two requirements for unpaid workers, as set by the U.S. Department of Labor: Interns must be assigned different work than paid employees and must receive training in an educational environment.

Enlightened organizations are mindful of the many other benefits they reap when employing interns, paid and unpaid. They are often rewarded with a highly educated or highly trained workforce. Taking on young workers can also help a company stay connected to younger and more diverse populations and may provide them with some new perspectives and ideas. Organizations also realize that providing internships can create goodwill—from the students who intern with them, from the universities through which the internships are organized, and even from the general public.

transnational movement of capital. However, they also do not enjoy the same consumption patterns that capitalist economies encourage. Socialism cannot provide capitalism's middle-class luxuries. Though class division is reduced, it is still present. Many socialist nations have political elites who enjoy a higher class of living than workers, and urban workers often benefit from having closer access to resources than rural workers. Further, reduction of class inequalities does not guarantee a reduction in other types of inequalities, such as racism, sexism, and ageism.

The U.S. Economy

To understand the political economy of various nations, think of capitalism and socialism as opposite ends of a continuum, with nations placed along its span as being more capitalist or more socialist. The United States would undoubtedly lie closer to the capitalist side than a country like Sweden would, but even U.S. capitalism is not a pure form.

While the United States is a capitalist nation, it also has socialist elements. Although capitalist businesses are privately owned, many benefit from government subsidies—grants, tax incentives, and special contracts. This is often referred to as "corporate welfare." In pure capitalism, such support would not exist. The U.S. government intervenes in the economy in other ways as well. Agencies such as the Federal Reserve Board often manipulate interest rates to stimulate the economy and control inflation. The Emergency Economic Stabilization Act of 2008 (also referred to as the "bailout bill") funneled more than $700 billion in government funds into banks, insurance companies, and other struggling private corporations in order to prop up the U.S. economy. Such government interventions constitute forms of socialism.

If the United States were purely capitalist, such institutions as education and health care would all be privately owned. However, most schools and many universities are publicly owned and operated. Even private universities get government monies, usually in the form of grants and federal financial aid. Health care is a trickier example, as much change is taking place in this arena. Medicare and Medicaid are long-standing federal programs that provide subsidized health care for the elderly and the poor. The Affordable Care Act ushered in more federally mandated and subsidized health-care coverage for millions of Americans. But many individuals and their employers still buy health insurance from for-profit insurers, and hospitals are often run for profit as well.

The government also spends millions of dollars annually for other general assistance or public aid programs for low-income families, including the Supplemental Nutrition Assistance Program (or SNAP—previously known as food stamps) and Temporary Assistance to Needy Families (TANF), often referred to as "entitlements." Thus, public

services are available to meet some of the basic needs of the poor, elderly, and disabled; current and former armed forces personnel; and expectant mothers, infants, and children. Our Social Security system, though partially funded through payroll taxes, is a public system providing retirement, survivorship, and disability benefits to eligible Americans. And even the wealthiest among us get public subsidies in the form of tax deductions—for home ownership, investments, inheritances, and for sheltering monies in corporations. Debates continue about whether these services satisfactorily meet the needs of low-income Americans and whether it's the government's responsibility to provide them. Conservative politicians who periodically accuse their rivals of "socialist" tendencies may need to be reminded that things they enjoy every day—like streetlights and highway maintenance, police protection and firefighters, libraries and public schools—are all part of a system of centrally funded and regulated services they likely would not want to do without.

In theory, capitalism and socialism are opposites. In reality, there is no pure form of either capitalism or socialism; rather, nations typically have some features of both economic systems. Each system represents a different political ideology and economic reality for the people and workers in its economy. Economic systems evolve and change over time, and with them, the institution of work.

THE NATURE OF WORK

Historical and technological changes leading to the Agricultural, Industrial, and Information Revolutions fundamentally changed societies across several centuries. Societies have also adopted economic systems—capitalist, socialist, or a combination of both—that influence the types of work available, as well as our patterns of working.

The Agricultural Revolution and Agricultural Work Today

Perhaps the earliest form of economy in North America was found in pre-sixteenth-century Native American societies. An estimated 2 million to 10 million indigenous people inhabited the continent prior to colonization by Europeans. Some were hunting-and-gathering societies, which had to be highly mobile, relocating for food and weather conditions. In these societies, the division of labor revolved around survival, with the men hunting animals or foraging for plant sources of food, and the women, children, and elderly doing the cooking, sewing, and other tasks at the campsite. Others were horticultural societies based on the domestication of animals, farming, and generating a surplus of resources. They had more permanent settlements and a greater diversification of labor because different types of workers, such as farmers, craftspeople, and traders, were all necessary to the economy.

The **Agricultural Revolution** continued some of the social and economic trends that began with horticultural societies. Better farming and ranching techniques allowed larger groups to thrive and remain in one location for longer periods of time. Agricultural work involves farming in groups, families, or communities to grow the food and materials necessary for sustenance. Instead of buying flour at a store, for example, you would sow, maintain, grow, and harvest wheat, and mill your own flour to then cook with in your home. This was in addition to weaving fabrics and caring for livestock. The Agricultural Revolution lasted for many centuries, but in the eighteenth century, food production was greatly increased by new innovations in farming and animal husbandry. Among those developments were the invention of new types of plows and mechanized seed spreaders, new techniques of crop rotation and irrigation, and advancements in the selective breeding of livestock.

Anthropologists have contended that the shift from hunting and gathering to agricultural work increased the amount of labor individuals had to perform daily, which led to divisions of labor, and, eventually, to slave labor. In the agricultural economy that flourished in the early United States, large plantation owners, in order to accumulate wealth from cotton or sugar-cane crops, depended on cheap, plentiful labor. This division of labor fell largely along race, gender, and class lines (Amott and Matthaei 1996). In the pre–Civil War era, many of the plantations of the South that were owned by whites were farmed by black slaves brought from Africa (Davis 2001). Slave labor was essentially free, which increased owners' profits. Poor white people sometimes owned small farms or worked as tenant farmers or sharecroppers. White men were usually owners of land and small businesses, while white women were usually household managers. Though slavery was abolished in the United States in 1865, in other parts of the world today, agricultural work still utilizes forced labor.

While agricultural work continues to be a large part of the U.S. and global labor market today, it looks significantly different as a result of industrial and postindustrial changes. For example, farmers now utilize technologies such as crop rotation, irrigation, mass production, and transportation. These elements are part of what is termed the "agribusiness" system, a marriage of agriculture and business, which refers to an integrated and interdependent system that includes the actual labor of farming as well as developing and selling farm equipment, food processing, marketing, and sales. Agricultural work, which was once a family or small community endeavor, is becoming less and less common as large agribusiness corporations such as DowDuPont, and Monsanto are able to push smaller farms out of the market. Agricultural work is also becoming increasingly stratified, with numerous hierarchical positions ranging from contract fieldworkers to farm executives (Holmes 2011).

AGRICULTURAL REVOLUTION the social and economic changes, including population increases, that followed from the domestication of plants and animals and the gradually increasing efficiency of food production

INDUSTRIAL REVOLUTION the rapid transformation of social life resulting from the technological and economic developments that began with the assembly line, steam power, and urbanization

The Industrial Revolution and Industrial Work Today

The **Industrial Revolution** was a time of rapid technological, social, and economic change that almost completely transformed life in modern times—a radical break from the past, disrupting social patterns that had been relatively stable for centuries. The Industrial Revolution began in England with the invention of the steam engine in 1769, which was first used to power machinery, initially for the manufacture of textiles. By the end of the eighteenth century, steam-powered factories had spread to the United States and other nations (Hughes and Cain 1994). With more mechanized machinery such as the cotton gin, the American economy moved from manual labor to machine manufacturing. Even farming would change, with the introduction of mechanical plows and reapers. The nineteenth century brought steam-powered ships and railways, the internal combustion engine, electrical power generation, and new tools and appliances. By the end of the 1800s, the modern corporation had emerged—a business that could manage a range of activities across geographic regions.

The spread of industrialism in the eighteenth and nineteenth centuries created "work" in the modern sense. Before the Industrial Revolution, most of the population engaged

Slaves at Work in the Field The agricultural economy in the South depended on slave labor to grow cotton and tobacco.

in agriculture, and the production of goods was organized around the household or small craft shops. Employment in manufacturing meant that people no longer worked in or around their homes as artisans or craftsmen but instead went off into the industrial districts of large cities to work in factories. Wage labor replaced the household subsistence model of the agricultural society. Wage labor took place in factories, and then wages were used to buy goods (like food and clothing) that had previously been produced at home.

With the shift to a manufacturing economy, vast numbers of people migrated into cities from rural areas in search of work. There was a great influx of immigrants, primarily from Europe, who provided a steady source of cheap, easily exploitable labor. Densely populated neighborhoods sprang up to accommodate the masses, housing was often substandard, such as tenement apartments in crowded ghettos with no land or greenspace, and many families lived in poverty. At the same time, discoveries in science and medicine around this time led to increased life expectancy and decreased infant mortality. Many more people had access to dependable food and water sources and some form of health care. Laws giving some protections to workers, such as child labor reforms, also emerged as an important aspect of the overall health of working populations.

The industrial economy helped create robust growth in the United States for many decades (with periodic downturns such as the Great Depression in the 1930s and the more recent recessions of the 1980s and 2000s). Plentiful manufacturing and industrial jobs meant that high school graduates could enter the job market making a good wage. They could buy houses and raise families with their manufacturing paychecks and become solid members of the middle class.

The industrial economy increased stratification of the workforce along class, race, and gender lines (Amott and Matthaei 1996). Wealthy white families owned the means of production, such as factories, energy sources, or land, and the financial institutions that supported the accumulation of wealth; the men were in the workplace, while the women ran the household. A middle class of educated, skilled workers emerged, often in managerial professions. Working-class white men now earned a "family wage" at the factory, while women worked without pay in the home. But for families that needed more than one income, women and even children joined the workforce. Poor women, immigrant women, and women of color increasingly performed domestic labor in white women's households (Amott and Matthaei 1996). But they also worked at factory jobs that were reserved for women, such as millwork and sewing in textile factories, for meager wages and under dangerous conditions.

The industrial economy revolved around the mass production of goods, and as a result, workers were often exploited and exposed to unsuitable working conditions. The use of the assembly line, for example, in which parts were added to a product in sequential order, aided the mass production of goods, but often at the expense of workers' well-being. In contrast to the artisan mode, in which one worker or a team of workers would produce an item in its entirety from start to finish, on an assembly line each worker would do one or two specific tasks over and over again. Many workers disliked the assembly line because they never had the satisfaction of seeing the finished product, and they were also frustrated with the unsafe, exhausting working conditions.

The theories of Karl Marx are most often associated with the spread of industrialization, the capitalist economies and class systems that it produced, and the workers who toiled in factories. According to Marx, the powerful have always

Women Working in a Shoe Factory Many factory jobs that were reserved for women paid meager wages and required working under dangerous conditions.

exploited workers. As he asserted in *The Communist Manifesto,* "oppressor and oppressed stood in constant opposition to one another" in a perpetual struggle for economic resources, as all history "is the history of class struggles" (Marx 2001, p. 245). The proletariat, or workers, in an industrial economy possess only one thing of economic value, and that is their time, which they sell to capitalists who own the means of production. Workers are paid for their time and labor, but their wages do not represent the full profit from the sale of the goods they produce. The sale of the goods not only covers the workers' wages and the expenses of running the factory but also generates additional revenue or "surplus value," which then belongs to the owner.

Marx believed that workers in capitalist societies experienced **alienation** in many ways as a result of that system. Workers are alienated, Marx argued, because they are paid for their labor but do not own the things they produce. Unlike the farmers and craft workers of prior eras in traditional, precapitalist societies, industrial workers feel no sense of personal satisfaction, joy, or fulfillment in producing goods that are owned and controlled by someone else; instead, work is merely a means of making a living. The worker is alienated from other people, "the alienation of man from man," as Marx called it. Instead of cooperating, workers are forced to compete for scarce jobs and resources, turning other workers into rivals rather than partners. Workers are also alienated from the owners, as they recognize work as "an activity that is under the domination, oppression, and yoke of another man" (Marx 2001, p. 92). Finally, Marx argued, the worker is alienated from his own basic humanity as a result of his placement in the class system.

Marx was describing work in the industrial era of the nineteenth century, but his analyses can apply to today's industrial workers as well. While some firms may allow workers greater autonomy, dignity, and a personal stake in the process and in the goods they produce, many workers still toil in the same conditions of exploitation, alienation, and class struggle that Marx thought needed to change.

The Information Revolution and Postindustrial Work Today

The **Information Revolution** is the most recent of the historical and technological changes that have led to new economic and working conditions in the United States and around the world. Also referred to as the Digital Revolution, Digital Age, or Postindustrial Age, it is expected to bring about as dramatic a transformation of society as the revolutions that preceded it (Castells 2000). We may not recognize how truly radical this change is, partly because we are at the beginning of a revolution that will continue to evolve over our lifetimes. Manufacturing is becoming more automated (using robots instead of people), and jobs are moving "offshore" to countries where labor is cheaper. Manufacturing jobs in the United States have plummeted, with about 7.5 million jobs lost since 1980 (Hernandez 2018; Wilson 2014). Even in the states with the highest proportion of manufacturing jobs (Indiana, Wisconsin, Michigan, and Iowa), the percentages range from only 13 percent to 17 percent (Center for Manufacturing Research 2016).

The Information Revolution began in the 1970s with the development of the microchip or microprocessor used in computers and other electronic devices. When computers were coupled with the introduction of the Internet in the early 1990s and became more affordable, they were soon widely used. Other technologies associated with the Information Revolution include computer networking and all types of digital media, satellite and cable broadcasting, and telecommunications. These technologies have become a ubiquitous part of everyday life in the twenty-first century.

The Information Revolution brought a profound shift from an economy based on the production of goods to one based on the production of knowledge and services (Castells 2000). Of course, the United States is still involved in agriculture and manufacturing, but these are shrinking parts of our economy. According to the Department of Labor, the U.S. economy currently consists of ten "supersectors" (or areas in which people work) that fall under two broad categories: goods-producing industries and service-providing industries (U.S. Bureau of Labor Statistics 2015b). These supersectors include construction; education and health services; financial activities; information; leisure and hospitality; manufacturing; natural resources and mining; other services; professional and business services; and trade, transportation, and utilities. Fully two-thirds of these supersectors deal in knowledge or service work, but these two kinds of workers have very different experiences on the job.

ALIENATION the sense of dissatisfaction the modern worker feels as a result of producing goods that are owned and controlled by someone else

INFORMATION REVOLUTION the recent social revolution made possible by the development of the microchip in the 1970s, which brought about vast improvements in the ability to manage information

SERVICE WORK work that involves providing a service to businesses or individual clients, customers, or consumers rather than manufacturing goods

SERVICE WORK The service sector, or service industry, has experienced tremendous growth in the postindustrial economy and is now the dominant form of employment. **Service work** is done by anyone who provides a service to businesses or individual clients. Services may entail the distribution or sale of goods from producer to consumer (wholesaling and retailing), transformation of goods in the process of delivering them (the restaurant business), or no goods at all (massage therapy, housecleaning). Service work can be found in

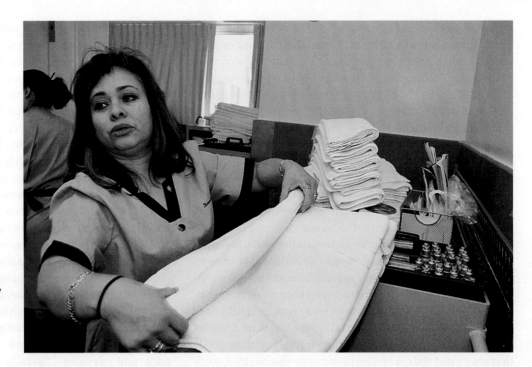

Nickel and Dimed Barbara Ehrenreich found that many service workers barely scrape by, working long hours for minimum wage and no benefits. Because many service workers live paycheck to paycheck, they often have trouble asserting their rights or taking time off for illnesses because of fear of losing their jobs.

such industries as banking, consulting, education, entertainment, health care, insurance, investment, legal services, leisure, news media, restaurants (including fast food), retail, tourism, and transportation.

All service work has a focus on serving and interacting with people. It often involves direct contact with clients, customers, patients, or students by those rendering the service, whether they are waiters, cashiers, nurses, doctors, teachers, or receptionists. In service work, situations arise when the worker's concerns, standards, and expectations conflict with those of clients. For example, you have a toothache, but the dentist doesn't have an open appointment until tomorrow. It's not the dentist who has to give you the bad news but the receptionist who must try to convince you to wait until then. At the same time, service workers are subject to the scrutiny and critique of a manager or supervisor, so in addition to the potential clash between workers and clients, there are also issues of autonomy and control over their work. This can create distinctive tensions in service work interactions, and power relationships both subtle and more obvious are clearly present in this type of work.

Some service work pays well, particularly at the management and executive levels, and in certain fields, such as banking, entertainment, and law; but much service sector employment is unstable, part-time or temporary, low paying, and often without such benefits as health care or retirement. Women, persons of color, and the poor are likely to be found in the service sector, thus perpetuating a lower-class status among those holding such positions (Fisher 2015).

One case study provides a classic—and highly personal—analysis of service work. Barbara Ehrenreich explored some of the issues of power and work in her book *Nickel and Dimed: On (Not) Getting By in America* (2001). As research for the book, Ehrenreich took minimum-wage service jobs in three different cities—as a waitress in Florida, a hotel maid in Maine, and a Walmart employee in Minnesota—and experienced the difficulties of trying to make ends meet and maintain her self-respect in low-wage service positions.

Ehrenreich found that service workers in these types of jobs are likely to be exploited in a number of ways. First, the low wages, lack of benefits, and grueling hours make it difficult to pay even the most basic bills. She discovered this herself when she couldn't scrape up enough money for a deposit on an apartment and ended up living in a sleazy hotel and getting her dinner from the local charity's food pantry. Her co-workers lived in flophouses, in their cars, or in small apartments crowded with family, friends, and strangers, and one ate nothing but a small bag of Doritos every day for lunch. They were fired for asserting their rights or for getting ill or injured, and they developed chronic health problems because of the stress and poor conditions under which they labored. And yet, they couldn't stop—they were all reliant on the next paycheck to get by (or not get by, as Ehrenreich argues), and so they had to endure abuse, exploitation, and all sorts of risks for the tenuous security of serving, scrubbing, and selling. Ehrenreich argues that there's no way to "make it" under these circumstances, and her experiences illustrate this argument with chilling clarity.

Inequalities of power in service work have many sources—gender, race, age, and immigration status—and those with greater power (clients, managers) may take advantage without even realizing it. Ehrenreich reminds us that even in "respectable" forms of service work, exploitation is common. What about jobs that are illegal—such as prostitution or the work of undocumented farm laborers? These workers lack the legal protections that even Walmart employees or chain restaurant waitstaff have access to, and they may be subject to prosecution and punishment merely for doing their jobs.

KNOWLEDGE WORK **Knowledge work** is done by anyone who works primarily with information or who develops and uses knowledge in the workplace (Drucker 2003; Loo 2017). For such workers, information and knowledge are both the raw material and the product of their labor. Knowledge workers create value in the economy through their ideas, creativity, judgments, analyses, designs, and innovations. Some examples of knowledge work include advertising, engineering, marketing, product development, urban planning, and web design. Many knowledge workers are employed in traditional fields as teachers, accountants, lawyers, or scientists, but knowledge work also includes people who work in newer areas such as wireless communications, network systems analysis, computer programming, software development, account management, information security, and database administration.

In the twenty-first century, knowledge or information work is increasingly common, while manual labor is increasingly rare (Adelstein 2011). The massive changes wrought by information technologies—sometimes referred to as the "new economy"—have transformed the nature of work again in ways that are not yet fully understood (Loo 2017). While many of these technologies purport to increase productivity and save time, the average worker is now working more hours in a week than their predecessor in the pre–Information Age workplace.

A look at telecommuting reveals more about the nature of knowledge work. More and more workers are doing telework, or **telecommuting**. They stay at home rather than commute to the office, and they are connected to their workplace through communications technology. According to Gallup, fully 43 percent of workers spend at least some of their time working remotely, meaning in a location different from that of their co-workers, including 57 percent of workers in computer and information systems and 48 percent of those working in the arts, design, entertainment, and the media (Gallup 2017).

Supporters claim that telecommuting has many benefits for the worker, the business, and society at large. Employees get flexible work schedules. Traffic delays, parking problems, and time wasted commuting don't exist for the telecommuter. Businesses get increased productivity and fewer sick days when they allow employees to telecommute. In traditional office environments, the only measure of employee value is the number of hours present in the office, regardless of

what gets done, whereas telecommuters must demonstrate their accomplishments more concretely. According to studies, telecommuting decreases workplace distractions and boosts worker productivity; telecommuters often work longer hours and are more efficient than their in-office peers and co-workers (Wisenberg Brin 2013). Telecommuting has also made it easier for a wider range of employees to participate in the workforce; this helps many groups, including single parents, seniors, or workers with disabilities, stay employed full-time (Tugend 2014).

As technology develops, debates remain about the positive and negative aspects of physically and geographically separating workers from one another. Some suggest that new technologies will actually increase the need for face-to-face contact and tightly knit workplaces. For example, workers who write code for computer software can do so anywhere they have a computer and instantly send the results to those who will package and market the software, but software companies are still the most geographically concentrated of any industry. The Internet giant Google, one of the world's largest publicly traded companies, refers to its home office in Mountain View, California, as "the Googleplex" and has gone to great lengths to make it an appealing place for employees to work. The campuslike atmosphere has beautiful grounds, interesting art and architecture, delicious meals served in friendly surroundings,

> **KNOWLEDGE WORK** work that primarily deals with information; producing value in the economy through ideas, judgments, analyses, designs, or innovations
>
> **TELECOMMUTING** working from home while staying connected to the office through communications technology

Pied Piper The coders on HBO's *Silicon Valley* are examples of knowledge workers. Information technology has ushered in a new economy dominated by knowledge work.

and volleyball nets for impromptu games. They do this precisely because the company still wants its workers together at the same location in order to foster greater creativity and group cohesion.

Google is just one of many tech firms that make up California's "Silicon Valley"; Apple, Intel, Facebook, HP, Oracle, PayPal, eBay, Netflix, Adobe, Yahoo, Twitter, Fitbit, Pandora, Shutterfly, Yelp, and Square are also based there. In the Information Age, more and more work requires the creative manipulation of knowledge, and for this workers need to brainstorm and share ideas in more interactive ways than technology currently allows. The tech industry suggests that even when work can be done anywhere, there will still be a real need to bring people together, at least some of the time.

The rise of new technologies may roll back many of the original effects of the Industrial Revolution. Manufacturing made it necessary for many people to work at the same location, causing the growth of cities and the decline of rural and small-town populations. However, with new technologies that let people work from anywhere, perhaps telecommuting will cause cities to shrink again as more people will be able to live without reference to the company that employs them. Small towns are now offering an attractive alternative to outsourcing. High-tech jobs are beginning to relocate to rural areas, where companies are finding it cheaper to do business and more attractive for their employees (Kotkin 2018). It's possible that information technology may one day reunite the worlds of work and home that the Industrial Revolution tore asunder.

DATA WORKSHOP

Analyzing Media and Pop Culture

The World of Work and Workers as Seen on TV

FBI agent, judge, nurse, salesperson, newscaster, football coach, city council member, firefighter, private investigator, district attorney, forensics expert, restaurant server, police officer, interior designer, school principal, military officer—these are just some of the jobs of characters you'd find on television's most popular dramas and sitcoms. As one of the most powerful sources of socialization in the lives of young people, television may contribute to our attitudes and ideas about the working world. Some jobs are totally absent from the TV landscape, some are shown as merely the butt of jokes, and others are made to seem impossibly hip, glamorous, and exciting. How real is any of it? Do the jobs on TV

accurately reflect those jobs in real life? How do TV jobs compare with those of your family, friends, or acquaintances? What kinds of work-related issues do characters on television experience compared to those of real people in those same types of jobs or industries? What are the underlying messages of the depictions of work and workers on TV?

Sociologists who are interested in the media often ask such questions when comparing media content to the real world. This Data Workshop asks you to look at how fictionalized TV dramas and sitcoms portray jobs and the realities of working life. Your instructor might want you to do both of the exercises, or just one of the two. For either exercise you will be using existing sources and doing a content analysis. Refer to Chapter 2 for a refresher on this research method.

EXERCISE ONE: WORKING CONDITIONS AND TV JOBS
Examine the modern workplace as depicted on a current TV drama or sitcom. You'll want to take notes as you view one episode of the program, and you may need multiple viewings to collect your data. Look at the way characters perform their jobs in the show. Often workers are shown socializing or engaging in other kinds of personal activities while on the job. How much real work gets done? And when characters are actually working, what aspects of that work are featured during the program? Often we see only the most unusual or glamorous aspects of work, while the day-to-day routine or behind-the-scenes aspects rarely appear. Another dimension is how characters relate to their jobs and to their co-workers. Are they happy and fulfilled by the work they do? Do they complain about work or experience other kinds of troubles with their jobs? How are power and resistance exercised in the workplace? Discuss your findings and assess the extent to which you believe the programs accurately reflect these professions in real life.

EXERCISE TWO: MAKING A LIVING ON TV
Examine the modern worker as depicted on a current TV drama or sitcom. View an episode of your chosen program and do a content analysis. Take written notes and describe in as much detail as possible the characters' work and lifestyles to answer the following prompts. What kinds of lessons do we learn about work and money from a TV show? We rarely get much information about how characters have gotten their jobs or what kind of training or experience got them to their positions. We also know very little about how hard they work or what they get paid. TV characters often seem to live extravagant lifestyles with little relationship between actual

Working in Prime Time How do television shows like *Brooklyn Nine-Nine* (left) and *Workaholics* (right) represent working life?

salaries and what they can afford to buy. Provide examples from the show and discuss the characters' standard of living. Could real people working comparable jobs afford the same lifestyle that the television characters seem to enjoy? Finally, how do television characters influence our own career goals and aspirations?

There are two options for completing this Data Workshop:

PREP-PAIR-SHARE Complete one or both of the exercises provided and follow the instructions as outlined. Bring your notes to class and get together with one or two students to discuss. (Your instructor may organize groups according to which exercises were completed.) Compare your findings with those of other members of the group. What conclusions do you share?

DO-IT-YOURSELF Choose one of the exercises provided (or your instructor may assign a specific exercise) and follow the instructions as outlined. Write a three- to four-page essay analyzing your findings. Make sure to attach your notes to the paper.

RESISTANCE STRATEGIES: HOW WORKERS COPE

Individuals and groups cope with their working conditions in a variety of ways, called **resistance strategies**. These are tactics that let workers take back a degree of control over the conditions of their labor and feel that they have some sense of autonomy even in the face of dehumanizing, alienating constraints imposed by the terms and demands of their employment.

Individual resistance can range from the fairly benign, such as using work time to surf the web, to the truly dangerous, such as sabotaging the assembly line. More often,

individual resistance may be simply personalizing the workspace with photos or daydreaming on the job as a type of escape. Collective forms of resistance that seek solutions to shared workplace problems include union organizing and membership, strikes, walkouts, and work stoppages.

This discussion begins with an examination of individual resistance strategies within service work. We bring Max Weber's theory of bureaucracy into the present to see how workers today are coping with the constraints of those organizations. Last, we look at collective resistance strategies—union organization, both past and present.

Individual Resistance: Handling Bureaucracy

Bureaucratic organizations are found in almost every sector of the economy. In Weber's theory of bureaucracies, he highlighted the rational, impersonal, and coldly efficient nature of this form of social organization (refer to Chapter 5 for a review). Workers in highly bureaucratic organizations often feel the lack of autonomy—the ability to direct one's individual destiny and have the power to control the conditions of one's labor—in their everyday work lives. In highly structured, rule-bound, and depersonalized environments, workers' daily tasks are structured by external forces; for example, the pace of the assembly line is decided for them and they cannot slow it down or speed it up if they need to take a break or want to finish work early.

> **RESISTANCE STRATEGIES** ways that workers express discontent with their jobs and try to reclaim control of the conditions of their labor

In many corporate settings, employees at all levels are under various types of surveillance: Electronic key cards monitor their comings and goings, cameras record their activities, computer transactions are screened, and phone calls are recorded. In retail sales, workers' interactions with customers are often scripted, so that even what they say to others is outside their control. Not only is there a lack of autonomy, but there is also a lack of individuality in these workplaces. Workers are treated more like robots than people. Unlike a robot, however, human workers can resist and undermine the bureaucratic constraints that limit their autonomy in the workplace—and they do so in a wide variety of ways.

A fascinating example of workers resisting the bureaucratic constraints of their workplaces occurred in the early days of the Trump administration. As the new president took office, he began imposing gag orders on career federal employees in government agencies such as the Environmental Protection Agency and the Department of the Interior. These employees, whose agencies are closely tied to government policies involving resource use and climate change, were ordered to stop talking to the media about issues like scientific research findings, grant-funding opportunities, and environmental policy. The workers perceived the new president as being hostile to their agencies' missions of preserving and protecting natural resources. But as faceless, nameless employees of huge bureaucracies, how could they express serious disagreement with their boss, the president of the United States, without losing their jobs?

The answer soon became visible to millions on Twitter: New "rogue" agency accounts were used to deliberately leak the information the president wanted to suppress. It started when the National Park Service retweeted a *New York Times* reporter's feed of side-by-side photos comparing crowds at Trump's inauguration with those at Obama's 2009 inauguration. This image made President Trump so angry that the Department of the Interior (which includes the National Park Service) deactivated all of its Twitter accounts. Over the next few days and weeks, however, "rogue" accounts began to appear that were not officially linked to the agencies they represented but were clearly maintained by current employees who knew what was happening inside the agencies and who wanted the public to know, too. Accounts with names like Alt EPA, Alt FDA, Rogue NASA, Alt USDA, Angry National Park, and Alternative NOAA started "leaking" information about climate change, federal funding cuts, and censorship by the administration. Highly politicized, discrediting, and embarrassing information about the administration flowed from insiders to the public via these anonymous online channels, and there wasn't much President Trump could do about it.

But you don't have to be a high-ranking government knowledge worker to find opportunities for on-the-job resistance. Robin Leidner's study *Fast Food, Fast Talk* (1993) provides an in-depth look at individual resistance strategies in the service sector. The study focused on McDonald's employees and the routinized nature of their interactions with customers. Under the golden arches, every contact between the counter staff and the hungry consumer is strictly scripted, seemingly with no room for improvisation or creativity. Or is there?

McDonald's workers are trained to interact with customers using "The Six Steps": greeting, taking orders, assembling food, presenting it, receiving payment, and thanking them for

Resistance Strategies Photos from *The New York Times*, retweeted by the National Park Service, comparing crowds at Obama's 2009 inauguration (top) and Trump's in 2017 (bottom) enraged the White House. When the administration deactivated the National Park Service's official Twitter accounts, workers surreptitiously created "rogue" accounts in their place.

their business. As monotonous as these steps are, workers don't necessarily resent routinization—it helps them do their jobs effectively. One of the functions of the McDonald's service script is to regulate the power relationship between customer and worker: Customers' demands can be delivered with all types of attitude, but workers must always serve customers with a smile. The script constrains workers' responses. If they have rude or even abusive customers, they must still stick to the script. As one worker put it:

> You have to take their crap. [Laughs.] I'm not the type of person to say, "OK, have it your way." I mean, I have to admit, I'm tempted to backtalk a lot. That gets me in a lot of trouble. So I mean, when a customer's rude to me I just have to walk away and say, "Could you take this order please, before I say something I'm not supposed to say?" (p. 133)

Leidner proposes that submitting to scripted interactions all day long suppresses the real self and that this sort of tightly

IN RELATIONSHIPS
The Value of Break Time

If the model employee is someone who is supposed to be singularly focused on his or her job, it might seem like a contradiction to say that taking breaks or socializing with others at work is actually a sign of a healthy work environment. According to recent research, however, coffee breaks should not be considered a waste of time or productivity; instead, they have important social as well as financial value for organizations (Stroebaek 2013). Other studies have confirmed that the social bonds that are formed when sharing coffee breaks help create a positive group climate, which, in turn, has the potential to increase productivity within the organization (Waber et al. 2010). The proverbial coffee break is a subject that sociologists take very seriously.

Let's face it, work can be stressful. Whether you work in an office, in retail, or on a factory floor, the workplace is fraught with difficulties and demands. Coffee breaks are an important social practice within workplace culture, as they provide a crucial coping mechanism for workers. The kind of casual, informal encounters that take place during breaks in the workday are essential in promoting the professional and personal well-being of employees. This is especially true of difficult or stressful jobs. One study found that job stress was relieved by forming "communities of coping" during coffee breaks with co-workers.

Collegial relations are created during coffee breaks because "when having a coffee break, employees talk about themselves, their lives, and each other with symbols and stories not necessarily related to work relationships or organizational membership" (Stroebaek 2013, p. 383). These communities provide a space for social interaction with fellow employees, allowing them to share both professional opinions and personal frustrations about their work. Co-workers thus nurture a shared sense of investment in their jobs and in one another as a community.

This is not the first time that a sociologist has essentially endorsed goofing off with your co-workers. Play can be understood as resistance or opposition to work, but it is also an integral part of making work more enjoyable and, in the long run, more productive. Paradoxically, we find that play emerges in even the most harsh and strenuous work environments, demonstrated by Donald Roy in his classic study of "banana time," a short break in the day where workers use play to subvert the monotony of factory work (Roy 1959). If work is seen as unpleasant and painful, then workers must find ways to make it more tolerable. Roy, quoting social theorist Henri de Man, related that even in a factory system, it was "psychologically impossible to deprive any kind of work of all its positive emotional elements ... the instinct for play and the creative impulse" (Roy 1959, p. 160).

Play, then, helps workers reclaim and assert their identity when the workplace seems otherwise devoid of positive meaning. Informal interactions with co-workers while on the job are not just distractions from the workload at hand. Instead, these shared breaks turn out to be crucial to job satisfaction. And that's good for the employee and the company alike.

Banana Time Is Play Time Studies show that the "communities of coping" that workers form during coffee breaks reduce stress and promote a positive group climate.

controlled work environment can actually be damaging to the individual. She found that some workers improvised on the steps, personalizing them in tiny but still noticeable ways. She observed that there were limits within which workers could

> use the script as a starting point and inject [their] own personality into the interactions. Thus, some window workers joked or chatted with customers and tried to make the exchanges enjoyable for both parties. This stance implied an assertion of equality with customers and a refusal to suppress the self completely. (p. 190)

When engaging in these actions on the job, workers may be inviting a reprimand from their supervisor, or worse. But they are also engaging in resistance, asserting their own identities in the face of a depersonalizing routine or an administration whose policies they oppose. They are being active rather than passive, controlling the situation rather than being controlled by it; they are asserting their own autonomy on the job.

It is difficult to think of a form of employment that would allow us to avoid bureaucratic constraints altogether. What types of resistance strategies have you used to regain a bit of independence and power in the workplace?

Collective Resistance: Unions

Although individual resistance strategies may provide a small measure of autonomy for some workers, they don't fundamentally change the working conditions or make permanent improvements to the terms of employment for all workers. That is why workers sometimes seek more lasting solutions to their problems by organizing to instigate collective resistance strategies. They do so by forming unions.

A **union** benefits workers in various ways and serves to counterbalance the power of employers. A labor union is an association of workers who come together to improve their economic status and working conditions. The two main types of unions are craft unions, in which all the members are skilled in a certain craft (e.g., the International Brotherhood of Carpenters and Joiners), and industrial unions, in which all the members work in the same industry regardless of their particular skill (e.g., the Service Employees International Union). Some unions are local, with small memberships; others are large national organizations representing millions of workers.

Union negotiations with employers about the terms of employment and working conditions are coordinated through collective bargaining, in which contract decisions between management and union representatives must be mutually agreed upon rather than imposed unilaterally. When disagreements arise between management and employees, unionized workers may threaten to or actually stage a temporary walkout, work stoppage, or strike to express their grievance and force corporate managers and owners to negotiate. Often the striking workers will try to discourage the public from patronizing the businesses implicated in the labor dispute and try to prevent other, outside replacement workers (sometimes called "scab labor") from taking their jobs while they are out on strike.

Unions have a long history in the United States. At various times, they have existed on the margins of society and been vigorously opposed by capitalists and other free-market supporters. Unions in the nineteenth and early twentieth

Lawrence, Massachusetts, 1912 During the textile mill strike, workers demanded "bread and roses," eloquently capturing their desire for something more than just the wages needed to survive.

centuries were brutally suppressed by capitalists, and union organizers were frequently arrested and jailed. Often they were charged with conspiracy because attempts to form unions were illegal for much of U.S. history. The Typographical Union (representing print typesetters), which formed in 1852, is usually considered the "first durable national organization of workers" in the United States.

Unions of this era fought for a variety of workplace reforms. During the 1912 textile mill strikes in Lawrence, Massachusetts, the workers' slogan was "bread and roses," emphasizing their desire for something more than wages sufficient to survive. Unions also led campaigns to end child labor, to establish an eight-hour workday and a five-day workweek, and to increase workplace safety. For this reason, unions are still sometimes referred to as "the people who brought you the weekend." We now take for granted much of what the early unions won to improve the lives of American workers. It is not surprising that many were willing to fight for unionization even in the face of extreme opposition.

At the same time that unions were growing in strength and numbers, challenges came from industry and government, beginning with the Taft-Hartley Act of 1947, which placed limits on the power of unions and the activities of members. Union membership reached its peak in the 1950s and has since been in steep decline. In 1955, approximately 35 percent of the labor force was unionized; by 2018, only 10.5 percent of the workforce belonged to a union (U.S. Bureau of Labor Statistics 2019e). As of 2018, twenty-seven states have passed "right-to-work" laws that prohibit workplaces from making union membership a requirement of all employees. With a shift in the U.S. economy from manufacturing to the service sector, the only unions to grow since the early 1970s have been public sector employees' unions. Compared to private sector workers, public sector workers are five times more likely to be a part of a union.

The number of actions taken by laborers has also been on the decline. In the 1950s, an average of 352 major strikes occurred each year; by 2017, that number had fallen to just seven (U.S. Bureau of Labor Statistics 2019a). A dramatic exception to the trend in declining work stoppages occurred in 2018, however, when the number of major strikes surged across the nation. More than 485,000 workers were involved in some 20 strikes, the highest number since 1986 (U.S. Bureau of Labor Statistics 2019f). There were work stoppages in both the public and private sectors, including hotel workers striking against Marriott, patient-care workers striking against the University of California medical centers, communications workers striking against AT&T, and tech workers striking against Google. But perhaps what characterized the "year of the strike" most were the massive walkouts of hundreds of thousands of teachers in Arizona, West Virginia, Oklahoma, Colorado, Kentucky, and North Carolina. At issue were lack of funding, low pay, teacher

Los Angeles, 2019 Massive teacher strikes, like this one in Los Angeles in 2019, reverse a trend in declining work stoppages. Protesters demonstrate for better conditions for students and teachers.

shortages, large class sizes, and challenges to traditional public education from charter schools. Teacher strikes continued in 2019, most notably when more than 30,000 public school staff and teachers walked out in Los Angeles (the second-largest school district in the country). In all these cases, unions won important concessions for their members, including wage increases, lower caps on class size, and the hiring of more school nurses, counselors, and librarians.

Unions have also shifted their focus in recent decades. When the economy faltered in the 1970s, American corporations found it was cheaper to move production overseas to countries whose working conditions were practically unregulated. Industries that leave the United States, referred to as "runaway shops," have been especially prevalent in manufacturing, where firms take advantage of cheap labor and lax environmental laws in other countries. More recently, an increasing number of service sector jobs have also been moved overseas. As a result, some unions have changed their efforts from fighting for better wages and working conditions to keeping jobs in this country.

THE CONSCIENCE OF CORPORATE AMERICA

From a Weberian perspective, we can see that large bureaucracies laden with rules and procedures can deprive employees of a sense of autonomy, individuality, and control. From

IN THE FUTURE
Will Your Job Be "Uber-ized"?

On-demand app-based services have emerged and boomed in the last few years, and it seems no industry is immune to their pull. A few years ago it might have seemed weird—even dangerous—to get a ride to the airport from a stranger driving a nondescript late-model minivan; indeed, your parents would probably still balk at this and instead take a traditional, centrally dispatched yellow taxi.

The workers who drive your Ubers, shop for your groceries, and show up at your house to hang your pictures are part of what's known as the "gig economy." This refers to a way of working that doesn't involve stable, full-time employment with one company but rather a series of freelance jobs ("gigs") that may take advantage of individuals' unique skill sets but that provide neither stability nor benefits. While the gig economy is currently concentrated in the "rides and rooms" industries, the "taskification" of work has spread to other areas as well, including housecleaning (Neatso), laundry (Washio), and grocery shopping (Instacart).

According to the Pew Research Center, fully 72 percent of Americans have used some type of "on-demand" online service; usage is highest among the young, the college educated, and those with household incomes above $100,000. Nearly a quarter of Americans reported earning money in the gig economy, either by renting out a property, selling something online, or completing a task or job via a digital platform (Smith 2016a, 2016b).

There have always been "gig" workers, and even very successful ones (Dr. Ferris's dog-sitter, who also sells handmade jewelry, styles hair, delivers pizza, and plays bagpipes in parades, recently bought her own home with her earnings). What has changed about this kind of labor is the way technology facilitates it. Before the Internet, freelancers advertised through newspapers, hung posters on telephone poles, or just relied on word of mouth. They remained their own bosses, set their own rates, and made their own decisions about when they should, could, and would work. But with the proliferation of smartphones that put web connectivity and applications at just about everyone's fingertips, services have popped up that do the work of electronic intermediaries, connecting gig workers with clients. Apps also modulate pricing, charging what the market will bear given the type of service, location, and even time of day.

For busy people with little time for mundane chores but with money to pay others to do them, these services take the effort out of searching for the right provider at the right price, right now! But for the workers who provide those services, it isn't always such a great deal (Heller 2017). Uber drivers, for example, don't get overtime pay or health benefits, nor do they qualify for worker's compensation, unemployment insurance, or retirement benefits. They do not currently have the right to unionize, and the company can lower their pay and "switch off" drivers (take them out of service) without notice. Do the

---

a Marxist perspective, we can see how large capitalist corporations sometimes exploit their workers and cause alienation and how their power hierarchies often exclude women and minorities. These criticisms are true in the aggregate. Money, power, and influence converge in corporate America, and with these come opportunities for greed, exploitation, and abuse.

Negative stories about corporate America abound, whether they concern oil and energy firms, pharmaceutical companies, health insurance providers, or the world of high finance. Cases of corporate malfeasance continue to occur as they have throughout the history of capitalism. Some involve illegal activities, while others are characterized by unethical, if not criminal, behaviors. There can be devastating and deadly consequences when corporations privilege

profit-making above any costs or damage done to individuals, society, or the planet.

The emissions scandal and subsequent cover-up surrounding Volkswagen is a case in point of corporate malfeasance. In essence, the German automaker rigged its diesel engine cars with a mechanism that allowed them to pass stringent U.S. emissions standards in stationary tests, while on the road those same vehicles emitted up to 40 times the legal limits of nitrogen oxides, gases that contribute to air pollution. More than 500,000 cars were sold in the United States with "defeat devices" designed to bypass regulatory emissions tests. This allowed VW-model cars to achieve better real-world performance than would be possible by adhering to the required emissions standards. The scheme began to unravel in 2015, after a company whistle-blower revealed

benefits outweigh the costs? Some say yes: As giggers they can work and earn when they want, and someone else takes care of the paperwork. A Pew Research Center survey shows that almost 70 percent of respondents cite flexible time as the top benefit of gig work (Smith 2016a). They also see this type of work as good for those who don't need a full-time job (54 percent) and for those just entering the job market (37 percent). But the respondents also acknowledge the downside of gig work: Nearly a quarter of Americans believe these arrangements allow companies to take advantage of workers and another 21 percent believe that gig work places too large a financial burden on workers. They also recognize that this may not be the kind of work upon which one can build a career.

Others note that this way of organizing work can be detrimental to those who still rely on traditional employers and employment: The more on-demand, app-based ride services there are, the lower the demand is for traditional, centrally dispatched taxicabs and drivers. In an effort to address low wages, states such as New York have taken action to limit the number of Uber vehicles that can be in service at any particular time, thus giving all drivers better odds of earning fares. Airbnb creates a similar problem: When people rent out their own apartments to tourists, traditional hotels make less money, generate fewer tax dollars, and produce less employment for their housekeepers, valets, front desk clerks, and catering staff. App-based gig work undercuts the conventional low-wage job market, which may make it harder for already vulnerable workers to get a paycheck. This trickle-down underemployment may magnify inequalities that already exist in our society (Schor et al. 2016).

The Gig Economy Uber, the ride-sharing service, has been accused of exploiting its workers, discriminating against riders with disabilities, sexism, and predatory pricing.

Could your career be "Uberized," meaning taskified, gigged-out, broken down into parts that could be done by separate, lower-paid service providers? Maybe. It isn't just less-skilled labor like housecleaning or driving that is subject to taskification. Professional work is giggable too: Doctors make house calls through Medicast; massage therapists seek clients on Soothe and Zeel; attorneys UpCounsel; on-the-spot child care can be found on KangaDo; and the so-called "one-on-one" education model turns teachers into freelancers and students into customers in some private schools (Spencer 2017). Maybe the next revolution in work will be known as the Gig Revolution.

that top VW executives had tried to conceal their knowledge of the devices. The Environmental Protection Agency (EPA) issued a notice against the company citing its violation of the Clean Air Act, and the U.S. Department of Justice initiated an investigation into the wrongdoing. The company responded with recalls, vouchers, and trade-in incentives to mollify VW owners and attempt to repair its reputation as a carmaker. In 2017, a U.S. federal judge slapped the company with a $2.8 billion criminal fine for rigging its diesel engine cars to cheat on government emissions tests.

But not all corporations are bad actors, and sometimes we see major corporate players transcend self-interest and act with great altruism. In recent years a growing number of organizations have taken it upon themselves to become good corporate citizens. In an effort to bolster their reputations,

and perhaps to avoid outside intervention, corporations are adopting new forms of self-regulation and taking proactive measures to integrate social and ethical concerns into their business models. Corporate social responsibility, or CSR (also called corporate conscience or citizenship), is a relatively new movement but one that is spreading. At best, this shift is leading more corporations to take steps toward making a more positive impact on society and the world. Corporations engage in good citizenship in a number of ways; some are focused on environmental issues or workers' rights, others on a range of social programs and philanthropic giving.

Bill Gates, the founder and former CEO of Microsoft, is one of the wealthiest people in the world and, along with his wife, Melinda, one of the most generous as well. In 2017, they ranked as the top charitable donors in the country, having given $4.7 billion to the Bill & Melinda Gates Foundation, a private philanthropic organization with a $50 billion endowment. Established in 2000, the foundation has allocated more than $46 billion to tackle critical problems in the United States and worldwide. For instance, one of its global nonprofits has provided more than 440 million vaccinations against such diseases as smallpox, measles, and polio, an achievement that is estimated to have already prevented over 6 million deaths (Bustreo, Okwo-Bele, and Kamara 2015). The foundation has also worked to empower some of the world's poorest women to become a greater part of their local economies by using cell phones and other digital technologies to access financial services and payment exchange systems.

Despite its great number of successes, the Gates Foundation is not without critics. Some believe that, as a privately run organization, it is far too powerful. Others have questioned the foundation's funding priorities or worry about its encroachment into parallel program areas already being addressed by other public agencies. Some of the most intense scrutiny relates to the foundation's interests in U.S. education and, more specifically, its efforts to implement the highly controversial Common Core standards in schools. These criticisms aside, the Bill & Melinda Gates Foundation continues to enjoy widespread public support for the remarkable strides it has made in addressing some of the world's most pressing problems.

> **GLOBALIZATION** the cultural and economic changes resulting from dramatically increased international trade and exchange in the late twentieth and early twenty-first centuries

Another example of good corporate citizenship is the role of various companies in upholding the Paris climate accord. In June 2017, President Trump announced his intention to withdraw the United States from the world's most important treaty to combat climate change. For perspective, only two other countries, Syria and Nicaragua, are not part of the accord. His justification was that it was bad for businesses to be forced to adhere to regulations designed to reduce global warming. But hundreds of U.S. businesses disagreed and responded to Trump's withdrawal with their own statement announcing that they will continue to support actions to meet the Paris Agreement goals. Titled "We Are Still In," the letter was signed by heads of Google, Apple, Microsoft, eBay, IBM, Target, IKEA, Timberland, North Face, Starbucks, Gap, Levi Strauss, and even the 800-pound gorilla of global retailing, Walmart. Their commitment to upholding the Paris Agreement—no matter what policies a president may adopt—is a way of recognizing that business can be good for the planet. Whether it's based on altruism or just good for business, big corporations are suddenly part of the national conversation about climate change and social justice in a way they never have been before.

THE ECONOMICS OF GLOBALIZATION

Globalization describes the cultural and economic changes that have occurred as a result of dramatically increased international trade and exchange in the late twentieth and early twenty-first centuries. Although there has always been some global economic trade—East Asia's ancient spice and silk trade routes and the sixteenth-century English and Dutch shipping empires are early examples—the effects of globalization have become more highly visible since the 1970s. Globalization has been fostered through the development of international economic institutions; innovations in technology; the movement of money, information, and people; and infrastructure that supports such expansion. Today, it is possible to view the world as having one global economy, with huge corporations whose production processes span national borders, international regulatory bodies such as the World Trade Organization (WTO), financial bodies such as the International Monetary Fund (IMF), and transnational trade agreements such as the North American Free Trade Agreement (NAFTA) redefining economic relationships between and among nations.

Supporters of globalization believe that "free trade" can lead to more efficient allocation of resources, lower prices, more employment, and higher output, with all countries involved in the trade benefiting. Critics believe that free trade promotes a self-interested corporate agenda and that powerful and autonomous multinational corporations can exploit workers and increasingly shape the politics of nation-states. And the recent global recession, marked by financial crises in the United States, Europe, and China, shows us that all world economies are connected, for better or for worse.

International Trade

To explain economic globalization, social scientists have used the terms "shallow integration" and "deep integration" (Dicken 1998). Shallow integration refers to the flow of goods and services that characterized international trade until several decades ago. In a shallow integration model, a national company would arrange with a foreign company to either import or export products exclusively within that single nation's economy. For example, thirty years ago, a Japanese car would have been made almost entirely in Japan, and a pair of American jeans would have been made in the United States. Thus, Japan would export cars to the United States, and the United States would import these Japanese cars. Likewise, the United States would export jeans to Japan, and Japan would import the American jeans. To protect their interests, nations would impose taxes on imports, sometimes making those imports more expensive to buy than similar products made at home.

Deep integration refers to the global flow of goods and

services in today's economy. While companies still make arrangements with other companies for imports and exports, their relationships are far more complex. Most significantly, companies are no longer national; they are multinational, with major decision making, production, and/or distribution branches of a particular company spread all over the world. When we look at the labels on our clothing, the global nature of their origin is often concealed. The label may say "Made in...," but the raw materials or other parts may have originated somewhere else.

When nations make laws to protect national economic interests, they must often do so with a host of other nations in mind. NAFTA, which was signed into law in 1993, is an excellent example of this complex web of global relationships. Many major apparel companies, such as Nike and Gap, have marketing and design headquarters in the United States, but many of their garment factories are in Mexico, another country in NAFTA. Under NAFTA, U.S. companies can avoid paying taxes when they export raw materials to Mexico and then import the finished products. Global trade agreements like NAFTA often benefit private industry much more than they do nations and sometimes remain controversial even after they have become law.

Transnational Corporations

Transnational corporations (TNCs) are another part of the global economy. These firms purposefully transcend national borders so that their products can be manufactured, distributed, marketed, and sold from many bases all over the world. We may think of companies like Coca-Cola or General Electric as quintessentially American, but they are more accurately understood as global or transnational corporations. What is distinctive about today's TNCs is the way they shape the global economy. In the past fifty years, they have experienced unprecedented growth in both numbers of firms and amount of economic impact.

The United Nations' list of the world's top 100 non-financial TNCs assigns firms a "transnationality index" by assessing the ratios between foreign employment and total employment, foreign investments and total investments, and foreign sales and total sales (United Nations Conference on Trade and Development 2018). Among the top twenty-five "transnational" firms are six U.S. companies: Exxon Mobil (7), General Electric (9), Chevron (10), Apple (14), DowDuPont (19), and Johnson & Johnson (22). The petroleum industry is the most transnational, followed by electronics and pharmaceuticals. All of the above-listed firms make products that are marketed strongly as "American" brands, yet they are clearly global organizations.

TNCs exert tremendous influence in the global economy. They can be found among the top global economies ranked by either gross domestic product (GDP) or total sales. In 2017, Walmart was actually the twenty-fourth-largest

Coca-Cola and the Global Economy An employee oversees production at a new Coca-Cola plant in Indonesia. While Coca-Cola is headquartered in Atlanta, Georgia, the company has plants that span the globe.

economy according to its earnings, larger than the economies of Belgium and Thailand. Toyota, which was the forty-seventh-largest economy in 2017, ranked higher than Finland (see Table 11.1). As corporations grow, new TNCs have been added to the list. When we consider that firms have the economic weight of nations, we can understand just how much political clout TNCs wield in terms of global governance. For instance, an American TNC can exercise powerful influence by donating huge amounts of money to lobbyists and political campaigns. Further, in international regulatory bodies, such as the World Trade Organization, TNCs are often able to influence trade law at a global level.

Another manifestation of the ever-increasing economic power of TNCs is competition in the global market. Because TNCs can take advantage of cheap pools of labor by either relocating their own factories or outsourcing the work, nations compete with each other for these contracts by undercutting their citizens' wages and offering incentives, such as tax-free zones. Scholars, politicians, activists, and commentators have called this the "race to the bottom." These kinds of policies hurt the local populations, often depriving workers of decent wages and the potential benefits, such as schools and hospitals, that would have been derived from taxes.

Global Sweatshop Labor

One way the race to the bottom hurts workers in their own countries is by creating an environment where sweatshop labor can exist. A **sweatshop** is a workplace where workers are subjected to extreme exploitation, including below-standard wages, long hours, and poor working conditions that may pose health or safety hazards. Sweatshop workers are often

> **SWEATSHOP** a workplace where workers are subject to extreme exploitation, including below-standard wages, long hours, and poor working conditions that may pose health or safety hazards

TABLE 11.1 Ranking the World's Economies

Rank 2017	Company/Country	GDP/Revenue (millions)	Rank 2017	Company/Country	GDP/Revenue (millions)
1	United States	$19,390,604	26	Thailand	$455,303
2	China	$12,237,700	27	Iran	$454,013
3	Japan	$4,872,137	28	Austria	$416,596
4	Germany	$3,677,439	29	Norway	$398,832
5	United Kingdom	$2,622,434	30	United Arab Emirates	$382,575
6	India	$2,600,818	31	Nigeria	$375,745
7	France	$2,582,501	32	Israel	$350,851
8	Brazil	$2,055,506	33	State Grid	$348,903
9	Italy	$1,934,798	34	South Africa	$348,872
10	Canada	$1,653,043	35	Hong Kong	$341,449
11	Russian Federation	$1,577,524	36	Ireland	$333,731
12	Republic of Korea	$1,530,751	**37**	**Sinopec Group**	**$326,953**
13	Australia	$1,323,421	**38**	**China National Petroleum**	**$326,008**
14	Spain	$1,311,320	39	Denmark	$324,872
15	Mexico	$1,150,888	40	Singapore	$323,907
16	Indonesia	$1,015,539	41	Malaysia	$314,710
17	Turkey	$851,549	42	Colombia	$314,458
18	Netherlands	$826,200	43	Philippines	$313,595
19	Saudi Arabia	$686,738	**44**	**Royal Dutch Shell**	**$311,870**
20	Switzerland	$678,887	45	Pakistan	$304,952
21	Argentina	$637,430	46	Chile	$277,076
22	Sweden	$538,040	**47**	**Toyota Motor Company**	**$265,172**
23	Poland	$526,466	**48**	**Volkswagen**	**$260,028**
24	**Walmart**	**$500,343**	49	Finland	$251,885
25	Belgium	$492,681	50	Bangladesh	$249,724

SOURCES: *Fortune* 2018; World Bank 2019a.

intimidated with threats of physical discipline and are prevented from forming unions or other workers' rights groups. Historically, sweatshops originated during the Industrial Revolution as a system where middlemen earned profits from the difference between what they received for delivering on a contract and the amount they paid to the workers who produced the contracted goods. The profit was said to be "sweated" from the workers, because they received minimal wages and worked excessive hours under unsanitary and dangerous conditions.

Sweatshops, however, are not a thing of the past. Unfortunately, there are many in the world today making large numbers of the goods that we unknowingly consume. Though perhaps more prevalent overseas, sweatshops exist in the United States as well. The General Accounting Office (GAO) defines a sweatshop as "an employer that violates more than one federal or state labor law governing minimum wage and overtime, child labor, industrial homework, occupational safety and health, workers' compensation, or industrial regulation" (Ross 1997, p. 12). In 2016, the U.S. Department of Labor investigated 77 Los Angeles garment factories and discovered labor violations at 85 percent of them. Most garment workers are paid by the piece rather than by the hour. This is legal as long as the employers guarantee a minimum wage. But it doesn't always work out that way. The investigation found that some workers were being paid as little as $4 per hour, and most only an average of $7 per hour, far below the $12 minimum wage for Los Angeles at that time. Factories producing garments for such retailers as Ross Dress for Less, Marshalls, and T.J. Maxx were ordered to pay $1.3 million in back wages, lost overtime, and damages. But the brands themselves faced no liability, though their own business model is built on selling low-cost clothing. Big retailers can take the position that they are not involved in manufacturing or in employing factory workers, even if those workers sew that brand's labels into the garments they produce. This is part of the reason why sweatshop conditions persist, despite laws against them.

American companies may also manufacture goods overseas using foreign sweatshop labor. Nike, Gap, and clothing lines associated with Mary-Kate and Ashley Olsen, Jay-Z, Ivanka Trump, and Sean "Diddy" Combs have all been charged with using sweatshop labor in Southeast Asia, Central America, and elsewhere and have been pressured to reform their practices. Factory fires in 2012 killed 289 garment workers in Pakistan and 117 in Bangladesh, and in April 2013, over 1,000 garment workers in Bangladesh were killed when their factory building collapsed. In the first two cases, workers were trapped without proper emergency exits in buildings where clothing was made for American companies such as Walmart, J. C. Penney, and Kohl's (Ahmed 2012). In the last case, the deadliest garment-industry accident in history, the building was made of shoddy materials and constructed on unstable ground and thus could not withstand the vibrations of machinery within (Associated Press 2013).

Many universities have also been in the practice of purchasing their logo apparel from clothing manufacturers that use sweatshop labor. Students at schools like the University of Michigan, University of North Carolina, University of Wisconsin–Madison, University of California, Duke University, and Georgetown University have all acted to pressure their respective administrators into changing university purchasing policy to seek out union-made and verifiably sweatshop-free products. We encourage you to do your own research on whether sweatshop products have reached the student store on your campus or wherever you shop for clothing—and whether such items are in your own closet already.

Blood, Sweat, and Tears Activists lead a demonstration outside an H&M store in protest of working conditions at a factory in Bangladesh used by the company (left). People crowd outside the ruins of Rana Plaza, an eight-story garment factory that collapsed in April 2013, killing more than a thousand workers (right).

DATA WORKSHOP

Analyzing Everyday Life

Are Your Clothes Part of the Global Commodity Chain?

You probably own and consume a large number of products that originated in faraway countries, including your car, clothing, or shoes. These items have traveled widely during the process from production to consumption. Food, pharmaceuticals, and electronics are other examples of globally made products. Social scientists call such international movements of goods "global commodity chains" (Dunaway 2014; Gereffi and Korzeniewicz 1994).

Global commodity chains are networks of corporations, product designers and engineers, manufacturing firms, distribution channels (such as ocean freightliners, railroads, and trucking firms), and consumer outlets (such as Walmart). Global commodity chains start with a product design and brand name and end with the consumer making a purchase. But between start and finish is often a complex global process involving many different people, in many different nations, all contributing to the final product.

The manufacturing of goods, from garments to electronics to automobiles, used to happen primarily in the United States and other Western nations; today's manufacturing centers are located primarily in poorer nations, such as the Philippines, China, Indonesia, and many Latin American countries. American corporations such as Nike, Gap, and Levi Strauss have closed all their U.S. manufacturing plants and hired contractors and subcontractors from East Asia and Latin America to make their products at substantially lower prices. Now these companies focus large amounts of financial resources on "branding" their products (Klein 2000). Branding is the process, usually accomplished through advertising, by which companies gain consumers' attention and loyalty. Much of the money you pay for some products goes toward financing these branding campaigns, while a much smaller sum pays the workers who actually make the products.

In this Data Workshop you will be using existing sources in your research and analysis. Return to the section in Chapter 2 for a review of this method. The following three exercises will help you better understand where the things that you buy come from and the continuing disparity between product values and workers' wages. Document what you find in written notes. (You can also take photos of the items.)

EXERCISE ONE: THE GLOBAL CLOSET

Pick out five to ten items of clothing from your closet. Now check the labels. Where were your clothes made? Make a list of the nations represented in your closet. How many nations are in East Asia or Latin America or other parts of the globe? Is there a difference between where an item is made and where it is assembled? Does the label indicate where the fabric originated?

EXERCISE TWO: ONCE "MADE IN THE U.S.A."

Ask your parents, aunts or uncles, or grandparents if you can look at the labels of their older clothes. Or go to a thrift store or secondhand store and look for older or vintage clothes there. Again pick out five to ten items of clothing. How many of those items were made in the United States? How many were made elsewhere? What does this tell you about the globalization of the garment manufacturing industry over the past several decades?

EXERCISE THREE: ARE YOUR FAVORITE BRANDS "SWEAT FREE"?

Choose one or more of your favorite brands of clothing, shoes, or other fashion accessories. What is your brand's stance on sweatshop labor? Do workers who make your favorite products earn a living wage? You can check many corporations' ethics regarding labor conditions by doing a simple search on the Internet. Or visit the website of one of the following pro-labor organizations to see how your brands score:

- Fair Labor Association: www.fairlabor.org

- CorpWatch: www.corpwatch.org

- Global Exchange: www.globalexchange.org

There are two options for completing this Data Workshop:

PREP-PAIR-SHARE Complete the exercises provided, following the instructions as outlined. Bring your notes to class to discuss with other students in pairs or small groups. Your instructor may organize groups so that all members have done the same exercise or all members have done a different exercise. Compare your findings as a group. Did you find similar or different results?

DO-IT-YOURSELF Complete the exercises provided and follow the instructions as outlined. Write a three- to four-page essay analyzing your findings. Attach any written notes or other documentation to your paper.

Outsourcing

The U.S. economy is increasingly affected by globalization, and as a result, American companies have sought out new business models to reduce costs and remain competitive. One increasingly popular approach is outsourcing or offshoring. **Outsourcing** involves "contracting out" or transferring to another country the labor that a company might otherwise have employed its own staff to perform. Typically, a company's decision to outsource is made for financial reasons and is usually achieved by transferring employment to locations where the cost of labor is much cheaper.

A variety of jobs are suitable for outsourcing. Manufacturing jobs were some of the first to go, but an increasing number of service jobs have followed in the last couple of decades. Among them are office and clerical staff, purchasing, finance, and human resources workers. Offshoring is also happening in other service areas requiring highly skilled workers. Jobs in information technology–producing industries, such as data entry, communication services, communication equipment, and computer hardware, software, and services, are some of the main jobs involved in outsourcing. Although countries in Southeast Asia, such as the Philippines, and those in Eastern Europe are key sites for information technology offshoring, India has become the primary location for this practice because of the shared English language and cheap employment. It makes sense to employ workers abroad if, for instance, a company can hire a computer engineer in India for less than $10,000 a year compared with one who does the same work but costs $90,000 on average in the United States.

When we think about outsourcing, we may picture a foreign worker assembling an American-model automobile, or we may remember the foreign accent of someone we spoke with at a help desk or call center who provided us with tech support or customer service. Although outsourcing is still most common in areas such as manufacturing and information services, it has spread into new and what might seem like far less likely types of employment. For example, there has been an upsurge in medical outsourcing, particularly health-care business processing for such things as medical transcription, coding, and billing services. But even more sophisticated medical work is outsourced as well. Teleradiology has been widely implemented by hospitals, clinics, and specialized imaging facilities. Teleradiology allows for images such as X-rays, ultrasounds, and MRIs to be taken in one location and then viewed by a radiologist at a remote site for the purposes of interpretation and diagnosis. Increasingly, these referrals are made to India. The practice is not only about saving money; it can also result in significant benefits to patient care, especially when a radiological specialist is needed. Teleradiology is open 24/7 to respond to emergencies, and it allows a highly trained radiologist to provide medical expertise without having to be in the same location as the patient.

> **OUTSOURCING** "contracting out" or transferring to another country the labor that a company might otherwise have employed its own staff to perform; typically done for financial reasons

Sociologist France Winddance Twine (2011a) has researched another medical trend: outsourcing the womb. For the past several decades, infertile couples who wish to have biological children have been hiring women to serve as surrogates. These woman are impregnated in vitro with the egg and sperm of a couple who are unable to conceive on their own. Although this practice is legal in the United States, it has been outlawed in other Western countries. For more than a decade, there was a surrogate baby boom in places such as India. Outsourcing occurred in this market for the same reasons as in other industries: There was an available workforce overseas where the costs were much cheaper than

TABLE 11.2 Theory in Everyday Life

Perspective	Approach to Work and the Economy	Case Study: Outsourcing of Work
Structural Functionalism	Different types of work (high prestige and pay to low prestige and pay) are necessary to the economy and have functions that help maintain social order.	Outsourcing is necessary to keep both national and global economies stable in the current market.
Conflict Theory	A stratified labor market creates intergroup conflict—wealthier capitalists may exploit less powerful workers.	Outsourcing exploits poor and developing nations and laid-off local workers, all while enriching corporations.
Symbolic Interactionism	Work is central to our self-concept. We are intensely identified with our work, both by ourselves and by others.	Workers whose jobs are outsourced may come to see themselves as worthless and expendable because it seems that others see them that way too.

GLOBAL PERSPECTIVE

World of Warcraft and "Gold Farming" in China

Many people are familiar with the concept of sweatshops, where cheap labor is exploited to make clothing and goods for people in industrialized nations. While people easily understand how labor can be exploited for the production of material goods, a more difficult concept to grasp is how labor can be exploited in the market for virtual goods. Rather than working long hours under inhumane conditions for little pay in order to produce luxury items such as Nikes and Ray-Bans, "gold farmers" are exploited in order to create the ultimate luxury product—status in an online computer game.

Some of the most popular forms of video games are massively multiplayer online role-playing games (MMORPGs) such as *World of Warcraft* (WoW), *Ultima Online*, and *Everquest*. *WoW* is the most popular of these games, with approximately 10 million subscribers, or about 35 percent of the market; it earned over $1 billion in revenues in 2013 (Tassi 2014). As with many MMORPGs, players make an initial investment to purchase the software for the game, and they are also charged a monthly subscription fee in order to play. In *WoW*, players use a character avatar through which they explore the virtual world, complete quests, and interact with other players or nonplayer characters (NPCs). Quests are assignments given by an NPC that usually involve killing a monster, gathering resources, or finding a difficult-to-locate object. Successful quests are rewarded with in-game money

and experience points that a character can use to buy new skills and equipment. Because of the interactive nature of *WoW*, advancing in the game isn't just a matter of personal achievement but also a matter of reputation and status in the community.

"Gold farms" profit from the importance of advancement in an MMORPG. According to estimates, around 100,000 people in China are employed as gold farmers, making $120 to $250 (U.S.) per month playing *WoW* for twelve- to eighteen-hour shifts (Vincent 2011). These Chinese gold farmers carry out in-game actions so that they can earn virtual money to buy equipment, skills, and status. These virtual assets are sold to real (recreational) players for real-world money, creating a unique intersection of virtual and real-world economies. Literally, a player can spend real-world money to buy status and reputation in an online game. Since many of the beginning levels of *WoW* involve spending long hours doing repetitive and dull virtual tasks, the idea of being able to bypass this tedium to start at more advanced levels appeals to many players. Creating characters requires time and effort that players who use the services of gold farmers are unable or unwilling to devote to the game.

Many of the criticisms of manufacturing sweatshops can be applied to the gold-farming phenomenon. Gold farmers labor for the benefit of middle-class gamers in industrialized

in the United States. Understandably, there were also concerns about surrogacy exploiting young, poor women, and so in 2018 the Indian government passed a law prohibiting foreign parents from hiring Indian surrogates. But it remains legal in other places, including Thailand, the Ukraine, and Georgia. If we can now outsource pregnancy, what other jobs might be next?

DIFFERENT WAYS OF WORKING

There are alternative ways of working, not all of which fit into typical categories of work. First we look at professional socialization, the process by which new members learn and internalize the norms and values of their group, examining case studies of workers in three unusual fields. Then

we examine the contingent workforce—those who work in positions that are temporary or freelance or who work as independent contractors. Finally, we take a look at nonprofit corporations—private organizations whose missions go beyond the bottom line—and volunteerism, the work of people who seek no compensation for their investment of time and energy.

Professional Socialization in Unusual Fields

Every new job requires some sort of training for the prospective employee. Anyone in a new position confronts an unfamiliar set of expectations and workplace norms that must be learned so the new person can fit into the environment. This process, called professional socialization, involves learning not only the social role but also the various details about how

nations. Ge Jin (2006), a PhD student at the University of California, San Diego, has documented working conditions in gold-farming "sweatshops," where he filmed workers crowded into an airport hangar, bleary eyed, chain-smoking, and sleeping two to a single mat on the floor. Are bad jobs better than no jobs? Though most people in developed nations would view $3 a day as extremely low pay, in impoverished communities "$1 or $2 a day can be a life-transforming wage" (Kristof and WuDunn 2000). While there are those who argue that playing a computer game takes less of a physical toll than subsistence farming or factory work, it is evident that there is an imbalance between the amount of money that workers are paid to produce these virtual resources and the prices that gamers pay to buy them. The sum of $200 can buy 500 pieces of online gold in *WoW*, which would take an estimated 100 hours of playing to earn.

The gaming world is up in arms about the gold-farming phenomenon. While some gamers find that the opportunity to buy gold augments their playing experience, other gamers hold that buying from gold farmers confers an unfair advantage to those with expendable income. Purists argue that MMORPGs should be free of the corruption of the real world and that escapism is not possible with people buying status and reputation. Players who use the services of gold farmers affect the virtual economy by driving up the prices of the rarest items. Traditional players then become resentful, as these price increases require them to work longer for items that players with real-world cash can purchase with little effort.

Strategies for retaliation against players identified as gold

Chinese Gold Farmers How has the popularity of online games such as *World of Warcraft* led to the rise of new types of sweatshops?

farmers include verbal harassment inside the game. Rather than taking out their frustrations on the gold farm brokers who benefit from the process, some players will follow suspected gold farmers within the game and bombard them with racist comments. Gold farming then becomes a matter not just of class and economics but also of race and racism.

Are gold farms good or bad? Should the virtual world be free of the corruption of the real world? Are gamers just too invested in their games? These are all questions to ask when pondering the intersections of the virtual world and real world that collide in the gold-farming sweatshops.

to do the job. Several sociological studies have explored the process of professional socialization, focusing on medical students (Becker et al. 1961; Fox 1957; Haas and Shaffir 1977, 1982), teachers (Lortie 1968), clergy (Kleinman 1984), nurses (Stimson 1967), social workers (Loseke and Cahill 1986), and lawyers (Granfield 1992).

Spencer Cahill's study of students preparing to become funeral directors, for example, focused not only on the practical skills developed by mortuary science students but also on the "emotional labor" (Hochschild 1983) involved in this occupation. Most social interaction within the mortuary science program revolved around death; as a result, students learned how to engage in the practice of "normalizing talk." "Mortuary science education requires students to adopt an occupational rhetoric and esoteric language that communicate professional authority and a calm composure towards matters that most of the lay public finds emotionally upsetting"

(Cahill 1999, p. 106). In addition, students were required to control their own emotional responses to the work. "Some students told me that they found 'cases' of young children emotionally disturbing.... Yet, these students reportedly did 'get used to it,' 'keep it down,' and deal with emotionally distressing 'cases'" (pp. 108–109). Cahill found that successful mortuary science students were those who could best deal with the emotional component of the work.

In his study of wildland firefighters in the Southwest, Matthew Desmond (2006) found that the socialization process begins years—and sometimes generations—before the men even apply for the job. While fighting fire is intensely physical work, it also requires a special quality of mind and self-identity as well. Many of the men who do this work come from rural working-class backgrounds. This often means that they have spent time working and playing outdoors—on a farm, perhaps, or hunting and fishing with their fathers and

On the Fireline While many occupations require on-the-job socialization into the workplace's culture and norms, others, like wildland firefighting, have a much longer socialization process that begins well before the first day of work.

brothers (who may have served as wildland firefighters themselves). They can shoot and sharpen tools and drive off-road vehicles, and they can take care of themselves in the woods or on the trail in ways that those from large urban environments usually cannot. They may have grown up in relatively isolated communities—in small towns, on Native reservations, or on ranchland. They have been socialized into what Desmond calls "country masculinity," and as a result, they have already acquired certain competencies and qualities that provide good preparation for the rigors of wildland firefighting. So while the Forest Service does train its new recruits, the success of any new hire is likely to be based more on his experiences before joining the organization.

Jacqueline Lewis (1998) examined the socialization of exotic dancers and what goes into learning their job. "For exotic dancers, achieving job competence involves getting accustomed to working in a sex-related occupation and the practice of taking their clothes off in public for money" (Lewis 1998, p. 1). On-the-job socialization was essential for the women who entered this line of work: "Similar to the socialization experiences of individuals in other occupations, novice dancers learn through interaction and observation while on the job.... Since there is no formal certification structure, peers play an important role in this transformation process" (p. 5). Lewis found that several women felt the socialization process "inadequately prepared them for some of the realities of the life of an exotic dancer"

CONTINGENT AND ALTERNATIVE WORKFORCE
those who work in positions that are temporary or freelance or who work as independent contractors

(p. 12)—mainly the negative impact it would have on their private lives and the difficulties of having long-term heterosexual relationships with men outside the industry.

The Contingent and Alternative Workforce

Traditionally, most Americans have hoped to find a job they would keep their whole lives, one that would provide forty-hour workweeks along with vacations and health and retirement benefits. Increasingly, this sort of job is becoming rare. A growing percentage of Americans have less steady work arrangements that could be defined as work that does not involve explicit or implicit contracts for long-term employment. These workers are referred to as the **contingent and alternative workforce**. It is made up of four categories: temporary workers, independent contractors, on-call workers, and contract company workers—sometimes called "temps" or "freelancers." During the past couple of decades, contingent and alternative work has become an important segment of the labor market, in some cases replacing long-term, full-time employment. According to the U.S. Bureau of Labor Statistics (2018d), the contingent and alternative workforce totaled 21 million workers in 2017, making up about 14 percent of the U.S. workforce.

Many see this situation as a potential disaster, as inferior jobs are created by corporations seeking to slash overhead, especially those costs associated with health benefits, which are almost never available to contingent workers. Employers have a number of financial and legal responsibilities to their regular workers—overtime pay, health insurance, Social Security, disability, and workers' compensation benefits—that don't apply to temps or independent contractors. Many fear businesses will increasingly turn to these employment arrangements solely to cut costs, to the distinct disadvantage of their employees.

The case histories of two giant firms show the potential for the exploitation of contingent and alternative workers. Sometimes businesses will classify workers as "independent contractors" even though they do the same work in the same place as regular workers. In an infamous example in the late 1990s, Microsoft was forced to pay $97 million to settle a lawsuit alleging it had wrongly classified a group of employees as independent contractors, making them ineligible for benefits. These workers had been hired as freelancers to work on specific projects, but "the workers were fully integrated into Microsoft's workforce, working under nearly identical circumstances as Microsoft's regular employees...the same core hours at the same location and the same supervisors as regular employees" (Muhl 2002).

A different, though equally exploitative, tactic was used by the contractors hired to clean Walmart stores. In 2003, federal agents arrested 245 undocumented workers in sixty different Walmart stores around the country. The workers came from eighteen nations, but very few of them actually worked for Walmart. Instead, they were employed by independent contractors hired by Walmart to do its nightly cleaning (Bartels 2003). Although companies are not responsible for the actions of subcontractors they hire, they can be held responsible if it is proven they knew something illegal was going on. This is especially important when the jobs that are offered to undocumented workers are exploitative or abusive. When contractors hire employees who work seven days a week and receive no overtime pay or benefits, then those contractors are in violation of overtime, Social Security, and workers' compensation laws. Furthermore, it is much harder for legitimate contractors to win bids for contracts when their competition can offer lower prices by illegally underpaying their workers.

It is not surprising to discover a lack of job satisfaction among temporary workers, mainly clerical and manufacturing workers and on-call workers, such as construction workers, nurses, adjunct instructors, and truck drivers (Dickson and Lorenz 2009). Many temporary workers hope they will be able to use their temp job as a springboard to a permanent one, but often this does not happen. However, the flexibility and freedom of such work arrangements may appeal to a substantial number of workers, such as students, parents with children at home, and retirees.

Of the categories of alternative workers tracked by the Bureau of Labor Statistics, independent contractors make up the largest group—more than 10 million in total. In contrast to the traditional worker, the occupational profile of the independent contractor is skewed toward several high-skilled fields, including writers and artists, insurance and real estate agents, construction trade employees, and other technical and computer-related professions. They tend to be better paid than the average worker and prefer their employment

The Just-in-Time Professor The postsecondary academic workforce has experienced a shift away from full-time tenured or tenure-track faculty to part-time adjunct instructors. Adjunct instructors now represent half of all higher education faculty, up from 20 percent in 1970.

situation for the flexibility and freedom it offers (Fishman 2011). However, even in this category, a significant minority of workers, especially women, make less money and are less satisfied with their situation. Some also suffer from alienation, disenchantment, and burnout.

The Third Sector and Volunteerism

Not all corporations seek a profit, nor do all workers get paid a wage for their labor. Numerous organizations engage in social welfare, social justice, or environmental services. Typically, these are churches, schools, hospitals, philanthropic foundations, art institutions, scientific research centers, and a multitude of other organizations, both permanent and temporary. They are private, rather than government, organizations and are devoted to serving the general welfare, not their own financial interests. They are nonprofit organizations, designed to run as cost-effectively as possible and to direct any gains or earnings, above basic operating expenses, back into the causes they support. Together, these organizations and the workers who staff them constitute what social scientists call the **Independent (or Third) Sector** of the economy. Nonprofits contributed an estimated $985 billion to the U.S. economy in 2015, which amounted to more than 5 percent of the nation's gross domestic product (McKeever 2019).

INDEPENDENT (OR THIRD) SECTOR the part of the economy composed of nonprofit organizations; their workers are mission driven, rather than profit driven, and such organizations direct surplus funds to the causes they support

The Third Sector helps society in a number of ways. First, these organizations play a significant part in the American system of pluralism, operating alongside the first two sectors of government and business while helping to strengthen them and make them work better. Although we think of nonprofits, business, and government as separate, they are really interconnected through their impact on public policy. Second, nonprofit organizations deliver a wide range of vital services to millions of people in almost every social category. Last, they are a humanizing force in American society, allowing an important avenue of expression for altruism.

While most nonprofits have some paid employees, they also rely on volunteers to deliver their services to the public. Volunteerism reflects a profound and important American value—that citizens in a democracy have a personal responsibility to serve those in need. An estimated 77 million Americans, or about 30 percent of the total population, engaged in some form of volunteer work in 2017. Women tend to volunteer in larger numbers: More than 34 percent of all U.S. women, compared to 27 percent of men, volunteered in 2017. Volunteers come from every socioeconomic level, but members of the middle and upper-middle classes are most likely

The Third Sector A Williams College student volunteers at a local high school, where she tutors English language learners.

to volunteer, as are those with a higher level of educational attainment. The estimated total value of donated hours in 2017 was $167 billion (Corporation for National & Community Service 2019).

People engage in volunteer work for many reasons—for social justice, social change, religious values, work experience, and participation in clubs and social groups, and even out of boredom. Not only does volunteering satisfy our most altruistic ideals; it can also be a way to enhance our careers, strengthen our relationships, and even let us live out fantasies or dreams that are not part of our normal, everyday lives. And in so doing, volunteers help create a different world for themselves and others. There are many ways of working—some conventional, some alternative. Not all workers have jobs in traditional fields; not all workers have permanent or full-time jobs; and not all workers do it for a paycheck.

TIME FOR A VACATION?

Americans like to think we're hard workers. We are, of course. But we might be working *too* hard. Compared to European Union (EU) countries and other developed countries around the globe, we work up to eight weeks more each year. According to the Center for Economic and Policy Research (Ray, Sanes, and Schmitt 2013), most of the world's wealthiest nations mandate a certain amount of paid vacation time—from ten days in Japan to thirty-eight in Austria (Figure 11.1). The United States? Zero. That's right: U.S. workers are not legally entitled to any paid vacation. Your employer may offer it—about 75 percent of U.S. employers do—but if you're a part-time or low-wage worker (in food service and retail jobs, for instance), you probably don't get any paid vacation, and you don't have any legal way to get it, either.

So, we definitely work more...but is that better? Does working more days per year necessarily translate into higher productivity? Not necessarily:

> Because the United States is the second-most productive developed country as measured by GDP per capita and has no mandatory vacation time, some might argue that vacation reduces productivity. However, in another

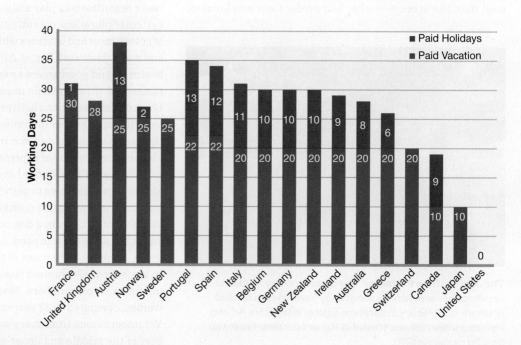

FIGURE 11.1 Paid Vacation and Paid Holidays

SOURCE: Ray, Sanes, and Schmitt 2013.

measure of labor productivity—GDP per hour worked—the U.S. was only marginally better than Germany and France, both developed countries that guarantee among the most vacation time. (Hess 2013)

So maybe we Americans shouldn't work so much after all? Mandatory paid vacation allows workers to engage in self-care, spend time with family, and travel the world without having to give up salary. In fact, some EU countries actually give vacation pay to their workers in order to help them meet the extra costs of travel during their time off! Sounds crazy to American ears but think about it: More time off plus more money to spend during that time off generates more economic activity and may mean more productivity once you're back on the job (Mohn 2014). So if you're one of the lucky Americans whose employer offers paid vacation time, by all means use it. It's your patriotic duty!

Closing Comments

You may never have imagined that work was such a big part of life. You might have had a job of some kind, but now you probably have a better idea of just how important work is on both a collective and an individual level. We hope that you have gained some insight into the structure and meaning of work in your own lives and the lives of others in society. Work is such an important topic that sociologists have devoted much of their own work to studying it. While we can be fairly certain that work will remain a major reality in the human experience, the nature and kind of work that we do are likely to keep changing with the times. What will work look like in the near or distant future? Surely sociologists (if they still exist as an occupational group) will be most interested to learn. Perhaps you, too, now share this interest.

APPLYING WHAT YOU'VE LEARNED

Let's Talk More

1. Thinking of the United States as a capitalist nation with some socialist elements, are there any ways that you directly benefit from government intervention in the economy?

2. Resistance strategies are ways that workers can assert some degree of autonomy in a workplace that increasingly exerts control and keeps workers under surveillance. What sorts of actions qualify as individual resistance strategies? Have you ever done anything like this?

3. Almost every job requires some degree of professional socialization. Have you ever experienced anything like this? Did you engage in any anticipatory socialization first?

Let's Explore More

1. **Film** Meyers, Nancy, dir. *The Intern*. 2017.

2. **Book** Rivera, Lauren. 2015. *Pedigree: How Elite Students Get Elite Jobs*. Princeton, NJ: Princeton University Press.

3. **Blog Post** Sternheimer, Karen. "Inequality and the Cashless Economy." *Everyday Sociology* (blog). August 13, 2018.
   http://WWNorton.com/rd/x4W7G.

CHAPTER 12

Life at Home: Families and Relationships

Tomas, a single doctor in his sixties, has lived in the same home in Houston for thirty years, and always with three much-loved dogs: two boxers named Blaze and Pepe, and a Boston terrier named Brownie. They are his devoted companions. When one of the dogs dies, Tomas gets a new dog of the same breed and keeps the dog's name. Thus, if Pepe died, the new boxer would be named Pepe; if Brownie died, the new Boston terrier would also be Brownie. Tomas's relationship with his dogs has lasted for thirty years. Are Tomas and the dogs a family?

Stacie and Eric met in college and married a year after they graduated. Their job hunts, however, led them in different directions: Stacie took a job with an international policy agency

in Washington, DC, and Eric went to work for a major corporation in Miami. Living in their respective cities, they spend lots of time Facetiming and lots of money on weekend plane tickets. After about five years, Stacie became pregnant, and the baby is due in a few months. Are Stacie and Eric a family?

Jeannie and Elena met in graduate school—almost twenty years ago. They are both professors in Manhattan, Kansas, and together they bought and fixed up an old house. They had wanted to formalize their commitment to one another, but they could not do so for many years because of a ban on same-sex marriage in Kansas. Nevertheless, they adopted a little boy named Conor, who is now in his teens. Are Jeannie, Elena, and Conor a family?

For some of you, the answers may come easily, but others may find yourselves wondering—are these groups really families? Tomas loves Brownie, Blaze, and Pepe, but can you really be a family if most of your members aren't human? And is Tomas's replacement policy similar to or different from the practice of remarrying when a spouse dies? What about Stacie and Eric? They're married and are having a biological child, which seems to make them easily definable as a family. Yet they don't live under the same roof or even in the same state. What does that make them? Even Tomas and the dogs live together. And so do Jeannie and Elena, who own their home together. And they're raising their son Conor together, even though they couldn't jointly adopt him as a married heterosexual couple could. Instead, Elena had to adopt him on her own first, with Jeannie becoming his second parent later. With same-sex marriage now legal across the United States, they are thinking about tying the knot. Do these complications mean that they aren't a real family?

It all depends on how you define family. If emotional bonds and mutual support are the only criteria, then all of these groups are families. But if a marital bond is required, then only Stacie and Eric are a family. If other legal ties are included, then Elena, Jeannie, and Conor can be a family too. If you have to be heterosexual, then Jeannie and Elena are out, and we really don't know about Tomas, do we? If the longevity of the relationships is the key, then Tomas and the dogs win over both of these other potential families. But if you have to be human and irreplaceable, then all those Brownies, Blazes, and Pepes don't qualify. And if a shared residence must be part of the equation, then Tomas and the dogs are in and so are Jeannie and Elena, but Stacie and Eric are out. While the archetypal image of the nuclear family endures, sociologists who study families are astonished by how rapidly our ideas about the ideal family have changed in recent years. So how do you define family?

How to Read This Chapter

In this chapter, we examine society's most basic social group—the family. Yet what makes a family is subject to debate. Sociology doesn't define a family by who its members are but by what they do, how they relate to one another, and what their relationship is to the larger society. You will probably see some of your own family's story in these discussions. We'll look at the dynamic diversity of family forms in the contemporary United States, the functions of family for society, the hierarchies of inequality that shape family life, the work that gets done by and in families, the kinds of troubles families experience, and the political and cultural controversies that affect families. You will learn that when it comes to family life, change is the only constant.

WHAT IS THE FAMILY?

The U.S. Census Bureau defines "family" as two or more individuals related by blood, **marriage**, or **adoption** living in the same household. This definition is a starting point, but it's too limited to encompass even the family arrangements described in the opening vignette. Contemporary sociologists use the word **family** to mean a social group whose members are bound by some type of tie—legal, biological, emotional, or a combination of all three. They may or may not share a household, but family members are interdependent and have a sense of mutual responsibility for one another's care. We don't define family by specific types of people (parents or children) or specific types of ties (marriage or biology) because we believe the definition should be broad enough to encompass a variety of forms. However, this very variety is the source of controversy both within and outside academia. Regardless of the definition, most people recognize family as an integral social institution found in every society.

The family as an institution has always changed in response to its social, cultural, political, and economic milieu. Before the Industrial Revolution, "family" tended to mean **extended family**—a large group of **kin**, or relatives, which could include grandparents, uncles, aunts, and cousins, living in one household. After the Industrial Revolution, this configuration was largely superseded by the **nuclear family**—a heterosexual couple, usually married, living in their own household and raising children. Along the way, the family moved from a more public social institution to a private one, as many functions formerly associated with the family were transferred to other institutions. For example, work and production moved from the family to the factory, education moved from the family to the school, and government took over a variety of social welfare and support services formerly taken care of by the extended family.

Subsequent waves of social change, such as the women's liberation movement and the move toward individual independence and self-fulfillment, have begun to erode the dominance of the married, heterosexual nuclear family, as increased divorce rates, working mothers, single parents, same-sex marriage, LGBTQ families, and other alternative family arrangements become more common. Many sociologists speak of the sociology not of *the* family but rather of *families*. "Family situations in contemporary society are so varied and diverse that it simply makes no sociological sense to speak of a single ideal-type model of 'the family' at all" (Bernardes 1985, p. 209).

Even though a two-heterosexual-married-parent household with a stay-at-home mother, a breadwinning father, and their two biological children is no longer the norm, this type of family remains the model by which new forms of family are judged. However, there are exceptions, as commonsense definitions of family reflect the changes occurring in the larger society at any given moment. Marriage still equates with family, and about half of Americans ages eighteen and older are married. But other ways of coupling and cohabiting are also embraced. Children seem to be important in our customary definitions of family: One study found that unmarried couples, both gay and heterosexual, are more likely to be considered a family if children are present (Powell et al. 2010). Still, family is not always about children; 6 percent of married women are childless by choice (Reyes 2013).

As you will see as you read this chapter, what constitutes the model or hypothetical family may be very different from how families define themselves "on the ground."

SOCIOLOGICAL PERSPECTIVES ON FAMILIES

Among the sociological perspectives on the family, structural functionalists view family as a cultural universal and try to identify its functions for society. Conflict theorists argue that there are inherent inequalities both within and between families. Symbolic interactionists focus on the family as the product of interactional processes, while feminist and queer theoretical perspectives question male dominance and heteronormativity as yardsticks for determining what

> **MARRIAGE** a formally recognized bond between two spouses, establishing contractual rights and obligations between them
>
> **ADOPTION** the legal process of acquiring parental responsibilities for a child other than one's biological offspring
>
> **FAMILY** a social group whose members are bound by legal, biological, or emotional ties, or a combination of all three
>
> **EXTENDED FAMILY** a large group of relatives, usually including at least three generations living either in one household or in close proximity
>
> **KIN** relatives or relations, usually those related by common descent
>
> **NUCLEAR FAMILY** a heterosexual couple with one or more children living in a single household

Families on TV Functionalists might say that the traditional roles of Fred and Wilma Flintstone provided a validation of the prevailing social norms of the 1960s, while symbolic interactionists would find much to analyze in the quirky relationships of the Belcher family from *Bob's Burgers*.

is "normal" when it comes to family. Each of these theories offers useful insights into our understanding of family units.

Structural Functionalism

In *Suicide*, Émile Durkheim (1897/1951) argued that the Industrial Revolution and the division of labor had undermined the older social institutions that formerly regulated society, leaving some people suffering from anomie, or normlessness, that sometimes resulted in suicide. He found that marriage and family, at least for men, decreased the chances of suicide because they provide the structure and regulation that Durkheim believed people require to be happy. Durkheim hypothesized that men who were married and had children were less likely to kill themselves because of their obligations to their families, while single men had less to tether them to this mortal coil, and hence would be more likely to succumb to suicidal impulses.

The structural functionalists who followed Durkheim argued that society's survival requires institutions that can serve its essential functions: economic production, the socialization of children, instrumental and emotional support, and sexual control. Although the family is no longer directly involved in economic production, it performs the functions that allow production to happen. Talcott Parsons (1955) argued that "the modern nuclear family was especially complementary to the requirements of an industrial economy" because it freed individuals from onerous obligations to extended family members and made possible the geographic and social mobility demanded by the modern economy (Mann et al. 1997).

In the most basic sense, the family is responsible for the reproduction of society, as it produces and socializes children who will in turn become future workers and produce and socialize more new members of society. This is what Parsons

referred to as "pattern maintenance," whereby the values and norms of a society are passed on to the next generation. Family also, ideally, brings emotional support for its members by providing us with significant others such as spouses, parents, and siblings, and regulates sexuality by helping define with whom we can and cannot mate (in most societies, the ineligible list includes our brothers, sisters, and parents). These patterns, according to functionalists, help society run smoothly and maintain stability and order, and family as a social institution contributes to social order as a result.

Conflict Theory

Conflict theorists recognize that the family produces and socializes children to function efficiently in a capitalist economy, but they see this function as problematic. The nuclear family, a relatively recent historical invention, acts as the primary economic unit in modern capitalist society, and since conflict theorists see capitalism as oppressive, they claim that this form of family contributes to that oppression—and is often understood as an oppressive institution in itself. Conflict theorists believe that society revolves around conflict over scarce resources and that conflict within the family is also about the competition for resources: time, energy, and the leisure to pursue more interesting recreational activities.

In this analysis, conflict theorists see exploitation in the family through a sex-based, rather than a class-based, division of labor. Conflict perspectives overlap with feminist perspectives on the family, as feminists assume that the family is a gendered social institution and that men and women experience family differently. In patriarchal societies, men wield greater power than women, both within and outside the family, and women's contribution to family and society (such as household labor, child rearing, and other traditionally female work) is devalued and unpaid or underpaid (Bianchi et al.

2012). Considering men to be "heads of household" and providing them with legal rights that women don't have (which in some countries include the right to inherit property or to seek a divorce) means that families themselves are places in which women are discriminated against.

Gender is not the only system of stratification that shapes our experience in families. Age and ability may be the basis for inequality, conflict, and even violence within families and will be discussed in more detail later in the chapter.

Symbolic Interactionism

As Jim Holstein and Jay Gubrium point out in their book *What Is Family* (1990), the *family* does not exist, only *families*. By this, these symbolic interactionists mean that they consider it more effective to look at how family relations are created and maintained in interaction with one another, rather than how families are structured. Even though the legal bond of marriage has the same technical meaning for every couple, individual marriages may have very different expectations and rules for behavior. One couple may require sexual monogamy within their marriage, while their neighbors may not; one couple may pool their finances, while their neighbors may keep separate bank accounts. This approach conceives of family as a fluid, adaptable set of concepts and practices that people use "for constructing the meaning of social bonds" (Holstein and Gubrium 1995), a set of vocabularies to describe particular relationships.

Consider the number of relatives, defined by blood or marriage, most people have who play no meaningful role in their lives, who "aren't really family." When we describe people in terms of family, we are making claims about the "rights, obligations, and sentiments" that exist within their relationships (Gubrium and Buckholdt 1982). Consequently, we are constantly evaluating and reevaluating the attitudes and behaviors of those around us, assigning family status to new people and dismissing others from our circle of meaningful family

relations. In *All Our Kin*, an ethnography of kinship relations in an urban African American community, Carol Stack (1974) found this dynamic at work in the way people talked about family—including this woman, who explained,

> Most people kin to me are in this neighborhood . . . but I got people in the South, in Chicago, and in Ohio too. I couldn't tell most of their names and most of them aren't really kinfolk to me. . . . Take my father, he's no father to me. I ain't got but one daddy and that's Jason. The one who raised me. My kids' daddies, that's something else, all their daddies' people really take to them—they always doing things and making a fuss about them. We help each other out and that's what kinfolks are all about. (p. 45)

A symbolic interactionist might say that "family members do not merely passively conform to others' expectations" but rather "actively and creatively construct and modify their roles through interactions" (Dupuis and Smale 2000, p. 311)—that is, the people who help each other out, who care for each other, and who express that care are family, whether or not they are legally or biologically related. Sociologist Philip Cohen (2014) has coined the term "personal family" to describe some of these relationships.

Feminist and Queer Theory

Feminist and queer theoretical perspectives on family address what other sociological perspectives overlook: the interplay of gender and sexuality in family and society. Feminist theorists question male dominance, both within and outside families (hooks 2003, 2005; MacKinnon 2005, 2006). Why, for example, when heterosexual partners share a home, do we refer to the male partner as the "head of household"? This simple and often taken-for-granted designation bestows upon men the power to make decisions, control financial and other resources, and expect domestic

TABLE 12.1 Theory in Everyday Life

Perspective	Approach to Family	Case Study: Marriage
Structural Functionalism	Family performs necessary functions, such as the socialization of children, that help society run smoothly and maintain social order.	Marriage regulates sexuality and forms the basis for family, with all its other functions.
Conflict Theory	Family is a site of various forms of stratification and can produce and reproduce inequalities based on these statuses.	Marriage as a civil right was not extended to all same-sex couples in the United States until 2015. Nontraditional families are still marginalized in many ways, while the nuclear family remains the standard.
Symbolic Interactionism	Family is a social construction; it is created, changed, and maintained in interaction.	Marriage is not made solely by completing a legal contract but is also constructed through the accumulation of everyday interactions between partners over the years. Rules and expectations may vary from one marriage to another.

labor and emotional support from the women in their families. This is just one of many elements of family and social structure that tend to privilege men and exploit women, and assumptions like this about gender in families affect us all. That includes the authors of this textbook. When Dr. Ferris married her husband, she did not take his last name, but they did want to share joint access to each other's bank accounts. She arranged with her bank to add her husband's name to her account, giving them both the authority to sign checks. When the next month's bank statement was posted, it showed just her husband's name! Dr. Ferris's name had been removed from her own financial life once she acquired a male "head of household." As you might imagine, the bank president got an earful about this error.

Queer theorists further critique traditional perspectives on family by resisting heteronormativity as well as sexism in their analyses (Butler 1999, 2004; Sedgwick 1990, 2014). The male head of household example works here, too. If men are assumed to be "heads" of families, who, then, heads nonheterosexual families? How would gay or lesbian couples determine who is the "head"? What about single women—who heads their households? Neither masculinity nor heterosexuality should be a requirement for individuals to have power and autonomy within families (or outside them). Feminist and queer theories help us see that more diverse and egalitarian family structures are possible (Oswald et al. 2009).

MATE SELECTION

You may think that you are attracted to certain people because of their unique individual characteristics or something intangible called "chemistry." In reality, however, Cupid's arrow is aimed largely by society. Two time-tested concepts in social science—homogamy and propinquity—tell us a lot about how the mate-selection process works. **Homogamy** literally means "like marries like": We tend to choose mates who are similar to us in class, race, ethnicity, age, religion, education, and even levels of attractiveness. Indeed, some groups encourage and even enforce the practice of **endogamy** by requiring that their members choose mates only from within the group. Such groups may even impose harsh punishments for **exogamy**, or "marrying out." You can certainly find examples of people whose romantic relationships cross group and category lines—interracial or interreligious couples, or

"All of Me" It wasn't until 1967 that the Supreme Court ruled antimiscegenation laws unconstitutional in the landmark *Loving v. Virginia*. In 2015, 17 percent of newlyweds were in interracial marriages.

"May/December" romances—but these relationships are often viewed with disapproval by others in the couples' social circles. There are considerable social pressures to adhere to homogamy.

Propinquity refers to geographical proximity: We tend to choose people who live nearby. This is logical; we are likely to find possible mates among the people in our neighborhood, at work, or at school. The Internet makes courtship and romance possible across much greater geographical distances, as we can now meet and converse with people in all parts of the world, so our pool of potential mates moves beyond local bounds. But this technology, while it can weaken the effects of propinquity, can also intensify the effects of homogamy by bringing together people with very specific interests and identities. Examples include online dating services such as Christian Mingle for Christian singles; OurTime.com for people over age fifty; and Athletic Passions for people into fitness and sports. Online dating giant eHarmony hosts special subsites for black, Hispanic, Asian, and Jewish daters who wish to meet people like themselves. There's even a service for rural daters called FarmersOnly.com!

Courtship, romance, and intimacy are all influenced by the larger culture—and are also historically specific. As an example of how the forms and definitions of family change over time, marriage between people of different racial, ethnic, or national backgrounds was actually prohibited for

HOMOGAMY the tendency to choose romantic partners who are similar to us in terms of class, race, education, religion, and other social group membership

ENDOGAMY marriage to someone within one's social group

EXOGAMY marriage to someone from a different social group

PROPINQUITY the tendency to partner with people who live close by

most of U.S. history. From the time of slavery through the 1960s, mixed-race relationships were considered criminal and were also punished outside the law. Fears of interracial relationships led to the lynching of African American men and the creation of **antimiscegenation** laws in several states that prohibited the mixing of racial groups through marriage, cohabitation, or sexual interaction (Messerschmidt 1998). The most significant of these laws fell after the 1967 Supreme Court declared that Virginia's law banning marriage between persons of different races was unconstitutional under the Fourteenth Amendment (*Loving v. Virginia* 1967).

While once uncommon, mixed-race unions are becoming more commonplace. In 1980, just 3 percent of all married people had a spouse of a different race or ethnicity. That share had more than tripled—to 10 percent of all married people—by 2015. As Figure 12.1 shows, interracial marriage rates are even higher among newlyweds: In 2015, 17 percent of newlyweds had a spouse of a different race (Livingston and Brown 2017). The most dramatic increases are seen among black newlyweds; from 1980 to 2015, the share who married someone of a different race rose from 5 percent to 18 percent. Whites, too, are intermarrying more often, with their rates rising from 4 percent to 11 percent. Asians and Hispanics are the most likely to intermarry: 29 percent of Asian and 27 percent of Hispanic newlyweds in 2015 were married to someone of a different race.

Attitudes about interracial marriage are changing as well. The number of Americans who say that marrying someone of a different race is good for society rose from 24 percent in 2010 to 39 percent in 2017 (Livingston and Brown 2017).

Younger Americans are even more positive about people of different races marrying each other; roughly half of all Millennials view this as a positive trend (Pew Research Center 2014a). Mixed-race couples still face prejudice and discrimination, but opposition to interracial marriage has decreased dramatically.

As one of the most high-profile issues of the past decade, same-sex marriage has undergone a similar transformation. The United States was deeply divided over the issue, with some states passing bans on same-sex marriage and others making it legal. In 2015, the Supreme Court ruled that such bans were unconstitutional, effectively allowing gays and lesbians to marry nationwide. Of course, not all gay and lesbian partners will want to marry. And some queer couples were already able to marry without any changes in the law—a cisgender woman and her transgender male partner, for example (Pfeffer 2012). Finally, neither LGBTQ nor heterosexual persons need legal marriage to form romantic relationships or establish families. So the notion that marriage is the basis for family—as well as the traditional definitions of marriage and family—are called into question by modern family trends.

Monogamy, or marrying only one individual at a time, is still considered the only legal form of marriage in modern Western culture. **Polygamy**, or having multiple spouses, may be practiced among some subcultures around the world but is not widely acknowledged as a legitimate form of marriage. The more commonly known form of polygamy is **polygyny**, in which a man is married to multiple wives. **Polyandry**, in which a woman has multiple husbands, has been documented in Tibet but is the rarer form of polygamy. **Polyamory** is a type of multiple-person partnership defined by sociologist Elisabeth Sheff as "consensual and emotionally intimate nonmonogamous relationships in which both men and women can negotiate to have multiple partners" (Sheff 2014).

While we experience courtship at an individual, interactional level, it will always be shaped by macro-structural forces in the larger society, such as racial, ethnic, or religious prejudices and gendered role expectations. But courtship changes as other aspects of the surrounding culture change. As our society becomes less racist, sexist, and heterosexist, romantic options will expand as well. The development of intimate romantic relationships is not something "natural"; it is socially constructed to *appear* natural.

ANTIMISCEGENATION the prohibition of interracial marriage, cohabitation, or sexual interaction

MONOGAMY the practice of marrying (or being in a relationship with) one person at a time

POLYGAMY a system of marriage that allows people to have more than one spouse at a time

POLYGYNY a system of marriage that allows men to have multiple wives

POLYANDRY a system of marriage that allows women to have multiple husbands

POLYAMORY a system of multiple-person partnership

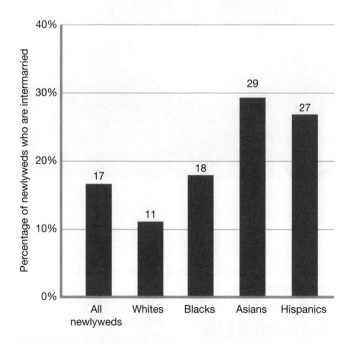

FIGURE 12.1 Intermarriage Rates by Race

SOURCE: Livingston and Brown 2017.

GLOBAL PERSPECTIVE
Talking about Kin

In P. D. Eastman's children's book *Are You My Mother?* a newly hatched bird wanders about asking everyone—and everything—he encounters, "Are you my mother?" Sadly for the newborn, neither the construction crane, nor the cow, nor the cat is the parent he is searching for. On the last page of the book, however, the tiny bird is serendipitously returned to his nest and reunited with a maternal-looking chickadee.

FICTIVE KIN close relations with people we consider "like family" but who are not related to us by blood or marriage

When reading something like *Are You My Mother?* most people in the Western world would assume that the word "mother" means "female parent." However, in the Hawaiian language, *makuahine* means both "mother" and "aunt" and refers to any female relative in the generation of that person's parents; *makuakane* is the equivalent term for men (Schwimmer 2001; Stanton 1995). In Hawaiian, then, "Are you my mother?" could just as easily mean "Are you my father's brother's wife?" In China, though, kinship terms are very precise. There are particular terms for a "father's brother's wife" that vary depending on whether the wife is married to the older brother or the younger one (Levi-Strauss 1949/1969)!

One reason we name our kin is to delineate the relationships and obligations we share. In some cases, we use the term **fictive kin** to refer to people who are not related to us through blood or through marriage. Such kin are created through closely knit friendships to the family. You may have a family friend you call Auntie So-and-So. In other societies, fictive kin may be culturally prescribed. In Jordan, it is perfectly normal for adult strangers to address one another with the Arabic equivalents of brother/sister, maternal aunt/uncle, and paternal aunt/uncle. In addition, an older Jordanian woman may affectionately refer to a child (of either gender) as "mother" (Farghal and Shakir 1994).

Sometimes fictive kinship ties are formalized through ceremony, as when a female in India ties a sacred thread around the wrist of an unrelated close male friend to indicate that she considers him a brother. In Latin America, godparents (or *compadres*, a word that can be translated as "co-parent" rather than "godparent") are considered permanent members of their godchildren's family. Not surprisingly, the Spanish words for "daughter" and "son" are very close to the words for "goddaughter" and "godson" (Davila 1971; van den Berghe 1979).

Examining kinship terms is one way to understand the diversity of families and how kin fulfill their social roles. As you can see, aunts, elder brothers, godparents, and family friends can all be important family members.

RELATIONSHIP TRENDS

Family relationships can take a number of different forms. From being single, to married with—or without—children, to divorced and then remarried, when it comes to modern family relationships, there are many possible outcomes. Relationship trends may also change over time, with some arrangements becoming more widespread while others become less so.

Unmarried Life

There's a pervasive idea in American society that puts marriage and family at the center of everyone's lives, when in fact it's becoming less and less so. Many people live outside such arrangements. The average American now spends the majority of their life as unmarried because people live longer, delay marriage, or choose a single lifestyle (Klinenberg 2012b).

The term "single" often implies a young heterosexual adult who is actively seeking a partner for a relationship or marriage. But singles may also include people of any sexual orientation who live together or are in a relationship without opting to get married, people living alone who are in long-distance relationships, people living in communes, widows and widowers, and some clergy members as well as those who are single as a result of divorce or who simply choose not to have a partner.

Married couples were the dominant model through the 1950s, but their numbers have slipped from nearly 80 percent of households in 1960 to 48 percent in 2018 (U.S. Census Bureau 2018c). Married couples with children—the traditional model of family—totaled less than 20 percent of households in 2018, and that number is projected to drop. The remaining households are single parents, cohabiting partners, or others. A stunning 28 percent of all households in 2018 consisted of people who live alone (Figure 12.2).

Some unmarried couples live together before or instead of being married. Demographers call this **cohabitation**. Cohabitation has become increasingly commonplace: In 1996, just 3 percent of U.S. adults lived with an unmarried partner. Today, nearly 8 percent of U.S. adults are living with an unmarried partner (Gurrentz 2018). While this proportion is still relatively small compared to the 51 percent of U.S. adults who are married, it represents a 30 percent increase in the number of U.S. adults cohabiting just in the last ten years (Stepler 2017). A possible reason for this rise in cohabitation may be the growing economic independence of individuals today, resulting in less financial motivation for marriage as a legal contract. Changing attitudes about religion have also made sexual relationships outside marriage more socially acceptable. In addition, marriage is no longer viewed as a prerequisite for childbearing. In 2017, nearly 40 percent of all births were to unmarried women (Martin et al. 2018). A significant majority (58 percent) of premarital births are to cohabiting couples (Curtin, Ventura, and Martinez 2014).

Cohabitation is most common among young adults twenty-five to thirty-four years of age. In 2018, 15 percent of young adults in this age group were living with an unmarried partner (Gurrentz 2018). It's worth noting that cohabitation is also growing among older Americans; adults fifty years of age or older make up 23 percent of all cohabiting couples (Stepler 2017). Cohabitors also comprise the largest number of interracial couples: 18 percent of cohabiting adults live with a partner of another race or ethnicity (Livingston 2017).

Because marriage has for so long been seen as the normative basis for families and households, unmarried people

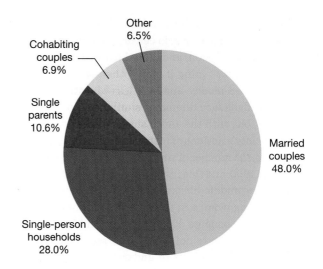

FIGURE 12.2 Households by Type, 2018
SOURCE: U.S. Census Bureau 2018x.

can sometimes feel as if the world is organized specifically to exclude them. Indeed, single people are usually charged more for auto and health insurance than married people, some tax breaks are available only to married couples, and even hotel rooms and vacation packages are usually advertised with "double occupancy" rates. Single people routinely grumble about relatives who ask when they are going to "settle down and get married." Since those who live alone are more likely to be older women (Klinenberg 2012b, p. 5), they may experience multiple forms of discrimination at once.

But as the number of people who live alone increases, so does their potential power to change a society in which they are no longer a minority. Among the growing movement of activists promoting the rights of unmarried people in the United States is the nonprofit group Unmarried Equality. The group engages in research, education, and advocacy for unmarried and single adults of all types and is concerned about the discrimination that is built into the American social system, especially at an economic and political level but also in terms of culture and values. One of its efforts is to increase the recognition of unmarrieds and singles as a constituency of voters, workers, taxpayers, and consumers worthy of equal rights and protection.

COHABITATION living together as a romantic couple without being married

Single and Solo Parenting

Although some people become single parents through divorce or death, others choose to go solo and have children without the support of a committed partner—through adoption, artificial insemination, or surrogacy. Attitudes about solo mothers vary greatly and often depend on the mother's age, race, education level, occupation, income, and support network of friends and extended family members. Women with more of these resources, including solo celebrity moms like Sandra Bullock, Charlize Theron, and Sheryl Crow, may be subject to less criticism for "going it alone" than women who are younger, earn less money, and have less education or social support. Solo dads face dilemmas similar to those faced by single moms, but with the added suspicion and stigma surrounding society's notions of men who spend time with children. Even so, the number of single dads has increased almost tenfold since 1960, and this increase seems likely to continue.

A prevailing middle-class assumption about single mothers is that young women in the inner city become mothers to access welfare benefits. Kathryn Edin and Maria Kefalas (2005) spent five years doing in-depth research with 162 low-income single mothers to understand their attitudes about parenthood and marriage. They dispelled the myth that such women become mothers to cash in on welfare benefits and instead found that for these young women, having a baby was a symbol of belonging and being valued. While becoming a lawyer or a CEO may seem like a pipe dream, being a good mother is an accessible role that can generate respect and admiration in the community.

Single-parent households vary significantly by race. In 2018, 26 percent of white families with children under eighteen were single-parent families compared with 60 percent of black families (U.S. Census Bureau 2018b). This means that black children are much more likely to be raised by a single parent: In 2018, 22 percent of white children were living with a single parent compared to 53 percent of black children.

Regardless of the circumstances of single parenting, raising children without the help of a partner is challenging. Financially, physically, and emotionally, single parents must perform a task that was traditionally undertaken by a community rather than an individual.

Blended Families

Most divorced people will eventually marry someone else. In fact, four in ten new marriages involve at least one partner who was married before (Livingston 2014). Consequently, about one in six children today is living in a blended family or stepfamily (Pew Research Center 2015f). However, statistics about stepfamilies are inconsistent and often contradictory, because it is difficult to quantify and define the intricate relationships involved in a stepfamily. The U.S. Census has not routinely accounted for them in its data gathering.

There are no traditional norms or models for stepfamilies, and our firmly held notions of the "traditional" family lead many in stepfamilies to find the transition to a new family situation difficult. Stepfamilies face special challenges, for example, when there are children in different stages of the life cycle. The needs and concerns of teenagers may be vastly different from those of their infant half brother or half sister, and it may take more work to adjust to the new living situation. With the added challenges of blending in-laws, finances, and households, remarriages are even more likely to end in divorce than first marriages. However, in successful remarriages, partners are usually older and have learned important

Modern Families The Pritchett-Dunphy-Tucker clan on *Modern Family* is a large blended family of stepparents, stepsiblings, half siblings, adopted children, and stepchildren. Today, about one in six children is living in a blended family.

lessons about compatibility and relationship maintenance from the failure of their first marriages.

Some partners in gay and lesbian couples have a heterosexual marriage (and divorce) in their past. While it is difficult to estimate, one study hypothesized that approximately 4 percent of heterosexual marriages have one gay or bisexual partner (Laumann et al. 1994). While not all these marriages end in divorce, when they do, the gay partner becomes free to form a new family with the partner of his or her choice, just as the heterosexual partner does. So while the majority of blended families are heterosexual, some will be "mixed orientation" and include stepparents of more than one sexual orientation.

Childfree Living

Having children used to be seen as a mandate and being childless a tragedy—especially for women. We still cling to this imperative: 86 percent of adults surveyed in a recent poll either had children or wanted them (Gallup 2018). But because men and women (gay and straight, married and unmarried) now have more choice than ever about whether to have children, some are choosing to live "childfree" rather than "childless." In 2016, 14 percent of women between the ages of forty and forty-four had never given birth, up from 10 percent in the mid-1970s (Livingston 2018). Bear in mind that never having given birth does not always mean a woman is childless; she may have stepchildren or adopted children.

There are many reasons people opt out of parenthood: Children are expensive and exhausting and raising them takes energy away from other things that individuals may value more, such as careers, avocations, and other relationships. Others describe not having children as an ethically responsible decision not to add to the world's growing population (Blackstone 2014). Childfree adults field all sorts of exasperating questions about their lives, from "Wait, don't you like kids?" to "Oh, that's too bad you can't get pregnant" to "Who is going to take care of you when you get old?" and the classic, "Well, that's just selfish." In fact, people who remain childfree may love kids, be quite fertile, be generous with others, and have a perfectly good plan in place for their retirement years; they just don't want to raise kids. But childfree people—especially women—are stigmatized for their choice and are often the object of pity, suspicion, and discrimination. Researcher Laura Scott (2009) describes our society as "pronatalist," meaning that our cultural values support childbearing and child rearing as the normative and preferred practice, and those who choose to remain childfree must battle against the judgments others make about them based on their nonconformity.

Despite the pervasive idea that parenthood brings greater joy to life, in reality, having a child can have a fairly strong negative impact on a person's happiness. The effect of a new baby during the first two years of its life can be more devastating to parents than a divorce, unemployment, or even the death of their partner (Margolis and Myrskylä 2015). Only about 30 percent of parents remained at about the same state of happiness or better after they had a baby, while the rest experienced some drop in their overall well-being. Another study showed that childfree couples are happier in their relationships and more satisfied with their partners than couples with children (Gabb et al. 2013).

BREAKING UP

Although many people stay in unsatisfying marriages or other relationships, couples break up every day. In this section, we consider the changing patterns of breakups, divorces, and remarriages as they affect children and adults. We also look at the resulting issues of custody, visitation, and child support.

In 2018, about 55 percent of the population over age eighteen was married while about 10 percent was divorced (U.S. Census Bureau 2018e). The percentage of married people who have divorced has greatly increased since 1950, but it is not accurate to say that approximately 50 percent of all marriages now end in divorce, although that myth persists (Miller 2014). In fact, the divorce rate actually decreased by 18 percent from 2008 to 2016 despite more permissive attitudes toward divorce. Sociologist Philip Cohen (2019) expects divorce rates to continue to decline, with marriage becoming both rarer and more stable.

About 57 percent of those who divorce will eventually marry other people (Livingston 2014). There is a gender gap in remarriage patterns, with 64 percent of previously married men having remarried compared to 52 percent of previously married women. This gender gap may be explained by the fact that married women are less happy than single women and their married male husbands. According to sociologist Lisa Wade (2017b), women are more likely to file for divorce, and when they do, they are happier as divorcees than they were when married (while the opposite is true for men). Remarriage rates among younger Americans in the United States are actually significantly lower now than they were in 1960; the opposite is true of older adults (Livingston 2014). This may be due to a number of factors, including an increase in cohabitation among unmarried couples.

The work of sociologist Nicholas Wolfinger (2005) has focused on studying the divorce cycle, or the tendency of divorce to run in families. In the early 1970s, the children of divorced parents were more than three times more likely to divorce than their peers from intact families, but those figures dropped to about one and a half times by the mid-1990s. Still, this seemed to indicate a strong pattern of intergenerational transmission of divorce. Wolfinger and others have speculated that every family structure transition (such as divorce or remarriage) that children experience in their family of

ON THE JOB
When Building Families Is Part of Your Job

If you've read this far in this chapter, you've probably already gotten the sociological message: Families don't "just happen." They are the product of interactional work. When most people say it takes "work" to make a family, they just mean it takes effort. But for the social workers, caregivers, child psychologists, lawyers, and others who are employed in the foster care and adoption systems, "making" families is what they do for a living.

In the United States today there are more than 425,000 children in foster care and more than 2 million adopted children. These children come from an extraordinarily diverse set of circumstances and backgrounds. They are different ages, have different racial and ethnic backgrounds, and are even from different parts of the world. What they all have in common is that a social worker or someone else from the helping professions worked to make them part of a family. For about 55 percent of the children in foster care the case plan is to reunite them with their parents or guardians. Another 25 percent are awaiting adoption, and the rest have less common case plans, like emancipation (U.S. Department of Health and Human Services 2016). For these kids, a social worker is going to play an important role in their lives.

Judith Schagrin, who spent her career working for Baltimore County Children's Services, compares a foster care placement to an "arranged marriage" and says that "like arranged marriages, sometimes they work out and sometimes they're just a bad match" (Green 2016). Social workers must spend time getting to know the children they represent as well as the prospective foster families while often juggling very full caseloads. When people think about the problems associated with foster care, usually they think about children being abused by foster parents. Such abuse is always tragic, but it is also quite rare. On an everyday basis, social workers are focused on finding foster parents who are a good fit and can provide children with safety and stability.

According to the 2010 Census, 2.3 percent of all children in the United States are adopted. Some of these adoptions involve stepparents who adopt the children of a new spouse, but there are still about 1.8 million adopted children who live in a household without either of their biological parents (Vandivere, Malm, and Radel 2009). Although the numbers have slowed in recent years, as many as 25 percent of those children were adopted internationally. Not all international adoptions result in interracial families, but they often do: 40 percent of adoptive families "were involved in a transracial, transethnic, or transcultural adoption" (Kreider and Lofquist 2010).

origin cumulatively increases the likelihood of negative outcomes for those children. Other research has quantified this factor, noting that each parental breakup experienced while growing up increases the odds of those children dissolving their own adult relationships by 16 percent (Amato and Patterson 2016). According to Wolfinger (2017), "If you experience relationships as transitory while growing up, that's what you'll do as an adult." It is important to note, however, that transitions in the structure of one's family of origin are but one of many factors that determine how children of divorce fare in their own marriages.

Legalization of same-sex marriage now presents the possibility of divorce for gay and lesbian couples as well. Since all U.S. states and territories recognize such marriages, they should also allow for legal reciprocity when it comes to divorce. Because same-sex marriage is relatively new, there is not as yet a lot of data on divorce rates. Early research indicates that about 1 percent of same-sex couples divorce per year, compared with 2 percent of heterosexual couples (Badgett and Mallory 2014). However, alternate analyses of the same data (Gelman 2014) found that same-sex marriages are about as likely as heterosexual marriages to end in divorce.

Divorce isn't the only way to break up, of course. And since not all couples opt to marry, their breakups are not required to occur within the legal framework of divorce. Divorce laws can help streamline the process for those who are married, while those who are not married must cobble together a package of separate legal contracts that meets their needs as well as their children's needs.

Custody, Visitation, and Child Support

Reviewing the legal policies that address the consequences of parental breakups for children, sociologists are concerned with whether custody, visitation, and child support effectively replace the resources, both emotional and financial, of a two-parent household. Do they help children?

Transracial adoptions (where the race or ethnicity of the adopted child is different from the race or ethnicity of the parents) illustrate the challenges faced by social workers who facilitate and monitor adoptions. While everyone agrees that social workers should be screening adoptive parents to make sure they'll provide a loving, supportive, and welcoming home, the situation gets more complicated when you have to define terms like "supportive." For instance, should parents be encouraged to adopt across racial or ethnic lines? The Multiethnic Placement Act of 1995 made it easier to match prospective adoptees with parents from a different racial background, but debate remains over whether race and culture should be considered when building families (Kreider and Lofquist 2010).

The adoption process is long and complicated and social workers are there from start to finish. They start by leading training sessions in which families learn about adoption and the important issues surrounding it—for example, how to talk about adoption with children and other family members, what to expect in cases of international or interracial adoption, or how to maintain an open relationship with an adopted child's birth family. Then they screen the prospective parents and take them through the extensive state licensing procedures that will qualify them to adopt a child. They interview prospective parents about their desire to adopt, their family life, and their hopes for the future. This stage of the process includes visiting their homes to make sure they can provide

Fostering Families The TV show *The Fosters* features a multiethnic blended family of a biological child, adopted twins, and two foster children.

a safe environment, collecting letters of recommendation from friends and employers, and even obtaining veterinary clearances on the family pets!

Despite the vital importance of this work, social workers are perpetually in short supply. It is estimated that over the next fifteen to twenty years the United States will experience a shortfall of more than 195,000 social workers (Lin, Lin, and Zhang 2016). So if you're interested in the helping professions, you can have an incredibly rewarding profession and job security.

Custody is the physical and legal responsibility for the everyday life and routines of children. In previous decades it was mothers who were disproportionately awarded sole custody of children. But more recently there has been a dramatic shift toward shared custody between both parents (Cancian and Meyer 1998; Cancian, Brown, and Cook 2014), and research shows that this arrangement might be better for children's health (Bergström et al. 2015). By 2008, mother sole-custody had declined from a high of 80 percent to just 42 percent. This decline reflects an increase in shared custody from 5 percent to 27 percent of all cases. There has been little change in father sole-custody, which has remained at about 10 percent.

Courts award visitation to noncustodial parents to protect parent–child relationships. Generally, parents with regular visitation patterns are better able to meet the psychological and financial needs of their children. Fathers who visit regularly are more likely to maintain strong relationships with their children and to pay child support (Seltzer, Schaeffer, and Charng 1989), and research shows that this is good for kids'

academic success and may help reduce risky behaviors (Jones and Mosher 2013). Despite increased vigilance of courts and lawmakers regarding mandated child support policies, noncustodial parents often fail to make regular payments to custodial parents. Sociologists have found that many parents make informal arrangements or decisions about child support schedules, without the mediation of the legal system, soon after the divorce (Grall 2018; Peters et al. 1993) and that the stability of payments varies substantially, even among the most reliable payers (Meyer and Bartfeld 1998).

> **CUSTODY** the physical and legal responsibility of caring for children; assigned by a court for divorced or unmarried parents

As children are more likely to live in poverty after their parents' divorce, child support policies are important. Women are more likely to suffer downward economic mobility after divorce, especially if they retain custody of their children. In 2015, the poverty rate for custodial-mother families was 29 percent, compared to 17 percent for custodial-father families (Grall 2018). Furstenberg, Hoffman, and Shrestha (1995) found that women experience on average a 25 percent decline in their economic well-being after a divorce. Accompanying this postdivorce decline in financial resources are often scholastic failure, disruptive conduct, and troubled relationships in children of divorced families (Keith and Finlay 1988; Morrison and Cherlin 1995). However, it is not clear whether these behavior problems are the effect of the divorce itself or of the problems that led up to the divorce. Researcher Jui-Chung Allen Li (2007) found that if the behavior of children is compared before and then after divorce, the divorce itself is shown to have had very little impact on their grades or conduct.

THE WORK OF FAMILY

When we think of work, we usually think of activities done for a paycheck. But paid labor is not the only type of work that sociologists are interested in—especially in the study of family. Many types of work—both paid and unpaid—are necessary to keep a family operating: child care, housecleaning, car maintenance, cooking, bill paying, helping with homework, and doing laundry—the list seems endless, especially when you are the one doing the work!

These tasks can be instrumental or expressive. **Instrumental tasks** generally achieve a tangible goal (washing the dishes, fixing the gutters), whereas **expressive tasks** generally achieve emotional or relational goals (remembering relatives' birthdays, playing Chutes and Ladders with the kids). In a real-world family, however, much of the work has both instrumental and expressive elements. The expressive work of remembering and celebrating birthdays, for example, includes all sorts of instrumental tasks, such as buying presents, writing cards, and baking cakes (Di Leonardo 1987; Pleck 2000).

Instrumental tasks, such as cooking dinner, include expressive elements as well. As a social scientist committed to making the invisible labor of family visible, Marjorie DeVault (1991/1994) excavates all the knowledge, skills, and practices—both instrumental and expressive—we take for granted when we feed our families. Not only is the knowledge of cooking needed, but also the necessary shopping must be done to stock the kitchen; to make meals that account for family members' likes, dislikes, and allergies; and to create varied and balanced menus. Producing meals that please, satisfy, and bring individuals together is just one of the ways that family is created and sustained through interactional work—both instrumental and expressive. We constitute family in and through meals and every other mundane activity of everyday life.

INSTRUMENTAL TASKS the practical physical tasks necessary to maintain family life

EXPRESSIVE TASKS the emotional work necessary to support family members

Analyzing Everyday Life

Comparative Mealtime

Some of us carry a strong and positive image of our family gathered around the dining room table for dinner each evening. While we were growing up, dinner may have been the one time in the day when the whole family was together and shared food, stories, lessons, and news. For many of us, a great deal of socialization took place around the dinner table; we learned about manners ("Sit up straight," "Don't speak with your mouth full") as well as morality, politics, or anything else that seemed important to the adults raising us. Some of us, on the other hand, may have different memories of family mealtimes. Perhaps they were a time of tension and arguments, or perhaps the family rarely ate a meal together.

In this Data Workshop, you will be doing participant observation research and writing a short ethnography on mealtime activity. See Chapter 2 for a review of this research method. You will pick two different mealtime settings or situations to examine. You can choose from among a range of possibilities, including the following:

- Which meal you study—breakfast, lunch, or dinner

- Where the meal takes place—in your family home, at a friend's or a relative's house, at your own apartment or dormitory dining hall, or at a workplace lunchroom, picnic in the park, or restaurant

- Who is eating the meal—family members, roommates, friends, co-workers, or strangers

What's for Dinner? What do our mealtime practices tell us about contemporary American families?

After you do the participant observation at the two meal-times, write some field notes and answer the following questions in as much detail as you can. These field notes will serve as data for your analysis:

- What are the prevailing rules, rituals, norms, and values associated with the setting and situation? For example, does everyone sit down to eat at the same time? Do people leave after they finish even if others are still eating? Do you need to get in line to order or pay for food?

- What kinds of complementary roles are the various participants engaged in? Who cooks the food, sets the table, clears the table, does the dishes, and so forth? Or are you served in a cafeteria or restaurant?

- What other types of activities (besides eating) are taking place at mealtime? Are people watching TV, listening to music or a ballgame, reading the newspaper, or texting?

- What social purposes does the setting or situation serve other than providing a mealtime environment for the participants? For example, what do the participants talk about? If children are involved, do they talk about school or their friends? Are family activities or problems discussed? What kinds of interactions do you see among co-workers or roommates?

Further analyze your field notes to identify patterns within each setting and meal. What are the similarities and differences between settings and meals? How do participants make these mealtimes meaningful as social events?

There are two options for completing this Data Workshop:

PREP-PAIR-SHARE Make the mealtime observations and prepare some written notes about your preliminary findings that you can refer to during class. Get together with one or two other students and discuss your research. Compare the analyses of the different meals observed by the group members. What are the similarities and differences in your findings? What patterns emerge from the data gathered by the entire group?

DO-IT-YOURSELF Complete the research process. Write a three- to four-page essay answering the questions provided and reflecting on your own experience in conducting this study. What do you think your observations tell us about contemporary Americans and the practices and functions of mealtimes? Don't forget to attach your field notes to your essay.

Gender, Sexuality, and Family Labor

Imagine working a labor-intensive forty to sixty hours waiting tables, making automobile parts, doing data entry, or teaching second graders. Each day you arrive home feeling tired, hungry, and worn out, but you cannot sit down to relax. You still need to cook a meal, do some laundry and cleaning, and take care of your children or perhaps your elderly parents. Who is more likely to come home to this scenario? When you ask young couples, 67 percent say that sharing household chores is key to a successful marriage (Geiger 2016). But is that what's actually happening? Let's look at the division of labor within the household.

Men and women have always performed different roles to ensure the survival of their families, but these roles were not considered unequal until after the Industrial Revolution. At that time, men began to leave their homes to earn wages working in factories. Women remained at home to take care of children and carry out other domestic responsibilities. As men's earned wages replaced subsistence farming—in which women had always participated—these wages became the primary mechanism for providing food, clothing, and shelter for families, thus giving men economic power over women. In more recent decades, however, most families require a two-person income in order to make ends meet. So now most women work too.

Despite women's increasing participation in the paid workforce, they are still more likely to perform the bulk of household and caregiving labor. A study of working couples and parents by Arlie Hochschild and Anne Machung (1989) found that women were indeed working two jobs: paid labor outside the home, or the first shift, and unpaid labor inside the home, or the **second shift**. In a few cases, men share household chores equitably or even do more than their partners (Coltrane 1997), but in most cases women bear the brunt of unpaid household labor.

SECOND SHIFT the unpaid housework and child care often expected of women after they complete their day's paid labor

Hochschild and Machung's observations were groundbreaking in their analysis of post-feminist families. Despite the gains of the women's movement, couples were still dividing the household labor along traditional gender lines. Stereotypical "women's work" is usually more labor intensive, consisting of chores such as grocery shopping, washing dishes, cooking, laundry, and child care, while men tend to do more occasional or sporadic outdoor (yard) work and auto and home repairs. The women in the study tried numerous strategies to achieve balance between work and home: hiring other women to clean their houses and care for their children; relying on friends or family members for help; refusing to do certain chores, especially those considered to be generally "men's work"; lowering their expectations for cleanliness or quality of child care; or reducing the number of hours they worked outside the home. But some women accepted their dual workloads without any help to avoid conflicts with spouses and children. Hochschild and Machung called these women "Supermoms" but also found that these "Supermoms" often felt unhappy or emotionally numb.

It's important to note that their concept of the "Supermom" has been applicable to working-class mothers all along. The stay-at-home parent is possible only when one salary can support the entire family. Before college-educated women were encouraged to work in the paid labor force, working-class women were there out of necessity. The strategies that middle-class women use to negotiate their second shift are available only to wealthier families. After all, a woman who cleans another family's house and takes care of their children rarely has the financial resources to hire someone to do the same for her. And so the second shift is present in working-class homes as well (Miller and Sassler 2012), with women rarely getting the privilege of "downtime."

More recent studies have found little change: Traditional gender roles still influence the domestic lives of working families. Among dual-earner couples, gender, income, and the number of hours worked outside the home were all predictive of how housework was divided (Matos 2015). Women,

Supermom For many women, "work" doesn't end when they leave the workplace. On returning home, many begin what Arlie Hochschild calls "the second shift," doing the unpaid work of running a household, including doing laundry, preparing dinner, and helping with homework.

lower earners, and those who spend less time in paid work tend to take responsibility for stereotypical female chores, whereas men, higher earners, and those who spend more time in paid work tend to take responsibility for stereotypical male chores. Perhaps it indicates progress that there is growing dissatisfaction with these arrangements, although more so among women than among men (Forste and Fox 2012).

With the increasing visibility of same-sex couples, alternative models are now available for comparison. In same-sex couples, the household chores can't be unequally distributed by gender, but they aren't always divided equally, either. We might ask, then, what principle do they use to divide responsibilities? In some respects, same-sex couples have already broken out of the normative family structure that still applies to hetero couples. This may allow them to be more creative in determining how the work of family gets done. Research indicates that same-sex couples tend to communicate better, share duties more fairly, and assign chores based on personal preference rather than by gender, income, or hours worked (Matos 2015). Importantly, same-sex couples are more likely to share equally the most time-consuming work of child care.

And while there is very little sociological research on trans families, scholar Carla Pfeffer's (2012, 2014) studies of cisgender women in partnership with transgender men complicate things even further. In these queer families, the designations of gay/straight, male/female, wife/husband, and mother/father are nonnormative, making it problematic to ask if the women/wives/mothers are disproportionately taking on the "second shift." How do we categorize the labor of a child's biological mother (childbearing, breastfeeding, and other child-care activities, especially in the early months) when the same person may also be the child's legal father? Same-sex and trans families can help us reframe the work of family and perhaps organize it differently in the future. After all, everybody's time is valuable.

FAMILY AND THE LIFE COURSE

As an agent of socialization and the most basic of primary groups, the family molds everyone—young children, teenagers, adults, and senior citizens—and its influences continue throughout the life course.

When we are children, our families provide us with our first lessons in how to be members of society. Children's experiences are shaped by family size, birth order, presence or absence of parents, socioeconomic status, and other sociological variables. Dalton Conley's 2004 work, *The Pecking Order*, maintains that inequality between siblings; things outside the family's control, such as the economy, war, illness, and death; and marital discord affect each child at different stages in their life, resulting in different experiences for each child.

IN RELATIONSHIPS
From Boomerang Kids to the Sandwich Generation

When people talk about the disappearance of the nuclear family, they are usually referring to the divorce rate, but, especially for the Baby Boom generation, families are changing in other ways as well. Increasing numbers of middle-aged people are becoming members of a "sandwich generation," adults who provide material and emotional support for both young children and older living parents (Lachman 2004, p. 322). This effect is magnified by the increasing number of so-called boomerang kids, who leave home at eighteen to attend college but then return home for at least a short period of time afterward.

Both of these dynamics are being driven less by choice than by demographic and economic necessity. In 1970, the average age at first marriage was less than twenty-one for women and a little over twenty-three for men. In 2018, the median age at first marriage for women was 27.8, and for men it was 29.8 (U.S. Census Bureau 2018e). As a result, people are having children later, increasing the chances that child rearing and elder care will overlap. Advances in life expectancy also contribute to the sandwich effect; many of the medical advances that allow people to live longer also increase their need for material support.

While there have always been adults caring for their elderly parents, never before have there been this many elderly. In fact, by 2035, older adults are projected to outnumber children for the first time in U.S. history (Vespa 2018). Meanwhile, between tuition increases, student loans, and a challenging job market, students leaving college are more likely to need help from their parents than ever before. In 1980, less than 9 percent of all individuals between twenty-five and thirty-four lived with their parents. By 2016, this proportion had increased to 15 percent, still a small group but one that has increased significantly during the past three decades (Fry 2017).

Members of the sandwich generation have found themselves with more responsibilities than ever before. Not only are their parents living longer, but medical costs associated with old age are growing rapidly, and often they have children, of all ages, still dependent on them as well. Never before has there been a substantial cohort of Americans so directly burdened with such a wide range of family responsibilities. However, in some ways, the more the sandwich generation adults and the boomerang kids change the family, the more

Sandwiched With four generations under one roof, the LaRock and Bruno families are an extreme example of the sandwich generation, where adults provide support for both children and aging parents.

the family stays the same, especially in the way that gender roles manifest themselves. Even among eighteen- to twenty-four-year-olds, boys are more likely to live at home than girls. While men and women might be driven by the same financial troubles, moving back in with her parents has different consequences for a woman. She is likely to be asked to take on more domestic responsibilities, and typically she feels a greater loss of independence.

Gender functions in similar ways for the sandwich generation, as it is still mostly women who are called on to provide the emotional and instrumental support for elderly parents, even when those women also work. In fact, "working women who do take on caregiving tasks may reduce their work hours" (Velkoff and Lawson 1998, p. 2), finding themselves having to prioritize family over career in ways men often do not.

Despite the costs associated with being a member of the sandwich generation, there is good news as well. Although it is challenging to assume "dual responsibilities," these are mostly experienced as "a 'squeeze' but not stress," and these relationships can also be a source of happiness and well-being (Lachman 2004, p. 322). And while there is still a certain stigma associated with moving back in with your parents, the fact that so many are willing to do so suggests that today's boomerang kids may enjoy closer relationships with their parents than did the kids of previous generations.

Conley argues that family proves not to be the consistent influence many people view it to be.

In addition, the presence of children shapes the lives of parents. Relationship satisfaction tends to decline when there are small children in the house, and heterosexual couples' gendered division of labor becomes more traditional when children are born, even if it has been nontraditional up to that point. As children get older, they may exert other types of influence on their parents—for example, children can pressure their parents to quit smoking or eat healthier food. And, of course, later in life, they may be called on to care for their elderly parents as well as their own offspring—a phenomenon known as "the sandwich generation" effect.

Aging in the Family

The American population is aging. The number of Americans sixty-five or older is growing twice as fast as the population as a whole (Werner 2011) and is expected to nearly double by 2060 (Administration for Community Living 2018). This is because the Baby Boom generation (the large number of Americans born in the two decades after World War II) is moving into middle age and beyond, concurrent with advances in medical technology. Average life expectancy in the United States is nearly seventy-nine (with women living an average of five years longer than men). More people are living longer, and that has an impact on families and society.

Planning for an aging population means taking into account both the basic and special needs of older individuals. Retirement income is an important part of this planning. Social Security benefits are the major source of income for most of the elderly in the United States. Without other sources of income, retired citizens may find themselves with limited resources; in 2016, 9.3 percent of adults sixty-five and older lived below the poverty line (Semega, Fontenot, and Kollar 2017). Some seniors solve the problem by living with their adult children or with nonfamily members; even so, in 2017, 34 percent of women and 20 percent of men age sixty-five and older lived alone. The proportion of older adults living alone increases with age, with nearly half (45 percent) of women age seventy-five and older doing so in 2017 (Administration for Community Living 2018).

Like other traditional functions of the family (such as educating children), care of the elderly is no longer a primary duty of family and has been taken over by other institutions: Some senior citizens will spend time in a nursing home, being housed and cared for by people other than their family members. In 2017, approximately 1.5 million seniors ages sixty-five and older, or about 3 percent, lived in institutional settings such as nursing homes. These numbers increase dramatically with age; approximately

Gray Divorce Divorced seniors become roommates in the Netflix show *Grace and Frankie*. Between 1990 and 2010, the divorce rate for adults over fifty doubled (Brown and Lin 2012).

9 percent of people ages eighty-five and older live in such institutional settings (Administration for Community Living 2018).

Coping with the transitions of retirement, loss of one's partner, declining health, and death are central tasks for seniors. However, as the average life span extends, the elderly are also taking on new roles in society. Many live healthy, vibrant, active lives and are engaged with their families and communities in ways that are productive for both the individual and the person's groups.

TROUBLE IN FAMILIES

While families are often a place of comfort, support, and unconditional love, some are not a "haven in a heartless world" (Lasch 1977). The family may be where we are at the greatest risk—emotionally, socially, and physically. "People are more likely to be killed, physically assaulted, sexually victimized . . . in their own homes by other family members than anywhere else, or by anyone else, in our society" (Gelles 1995, p. 450). Because of current social norms about the privacy of family life, and because the family is the site of unequal power relations and intense feelings, the circumstances are ripe for trouble and violence.

Domestic abuse is an umbrella term for a variety of behaviors that involve violence or abuse within a household setting. Domestic abuse may be aimed at an intimate partner or at other members of the family, especially children or elders. Abusers use a variety of behaviors to gain and maintain control over their victims. These behaviors fall into five main categories: physical (slapping, punching, kicking, choking, shoving, restraining), verbal (insults, taunts, threats, degrading statements), financial (insisting on complete control of all household finances, including making decisions about who will work and when), sexual (rape, molestation),

DOMESTIC ABUSE any physical, verbal, financial, sexual, or psychological behaviors abusers use to gain and maintain power over their victims

and psychological or emotional abuse (mind games, threats, stalking, intimidation). Although not all abusers are physically violent toward their partners, any one type of abuse increases the likelihood of the others. In an abusive relationship, it is extremely rare to find only one form of abuse.

Intimate Partner Violence

Imagine that tomorrow's newspapers ran front-page headlines about a newly discovered disease epidemic that could potentially kill one-quarter of all American women. Between 1 million and 4 million women would be afflicted in the next year alone. What kind of public reaction would there be?

Let's reframe the scenario: In the United States, nearly one out of every four women has suffered severe physical violence at the hands of an intimate partner (Smith et al. 2017). Intimate partner violence (IPV) refers to violence that occurs between two people in a close relationship, including current and former spouses and dating and sexual partners. IPV includes five main types of behavior: physical violence, sexual violence, stalking, psychological aggression, and control of reproductive or sexual health (Smith et al. 2017). More than one in three women (37 percent) have experienced sexual violence, physical violence, or stalking by an intimate partner during her lifetime and nearly 7 percent of women in just the last year. Nearly half of women reported psychological aggression by an intimate partner in their lifetimes.

Rates of intimate partner violence vary somewhat across groups. American Indian/Alaska Natives are most often victimized by partners, followed by blacks, whites, and Hispanics; Asian women are victimized least often (Smith et al. 2017). Among LGBTQ partners, 43 percent of gay men and 19 percent of lesbian women experience relationship violence compared with 16 percent of heterosexual couples; 10 percent of bisexuals and 9 percent of queer partners experience intimate partner violence (Waters 2016).

Women are certainly not the only victims of intimate partner violence, but statistically, they are more likely than men to be victimized by an intimate partner: According to the Department of Justice, between 2003 and 2012, 82 percent of intimate partner violence was committed against women (Catalano 2013; Truman and Morgan 2014). Women between the ages of eighteen and twenty-four are victims of abuse at the hands of an intimate partner more frequently than women (and men) in any other age group. Women with lower household earnings are also more likely to be abused than those in higher socioeconomic groups. Age and economic security, however, do not make someone immune to abuse.

Contrary to popular opinion, most abusive partners are neither "out of control" nor have "anger management problems" in the traditional sense. They often seem charming and calm to co-workers, friends, and police officers; they deliberately decide to be violent with those least likely to report the crime and over whom they maintain the most control:

their family members. IPV results from the abuser's desire for power over the victim, and abusers often blame their victims: I wouldn't have beaten you if dinner had been on time, or if you hadn't been "flirting" with the sales associate at the mall. One abuser is reported to have said to police officers, "Yes, I hit her five or six times, but it was only to calm her down" (Scutt 2003).

A four-stage **cycle of violence** seems to occur in almost every abusive relationship. In the first stage, the abusive partner is charming, attentive, and thoughtful; disagreements are glossed over and the relationship looks stable and healthy. However, tension is building to the second stage, often described as "walking on eggshells." Here, both parties sense that something will happen no matter what the victim may do to try to avoid it. During the third stage, acute abuse and violence occur, lasting for seconds, hours, or even days. Whatever

CYCLE OF VIOLENCE a common behavior pattern in abusive relationships; the cycle begins happily, then the relationship grows tense, and the tension explodes in abuse, followed by a period of contrition that allows the cycle to repeat

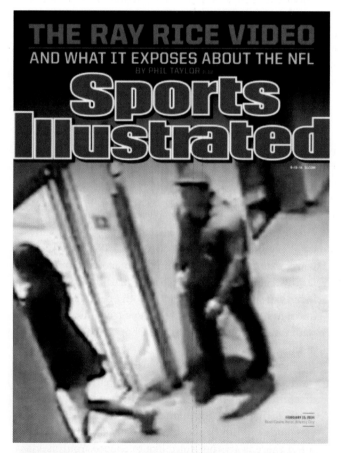

IPV and the NFL Former Baltimore Ravens running back Ray Rice was caught on an Atlantic City surveillance camera as he coldcocked his fiancée, now his wife, and dragged her out of an elevator. This incident set in motion an investigation that effectively ended Rice's NFL career and shined a light on professional football as a game that involves violence both on and off the field.

happens, the abuser will invariably blame the victim for the incident. The fourth stage, often referred to as "loving contrition," is the "honeymoon" phase and is one of the reasons victims remain in abusive relationships. After the violence, the abuser will apologize profusely and promise that it will never happen again. The abuser may buy the victim gifts, beg forgiveness, and talk about getting help or making a change. Most abusers, however, have no interest in changing because they don't want to give up their control over their victims. Soon the cycle starts again, with flowers and gifts giving way to tension, uneasiness, and another battering.

Victims of intimate partner violence stay with their abusers for many reasons. After years of abuse, victims often believe what their abusers tell them: that they can't make it on their own and are somehow responsible for the abuse. If they have not been allowed to attend school or to work, they may not have employment skills. Often children are involved, or abusers threaten to harm other family members. Many victims have been isolated from friends and family and are afraid to speak of the abuse to anyone, and they see no options but to remain where they are. Survivors who do manage to leave may find that their abusive partners present an even greater risk to their safety after they have exited the relationship (Dunn 2002).

DATA WORKSHOP

Analyzing Media and Pop Culture

Family Troubles in Film

Family relations have long been the basis of good comic, tragic, and dramatic films. This Data Workshop asks you to examine family dynamics and, more specifically, family troubles, as depicted in a feature film. You will be using existing sources and doing both a content analysis and a historical comparative analysis of a film dealing with family troubles. Return to Chapter 2 for a review of this research method.

The following films depict a variety of family troubles: marital issues, divorce, domestic abuse, parental neglect, disabilities and illnesses, sex and dating, pregnancy, death, delinquency, and financial difficulties. Other movies could certainly be added to this list; ask your instructor, if there is another you'd like to choose. Your movie should be available on DVD or online so that you can view (and review) it carefully. Please be aware of MPAA ratings and watch only those movies that are appropriate for your age and that you are comfortable viewing:

American Beauty	*My Big Fat Greek Wedding*
Amreeka	*Ordinary People*
August: Osage County	*Precious*
The Big Sick	*Rachel Getting Married*
Boyhood	*Roma*
Crazy Rich Asians	*The Royal Tenenbaums*
The Descendants	*Saving Face*
The Ice Storm	*The Squid and the Whale*
In America	*A Star Is Born*
In the Bedroom	*Stepmom*
The Joy Luck Club	*Still Alice*
The Kids Are All Right	*Terms of Endearment*
Kramer vs. Kramer	*We Don't Live Here Anymore*
Lion	*What's Eating Gilbert Grape*
Manchester by the Sea	*You Can Count on Me*

Choose a movie that is primarily about contemporary family relations and problems; then read through the workshop prompts and keep them in mind while viewing. Watch the film closely and pay attention to the plotlines, scenes, characters, and dialogues in which family troubles are depicted. Take notes as you watch the movie; you may need to review certain segments several times to do a thorough content analysis. As part of the process, you will also be doing an Internet search to gather more data about the family problems and their incidence in contemporary society. Be sure to note the source of your web references.

Respond to the following points and questions:

- Give some background information on the film and why you chose it.

- Describe the family troubles that are the focus of the film. How are these problems manifested in the lives of the family members?

- How do the various characters deal with their problems? What solutions do they propose through their talk or actions? How effective are these solutions in addressing the family's troubles?

- Put the family's problems in a broader sociological context. In what ways are the individual troubles of family members linked to larger social patterns and problems?

- Gather some recent data from the U.S. Census Bureau, other government or private agencies, or various news sources. How widespread are these problems in the real world? How are they being discussed and dealt with at a public level?

- How accurately do you think the family's troubles, and their possible solutions, were depicted in the film? What kind of a role, if any, do you think the

Family Troubles In the film *Crazy Rich Asians*, Nick introduces his girlfriend, Rachel, to his mother, which stirs up trouble, while in *A Star Is Born*, Jack's alcoholism causes problems in his marriage to Ally.

media can play in helping to improve family troubles and associated social problems?

There are two options for completing this Data Workshop:

PREP-PAIR-SHARE Complete the research activities and develop some preliminary analyses. Prepare some informal notes that you can refer to during in-class discussions. Pair up with one or more classmates and discuss your insights. Compare and contrast the analyses of the films observed by participants in your group.

DO-IT-YOURSELF Complete the research activities described and develop some preliminary answers to the questions. Write a three- to four-page essay about the film's relevance. What do you think your observations tell us about contemporary American families and the ways in which family troubles are portrayed on film? Remember to include your notes and provide any references you used.

Child and Elder Abuse

Children and the elderly also suffer at the hands of abusive family members—and can suffer in distinctive ways that are linked to their special status in the family. Child abuse and elder abuse, which fall under the umbrella term of "domestic abuse," are likely to be underreported, partly because of the relative powerlessness of the victims and the private settings of the abuse. Official statistics show that about 1 percent of children in the United States are abused in some way, though, given underreporting, the number is likely much higher (U.S. Department of Health and Human Services 2017). Children under the age of one and black children suffer from the highest rates of abuse.

In addition to physical violence and verbal, emotional, and sexual abuse, children may experience a distinctive type of abuse known as **neglect**—inadequate nutrition, insufficient clothing or shelter, and unhygienic or unsafe living conditions. Three-fourths of child abuse victims suffer from neglect (U.S. Department of Health and Human Services 2017). Because children depend on adults for their care and well-being, they suffer when those adults abandon or corrupt that responsibility. Sexual abuse is another form of child abuse that exploits the trust that children must place in their caregivers. Inappropriate sexual relationships between parents and children have devastating, lifelong consequences for child victims, which may include self-destructive behavior, such as eating disorders and substance abuse, and the inability to form trusting relationships later in life. In addition, those who were physically or sexually abused as children have a much higher likelihood of becoming abusers themselves.

> **NEGLECT** a form of child abuse in which the caregiver fails to provide adequate nutrition, sufficient clothing or shelter, or hygienic and safe living conditions

Elder abuse is another form of domestic abuse. It is estimated that about 10 percent of older adults have been subjected to elder abuse (Lachs and Pillemer 2015). Like child abuse, elder abuse can take distinctive forms. As well as physical, verbal, emotional, and sexual abuse, there is financial exploitation or theft; relatives or other caregivers may steal or misuse the elder's property or financial resources. Another form is neglect and abandonment. Some elders are dependent on others to care for them. Refusal to provide food, shelter, health care, or protection can be as devastating to an elder as it is to a child. Both elder abuse and child abuse exploit the special powerlessness of victims and are difficult to monitor and control.

POSTMODERN FAMILIES: THE NEW NORMAL

In 1960, over two-thirds of families consisted of a married couple with a male breadwinner, a stay-at-home mom, and their children. By 2012, less than one-quarter of families

IN THE FUTURE
Trends in Baby Making: Back to the Future?

The first successful progeny of in vitro fertilization, or IVF (referred to disparagingly as a "test-tube baby"), was born in 1978. Louise Brown Mullinder is now a parent herself, and millions of "test-tube babies" have been conceived, born, and raised all over the world. Assisted reproductive technology has come a long way since the experiment that resulted in Louise's birth. Now would-be parents have many options: Fertility treatments, IVF, egg and sperm donations, and gestational surrogacy are all growing in popularity. And artificial wombs are being developed that would allow the entire gestation process to occur "in vitro"—no actual human pregnancy required (Mejia 2014). What do these developments mean for the future of the family?

Some of the benefits are already clear: People who were once unable to have biological children now can do so. Single people, LGBTQ people, infertile people, and postmenopausal women can access these ways of creating family—if they have the necessary financial resources. A round of IVF costs between $10,000 and $15,000, and a woman typically has to go through two to three rounds before getting pregnant, while expenses for surrogate birth can reach $100,000 or more. These costs are prohibitive for many people, meaning only people of a certain SES can make use of these reproductive technologies. In other words, in addition to creating new ways of forming families, these technologies are creating new forms of inequality.

Advances in technology have also made a variety of genetic screenings possible, allowing parents to determine whether an embryo carries certain diseases or disorders or provides the genetic match necessary to be a "savior sibling" for an older child in need of a transplant. Technologies like these make it possible to imagine a future of "designer" children whose genetic characteristics, such as gender, intelligence, or disease susceptibility, can be manipulated by parents and doctors. The ethics of such a scenario are problematic to say the least.

At the same time that baby-making technologies depart for the future (while leaving cultural ethics struggling to catch up), there is a countermovement to return to practices of the past when it comes to pregnancy and childbirth. In the past, and in other cultures, women often labored and gave birth at home, surrounded by experienced and supportive female friends and family members. Hospital birthing practices have made that rarer now, especially in the United States. In 2017, just 1 percent of births occurred at home (Martin et al. 2018).

Additionally, a growing number of mothers-to-be are employing "doulas"—birth support professionals who help pregnant women through labor and delivery, providing assistance, encouragement, and care that medical staff and co-parents can't always provide. The rise in popularity of doulas is linked to women wanting to have a more pleasurable birth experience, along with growing criticism of hospital birth (Port 2014; Declercq et al. 2007). And those who use doula services, within or outside of hospitals, are almost unanimously satisfied with them, giving doulas higher ratings as birth attendants than they give friends, family members, partners, doctors, or nurses. Research shows that women assisted by doulas are less likely to have low-birth-weight babies or experience a birth complication and more likely to engage in breastfeeding (Gruber, Cupito, and Dobson 2013). Until recently, the practices of doulas had been predominantly passed down within family/communal traditions; now, more formal training is provided, with several organizations offering training and certification for doulas.

Despite the inevitable bureaucratization of even this traditional practice, the popularity of doulas indicates that the future of childbirth is not all about cutting-edge technology. Doulas take us "back to the future," with time-honored practices that women have used for centuries. And indeed, there is no reason why doulas can't coexist with assisted reproductive technologies. The past always has something to offer the future.

CRISPR and Designer Babies Chinese researcher He Jiankui claims to have used CRISPR gene-editing technology to produce twins who are resistant to the human immunodeficiency virus carried by their father.

looked like this, and there was no single arrangement that could be used to describe the majority of families (Cohen 2014). Instead, we are looking at a growing diversity of family forms, including unmarried parents, childfree families, blended families, multiracial families, LGBTQ families, and extended family households. This diversity is a result of a number of social changes over the past half-century, including technological innovations in household labor, improved birth control, greater employment opportunities and increasing educational attainment for women, easier access to divorce, increasing acceptance of mixed-race and LGBTQ persons and households, and changes in social welfare programs and laws. Families respond to these social-structural changes in ways that best fit and meet their needs. Indeed, diverse family forms are not especially new; they are merely new to mainstream working- and middle-class families. Minority families, those living in poverty, and LGBTQ families have always had to improvise to fit into a society that ignored or devalued their needs and activities (Edin and Lein 1997; Pfeffer 2017; Stacey 1998; Stack 1974; Weston 1991). Diverse, improvisational postmodern family forms will become more and more familiar to the rest of society as we all cope with the social and cultural changes of the twenty-first century.

Closing Comments

When sociologists study the dynamics of family, they must define the subject of their interest. What exactly is family? This process sometimes leads to definitions that lie outside the traditional notions of biological or legal relations that have historically defined family. Certainly, this is true if one looks outside the United States at the astonishing variety of customs and practices that define family around the world. Here, too, the nature of the nuclear family is changing, while new types of family groupings are becoming more commonplace. The emergence of these "brave new families" has led to a sea change in the study of families, with an increasing recognition of the diversity and plurality that characterize family arrangements.

APPLYING WHAT YOU'VE LEARNED

Let's Talk More

1. What do sociologists mean when they say that instead of the sociology of the *family*, we should have a sociology of *families*? Why do we think of particular people (or even pets) as family members?

2. Homogamy helps explain a lot about mate selection in contemporary society: We tend to date and marry people who are similar to us in culturally meaningful ways. What cultural factors influence your relationship choices?

3. Women who work outside the home often face a "second shift" of housework when they get home. How do men avoid doing their share of this work?

Let's Explore More

1. **Film** Mendes, Sam, dir. *Away We Go*. 2009.

2. **Book** Sassler, Sharon; and Miller, Amanda. 2017. *Cohabitation Nation: Gender, Class, and the Remaking of Relationships*. Oakland: University of California Press.

3. **Blog Post** Innis, Janis Prince. "Family Rules: What Is a Family?" *Everyday Sociology* (blog). November 4, 2010. *http://WWNorton.com/rd/Lr5j8*.

CHAPTER 13

Leisure and Media

You're sitting in a darkened theater watching a movie unfold on the big screen. Two young lovers meet, woo, and marry. They honeymoon at a mountain resort—where, unfortunately, they are kidnapped by political rebels who break into song, swinging their rifles in unison as they dance in camouflage fatigues. After the ransom is paid, the couple return to the city, where they shop for housewares—at a store where clerks croon and shoppers dance in the aisles. But before they are allowed to live happily ever after, their baby is switched at birth with another infant, and they must track down their child with the help of a singing police detective/spiritual advisor. The film lasts more than three hours; during that time, audience members (men in one section, women and children in another) come and go,

fetching delicious snacks that extend far beyond prosaic popcorn and soda. They yell, groan, sing, talk back, and even throw things at the screen—but nobody shushes them. Where are you? You're in "Bollywood."

This term, an obvious play on the American film capital, is used to describe a particular class of movies produced in Mumbai (or Bombay). The Indian film industry is the most prolific in the world, and the movies it produces are very different from those Americans are used to. A typical film usually includes romance, political intrigue, and dramatic events such as kidnappings, military battles, or natural disasters—and there is always lots of singing and dancing! In other words, Indian films are a mixture of what American audiences understand to be separate genres: romance, musical, action, thriller, and so on. As a result, Americans often react to Indian films as strange, exhausting, and disorganized, while Indians find American movies boring, unemotional, and too short (Srinivas 1998).

Some American audiences got their first taste of Bollywood from British director Danny Boyle's *Slumdog Millionaire*, a film that borrowed some of the same stylistic elements and won the Best Picture Academy Award in 2009. You might have seen *La La Land* in 2016—it won Oscars for directing and acting, and it, too, borrowed elements from Bollywood, including dazzling sets, bright colors, romance, and song-and-dance numbers. Still, it's unlikely that the theatergoing experience for U.S. audiences was anything close to what is typical in India. In Indian theaters, silence is not the norm; audience members respond to what's on-screen in ways that seem startling or even wrong to Americans. The only American film experience that resembles the Bollywood model is the midnight showings of *The Rocky Horror Picture Show*, where enthusiastic fans dress up, sing along, talk back, throw toast, and shoot squirt guns at the screen. (Never heard of *The Rocky Horror Picture Show*? Look it up. We bet there's a screening in your area!) In Bollywood, though, this type of behavior is the rule rather than the exception.

How to Read This Chapter

In this chapter, we will look at leisure and some of the many things we do for fun. This does not mean that the chapter is any less important than others that cover more traditional ground. In fact, we can and should treat topics such as the media and entertainment, sports and recreation, tourism, and hobbies with the same analytic approaches we use to examine other core aspects of culture and society. The production and consumption of leisure activities may seem light-weight or trivial at first glance, but they are worthy of serious sociological consideration. As social institutions, the media and leisure industries play a key role in contemporary life. We will look at the structure and meaning of leisure, its impact on society, and its ubiquitous place in our everyday experiences. Paying attention to your own leisure activities and media usage will add to your understanding of the chapter.

A SOCIOLOGY OF LEISURE

Leisure is time that can be spent doing whatever you want—or nothing at all. It can include any activity that is satisfying or amusing, experienced as refreshing for body and mind. This means that just about any activity could fall under this heading, depending on individual preference, and that people can spend their leisure time engaged in all sorts of activities. Leisure is broad enough, then, to encompass a wide variety of pastimes: playing volleyball, traveling to Italy, gardening, woodworking, doing needlepoint, gaming, listening to music, sleeping in, watching television, reading, shopping, writing poetry, hiking, building houses for Habitat for Humanity, baking cookies—the possibilities are endless. For some people, watching TV is a leisure activity. For others, leisure means such activities as skydiving or snowboarding. For many, it's both. It's important to note that what makes something a leisure activity is not its appearance on this or any other list but rather the experience of the activity itself. Does it feel enjoyable, liberating, even transformative? Then we can call it leisure.

What Is Leisure?

The study of leisure is somewhat new in sociology, but there are many reasons why it has become an important area of interest. The term "leisure" is primarily defined in contrast to paid labor or other obligatory activities, or as the opposite of work. Work has typically been understood as serious and consequential, while leisure activities are seen as minor or trivial. Leisure activities, though, absorb so much time, energy, and resources that they must represent "important developmental goals and meet other personal needs of both children and adults" (Kraus 1995). In many ways, it is leisure that provides the most "meaningful experiences" and allows people "opportunities to reveal their true selves" (Havitz and Dimanche 1999). This suggests that leisure is well worth studying. Indeed, leisure studies has become established as a separate academic discipline within the social sciences.

The idea of leisure itself is rather new historically. In the premodern world, the line between work and play was not nearly as clearly defined as it is today—in part because there was an awful lot of work to be done and there were fewer options for entertainment, especially among the working classes. Activities we now engage in almost exclusively as a form of **recreation** (like gardening, hunting and fishing, or knitting) were necessities in the past, and common pastimes like going to the movies and watching television didn't even exist. Even in the late nineteenth century, low wages and long hours meant that only the wealthy had the time and resources to pursue recreational activities with any consistency.

This situation began to change between 1890 and 1940, as the amount of time that the middle class could devote to leisure activities grew rapidly (Fischer 1994). The increase in leisure time was largely fueled by industrialization and technological progress that increased work productivity and spurred time-saving inventions for the home such as the washing machine, dishwasher, and vacuum cleaner. While contemporary Americans still work more hours than their counterparts in other developed nations, on an average day we manage to find just over five hours of leisure time. While this is true for the majority, not everyone has the same amount of time, money, or inclination to participate in leisure pursuits. For example, men have more leisure time than women, due in large part to women's disproportionate responsibility for household labor (Sayer 2016).

LEISURE a period of time that can be spent relaxing, engaging in recreation, or otherwise indulging in freely chosen activities

RECREATION any satisfying, amusing, and stimulating activity that is experienced as refreshing and renewing for body, mind, and spirit

Many people think of their nonwork time as "free time" or leisure, using the terms interchangeably. But it's not always easy to determine whether an activity counts as leisure. Sometimes work and leisure may seem to blend or overlap, especially now that devices like smartphones, tablets, and laptops keep us plugged in virtually 24/7. And free time is not always the same thing as leisure time. Sociologist Chris Rojek (1985, 1995, 2000) warns us not to equate free time (or nonworking time) with leisure time. He argues that leisure, by its very definition, constitutes some kind of choice about how to spend one's time. Let's look at a couple of examples.

In one scenario, Amber, Zack, and Juan—all taking the same sociology class—plan an evening study session at a local café. The café is bustling with other students studying too. Amber arrives late from her job as a sales clerk. Zack and

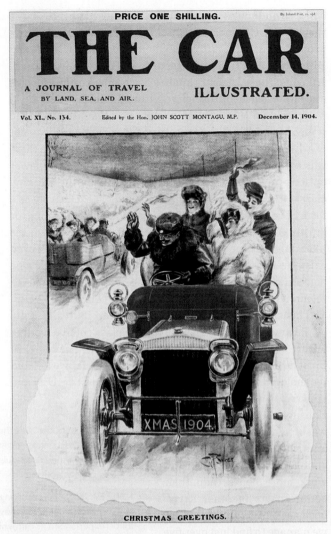

Rise of the Leisure Class Around the turn of the twentieth century, industrial productivity and new technologies created new opportunities for leisure among the middle and upper classes. Note this early travel magazine.

Juan have already outlined a few chapters and drunk a few cups of coffee. The three chat for a while before continuing to study. Periodically, they check their cell phones and send text messages. At the end of the night, they plan to meet again the following day. When does work end and leisure begin? In this scenario, it is difficult to decide which is which. Meeting at a café to study seems more like a leisure activity than doing retail sales at a store. However, studying at a café seems more like work than merely meeting friends to chat.

In another scenario, Cheryl finishes work for the day, picks up her children from school, cooks her family an evening meal, helps her children with their schoolwork, and then puts them to bed. You could say that Cheryl leaves one workplace (her job) only to enter another (her home and family). When has she had any free time?

CONSUMPTION the utilization of goods and services, either for personal use or in manufacturing

Arguably, Cheryl continues to work after she leaves her job at 5:00 p.m. and thus has no free time. She, however, may think of spending time with her family as her free time. Or is free time when we have "nothing" to do? If so, what constitutes "nothing"?

Because leisure is hard to define, it's also difficult to measure. Rather than understanding leisure as the opposite of work, sociologists see the two as complementary activities within a capitalist economic system—two activities linked by **consumption** (Rojek 1985, 1995). Thus, we work for wages to consume a variety of goods and services, including leisure. As we consume more leisure, we must earn more wages to pay for it. We choose leisure time to supplement our working lives, and the connection between the two is more than merely oppositional.

Trends in Leisure

Many discussions of modern leisure-time activities emphasize three related trends that have changed the ways in which we engage in these activities. We now look at these developments in turn: the decline of public life, the digitization of leisure and recreation, and the commodification of leisure.

THE DECLINE OF PUBLIC LIFE Sociologist Richard Sennett argues that modernity has seen the "fall of public man," as people increasingly seek refuge in "ties of family or intimate association" (Sennett 1977, p. 3). This decline in public life has affected leisure in far-reaching ways. After World War II, the mass migration to the suburbs and the introduction of television encouraged people to stay home and even usurped shared, public activities such as moviegoing (Fischer 1994). Television in particular has been called "the 800-pound gorilla of leisure time" (Putnam 1995). Despite the development of the Internet and its many options for online activities, TV watching remains an enduring and popular pastime. The average American still spends just over half of their leisure time watching TV (Figure 13.1; U.S. Bureau of Labor Statistics 2018b).

One large-scale longitudinal study sponsored by the National Endowment for the Arts found that "Americans are increasingly less likely to go out for a dose of the arts, and more likely to stay home and enjoy performances in front of their home entertainment centers" (Yin 2003). The effect has been most obvious in music and theater, but even the visual arts are starting to see a change. People still visit museums and galleries, but a growing number are also looking at pictures online or in books and magazines.

If television began this process, then more recent developments have only intensified it. Digital entertainment across a variety of platforms has made the private home an even more attractive site for leisure. Critics fear that the Internet has further isolated individuals from the outside world and also from one another. Technology can divide us even

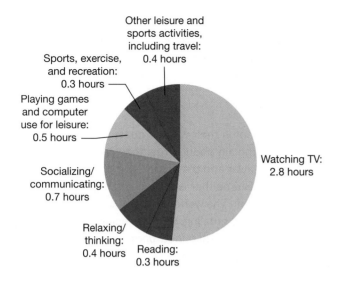

FIGURE 13.1 Leisure Time on an Average Day

NOTE: Data include all days of the week and are annual averages for 2017.

SOURCE: U.S. Bureau of Labor Statistics 2018b.

Pie chart labels:
- Other leisure and sports activities, including travel: 0.4 hours
- Sports, exercise, and recreation: 0.3 hours
- Playing games and computer use for leisure: 0.5 hours
- Socializing/communicating: 0.7 hours
- Relaxing/thinking: 0.4 hours
- Reading: 0.3 hours
- Watching TV: 2.8 hours

when we're together. With everyone glued to small and big screens alike, are we losing our sense of civic and interpersonal engagement?

DIGITIZATION OF LEISURE The impact of new technologies on leisure over the past two decades has been great: The Internet, smartphones, and social media, especially, have transformed our experience of leisure and recreation in what were once unimaginable ways. Consider our digital devices: Televisions, computers, tablets, smartphones, and other equipment allow us to access information and activities in digital spaces. These devices keep us connected to the Internet and allow us to spend our leisure time consuming online content and interacting with others who are not physically copresent. When online, we can play games, watch movies, listen to podcasts, or post and enjoy others' posts on social media. We spend about four hours per day on our computers, tablets, and smartphones—that's 25 percent of our waking hours (Nielsen 2019).

What were once solely analog activities, like sports, crafting, and just hanging out in nature, have become digitized in multiple ways. For example, we now have smartwatches and digital activity trackers that will monitor the number of steps we take on a hike, the miles we run in a workout, or the speed we maintain on our bicycle. These devices can also calculate our heart rates, calories burned, and hours of REM sleep. This means that our leisure moments are digitally surveilled and translated into data instead of just experienced as something enjoyable. There are now a myriad of digital-only activities that we obsessively engage in—like gaming, interacting with social media, and browsing Pinterest; these activities take up hours of our day that were once spent engaging in real-world recreation. And there is even the phenomenon of

pop-up "experiences" or "Instagram Museums"—interactive exhibits designed solely to provide interesting backdrops for photos destined for social media.

Finally, digital media and devices allow us to connect to people in ways we couldn't before: We may now maintain friendships (an important locus of leisure activity) with people around the world whom we would never have crossed paths with in the nondigital past. Some of our online connections can and do translate into real-world relationships—for example, sites like Meetup.com are tools for organizing real-life get-togethers, and someone can start a Meetup group around almost any interest that they want to share with others: play board games, walk dogs, or learn to cook. The digitization of leisure influences the tools we use, the activities we engage in, and the people we connect with as we pursue leisure in the Internet age.

> **COMMODIFICATION** the process by which it becomes possible to buy and sell a particular good or service

COMMODIFICATION OF LEISURE One development that is making an enormous impact on our lives is the massive increase in the **commodification**, or commercialization, of leisure activities. Where people formerly made their own fun, they now purchase it in the form of goods and services. In 2017, the average American spent over $3,200 on entertainment, representing 5 percent of all expenditures that year (U.S. Bureau of Labor Statistics 2018c). Much of that is spent on media products (music, movies, video games, apps, books, magazines, newspapers, and so on), but it also includes

Do It for the 'Gram The Museum of Ice Cream isn't a museum. It's a made-for-Instagram playground for adults, an installation designed to provide pretty backgrounds for social media selfies. And yes, yummy treats are included.

ON THE JOB
Professional Musicians: Playing Is Work

Who wouldn't want to be a rock star? Lear-jetting from city to city, mobbed by adoring fans, staying in four-star hotel suites, partying backstage with celebrities, and getting paid tons of money to play—and the operative word is "play"—music. Such are the stereotypes of the professional musician's life. But a closer look at the real work they do reveals some underlying contradictions to the public images we see of their fame and success.

The casual observer is likely to underestimate what it takes to "make it" as a professional musician. Regardless of how talented, naturally gifted, or even lucky a musician might be, it's going to take a lot of hard work to succeed. We don't ordinarily appreciate all the seemingly endless hours musicians must devote to learning and perfecting their craft. In fact, it takes something like 10,000 hours to become an expert in any field, according to Malcolm Gladwell (2008), who studied "outliers," or exceptionally successful people. Gladwell claims that greatness takes an enormous amount of time, and that the "10,000 Hour Rule" applies to understanding how the Beatles honed their skills in the years prior to becoming famous. This dispels the notion that anybody can become an "overnight success" and upholds the truism that everybody must "pay their dues" in order to make it in the music business.

Of course, there are also many different versions of success as a professional musician, and some of them are a lot less glamorous than what we might imagine. Not every successful musician becomes rich and famous. Many work in relative obscurity as band members, backup singers, session players, songwriters, or producers. Their careers can be tenuous, uneven, and short-lived. The recent films *20 Feet from Stardom* and *The Wrecking Crew* document the lives of such professionals, giving greater recognition to those who toil just outside the brightest spotlight. Still, most musicians love what they do and feel fortunate if they can make a living at it.

While professional musicians readily acknowledge the benefits inherent in their work, it doesn't mean they have nothing to complain about. True, they aren't doing strenuous manual labor and they aren't stuck in a cubicle from 9:00 to 5:00. But neither is what they do as fun and easy as it might appear. The work conditions can be difficult and the days long and grueling. Writing, recording, rehearsing, and touring require sustained concentration, teamwork, and stamina. The work is often characterized by drudgery and repetition rather than spontaneity and creativity. After years in the business, some musicians suffer from the same kind of disenchantment with their careers that workers in other fields experience, despite whatever notions of romance might have attracted them to the music business in the first place (Stein 1997).

The rewards of working in any glamorous profession, whether it's music, show business, or sports, probably seem well worth any of these difficulties. As social observers, however, we need to consider what goes on behind the scenes and remember that what looks like play to one person might feel a whole lot more like work to another.

20 Feet from Stardom Backup singers Jo Lawry, Judith Hill, and Lisa Fischer take the spotlight in the 2013 documentary.

---

spending on toys, hobbies, sporting equipment, and admissions fees to a variety of attractions.

Simple, inexpensive, and spontaneous outdoor activities like hiking are still popular, but they increasingly compete with formally organized and "technologically innovative forms of play such as scuba diving, parasailing, skydiving and hang-gliding, snowmobiling, and other kinds of off-road travel [that] have opened up new environments for the play experience" (Kraus 1995). Even those activities that were once necessities, like hunting and fishing, now come with a dizzying array of commodities. Sport fishing relies on expensive boats, lures, rods, and sonar to help locate the fish. Hunting seems to demand special clothing, scent blockers, calls and decoys, infrared vision enhancement, and even special hearing aids that allow hunters to tune in to specific frequencies while stalking particular animals. Instead of visiting the local swimming hole, we pay to visit water parks. Instead of playing softball or soccer, we may simply watch sports on TV, played by professionals. In almost every case, our recreation is mediated by goods and services that we seem to "require" in order to have fun.

The ultimate example of the commercialization of leisure, however, is shopping: where the purchase of commodities becomes an end in itself. Recreational shopping is a recent historical development. Until the mid-twentieth century, people shopped mainly to acquire food, clothing, fuel, tools, and other essential goods. In addition, we have become aspirational shoppers; we shop to live out our fantasies and dreams, and the shopping experience itself delivers a "sensual and emotional high" (Zukin 2004, p. 220). Shopping is no longer just about "bread"—it has also become its own "circus."

In recent years, the shopping mall has undergone changes. The old-style enclosed shopping center has declined in popularity, and the country is littered with shuttered and empty malls. Some blame the mall's demise on the Internet and the ease and convenience of shopping online, but Americans still do most of their spending in brick-and-mortar stores. At the same time, new (or refurbished) malls are offering more than just a place to buy things. In order to attract and captivate shoppers, malls are becoming "lifestyle" centers for entertainment and social gathering (Nielsen 2013).

Leisure, money, and business intersect in other ways as well. Almost any kind of activity we enjoy must be supported in some way by others. From hiking in the local foothills (consider how the Parks and Recreation Department might be involved in maintaining trails) to eating an ice cream cone (consider the manufacturing, delivery, and service involved in getting the cone to your hand), many people work to make these activities possible. When you go to a professional baseball or basketball game, chances are that you're there to root for your favorite team, eat hot dogs and drink soda or beer, and generally have a good time with family or friends. Work is probably the last thing on your mind. But what about the people who help provide that experience for you—the parking attendants, ticket-takers, security officers, ushers, food and souvenir vendors, janitors, and maintenance workers? What about the team owners, talent scouts, agents, managers, coaches, trainers, and players themselves? If the game is covered by the media, then you can add announcers, reporters, sportscasters, photographers, camera crews, producers, editors, publishers, advertisers, and others. According to the U.S. Department of Labor, nearly 17 million people work in the leisure and hospitality sector of the economy. That includes jobs in the arts, in entertainment, and in recreation as well as in the lodging and food services that often go along with them (U.S. Bureau of Labor Statistics 2019b).

Clearly, leisure is big business. Let's take the National Basketball Association (NBA) as an example. In 2019, the New York Knicks were the top-grossing team, worth an estimated $4 billion. The average NBA team is now valued at nearly $1.9 billion. All told, the NBA's thirty teams raked in $8 billion in the 2017–2018 season (Badenhausen and Ozanian 2019). According to the Entertainment and Sports Programming Network (ESPN), the Philadelphia 76ers boasted the highest attendance of any team in 2018–2019, with more than 830,000 people attending forty-one home games, an average of about 20,400 spectators per game (ESPN 2019). Many more millions of fans tuned in to NBA games on radio and TV or watched online. Overall, the businesses that could be broadly classified as providing leisure or entertainment are easily worth trillions of dollars. As such, these industries account for a major part of the U.S. and global economies.

THE STUDY OF MEDIA

Any study of leisure must necessarily consider media. As we have seen, people spend their leisure time engaged in a wide variety of activities. For many Americans, consuming media—reading the newspaper, watching TV, listening to the radio, or browsing the Internet—accounts for a large portion of this time. Clearly, the media have extensive reach. They are a major social institution and one with increasing power and importance in the digital age. At first glance, we might conclude that the media's purpose is simply to supply information, educate, or entertain. While this is not incorrect, it is a somewhat incomplete view of a complex and sophisticated social institution.

The Media and Democracy

One of the first things to remember about the media is their intimate relationship to a democratic system of government. The media have always been seen as both an instrument of the state and a tool for social change. Some of the original struggles during the fight for American independence were waged around these very issues. Early American leaders recognized the importance of news in educating and mobilizing the new citizenry. They were opposed to European governments' control over the media (which consisted at that time of books and newspapers) and sought instead to free the press so that it could be used as a voice of the people. That is precisely why the framers of the U.S. Constitution included guarantees to freedom of expression and freedom of the press in the First Amendment:

> Congress shall make no law respecting an establishment of religion, or prohibiting the free exercise thereof; or

abridging the freedom of speech, or of the press; or the right of the people peaceably to assemble, and to petition the Government for a redress of grievances.

These are among our most precious and fiercely defended rights as Americans. The press was also intended to serve as a kind of watchdog for government, independently examining political leaders and giving the people another means of checks and balances against the three branches of the government. It would ensure that no branch, whether the executive, legislative, or judicial, amassed too much power. Thus, the media are a last defense of an open, democratic system. They play a critical role in uncovering and exposing all kinds of government malfeasance, corruption, and incompetence.

Interestingly, social media have made it possible for politicians to bypass traditional media outlets (like news channels) and communicate directly with the people. President Donald Trump has famously used his Twitter account to do this, tweeting explicitly about his desire to silence the mainstream media and limit their First Amendment freedoms. In a February 2017 tweet he even pronounced that CNN, *The New York Times*, and the three major networks (ABC, NBC, and CBS) were "the enemy of the American People!" He has accused media outlets on numerous occasions of disseminating "fake news" when he has disliked or disagreed with what they broadcast.

CONGLOMERATION the process by which a single corporation acquires ownership of a variety of otherwise unrelated businesses

SYNERGY a mutually beneficial interaction between parts of an organization that allows it to create something greater than the sum of its individual outputs

MERGER the legal combination of two companies, usually in order to maximize efficiency and profits by eliminating redundant infrastructure and personnel

While the principle of a free press still stands today, it is worth considering just who is free to own what we currently refer to as "the press," in other words, a media outlet. Who has access to the media, who controls media products, whose voice is reaching a mass audience, and what kind of message is being sent by these powerful instruments of "free speech"?

The Structure of Media Industries

Media companies are among the many big businesses that drive the U.S. economy, and their profits and losses are closely followed by investors in the stock market. Media products are among the country's biggest exports, fueling a worldwide demand for information and entertainment. The number of these companies seems to constantly expand, and there are almost too many publishing houses, production companies, TV networks, film studios, radio stations, record labels, and website and game developers to name. Then there are also the companies that make the hardware, software, and digital devices on which we consume it all. As the media industries grow, so does their power. Let's look at some interrelated trends in the structure of media industries.

CONGLOMERATION What is not readily evident from this seeming proliferation of media is that the businesses are often owned by the same large parent companies. The trend toward **conglomeration** began growing in the 1990s (McChesney 2000). Huge corporations were acquiring media companies as part of their larger holdings. This is why a company like Seagram's, which manufactures alcoholic beverages, bought (and later sold) Universal (then MCA), which produces film, television, and music. Or how General Electric, which makes everything from light bulbs to jet engines, came to own the NBC television network. Now Comcast owns both NBC and Universal. Buying successful media companies makes good sense as an economic investment, so it is not surprising that other corporations might want to share in the huge profits generated by the entertainment industry.

A typical media conglomerate might comprise many divisions: book and magazine publishing, radio and TV broadcasting, a cable network, a movie studio and theaters, record labels, video game distribution, websites, a theme park, even a sports franchise. Also referred to as horizontal integration, this allows the company to take advantage of its own organizational structure and market its products across a wide range of media formats and outlets. Media companies favor products they can "cross-promote" along their various divisions, thus creating what is called **synergy**. For example, a company might produce a movie that is adapted from a book it published; distribute the film to theaters it owns; advertise and review it in company newspapers, magazines, and TV programs; put the soundtrack on its record label; create recognizable characters that appear in commercials or at its theme park; release the movie on its DVD label; and later broadcast it on the company's cable channel and television network.

The cornucopia of media choices is thus somewhat deceiving. Many brands and labels are really just different company identities within a larger structure. There are actually very few "independent" media producers that can remain viable in such a marketplace. Often, once an independent becomes successful, it is quickly bought out by a larger conglomerate, which is searching for ways to increase revenues. Another trend consists of a **merger** between two or more companies to create an even bigger media giant. The model for this trend took place in 2000 with the merger between a new media company, AOL (America Online), and an older one, Time Warner. In 2017, wireless carrier Verizon bought Internet provider Yahoo in a deal that merged two of the nation's largest tech providers. Mergers like this one typically require the approval of relevant federal agencies; for example, AT&T won the right to buy Time Warner after a court battle with the Department of Justice's antitrust arm.

DATA WORKSHOP

Analyzing Media and Pop Culture

Blockbuster Hits and the Business of Movies

When the Walt Disney Company bought 21st Century Fox for over $70 billion in 2019, the acquisition made headlines. As part of the deal, Disney acquired Deadpool, the X-Men, and the Fantastic Four as well as a controlling share of Hulu. In just the last ten years, the media giant has acquired Lucasfilm (the original home of *Star Wars*) and pulled off an aggressive buyout of Marvel—the comic book and movie studio. Taken together, these three deals presented some of the most lucrative possibilities ever in terms of Disney's added ability for synergy, marketing, and future growth, particularly in the area of streaming (Schwartz 2019; Gabler 2012). Disney now owned some of the most recognizable and bankable brands in entertainment and was poised to translate them into greater successes and profits, a situation to which any media company would aspire.

Most people think of movies as primarily a form of entertainment. But in this Data Workshop we want you to consider them as a business. And the movie business is big business, especially when it comes to those mega-blockbuster hits. Making movies for a mass audience is expensive (and risky), but it can also be highly profitable. The major studios that make these kinds of movies must come up with strategies to help maximize the potential for profits and minimize the potential risks of financing a costly "flop." How can media companies ensure that their biggest movies become their biggest hits? This is where their corporate practices and structures can benefit the bottom line.

Big media companies like Disney have an advantage when it comes to producing and distributing their products. When a parent company owns many subsidiaries, it can market its properties across a variety of media outlets. In other words, such companies can benefit from cross-promotion. The greater the diversity and reach of a company's divisions, the more opportunities there are to create synergy. The most attractive properties are those that might start as a comic book but can then be turned into a movie and a video game, where the stars of the movie can be featured on TV talk shows or magazine covers and where fans will be able to follow additional story lines and interact on websites, through social media, or at fan conventions. Think of all the avenues for promotion that a media giant might own and exploit.

One common practice in filmmaking follows the adage that "nothing succeeds like success." Studio execs favor movie "franchises" from which many hits can be spawned. Think *James Bond, The Avengers, Mission Impossible, X-Men, Spider-Man, The Fast and the Furious, Transformers, Harry Potter, Batman*, and such. These films were the basis for producing many other, sometimes even more successful, films in the form of prequels, sequels, and spinoffs. A related approach is to do remakes by producing an updated version of an older film or show that was successful before, for instance, *Ocean's Eleven* or *A Star Is Born*, or, in a new twist, producing live-action versions of what were originally animated films, like *The Lion King* and *Aladdin*.

Another strategy for increasing the odds of a hit, or at least diminishing the losses that might incur from a flop, is to partner with an outside company and engage in what is referred to as "co-promotion." In these relationships, the partner company invests in the film for some kind of consideration, primarily rights to promote its products in conjunction with the film. This takes several forms. The partner can provide product placement within the film to more covertly "advertise" its particular brand (whether it's an automobile, cell phone, or soda) to audiences. Or the partner might be involved in merchandising tie-ins with the film, as when a fast-food chain offers customers a free toy or collector's cup with purchase. Many companies also create merchandise such as action figures, posters, T-shirts, or hats to further promote and profit from their films.

For this Data Workshop you will be asked to use existing sources to investigate the marketing and promotion for a recent blockbuster movie. Refer to Chapter 2 for a review of this research method. Choose a movie that exemplifies the strategies of hit making. It's not necessary that you see the film yourself (but you may) in order for you to analyze the corporate economics behind making it. There are a variety of sources and materials you can examine online. All the major studios create official websites for their movie releases. Or you can visit IMDb.com, the Internet Movie Database site that provides detailed information on every film made. Look for company credits like who produced and distributed the film and its soundtrack. Review the box office receipts, and note the film's costs and profits. Check out the studio's site for links to merchandise and related social media campaigns. Read some business news articles about the movie's success. There are likely to be other sites where you can find out more about how your blockbuster did business.

Once you have the data, consider these questions:

- How many elements from the strategies described here can you find to help account for your film's success?

- Did the movie studio take advantage of all possible avenues to reap the greatest profits, or can you suggest other ways the studio could have improved or expanded its sales campaigns?

- How does the corporate business model shape the kinds of movies that get made?

- What makes blockbusters popular with audiences, and why?

There are two options for completing this Data Workshop:

PREP-PAIR-SHARE Choose a blockbuster film to examine. Look at how the movie was marketed. Make notes about what you find to bring to class. Discuss with others in small groups, comparing the different films and their promotional campaigns.

DO-IT-YOURSELF Write a three- to four-page essay addressing the questions provided and the various ways that movie studios attempt to produce hits. Make reference to the data you collected about the marketing campaigns.

CONCENTRATION Mergers and acquisitions associated with conglomeration result in yet another major trend: **concentration**. The ownership of media companies of all kinds is now concentrated in the hands of fewer and fewer large conglomerates. Communication researchers who follow media ownership saw a consistent trend through the 1980s and 1990s characterized by mergers and buyouts and resulting in fewer but larger media companies in the 2000s (Bagdikian 2004; McChesney 1997, 2004). Researchers often refer to the big five or six global media conglomerates, down from more than twenty-five such companies just a decade or two ago, that now dominate the media industries (Free Press 2017; Klinenberg 2007; Shah 2007). The current list includes Comcast, the Walt Disney Company, AT&T, Viacom, and CBS, as shown in Table 13.1. While few in number, these media giants keep getting bigger. As you learned in the Data Workshop, in 2019, the Walt Disney Company bought 21st Century Fox for more than $70 billion. That leaves only a small percentage of media companies truly independent from this corporate reality.

Two government agencies, the Federal Communications Commission (FCC) and the Securities and Exchange Commission (SEC), are charged with regulating the large conglomerates. The FCC has established some restrictions on media-outlet ownership by any single company in order to avoid a **monopoly** in any one market. Otherwise, one media giant might be able to own all the newspapers and TV and radio stations in a region, effectively stifling any competition and potentially providing a single voice for information where several voices serve a democracy better. And the SEC is involved in **antitrust legislation**, governing mergers between companies and further discouraging monopolies from forming. However, in recent years, increasing **deregulation**, the reduction or removal of government restrictions on the media industry, has allowed companies to gain control of ever-larger chunks of the media market.

These decisions are often fiercely debated by the U.S.

Blockbuster Merger When it purchased 21st Century Fox in 2019, Disney gained creative and financial control of some of the most successful and highest-grossing film and TV assets, including *Deadpool*, *Avatar*, and *The Simpsons*.

TABLE 13.1   The Concentration of Media Outlets

Corporation	Principal Holdings
Comcast	NBC, Xfinity, Telemundo, MSNBC, CNBC, Bravo, USA Network, Syfy, E!, Universal Pictures, Philadelphia Flyers, University Pictures, DreamWorks Animation, Focus Features, Oxygen, Golf Channel, University Studios and other parks and resorts
Walt Disney Company	ABC, ESPN, Disney Channel, Freeform, FOX, National Geographic, FX, Twentieth Century Fox Film, Fox Searchlight Pictures, Blue Sky Studios, Walt Disney Studios, Lucasfilm, Pixar, Marvel Studios, Touchstone Pictures, Polaris, Walt Disney Parks and Resorts
AT&T	AT&T, DirecTV, Cricket Wireless, U-verse, YP.com, HBO, CNN, DC Comics, Cartoon Network, TNT, TBS, Cinemax, TMZ.com, NCAA.com, Adult Swim, Warner Brothers (Entertainment, Motion Pictures, Television, Records)
CBS	CBS, Showtime, Simon & Schuster, CNET, TVGuide.com, Metacritic, GameSpot
Viacom	Paramount Pictures, Comedy Central, BET, MTV, VH1, Nickelodeon, Spike, TV Land

SOURCE: Selyukh et al. 2017.

Congress, media companies, and media watchdog groups. Social critics are concerned about increasing concentration and its possible consequences for a democratic society that values freedom of the press and a plurality of voices. "Net neutrality" has become an important frontier in the battle for control over the delivery of data over the Internet. And this battle is ongoing: In 2017, the FCC repealed net neutrality, reversing legislation passed in 2015 that barred service providers like Verizon and Comcast from blocking or throttling Internet traffic or creating paid "fast lanes." Proponents of net neutrality want to ensure that Internet providers treat all data equally and that they don't discriminate among different companies, allowing some but not others faster or cheaper services. If the largest companies are allowed to control the dissemination of information, does that undermine the constitutional rights of average citizens to have their voices heard?

Even in today's heavily concentrated media market, there are still opportunities for alternative voices to be heard. This is thanks, in part, to a proliferation of digital technology. These alternative voices, though, are typically confined to small, marginal outlets. Still, almost everyone can now find a platform on which to express themselves. For instance, bloggers and podcasters are able to circumvent the constraints of commercial radio and print journalism to transmit their political opinions or musical sensibilities to an (admittedly small) audience online. Artists of all types can build their own websites to promote (and sometimes sell) their work, while YouTube allows individuals to upload homemade videos to their own channels. In fact, some big-time musical artists got their start on YouTube, including Justin Bieber and Carly Rae Jepsen. Someone else may garner thousands, or tens of thousands, of followers on Twitter or Instagram,

like Cardi B. With the rapid development of faster, cheaper, and more user-friendly digital media, more people now have access to technologies that allow them to produce and distribute their own work in the global marketplace. It's worth asking, though: Whose voices get heard in a saturated media landscape? Can an individual, or small enterprise, really hope to compete?

POWER SHIFTS The past decade has seen unprecedented change in the structure and organization of media industries. So-called new media have exploded. Technology and communications companies have become key players in a marketplace once dominated by more traditional media leaders. We see many cases where new and old media firms combine forces to create the emerging giants of an evolving industry. These giants are increasingly structured around horizontal integration, a type of organization where the company can control other companies that produce or distribute the same product and use its various subsidiaries and divisions to market products more widely. This may allow companies to effectively monopolize a particular industry—for example, AMC became the biggest movie theater chain in the United

CONCENTRATION the process by which the number of companies producing and distributing a particular commodity decreases, often through mergers and conglomeration

MONOPOLY a situation in which there is only one individual or organization, without competitors, providing a particular good or service

ANTITRUST LEGISLATION laws designed to maintain competition in the marketplace by prohibiting monopolies, price fixing, or other forms of collusion among businesses

DEREGULATION reduction or removal of government controls from an industry to allow for a free and efficient marketplace

Prime Video In addition to selling everything under the sun, Amazon produces shows such as *The Marvelous Mrs. Maisel*, a series about a 1950s divorcee who becomes a stand-up comedienne.

States after acquiring several other, smaller theater chains (including Carmike Cinemas and Odeon Cinemas) in 2016. The idea is always to reach a bigger share of audiences and consumers. Companies might also seek vertical integration, in which they own the entire supply chain of a particular product. For example, Live Nation merged with Ticketmaster to create a company that now manages and represents performers, books and produces their shows, and sells the tickets for those shows (complete with a steep "convenience" fee).

New and converging media and communications technologies have revolutionized the way these industries work. Power has shifted from companies that produce products to companies that distribute them. What is becoming clear is that in a digital age, the companies that provide access to entertainment and media will be at least as important as the companies that actually make the entertainment. And many companies, such as Netflix, Hulu, and Amazon, will try to do both: They create content (TV shows, movies, etc.) and distribute it on their own streaming platforms. In fact, in 2019, Netflix made history when its film *Roma* took home three Academy Awards, including Best Foreign Language Film.

A look at Amazon can help us better understand some of the key trends in the structure of the media industries. While Amazon used to just sell books and still does, the company has expanded its products and services and furthered its reach in significant ways. Amazon now sells everything under the sun, from clothing to cloud computing. Over the years Amazon has gobbled up other Internet retailers like Zappos.com (shoes), Diapers.com (baby gear), and, most recently, the grocery store chain Whole Foods. Further, Amazon has perfected the art of speedy delivery, now offering next-day and even same-day services in some locations. Amazon also offers ebooks, audiobooks, and streaming video and music as well as the necessary tech devices for enjoying them, including the Kindle e-reader, Fire tablet and TV, and the Echo and Alexa smart devices. Most notably, Amazon also develops its own original content, including award-winning shows like *The Marvelous Mrs. Maisel* and *Mozart in the Jungle*. So, you can watch your Amazon-produced TV show on your Amazon Fire while eating a tasty Whole Foods treat and waiting for the flying drone to deliver your new shoes, which you can see coming via your Ring video doorbell (which Amazon also owns)—just tell Alexa to cross that off your to-do list! Buying up other companies and developing more products and services allow Amazon to better compete with other online shopping companies, as well as with brick-and-mortar stores. The goal, as always, is to increase Amazon's market share and the profits of its stockholders.

Another area of change involves the astronomical growth in mobile media. Seemingly everyone now carries a smartphone, and these devices are not only being used to make phone calls or text. We use them to do all sorts of things online—things that we used to do on a computer just a handful of years ago. This has translated into enormous economic power for the telecommunications industry, companies like Samsung that make the devices, and wireless carriers like AT&T and Verizon. The other big winners are tech companies like Google and social media sites like Facebook and Snapchat. We're talking about a current consumer base of several billion users. As more people take their media on the go, these companies will be vying for consumers and looking to boost profits with ad revenues and sales. There will be more mergers, such as the 2017 deal between Verizon and Yahoo, as media giants adjust to and prosper from new technologies and new business trends. This increased consolidation is bound to affect users in numerous ways.

The Regulation of Media Content

Another area of intense debate about media industries revolves around the content they produce and government censorship. Some claim that media content, especially when it is violent or sexual in nature, has a negative effect on society and should therefore be restricted; others believe that the right to free speech or artistic freedom should in no way be infringed upon and support a media free market. What role, if any, should the government play in negotiating these competing interests?

The FCC imposes regulations on what the media may produce, once again qualifying the notion of absolute freedom of expression. As you may be aware, certain types of speech are not protected under the Constitution. Material considered to be obscene, for example, is illegal. The criteria used to define obscenity are based on a momentous 1959 Supreme Court decision, *Roth v. United States*. According to the ruling, child pornography and other "material which deals with sex in a manner appealing to prurient interest" are considered obscene. However, the line between obscene material and "indecent" material, which is restricted but not forbidden, is sometimes hard to draw.

RATINGS AND WARNINGS Over the past several decades, various media industries have turned to self-regulation of the materials they produce, often in the face of threats of censorship and in an effort to avoid outside regulation by government agencies. These efforts first began in 1968 when the Motion Picture Association of America (MPAA) established the movie ratings with which you are likely familiar. Those ratings are G, PG, R, and more recently PG-13 and NC-17, the latter to distinguish material unfit for anyone under seventeen from adult or pornographic material carrying an X rating. Next was the music business in 1985, when the Recording Industry Association of America agreed to place warning stickers on certain albums containing songs about drugs, sex, violence, and other potentially objectionable subjects. These labels ("Parental Advisory: Explicit Lyrics") were the recording industry's response to pressure from U.S. Senate hearings and lobbying from the Parents' Music Resource Center, headed by Tipper Gore (former wife of then senator and future vice president Al Gore).

The 1990s ushered in self-regulation for other media industries eager to avoid government restrictions on their products. The Entertainment Software Rating Board established a rating system for video games in 1993 based on age appropriateness. In 1997, television programs began featuring a ratings system that not only suggests the appropriate age for viewers but also warns of violence (real-life or cartoon), sex (including dialogue with sexual innuendo), and offensive language. The "V-chip" was added to TV receivers to allow parents to block violent programs altogether. More means of controlling content appeared as digital media spread to new devices. In the 2000s, software programs were developed to limit access to certain types of websites. Parents could now choose to block or filter not only websites but also instant messaging, game apps, file transfers, and downloads. By the 2010s, parents had options to control mobile devices and even to do remote tracking of their children's activities.

These voluntary measures at regulating content, self-imposed by media industries, acknowledge the concern that some material is unsuitable, especially for children. Some studies of the effectiveness of these measures indicate that children are still being exposed to objectionable material and that parents may be misled if they believe ratings systems or blocking software are preventing their children from having access to those materials (AV Comparatives 2014; Garry and Spurlin 2007). With the massive proliferation of adult material that is available online, it has become increasingly difficult to police content and the possibility of exposure. As researcher Gail Dines (2017) explains, "Porn sites get more visitors each month than Netflix, Amazon, and Twitter combined, with Pornhub alone receiving 21.2 billion visits in 2015."

WHO REGULATES THE INTERNET? No one owns the Internet, but your ISP (Internet Service Provider) owns the lines through which Internet content is delivered to your device. Until recently, "net neutrality" was the law of the land, meaning that no Internet-based service or content could be privileged over another. Net neutrality ensured that the Internet functioned the same way no matter who was using it and no matter what they were using it for. The Internet was seen as a public good that should be available equitably to all, no matter what content was accessed. Without government regulation, your ISP could impose caps on your data use at any given time in order to limit your streaming of certain online products.

TABLE 13.2 Theory in Everyday Life

Perspective	Approach to Recreation and Leisure	Case Study: Spectator Sports in America
Structural Functionalism	Social institutions such as recreation and leisure provide for the needs of society and its members and help to maintain social cohesion and unity.	Participation in spectator sports helps to reaffirm social bonds; rooting for a team underscores the value of performance and competition.
Conflict Theory	Social institutions such as recreation and leisure reflect the existing power structures in society and thus create and maintain social inequalities.	Participation in spectator sports legitimizes conflict between groups in society and the belief in winners and losers.
Symbolic Interactionism	Social institutions such as recreation and leisure are produced when people act together; they play a meaningful role in the everyday lives of members.	Participation in spectator sports provides members with a sense of group affiliation and personal identification.

In the age of media conglomeration, this could mean "throttling" your streaming speed when you're accessing the competitor's content. This would allow corporate (and individual) customers to pay for "better" (more, faster, smoother) Internet service if they have the resources to do so, while those without such resources (smaller companies, less wealthy individuals) could experience slowdowns or even become unable to access certain types of content. Dismantling net neutrality gives wealthy and powerful interests fuller access to online content while effectively censoring access for those with fewer resources.

On the other hand, some Internet content may need to be more closely regulated. For example, Facebook, which for years exerted little oversight over the content posted on the site, expressed shock when it learned that Russian agents had purchased ads and created "bot" accounts that reached millions of users in a coordinated and systematic attempt to sway the 2016 election. The social media company then embarked on a campaign of identifying and deleting posts and accounts associated with Russian misinformation efforts. The debate on whether Facebook should regulate content has since expanded to include hate speech and known white supremacist individuals and organizations, putting Facebook at the center of a debate over social and political speech and the First Amendment rights of all.

Is This Art? The 1998 show "The Art of the Motorcycle" at the Guggenheim Museum in New York broke attendance records but attracted negative reviews from art critics for "sucking down to our lowest impulses."

CULTURE AND CONSUMPTION OF MEDIA

Conflicts about the appropriateness of this or that cultural product often hinge on perceived differences in the value of one kind of cultural consumption over another. For instance, is opera "better" for you, or for society, than heavy metal music? Does one elevate and the other debase? And if so, why, and who decides? Perhaps it's not even a question of either/or, but rather a matter of taste, time, and context.

High, Low, and Popular Culture

"Culture wars" about audiences and the appropriateness of material can be fought just about anywhere. In the summer of 1998, an exhibit opened at the Guggenheim Museum in New York City that was uniformly panned by the critics. The *New Republic* called the exhibit "a pop nostalgia orgy masquerading as a major artistic statement," and *Salon's* art critic accused the Guggenheim of "wear[ing] its cultural pants around its ankles" and "sucking down to our lowest impulses." What were they so upset about? The exhibit was titled "The Art of the Motorcycle," and the critics were upset because motorcycles were not, in their opinion, art. The public, on the other hand, loved it—the exhibit broke all previous museum attendance records. People who might never otherwise have set foot in the museum came to view this colorful collection of motorcycles dating back to 1868.

The motorcycles at the Guggenheim stirred up a longstanding debate over the very definitions of art and culture. The critics' objections were based on their perception that **popular culture**, or mass culture (motorcycles), had invaded a **high culture** venue (the Guggenheim Museum). In this case, popular culture was seen as unsavory and even dangerous—the implication being that pop culture is a mass phenomenon that somehow threatens the position of the elites by challenging their preferences. As with so many sociological concepts, these terms come originally from the German: in this case, *kultur* (the culture of the elite classes) and *massenkultur* (the culture of the masses). But are these two categories really so separate? As you may have noticed in your own everyday experiences, the distinctions between the two categories are beginning to blur and relax.

First, there are multiple high cultures and multiple pop cultures, based on differences in taste and aesthetics. Also, each category has its own set of hierarchies. For example, rap and hip-hop music are definitely pop culture phenomena. Produced by mostly minority artists for whom "street credibility" is one of the most important qualifications, these musical forms have widespread popular appeal, especially among teenagers and young adults. But rap and hip-hop have their own elites, artists who are at the top of the charts and who have a great deal of influence within and outside their pop culture domain. Artists such as Kanye West, Jay-Z,

GLOBAL PERSPECTIVE
The Other Football

Do you know the rules for cricket, that complicated ball and bat sport so popular in India? What's up with the Canadians and their love of curling, you know, the game played on ice with the brooms? How about jai alai, what Spain proclaims is the world's fastest sport, the one with the three-walled court? Every country seems to have its favorite sport, but there is one that is most beloved the world over—football. No, not *that* football—the other one. What Americans call soccer but everyone else calls football is wildly popular internationally, but it is just beginning to take off among U.S. sports fans. American interest in soccer seems to spike every four years when the World Cup rolls around; otherwise, major league soccer still lags well behind the professional sports behemoths of football, baseball, and basketball.

The rest of the world, however, thinks Americans are crazy. In almost every other country around the world, football (soccer) is a major sport. There are local and national competitions between teams and international competitions between national teams. Salaries for top players often surpass deals made with elite American athletes, with tens of millions of dollars going to heavyweights like Cristiano Ronaldo, Lionel Messi, and Neymar Jr.

While soccer has a lackluster fan base in the United States, the sport inspires intense devotion from fans across the globe. But sometimes that passion has a downside. More specifically, it's the rowdy and sometimes violent fans, often referred to as "hooligans," who have garnered attention from their association with soccer. The British, especially, are infamous for the mobs of "yobs" (slang for hooligans) that cause mayhem both in Great Britain and elsewhere in the soccer-playing world as they follow and fight over their teams. Violence typically breaks out between fans of rival teams. Brawls may escalate into riots and stampedes, leading to injury, death, and destruction of property. Soccer, like many sports, has a violent history: In the medieval period, entire towns would participate in soccer matches to resolve disputes, and kings and queens at times had the game banned because of violence. In those days, it was the players who had to be concerned for their safety; since the rise of contemporary hooliganism, it's the spectators who need to be wary.

Hooliganism began in England in the 1960s and then quickly spread to many other European nations and beyond (Buford 1993). As the popularity of soccer increased, injuries and even fatalities mounted. Fortunately, there has been a marked reduction in the number of violent incidents in recent years. This is due to a number of factors, including more self-regulation among fans, better stadium designs, more intervention by security personnel, and increased efforts on the part of police forces (Morris 2014). These measures have not eliminated hooliganism, but every year fewer people are injured at soccer matches around the world.

Why does soccer spur violence in some of its fans? Some theories speculate that the fanaticism of hooligans is only an excuse to be violent (this argument has been applied to violence in other sports as well). Skinheads, for example, have used soccer matches to broadcast their beliefs. Others assert that fandom can develop into a nationalistic fervor that increases the likelihood of violence (Brimson 2010). For example, for British fans who feel united against a foreign team while in a foreign country, it may be easy to feel both isolated and compelled to defend the honor of their team and country—especially when emotions are already heightened with the fury of athletic competition (King 1995). This argument can be levied at other sports and their fans as well. Think of the riots that often ensue in college towns after a big victory for the home team.

Although fan violence at U.S. sporting events is certainly not unheard of, so far nothing on the scale of soccer hooliganism has occurred. Why is such behavior rarer in the United States? Is it because U.S. teams are seldom involved in truly international competition? Or is it because there are so many different professional sports and teams to follow? As soccer—the real football—grows in popularity in the United States, will the sport's hooligans come with it, too?

A History of Violence Russian fans riot during a football match between FK Austria Wien and Zenit St. Petersburg.

Young, Scrappy, and Hungry
Hit Broadway musical *Hamilton* effectively blends high and low culture. Creator Lin-Manuel Miranda (center) credits Biggie Smalls, *The West Wing*, Jay-Z, and classic musicals such as *Jesus Christ Superstar* and *Evita* as influences.

Nicki Minaj, Beyoncé, and Pulitzer Prize winner Kendrick Lamar, the elites of the rap and hip-hop worlds, show that the distinction between mass and elite is a fuzzy one.

The boundaries between high culture and popular culture are often permeable, so the way we categorize any particular type of art or artist can change over time. We usually consider the works of Shakespeare as the pinnacle of high culture, but this was not always so; in previous eras, his plays were performed before commoners and aristocrats alike. The director Alfred Hitchcock is among the most revered filmmakers of all time, but he was not always held in such high esteem. Early on, critics dismissed his films as schlock; now they are considered pillars of the film canon. Even television is shedding its reputation as disposable fluff. Shows like *Westworld* and *Game of Thrones* are the subject of serious literary criticism once reserved for high art.

There is another way in which these kinds of distinctions are problematic. In the real world, most cultural products contain elements of both mass and high culture. Why do you think we call certain TV programs soap "operas"? The story lines and intense emotions of *The Young and the Restless* parallel and sometimes rival those of Puccini's *Madama Butterfly* and Wolfgang Amadeus Mozart's *Don Giovanni*. Led Zeppelin and Van Halen songs, when written out in standard musical notation, show a recognizable symphonic structure. Some of their compositions are as complex as those found in classical music. Rap and hip-hop overtly draw on other types of music in the practice of sampling, and

Ludwig van Beethoven, Georges Bizet, and Béla Bartók have all been sampled by R&B artists. Lin-Manuel Miranda's *Hamilton*, a hip-hop musical about the United States' first secretary of the treasury, won eleven Tony Awards (just shy of the record twelve Tonys won by *The Producers*) for successfully combining high and pop culture. These examples, and many others, indicate that high culture and pop culture are not mutually exclusive and can coexist within the same product.

TASTES AND MEANING The distinctions between high and popular culture are based on the characteristics of their audiences. Differences of class, education, race, and even religion help create these categories. Sociologist Herbert Gans (1999) calls the groups of people who share similar artistic, recreational, and intellectual interests **taste publics**. Taste publics aren't necessarily organized groups, but they do inhabit the same aesthetic worlds, which Gans calls **taste cultures**; that is, people who share the same tastes will also usually move in the same cultural circles. For example, sociologist David Halle (1993) found that members of the upper class are more likely to have abstract paintings hanging in their homes, while members of the working class are more likely to display family photographs in their homes.

The music, movies, clothes, foods, art, books, magazines, cars, sports, and television programs you enjoy are influenced at least in part by your position in society (e.g., Reeves 2015). Unknowingly, you belong to a number of taste publics and inhabit a number of taste cultures, in that you share your interests with others who are similar to you demographically. What you think of as your own unique individual preferences are in some ways predetermined by your age, race, gender, class, level of education, and regional location.

TASTE PUBLICS groups of people who share similar artistic, literary, media, recreational, and intellectual interests

TASTE CULTURES areas of culture that share similar aesthetics and standards of taste

MEDIA EFFECTS AND AUDIENCES

Media researchers have sought to understand whether popular culture can influence certain types of behavior (Anderson et al. 2010; Gerbner and Gross 1976; Malamuth and Donnerstein 1984; Weinstein 1991, 2000). Do TV crime shows increase our propensity to violence? Does pornography lead to the abuse of women? Does heavy metal music make teenagers suicidal? Such questions suggest that cultural products impose their intrinsic meanings on their audiences in a simplistic, stimulus-and-response fashion. But while it is true that media are potentially powerful transmitters of cultural values and norms, the process is neither immediate nor uncomplicated.

Sometimes dramatic events like the 2012 mass shooting of audience members during a midnight showing of *The Dark Knight Rises* raise concerns about the relationship between media content and real life. The influence or effects of the media on society have been studied for many decades by scholars in a range of disciplines, including psychology, communications, and sociology. The theories they have generated run along a spectrum, from the media having great power and influence over audiences, to their having little or none, to audiences themselves being central in the creation of meaning. It is worth examining what each of these theories has to say about the effects of media on society and the individual and to consider the applicability of any theory to the postmodern, digital world in which we now live.

Early Theories of Media Effects

In the early years of mass media, it was thought that audience members of all sorts (including readers) were passive recipients of content and that the meaning (if any) of the "texts" they consumed was transmitted unaltered and absorbed straight into their consciousness. (The term "text" is a general one that can include sound and image as well as print.) This notion was contained in the model known as the **hypodermic needle theory** (or **magic bullet theory**). The assumption was that, like an injection, media content was shot directly into the audience members, who responded instantaneously to its stimulus (Lazarsfeld and Katz 1955).

One of the key examples often cited to support this theory was the 1938 radio broadcast of H. G. Wells's short story "War of the Worlds" narrated by Orson Welles. The radio show used a mock news-bulletin format and was played uninterrupted by commercial breaks. Listeners who tuned in after the beginning of the show did not realize it was merely a dramatization of a Martian invasion. It was reported that audience members numbering in the millions actually believed the "news" was true and were so frightened as to have sparked widespread panic. Though this might seem rather exaggerated now, the

War of the Worlds A radio broadcast of H. G. Wells's short story "The War of the Worlds" caused widespread panic when listeners misinterpreted the mock news bulletin as an account of a real Martian invasion.

theory still points to an important principle about the media's potential to directly influence behavior.

Active Audiences: Minimal Effects Theories

Media scholars quickly realized that the hypodermic needle theory was not accurate or applicable for the most part—that audience members were not as passive or easily persuaded as first believed and that the various forms of media themselves were not as all-powerful in their influence over individuals. A number of related theories were developed during the 1960s and 1970s that proposed the media had limited or minimal effects. This research supported the

> **HYPODERMIC NEEDLE THEORY (MAGIC BULLET THEORY)**
> a theory that explains the effects of media as if their contents simply entered directly into the consumer, who is powerless to resist their influence

idea of **active audiences**. Instead of asking, "What do media do to people?" scholars began to ask, "What do people do with media?" (Severin and Tankard 1997).

For example, the **uses and gratifications paradigm** contains several theories that emphasize a more actively engaged audience member (Katz 1959). Blumler and Katz (1974) highlighted five areas in which audiences sought gratification and fulfilled needs through their use of the media. First, audiences could achieve some sense of escape from reality; second, audiences could use media for social interaction, forming relationships to characters, or conversing with others about products and programs; third, audiences could gain some aspect of personal identity by incorporating elements found in the media into their everyday lives; fourth, the media could serve to inform and educate audiences; and fifth, audience members could consume media purely for the sake of entertainment.

Many media scholars have been interested in the persuasive powers of the media, whether used in advertising to get consumers to buy products or used in the political arena to sway public opinion or to garner votes. Two related theories suggest that the influence of the media is more limited than marketing executives or campaign managers might wish. **Reinforcement theory** argues that individuals tend to seek out and listen to only those messages that align with their existing attitudes and beliefs. This theory has new resonance in the age of the Internet and "filter bubbles." According to the theory, audience members typically tune out anything that might seem too challenging and instead prefer only those messages that support what they already believe (Atkin 1973, 1985; Klapper 1960).

The **agenda-setting theory** focuses on how the mass media can influence the public by the way stories are presented in the news (McCombs and Shaw 1972, 1977). Depending on which stories are chosen as newsworthy and how much time and space are devoted to their coverage, the public gets a sense of the value or importance of any given event. The media may not be able to tell audiences what to think, but they do set the agenda for what (stories) to think about. Finally,

the **two-step flow model** of communication suggests that audiences get much of their information from "opinion leaders" who can convey and explain important news rather than from more direct or firsthand sources (Lazarsfeld and Katz 1955). Certainly someone like Oprah Winfrey exemplifies this; she is known for her widespread ability to influence and can introduce millions of her audience members to whatever is her latest concern.

Interpretive Strategies and Communities

Media research in the 1980s and 1990s maintained its focus on active audiences. Theorists proposed that media consumers bring to the experience different **interpretive strategies**. This approach argues that different individuals, because of their different experiences, perspectives, and personalities, may respond to media content in unique and idiosyncratic ways. This means that whatever meanings may be inherent in texts, consumers may read them in the intended ways but can also modify and even invert the meanings of texts depending on their own backgrounds and purposes. Different interpretive strategies mean that any given text may have multiple meanings.

Working within the cultural studies perspective, Stuart Hall's **encoding/decoding model** (1980, 1997) combines elements of the hypodermic needle/magic bullet and active audience theories. This model assumes on the one hand that specific ideological messages are loaded, or encoded, into cultural products and that they therefore have the potential to influence individuals, especially with regard to promoting the interests of capitalist elites. On the other hand, individuals may respond to messages embedded in the media in a variety of ways. In fact, when faced with ideologically encoded cultural products like movies or music, for example, we may decode them in novel ways. Further, we can engage in "cultural resistance" or choose "oppositional" or "against the grain" readings of products, subverting their original or dominant meaning.

For example, Beyoncé's recent visual album, *Lemonade*, can be read in a number of ways. Millions of fans (and many reviewers and cultural commentators) saw it as a manifesto of black feminist empowerment, while a small subgroup of critics—like feminist theorist bell hooks (2016)—were disappointed with the video's familiar commodification of the female body and felt it didn't go far enough in condemning the exploitation of women, African Americans, and other subordinated groups. This type of split in the interpretation of cultural texts is actually common and is visible across the artistic spectrum. It helps explain why your mom loved Madonna's "Like a Virgin" as ardently as your grandma hated it.

Henry Jenkins (1992) extends the model to something he calls **textual poaching**, wherein audience members take

ACTIVE AUDIENCES a term used to characterize audience members as active participants in "reading" or constructing the meaning of the media they consume

USES AND GRATIFICATIONS PARADIGM approaches to understanding media effects that focus on how the media fulfill individuals' psychological or social needs

REINFORCEMENT THEORY theory that suggests that audiences seek messages in the media that reinforce their existing attitudes and beliefs and are thus not influenced by challenging or contradictory information

AGENDA-SETTING THEORY theory that the media can set the public agenda by selecting certain news stories and excluding others, thus influencing what audiences think about

TWO-STEP FLOW MODEL theory on media effects that suggests audiences get information through opinion leaders who influence their attitudes and beliefs, rather than through direct, firsthand sources

Interpreting Beyoncé's *Lemonade* Media theorists propose that we respond to media content in unique ways based on our backgrounds and personalities. Is *Lemonade* a black feminist manifesto or just another example of the commodification of the female body? Depends who you ask.

the original product and manipulate it themselves—often to tell stories or express ideologies very different from the original. For example, fans of the TV show *Star Trek* have taken episodes of the program, then deconstructed and re-edited them to create new stories (called "K/S," or "Slash") in which Captain Kirk and Mr. Spock are not just best friends and co-workers but also passionate gay lovers. This oppositional restructuring indicates that viewers can read different meanings into the text than were intended by the producers—indeed, can reproduce the text in order to make those meanings central. Jenkins's ideas have also been applied to new forms of digital media that provide fans with more control over content and more opportunities for engaging in what he calls participatory culture (Jenkins 2006). New technologies have made textual poaching much easier: Social media connect fans to one another while providing easier access to the original textual content (via YouTube, for example) and user-friendly photo- and video-editing software. Not all artists appreciate their fans' textual poaching, but some, like Harry Potter author J. K. Rowling, are flattered that people love their characters enough to imagine new stories for them.

Responding to cultural texts is thus an exercise in the distribution of power. The more active the audience is in interpreting the text, the less control the producers have over the messages that are communicated. While you may not go so far as one of Jenkins's "textual poachers," neither are you a passive recipient of predigested pop-culture pabulum. Your consumption of media (film, television, music, books) and live performance (concerts, theater, sports) is active in the sense that you contribute your own interpretive resources—context, experience, and perspective. And to the extent that you share these experiences with others, you may find that you are part of an **interpretive community**—a group of like-minded people who enjoy cultural products in the same way.

The concept of the interpretive community is usually attributed to literary theorist Stanley Fish (1980), who contended that although an author might have intended a certain meaning in a text, it is individual readers who inevitably interpret the text in their own ways, thus creating the potential for an almost infinite number of meanings of the same text. Sociologists use the term **polysemy** to describe how any cultural product is subject to multiple interpretations and hence has many possible meanings (Fiske 1989; Hall 1980). For instance, an animated show like *The Simpsons* or *We Bare Bears* can be enjoyed on a variety of levels, by children for its humor alone and by adults for its social commentary. Polysemy helps us understand how one person can absolutely love the same movie (or song, painting, cartoon, necklace, car, meal, or tattoo) that another person absolutely hates. When audiences are made up of people from different backgrounds, it is more likely that polysemy will come into play, that is, that audience members will interpret the same texts in different ways. Meaning is not a given, nor is it entirely open—we make meaning individually and together, as audiences and consumers of culture.

The fact that we usually end up interpreting the same texts in the same ways has to do with shared culture and frameworks that members of the same interpretive communities have in common. Janice Radway (1991), in her ethnography of romance-novel readers, argued that cultural context is the reason that readers share similar sets of reading strategies and interpretive codes. In the case of her romance readers, it is the need to escape from the constraints of a life devoted to caring for others. Whether visiting a museum exhibit, going to a concert, or watching a TV show, members of interpretive communities bring with them shared sensibilities about understanding cultural products through their own particular lenses.

INTERPRETIVE STRATEGIES the ideas and frameworks that audience members bring to bear on a particular media text to understand its meaning

ENCODING/DECODING MODEL a theory on media that combines models that privilege the media producer and models that view the audience as the primary source of meaning; this theory recognizes that media texts are created to deliver specific messages and that individuals actively interpret them

TEXTUAL POACHING Henry Jenkins's term for the ways that audience members manipulate an original cultural product to create a new one; a common way for fans to exert some control over the media they consume

INTERPRETIVE COMMUNITY a group of people dedicated to the consumption and interpretation of a particular cultural product and who create a collective, social meaning for the product

POLYSEMY having many possible meanings or interpretations

IN RELATIONSHIPS
Fan–Celebrity Relations

It is simply taken for granted that an American will know about a huge swarming throng of unmet figures through his [sic] consumption of the various media. (Caughey 1984, p. 32)

Who is this "huge swarming throng"? Celebrities—people with whom few of us have actual face-to-face interactions but whom many of us feel we know, sometimes intimately. Celebrities can be important in the lives of ordinary people—as role models, objects of desire, or just friendly figures encountered daily on the TV or computer screen. And just because these relationships are one-sided doesn't mean that they aren't relationships.

Most of us put very little energy into developing these types of relationships. Frankly, we don't have to, as we are constantly bombarded with information about celebrities all the time. We can't help but acquire information about their professional and personal lives, even if it's just while standing in line at the supermarket (Ehrenreich 1990). But some fans deliberately pursue information about and contact with celebrities in more active ways. Maybe you read a magazine article or watched a TV show to learn more about your favorite athlete; maybe you bought a ticket to a performance with the hopes of seeing your favorite musician after the show. Maybe you serendipitously crossed paths with your favorite actor at the airport or in line at the post office. Encounters like these, while exciting, can also be expensive and unpredictable, and the contact between fan and celebrity is largely outside the fan's control (Ferris 2001, 2004; Ferris and Harris 2010).

The Internet has made it easier for fans to engineer encounters with celebrities. TMZ, Popsugar, and PerezHilton are a few of the websites that are making big business out of celebrity watching. They all carry the latest gossip and prized candid photos of stars that generate millions of web hits every month. With more people using smartphones, news about celebrities travels fast, as do those wishing to pursue them. And sometimes, fan expectations and senses of entitlement to celebrity contact go dangerously awry.

Security experts usually try to keep the details under wraps, but it is safe to say that most public figures have a number of potentially dangerous fans whose activities are monitored by both public law enforcement and private security firms. Several celebrities have been killed (Beatle John Lennon, actress Rebecca Schaeffer, Tejano star Selena) or

LEISURE AND RELATIONSHIPS

As spectators, we have many choices for how to watch sports or other events. We can attend a live game if we can afford the tickets or watch it on TV or stream it online, or we can hear the play-by-play over radio or satellite. At the same time, we can participate through social media and weigh in on the action along with other commentators and fans. We can watch the game alone or with others, at home, in dorm lounges, or at a sports bar. We can also choose to record the game and watch it at a later time. With so many ways to follow our favorite teams and players, it's not surprising to find how important they are to our sense of self and belonging to a community.

Our recreational choices can lead us to form unique bonds with others. Some of those bonds take the form of **role model** relationships, in which more prominent members of a leisure subculture serve as examples for us to strive toward. It is a widely accepted practice to look up to, admire, and mold ourselves after exceptional people and celebrities of all types.

Let's look at the influence of sports figures. Athletes have always been role models, but they have never been as visible as they are now. Sports media are a constant, making it easier to follow our favorite players both on and off the court (or field). All that exposure can turn them into superstars, but it can also reveal their feet of clay. In the 1990s, for instance, kids chanted "I wanna be like Mike" to communicate their admiration for Chicago Bulls player Michael Jordan. Tiger Woods, who in 1997 became the youngest golfer and first person of color ever to win the Masters Tournament, generated the same type of hero worship among youngsters, who intoned "I am Tiger Woods" as they stepped up to the tee in record numbers.

ROLE MODEL an individual who serves as an example for others to strive toward and emulate

seriously wounded (actress Theresa Saldana) by obsessed fans. Others have endured repeated home break-ins (Sandra Bullock, Justin Timberlake, Mila Kunis, Madonna, and Brad Pitt), and many are plagued by "pop-up" visits from fans who follow them surreptitiously and then reveal themselves in airports, restaurants, or public restrooms. Threatening letters are sometimes sent to the stars' management offices and even delivered to their home addresses. In order to protect Hollywood celebrities and other public figures from dangerous fans, the Los Angeles Police Department has created a division called the Threat Management Unit, and California further led the nation in passing anti-stalking laws in 1990 that have served as models for those in other states. Unfortunately, legislation doesn't deter all stalkers.

For some, celebrity stalking is a professional obligation. These people include members of the press, and especially the paparazzi—freelance photographers who pursue celebrities in order to get candid shots. Paparazzi may charter helicopters, hack through forests, or scale castle walls in daring stunts in order to capture images of celebrity dates, weddings, and newborn babies. Their intrusiveness can even provoke violence from celebrities, as witnessed when former NBA star Lamar Odom ripped open the car doors of members of the paparazzi who were following him, pulled their equipment out onto the street, and smashed it with a crowbar. In some instances, it is actually the photographer who is

Photo Op Emma Stone and Andrew Garfield hold notecards with the names of nonprofit organizations in front of their faces.

assaulted, as in the case of one who took a punch in the jaw from actor Alec Baldwin.

While paparazzi can be annoying to celebrities, fans consume their products every day. When we read supermarket tabloids, watch TV entertainment news shows, or scan headlines on gossip blogs, we support the paparazzi's activities—because they support ours. They feed our imaginations, provide us with information about celebrities, and help us envision the worlds of those who are part of our everyday lives but have no idea who we are.

Role models like Jordan and Woods may inspire us to excel in sports and in other areas as well, since both of them have excelled in business and in charity. But their personal failures (both men admitted to marital infidelity) make us wonder what kinds of role models they really are. Some would argue that sports figures are not appropriate role models: Even though they must work hard in order to excel, they still possess unique skills and talents that the rest of us don't have. In fact, another basketball player, Charles Barkley, who played with the Phoenix Suns at the time, famously asserted "I am not a role model," arguing that parents and teachers were more appropriate examples for children to follow. And interestingly, each of the above quotes ("I wanna be like Mike," "I am Tiger Woods," *and* "I am not a role model") was eventually used in Nike commercials—all to inspire consumers to buy expensive sporting goods. In a commercial for Nike, Cleveland Cavalier star LeBron James riffed on the "I am not a role model" theme by asking "What should I do?" of his audience.

"Should I be who you want me to be?" or should he just be himself and not worry about what fans think of him? Can any celebrity afford to do that?

Sports and entertainment role models aside, we also build relationships with people who share our interests—our soccer teammates, fellow collectors of *Star Wars* memorabilia, bluegrass aficionados, or backgammon players. These are important members of our social world.

Leisure and Community

When it comes to the people you play pickup basketball with every Thursday evening, the members of your gardening club, or the folks you watch *Stranger Things* with, your friendship is unlikely to be confined solely to a love of basketball, gardening, or television; your bonds probably extend into other areas of your lives as well. But it is your shared interests that have brought you together, and these activities speak to the

Creative Cosplay Events like Comic Con draw together fans of comic books, video games, anime, and sci-fi films. The Internet has made it easier for people with shared interests to find each other.

heart of Émile Durkheim's pioneering sociological questions about community and social cohesion, first asked more than a hundred years ago and still central today.

Some scholars argue that a critical problem has emerged in contemporary society that undermines social cohesion. They contend that group values in important social groups such as the family, the church, or a labor union have been eclipsed by a rhetoric that espouses radical individual rights first and foremost. For instance, dinner with the family might be passed up in favor of a mother's Pilates lesson or a brother's going to a friend's house to watch the fight on TV. Or the Catholic requirement to attend Mass each week might be fulfilled only on Christmas and Easter.

Sociologist Amitai Etzioni is the leading proponent of a movement that seeks to remedy this problem: **Communitarianism** argues that individual rights do not cancel out collective responsibility. The movement is an attempt to rebuild a sense of group values that benefit all rather than merely the individual. Etzioni's version of communitarianism (1996) is specific in its proposals about how to balance individual rights with social responsibilities—for example, by explicitly teaching positive values in schools. But the question for us here is this: Are bonds based on shared leisure interests enough to constitute a sense of group responsibility compatible with communitarian aims? Or are basketball, gardening, television, and the like just too flimsy a basis for real group identity?

COMMUNITARIANISM a political and moral philosophy focused on strengthening civil society and communal bonds

LIFESTYLE ENCLAVES groups of people drawn together by shared interests, especially those relating to hobbies, sports, and media

Robert Bellah, whose work has examined group values in the United States, supplies another critique but also hints at a potential answer for us. He argues that bonds based on shared interests like those mentioned earlier don't create real community. Rather, such groups constitute **lifestyle enclaves**, which are different from real communities in that they are likely to remain private and segmented, focused on their own shared interests rather than involved in the larger group life (Bellah, Sullivan, and Tipton 1985). So you and your fellow ballplayers, knitters, or TV fans may find your connections to each other to be personally rewarding, but you aren't necessarily contributing to the common good. Or are you?

In Kerry Ferris's (2001) research on *Star Trek* and soap opera fan clubs, she found that while people in these clubs did initially bond solely because of their dedication to particular TV shows, these bonds developed over time in ways that Bellah might not have predicted. Eventually, the groups branched out from their narrow focus and began to pursue things like charitable fund-raising and community service projects that expanded the boundaries of their lifestyle enclave. One *Star Trek* fan club, for example, raised money to help an animal welfare organization that was sponsored by *Trek* actor William Shatner; while their contributions were guided by their specific interests (how many other people even know what Shatner's favorite charity is?), their community spirit was obvious. So perhaps a sense of shared mission within a small group of TV viewers or tulip enthusiasts is not incompatible with a larger sense of social responsibility after all. You can indulge your individual sense of play and work for the common good as well.

Collectors and Hobbyists

Sports are not the only recreational pursuits that draw people together. Many collectors' groups organize annual conventions so that members with shared interests can hobnob with one another for one intensive weekend (Rubel and Rosman 2001). Collectors of Dolly Parton memorabilia, for example, meet once a year in Pigeon Forge, Tennessee, to buy, sell, and trade Dolly-related items and share their love of the country music diva. Fans of a different kind of dolly, Barbie, also meet annually to connect with others who collect Barbie, her friends, and all their accessories. You'll find her on-again, off-again boyfriend Ken there as well, although he now has his own convention, or "Kenvention." And at yet another weekend convention, collectors gather together to "keep history alive" and honor real military heroes both past and present, by buying, selling, and trading twelve-inch action figures die-cast in the image of notable members of the armed forces.

But collectors and hobbyists are no longer limited to meeting face-to-face at an annual convention or weekend workshop. The Internet has helped spawn myriad virtual communities where enthusiasts can interact online. Do-it-yourselfers and garage woodworkers who might normally work alone have found compatriot crafters with whom they can converse. Connecting with others who share the same interests is facilitated by a plethora of websites and social media. Blogs, Facebook, YouTube, Instagram, Pinterest, eBay, and Etsy allow collectors and hobbyists to meet, organize activities, swap tips, show off their wares, and search for the perfect purchases. In some cases, like online gaming, the Internet is the sole source of the hobby.

Hangouts: The Third Place

Away from work or school, where else do you spend your time? Researcher Robert Putnam (2000) laments that, in the United States at least, you will probably be watching TV at home rather than gathering in a public place to socialize with others. But if you lived in France, you might head to the corner café; in Germany, the neighborhood *Bierstube*; in Greece, the local *taverna*. Establishments such as these bear the label **third place** (after home and work, which are first and second). They are informal public places where people come together regularly for conversation and camaraderie. Sociologist Ray Oldenburg (1999, 2002) calls these "great good places" at the heart of community. He is among a growing number of critics who have begun to worry that there are few such places left in the United States—and that we might be suffering as a society because of it.

You know the place—the local diner with a counter that's always full of old men talking about fishing for bluegill, complaining about the cost of prescription medications, or bemoaning the irresponsibility of youth. You might have thought such talk trivial or silly, but the interactions and relationships that develop in third places are important far beyond any specific conversational content. Coffeehouse, bar, or barbershop—third places are more than just hangouts. Oldenburg argues that they are core settings for informal but essential aspects of public and community life. They provide opportunities to connect with others in ways that relieve alienation and anomie, problems Durkheim attributed to modern society. And there are more generalized benefits to society as well—the feeling of public spirit generated in third places can strengthen **civil society**, increase political awareness and participation, and sustain democracy from

> **THIRD PLACE** any informal public place where people come together regularly for conversation and camaraderie when not at work or at home
>
> **CIVIL SOCIETY** those organizations, institutions, and interactions outside government, family, and work that promote social bonds and the smooth functioning of society

Where's Your Third Place? Whether it's a coffeehouse, diner, barbershop, or neighborhood pub, third places are informal public places where people come together regularly for conversation and camaraderie.

the ground up. So that local hangout spot is more important than it appears to be. It helps maintain social cohesion and links the individual to the community.

In the years since Oldenburg coined the term, third places have not disappeared, but they have changed. Gone are the local bookstores where many once gathered. But new technology has also drawn people to new hot spots, as they huddle around free Wi-Fi wherever it may be. Some may bemoan that we have become a nation of isolated screen gazers, even when we're occupying the same space. But the Internet is also making it easier for people to find each other, and mobile apps like Meetup and Foursquare may actually support community building and bringing people back together.

DATA WORKSHOP

Analyzing Everyday Life

Now Go Hang Out

Third places are important to a sense of community and belonging. Are they at risk of disappearing, or are they still attracting people who want to hang out somewhere together? For this Data Workshop you will be doing a short ethnography of a third place. You'll investigate the social setting of a local hangout using participant observation. Refer to Chapter 2 for a review of this research method. You are encouraged to pick a place where you, or others you know, hang out for real, as this background knowledge can help with your analysis; in this case, you'll also be doing an autoethnography.

It doesn't matter which kind of hangout you choose; it could be a bar, restaurant, gym, park, student union, or bookstore. What's important is to make sure that it's a real hangout, someplace where people linger, that they return to regularly to socialize. Part of your work will be to determine just what constitutes a good hangout. So think a bit about your own habits and those of your friends, and choose what you think is a good hangout to study where you'll be both a participant and an observer.

Begin by spending about a half hour or more at the third place you've chosen to study. Even if you're already familiar with the setting, try to have a beginner's mind and take in as much detail about what's happening as possible. Be prepared to write some informal ethnographic field notes describing both the physical and social settings. Examine the items of material culture and the physical layout of the space. Watch the people and note how they interact around (and perhaps with) you, listen for snippets of conversation, and be aware of your own role as both a participant and an observer.

Once you've completed your field notes, you're ready for some analysis. Consider these questions:

- What is the physical space like, and why is it conducive to people hanging out?

- What makes this place a good hangout for the people there?

- Can you distinguish who are the "regulars" and who are not? How do you tell a one-time visitor from a regular?

- How do people establish themselves as regulars?

- What kinds of interactions take place at the hangout? Are people congregated in pairs or small groups, or are they mostly alone?

- What kinds of activities are people engaged in at the hangout?

Finally, approach one or two people you think are regulars and ask them the following questions. Alternatively, if you're a regular, you can answer these questions yourself:

- What does the third place mean to the regulars who go there?

- How does the hangout function in the course of their everyday lives?

- In what respect is being a regular at the hangout a part of someone's identity?

In writing up your analysis, include some examples of the particular **idioculture** you find—the distinctive customs, values, and language expressed in the place and in the interactions of the people who hang out there.

There are two options for completing this Data Workshop:

PREP-PAIR-SHARE Visit a third place and prepare written field notes that you can refer to in class. Partner with one or two other students and discuss your findings. Listen for any differences or variations in each other's experiences and insights.

DO-IT-YOURSELF Conduct ethnographic research at a field site. Write a three- to four-page essay answering the questions provided. Use specific excerpts from your field notes to support your analysis and make sure to attach your field notes to your finished paper.

Travel and Tourism

While some people find respite in hangouts close to home, others relax and rejuvenate by seeing the world. The travel and tourism industries (which include airlines, hotels, car-rental agencies, restaurants, theme parks, resorts, and other attractions) are multibillion-dollar businesses and play an important part in the U.S. economy. And it's a sector that keeps growing. In 2017, the travel and tourism industries in the United States employed 5.5 million workers directly and helped support another 2.3 million jobs in related industries. Travel and tourism sales generated a total of $1.6 trillion. The nearly 77 million international visitors to the United States in 2017 spent over $250 billion on travel- and tourism-related goods and services. These dollar figures are important to the overall economy: Travel and tourism account for about 32 percent of all service exports and 11 percent of total exports (U.S. Department of Commerce 2018).

The impact of tourism on a place is more than just economic. Tourism can have a profound effect on a culture as well. While we may travel to learn to appreciate different cultures, we may also exoticize or even mistreat other groups as we fit them into our own recreational needs, rather than learning about them on their own terms (Urry 1990, 1992, 2002). Travel and tourism shape not just our individual relations with others but also political relations between nations on a global scale. One area of contention concerns the environmental impact of travel and tourism.

For example, America's National Parks were established to preserve unique natural beauty and critical ecosystems so that our citizens could continue to benefit from them. We learn about them through books (like Bill Bryson's *A Walk in the Woods*), photos (like Ansel Adams's pictures of Yosemite), and documentary films (like Ken Burns's PBS series *America's Best Idea*). If we're lucky, we get to visit them, too. San Francisco's Golden Gate Recreational Area is the most popular, but the Great Smoky Mountains, the Grand Canyon, and Yellowstone are also favorites. The National Park Service promotes visits by issuing free passes to all fourth graders in the United States and selling $80 lifetime passes to travelers who are sixty-two years old and older. Visitors, though, mean traffic, trash, and threats to the ecosystems within each park. Human impacts include pollution from cars and boats, tons of garbage from campers and picnickers, and even graffiti on boulders and historic structures. Tourists trample delicate vegetation and interfere with the lives of birds and animals, often without intending to do so. The National Park Service sponsors ongoing preservation and conservation programs, but the necessary funding is not always provided, and the tension between use and abuse of the parks is a constant struggle.

One response to the impact of tourism on places is the phenomenon of **ecotourism**. Ecotourism is characterized by the efforts of tourists and the travel industry to lessen

America the Beautiful In 2018 more than 318 million people visited National Parks such as Yellowstone, Zion, the Grand Canyon, and Shenandoah.

the negative consequences of tourism on the environment as well as on local cultures. Ecotourism promotes a consciousness about environmentally and culturally sensitive travel options. Ecotourists are often from highly industrialized nations and are usually visiting less developed nations. But if they are truly aware of their potential to cause harm, shouldn't they avoid environmentally sensitive locations such as rain forests or the habitats of endangered species?

Sociologists who study ecotourism have mixed views about its effectiveness. Some argue that it is merely consumerism with a "green" wrapping, that the "eco" part of the label is a marketing technique to make tourists feel less guilty about traveling to places where they can't help but make a negative impact. Other sociologists argue that ecotourism, if effectively managed, *can* make positive contributions to both the environment and local communities (Bandy 1996; Scheyvens 2000; Wearing and Wearing 1999; Weinberg, Bellows, and Ekster 2002; Wood 2002). Tourists and travel companies must actively attempt to counterbalance their impact

ECOTOURISM foreign travel with the goal of minimizing the environmental consequences of tourism as well as its possible negative effects on local cultures and economies, typically involving people from highly industrialized nations traveling to less developed countries

IN THE FUTURE
When Your DNA Is Your Travel Guide

With the appearance of websites such as Ancestry.com, television shows like TLC's *Who Do You Think You Are?*, and DNA testing services like 23andMe, many of us have become increasingly interested in our genealogical and biological makeup. The process of tracing our roots through our DNA can help us answer important questions about both our ancestors and ourselves. Many who make use of these services find that their experience is not just a journey through family history, but a voyage of self-discovery as well. And in some cases, "journey" and "voyage" are not just figures of speech.

As global travel becomes easier, faster, and more affordable, a phenomenon called "DNA tourism" (sometimes also referred to as "heritage tourism") has been on the rise. DNA tourism is related to the idea of the pilgrimage—a journey to a geographical location of significance to one's religion. One type of traditional pilgrimage is the *hajj*, an excursion to Mecca in Saudi Arabia, which is required of all Muslims once in their lifetime. Catholics may travel to the Vatican or to other important sites such as the grotto and sanctuary at Lourdes in France or the Cathedral of Santiago de Compostela in Spain. But DNA tourism is less about religion and more about the biological and cultural legacies of different racial and ethnic groups. Since DNA kits like 23andMe are able to identify the geographical areas associated with our genetic origins, members of racial and ethnic groups who live outside the countries of their ancestors can now entertain the possibility of traveling to the "old country," wherever that may be.

Tourism ministries worldwide market their countries and cultures as must-see places for members of their DNA diaspora—people whose ancestors may have migrated generations ago. Travel agencies are putting together DNA group tours, complete with DNA testing and an expert genealogist along for the ride. Ancestry.com can hook you up with living relatives in-country. And Airbnb has partnered with 23andMe to help people plan heritage trips: your DNA results now come with suggested rentals, tours, and classes in your countries of origin (Spurrell 2019). Even airlines are getting in on the trend: Aeroméxico recently offered discounts to Americans flying to Mexico based on the percentage of Mexican heritage shown in their DNA tests.

The most common destinations for U.S.-based DNA travelers are in Europe, with Ireland topping the list. The U.S. Census reports that approximately 10 percent of the American population—or more than 32 million people—claimed Irish heritage in 2017 (U.S. Census Bureau 2019c). That's a lot of potential tourists from America (almost seven times the population of Ireland itself), and the official Irish tourist bureau caters specifically to those who wish to investigate their Irish ancestry. The tourism industry in Ireland encourages people with Irish DNA to take tours that trace their family's heritage. The country's tourism office, in association with the Irish Genealogical Project, entices travelers to visit Irish Family History Foundation centers around the country and promises "a personal and emotional journey... of discovery" as travelers discover the roots of their family trees.

Even more Americans—13 percent, or about 40 million people—identify as having African heritage. Because of the historical brutalities of slavery, it has often been difficult for many African Americans to pinpoint their cities or countries of ancestral origin; often, all they knew was that most African slaves were taken from the west coast of the continent. The new DNA-testing technologies now offer a narrower, more accurate estimate of the area from which a family hails. Some countries in western Africa have begun exploring the touristic implications of slavery's tragic legacy. Ghanaian tourism officials, for example, want the far-flung diasporan descendants of American, European, and Caribbean slaves to think of Africa as home and to consider making a pilgrimage to the land of their ancestors. They even labeled 2019 "The Year of Return" for African Americans to Ghana. They offer tours that focus on slave-trade sites, such as the forts in which newly enslaved Africans were imprisoned before being shipped to the New World (which most visitors find both deeply moving and disturbing). But they also entertain visitors and educate them about Ghanaian culture and customs with colorful festivals, dancing, and feasting. Ghanaian officials, hoping that some visitors will choose to make Ghana their permanent home, are offering special visas for diasporans to make it easy to travel to and from the homeland.

As DNA kits get more affordable, more people will be able to pinpoint the location of their family roots and more may be able to consider a trip to their ancestral homes around the globe. Whether you pay thousands for a private tour, or do it on the cheap, DNA tourism is a growing travel trend and points to a future in which we know more about ourselves and understand better our connections with each other.

with sensitivity to the environment as well as to the values of local communities. The question remains whether ecotourism can live up to its claims and place environmental and cultural concerns before profits.

Closing Comments

Who would have thought that the things you do for fun might actually be important? The many activities considered part of leisure—travel, entertainment, sports, hobbies—while prevalent features of our everyday lives, play an increasingly significant role in the shape of society. We hope we haven't spoiled their pleasure by asking you to examine their various structures and meanings. You can still enjoy your leisure activities even after you've learned to view them from a critical, sociological perspective!

APPLYING WHAT YOU'VE LEARNED

Let's Talk More

1. Sociologists associate types of leisure with different social classes. Which leisure activities are associated with wealthy elites? With working-class people? Which leisure activities, if any, have no particular class associations?

2. How powerful are the media in persuading us to buy certain products or hold particular beliefs? Discuss reinforcement theory, agenda setting, or the two-step flow model. Which of these theories best explains the influence of the media?

3. Are bonds based on shared leisure interests sufficient to constitute a sense of group identity? Or are recreational activities too inconsequential to create true group belonging? Think about people you know through shared recreation or leisure pursuits. Are they part of your primary group, or are they more like secondary group members or part of your "lifestyle enclave"?

Let's Explore More

1. **Film** Smith, Chris, dir. *Fyre*. 2019.

2. **Article** Rafalow, Matt. 2018. "Disciplining Play: Digital Youth Culture as Capital at School." *American Journal of Sociology*, vol. 123, no. 5: 1416–1452.

3. **Blog Post** Kaufman, Peter; and Bente, Richard. "Red Card! The Exclusion of Sports in Sociology." *Everyday Sociology* (blog). July 3, 2014.

   http://WWNorton.com/rd/Aq9t6.

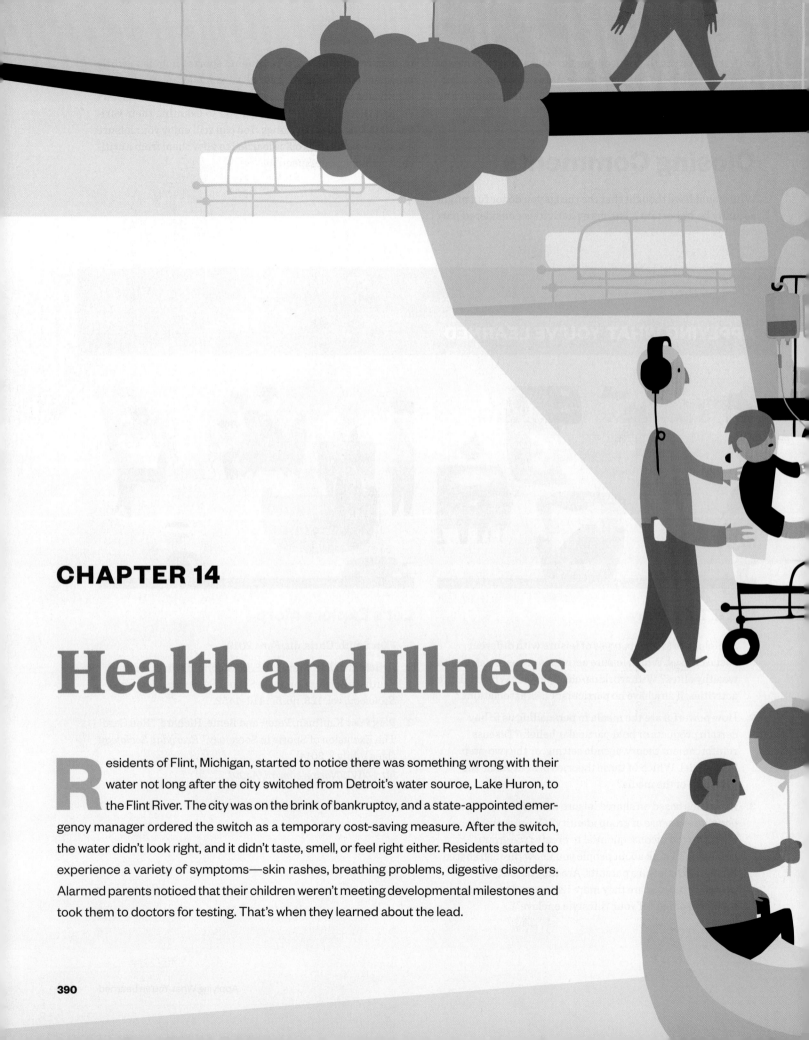

CHAPTER 14

Health and Illness

Residents of Flint, Michigan, started to notice there was something wrong with their water not long after the city switched from Detroit's water source, Lake Huron, to the Flint River. The city was on the brink of bankruptcy, and a state-appointed emergency manager ordered the switch as a temporary cost-saving measure. After the switch, the water didn't look right, and it didn't taste, smell, or feel right either. Residents started to experience a variety of symptoms—skin rashes, breathing problems, digestive disorders. Alarmed parents noticed that their children weren't meeting developmental milestones and took them to doctors for testing. That's when they learned about the lead.

The new water source was more corrosive, and it damaged the protective coating inside the city's aging lead pipes that delivered water to residents. Lead from the pipes leached into the water system, creating a massive public health crisis. No amount of lead in water is safe for drinking, and the health repercussions can be devastating. Lead poisoning can cause brain damage and other serious health problems. The effects can be long-lasting and irreversible and are especially dangerous to children under the age of five. Young children exposed to lead are at greater risk for developmental delays, attention-deficit/hyperactivity disorder (ADHD), and lower IQ scores. Even low levels of lead can be damaging if exposure continues over many months, which is what happened in Flint.

State officials should have known there was something wrong, too, but they were slow to address the problem. Environmental regulators insisted that the water was safe, despite obvious evidence to the contrary. It took more than eighteen months for Michigan governor Rick Snyder to acknowledge the lead problem and to coordinate a response. Worse still, the water supply was found to have other contaminants as well, including bacteria responsible for Legionnaires' disease. The daily routines of cooking and cleaning were no longer a simple matter. The stress of living under these conditions—the worry, anger, and frustration—took an additional toll.

Even after the governor declared a state of emergency in Flint and asked the federal government to step in, relief efforts were slow and often inadequate. The majority of Flint's residents are black and 40 percent of the residents live in poverty. Would the response have been different if the city was more affluent—or white? To many observers and researchers, Flint is an object lesson in environmental racism. Numerous studies have shown that communities of color are disproportionately burdened by environmental hazards; deep racial disparities exist when it comes to the likelihood of exposure to pollution and toxic chemicals such as lead (Sampson and Winter 2016). Sadly, many in Flint will face costly health consequences for years, and possibly generations, to come.

The public health crisis in Flint is just one example of how social status and environment can intersect with health and illness. Elsewhere we find similar examples that illustrate this key sociological insight. For instance, researchers recently determined that living anywhere close to heavy traffic (such as a freeway or busy highway) is associated with a higher incidence of dementia (Chen et al. 2017). The city of Las Vegas presents another case. According to sociologist Matt Wray and his colleagues (2008), merely being in Las Vegas, as either a resident or a tourist, increases one's suicide risk. Such research recognizes what we will be exploring in this chapter: Although health, illness, and mortality are physiological phenomena, they are also unquestionably shaped by social factors.

How to Read This Chapter

Health and illness are constants of human existence, a natural part of having a physical body that is subject to injury, disease, aging, and death. Health and illness are not just physical states—they also include aspects of our mental well-being and are influenced by shifting cultural beliefs about what is ideal and desirable. As a society, we have established the social institution of medicine to address the challenges of our physical existence. Sociologists ask you to consider how larger social forces help shape this institution and your own embodied experience of health or illness.

THE SOCIOLOGY OF MEDICINE, HEALTH, AND ILLNESS

Why is sociology interested in topics that might seem more at home in a medical school textbook? Well, for one thing, our bodies (where health and illness are ostensibly located) are social objects. Our physical selves have socially constructed meanings and are affected by social forces. This means that the very definition of health is social; our individual health is subject not just to cross-cultural or historically specific interpretive differences but also to different influences depending on where and when we live, as well as what statuses we hold in our society.

Let's look at a couple of examples where the nature of health is defined by its social rather than biological context. Think about what having a healthy body means in a developed country like the United States. We value slim, athletic builds

and bodies with just the right amount of curviness and consider people with these body types to be healthier than people with more fleshy builds. But in Dakar, Senegal, people tend to value body types that in the United States would be considered clinically overweight. Senegalese women in particular associate these body types with health (and by extension with wealth enough to eat well); slimmer women actually want to gain weight in order to attain the "desirable," "healthy" build (Holdsworth et al. 2004). Another example: In the United States, "healthy" teeth are not just free of cavities but also straight and white. So in addition to brushing teeth daily and visiting the dentist regularly, Americans spend big money on orthodontic and whitening procedures. Meanwhile, in many other parts of the world, irregularly shaped or unevenly colored teeth are not necessarily seen as "bad" or "unhealthy," and cosmetic dentistry is far less common. These examples indicate that our definitions of health (and beauty as a sign of health) are determined at least in part by our cultural context and not always by a biological bottom line.

Another important aspect of health as a social phenomenon involves the spread of disease. Think about it: You've caught a good number of illnesses from other people. Someone behind you in the movie theater coughed, and you got a cold (if you were lucky) or tuberculosis (if you were unlucky). Someone flipping burgers at a fast-food restaurant forgot to wash her hands, and you got an upset stomach (if you were lucky) or hepatitis A (if you were unlucky). If you have young children in school or day care, you know that kids are like family disease vectors—they catch bugs from other kids, bring them home, and spread them around to family members.

Social milieu affects your risk of disease. Take, for example, the recent measles outbreaks across the United States. Measles is a highly contagious disease that causes fever, a full-body rash, and sometimes other complications. Death from measles is rare in developed countries like the

Health in a Cultural Context Senegalese women live in a society that values fuller body types that might be classified as overweight in other cultures. The United States puts such a strong emphasis on straight, white teeth that many people spend thousands of dollars on cosmetic dental procedures.

Outbreak in Brooklyn Measles cases in the United States have increased sharply, due in large part to a growing number of vaccine resisters. In 2019, New York City experienced the worst outbreak of measles since 1992, with nearly all cases occurring in a tightly knit ultra-Orthodox Jewish community in Brooklyn.

United States, with widespread vaccination programs and high-quality health care, but fatality rates can be as high as 30 percent in places without such amenities, or in populations that cannot receive vaccines, such as infants under twelve months of age or people with compromised immune systems such as AIDS or chemotherapy patients.

In 2019, measles reached a major milestone, infecting more people in the United States than in any other year since 1994, despite the disease being declared eradicated in 2000. The increase in cases was driven in part by lingering outbreaks in several concentrated areas, but cases were confirmed in a total of twenty-six states. The Centers for Disease Control and Prevention (CDC) linked the outbreaks to two primary sources: travelers who brought measles back from other countries where large outbreaks were occurring, and the further spread in U.S. communities with pockets of unvaccinated people (CDC 2019).

One such pocket of unvaccinated people was an insular enclave of ultra-Orthodox Jews in Brooklyn, New York. In 2019, Israel was in the midst of a years-long measles epidemic. American travelers visiting the country brought back the virus to the Brooklyn community. A large number among those community members were vaccine resisters who hadn't immunized their children. The main reason for this was a largely secular, rather than religious, concern about a link between the measles vaccination and autism. There is, it should be noted, no scientific evidence to support such a link, and this has been thoroughly researched. In an effort to stop the spread of infection in New York, city officials declared a public health emergency and imposed a mandatory vaccination order on residents in the Williamsburg area of Brooklyn.

A highly vaccinated community maintains what is called "herd immunity," a kind of group resistance that helps protect even the unvaccinated from contracting the disease (herd immunity for measles requires about a 95 percent vaccination rate). Those who voluntarily decline vaccinations, though, put both themselves and the rest of the "herd" at risk. The lower the vaccination rate of a community (residents of a town, for example, or students at a school, or visitors to a theme park), the lower the group's collective immunity and the more vulnerable to infection members become.

Our bodies are social objects, and our social experiences and social location shape our prospects for health and risks of disease. These are only some of the reasons that health and illness are social phenomena. As you read this chapter, you'll find that there are social, cultural, and subcultural factors affecting just about everything having to do with health and illness.

DEFINING HEALTH AND ILLNESS

Terms such as "healthy" and "sick" may seem straightforward, but their meanings are not absolute or universal. The World Health Organization (WHO), a division of the United Nations charged with overseeing global health issues, defines health as "a state of complete physical, mental, and social well-being and not merely the absence of disease or infirmity" (WHO 1946). Let's look further at how illnesses are defined and treated in the United States.

Types of Illnesses

Diseases and illnesses are commonly categorized as either acute or chronic. **Acute diseases** have a sudden onset, may be briefly incapacitating, and are either curable or fatal. These illnesses are often caused by an organism such as a germ, virus, or parasite that infects the body and disrupts the normal functioning of one or more areas. Many acute illnesses are contagious and can spread from one person to many people. The common cold, pneumonia, and measles could all be considered acute illnesses. **Chronic diseases** develop over a longer period of time and may not be detected until later in their progression. They can sometimes be related to environment, lifestyle, and personal choices. Many chronic diseases are manageable, but others progress and eventually become

ACUTE DISEASES diseases that have a sudden onset, may be briefly incapacitating, and are either curable or fatal

CHRONIC DISEASES diseases that develop over a longer period of time and may not be detected until later in their progression, when symptoms occur

CURATIVE or **CRISIS MEDICINE** type of health care that treats the disease or condition once it has manifested

The Crown Juul Chronic diseases can be linked to lifestyle and personal choices such as smoking or vaping. According to the CDC, one in five high school students has used e-cigarettes (Gentzke 2019).

fatal. Cancer, cardiovascular disease, and some forms of diabetes can all be considered chronic diseases.

The kinds of diseases that affect us can vary over time and by place. For most of history, humans worried about becoming afflicted with acute diseases. Indeed, prior to 1900, the leading causes of death in the United States were influenza, pneumonia, tuberculosis, and gastroenteritis. Over the past century, drastic changes in medicine and public health have all but wiped out certain acute diseases (such as polio), while chronic ones (such as diabetes and heart disease) have grown vastly in proportion (CDC 2017a). Chronic diseases have become among the most important factors governing health and illness today. A majority of the top ten causes of death in the United States are chronic diseases; the top three causes of death in 2017 were heart disease, cancer, and unintentional injuries, with chronic respiratory illnesses like asthma and emphysema not far behind at number four (Murphy et al. 2018; Hoyert and Xu 2012). However, acute diseases continue to pose significant threats to people living in the developing world, where the top killers still include respiratory infections, diarrheal diseases, tuberculosis, and malaria (WHO 2018a).

Approaches to Medical Treatment

The health-care system in the United States is characterized by three approaches: curative or crisis, preventive, and palliative. **Curative** or **crisis medicine** treats the disease once it has become apparent. Sometimes this works well, especially in the case of acute illnesses like food poisoning, or sports injuries like a torn ligament, that have no early treatment option. But in the case of chronic illnesses, a delay in recognizing causes or symptoms before the disease advances may mean the difference between recovery and death. **Preventive**

medicine aims to avoid or forestall the onset of disease by making lifestyle changes: regular exercise, proper diet and nutrition, smoking cessation, stress reduction, and other measures to maintain or improve one's health. Lifestyle changes are often the most effective and least costly ways to prevent a range of chronic conditions. **Palliative care** focuses on symptom and pain relief and on providing a nurturing and supportive environment to those suffering from a serious illness or at the end of life, either in addition to or in place of fighting the illness or disease.

PREVENTIVE MEDICINE type of health care that aims to avoid or forestall the onset of disease by taking preventive measures, often including lifestyle changes

PALLIATIVE CARE type of health care that focuses on symptom and pain relief and providing a supportive environment for critically ill or dying patients

DATA WORKSHOP
Analyzing Everyday Life
Student Health Issues Survey

For many young people, moving away from home and going to college mark the beginning of their independent lives as adults. While there is much to celebrate at this milestone, it can also be a time full of new demands and challenges. Perhaps you or someone you know is dealing with homesickness, an abusive relationship, or stress and anxiety. As a college student, you can learn to become more responsible and disciplined and more conscientious about taking care of yourself. But you can also be threatened by alcohol or substance abuse, eating disorders, or depression. The college years are an important phase of development and one in which many young people struggle to some degree with their newfound adult lives.

The American College Health Association (ACHA) is an organization that partners with colleges and universities to conduct large-scale surveys on the habits, behaviors, and perceptions affecting the health and well-being of students. In fall 2018, the ACHA surveyed more than 26,000 students at forty institutions. They found some interesting trends; for instance, 45 percent of students said they had experienced "more than average stress" within the last twelve months, while another 13 percent said they had experienced "tremendous stress." Women reported higher levels of stress than men. Results from the ACHA survey are helping schools offer education and support services regarding a variety of issues (ACHA 2018).

For this Data Workshop you will be conducting your own small-scale survey study of health and wellness issues. Refer to Chapter 2 for a review of survey research. You will be designing a questionnaire, distributing surveys to a sample of your target population, and then analyzing the responses.

Begin by thinking about whom you would like to study and what kinds of questions you would like to ask them. Your respondents should all be college students; remember to ask for their consent to participate. You'll want to gather some basic demographic background from each respondent. Consider such variables as race and ethnicity, class, national background, gender, religion, and/or age of your sample. There are many possibilities for comparing and contrasting within or across categories. Because this is only a pilot study, the number of people you can survey will necessarily be small. You'll probably have to draw from what is referred to as a "convenience sample" of respondents rather than using a more scientific random sample. How many people you include in your sample may also depend on how many questions you'd like to ask each respondent.

Typically, survey questions are closed-ended with preset response options, usually yes or no or agree/disagree (Likert scale). You may also want to include open-ended questions that allow respondents to answer in their own words. The kinds of questions you ask may also help to determine the number of questions to include. There's no one right way to structure a survey, but do keep the questionnaires as clear and simple as possible. Here is a list of possible topics for your study. Feel free to add your own topics.

anger	peer pressure
body image	pregnancy
depression	relationships
drugs and alcohol	sexual assault
eating disorders	sexually transmitted diseases
exercise	sleep difficulties
financial issues	stress and anxiety
gambling	suicide
grades and studying	tobacco use
grief and loss	violence
homesickness	

Questions about daily habits, relationships, and emotions can tell you something about an individual's mental and physical health. You might ask students about their lifestyles—what they eat, how much they sleep, whether they exercise, drink or smoke, or practice safe sex. Do they play a musical instrument, are they on a sports team, or do they belong to any campus clubs? You might ask about their physical health—how often they get sick, or what they do to stay healthy. Or you might ask about their mental health—whether they experience stress, depression, and/or anxiety, what causes them to feel it, and what they do to alleviate it. Some topics may be too sensitive or personal in nature, so use good judgment. Let your respondents know that they can decline to answer any questions that make them uncomfortable. Remember that you must also respect the privacy and confidentiality of your respondents. Once you've finalized the questions, you're ready to distribute the surveys.

After gathering data, you'll want to begin to analyze your findings. Sift through your completed surveys and compile some notes about what you find. See what kinds of patterns you can find—similarities, differences, comparisons, and contradictions. What do you think these data reveal about how your respondents cope with the health issues they encounter at school?

There are two options for completing this Data Workshop:

PREP-PAIR-SHARE Design a questionnaire and distribute surveys to a small sample from your target population (perhaps three or four people). Look over their answers, make notes about any preliminary results, and bring them with you to class. Get together with one or two other students and discuss your findings. Look for similarities and differences in both your own findings and those of your fellow discussion group members. See if you can identify any patterns that emerge from the data gathered by the entire group.

DO-IT-YOURSELF Design a questionnaire and distribute surveys to a small group of respondents from your target population (perhaps six or seven people). Write a two- to three-page essay describing the research process and analyzing your findings. Be sure to attach to your paper a copy of your questionnaire and any notes you took. How do your findings confirm or refute any hypotheses you might have had before beginning the study? What do your data suggest about the relationship between college life and student health?

THE PROCESS OF MEDICALIZATION

Because what constitutes illness can be socially constructed, it's interesting to look at how some problems that were once not considered medical conditions have been transformed into illnesses over time. This process is known as

medicalization, and it has affected our perspective on a variety of behaviors and conditions. A half century ago, we thought of alcoholism and addiction as the result of weak will or bad character, but we now see them as diseases that respond to medical and therapeutic treatment. Kids who might have been written off as "unruly" or "incorrigible" in the 1950s are now diagnosed with attention-deficit/hyperactivity disorder, or ADHD, and given drugs to keep them calm and focused (Conrad 2006). Obesity, once seen as a failure of willpower, can now be treated with surgery and drugs.

Even birth and death have been medicalized. In the early years of the twentieth century, more than half of American women gave birth at home, attended only by family, friends, or midwives, without drugs or surgeries. By 1955, that number had declined steeply, to about 1 percent of American women (Cassidy 2006). While home births have increased in the past decade, they still account for less than 2 percent of births in the United States (CDC 2014b). We now see pregnancy as a "medical condition" for which a hospital birth—and, often, a doctor's intervention in the form of an episiotomy or caesarean section—is the "treatment."

Death has undergone the same transformation: Once a natural (though sad) part of family life, it is now something that we will go to great medical lengths to delay (though we can never stave it off forever). Death also used to occur at home, but today about 70 percent of patients die in other settings (CDC 2018a), despite the fact that studies show it is less stressful for terminally ill patients to die at home (Searing 2010). For many people living great distances away from relatives, dying at home is no longer even an option.

Medicalization changes both the meaning of a condition and the meaning of the individual who suffers from it. In the case of birth and death, it turns a natural part of the human life cycle into something unfamiliar that we fear we can't handle on our own. We therefore turn to medical experts who may or may not intervene in ways that actually help and may in fact further traumatize patients and their families. In other cases, such as with conditions like addiction, obesity, or mental or emotional problems, medicalization takes the pressure off individual people. The fact that they drink too much, eat too much, can't concentrate, or are sad all the time is no longer their fault as individuals—it is the fault of the disease. We would never advise someone to "just get over" pneumonia or a broken leg—and as the process of medicalization continues, we are less likely to think of addiction, obesity, and depression as conditions people should "just get over" on their own.

The Social Construction of Mental Illness

Understanding that disease can be socially constructed allows us to see how its meanings can change over time. For example, take the social meaning of mental illness. Over the course of history and in different societies, theories of the causes of mental illness have varied widely. Each new theory led to a different type of treatment (and justification for that treatment), some of which seem shockingly inhumane to us now. For example, in fourteenth-century London, Bethlem Royal Hospital (which is still in operation today) became a kind of prison for those suffering from mental illnesses. Based on the theory that mental illness was a moral failing caused by demonic possession or individual weakness, the "treatment" for those who suffered was removal from society. Bethlem, or Bedlam as it came to be known, warehoused the mentally ill under the most horrifying of conditions, which included overcrowding; lack of food, water, and sanitation; whippings; and "exorcisms."

In Colonial America, the prevailing theory was that mental illness was caused by the astrological position of the moon at the time of the individual's birth; hence the term "lunatic." According to this theory, mental illness was located inside a lunatic's body, and the only possible cures involved treatments meant to release the illness, such as bleeding (which often killed the patients) and long-term induced vomiting (also potentially fatal). In the 1930s, the cause of mental illness was believed to be located in a particular portion of

> **MEDICALIZATION** the process by which behaviors or conditions that were once seen as personal problems are redefined as medical issues

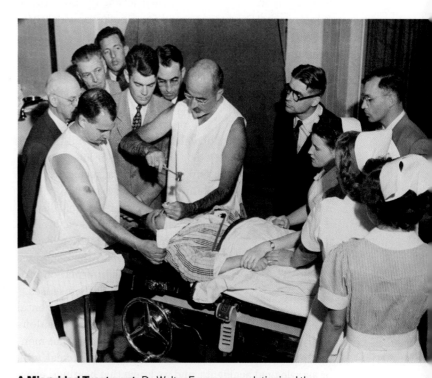

A Misguided Treatment Dr. Walter Freeman revolutionized the lobotomy procedure, which he performed with an ice pick–like instrument that severed nerve connections in the front part of the brain.

IN THE FUTURE
Treating America's Opioid Epidemic

We are in the grip of a devastating public health crisis—the opioid epidemic is growing rapidly and shows no signs of slowing down. The number of overdose deaths involving opioids was six times higher in 2017 than in 1999, according to the Centers for Disease Control and Prevention (2018b). Drug overdose is now the leading cause of death for Americans under the age of 50. On average, 130 Americans die every day from an overdose involving opioids, including prescription drugs and illicit substances like heroin. With the spike in opioid-related deaths, life expectancy in the United States has actually declined in recent years, an unprecedented reversal of longtime trends in mortality.

The epidemic can be traced to the 1990s, when Purdue Pharma introduced OxyContin. The drug was touted as a safer, more effective pain medication that was nonaddicting, even when taken long term. Purdue marketed the drug aggressively and put unprecedented resources toward outreach to doctors, sometimes lavishing them with gifts and free vacations. Family doctors and general practitioners became increasingly willing to treat their patients with this new pain medication, all the while following the prescribing guidelines that Purdue endorsed. OxyContin was widely prescribed for post-operative pain, sports injuries, accidents, dental surgeries, and other conditions.

As it turned out, OxyContin was highly addictive, contrary to Purdue's claims. By the time this became clear, large numbers of people were already hooked. Contrary to the stereotype, many people who became drug addicts did not start out using opioids for recreational purposes. They were given painkillers for legitimate purposes and told to take them by doctors who were supposed to be authorities on such matters. At the outset, the opioid crisis was concentrated in certain populations—particularly low-income and predominantly white communities. Doctors may have been more willing to prescribe painkillers to white patients and, conversely, to withhold them from nonwhites. Such racial bias also means that the epidemic has been framed as a public health issue rather than a criminal justice issue.

Some of the hardest-hit populations were in places that were experiencing economic hardship. The story of Roanoke, Virginia, as chronicled in Beth Macy's *Dopesick* (2018), served as a harbinger of what would later happen in many other places around the country and of how opioid addiction could quickly spread through and decimate a community. Following the 2008 recession, Roanoke, a largely white, working-class area in Appalachia, was reeling from a flagging economy, high unemployment, and a lack of opportunities—a backdrop for what demographers have called "deaths of despair" by

---

the brain, the removal of which would thus provide the cure. The lobotomy, in which a bit of the brain (or lobe) was surgically removed, often without anesthesia, seemed to work nicely; patients became calm enough to leave the hospital and return home. We now know that lobotomies merely disconnected two critical parts of the brain from each other, leaving patients unable to feel emotions or act on the information provided to them by their senses.

These approaches to mental illness now seem ridiculous and cruel. We know that mental illness is not caused by demonic possession, a weak will, or astrological accidents, and we know that beatings, exorcisms, and lobotomies cannot restore mental health. We are certain (aren't we?) that mental illness is caused by problems of brain chemistry and that proper treatment involves medications that restore that chemistry to its healthy balance. But given the history of changing meanings and treatments, we have to ask: What makes this theory any better than the others? How can we be sure that this time we've gotten it right? Isn't it possible that, a hundred years from now, we'll discover the "real" cause of mental illness and that drug treatments will seem as useless and inhumane as surgeries and bleedings do now?

EPIDEMIOLOGY AND DISEASE PATTERNS

As we have noted, sociologists are interested in the social aspect of disease patterns. The study of these patterns is known as **epidemiology**. Epidemiologists collect and analyze data in order to understand the causes of a particular illness, how it is communicated, the factors affecting its

EPIDEMIOLOGY the study of disease patterns to understand the cause of illnesses, how they are spread, and what interventions to take

alcohol, suicide, and drug overdose. Such communities often lack adequate resources, including education and jobs, to help support vulnerable and disadvantaged residents so that they don't lapse into drug abuse, or to offer them treatment options when they become addicted.

A new phase of the opioid epidemic began in 2010, characterized by rapid increases in overdose deaths involving heroin. As a growing number of people became addicted to prescription opiates, many of them had trouble acquiring the drug after the prescriptions ran out. Faced with the prospect of excruciating withdrawal symptoms, some addicts turned to the black market, while others resorted to taking cheaper, more readily available illicit drugs such as heroin. By 2013, many addicts were turning to synthetic opioids, particularly fentanyl, which is cheaper and more potent than heroin. Fentanyl can be easily manufactured in a black-market lab, and it has flooded the illicit drug trade. The drug, which has already surpassed heroin and other opiates in usage, has been involved in nearly one half of all opioid-related deaths (Jones, Einstein, and Compton 2018).

The opioid epidemic has become a part of daily reality for an increasing number of people. Fully 42 percent of Millennials say they personally know someone who has dealt with opioid addiction. By race, 54 percent of whites know such a person, while this is true of 30 percent of blacks, 26 percent of Asians, and 23 percent of Latinos (Perry and Arenge 2018). Sadly, it is one of the most difficult addictions to recover from, even when treatment is available. And the toll has already

The Toll of the Opioid Epidemic The Gilbert family of Roanoke, Virginia, mourns the loss of Jordan Gilbert, who died of an opioid overdose at twenty-seven. Life expectancy in the United States has recently declined due to the rise in overdose deaths.

been taken in so many communities, families, businesses, and individual lives. Unfortunately, solving this crisis is not as easy as just ceasing to prescribe opioids; there are patients who have real needs for such drugs. The opioid epidemic is a massive public health problem that is unlikely to be solved in the near term because eliminating the disease will require attacking root causes, including biases in prescribing practices, mental health issues, and poverty.

development and distribution in a population, where it is likely to spread, and what the most effective interventions might be. Over many centuries of human history, major illnesses such as cholera, typhus, yellow fever, and smallpox would sweep across vast stretches of the globe and decimate populations from practically every continent. More recently, such illnesses as tuberculosis, malaria, and measles continue to kill millions around the world. What future illnesses might threaten humanity next, and can we identify them before widespread devastation occurs? Epidemiologists combine data and methods from the biological and social sciences with a public health orientation to answer important questions about the origins and spread of disease.

Epidemiologists swing into action whenever a new disease emerges or an unexpected outbreak of a previously eradicated disease occurs. For example, in the West African Ebola outbreak of 2014, epidemiological researchers established the connection among hundreds and then thousands of patients,

analyzed the genetic makeup of the virus that had infected them, and confirmed that the patients were suffering from a strain of Ebola that was evolving as it was being transmitted. As a result of this research, widespread public health awareness campaigns were put in place to educate people about the transmission, prevention, and treatment of the disease. In particular, traditional burial practices, including washing, touching, and kissing the body of the deceased, were targeted as the primary modes of transmission, since it was through these practices that the disease could devastate entire families and communities. Health-care workers were also at high risk due to their close contact with infected patients, and so Ebola prevention protocols were developed to help keep them safe. Despite these attempts at intervention, the disease spread quickly and eventually killed over 11,000 people, approximately 50 percent of those infected.

The Ebola epidemic spread to ten countries, but it never officially became what is known as a pandemic. What are the differences between the two terms? An **epidemic** occurs when the number of cases of a particular disease during a particular time period is significantly higher than might otherwise be expected. The term **pandemic** is used when cases of the disease also cover an especially large geographical region (say, a continent or the entire globe). What constitutes an epidemic is usually determined by national public health organizations—in the United States, that would be the Centers for Disease Control and Prevention (CDC) in Atlanta (Koerner 2003). The World Health Organization (WHO) in Geneva, Switzerland, monitors and defines pandemics.

Human immunodeficiency virus (HIV) and the disease it causes, acquired immunodeficiency syndrome (AIDS), is an example of a pandemic. More than 77 million people have been infected with HIV/AIDS since the virus was first identified in the early 1980s, and more than 35 million have died from it. Currently there are more than 36 million people living with HIV/AIDS (UNAIDS 2018). This makes HIV/AIDS a global phenomenon, but it can also be looked at as a series of epidemics. AIDS is always the same disease, but it is a very different epidemic depending on where it is.

In many places, HIV/AIDS is a concentrated epidemic, with the majority of cases transmitted by a particular method and among a particular subpopulation within a given country. In Central Europe and Central Asia, intra-venous drug use is responsible for the majority of cases (O'Neill 2007). In Latin America, the routes by which HIV is transmitted are more diverse, but same-sex male intercourse is the most common. In Southeast Asia, commercial sex workers make up a much larger percentage of the HIV-positive population. In sub-Saharan Africa, HIV/AIDS is a generalized epidemic spread through the entire population, such that in some countries more than 30 percent of adults are infected.

As a pandemic, HIV/AIDS is distributed disproportionately: Only about 6 percent of all cases are in wealthy industrialized nations in Western and Central Europe and North America, whereas more than two-thirds of cases occur in African nations (Kaiser Family Foundation 2019a). In the developed world the vast majority of HIV/AIDS sufferers have access to antiretroviral drugs, which transform the disease into something much closer to a chronic condition and significantly improve patient outcomes. For a long time these drugs were prohibitively expensive in the developing world, so the vast majority of patients could not receive them. Since 2010 there has been a surge in access to antiretroviral drugs in precisely the world's most infected regions. By 2017, 59 percent of people living with HIV worldwide were accessing antiretroviral therapy, making their prognosis considerably better (UNAIDS 2018).

Epidemiologists are now identifying the role of global climate change in spreading some of the most important diseases afflicting the world, and they are tracking how this process occurs (Barrett, Charles, and Temte 2015). Because climate affects things like the availability of fresh water and "arable" (or farmable) land, it also affects where people live and their patterns of migration. As people leave places where

EPIDEMIC occurs when the number of cases of a particular disease during a particular time period is significantly higher than might otherwise be expected

PANDEMIC occurs when a significantly higher number of cases of a disease also spreads through an especially large geographical region spanning many countries or even continents

A Modern-Day Epidemic
A sign in Freetown, Sierra Leone, warns of the dangers of Ebola. The 2014 Ebola outbreak in West Africa claimed more than 11,000 lives.

TABLE 14.1 Theory in Everyday Life: Explanations of Addiction

Perspective	Approach to Medicine and Health	Case Study: Drug and Alcohol Addiction
Structural Functionalism	Disease is a threat to social order, and sick people cannot fulfill their roles and contribute to society; the health-care system should return patients to health and normal functioning as members of society.	People who become addicted to drugs and alcohol may be responding to strains in the social system and their own lives; they may adapt by retreating or escaping through drugs and alcohol.
Conflict Theory	Health and the health-care system are valuable resources that are unequally shared in society; conflict may arise among different groups seeking access to and control over these resources.	Those in power can define social policy and create laws regarding medicine and health care; people of lower social status are more likely to be scrutinized as problem drinkers or drug addicts and may be unduly punished.
Symbolic Interactionism	The meanings of health and illness are dependent on historical, cultural, and situational contexts. Stigma may be attached to certain disease states and to those who suffer from them.	People learn to use alcohol and drugs in social interaction and are influenced by peers and other groups; they may attach different meanings and values to substances and behaviors.

climate change has made food, water, and other resources scarce, they crowd into other areas that may then experience overpopulation. When people live in very close quarters, the risks rise for malnutrition and the spread of infectious diseases, including waterborne illnesses such as cholera (Khasnis and Nettleman 2005).

Global climate change can also affect animal populations that spread diseases among humans. Even small increases in temperature can multiply the numbers of **vector organisms** that carry and spread pathogens (infectious agents) in a given area. Mosquitoes carrying malaria, for example, used to be limited to sub-Saharan Africa and other hot or tropical regions. But in Kenya, malaria has recently penetrated mountainous regions that were once too chilly for mosquitoes to survive, and similar reports have come from parts of Europe and as far north as Moscow, Russia (Bouzid et al. 2014; Caminade et al. 2014). The United States is also at risk. Other illnesses such as Lyme disease (carried by ticks), yellow and dengue fevers and West Nile virus (carried by mosquitoes), avian influenza (carried by birds), and even bubonic plague (carried by fleas on rodents) may skyrocket as climate change drives these vector animals out of their customary territories and into new ecosystems (Dell'Amore 2008; Morin, Comrie, and Ernst 2013; Randall 2019).

SOCIAL INEQUALITY, HEALTH, AND ILLNESS

As we have seen in previous chapters, a person's socioeconomic status, race, and gender also shape their experiences of health and illness. Answers to such questions as "Who gets sick?" "What kinds of diseases do they get?" "Who gets treatment?" and "What kind of treatment do they get?" are all influenced by social hierarchies and structures of inequality.

Intersections of Class

It's easy to see how one's social class might have an effect on one's health. People of higher socioeconomic status (SES) not only can afford more and better health-care services (insurance plans, doctor visits, diagnostic tests and treatments, prescription medications) but also may have greater access to other resources (better nutrition, cleaner neighborhoods, more preventive practices like exercise) that positively influence their health. As a group, people with higher SES are better informed health consumers and they generally enjoy more physical well-being than those of lower SES (Blackwell and Villarroel 2016). In fact, people with higher incomes can even expect to live longer lives. This is true throughout the income distribution, but it is most stark when comparing those at the very top with those at the very bottom. A recent study found that the gap in life expectancy between the richest 1 percent and the poorest 1 percent was 14.6 years for men and 10.1 years for women (Chetty et al. 2016b).

People with lower SES have substantially higher rates of various diseases and chronic illnesses, along with higher death rates and shorter life expectancy (Chokshi 2018; Blackwell and Villarroel 2016; Lynch, Kaplan, and Shema 1998). They may have little regular access to health-care providers, lack the ability to participate in preventive practices, or

VECTOR ORGANISMS animals like mosquitoes, ticks, and birds that carry and spread pathogens (germs or other infectious agents) in a given area

have trouble affording prescription medications and other recommended procedures (Lynch, Kaplan, and Shema 1997). The effects of poverty consistently correlate with higher incidences of mental health problems (Groh 2007). People living in poverty are twice as likely to suffer from depression as those who are not (Brown 2012).

Educational attainment is a key factor linking SES and disparate health outcomes. Sociologists believe that education is a root cause of good health (Hummer and Hernandez 2013). Individuals with more education are less likely to be obese and are less likely to smoke: In 2017, 37 percent of people with a GED smoked cigarettes compared to just 7 percent of people with a bachelor's degree (Wang et al. 2018). Highly educated adults have lower mortality rates than those who are less educated, and this holds across racial/ethnic, gender, and age groups. Remaining life expectancy at age twenty-five is about a decade shorter for those who have not completed high school compared to those who have a college degree (Hummer and Hernandez 2013).

Intersections of Race

Disparities by race and ethnicity persist in almost every key measurement of health. One of the largest and most persistent health disparities among different racial and ethnic groups is the infant mortality rate, which is considered a key measure of public health. While infant mortality rates have improved markedly in recent years, there remain stark racial and ethnic disparities. Black women in particular experience much higher infant mortality rates—more than two times higher than white women. This is largely due to the fact that black women are much more likely than women of other races to give birth preterm (MacDorman and Mathews 2011; Mathews and Driscoll 2017). Rates of diabetes also vary across race and ethnicity: African Americans have the

highest prevalence, at 13 percent, while the rate is 12 percent for Hispanics, 8 percent for Asians, and 7 percent for whites (CDC 2017d; Spanakis and Golden 2013). We even see disparities when it comes to life expectancy: In 2016, life expectancy for white men (76.1 years) was 4.5 years longer than for black men (71.5 years); similarly, life expectancy for white women (81.0) was 3 years longer than for black women (77.9). Notably, Hispanics have the longest life expectancy at birth: 79.1 years for men and 84.2 years for women (CDC 2018a).

African Americans and Hispanics are less likely to be able to afford health insurance and, consequently, to have access to health care or to engage in regular health practices (Artiga, Orgera, and Damico 2019). Minorities are also more often exposed to unhealthful surroundings, whether in the workplace or in residential neighborhoods. A recent study by scientists at the Environmental Protection Agency (EPA) found that people of color are more than 30 percent more likely to live near pollution-emitting facilities than whites and that these emissions are linked to higher rates of asthma and heart attacks and overall lower life expectancy (Mikati et al. 2018). What happened to the water supply in Flint, Michigan, is evidence of this kind of environmental racism, which refers to how environmental hazards disproportionately affect racial minorities. In another example, Emily Rosenbaum (2008) found that Hispanics and blacks in New York City tended to live in poorer-quality housing in lower-income neighborhoods and to suffer much higher incidences of asthma than their Asian, white, and higher-SES counterparts.

While socioeconomic status is a factor, that is only part of the story: Public health researchers have found compelling evidence that some of these disparities are linked to systemic racism and discrimination, especially among African Americans (Paradies et al. 2015). The idea of "weathering" was first proposed by public health researcher Arline Geronimus to

Racial Disparities in Health (Left) Racial minorities are much more likely to live near polluting facilities, which is linked to higher rates of asthma and heart attacks. (Right) Black women die of complications from pregnancy far more often than do white women. The stresses of racism can create a "weathering" effect and lead to deleterious health outcomes for blacks.

describe the subtle but cumulative effects of "lifelong physiological stress-mediated wear and tear" that results in worse mental and physical health outcomes (Geronimus 1992; Geronimus et al. 2006). As a metaphor, weathering suggests erosion through incremental but sustained stress in one's environment. Because of repeated exposure to the stresses of racism and poverty, the health of African Americans begins to deteriorate as soon as early adulthood.

One telling sign of weathering is higher maternal mortality rates among African Americans than those in other ethnic or racial groups. Black women are more than three times more likely to die from complications from pregnancy than white women (Petersen et al. 2019). Only a small part of this can be explained by a lack of health insurance or access to prenatal care. Even someone like Serena Williams, who nearly died following the birth of her daughter in 2017, is at risk. Research suggests that even when African Americans have higher SES and education levels, they must still deal with racism and the stress of interacting with people outside their racial groups (Purnell, Camberos, and Fields 2014). No matter how successful, African Americans still suffer from significant stigma associated with their identity. And that has real implications for their overall health.

Intersections of Gender

Gender is another source of inequality that complicates the health picture for men and women. Health is one place where gender inequality typically benefits women over men, as women are generally healthier and enjoy a longer life expectancy in spite of having a lower SES than men. In 2016, the average life expectancy for women (81.1 years) was five years longer than the average life expectancy for men (76.1 years). Traditional male gender-role expectations may result in men who work in more dangerous occupations and engage in more risky lifestyle behaviors (such as smoking, drinking, doing drugs, and driving fast). The more strongly men identify with stereotypical ideas about masculinity, the more likely they are to avoid preventive health care, regardless of their level of SES (Springer and Mouzon 2011).

Despite the fact that women tend to live longer than men, women still suffer from inequalities in other areas of health care. Men and women suffer from some diseases, such as cancer and diabetes, in about equal numbers. Even though heart disease has long been thought of as a "man's disease," about the same number of men and women die from it each year (Xu et al. 2016). But historically women have not been screened and treated for heart disease as early or as aggressively as are men. In addition, much of the research on cardiovascular disease has historically focused on men. It wasn't until recently that researchers recognized that women often experience different heart attack symptoms than men (Leifheit-Limson et al. 2015). This has resulted in higher death rates from heart attacks among women.

In medical research, the male body has always been treated as the standard, while women have often been ignored. This was the case with the sleep medication Ambien. The adult dosage of the drug was designed for the average man, so women taking it were still under the influence when they awoke in the morning, which resulted in their getting into more accidents. The Food and Drug Administration had to step in to advise women to cut their dose in half because they were metabolizing the medication more than twice as slowly as men. Recent research suggests that women also have more adverse reactions to drugs than men, and one of the most prevalent of those reactions is simply that the medications don't work at all. And some medications that are beneficial to men are actually harmful to women (Perez 2019).

When it comes to mental health, women are 40 percent more likely than men to develop mood or anxiety disorders such as depression. They are also more vulnerable to trauma and stress-related disorders (Li and Graham 2017). Researchers have speculated that female sex hormones may play a role. But women are also more likely to seek out mental health care than men, which may mean that there is a discrepancy in the rates of reporting and diagnosis of mental illness between women and men, rather than a discrepancy in the rates of occurrence.

Inequality and the Problem of Food Deserts

When the residents of Flint, Michigan, were hit by the water crisis in 2014, they were already dealing with another big problem: getting healthy food. Much of the city of Flint qualifies as a **food desert**, a predominantly low-income community in which the residents have little or no access to fresh, affordable, healthy foods. Most food deserts are located in densely populated urban areas that may have convenience stores and fast-food restaurants but no grocery stores or other outlets for fresh fruits, vegetables, meats, and other healthy foods. Sparsely populated rural areas, where stores are far away and hard to access, can also be considered food deserts. The United States Department of Agriculture (USDA) estimates that more than 23 million Americans live in food deserts (USDA 2012). This means that they may have to shop at drugstores, liquor stores, or corner mini-marts for food items or subsist on the chicken nuggets, burritos, or burgers and fries from the takeout chain on the corner. People who live in food deserts may have few meal choices that aren't highly processed and loaded with fat, sugar, and chemicals.

FOOD DESERT a community in which the residents have little or no access to fresh, affordable, healthy foods, usually located in densely populated urban areas

Food deserts are often in neighborhoods that are predominantly low income or nonwhite in population. This means that the effects of food deserts are experienced disproportionately

GLOBAL PERSPECTIVE
Zika Virus: Women and Children Last

In 1947, a virus was discovered in Uganda's Zika Forest. Researchers isolated the virus, determined that it could be mosquito-borne, and noted that its symptoms seemed limited to fever, mild discomfort, and sometimes a rash. Over the years, a number of articles about the Zika virus were published in medical journals, and cases of Zika infection were identified in mostly tropical locations where the carrier mosquitoes were located: Central Africa, Southeast Asia, and some Pacific Island nations. Then, in 2013, a large outbreak hit French Polynesia; at the same time, cases started showing up in less tropical, more developed regions such as Australia, Japan, North America, and Europe (Cohen 2016). Along with its growing epidemiological footprint, Zika also became associated with more serious symptoms, such as Guillain-Barre syndrome, a neurological problem that can cause temporary paralysis.

Then, in 2015, Brazil was hit with the largest Zika outbreak ever recorded. Over an eighteen-month period, more than 300,000 Brazilians were diagnosed with Zika. Given the sometimes mild symptoms, it is possible that many more were infected but did not realize it at the time. But a devastating complication soon became visible: Brazilian women who contracted Zika while pregnant began giving birth to microcephalic babies. Microcephaly is a congenital defect in which babies are born with smaller than normal brains and skulls; it causes developmental and medical complications throughout the life course. Over 6,000 babies were born with microcephaly during the almost two-year period of Brazil's Zika emergency, compared to an average rate of about 160 microcephaly cases per year before the Zika epidemic.

This connection turned what had been seen as a mild illness into a serious national—and international—health crisis, as Rio de Janeiro was scheduled to host the Summer Olympic Games in August 2016. That meant that tens of thousands of athletes and over half a million tourists would soon descend on a country with a serious outbreak of a mosquito-borne disease that had horrifying outcomes for the babies of women who contracted it during pregnancy. To make matters worse, it was becoming evident that Zika could also be transmitted sexually. The potential for a global Zika explosion made tourists, Brazilian bureaucrats, Olympic teams, and international health officials extremely wary. Some called for boycotts and even cancellation of the Games. Instead, community prevention campaigns focused on mosquito control; advisories were issued to residents, athletes, and tourists; and the 2016 Games went on.

The central advisory issued by the WHO was, basically, "If you live in or travel to a Zika-affected area, don't get pregnant." Logical from a health perspective and easy enough if you're a man. But it is not always possible for women to avoid or end potentially disastrous pregnancies, especially in places where contraceptives are expensive or difficult to access, levels of sexual violence are high, and abortion is illegal or hard to get. Where are these places? The same places that are high risk for the Zika virus. Brazil, for example, criminalizes abortion, as do several other Latin American countries. Abortion is criminalized in Puerto Rico, a Zika-affected U.S. Territory, despite federal laws that should supersede. No matter where one lives, contraception can be expensive or otherwise hard to access, especially for those in poverty.

So while the mosquitoes carrying the Zika virus may infect men and women equally, the burden of the disease and the onus of preventing its worst consequences fall unequally on women, and specifically women who are likely to have restricted access to the tools of prevention. That makes Zika a gender issue. For most who contracted it, Zika wasn't much worse than a common cold, and quick response to the 2015–2016 outbreak has helped limit the number of those seriously affected. But Zika's long-term effects on the babies of women who contracted it while pregnant will continue for decades. Prevention efforts across the globe have limited Zika's spread so far, and a possible vaccine is currently in clinical trials (Mukherjee 2016). But Brazil will have a cohort of thousands of microcephalic children who will require a lifetime of services and support.

The Face of Microcephaly Babies with microcephaly, a serious complication of the Zika virus, have smaller brains and skulls.

Food Deserts The absence of grocery stores contributes to the lack of healthy food options available in urban and poor neighborhoods.

by the poor and by African Americans, Hispanics, and other minority groups. The health effects of living in a food desert are significant: The risk of obesity, diabetes, and heart disease for African Americans increases by half and for Hispanics by two-thirds (Powell et al. 2007; Whitacre et al. 2009). So, while any given individual may be at risk for obesity, diabetes, or heart disease, living in a food desert increases those risks.

Why do food deserts exist? They are not a new phenomenon. Grocery chains began leaving urban areas for the suburbs in the 1960s and 1970s as a result of perceived problems with security, profitability, real-estate costs, and parking (Ferguson and Abell 1998). In their place, bodegas, liquor stores, and fast-food chains popped up, leaving central urban populations with far fewer healthy food options. Some city and state governments are trying to entice supermarkets back to these neighborhoods with programs like tax incentives, grants, or loans for big food retailers and subsidies for farmers' markets (Haber 2010).

As we have seen, our individual health is shaped by our neighborhood context, which is itself shaped by race and class inequality, the actions of big corporations, and the responses of governmental bodies at all levels. This phenomenon is known as **deprivation amplification**, meaning that our individual disease risks (based on our heredity and physiology) may be amplified by social factors (Macintyre, MacDonald, and Ellaway 2008). The solutions to these health problems are not going to be found merely at the individual level—they must incorporate social action as well. Yes, you need to eat more healthfully in order to control your diabetes, but you must be able to find healthy foods close by and at affordable prices in order to do so.

MEDICINE AS A SOCIAL INSTITUTION

For proof that medicine is a social institution, take a look at the American Medical Association (AMA). The AMA is usually thought of as an organization that makes health recommendations on such topics as childhood obesity and cancer prevention to benefit the general public. But physicians and other medical professionals know the AMA as a trade union that creates the rules and regulations governing medical licensure. Almost all issues concerning medicine in both public health and professional regulation are governed by the AMA.

Milton Friedman (1994), the winner of the 1976 Nobel Prize in Economics and a vocal critic of the AMA, argued that the AMA limits admissions to medical schools and restricts medical licensing to advance the interests of physicians. He viewed the AMA as a monopolizing organization that reduced the quantity and quality of medical care by forcing the public to pay more for medical services because of the lack of qualified physicians. For example, the AMA does not allow physicians who are trained in foreign countries to practice in the United States without passing the United States Medical Licensing Exam (USMLE). For many of these physicians, fulfilling the requirements of the USMLE is a lengthy and arduous process that often necessitates repeating medical

> **DEPRIVATION AMPLIFICATION** when our individual disease risks (based on our heredity and physiology) are amplified by social factors

ON THE JOB
Cultural Competence in Health Professions

Lia Lee was a baby when her epileptic seizures began. When she was three years old, she had an especially serious attack, and her parents, Hmong immigrants living in California's Central Valley, took her to the Merced County Medical Center for treatment. What happened to Lia, her family, and her doctors during the next two years is the subject of journalist Anne Fadiman's book *The Spirit Catches You and You Fall Down (1998)*.

The book's title refers to the way the Hmong, a Southeast Asian ethnic group, view Lia's affliction. Indeed, their understanding of all health problems involves malevolent attempts by evil spirits, known as *dabs*, to meddle with human souls. The differences between Hmong understandings of epilepsy and its appropriate treatment and those of the Western medical establishment created the conflict in which Lia Lee was trapped.

> **CULTURAL COMPETENCE** the concept of acknowledging and incorporating a patient's cultural background as part of the treatment process; the recognition that patients' beliefs shape their approach to health care

The details of Lia's case are heart-wrenching: Both her parents and her doctors tried their best to heal her. But because of cultural and language differences, they were unable to understand each other's perspective. They became suspicious and mistrustful of each other, which made collaboration even harder. The doctors firmly believed in Western biomedical approaches to epilepsy; they thought that if the Lees gave Lia the right medicines at the right times, she would be fine. Meanwhile, the Lees firmly believed that the *dab* had Lia's soul in its grip and that traditional Hmong procedures (such as shamanic healing ceremonies) should be part of her treatment.

Both parties saw the other side's actions as counterproductive; they resisted cooperating because they each believed the other's approach would make Lia's condition worse. Caught in this standoff between Western medicine and Hmong tradition, Lia did get worse, eventually suffering "The Big One," a seizure that left her with severe and permanent brain damage. After decades spent in a vegetative state, tended lovingly by her family, Lia died in 2012.

Lia Lee's case has been a touchstone for a number of more recent attempts to increase the cultural awareness of health-care professionals, with the hopes of avoiding future cases like hers. This movement has coined the term **cultural competence** to describe the concept of acknowledging and incorporating a patient's cultural background as part of the treatment process. Cultural competence refers to the ability of health practitioners and organizations to effectively deliver health-care services that meet the social, cultural, and linguistic needs of patients (Betancourt, Green, and Carrillo 2012). As the U.S. population continues to grow in diversity, it becomes increasingly important that health-care professionals be adept at interacting with patients from a wide variety of backgrounds. Because such skills can have life-and-death consequences, many health-care organizations such as hospitals and clinics have implemented cultural-competence policies, programs, and training. These initiatives help foster cross-cultural communication and improve the delivery of

residency before they are allowed to practice medicine—even though they were fully licensed and practicing physicians in their country of origin.

The AMA enforces these restrictions despite a serious shortage of physicians in the United States. Overall, it is estimated that there will be a deficit of between 61,700 and 94,700 physicians by 2025. You might think this is because fewer students are interested in medical careers, but in fact, in 2014, only 43 percent of all medical school applicants were admitted to traditional U.S. medical schools (USMDs). The scarcity of USMD physicians translates to greater professional status relative to international or non-USMD physicians. By being underproduced, USMD physicians remain in high demand.

This phenomenon, known as degree rationing, has been happening since the 1950s (Jenkins and Reddy 2017).

The AMA also delineates the professional boundaries for the practice of medicine. For instance, surgery is the exclusive territory of physicians, making their services highly valued. If physical therapists could also perform surgery, it would undercut the authority and status of physicians. Competition from alternative service providers might also challenge what physicians could charge for surgical procedures. The medical profession has been quite successful at staving off incursions into physicians' territories. As another example, the AMA and the American College of Obstetricians and Gynecologists also restrict such practices as home births.

services that meet the needs of patients. Cultural competence has also emerged as a way for institutions to address factors that contribute to health disparities for minority group members.

Training in the area of cultural competence is now becoming part of the standard curriculum for pre-med and medical students. For example, the Association of American Medical Colleges (AAMC) has produced a set of curriculum recommendations for medical schools and provides evaluation tools for assessing the impact of cultural-competence initiatives once they are in place (2017). The goal is to train new physicians to recognize the importance of cultural knowledge and beliefs—their patients' and their own—in health-care encounters and to provide them with strategies for effective diagnosis, treatment, and interaction in cross-cultural encounters.

As part of the AAMC's plan, students are encouraged to examine their own cultural backgrounds, assumptions, and biases and to exercise nonjudgment when asking questions and listening to patients discuss their own health beliefs. They are trained to respect patients' diverse ideas about health and illness, to recognize when to use interpreters, and even to collaborate with traditional healers from their patients' cultures. They are also urged to appreciate the power imbalances between doctors and patients and to work to eliminate racism and stereotyping from health-care practices.

Undergraduate students often assume that they should major in a "hard" science such as biology if they want to go into a health profession. But given the rising importance of cultural competence in health professions, this may not be the ideal foundation. A student with a social science background, like sociology, may be even better prepared for working in the medical field than a biologist. An understanding of

Culture Clash Foua Yang holds a photo of her daughter Lia Lee, who fell into a vegetative state at the age of five after a catastrophic seizure. The heartbreaking case of this Hmong family and their experience with Western medicine inspired a movement to increase the cultural competence of health-care professionals.

such issues as ethnocentrism, inequality, and the importance of culture in the lives of individuals means that students of sociology are already ahead of bio majors when it comes to issues of cultural competence in the practice of medicine. Indeed, as of 2015, the Medical College Admissions Test (MCAT) now includes questions in psychology and sociology.

Even though trained midwives and doulas (who provide emotional support) can safely assist at home births, pregnant women have their options limited by the pressure that the AMA places on women to have labor and delivery at a hospital attended by physicians. As a result, midwives and doulas are forced to operate on the margins of the industry, while physicians and hospitals are able to increase their profits from hospital births.

Institutional Contexts

The institutional context can have a powerful effect on the interactions that occur within it. You might remember David

Rosenhan's study "On Being Sane in Insane Places" (1973) from Chapter 6, in which "pseudo-patients" who were admitted to a mental hospital were unable to convince hospital staffers of their sanity. In this case, the place itself overrode the individuals' claims to normalcy: Once they were defined by and situated within the institution, they could no longer exert any power over their own status, and every one of their interactions served as "proof" of their presumed mental illness. Erving Goffman (1961) found something similar in his study of hospitalized mental patients, *Asylums*: Psychiatric patients frequently offered explanations for being there that highlighted their normalcy and attempted to reframe their selves as sane and healthy. They inevitably failed to change

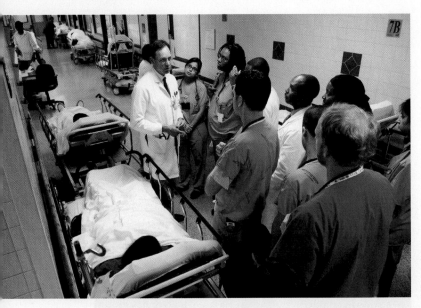

Medicine as a Social Institution Medical students shadow a doctor in an ER. The path to becoming a doctor is highly regimented.

anyone's mind, however, since the power of their institutionally inflicted diagnoses was indisputable.

Sociologist Elaine Feder-Alford's (2006) ethnomethodological analysis of her own hospitalization (for streptococcal pneumonia) shows that these social processes are still at work in medical institutions. She describes being treated like a "piece of meat," an object, or an "incompetent child" by hospital staff during her illness. She felt dehumanized and powerless, as if they saw her as a diagnosis rather than as a human being. Medical professionals plunged long syringes into her stomach without explaining why and accused her of being an alcoholic because she contracted a liver infection. The institution she inhabited as a patient defined her very differently than she defined herself, creating conflict at just the point in time when she was most ill and least able to defend her definition of herself and the situation. As her condition improved, so did her ability to assert her humanity and negotiate for better treatment within the institutional setting. Her experience left her dismayed at the power of the hospital to reduce the patient to an object and led her to promote "proposals that acknowledge patients in a hospital setting as human beings with individual needs and feelings" (p. 618).

Doctor–Patient Relations

The institutional context of medicine shapes the interactions among individuals within it. But those interactions also contribute to the shape of the institution itself. Sociologists have long been interested in studying interactions in health-care settings. Studies of doctor–patient interactions have shown that while we may think that doctors automatically have more status (and hence more power) than patients, this power dynamic actually has to be established in the interaction; it

is not an inevitable feature of medical settings. The "smallest details of the way in which participants talk to one other can have sizable impacts on the eventual outcomes," and outcomes depend on who participates in the interaction (doctors, pharmacists, physical therapists, patients, parents, kids) and in what kind of setting the interaction takes place (office visits, phone consultations, surgical theaters) (Pilnick, Hindmarsh, and Teas Gill 2009, p. 11).

There are, however, institutional, social, and geographic influences on these kinds of interactions. Doctors in rural settings are more likely to spend time engaging in emotional labor with their patients than are doctors in urban settings, even when accounting for time spent per patient and number of patients seen per day. Doctors in rural settings are more likely to know their patients from their community and interact with them in less instrumental ways, which studies have demonstrated leads to improved patient outcomes (Desjarlais-deKlerk and Wallace 2013).

Doctor–patient relationships also produce disparities in health care for women and other minority group members. The treatment and management of pain makes a case in point. About 20 percent of the U.S. population suffers from chronic pain (Dahlhamer et al. 2018). But not all patients are treated equally. Research shows that women are at greater risk for many pain conditions and that they are more pain-sensitive in some instances compared to men, yet their complaints are more likely to be dismissed (Fillingim et al. 2009). Bias and long-standing gender stereotypes still influence how doctors and other caregivers respond to women in pain. They are more likely to see women as overly emotional (hysterical) and to prescribe sedatives rather than pain medication (Institute of Medicine 2011). The inverse is true for male patients, who are considered more stoic and resistant to treatment and who must therefore be given more pain medication.

Studies have also found that a substantial number of medical students and residents still hold false beliefs about biological differences between whites and African Americans. This racial bias shapes the way that doctors perceive African American patients; their pain is more likely to be underestimated and undertreated compared with that of white patients (Hoffman et al. 2016). This disparity holds true even in cases such as young children with appendicitis and adults with extremity fractures in the ER. Upwards of 65 million Americans suffer from pain, but if you are African American or a woman, you'll also face racism and sexism when you seek treatment for it.

Recent research on doctor–patient interactions has uncovered some surprising, possibly life-changing findings. A 2016 study found that elderly hospitalized patients treated by female doctors had better outcomes than those treated by male doctors (Tsugawa et al. 2016). If treated by a female doctor, patients had a 4 percent lower risk of dying prematurely and a 5 percent lower risk of being rehospitalized within thirty days. This was true across a range of medical conditions.

When applied over a large population, these effects make a significant difference. The researchers estimated that if male doctors could achieve the same outcomes as their female colleagues, there would be 32,000 fewer deaths each year among Medicare patients alone.

While other studies have documented differences in the way men and women practice medicine, this study is the first to link these gender disparities in care to actual patient outcomes. Previous studies confirmed that female doctors are more likely to adhere to clinical guidelines, to order preventive tests, and to provide more patient-centered care (Lurie et al. 1993). Female doctors have a different communication style with their patients; they are often more encouraging and reassuring. They also spend more time on patient visits than do male doctors. The results show that's good for patients, but it's also good for hospitals and insurance companies. Unfortunately, only about a third of practicing doctors in the United States are female (although they make up half of all graduates from medical schools). Gender discrimination may be a part of why there aren't more female doctors in the workforce; on average, female doctors are still paid less and promoted less often than their male colleagues.

Additional research on medical interaction has moved beyond focusing merely on doctor–patient interaction, acknowledging that there are other important dyads (and triads and groups) in medical institutions that are worth examining. Interactions between patients and therapists, pharmacists, or dentists are structured differently and address different issues than those between patients and physicians. And interactions between health-care practitioners (such as doctor–nurse, surgeon–anesthetist, or teacher–trainee), either within or outside of patients' presence, are equally important. So are interactions facilitated by medical technologies, such as ultrasound screenings, which place nurse practitioners into complex scenarios where their expertise is in tension with the technology's forced standardization (Pilnick, Hindmarsh, and Teas Gill 2009). One powerful analysis of an emergency-services call shows what happens "when words fail," as the dispatcher becomes irritated with the panic-stricken caller, and their clash about what constitutes an appropriate call for help results in the victim's death (Whalen, Zimmerman, and Whalen 1988). Studies such as this one indicate that rules, roles, and other elements of institutional order are emergent and situational. They are not necessarily written down somewhere for the rest of us to follow but instead are created and maintained (and sometimes distorted) in interaction.

The Sick Role

Of course, in addition to being shaped in interaction, rules and roles in medical institutions are influenced by external social structures as well. One example of this is the **sick role**. This concept, advanced by functionalist Talcott Parsons (1951), was a way of encapsulating the actions and attitudes that society expects from someone who is ill, as well as the actions and attitudes that a person might expect from other members of society. Being ill is, from a functionalist perspective, a form of deviance; it violates norms about health and productivity. So, as part of the sick role, a patient is exempted from their regular responsibilities (such as work, child care, or other, less tangible obligations) and is not held responsible for their illness. However, the patient also has a new set of duties, which include seeking medical help as part of an earnest effort to recuperate and get back to normal. If the sick person abides by these requirements, they will not be treated as deviant by society; but if the sick person languishes for too long, doesn't do much to improve their condition, or seems too interested in staying sick, that person is likely to experience negative sanctions from society.

As you might imagine, the concept of the sick role has changed over the many decades since Parsons first proposed it, in part because of advances in diagnostic technology. For example, with genetic testing, we can now identify people who are at risk of certain diseases before they ever become ill (indeed, not everyone who is at risk becomes ill). What does this new diagnostic label—"at risk"—mean for the performance of the sick role? Those people with genetic risk factors but no symptoms of disease exist in a liminal space between

SICK ROLE the actions and attitudes that society expects from someone who is ill

Sick Role and Genetic Risk How might people who have a genetic risk of certain diseases but who show no symptoms exist in a space between the healthy and the sick?

the healthy and the sick. They inhabit a "potential sick role," with a different set of expectations than in Parsons's traditional model. One particularly interesting finding is that those who are in the lowest risk category sometimes try to get themselves recategorized as high risk. This may be because it is easier to determine the expectations for a high-risk patient (getting regular screenings, warning family members that they might be at risk, etc.) than for a low-risk patient. This suggests a more dynamic, nuanced definition of the "sick role" and provides for the possibility that the experience of health and illness is not as straightforward as Parsons originally hypothesized.

DATA WORKSHOP

Analyzing Media and Pop Culture

Medicine on Television

From *M*A*S*H* to *St. Elsewhere*, from *Dr. Kildare* to *Doogie Howser* and *House*, television shows about hospitals have long captivated American audiences. Medical dramas and comedies have been some of the most critically acclaimed and highest-rated prime-time television shows over the years. Many medical shows have multiple fan sites for discussing every detail of every episode. And because these shows are so prevalent and popular, they influence America's perception of different diseases and treatments, the roles of patients and medical staff, and the nature and function of the medical institution.

In conventional American television, the medical problems faced by the protagonists are easily solved.

There is generally a patient or multiple patients with medical conditions that are triaged, diagnosed, treated, and healed within a single episode. Anyone who has dealt with a serious illness or accident knows that the reality of health care in the United States is a prolonged process that involves long waits, multiple visits to multiple doctors and different facilities for testing, and complicated interactions with insurance providers. But on TV, the anger, sadness, and frustration of the patient's experience are generally glossed over in favor of the viewpoint of the medical professionals involved in the process.

For this Data Workshop, you will be using existing sources to do a content analysis comparing the world of TV with the real world. Refer back to Chapter 2 for a refresher on this research method. Select a scripted medical drama or comedy (not a reality or documentary show), using the following list as inspiration. Choose a show that is fairly recent so that it is up-to-date with what's happening in medicine. And make sure that it is available for multiple viewings:

Chicago Hope	*New Amsterdam*
Chicago Med	*The Night Shift*
Children's Hospital	*Nurse Jackie*
Code Black	*Private Practice*
ER	*The Resident*
The Good Doctor	*Rosewood*
Grey's Anatomy	*Royal Pains*
House, M.D.	*Scrubs*

Select an episode that deals with a specific disease or condition. Watch the episode closely and pay attention to the plot lines, scenes, characters, and dialogues in which the specific disease or medical condition is depicted. Take notes as you watch and include specific details; you may have to review some scenes several times before you can do a thorough content analysis.

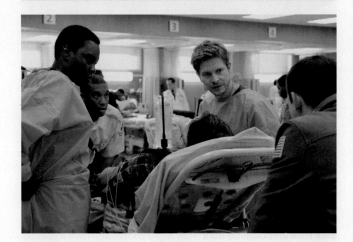

Medicine on Television *The Resident* and *The Good Doctor* are both medical dramas that portray hospitals in ways that don't always resonate with real life.

Next, look up the epidemiology of that disease or condition. You may start with a web search, but make sure you are consulting a medical journal site or an organization such as the Mayo Clinic or Centers for Disease Control and Prevention rather than Wikipedia or WebMD. For example, articles from the *New England Journal of Medicine*, the American Medical Association, or the American Association of Family Physicians will yield more thorough and accurate data for the purposes of this exercise.

You may want to consider the following questions when looking at the disease's epidemiology:

- How common is the disease or condition?

- What are the causes of and contributing factors to the disease or condition?

- Does it affect different groups (for example, men and women, or patients of different races or ethnicities) in different ways?

- Which groups are more likely to contract the disease or condition? Why?

- Who is involved in the diagnosis and treatment of the disease or condition?

- How expensive, rare, dangerous, and/or available are the treatments, and are there any side effects?

- How rich, lucky, or well insured would a patient have to be to undergo treatments?

Compare and contrast the show's treatment of the disease or condition to the statistics your research has revealed. How accurate was the portrayal? How does the show's treatment of illness reflect the average experience of an American patient with the same illness? And most important, what kinds of effects would any discrepancies have on the perceptions of audiences, patients, and even physicians regarding the disease or condition and its treatment? How does this affect American viewers' understanding of the health-care system?

There are two options for completing this Data Workshop:

PREP-PAIR-SHARE Conduct a content analysis of one episode of your chosen TV show and develop some preliminary answers to the questions posed. Prepare written notes that you can refer to during in-class discussions. Pair up with one or more classmates and discuss your findings in small groups. Compare and contrast the analyses of actual and fictional disease experiences as observed by participants in your group.

DO-IT-YOURSELF Complete your content analysis and develop some preliminary answers to the questions posed. Then write a three- to four-page essay discussing your answers and reflecting on your observations of the differences between fictional depictions of disease and treatment and real-world data. What do you think your observations tell us about the contemporary U.S. health-care system and the ways in which it is depicted in television?

ISSUES IN MEDICINE AND HEALTH CARE

The fields of medicine and health care have continued to evolve and advance, often affecting individual lives in profound ways and addressing some of the most pressing problems facing humanity. While much of the progress over the last decades has been tremendously positive, there are still unfulfilled promises and new questions to resolve. In this last section, we examine some of the current trends and future challenges in medicine and health care.

Health-Care Reform in the United States

In 1974, when Richard Nixon gave his final State of the Union address before a joint session of Congress, he called for "a new system that makes high-quality health care available to every American in a dignified manner and at a price he can afford" (1974). Nixon, a Republican, had previously described comprehensive health-care reform as the highest priority on his unfinished agenda for the United States. It would remain a national priority that eluded many other politicians for many more decades until 2010, when the Patient Protection and Affordable Care Act was signed into law. This legislation, commonly known as the ACA or "Obamacare," finally brought something like universal health-care coverage to all U.S. citizens. Yet the act was not met with universal approval. It frustrated many longtime advocates of health-care reform by not going far enough, while simultaneously infuriating others by going too far.

The ACA included major insurance reforms, such as allowing children to remain on their parents' insurance plan through age twenty-six, rather than the previous limit of age twenty-one or after college graduation. Also, insurance companies could no longer deny coverage to anyone with preexisting conditions such as diabetes or epilepsy. Importantly, the law closed loopholes that once allowed insurance companies to deny or limit coverage to people who became ill. Insurers were no longer allowed to impose lifetime spending caps—allotting a certain amount of money for a given patient over that patient's lifetime—a limit surpassed by many who have serious illnesses. Additionally, the law banned **rescission**—canceling coverage only after a person gets sick. Women could no longer be charged more than men for their health insurance, Medicare recipients could get additional discounts on prescription drugs, and insurers could not raise their rates more than 10 percent per year without justification.

One of the most important provisions was the creation of federal and state-run insurance exchange systems to cover the unemployed, self-employed, and anyone else without insurance. The law included a requirement, called the individual mandate, that most Americans purchase at least a basic level of health insurance to avoid a fine. By requiring people with generally low healthcare costs, such as healthy people and the young, to purchase coverage, the individual mandate helped keep premiums down and markets stable so that it was possible to require insurance companies to cover people with preexisting conditions. There were some exceptions to the individual mandate for the poor, and subsidies were offered for other low-income individuals and families to help in purchasing insurance. Companies that employed more than fifty people had to provide health insurance or suffer fines, but new small-business exchanges were created to help companies comply; there were also tax credits available to support small businesses in covering their employees.

In many ways, the ACA delivered on its promises. Indeed, in 2016 the number of uninsured Americans fell to a record low of just 8.8 percent, or 28.2 million people (Martinez, Zammitti, and Cohen 2017). When the ACA's provisions first began taking effect in 2010, the uninsured rate was 16 percent. That means there were 20.4 million fewer people who lacked health insurance coverage in 2016 compared with 2010.

Even before the legislation had passed, opponents began organizing to repeal the law. They believed that it would cost too much, raise taxes, hurt businesses, and lead to a government takeover of health care, among other complaints. Opponents also challenged the constitutionality of the law and took their cause to state and federal courts. Republican leaders in Congress took steps to repeal the ACA and replace it with new legislation, while Democratic leaders proposed bills to modify and strengthen it. Americans remain divided over Obamacare, but support has grown since its inception. In 2019, 50 percent of all adults had a favorable opinion of the ACA, compared to 39 percent who had an unfavorable opinion (Kaiser Family Foundation 2019b).

Health-care reform is likely to remain a battleground. There are many disagreements about how best to design and implement a national health-care plan for Americans, but few would argue we don't need one. Until the ACA, the United States was the last wealthy, industrialized nation in the world without some form of universal health coverage for its citizens. While we haven't exactly caught up to our peers, the ACA undeniably constitutes a major change to the U.S. health-care system.

Complementary and Alternative Medicine

In all likelihood, you or someone you know has participated in some form of alternative medicine. If you've ever tried deep breathing for relaxation, a nutritional supplement to gain or lose weight, or an herbal remedy for a cold, if you've gone to a chiropractor, had a massage, or taken a yoga class, then you've made use of alternative medicine. Complementary and alternative medicine (CAM) is a group of medical treatments, practices, and products that includes acupuncture, homeopathy, hypnosis, and meditation, as well as traditional healers like shamans and movement therapies like Pilates. **Complementary medicine** can be used in conjunction with conventional Western medicine, whereas **alternative medicine** is used instead of it. Some of these practices or products are ancient (such as acupuncture and herbs), while others are new only to the Western world or arose in the past few decades (such as biofeedback, fasting, and "juice cleanses").

Complementary and alternative medicine has generated both enthusiasts and critics. Some skeptics call this type of medicine "quackery," nothing more than modern-day "snake oil" that promotes false hopes to a vulnerable public. Others who may have found few satisfactory answers within the medical establishment become staunch believers in the benefits of various CAM treatments. Indeed, some CAM practices and practitioners are slowly gaining legitimacy (and popularity), and **integrative medicine** is a burgeoning part of the field that combines conventional medicine with particular CAM practices that have proven safe and effective. Scientific studies of CAM practices lag behind those done on conventional medicine, and more evidence is needed about whether and how CAM practices work and on which patients with what conditions. It's possible that some forms of alternative medicine may one day prove better at treating some conditions than conventional medicine. But it is still rare for insurers to cover alternative medicine, so patients currently seeking those treatments typically have to pay out of pocket.

The increasing number of people who have turned to CAM practices is remarkable. In the United States, 38 percent of adults age eighteen and over and nearly 12 percent of children have used one or more forms of CAM within the

IN RELATIONSHIPS
Solving the Mystery of Autism

Autism Spectrum Disorder (ASD), as defined by the American Psychiatric Association (2017), is a "complex developmental disorder that can cause problems with thinking, feeling, language and the ability to relate to others." The disorder can also feature repetitive behaviors and restricted interests. These symptoms can range from severe to very mild, and thus are categorized as a "spectrum." ASD symptoms generally become evident before the age of three and last throughout a person's life, though many do improve over time with social skills training, behavioral therapy, and other interventions (Dawson and Bernier 2013).

What causes ASD remains unclear. It's presumed to have a genetic link, but that doesn't tell the whole story. A widely accepted hypothesis is that ASD is multifactoral, meaning that both genetics and environment influence its prevalence. A number of studies indicate that advanced maternal age (King et al. 2009), closely spaced pregnancies, birth weight, prematurity, and birth order (Cheslack-Postava, Liu, and Bearman 2011) could play a role. Environmental factors such as air pollution and exposure to toxins may also be contributing to ASD (Raanan et al. 2015). There has been a great deal of controversy around the issue of vaccines and ASD. Despite overwhelming evidence and the fact that all the major medical boards and organizations have discredited any link, there are still parents who refuse to vaccinate their children. Paradoxically, anti-vaxxers may be putting their own and others' children at greater risk for other disabling or deadly diseases (such as mumps or measles), while trying to "protect" them from ASD.

How we understand disabilities is socially constructed and thus has important ramifications for how a group of people is medically and socially treated. A change in the definition of ASD can have significant consequences. For example, Asperger's syndrome first appeared in the fourth edition of the *Diagnostic and Statistical Manual of Mental Disorders* (DSM) in 1994 as a separate disorder, but by the time the fifth edition was released in 2013, Asperger's had been folded into the larger umbrella category of ASD. These changes are not simply a matter of categorization; diagnosis, treatment, and access to services often rest on the ability to identify and differentiate particular aspects of the disorder. Research shows that in the years when diagnostic criteria are changed, the odds of a patient's being diagnosed with ASD increases (King et al. 2009).

For several decades, rates of ASD in the United States continued to rise. It was uncertain whether the increase was due to greater detection and diagnosis or to actual prevalence in the population. More recently, research indicates that this rise has leveled off. According to the CDC, one in fifty-nine children has ASD. Boys are four times as likely to be identified with ASD as girls. Some researchers suspect that this disparity can be partly explained by the fact that girls tend to exhibit milder symptoms than boys and are thus less often diagnosed. The prevalence of ASD varies by socioeconomic status, with greater rates in high-income neighborhoods. We also see disparities by race: Roughly one in fifty-eight white children has ASD compared to one in sixty-three black children and one in seventy-one Hispanic children (Baio et al. 2018). It's likely that all racial groups have a similar prevalence but that black and Hispanic children are not diagnosed as often.

Advances in brain imaging now make it possible to identify high-risk children much earlier in infancy. This is important because research shows that treatment for ASD is more successful the sooner it begins, while the brain is still developing. Brain imaging is already helping us to better understand why children with ASD have trouble navigating the social world, and also why they often have extraordinary talents in areas such as math, music, and art. Research is ongoing and may bring us better ways to treat and even prevent ASD in the future. Until the mystery of autism is solved, early diagnosis and intervention is crucial, and so is providing support and social services to those with ASD and to their families.

On the Spectrum These twin boys function on opposite ends of the autism spectrum. How is our understanding of ASD socially constructed?

past year (Nahin, Barnes, and Stussman 2016). Natural supplements (nonvitamin products such as fish oil/omega-3, glucosamine, echinacea, flaxseed, and ginseng), deep breathing, meditation, chiropractic, yoga, acupuncture, and massage are some of the most frequently used forms of CAM. Americans are most likely to seek these treatments for neck, back, joint, and headache pain but may also use them for anxiety, high cholesterol, head and chest colds, and insomnia. Celebrities and professional athletes often attribute successful recoveries from illnesses or injuries to CAM therapies. Both the San Diego Padres and San Francisco Giants baseball teams employ a staff acupuncturist for their players.

Medical Ethics

Medical science continues to progress at a rapid pace, bringing new discoveries and producing innovations that are bound to change human health in the future. We tend to think of these advancements as having a uniformly positive impact on society, but this is not always true. In many cases, new advancements bring new and sometimes troubling issues to the fore. **Bioethics** is the study of controversial moral or ethical issues related to scientific and medical advancements. Among hot topics are questions about extending life through artificial means, stem cell research, the use of animals in medical experiments, and even the idea of human cloning.

The Human Genome Project (HGP) is a scientific endeavor that seeks to identify and map the 20,000 to 25,000 genes that make up human DNA from both a physical and functional perspective. The project began in 1990, and the first version of the genome was completed in 2003. Scientists hope that decoding DNA will help elucidate how the human body works, providing clues for how to treat and possibly prevent serious illnesses. One of the results of the HGP is the ability to identify predispositions to hereditary diseases such as certain types of cancer, cystic fibrosis, and liver disease through genetic testing. Results from the HGP may also provide the key to the management of diseases such as Alzheimer's.

The rapid advancement of medical technologies like the HGP also brings numerous ethical issues to the table. One of the more controversial aspects of these advances is genetic testing in utero and at birth. For example, preimplantation genetic diagnosis allows doctors to test DNA samples from embryos that are grown in vitro. These tests can tell whether a baby will be born with certain disorders and allow for the selection of only certain embryos for implantation, potentially allowing parents to choose whether to have a disabled child. There are ethical concerns about genetic testing becoming a modern-day form of **eugenics**, in which the human gene pool is "improved" through science.

In cases where genetic testing reveals future susceptibility to disease for otherwise healthy individuals, there are ethical issues about the use of the genetic profiles. Can a person be stigmatized because of their genetic profile? Will insurance companies be able to deny coverage or even treatment of illnesses that can now be revealed through in utero genetic testing? Will parents be encouraged to end pregnancies if the fetus's genetic profile reveals a torturous, expensive, or stigmatizing condition? Certainly, medical technology is advancing rapidly enough to cause a cultural lag or delay in the legal, ethical, and social issues surrounding its use.

End of Life

Another area in which ethics may lag behind science is end-of-life care. On the one hand, we now possess the technologies and treatments to prolong the lives of patients who in prior eras would have died much more rapidly than they now do from traumatic injuries and from diseases such as ALS (Lou Gehrig's disease), Alzheimer's disease, cystic fibrosis, and certain cancers. In addition, hospice and palliative care can now make terminally ill patients more comfortable and give them more time to prepare for the inevitable. On the other hand, this ability to prolong life can sometimes make it more difficult to distinguish between "living" and "dying" (such as in cases of patients in persistent vegetative states) and hence to respond appropriately to those who are close to death (Kaufman 2005). The ability to rescue patients from the brink of death and to keep on life support those who would otherwise pass away raises the question: Just because we can keep someone alive, does that mean that we should always do so?

Organizations such as Compassion and Choices and Final Exit promote the right of terminally ill patients to invoke medically assisted suicide and the ability to "die with dignity," that is, to die while they are still in control of their bodies and minds. But critics worry that this approach will encourage ending life for the "wrong" reasons, such as treatable depression or disability. This often leaves critically ill patients and their families wondering what to do and when to do it. How to approach death and dying has always challenged us and there is every indication that, even in our age of advanced medical technology, it will continue to do so.

Take the example of Brittany Maynard, who was diagnosed with terminal brain cancer at the age of twenty-nine and given six months to live. Maynard decided that, when the time came, she wanted to have control over when and how she died. She knew that, as a resident of California, she would not be legally allowed to do this, so she and her husband, Dan, packed up and moved to Oregon, where a "death with dignity" law allows doctors to prescribe medication that terminally ill patients can use to end their own lives when they see fit. Maynard did so on November 1, 2014, but not before becoming an activist for doctor-assisted suicide and voicing strong support for aid-in-dying legislation. The passage of California's End of Life Option Act in June 2016 may be owed in part to Maynard's legacy.

Closing Comments

Concerns about health and illness are a constant part of human existence. As individuals, we will each face the pleasures and frustrations of living in a physical body that is affected by our lifestyles and life chances. A sociological approach is especially helpful in allowing us to understand the links between social structures and processes on one side and health outcomes on the other. We recognize that health is not merely a biological state but rather another important area of human life affected by social institutions and social inequalities. Medicine and health care are rapidly advancing, and as a result, we may someday live longer and healthier lives, but we will always be shaped by the social contexts in which our lives take place. Science may soon discover new treatments for old diseases, but it is just as likely that we will have to continue dealing with current challenges to our health, along with as-yet-unknown ones, in the future. It is certain that there will be cultural changes in our values and beliefs that bring about new understandings and practices regarding the relationship between society and the health of both people and the planet.

APPLYING WHAT YOU'VE LEARNED

Let's Talk More

1. Hyperactivity, addiction, and obesity are now viewed as medical conditions as opposed to behavioral problems. Can you think of other kinds of behaviors or conditions that are becoming "medicalized"? Should we consider internet or video game addiction a medical condition?

2. Think about the last time you were ill or injured. Describe what it was like to be cast in the "sick role." What kind of special privileges or excuses from obligations could you claim? What kind of sympathy or special care did you receive? What kind of expectations did others have about you taking care of yourself?

3. As science and medicine continue to advance, what kinds of ethical issues will arise in the future? Is all medical progress positive or are there some areas of research that should be forbidden?

Let's Explore More

1. **Film** Russell, David O., dir. *Silver Linings Playbook*. 2012.

2. **Book** Reich, Jennifer. 2016. *Calling the Shots: Why Parents Reject Vaccines*. New York: New York University Press.

3. **Blog Post** Sternheimer, Karen. "The Social Geography of Health." *Everyday Sociology* (blog). June 1, 2017. *http://WWNorton.com/rd/a6C8A.*

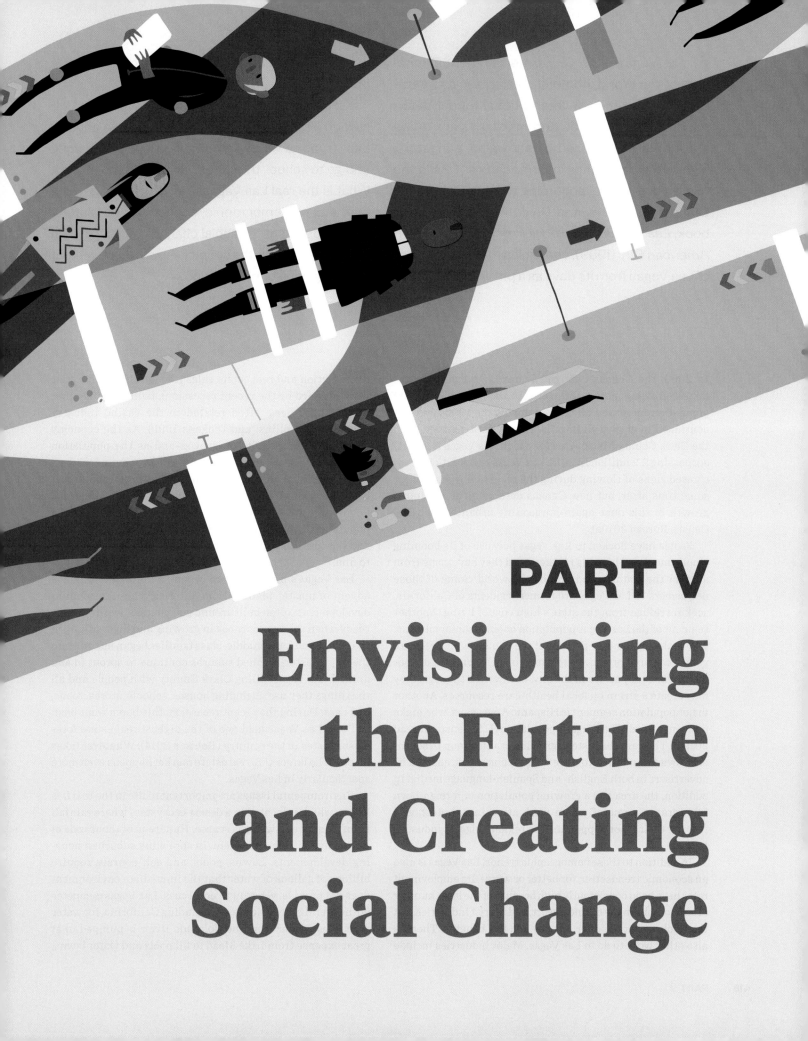

PART V
Envisioning the Future and Creating Social Change

L as Vegas—Sin City, Entertainment Capital of the World, home of glitz, glitter, and gambling; fantasy mecca, international tourist destination where fortunes and marriages are made and broken; populated by showgirls, gangsters, high-rollers, and Elvis impersonators. This is the "Hollywood Vegas" according to Mark Gottdiener, Claudia C. Collins, and David R. Dickens. Their book, *Las Vegas: The Social Production of an All-American City* (1999), chronicles the development of Las Vegas from its days as a pit stop for Spanish explorers in the early 1800s to the neon marvel it has become.

Gottdiener, Collins, and Dickens analyze the Hollywood Vegas, but they argue that there is another Las Vegas as well, where regular people live, work, and go to school, the supermarket, and the movies. What is the real Las Vegas like? It's big, it's growing fast, and its demographic, economic, and cultural trends represent the social changes taking place in many cities across the country—even those without pulsating neon or posh casinos.

In 2000, the Census confirmed that Las Vegas was the fastest-growing metropolitan area in the United States. Its population increased 83 percent during the 1990s and has continued to grow well into the twenty-first century, with the Clark County Metro Area (of which Las Vegas is a part) surpassing 2.2 million in 2018. Las Vegas's population boom showed signs of slowing during the recession years and for some time after, but new Census data confirm continued growth in this once again burgeoning urban locale (U.S. Census Bureau 2019e).

People have flocked to Las Vegas because of its booming employment and housing markets, and they have come from all over the country and around the world. Some of those newcomers to Las Vegas are former residents of California, seeking refuge from the state's high cost of living. Another segment of the Las Vegas population boom is senior citizens, who make up about 14 percent of the populace. Retirees are valued consumers who spend money on new homes and other items when they arrive in the city; however, as they age, they may create a strain on local health-care resources. Another major population segment is Hispanic Americans, who make up about a third of Las Vegas's population (U.S. Census Bureau 2019g). They are the fastest-growing ethnic group in southern Nevada, and they, too, are valued consumers, courted by advertisers in both English- and Spanish-language media. In addition, the area has a growing population of foreign-born immigrants, some of whom work at casinos, hotels, and resorts, their labor supporting the region's biggest industry, tourism.

In addition to these demographic trends, Las Vegas is also an economic trendsetter, for better or worse. Its employment rates have been consistently high because of the large number of service jobs in the casino, resort, and tourist industries, but these jobs generally offer low pay and few benefits. There is also other work to do in Las Vegas. Major industries include construction and real estate sales (though these industries were hit hard by the recent recession), banking, and other financial services, often related to the casino industry (Gottdiener, Collins, and Dickens 1999). As the economy diversifies, the population grows—and as the population grows, more services and other work become necessary. Cards must be dealt, meals must be cooked, hotel rooms must be cleaned, children must be taught, cars must be repaired, and houses must be built, sold, and financed. However, if a population begins to decline, the market for all those goods and services diminishes, and jobs of all sorts become harder to find.

Las Vegas's housing boom began in the 1970s with the advent of master-planned communities. These residential developments, often built around golf courses, were move-in ready when the economy began growing and diversifying in the 1980s, and more middle-class families began moving into the city. Master-planned suburbs continue to sprout in and around Las Vegas, filling Clark County with people and all the things they use, including houses, schools, stores, roads, and cars. During the recent recession, this boom went bust. In 2014, Las Vegas held one of the highest real estate foreclosure rates in the country (Robison 2014). Whatever takes place in the larger U.S. real estate market happens even more spectacularly in Las Vegas.

Environmental issues are important to life in the real Las Vegas, which is located in a desert ecosystem where rainfall is infrequent and water is scarce. Hundreds of thousands of people live in this ecosystem, in sprawling suburban housing developments. Lawns, pools, and golf courses require billions of gallons of water that the immediate environment does not provide, yet growth continues. Las Vegas competes with several other arid states, including California, for water resources. Water from the Colorado River is pumped in at great expense from Lake Mead to fill pools and water lawns, as well as for household use. Lake Mead is also the destination for all of Las Vegas's outgoing effluent—treated sewage and runoff full of lawn chemicals. These environmental toxins cycle back into the drinking water consumed by the area's residents.

Water isn't the only environmental issue that Las Vegas faces. Atomic test sites from the 1950s and 1960s, located in the Mojave Desert, were once in the middle of nowhere—but suburban sprawl continues to draw closer to these areas. The same is true of a number of desert chemical plants in areas that are also being encroached upon by residential development. Recently, environmental activists have successfully prohibited nuclear waste transport and dumping in the Las Vegas area.

A fluctuating population, an economy dominated by service-industry work, a natural environment strained to its limits by desert sprawl—this is the real Las Vegas. Add the glittery, neon-lit Hollywood fantasy town, and you have a vanguard city for the twenty-first century. Economic, environmental, and demographic trends that already appear in Las Vegas—including the booms and busts of the larger economy—will become increasingly visible in other U.S. cities.

Cultural and social changes occurring in Las Vegas may also be visible where you live—including the legalization of gambling. While Las Vegas was once the center of a gambling industry dominated by organized crime, legal casinos are now operated all over the country by groups of all sorts, including state governments and Native American tribes. Gambling boats float on many Midwestern lakes and rivers,

and resort casinos continue to spring up on Indian reservations in almost half the U.S. states.

Las Vegas is also the site of unusually powerful labor unions, which represent many of the service employees—cooks, waiters, musicians, hotel employees—whose work keeps the city running. At a time when union membership is down in the rest of the country, Las Vegas is a strong union city—ironically located in Nevada, a right-to-work state. Union laborers tend to have higher wages and more benefits than nonunion workers because of the power of collective bargaining. The resurgence of union membership in Las Vegas's service industries may inspire workers in other cities with service- and tourism-dominated economies.

Gottdiener and his coauthors argue that "in many ways Las Vegas represents, though often in exaggerated form, several important trends in contemporary American society as a whole" (1999, p. xi). In Part V, we examine many of those trends from a sociological perspective as part of our focus on social change. In Chapter 15, we examine a variety of demographic and environmental trends, such as suburbanization, migration, and aging. And we consider processes of cultural and social change, such as activism by labor unions and environmentalists, in Chapter 16. As you read these chapters, think about your own city or town and the trends you have observed close to home. Also think about the changes you would like to see in your surroundings; a sociological perspective can help you strategize to make those changes happen. In any case, keep an eye on Las Vegas for changes yet to come—because, as research demonstrates, what happens in Vegas doesn't necessarily stay in Vegas!

CHAPTER 15

Populations, Cities, and the Environment

Chris McCandless was the picture of success. The son of upper-middle-class professionals in Washington, DC, he had just graduated from Emory University in Atlanta and was headed for law school. Nonetheless, he felt constrained and even betrayed by a society that perpetuated poverty and inequality and often seemed to care so little for its individual members. He wanted to experience the personal freedom of being untethered from obligations to family, school, and work—even though that meant letting go of the emotional and material security they provide.

After graduation, Chris headed for the wilderness, which he saw as pure and untainted while he viewed society as corrupt and damaged. Chris moved in and out of the social world during the next two years; he lived in the wilderness successfully for long stretches of time but always came back to civilization for supplies, to earn a little money, and to make some human connections. After spending months alone in the deserts of the Southwest, he arrived in Bullhead City, Arizona, and took a job at a McDonald's. He was leather-skinned and malnourished, had no money or belongings, and had lost his car in a flash flood—but he was still alive, and after a brief stint in what he considered the most sinister of all social institutions (the fast-food industry), he disappeared back into nature again, this time headed to the great unspoiled expanses of Alaska.

Chris did a lot of reading in preparation for his journey, and he seemed able to endure the physical and emotional hardships of being alone in the wilderness for months at a time. His journal entries reveal that he often felt exhilarated and truly believed that his was the superior way of life. But Chris's story did not end happily. Two years after he left his hometown of Atlanta, his body was found on the Alaskan tundra many miles outside Fairbanks by a group of moose hunters.

In his book *Into the Wild*, Jon Krakauer reconstructed Chris's journey through diaries and interviews. Krakauer determined that while living on the tundra for four months alone, Chris inadvertently ate something that may have poisoned him. Realizing how sick he was, he began to yearn for the saving presence of other humans—for both assistance and companionship. At the very end, Chris's journal entries reveal a desire to return to the social world and a recognition of the protection society offers from the rigors of nature. Chris did not get to reenter society with his newfound insight, but perhaps we can learn more about our own relationship to both the natural and the social worlds from his story.

How to Read This Chapter

This chapter covers three big and deeply connected topics in sociology: population, urbanization, and the environment. To this point, we have focused mostly on society—on people and their effect on each other. But humans live in a natural as well as a social world, and their environment is another key factor in their lives. We are affected by and have a profound effect on the planet earth. The number of humans who live on the planet has nearly tripled since the middle of the last century, from 2.5 billion in 1950 to more than 7.5 billion today. Population studies show that ever-greater numbers of people are settling into large, sprawling cities—a trend called urbanization. Growing populations and increased urbanization create new demands and pressures on the global environment as more natural resources are consumed and more pollution and waste are produced. Remember that these huge global shifts are the result of the cumulative actions of many individuals over time.

POPULATION

If we want to understand the relationship between the social world and the natural world, we must examine human population. The next sections look at how sociologists study population and its related issues. To paraphrase sociologist Samuel Preston, the study of population has something for everyone: the confrontations of nature and civilization; the dramas of sex and death, politics and war; and the tensions between self-interest and altruism.

Demography

Demography is the study of the size, composition, distribution, and changes in human population. Sociologists and others who study population are called demographers. Demography is essentially a macro-level, quantitative approach to society, but it is more than just simply counting heads. Population dynamics are influenced not only by biological factors such as births and deaths but also by sociological factors such as cultural values, religious beliefs, and political and economic systems. People are not just animals who reproduce by instinct; they are subject to structural constraints as well as individual agency, all of which affect their behavior and ultimately the world in which they live.

The U.S. government has long been interested in keeping track of those residing within its geographic boundaries. The U.S. Constitution mandates that a census be taken every ten years. The U.S. Census Bureau, a part of the Department of Commerce, regularly conducts these studies of the population, going back to the first such attempt in 1790. At the beginning of every new decade, census takers try to contact every person living in the country. Surveys, either short or long form, are sent to every household to gather a range of demographic information, from household size and age of family members to their gender, education level, income, and ethnic background. In the years between the decennial census, smaller-scale studies are continuously conducted by the Census Bureau. Other countries are less systematic at gathering data, so many statistics that refer to global population are necessarily based on scientific estimates.

Three basic demographic variables are crucial to understanding population dynamics. The first is **fertility rate**—the average number of births per 1,000 people in the total population. The total fertility rate is the average number of children a woman would be expected to have during her childbearing years. The fertility rate in the United States is approximately 1.8. Fertility rates vary across the globe, with some of the highest rates in sub-Saharan Africa, with Niger at 7.2, and some of the lowest in Southeast Asia, with Singapore at 1.2 (World Bank 2019b).

The next demographic variable is **mortality rate** (or death rate)—the number of deaths that can be expected per 1,000 people per year. This statistic is usually modified by other factors, so the mortality rate within a particular country varies within age, sex, ethnic, and regional groups. A related concept is **infant mortality** rate, or the average number of deaths per 1,000 live births. The death rate in the United States is approximately 9 and the infant mortality rate is approximately 6. Mortality and infant mortality rates vary across the globe, some of the highest being in African countries, with a death rate of 13 in the Central African Republic, for example, and an infant mortality rate of 88. Some of the lowest mortality rates are found in wealthier Middle Eastern countries such as Qatar with 2, and some of the lowest infant mortality rates are found in Asian countries such as Japan and Singapore with 2 (World Bank 2019c).

Another related concept is **life expectancy**, or the average age to which a person can expect to live. Here, too, other factors are involved, so life expectancy of people within a particular country varies by sex, ethnicity, and social class. In general, life expectancy rose dramatically in the twentieth century. The life expectancy for a person born in the United States in 2016 is approximately 78.6 years of age; the average

---

DEMOGRAPHY study of the size, composition, distribution, and changes in human population

FERTILITY RATE a measure of population growth through reproduction; often expressed as the number of births per 1,000 people in a particular population or the average number of children a woman would bear over a lifetime

MORTALITY RATE a measure of the decrease in population due to deaths; often expressed as the number of deaths per 1,000 people in a particular population

INFANT MORTALITY average number of infant deaths per 1,000 live births in a particular population

LIFE EXPECTANCY average age to which people in a particular population are expected to live

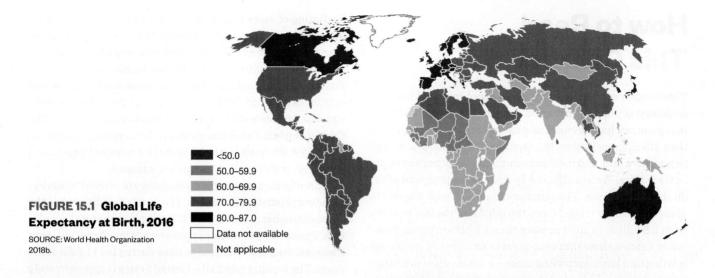

FIGURE 15.1 Global Life Expectancy at Birth, 2016

SOURCE: World Health Organization 2018b.

■	<50.0
■	50.0–59.9
■	60.0–69.9
■	70.0–79.9
■	80.0–87.0
□	Data not available
■	Not applicable

for men is 76.1, while for women it is 81.1 (Centers for Disease Control and Prevention 2018a). Life expectancy in the United States varies by social location, as noted in several earlier chapters: Race, class, gender, and other factors influence our health, the types of illness we suffer, our access to care, and hence the age at which we die. As Figure 15.1 shows, life expectancy also varies greatly across the globe, with some of the highest averages in wealthier nations such as Japan at 84, and some of the lowest in African countries such as Sierra Leone at approximately 53 years—in large part because of the AIDS epidemic (World Health Organization 2018b). **Life span**, or **longevity**, is a measure of the maximum age to which humans can live. This has also increased dramatically—again, depending on where you live. More people around the globe are living to 100 years of age, and some even longer. There is some controversy over the holder of the world record for oldest person to ever live: Jeanne Calment of France is purported to have reached 122 years and 164 days (Rosenberg 2019). There are well-documented cases of people living to 115, 116, 117, and even 119, and the majority of these supercentenarians—people over 110 years of age—are women (Epstein et al. 2019).

The last demographic variable that we will consider is **migration**—the movement of people from one geographic area to another for the purposes of resetting. Migrations have occurred throughout human history and have played an important part in populating the planet. As a demographic variable, migration neither adds to nor subtracts from the total number of people on the planet; it simply refers to their relocation from place to place. Related concepts are **immigration** and **emigration**. Immigrants are those people coming into a country or region to which they are not native. Emigrants are those departing from a country or region with the intention of settling permanently elsewhere. **Internal migration** refers to patterns within a country, where the movement is generally from rural to urban areas.

The **net migration** for any country is the difference between the number of persons entering and leaving a country during the year. The net migration rate in the United States was 2.9 in 2016, which means that there was an increase of 2.9 persons for every 1,000 inhabitants in the United States. Migration patterns can sometimes be controversial: In the United States, for example, illegal immigration from Latin America has been a point of political conflict for several decades. In general, worldwide migration patterns show that people are moving from least-industrialized to most-industrialized countries. There are often other economic or political reasons for migration, with refugees pouring in and out of some countries depending on patterns of war, famine, or other problems. Countries with the highest net migration rates include Qatar and the British Virgin Islands (both have very small populations to start with, so it takes only a few immigrants to increase their net migration rate), while those with the lowest rates include the war-torn countries of Central African Republic and Syria (United Nations Department of Economic and Social Affairs 2017).

The study of population dynamics involves the interplay among these three sources of population change: fertility, mortality, and migration. These variables are used to construct current population models and future projections. We can apply demographic variables to the global population or to a population within a particular region or country.

LIFE SPAN or LONGEVITY the uppermost age to which a person can potentially live

MIGRATION movement of people from one geographic area to another for the purpose of resettling

IMMIGRATION entering one country from another to take up permanent residence

EMIGRATION leaving one country to live permanently in another

INTERNAL MIGRATION movement of a population within a country

NET MIGRATION net effect of immigration and emigration on a particular population; expressed as an increase or decrease

IN THE FUTURE
Living to 150

Author Sonia Arrison (2011) predicts that her own son, born in 2010, may very well live to be 150 years old. This preschooler and his generational cohort are poised to reap the benefits of advances in health and technology that promise to extend their lifetimes far beyond those of their ancestors.

You are probably already familiar with some of the developments contributing to our increased life spans. Medical advances have conquered (or at least controlled) many of the diseases that once kept us from growing old, such as smallpox, measles, polio, and tuberculosis. Injuries that were once guaranteed to be fatal are now treatable and survivable through advanced surgical techniques. Public health measures have improved sanitation, food and water safety, and community education. New concerns with environmental degradation, pollution, pesticides, and chemicals are leading to less toxic exposure. Of course, all these things are more likely to be true in wealthier, developed regions such as the United States and Europe; life spans are still much shorter in areas where these advances are not widely available.

Even so, centenarians—people who live to be over 100 years of age—are getting to be more common worldwide. The United Nations estimated there were about 451,000 centenarians in 2015, compared to fewer than 100,000 in 1900, with the United States, Japan, and China in the top three positions (Stepler 2016). And in the United Kingdom, one-third of all babies born in 2013 are expected to live to 100 (Christensen and Willingham 2014). Most current centenarians are women. And our current centenarians got old the old-fashioned way: clean living, healthy food, exercise, stress management, and good genes. Arrison's son and his friends may have the assistance of technological advances that sound like science fiction but are or will soon be reality.

Drugs to treat chronic illnesses such as diabetes, heart disease, and even inflammation may have the side effect of extending life spans (Duncan 2012). Stem cell research may allow for the regeneration of damaged cells, organs, and other body parts. Gene therapy may eradicate killers such as sickle cell disease, cystic fibrosis, various cancers, and other hereditary diseases (Glor 2012). Technology that replaces human body parts with machines and connects those machines directly to our brains may expand the number of "cyborgs," or partially bionic humans, in addition to expanding our definition of what constitutes "natural" life (Duncan 2012).

These possibilities sound fascinating, don't they? But they all focus solely on keeping individuals healthy and alive.

What happens to society if people start living much longer, healthier lives? For one thing, longer lives mean that we must reconsider the whole notion of retirement. Retirement itself is a product of increasing life spans: In 1900, when life expectancy in the United States was less than fifty years, people didn't have a chance to "retire" at all. Retiring at sixty-five, our current average age, seems ridiculous (not to mention boring) if you'll be living another eighty years or so. The prospect arises, then, of people pursuing multiple careers (including the multiple educations necessary to prepare for them) in one lifetime. So people may find themselves retiring two, three, or more times in their 100-plus years.

Dessert with Every Meal
Jeanne Calment of France was the oldest human being whose age was well documented. She died at 122 in 1997.

Our current notion of marriage as a "'til death do us part" contract also may deserve some revision if we're going to live to 150. Will we just marry later? Or will multiple marriages over the course of a lifetime become more common and acceptable? Will marriage contracts have to include "sunset clauses" or expiration dates, at which time we may renew them if we choose? Don't laugh—this has already been proposed by lawmakers in Mexico! And what about family planning? Will we push the boundaries of fertility as we push the boundaries of longevity? If so, will nuclear families be larger? Will extended family living or communal child care become more common?

Finally, what will happen to our values, morals, and beliefs? So many of the social rules about marriage, family, and life in general are rooted in religion—how will religion respond if and when we find ourselves living longer and hence calling some of these rules into question? We already worry that attempts to extend life and stave off death amount to "playing God." If we live longer, will religion be forced to pay more attention to this life and less to the afterlife?

All we can say in answer to these questions is that if you eat right, exercise, and have good genes, you can stick around to see for yourselves…

If we focus on the United States, we can track several interesting population trends. The United States is currently the third most populous nation (after China and India), with about 326 million people. It is also one of the fastest-growing industrialized nations. According to the Census Bureau, the U.S. population is projected to grow by 78 million between 2017 and 2060—an average increase of 1.8 million people per year. The native population is projected to increase by 20 percent while the foreign-born population is expected to grow by an astounding 58 percent (Vespa, Armstrong, and Medina 2018). While the overall trend sees people moving to the "sunbelt" states in the South and West from "rustbelt" states in the North and East, there are notable exceptions: In recent years, North Dakota—fueled by an oil boom—has had one of the highest growth rates in the country. In contrast, Illinois, West Virginia, Connecticut, and Vermont are experiencing the biggest declines in population (U.S. Census Bureau 2018f). A final key population trend is the rapid "graying," or aging, of the U.S. population. The Census Bureau projects that by 2030, one in five Americans will be sixty-five or older, and by 2035, older adults will outnumber children for the first time in U.S. history (Vespa, Armstrong, and Medina 2018).

Theories of Population Change

Concerns about population growth first emerged in the eighteenth century during the Industrial Revolution. Many demographic variables at that time contributed to rapid growth in the newly burgeoning urban areas of Europe. Mechanization, which increased agricultural production, and the introduction of a hearty new staple from South America—the potato—made available enough food for people to sustain themselves and support larger families. Other technological and scientific advances helped decrease infant mortality rates while increasing fertility and extending life expectancy. As a result, the first real population boom in human history occurred.

THE MALTHUSIAN THEOREM Thomas Malthus, a British clergy member turned political economist, was one of the first scholars to sound the alarm on overpopulation. Although he lived at a time when people believed in technology and progress, the promise of prosperity and abundance, and the perfectibility of human society, he himself was less than optimistic about the future. Based on his observation of the world around him, Malthus wrote a book in 1798 called *An Essay on the Principle of Population*, in which his basic premise, the **Malthusian theorem**, stated that the population would expand at a much faster rate than agriculture; inevitably, at some future point, people would far outnumber the available land and food sources. If population increases surpassed the ability of the earth to provide a basic

MALTHUSIAN THEOREM the theory that exponential growth in population will outpace arithmetic growth in food production and other resources

level of subsistence, then massive suffering would follow. His theory has two simple principles: that population growth is exponential or geometric (1, 2, 4, 8, 16, 32 . . .) and that production is additive or arithmetic (1, 2, 3, 4, 5, 6 . . .).

According to his calculations, society was headed for disaster, or what is called the Malthusian trap. To avoid such a catastrophe, Malthus (1798/1997) made several rather radical policy recommendations. He may have been the first to propose that humans should collectively limit their reproduction to save themselves and preserve their environments. He urged "moral restraint" in sexual reproduction to curtail overpopulation. If human beings were unable to restrain themselves (by postponing marriage or practicing abstinence), nature would exert "positive checks" on population growth through famine, war, and disease. Malthus also advocated state assistance to the lower classes so they could more readily achieve a middle-class lifestyle supported by decent wages and benefits and adopt the values associated with later marriage and smaller families (New School 2004).

Malthus's ideas were not always popular, though they were influential and widely read. Charles Darwin noted that Malthusian theory was an important influence on his own theory of evolution and natural selection. Malthus also influenced whole new generations of social thinkers, not just demographers but others as well, and their respective ideas on population growth.

NEW MALTHUSIANS More than 200 years later, some people, the neo-Malthusians, or New Malthusians, essentially still agree with him. Among the notable modern voices looking at the problem of overpopulation are William Catton (1980), Paul and Ann Ehrlich (1990), and Garrett Hardin (1993). They worry about the rapid pace of population growth and believe that Malthus's basic prediction could be true. In some respects, they claim, the problem has even gotten worse. There are a lot more people on the planet in the twenty-first century, so continued reproduction expands even more quickly than in Malthus's time. And with continued technological advancements—such as wars that use "surgical strikes," modern standards of sanitation, and the eradication of many diseases—people are living much longer than before. When Malthus was alive, there were approximately 1 billion people on the planet; it was the first time in recorded history that the population reached that number. The time required for that number to double and for each additional billion to be added has continued to decrease (Figure 15.2). Today there are more than 7.5 billion people on the planet—and counting. The United Nations predicts that world population will surpass 9.5 billion by 2050 and continue to grow to more than 11 billion by the end of the century (United Nations Department of Economic and Social Affairs 2017).

The New Malthusians also point to several sociological factors that influence the reproductive lives of many and promote large families. Religion still plays a role in many

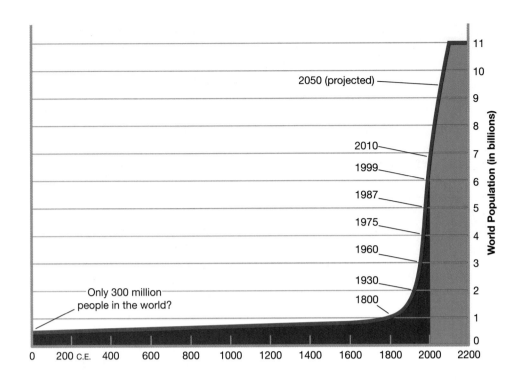

FIGURE 15.2
World Population Growth over 2,000 Years

SOURCE: Population Reference Bureau 2010.

societies: The Catholic Church still forbids members to practice any birth control besides the rhythm method, even though 77 percent of American Catholics surveyed in a poll said the church should allow them to use some form of artificial contraception (Pew Research Center 2014c). In many poorer nations, more children mean more financial support for the family. They work various jobs in their youth to help sustain the household, and for parents, children may be the only source of support they have in old age. Some governments encourage the expansion of their population base and promote the addition of new citizens who can become taxpayers or soldiers. Governments may even provide incentives to parents, such as tax deductions for each child. Finally, cultural influences, from "family values" to "machismo," sometimes confer more prestige on those with children; women gain status in the valued role of mother, while men gain status for their perceived virility.

ANTI-MALTHUSIANS Not everyone agrees with Malthus's argument, even today. Economists such as Julian Simon (1996, 2000) and demographers such as William Peterson (2003) believe that Malthus reached faulty conclusions and that he couldn't have envisioned the many modern developments that would influence population dynamics. In fact, the anti-Malthusians are more concerned about the population shrinking and the possibility of a demographic free fall. Some countries, such as Japan, are already dealing with new problems caused by a rapidly shrinking population. The United States may soon face a similar dilemma as the birth rate falls below replacement levels (usually calculated as 2.1). Demographers don't anticipate a widespread free fall in population

happening just yet, but they forecast a very different future when the pattern of demographic transition, now occurring in many industrialized nations, spreads to the rest of the developing world.

Demographic transition theory is an alternative to the Malthusian perspective that takes more recent historical patterns into account and looks at countries and their populations based on the stages of economic development they experience (see Figure 15.3). In Stage 1, during a country's preindustrial period, fertility and mortality rates are high while production is low; this means that population growth is low as well, since births and deaths cancel each other out, and resources cannot support higher populations. In Stage 2, as a country is developing economically, improvements in sanitation and food supplies mean that the death rate decreases drastically. However, birth rates stay high at this stage, which leads to rapid population growth. Countries currently in Stage 2 include Laos, Afghanistan, and Angola. In Stage 3, industrialized countries see birth rates fall in response to the decrease in mortality as well as to improvements in technology that require fewer people to keep things running smoothly. In this stage, populations start stabilizing, as has occurred in places like Mexico, Sudan, and the Philippines, as well as South Africa, Egypt, and a number of Central American and South Asian nations. In Stage 4, as economic development is achieved, countries see low birth rates, low death rates, and low rates of population growth. The United States, Canada, China, Brazil, and

> **DEMOGRAPHIC TRANSITION**
> a theory about change over time from high birth and death rates to low birth and death rates, resulting in a stabilized population

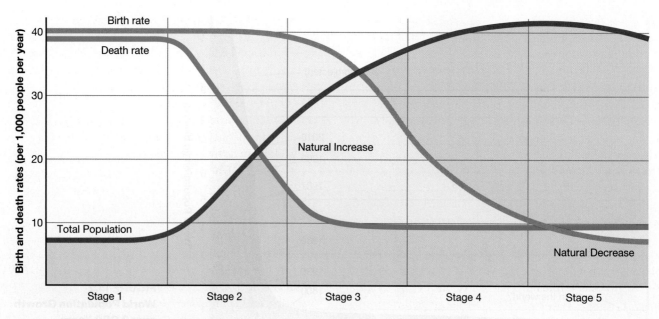

FIGURE 15.3 **Demographic Transition**

much of Europe are currently in Stage 4. In some cases, population growth dips below replacement levels in this stage, which has led theorists to propose a possible Stage 5, in which populations of highly developed countries begin to decline, as has happened in places like Japan and Hungary.

The important insight of demographic transition theory is that the relationship between population and resources changes in each stage of economic and industrial development, and not all countries experience those stages at the same historical time. It is also important to note that, even in Stage 4 (or 5), resources can still be unequally distributed, resulting in deprivation for some residents of even the richest, most developed nations, such as the United States. For example, in the United States, nearly 12 percent of households experience hunger or food insecurity, that is, the limited or uncertain ability to acquire adequate and safe foods (U.S. Department of Agriculture 2018).

So who is right? Will the world population eventually stabilize, or will it continue to spiral out of control? Will technological advances allow us to get needed resources to a growing global populace? We may not know the answer to those questions for many years, so in the meantime we continue to speculate about what may happen as new countries join the ranks of the developed world. Will fertility decrease? Will death rates continue to slow? Science constantly brings technological advancements that enhance health and prolong life, but new and deadly diseases such as AIDS, Zika, and Ebola may claim an ever-greater death toll in nations

RURAL relating to sparsely settled areas; in the United States, any county with a population density between 10 and 59.9 people per square mile

URBAN relating to cities; typically describes densely populated areas

too poor to afford the medicines needed for treatment. As the world's current occupants, we have to live now with the consequences of our choices. Many policy and advocacy groups concerned with population issues have been established in the past few decades, including Zero Population Growth, World Overpopulation Awareness, the Population Institute, and the Population Reference Bureau. To find out more, visit their websites.

CITIES

The dynamics of population growth (and sometimes shrinkage) throughout human history have been accompanied by the development of larger cities, in which more people are now living. Cities, however, are not a modern development. They have been in existence for thousands of years. We find evidence of ancient cities in the Middle East, Africa, Asia, and South America. By comparison to today's standards, these early cities would be considered quite small. They generally had just several thousand residents and were typically agricultural centers along major trade routes. Some much larger cities, however, had hundreds of thousands of residents, such as the Mediterranean cities of Athens and Rome. One reason cities were able to thrive was advances in agriculture that allowed surpluses of food to be readily available to support a population that was not directly involved in its production. People were thus freed to engage in other activities necessary for the functioning of the city and its residents.

Cities were not the prevalent residential areas until well into the nineteenth and twentieth centuries. Until then, the vast majority of people worldwide lived in **rural**, or country, areas. The wide-scale development of cities, or **urban** areas, was made possible by the significant social, economic, and political changes accompanying the Industrial Revolution, when masses of people were drawn into cities to find housing and the manufacturing jobs they needed to earn a living. Fewer families were involved in farming, as large companies, or agribusiness, began to emerge. Cities were populated not only by migrants from rural areas but also by immigrants from other countries, seeking opportunity and a better way of life. Industrialization provided the jobs and the means of communication and transportation to build the burgeoning city infrastructure that could support growing numbers of residents. This process in which growing numbers of people move from rural to urban areas is called **urbanization**.

The term "city" is currently used to refer to an urban settlement with a large population, usually at least 50,000 to 100,000 people. Although a few states, including Wyoming, West Virginia, Delaware, Maine, and Vermont, have no cities with populations of 100,000 people or more, California has seventy cities with more than 100,000 people, followed by Texas with thirty-six and Florida with twenty-one. Urban demographers use the word **metropolis** to refer to an urban area with an even larger population—usually at least 500,000 people—that typically serves as the economic, political, and cultural center for a region. The U.S. Census Bureau defines the term **Metropolitan Statistical Area (MSA)** as a metropolitan area that includes a single large city of at least 50,000 residents that is surrounded by an adjacent area that is socially and economically integrated with the city. As of 2018, the United States contained 384 MSAs (Office of Management and Budget 2018). Many of the largest American cities, such as Los Angeles, Dallas, San Antonio, Phoenix, and San Diego, have continued to grow in the past decade.

Largest of all is a **megalopolis**, also sometimes called a megacity—a group of densely populated metropolises (or agglomerations) that grow contiguous to each other and eventually combine to form a huge urban complex (Gottman 1961). One American megalopolis is referred to as "ChiPitts," or the Great Lakes megalopolis, a group of metropolitan areas in the Midwest, extending from Pittsburgh to Chicago (and including Detroit, Cleveland, Columbus, Cincinnati, and Indianapolis), with a total population of almost 60 million. The ChiPitts metro areas are linked not only by geographic proximity but also by economics, transportation, and communications systems (Gottman and Harper 1990). Another megalopolis is "BosWash," or the Northeast megalopolis, extending from Boston to Washington, DC, and including twenty-two other metropolises such as New York City and Philadelphia. BosWash has a total population of almost 50 million, or approximately 17 percent of the entire U.S. population. Megalopolises are found worldwide in countries including Brazil, Mexico, Indonesia, India, China, and Japan (Castells and Susser 2002). These are sometimes called megaregions or **global cities** to emphasize their position in

URBANIZATION movement of increasing numbers of people from rural areas to cities

METROPOLIS an urban area with a large population, usually 500,000 to 1 million people

METROPOLITAN STATISTICAL AREA (MSA) an area with at least one major city of 50,000 or more inhabitants that is surrounded by adjacent counties that are socially and economically integrated with the city core

MEGALOPOLIS a group of densely populated metropolises that grow dependent on each other and eventually combine to form a huge urban complex

GLOBAL CITIES a term for megacities that emphasizes their global impact as centers of economic, political, and social power

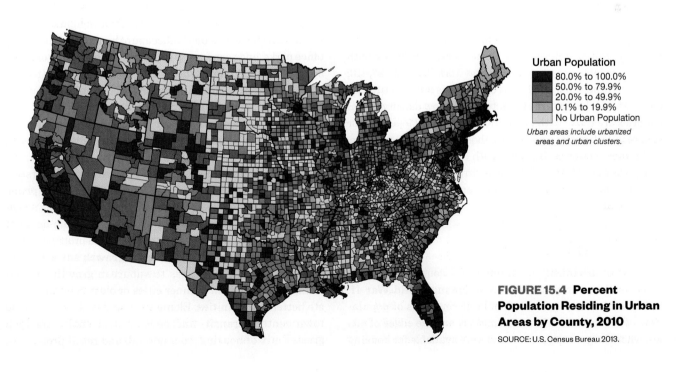

Urban Population
- 80.0% to 100.0%
- 50.0% to 79.9%
- 20.0% to 49.9%
- 0.1% to 19.9%
- No Urban Population

Urban areas include urbanized areas and urban clusters.

FIGURE 15.4 Percent Population Residing in Urban Areas by County, 2010

SOURCE: U.S. Census Bureau 2013.

an increasingly globalized world as centers of economic, political, and social power (Sassen 1991).

In the early 1800s, only about 3 percent of the world's population lived in urban areas and only one city had a population greater than 1 million people: Peking, China (now called Beijing). In the early 1900s, almost 14 percent of the world's population lived in urban areas, and a dozen or so cities around the world (including New York City, London, Paris, Moscow, and Tokyo) had 1 million or more residents. By the early 2000s, more than 50 percent of the world's population was living in urban areas, and we now have to count as large cities those with 10 million people or more; there were thirty-three of these megacities in the world in 2018—home to around one in eight people worldwide (UN Department of Economic and Social Affairs 2018).

A similar pattern can be seen in the United States. In the early 1800s, just 6 percent of the population lived in urban areas, whereas 94 percent lived in rural areas. In the early 1900s, the split was 40 percent urban and 60 percent rural. Today, 81 percent of the population is urban and 19 percent is rural. Ten American cities have populations over 1 million; the largest, New York City, has a population of over 8.3 million (U.S. Census Bureau 2019b).

Cities are often characterized by **urban density**, measured by the total number of people per square mile. Some of the most densely populated cities in the United States include Guttenberg, New Jersey, with 58,821 residents per square mile; New York City with 27,016; and San Francisco with 17,246 (U.S. Census Bureau 2013). By contrast, rural areas are characterized by low density. Rural counties are those with populations of 10 to 59.9 people per square mile; frontier counties are those with 0.5 to 9.9 people; and remote counties are those with 0.04 people per square mile or fewer. Alaska is the most rural state in the United States, followed by Wyoming, Montana, North Dakota, and South Dakota.

Trends in Urbanization

Along with urbanization, an important countertrend surfaced in the years immediately following World War II. **Suburbanization** is the shift of large segments of population away from the urban core and toward the edges of cities, where larger expanses of land were available for housing

developments that provided families with a chance to buy a home of their own and avoid the overcrowding of inner-city life. One of the first significant suburbs was called Levittown (based on the name of the builders), a community of 17,450 tract houses for 75,000 people built in Hempstead, New York, in the late 1940s. The simply designed homes were mass-produced and sold at prices affordable to returning veterans and the newly growing middle class (Wattel 1958). In the 1950s, a second Levittown was built near Philadelphia, and in the 1960s a third in New Jersey. Herbert Gans's study *The Levittowners* (1967) found that homeownership gave suburbanites a sense of pride and more privacy and space, which they valued greatly.

Suburbanization also reflected a retreat from some of the problems associated with city living—crowding, noise, and crime. As more families were able to afford single-family homes, large yards with the proverbial white picket fence and a two-car garage became the image of the "American Dream" (Fava 1956; Kelly 1993). The decades-long shift of populations to the suburbs has accelerated and expanded throughout the nation, with more families moving farther and farther away into what's been called the "exurbs" (Berube et al. 2006; Frey 2003).

Suburban life has its own problems: long commutes, little contact among neighbors, and de facto racial segregation in housing and schools. Some observers have also criticized the monotonous uniformity of the new suburbs, claiming that they promote listless personalities, conformity, and escapism (Jackson 1985; Riesman 1957; Whyte 1956). Another problem related to suburbanization is **urban sprawl** (sometimes also called suburban sprawl). This phenomenon has to do with how cities and suburbs grow. It is often a derogatory term applied to the peripheral expansion of urban boundaries and is associated with irresponsible or poorly planned development. Critics say that such areas are often unsightly, characterized by a homogeneous landscape of housing subdivisions, office parks, and corner strip malls lacking character or green space (Duany, Plater-Zyberk, and Speck 2001; Gutfreund 2004; Kunstler 1993) and bringing problems of traffic, pollution, crowded schools, and high taxes.

While most suburbs remain "bedroom communities," or primarily residential, others have become **edge cities** with their own centers of employment and commerce (Garreau 1992). Edge cities are usually in close proximity to intersecting highways and urban areas. "Silicon Valley" is a prime example: The once sleepy suburb of San Jose became a center of the high-tech industry during the dot-com boom of the 1990s. Edge cities are one answer to the problems associated with suburbanization. **Smart growth** advocates are also promoting alternatives to suburban growth, emphasizing redevelopment of inner cities or older suburbs to create better communities. Elements of smart growth include town centers; transit- and pedestrian-friendly streets; a greater mix of housing, commercial, and retail properties;

URBAN DENSITY concentration of people in a city, measured by the total number of people per square mile

SUBURBANIZATION the shift of large segments of population away from the urban core and toward the edges of cities

URBAN SPRAWL a derogatory term for the expansion of urban or suburban boundaries, associated with irresponsible or poorly planned development

EDGE CITIES centers of employment and commerce that began as suburban commuter communities

SMART GROWTH term for economic and urban planning policies that emphasize responsible development and renewal

ON THE JOB
Agriculture: From the Country to the City

John Peterson is not your average Midwestern farmer. First of all, he's an organic farmer: No pesticides or chemical fertilizers are allowed at Angelic Organics, a 100-acre biodynamic farm located almost two hours west of Chicago. Angelic Organics is also one of the largest community supported agriculture (CSA) farms in the nation: The farm is supported in part by local shareholders, who buy a share of the farm and then receive a portion of its harvest, meaning that no supermarkets or cross-country truck travel stands between the shareholders and their weekly boxes of onions, kale, squash, tomatoes, peppers, basil, and rutabagas. John's unique and colorful story of saving his family's failing conventional farm by transforming it into a thriving organic CSA was featured in the critically acclaimed documentary *The Real Dirt on Farmer John*. Farmer John is an eccentric, biodynamic, community-supported vegetable and herb farmer in Caledonia, Illinois. And he's a man on a mission.

Understanding the need for education and outreach, Farmer John teamed up with Tom Spaulding and other Chicago-area shareholders to create a learning center at Angelic Organics. Angelic Organics Learning Center (AOLC) is dedicated to spreading the word about organic food production throughout the greater Chicago area. AOLC recognizes that while not everyone is destined to become a real rural farmer, even city dwellers can incorporate some of Farmer John's practices into their own backyard gardening endeavors and everyday household practices. Classes in soap making, chicken care, beekeeping, cheese making, and composting teach urban gardeners skills that help them save money, care for their families' health, and become more responsible stewards of their little patches of earth.

Angelic Organics Learning Center also sponsors an "urban initiative" that brings community gardening to the inner city. For example, their Roots and Wings program in Rockford, Illinois, involves local youth in growing organic produce in city plots. The kids also learn to cook, serve, and eat the fresh food they have produced themselves, and they sell their surplus at local farmers' markets so that their neighbors can enjoy the bounty as well. The youth participants don't just reap the benefits of learning about food and urban agriculture—they also become skilled at business, leadership, and problem solving. AOLC runs similar programs with city partners in the Chicago neighborhoods of Englewood and Little Village.

Urban farming like the type that Farmer John and the Angelic Organics Learning Center advocate and teach is becoming more popular in the United States. Gardeners lay sod on top of skyscrapers in New York City, Washington, DC, Chicago, Detroit, and San Francisco to grow vegetables and herbs for local chefs (Burros 2009). These rooftop gardens also provide insulation and drainage for the buildings and contribute to cooler cities (temperature-wise, that is). At ground level, community gardens provide space for apartment dwellers to grow their own healthy fruits and vegetables as well as save money and make connections with others by doing so.

In some cases, urban gardening requires real rebellion: "Gangsta gardener" and community leader Ron Finley planted vegetables in the strips of earth between the sidewalk and the street in his South Los Angeles neighborhood and ended up with multiple citations for "gardening without a permit" on what were tiny plots of city-owned land. But Finley persisted and has built a movement around turning unused urban spaces into productive mini-farms, or "food forests," as Finley calls them.

There is probably an urban farm in your city or town. There may even be an urban farmer in your neighborhood. And anyone who recognizes the benefits—for individuals, society, and the environment—can try their hand at urban farming. All it takes is a little dirt.

Guerilla Gardening Self-described "gangsta gardener" Ron Finley turns unused spaces in his South Los Angeles neighborhood into mini-farms.

TABLE 15.1 Theory in Everyday Life

Perspective	Approach to the Natural Environment	Case Study: Urban Sprawl
Structural Functionalism	The natural world exists in order to keep the social world running smoothly. The environment provides raw materials and space for development in order to meet society's needs.	As population increases, cities must grow in order to accommodate the growing population, so urban sprawl is functional for society.
Conflict Theory	Not all groups or individuals benefit equally from society's use of the natural environment.	Urban sprawl creates largely white upper- and middle-class suburbs around cities whose residents are minorities, seniors, immigrants, working class, and/or poor. This means that suburban residents may have access to resources, like well-funded schools, that urban dwellers may not.
Symbolic Interactionism	The meanings assigned to the natural environment will determine how society sees and uses it.	Redefining open land as a scarce resource, and redefining urban areas as valuable spaces, may lead to the reduction of urban sprawl: Open land could be conserved, while urban spaces could be rehabilitated and revitalized.

and the preservation of open space and other environmental amenities.

Many long-established cities suffered when populations began moving to the suburbs—including Detroit, Chicago, and Philadelphia in the North and East (the rustbelt) as well as New Orleans, St. Louis, and San Francisco in the South, Midwest, and West (U.S. Census Bureau 2005). Since the 1950s and 1960s, people have left cities not only to find more space and bigger homes in the nearby suburbs but also to flee other problems endemic to the city. Largely, those escaping the cities were upper- and middle-class whites who could afford to leave—a trend often referred to as **white flight** (or sometimes "suburban flight"). Those remaining in cities were predominantly minorities, seniors, immigrants, the working class, or the poor. White flight left urban areas abandoned by businesses and financial institutions, leading to broken-down and boarded-up shops and streets and creating ghettos that further exacerbated the problems associated with inner cities (Wilson 1996). Although suburbs are starting to diversify (Frey 2014b), they still carry the symbolic blemish of white flight.

In the 1960s and 1970s, to address the problem of decaying inner cities, local city governments and private investors took advantage of **urban renewal** efforts that included renovation, selective demolition, commercial development, and tax incentives aimed at revitalizing business districts and residential neighborhoods (Frieden and Sagalyn 1992). Urban renewal has been a limited success. While it did revitalize many areas, it often came at a high cost to existing communities. In many cases, it resulted in the destruction of vibrant, if run-down, neighborhoods (Mollenkopf 1983).

Urban renewal is linked to another trend that has also changed many formerly blighted cities: **gentrification**. This is the transformation of the physical, social, economic, and cultural life of formerly working-class or poor inner-city neighborhoods into more affluent middle-class communities as wealthier people return to the cities (Glass 1964). This trend, which took off in the 1990s, is evident in some of the nation's largest cities, such as Boston, New York, Philadelphia, Chicago, and San Francisco (Mele 2000). Various higher-income individuals, whether they were young professionals ("yuppies"), artists, or retirees, recognized the potential for rehabilitating downtown buildings (Castells 1984). They valued the variety and excitement of urban living more than the mini-malls of sleepy suburbia (Florida 2004). The term "gentrification" carries a distinct class connotation, and often a racial one as well (Hwang and Sampson 2014). While converting, renovating, remodeling, and constructing new buildings beautifies old city neighborhoods and brings new amenities and businesses to an area, it also increases property values and tends to displace lower-income residents (Zukin 1987, 1989, 2016). Gentrification, then, does not eradicate the problems of poverty; it too often leaves racial minorities and lower-income Americans with few options other than to move elsewhere.

In both cities and suburbs, affordable housing has become increasingly scarce over the last few decades. Sociologist Matthew Desmond has called this shortage a national crisis. The United States has a deficit of 7 million rental units for

WHITE FLIGHT movement of upper- and middle-class whites who could afford to leave the cities for the suburbs, especially in the 1950s and 1960s

URBAN RENEWAL efforts to rejuvenate decaying inner cities, including renovation, selective demolition, commercial development, and tax incentives

GENTRIFICATION transformation of the physical, social, economic, and cultural life of formerly working-class or poor inner-city neighborhoods into more affluent middle-class communities

UTOPIA literally "no place"; an ideal society in which all social ills have been overcome

DYSTOPIA opposite of a utopia; a world where social problems are magnified and the quality of life is extremely low

the lowest-income households; nearly 11 million households are severely rent burdened, spending more than half of their income on housing and utilities (National Low Income Housing Coalition 2019). Older public housing projects are being vacated and demolished by officials who believe that concentrated poverty is bad for neighborhoods and neighbors, but affordable housing units often have long waiting lists. Low-income families have a hard time keeping up with high rents in more expensive areas, even when they receive government subsidies. Cities are often reluctant to support the construction of inexpensively priced housing units. Neighbors often don't want "those people" (the poor, new immigrants, or racial minorities) on their blocks, and developers just go where the money is.

DATA WORKSHOP

Analyzing Media and Pop Culture

Imagining the Cities of Tomorrow

People have always been interested in the future. Storytellers, inventors, scientists, politicians, and daydreamers have tried to imagine and, in some instances, create a vision of what will come.

Imagining the city of tomorrow is an almost constant theme in contemporary popular culture—books and comics, radio and TV, movies, and video games. Some of these represent a brighter vision of tomorrow, a **utopia** where humankind is finally freed from drudgery and disease, strife, and suffering. Some represent a darker vision of tomorrow, a **dystopia** where humankind is trapped in a ruthless, apocalyptic world of machines and nature gone mad.

Although examples of the city of the future appear in many different media, this Data Workshop asks that you focus on film. You may have a favorite movie depicting the future, whether it's in the genre of science fiction, action adventure, thriller, horror, drama, or comedy. In deciding which movie to choose for your content analysis, consider whether the movie proposes a serious or realistic possibility of the future and avoid anything too far out in terms of monsters, aliens, or fantasy worlds.

The following is a partial list of movies that could satisfy the assignment. This list is not exhaustive, and you may prefer to use a film not in the list. (Please be aware of MPAA ratings for movies and select appropriate material for your age group.)

12 Monkeys	*Idiocracy*
1984	*Independence Day*
A.I. (Artificial Intelligence)	*Left Behind*
Back to the Future	*Mad Max*
Black Panther	*The Matrix*
Blade Runner	*Metropolis*
Blade Runner 2049	*Minority Report*
Brazil	*Oblivion*
Chappie	*The Purge*
Children of Men	*Road Warrior*
The Day after	*Slaughterhouse Five*
Tomorrow	*Snowpiercer*
Demolition Man	*Solaris*
District 9	*Strange Days*
Divergent	*The Terminator*
Elysium	*Terminator 2:*
eXistenZ	*Judgment Day*
Fahrenheit 451	*Total Recall*
The Fifth Element	*Tron*
Gattaca	*The Truman Show*
Her	*V for Vendetta*
The Hunger Games	*Videodrome*

Wakanda Forever The fictional nation from *Black Panther* is a vision of an uncolonized African utopia.

For this Data Workshop, you will be using existing sources and doing a content analysis. Refer to Chapter 2 for a review of this research method. Now watch the movie while keeping in mind the concepts you have learned from this chapter, especially with regard to urbanization. Take notes about the settings and environments in the movie. Identify and capture key scenes or dialogue that address the city and city life in the film. In conducting your content analysis, consider some of the following questions:

- At what point in the future does the movie take place?

- What is the major theme of the movie? What is its overall message?

- Does the movie represent a utopian or dystopian vision of the future? Does it represent positive or negative changes to society?

- What sorts of futuristic elements are included in the movie, such as time travel, virtual reality, mind control, wars between humans and machines, or apocalyptic destruction?

- How is the modern city or landscape of the future depicted? What are its structural features in both public and private realms?

- Compare the future with the present. How is the future the same or different? How is it better or worse?

- What are people like in the future? How are they affected by their environment? How does their environment affect their lives?

- Could this version of the future realistically occur? Would you like to live in such a future?

There are two options for completing this Data Workshop:

PREP-PAIR-SHARE Conduct your content analysis and develop some preliminary answers to the questions provided. Prepare some written notes that you can refer to during in-class discussions. Pair up with one or more classmates and discuss your findings in small groups. Compare and contrast the analyses of the films observed by participants in your group.

DO-IT-YOURSELF Complete the research activities described and develop some preliminary answers to the questions provided. Then write a three- to four-page essay discussing your answers and reflecting on your observations of the film. What do you think your observations tell us about our society's hopes and fears for the future of cities and city life?

Living in the City

Who lives in cities? What about city life continues to attract droves of people? Big cities offer residents bright lights, a fast pace, excitement, and opportunity. They differ from small rural towns and suburban neighborhoods, so a certain type of person is more likely to be found living there.

Louis Wirth, a member of the Chicago School of sociology, proposed the idea of "urbanism as a way of life." He believed that cities affected the outlook, mentality, and lifestyle of their residents. While cities offer personal freedom, relaxed moral restraints, relative anonymity, variety, and diversity, there is also a certain social cost involved. People tend to belong to more formal organizations with more narrow goals and to engage less frequently in intimate interaction with one another. Wirth's (1938) analysis was in line with the belief that cities cause **social atomization**—that they are filled with free-floating individuals rather than members of a community. Another sociologist, Claude Fischer (1976), found that people create a sense of community by dividing the city into little worlds within which they feel familiar and involved. These groups allow for informal and close relationships, giving city dwellers more intimacy and a feeling of belonging.

In 1962, Herbert Gans published a major ethnographic study, *The Urban Villagers*, in which he identified distinct categories of **urbanites**, or people who live in urban areas. The first are called "cosmopolites"—students, intellectuals, artists, entertainers, and other professionals who are drawn to the city because of its cultural benefits and convenience to their lifestyles. The next group are the "singles," unmarried people seeking jobs, entertainment, and partners with whom to settle down. Singles may include cosmopolites as well. When singles do find a marriage partner or mate, they tend to move to the suburbs, often in preparation to starting a family.

Another group of city dwellers are the "ethnic villagers," often recent immigrants to the area. They tend to settle near others with whom they share a common racial, ethnic, national, religious, or linguistic background; these are often distant relatives or others with whom they have a connection. This is why many major cities still have Chinatowns, Little Italys, and other ethnic neighborhoods. Once here, immigrants form tightly knit ethnic enclaves that resemble the villages of their home countries.

The last group of urban dwellers are the "deprived" and the "trapped." These are the people at the bottom of the social hierarchy—the poor, homeless, disabled, elderly, and mentally ill. Without resources and means of support, they cannot afford to leave the city, even if they could find jobs, services, or housing elsewhere; they are inescapably stuck where they are. This perpetuates a cycle of poverty and despair.

ALIENATION AND ALTRUISM: THE CASE OF NEW YORK CITY As products of the Industrial Revolution, cities are celebrated for providing unprecedented degrees of freedom for individuals. Life in rural agricultural communities was much more restrictive, with family and neighbors placing tight constraints on behavior. However, sociology has been suspicious of cities, seeing this very freedom as a source of **alienation**. Early sociologist Georg Simmel argued that while urban environments "allowed a much greater degree of individual liberty," they did so only "at the expense of treating others in objective and instrumental terms" and relating to others only through a "cold and heartless calculus" (Harvey 1990). In short, except for their chosen subcultures, city dwellers fail to develop community, feel little connection with neighbors, have relationships that are largely shallow and impersonal, and fail to care about one another (Simmel 1950).

The murder of Catherine "Kitty" Genovese in New York City has come to represent all such fears about modern urban life. Late on March 13, 1964, Genovese was returning home from her job as a bar manager when she was attacked by a man named Winston Moseley. He first attacked Genovese after she parked her car outside the Kew Gardens apartment building where she lived. She was stabbed several times before her attacker was frightened off when lights went on in nearby apartments. Badly wounded and bleeding, Genovese was later reported to have shouted, "Oh, my God, he stabbed me! Please help me! Please help me!" (Gansberg 1964). Somehow, she then made her way to the back of the building, apparently trying to get to the staircase that led to her apartment. However, her assailant returned and stabbed and beat her to death, before sexually assaulting her. The entire attack, although intermittent, was reported to have lasted nearly thirty minutes.

Kitty Genovese The original account of the twenty-eight-year-old's murder outside her Queens apartment building claimed that there were thirty-eight witnesses—none of whom intervened.

As horrible as this was, it wouldn't be remembered today if it were just a tragic murder. What has made this case memorable was the story that developed in the aftermath about the number of bystanders who must have heard the crime taking place but failed to take action. *The New York Times* reported that thirty-eight people witnessed Genovese getting attacked and yet no one came to her aid. For many, this seemed to be the ultimate indictment of big cities in general, and New York City in particular, and much of the press coverage seemed to demonize the individuals who failed to "get involved." While we now know that some neighbors did in fact try to intervene (Cook 2015), it was not enough to change the outcome.

In the aftermath of the Genovese murder, John Darley and Bibb Latané (1968) conducted several experiments on **altruism** and helping behaviors. These experiments were designed to test what came to be called the **bystander effect**, or the **diffusion of responsibility**. In one experiment, different-sized groups of test subjects heard what sounded like a woman having an accident in the next room. Darley and Latané found that the higher the number of bystanders present, the lower the chances that any of them would attempt to help. Basically, the researchers theorized that the responsibility "diffused" throughout the crowd so that no one person felt responsible enough to do anything, most assuming that someone else would help. However, when groups were small, the chances that someone would do something to help increased greatly.

In a similar experiment, they placed different-sized groups of subjects in a room, under the pretense of taking a test, and gradually filled the room with smoke. Again, they found that the greater the number of subjects in a room, the lower the chances that anyone would mention the smoke. Here, along with the diffusion of responsibility, they argued that **pluralistic ignorance** was at work. When large groups of people encounter an ambiguous or unusual situation, they tend to look to each other for help in defining the situation. If no member of the group decides that it is an emergency, and therefore worthy of reacting, it is likely that all members will continue to ignore the situation.

SOCIAL ATOMIZATION a social situation that emphasizes individualism over collective or group identities

URBANITES people who live in cities

ALIENATION decreasing importance of social ties and community and the corresponding increase in impersonal associations and instrumental logic

ALTRUISM unselfish concern for the well-being of others and helping behaviors performed without self-interested motivation

BYSTANDER EFFECT or **DIFFUSION OF RESPONSIBILITY** the social dynamic wherein the more people who are present in a moment of crisis, the less likely any one of them is to take action

PLURALISTIC IGNORANCE a process in which members of a group individually conclude that there is no need to take action because they see that other group members have not done so

IN RELATIONSHIPS
Encounters with Strangers

Cities are places where strangers come together. Before there were cities, there were also no strangers; those who were unknown were driven off, killed, or quickly assimilated into the clan, tribe, or group (Lofland 1973). With the advent of cities came the prospect of living life in close proximity to hundreds, thousands, or even millions of people we will never know and from whom we cannot be completely segregated. City life would seem to bring the prospect for all sorts of chaos and conflict—and yet every day, in contemporary cities, millions of people go about their business in relative harmony, brushing elbows with one another on the sidewalk or subway in encounters that are neither friendly nor unfriendly but merely orderly.

What are the interactional structures that order urban life? Public interactions with strangers can be treacherous, as we encounter people we do not know and whose reactions we cannot predict. For the most part, we are not talking about the danger of physical attack. More common than getting mugged is being "looked at funny," getting "goosed," or being the target of "cat calls." These are threats to self more than anything else—being treated as a nonperson, or as a piece of meat. How do we guard against these minor molestations when we walk down the street every day?

CIVIL INATTENTION
an unspoken rule governing interactions in public places, whereby individuals briefly notice others before ignoring them

A specific way we deal with strangers in public is by practicing what Erving Goffman (1971) called **civil inattention**. This is a taken-for-granted rule of public place interaction, a basic public courtesy we extend to one another that helps guard against unpleasant interactions with strangers. About eight or ten feet away from each other, we tend to look at and then away from the person we are approaching—all in one sweep of our gaze. We have looked, but not too intently or for too long. This allows us to navigate through urban spaces without bumping into strangers and to avoid the kinds of interactions that might lead to trouble.

The practice of civil inattention is so commonplace that you may not realize you do it every day. Now, walk down the street and notice your own gazework and that of others—with full comprehension of how this simple act helps avoid conflict, enables smooth interactions between strangers, and basically makes city life possible.

What might move us to violate civil inattention—to interact with strangers in ways that might otherwise be forbidden? Anything, Goffman suggests, that makes us more "open." Open persons are those whose identities expose them to the overtures of others. Examples of open persons are police officers (and others in uniform), pregnant women, small children, the disabled, those with unusual physical characteristics such as height or hair color, same-sex couples... the list goes on and on. One type of open person you have probably encountered is a person walking a dog. Dogs serve as what Goffman called "bridging devices"—excuses for strangers to begin conversations that the rules of civil inattention would otherwise prevent. Dogs facilitate interactions in public places—indeed, dogs serve as (perhaps unwitting) team members in their masters' performances (Robins, Sanders, and Cahill 1991). They can be referred to by others as a kind of icebreaker as well (Wood et al. 2007). We've all found ourselves exclaiming, "Cute puppy!" or "Wow, that's a big dog" as we pass dogwalkers on the street, and sometimes those utterances develop into longer conversations.

And, of course, there's the classic notion of the dog as "chick magnet" or "dude magnet," helping its owner attract, converse with, and pick up women or men for romantic purposes. So perhaps we should give our pooches more credit for helping to connect us with each other and to make city life more humane.

Don't Talk to Strangers, Unless They're with a Dog Erving Goffman observed that dogs facilitate interactions among strangers by serving as bridging devices.

These conclusions can also help explain a time when New Yorkers did come to each other's aid out of a sense of belonging and **community**: in the wake of the September 11, 2001, attacks on the World Trade Center. In the hours and days after the attacks, Americans rushed to help however they could. "Tens of thousands of patriotic Americans rolled up their sleeves and gave blood," monetary donations poured in, and ordinary New Yorkers rushed to pitch in (Stapleton 2002). Some of the most heroic rescue efforts at the World Trade Center were made by ordinary people who rushed to help as soon as they heard. Two Port Authority police officers, Will Jimeno and John McLoughlin, were the last people to be found alive in the collapsed remains of the World Trade Center towers. They were discovered by Charles Sereika, a former paramedic, and David Karnes, an accountant from Connecticut who "had changed into his Marine camouflage outfit" and driven down to Manhattan as soon as he heard the news (Dwyer 2001). The movie *World Trade Center* (2006) by Oliver Stone depicts their story. And even if things have somewhat returned to normal (meaning people are less friendly now), almost everyone agrees that New Yorkers "were wonderful during the crisis, and we were tender to each other.... Volunteers streamed to the site" and "after only a few days there were so many, they were turned away by the hundreds.... Strangers spoke to each other in the street, in stores, and on the subway" (Hustvedt 2002).

So what made the difference in the two events? Many of those who heard Kitty Genovese being murdered may have believed that it was a bar fight or a lover's quarrel. Not knowing what was happening, they were unsure how to respond; there was no emergency telephone system the way there is now, and many people were reluctant to get personally involved with the police. In the aftermath of the Kitty Genovese murder, the "911" emergency system was created, neighborhood watch groups were formed, and Good Samaritan laws were passed to protect bystanders from liability in emergencies. So now, whenever bystanders do jump in to help, it is in part because of the changes that Genovese's murder provoked. While alienation is part of life in cities, so is altruism. Both are part of our shared social worlds.

THE ENVIRONMENT

The final section of this chapter once again considers the connection between the social and the natural worlds. Human populations have grown tremendously, as have the cities in which most of them live. Now how do those people interact with the natural environment and what impact does the environment have on how they live? Whether we go camping, surfing, or just take a walk through Central Park, we all go to nature to escape, to recreate, to relax. It is ironic that we now seek out nature as a retreat from the demands of society, because society itself originated and evolved at least in part to protect us against the demands of nature.

The cooperation and interdependence that characterize most social groups allow individuals to withstand the risks of the natural environment. The products of culture—clothing, architecture, automobiles, and many others—contribute to our ability to live in what would otherwise be inhospitable surroundings. Without her insulated house and its furnace, her layers of clothing topped with a Gore-Tex parka, and her car with a remote starter and all-weather tires, Dr. Ferris would have a hard time surviving the harsh winters in northern Illinois. And all these survival tools are supplied because she is part of a society whose other members have created what she needs to be safe and warm in the elements. Society provides all of us with a buffer against nature; without it, we wouldn't last very long in the ocean, the snowdrifts, or the desert.

The environment is a somewhat recent area of interest among sociologists, coinciding with the general public's concern about environmental issues (Guber 2003). When sociologists use the term **environment**, it encompasses aspects of both the natural and the human-made environments and includes everything from the most micro level of organisms to all the parts of the earth that support life. Sociologists study the ways that societies are dependent on the natural world; how cultural values and beliefs shape views about and influence usage of the environment; the politics and economics of natural resources; and the social construction of conflicts, problems, and solutions that are a result of our relationship to the natural world.

First, we will look at environmental problems as social problems. This discussion encompasses two big areas: problems of consumption and problems of waste. Sociologists, however, must look beyond descriptions of problems and attempt to apply analytic frameworks for understanding the social complexities underlying the problems.

Environmental Problems

Many students first become acquainted with the subject of the environment through the lens of social problems. Learning the "three Rs" in school has now come to mean reduce, reuse, recycle. We need to help "save" the environment because it is under threat from consumption and waste.

PROBLEMS OF CONSUMPTION The planet earth provides an abundance of natural resources, including air, water, land, wildlife, plants, and minerals. We have learned to exploit these resources not only for basic survival but also to build

> **COMMUNITY** a group of people living in the same local area who share a sense of participation, belonging, and fellowship
>
> **ENVIRONMENT** in sociology, the natural world, the human-made environment, and the interaction between the two

GLOBAL PERSPECTIVE
Water, Water Everywhere but Not a Drop to Drink

As the worldwide population continues to grow, water accessibility has become a central issue with a global context. With global population projected to grow by approximately 2 to 3 billion people over the next forty years, the worldwide demand for food is consequently expected to skyrocket. While water is considered a "renewable resource," massive population growth matched with an ever-increasing demand for food has threatened the global water supply. Agriculture and food production make up the largest sources of freshwater consumption, with 70 percent of global freshwater being used directly for food consumption (Khokhar 2017). With accessibility expected to decrease in many areas of the world, water has become a new battleground as many regions continue to struggle to secure clean water and maintain control of local water supplies.

At the forefront of the global water crisis are the nations of Africa, whose water supplies have been contentiously sought after by international corporations and wealthy investors alike (Bienkowski 2013). Unlike the national borders that divide countries, water is frequently a "transboundary" resource in that rivers can cross political boundaries (United Nations 2014b). Wealthy countries often exploit natural resources, such as water, from less developed countries—often to the detriment of the local population. With around one-third of the world's transboundary water basins, Africa has become a hot spot for land grabs, or water grabs, by wealthy countries seeking more affordable access to supplies of water (GRAIN 2012). Despite the fact that Africa is one of the driest regions in the world, wealthier countries also facing water scarcity—such as Saudi Arabia—have created incentives for corporations to capitalize on the continent's water supply and divest from using domestic water supplies.

While Saudi Arabia has been able to save millions of gallons of water each year and avoid depleting its own natural water sources by tapping into Africa's water supply, Africa continues to face water scarcity alongside poverty and hunger. The Alwera River in Ethiopia provides water to thousands of people within the surrounding area and has recently become a site of water grabbing. Billionaire Mohammed al-Amoudi is one of the many wealthy Saudi investors who have established plantations in Africa with the intention to divest from nearby water sources (GRAIN 2012). Saudi companies have purchased millions of hectares of land in Africa

to obtain access to water, including efforts to acquire the headwaters of the Nile River (Pierce 2012).

Take the case of Bolivia. In 2000, Bolivia's municipal water system was sold to a transnational consortium in exchange for debt relief, prompting the infamous Cochabamba Water War. Farmers, factory workers, students, and middle-class professionals all came together in opposition to water privatization, organizing strikes, road blockages, and protests and eventually forcing the return of the country's water supply to popular control. Despite this happy ending, Bolivia still struggles to control and monitor the activities of the country's 28,000 local water and sanitation providers, many of which are plagued by deteriorated systems and community conflicts (Achtenberg 2013).

Ultimately, the struggles for water in the United States and throughout the world signal larger issues around accessibility, rights, and control of natural and vital resources. In 2010, the United Nations created a resolution that officially recognized access to clean water as a human right; however, little has been resolved to combat water grabbing and privatization efforts within vulnerable developing countries (United Nations 2014a). While people in developing countries struggle to maintain control of their valuable water resources, threats of privatization and water grabbing have only escalated as the global population and demand for food production continue to increase.

Water Scarcity The UN estimates that 1.8 billion people will be living in areas with absolute water scarcity by 2050.

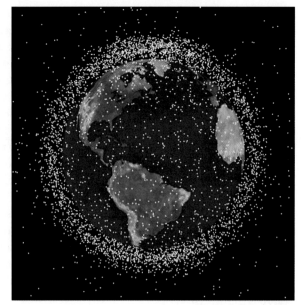

The Social World and the Natural World Society affects nature even in the remotest places—including in our oceans and in outer space! Garbage floats off the shore of Manila Bay (left), and NASA illustrates the objects orbiting Earth (right).

everything in material culture that is part of the modern world. Humans have long been presented with the challenge of managing their use of natural resources, but those challenges have changed in the postindustrial era.

Renewable resources are natural resources that can be regenerated; for instance, oxygen is replenished by plants and trees, water by evaporation and rain clouds, trees and plants by pollen and seeds, and animals by mating and reproduction. The wind blows and the sun shines in ample abundance. **Nonrenewable resources** are those that cannot be replaced (except through tens of thousands of years of geological processes); they include fossil fuels such as oil and minerals such as coal, copper, and iron. All natural resources are susceptible to overuse or overconsumption and eventually to depletion or even exhaustion. As a result of rising demands, we have already seen rising costs or outright shortages for such commodities as seafood, timber, and gasoline.

One of the world's most pressing problems is how to meet enormous and growing demands for energy. We need energy—gas, electric, or nuclear—to help power everything from cars and televisions to factories and airplanes. But these forms of energy are not inexhaustible. We have relied primarily on nonrenewable sources, such as coal and fossil fuels, to meet our needs. The current mix of fuel sources comes from 37 percent petroleum, 29 percent natural gas, 14 percent coal, 9 percent nuclear, and only about 11 percent renewable energy sources (U.S. Energy Information Administration 2018). Renewable sources such as wind and solar power are being developed, but they are not sufficient yet to provide the substantial quantities of energy we will need in the future.

Industrialized nations are the largest consumers of energy, using approximately 70 percent of the total energy produced in the world; of those nations, the United States' share is 18 percent, Saudi Arabia's is 12 percent, Russia's is 11 percent, and Canada and China use 5 percent each (U.S. Energy Information Administration 2019). Developing nations that now use the remaining 30 percent are becoming more industrialized, and consequently their energy needs will also increase, thus closing the energy usage gap among nations during the next twenty-five years. Total worldwide energy consumption is projected to grow approximately 28 percent by 2040 (U.S. Energy Information Administration 2017).

Oil is a finite resource, and at some point the supply will be exhausted. For many decades the United States has relied heavily on foreign oil imports. More recently there has been high demand for more domestic oil exploration and production. Hydraulic fracturing, or "fracking," involves drilling thousands of feet underground to extract natural gas stores from shale. Fracking has released vast new quantities of oil and natural gas in the United States; it accounts for two-thirds of all natural gas production and about half of crude oil production (U.S. Energy Information Administration 2016). The practice is not without dangers and controversy: Fracking has been proven to contaminate groundwater and is starting to cause earthquakes in regions without active faults.

Another critical area of consumption is the rain forests in South America, Central America, Australia, Africa, and Southeast Asia. Rain forests are ecosystems located in tropical and temperate regions that are home to diverse plant and animal life (as well as indigenous peoples). Although rain forests cover only about 6 percent of the earth's landmass, they contain close to 50 percent of all microorganisms and plant and animal species in the world (Mittermeier, Myers, and Mittermeier 2000; Nunez 2019). Previously unknown life forms are being discovered there every year, while thousands are being driven to extinction. Products derived from the rain forest include not only foods and woods but also pharmaceuticals: More than 7,000 medical compounds are derived from native plants. Rain forests also play a key role in global climate control, evaporation and rainfall, and clearing the air of carbon dioxide.

In 1950, rain forests covered twice as much area as they do today, and they are disappearing at an alarming rate. In just the last fifty years, about 17 percent of the Amazonian rain forest has been destroyed (Nunez 2019). Destruction of the rain forests is of sociological import because it results from collective human behavior. The immediate cause of this destruction is to accommodate the logging, mining, and ranching industries. Although these industries may benefit the peoples of those regions, they are primarily providing for the consumption demands of the more developed nations of the world.

BIODIVERSITY the variety of species of plants and animals existing at any given time

POLLUTION any environmental contaminant that harms living beings

In addition to rain forests, worldwide **biodiversity** is in dangerous decline. In a shocking report by an intergovernmental panel on biodiversity and ecosystem services, the United Nations (2019) asserted that humans are speeding extinction and transforming the natural world at a rate "unprecedented in history." According to the report, the most comprehensive of its kind, the average abundance of plant and animal life has fallen by at least 20 percent, mostly since 1900. Up to a million plant and animal species are threatened with extinction, many within just decades, including more than 40 percent of amphibians and more than a third of marine mammals. These mass die-offs are being driven by human activities, including the destruction of habitats, pollution, the introduction of nonnative species, and overuse.

PROBLEMS OF WASTE Problems of consumption are linked to problems of waste, often two sides of the same coin. Consider water and air. Water is another natural resource that can be overused; we understand what happens during a drought, or when lakes, rivers, or underground aquifers are drained and then go dry. But water can also be damaged by what we put into it. And while we don't normally think of consuming air, it is an essential natural resource, and we can damage its quality and change for the worse the very atmosphere of the planet. Let's look at these examples of **pollution**.

Water is indispensable for life. About 71 percent of the earth's surface is covered with water (U.S. Geological Survey 2014). Almost 97 percent of it is in oceans of saltwater, home to a vast array of sea creatures and plants. Only 1 percent of the total is freshwater, found in lakes, rivers, and underground aquifers; the other 2 percent is in polar ice caps and glaciers. This is a small percentage to meet human needs—from drinking water to water for agricultural and ranching purposes. The world's oceans and freshwater supplies have been under increased threat from pollution by industrial development and population growth—mostly by allowing contaminants to enter oceans, lakes, rivers, and underground water supplies. The sources of this pollution are many: factories dumping chemical and solid wastes; agricultural runoff of manure, pesticides, and fertilizers; human sewage and urban runoff; and toxic chemicals falling from the skies in

Threats to Biodiversity and the Climate Rain forests, which play a key role in regulating the global climate and are home to almost 50 percent of the world's plant and animal species, are being destroyed at a rate of millions of acres each year. The Amazon experienced an alarming uptick in fires in 2019, sparking an international outcry.

Climate Change Maldivian Minister of Fisheries and Agriculture Ibrahim Didi calls attention to the threat of global warming to low-lying countries by holding an underwater meeting to sign a document calling on all nations to cut down their carbon dioxide emissions.

rain. Groundwaters and aquifers are also threatened by overuse and by pollutants that seep through the soil.

Access to freshwater is not equal throughout the world. About 4 billion people, which is nearly two-thirds of the world population, deal with severe water scarcity at least one month of the year (Mekonnen and Hoekstra 2016). There is a definite link between water scarcity and poverty. In developing nations, unclean water is a significant cause of disease and death. Access to clean, affordable water is also an issue in the United States. Although the **Environmental Protection Agency (EPA)** claims that the United States has one of the safest supplies of drinking water, about 10 percent of water systems in the nation don't meet EPA standards (Environmental Protection Agency 2016). As explored in Chapter 14, residents of Flint, Michigan, found out in 2015 that their tap water was contaminated with dangerously high levels of lead from aging, corroded pipes. In addition, agricultural runoff taints waterways with fertilizers and animal effluent, creating algae blooms and undrinkable water in the Midwest, South, and other farming areas. California and the Southwest are in almost constant states of crippling drought, importing water from other parts of the country at great expense.

Perhaps even more taken for granted than the water we drink is the air we breathe, but it, too, is a resource whose quality and quantity must be carefully guarded. The atmosphere is made up of thin layers of gases surrounding the planet and making life possible. It interacts with the land, oceans, and sun to produce the earth's climate and weather. The air that we breathe is ubiquitous, so we might not even think of it as a natural resource. But the earth's atmosphere

and its ability to sustain life are at risk from pollution. Not all threats come from humans; for instance, volcanoes or forest fires started by lightning can emit massive clouds of smoke, ash, and debris into the atmosphere. Human activity, however, accounts for a tremendous amount of air pollution, especially emissions from factories, power plants, and automobiles. A considerable amount of the polluting chemicals emitted into the atmosphere comes from a surprising source: livestock (Environmental Protection Agency 2017). The most common air pollutants include carbon monoxide, carbon dioxide, lead, nitrogen dioxide, ozone, sulfur dioxide, and particulates such as soot, smoke, and dust. Gases such as water vapor, carbon dioxide, methane, nitrous oxide, ozone, and fluorocarbon are called greenhouse gases. Together, these gases and pollutants not only create ugly smog and haze but also are hazardous to the health of humans and other species.

Greenhouse gases are also contributing to a change in the makeup of the earth's atmosphere. Scientists call this the **greenhouse effect**. The earth's climate is regulated through a process in which some of the sun's heat and energy are retained within the atmosphere. Naturally occurring gases (such as water vapor and carbon dioxide) help trap some of the earth's outgoing heat, which in turn maintains a

ENVIRONMENTAL PROTECTION AGENCY (EPA) a U.S. government agency established in 1969 to protect public health and the environment through policies and enforcement

GREENHOUSE EFFECT the process in which increased production of greenhouse gases, especially those arising from human activity (e.g., carbon dioxide, nitrous oxide, and methane) causes changes to the earth's atmosphere

stable, livable climate. An increase in greenhouse gases from air pollution results in greater retention of heat within the earth's atmosphere, leading to **global warming**, an increase in the world's average temperature. Global warming of only a few degrees can cause catastrophic consequences for the world and its inhabitants. One effect of global warming is **climate change**, in which weather patterns shift and become more extreme as a result of the increased tempera-

ture. Problems such as more severe droughts and wildfires; stronger and more frequent hurricanes and tornadoes; and increased rain and flooding are all part of climate change.

A landmark 2018 report by the United Nations' scientific panel on climate change—a group of scientists brought together by the UN to advise world leaders—paints a dire picture of the immediate threats of climate change. According to the report, human activity has caused the average temperature of the earth to rise about 1.8 degrees Fahrenheit since early industrialization in the 1850s. If greenhouse gas emissions continue at the current rate, the atmosphere is expected to warm by as much as 2.7 degrees by 2040, causing disastrous and irreversible changes. Initially, scientists believed the most severe effects of climate change wouldn't occur until the planet warmed by 3.6 degrees, but this newest report lowered that threshold to 2.7 degrees, meaning we are likely to reach crisis levels much sooner than expected. The report maintains that tens of millions of people, in the United States, China, India, Indonesia, Japan, and many other island nations, will be displaced because of coastal flooding, requiring an unprecedented evacuation and relocation of climate refugees. Elsewhere, changing global weather patterns will alter ecosystems that support life on earth, causing widespread habitat die-offs and threatening food and water supplies. While scientists believe it is technically possible to avoid a 2.7-degree increase, many doubt whether we have the political and economic willpower to do so in time.

GLOBAL WARMING gradual increase in the earth's temperature, driven recently by an increase in greenhouse gases and other human activity

CLIMATE CHANGE the increase in extreme weather patterns linked to global warming

ENVIRONMENTAL SOCIOLOGY the study of the interaction between society and the natural environment, including the social causes and consequences of environmental problems

TREADMILL OF PRODUCTION term describing the operation of modern economic systems that require constant growth, which causes increased exploitation of resources and environmental degradation

NEW ECOLOGICAL PARADIGM a way of understanding human life as just one part of an ecosystem that includes many species' interactions with the environment; suggests that there should be ecological limits on human activity

ANTHROPOCENTRIC literally "human centered"; the idea that needs and desires of human beings should take priority over concerns about other species or the natural environment

HUMAN EXCEPTIONALISM the attitude that humans are exempt from natural ecological limits

Environmental Sociology

To analyze problems of the environment, sociologists have developed **environmental sociology**, a distinct subfield of sociology that tackles environmental issues and examines the reciprocal interactions among the physical environment, social structure (including technology), and human behavior.

Contemporary industrial societies have been built on the premise of progress—on conquering nature and using natural resources to fuel production and increase profits (Schnaiberg and Gould 1994). Government policies and economic systems have frequently supported this belief. While progress has usually meant great wealth for some and goods and services for many, it has come at a price: environmental degradation and the accompanying social problems.

Environmental sociologists refer to this process as the **treadmill of production** (Schnaiberg 1980). They assert that the drive for economic growth in capitalist societies persists, even at the expense of the environment and despite opposition from activists and other groups, because corporate expansion provides critical taxable wealth and the jobs essential to the economic life of a society. Large corporations can typically defend themselves against calls for accountability for damages and exercise considerable influence through political lobbying and campaign contributions as well as appeals to change public opinion. Attacking the practices of these corporations can also be detrimental to the workers who need their jobs and to governments that depend on these industries for products critical to the nation's well-being and security (Schnaiberg and Gould 1994). This is why people's attitudes about the environment can be shaped by economic and political forces. The treadmill of production is not an environmentally friendly process; nevertheless, numerous societies are invested in its continued existence, and we will likely see enduring conflict between the economy and the environment at the international, national, regional, and local levels.

Understanding societal attitudes about the environment is an essential part of environmental sociology (Dunlap and Brulle 2015). In the 1970s, William Catton and Riley Dunlap (1978, 1980) developed the **new ecological paradigm**. Historically, Westerners have had a particularly **anthropocentric**, or human-centered, relationship with the environment, perceiving nature as something to master. Nature is believed to be inexhaustible and hence able to be used with impunity to serve humankind. Consumption is equated with success. This is consistent with the Judeo-Christian belief in humanity's dominion over the earth. Western culture thus perpetuates **human exceptionalism**, an attitude that humans are exempt from natural ecological limits (Dunlap and Catton 1994). Much of our progress through industrialization supports this notion that technology will allow us to overcome any environmental challenge. In contrast, the new ecological paradigm treats humans as part of the ecosystem or biosphere, one of many species that interact with the natural environment. Nature has limits that we must respect, and this may constrain economic development. The new ecological paradigm recognizes that human activity can have both intended and unintended consequences that shape social life and life on the planet.

Sometimes there are disagreements among scientists, businesses, interest groups, and policy makers over environmental issues such as climate change. How such problems as global warming are defined, interpreted, and understood depends on underlying cultural beliefs and values. On the far extreme is a small minority of climate deniers who question climate science or argue that global warming is part of the natural progression of the earth. You might not consider global climate change so bad if you also thought that extinction of some plant and animal life was an acceptable part of the evolutionary process of natural selection. Or if you thought that clean air, fossil fuels, or other natural resources were commodities in a free market and that nations must compete to use them and take responsibility for their consequences. For the most part, however, there is growing consensus that climate change is real and that it presents a pressing problem for humanity and the planet. A large majority of Americans, some 73 percent, believe that global warming is happening (Leiserowitz et al. 2018). About 62 percent also understand that global warming is caused primarily by human activity. These attitudes represent a marked change in public opinion from just a few years ago.

Environmental sociologists are interested in the processes that create attitude change and the relationship between attitudes and behavior. They want to understand why certain groups have become more "biocentric" (as opposed to anthropocentric), or more environmentally sensitive, and what inspires great numbers of people to participate in environmental movements.

DATA WORKSHOP

Analyzing Everyday Life

Student Attitudes on Environmentalism

"Sustainability," "environmentalism," and "being green" are all terms that refer to reducing human impact on the environment. Even though environmentally based social movements have become so mainstream that there is now an entire television channel, Planet Green, devoted to the topic, there are those who believe that environmentalists are alarmists who have invented issues like global warming, resource depletion, and growing landfills.

This Data Workshop asks you to examine the attitudes of your fellow college students in order to determine the extent of their environmental beliefs and behaviors. Do they believe that climate change has human causes? Do they recycle or conserve various resources and, if so, how? Do they worry about things like their "ecological footprint"?

For this Data Workshop you will be creating a survey about environmental attitudes and actions, administering it to your fellow students, and analyzing the findings. Refer to Chapter 2 for a review of this research method. Because this is a preliminary or pilot study, your sample population will be small, between five and ten respondents. Make sure to collect some demographic data such as age, gender, class, race/ethnicity, GPA, and major so that you can determine whether there is any relationship between backgrounds and attitudes.

In constructing the survey, consider using a Likert scale (agree–disagree format) to collect data on attitudes, as doing so will help streamline your analysis. Survey respondents can select the degree to which they agree or disagree with statements. Use the following statements as a starting place:

- Eating facilities on campus should use environmentally friendly products.

- I use environmentally friendly products at home as much as I can.

- I feel motivated to recycle.

- I use the recycling bins on campus.

- There are enough recycling bins on campus.

- If I see a piece of trash on the ground when I am outside, I will pick it up and dispose of it properly.

- Global warming is a threat to our planet.

- Humans and industry have contributed to global warming.

- I make attempts to reduce my carbon footprint by driving less and conserving energy in my daily life.

- Sustainability is an important issue for the entire world.

- If we don't reduce, reuse, and recycle, our world will face serious consequences.

- Environmentalism is a worthwhile cause.

There are two options for completing this Data Workshop:

PREP-PAIR-SHARE Once you have administered the survey, analyze your findings. What kinds of patterns can you identify? Are college students concerned about the environment? Does this concern translate into action? How do your findings confirm or refute any hypotheses that you might have had before beginning this study? What do you think your data reveal overall? Note the similarities and differences in your findings and those of your fellow group members. See if you can come up with a statement that identifies and incorporates the general patterns found in the data gathered by the entire group.

DO-IT-YOURSELF Compose and administer a survey to your sample population. Write a three- to four-page essay describing your research project and analyzing your findings. Attach your completed surveys and any notes to your paper.

THE ENVIRONMENTAL MOVEMENT

People have long been concerned about the relationship between humans and nature and about the impact of society on the environment. When people organize around these concerns, their collective efforts can have profound effects. When sociologists study the **environmental movement**, topics of interest include the origins of the groups involved, their internal organization and social network formation, their political role, and their presence at local, regional, national, and international levels. In this section, we will trace the four major eras in the history of the environmental movement in the United States while discussing major flashpoints in its development.

Most social scientists and historians date the beginning of the American environmental movement to the writings of Henry David Thoreau in the mid-1800s, especially *Walden; or, Life in the Woods*, concerning the rejection of urban materialism and the virtues of simple living (1854/1993). Thoreau has inspired many generations, and his central argument, about how humans affect the natural

ENVIRONMENTAL MOVEMENT a social movement organized around concerns about the relationship between humans and the environment

CONSERVATION ERA earliest stage of the environmental movement, which focused on the preservation of "wilderness" areas

MODERN ENVIRONMENTAL MOVEMENT beginning in the 1960s, the second major stage of the environmental movement; focused on the environmental consequences of new technologies, oil exploration, chemical production, and nuclear power plants

environment and thus must actively choose to preserve it, continues to be the backbone of environmental activism in the United States. While preservation or conservation remains a key focus, the environmental movement has become increasingly interested in how to respond to or prevent ecological disasters.

The late nineteenth and early twentieth centuries are often referred to as the **conservation era**; environmentalism in that time tended to reflect Thoreau's preservation argument. In this time, state and national parks, such as Yosemite (1864), Yellowstone (1872), and the Grand Canyon (1906), were established through legislative protection and funding. Congress approved the creation of the National Park Service in 1916 and continued to pass environmental laws to protect the wilderness and to regulate industries that impinged on it, such as mining and logging. Early environmental groups such as the Audubon Society (1886) and the Sierra Club (1892) that emphasized the conservation of wildlife and nature were also established around that time and are still in existence today.

From the mid-twentieth century on, environmentalism changed in response to several ecological disasters. For example, in 1948, in the town of Donora, Pennsylvania, twenty people died and more than 7,000 others were hospitalized when industrial waste that formed concentrated smog was released into the atmosphere and settled over the town, severely compromising the air quality for its residents. Congress responded to that ecological disaster (albeit late) by passing some of the first environmental legislation of the modern era, the Air Pollution Control Act of 1955.

The second era, the **modern environmental movement**, began in the 1960s in part as a response to Rachel Carson's landmark book *Silent Spring* (1962). Her book was an impassioned critique of the effects of pesticide use, specifically dichloro-diphenyl-trichloroethane, commonly known as DDT. The 1950s had witnessed an explosion of development

John Muir An early conservationist, Muir led the movement to establish national parks such as Yosemite.

Nuclear Disaster Evacuees from Fukushima, Japan, receive radiation scans. This nuclear plant suffered severe damage from an earthquake-generated tsunami in 2011.

in new chemicals such as fertilizers and pesticides, often hailed as revolutionary and miraculous in the practice of agriculture. But these same chemicals harmed or killed beneficial organisms and wildlife such as songbirds (hence the title of the book). There was even speculation that they could work their way up the food chain, becoming carcinogens in humans. Although the companies manufacturing DDT and other chemicals vigorously fought such allegations, public outcry eventually led to government hearings and an EPA ban on DDT in the United States and other countries (Bailey 2002). While there has been considerable debate about the validity of the science behind the DDT scare, it drew unprecedented public attention to environmental issues that had never been addressed before. As a result, environmentalism was able to find credibility in American society, and its practice has become an enduring force in public policy.

Unfortunately, many other ecological disasters occurred in the decades that followed. Some of the most notable were an oil spill in Santa Barbara in 1969 (Molotch 1970); the discovery of toxic waste in the Love Canal in 1978; the nuclear accident at Three Mile Island in 1979; the *Exxon Valdez* oil spill off the coast of Alaska in 1989; the discovery of a thirty-year oil spill at the Guadalupe Dunes in California in 1994 (Beamish 2002); and an even larger oil spill in the Gulf of Mexico in 2010. Each of these events elicited public outrage. Through a series of amendments and executive orders, the EPA was given broader powers that included the means to investigate ecological crises, organize cleanups, punish offenders, establish further regulations, and research environmentally friendly technologies.

The third era of the environmental movement, referred to as **mainstream environmentalism**, began in the 1970s. It emerged, in part, as a response to the Reagan administration's anti-environmental deregulation policies. National and international environmental organizations, such as the Sierra Club and Greenpeace as well as other watchdog groups, were becoming increasingly institutionalized. They began using well-crafted promotional campaigns and sophisticated political tactics to gain the attention of legislators and secure victories in their ongoing battles. Mainstream environmentalism evolved into a cluster of public interest groups, many of which had their own political action committees, or PACs, to lobby for positive legislative change. In addition to legal expertise, they developed economic and scientific expertise to support research, generate grants, and acquire land for preservation.

A link between the modern era and the mainstream era of environmentalism is **Earth Day**. The original event was conceived of by environmental activist and then senator Gaylord Nelson as both a "teach-in" and a protest gathering to express concerns about environmental issues. On the first Earth Day—celebrated April 22, 1970—20 million people participated. Earth Day is still celebrated nationally and internationally. Typically, it includes a variety of groups—environmentally friendly businesses, nonprofit organizations, local government agencies, and others—teaching people about ways to help the environment while celebrating their relationship to it.

MAINSTREAM ENVIRONMENTALISM beginning in the 1970s, the third stage of the environmental movement; characterized by enhanced organization, improved promotional campaigns and political tactics, and an increased reliance on economic and scientific expertise

EARTH DAY an annual event conceived of by environmental activist and former senator Gaylord Nelson to encourage support for and increase awareness of environmental concerns; first celebrated on April 22, 1970

Contemporary environmentalism, with its emphasis on grassroots efforts, represents a fourth era of the environmental movement. This movement emerged in the 1980s amid criticism that although mainstream environmental organizations were serving important functions in the overall effort, they were too accommodating to industry and government (Gottlieb 1997). **Grassroots environmentalism** is distinguished from mainstream environmentalism by its belief in citizen participation in environmental decision making. Its focus is often regional or local, and it can include both urban and rural areas. Grassroots groups are often less formally organized than their mainstream counterparts, which, in some instances, frees members from ineffective bureaucratic structures as they fight for issues of great importance to them. Grassroots environmentalism draws on a variety of ideologies, including feminist, Native, and spiritual ecologies, and cuts across ethnic, racial, and class lines.

NIMBY, which stands for "not in my back yard," was originally a derogatory term applied to those who complained about any kind of undesirable activity in their neighborhoods that would threaten their own health or local environment but were not concerned if it happened to people somewhere else. Now the term "NIMBY" has been appropriated by the contemporary grassroots environmental movement for the people "somewhere else" who are fighting against environmental degradation on their home turf, often without significant resources, to protect their families and surrounding communities.

Another expression of grassroots environmentalism is the **Green Party**. Established in 1984, the basic Green Party platform of ten principles includes a commitment to environmentalism, social justice, decentralization, community-based economics, feminism, and diversity. The environmental goal is a sustainable world in which nature and human society coexist in harmony. The Green Party seeks to be an alternative voice in political and policy debates that often challenges the mainstream Republican and Democratic parties and rejects corporate backing. The Green Party was among the first groups to endorse the Green New Deal, an ambitious proposal to transform the economy and tackle two big problems at once: social inequality and climate change. The Green New Deal aims to reduce greenhouse gases and shift from a reliance on nonrenewable energy sources to the use of renewable ones while also creating public works projects in the new green economy and employing workers from underserved communities.

The Future of the Environmental Movement

The **environmental justice** movement emerged as a response to environmental inequities, threats to public

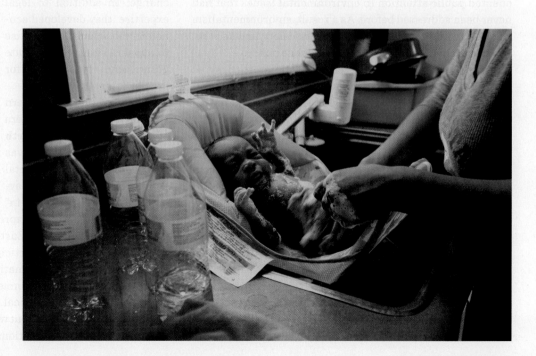

Flint Water Crisis A resident of Flint, Michigan, bathes her three-week-old baby son in bottled water after she learned that the city's tap water was contaminated with lead.

health, and the differential enforcement and treatment of certain communities with regard to ecological concerns. Those living in poverty and other minority communities are disproportionately at risk and bear a greater portion of the nation's environmental problems. For example, Flint, Michigan, which is still dealing with the consequences of lead-contaminated water, is a majority African American city whose population has a poverty rate of over 40 percent. The term **environmental racism** is applied when an environmental policy or practice negatively affects individuals, groups, or communities based on class, race, or ethnicity (Bullard 1993). For example, polluting facilities, including landfills and industrial facilities, are often located in low-income or minority neighborhoods (Mikati et al. 2018). Such communities may lack the political clout or economic means to buffer or defend themselves from such exposure. Those fighting against environmental racism maintain that access to environmental equality, or living in a healthy environment, is a basic human and civil right.

The Dakota Access Pipeline (DAPL) protests are an example of a movement for environmental justice. The pipeline was a project of a Texas-based oil company, Energy Transfer Partners, and was meant to carry oil from a North Dakota fracking field to a storage facility in southern Illinois. The original plan was to have the pipeline go through Bismarck, North Dakota. The Army Corps of Engineers, however, altered the route because of its additional length and the potential for serious consequences in the event of a spill; it was too close to municipal water sources, homes, and protected wetlands. So the route was revised to instead pass under the Missouri River near the water sources for the Standing Rock Reservation, home of several bands of Sioux Nation natives.

This did not sit well with the Standing Rock Sioux. Why should their community shoulder the risk of a spill? In protest, one family set up camp at the proposed construction site in April 2016. Soon hundreds and eventually thousands of protesters made Sacred Stone Camp their home. In addition, millions of Americans signed petitions seeking a halt to construction. Lawsuits and injunctions were filed, environmental impact statements were requested, and demonstrators chained themselves to pieces of heavy equipment, all in hopes that they would be able to reroute the pipeline away from the tribes' water supplies. Standing Rock protesters and their supporters (including senators Bernie Sanders and Dianne Feinstein, as well as activists such as the Rev. Jesse Jackson and actress Shailene Woodley) saw this as an unmistakable case of environmental racism: A heavy-polluting industry prevailed over a long-suffering Native community because of the political and economic power of its largely white allies, including a "pro-business" president.

Research on environmental justice is growing in importance as an area of scholarship within environmental sociology (Harlan et al. 2015). Sociologist Robert Bullard is considered the founding figure in this area. His landmark

Stand with Standing Rock Thousands of people gathered on the Standing Rock Reservation in North Dakota to protest the construction of a 1,200-mile oil pipeline that would pass underneath the Missouri River, the primary water source for a number of Native American tribes.

book *Dumping in Dixie: Race, Class, and Environmental Quality* (1990) examined the economic, social, and psychological effects associated with locating noxious facilities (such as landfills, hazardous-waste dumps, and lead smelters) within lower-income African American communities, where significant opposition was less likely. Bullard's work provided the foundation for environmental justice and has inspired a new generation of researchers seeking to advance the cause.

Environmental justice groups are making significant headway in changing government and industry policy and have won important court victories (Bullard, Johnson, and Wright 1997; Kaczor 1996). The EPA was charged with creating the Office of Environmental Justice (OEJ) to address the disproportionate impact of environmental hazards on vulnerable and overburdened communities. In 2019, the U.S. Senate formed the first Environmental Justice Caucus, led by senators Tammy Duckworth, Cory Booker, and Tom Carper. Recently, a lawsuit arguing for the constitutional right for a safe and livable climate has been making its way through the federal court system. The case of *Juliana v. United States* alleges that the government has violated the rights of twenty-one young plaintiffs by allowing for the continued use of fossil fuels, which contribute to climate change (Rosen 2019). Whatever the decision, it marks a new era of awareness and activism for climate justice.

ENVIRONMENTAL RACISM
any environmental policy or practice that negatively affects individuals, groups, or communities because of their race or ethnicity

Sustainability

The study of **sustainability** (or sustainable development) is among the most recent areas of environmental sociology, having emerged in the 1990s, and it continues to generate some controversy (McMichael 1996). The idea of sustainability was popularized in a United Nations World Commission on Environment and Development (1987) report titled "Our Common Future," often referred to as the Brundtland Report. Sustainability is a broad concept that tries to reconcile global economic development with environmental protection. It is based on the premise that the development aspirations of all countries cannot be met by following the path already taken by industrialized nations; the world's ecosystems cannot support it. Yet, since improving the conditions of the world's poor is an international goal, we must find ways to promote economic growth that both respect social justice and protect the environment, not only in the present but for future generations as well (Agyeman, Bullard, and Evans 2003; Humphrey, Lewis, and Buttel 2002).

One way to grasp the magnitude of supporting humans on the planet is the **ecological footprint**, an estimation of how much land and water area is required to produce all the goods we consume and to assimilate all the waste we generate (Wackernagel and Rees 1996). The current ecological footprint of the average American, approximately 20 acres, represents about five times the global average share of the earth's resources (for more information, check out the online Ecological Footprint Explorer). Compare that to someone from China, whose ecological footprint is approximately 8 acres, or someone from Haiti, with a little over 1.5 acres. Modern industrialized countries are overusing resources at an alarming rate: We would need 1.7 planet earths to support the world's population if everyone else were to adopt the consumption habits of the average American (Lu 2017).

Working toward sustainable development is a challenge. We have to find ways to meet the needs of a growing world population—for food, shelter, health care, education, and employment—while ensuring we sustain nature and the environment, whether that is freshwater, clean air, wildlife populations, natural resources, or nontoxic communities. It is even more important to work toward sustainability as we become increasingly globalized and have to think about the rest of the world and far into the future (Holdren, Daily, and Ehrlich 1995).

Some solutions toward sustainability are already being implemented. These include lifestyle modifications such as engaging in voluntary simplicity, recycling, practicing vegetarianism and veganism, buying organic foods, and using goods or services from environmentally friendly and fair trade companies. Others are modifications to our infrastructure, such as green building, ecological design, xeriscape (water-conserving) gardening, and land conservation. Digital technology is being employed to measure soil conditions from satellite data and to track fish populations through facial recognition ("fishface") software—all to better manage and enhance sustainable food production (McPeek 2018). Meanwhile, some state and local governments are enforcing stricter environmental standards and regulations than those imposed at the federal level. The United States Climate Alliance is one such bipartisan coalition; member states are committed to upholding the goals of the Paris Agreement and reducing greenhouse gas emissions. Every little bit makes a difference: Northern Illinois University, like many other colleges, gives entering first-years their own reusable water bottles to refill at "hydration stations" all over campus, keeping tons of plastic out of landfills.

SUSTAINABILITY economic development that aims to reconcile global economic growth with environmental protection

ECOLOGICAL FOOTPRINT an estimation of the land and water area required to produce all the goods an individual consumes and to assimilate all the waste an individual generates

Closing Comments

In this chapter, we have crossed a huge terrain—from population through urbanization to the environment. We hope that you can now see the connection among these three seemingly disparate areas of study. Human population has grown throughout history, particularly in the past 200 years. The rate at which the population increases is influenced by both biological and social factors. Where all these people live has also changed over time. As more of them locate in urban areas, cities play a key role in how we inhabit the world and what kind of world that becomes. The billions of people inhabiting the planet are part of an ecosystem, and they continue to have an impact on it. The natural environment both affects and is affected by human activity. So population, urbanization, and the environment are intimately related. There is a mutual effect and interdependence among them, where trends and changes in one reverberate through the others. As residents of planet earth, we all take part in the dynamic, not only enjoying or suffering current realities but also creating future ones.

Let's Talk More

1. Predictions about population growth or shrinkage vary sharply between neo-Malthusians and anti-Malthusians. How many children would you like to have? What kinds of social conditions lead to people having larger or smaller families?

2. Do you prefer to live in a dense urban area or a more lightly populated suburban one? What are some of the advantages and disadvantages of each?

3. Sociologists describe the problems associated with the environment in terms of consumption and waste. How are these two types of environmental problems connected? Describe something you've consumed recently in terms of the resources used to produce it and the waste (or pollution) it created.

Let's Explore More

1. **Film** Andersen, Kip; and Kuhn, Keegan, dirs. *Cowspiracy: The Sustainability Secret*. 2014.

2. **Article** Lequieu, Amanda McMillan. 2017. "'We Made the Choice to Stick It Out': Negotiating a Stable Home in the Rural, American Rust Belt." *Journal of Rural Studies*, vol. 53: 202–213.

3. **Blog Post** Sternheimer, Karen. "Micro Meets Macro: Gender Selection and Population Problems." *Everyday Sociology* (blog). July 2, 2018. *http://WWNorton.com/rd/b3Z7Y.*

CHAPTER 16

Social Change

Have you ever wanted your own personal robot that could order groceries, do your laundry, or drive you safely home from a party? Well, you're about to get your wish. This future is coming thanks to a few related technological advancements. It starts, of course, with the Internet and all of us having the ability to be online all the time. We use the Internet to do a dizzying array of things, from networking on social media, to shopping, to doing business and schoolwork, to streaming movies, TV, and music. Cloud computing is increasingly how we access, store, and manage our digital lives. You no longer need a computer or a hard drive when everything is hosted on a remote server like Apple iCloud or Google Drive. Now your term paper is safe in the cloud, no excuses.

Along with the Internet, we now have the Internet of Things (IoT). It's a system in which technological devices, such as smartphones and household gadgets, are able to "talk" to each other and exchange information. There's a huge market for "smart" consumer goods, such as thermostats that auto-adjust to the user's preferred temperature, lights that go on and off at preprogrammed times, and washer and dryer machines that communicate to coordinate their cycles. There are already way more "things" connected to the Internet than there are people in the world. Approximately 18 billion devices were connected to the Internet in 2017, and an estimated 30 billion will be connected by 2022 (Ericsson 2017).

Developers have found more and more ways to utilize smart technology, which relies on inter-device communication, creating endless possibilities for the IoT. For example, there's been an explosion of interest and investment in developing self-driving cars that communicate with GPS systems for navigation and are equipped with external sensors to assess driving hazards and weather conditions. Tesla was an early leader in the race to bring the driverless car to market. Tech firms such as Google and Intel and ride-sharing company Uber have also jumped into the race (Davies 2017).

Of course, when you interact with your smart home or driverless car, you won't need an actual life-sized robot anymore; instead, you'll be talking with a chatbot, your digital personal assistant. A chatbot is software that you chat with to help get complex tasks done. It will replace a lot of your current technology, like web browsers and apps, and will work across all platforms and devices, including the IoT. You might be utilizing an early version of this technology already, but Apple's Siri and Amazon's Alexa are just the beginning. Eventually, chatbots will become master-bots, able to connect and coordinate many aspects of your life and revolutionize your relationship to smart devices.

If you're like a lot of people, you welcome this onslaught of innovation. But it's important to stop to consider where all this technology is leading us. Our connectedness, what people appreciate so much about the Internet and their smart devices, is also creating new forms of risk. We are already confronting some of the problems of living online—viruses, ransom ware, invasions of privacy, cyberbullying, and credit card and identity theft. But a new class of problems linked to technology may be even more dangerous. Large-scale cyberattacks in the form of data breaches, leaks, or malware pose a serious threat to our social institutions and infrastructure. Hackers have already infiltrated major corporations (Sony and Verizon), universities (UCLA and New York University), social networks (LinkedIn and Yahoo), and federal agencies (the CIA, FBI, and NSA).

So what does all this mean? We're still finding out. As new technologies are being developed and adopted at an increasingly rapid pace, we can see both the promise and the risk of social change. Your automated home and driverless car have the potential to revolutionize your world—or bring it to a screeching halt. It all depends on whose orders the bots are following. Social change is always happening, but due to the amazing technological advances of the twenty-first century, it's happening quite rapidly at the moment. Can the rest of society keep up with these technology-driven social changes? Do we even have a choice?

How to Read This Chapter

There are a couple of reasons why we are ending this book with a chapter on social change. The first is that, to paraphrase an old cliché, change is the only constant. It is happening everywhere, all the time, in myriad variations. One of your challenges after reading this chapter will be to identify some of these social changes and to understand their patterns, causes, and consequences.

The other reason is more personal: We hope that reading this chapter will motivate you to work for social change yourself. The study of sociology can sometimes be a bit disheartening, as we learn the many ways in which our lives are constrained by social forces and institutional structures. But this chapter helps us remember that C. Wright Mills's "intersection of biography and history" is a two-way street: While society shapes the individual, the individual can shape society. You have the power to bring about social change, especially when you work together with others who share your views, values, and visions for a better world. So we want you to read this chapter with optimism; by understanding the processes of social change, you will be better qualified to make it happen yourself.

WHAT IS SOCIAL CHANGE?

No doubt you've heard your parents, grandparents, or other older family members reflect on "the way things were" when they were children. Hard-to-imagine times such as those before indoor plumbing or television, or during the Great Depression or World War II, undeniably made older Americans' lives very different from your own. People born even one generation apart can have different overall life experiences as a result of ongoing processes of social change. Consider how different life was for your professors who grew up during the Cold War versus your own childhood experiences in a post–9/11 America, or how different you feel from your grandparents, who came of age without the Internet and smartphones. Our culture evolves over time, as do our social institutions—the family, work, religion, education, and political systems. Sociologists define the transformation of culture over time as **social change**.

It's easy to identify particular historical periods where major social transformation was unmistakable: the Renaissance, the French Revolution, the Civil War, the women's rights movement. But it's important to realize that social change is occurring at all times, not just at moments of obvious cultural or political upheaval. The rate at which it happens, however, varies over time, with some historical periods experiencing rapid social change and others experiencing more gradual change. Social scientists recognize several major "social revolutions"—periods of time during which large-scale social change took place so rapidly that the whole of human society was dramatically redefined. The Agricultural Revolution made it possible for previously nomadic peoples to settle in one place, store surplus food for future use, and sustain larger populations with the products of their farms, herds, and flocks. The Industrial Revolution altered the way people worked, produced, and consumed goods and lived together in cities. And the Information Revolution (which is ongoing) has launched us into cyberspace thanks to digital technology and the Internet, and again society is being transformed because of it (Castells 2014; Rainee and Wellman 2012).

In addition to the pace, other elements of social change vary as well. Some changes are deliberate or intended, while others are unplanned or unintentional. For example, the invention of the automobile brought about intended changes—like the ability to travel greater distances more efficiently—yet it also brought about unforeseen events, such as the pollution of the atmosphere and the deaths of more than 30,000 people every year in car accidents. Some social

> **SOCIAL CHANGE** the transformation of a culture over time

Little Rock Nine Some social changes, such as the integration of public schools, cause outcry.

ON THE JOB
Helping Professions: Agents of Social Change

Does it sometimes seem as though there's no possible way you could ever make a contribution to changing the world? You're just one person, after all, and you may not be rich, famous, or all that influential. Right now, your primary concerns probably include graduating and perhaps getting your teaching credential (or social work certification or nursing license) so you can get a job! Also possibly on the to-do list: find a life partner, start a family, maybe buy a house. But don't think that focusing on your personal goals means that you're totally out of the social change loop. The way you live your life can make a difference all by itself.

Many sociology majors enter what are termed helping professions; these include nursing, counseling, and teaching and can also include careers in the social service, nonprofit, and law enforcement sectors. If you do go into this type of profession, you will find that every individual encounter you have with a client, student, patient, or offender will be an opportunity to make a tiny step toward social change.

As a first-grade teacher, for example, you will be able to introduce students to the joys of reading—a contribution to overcoming illiteracy, even if it involves only twenty kids. As a public health nurse, you urge patients with tuberculosis to finish their courses of antibiotics or you vaccinate children against polio, diphtheria, and measles—and in doing so, you protect the community's health as well as the health of your patients. When, as a social worker or psychologist, you lead a therapy group for husbands who batter their wives, you have the opportunity to help change the behavior of these men—and to protect their children from continuing a generational cycle of violence. When, as a police officer, you help run your neighborhood's after-school youth programs, you give teenagers alternatives to crime and delinquency, and their choices affect the entire community. When, as a lawyer, you donate your services to a legal clinic that helps undocumented workers gain residency, work permits, and citizenship, you contribute to solving the problems associated with illegal immigration and help change the demographic makeup of your city, state, and country. And even when you volunteer at the adult education center, teaching a computer-training class just once a week, you give your students the opportunity to add a new set of skills to their résumés, find new jobs, and reduce your county's unemployment figures, even if minutely.

Your contributions to social change don't stop here—if you marry, where you choose to live, and what you teach your children or students all contribute to the ever-present, ongoing processes of social change. So you don't have to sail away on Greenpeace's *Rainbow Warrior* ship or join the Peace Corps to make a difference in the world—you can do so in your everyday life as a member of a helping profession, as a community volunteer, and as a parent.

 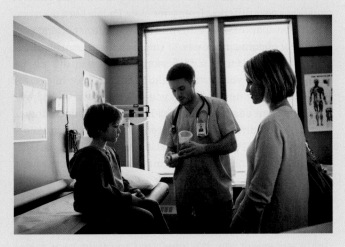

Helping Professions Teachers and nurses engage in small acts of social change in their everyday encounters with students and patients.

What Are the Sources of Social Change? Disasters such as the hurricane that ravaged Puerto Rico in 2017 can radically change the structures and cultures of the communities they destroy, and their impact can last for years.

changes are more controversial than others—the racial integration of public schools, for example, versus salsa's overtaking ketchup as America's top condiment—and some are more important than others. Most fashion trends have little lasting impact—remember the acid-washed jeans of the 1980s or grunge in the 1990s? Probably not. But some—like pants for women, miniskirts, and the bikini—have been extremely influential in their impact on gender roles in society.

So society is always changing, and the rates, intentionality, controversy, and importance of individual changes vary. But how does social change occur? One way is through a major physical event: Tornadoes, hurricanes, earthquakes, tsunamis, and volcanic eruptions can radically alter the structures and cultures of the communities they strike. Demographic factors also come into play; for instance, as the Baby Boomers have aged, American society has had to build schools and colleges (in the 1950s and 1960s), suburbs (in the 1960s, 1970s, and 1980s), retirement facilities (in the 1990s and 2000s), and long-term care facilities and hospitals (in the 2010s) to accommodate this huge population bulge. Another source of social change lies in discoveries and innovations, such as fire and the wheel. Try to imagine what your life would be like if humans had not figured out how to generate light and heat by striking sparks into kindling. Or, for that matter, imagine if the smartphone had never been invented.

Social change is often the result of human action. Jonas Salk, for example, developed a cure for polio, and Helen Keller overcame her own physical limitations to advocate for the rights of people living with disabilities. But our most important contributions to social change are made through the collective action of many: The civil rights movement, for example, fundamentally reshaped American society, as did the women's movement and the LGBTQ rights movement.

For this reason, we will spend a good portion of this chapter examining social movements, along with other types of collective behavior.

COLLECTIVE BEHAVIOR

When we join a group, we don't disappear as individuals. But we do tend to act differently in groups than we might alone. **Collective behavior** occurs when individuals converge, thus creating a group or crowd, whose members join in some sort of shared action. Crowds may form for different reasons, and people may gather for different purposes, but there is a common pattern to their behavior. While crowds may seem disorderly from the outside, collective behavior theories suggest that such occurrences are often organized and do maintain a certain amount of order.

Gustave Le Bon (1896) was one of the first social theorists to focus on the phenomenon of crowd behavior and what he called the "popular mind." He coined the term **contagion theory**, which suggests that when people come together, they get swept up in a crowd, which develops a "mob mentality." Le Bon likened such groups to herds of animals, where individuality and rational thought disappear and the external stimulus of the collective action takes over. So, in the case of rampaging soccer hooligans, contagion theory would argue that these fans have given their

COLLECTIVE BEHAVIOR behavior that follows from the formation of a group or crowd of people who take action together toward a shared goal

CONTAGION THEORY one of the earliest theories of collective action; suggests that individuals who join a crowd can become "infected" by a mob mentality and lose the ability to reason

rational thought over to a mob impulse and can no longer make independent decisions about their actions. But while the theory may seem useful when looking at cases like soccer hooliganism, it doesn't fully explain the wide range of collective behavior beyond the mindless mob.

A more recent idea gives us a better understanding. **Emergent norm theory** (Turner and Killian 1987) argues that collective behavior is not as uniform as Le Bon suggested, and that any number of factors can motivate people to participate in crowd activities. The underlying assumption here is that a group is guided by *norms* (shared cultural expectations for behavior) that emerge in interaction as the group responds to a situation and, as a result, the behavior of those in the crowd develops into collective action. An example of emergent norm theory in action is the recent ALS Ice Bucket Challenge, where people posted online videos in which they poured a bucket of ice on their own heads and challenged others to do the same as a fundraising ploy for medical research into amyotrophic lateral sclerosis (ALS). Millions participated, and their reasons likely varied—some had a personal connection to ALS, while others may have been motivated by merely wanting to look good on social media. So while it may appear that a group is one large, indistinguishable mass, the individuals who make it up can have varying understandings of what their roles are within the group as well as the meaning of their actions.

Collective behavior generally takes three forms: crowd behavior, mass behavior, and social movements. While these three types are discussed separately here, they are not mutually exclusive. In the real world, they may overlap whenever collective behavior actually occurs.

EMERGENT NORM THEORY a theory of collective behavior that assumes individual members of a crowd make their own decisions about behavior and that norms are created through others' acceptance or rejection of these behaviors

CROWD a temporary gathering of people in a public place; members might interact but do not identify with one another and will not remain in contact

Crowds

A **crowd** is formed when a large number of people come together, either on purpose or randomly. If you have ever strolled around a large city, you may have noticed a street performer (such as a mime, musician, or break dancer) trying to entertain passersby. In time, a crowd starts to develop. So despite the fact that those who stopped to watch had different reasons for walking down that street at that particular time, they have now become part of a crowd whose purpose is to be an audience for a street performer. As a crowd, they must adjust their behavior somewhat: Perhaps they stop conversing or put away their cell phones so as not to disturb the performer or those around them, clapping at the end of the performance. Even with this conformity of behavior, however, the fact remains that the individual motivation for joining the onlookers may vary. One person may have stopped because he was struck by the performer's talent, another because her feet hurt from walking. At a certain point, others may pause simply because they see the existing crowd and are curious.

While the street performer type of crowd comes about in a somewhat random way and is most often benign and temporary, other types of crowds can form in a more deliberate manner and lead to more highly expressive and consequential action. Let's look at two recent examples with very different trajectories: a street party in Isla Vista, California, and a protest rally in Baltimore, Maryland.

"Floatopia" began as a social gathering mostly for college students attending the University of California, Santa Barbara, and quickly grew into a popular annual event. The idea was for partygoers to bring rafts and other flotation devices to adjacent beaches for a day (and night) of fun. By 2011 the event was attracting over 10,000 people (thanks to Facebook), a number

A Tale of Two Cities While the people involved gathered together for different reasons, the events in both Isla Vista, California, and Baltimore, Maryland, illustrate how collective behavior can evolve into riots.

that overwhelmed the scarce facilities, leaving behind a massive amount of trash and human waste sullying the shore. As university officials moved to close the beaches, the event relocated to Del Playa, the bluff-top street above the beach. "Deltopia," as the event was renamed, grew even bigger, and in 2014, it erupted in violence when partygoers clashed with police trying to control the scene. Fires broke out, cars were demolished, bottles and bricks became weapons. The ensuing melee led to dozens of injuries (both students and police) and over a hundred arrests (Duke 2014). Such collective action can be characterized as a **riot**: a group of people engaged in disorderly behavior directed toward other people and/or property that results in disturbing the peace. After the riot in 2014, new strategies for crowd control were put into place. Deltopia still rages, but it is a smaller, more orderly event.

Not all examples of crowd behavior are fun and frivolous—some are serious and socially significant. On April 12, 2015, three white police officers in Baltimore pursued and apprehended twenty-five-year-old Freddie Gray after he reportedly made eye contact with the officers. Finding what they deemed an illegal switchblade knife clipped to Gray's pants, the officers proceeded to arrest Gray. Using her cell phone, a civilian onlooker captured the arrest on video, which showed officers dragging Gray, who was screaming in pain, into a police van. Upon arrival at the police station, Gray was already in a coma, having suffered a severe spinal injury. He died a week later in a local hospital.

When news of Gray's death became public, Baltimore residents gathered to protest outside the police station. In the days that followed, the protests escalated; what was initially a demonstration against a specific case of alleged police brutality became an expression of frustration about the city's wider set of social problems, including poverty, racism, crime, and years of unaddressed complaints about police abuse of communities of color. Eventually a full-scale riot developed, with looters breaking windows and throwing rocks while police and National Guard troops advanced and a state of emergency was declared. The violence lasted for ten days, finally quieting after Gray's funeral was held and a curfew was put in place. Citizens awoke to relative quiet on April 29 and began the work of cleaning up their neighborhoods, while still expressing a desire to see justice done in Freddie Gray's case. Supporters in cities such as Chicago, New York, and Philadelphia also held anti-police-brutality demonstrations. On May 1, Gray's death was ruled a homicide, and charges were filed against the three arresting officers, as well as three more officers (all black) who had participated in transporting Gray in the police van. While none of the officers was ultimately convicted, the case led to important policing reforms: Baltimore police now wear body cameras and their vehicles are equipped with cameras as well.

The events in both Isla Vista and Baltimore demonstrate how collective behavior can develop into riots. Furthermore,

they show how collective behavior can be both organized and chaotic, depending on the shared norms that emerge (McPhail 1991).

Mass Behavior

Mass behavior occurs when large groups of people not necessarily in the same geographical location engage in similar behavior. Mass behavior can range from buying a certain type of sneakers or getting a tattoo to playing Candy Crush Saga on your phone. Sociologists have focused on three areas of mass behavior in particular. Two areas, fads and fashions, should be familiar to you. The third too often goes unrecognized by those involved: social dilemmas.

FADS AND FASHIONS **Fads** are interests that are followed with great enthusiasm for a period of time. They can include products (such as electric cars or iPads), words or phrases ("selfie" or "lit"), clothing styles (aviator sunglasses or Supreme streetwear), hair styles (the fade or man bun), activities (goat yoga or juuling), gadgets (the Fitbit or AirPods), foods ("Impossible Burgers" or avocado toast), or even pets (purse-sized toy dogs or anything mixed with a poodle). For fads to continue for any length of time, social networks are necessary to spread the enthusiasm (Aguirre, Quarantelli, and Mendoza 1988; Gladwell 2000; Jones 2009). While fads tend not to result in lasting social change, they do follow certain social norms and can create a unified identity for those who practice them (Best 2006).

Dieting is a good example. Many Americans have followed such fad diets of the past as the all-grapefruit or the no-white-food diet; others have joined the low-carbohydrate fad of the Atkins and South Beach diets. During their heyday in the mid-2000s, the low-carbohydrate diets in particular had an impact on food industries, with grocery stores and fast-food chains trying to cater to the needs of their customers. Now, the paleo diet is the new low-carb approach, with adherents eating like "cavemen" did, which means lots of burgers but no buns. Gluten-free diets seem to be a more lasting trend. And juice cleanses and intermittent fasting are currently in vogue. Whatever comes next, it is likely that in wealthy countries like the United States, diet fads are sure to continue.

Another type of mass behavior is **fashion**: a widespread style of behavior and appearance. Fashion can mark you as belonging to a certain group; military fatigues and school

RIOT continuous disorderly behavior by a group of people that disturbs the peace and is directed toward other people and/or property

MASS BEHAVIOR similar behaviors engaged in by large groups of people without their necessarily being in the same place

FADS interests or practices followed enthusiastically for a relatively short period of time

FASHION the widespread custom or style of behavior and appearance at a particular time or in a particular place

A Fashion Empire Taraji P. Henson's character, Cookie, from the hit show *Empire*, is known for her high-fashion ensembles by designers like Gucci, Alexander McQueen, and Balmain.

uniforms are two examples. Like fads, certain fashions (such as extremely baggy clothes for boys and leggings for girls) can enjoy huge popularity for a time. Fashions come and go—and come back again. Fashion trends may take a cue from New York fashion week, the street styles of Miami, or the summer music festival scene. Photos of Kendall Jenner and Bella Hadid at Coachella have made festival wear such as wide bell bottom pants, fringe, and the cold-shoulder top the most de rigueur items for young women to rock.

Popular culture can also influence fashion. A look at two hit TV series is instructive. *Mad Men* (2007–2015) became popular not only for its great writing and acting but also for its celebration of the fashions of the 1950s and 1960s. The men's dapper suits and the women's full skirts and cinched waists brought retro glamour back to the world of fashion. When the hip-hop drama *Empire* debuted in 2015, it became an overnight sensation, as much for its story lines as for its fashionable music-biz characters. And it's not just the women who flaunt the flashy designer clothes; the men in the series are equally noticeable for their style. The real-life actors who play roles in these TV series are often closely followed in the tabloids, fashion magazines, and blogosphere, where fans like to critique or emulate their styles, both on-screen and off.

A whole industry has grown up around the consumer's desire to have those same looks the same moment they become popular. Fast-fashion brands such as Zara, Forever 21, H&M,

SOCIAL DILEMMA a situation in which behavior that is rational for the individual can, when practiced by many people, lead to collective disaster

TRAGEDY OF THE COMMONS a type of social dilemma in which many individuals' overexploitation of a public resource depletes or degrades that common resource

Topshop, and Uniqlo quickly produce inexpensive knock-offs of the most current fashion trends for the mass market. These brands take advantage of a global supply chain that enables them to inexpensively manufacture trendy, up-to-date clothes, right when they're most popular. So if you can't make it to Bonnaroo, you can always buy what the festival-goers were wearing at your local fast-fashion retail store just a week or two later.

SOCIAL DILEMMAS In the third category of mass behavior, called a **social dilemma**, behavior that is rational for an individual can lead to collective disaster. Let's take an example that's familiar to everyone: getting stuck in a traffic jam. You creep along slowly for what seems like forever and finally arrive at the source of the holdup. It's an accident, with two cars, a police cruiser, and an ambulance pulled over to the shoulder. But the accident isn't even on your side of the freeway, and there's nothing blocking your lanes of traffic. The holdup on your side is a result of everybody slowing down to get a good look. If they had just kept on driving at their normal speed, there wouldn't be a traffic jam. So what do you do when you finally get up to the scene of the accident? You slow down and take a look, too.

When many people make that same (seemingly) rational decision (to slow down for only a few seconds), the cumulative effect causes a kind of collective disaster (a traffic jam). As social beings, we deal with such situations almost daily, yet rarely do we see how best to handle them. According to many social thinkers, going all the way back to philosopher Thomas Hobbes (1588–1679), we live in a world governed by self-interest. How is our self-interest balanced with the interests of the collective? Social dilemmas help us understand this calculation.

There are two classes of social dilemmas. The first is known as a **tragedy of the commons**. In 1968, Garrett Hardin wrote an essay describing why this kind of dilemma emerges in society. He begins with the classic example of the "commons," which in the past served as a pasture shared by the whole community and on which everyone could graze their livestock. Because access to the commons was free and without restriction, each individual had an incentive to put as many head of livestock on the commons as possible, thereby increasing his own personal gain. But as everyone made that same decision, the commons inevitably became overgrazed. When a common resource is used beyond its carrying capacity, it eventually collapses, becoming totally incapable of supporting any life at all. This is the tragedy—when the commons is ruined. In a tragedy of the commons, the benefit is to the individual but the cost is shared by all.

The tragedy of the commons applies to recent history as well. Our natural resources, such as water, air, fossil fuels, forests, plants, and animals, might all be considered similar to a commons. In the case of the U.S. fishing trade, especially, we have seen how, as Hardin put it, "freedom in a commons

Tragedy of the Commons Abalone divers rest after climbing up a cliff. Since the 1990s, abalones have all but disappeared from the central coast of California due to overfishing.

brings ruin to all" (1968, p. 1244). For example, Dr. Stein remembers living in Santa Barbara in the late 1970s, when local abalones were plentiful. Divers off the California coast and around the Channel Islands could make a good living harvesting these mollusks along rocky shorelines. Any good seafood restaurant regularly offered abalone steaks on its menu, and a casual beachgoer might find abalone shells strewn along the sand. By the 1990s, however, abalones had all but disappeared. As each diver reached the same conclusion—that catching as many abalones as possible would increase his own profits—and more divers moved into the same fishing territory, the abalones were no longer able to regenerate their stocks and were eventually depleted to near extinction.

A partial solution is now in place with the designation of the Channel Islands National Marine Sanctuary, a federally protected area where commercial fishing is prohibited. In a variety of similar cases, such as the lobster trappers off the New England coast, regulatory agencies have had to step in and place restrictions on the territories and amount of yields allowed. Otherwise, a tragedy of the commons is likely to ensue. We might also consider social as well as natural resources as similar to a commons. For example, when too many people crowd the freeways at rush hour or throw litter out the window of their cars, the result is the commons in ruin.

So what can we do to solve these problems? If we could somehow increase the number of abalones in the sea or the number of lanes on the freeway, that would help solve two of them, but only temporarily. At some point, use overwhelms supply. To Hardin, social dilemmas are a "class of human problems which can be classified as having 'no technical solution'" (1968, p. 1243). What he means is that science or technology alone cannot solve the problems. The solutions must come from members of society: People will have to change their behavior.

The other class of social dilemmas is called a **public goods dilemma**, in which individuals must contribute to a collective resource from which they may not ever benefit. Blood banks are a good example. Because human blood can't be stored for much longer than a month at a time, many people must volunteer to donate blood regularly in order to keep supplies steady. Blood donors can be viewed as helping to create what is referred to as a "public good," in this case a blood bank. What motivates these people, on average some 9.5 million a year, to contribute something vital to themselves for which they may never receive anything in return? Everyone is equally entitled to draw from the blood bank regardless of whether they have ever given blood. People who take advantage of a public good without having contributed to its creation are called "free riders." In a public goods dilemma, unlike a tragedy of the commons, the cost is to the individual but the benefit is shared by all.

So how do we get people to contribute to a public good if they are not required to do so? There are numerous examples of this social dilemma in everyday life, as you know if you've ever witnessed a membership drive on public radio or public television. These noncommercial networks must appeal to individuals to contribute money so that they can continue to produce and broadcast programs. But regardless of whether people respond to the pledge drive, as free riders they can still tune in to the station anytime at no cost. Public goods dilemmas are also a class of human problems for which there are no technical solutions. This is why the government requires us to make certain contributions, in the form of taxes, in order to create such public goods as roads, schools, and fire departments. But there are many other types of public goods, such as blood banks, that only individuals can create through their own voluntary contributions.

> **PUBLIC GOODS DILEMMA** a type of social dilemma in which individuals incur the cost to contribute to a collective resource, though they may never benefit from that resource
>
> **SOCIAL MOVEMENT** any social group with leadership, organization, and an ideological commitment to promote or resist social change

By examining social dilemmas, we are presented with a dramatic example of mass behavior. We begin to see how seemingly small individual acts add up and cumulatively shape society. So the next time you are faced with a problem like where to throw your litter or whether to give blood, ask yourself what kind of collective outcome you would like your behavior to contribute to.

SOCIAL MOVEMENTS

Social movements are another form of collective behavior. Because they typically involve more resources and last a longer time, social movements are a particularly important part of social change. For many Americans, the term **social movement** is inextricably linked to thoughts of long-haired hippies, Volkswagen buses, and the antiwar protests of the

Emerging Social Movements
Black Lives Matter, an example of a new progressive social movement, was formed in 2013 in the wake of the acquittal of George Zimmerman in the shooting death of unarmed black teenager Trayvon Martin.

1960s. They may not think of the Nineteenth Amendment to the U.S. Constitution (giving women the right to vote), women's lib, the AFL-CIO workers union, Pentecostalism, the Revolutionary War, or Nazism—and yet all of these were, at the time of their inception, rightly termed "social movements."

So what precisely is a social movement? Does the term as accurately describe the efforts of liberals to elect a Democrat to Congress as it does the efforts of peace activists to end a war? The answer is no. According to Perry and Pugh (1978), "Social movements are collectives with a degree of leadership, organization, and ideological commitment to promote or resist change" (p. 221); Meyer (2000) adds that social movements "challenge cultural codes and transform the lives of their participants" (p. 39). A political campaign cannot usually be described as a social movement, because although it may be considered an organized collective with leadership and (sometimes) ideological commitment, and may indeed transform the lives of its participants, its purpose is not to fundamentally alter the status quo. Antiwar protesters, on the other hand, are usually trying not only to stop a specific violent conflict but also to change cultural support of war as an accepted means of solving disputes.

Promoting and Resisting Change

Because society is constantly changing, new social movements are always on the horizon, and even long-standing ones change their goals, strategies, and organizational forms over time. For example, American feminism has taken multiple forms during the past 150 years. Contrast the focus in the early twentieth century on voting rights for women with the

1960s era's broader concerns with equal opportunity and "liberation" from the constraints of sexism, and then with the crusade in the 1990s to include previously excluded groups like minority women. Greater emphasis on international women's rights followed in the 2000s, and finally, in the 2010s, some feminists started to agitate over transwomen's rights as part of the movement. Feminism's self-definition, public profile, objectives, and tactics have changed over time in response to the movement's own successes and failures, and in response to issues in the larger society—for example, in 2017, the #MeToo movement arose to combat sexual assault and harassment in response to some high-profile cases in Hollywood.

You may be involved yourself in social movements that didn't even exist in your grandparents' or parents' generation (or even ten years ago). For example, Critical Mass (cyclists who ride through city streets in large groups each month to protest an automobile-centric society), Straight Edge (nonviolent, drug-free, politically aware, and sometimes even vegan punk rockers who reject promiscuous youth cultures), PETA (People for the Ethical Treatment of Animals, which campaigns against meat, leather and furs, animal experimentation, and other forms of cruelty), and anti-vaxxers (a movement of parents who claim health reasons as justification for their refusal to vaccinate their children against preventable diseases like mumps and measles)—these movements have taken shape in just the past few decades. Hacktivists (hackers who use technology to spread subversive messages) have emerged as a social movement more recently; groups such as WikiLeaks, Anonymous, and LulzSec are among the most visible. The Black Lives Matter (BLM) movement came onto the scene in 2013 with a hashtag on social media in response to the acquittal of George Zimmerman in the shooting death of black teenager Trayvon Martin. Since then, BLM has grown in influence and numbers, becoming a nationwide movement. You have different opportunities for **activism** because you live in a different world than your parents did—even if you're still living in the same town.

Some emerging social movements are actually **regressive**, or reactionary; that is, they explicitly resist certain social changes, working to make sure things stay the same or even move backward to earlier forms of social order. Further along the extreme right are some reactionary hate groups like the Council of Conservative Citizens, a white supremacist group that wants to stop the ethnic and religious integration of American society and create a homogeneous, all-white society. Dylann Roof—the perpetrator of a brutal attack on a historic black church in Charleston, South Carolina, that claimed the lives of nine parishioners in June 2015—was reportedly inspired by the Council of Conservative Citizens and the white supremacist website the Daily Stormer. That website has been credited with inspiring others to commit hate crimes, including James Alex Fields Jr., who drove into a crowd of counterprotesters at a Unite the Right rally in Charlottesville, Virginia, killing one and injuring many others. The American Border Patrol is a militia group of private citizens who patrol and surveil the U.S.-Mexico border in an attempt to deter and disrupt the passage of illegal immigrants; they are characterized as an extremist group that blames immigrants for a slew of contemporary problems in the United States.

Other regressive movements aren't necessarily motivated by prejudice or hatred of diversity. The voluntary simplicity movement urges members to downsize in all areas of their lives—consumption, time at work, hours in front of the TV or computer screen, impact on the environment—in the belief that returning to a simpler approach to life will allow them more personal freedom and will benefit society in the long run by conserving resources and reducing stress. Similarly, the Slow Food movement was founded as a radical response to the "McDonaldization" of world cuisines. It now focuses on fresh, local, traditional foods, ethically sourced, prepared with care, and served in an atmosphere of calm and hospitality—the polar opposite of overprocessed, reheated burgers and fries served in a paper bag and eaten in the car. Slow Food has even influenced the Chipotle restaurant chain, whose corporate philosophy—and menu—try to align with the values of that movement.

The "rural rebound" that started in the 1990s, in which urban residents moved to nonmetropolitan areas in unprecedented numbers, is a type of demographic change that seems, on its face, to represent a regressive, back-to-basics movement as well (Johnson 1999). But a rural rebound doesn't necessarily mean that people have returned to declining rural industries, such as farming or mining. The rebound occurred, and still continues today, at least in part because of **progressive**, or forward-thinking, social change. New technologies have made rural living less isolating and facilitated new ways of working. The Internet allows people to work from anywhere in the world, which means that high-powered stockbrokers don't need to live in Manhattan and work in a "pit" on Wall Street. They can move to Eagle County, Colorado, or Walworth County, Wisconsin, and enjoy cheaper real estate, less traffic and crime, and more natural beauty while still performing their jobs. Along with better broadband service, federal assistance and investment in rural communities have increased home ownership and added infrastructure such as schools, hospitals, and public spaces that likewise improve rural quality of life (Vilsack 2016).

Emerging social movements, whether progressive, regressive, or some combination of both, will undoubtedly change the social landscape over time. If your activism is successful—and even if it isn't—then the social world will be a different place by the time the next generation comes of age. Imagine what kinds of activism they will be able to engage in then.

> **ACTIVISM** any activity intended to bring about social change
>
> **REGRESSIVE** term describing resistance to particular social changes, efforts to maintain the status quo, or attempts to reestablish an earlier form of social order
>
> **PROGRESSIVE** term describing efforts to promote forward-thinking social change
>
> **MASS SOCIETY THEORY** a theory of social movements that assumes people join not because of the movement's ideals but to satisfy a psychological need to belong to something larger than themselves

Theories of Social Movements

We can safely say that most of the institutions with which we are familiar began as social movements. How did they arise? Why do people join them? And how do today's radicals become tomorrow's establishment? Several theories attempt to address these questions, but the assumptions behind them have evolved over time.

MASS SOCIETY THEORY Scholars working in the 1940s, 1950s, and early 1960s generally viewed social movements with suspicion—as "dysfunctional, irrational, and exceptionally dangerous" (Meyer 2000, p. 37). People who joined a movement were thought to be attracted not by its ideals but by the refuge it offered "from the anxieties, barrenness, and meaninglessness of an individual existence" (Zirakzadeh 1997, p. 9). This explanation, labeled by sociologists as **mass society theory**, was not so remarkable when you consider that researchers in those decades had witnessed the effects of Nazism, Fascism, Stalinism, and McCarthyism, all of which originated as social movements and eventually devastated millions of lives (Zirakzadeh 1997).

RELATIVE DEPRIVATION THEORY By the 1960s, however, a sea change had occurred, and a new generation of scholars

IN RELATIONSHIPS
Hashtag Activism: #NeverAgain and #EnoughIsEnough

Valentine's Day will never be the same for students at Marjory Stoneman Douglas (MSD) High School. On February 14, 2018, a former student walked onto the campus in Parkland, Florida, and started shooting, killing fourteen students and three staff members and wounding seventeen others. It was the deadliest high school shooting in U.S. history; it also sparked a widespread social movement to reduce gun violence by supporting gun-control legislation at the state and federal levels.

Founded the day after the shooting by MSD survivors Cameron Kasky, Alex Wind, and Sofie Whitney, the grassroots student group called Never Again MSD quickly added others who would become well-known activists, including fellow survivors Emma González and David Hogg. Within days of the shooting, they had recruited thousands of supporters on social media and had begun planning a national day of action, all under the hashtag slogans #NeverAgain and #EnoughIsEnough. Core members of the group conducted countless media interviews in which they criticized politicians who responded with "thoughts and prayers," demanding instead that those same politicians take legislative action to make guns harder to get. The activists also emphasized that political leaders should stop taking contributions from the National Rifle Association (NRA), a powerful national gun-rights lobbying group.

Twitter and Facebook spread the group's hashtags like a virus. Less than a week after the shooting, the students had organized a march on the Florida statehouse while legislators inside voted down an assault weapons ban. A rally occurred at the state capitol the next day, starting with just over 100 people and soon swelling to over 3,000 as the MSD students were joined by other students and supporters from around the state, all expressing their disgust with their state representatives and chanting, "Enough is enough." The momentum continued from there. Never Again MSD has been credited with pressuring a number of big corporations to dissociate themselves from the NRA (many, such as Hertz and Budget car rental companies and Delta and United Airlines, had offered discounts to NRA members). They hosted gun-control rallies, town halls, and voter registration events all over the United States and continued to put pressure on elected representatives by calling their offices, meeting with them, and asking pointed questions of them in televised debates.

Never Again's biggest event was the national March for Our Lives, held in Washington, DC, on March 24, 2018. In addition to the DC march there were hundreds of companion marches held around the country and the world that day, with total attendance estimated in the millions. In the aftermath of the march, Never Again claimed a number of legislative victories, including in Florida, which in May 2018 passed a package of gun-restriction laws for the first time in decades.

Never Again MSD went from online expression to real-life movement in a remarkably short period of time. The group's viral spread could be accomplished only in the Digital Age, but its other strategies and tactics were remarkably old-fashioned: marching, registering voters, and engaging with political representatives. Taking to Facebook and Twitter within hours of the shooting, these young people were able to mobilize an amazing array of social movement resources quickly and effectively. Those who question the efficacy of hashtag activism can no longer doubt that the Internet can successfully connect us to millions of others who share our vision (whatever that vision may be—you don't have to be a gun-control activist to use these types of tactics) and that social media have arrived as an invaluable resource in the process of social change.

Activists Too Young to Vote Parkland shooting survivors Emma González and David Hogg participate in a panel discussion titled "#NeverAgain: How Parkland Students are Changing the Conversation on Guns."

researching the whos, hows, and whys of social movements were inclined to be more sympathetic. After all, the 1960s saw the rise and relative success of the antiwar and civil rights movements. Studies done on student protesters in the 1960s showed that the protesters "were more likely than their less active colleagues to be politically oriented, socially engaged, and psychologically well adapted" and that "participation in nonconventional politics tend[ed] to be an addition rather than an alternative to conventional means of participation" (Meyer 2000, pp. 37, 42). In other words, despite the assumptions of theorists working in the mid-twentieth century, activists were not disaffected loners but were instead highly engaged individuals seeking to address perceived injustices on several fronts. While people of color may have been alienated from the larger white society, they were certainly not isolated "joiners" who took up with social movements simply to "satisfy some kind of psychological need" (Meyer 2000, p. 37). The civil rights movement and others were practical political responses to inequality and oppression and provided opportunities for the oppressed to "redistribute political and economic power democratically and fairly" (Zirakzadeh 1997, p. 15). This explanation is called **relative deprivation theory** because it focuses on the actions of deprived or oppressed groups seeking rights already enjoyed by others in society; they are deprived relative to other groups.

Interestingly, the poorest and most oppressed people tend not to participate in social movements, despite their relative deprivation. For these individuals, the consequences of participation may be too high, and they may not have the resources necessary to join in (Perry and Pugh 1978; Zirakzadeh 1997). After all, if someone is working three jobs to support her family, it is unlikely that she has the time or energy to carry a sign in a street protest. There have been notable exceptions to this trend. In the American West during the 1960s and 1970s, migrant farm workers organized successfully under the leadership of Cesar Chavez. In the 1980s and 1990s, thousands of low-income janitors across the United States gained fairer wages and benefits by organizing unions as part of a Justice for Janitors campaign. And in the 2010s, low-wage workers in New York City (in industries such as retail, fast food, airport, and car washing) have continued to demand fair wages and the right to unionize (Lewis 2013; McGeehan 2015). The battle to establish a "living wage" (adequate to afford a decent standard of living) has spread to many other cities, including Seattle, San Francisco, and Los Angeles. At the same time, successful efforts have been countered in cities such as St. Louis, where new legislation has reinstated the (lower) minimum wage (Noguchi 2017), and by numerous states, such as Arizona, which recently attempted (but failed) to institute a lower minimum wage for students and younger workers.

A look at the history of voting rights in the United States shows the power of relative deprivation theory to explain certain types of social movements. For more than a hundred years, women and persons of color lobbied hard for the right to vote. (We could also turn this claim on its head by saying that for more than a hundred years, many white men fought hard to exclude women and persons of color from voting.) Women won the right to vote in 1919 with passage of the Nineteenth Amendment. To reach this point, suffragists spent decades protesting male-only voting through parades, written propaganda, debates, sit-ins, and hunger strikes. The suffrage movement, however, was primarily a white women's battle. At a rally in 1851, Sojourner Truth gave a famous speech ("Ain't I a Woman?") highlighting the exclusion of women of color from the movement. These women would have to wait until the Voting Rights Act of 1965 before they could legally vote.

Officially, African American males were granted the right to vote with the Fifteenth Amendment in 1870, but individual states effectively nullified this right by passing regulations requiring literacy tests, prohibitive poll taxes, and grandfather clauses (you could vote only if your grandfather had voted too) that specifically excluded them from voting. It wasn't until the 1965 Voting Rights Act was passed that all African American citizens gained the ability to exercise their constitutionally protected right to vote. The Voting Rights Act achieved significant inroads in protecting African Americans' right to vote, in part by requiring certain states to seek federal approval to change voting laws. In fact, it was so successful that the Supreme Court decided to remove that requirement in 2013. Not everyone has been in favor of that move: Critics of the decision argue that policies like voter ID, proof of citizenship, strict voter registration requirements, and limited early or mail-in voting discriminate against minority voters (Hurley 2013; Liptak 2013).

Still, neither the Voting Rights Act nor the Nineteenth Amendment is enough to secure voting rights for all Americans. To become a registered voter, you must be a U.S. citizen (either native born or naturalized), be at least eighteen years old, legally reside in the state in which you vote, and have an address of some kind. Most states do not allow ex-offenders, prisoners, or those designated mentally ill or incapacitated to vote.

Another tool that can be used to enhance or suppress the effects of various groups of voters is **gerrymandering**, or redistricting, whereby the officials in power at the state level deliberately redraw the borders of voting districts in order to advantage their political party. One type of gerrymandering, called "packing," is basically the voting equivalent of segregation: Put as many of the opposing party's voters in as few districts as possible, thereby limiting the

RELATIVE DEPRIVATION THEORY a theory of social movements that focuses on the actions of the oppressed groups seeking rights or opportunities already enjoyed by others in the society

GERRYMANDERING redrawing the boundary lines of state voting districts in order to advantage one political party over another

RESOURCE MOBILIZATION THEORY a theory of social movements that focuses on the practical constraints that help or hinder social movements' action

number of seats they will win. Another type, called "cracking," accomplishes the same goal by spreading the opposition voters thinly throughout a larger number of districts: In this case, their influence is diluted and the dominant party can win more seats. Both packing and cracking make for some oddly shaped districts. Michigan has one district that some have described as "Bart Simpson holding a fishing pole," and there's one in Maryland labeled the "Pinwheel of Death." These weird shapes string together neighborhoods that may have nothing at all in common in order to create voting blocs that advantage the party in power.

Gerrymandering is a creative—and legal—way to effectively disenfranchise one party and its associated demographic groups. If gerrymandering reduces the voting power of Democrats, that disproportionately disenfranchises women, people of color, and young people; if the voting power of Republicans is limited by gerrymandering, that disproportionately disenfranchises whites, men, and seniors.

RESOURCE MOBILIZATION Another way to look at social movements is by using **resource mobilization theory**. Here the focus is on how practical considerations such as recruitment, fundraising, and media coverage help or hinder social movements. The kind of society we live in has a lot to do with whether we are likely to join social movements, the tactics those movements will use, and whether the movements will succeed. For example, in a country like the United States,

with strong free-speech protections, anyone wanting to support reproductive rights can publish books and articles, march in the streets (with some restrictions), promote his or her views on social media, or start a letter-writing campaign to pressure lawmakers.

On the other hand, resource mobilization theory would hold that under a restrictive regime like that of the Taliban in Afghanistan, where peaceful protest is not an option, people are less likely to form and join social movements, and if they do, their tactics will look very different from those of activists in the United States and will be received very differently. In 2012, the Pakistani Taliban shot fourteen-year-old Malala Yousafzai in the head because she spoke out in favor of educating girls. She survived the attack and has since become an international symbol for women's rights, continuing her activism—from afar; it is too dangerous for her to return to her home country, where she is still wanted by the Taliban (Walsh 2013). In 2014, at just seventeen years old, Yousafzai became the youngest person to win the Nobel Peace Prize for her work. She continues to be a strong advocate for girls' education on the global stage.

In addition to a tolerant society, what social movements need is a long list of practical and human resources, without which it would be impossible to accomplish their goals. This list includes volunteers, funding, office space, phone banks, computers, Internet access, copy machines, and pens and pencils—as well as the know-how to put these resources into action. Social movements need participants, so recruitment is an important consideration. They also need money. Funding may go to support staff or pay for overhead, but much of what is raised will be spent on producing and soliciting media coverage to get the message out. Social media have become an important resource both for fundraising and for spreading the word. Small start-ups can use crowdfunding sites like Indiegogo and Kickstarter to raise money to get their business off the ground. A nascent social movement can begin organizing online, raising money via crowdfunding to run its operations while simultaneously raising awareness and support through social networks. For example, the Time's Up movement has raised more than $20 million on GoFundMe—the crowdfunding site's most successful campaign ever—for legal expenses for women and men who were subject to workplace sexual harassment.

Resource mobilization theory would say that however interesting or important a type of social change may be, no progress will be made unless certain practical resources are available. So if we consider the plight of women in Taliban-ruled parts of Pakistan or Afghanistan, for instance, we realize that some of the most basic human activities, such as reading and meeting together freely, are actually social movement resources that not everyone can take for granted. Protest and social movements have always been at the heart of American society and are likely to continue to define it in the future.

Malala Yousafzai While boarding the bus to school, Pakistani teenager Malala Yousafzai was shot by Taliban gunmen. In 2014, she was awarded the Nobel Peace Prize for her efforts to promote the education of women and girls across the globe.

DATA WORKSHOP

Analyzing Everyday Life

Activist Groups Get Organized

The day after Thanksgiving is also known as "Black Friday," the biggest shopping day of the year. On that day, which is thought of by many as the kickoff day to the holiday shopping season, retailers give incentives to customers by offering extended hours, tremendous discounts, and gifts. Customers sleep in parking lots waiting for the stores to open (often as early as 4 a.m.) and are so eager to buy merchandise at discounted prices that injuries and even deaths have resulted. Every year seems to bring another extreme case where someone is trampled to death by crowds rushing through the doors. From 2006 to 2016, ten deaths and 105 serious injuries were attributed to Black Friday.

In protest of the rampant consumerism of Black Friday, a group of social activists started "Buy Nothing Day." Adbusters, an anticonsumerist organization, promotes the event as "a day for society to examine the issue of overconsumption." The basic goal of Buy Nothing Day is to actually spend no money purchasing items on Black Friday, in order to raise awareness of the dangers of consumerism and overconsumption. For some, the idea of Buy Nothing Day has grown into a Buy Nothing Year. The Compact is an anticonsumerist group whose members pledge to go a year without buying anything new. Members are only allowed to purchase new underwear, food, and health and safety items, such as brake fluid and toilet paper. Other groups, like the Freegans, take a radical approach to consumerism and try to find everything for free. Websites like Freecycle and Buy Nothing Project help in the cause.

Such groups have much in common: They wish to counteract the negative global environmental and socioeconomic effects of U.S. consumerist culture and to simplify their lives. While it might seem extreme to most Americans to go an entire year without buying new items, many people find multiple benefits to living simply and, through their example, they are able to raise other people's consciousness about consumption, waste, and carbon footprints.

This Data Workshop asks you to analyze any activist group that is working for some kind of social change. You will be using existing sources to do a content analysis of various materials developed by the organization. Refer to Chapter 2 for a review of this research method. In

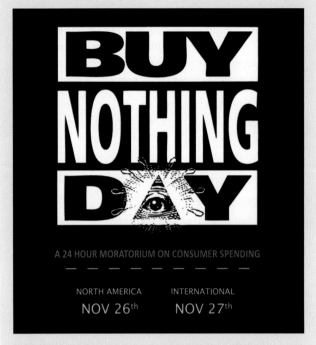

Anticonsumerism How do activist groups protest the excesses of consumerism?

particular, you will be looking at how the group works to promote and advance its agenda. Examine the group's use of various forms of media—including websites and social media as well as the more traditional radio, television, newspapers, magazines, brochures, or direct mail. Gather data by bookmarking links, taking screenshots or photos, making printouts, or composing informal notes about what you find. Once you have enough data to analyze, follow these steps:

1. Describe the activist group you chose. Identify the group's commitment to a larger social movement or cause, and discuss its particular goals.

2. How is the group attempting to use resource mobilization for its cause? What are its strategies regarding these three important activities?

   a. recruiting members and organizing supporters

   b. raising funds

   c. transforming public opinion and/or achieving change

3. Describe the group's media campaign. What different forms of media does the group use to convey its message? Which do you think is most successful? Least successful? Why?

4. In addition to the use of media, what other strategies does the group use to achieve its goals? For instance,

does the group organize rallies or protests or participate in community events? (These activities may be connected to larger media strategies; for example, a film screening or protest march might be advertised to attract greater support or news coverage.)

5. How effective is the group at convincing others to join the cause? What kind of reaction did the group elicit from you? How might the group improve its recruiting efforts?

There are two options for completing this Data Workshop:

PREP-PAIR-SHARE Collect your data and write some informal notes addressing the steps outlined earlier; bring these notes to class for reference. Partner with one or more students and present your findings. Compare your analyses and insights with others in your group.

DO-IT-YOURSELF Collect existing source data on your chosen activist group and follow the steps outlined earlier. Write a three- to four-page paper about the group's strategies, making specific reference to the materials it developed. Attach photos, screenshots, prints, links, or other relevant data to your paper.

Stages in a Social Movement

Social movements begin with a few ideas and some people who believe in them. How do they reach the point of marching in the streets (or recruiting members online)? They develop in stages, as identified by Armand Mauss (1975). Mauss described the first one as the "incipient" stage, when the public takes notice of a situation and defines it as a problem (Perry and Pugh 1978). People do not start organizing because they are content; rather, they "see a discrepancy, either real or perceived, between what they are getting and what they believe they should be getting" and decide to take action (Perry and Pugh 1978, p. 237).

For example, in the late nineteenth and early twentieth centuries, many laborers were frustrated over their long working hours, low wages, lack of free weekends, and unsafe working conditions. In response, they began to organize—or, in Mauss's words, to "coalesce," which is the second stage—and their movement gained momentum. Laborers, long an exploited segment of the workforce, drew on both traditionally accepted means of dissent, such as pushing for legislation that would improve working conditions, and tactics that were (at the time) "at the edges of political legitimacy," such as striking (Meyer 2000, p. 40).

Today, working conditions have greatly improved for many (though by no means for all) blue-collar workers, and unions, once considered marginal or radical, are now seen as part of the establishment. Mauss and others would argue that all successful social movements are eventually incorporated into institutions—that they become "bureaucratized" (third stage). Perry and Pugh assert that "in order to survive, social movements must adapt to their host society or succeed in changing it. When they are successful, they become social institutions in their own right" (1978, p. 265). To take another example, early American colonists rebelling against British rule were part of a social movement, but by the late 1700s, they had ceased to be radicals and had become part of the new nation's government.

A social movement's development can sometimes look a lot like failure; that is, one way or another, the movement will eventually "decline" (fourth stage). If it succeeds, it is

TABLE 16.1 Theory in Everyday Life

Perspective	Approach to Social Change	Case Study: The Environmental Movement
Structural Functionalism	Sometimes social change is necessary to maintain equilibrium and order in society.	Natural resources are necessary for the survival of society, so the growth of a social movement dedicated to the wise use and conservation of natural resources is functional for society.
Conflict Theory	Social change is the inevitable result of social inequality and conflict between groups over power and resources.	Environmental privileges (such as scenic natural vistas, clean water, and unpolluted air) are unequally distributed among groups in society. The environmental movement works to secure the rights of all citizens, rich and poor, to a clean, healthy, beautiful, and sustainable world.
Symbolic Interactionism	Social change involves changes in the meaning of things as well as changes in laws, culture, and social behavior.	The environmental movement works to safeguard animal species by having them declared "endangered" or "threatened." Redefining groups of animals in this way allows for their protection through endangered species laws rather than their decimation through hunting or habitat reduction.

IN THE FUTURE
Utopia—or Doomsday?

So what's next? What kind of future are we headed for? We have already experienced so much social change to get here today; the world is a very different place now than it was a generation—even a decade—ago. We are always on the brink of something new and revolutionary, and it's possible to see glimpses on the horizon. But there's a lot of disagreement about whether we're heading toward utopia or if doomsday is around the corner. Either way, change is coming, brought on by some combination of natural, technological, and social processes.

There have always been optimists and dreamers who see a bright future filled with promise. We'll have greater health and longer life expectancy with new treatments for disease and new ways of practicing and delivering health care. There will be more abundance with better ways to produce food, energy, and the consumer goods and services that people need. We'll work less and play more in better designed communities. With more access to more resources, inequality will diminish, and we can finally find more ways to get along with each other. We'll live in a totally wired world, where technological advances like artificial intelligence and virtual reality free us from drudgery and open up endless possibilities for the edification and transformation of humans. We'll travel around in driverless cars and high-speed hyperloops, vacation in space, and colonize Mars. These are just some of the promises that tomorrow's pioneers and innovators are working on at this very moment.

On the other end of the spectrum, there are the pessimists and doomsayers who take a dim view of the future ahead. They predict a time when the world gives out and society collapses and are making plans for how to ride out the apocalypse. It may come in the form of nuclear war, destruction at the press of a button. Or it may come in the form of dirty bombs or chemical and biological warfare that will wipe out great centers of human population, leaving whole swaths of continents barren and uninhabitable. Conflict might play out on a smaller scale, with warring factions turning to armed resistance and insurrection in our towns and cities.

Nature may wreak havoc on us, triggered by physical events such as earthquakes, droughts, and raging wildfires. Global climate change could cause more ice shelves to drift and melt away, raising sea levels and inundating coastlines worldwide. The food chain may collapse if honeybees die off or if genetically modified plants stop producing seeds. Humans may succumb to old diseases and new plagues we don't know how to fight. Hackers may turn connectivity against us, infecting and dismantling our means of communication, commerce, and governance. Or we may all get outsmarted by technology, once it knows how to learn without us. Survivalists and billionaires alike are stockpiling reinforcements or building self-contained bunkers underground, while others seek out Mars as an alternative to life on Earth.

What's going to happen in the future? How will things change? If you've been practicing to be a sociologist, then you've acquired some tools that might be useful as social change unfolds. You'll have developed a sociological imagination, which allows you to see the connections between what's happening in your own individual life and the larger public issues. And once you start seeing things like a sociologist, you can't un-see them. Your newfound awareness makes you a more astute social analyst and actor. Hold on to the sociological perspective and you'll have a better chance of contributing to the kind of positive social change you'd like to see in the world. Remember that the future doesn't happen on its own; it's made by people doing things together, just like us.

Doomsday Preppers Perhaps more valuable than a gas mask or canned food is a well-developed sociological imagination.

incorporated into the dominant culture; if it fails, it ceases to exist as an active movement—but it may have left an indelible mark on its host society nevertheless. Prohibitionists are an excellent case in point. Although those who wished to outlaw alcohol in the United States eventually failed, after the Eighteenth Amendment (Prohibition) was repealed in 1933, their efforts had a huge impact on American culture. There are still hundreds of "dry" municipalities where alcohol is not sold, for example, and laws about what time of day (or night) you can purchase alcohol, as well as the legal age (now twenty-one in all states) for consumption.

It is perhaps impossible to overstate the importance of social movements in any given society; life as we know it has been shaped by the rise and fall of all sorts of such movements. Imagine what the religious makeup of the world would be like if Martin Luther and his followers had not rebelled against the Catholic Church in the early sixteenth century, or what American culture would be like if Martin Luther King Jr. and the civil rights movement hadn't successfully organized. What would world politics have been like if the Nazis hadn't come to power in the 1930s or the Soviet Union hadn't broken up in 1991? What would the United States look like if the environmental movement hadn't spawned our national and state park systems? The list is endless. Take a moment to consider a few ideas and movements that in today's culture seem radical. Regardless of whether those movements succeed in the traditional sense of the word, it is a pretty safe bet that they will help shape the world for generations to come. And while the progress made by any social movement tends to happen slowly, the possibility for change and a better society for those future generations is the driving force for those who participate.

CULTURAL DIFFUSION the dissemination of material and symbolic culture (tools and technology, beliefs and behavior) from one group to another

TECHNOLOGICAL DETERMINISM a theory of social change that assumes changes in technology drive changes in society, rather than vice versa

CULTURAL LAG the time between changes in material culture or technology and the resulting changes in the broader culture's relevant norms, values, meanings, and laws

TECHNOLOGY AND SOCIAL CHANGE

As we have already seen, revolutionary social change is often the result of a technological development, whether that technological development is the plow, the assembly line, or the microchip. When new inventions spread from one society to another we call this process **cultural diffusion**. Social movements can also arise as a result of the diffusion of technological advancements: Labor unions multiplied in the factories of the Industrial Revolution, and today the Internet can bring more people together to work for social change than ever before. As you might imagine, then, sociologists have generated theories that seek to explain the particular influence of technology in creating social change (Kurzweil 1990; Pool 1997). One common characteristic of these theories is an emphasis on **technological determinism**—the idea that technology plays a defining role in shaping society. As one of the earliest proponents of this approach, William Ogburn (1964) described the process of social change as beginning with invention or discovery and proceeding when the invention is spread from one group or society to another. In the remainder of the chapter, we look at the relationship between technology and social change.

With so many amazing technological advances happening in the world today, we tend to think that technology is the answer to all our problems. But is it? Often those same advances come with issues of their own. At the beginning of this chapter, we saw how emerging technologies such as the Internet of Things are transforming our everyday lives for the better while also exposing us to new forms of risk. It seems that no social change is without its unforeseen, unintentional outcomes, some of which are positive and some of which are not.

We may welcome the invention of e-commerce, in vitro fertilization, or sport utility vehicles (SUVs) and notice only later that they bring unanticipated problems. For example, the Internet gives us access to an unprecedented number of goods and services that are just a click away. That's good news for consumers, but less so for brick-and-mortar stores that struggle to stay in business as individuals order the products they need—from books to clothing to groceries to toilet paper—online. Similarly, in vitro fertilization has allowed countless infertile couples to conceive. But it has also led a race to genetically modify embryos. Scientists using CRISPR, a new gene-editing technology, have already succeeded in repairing disease-causing mutations in human embryos. While this might lead to a future cure for cancer, it could also be used to create "designer babies." Technologies such as CRISPR open up a Pandora's box of ethical and moral questions about intervening in human DNA. And SUVs not only guzzle gasoline but also are more likely than other cars to kill or injure people when involved in an accident.

As a society, how do we respond to technological developments that seem to solve one set of problems (such as disease, infertility, communication, or transportation) while creating new ones? Often we must play "catch-up," scrambling to fix a problem once it manifests itself, rather than being able to plan ahead and prevent it in the first place. **Cultural lag** is the term sociologists use to describe this disconnect between a changing social condition and cultural adjustment to that change. Material culture (such as the technologies just discussed) often changes faster than nonmaterial culture (such as beliefs and laws), and we struggle to create new values and norms that correspond with new technologies.

DATA WORKSHOP

Analyzing Media and Pop Culture

The "Unplug" Experiment

Zen sociologist Bernard McGrane (1994; McGrane and Gunderson 2010) is noted for having designed a series of experiments widely used in teaching sociology students. This includes the "Doing Nothing" Data Workshop featured in Chapter 1. The "Un-TV" experiment is another of his most popular, in which he asks students to "watch" TV without turning it on. While these experiments may appear simple at first, the ideas they highlight are very sophisticated. Participants are required to use "beginner's mind" (setting aside all their prior judgments, opinions, and even experiences) to achieve an unusual level of consciousness about a particular aspect of their everyday lives.

This Data Workshop is inspired by the "Un-TV" experiment but lets you decide which form of media technology you'd like to unplug from. It should be something that regularly takes up your time and attention and that might actually be hard for you to give up. For most people, the most ubiquitous device in their world is a cell phone, but you could also choose a computer, music player, or tablet, or some other media format you use a lot, like cable TV, radio, or video games. Think about how long you can go without using this technology or device on a typical day (or longer). If you're like many people, even a few hours away from your cell phone or computer screen might seem like a very long time.

How are you going to feel when you can't text-message, watch videos on YouTube, post pictures on Instagram, or check your newsfeed on Facebook? We take these technologies for granted and cannot imagine our lives without them—but maybe life would be better! What are some of the benefits of unplugging? When we detach from our devices, we also get to disconnect from the overstimulation that comes from living in a media-saturated world. Can just a few hours of being unplugged reduce anxiety, dependency, fatigue, and information overload? Or does unplugging make you feel even more stressed out? That's what this experiment is designed to reveal. A great part of the difficulty of this experiment is actually getting yourself to do it. But even more so, it can be a challenge to confront your own habits and dependencies on a deep level. The "Unplug" experiment asks you to do just that.

In this Data Workshop, you will be doing participant observation research while also preparing to write an autoethnography of your experience. Return to Chapter 2 for a review of these research methods. You will be writing detailed field notes of what you observe during the experiment. Remember that you are attempting to use a beginner's mind. Don't try to figure out what will happen before you begin. Just "see what you can see." The idea is for you to notice the way the technology permeates your everyday life and what happens when you try to resist using it. Follow the numbered prompts below.

1. Choose a media technology for the experiment. This should be something you use regularly but that you can safely turn off for a period of time. Why did you choose this technology, and how does it represent an interesting experiment?

2. Determine how long you will go without this technology; it could be for an hour, an afternoon, or three days, depending on how often you use it. What's important is to create an impact by turning it off. Is the time period you determined adequate in length to produce meaningful results?

3. Go about your daily business while you refrain from using your chosen technology during the designated period. Don't become distracted. Keep a part of your focus on what's happening with the experiment and check in on yourself frequently. Take field notes at points during the research process or immediately upon completing it.

4. What happens as the experiment unfolds? Are you having any difficulties? When and why? What are your thoughts, feelings, and sensations? How attentive are you to the details of your reactions?

5. What happens as time progresses? How is it different as you get closer to the end of the allotted time for the experiment? Are you relieved to turn on your device again? Or were there some unexpected benefits of turning it off? What do you see now about using the technology that you did not notice before? Does it feel any different to resume using the technology after having conducted the experiment?

There are two options for completing this Data Workshop:

PREP-PAIR-SHARE Complete your observations, and prepare some field notes about the experiment that you can refer to in class. Get together with one or more students. What devices or technologies did you unplug from? Who had more or less difficulty with the experiment? Compare your insights and experiences with each other.

Technology in the Global Village

Over the years, social thinkers have expressed concerns about the effects of new technology. Some believed that electronic media would prove to be a dangerous, divisive, and degrading force in modern culture. Marshall McLuhan (1964), a Canadian communications researcher who also subscribed to the notion of technological determinism, expressed a degree of optimism that amounted to a utopian vision of what the various media could do for human society. McLuhan was particularly interested in television, which in the early 1960s was just then infiltrating households in North America. He imagined that television could re-create a sense of intimate community by linking people in disparate locations around the world through its broadcasts. Just as tribe members had once gathered to share stories around the light of a campfire, people would now sit in the glow of their TV screens, making television a kind of "virtual campfire" and those watching together members of a **virtual community**. McLuhan coined the term **global village** to capture that notion. He did not live to see the advent of the Internet a few decades later, but he certainly understood the potential for media to extend the human senses and join us to one another in unprecedented ways.

The intervening years have not totally confirmed McLuhan's utopian vision. New technologies have in fact had a profound impact on society, but in what ways and whether this impact has been positive or negative are still to be determined. What we do know is that media technology has become a global reality. Social scientists use the term **globalization** to refer to social structures and institutions such as politics and commerce that must now be conceived on a global rather than national scale. We can no longer remain isolated from social and political forces that reverberate around the world. There are now billions of people who have access to television and the Internet. More than 1 billion were estimated to have watched the first walk on the moon in 1969. Since then, other live events have attracted even larger global audiences, such as the funerals of Princess Diana in 1997 and Michael Jackson in 2009, the catastrophic attacks of September 11, 2001, and the Syrian refugee crisis. These are among the most significant images burned into our collective minds. But would it be a surprise to know that some of the most watched broadcasts of all time are international sporting events like the FIFA World Cup, the Tour de France, and the Olympics? No, the Super Bowl does not top the list (Clark 2014).

While news and sports attract the largest audiences, entertainment media are not far behind. Television produced in the West dominates the global market. The world's most valuable television networks, including CNN, MTV, Disney, FOX, and ESPN, all belong to U.S. media conglomerates. These networks produce programs that are aired to audiences in hundreds of other countries. In 2018, CBS's *The Big Bang Theory* was the most popular television series in the world, according to the data firm Parrot Analytics, and HBO's *Game of Thrones* was number two (*NZ Herald* 2018). In the last several years, there has also been an explosion of streaming content produced by Netflix, Amazon, and Hulu—all American companies. Very few other countries have the infrastructure or budgets to produce similar shows with the same technical quality. This makes it hard to compete with the most popular programs, which set world tastes.

With this proliferation of Western media, we also find that the contents tend to reflect Western values. Communication researchers often talk about the "politics of information flow," and we can see that the message, or ideology, embedded in TV shows or films tends to flow from industrialized countries like the United States to the rest of the world (Schiller 1976, 1992, 1996; Tomlinson 1991). Americans brought up on the principle of a free press and living in a media-saturated society are not typically alarmed by the proliferation of our popular culture to other parts of the globe. In fact, we might assume that ours is the voice of freedom and democracy, a force for positive change in places marked by censorship and disinformation (Rasmussen 2014; Rothkop 1997). But others question this flood of ideas, especially ideas about individualism and consumerism, coming from the West.

And Western ideas can cross cultural boundaries all too easily: It is almost impossible to block the reception of satellite and Internet communications to audiences anywhere in the world. This sets up a new kind of tension in the struggle for power and influence. It is now possible for a country to be "occupied" by an invisible invader that arrives through the airwaves or by satellite and wireless networks—think of Russia's use of social media to interfere in the 2016 U.S. presidential election. A country can be conquered by ideas rather than by force, a phenomenon known as **cultural imperialism**.

VIRTUAL COMMUNITIES social groups whose interactions are mediated through information technologies, particularly the Internet

GLOBAL VILLAGE Marshall McLuhan's term describing the way that new communication technologies override barriers of space and time, joining together people all over the globe

GLOBALIZATION the cultural and economic changes resulting from dramatically increased international trade and exchange in the late twentieth and early twenty-first centuries

CULTURAL IMPERIALISM the imposition of one culture's beliefs and practices on another culture through media and consumer products rather than by military force

Cultural Imperialism?
U.S. media products cross international borders and carry Western ideas and values with them. Hollywood blockbuster *Avengers: Endgame* recently passed *Avatar* as the highest-grossing movie of all time, largely due to strong ticket sales overseas.

Some consider the Western media's powerful influence as a kind of cultural domination. The result of this domination is often **cultural leveling**, a homogenizing process whereby societies lose their particular uniqueness as they all start to resemble one another.

As media technology makes possible a multiplicity of voices, Westerners have also been influenced by Eastern ideas (witness the popularity of yoga). Yet Western values continue to dominate and to shape the "village" that is the global village. They sometimes conflict with the values of other nations, some of which have tried to resist the Western media stranglehold and maintain their own distinctive cultural identity (see the case of Bhutan in this chapter's Global Perspective box). Challenges persist as to whether meaningful and egalitarian communication on a global level can really take place (Fortner and Fackler 2011; Gozzi 1996). Perhaps as technology advances, cultural distinctions can be maintained and divisions eliminated, thus approaching McLuhan's vision of a world united.

Living in a Postmodern World

Today, the Digital Age is but a few decades old, and already most of you probably cannot remember a time when you did not have a remote control, game controller, mouse, or cell phone in hand. And you cannot imagine living without them. It is safe to assume that we will see many more scientific and technological advancements in the near future. In particular, media technologies are likely to become cheaper, lighter, easier to use, faster, more flexible, more interactive, and capable of carrying more information. Despite what some call the "digital divide" (the uneven distribution of technology among different groups of people), technologies will play an increasingly important role in almost every aspect of our lives, and technological literacy will be a necessary skill for anyone participating in contemporary society.

Is all progress good? Is every technological advance beneficial? These questions arise because our society is in the midst of a major transformation: We are moving from a modern society to a postmodern society. **Modernity** refers to the social conditions and attitudes characteristic of industrialized societies, which include the decline of traditional community, an increase in individual autonomy and diversity of beliefs, and a strong belief in the ability of science and technology to improve our quality of life (Berger 1977). In many ways, this last promise of modernity has in fact been fulfilled. Since the Industrial Revolution, rates of infant mortality have declined, life expectancies have increased, and a number of common diseases have been cured or controlled. However, along with these advances have come increases in income inequality, violent crime, and child poverty (Miringoff and Miringoff 1999). So while modern society has its benefits, there are also problems, which is where the postmodern critique begins.

> **CULTURAL LEVELING** the process by which cultures that were once unique and distinct become increasingly similar
>
> **MODERNITY** a term that characterizes industrialized societies, including the decline of tradition, an increase in individualism, and a belief in progress, technology, and science

GLOBAL PERSPECTIVE
Bhutan and Gross National Happiness

While change may be inevitable, perhaps we can determine the direction, elements, and pace of that change. That is exactly what the current leaders of Bhutan are attempting to do. They provide an example of how to hold on to tradition, maintain a unique cultural identity, and exercise control over the pace of social change.

Bhutan is a tiny country of fewer than 1 million people, precariously perched at the "roof of the world" in the Himalayan Mountains. Despite its remote location between two of the world's most powerful and populous nations—China to the north and India to the south—Bhutan has remained a sovereign, independent nation throughout its history. In this ancient land, it seems almost as if time has stood still. It is only in the past few decades that Bhutan has emerged from its almost total isolation and taken some cautious steps into the postmodern era.

Bhutan is a predominantly Buddhist country that until recently was ruled by a king who had four wives (who were all sisters!) along with a cadre of mostly Western-educated officials. In 2008, at the behest of its enlightened monarch, Bhutan held its first democratic elections. Despite that political change, it may still be the only country in the world where the government's number-one concern is something it calls "Gross National Happiness": a blend of economic development and cultural richness; food, clothing, and shelter; health care and education; spiritual values; and individual contentment.

The government hopes to achieve Gross National Happiness by carefully identifying and adopting what the West is doing right while also rejecting its cynicism and consumerism. For example, the Bhutanese do not allow exploitation of their natural resources. There is no lumber industry in their millions of acres of lush forests, which instead have been designated national parks. Although Mt. Everest is nearby in Nepal, mountain climbers are forbidden to ascend the peaks of Bhutan's mountains. The Bhutanese have, however, taken advantage of one natural resource originating in the snowcap—immense, fast-flowing rivers that generate hydroelectric power, which is then exported to neighboring countries. Tourism to Bhutan could also have become a lucrative trade. But here, too, the government has limited the number of visitors who can enter the country each year.

For the most part, Bhutan has managed to avoid being overwhelmed by the forces of globalization and cultural leveling. While some Bhutanese enjoy basic modern conveniences like cell phone service and wireless Internet, in the capital city of Thimphu there are still no chain stores—no Starbucks, Targets, or Burger Kings. Especially remarkable is that the Bhutanese have so far been able to defend themselves against what might be the most powerful global intruder of all—television. For many years Bhutan was the only country in the world to ban TV. It was not until 2006 that television service was widely available across the country. Even so, programming was strictly limited. Because networks like MTV and CNN were also sneaking in via satellite, the government created its own national television network, the Bhutan Broadcasting Service (BBS), to provide a counterbalance to Western programs (Schell 2002).

At first, the BBS produced only a daily half-hour newscast in both English and the native language of Dzongkha,

Postmodernity refers to the social conditions and attitudes characteristic of postindustrialized societies, which include a focus on ideas and cultural debates rather than material things and a questioning of the achievements of science and technology. According to postmodern thought, the progress promised by modernity has failed to solve important social problems (such as income, gender, and racial inequality), and modern institutions (families, schools, workplaces, governments) are implicated in this failure. Although change is forecast in all these areas, there is no agreed-upon blueprint for what that change might look like.

The Industrial Revolution transformed Western society from traditional to modern. The Information Revolution is transforming Western society from modern to postmodern. While we are not yet certain what this particular transformation will mean in our everyday lives, we can be sure that it

POSTMODERNITY a term that characterizes postindustrial societies, including a focus on the production and management of information and skepticism of science and technology but soon it added documentaries and entertainment shows. Most of the BBS's programming is geared toward the distinct tastes and interests of the Bhutanese audience, while still being aligned with the guiding principles of their country. The Bhutanese broadcasters see audience members not as primarily consumers but as citizens in need of knowledge that can help them in their pursuit of Gross National Happiness.

Still, some worry about the homogenizing effects of television, especially for a new generation of children growing up with it. The arrival of the Internet has compounded such problems and may be much harder to withstand. Today, more than half of the global population has Internet access (International Telecommunications Union 2018). While this means that the Bhutanese can now access BBS programming on YouTube, it is the plethora of media from outside their own borders that may pose the greatest threat to their way of life. It is important not to romanticize life in Bhutan or even the pursuit of Gross National Happiness. Although the country is now a democracy, it still endures high rates of infant mortality, poverty, and illiteracy. Life expectancies are low, and women's opportunities are limited. Certain types of social change would seem to be necessary and inevitable. However, as they prepare for change, Bhutanese leaders remain idealistic about the ability of their traditional culture to resist Western values and to avoid the social problems that are so commonplace in other parts of the world.

Gross National Happiness
Global networks like MTV and CNN that cross borders via satellite concern Bhutanese leaders who see their children emulating foreign television programs. To counterbalance Western influence, the government created a national television network, the Bhutan Broadcasting Service (BBS).

will not be the final transformation our society will undergo. Society will continue to be shaped by technology, not only at the macro level of culture and social institutions but also at the micro level of groups and individuals. Technology will change what the world looks like as well as how we perceive it. It will greatly extend our abilities to obtain information and will influence the way we use it. We will become more comfortable with multitasking; navigating through nonlinear hyperspace; dealing with symbols, images, and sound as well as text; moving at a rapid pace; coping with a fractured sense of self; socializing online; experimenting with game strategies; and accepting the unpredictable.

Should we call such developments progress? What will we gain, and what do we stand to lose? Your parents and grandparents will not understand the postmodern, digital era in the same way that you do. So it is you who will be engineering the terms of the future. Perhaps now would be a good time to ask yourself what you can do as part of this new social revolution. Can you risk just sitting back and watching what will happen? Or are you willing to take what you have learned and go out and make a difference? We hope this chapter has inspired you to take an active role in creating whatever positive social change you envision.

Closing Comments

Throughout this text, we have focused on the sociological features of everyday life, including the role of the media and popular culture in society. The media are often the place where new developments, trends, and social changes first become visible. And our everyday lives are the places where we experience both social constraints and social change at the most fundamental level. You now have the tools necessary to understand these phenomena, because you now possess the sociological perspective.

The sociological perspective sometimes highlights distressing facts—the persistence of poverty and prejudice, for example, or the realities of crime. But it allows for optimism

as well. This is because the intersection of biography and history goes both ways: Society shapes individual lives, but individuals influence their society as well. Any disconcerting realizations you may have had during the course of this semester should be tempered by your knowledge that change is possible, and that *you* are its primary source.

Ultimately, this should be the most relevant element of your education in sociology. Years from now, no one will care whether you remember the details of labeling theory or the difference between organic and mechanical solidarity. What will continue to matter is your sense of investment in your society—your commitment to your family, your workplace, your community, and your world. Your mindful involvement in all of these areas can make each of them a better place—to raise children, to live, to work, to collaborate with others. Armed with the sociological perspective, you now have a new set of responsibilities: to investigate and participate in your social world, both locally and globally. We hope you do so with optimism and persistence, and in partnership with others.

Let's Talk More

1. Fashion can be a marker of social status and group identity. Do you wear any clothing, jewelry, shoes, or other accessories that indicate your membership in a group? Describe the item(s) and what they signify.

2. Mass society theory and relative deprivation theory offer two basic explanations for why people join social movements. Think of someone you know who is active in a social movement. Which theory do you think more accurately characterizes this person's motivations? How can you tell?

3. Some social changes are deliberate, while others are unplanned. Many influential technologies, like the automobile, create both kinds of change. For example, what kinds of changes were cell phones designed to bring about? What changes did they cause unexpectedly?

Let's Explore More

1. **Film** Gibney, Alex, dir. *The Inventor: Out for Blood in Silicon Valley*. 2019.

2. **Book** Rushkoff, Douglas. 2019. *Team Human*. New York: W. W. Norton.

3. **Blog Post** Kaufman, Peter. "Slacktivists, Hacktivists, and the New Faceless Agents of Social Change." *Everyday Sociology* (blog). December 15, 2015. *http://WWNorton.com/rd/x6FQf.*

Glossary

absolute deprivation an objective measure of poverty, defined by the inability to meet minimal standards for food, shelter, clothing, or health care

access the process by which an ethnographer gains entry to a field setting

achieved status a status earned through individual effort or imposed by others

action research a type of research aimed at creating social change, in which the researcher works closely with members of a community who participate in the research process and collaborate toward the goal of social change

active audiences a term used to characterize audience members as active participants in "reading" or constructing the meaning of the media they consume

activism any activity intended to bring about social change

acute diseases diseases that have a sudden onset, may be briefly incapacitating, and are either curable or fatal

adoption the legal process of acquiring parental responsibilities for a child other than one's biological offspring

agency the ability of the individual to act freely and independently

agenda-setting theory theory that the media can set the public agenda by selecting certain news stories and excluding others, thus influencing what audiences think about

agents of socialization social groups, institutions, and individuals (especially the family, schools, peers, and the mass media) that provide structured situations in which socialization takes place

aggregates collections of people who share a physical location but do not have lasting social relations

Agricultural Revolution the social and economic changes, including population increases, that followed from the domestication of plants and animals and the gradually increasing efficiency of food production

alienation decreasing importance of social ties and community and the corresponding increase in impersonal associations and instrumental logic; also, according to Marx, the sense of dissatisfaction the modern worker feels as a result of producing goods that are owned and controlled by someone else

alternative medicine a group of medical treatments, practices, and products that are used instead of conventional Western medicine

alternative workforce see *contingent workforce*

altruism unselfish concern for the well-being of others and helping behaviors performed without self-interested motivation

anomie "normlessness"; term used to describe the alienation and loss of purpose that result from weaker social bonds and an increased pace of change

anthropocentric literally "human centered"; the idea that needs and desires of human beings should take priority over concerns about other species or the natural environment

antimiscegenation the prohibition of interracial marriage, cohabitation, or sexual interaction

antiracist allies whites and others working toward the goal of ending racial injustice

antithesis the opposition to the existing arrangements in a dialectical model

antitrust legislation laws designed to maintain competition in the marketplace by prohibiting monopolies, price fixing, or other forms of collusion among businesses

apartheid the system of segregation of racial and ethnic groups that was legal in South Africa between 1948 and 1991

applied research the search for knowledge that can be used to create social change

ascribed status a status that is inborn; usually difficult or impossible to change

asexuality the lack of sexual attraction of any kind; no interest in or desire for sex

assimilation a pattern of relations between ethnic or racial groups in which the minority group is absorbed into the mainstream or dominant group, making society more homogeneous

authoritarianism a system of government by and for a small number of elites that does not include representation of ordinary citizens

authority the legitimate right to wield power

autoethnography a form of participant observation where the feelings and actions of the researcher become a focal point of the ethnographic study

backstage the places where we rehearse and prepare for our performances

basic research the search for knowledge without an agenda or practical goal in mind

beginner's mind approaching the world without preconceptions in order to see things in a new way

belief a proposition or idea held on the basis of faith

bias an opinion held by the researcher that might affect the research or analysis

biodiversity the variety of species of plants and animals existing at any given time

bioethics the study of controversial moral or ethical issues related to scientific and medical advancements

bisexuality sexual attraction toward members of both genders

blue collar a description characterizing skilled and semi-skilled workers who perform manual labor or work in service or clerical jobs

bourgeoisie owners; the class of modern capitalists who own the means of production and employ wage laborers

bureaucracy a type of secondary group designed to perform tasks efficiently, characterized by specialization, technical competence, hierarchy, written rules, impersonality, and formal written communication

bystander effect or **diffusion of responsibility** the social dynamic wherein the more people who are present in a moment of crisis, the less likely any one of them is to take action

capital punishment the death penalty

capitalism an economic system based on the laws of free market competition, privatization of the means of production, and production for profit

caste system a form of social stratification in which status is determined by one's family history and background and cannot be changed

category people who share one or more attributes but who lack a sense of common identity or belonging

causation a relationship between variables in which a change in one directly produces a change in the other

charismatic authority authority based in the perception of remarkable personal qualities in a leader

charter schools public schools run by private entities to give parents greater control over their children's education

Chicago School a type of sociology practiced at the University of Chicago in the 1920s and 1930s that centered on urban settings and field research methods

chronic diseases diseases that develop over a longer period of time and may not be detected until later in their progression, when symptoms occur

cisgender term used when gender identity and/or expression aligns with the sex assigned at birth

cisgenderism belief in the superiority of cisgender persons and identities

civil inattention an unspoken rule governing interactions in public places, whereby individuals briefly notice others before ignoring them

civil society those organizations, institutions, and interactions outside government, family, and work that promote social bonds and the smooth functioning of society

class consciousness the recognition of social inequality on the part of the oppressed, leading to revolutionary action

climate change the increase in extreme weather patterns linked to global warming

climate justice a perspective that frames global warming as a moral issue, proposing that those who are least responsible for climate change tend to suffer its worst consequences

closed-ended question a question asked of a respondent that imposes a limit on the possible responses

closed system a social system with very little opportunity to move from one class to another

code of ethics ethical guidelines for researchers to consult as they design a project

coercive power power that is backed by the threat of force

cohabitation living together as a romantic couple without being married

collective behavior behavior that follows from the formation of a group or crowd of people who take action together toward a shared goal

collective conscience the shared morals and beliefs that are common to a group and that foster social solidarity

collective effervescence an intense energy in shared events where people feel swept up in something larger than themselves

color-blind racism an ideology that removes race as an explanation for any form of unequal treatment

coming out openly declaring one's true identity to those who might not be aware of it; short for "coming out of the closet," a phrase used to describe how LGBTQ persons have felt compelled to keep their sexual orientation or gender identity secret

commodification the process by which it becomes possible to buy and sell a particular good or service

communism a system of government that eliminates private property; it is the most extreme form of socialism, because all citizens work for the government and there are no class distinctions

communitarianism a political and moral philosophy

focused on strengthening civil society and communal bonds

community a group of people living in the same local area who share a sense of participation, belonging, and fellowship

community college two-year institution that provides students with general education and facilitates transfer to a four-year university

comparative historical research research that uses existing sources to study relationships among elements of society in various regions and time periods

complementary medicine a group of medical treatments, practices, and products that can be used in conjunction with conventional Western medicine

concentration the process by which the number of companies producing and distributing a particular commodity decreases, often through mergers and conglomeration

confidentiality the assurance that no one other than the researcher will know the identity of a respondent

conflict theory a paradigm that sees social conflict as the basis of society and social change and that emphasizes a materialist view of society, a critical view of the status quo, and a dynamic model of historical change

conglomeration the process by which a single corporation acquires ownership of a variety of otherwise unrelated businesses

conservation era earliest stage of the environmental movement, which focused on the preservation of "wilderness" areas

constructionists those who believe that notions of gender are socially determined, such that a binary system is just one possibility among many

consumption the utilization of goods and services, either for personal use or in manufacturing

contagion theory one of the earliest theories of collective action; suggests that individuals who join a crowd can become "infected" by a mob mentality and lose the ability to reason

content analysis a method in which researchers identify and study specific variables or themes that appear in a text, image, or media message

contingent workforce those who work in positions that are temporary or freelance or who work as independent contractors

control group the members of a test group who are allowed to continue without intervention so that they can be compared with the experimental group

conversation analysis a sociological approach that looks at how we create meaning in naturally occurring conversation, often by taping conversations and examining their transcripts

cooling the mark out behaviors that help others to save face or avoid embarrassment, often referred to as civility or tact

copresence face-to-face interaction or being in the presence of others

correlation a relationship between variables in which they change together and may or may not be causal

counterculture a group within society that openly rejects or actively opposes society's values and norms

credential society a society that emphasizes the attainment of degrees and certificates as necessary requirements for the job market and social mobility

crime a violation of a norm that has been codified into law

criminal justice system a collection of social institutions, such as legislatures, police, courts, and prisons, that creates and enforces laws

criminology the systematic scientific study of crime, criminals, and criminal justice

critical race theory the study of the relationship among race, racism, and power

critical theory a contemporary form of conflict theory that criticizes many different systems and ideologies of domination and oppression

crowd a temporary gathering of people in a public place; members might interact but do not identify with each other and will not remain in contact

cultural appropriation the adoption of cultural elements belonging to an oppressed group by members of the dominant group, without permission and often for the dominant group's gain

cultural assimilation the process by which racial or ethnic groups are absorbed into the dominant group by adopting the dominant group's culture

cultural capital the tastes, habits, expectations, skills, knowledge, and other cultural assets that help us gain advantages in society

cultural competence the concept of acknowledging and incorporating a patient's cultural background as part of the treatment process; the recognition that patients' beliefs shape their approach to health care

cultural diffusion the dissemination of material and symbolic culture (tools and technology, beliefs and behavior) from one group to another

cultural imperialism the imposition of one culture's beliefs and practices on another culture through media and consumer products rather than by military force

cultural lag the time between changes in material culture or technology and the resulting changes in the broader culture's relevant norms, values, meanings, and laws

cultural leveling the process by which cultures that were once unique and distinct become increasingly similar

cultural relativism the principle of understanding other cultures on their own terms, rather than judging or evaluating according to one's own culture

culture the entire way of life of a group of people (including both material and symbolic elements) that acts as a lens through which one views the world and that is passed from one generation to the next

culture of poverty entrenched attitudes that can develop among poor communities and lead the poor to accept their fate rather than attempt to improve their lot

culture shock a sense of disorientation that occurs when entering a radically new social or cultural environment

culture wars clashes within mainstream society over the values and norms that should be upheld

curative or **crisis medicine** type of health care that treats the disease or condition once it has manifested

custody the physical and legal responsibility of caring for children; assigned by a court for divorced or unmarried parents

cyberbullying the use of electronic media (web pages, social networking sites, e-mail, Twitter, cell phones) to tease, harass, threaten, or humiliate someone

cybercrime crimes committed via the Internet, including identity theft, embezzlement, fraud, sexual predation, and financial scams

cycle of violence a common behavior pattern in abusive relationships; the cycle begins happily, then the relationship grows tense, and the tension explodes in abuse, followed by a period of contrition that allows the cycle to repeat

deception the extent to which the participants in a research project are unaware of the project or its goals

deconstruction a type of critical postmodern analysis that involves taking apart or disassembling old ways of thinking

deductive approach an approach whereby the researcher formulates a hypothesis first and then gathers data to test that hypothesis

definition of the situation an agreement with others about "what is going on" in a given circumstance; this consensus allows us to coordinate our actions with others and realize goals

democracy a political system in which all citizens have the right to participate

demographic transition a theory about change over time from high birth and death rates to low birth and death rates, resulting in a stabilized population

demography study of the size, composition, distribution, and changes in human population

dependent variable the factor that is changed (or not) by the independent variable

deprivation amplification when our individual disease risks (based on our heredity and physiology) are amplified by social factors

deregulation reduction or removal of government controls from an industry to allow for a free and efficient marketplace

deterrence an approach to punishment that relies on the threat of harsh penalties to discourage people from committing crimes

deviance a behavior, trait, belief, or other characteristic that violates a norm and causes a negative reaction

deviance avowal process by which an individual self-identifies as deviant and initiates their own labeling process

dialectical model Karl Marx's model of historical change, whereby two extreme positions come into conflict and create some new outcome

differential association theory Edwin Sutherland's hypothesis that we learn to be deviant through our associations with deviant peers

diffusion of responsibility see *bystander effect*

digital divide the unequal access to computer and Internet technology, both globally and within the United States

discrimination unequal treatment of individuals based on their membership in a social group; usually motivated by prejudice

disenchantment the rationalization of modern society

disenfranchised stripped of voting rights, either temporarily or permanently

disenfranchisement the removal of the rights of citizenship through economic, political, or legal means

domestic abuse any physical, verbal, financial, sexual, or psychological behaviors abusers use to gain and maintain power over their victims

dominant culture the values, norms, and practices of the group within society that is most powerful (in terms of wealth, prestige, status, influence, etc.)

double-barreled questions questions that attempt to get at multiple issues at once, and so tend to receive incomplete or confusing answers

double-consciousness W. E. B. DuBois's term for the divided identity experienced by blacks in the United States

dramaturgy an approach pioneered by Erving Goffman in which social life is analyzed in terms of its similarities to theatrical performance

dual enrollment programs that allow high school students to simultaneously enroll in college classes, earning credit for both high school and college degrees

dual nature of the self the idea that we experience the self as both subject and object, the "I" and the "me"

dyad a two-person social group

dysfunction a disturbance to or undesirable consequence of some aspect of the social system

dystopia opposite of a utopia; a world where social problems are magnified and the quality of life is extremely low

early college high schools institutions in which students earn a high school diploma and two years of credit toward a bachelor's degree

Earth Day an annual event conceived of by environmental activist and former senator Gaylord Nelson to encourage support for and increase awareness of environmental concerns; first celebrated on April 22, 1970

ecological footprint an estimation of the land and water area required to produce all the goods an individual consumes and to assimilate all the waste an individual generates

ecotourism foreign travel with the goal of minimizing the environmental consequences of tourism as well as its possible negative effects on local cultures and economies, typically involving people from highly industrialized nations traveling to less developed countries

edge cities centers of employment and commerce that began as suburban commuter communities

education the process by which a society transmits its knowledge, values, and expectations to its members so they can function effectively

embodied identity those elements of identity that are generated through others' perceptions of our physical traits

embodied status a status generated by physical characteristics

emergent norm theory a theory of collective behavior that assumes individual members of a crowd make their own decisions about behavior and that norms are created through others' acceptance or rejection of these behaviors

emigration leaving one country to live permanently in another

emotion work (emotional labor) the process of evoking, suppressing, or otherwise managing feelings to create a publicly observable display of emotion

empirical based on scientific experimentation or observation

encoding/decoding model a theory on media that combines models that privilege the media producer and models that view the audience as the primary source of meaning; this theory recognizes that media texts are created to deliver specific messages and that individuals actively interpret them

endogamy marriage to someone within one's social group

environment in sociology, the natural world, the human-made environment, and the interaction between the two

environmental justice a movement that aims to remedy environmental inequities such as threats to public health and the unequal treatment of certain communities with regard to ecological concerns

environmental movement a social movement organized around concerns about the relationship between humans and the environment

Environmental Protection Agency (EPA) a U.S. government agency established in 1969 to protect public health and the environment through policies and enforcement

environmental racism any environmental policy or practice that negatively affects individuals, groups, or communities because of their race or ethnicity

environmental sociology the study of the interaction between society and the natural environment, including the social causes and consequences of environmental problems

epidemic occurs when the number of cases of a particular disease during a particular time period is significantly higher than might otherwise be expected

epidemiology the study of disease patterns to understand the cause of illnesses, how they are spread, and what interventions to take

essentialists those who believe gender roles have a genetic or biological origin and therefore cannot be changed

ethnicity a socially defined category based on a common language, religion, nationality, history, or some other cultural factor

ethnocentrism the principle of using one's own culture as a means or standard by which to evaluate another group or individual, leading to the view that cultures other than one's own are abnormal or inferior

ethnography a naturalistic method based on studying people in their own environment in order to understand the meanings they attribute to their activities; also, the written work that results from the study

ethnomethodology the study of "folk methods" and background knowledge that sustain a shared sense of reality in everyday interactions

eugenics an attempt to selectively manipulate the gene pool in order to produce and "improve" human beings through medical science

Eurocentric the tendency to favor European or Western histories, cultures, and values over those of non-Western societies

evangelical a term describing conservative Christians who emphasize converting others to their faith

everyday actor someone who approaches the world by using knowledge that is practical or taken for granted

everyday class consciousness awareness of one's own social status and that of others

existing sources materials that have been produced for some other reason but that can be used as data for social research

exogamy marriage to someone from a different social group

experimental group the members of a test group who receive the experimental treatment

experiments formal tests of specific variables and effects, performed in a setting where all aspects of the situation can be controlled

expressions given expressions that are intentional and usually verbal, such as utterances

expressions given off observable expressions that can be either intended or unintended and are usually nonverbal

expressions of behavior small actions such as an eye roll or head nod that serve as an interactional tool to help project our definition of the situation to others

expressive leadership leadership concerned with maintaining emotional and relational harmony within the group

expressive role the position of the family member who provides emotional support and nurturing

expressive tasks the emotional work necessary to support family members

extended family a large group of relatives, usually including at least three generations living either in one household or in close proximity

extrinsic religiosity a person's public display of commitment to a religious faith

fads interests or practices followed enthusiastically for a relatively short period of time

false consciousness a denial of the truth on the part of the oppressed when they fail to recognize that the interests of the ruling class are embedded in the dominant ideology

family a social group whose members are bound by legal, biological, or emotional ties, or a combination of all three

fashion the widespread custom or style of behavior and appearance at a particular time or in a particular place

federal poverty line federal index that defines "official" poverty in the United States based on household income; updated annually

feeling rules norms regarding the expression and display of emotions; expectations about the acceptable or desirable feelings in a given situation

feminism belief in the social, political, and economic equality of the sexes; also the social movements organized around that belief

feminist theory a theoretical approach that looks at gender inequities in society and the way that gender structures the social world

feminization of poverty the economic trend showing that women are more likely than men to live in poverty, caused in part by the gendered gap in wages, the higher proportion of single mothers compared to single fathers, and the increasing costs of child care

feral children in myths and rare real-world cases, children who have had little human contact and may have lived in social isolation from a young age

fertility rate a measure of population growth through reproduction; often expressed as the number of births per 1,000 people in a particular population or the average number of children a woman would bear over a lifetime

feudal system a system of social stratification based on a hereditary nobility who were responsible for and served by a lower stratum of forced laborers called serfs

fictive kin close relations with people we consider "like family" but who are not related to us by blood or marriage

field notes detailed notes taken by an ethnographer describing their activities and interactions, which later become the basis of the analysis

first wave the earliest period of feminist activism, from the mid-nineteenth century until American women won the right to vote in 1920

focus group a process for interviewing a number of participants together that also allows for interaction among group members

folkways loosely enforced norms involving common customs, practices, or procedures that ensure smooth social interaction and acceptance

food desert a community in which the residents have little or no access to fresh, affordable, healthy foods, usually located in densely populated urban areas

front in the dramaturgical perspective, the setting or scene of performances that helps establish the definition of the situation

frontstage the places where we deliver our performances to an audience of others

fundamentalism the practice of emphasizing literal interpretation of texts and a "return" to a time of greater religious purity; represented by the most conservative group within any religion

game stage the third stage in Mead's theory of the development of self wherein children play organized games and take on the perspective of the generalized other

gender the physical, behavioral, and personality traits that a group considers normal for its male and female members

gender binary a system of classification with only two distinct and opposite gender categories

gender expression an individual's behavioral manifestations of gender

gender identity an individual's self-definition or sense of gender

gender nonconforming term used when gender identity and/or expression differs from societal expectations about gender roles

gender role socialization the lifelong process of learning to be masculine or feminine, primarily through agents of socialization

generalized other the perspectives and expectations of a network of others (or of society in general) that a child learns and then takes into account when shaping his or her own behavior

genocide the deliberate and systematic extermination of a racial, ethnic, national, or cultural group

gentrification transformation of the physical, social, economic, and cultural life of formerly working-class or poor inner-city neighborhoods into more affluent middle-class communities

gerrymandering redrawing the boundary lines of state voting districts in order to advantage one political party over another

gestures the ways in which people use their bodies to communicate without words; actions that have symbolic meaning

global cities a term for megacities that emphasizes their global impact as centers of economic, political, and social power

global village Marshall McLuhan's term describing the way that new communication technologies override barriers of space and time, joining together people all over the globe

global warming gradual increase in the earth's temperature, driven recently by an increase in greenhouse gases and other human activity

globalization the cultural and economic changes resulting from dramatically increased international trade and exchange in the late twentieth and early twenty-first centuries

government the formal, organized agency that exercises power and control in modern society, especially through the creation and enforcement of laws

grassroots environmentalism beginning in the 1980s, the fourth stage of the environmental movement; distinguished by the diversity of its members and belief in citizen participation in environmental decision making

Green Party a U.S. political party established in 1984 to bring political attention to environmentalism, social justice, diversity, and related principles

greenhouse effect the process in which increased production of greenhouse gases, especially those arising from human activity (e.g., carbon dioxide, nitrous oxide, and methane) causes changes to the earth's atmosphere

grounded theory an inductive method of generating theory from data by creating categories in which to place data and then looking for relationships among categories

group a collection of people who share some attribute, identify with one another, and interact with each other

group cohesion the sense of solidarity or loyalty that individuals feel toward a group to which they belong

group dynamics the patterns of interaction between groups and individuals

groupthink in very cohesive groups, the tendency to enforce a high degree of conformity among members, creating a demand for unanimous agreement

Hawthorne effect a specific example of reactivity, in which the desired effect is the result not of the independent variable but of the research itself

hegemonic masculinity a masculine ideal that promotes characteristics such as independence, aggression, and toughness, and rejects any alternate qualities in men

hegemony term developed by Antonio Gramsci to describe the cultural aspects of social control, whereby the ideas of the dominant group are accepted by all

heterogamy the tendency to choose romantic partners who are dissimilar to us in terms of class, race, education, religion, and other social group membership

heteronormativity the belief that heterosexuality is and should be the norm

heterosexism belief in the superiority of heterosexuality and heterosexuals

heterosexuality sexual attraction toward members of the other gender

hidden curriculum values or behaviors that students learn indirectly over the course of their schooling

high culture those forms of cultural expression usually associated with the elite or dominant classes

homeschooling the education of children by their parents, at home

homogamy the tendency to choose romantic partners who are similar to us in terms of class, race, education, religion, and other social group membership

homophobia fear of or discrimination toward gay, lesbian, and bisexual people

homosexuality sexual attraction toward members of one's own gender

honor killing the murder of a family member—usually female—who is believed to have brought dishonor to the family

horizontal social mobility the movement of individuals or groups within a particular social class, most often a result of changing occupations

human exceptionalism the attitude that humans are exempt from natural ecological limits

hypergamy marrying "up" in the social class hierarchy

hypodermic needle theory (magic bullet theory) a theory that explains the effects of media as if their contents simply entered directly into the consumer, who is powerless to resist their influence

hypogamy marrying "down" in the social class hierarchy

hypothesis a theoretical statement explaining the relationship between two or more phenomena

id, **ego**, and **superego** according to Freud, the three interrelated parts that make up the mind: the id consists of basic inborn drives that are the source of instinctive psychic energy; the ego is the realistic aspect of the mind that balances the forces of the id and the superego; the

superego has two components (the conscience and the ego-ideal) and represents the internalized demands of society

ideal culture the norms, values, and patterns of behavior that members of a society believe should be observed in principle

ideology a system of beliefs, attitudes, and values that directs a society and reproduces the status quo of the bourgeoisie

idioculture the customs, practices, and values expressed in a particular place by the people who interact there

immigration entering one country from another to take up permanent residence

implicit bias attitudes or stereotypes that are embedded at an unconscious level and may influence our perceptions, decisions, and actions

impression management the effort to control the impressions we make on others so that they form a desired view of us and the situation; the use of self-presentation and performance tactics

incapacitation an approach to punishment that seeks to protect society from criminals by imprisoning or executing them

incest sexual contact between family members; a form of child abuse when it occurs between a child and a caregiver

Independent (or Third) Sector the part of the economy composed of nonprofit organizations; their workers are mission driven, rather than profit driven, and such organizations direct surplus funds to the causes they support

independent variable the factor that is predicted to cause change

individual discrimination discrimination carried out by one person against another

inductive approach an approach whereby the researcher gathers data first, then formulates a theory to fit the data

Industrial Revolution the rapid transformation of social life resulting from the technological and economic developments that began with the assembly line, steam power, and urbanization

infant mortality average number of infant deaths per 1,000 live births in a particular population

influential power power that is supported by persuasion

Information Revolution the recent social revolution made possible by the development of the microchip in the 1970s, which brought about vast improvements in the ability to manage information

informed consent a safeguard through which the researcher makes sure that respondents are freely participating and understand the nature of the research

in-group a group that one identifies with and feels loyalty toward

in-group orientation among stigmatized individuals, the rejection of prevailing judgments or prejudice and the development of new standards that value their group identity

innovators individuals who accept society's approved goals but not society's approved means to achieve them

institutional discrimination discrimination carried out systematically by institutions (political, economic, educational, and others) that affects all members of a group who come into contact with it

institutional review board a group of scholars within a university who meet regularly to review and approve the research proposals of their colleagues and make recommendations for how to protect human subjects

instrumental leadership leadership that is task or goal oriented

instrumental role the position of the family member who provides material support; often an authority figure

instrumental tasks the practical physical tasks necessary to maintain family life

integrative medicine the combination of conventional medicine with complementary practices and treatments that have proven to be safe and effective

intergenerational mobility movement between social classes that occurs from one generation to the next

internal colonialism the economic and political subjugation of the minority group by the dominant group within a nation

internal migration movement of a population within a country

interpretive community a group of people dedicated to the consumption and interpretation of a particular cultural product and who create a collective, social meaning for the product

interpretive strategies the ideas and frameworks that audience members bring to bear on a particular media text to understand its meaning

intersectionality a concept that identifies how different categories of inequality (race, class, gender, etc.) intersect to shape the lives of individuals and groups

intersex used to describe a person whose chromosomes or sex characteristics are neither exclusively male nor exclusively female

intervening variable a third variable, sometimes overlooked, that explains the relationship between two other variables

interviews person-to-person conversations for the purpose of gathering information by means of questions posed to respondents

intragenerational mobility movement between social classes that occurs during the course of an individual's lifetime

intrinsic religiosity a person's inner religious life or personal relationship to the divine

iron cage Max Weber's pessimistic description of modern life, in which we are caught in bureaucratic structures that control our lives through rigid rules and rationalization

just-world hypothesis argument that people have a deep need to see the world as orderly, predictable, and fair, which creates a tendency to view victims of social injustice as deserving of their fates

kin relatives or relations, usually those related by common descent

knowledge work work that primarily deals with information; producing value in the economy through ideas, judgments, analyses, designs, or innovations

labeling theory Howard Becker's idea that deviance is a consequence of external judgments, or labels, that modify the individual's self-concept and change the way others respond to the labeled person

language a system of communication using vocal sounds, gestures, or written symbols; the basis of symbolic culture and the primary means through which we communicate with one another and perpetuate our culture

latent functions the less obvious, perhaps unintended functions of a social structure

laws types of norms that are formally codified to provide an explicit statement about what is permissible or forbidden, legal or illegal in a given society

leading questions questions that predispose a respondent to answer in a certain way

legal-rational authority authority based in laws, rules, and procedures, not in the heredity or personality of any individual leader

leisure a period of time that can be spent relaxing, engaging in recreation, or otherwise indulging in freely chosen activities

LGBTQ lesbian, gay, bisexual, transgender, and queer (sometimes "I" is added for "intersex" and "A" for "asexual")

liberation theology a movement within the Catholic Church to understand Christianity from the perspective of the poor and oppressed, with a focus on fighting injustice

life expectancy average age to which people in a particular population are expected to live

life history an approach to interviewing that asks for a chronological account of the respondent's entire life or some portion of it

life span or **longevity** the uppermost age to which a person can potentially live

lifestyle enclaves groups of people drawn together by shared interests, especially those relating to hobbies, sports, and media

Likert scale a way of formatting a survey questionnaire so that the respondent can choose an answer along a continuum

literature review a thorough search through previously published studies relevant to a particular topic

looking-glass self the notion that the self develops through our perception of others' evaluations and appraisals of us

lower-middle class see *working class*

macrosociology the level of analysis that studies large-scale social structures in order to determine how they affect the lives of groups and individuals

mainstream environmentalism beginning in the 1970s, the third stage of the environmental movement; characterized by enhanced organization, improved promotional campaigns and political tactics, and an increased reliance on economic and scientific expertise

Malthusian theorem the theory that exponential growth in population will outpace arithmetic growth in food production and other resources

manifest functions the obvious, intended functions of a social structure for the social system

marriage a formally recognized bond between two spouses, establishing contractual rights and obligations between them

mass behavior similar behaviors engaged in by large groups of people without their necessarily being in the same place

mass society theory a theory of social movements that assumes people join not because of the movement's ideals but to satisfy a psychological need to belong to something larger than themselves

master status a status that is always relevant and affects all other statuses we possess

material culture the objects associated with a cultural group, such as tools, machines, utensils, buildings, and artwork; any physical object to which we give social meaning

McDonaldization George Ritzer's term describing the spread of bureaucratic rationalization and the accompanying increases in efficiency and dehumanization

means of production anything that can create wealth: money, property, factories, and other types of businesses, and the infrastructure necessary to run them

mechanical solidarity the type of social bonds present in premodern, agrarian societies, in which shared traditions and beliefs created a sense of social cohesion

medicalization the process by which some behaviors or conditions that were once seen as personal problems are redefined as medical issues

megalopolis a group of densely populated metropolises that grow dependent on each other and eventually combine to form a huge urban complex

men's liberation a movement that originated in the 1970s to discuss the challenges of masculinity

men's rights movement an offshoot of male liberation whose members believe that feminism promotes discrimination against men

merger the legal combination of two companies, usually in order to maximize efficiency and profits by eliminating redundant infrastructure and personnel

meritocracy a system in which rewards are distributed based on merit

metropolis an urban area with a large population, usually 500,000 to 1 million people

Metropolitan Statistical Area (MSA) an area with at least one major city of 50,000 or more inhabitants that is surrounded by adjacent counties that are socially and economically integrated with the city core

microaggressions everyday uses of subtle verbal and nonverbal communications that convey denigrating or dismissive messages to members of certain social groups

microsociology the level of analysis that studies face-to-face and small-group interactions in order to understand how they affect the larger patterns and structures of society

middle class social class composed primarily of white collar workers with a broad range of education and incomes; they constitute about 30 percent of the U.S. population

midrange theory an approach that integrates empiricism and grand theory

migration movement of people from one geographic area to another for the purpose of resettling

minority group a social group that is systematically denied the same access to power and resources available to society's dominant groups though its members are not necessarily fewer in number than the dominant groups

miscegenation romantic, sexual, or marital relationships between people of different races

misogyny an ingrained prejudice against women; dislike, contempt, or hatred of women

modern environmental movement beginning in the 1960s, the second major stage of the environmental movement; focused on the environmental consequences of new technologies, oil exploration, chemical production, and nuclear power plants

modernism a paradigm that places trust in the power of science and technology to create progress, solve problems, and improve life

modernity a term that characterizes industrialized societies, including the decline of tradition, an increase in individualism, and a belief in progress, technology, and science

monarchy a government ruled by a king or queen, with succession of rulers kept within the family

monogamy the practice of marrying (or being in a relationship with) one person at a time

monopoly a situation in which there is only one individual or organization, without competitors, providing a particular good or service

monotheistic a term describing religions that worship a single divine figure

moral holiday a specified time period during which some norm violations are allowed

mores norms that carry great moral significance, are closely related to the core values of a cultural group, and often involve severe repercussions for violators

mortality rate a measure of the decrease in population due to deaths; often expressed as the number of deaths per 1,000 people in a particular population

multiculturalism a policy that values diverse racial, ethnic, national, and linguistic backgrounds and so encourages the retention of cultural differences within the larger society

nature vs. nurture debate the ongoing discussion of the respective roles of genetics and socialization in determining individual behaviors and traits

negative questions survey questions that ask respondents what they don't think instead of what they do think

neglect a form of child abuse in which the caregiver fails to provide adequate nutrition, sufficient clothing or shelter, or hygienic and safe living conditions

net migration net effect of immigration and emigration on a particular population; expressed as an increase or decrease

new ecological paradigm a way of understanding human life as just one part of an ecosystem that includes many species' interactions with the environment; suggests that there should be ecological limits on human activity

NIMBY short for "not in my back yard"; originally referred to protests aimed at shifting undesirable activities onto those with less power; now sometimes used without negative connotations to describe local environmental activists

nonrenewable resources finite resources that can become exhausted; includes those that take so long to replenish as to be effectively finite

norms rules or guidelines regarding what kinds of behavior are acceptable and appropriate within a particular culture; these typically emanate from the group's values

nuclear family a heterosexual couple with one or more children living in a single household

objectivity impartiality; the ability to allow the facts to speak for themselves

oligarchy political rule by a small group of people, usualy members of a wealthy or otherwise dominant class

online education any educational course or program in

which the teacher and the student meet via the Internet, rather than meeting physically in a classroom

open system a social system with ample opportunities to move from one class to another

open-ended question a question asked of a respondent that allows the answer to take whatever form the respondent chooses

operational definition a clear and precise definition of a variable that facilitates its measurement

opinion leaders high-profile individuals whose interpretation of events influences the public

organic solidarity the type of social bonds present in modern societies, based on difference, interdependence, and individual rights

out-group a group toward which an individual feels opposition, rivalry, or hostility

outsiders according to Howard Becker, those labeled deviant and subsequently segregated from "normal" society

outsourcing "contracting out" or transferring to another country the labor that a company might otherwise have employed its own staff to perform; typically done for financial reasons

palliative care type of health care that focuses on symptom and pain relief and providing a supportive environment for critically ill or dying patients

pandemic occurs when a significantly higher number of cases of a disease also spreads through an especially large geographical region spanning many countries or even continents

paradigm a set of assumptions, theories, and perspectives that makes up a way of understanding social reality

paradigm shift a major change in basic assumptions of a particular scientific discipline

participant observation a methodology associated with ethnography whereby the researcher both observes and becomes a member in a social setting

particular or significant other the perspectives and expectations of a particular role that a child learns and internalizes

passing presenting yourself as a member of a different group than the stigmatized group to which you belong

patriarchy literally meaning "rule of the father"; a male-dominated society

personal front the performance tactics we use to present ourselves to others, including appearance, costume, and manner

pilot study a small-scale study carried out to test the feasibility of conducting a study on a larger scale

play stage the second stage in Mead's theory of the development of self wherein children pretend to play the role of the particular or significant other

pluralism a cultural pattern of intergroup relations that encourages racial and ethnic variation and acceptance within a society

pluralist model a system of political power in which a wide variety of individuals and groups have equal access to resources and the mechanisms of power

pluralistic ignorance a process in which members of a group individually conclude that there is no need to take action because they see that other group members have not done so

political action committees (PACs) organizations that raise money to support the interests of a select group or organization

politics methods and tactics intended to influence government policy, policy-related attitudes, and activities

pollution any environmental contaminant that harms living beings

polyamory a system of multiple-person partnership

polyandry a system of marriage that allows women to have multiple husbands

polygamy a system of marriage that allows people to have more than one spouse at a time

polygyny a system of marriage that allows men to have multiple wives

polysemy having many possible meanings or interpretations

popular culture forms of cultural expression usually associated with the masses, consumer goods, and commercial products

population transfer the forcible removal of a group of people from the territory they have occupied

positive deviance actions considered deviant within a given context but later reinterpreted as appropriate or even heroic

positivism the theory that sense perceptions are the only valid source of knowledge

postmodernism a paradigm that suggests that social reality is diverse, pluralistic, and constantly in flux

postmodernity a term that characterizes postindustrial societies, including a focus on the production and management of information and skepticism of science and technology

power the ability to control the actions of others

power elite a relatively small group of people in the top ranks of economic, political, and military institutions who make many of the important decisions in American society

pragmatism a perspective that assumes organisms (including humans) make practical adaptations to their environments; humans do this through cognition, interpretation, and interaction

praxis the application of theory to practical action in an effort to improve aspects of society

prejudice an idea about the characteristics of a group that is applied to all members of that group and is unlikely to change regardless of the evidence against it

preparatory stage the first stage in Mead's theory of the development of self wherein children mimic or imitate others

prestige the social honor people are given because of their membership in well-regarded social groups

preventive medicine type of health care that aims to avoid or forestall the onset of disease by taking preventive measures, often including lifestyle changes

primary deviance in labeling theory, the initial act or attitude that causes one to be labeled deviant

primary groups groups composed of the people who are most important to our sense of self; members' relationships are typically characterized by face-to-face interaction, high levels of cooperation, and intense feelings of belonging

primary sex characteristics biological factors, such as chromosomes, hormones, and reproductive organs, that distinguish males from females

privilege unearned advantage accorded to members of dominant social groups (males, whites, heterosexuals, the physically able, etc.)

probability sampling any sampling procedure that uses randomization

profane the ordinary, mundane, or everyday

pro-feminist men's movement an offshoot of male liberation whose members support feminism and believe that sexism harms both men and women

progressive term describing efforts to promote forward-thinking social change

proletariat workers; those who have no means of production of their own and so are reduced to selling their labor power in order to live

property crime crime that does not involve violence, including burglary, larceny-theft, motor vehicle theft, and arson

propinquity the tendency to partner with people who live close by

psychosexual stages of development four distinct stages of the development of the self between birth and adulthood, according to Freud; personality quirks are a result of being fixated, or stuck, at any stage

public goods dilemma a type of social dilemma in which individuals incur the cost to contribute to a collective resource, though they may never benefit from that resource

qualitative research research that works with nonnumerical data such as texts, field notes, interview transcripts, photographs, and tape recordings; this type of research more often tries to understand how people make sense of their world

quantitative research research that translates the social world into numbers that can be treated mathematically; this type of research often tries to find cause-and-effect relationships

queer theory social theory about gender and sexual identity; emphasizes the importance of difference and rejects ideas of innate identities or restrictive categories

race a socially defined category based on real or perceived biological differences between groups of people

race consciousness an ideology that acknowledges race as a powerful social construct that shapes our individual and social experiences

racial assimilation the process by which racial minority groups are absorbed into the dominant group through intermarriage

racism a set of beliefs about the claimed superiority of one racial or ethnic group; used to justify inequality and often rooted in the assumption that differences among groups are genetic

rape culture a set of beliefs, norms, and values that normalizes sexual violence against women

rapport a positive relationship often characterized by mutual trust or sympathy

rationalization the application of economic logic to human activity; the use of formal rules and regulations in order to maximize efficiency without consideration of subjective or individual concerns

reactivity the tendency of people and events to react to the process of being studied

real culture the norms, values, and patterns of behavior that actually exist within a society (which may or may not correspond to the society's ideals)

rebels individuals who reject society's approved goals and means and instead create and work toward their own (sometimes revolutionary) goals using new means

recreation any satisfying, amusing, and stimulating activity that is experienced as refreshing and renewing for body, mind, and spirit

reference group a group that provides a standard of comparison against which we evaluate ourselves

reflexivity how the identity and activities of the researcher influence what is going on in the field setting

region the context in which the performance takes place, including location, décor, and props

regressive term describing resistance to particular social changes, efforts to maintain the status quo, or attempts to reestablish an earlier form of social order

rehabilitation an approach to punishment that attempts to reform criminals as part of their penalty

reinforcement theory theory that suggests that audiences seek messages in the media that reinforce their existing attitudes and beliefs and are thus not influenced by challenging or contradictory information

relative deprivation a relative measure of poverty based on the standard of living in a particular society

relative deprivation theory a theory of social movements that focuses on the actions of the oppressed groups seeking rights or opportunities already enjoyed by others in the society

reliability the consistency of a question or measurement tool; the degree to which the same questions will produce similar answers

religion any institutionalized system of shared beliefs and rituals that identify a relationship between the sacred and the profane

religiosity the regular practice of religious beliefs, often measured in terms of frequency of attendance at worship services and the importance of religious beliefs to an individual

renewable resources resources that replenish at a rate comparable to the rate at which they are consumed

replicability the ability of research to be repeated and, thus, later verified by other researchers

representative sample a sample taken so that findings from members of the sample group can be generalized to the larger population; also referred to as a stratified sample

representativeness the degree to which a particular studied group is similar to, or represents, any part of the larger society

rescission the practice by insurance companies of canceling coverage only after a person gets sick

residential segregation the geographical separation of the poor from the rest of an area's population

resistance strategies ways that workers express discontent with their jobs and try to reclaim control of the conditions of their labor

resocialization the process of replacing previously learned norms and values with new ones as a part of a transition in life

resource mobilization theory a theory of social movements that focuses on the practical constraints that help or hinder social movements' action

respondent a participant in a study from whom the researcher seeks to gather information

response rate the number or percentage of surveys completed by respondents and returned to researchers

retreatists individuals who renounce society's approved goals and means entirely and live outside conventional norms altogether

retribution an approach to punishment that emphasizes retaliation or revenge for the crime as the appropriate goal

reverse racism the claim by whites that they suffer discrimination based upon their race and, therefore, experience social disadvantages

riot continuous disorderly behavior by a group of people that disturbs the peace and is directed toward other people and/or property

ritual a practice based on religious beliefs

ritualists individuals who have given up hope of achieving society's approved goals but still operate according to society's approved means

role the set of behaviors expected of someone because of their status

role conflict experienced when we occupy two or more roles with contradictory expectations

role exit the process of leaving a role that we will no longer occupy

role model an individual who serves as an example for others to strive toward and emulate

role strain experienced when there are contradictory expectations within one role

role-taking emotions emotions such as sympathy, embarrassment, or shame that require that we assume the perspective of another person or group and respond accordingly

rural relating to sparsely settled areas; in the United States, any county with a population density between 10 and 59.9 people per square mile

sacred the holy, divine, or supernatural

same-sex marriage federally recognized marriage between members of the same sex; made legal in the United States in 2015

sample the members of the target population who will actually be studied

sanctions positive or negative reactions to the ways that people follow or disobey norms, including rewards for conformity and punishment for violations

Sapir-Whorf hypothesis the idea that language structures thought and that ways of looking at the world are embedded in language

saturated self a postmodern idea that the self is now developed by multiple influences chosen from a wide range of media sources

school vouchers payments from the government to parents whose children attend failing public schools; the money helps parents pay private school tuition

scientific method a procedure for acquiring knowledge that emphasizes collecting concrete data through observation and experimentation

second shift the unpaid housework and child care often expected of women after they complete their day's paid labor

second wave the period of feminist activism during the 1960s and 1970s, often associated with the issues of women's equal access to employment and education

secondary deviance in labeling theory, the subsequent

deviant identity or career that develops as a result of being labeled deviant

secondary groups groups that are larger and less intimate than primary groups; members' relationships are usually organized around a specific goal and are often temporary

secondary sex characteristics physical differences between males and females, including facial and body hair, musculature, and bone structure, that are unrelated to reproduction

secular nonreligious; a secular society separates church and state and does not endorse any religion

segregation the physical and legal separation of groups by race or ethnicity

self the individual's conscious, reflexive experience of a personal identity separate and distinct from others

self-fulfilling prophecy an inaccurate statement or belief that, by altering the situation, becomes accurate; a prediction that causes itself to come true

service work work that involves providing a service to businesses or individual clients, customers, or consumers rather than manufacturing goods

sex an individual's membership in one of two categories—male or female—based on biological factors

sexism the belief that one sex, usually male, is superior to the other

sexual orientation or **sexual identity** the inclination to feel sexual desire toward people of a particular gender

sexuality the character or quality of being sexual

sick role the actions and attitudes that society expects from someone who is ill

signs symbols that stand for or convey an idea

simple random sample a particular type of probability sample in which every member of the population has an equal chance of being selected

simplicity movement a loosely knit movement that opposes consumerism and encourages people to work less, earn less, and spend less, in accordance with non-materialistic values

simulacrum an image or media representation that does not reflect reality in any meaningful way but is treated as real

situational ethnicity an ethnic identity that can be either displayed or concealed depending on its usefulness in a given situation

slavery the most extreme form of social stratification, based on the ownership of people

smart growth term for economic and urban planning policies that emphasize responsible development and renewal

social analyst someone who approaches the world by using reasoning and questions to gain deeper insights

social atomization a social situation that emphasizes individualism over collective or group identities

social change the transformation of a culture over time

social class a system of stratification based on access to such resources as wealth, property, power, and prestige

social construction the process by which a concept or practice is created and maintained by participants who collectively agree that it exists

social control the formal and informal mechanisms used to elicit conformity to values and norms and thus promote social cohesion

social control theory a theory of crime, proposed by Travis Hirschi, that posits that strong social bonds increase conformity and decrease deviance

social Darwinism the application of the theory of evolution and the notion of "survival of the fittest" to the study of society

social dilemma a situation in which behavior that is rational for the individual can, when practiced by many people, lead to collective disaster

social identity theory a theory of group formation and maintenance that stresses the need of individual members to feel a sense of belonging

social inequality the unequal distribution of wealth, power, or prestige among members of a society

social influence group impact on others' decisions

social institutions systems and structures within society that shape the activities of groups and individuals

social learning the process of learning behaviors and meanings through social interaction

social loafing the phenomenon in which each individual contributes a little less as more individuals are added to a task; a source of inefficiency when working in teams

social mobility the movement of individuals or groups within the hierarchical system of social classes

social movement any social group with leadership, organization, and an ideological commitment to promote or resist social change

social network the web of direct and indirect ties connecting an individual to other people who may also affect the individual

social reproduction the tendency of social classes to remain relatively stable as class status is passed down from one generation to the next

social sciences the disciplines that use the scientific method to examine the social world

social stratification the division of society into groups arranged in a social hierarchy

social ties connections between individuals

socialism an economic system based on the collective ownership of the means of production, collective distribution of goods and services, and government regulation

socialization the process of learning and internalizing the values, beliefs, and norms of our social group, by which we become functioning members of society

society a group of people who shape their lives in

aggregated and patterned ways that distinguish their group from others

sociobiology a branch of science that uses biological and evolutionary explanations for social behavior

socioeconomic status (SES) a measure of an individual's place within a social class system; often used interchangeably with "class"

sociological imagination a quality of the mind that allows us to understand the relationship between our individual circumstances and larger social forces

sociological perspective a way of looking at the world through a sociological lens

sociology the systematic or scientific study of human society and social behavior, from large-scale institutions and mass culture to small groups and individual interactions

solidarity the degree of integration or unity within a particular society; the extent to which individuals feel connected to other members of their group

special interest groups organizations that raise and spend money to influence elected officials and/or public opinion

spurious correlation the appearance of causation produced by an intervening variable

status a position in a social hierarchy that carries a particular set of expectations

status inconsistency a situation in which an individual holds differing and contradictory levels of status in terms of wealth, power, prestige, or other elements of socioeconomic status

stereotype promise a kind of self-fulfilling prophecy in which positive stereotypes, such as the "model minority" label applied to Asian Americans, lead to positive performance outcomes

stereotype threat a kind of self-fulfilling prophecy in which the fear of performing poorly—and confirming stereotypes about their social groups—causes students to perform poorly

stereotyping judging others based on preconceived generalizations about groups or categories of people

stigma Erving Goffman's term for any physical or social attribute that devalues a person or group's identity and that may exclude those who are devalued from normal social interaction

structural functionalism a paradigm based on the assumption that society is a unified whole that functions because of the contributions of its separate structures

structural mobility changes in the social status of large numbers of people as a result of structural changes in society

structure a social institution that is relatively stable over time and that meets the needs of a society by performing functions necessary to maintain social order and stability

subculture a group within society that is differentiated by its distinctive values, norms, and lifestyle

suburbanization the shift of large segments of population away from the urban core and toward the edges of cities

suffrage movement the movement organized around gaining voting rights for women

surveys research method based on questionnaires that are administered to a sample of respondents selected from a target population

sustainability economic development that aims to reconcile global economic growth with environmental protection

sweatshop a workplace where workers are subject to extreme exploitation, including below-standard wages, long hours, and poor working conditions that may pose health or safety hazards

symbolic culture the ideas associated with a cultural group, including ways of thinking (beliefs, values, and assumptions) and ways of behaving (norms, interactions, and communication)

symbolic ethnicity an ethnic identity that is relevant only on specific occasions and does not significantly affect everyday life

symbolic interactionism a paradigm that sees interaction and meaning as central to society and assumes that meanings are not inherent but are created through interaction

synergy a mutually beneficial interaction between parts of an organization that allows it to create something greater than the sum of its individual outputs

synthesis the new social system created out of the conflict between thesis and antithesis in a dialectical model

taboo a norm ingrained so deeply that even thinking about violating it evokes strong feelings of disgust, horror, or revulsion

target population the entire group about which a researcher would like to be able to generalize

taste cultures areas of culture that share similar aesthetics and standards of taste

taste publics groups of people who share similar artistic, literary, media, recreational, and intellectual interests

technological determinism a theory of social change that assumes changes in technology drive changes in society, rather than vice versa

technology material artifacts and the knowledge and techniques required to use them

telecommuting working from home while staying connected to the office through communications technology

tertiary deviance redefining the stigma associated with a deviant label as a positive phenomenon

textual poaching Henry Jenkins's term for the ways that audience members manipulate an original cultural product to create a new one; a common way for fans to exert some control over the media they consume

theories abstract propositions that explain the social world and make predictions about the future

thesis the existing social arrangements in a dialectical model

thick description the presentation of detailed data on interactions and meaning within a cultural context, from the perspective of its members

third place any informal public place where people come together regularly for conversation and camaraderie when not at work or at home

third wave the most recent period of feminist activism, focusing on issues of diversity, globalization, and the variety of identities women can possess

Thomas theorem classic formulation of the way individuals determine reality, whereby "if people define situations as real, they are real in their consequences"

total institutions institutions in which individuals are cut off from the rest of society so that they can be controlled and regulated for the purpose of systematically stripping away previous roles and identities in order to create new ones

toxic masculinity a masculine ideal that espouses extreme and harmful attitudes and behaviors and may lead to various negative effects for women and men

tracking the placement of students in educational "tracks," or programs of study (e.g., college prep, remedial), that determine the types of classes they take

traditional authority authority based in custom, birthright, or divine right

tragedy of the commons a type of social dilemma in which many individuals' overexploitation of a public resource depletes or degrades that common resource

transgender term used when gender identity and/or expression is different from the sex assigned at birth

transphobia fear of or discrimination toward transgender or other gender-nonconforming people

treadmill of production term describing the operation of modern economic systems that require constant growth, which causes increased exploitation of resources and environmental degradation

triad a three-person social group

two-step flow model theory on media effects that suggests audiences get information through opinion leaders who influence their attitudes and beliefs, rather than through direct, firsthand sources

unchurched a term describing those who consider themselves spiritual but not religious and who often adopt aspects of various religious traditions

underclass the poorest group, comprising the homeless and chronically unemployed who may depend on public or private assistance; they constitute about 12 percent of the U.S. population

Uniform Crime Report (UCR) an official measure of crime in the United States, produced by the FBI's official tabulation of every crime reported by more than 18,000 law enforcement agencies

union an association of workers who bargain collectively for wages and benefits and better working conditions

unobtrusive measures research methods that rely on existing sources and where the researcher does not intrude upon or disturb the social setting or its subjects

unschooling a homeschooling alternative that rejects the standard curriculum in favor of student-driven types of learning

upper class an elite and largely self-sustaining group who possess most of the country's wealth; they constitute about 1 percent of the U.S. population

upper-middle class social class consisting of mostly highly educated professionals and managers who have considerable financial stability; they constitute about 14 percent of the U.S. population

urban relating to cities; typically describes densely populated areas

urban density concentration of people in a city, measured by the total number of people per square mile

urban renewal efforts to rejuvenate decaying inner cities, including renovation, selective demolition, commercial development, and tax incentives

urban sprawl a derogatory term for the expansion of urban or suburban boundaries, associated with irresponsible or poorly planned development

urbanites people who live in cities

urbanization movement of increasing numbers of people from rural areas to cities

uses and gratifications paradigm approaches to understanding media effects that focus on how the media fulfill individuals' psychological or social needs

utopia literally "no place"; an ideal society in which all social ills have been overcome

validity the accuracy of a question or measurement tool; the degree to which a researcher is measuring what they think they are measuring

value-free sociology an ideal whereby researchers identify facts without allowing their own personal beliefs or biases to interfere

values ideas about what is right or wrong, good or bad, desirable or worthy in a particular group; they express what the group cherishes and honors

variables two or more phenomena that a researcher believes are related; these will be examined in the experiment

vector organisms animals like mosquitoes, ticks, and

birds that carry and spread pathogens (germs or other infectious agents) in a given area

verstehen "empathic understanding"; Weber's term to describe good social research, which tries to understand the meanings that individuals attach to various aspects of social reality

vertical social mobility the movement between different class statuses, often called either upward mobility or downward mobility

violent crime crime in which violence is either the objective or the means to an end, including murder, rape, aggravated assault, and robbery

virtual communities social groups whose interactions are mediated through information technologies, particularly the Internet

wealth a measure of net worth that includes income, property, and other assets

wealth gap the unequal distribution of assets across a population

white collar a description characterizing lower-level professional and management workers and some highly skilled laborers in technical jobs

white collar crime crime committed by a high-status individual in the course of their occupation

white flight movement of upper- and middle-class whites who could afford to leave the cities for the suburbs, especially in the 1950s and 1960s

white nationalism the belief that the nation should be built around a white identity that is reflected in religion, politics, economics, and culture

working class or **lower-middle class** social class consisting of mostly blue collar or service industry workers who are less likely to have a college degree; they constitute about 30 percent of the U.S. population

working poor poorly educated manual and service workers who may work full-time but remain near or below the poverty line; they constitute about 13 percent of the U.S. population

References

Abel, Jaison R.; and Deitz, Richard. 2014. "Do the benefits of college still outweigh the costs?" *Current Issues in Economics and Finance*: Federal Reserve Bank of New York. http://www.newyorkfed.org/research/current_issues/ci20-3.pdf.

Achtenberg, Emily. 2013. "From water wars to water scarcity: Bolivia's cautionary tale." North American Congress on Latina America, June. https://nacla.org/blog/2013/6/5/waterwars-water-scarcity-bolivia's-cautionary-tale.

Acierno, R.; Hernandez, M. A.; Amstadter, A. B.; Resnick, H. S.; Steve, K.; Muzzy, W.; et al. 2010. "Prevalence and correlates of emotional, physical, sexual, and financial abuse and potential neglect in the United States: The national elder mistreatment study." *American Journal of Public Health*, vol. 100, no. 2: 292–297.

ACLU. 2003. "Inadequate representation." American Civil Liberties Union online publication, October 8. https://www.aclu.org/capital/unequal/10390pub20031008.html.

———. 2017. "Fact sheet on voter ID laws." https://www.aclu.org/other/oppose-voter-id-legislation-fact-sheet.

Adelstein, Jennifer. 2011. "What makes a knowledge society? Privileging discourses." In Katerina Nicolopoulou, Mine Karatas-Özkan, Ahu Tatli, and John Taylor, eds., *Global Knowledge Work: Diversity and Relational Perspectives.* Cheltenham: Edward Elgar Publishing, pp. 3–21.

Adler, Patricia A.; and Adler, Peter. 1991. *Backboards and Blackboards: College Athletes and Role Engulfment.* New York: Columbia University Press.

Administration for Community Living. 2018. "2017 profile of older Americans." https://acl.gov/sites/default/files/Aging%20and%20Disability%20in%20America/2017OlderAmericansProfile.pdf.

Administration on Aging. 2016. "A profile of older Americans: 2016." https://www.acl.gov/sites/default/files/Aging%20and%20Disability%20in%20America/2016-Profile.pdf.

Adorno, T.; and Horkheimer, M. 1979. "The culture industry: Enlightenment as mass deception." In T. Adorno and M. Horkheimer, eds., *Dialectic of Enlightenment.* London: Verso.

Aguirre, Benigno; Quarantelli, Enrico; and Mendoza, Jorge L. 1988. "The collective behavior of fads: The characteristics, effects and career of streaking." *American Sociological Review*, vol. 53: 569–589.

Agyeman, Julian; Bullard, Robert D.; and Evans, Bob; eds. 2003. *Just Sustainabilities: Development in an Unequal World.* Cambridge, MA: MIT Press.

Ahmed, Farid. 2012. "At least 117 killed in fire at Bangladeshi clothing factory." *CNN*, November 25. http://www.cnn.com/2012/11/25/world/asia/bangladesh-factory-fire/index.html.

Alatas, Syed Farid; and Sinha, Vineeta. 2001. "Teaching classical sociological theory in Singapore: The context of Eurocentrism." *Teaching Sociology*, vol. 29, no. 3: 316–331.

Alcoholics Anonymous. 2001 (orig. 1939). *Alcoholics Anonymous: The Story of How Many Thousands of Men and Women Have Recovered from Alcoholism*, 4th ed. New York: Alcoholics Anonymous World Service.

Alexander, Michelle. 2011. *The New Jim Crow: Mass Incarceration in the Age of Colorblindness.* New York: The New Press.

Allen, Drew; and Dadgar, Mina. 2012. "Does dual enrollment increase students' success in college? Evidence from a quasi-experimental analysis of dual enrollment in New York City." *Wiley Periodicals, Inc.* June. http://onlinelibrary.wiley.com/doi/10.1002/he.20010/abstract.

Allen, I. Elaine; and Seaman, Jeff. 2013. "Changing course: Ten years of tracking online education in the United States." Wellesley, MA: Babson College/Quahog Research Group. http://www.onlinelearningsurvey.com/reports/changingcourse.pdf.

Allport, G.; and Ross, M. 1967. "Personal religious orientation and prejudice." *Journal of Personality and Social Psychology*, vol. 5, no. 4: 432–443.

Almaguer, Tomas. 2008. *Racial Fault Lines: The Historical Origins of White Supremacy in California.* Berkeley: University of California Press.

Altermatt, Ellen Rydell; and Pomerantz, Eva M. 2005. "The implications of having high-achieving versus low-achieving friends: A longitudinal analysis." *Social Development*, vol. 14, no. 1: 61–81.

Amato, Paul R.; and Patterson, Sarah E. 2016. "The intergenerational transmission of union instability in early adulthood." *Journal of Marriage and Family*, vol. 79, no. 3. December 5. http://onlinelibrary.wiley.com/doi/10.1111/jomf.12384/full.

American Association of Community Colleges. 2011. http://aacc.nche.edu/pages/default.aspx.

———. 2017. "Fast facts 2017." https://www.aacc.nche.edu/research-trends/fast-facts/.

American Civil Liberties Union. 2008. "A study of racially disparate outcomes in the Los Angeles Police Department." https://www.aclusocal.org/sites/default/files/wp-content/uploads/2015/09/11837125-LAPD-Racial-Profiling-Report-ACLU.pdf.

American College Health Association. 2018. "American College Health Association—National college health assessment II: Reference group executive summary fall 2018." https://www.acha.org/documents/ncha/NCHA-II_Fall_2018_Reference_Group_Executive_Summary.pdf.

American Psychiatric Association. 2017. "What is Autism Spectrum Disorder?" https://www.psychiatry.org/patients-families/autism/what-is-autism-spectrum-disorder.

Ananat, Elizabeth Oltmans. 2005. "The wrong side of the tracks: Estimating the causal effects of racial segregation on city outcomes." Unpublished working paper. MIT Department of Economics.

Anderson, Craig A.; et al. 2010. "Violent video game effects on aggression, empathy, and prosocial behavior in Eastern and Western countries: A meta-analytic review." *Psychological Bulletin*, vol. 136, no. 2: 151–173.

Anderson, Doug. 2009. "The changing face of unemployment." *Nielsenwire.* March 1. blog.nielsen.com/nielsenwire/consumer/the-changing-face-of-unemployment.

Anderson, Elijah. 1990. *Streetwise: Race, Class and Change in an Urban Community.* Chicago: University of Chicago Press.

Anderson, Kristin J.; and Leaper, Campbell. 1998. "Meta-analysis of gender effects on conversational interruption: Who, what, when, where, and why." *Sex Roles*, vol. 39, no. 3-4: 225–252.

Anderson, L. R. 2016. "Divorce rate in the U.S.: Geographic variation, 2015." *Family Profiles, FP-16-21.* Bowling Green, OH: National Center for Family & Marriage Research.

Anderson, M. 2017. "Digital divide persists even as lower-income Americans make gains in tech adoption." Pew Research Center, March 22. https://www.pewresearch.org/fact-tank/2017/03/22/digital-divide-persists-even-as-lower-income-americans-make-gains-in-tech-adoption/.

———. 2018. "A majority of teens have experienced some form of cyberbullying." Pew Research Center. https://www.pewinternet.org/2018/09/27/a-majority-of-teens-have-experienced-some-form-of-cyberbullying/.

———; and Kumar, M. 2019. "Digital divide persists even as lower-income Americans make gains in tech adoption." Pew Research Center, May 7. https://www.pewresearch.org/fact-tank/2019/05/07/digital-divide-persists-even-as-lower-income-americans-make-gains-in-tech-adoption/.

Anderson, Steven W.; Bechara, Antoine; Damasio, Hann; Tranel, Daniel; and Damasio, Antonio R. 1999. "Impairment of social and moral behavior related to early damage in human prefrontal cortex." *Nature Neuroscience*, vol. 2, no. 11: 1032–1037.

Anzaldúa, Gloria. 1987. *Borderlands/La Frontera: The New Mestiza.* San Francisco: Aunt Lute Books.

Arendt, Hannah. 1958. *The Origins of Totalitarianism.* London: Allen and Unwin Press.

Armitage, Angus. 1951. *The World of Copernicus.* New York: Mentor Books.

Armstrong, Elizabeth A.; Hamilton, Laura; and Sweeney, Brian. 2006. "Sexual assault on campus: A multilevel, integrative approach to party rape social problems," *Social Problems*, vol. 53, no. 4: 483–499.

Arrison, Sonia. 2011. *One Hundred Plus: How the Coming Age of Longevity Will Change Everything, from Careers and Relationships to Family and Faith.* Boston: Basic Books.

Artiga, Samantha; Orgera, Kendal; and Damico, Anthony. 2019. "Changes in health coverage by race and ethnicity since implementation of the ACA, 2013–2017." Kaiser Family Foundation, February 13. https://www.kff.org/disparities-policy/issue-brief/changes-in-health-coverage-by-race-and-ethnicity-since-implementation-of-the-aca-2013-2017/.

Asch, S. 1958. "Effects of group pressure upon the modification and distortion of judgments." In E. E. Maccoby, T. M. Newcomb, and E. L. Hartley, eds., *Readings in Social Psychology.* New York: Holt, Rinehart, & Winston.

Associated Press. 2013. "Bangladesh factory collapse blamed on swampy ground and heavy machinery." http://www.guardian.co.uk/world/2013/may/23/bangladesh-factory-collapse-rana-plaza.

———. 2015. "Supermarkets in food deserts." http://interactives.ap.org/2015/food-deserts/.

Association of American Medical Colleges. 2009. "Scientific foundations for future physicians." http://www.hhmi.org/grants/pdf/08-209_AAMC-HHMI_report.pdf.

———. 2017. "Promoting a diverse and culturally competent health care workforce." *AAMC News*, May 30. https://news.aamc.org/for-the-media/article/diverse-healthcare-workforce/.

Association of Certified Fraud Examiners. 2012. *2012 Report to the Nations: Key Findings and Highlights.* http://www.acfe.com/rttn-high lights.aspx.

Association of Statisticians of American Religious Bodies. 2012. "Second largest religious tradition in each state, 2010."

Astin, Alexander W.; Astin, Helen S.; and Lindholm, Jennifer A. 2010. "National study of spirituality in higher education: Students' search for meaning and purpose." UCLA Higher Education Research Institute. http://spirituality.ucla.edu/findings/.

Atauhene, B. 2011. "South Africa's land reform crisis: Eliminating the legacy of apartheid." *Foreign Affairs*, vol. 90, no. 4: 121–129.

Atkin, C. 1973. "Instrumental utilities and information seeking." In P. Clark, ed., *New Models for Mass Communication Research.* Beverly Hills, CA: Sage.

———. 1985. "Informational utility and selective exposure." In D. Zillmann and J. Bryant, eds., *Selective Exposure to Communication.* Hillsdale, NJ: Erlbaum.

AV Comparatives. 2014. "Parental control test and review 2014." September 14. http://www.av-comparatives.org/wp-content/uploads/2014/09/Parental_Control_Report_2014.pdf.

Avishai, Orit. 2008. "Doing religion in a secular world: Women in conservative religions and the question of agency." *Gender and Society*, vol. 22, no. 4: 409–433.

Ayers, John W.; Althouse, Benjamin M.; Leas, Eric C.; Dredze, Mark; and Allem, Jon-Patrick. 2017. "Internet searches for suicide following the release of *13 Reasons Why.*" *JAMA Internal Medicine*, vol. 177, no. 10: 1527–1529. https://doi.org/10.1001/jamainternmed.2017.3333.

Babiak, T. 2004. "Everything goes at Burning Man: Counterculture fest is everything that North America isn't." *National Post*, September 6, p. B10.

Baca Zinn, Maxine; and Eitzen, D. Stanley. 2002. *Diversity in Families.* Boston: Allyn and Bacon.

Badenhausen, Kurt; and Ozanian, Mike. 2019. "NBA team values 2019: Knicks on top at $4 billion." *Forbes*, February 6. https://www.forbes.com/sites/kurtbadenhausen/2019/02/06/nba-team-values-2019-knicks-on-top-at-4-billion/.

Badgett, M. V.; and Mallory, C. 2014. "Patterns of relationships for same-sex couples: Divorce and terminations." http://williamsinstitute.law.ucla.edu/wp-content/uploads/Badgett-Mallory-Divorce-Terminations-Dec-2014.pdf.

Bagdikian, Ben H. 2004. *The New Media Monopoly.* Boston: Beacon Press.

Bailey, Holly. 2010. "ABC News/Yahoo! News Poll: People are losing faith in the American Dream." *Yahoo! News*, September 21. www.news.yahoo.com.

Bailey, Martha J.; and Dynarski, Susan M. 2011. "Inequality in postsecondary attainment." In Greg Duncan and Richard

Murnane, eds., *Whither Opportunity: Rising Inequality, Schools, and Children's Life Chances*, 117–132. New York: Russell Sage Foundation.

Bailey, Ronald. 2002. "*Silent Spring* at 40: Rachel Carson's classic is not aging well." *Reason Online Magazine*, June 12. http://reason.com/rb/rb061202.shtml.

Baio, J.; Wiggins, L.; Christensen, D. L.; et al. 2018. "Prevalence of autism spectrum disorder among children aged 8 years—Autism and Developmental Disabilities Monitoring Network, 11 sites, United States, 2014." *Morbidity and Mortality Weekly Report Surveillance Summaries*, vol. 67, no. SS-6: 1–23.

Baker, J. P.; and Crist, J. L. 1971. "Teacher expectancies: A review of the literature." In J. D. Elashoff and R. E. Snow, eds., *Pygmalion Reconsidered: A Case Study in Statistical Inference: Reconsideration of the Rosenthal-Jacobson Data on Teacher Expectancy*. Worthington, OH: Charles A. Jones.

Bales, Kevin. 2000. *Disposable People: New Slavery in the Global Economy*. Berkeley: University of California Press.

———; and Soodalter, Ron. 2009. *The Slave Next Door: Human Trafficking and Slavery in America Today*. Berkeley: University of California Press.

Bandura, A. 1965. "Influence of models' reinforcement contingencies on the acquisition of imitative response." *Journal of Personality and Social Psychology*, vol. 1: 589–595.

Bandy, Joe. 1996. "Managing the other of nature: Sustainability, spectacle, and global regimes of capital in ecotourism." *Public Culture*, vol. 8, no. 3: 539–566.

Banfield, E. C. 1970. *The Unheavenly City*. Boston: Little, Brown and Co.

Banks, Ingrid. 2000. *Hair Matters: Beauty, Power, and Black Women's Consciousness*. New York: New York University Press.

Barnard, Alex V. 2016. Freegans: *Diving into the Wealth of Food Waste in America*. Minneapolis, MN: University of Minnesota Press.

Barner, Mark R. 1999. "Sex-role stereotyping in FCC-mandated children's educational television." *Journal of Broadcasting & Electronic Media*, vol. 43, no. 4: 551.

Barnes, Brooke. 2009. "Disney swoops into action buying Marvel for $4 billion." *The New York Times*, August 31. http://www.nytimes.com.

Barnett, Jessica C.; and Berchick, Edward R. 2017. "Health insurance coverage in the United States: 2016." U.S. Census Bureau. https://www.census.gov/content/dam/Census/library/publications/2017/demo/p60-260.pdf.

Barocio, Jacqueline; and Shaefer, H. Luke. 2016. "The number of American households seeking help at food pantries hits highest point in two decades in 2014." *$2 a Day*, August 16. http://www.twodollarsaday.com/blog/2016/8/16/the-number-of-american-households-seeking-help-at-food-pantries-hits-highest-point-in-two-decades-in-2014.

Barrett, Bruce; Charles, Joel W.; and Temte, Jonathan L. 2015. "Climate change, human health, and epidemiological transition." *Preventive Medicine,* vol. 70: 69–75.

Barry, Dave. 1987. *Dave Barry's Bad Habits: A 100% Fact-Free Book*. New York: Holt, p. 203.

Bartels, Chuck. 2003. "Wal-Mart starting to look at all its 1.1 million U.S. workers." *Times-Picayune* (New Orleans, LA), October 25, "Money," p. 1.

Bartkowski, John P.; and Read, Jen'nan Ghazal. 2003. "Veiled submission: Gender, power, and identity among evangelical and Muslim women in the United States." *Qualitative Sociology*, vol. 26: 71–92.

Batan, Clarence M. 2004. "Of strengths and tensions: A dialogue of ideas between the classics and Philippine sociology." *UNITAS*, vol. 77, no. 2: 163–186.

Baudrillard, Jean. 1994 (orig. 1981). *Simulacra and Simulation*. Trans. Sheila Glaser. Ann Arbor: University of Michigan Press.

Bauer, Martin W.; and Gaskell, George, eds. 2000. *Qualitative Researching with Text, Image and Sound*. London; Thousand Oaks, CA: Sage.

Baum, Sandry; Ma, Jennifer; and Payea, Kathleen. 2013. "Education pays: The benefits of higher education for individuals and society." https://trends.collegeboard.org/sites/default/files/education-pays-2013-full-report-022714.pdf.

BBC News. 2013. "'Urgent need' to remove space debris." April 25. http://www.bbc.co.uk.

Beamish, Thomas. 2002. *Silent Spill: The Organization of an Industrial Crisis*. Boston: MIT Press.

Beard, Jennifer; Feeley, Frank; and Rosen, Sydney. 2009. "Economic and quality of life outcomes of antiretroviral therapy for HIV/AIDS in developing countries: A systematic literature review." *AIDS Care*, vol. 21, no. 11: 1343–1356.

Bearman, Peter S. 2010. "Just so stories: Vaccines, autism, and the single-bullet disorder." *Social Psychological Quarterly*, vol. 73, no. 2: 112–115.

Becker, A.; Burwell, R.; Herzog, D.; Hamburg, P.; and Gilman, S. 2002. "Eating behaviours and attitudes following prolonged exposure to television among ethnic Fijian adolescent girls." *The British Journal of Psychiatry*, vol. 180: 509–514.

Becker, Howard S. 1963. *Outsiders: Studies in the Sociology of Deviance*. Chicago: University of Chicago Press.

———. 1986. *Doing Things Together: Selected Papers*. Evanston, IL: Northwestern University Press.

———; Greer, Blanche; Hughes, Everett C.; and Strauss, Anselm L. 1961. *Boys in White: Student Culture in Medical School*. Chicago: University of Chicago Press.

Beckett, K.; and Evans, H. 2014. "The role of race in Washington State capital sentencing, 1981–2014." https://deathpenaltyinfo.org/documents/WashRaceStudy2014.pdf.

———. 2016. "Race, death, and justice: Capital sentencing in Washington State, 1981–2014." *Columbia Journal of Race and Law*, vol. 6, no. 2.

Bell, Daniel. 1976. *The Coming of Post-Industrial Society: A Venture in Social Forecasting*. New York: Basic Books.

Bell, Derrick A., Jr. 1980. "*Brown v. Board of Education* and the interest-convergence dilemma." *Harvard Law Review*, vol. 93, no. 3: 518–533.

Bellah, Robert; Sullivan, William; and Tipton, Steven. 1985. *Habits of the Heart: Individualism and Commitment in American Life*. Berkeley: University of California Press.

Bengali, Leila; and Daly, Mary C. 2014. "Is it still worth going to college?" *FRBSF Economic Letter*, May 5. http://www.frbsf.org/economic-research/publications/economic-letter/2014/may/is-college-worth-it-education-tuition-wages/.

Berchick, E. R.; Hood, E.; and Barnett, J. C. 2018. "Health insurance coverage in the United States: 2017." U.S. Census Bureau. https://www.census.gov/library/publications/2018/demo/p60-264.html.

Berger, Andrea; Turk-Bicakci, Lori; Garet, Michael; Knudson, Joel; and Hoshen, Gur. 2014. "Early college, continued success: Early college high school initiative impact study." *American Institutions for Research,* January 15. http://www.air.org/resource/early-college-continued-success-early-college-high-school-initiative-impact-study-2014.

Berger, Peter. 1963. *Invitation to Sociology: A Humanistic Perspective*. New York: Doubleday.

_____. 1977. *Facing Up to Modernity: Excursions in Society, Politics, and Religion*. New York: Basic Books.

_____; and Luckmann, T. 1966. *The Social Construction of Reality: A Treatise in the Sociology of Knowledge*. Garden City, NY: Anchor Books.

Bergström, Malin; Fransson, Emma; Modin, Bitte; Berlin, Marie; Gustafsson, Per A.; and Hjern, Anders. 2015. "Fifty moves a year: Is there an association between joint physical custody and psychosomatic problems in children?" *Journal of Epidemiology and Community Health*, vol. 69, no. 8: 769–774.

Berman, A. 2017. "How Google is revealing unmapped areas of the world in virtual reality." March 10. https://singularityhub.com/2017/03/10/how-google-is-revealing-unmapped-areas-of-the-world-in-virtual-reality/.

Berman, Mark. 2014. "Horror and few answers in small Florida town after man kills his daughter and six grandchildren." *The Washington Post*, September 19.

Bernardes, Jon. 1985. "Do we really know what the family is?" In P. Close and R. Collins, eds., *Family and Economy in Modern Society*. New York: Macmillan.

Bertrand, Marianne; and Mullainathan, Sendhil. 2004. "Are Emily and Greg more employable than Lakisha and Jamal? A field experiment on labor market discrimination." *American Economic Review*, vol. 94, no, 4: 991–1013.

Berube, A.; Singer, A.; Wilson, J. H.; and Frey, W. H. 2006. "Finding exurbia: America's fast-growing communities at the metropolitan fringe." Washington, DC: The Brookings Institution.

Best, Joel. 2006. *Flavor of the Month: Why Smart People Fall for Fads*. Berkeley: University of California Press.

Best, Samuel J.; and Krueger, Brian S. 2004. *Internet Data Collection*. Sage University Paper Series no. 141. Thousand Oaks, CA: Sage.

Betancourt, Joseph R.; Green, Alexander R.; and Carrillo, J. Emilio. 2012. "Cultural competence in health care: Emerging frameworks and practical approaches." The Commonwealth Fund, October. http://www.commonwealthfund.org/usr_doc/betancourt_culturalcompetence_576.pdf.

Bianchi, Suzanne M.; Sayer, Liana C.; Milkie, Melissa A.; and Robinson, John P. 2012. "Housework: Who did, does or will do it, and how much does it matter?" Social Forces, vol. 91, no. 1 (September 1): 55–63.

Bienkowski, Brian. 2013. "Corporations grabbing land and water overseas." *Scientific American*, February. http://www.scientificamerican.com/article/corporations-grabbing-land-and-water-overseas/.

Blackstone, A. 2014. "Childless… or childfree?" *Contexts*, vol. 13, no. 4: 68–70.

Blackwell, D. L.; and Villarroel, M. A. 2016. "Summary health statistics for U.S. adults: 2015, Table A-11a, National Health Interview Survey." National Center for Health Statistics. http://www.cdc.gov/nchs/nhis/SHS/tables.htm.

Blau, F. D.; and Kahn, L. M. 2016. "The gender wage gap: Extent, trends, and explanations." IZA Discussion Paper Series, 9656. Bonn, Germany: Institute for the Study of Labor. http://ftp.iza.org/dp9656.pdf.

Blau, Melinda; and Fingerman, Karen. 2009. *Consequential Strangers: The Power of People Who Don't Seem To Matter… But Really Do*. New York: W. W. Norton.

Bliss, Catherine. 2018. *Social by Nature: The Promise and Peril of Sociogenomics*. Stanford, CA: Stanford University Press.

Bloom, Allan. 1987. *The Closing of the American Mind*. New York: Simon & Schuster.

Blumer, Herbert. 1969. *Symbolic Interactionism: Perspective and Method*. Berkeley: University of California Press.

Blumler, J. G.; and Katz, Elihu. 1974. *The Uses of Mass Communication: Current Perspectives on Gratifications Research*. Beverly Hills, CA: Sage.

Bly, Robert. 1990. *Iron John: A Book About Men*. Upper Saddle River, NJ: Addison-Wesley.

Bobo, Lawrence; Charles, Camille Z.; Krysan, Maria; and Simmons, Alicia D. 2012. "The real record on racial attitudes." In Peter V. Marsden, ed., *Social Trends in American Life: Findings from the General Social Survey since 1972*. Princeton, NJ: Princeton University Press, pp. 38–83.

Bogaert, Anthony F. 2004. "Asexuality: Prevalence and associated factors in a national probability sample." *Journal of Sex*, vol. 41, no. 3: 279–287.

Bohner, Gerd; Siebler, Frank; and Schmelcher, Jurgen. 2006. "Social norms and the likelihood of raping: Perceived rape myth acceptance of others affects men's rape proclivity." *Personality and Social Psychology Bulletin*, vol. 32, no. 3: 286–297.

Bonacich, Edna. 1980. *The Economic Basis of Ethnic Solidarity: Small Business in the Japanese American Community*. Berkeley: University of California Press.

Bond, Rod; and Sussex, Peter B. 1996. "Culture and conformity: A meta-analysis of studies using Asch's (1952b, 1956) line judgment task." *Psychological Bulletin*, vol. 119, no. 1: 111–137.

Bonilla-Silva, Eduardo. 2013/2017. *Racism Without Racists: Color-Blind Racism and the Persistence of Racial Inequality in America*. New York: Rowman & Littlefield.

_____. 2015. "More than prejudice: Restatement, reflections, and new directions in critical race theory." *Sociology of Race and Ethnicity*, vol. 1, no. 1: 75–89.

Bordo, Susan. 1995. *Unbearable Weight: Feminism, Western Culture, and the Body*. Berkeley: University of California Press.

Borm, Brigitte. 2017. "Welcome home: An ethnography on the experiences of Airbnb hosts in commodifying their homes." In Urte Undine Frömming, Steffen Köhn, Samantha Fox, and Mike Terry, eds., *Digital Environments: Ethnographic Perspectives across Global Online and Offline Spaces*, 39–52. Germany: Transcript Verlag.

Boudon, Raymond. 1991. "What middle-range theories are." *Contemporary Sociology*, vol. 20, no. 4: 519–522.

Bourdieu, Pierre. 1973. "Cultural reproduction and social reproduction." In Richard Brown, ed., *Knowledge, Education, and Social Change: Papers in the Sociology of Education*. London: Tavistock.

_____. 1984. *Distinction: A Social Critique of the Judgement of Taste*. Cambridge, MA: Harvard University Press.

Bouzid, M.; Colon-Gonzalez, F. J.; Lung, T.; Lake, I. R.; and Hunter, P. R. 2014. "Climate change and the emergence of vector-borne diseases in Europe: Case study of dengue fever." *MBC Public Health*, vol. 14: 781.

Bowles, Samuel; and Gintis, Herbert. 1977. *Schooling in Capitalist America: Educational Reform and the Contradictions of Economic Life*. New York: Basic Books.

boyd, danah. 2014. *It's Complicated*. New Haven, CT: Yale University Press.

Boyle, Brendan. 2009. "Income gap is growing: The rich are getting richer—and rich whites quicker than rich blacks." *South African Times*, October 8. http://www.timeslive.co.za/business/article143706.ece.

Bozick, Robert; Alexander, Karl; and Entwisel, Doris; et al. 2010.

"Framing the future: Revisiting the place of educational expectations in status attainment." *Social Forces*, vol. 88, no. 5: 2027–2052.

Bradley, Graham; and Wildman, Karen. 2002. "Psychosocial predictors of emerging adults' risk and reckless behaviors." *Journal of Youth and Adolescence*, vol. 31, no. 4: 253–265.

Brennan Center for Justice. 2017. "Debunking the voter fraud myth." https://www.brennancenter.org/analysis/debunking -voter-fraud-myth.

Bridge, J. A.; Greenhouse, J. B.; Ruch, D.; Stevens, J.; Ackerman, J.; Sheftall, A. H.; Horowitz, L. M.; Kelleher, K. J.; Campo, J. V. 2019. "Association between the release of Netflix's *13 Reasons Why* and suicide rates in the United States: An interrupted times series analysis," *Journal of American Academy of Child & Adolescent Psychiatry* (in press; available online April 28).

Brief, Arthur P.; Buttram, Robert T.; Elliott, Jodi D.; Reizenstein, Robin M.; and McCline, Richard L. 1995. "Releasing the beast: A study of compliance with orders to use race as a selection criterion." *Journal of Social Issues*, vol. 51, no. 3: 177–193.

Brimson, Dougie. 2010. *March of the Hooligans: Soccer's Bloody Fraternity.* London: Virgin Books.

Brinkley-Rogers, Paul. 2002. "Pledge of allegiance reflects timeline of nation's history." *Columbus Dispatch*, June 28, p. 2A.

British Broadcasting Corporation. 2016. "Pakistan honour killings on the rise, report reveals." April 1. http://www.bbc.com/news /world-asia-35943732.

Brodkin, Karen. 1999. *How Jews Became White Folks and What That Says About Race in America.* New Brunswick, NJ: Rutgers University Press.

Bronson, Jennifer; and Carson, E. Ann. 2019. "Prisoners in 2017." U.S. Department of Justice. https://www.bjs.gov/content/pub /pdf/p17.pdf.

Brooks, James F. 2002. *Confounding the Color Line: The Indian-Black Experience in North America.* Lincoln: University of Nebraska Press.

Brooks-Gunn, Jeanne; Duncan, Greg J.; Klebanov, Pamela Kato; and Sealand, Naomi. 1993. "Do neighborhoods influence child and adolescent development?" *American Journal of Sociology*, vol. 99, no. 2: 353–395.

Broton, K. M. 2017. "The evolution of poverty in higher education: Material hardship, academic success, and policy perspectives." Unpublished doctoral dissertation. University of Wisconsin–Madison.

Brown, Alyssa. 2012. "With poverty comes depression, more than other illnesses." Gallup Well-Being Index. October 30. http:// www.gallup.com/poll/158417/poverty-comes-depression -illness.aspx?utm_source=tagrss&utm_medium=rss&utm _campaign=syndication.

Brown, S. L.; and Lin, I. F. 2012. "The gray divorce revolution: Rising divorce among middle-aged and older adults 1990–2010." *The Journals of Gerontology, Series B: Psychological Services and Social Services*, vol. 67, no. 6: 731–741.

Browning, Lynnley. 2014. "Do team games for employees really improve productivity?" *Newsweek*, October 26.

Buford, Bill. 1993. *Among the Thugs.* New York: Vintage.

Buitrago, K.; Rynell, A.; and Tuttle, S. 2017. "Cycle of risk: The intersection of poverty, violence, and trauma in Illinois." Heartland Alliance. https://www.heartlandalliance.org /povertyreport.

Bullard, Robert. 1990. *Dumping in Dixie: Race, Class and Environmental Quality.* Boulder, CO: Westview Press.

———. 1993. *Confronting Environmental Racism: Voices from the Grassroots.* Boston: South End Press.

———; Johnson, Glenn S.; and Wright, Beverly H. 1997. "Confronting environmental injustice: It's the right thing to do." *Race, Gender & Class*, vol. 5, no. 1: 63–79.

———; and Wright, Beverly H. 1990. "The quest for environmental equity: Mobilizing the African-American community for social change." *Society and Natural Resources*, vol. 3: 301–311.

Burger, Jerry M. 2009. "Replicating Milgram: Would people still obey today?" *American Psychologist*, vol. 64, no. 1: 1–11.

Burr, Ty. 2017. "Is 'Ghost in the Shell' an act of Hollywood whitewashing? Yes. And no." *Boston Globe*, March 31. https://www.bostonglobe.com/arts/movies/2017/03 /30/ghost-shell-act-hollywood-whitewashing-yes-and /o2qlxojR8iVe45DNeTQEWN/story.html.

Burros, Marian. 2009. "Urban farming, a bit closer to the sun." *The New York Times*, June 16.

Burton, Neel. 2012. "Compared to men, women are twice as likely to develop depression." *Psychology Today*, May 17. http:// archpsyc.jamanetwork.com/article.aspx?articleid=1733742.

Bustreo, F.; Okwo-Bele, J. M.; and Kamara, L. 2015. "World Health Organization perspectives on the contribution of the Global Alliance for Vaccines and Immunization on reducing child mortality." *Archives of Disease in Childhood*, vol. 100, Suppl. 1: s34–s37.

Butler, Judith. 1993. *Bodies That Matter: On the Discursive Limits of "Sex."* New York: Routledge.

———. 1999. *Gender Trouble.* New York: Routledge.

———. 2004. *Undoing Gender.* New York and London: Routledge.

Buttel, Frederick H. 1987. "New directions in environmental sociology." *Annual Review of Sociology*, 13: 465–488.

Byrne, D. G. 1981. "Sex differences in the reporting of symptoms of depression in the general population." *British Journal of Clinical Psychology*, vol. 20: 83–92.

Cahill, Spencer. 1999. "Emotional capital and professional socialization: The case of mortuary science students (and me)." *Social Psychology Quarterly*, vol. 62 (June): 101–116.

Calahan, M.; Perna, L. W.; Yamashita, M.; Wright-Kim, J.; & Jiang, N. 2019. "2019 indicators of higher education equity in the united states: Historical trend report." Washington, DC: The Pell Institute for the Study of Opportunity in Higher Education, Council for Opportunity in Education (COE), and Alliance for Higher Education and Democracy of the University of Pennsylvania (PennAHEAD).

Califano, Joseph A., Jr. 1999. "What was really great about the Great Society?" *Washington Monthly*, October.

California Community Colleges Chancellor's Office. 2015. "Key facts about California community colleges," January. http:// californiacommunitycolleges.cccco.edu/PolicyInAction /KeyFacts.aspx.

Calvey, David. 2018. "The everyday world of bouncers: A rehabilitated role for covert ethnography." *Qualitative Research*, 1–16.

Caminade, Cyril; et al. 2014. "Impact of climate change on global malaria distribution." *Proceedings of the National Academy of Sciences*, vol. 111, no. 9: 3286–3291.

Cancian, Maria; Brown, P. R.; and Cook, S. T. 2014. "Who gets custody now? Dramatic changes in children's living arrangements after divorce." *Demography*, vol. 51, no. 4: 1381–1396.

———; and Meyer, Daniel R. 1998. "Who gets custody?" *Demography*, vol. 35, no. 2: 147–157.

Cappelli, Peter. 2015. *Will College Pay Off? A Guide to the Most*

Important Financial Decision You'll Ever Make. New York: Public Affairs.

Carnevale, A.; Cheah, B.; and Hanson, A. R. 2015. "The economic value of college majors." Georgetown University Center on Education and the Workforce. https://cew.georgetown.edu/cew-reports/valueofcollegemajors/.

———; Rose, S. J.; and Cheah, B. 2011. "The college payoff: Education, occupations, lifetime earnings." Georgetown University Center on Education and the Workforce, August 5. http://www.cew.georgetown.edu/collegepayoff.com.

Carpenter, Sandra; and Meade-Pruitt, S. Maria. 2008. "Does the Twenty Statements Test elicit self-concept aspects that are most descriptive?" *World Cultures eJournal*, vol. 16, no. 1.

Carson, Ann E. 2018. "Prisoners in 2016." U.S. Department of Justice. https://www.bjs.gov/content/pub/pdf/p16.pdf.

Carson, Rachel. 1962/1994. *Silent Spring.* New York: Houghton Mifflin.

Cassidy, Tina. 2006. *Birth.* New York: Atlantic Monthly Press.

Castells, Manuel. 1984. "Cultural identity, sexual liberation and urban structure: The gay community in San Francisco." In *The City and the Grassroots: A Cross-Cultural Theory of Urban Social Movements.* Berkeley: University of California Press.

———. 2000. *The Rise of the Network Society*, vol. 1. 2nd ed. Malden, MA: Blackwell.

———. 2014. "The impact of the Internet on society: A global perspective." OpenMind. https://www.bbvaopenmind.com/en/article/the-impact-of-the-internet-on-society-a-globalperspective/?utm_source=views&utm_medium=article07&utm_content=Internet-society.

———; and Susser, Ida. 2002. *The Castells Reader on Cities and Social Theory.* Malden, MA: Blackwell.

Catalano, S. 2013. "Intimate partner violence: Attributes of victimization, 1993–2011." U.S. Bureau of Justice Statistics. https://www.bjs.gov/content/pub/pdf/ipvav9311.pdf.

Catalyst. 2013. "Women on boards." May 31. http://catalyst.org/knowledge/women-boards.

Catholics for a Free Choice. 2002. "Student bodies: Reproductive health care at Catholic universities." http://www.catholicsforchoice.org/topics/healthcare/documents/2002studentbodies.pdf.

Catton, William R., Jr. 1980. *Overshoot: The Ecological Basis of Revolutionary Change.* Urbana: University of Illinois Press.

———; and Dunlap, Riley E. 1978. "Environmental sociology: A new paradigm." *American Sociologist*, vol. 13: 41–49.

———; and Dunlap, Riley E. 1980. "A new ecological paradigm for post-exuberant sociology." *American Behavioral Scientist*, vol. 24, no. 1: 15–47.

Caughey, John L. 1984. *Imaginary Social Worlds: A Cultural Approach.* Lincoln: University of Nebraska Press.

———. 1999. "Imaginary social relationships." In Joseph Harris and Jay Rosen, eds., *Media Journal: Reading and Writing About Popular Culture.* Boston: Allyn and Bacon.

Cellini, S. R.; and Darolia, R. 2016. "Brown Center on education policy." Brookings Institute. https://www.brookings.edu/wp-content/uploads/2016/07/cellini.pdf.

———; and Turner, N. 2016. "Gainfully employed? Assessing the employment and earnings of for-profit college students using administrative data." NBER Working Paper No. 22287. http://www.nber.org/papers/w22287.

Center for Manufacturing Research. 2016. "Manufacturing employment by state." http://www.nam.org/Data-and-Reports/State-Manufacturing-Data/State-Manufacturing-Data/Manufacturing-Employment-by-State-March-2016/.

Center for Responsive Politics. 2016a. "2016 outside spending, by Super PAC." https://www.opensecrets.org/outsidespending/summ.php?chrt=V&type=S.

———. 2016b. "Reelection rates over the years." https://www.opensecrets.org/overview/reelect.php.

———. 2017. "Lobbying: Top spenders, 1998–2017." https://www.opensecrets.org/lobby/top.php?showYear=a&indexType=s.

———. 2018. "Reelection rates over the years." https://www.opensecrets.org/overview/reelect.php.

———. 2019. "Lobbying: Top spenders." https://www.opensecrets.org/lobby/top.php?indexType=s.

Center on Budget and Policy Priorities. 2019. "Policy basics: Where do our federal tax dollars go?" January 29. https://www.cbpp.org/research/federal-budget/policy-basics-where-do-our-federal-tax-dollars-go.

Centers for Disease Control and Prevention. 2013a. "Health behavior of adults: United States, 2008–2010." http://www.cdc.gov/nchs/data/series/sr_10/sr10_257.pdf.

———. 2013b. "Health, United States, 2013." http://www.cdc.gov/nchs/data/hus/hus13.pdf#068.

———. 2014a. "Sexual orientation and health among U.S. adults: National Health Interview Survey, 2013." http://www.cdc.gov/nchs/data/nhsr/nhsr077.pdf.

———. 2014b. "Trends in out-of-hospital births in the United States, 1990–2012." http://www.cdc.gov/nchs/data/databriefs/db144.htm.

———. 2015. "National health interview study. Table 1: Sexual orientation among U.S. adults aged 18 and over, by sex and age group: United States, 2015." https://www.cdc.gov/nchs/data/nhis/sexual_orientation/asi_2015_stwebsite_tables.pdf.

———. 2016. "Deaths: Leading causes for 2014." www.cdc.gov/nchs/data/nvsr/nvsr65/nvsr65_05.pdf.

———. 2017a. "Chronic disease overview." https://www.cdc.gov/chronicdisease/overview/index.htm#ref1.

———. 2017b. "Health in the United States, 2016: With chartbook on long-term health trends." https://www.cdc.gov/nchs/data/hus/hus16.pdf.

———. 2017c. "Health in the United States, 2016: With chartbook on long-term health trends. Table 15." https://www.cdc.gov/nchs/data/hus/hus16.pdf#015.

———. 2017d. "National diabetes statistics report, 2017." https://www.cdc.gov/diabetes/pdfs/data/statistics/national-diabetes-statistics-report.pdf.

———. 2018a. "Health, United States, 2017: With special feature on mortality." https://www.cdc.gov/nchs/data/hus/hus17.pdf.

———. 2018b. "Opioid overdose: Understanding the epidemic." December 19. https://www.cdc.gov/drugoverdose/epidemic/index.html.

———. 2019. "Measles cases and outbreaks." June 3. https://www.cdc.gov/measles/cases-outbreaks.html.

Central Intelligence Agency. 2017. "The world factbook: Swaziland." https://www.cia.gov/library/publications/the-world-factbook/geos/wz.html.

———. 2019. "The world factbook 2019–20." Washington, DC. https://www.cia.gov/library/publications/the-world-factbook/index.html.

Cha, Youngjoo; and Weeden, K. A. 2014. "Overwork and the slow convergence in the gender gap in wages." *American Sociological Review*, vol. 79, no. 3: 457–484.

Champagne, Duane. 1994. *Native America: Portrait of the People.* Canton, MI: Visible Ink Press.

Charles, Camille Zubrinsky. 2001. "Processes of racial residential segregation." In Alice O'Connor, Chris Tilly, and Lawrence Bobo, eds., *Urban Inequality: Evidence from Four Cities.* New York: Russell Sage Foundation.

Chen, Hong; et al. 2017. "Living near major roads and the incidence of dementia, Parkinson's disease, and multiple sclerosis: A population-based cohort study." *The Lancet,* vol. 389, no. 10070 (January): 718–726. doi: http://dx.doi.org/10.1016 /S0140-6736(16)32399-6.

Chen, Katherine K. 2004. "The Burning Man organization grows up: Blending bureaucratic and alternative structures." Doctoral Dissertation. Harvard University.

Cherlin, Andrew J.; and Furstenberg, Frank F., Jr. 1994. "Stepfamilies in the United States: A reconsideration." *Annual Review of Sociology*, vol. 20: 359–381.

Cheslack-Postava, Keely; Liu, Kayuet; and Bearman, Peter S. 2011. "Closely spaced pregnancies are associated with increased odds of autism in California sibling births." *Pediatrics*, vol. 127, no. 2: 246–253.

Chesler, Phyllis. 2010. "Worldwide trends in honor killings." *Middle East Quarterly,* Spring: 3–11.

Chesley, Noelle. 2011. "Stay-at-home fathers and breadwinning mothers." *Gender & Society*, vol. 25, no. 5: 642–664.

Chetty, R.; Grusky, D.; Hell, M.; Hendren, N.; Manduca, R.; and Narang, J. 2016a. "The fading American dream: Trends in absolute income mobility since 1940." http://www.equality-of -opportunity.org/assets/documents/abs_mobility_summary .pdf.

———; Stepner, M.; Abraham, S.; Lin, S.; Scuderi, B.; Turner, N.; Bergeron, A.; and Cutler, D. 2016b. "The association between income and life expectancy in the United States, 2001–2014." *Journal of the American Medical Association,* vol. 315, no. 16: 1750–1766. doi:10.1001/jama.2016.4226. http:// jamanetwork.com/journals/jama/article-abstract/2513561.

Chetty, Raj; Hendren, Nathaniel; Jones, Maggie R.; and Porter, Sonya. 2018. "Race and economic opportunity in the United States: An intergenerational perspective." Working Paper. http://www.equality-of-opportunity.org/assets/documents /race_paper.pdf.

Chetty, Raj; Hendren, Nathaniel; Kline, Patrick; and Saez, Emmanuel. 2014a. "Where is the land of opportunity? The geography of intergenerational mobility in the United States." *Quarterly Journal of Economics*, vol. 129, no. 4: 1553–1623.

———; Turner, Nicholas. 2014b. "Is the United States still a land of opportunity? Recent trends in intergenerational mobility." *National Bureau of Economic Research*. January. http://www .nber.org/papers/w19844.

Child Trends Databank. 2018. "Family structure." https:// www.childtrends.org/indicators/family-structure.

Chodorow, Nancy. 1978. *The Reproduction of Mothering: Psychoanalysis and the Sociology of Gender*. Berkeley: University of California Press.

———. 1994. *Femininities, Masculinities, Sexualities: Freud and Beyond*. Lexington: University Press of Kentucky.

———. 2009. *The Reproduction of Mothering*. Berkeley: University of California Press.

Chokshi, Dave A. 2018. "Income, poverty, and health inequality." The JAMA Forum, April 3. *Journal of the American Medical Association*, vol. 319, no. 13: 1312–1313. https://doi.org/10.1001 /jama.2018.2521.

Christakis, N. A. 1995. "The similarity and frequency of proposals to reform U.S. medical education: Constant concerns." *Journal of the American Medical Association*, vol. 274: 706.

———; and Fowler, James. 2009. *Connected: The Surprising Power of Our Social Networks and How They Shape Our Lives*. New York: Little, Brown and Company.

———; and Fowler, James H. 2013. "Social contagion theory: Examining dynamic social networks and human behavior."

Statistics in Medicine, vol. 32, no. 4 (February): 556–577. doi:10 .1002/sim.5408.

Christensen, Jen; and Willingham, Val. 2014. "Live to 100: Number of centenarians has doubled." *CNN*. June 4. http://www.cnn .com/2014/06/04/health/centenarian-death/.

Cialdini, Robert B. and Trost, M. R. 1998. "Social influence: Social norms, conformity, and compliance." In D. T. Gilbert, S. E. Fiske, and G. Lindzey, eds., *Handbook of Social Psychology*, vol. 2. 4th ed. Boston: McGraw-Hill.

Cicourel, Aaron V. 1972. "Basic and normative rules in the negotiation of status and role." In D. Sudnow, ed., *Studies in Social Interaction*. New York: Free Press.

Clark, Meagan. 2014. "What is the world's most-watched TV program? Hint: It's not in the US." *International Business Times*, February 6. http://www.ibtimes.com/what-worlds-most -watched-tv-program-hint-its-not-us-1553678.

Clayman, Steven E. 2002. "Sequence and solidarity." *Advances in Group Processes*, vol. 19: 229–253.

Clinton, Catherine; and Gillespie, Michelle, eds. 1997. *The Devil's Lane: Sex and Race in the Early South*. New York: Oxford University Press.

Coates, Ta-Nehisi. 2015. *Between the World and Me*. New York: Spiegel & Grau.

Cohen, Cathy J. 2005. "Punks, bulldaggers, and welfare queens: The radical potential of queer politics?" In *Black Queer Studies: A Critical Anthology*, ed. by E. Patrick Johnson and Mae G. Henderson, 21–51, Durham/London: Duke University Press.

Cohen, Jon. 2016. "Zika's long strange trip into the limelight." *Science,* February 8. http://www.sciencemag.org/news/2016/02 /zika-s-long-strange-trip-limelight.

Cohen, Philip. 2014. *The Family: Diversity, Inequality and Social Change*. New York: W. W. Norton.

———. 2019. "The coming divorce decline." Presented at the 2019 Population Association of America meetings.

Cohen, S. P. 2001. *India: Emerging Power*. Washington, DC: Brookings Institution Press.

Coleman, James S. 1966. "Equality of Educational Opportunity (COLEMAN) Study (EEOS)." Ann Arbor, MI: Inter-university Consortium for Political and Social Research. http://doi.org/10 .3886/ICPSR06389.v3.

Coleman, John R. 1983. "Diary of a homeless man." *New York Magazine*, February.

College Board. Annual Survey of Colleges. 2016. "Trends in college pricing 2016." https://trends.collegeboard.org/sites/default /files/2016-trends-college-pricing-web_1.pdf.

Collins, Patricia Hill. 2006. *From Black Power to Hip Hop: Racism, Nationalism, and Feminism*. Philadelphia: Temple University Press.

Collins, R. L. 2011. "Content analysis of gender roles in media: Where are we now and where should we go?" *Sex Roles*, vol. 64: 290.

Collins, Randall. 1979. *The Credential Society: An Historical Sociology of Education and Stratification*. New York: Worthington Press.

Coltrane, Scott. 1997. *Family Man: Fatherhood, Housework and Gender Equity*. New York: Oxford University Press.

Common Core State Standards Initiative. 2015. "About the Standards." http://www.corestandards.org/about-the -standards/.

Community Organizing and Family Issues (COFI). 2009. "Why isn't Johnny in preschool?" http://www.cofionline.org/files /earlylearningre port.pdf.

Comte, Auguste. 1988 (orig. 1842). *Introduction to Positive Philosophy*. Frederick Ferré, ed. and tr. Indianapolis, IN: Hackett.

Congressional Budget Office. 2018. "The distribution of household income, 2015." November 8. https://www.cbo.gov/publication/54646.

Conley, Dalton. 2000. *Honky.* Berkeley and Los Angeles: University of California Press.

———. 2002. *Wealth and Poverty in America: A Reader.* Malden, MA: Blackwell.

———. 2004. *The Pecking Order: Which Siblings Succeed and Why.* New York: Pantheon.

———. 2009. *Elsewhere, U.S.A.: How We Got from the Company Man, Family Dinners and the Affluent Society to the Home Office, BlackBerry Moms and Economic Anxiety.* New York: Pantheon.

———. 2016. "Socio-genomic research using genome-wide molecular data." *Annual Review of Sociology,* vol. 42: 275–299.

———; and Fletcher, J. 2017. *The Genome Factor: What the Social Genomics Revolution Reveals about Ourselves, Our History, and the Future.* Princeton, NJ: Princeton University Press.

Connell, R. W. 1995. *Masculinities.* Berkeley: University of California Press.

———; and Messerschmidt, James W. 2005. "Hegemonic masculinity: Rethinking the concept." *Gender and Society,* vol. 19, no. 6: 829–859.

Conrad, Peter. 2006. *Identifying Hyperactive Children: The Medicalization of Deviant Behavior.* Burlington, VT: Ashgate.

Conti, Joseph. 2003. "Trade, power, and law: Dispute settlement in the World Trade Organization, 1995–2002." Unpublished Master's Thesis. University of California, Santa Barbara.

———. 2005. "Power through process: Determinants of dispute resolution outcomes in the World Trade Organization." Unpublished Dissertation. University of California, Santa Barbara, Department of Sociology.

———. 2010. "Learning to dispute: Repeat participation, expertise, and reputation at the World Trade Organization." *Law & Social Inquiry,* vol. 35, no. 1: 625–662.

Cook, Kevin. 2015. *Kitty Genovese: The Murder, the Bystanders, and the Crime That Changed America.* New York: W. W. Norton.

Cook, Noble David. 1998. *Born to Die: Disease and New World Conquest, 1492–1650.* Cambridge, UK: Cambridge University Press.

Cooley, Charles Horton. 1909. *Social Organization: A Study of the Large Mind.* New York: Scribner.

Coontz, Stephanie. 2000. *The Way We Never Were: American Families and the Nostalgia Trap.* New York: Basic Books.

Cooper, David; and Essrow, Dan. 2015. "Low-wage workers are older than you think." Economic Policy Institute, April 27. http://www.epi.org/publication/low-wage-workers-are-older-than-you-think/.

Cooper, H. 2014. "Pentagon study finds 50% increase in reports of military sexual assaults." *The New York Times,* May 1. http://www.nytimes.com/2014/05/02/us/military-sex-assault-report.html?_r=0.

Corporation for National & Community Service. 2016. "New report: Service unites Americans; Volunteers give service worth $184 billion." https://www.nationalservice.gov/newsroom/press-releases/2016/new-report-service-unites-americans-volunteers-give-service-worth-184.

———. 2019. "Volunteering in America: Research." https://www.nationalservice.gov/serve/via/research.

Correll, S. J.; Benard, S.; and Paik, I. 2007. "Getting a job: Is there a motherhood penalty?" *American Journal of Sociology,* vol. 112, no. 5: 1297–1339.

Cota, A. A.; Evans, C. R.; Dion, K. L.; Kilik, L. L.; and Longman, R. S. 1995. "The structure of group cohesion." *Personality and Social Psychology Bulletin,* vol. 21: 572–580.

Creanga, A. A.; Berg, C. J.; Syverson, C.; Seed, K.; Bruce, C.; and Callaghan, W. M. 2012. "Race, ethnicity and nativity differentials in pregnancy-related mortality in the United States: 1993–2006." *Obstetrics & Gynecology,* vol. 120, no. 2: 261–268.

CREDO. 2013. The National Charter School Study. Stanford University Center for Research on Education Outcomes. https://credo.stanford.edu/documents/NCSS%202013%20Final%20Draft.pdf.

Crenshaw, Kimberle. 1991. "Mapping the margins: Intersectionality, identity politics, and violence against women of color." *Stanford Law Review,* vol. 43, 6: 1241–1299.

———; Gotanda, Neil; Peller, Garry; and Thomas, Kendall, eds. 1996. *Critical Race Theory: The Key Writings That Formed the Movement.* New York: New Press.

Cronk, Terri M. 2017. "DoD releases latest military sexual assault report." https://www.defense.gov/News/Article/Article/1168765/dod-releases-latest-military-sexual-assault-report/.

Cunningham, M.; and Jones, J. W. 2010. "Attitude and behavior assessments versus personality tests for personnel selection: Impact on key business indicators." Human Capital Research Report. Chicago: General Dynamics Information Technology.

Curtin, Sally C.; Ventura, Stephanie J.; and Martinez, Gladys M. 2014. "Recent declines in nonmarital childbearing in the United States." NCHS Data Brief, No. 162. August. http://www.cdc.gov/nchs/data/databriefs/db162.pdf.

Dahl, Robert A. 1961. *Who Governs?* New Haven, CT: Yale University Press.

Dahlhamer, J.; Lucas, J.; Zelaya, C.; et al. 2018. "Prevalence of chronic pain and high-impact chronic pain among adults—United States, 2016." *Morbidity and Mortality Weekly Report,* vol. 67: 1001–1006. https://www.cdc.gov/mmwr/volumes/67/wr/mm6736a2.htm.

Darley, John; and Latané, Bibb. 1968. "Bystander intervention in emergencies: Diffusion of responsibility." *Journal of Personality and Social Psychology,* vol. 8: 377–383.

Darrow, Barb. 2017. "Turns out attendance at Women's March events was bigger than estimated." *Fortune.* January 23. http://fortune.com/2017/01/23/womens-march-crowd-estimates/.

Davey, Monica. 2017. "21 across U.S. are indicted in 'modern-day sex slave' ring." *The New York Times.* May 25. https://www.nytimes.com/2017/05/25/us/raid-sex-trafficking-thailand.html.

Davies, Alex. 2017. "Detroit is stomping Silicon Valley in the self-driving car race." *Wired,* April 3. https://www.wired.com/2017/04/detroit-stomping-silicon-valley-self-driving-car-race/.

Davila, M. 1971. "Compadrazgo: Fictive kinship in Latin America." In N. Graburn, ed., *Readings in Kinship and Social Structure.* New York: Harper & Row.

Davis, Angela Y. 2001. "Outcast mothers and surrogates: Racism and reproductive politics." In Laurel Richardson, Verta Taylor, and Nancy Whittier, eds., *Feminist Frontiers IV.* Boston: McGraw-Hill.

Davis, Georgiann. 2015. *Contesting Intersex: The Dubious Diagnosis.* New York: New York University Press.

Davis, Kingsley. 1940. "Extreme social isolation of a child." *American Journal of Sociology,* vol. 45 (January): 554–565.

———. 1947. "Final note on a case of extreme isolation." *American Journal of Sociology,* vol. 52, no. 5: 432–437.

———; and Moore, Wilbert. 1945. "Some principles of stratification." *American Sociological Review,* vol. 10, no. 2: 242–249.

Dawson, G.; and Bernier, R. 2013. "A quarter century of progress on the early detection and treatment of Autism Spectrum Disorder." *Development and Psychopathology*, vol. 25: 1455–1472.

De Alth, Shelley. 2009. "ID at the polls: Assessing the impact of recent state voter ID laws on voter turnout." *Harvard Law and Policy Review*, vol. 3: 185–202.

De Graaf, John; Waan, David; and Naylor, Thomas. 2002. *Affluenza: The All-Consuming Epidemic*. San Francisco: Berrett-Koehler.

Declercq, E. R.; Sakala, C.; Corry, M. P.; and Applebaum, S. 2007. "Listening to mothers II: Report of the second national U.S. survey of women's childbearing experiences." *The Journal of Perinatal Education*, vol. 16: 9–14.

DeFrancisco, Victoria Leto. 1991. "The sounds of silence: How men silence women in marital relations." *Discourse & Society*, vol. 2, no. 4: 413–423.

Del Fresno García, Miguel; and Peláez, Antonio López. 2014. "Social work and netnography: The case of Spain and generic drugs." *Qualitative Social Work*, vol. 13, no. 1: 85–107.

Delgado, Richard; and Stefancic, Jean. 2012. *Critical Race Theory: An Introduction*, 2nd ed. New York: New York University Press.

Dell'Amore, Christine. 2008. "'Deadly dozen' diseases could stem from global warming." *National Geographic News*, October 7. http://www.news.nationalgeographic.com/news/2008/10/081007-climate-diseases.html.

Department of Justice. 2015. "Investigation of the Ferguson police department." https://www.justice.gov/sites/default/files/opa/press-releases/attachments/2015/03/04/ferguson_police_department_report.pdf.

Desilver, Drew. 2014a. "College enrollment among low-income students still trails richer groups." Pew Research Center. January 15. http://www.pewresearch.org/fact-tank/2014/01/15/college-enrollment-among-low-income-students-still-trails-richer-groups/.

———. 2014b. "Voter turnout always drops off for midterm elections, but why?" Pew Research Center. http://www.pewresearch.org/fact-tank/2014/07/24/voter-turnout-always-drops-off-for-midterm-elections-but-why/.

Desjarlais-deKlerk, Kristen; and Wallace, Jean E. 2013. "Instrumental and socioemotional communications in doctor-patient interactions in urban and rural clinics." *BMC Health Services Research*, vol. 13: 261.

Desmond, Matthew. 2006. "Becoming a firefighter." *Ethnography*, vol. 7, no. 4: 387–421.

———. 2016. *Evicted: Poverty and Profit in the American City*. New York: Crown.

DeVault, Marjorie. 1994 (orig. 1991). *Feeding the Family: The Social Organization of Caring as Gendered Work*. Chicago: University of Chicago Press.

Di Leonardo, Micaela. 1987. "The female world of cards and holidays: Women, families, and the work of kinship." *Signs*, vol. 12, no. 3: 340–350.

DiAngelo, R. 2012. *What Does It Mean to Be White? Developing White Racial Literacy*. New York: Peter Lang.

Dicken, Peter. 1998. *The Global Shift: Transforming the World Economy*, 3rd ed. New York: Guilford Press.

Dickson, Kevin; and Lorenz, Alicia. 2009. "Psychological empowerment and job satisfaction of temporary and part-time nonstandard workers." Institute of Behavioral and Applied Management. http://www.ibam.com/pubs/jbam/articles/vol10/no2/JBAM_10_2_2.pdf.

Dines, Gail. 2017. "Growing up with porn: The developmental and societal impact of pornography on children." *Dignity: A Journal on Sexual Exploitation and Violence*, vol. 2, no. 3.

Dobbin, F.; and Kalev, A. 2016. "Why diversity programs fail." *Harvard Business Review*. https://hbr.org/2016/07/why-diversity-programs-fail.

Doherty, Brian. 2000. "Burning Man grows up." *Reason*, vol. 31: 24–33. http://www.reason.com/0002/fe.bd.burning.shtml.

———. 2004. *This Is Burning Man*. New York: Little, Brown and Company.

Domhoff, G. William. 1983. *Who Rules America Now? A View from the Eighties*. Englewood Cliffs, NJ: Prentice Hall.

———. 1987. *Power Elites and Organizations*. Newbury Park, CA: Sage.

———. 1990. *The Power Elite and the State: How Policy Is Made in America*. New York: de Gruyter.

———. 2002. *Who Rules America Now? Power and Politics in the Year 2000*, 3rd ed. Mountain View, CA: Mayfield.

———. 2013. *Who Rules America? The Triumph of the Corporate Rich*. New York: McGraw Hill.

Donnelly, Denise; and Finkelhor, David. 1993. "Who has joint custody? Class differences in the determination of custody arrangements." *Family Relations*, vol. 42, no. 1: 57–60.

Dover, Tessa L.; Major, Brenda; and Kaiser, Cheryl R. 2016. "Diversity policies rarely make companies fairer, and they feel threatening to white men." *Harvard Business Review*, January 4.

Drucker, Peter. 2003. *The Essential Drucker: The Best of Sixty Years of Peter Drucker's Writings on Management*. New York: Collins.

Duany, Andres; Plater-Zyberk, Elizabeth; and Speck, Jeff. 2001. *Suburban Nation: The Rise of Sprawl and the Decline of the American Dream*. New York: North Point Press.

DuBois, W. E. B. 1903. *The Souls of Black Folk*. Chicago: A.C. McClurg & Co.; [Cambridge]: University Press John Wilson and Son, Cambridge, U.S.A.

Duggan, Lisa. 2003. *The Twilight of Equality? Neoliberalism, Cultural Politics, and the Attack on Democracy*. Boston: Beacon Press.

Duke, Alan. 2014. "'Deltopia' party in California turns violent; dozens arrested." *CNN*, April 7. http://www.cnn.com/2014/04/06/us/california-street-party-melee/.

Dunaway, Wilma. 2014. *Gendered Commodity Chains: Seeing Women's Work and Households in Global Production*. Stanford, CA: Stanford University Press.

Duncan, David Ewing. 2012. "How long do you want to live?" *The New York Times Sunday Review*, August 25.

Duneier, Mitchell; and Carter, Ovie. 1999. *Sidewalk*. New York: Farrar, Straus and Giroux.

Dunlap, Riley E.; and Brulle, Robert J. 2015. "Climate change and society: Sociological perspectives." Oxford Scholarship Online. https://www.oxfordscholarship.com/view/10.1093/acprof:oso/9780199356102.001.0001/acprof-9780199356102.

Dunlap, Riley, E.; and Catton, William, Jr. 1979. "Environmental sociology." *Annual Review of Sociology*, vol. 5: 243–273.

———. 1994. "Struggling with human exemptionalism: The rise, decline and revitalization of environmental sociology." *The American Sociologist*, vol. 25: 5–30.

Dunn, A. 2018. "Partisans are divided over the fairness of the U.S. economy—and why people are rich or poor." Pew Research Center, October 4. http://www.pewresearch.org/fact-tank/2018/10/04/partisans-are-divided-over-the-fairness-of-the-u-s-economy-and-why-people-are-rich-or-poor/.

Dunn, J. L. 2002. *Courting Disaster: Intimate Stalking, Culture, and Criminal Justice*. New Brunswick, NJ: Transaction.

Dupuis, Sherry L.; and Smale, Bryan J. A. 2000. "Bittersweet journeys: Meanings of leisure in the institution-based caregiving context." *Journal of Leisure Research*, vol. 32, no. 3: 303.

Durkheim, Emile. 1895. *The Rules of Sociological Method.* New York: Simon & Schuster.

———. 1951 (orig. 1897). *Suicide: A Study in Sociology.* Trans. John A. Spaulding and George Simpson. Glencoe, IL: Free Press.

———. 1984 (orig. 1893). *The Division of Labor in Society.* Trans. W. D. Halls. New York: Free Press.

———. 1995 (orig. 1912). *The Elementary Forms of Religious Life.* Trans. Karen E. Fields. New York: Free Press.

Dutta, Soumitra; and Fraser, Mathew. 2008. "Barack Obama and the Facebook election." *U.S. News and World Report,* November 19. http://www.usnews.com/opinion/articles/2008/11/19/barack-obama-and-the-facebook-election.

Dwyer, Jim. 2001. "A nation challenged." *The New York Times,* November 6, p. A1.

Dye, Thomas R. 2002. *Who's Running America? The Bush Restoration,* 7th ed. Upper Saddle River, NJ: Prentice Hall.

Eagan, K.; et al. 2017. "The American freshman: National norms fall 2016." https://www.heri.ucla.edu/monographs/TheAmericanFreshman2016.pdf.

The Economist. 2017. "Climate change and inequality: The rich pollute, the poor suffer," July 13. https://www.economist.com/finance-and-economics/2017/07/13/climate-change-and-inequality.

Edgerton, Robert B. 1992. *Sick Societies: Challenging the Myth of Primitive Harmony.* New York: Free Press.

Edin, Kathryn. 2000. "Few good men." *American Prospect,* vol. 11, no. 4 (January 3).

———; and Kefalas, Maria. 2005. *Promises I Can Keep: Why Poor Women Put Motherhood Before Marriage.* Berkeley: University of California Press.

———; and Lein, Laura. 1997. *Making Ends Meet.* New York: Russell Sage Foundation.

———; and Shaefer, H. Luke. 2016a. *$2.00 a Day: Living on Almost Nothing in America.* New York: Houghton Mifflin.

———; and Shaefer, H. Luke. 2016b. "20 years since welfare 'reform.'" *The Atlantic,* August 22.

Edwards-Levy, Ariel. 2012. "Students at Catholic colleges protest lack of access to birth control." *The Huffington Post,* February 9. http://www.huffingtonpost.com/2012/02/09/catholic-college-students-birth-control_n_1265771.html.

Egelko, Bob. 2002. "Pledge of allegiance ruled unconstitutional; many say ruling by S. F. court hasn't a prayer after appeals." *San Francisco Chronicle,* June 27, p. A1.

Ehrenreich, Barbara. 1990. *The Worst Years of Our Lives: Irreverent Notes from a Decade of Greed.* New York: Pantheon.

———. 2001. *Nickel and Dimed: On (Not) Getting By in America.* New York: Metropolitan Books.

———. 2004. "All together now." *The New York Times,* July 15.

Ehrlich, Paul R.; and Ehrlich, Anne H. 1990. *The Population Explosion.* New York: Simon & Schuster.

Eisenstein, Zillah. 1979. "Capitalist patriarchy and the case for socialist feminism." *Monthly Review,* February.

Ellis, Carolyn. 1995. "Emotional and ethical quagmires in returning to the field." *Journal of Contemporary Ethnography,* vol. 24: 68–96.

———. 1997. "Evocative autoethnography: Writing emotionally about our lives." In W. G. Tierney and Y. S. Lincoln, eds., *Representation and the Text: Re-framing the Narrative Voice.* Albany, NY: SUNY Press.

———. 2007. "Telling secrets, revealing lives: Relational ethics in research with intimate others." *Qualitative Inquiry,* vol. 13, no. 3: 3–29.

———; Adams, Tony E.; and Bochner, Arthur P. 2010. "Autoethnography: An overview [40 paragraphs]." *Forum Qualitative Sozialforschung Forum: Qualitative Social Research,* vol. 12, no. 1, art. 10. http://nbn-resolving.de/urn:nbn:de:0114-fqs1101108.

Emerson, Robert. 2002. *Contemporary Field Research: Perspectives and Formulations,* 2nd ed. Long Grove, IL: Waveland Press.

England, Paula. 1992. *Comparable Worth: Theories and Evidence.* Edison, NJ: Aldine Transaction.

Enten, Harry. 2016. "'Shy' voters probably aren't why the polls missed Trump." *FiveThirtyEight.* November 16. https://fivethirtyeight.com/features/shy-voters-probably-arent-why-the-polls-missed-trump/.

Environmental Protection Agency. 2012. "Municipal solid waste." http://www.epa.gov/epawaste/nonhaz/municipal/.

———. 2014. "Climate change facts: Answers to common questions." http://www.epa.gov/climatechange/basics/facts.html.

———. 2016. "Moving forward for America's drinking water." *The EPA Blog,* April 26. https://blog.epa.gov/blog/2016/04/moving-forward-for-americas-drinking-water/.

———. 2017. "Inventory of U.S. greenhouse gas emissions and sinks: 1990–2015." https://www.epa.gov/sites/production/files/2017-02/documents/2017_complete_report.pdf.

Epstein, Louis; Young, Robert; Adams, Johnny; and Muir, Mark. 2019. "GRG world supercentenarian rankings list." Gerontology Research Group, January 20. http://supercentenarian-research-foundation.org/TableE.aspx.

Ericsson. 2017. "Ericsson mobility report." https://www.ericsson.com/assets/local/mobility-report/documents/2017/ericsson-mobility-report-june-2017.pdf.

ESPN. 2019. "NBA attendance report—2019." http://www.espn.com/nba/attendance/_/year/2018.

Etzioni, Amitai. 1996. "The responsive community: A communitarian perspective." *American Sociological Review,* vol. 61, no. 1: 1–11.

Evans, L. 2011. *Cabin Pressure: African American Pilots, Flight Attendants and Emotional Labor.* Lanham, MD: Rowman & Littlefield.

Everton, Sean F. 2012. *Disrupting Dark Networks.* Cambridge: Cambridge University Press.

Fabes, Richard A.; Martin, Carol Lynn; and Hanish, Laura D. 2003. "Young children's play qualities in same-, other-, and mixed-sex peer groups." *Child Development,* vol. 74, no. 3: 921.

Fadiman, Anne. 1998. *The Spirit Catches You and You Fall Down.* New York: Farrar, Straus and Giroux.

Fairbanks, C. 1992. "Labels, literacy and enabled learning: Glenn's story." *Harvard Educational Review,* vol. 62, no. 4: 475–493.

Falconer, Renee C.; and Byrnes, Deborah A. 2003. "When good intentions are not enough: A response to increasing diversity in an early childhood setting." *Journal of Research in Childhood Education,* vol. 17, no. 2: 188.

Faludi, Susan. 1999. *Stiffed: The Betrayal of the American Man.* New York: William & Morrow.

Farghal, M.; and Shakir, A. 1994. "Kin terms and titles of address as relational social honorifics in Jordanian Arabic." *Anthropological Linguistics,* no. 36: 240–253.

Farrell, Warren. 1975. *The Liberated Man.* New York: Bantam.

Fausto-Sterling, Anne. 2000. *Sexing the Body: Gender Politics and the Construction of Sexuality.* New York: Basic Books.

Fava, S. F. 1956. "Suburbanism as a way of life." *American Sociological Review*, vol. 21: 34–37.

Feagin, J. 2000. *Racist America: Roots, Current Realities, and Future Reparations*. New York: Routledge.

_____. 2017. "After Charlottesville: A contexts symposium." https://contexts.org/blog/after-charlottesville/#feagin.

Feder-Alford, Elaine. 2006. "Only a piece of meat: One patient's reflections on her eight-day hospital experience." *Qualitative Inquiry*, vol. 12, no. 3: 596–620.

Federal Bureau of Investigation (FBI). 2016a. "Crime in the United States, 2015." December 14. https://ucr.fbi.gov/crime-in-the-u.s/2015.

_____. 2016b. "2015 Crime in the United States. Expanded homicide." https://ucr.fbi.gov/crime-in-the-u.s/2015/crime-in-the-u.s.-2015/offenses-known-to-law-enforcement/expanded-homicide.

_____. 2016c. "Hate crime statistics: 2015." https://ucr.fbi.gov/hate-crime/2015/topic-pages/incidentsandoffenses_final.

_____. 2018a. "Crime in the United States 2017." https://ucr.fbi.gov/crime-in-the-u.s/2017/crime-in-the-u.s.-2017.

_____. 2018b. "Hate crime statistics, 2017." https://ucr.fbi.gov/hate-crime/2017/hate-crime.

Feingold, David. 2010. "Trafficking in numbers." In Peter Andreas and Kelly Greenhill, eds., *Sex, Drugs, and Body Counts*. Ithaca, NY: Cornell University Press.

Ferguson, Bruce; and Abell, Barbara. 1998. "The urban grocery store gap." *Commentary* (Winter): 6–14.

Ferris, Kerry. 2001. "Through a glass, darkly: The dynamics of fan-celebrity encounters." *Symbolic Interaction*, vol. 24, no. 1 (February): 25–47.

_____. 2004. "Seeing and being seen: The moral order of celebrity sightings." *Journal of Contemporary Ethnography*, vol. 33, no. 3: 236–264.

_____; and Harris, Scott R. 2010. *Stargazing: Celebrity, Fame and Social Interaction*. New York: Routledge.

Fillingim, R. B.; King, C. D.; Ribeiro-Dasilva, M. C.; Rahim-Williams, B.; and Riley III, J. L. 2009. "Sex, gender, and pain: A review of recent clinical and experimental findings." *Journal of Pain*, vol. 10, no. 5: 447–485. https://www.ncbi.nlm.nih.gov/pmc/articles/PMC2677686/.

Fine, Gary Alan. 1993. "The sad demise, mysterious disappearance, and glorious triumph of symbolic interactionism." *Annual Review of Sociology*, vol. 19: 61–87.

_____. 1996. *Kitchens: The Culture of Restaurant Work*. Berkeley: University of California Press.

_____. 2001. *Gifted Tongues: High School Debate and Adolescent Culture*. Princeton, NJ: Princeton University Press.

_____. 2010. *Authors of the Storm: Meteorology and the Culture of Prediction*. Chicago: Chicago University Press.

Finkel, M. 2014. "The strange and curious tale of the last true hermit." *GQ*, August 4. http://www.gq.com/story/the-last-true-hermit.

Fischer, Claude S. 1976. *The Urban Experience*. New York: Harcourt Brace Jovanovich.

_____. 1994. "Changes in leisure activities, 1890–1940." *Journal of Social History*, vol. 27, no. 3: 453.

_____. 2011. *Still Connected*. New York: Russell Sage Foundation.

Fischer, Mary J.; and Kmec, Julie A. 2004. "Neighborhood socioeconomic conditions as moderators of family resource transmission: High school completion among at-risk youth." *Sociological Perspectives*, vol. 47, no. 4: 507–527.

Fish, Stanley. 1980. *Is There a Text in This Class? The Authority of Interpretive Communities*. Cambridge, MA: Harvard University Press.

Fisher, Milia. 2015. "Women of color and the gender wage gap." Center for American Progress. https://www.americanprogress.org/issues/women/reports/2015/04/14/110962/women-of-color-and-the-gender-wage-gap/.

Fishman, Stephen. 2011. "Working as a consultant or independent contractor." *Consultant and Independent Contractor Agreements*. Berkeley, CA: NOLO.

Fiske, Jonathan. 1989. *Understanding Popular Culture*. London: Unwin Hyman.

FitzGerald, Frances. 1980. *America Revised: History Schoolbooks in the Twentieth Century*. New York: Vintage Books.

Florida, Richard. 2002. *The Rise of the Creative Class: And How It Is Transforming Work, Leisure, Community and Everyday Life*. New York: Basic Books.

_____. 2004. *Cities and the Creative Class*. New York: Routledge.

Fontenot, K.; Semega, J.; and Kollar, M. 2018. "Income and poverty in the United States: 2017." U.S. Census Bureau, September. https://www.census.gov/content/dam/Census/library/publications/2018/demo/p60-263.pdf.

Forbes. 2017. "Forbes releases 19th annual NBA team valuations." https://www.forbes.com/sites/forbespr/2017/02/15/forbes-releases-19th-annual-nba-team-valuations/#5b4deeed7f03.

Ford, Jessie; and England, Paula. 2015. "What percent of college women are sexually assaulted in college?" *Contexts*, Jan. 12. https://contexts.org/blog/what-percent-of-college-women-are-sexually-assaulted-in-college/.

Forste, Renata; and Fox, Kiira. 2012. "Household labor, gender roles, and family satisfaction: A cross-national comparison." *Journal of Comparative Family Studies*, vol. 43, no. 5 (September–October): 613–631.

Fortner, Robert S.; and Fackler, Mark P. 2011. *The Handbook of Global Communication and Media Ethics*. Hoboken, NJ: Wiley-Blackwell.

Fortune. 2017. "Global 500." *Fortune*. http://fortune.com/global500/.

_____. 2018. "Global 500." *Fortune*, July 19. http://fortune.com/global500/list/.

Fox, Renee. 1957. "Training for uncertainty." In Robert Merton, ed., *The Student Physician*. Cambridge, MA: Harvard University Press.

Fraga, Bernard L.; and Miller, Michael G. 2018. "Who does voter ID keep from voting?" (unpublished manuscript on file with the Harvard Law School Library, July 23, 2018), PDF file.

Frank, Nathaniel. 2012. "The Associated Press bans homophobia." *Slate*. November 27. http://www.slate.com/articles/double_x/doublex/2012/11/the_ap_bans_homophobia_is_the_word_really_inaccurate.html.

Frayer, Lauren. 2012. "Pakistan's transgenders in a category of their own." National Public Radio, September 3. http://www.npr.org/2012/09/03/160496712/pakistans-transgenders-in-a-category-of-their-own?sc=17&f=1001.

Free Press. 2017. "Who owns the media?" https://www.freepress.net/ownership/chart.

Freese, J. 2018. "The arrival of social science genomics." *Contemporary Sociology*, vol. 47, no. 5: 524–536. https://doi.org/10.1177/0094306118792214a.

Freud, Sigmund. 1955 (orig. 1900). *The Interpretation of Dreams*. London: Hogarth.

_____. 1905. *Three Essays on the Theory of Sexuality*. New York: Avon Books.

_____. 2010 (orig. 1930). *Civilization and Its Discontents*. New York: W. W. Norton.

Frey, William H. 2003. "The new migration equation." *Orlando Sentinel*, November 9.

———. 2014a. *Diversity Explosion: How New Racial Demographics Are Remaking America*. Washington, DC: The Brookings Institute.

———. 2014b. "The suburbs: Not just for white people anymore." *The New Republic*, November 24. https://newrepublic.com/article/120372/white-suburbs-are-more-and-more-thing-past.

———. 2018. "The US will become 'minority white' in 2045, Census projects." *The Avenue*, March 14. https://www.brookings.edu/blog/the-avenue/2018/03/14/the-us-will-become-minority-white-in-2045-census-projects/.

Fried, J.; and Hansson, D. H. 2013. *Remote*. New York: Crown Business.

Friedan, Betty. 1963. *The Feminine Mystique*. New York: W. W. Norton.

Frieden, Bernard; and Sagalyn, Lynne B. 1992. *Downtown, Inc.: How America Rebuilds Cities*. Cambridge, MA: MIT Press.

Friedkin, Noah E. 2004. "Social cohesion." *Annual Review of Sociology*, vol. 30: 409–425.

———; and Cook, Karen S. 1990. "Peer group influence." *Sociological Methods and Research*, vol. 19, no. 1: 122–143.

———; and Granovetter, Mark, eds. 1998. *A Structural Theory of Social Influence. Structural Analysis in the Social Sciences*. Cambridge, UK: Cambridge University Press.

———; Jia, P.; and Bullo, F. 2016. "A theory of the evolution of social power: Natural trajectories of interpersonal influence systems along issue sequences." *Sociological Science*, vol. 3: 444–472.

Friedman, Milton. 1994. "Medical licensure." *Freedom Daily*, January. http://www.fff.org/freedom/0194e.asp.

Fry, R. 2017. "It's becoming more common for young adults to live at home—and for longer stretches." Pew Research Center. http://www.pewresearch.org/fact-tank/2017/05/05/its-becoming-more-common-for-young-adults-to-live-at-home-and-for-longer-stretches/.

Fu, King-wa; and Yip, Paul. 2009. "Estimating the risk for suicide following the suicide deaths of 3 Asian entertainment celebrities: A meta-analytic approach." *Journal of Clinical Psychiatry*, vol. 70, no. 6 (June): 869–878. https://www.ncbi.nlm.nih.gov/pubmed/19573483.

Fuller, Robert C. 2002. *Spiritual but Not Religious: Understanding Unchurched America*. New York: Oxford University Press.

Furstenberg, Frank; Hoffman, Saul; and Shrestha, Laura. 1995. "The effect of divorce on intergenerational transfers: New evidence." *Demography*, vol. 32, no. 3: 319–333.

Fussell, Paul. 1983. *Class: A Guide Through the American Status System*. New York: Touchstone.

Gabb, Jacqui; Klett-Davies, Martina; Fink, Janet; and Thomae, Manuela. 2013. "Enduring love? Couple relationships in the 21st century." The Open University. November. http://www.open.ac.uk/researchprojects/enduringlove/sites/www.open.ac.uk.researchprojects.enduringlove/files/files/ecms/web-content/Final-Enduring-Love-Survey-Report.pdf.

Gabler, Neil. 2012. "It's a brand-news day in Hollywood." *Los Angeles Times*, November 10. http://www.latimes.com/entertainment/movies/moviesnow/la-et-mn-ca-disney-lucasfilm-marvel-20121111,0,7695955.story.

Gaffey, Conor. 2017. "Neo-Nazi site *The Daily Stormer* tried to go online in Albania. It failed." *Newsweek*, August 31. http://www.newsweek.com/daily-stormer-andrew-anglin-charlottesville-657468.

Gaither, Sarah E.; Apfelbaum, Evan P.; Birnbaum, Hannah J.; Babbitt, Laura G.; and Sommers, Samuel R. 2018. "Mere membership in racially diverse groups reduces conformity." *Social Psychological and Personality Science*, vol. 9, no. 4: 402–410.

Galbraith, Patrick W. 2012. *Otaku Spaces*. Seattle, WA: Chin Music Press.

Gallagher, Sally K. 2004. "The marginalization of evangelical feminism." *Sociology of Religion*, vol. 65, no. 3: 215–237.

———. 2019. "Americans' worries about race relations at record high." March 15. http://www.gallup.com/poll/206057/americans-worry-race-relations-record-high.aspx.

Gallup. 2017. "State of the American workplace." http://www.gallup.com/reports/199961/state-american-workplace-report-2017.aspx.

———. 2018. "Children." https://news.gallup.com/poll/1588/children-violence.aspx.

———. 2019. "Race relations." http://www.gallup.com/poll/206057/americans-worry-race-relations-record-high.aspx.

Gans, Herbert J. 1962. *The Urban Villagers*. New York: The Free Press of Glencoe, Inc., The Macmillan Company.

———. 1967. *The Levittowners: Ways of Life and Politics in a New Suburban Community*. New York: Columbia University Press.

———. 1971. "The uses of poverty: The poor pay all." *Social Policy*, July–August: 20–24.

———. 1999. *Popular Culture and High Culture: An Analysis and Evaluation of Taste*. New York: Basic Books.

Gansberg, Martin. 1964. "37 who saw murder didn't call the police: Apathy at stabbing of Queens woman shocks inspector." *The New York Times*, March 27.

Garber, Marjorie. 1997. *Vested Interests: Cross Dressing and Cultural Anxiety*. London: Routledge.

———. 1998. *The Symptoms of Culture*. New York: Routledge.

Gardner, Phil. 2011. "The debate over unpaid college internships." Intern Bridge, Inc. http://citeseerx.ist.psu.edu/viewdoc/download?doi=10.1.1.372.1710&rep=rep1&type=pdf.

Garfinkel, H. 1967/1984. *Studies in Ethnomethodology*. Cambridge: Polity Press.

Garr, Emily. 2008. "The unemployment trend by state." Economic Policy Institute Economic Snapshots. http://www.epi.org/content.cfm/webfeatures_snapshots_20080924.

Garreau, Joel. 1992. *Edge City: Life on the New Frontier*. New York: Anchor Books.

Garry, Patrick M.; and Spurlin, Candice J. 2007. "The effectiveness of media rating systems in preventing children's exposure to violent and sexually explicit media content: An empirical study." *Oklahoma City University Law Review*, vol. 32, no. 2. http://ssrn.com/abstract=1139167.

Garvin, Glenn. 2008. "Too pretty? That's when it got ugly." *The Miami Herald*, March 23.

Gates, Gary. 2012. "Gallup Special Report: The U.S. adult LGBT population." October. http://williamsinstitute.law.ucla.edu/research/census-lgbt-demographics-studies/gallup-special-report-18oct-2012/#sthash.61XZT5ub.dpuf.

———. 2014. "In US, LGBT more likely than non-LGBT to be uninsured." August 26. http://www.gallup.com/poll/175445/lgbt-likely-non-lgbt-uninsured.aspx.

———; and Herman, J. L. 2014. "Transgender military service in the United States." Williams Institute, UCLA School of Law. https://williamsinstitute.law.ucla.edu/wp-content/uploads/Transgender-Military-Service-May-2014.pdf.

Gee, Alastair; Barney, Liz; and O'Malley, Julia. 2017. "How America counts its homeless—and why so many are overlooked." *The Guardian*. https://www.theguardian.com/us-news/2017/feb/16/homeless-count-population-america-shelters-people.

Geertz, Clifford. 1973. "Deep play: Notes on the Balinese cockfight." In *The Interpretation of Cultures*. New York: Basic Books.

Geiger, Abigail. 2016. "Sharing chores a key to good marriage, say majority of married adults." Pew Research Center. November 30. http://www.pewresearch.org/fact-tank/2016/11/30/sharing-chores-a-key-to-good-marriage-say-majority-of-married-adults/.

Gelles, Richard J. 1995. *Contemporary Families: A Sociological View*. Thousand Oaks, CA: Sage.

Gelman, Andrew. 2014. "Same-sex divorce rate not as low as it seemed." *The Washington Post*, December 15. https://www.washingtonpost.com/news/monkey-cage/wp/2014/12/15/same-sex-divorce-rate-not-as-low-as-it-seemed/.

Gemar, K.; Zarkowski, P.; and Avery, D. 2008. "Hotel room suicide: Las Vegas and Clark County." *Social Psychiatry and Psychiatric Epidemiology*, 43:25–27.

Gentzke, A. S.; Creamer, M.; Cullen, K. A.; et al. 2019. "Vital signs: Tobacco product use among middle and high school students—United States, 2011–2018." *Morbidity and Mortality Weekly Report*, vol. 68: 157–164.

Gerbner, George; and Gross, L. 1976. "Living with television: The violence profile." *Journal of Communication* (Spring): 173–199.

Gereffi, Gary; and Korzeniewicz, Miguel, eds. 1994. *Commodity Chains and Global Capitalism*. Westport, CT: Praeger.

Gergen, Kenneth. 1991. *The Saturated Self*. New York: Basic Books.

Geronimus, Arline T. 1992. "The weathering hypothesis and the health of African-American women and infants: Evidence and speculations." *Ethnicity & Disease*, vol. 2, no. 3: 207–221. https://www.ncbi.nlm.nih.gov/pubmed/1467758.

——; Hicken, Margaret; Keene, Danya; and Bound, John. 2006. "'Weathering' and age patterns of allostatic load scores among blacks and whites in the United States." *American Journal of Public Health*, vol. 96, no. 5: 826–833. https://www.ncbi.nlm.nih.gov/pmc/articles/PMC1470581/.

Gibson, Campbell; and Lennon, Emily. 2001. "Historical census statistics on the foreign-born population of the United States: 1850–1990." U.S. Bureau of the Census, Population Division. http://www.census.gov/population/www/documentation/twps0029.html.

Gibson, W. 2001. "Modern boys and mobile girls." *The Guardian*, March 31. https://www.theguardian.com/books/2001/apr/01/sciencefictionfantasyandhorror.features.

Gilbert, Dennis. 2014. *The American Class Structure in an Age of Growing Inequality*. Thousand Oaks, CA: Sage. http://www.sagepub.com/upm-data/60307_Chapter_1.pdf.

Gladwell, Malcolm. 2000. *The Tipping Point: How Little Things Can Make a Big Difference*. New York: Little, Brown and Company.

——. 2008. *Outliers: The Story of Success*. New York: Little, Brown and Company.

Glaser, Barney G.; and Strauss, Anselm L. 1967. *The Discovery of Grounded Theory: Strategies for Qualitative Research*. Chicago: Aldine Publishing Company.

Glaser, Mark. 2007. "Your guide to the digital divide." *MediaShift*. PBS, January 17. http://www.pbs.org/mediashift/2007/01/digging_deeperyour_guide_to_th.html.

Glass, Ruth. 1964. "Aspects of change." In Centre for Urban Studies, ed., *London: Aspects of Change*. London: MacGibbon and Kee.

Glor, Jeff. 2012. "Could babies born today live to 150?" *CBS News*, February 9. http://www.cbsnews.com/8301-505269_162-57373788/could-babies-born-today-live-to-150.

Goffman, Alice. 2014. *On the Run: Fugitive Life in an American City*. New York: Picador.

Goffman, Erving. 1956. *Presentation of Self in Everyday Life*. Garden City, NY: Anchor Books.

——. 1961. *Asylums: Essays on the Social Situation of Mental Patients and Other Inmates*. Garden City, NY: Anchor Books.

——. 1962. *Stigma: Notes on the Management of Spoiled Identity*. Upper Saddle River, NJ: Prentice Hall.

——. 1971. *Relations in Public: Microstudies of the Public Order*. New York: Basic Books.

Goldberg, Herb. 1976. *The Hazards of Being Male*. New York: Nash.

Goldrick-Rab, S.; Richardson, J.; Schneider, J.; Hernandez, A.; and Cady, C. 2018. "Still hungry and homeless in college." Wisconsin HOPE Lab. https://hope4college.com/wp-content/uploads/2018/09/Wisconsin-HOPE-Lab-Still-Hungry-and-Homeless.pdf.

Goldstein, Dana. 2014. *The Teacher Wars: A History of America's Most Embattled Profession*. New York: Doubleday.

Goodacre, Daniel M. 1953. "Group characteristics of good and poor performing combat units." *Sociometry*, vol. 16, no. 2: 168–179.

Goode, Erich. 1997. *Deviant Behavior,* 5th ed. Upper Saddle River, NJ: Prentice Hall.

Goode, William J. 1982. *The Family*. Englewood Cliffs, NJ: Prentice Hall.

Gottdiener, Mark; Collins, Claudia C.; and Dickens, David R. 1999. *Las Vegas: The Social Production of an All-American City*. Malden, MA: Blackwell.

Gottfried, J.; Stocking, G.; and Grieco, E. 2018. "Partisans remain sharply divided in their attitudes about the news media." Pew Research Center. http://www.journalism.org/2018/09/25/democrats-and-republicans-remain-split-on-support-for-news-medias-watchdog-role/.

Gottlieb, Robert. 1997. "Reconstructing Environmentalism: Complex Movements, Diverse Roots, in Out of the Woods: Essays in Environmental History." In Char Miller and Hal Rothman, eds., *Environmental History Review*, 145–47.

Gottman, Jean. 1961. *Megalopolis: The Urbanized Northeastern Seaboard of the United States*. New York: Twentieth Century Fund.

——; and Harper, Robert. 1990. *Since Megalopolis: The Urban Writings of Jean Gottman*. Baltimore: Johns Hopkins University Press.

Gottschalk, Simon. 1993. "Uncomfortably numb: Countercultural impulses in the postmodern era." *Symbolic Interaction*, vol. 16, no. 4: 357–378.

Gould, Elise. 2014. "Why America's workers need faster wage growth—and what we can do about it." Economic Policy Institute. August 27. http://www.epi.org/publication/why-americas-workers-need-faster-wage-growth/.

——; Cooke, T.; and Kimball, W. 2015. "What families need to get by." Economic Policy Institute. http://www.epi.org/publication/what-families-need-to-get-by-epis-2015-family-budget-calculator/.

——; and Wolfe, J. 2018. "Household income growth slowed markedly in 2017 and was stronger for those at the top, while earnings declined slightly." Economic Policy Institute, Sept. 12. https://www.epi.org/blog/household-income-growth-slowed-markedly-in-2017-and-was-stronger-for-those-at-the-top-while-earnings-declined-slightly/.

Gozzi, Raymond, Jr. 1996. "Will the media create a global village?" *ETC: A Review of General Semantics*, vol. 53: 65–68.

Grady, Sarah. 2017. "A fresh look at homeschooling in the U.S." *National Center for Education Statistics Blog*, September 26. https://nces.ed.gov/blogs/nces/post/a-fresh-look-at-homeschooling-in-the-u-s.

Graham, Lawrence Otis. 1996. *A Member of the Club: Reflections on Life in a Racially Polarized World*. New York: Harper Perennial.

GRAIN. 2012. "Squeezing Africa dry: Behind every land grab is a water grab." June 11. http://www.grain.org/article/entries/4516 -squeezing-africa-dry-behind-every-land-grab-is-a-water-grab.

Grall, T. 2018. "Custodial mothers and fathers and their child support: 2015." U.S. Census Bureau. https://www.census.gov /content/dam/Census/library/publications/2018/demo/P60 -262.pdf.

Gramsci, Antonio. 1985. *Selections from Cultural Writings.* Cambridge, MA: Harvard University Press.

———. 1988. *An Antonio Gramsci Reader.* David Forgacs, ed. Boston: Schocken.

Granfield, Robert. 1992. *Making Elite Lawyers.* New York: Routledge.

Granovetter, Mark. 1973. "The strength of weak ties." *American Journal of Sociology,* vol. 78, no. 6: 1360–1380.

Green, Adrienne. 2016. "From social worker to foster parent and back." *The Atlantic.* August 11. https://www.theatlantic.com /business/archive/2016/08/social-worker/495533/.

Greenwood, Shannon; Perrin, Andrew; and Duggan, Maeve. 2016. "Social media update 2016: Facebook usage and engagement is on the rise, while adoption of other platforms holds steady." Pew Research Center. November 11. http://www.pewinternet.org /2016/11/11/social-media-update-2016/.

Grigsby, Mary. 2004. *Buying Time and Getting By: The Voluntary Simplicity Movement.* Albany, NY: SUNY Press.

Groh, Carla J. 2007. "Poverty, mental health, and women: Implications for psychiatric nurses in primary care settings." *Journal of the American Psychiatric Nurses Association,* vol. 13, no. 5: 267–274.

Gruber, K. J.; Cupito, S. H.; and Dobson, C. F. 2013. "Impact of doulas on healthy birth outcomes." *The Journal of Perinatal Education,* vol. 22, no. 1: 49–58. http://doi.org/10.1891/1058 -1243.22.1.49.

Guber, Deborah Lynn. 2003. *The Grassroots of a Green Revolution: Polling America on the Environment.* Cambridge, MA: MIT Press.

Gubrium, Jaber; and Buckholdt, D. R. 1982. "Fictive family: Everyday usage, analytic, and human service considerations." *American Anthropologist,* vol. 84, no. 4: 878.

Guo, Guang; Elder, Glen H.; Cai, Tianji; and Hamilton, Nathan. 2009. "Gene–environment interactions: Peers' alcohol use moderates genetic contribution to adolescent drinking behavior." *Social Science Research,* vol. 38, no. 1: 213–224. http:// dx.doi.org/10.1016/j.ssresearch.2008.04.002.

Guo, Guang; Tong, Yuying; and Cai, Tianji. 2008. "Gene by social-context interactions for number of sexual partners among white male youths: Genetics-informed sociology." *American Journal of Sociology,* vol. 114, Suppl: S36–S66.

Gurrentz, B. 2018. "Living with an unmarried partner now common for young adults." U.S. Census Bureau. https://www .census.gov/library/stories/2018/11/cohabitaiton-is-up -marriage-is-down-for-young-adults.html.

Gustafson, Krystina. 2015. "Wal-Mart pay hike starts wage war." *NBC News.* February 25. http://www.nbcnews.com/business /economy/wal-mart-pay-hike-starts-wage-war-n312671.

Gutfreund, Owen. 2004. *Twentieth Century Sprawl: Highways and the Reshaping of the American Landscape.* New York: Oxford University Press.

Haas, Jack; and Shaffir, William. 1977. "The professionalization of medical students: Development competence and a cloak of competence." *Symbolic Interaction,* vol. 1: 71–88.

———. 1982. "Taking on the role of doctor: A dramaturgical analysis of professionalization." *Symbolic Interaction,* vol. 5: 187–203.

Haber, Gary. 2010. "Bill tries to lure grocers to Maryland's poor areas." *Baltimore Business Journal,* March 26. http://baltimore .bizjournals.com/baltimore/stories/2010/03/29/story4.html.

Habermas, Jürgen. 1984. *The Theory of Communicative Action, Vol. 1: Reason and the Rationalization of Society.* Thomas McCarthy, trans. Boston: Beacon Press.

———. 1987. *The Theory of Communicative Action, Vol. 2: Lifeworld and System: A Critique of Functionalist Reason.* Thomas McCarthy, trans. Boston: Beacon Press.

Hakim, Danny. 2001. "Fidelity picks a president of funds unit." *The New York Times,* May 22, p. C1.

Hall, Stuart. 1980. "Encoding/decoding." In S. Hall, D. Hobson, A. Lowe, and P. Willis, eds., *Culture, Media, Language.* London: Hutchinson.

———. 1997. *Representation: Cultural Representations and Signifying Practices.* London and Thousand Oaks, CA: Sage in association with the Open University.

———. 2006. "Constructing difference: Creating 'other' identities." In Paula Rothenberg, ed., *Beyond Borders: Thinking Critically About Global Issues.* New York: Worth Publishers.

Halle, David. 1993. *Inside Culture: Art and Class in the American Home.* Chicago: University of Chicago Press.

Hampton, Keith N.; Goulet, Lauren Sessions; Rainie, Lee; and Purcell, Kristen. 2011. "Social networking sites and our lives." Washington, DC: Pew Research Center's Internet and American Life Project, June 16. http://pewinternet.org/~/media//Files /Reports/2011/PIP%20-%20Social%20networking%20sites %20and%20our%20lives.pdf.

Hancock, Adrienne B.; and Rubin, Benjamin A. 2015. "Influence of communication partner's gender on language." *Journal of Language and Social Psychology,* vol. 34, no. 1: 46–64.

Handel, Gerald; Cahill, Spencer; and Elkin, Frederick. 2007. *Children and Society: The Sociology of Children and Childhood Socialization.* New York: Oxford University Press.

Hao, Lingxin; and Cherlin, Andrew J. 2004. "Welfare reform and teenage pregnancy, childbirth, and school dropout." *Journal of Marriage and Family,* vol. 66: 179–194.

Hardin, Garrett. 1968. "The tragedy of the commons." *Science,* vol. 162: 1243–1248.

———. 1993. *Living Within Limits.* New York: Oxford University Press.

Harlan, Sharon L.; Pellow, David N.; Roberts, J. Timmons; Bell, Shannon Elizabeth; Holt, William G.; and Nagel, Joane. 2015. "Climate justice and inequality." In Riley E. Dunlap and Robert J. Brulle, eds., *Climate Change and Society: Sociological Perspectives.* https://www.oxfordscholarship.com/view/10.1093 /acprof:oso/9780199356102.001.0001/acprof-9780199356102 -chapter-5.

Harrell, Erika; Langston, Lynn; Berzofsky, Marcus; Couzens, Lance; and Smiley-McDonald, Hope. 2014. "Household poverty and nonfatal violent victimization, 2008–2012." U.S. Department of Justice. https://www.bjs.gov/content/pub/pdf /hpnvv0812.pdf.

Harris, David A. 1999. "Driving while black: Racial profiling on our nation's highways." Washington, DC: American Civil Liberties Union.

Hartung, Daniel M.; Bourdette, Dennis N.; Ahmed, Sharia M.; and Whitham, Ruth H. 2015. "The cost of multiple sclerosis drugs in the US and the pharmaceutical industry." *Neurology.* April 24. http://managedhealthcareexecutive.modernmedicine.com /managed-healthcare-executive/news/aarp-study-finds-sharp -rise-price-brand-name-prescription-drugs?page=full.

Harvard IOP. 2015. "Harvard IOP Fall 2015: Trump, Carson lead Republican primary; Sanders edging Clinton among Democrats, Harvard IOP poll finds," p. 207.

Harvard Magazine. 2008. "Race in a genetic world." May–June: 62–65.

Harvey, David. 1990. *The Condition of Postmodernity: An Enquiry into the Origins of Cultural Change.* Cambridge, MA: Wiley-Blackwell.

Hasenbush, Amira; Flores, Andrew R.; and Herman, Jody L. 2018. "Gender identity nondiscrimination laws in public accommodations: A review of evidence regarding safety and privacy in public restrooms, locker rooms, and changing rooms." *Sexuality Research and Social Policy,* vol. 16, no. 1 (March 2019): 70–83. Published ahead of print July 23, 2018. https://doi.org/10.1007/s13178-018-0335-z.

Hatzenbuehler, M. L; Bellatorre, A.; Lee, Y.; Finch, B. K.; Muennig, P.; and Fiscella, K. 2014. "Structural stigma and all-cause mortality in sexual minority populations." *Social Science & Medicine,* vol. 103: 33–41.

Havitz, Mark E.; and Dimanche, Frederic. 1999. "Leisure involvement revisited: Drive properties and paradoxes." *Journal of Leisure Research,* vol. 31, no. 2: 122.

Hawley, Amos H. 1950. *Human Ecology: A Theory of Community Structure.* New York: Ronald Press.

Hawley, Josh. 2018. "2017 annual report: Missouri vehicle stops." https://www.ago.mo.gov/docs/default-source/public-safety/2017vehiclesstops-executivesummary.pdf?sfvrsn=2.

Hayase, Nozomi. 2010. "Otaku: A silent cultural revolution." Cultureunplugged.com. http://truthseekers.cultureunplugged.com/truth_seekers/2010/07/otaku-a-silent-cultural-revolution-.html.

Hays, Sharon. 1996. *The Cultural Contradictions of Motherhood.* New Haven, CT: Yale University Press.

——. 2003. *Flat Broke with Children: Women in the Age of Welfare Reform.* New York: Oxford University Press.

Hegewisch, A.; and Hartmann, H. 2019. "The gender wage gap: 2018 earnings differences by race and ethnicity." Institute for Women's Policy Research. https://iwpr.org/publications/gender-wage-gap-2018/.

Heilprin, John. 2005. "FBI: Radical-activist groups are major threat." *Seattle Times,* May 19. http://seattletimes.nwsource.com/html/nationworld/2002280292_ecoterror19.html.

Heller, Nathan. 2017. "Is the gig economy working?" *The New Yorker,* May 15. http://www.newyorker.com/magazine/2017/05/15/is-the-gig-economy-working.

Hennigan, W. J. 2017. "The U.S. military is targeting Islamic State's virtual caliphate by hunting & killing its online operatives one-by-one." *Los Angeles Times,* May 5. http://www.latimes.com/world/middleeast/la-fg-isis-online-20170502-story.html.

Henninger, P.; Meredith, M.; Morse, M.; Damjanovic, N.; Gujar, K.; and Hsu, K. 2018. "Who votes without identification? Using affidavits from Michigan to learn about the potential impact of strict photo voter identification laws." SSRN. https://ssrn.com/abstract=3205769.

Herek, G. M. 1990. "The context of anti-gay violence: Notes on cultural and psychological heterosexism." *Journal of Interpersonal Violence,* vol. 5: 316–333.

Heritage, John; and Clayman, Steven E. 2010. *Talk in Action: Interactions, Identities and Institutions.* Boston: Wiley-Blackwell.

Hernandez, Richard. 2018. "The fall of employment in the manufacturing sector." Monthly Labor Review, Bureau of Labor Statistics, https://www.bls.gov/opub/mlr/2018/beyond-bls/the-fall-of-employment-in-the-manufacturing-sector.htm.

Heron, M. 2018. "Deaths: Leading causes for 2016." *National Vital Statistics Reports,* vol. 67, no. 6. https://www.cdc.gov/nchs/data/nvsr/nvsr67/nvsr67_06.pdf.

Herrnstein, R.; and Murray, C. 1994. *The Bell Curve: Intelligence and Class Structure in American Life.* New York: Free Press.

Hess, Alexander E. M. 2013. "On holiday: Countries with the most vacation days." *USA Today,* June 8. https://www.usatoday.com/story/money/business/2013/06/08/countries-most-vacation-days/2400193/.

Hetey, R. C.; Monin, B.; Maitreyi, A.; and Eberhardt, J. L. 2016. "Data for change: A statistical analysis of police stops, searches, handcuffings, and arrests in Oakland, Calif., 2013–2014." Stanford University, SPARQ: Social Psychological Answers to Real-World Questions.

Hewitt, John. P. 2000. *Self and Society: A Symbolic Interactionist Social Psychology.* Boston: Allyn and Bacon.

Hill, Peter; and Wood, Ralph. 1999. *Measures of Religiosity.* Birmingham, AL: Religious Education Press.

Hirschi, Travis. 1969. *Causes of Delinquency.* Berkeley: University of California Press.

Hochschild, Arlie Russel. 1975. "The sociology of feeling and emotion." In Marcia Millman and Rosabeth Moss Kanter, eds., *Another Voice.* Garden City, NY: Doubleday.

——. 1983. *The Managed Heart: The Commercialization of Human Feeling.* Berkeley: University of California Press.

——. 2018. *Strangers in Their Own Land: Anger and Mourning on the American Right.* New York: The New Press.

——; and Machung, Anne. 1989. *The Second Shift: Working Parents and the Revolution at Home.* New York: Viking.

Hochschild, Jennifer L. 1996. *Facing Up to the American Dream: Race, Class, and the Soul of the Nation.* Princeton, NJ: Princeton University Press.

Hodge, Robert; and Tripp, David. 1986. *Children and Television: A Semiotic Approach.* Cambridge, UK: Polity Press.

Hoffman, Kelly M.; Trawalter, Sophie; Axt, Jordan R.; and Oliver, M. Norman. 2016. "Racial bias in pain assessment and treatment recommendations, and false beliefs about biological differences between blacks and whites." *Proceedings of the National Academy of Sciences of the United States of America,* vol. 113, no. 16: 4296–4301. https://www.ncbi.nlm.nih.gov/pmc/articles/PMC4843483/.

Hoffman, Matt; and Torres, Lisa. 2002. "It's not only 'who you know' that matters: Gender, personal contacts, and job lead quality." *Gender and Society,* vol. 16, no. 6: 793–813.

Holdren, John P.; Daily, Gretchen; and Ehrlich, Paul R. 1995. "The meaning of sustainability: Biogeophysical aspects." In M. Munasinghe and W. Shearer, eds., *Defining and Measuring Sustainability: The Biogeophysical Foundations.* Washington, DC: World Bank.

Holdsworth, M.; Gartner, A.; Landais, E.; Maire, B.; and Delpeuch, F. 2004. "Perceptions of healthy and desirable body size in urban Senegalese women." *International Journal of Obesity and Related Metabolic Disorders,* vol. 28, no. 12: 1561–1568.

Holifield, E. B. 2015. "Why do Americans seem so religious?" *Sacred Matters.* https://sacredmattersmagazine.com/why-do-americans-seem-so-religious/.

Holmes, Seth M. 2011. "Structural vulnerability and hierarchies of ethnicity and citizenship on the farm, medical anthropology: Cross-cultural studies in health and illness." *Medical Anthropology,* vol. 30, no. 4: 425–449.

Holstein, James; and Gubrium, Jaber. 1990. *What Is Family?* Mountain View, CA: Mayfield Publishing Company.

——. 1995. "Deprivatization and the construction of domestic life." *Journal of Marriage and the Family,* vol. 57, no. 4: 894.

_____. 2000. *The Self We Live By: Narrative Identity in a Postmodern World*. New York: Oxford University Press.

Homans, George. 1951. *The Human Group*. New York: Harcourt Brace Jovanovich.

Hong, Victor; Foster, Cynthia J. Ewell; Magness, Christina S.; McGuire, Taylor C.; Smith, Patricia K.; and King, Cheryl A. 2018. "*13 Reasons Why*: Viewing patterns and perceived impact among youths at risk of suicide." *Psychiatric Services*, vol. 70, no. 2 (February 1, 2019): 107–114. Published ahead of print November 20, 2018. https://ps.psychiatryonline.org/doi/10.1176/appi.ps.201800384.

hooks, bell. 1990. *Yearning: Race, Gender and Cultural Politics*. Boston: South End Press.

_____. 2003. *We Real Cool: Black Men and Masculinity*. London: Routledge.

_____. 2005. *Soul Sister: Women, Friendship, and Fulfillment*. Cambridge, MA: South End Press.

_____. 2016. "Moving beyond pain." http://www.bellhooksinstitute.com/blog/2016/5/9/moving-beyond-pain.

Hopkins, Daniel J.; Meredith, Marc; Morse, Michael; Smith, Sarah; and Yoder, Jesse. 2017. "Voting but for the law: Evidence from Virginia on photo identification requirements." *Journal of Empirical Legal Studies*, vol. 14, no. 1: 79–128.

Hoyert, Donna; and Xu, Jiaquan. 2012. "Deaths: Preliminary data for 2011." *National Vital Statistics Reports*, vol. 61, no. 6. http://www.cdc.gov/nchs/data/nvsr/nvsr61/nvsr61_06.pdf.

Hsiang, Solomon; Kopp, Robert; Jina, Amir; Rising, James; Delgado, Michael; Mohan, Shashank; Rasmussen, D. J.; Muir-Wood, Robert; Wilson, Paul; Oppenheimer, Michael; Larsen, Kate; and Houser, Trevor. 2017. "Estimating economic damage from climate change in the United States." *Science*, vol. 356, issue 6345: 1362–1369.

Hudak, S. 2015. "FAMU settles hazing lawsuit spawned by death of drum major Robert Champion." *Orlando Sentinel*. http://www.orlandosentinel.com/news/famu-hazing-band/os-famu-hazing-robert-champion-settlement-20150918-story.html.

Huddleston, Tom. 2016. "NBC under pressure to cancel *Biggest Loser*." *Fortune*. May 23. http://fortune.com/2016/05/23/biggest-loser-nbc-contestants/.

Hughes, Jonathon; and Cain, Louis. 1994. *American Economic History*, 4th ed. New York: HarperCollins College Publishers.

Hull, Elizabeth. 2002. "Florida's former felons: You can't vote here." *Commonwealth*, vol. 129, no. 12: 16.

Hummer, Robert A.; and Hernandez, Elaine M. 2013. "The effect of educational attainment on adult mortality in the United States." *Population Bulletin*, vol. 68, no. 1.

Humphrey, Craig R.; Lewis, Tammy L.; and Buttel, Frederick H. 2002. *Environment, Energy, and Society: A New Synthesis*. Belmont, CA: Wadsworth.

Hunt, Abby. 2018. "Students for Sexual Health referendum gets 94 percent support." *The Heights*, February 17. http://bcheights.com/2018/02/17/students-for-sexual-health-wins-referendum/.

Hunt, Darnell; and Ramon, Ana-Christina. 2015. "Hollywood diversity report 2015." Ralph J. Bunche Center for African American Studies at UCLA. http://www.bunchecenter.ucla.edu/wp-content/uploads/2015/02/2015-Hollywood-Diversity-Report-2-25-15.pdf.

_____. 2017. "Hollywood diversity report 2017." Ralph J. Bunche Center for African American Studies at UCLA. http://www.bunchecenter.ucla.edu/wp-content/uploads/2017/04/2017-Hollywood-Diversity-Report-2-21-17.pdf.

Hunter, James D. 1991. *Culture Wars: The Struggle to Define America*. New York: Basic Books.

_____. 2006. "Is there a culture war? A dialogue on values and American public life." Washington, DC: The Brookings Press.

Hurley, Lawrence. 2013. "Supreme Court guts key part of landmark Voting Rights Act." Reuters. http://www.reuters.com/article/2013/06/25/us-usa-court-voting-idUSBRE95O0TU20130625.

Hustvedt, Siri. 2002. "9/11 six months on." *The Observer*, March 10. Special Supplement, p. 6.

Hwang, J.; and Sampson, R. J. 2014. "Divergent pathways of gentrification: Racial inequality and the social order of renewal in Chicago neighborhoods." *American Sociological Review*, vol. 79, no. 4: 726–751. https://doi.org/10.1177/0003122414535774.

Ignatiev, Noel. 1996, 2008. *How the Irish Became White*. London: Routledge.

Iftikhar, Arsalan. 2016. "Honor killings are a global problem." *Time*. July 29. http://time.com/4415554/honor-killing-qandeel-baloch/.

Institute for Health Metrics and Evaluation. 2016. "US health map." Seattle, WA: IHME, University of Washington. http://vizhub.healthdata.org/subnational/usa.

Institute of Medicine. 2011. *Relieving Pain in America: A Blueprint for Transforming Prevention, Care, Education, and Research*. Washington, DC: National Academies Press. https://www.ncbi.nlm.nih.gov/books/NBK92525/.

Insurance Institute for Highway Safety. 2018. "Fatality facts: Gender." https://www.iihs.org/iihs/topics/t/general-statistics/fatalityfacts/gender/2017.

International Labour Organization and Walk Free Foundation. 2017. "Global estimates of modern slavery: Forced labour and forced marriage." https://www.ilo.org/wcmsp5/groups/public/@dgreports/@dcomm/documents/publication/wcms_575479.pdf.

International Telecommunications Union. 2017. "ICT facts and figures 2017." https://www.itu.int/en/ITU-D/Statistics/Documents/facts/ICTFactsFigures2017.pdf.

_____. 2018. "New ITU statistics show more than half the world is now using the Internet." *ITU News*, Dec. 8. https://news.itu.int/itu-statistics-leaving-no-one-offline/.

Isikoff, Michael. 2004. "The dots never existed." *Newsweek*, July 19.

Iwamoto, Derek K.; Brady, Jennifer; Kaya, Aylin; and Park, Athena. 2018. "Masculinity and depression: A longitudinal investigation of multidimensional masculine norms among college men." *American Journal of Men's Health*, vol. 12, no. 6: 1873–1881.

Jackson, K. T. 1985. *Crabgrass Frontier: The Suburbanization of the United States*. New York: Oxford University Press.

Jackson, Phillip. 1968. *Life in Classrooms*. New York: Holt, Rinehart, and Winston.

Jackson-Jacobs, Curtis. 2004. "Taking a beating: The narrative gratifications of fighting as an underdog." In Hayward et al., eds., *Cultural Criminology Unleashed*. London: Glasshouse.

Jamieson, Kathleen Hall. *Cyberwar: How Russian Hackers and Trolls Helped Elect a President*. New York: Oxford University Press.

Jamieson, Patrick; and Romer, Don. 2014. "Violence in popular U.S. prime time TV dramas and the cultivation of fear: A time series analysis." *Media and Communication*, vol. 2, no. 2: 31–41.

Janus, Irving L. 1971. "Groupthink." *Psychology Today*, November.

_____. 1982. *Groupthink*. 2nd ed. Boston: Houghton-Mifflin.

Jay, M. 2003. "Critical race theory, multicultural education, and the hidden curriculum of hegemony," *Multicultural Perspectives*, vol. 5, no. 4: 3–9.

Jenkins, Henry. 1992. *Textual Poachers: Television Fans and Participatory Culture*. London. Routledge.

———. 2006. *Fans, Bloggers, and Gamers: Exploring Participatory Culture*. New York: New York University Press.

Jenkins, Tania M.; and Reddy, Shalini. 2017. "Revisiting the rationing of medical degrees in the United States." *Contexts*, January 11. https://contexts.org/articles/revisiting-the-rationing-of-medical-degrees-in-the-united-states/.

Jin, Ge. 2006. "Chinese gold farmers." http://www.we-make-money-not-art.com/archives/2006/03/ge-jin-a-phd-st.php.

Jobs for the Future. 2013. "Early college high schools get results." http://www.jff.org/sites/default/files/ECHS_get_results_040113.pdf.

Johnson, Kenneth M. 1999. "The rural rebound." *Population Reference Bureau Reports on America*, vol. 1, no. 3 (August).

———; and Beale, Calvin L. 1994. "The recent revival of widespread population growth in nonmetropolitan America." *Rural Sociology*, vol. 59, no. 4: 655–667.

Jones, Andrew R. 2009. *Fads, Fetishes, and Fun: A Sociological Analysis of Pop Culture*. San Diego, CA: Cognella.

Jones, C. M.; Einstein, E. B.; and Compton, W. M. 2018. "Changes in synthetic opioid involvement in drug overdose deaths in the United States, 2010–2016." *Journal of the American Medical Association*, vol. 319, no. 17: 1819–1821.

Jones, Greg. 2012. "Good workers gone bad: How to spot employee theft." *CNBC*, February 12. http://www.cnbc.com/id/46556452/Good_Workers_Gone_Bad_How_to_Spot_Employee_Theft.

Jones, Jeffrey M. 2017. "In US, 10.2% of LGBT adults now married to same-sex spouse." Gallup. http://www.gallup.com/poll/212702/lgbt-adults-married-sex-spouse.aspx?utm_source=alert&utm_medium=email&utm_content=morelink&utm_campaign=syndication.

Jones, Jo; and Mosher, William D. 2013. "Fathers' involvement with their children: United States, 2006–2010." *National Health Statistics Reports*, no. 71: 1–22. Hyattsville, MD: National Center for Health Statistics.

Jones, Nikki. 2012. *Between Good and Ghetto: African American Girls and Inner-City Violence*. New Brunswick, NJ: Rutgers University Press.

Jones, Robert P.; Cox, Daniel; and Banchoff, Thomas. 2012. *A Generation in Transition: Religion, Values, and Politics Among College-Age Millennials*. Washington, DC: Public Religion Research Institute, Georgetown University, 2012.

Jones, Robert P.; et al. 2016. "How immigration and concerns about cultural changes are shaping the 2016 election." Public Religion Research Institute (PRRI). June 23.

Jones, Steve. 1997. *Virtual Culture: Identity and Communication in Cybersociety*. Thousand Oaks, CA: Sage.

———; and Philip Howard, eds. 2003. *Society Online: The Internet in Context*. Thousand Oaks, CA: Sage.

Juergensmeyer, Mark. 2003. *Terror in the Mind of God: The Global Rise of Religious Violence*. Berkeley: University of California Press.

Kaczor, Bill. 1996. "Neighborhood blames years of woe on 'Mount Dioxin.'" *Charleston Gazette*, March 11.

Kadushin, Charles. 2012. *Understanding Social Networks: Theories, Concepts, and Findings*. Oxford: Oxford University Press.

Kaiser Family Foundation. 2019a. "The global HIV/AIDS epidemic." January 28. https://www.kff.org/global-health-policy/fact-sheet/the-global-hivaids-epidemic/.

———. 2019b. "KFF health tracking poll: The public's views on the ACA." April 24. https://www.kff.org/interactive/kff-health-tracking-poll-the-publics-views-on-the-aca/#?response=Favorable—Unfavorable&aRange=twoYear.

Kalev, Alexandra; Dobbin, Frank; and Kelly, Erin. 2006. "Best practices or best guesses? Assessing the efficacy of corporate affirmative action and diversity policies." *American Sociological Review*, vol. 71 (August): 589–617.

Kalleberg, Arne L. 2009. "Precarious work, insecure workers: Employment relations in transition." *American Sociological Review*, vol. 74, no. 1: 1–22.

Kalmijn, M. 1998. "Intermarriage and homogamy: Causes, patterns, trends." *Annual Review of Sociology*, vol. 24: 395–421.

Kang, Miliann. 2010. *The Managed Hand: Race, Gender, and the Body in Beauty Service Work*. Berkeley: University of California Press.

Kann, L.; Olsen, E. O.; McManus, T.; et al. 2016. "Sexual identity, sex of sexual contacts, and health-related behaviors among students in grades 9–12—United States and selected sites, 2015." *MMWR Surveillance Summaries 2016*, vol. 65, no. SS-9: 1–202.

Karau, S. J.; and Williams, K. D. 1993. "Social loafing: A meta-analytic review and theoretical integration." *Journal of Personality and Social Psychology*, vol. 65: 681–706.

Karp, Melinda Mechur. 2012. "'I don't know, I've never been to college!' Dual enrollment as a college readiness strategy." *New Directions for Higher Education*, vol 2012, issue 158.

Katz, Elihu. 1959. "Mass communication research and the study of popular culture." *Studies in Public Communication*, vol. 2: 1–6. http://repository.upenn.edu/asc_papers/165.

———; and Lazarsfeld, Paul F. 1955. *Personal Influence: The Part Played by People in the Flow of Mass Communications*. New York: Macmillan Free Press.

Katz, Jack. 1988. *Seductions of Crime: Moral and Sensual Attractions of Doing Evil*. New York: Basic Books.

———. 1997. "Ethnography's warrants." *Sociological Methods & Research*, vol. 25, no. 4: 391–423.

Kaufman, Sharon. 2005. *And a Time to Die: How American Hospitals Shape the End of Life*. New York: Scribner.

Keaton, Patrick. 2014. "Selected statistics from the public elementary and secondary education universe: School year 2012–13." National Center for Education Statistics, October 30. http://nces.ed.gov/pubs2013/2014098/findings.asp.

Keith, Verna M.; and Finlay, Barbara. 1988. "The impact of parental divorce on children's educational attainment, marital timing, and likelihood of divorce." *Journal of Marriage and the Family*, vol. 50, no. 3: 797–809.

———. 2005. *Media Spectacle and the Crisis of Democracy: Terrorism, War and Election Battles*. Boulder, CO: Paradigm.

Kelly, Barbara. 1993. *Expanding the American Dream: Building and Rebuilding Levittown*. Albany: State University of New York Press.

Kelman, H. 1958. "Compliance, identification, and internalization: Three processes of attitude change." *Journal of Conflict Resolution*, vol. 1: 51–60.

Kendi, Ibram X. 2016. *Stamped from the Beginning: The Definitive History of Racist Ideas in America*. New York: Nation Books.

Kephart, William. 2000. *Extraordinary Groups: An Examination of Unconventional Lifestyles*. New York: W. H. Freeman.

Kerstetter, Jackie. 2016. "The 2016 EdNext poll—including 10-year trends in public opinion." *Education Next*, August 23. https://www.educationnext.org/the-2016-ednext-poll-including-10-year-trends-in-public-opinion/.

Kessler, R. C. 2003. "Epidemiology of women and depression." *Journal of Affective Disorders*, vol. 74, no. 1: 5–13.

Khasnis, Atul A.; and Nettleman, Mary D. 2005. "Global warming and infectious disease." *Archives of Medical Research*, vol. 36, no. 6: 689–696.

Khokhar, Tariq. 2017. "Globally, 70% of freshwater is used for agriculture." *World Bank Data Blog*, March 22. https://blogs.worldbank.org/opendata/chart-globally-70-freshwater-used-agriculture.

Kilbourne, Jean. 1999. *Killing Us Softly 3*. Dir. Sut Jhally. Center for Media Literacy.

Killewald, Alexandra. 2013. "A reconsideration of the fatherhood premium: Marriage, residence, biology, and the wages of fathers." *American Sociological Review*, vol. 78: 96–116.

Kimmel, Michael. 1987. *Changing Men: New Directions in Research on Men and Masculinity*. Thousand Oaks, CA: Sage.

―――. 2009. *Guyland: The Perilous World Where Boys Become Men*. New York: Harper Perennial.

King, A. 1995. "Outline of a practical theory of football violence." *Sociology*, vol. 24: 635–652.

King, Marissa D.; Fountain, Christine; Dakhlallah, Diana; and Bearman, Peter S. 2009. "Estimated autism risk and older reproductive age." *American Journal of Public Health*, vol. 99, no. 9: 1673–1679.

Kingkade, Tyler. 2014. "Fewer than one-third of campus sexual assault cases result in expulsion." *Huffington Post*. September 29. http://www.huffingtonpost.com/2014/09/29/campus-sexual-assault_n_5888742.html.

Kinsey, Alfred C.; Pomeroy, Wardell B.; and Martin, Clyde E. 1998 (orig. 1948). *Sexual Behavior in the Human Male*. Bloomington: Indiana University Press.

―――; and Gebhard, Paul H. 1998 (orig. 1953). *Sexual Behavior in the Human Female*. Bloomington: Indiana University Press.

Kirkham, Chris. 2015. "U.S. is asked to forgive debt of Corinthian colleges students." *Los Angeles Times*, April 9. http://www.latimes.com/business/la-fi-corinthian-student-debt-20150410-story.html.

―――; and Hsu, Tiffany. 2014. "LA wage hikes spark fierce debate." *Los Angeles Times*, October 24. http://www.latimes.com/business/la-fi-minimum-wage-debates-20141025-story.html#page=1.

Kitsuse, John I. 1980. "Coming out all over: Deviants and the politics of social problems." *Social Problems*, vol. 28: 1–13.

Kitzinger, C. 1987. *The Social Construction of Lesbianism*. London: Sage.

Klapper, J. 1960. *The Effects of Mass Communication*. New York: Free Press.

Klein, Naomi. 2000. *No Logo: Taking Aim at the Brand Bullies*. New York: Picador.

Kleinman, Sherryl. 1984. *Equals Before God: Seminarians as Humanistic Professionals*. Chicago: University of Chicago Press.

Klinenberg, Eric. 2002. *Heat Wave: A Social Autopsy of a Disaster in Chicago*. Chicago: University of Chicago Press.

―――. 2007. "Breaking the news." *Mother Jones*, March/April. http://www.motherjones.com/news/feature/2007/03/breaking_the_news.html.

―――. 2012a. "Facebook isn't making us lonely." *Slate*, April 19. http://www.slate.com/articles/life/culturebox/2012/04/is_facebook_making_us_lonely_no_the_atlantic_cover_story_is_wrong_.single.html.

―――. 2012b. *Going Solo: The Extraordinary Rise of Living Alone*. New York: Penguin Press.

Knobloch-Westerwick, Silvia; and Lavis, Simon M. 2017. "Selecting serious or satirical, supporting or stirring news? Selective exposure to partisan versus mockery news online videos." *Journal of Communication*, vol. 67, no. 1: 54–81. https://doi.org/10.1111/jcom.12271.

Koerner, Brendan I. 2003. "Outbreaks vs. epidemics: Whether it's time to freak about the flu." *Slate*, December 19. http://www.slate.com/id/2092969.

Kolata, G. 2016. "After 'The Biggest Loser,' their bodies fought to regain weight." *The New York Times*, May 2. https://www.nytimes.com/2016/05/02/health/biggest-loser-weight-loss.html?_r=2.

Kollock, Peter; Blumstein, Philip; and Schwartz, Pepper. 1985. "Sex and power in interaction: Conversational privileges and duties." *American Sociological Review*, vol. 50, no. 1: 34–46.

Kosciw, Joseph G.; Greytak, Emily A.; Giga, Noreen M.; Villenas, C.; and Danischewski, David J. 2016. "The 2015 National School Climate Survey." https://www.glsen.org/sites/default/files/2015%20National%20GLSEN%202015%20National%20School%20Climate%20Survey%20%28NSCS%29%20-%20Full%20Report_0.pdf.

Koseff, Alexei. 2014. "Jerry Brown approves community college bachelor's degrees." *Sacramento Bee*, September, 29. http://www.sacbee.com/news/politics-government/capitol-alert/article2615016.html.

Kosmin, Barry A.; and Keysar, Ariela. 2013. "Religious, spiritual, and secular: The emergence of three distinct worldviews among American college students." Hartford, CT: Trinity College. http://www.trincoll.edu/Academics/centers/isssc/Documents/ARIS_2013_College%20Students_Sept_25_final_draft.pdf.

―――; Mayer, Egon; and Keysar, Ariela. 2001. "American religious identification survey." The Graduate Center of the City University of New York. http://www.gc.cuny.edu/faculty/research_briefs/aris/aris_index.htm.

Kotkin, J. 2018. "Where small town America is thriving." *Forbes*, March 8. https://www.forbes.com/sites/joelkotkin/2018/03/08/where-small-town-america-is-thriving/#3fc2ddfb38b8.

Kozol, J. 1991. *Savage Inequalities: Children in America's Schools*. New York: Crown Publishing.

Krakauer, Jon. 1997. *Into the Wild*. New York: Anchor Books.

Kramer, A. D. I.; Guillory, J. E.; and Hancock, J. T. 2014. "Experimental evidence of massive-scale emotional contagion through social networks." *Proceedings of the National Academy of Sciences of the United States*, vol. 111, no. 24.

Krashen, S. D. 1996. *Under Attack: The Case against Bilingual Education*. Culver City, CA: Language Education Associates.

Kraus, Richard G. 1995. "Play's new identity: Big business." *Journal of Physical Education, Recreation & Dance*, vol. 66, no. 8: 36.

Kreager, D. A.; and Haynie, D. L. 2011. "Dangerous liaisons? Dating and drinking diffusion in adolescent peer networks." *American Sociological Review*, vol. 76, no. 5: 737.

Kreider, Rose M.; and Lofquist, Daphne A. 2010. "Adopted children and stepchildren: 2010." *Adoption Quarterly*, vol. 13: 268–291.

Kristian, Sarah. 2018. "Social aspiration and traditional speech features among rural Newfoundland youth." In Elizabeth Seale and Christine Mallinson, eds., *Rural Voices: Language, Identity and Change across Place*, 143–164. Lanham, MD: Lexington Books.

Kristof, N.; and WuDunn, S. 2000. "Two cheers for sweatshops." *New York Times Magazine*, September 24. http://www.nytimes.com/library/magazine/home/20000924mag-sweatshops.html.

Krivickas, Kristy; and Lofquist, Daphne. 2011. "Demographics of same-sex couple households with children." http://www.census.gov/hhes/same sex/files/Krivickas-Lofquist%20PAA%202011.pdf.

Kroll, L.; and Dolan, K. 2018. "Forbes 400: The definitive ranking of the wealthiest Americans." *Forbes*, October 3. https://www.forbes.com/forbes-400/#61a863c07e2f.

Kuhn, Manfred; and McPartland, T. S. 1954. "An empirical investigation of self-attitude." *American Sociological Review*, vol. 19: 68–79.

Kuhn, Thomas S. 1970 (orig. 1962). *The Structure of Scientific Revolutions*. Chicago: University of Chicago Press.

Kunstler, J. H. 1993. *The Geography of Nowhere: The Rise and Decline of America's Man-Made Landscape*. New York: Simon & Schuster.

Kurtzleben, D. 2013. "Gay couples more educated, higher-income than heterosexual couples." *U.S. News and World Report*, March 1. http://www.usnews.com/news/articles/2013/03/01/gay-couples-more-educated-higher-income-than-heterosexual-couples.

———. 2018. "Electing more women would change Congress (but not make it more bipartisan)." National Public Radio, August 10. https://www.npr.org/2018/08/10/636258585/electing-more-women-would-change-congress-but-not-make-it-more-bipartisan.

Kurzweil, Ray. 1990. *The Age of Intelligent Machines*. Cambridge, MA: MIT Press.

Lachman, Margie. 2004. "Development in midlife." *Annual Review of Psychology*, vol. 55: 305–31.

Lachs, M.; and Pillemer, K. 2015. "Elder abuse." *New England Journal of Medicine*, vol. 373: 1947–1956. doi: 10.1056/NEJMra1404688.

Lacy, Karyn R. 2007. *Blue Chip Black: Race, Class, and Status in the New Black Middle Class*. Berkeley: University of California Press.

LaFraniere, Sharon; and Lehren, Andrew W. 2015. "The disproportionate risks of driving while black." *The New York Times*, October 25. https://www.nytimes.com/2015/10/25/us/racial-disparity-traffic-stops-driving-black.html?_r=0.

Laing, Aislinn. 2012. "South Africa's whites still paid six times more than blacks." *The Telegraph*, October 30. http://www.telegraph.co.uk/news/worldnews/africaandindianocean/southafrica/9643548/South-Africas-whites-still-paid-six-times-more-than-blacks.html.

LaMarre, Thomas. 2004. "An introduction to the otaku movement." *EnterText*, vol. 4, no. 1: 151–187.

Lane, J. Mark; and Tabak, Ronald J. 1991. "Judicial activism and legislative 'reform' of federal habeas corpus: A critical analysis of recent developments and current proposals." *Albany Law Review*, vol. 55, no. 1: 1–95.

Langer, Roy; and Beckman, Suzanne C. 2005. "Sensitive research topics: Netnography revisited." *Qualitative Market Research*, vol. 8, no. 2: 189–203.

Lareau, Annette. 2003. *Unequal Childhoods: Class, Race and Family Life*. Berkeley: University of California Press.

Laroche, Michel; Habibi, Mohammad Reza; and Richard, Marie-Odile. 2013. "To be or not to be in social media: How brand loyalty is affected by social media?" *International Journal of Information Management*, vol. 33: 76–82.

Larson, Doran. 2013. "Why Scandinavian prisons are superior." *The Atlantic*, September 24. http://www.theatlantic.com/international/archive/2013/09/why-scandinavian-prisons-are-superior/279949/.

Larson, R. W.; and Richards, M. H. 1991. "Daily companionship in late childhood and early adolescence: Changing developmental contexts." *Child Development*, vol. 62: 284–300.

Lasch, Christopher. 1977. *Haven in a Heartless World: The Family Besieged*. New York: Basic Books.

Laumann, Edward O.; Gagnon, John H.; Michael, Robert T.; and Michaels, Stuart. 1994. *The Social Organization of Sexuality*. Chicago: University of Chicago Press.

Lazar, D.; et al. 2009. "Computational social science." *Science*, vol. 323, no. 5915: 721–723.

Lazarsfeld, Paul; and Katz, Elihu. 1955. *Personal Influence*. New York: Free Press.

Le, Vanna. 2014. "Global 2000: The world's largest media companies of 2014." *Forbes*, May 7. http://www.forbes.com/sites/vannale/2014/05/07/global-2000-the-worlds-largest-media-companies-of-2014/.

Le Bon, Gustave. 1896. *The Crowd: A Study of the Popular Mind*. New York: Viking Press.

Leaper, Campbell; and Ayers, Melanie M. 2007. "A meta-analytic review of gender variations in adults' language use: Talkativeness, affiliative speech, and assertive speech." *Personality and Social Psychology Review*, vol. 11: 328–363.

Lederer, Edith. 2012. "U.N.: 4 million human trafficking victims." *Associated Press*, April 3. http://www.news.yahoo.com/un-2-4-million-human-trafficking-victims-004512192.html.

Lederman, D. 2018. "Who is studying online (and where)." *Inside Higher Ed*, January 5. https://www.insidehighered.com/digital-learning/article/2018/01/05/new-us-data-show-continued-growth-college-students-studying.

Lee, Jennifer; and Bean, Frank D. 2012. *The Diversity Paradox: Immigration and the Color Line in Twenty-First Century America*. New York: Russell Sage Foundation.

Lee, Jennifer; and Zhou, Min. 2014. "The success frame and achievement paradox: The costs and consequences for Asian Americans." *Race and Social Problems*, vol. 6, no. 1: 38–55.

———. 2015. *The Asian American Achievement Paradox*. New York: Russell Sage Foundation.

Leidner, Robin. 1993. *Fast Food, Fast Talk*. Berkeley: University of California Press.

Leifheit-Limson, Erica C.; D'Onofrio, Gail; et al. 2015. "Sex differences in cardiac risk factors, perceived risk, and health care provider discussion of risk and risk modification among young patients with acute myocardial infarction." *Journal of the American College of Cardiology*, vol. 66, no. 18, November. http://www.onlinejacc.org/content/66/18/1949.

Leiserowitz, A.; Maibach, E.; Rosenthal, S.; Kotcher, J.; Ballew, M.; Goldberg, M.; and Gustafson, A. 2018. "Climate change in the American mind: December 2018." Yale University and George Mason University. New Haven, CT: Yale Program on Climate Change Communication.

Lemert, Edwin M. 1951. *Social Pathology: A Systematic Approach to the Theory of Sociopathic Behavior*. New York: McGraw-Hill.

Lenhart, Amanda. 2015. "Teens, technology and friendships: Video games, social media and mobile phones play an integral role in how teens meet and interact with friends." Pew Research Center. August 6. http://www.pewinternet.org/2015/08/06/teens-technology-and-friendships/.

Lepowsky, Maria Alexandra. 1993. *Gender and Power from Fruit of the Motherland*. New York: Columbia University Press.

Lerner, Melvin. 1965. "Evaluation of performance as a function of performer's reward and attractiveness." *Journal of Personality and Social Psychology*, vol. 1, no. 4: 355–360.

———. 1980. *The Belief in a Just World: A Fundamental Delusion*. New York: Plenum Press.

Levi-Strauss, C. 1969 (orig. 1949). In R. Needham, ed., *The Elementary Structures of Kinship*. rev. ed. J. Bell and J. von Sturmer, trans. Boston: Beacon Press.

Levinson, David, ed. 2002. *Encyclopedia of Crime and Punishment.* Thousand Oaks, CA: Sage Publications.

Lewis, Christopher Alan; Shelvin, Mark; McGuckin, Conor; and Navratil, Marek. 2001. "The Santa Clara Strength of Religious Faith Questionnaire: Confirmatory factor analysis." *Pastoral Psychology*, vol. 49, no. 5. http://www.infm.ulst.ac.uk/~chris/64.pdf.

Lewis, Jacqueline. 1998. "Learning to strip: The socialization experiences of exotic dancers." *Canadian Journal of Human Sexuality*, vol. 7: 1–16.

Lewis, Jamie M.; and Kreider, Rose M. 2015. "Remarriage in the United States." U.S. Census Bureau, March 2015. https://www.census.gov/content/dam/Census/library/publications/2015/acs/acs-30.pdf.

Lewis, Jason. 2013. "New report details plans for low-wage worker justice." *The Village Voice*, February 14. http://blogs.villagevoice.com/runninscared/2013/02/new_report_deta.php.

Lewis, Michael. 2011. *The Big Short: Inside the Doomsday Machine.* New York: W. W. Norton.

Lewis, Oscar. 1959. *Five Families: Mexican Case Studies in the Culture of Poverty.* New York: Basic Books.

Lhamon, C. E.; and Samuels, J. 2014. "Dear colleague letter from the U.S. Department of Justice and the U.S. Department of Education." https://www2.ed.gov/about/offices/list/ocr/letters/colleague-201401-title-vi.html.

Li, J.; and Singelmann, J. 1998. "Gender differences in class mobility: A comparative study of the United States, Sweden, and West Germany." *Acta Sociologica*, vol. 41, no. 4: 315–333.

Li, Jui-Chung Allen. 2007. "The impact of divorce on children's behavior problems." *A Briefing Paper Prepared for the Council on Contemporary Families*, July 21. https://contemporaryfamilies.org/impact-divorce-childrens-behavior-problems/.

Li, Sophie H.; and Graham, Bronwyn M. 2017. "Why are women so vulnerable to anxiety, trauma-related and stress-related disorders? The potential role of sex hormones." *The Lancet Psychiatry*, vol. 4, no. 1: 73–82. http://www.sciencedirect.com/science/article/pii/S2215036616303583.

Liazos, Alexander. 1972. "The poverty of the sociology of deviance: Nuts, sluts and perverts." *Social Problems*, vol. 20: 103–120.

Lin, Vernon W.; Lin, Joyce; and Zhang, Xiaoming. 2016. "U.S. social worker workforce report card: Forecasting nationwide shortages." *Social Work*, vol. 61, no. 1: 7–11.

Lipka, Michael. 2013. "What surveys say about worship attendance—and why some stay home." Pew Research Center. September 13. http://www.pewresearch.org/fact-tank/2013/09/13/what-surveys-say-about-worship-attendance-and-why-some-stay-home/.

———. 2015. "A closer look at America's rapidly growing religious 'nones.'" Pew Research Center, May 13. http://www.pewresearch.org/fact-tank/2015/05/13/a-closer-look-at-americas-rapidly-growing-religious-nones/.

Liptak, Adam. 2013. "Supreme Court invalidates key part of voting rights act." *The New York Times*, June 25.

Livingston, Gretchen. 2013. "The rise of single fathers." July 2. http://www.pewsocialtrends.org/2013/07/02/the-rise-of-single-fathers/.

———. 2014. "Four-in-ten couples are saying 'I Do,' again." Pew Research Center. http://www.pewsocialtrends.org/2014/11/14/four-in-ten-couples-are-saying-i-do-again/.

———. 2015. "Childlessness falls, family size grows among highly educated women." Pew Research Center. May 7. http://www.pewsocialtrends.org/2015/05/07/childlessness-falls-family-size-grows-among-highly-educated-women/.

———. 2017. "Among U.S. cohabiters, 18% have a partner of a different race or ethnicity." Pew Research Center. June 8. http://www.pewresearch.org/fact-tank/2017/06/08/among-u-s-cohabiters-18-have-a-partner-of-a-different-race-or-ethnicity/.

———. 2018. "They're waiting longer, but U.S. women today more likely to have children than a decade ago." Pew Research Center. http://www.pewsocialtrends.org/2018/01/18/theyre-waiting-longer-but-u-s-women-today-more-likely-to-have-children-than-a-decade-ago/.

———; and Brown, A. 2017. "Intermarriage in the U.S. 50 years after *Loving v. Virginia*." Pew Research Center. May 18. http://www.pewsocialtrends.org/2017/05/18/intermarriage-in-the-u-s-50-years-after-loving-v-virginia/.

———; and Caumont, Andrea. 2017. "Five facts on love and marriage in America." Pew Research Center. February 13. http://www.pewresearch.org/fact-tank/2017/02/13/5-facts-about-love-and-marriage/.

Lofland, Lyn. 1973. *A World of Strangers: Order and Action in Urban Public Space.* New York: Basic Books.

Lombardo, Clare. 2019. "Why white school districts have so much more money." National Public Radio, February 26. https://www.npr.org/2019/02/26/696794821/why-white-school-districts-have-so-much-more-money.

Loo, Sai. 2017. *Creative Working in the Knowledge Economy.* Abingdon: Routledge.

Lopez, G. and Radford, J. 2017. "Facts on U.S. Immigrants." Pew Research Center. May 3. http://www.pewhispanic.org/2017/05/03/facts-on-u-s-immigrants-current-data/.

Lopez, Gustavo; Bialik, Kristen; and Radford, Jynnah. 2018. "Key findings about U.S. immigrants." Pew Research Center. November 30. http://www.pewresearch.org/fact-tank/2018/11/30/key-findings-about-u-s-immigrants/.

Lorenz, T. 2018. "Teens are being bullied 'constantly' on Instagram." *The Atlantic*, October 10. https://www.theatlantic.com/technology/archive/2018/10/teens-face-relentless-bullying-instagram/572164/.

Lortie, Dan. 1968. "Shared ordeal and induction to work." In Howard Becker, Blancher Greer, David Reisman, and Robert Weiss, eds., *Institutions and the Person.* Chicago: Aldine.

Loseke, Donileen; and Cahill, Spencer. 1986. "Actors in search of a character: Student social workers' quest for professional identity." *Symbolic Interaction*, vol. 9: 245–258.

Love, Adam; and Hughey, Matthew W. 2015. "Out of bounds? Racial discourse on college basketball message boards." *Ethnic and Racial Studies*, vol. 38, issue 6: 877–93.

Lu, Denise. 2017. "We would need 1.7 Earths to make our consumption sustainable." *The Washington Post*, May 4.

———; and Yourish, Karen. 2019. "The turnover at the top of the Trump administration is unprecedented." *The New York Times*, March 8. https://www.nytimes.com/interactive/2018/03/16/us/politics/all-the-major-firings-and-resignations-in-trump-administration.html.

Lubet, Steven. 2015. "Ethics on the run." *The New Rambler: An Online Review of Books.* May 26. http://newramblerreview.com/book-reviews/law/ethics-on-the-run.

Lurie, Nicole; Slater, Jonathan; McGovern, Paul; Ekstrum, Jacqueline; Quam, Lois; and Margolis, Karen. 1993. "Preventive care for women—does the sex of the physician matter?" *New England Journal of Medicine*, vol. 329: 478-482, August 12. doi: 10.1056/NEJM199308123290707.

Lynch, J. W.; Kaplan, G. A.; and Shema, S. J. 1997. "Cumulative impact of sustained economic hardship on physical, cognitive, psychological, and social functioning." *New England Journal of Medicine*, vol. 337, no. 26: 1889–1895.

_____. 1998. "Income inequality and mortality in metropolitan areas of the United States." *American Journal of Public Health*, vol. 88, no. 7: 1074–1080.

Lynd, Robert S.; and Lynd, Helen Merrell. 1937. *Middletown in Transition: A Study in Cultural Conflicts*. New York: Harcourt Brace.

_____. 1959 (orig. 1929). *Middletown: A Study in Modern American Culture*. San Diego, CA: Harvest Books/Harcourt Brace.

Maccoby, E. E.; and Jacklin, C. N. 1987. "Sex segregation in childhood." In H. W. Reese, ed., *Advances in Child Development and Behavior*. Orlando, FL: Academic Press.

MacDorman, M. F.; and Mathews, T. J. 2011. "Understanding racial and ethnic disparities in U.S. infant mortality rates." NCHS Data Brief, no. 74. Hyattsville, MD: National Center for Health Statistics. https://www.cdc.gov/nchs/data/databriefs/db74.pdf.

_____; and Declercq, E. 2014. "Trends in out-of-hospital births in the United States, 1990–2012." NCHS data brief, no 144. Hyattsville, MD: National Center for Health Statistics.

Macintyre, S.; MacDonald, L.; and Ellaway, A. 2008. "Do poorer people have poorer access to local resources and facilities? The distribution of local resources by area deprivation in Glasgow, Scotland." *Social Sciences & Medicine*, vol. 67, no. 6: 900–914.

MacKinnon, Catharine A. 2005. *Women's Lives, Men's Laws*. Cambridge, MA: Belknap Press.

_____. 2006. *Are Women Human? And Other International Dialogues*. Cambridge, MA: Belknap Press of Harvard University Press.

Macy, Beth. 2018. *Dopesick: Dealers, Doctors, and the Drug Company That Addicted America*. New York: Little, Brown and Company.

Maheshwari, Sapna. 2016. "How fake news goes viral." *The New York Times*, November 20.

Mahmood, Saba. 2004. *Politics of Piety: The Islamic Revival and the Feminist Subject*. Princeton, NJ: Princeton University Press.

Mai-Duc, Christine. 2015. "The world's new oldest person: Gertrude Weaver, 116, of Arkansas." *Los Angeles Times*, April 6. http://www.latimes.com/nation/nationnow/la-na-nn-arkansas-worlds-oldest-person-dies-20150406-story.html.

Malamuth, Neil; and Donnerstein, Edward, eds. 1984. *Pornography and Sexual Aggression*. New York: Academic Press.

Malthus, Thomas. 1997 (orig. 1798). *An Essay on the Principle of Population, as It Affects the Future Improvement of Society with Remarks on the Speculations of Mr. Godwin, M. Condorcet, and Other Writers*. London: J. Johnson, St. Paul's Churchyard. http://www.ac.wwu.edu/~stephan/malthus/malthus.0.html.

Manjoo, Farhad. 2013. "How Google became such a great place to work." *Slate*, January 21. http://www.slate.com/articles/technology/technology/2013/01/google_people_operations_the_secrets_of_the_world_s_most_scientific_human.html.

Mann, Susan A.; Grimes, Michael D.; Kemp, Alice Abel; and Jenkins, Pamela J. 1997. "Paradigm shifts in family sociology? Evidence from three decades of family textbooks." *Journal of Family Issues*, vol. 18, no. 3: 315.

Marche, Stephen. 2012. "Is Facebook making us lonely?" *The Atlantic*, May. http://www.theatlantic.com/magazine/archive/2012/05/is-facebook-making-us-lonely/8930.

Marcuse, Herbert. 1991 (orig. 1964). *One-Dimensional Man: Studies in the Ideology of Advanced Industrial Society*. Boston: Beacon Press.

Margolis, Jason. 2016. "Idaho's first Syrian refugee wants Americans to understand their country's vetting process." Public Radio International. October 20. http://www.pri.org/stories/2016-10-20/idaho-s-first-syrian-refugee-wants-americans-understand-their-countrys-vetting.

Margolis, Rachel; and Myrskylä, Mikko. 2015. "Parental well-being surrounding first birth as a determinant of further parity progression." *Demography*, vol. 52, no. 4: 1147–1166.

Marsh, Sarah. 2016. "Many suffer but no one talks about it: The rise of eating disorders in Japan." *The Guardian*. May 16. https://www.theguardian.com/world/2016/may/17/many-suffer-but-no-one-talks-about-it-the-rise-of-eating-disorders-in-japan.

Marshall, Alex. 2018. "Brown point shoes arrive, 200 years after white ones." *The New York Times*, November 4. https://www.nytimes.com/2018/11/04/arts/dance/brown-point-shoes-diversity-ballet.html.

Martin, J. A.; Hamilton, B. E.; Osterman, M. J. K.; et al. 2017. "Births: Final data for 2015." *National Vital Statistics Report*, vol. 66, no 1. Hyattsville, MD: National Center for Health Statistics.

_____. 2018. "Births: Final data for 2017." *National Vital Statistics Reports*, vol. 67, no. 8. Hyattsville, MD: National Center for Health Statistics. https://www.cdc.gov/nchs/data/nvsr/nvsr67/nvsr67_08-508.pdf.

Martin, Laura. 1986. "Eskimo words for snow: A case study in the genesis and decay of an anthropological example." *American Anthropologist*, vol. 88, no. 2: 418–423.

Martin, Lisa A.; Neighbors, Harold W.; and Griffith, Derek M. 2013. "The experience of symptoms of depression in men vs. women: Analysis of the National Comorbidity Survey Replication." *JAMA Psychiatry*, vol. 70, no. 10: 1100–1106.

Martin, Molly A. 2008. "The intergenerational correlation in weight: How genetic resemblance reveals the social role of families." Supplement, *American Journal of Sociology*, vol. 114: S67–105.

Martinelli, Marissa. 2015. "Cameron Crowe apologized for casting Emma Stone as a half-Asian character. Sort of." *Slate*, June 13. http://www.slate.com/blogs/browbeat/2015/06/03/cameron_crowe_apology_for_white_washed_casting_in_aloha.html.

Martinez, M. E.; Zammitti, E. P.; and Cohen, R. A. 2017. "Health insurance coverage: Early release of estimates from the National Health Interview Survey, January–September 2016." National Center for Health Statistics. CDC. February. http://www.cdc.gov/nchs/nhis/.

Martinez, Martha A.; and Aldrich, Howard. 2014. "Sociological theories applied to family business." In Leif Melin, Mattias Nordqvist, and Pramodita Sharma, eds., *The SAGE Handbook of Family Business*, 83–99. Thousand Oaks, CA: Sage.

Marullo, Sam. 1999. "Sociology's essential role: Promoting critical analysis in service learning." In J. Ostrow, G. Hesser, and S. Enos, eds., *Cultivating the Sociological Imagination: Concepts and Models for Service Learning in Sociology*. Washington, DC: American Association for Higher Education.

Marx, Karl. 1982 (orig. 1848). *The Communist Manifesto*. New York: International.

_____. 2001. *Selected Writings*. David McLellan, ed. Oxford: Oxford University Press.

_____. 2006 (orig. 1890). *Das Kapital*. Miami, FL: Synergy International of the Americas, Ltd.

Maslin Nir, Sarah. 2010. "Embracing a life of solitude." *The New York Times*, April 14.

Massey, D. S.; and Denton N. A. 1993. *American Apartheid: Segregation and the Making of the Underclass*. Cambridge, MA: Harvard University Press.

Mather, V. 2017. "Six New England Patriots say they will skip a

White House visit." *The New York Times*, February 8. https://www.nytimes.com/2017/02/08/sports/football/new-england-patriots-white-house-visit-donald-trump.html.

Mathews, T. J.; and Driscoll, A. K. 2017. "Trends in infant mortality in the United States, 2005–2014." NCHS Data Brief, no. 279. Hyattsville, MD: National Center for Health Statistics. https://www.cdc.gov/nchs/data/databriefs/db279.pdf.

Matos, Kenneth. 2015. "Modern families: Same- and different-sex couples negotiating at home." Families and Work Institute. http://www.familiesandwork.org/downloads/modern-families.pdf.

Matsuda, Mari J.; Lawrence, C. R.; Delgado, Richard; and Crenshaw, Kimberle. 1993. *Words That Wound: Critical Race Theory, Assaultive Speech and the First Amendment.* Boulder, CO: Westview Press.

Matza, David. 1969. *Becoming Deviant.* Englewood Cliffs, NJ: Prentice Hall.

Mauss, Armand L. 1975. *Social Problems as Social Movements.* Philadelphia: J. B. Lippincott.

Mayo, Elton. 1949. *Hawthorne and the Western Electric Company, The Social Problems of an Industrial Civilisation.* New York: Routledge.

Mbatha, A. 2018. "Why land seizure is back in the news in South Africa." *The Washington Post*, November 15. https://www.washingtonpost.com/business/why-land-seizure-is-back-in-news-in-south-africa/2018/08/01/7a0712f8-9585-11e8-818b-e9b7348cd87d_story.html?noredirect=on&utm_term=.abd86fc8e092.

McArdle, Megan. 2012. "Is college a lousy investment?" *Newsweek*, September 9.

McCaa, Robert. 1994. "Child marriage and complex families among the Nahuas of ancient Mexico." *Latin American Population History Bulletin*, 26: 2–11.

McCabe, Janice M. 2016. *Connecting in College: How Friendship Networks Matter for Academic and Social Success.* Chicago: University of Chicago Press.

McCall, L. 2001. "Sources of racial wage inequality in metropolitan labor markets: Racial, ethnic, and gender differences." *American Sociological Review*, vol. 66, no. 4: 520–541.

McCandless, David. 2009. *Information Is Beautiful.* New York: Harper Collins.

McChesney, Robert. 1997. *Corporate Media and the Threat to Democracy.* Open Media Pamphlet Series. New York: Seven Stories Press.

———. 2000. *Rich Media, Poor Democracy: Communication Politics in Dubious Times.* New York: New Press.

———. 2004. *The Problem of the Media: U.S. Communication Politics in the Twenty-First Century.* New York: Monthly Review Press.

McClintock, Elizabeth Aura. 2016. "It's a man's, and a woman's, world: The psychology of mansplaining." *Psychology Today*, March 31. https://www.psychologytoday.com/blog/it-s-man-s-and-woman-s-world/201603/the-psychology-mansplaining.

McCombs, Maxwell; and Shaw, Donald. 1972. "The agenda-setting function of mass media." *Public Opinion Quarterly*, vol. 36, no. 2: 176–187.

———. 1977. "The agenda-setting function of the press." In D. Shaw and M. McCombs, eds., *The Emergence of American Political Issues: The Agenda-Setting Function of the Press.* St. Paul, MN: West Publishing.

McCoy, Terrence. 2014. "In Pakistan, 1,000 women die in 'honor killings' annually. Why is this happening?" *The Washington Post*, May 28. https://www.washingtonpost.com/news/morning-mix/wp/2014/05/28/in-pakistan-honor-killings-claim-1000-womens-lives-annually-why-is-this-still-happening/?utm_term=.fa130c56f680.

McCune, J. 2014. *Sexual Discretion: Black Masculinity and the Politics of Passing.* Chicago: University of Chicago Press.

McDonald, Michael. 2014. "National general election VEP turnout rates, 1789–present." United States Elections Project. June. http://www.electproject.org/national-1789-present.

———. 2019. "National general election VEP turnout rates, 1789–present." United States Election Project. http://www.electproject.org/national-1789-present.

McGeehan, Patrick. 2015. "Cuomo moves to raise wages for New York fast-food workers." *The New York Times*, May 6. http://www.nytimes.com/2015/05/07/nyregion/cuomo-moves-to-raise-wages-for-new-york-fast-food-workers.html?_r=0.

McGhee, Paul E.; and Frueh, Terry. 1980. "Television viewing and the learning of sex-role stereotypes." *Sex Roles*, vol. 6, no. 2: 179.

McGrane, Bernard. 1994. *The Un-TV and the 10 MPH Car: Experiments in Personal Freedom and Everyday Life.* New York: Small Press.

———; and Gunderson, John. 2010. *Watching TV Is Not Required: Thinking About Media and Thinking About Thinking.* New York: Routledge.

McIntosh, Peggy. 1988. "White privilege and male privilege: A personal account of coming to see correspondences through work in women's studies." Working Paper No. 189. Center for Research on Women. Wellesley, MA: Wellesley College.

McKeever, B. 2019. "The nonprofit sector in brief." https://nccs.urban.org/project/nonprofit-sector-brief.

McLuhan, Marshall. 1964. *Understanding Media: The Extensions of Man.* New York: McGraw Hill.

McMichael, Philip. 1996. *Development and Social Change: A Global Perspective.* Thousand Oaks, CA: Pine Forge Press.

McNicol, Tony. 2006. "Meet the geek elite." *Wired Magazine*, vol. 14, no. 7. http://www.wired.com/wired/archive/14.07/posts.html?pg=5.

McPeek, Brian. 2018. "Smart solutions for sustainability." The Nature Conservancy, October 18. https://www.nature.org/en-us/what-we-do/our-insights/perspectives/smart-solutions-for-sustainability/.

McPhail, Clark. 1991. *The Myth of the Madding Crowd.* New York: de Gruyter.

Mead, George Herbert. 1934. *Mind, Self and Society.* Charles Morris, ed. Chicago: University of Chicago Press.

Mejia, P. 2014. "Fetuses in artificial wombs: Medical marvel or misogynist malpractice?" *Newsweek*, August 6.

Mekonnen, Mesfin M.; and Hoekstra, Argen Y. 2016. "Four billion people facing severe water scarcity." *Science Advances*, vol. 2, no. 2. https://advances.sciencemag.org/content/2/2/e1500323.

Mele, Christopher. 2000. *Selling the Lower East Side: Culture, Real Estate, and Resistance in New York City.* Minneapolis: University of Minnesota Press.

Menzel, Peter. 1995. *Material World: A Global Family Portrait.* Sierra Club Books.

Merton, Robert K. 1938. "Social structure and anomie." *American Sociological Review*, vol. 3, no. 5: 672–682.

———. 1948. "The self-fulfilling prophecy." *Antioch Review*, vol. 8, no. 2: 193–210.

———. 1949. "Discrimination and the American creed." In R. M. MacIver, ed., *Discrimination and National Welfare*, 99–126. New York: Institute for Religious Studies.

———. 1968. *Social Theory and Social Structure.* 2nd rev. ed. New York: Free Press.

———. 1996. *On Social Structure and Science.* Chicago: University of Chicago.

Messerschmidt, James W. 1993. *Masculinities and Crime: Critique and Reconceptualization of Theory.* Totowa, NJ: Rowman and Littlefield.

———. 1998. "Men victimizing men: The case of lynching: 1865–1900." In Lee H. Bowker, ed., *Masculinities and Violence.* Thousand Oaks, CA: Sage.

Messner, Steven F.; and Rosenfeld, Richard. 2012. *Crime and the American Dream,* 5th ed. Boston: Wadsworth Publishing.

Meyer, D. 2000. "Social movements: Creating communities of change." In R. Teske and M. Tetreault, eds., *Conscious Acts and the Politics of Social Change.* Columbia: University of South Carolina Press.

Meyer, Daniel R.; and Bartfeld, Judi. 1998. "Patterns of child support compliance in Wisconsin." *Journal of Marriage and the Family,* vol. 60, no. 2: 309–318.

Meyrowitz, Joshua. 1985. *No Sense of Place: The Impact of Electronic Media on Social Behavior.* New York: Oxford University Press.

Michener, Jamila. 2016. "Race, poverty, and the redistribution of voting rights." *Poverty and Public Policy,* vol. 8, no. 2: 106–128.

Mikati, Ihab; Benson, Adam F.; Luben, Thomas J.; Sacks, Jason D.; and Richmond-Bryant, Jennifer. 2018. "Disparities in distribution of particulate matter emission sources by race and poverty status." *American Journal of Public Health,* vol. 108, no. 4: 480–485. https://www.ncbi.nlm.nih.gov/pubmed/29470121.

Milgram, Stanley. 1963. "Behavioral Study of Obedience." *Journal of Abnormal Social Psychology,* vol. 67: 371–378.

———. 1974. *Obedience to Authority: An Experimental View.* New York: Harper & Row.

Miller, Amanda Jayne; and Sassler, Sharon. 2012. "The construction of gender among working-class cohabiting couples." *Qualitative Sociology,* vol. 35, no. 4: 427–446.

Miller, Claire Cain. 2012. "In Google's inner circle, a falling number of women." *The New York Times,* August 22.

———. 2014. "The divorce surge is over, but the myth lives on." *The New York Times,* December 2. http://www.nytimes.com/2014/12/02/upshot/the-divorce-surge-is-over-but-the-myth-lives-on.html?_r=0&abt=0002&abg=0.

Miller, Laura. 1997. "Women in the military." *Social Psychology Quarterly,* vol. 60, no. 10: 32–51.

Miller, Sarah A. 2016. "'How you bully a girl': sexual drama and negotiation of gendered sexuality in high school." *Gender and Society,* vol. 30, issue 5: 721–44. https://doi.org/10.1177/0891243216664723.

Mills, C. Wright. 1959. *The Sociological Imagination.* New York: Oxford University Press.

———. 1970 (orig. 1956). *The Power Elite.* New York: Oxford University Press.

Miner, Horace. 1956. "Body ritual among the Nacirema." *American Anthropologist,* vol. 58, no. 3: 503–507.

Miringoff, Marc; and Miringoff, Marque-Luisa. 1999. *The Social Health of the Nation: How America Is Really Doing.* New York: Oxford University Press.

Mishory, Jen. 2018. "The future of statewide college promise programs." The Century Foundation, March 6. https://tcf.org/content/report/future-statewide-college-promise-programs/?session=1.

Mitchell, Katharyne. 1993. "Multiculturalism, or the united colors of capitalism?" *Antipode,* vol. 25, no. 4: 263–294.

Mittermeier, Russell A.; Myers, Norman; and Mittermeier, Cristina Goettsch. 2000. *Hotspots: Earth's Biologically Richest and Most Endangered Terrestrial Ecoregions.* Arlington, VA: Conservation International.

Mohn, Tanya. 2014. "Take a vacation: It's good for productivity and the economy, according to a new study." *Forbes,* February 28. https://www.forbes.com/sites/tanyamohn/2014/02/28/take-a-vacation-its-good-for-productivity-and-the-economy-according-to-a-new-study/#5700a3955a33.

Mollenkopf, John. 1983. *The Contested City.* Princeton, NJ: Princeton University Press.

Molotch, Harvey. 1970. "Oil in Santa Barbara and power in America." *Sociological Inquiry,* vol. 40: 131–144.

Montagu, A. 1998. *Man's Most Dangerous Myth: The Fallacy of Race,* 6th ed. Thousand Oaks, CA: Altamira Press.

Morgan, Jacob. 2014. *The Future of Work: Attract New Talent, Build Better Leaders, and Create a Competitive Organization.* New York: Wiley.

Morin, C. W.; Comrie, A. C.; and Ernst, K. C. 2013. "Climate and dengue transmission: Evidence and implications." *Environmental Health Perspectives,* vol. 121: 1264–1272.

Morris, Bill. 2014. "What is it about soccer that brings out the hooligan in its fans?" *The Daily Beast,* June 25. http://www.thedailybeast.com/articles/2014/06/25/what-is-it-about-soccer-that-brings-out-the-hooligan-in-its-fans.html.

Morrison, Donna Ruane; and Cherlin, Andrew J. 1995. "The divorce process and young children's well-being: A prospective analysis." *Journal of Marriage and the Family,* vol. 57, no. 3: 800–812.

Mose, Tamara R. 2016. *The Playdate: Parents, Children, and the New Expectations of Play.* New York: New York University Press.

Muhl, Charles J. 2002. "What is an employee? The answer depends on the federal law; in a legal context, the classification of a worker as either an employee or an independent contractor can have significant consequences." *Monthly Labor Review,* vol. 125, no. 1: 3–11.

Mukherjee, Siddhartha. 2016. "The race for a Zika vaccine." *The New Yorker,* August 22. http://www.newyorker.com/magazine/2016/08/22/the-race-for-a-zika-vaccine.

Mullins, N. 1973. *Theories and Theory Groups in Contemporary American Sociology.* New York: Harper & Row.

Murphy, S. L.; Xu, J. Q.; Kochanek, K. D.; and Arias, E. 2018. "Mortality in the United States, 2017." NCHS Data Brief, no. 328. Hyattsville, MD: National Center for Health Statistics. https://www.cdc.gov/nchs/data/databriefs/db328-h.pdf.

Myers, Norman; and Kent, Jennifer. 2004. *The New Consumers: The Influence of Affluence on the Environment.* Washington, DC: Island Press.

———, eds. 2005. *The New Atlas of Planet Management.* Berkeley: University of California Press.

Nahin, R. L.; Barnes, P. M.; and Stussman, B. J. 2016. "Expenditures on complementary health approaches: United States, 2012." National Health Statistics Reports; no 95. Hyattsville, MD: National Center for Health Statistics.

NASA. 2014. "New NASA images highlight U.S. air quality improvement." http://www.nasa.gov/content/goddard/new-nasa-images-highlight-us-air-quality-improvement/.

National Association of Colleges and Employers. 2013a. "Class of 2013: Paid interns outpace unpaid peers in job offers, salaries." May 29. https://www.naceweb.org/s05292013/paid-unpaid-interns-job-offer.aspx.

———. 2013b. "Just 38 percent of unpaid internships were subject to FSLA guidelines." June 26. https://www.naceweb.org/s06262013/unpaid-internship-FLSA-guidelines.aspx.

———. 2016a. "The class of 2016 student survey report." http://www.naceweb.org/uploadedfiles/files/2016/publications

/executive-summary/2016-nace-student-survey-executive -summary.pdf.

———. 2016b. "Paid interns/co-ops see greater offer rates and salary offers than their unpaid classmates." http://www .naceweb.org/job-market/internships/paid-interns-co-ops -see-greater-offer-rates-and-salary-offers-than-their-unpaid -classmates/.

———. 2017. "The class of 2017 student survey report: Results from NACE's annual survey of college students." https://www .naceweb.org/uploadedfiles/files/2017/publication/executive -summary/2017-nace-student-survey-executive-summary.pdf.

———. 2019. "Job offers for class of 2019 grads impacted by internship experience." May 13. https://www.naceweb.org/job -market/trends-and-predictions/job-offers-for-class-of-2019 -grads-impacted-by-internship-experience/.

National Center for Charitable Statistics. 2016. "Quick facts about nonprofits." http://nccs.urban.org/data-statistics/quick -facts-about-nonprofits.

National Center for Education Statistics. 2016. "Student reports of bullying: Results from the 2015 School Crime Supplement to the National Crime Victimization Survey." U.S. Department of Education, December 2016. https://nces.ed.gov/pubs2017 /2017015.pdf.

———. 2018a. "Back to school by the numbers: 2018." NCES blog, August 20. https://nces.ed.gov/blogs/nces/post/back-to-school -by-the-numbers-2018.

———. 2018b. "Digest of education statistics, 2018, Table 306.20: Total fall enrollment in degree-granting postsecondary institutions, by control and classification of institution, level of enrollment, and race/ethnicity of student: 2017." https://nces.ed .gov/programs/digest/d18/tables/dt18_306.20.asp.

———. 2018c. "Table 318.10: Degrees conferred by postsecondary institutions, by level of degree and sex of student: Selected years, 1869–70 through 2027–28." *Digest of Education Statistics*, 2018. https://nces.ed.gov/programs/digest/d17/tables/dt17_318.10 .asp.

———. 2019a. "Annual earnings of young adults." *The Condition of Education*, February. https://nces.ed.gov/programs/coe /indicator_cba.asp.

———. 2019b. "The condition of education 2018." https:// nces.ed.gov/pubs2019/2019144.pdf.

National Center for Health Statistics. 2018. "Health, United States, 2017: With special feature on mortality." Hyattsville, MD. https://www.cdc.gov/nchs/data/hus/hus17.pdf.

National Center for the Study of Privatization in Education. 2015. "Charter schools." http://www.ncspe.org/publications_files /Charter%20Schools-FAQ.pdf.

National Employment Law Project (NELP). 2011. "Local living wage laws and coverage." http://www.nelp.org/index.php/site /issues/category/living_wage_laws/.

National Institutes of Health. 2014. "SEER cancer statistics review, 1975–2011." http://seer.cancer.gov/archive/csr/1975 _2011/.

National Law Center on Homelessness and Poverty. 2015. "Homelessness in America: Overview of data and causes." http://www.nlchp.org/documents/Homeless_Stats_Fact _Sheet.

National Low Income Housing Coalition. 2018. "The gap: A shortage of affordable rental homes." https://reports.nlihc.org /gap.

National Opinion Research Center. 2015. "General Social Surveys, 1972–2014: Cumulative Codebook." http://publicdata.norc.org /GSS/DOCUMENTS/BOOK/GSS_Codebook.pdf.

National Student Clearinghouse Research Center. 2017. "Term enrollment estimates, spring 2017." https://nscresearchcenter .org/wp-content/uploads/CurrentTermEnrollment-Spring2017 .pdf.

Nattras, Nicoli; and Seekings, Jeremy. 2001. "Two nations? Race and economic inequality in South Africa today." *Daedalus*, vol. 139 (winter): 45–70.

Neumark, David. 2004. "The economic effects of mandated wage floors." Public Policy Institute of California. http://www.ppic .org/content/pubs/op/OP_204DNOP.pdf.

New School. 2004. "Thomas Robert Malthus, 1766–1834." http:// cepa.newschool.edu/het/profiles/malthus.htm.

Newkirk II, Van R. 2017. "How voter ID laws discriminate." *The Atlantic*, February 18. https://www.theatlantic.com/politics /archive/2017/02/how-voter-id-laws-discriminate-study /517218/.

Newman, David M. 2000. *Sociology: Exploring the Architecture of Everyday Life*, 3rd ed. Thousand Oaks, CA: Pine Forge Press.

Newport, Frank. 2015. "Americans' perceived time crunch no worse than in past." *Gallup*, December 31. http://www.gallup .com/poll/187982/americans-perceived-time-crunch-no-worse -past.aspx.

Newton, Michael. 2004. *Savage Girls and Wild Boys: A History of Feral Children.* New York: Picador.

Nielsen. 2013. "State of the media: U.S. consumer usage report." January 7. http://www.nielsen.com/content/dam/corporate /us/en/reports-downloads/2013%20Reports/Nielsen-US -Consumer-Usage-Report-2012-FINAL.pdf.

———. 2017. "The state of traditional TV: Updated with Q1 2017 data." July 26. http://www.marketingcharts.com/featured -24817.

———. 2018. "Time flies: U.S. adults now spend nearly half a day interacting with media." July 31. https://www.nielsen.com /us/en/insights/news/2018/time-flies-us-adults-now-spend -nearly-half-a-day-interacting-with-media.html.

———. 2019. "The Nielsen total audience report: Q3 2018." https:// www.nielsen.com/content/dam/corporate/us/en/reports -downloads/2019-reports/q3-2018-total-audience-report.pdf.

Nixon, Richard. 1974. "Address on the State of the Union delivered before a joint session of the Congress," January 30. In J. T. Wooley and G. Peters, eds., *The American Presidency Project*. http://www.presidency.ucsb.edu/ws/index.php?pid=4327.

Noguchi, Yuki. 2017. "As cities raise minimum wages, many states are rolling them back." National Public Radio, July 18. http:// www.npr.org/2017/07/18/537901833/as-cities-raise-minimum -wages-many-states-are-rolling-them-back.

Nonprofit Vote. 2017. "America goes to the polls 2016: A report on voter turnout in the 2016 election." http://www.nonprofitvote .org/documents/2017/03/america-goes-polls-2016.pdf.

———. 2019. "America goes to the polls 2018: A report on voter turnout and election policy in the 50 states." https://www .nonprofitvote.org/documents/2019/03/america-goes-polls -2018.pdf/.

Nordberg, Jenny. 2014. *The Underground Girls of Kabul*. New York: Crown Publishing.

Nowland, Rebecca; Necka, Elizabeth A.; and Cacioppo, John T. 2017. "Loneliness and social internet use: Pathways to reconnection in a digital world." *Perspectives on Psychological Science*, vol. 13, no. 2: 1–18.

Nunez, C. 2019. "Rainforests, explained." *National Geographic*. https://www.nationalgeographic.com/environment/habitats /rain-forests/.

Nuwer, Hank. 1999. *Wrongs of Passage: Fraternities, Sororities, Hazing and Binge Drinking.* Bloomington: Indiana University Press.

_____. 2004. *The Hazing Reader.* Bloomington: Indiana University Press.

_____. 2018. *Hazing: Destroying Young Lives.* Bloomington: Indiana University Press.

_____. 2019. "Hazing deaths: 1737–2019." http://www.hanknuwer.com/hazing-deaths/.

NZ Herald. 2018. "World's most popular TV shows revealed." October 17. https://www.nzherald.co.nz/entertainment/news/article.cfm?c_id=1501119&objectid=12143757.

Oakley, Deirdre; and Burchfield, Keri. 2009. "Out of the projects, still in the hood: The spatial constraints on public housing residents' relocation in Chicago." *Journal of Urban Affairs*, vol. 31, no. 5: 589–614.

O'Brien, Jodi; and Kollock, Peter. 1997. *The Production of Reality: Essays and Readings on Social Interaction.* Thousand Oaks, CA: Pine Forge Press.

Ochs, Elinor. 1986. "Introduction." In Bambi B. Schieffelin and Elinor Ochs, eds., *Language and Socialization Across Cultures.* New York: Cambridge University Press.

Office of Management and Budget. 2015. "OMB Bulletin No. 15-01: Revised delineations of Metropolitan Statistical Areas, Micropolitan Statistical Areas, and Combined Statistical Areas, and guidance on uses of the delineations of these areas." https://www.whitehouse.gov/sites/whitehouse.gov/files/omb/bulletins/2015/15-01.pdf.

_____. 2018. "Revised delineations of metropolitan statistical areas, micropolitan statistical areas, and combined statistical areas, and guidance on uses of the delineations of these areas." September 14. https://www.whitehouse.gov/wp-content/uploads/2018/09/Bulletin-18-04.pdf.

Ogburn, William. 1964. *On Cultural and Social Change: Selected Papers.* Chicago: University of Chicago Press.

Oldenburg, Ray. 1999. *The Great Good Place: Cafes, Coffee Shops, Bookstores, Bars, Hair Salons, and Other Hangouts at the Heart of a Community.* Marlowe & Company.

_____. 2002. *Celebrating the Third Place: Inspiring Stories about the "Great Good Places" at the Heart of Our Communities.* De Capo Press.

Omi, Michael; and Winant, Howard. 1994. *Racial Formation in the United States: From the 1960s to the 1990s,* 2nd ed. New York: Routledge.

_____. 2015. *Racial Formation in the United States,* 3rd ed. New York: Routledge.

O'Neill, J. 2007. "HIV/AIDS in the developing world: What can we do?" In R. Gallo, ed., *Retroviruses: Biology, Pathogenic Mechanisms and Treatment, The Biomedical & Life Sciences Collection.* London: Henry Stewart Talks.

Online Learning Consortium. 2016. "Report: One in four students enrolled in online courses." February 25. https://onlinelearningconsortium.org/news_item/report-one-four-students-enrolled-online-courses/.

Oppenheimer, Mark. 2012. "Sociologist's paper raises questions on role of faith in scholarship." *The New York Times,* October 12. https://www.nytimes.com/2012/10/13/us/mark-regnerus-and-the-role-of-faith-in-academics.html.

Orthofer, A. 2016. "Wealth inequality in South Africa: Evidence from survey and tax data." Working Paper 15, Research Project on Employment, Income Distribution, and Inclusive Growth. http://www.redi3x3.org/sites/default/files/Orthofer%202016%20REDI3x3%20Working%20Paper%2015%20-%20Wealth%20inequality.pdf.

Oswald, R. F.; Blume, L; and Marks, S. 2005. "Decentering heteronormativity: A model for family studies." In V. L. Bengtson, A. C. Acock, K. R. Allen, P. Dilworth-Anderson, and D. M. Klein, eds., *Sourcebook of Family Theory and Research.* Thousand Oaks, CA: Sage.

Oswald, R. F.; Kuvalanka, K. A.; Blume, L. B.; and Berkowitz, D. 2009. "Queering 'the family.'" In Sally A. Lloyd and April L. Few, eds., *Handbook of Feminist Family Studies,* 43–55. Thousand Oaks, CA: Sage.

Paasonen, S.; et al. 2007. "Pornification and the education of desire." In S. Paasonen et al., eds., *Pornification: Sex and Sexuality in Media Culture.* Oxford, UK: Berg.

Pager, Devah. 2003. "The mark of a criminal record." *American Journal of Sociology,* vol. 108, no. 5 (March): 937–975.

_____. 2007. *Marked: Race, Crime, and Finding Work in an Era of Mass Incarceration.* Chicago: University of Chicago Press.

Papademetriou, Demetrios G.; Somerville, Will; and Sumption, Madeleine. 2009. "The social mobility of immigrants and their children." Migration Policy Institute, June. https://www.migrationpolicy.org/research/social-mobility-immigrants-and-their-children.

Paradies, Yin; Ben, Jehonathan; Denson, Nida; Elias, Amanuel; Priest, Naomi; Pieterse, Alex; Gupta, Arpana; Kelaher, Margaret; and Gee, Gilbert. 2015. "Racism as a determinant of health: A systematic review and meta-analysis." *PLoS One,* vol. 10, no. 9. https://www.ncbi.nlm.nih.gov/pmc/articles/PMC4580597/#pone.0138511.ref433.

Pariser, Eli. 2011. *The Filter Bubble: What the Internet Is Hiding from You.* New York: Penguin Press.

Park, Haeyoun; and Omri, Rudy. 2016. "U.S. reaches goal of admitting 10,000 Syrian refugees. Here's where they went." *The New York Times,* August 31. https://www.nytimes.com/interactive/2016/08/30/us/syrian-refugees-in-the-united-states.html.

Park, Robert Ezra. 1961. "Human ecology." Reprinted in G. A. Theodorson, ed., *Studies in Human Ecology.* New York: Row, Peterson & Company.

Parker, Kim; Cilluffo, Anthony; and Stepler, Renee. 2017. "6 facts about the U.S. military and its changing demographics." Pew Research Center. http://www.pewresearch.org/fact-tank/2017/04/13/6-facts-about-the-u-s-military-and-its-changing-demographics/.

Parker, Lonnae O'Neal. 1998. "Brand identities." *The Washington Post,* May 11.

Parlapiano, Alicia. 2013. "Movement on social issues." *The New York Times,* March 25.

Parsons, Christi. 2015. "Obama plan for free community college: U.S. would pay 75%, states 25%." *Los Angeles Times,* January. http://www.latimes.com/nation/la-na-obama-community-college-20150108-story.html.

Parsons, Talcott. 1951. *The Social System.* Glencoe, IL: Free Press.

_____. 1955. "The American family: Its relation to personality and social structure." In Talcott Parsons and R. Bales, eds., *Family Socialization and Interaction Process.* New York: Free Press.

_____; and Bales, R., eds. 1955. *Family, Socialization and Interaction Process.* New York: Free Press.

Pascoe, C. J. 2007. *Dude, You're a Fag: Masculinity and Sexuality in High School.* Berkeley: University of California Press, p. 5.

Patterson, Margot. 2004. "The rise of global fundamentalism." *National Catholic Reporter,* May 7.

Peavy, Linda; and Smith, Ursula. 1998. *Pioneer Women: The Lives of Women on the Frontier.* Norman: University of Oklahoma Press.

Perez, Caroline Criado. 2019. *Invisible Women: Data Bias in a World Designed for Men*. New York: Abrams Press.

Perlin, Ross. 2011. *Intern Nation: How to Earn Nothing and Learn Little in the Brave New Economy*. New York: Verso.

_____. 2012. "Today's internships are a racket, not an opportunity." *The New York Times*, February 2. http://www.nytimes.com/roomfordebate/2012/02/04/do-unpaid-internships-exploit-college-students/todays-internships-are-a-racket-not-an-opportunity.

Perls, T. T.; and Fretts, R. 1998. "Why women live longer than men." *Scientific American Presents: Women's Health: A Lifelong Guide*, vol. 9, no. 4: 100–104.

Perrin, S.; and Spencer, C. P. 1980. "The Asch effect: A child of its time." *Bulletin of the British Psychological Society*, vol. 32: 405–406.

_____. 1981. "Independence or conformity in the Asch experiment as a reflection of cultural and situational factors." *British Journal of Social Psychology*, vol. 20: 215–210.

Perry, Brea L.; Pescosolido, Bernice A.; Bucholz, Kathleen; Edenberg, Howard; Kramer, John; Kuperman, Samuel; Schuckit, Marc Alan; and Nurnberger, John. 2013. "Gender-specific gene-environment interaction in alcohol dependence: The impact of daily life events and GABRA2." *Behavioral Genetics*, vol. 43, no. 5: 402–414.

Perry, J.; and Pugh, M. 1978. *Collective Behavior: Response to Social Stress*. St. Paul, MN: West Publishing Company.

Perry, Stephanie; and Arenge, Andrew. 2018. "Millennial poll: 42 percent know someone who has dealt with opioid addiction." *NBC News*, June 15. https://www.nbcnews.com/politics/politics-news/millennial-poll-42-percent-know-someone-who-has-dealt-opioid-n883366?cid=sm_npd_nn_tw_ma.

Peters, H. Elizabeth; Argys, Laura M.; Maccoby, Eleanor E.; and Mnookin, Robert H. 1993. "Enforcing divorce settlements: Evidence from child support compliance and award modifications." *Demography*, vol. 30, no. 4: 719–735.

Petersen, E. E.; Davis, N. L.; Goodman, D.; et al. 2019. "Vital signs: Pregnancy-related deaths, United States, 2011–2015, and strategies for prevention, 13 states, 2013–2017." *Morbidity and Mortality Weekly Report*, vol. 68: 423–429.

Peterson, W. 2003. *From Persons to People: Further Studies in the Politics of Population*. New Brunswick, NJ: Transaction Publishers.

Petrosky, E.; Blair, J. M.; Betz, C. J.; Fowler, K. A.; Jack, S. P.; and Lyons, B. H. 2017. "Racial and ethnic differences in homicides of adult women and the role of intimate partner violence—United States, 2003–2014." *Morbidity and Mortality Weekly Report*, vol. 66: 741–746.

Pettigrew, Thomas F., and Tropp, Linda R. 2011. *When Groups Meet: The Dynamics of Intergroup Contact*. East Sussex, UK: Psychology Press.

Pettit, Becky; and Western, Bruce. 2004. "Mass imprisonment and the life course: Race and class inequality in U.S. incarceration." *American Sociological Review*, vol. 69: 151–169.

Pew Internet and American Life Project. 2012. "Privacy management on social media sites." http://www.pewinternet.org/2012/02/24/privacy-management-on-social-media-sites/.

Pew Research Center. 2008. "U.S. Religious Landscape Survey." http://religions.pewforum.org.

_____. 2012. "Religion and the unaffiliated." http://www.pewforum.org/2012/10/09/nones-on-the-rise-religion/#what-keeps-people-out-of-the-pews.

_____. 2014a. "Millennials in adulthood." http://www.pewsocialtrends.org/2014/03/07/millennials-in-adulthood/.

_____. 2014b. "The rising cost of not going to college." http://www.pewsocialtrends.org/2014/02/11/the-rising-cost-of-not-going-to-college/.

_____. 2014c. "U.S. Catholics view Pope Francis as a change for the better." March 6. http://www.pewforum.org/2014/03/06/catholics-view-pope-francis-as-a-change-for-the-better/.

_____. 2015a. "America's changing religious landscape." http://www.pewforum.org/2015/05/12/americas-changing-religious-landscape/.

_____. 2015b. "Beyond distrust: How Americans view their government." http://www.people-press.org/files/2015/11/11-23-2015-Governance-release.pdf.

_____. 2015c. "Latest trends in religious restrictions and hostilities." http://www.pewforum.org/2015/02/26/religious-hostilities/.

_____. 2015d. "Modern immigration wave brings 59 million to U.S., driving population growth and change through 2065." http://www.pewhispanic.org/2015/09/28/chapter-2-immigrations-impact-on-past-and-future-u-s-population-change/.

_____. 2015e. "Most say government policies since recession have done little to help middle class, poor." http://www.people-press.org/2015/03/04/most-say-government-policies-since-recession-have-done-little-to-help-middle-class-poor/.

_____. 2015f. "Parenting in America." http://www.pewsocialtrends.org/2015/12/17/1-the-american-family-today/.

_____. 2015g. "The American middle class is losing ground." http://www.pewsocialtrends.org/files/2015/12/2015-12-09_middle-class_FINAL-report.pdf.

_____. 2015h. "U.S. public becoming less religious." http://www.pewforum.org/2015/11/03/u-s-public-becoming-less-religious/.

_____. 2016a. "Campaign exposes fissures over issues, values, and how life has changed in the U.S." http://www.people-press.org/files/2016/03/3-31-16-March-Political-release-1.pdf.

_____. 2016b. "Election 2016: Campaigns as a direct source of news." http://www.journalism.org/2016/07/18/election-2016-campaigns-as-a-direct-source-of-news/.

_____. 2016c. "Low approval of Trump's transition but outlook for his presidency improves." http://assets.pewresearch.org/wp-content/uploads/sites/5/2016/12/08135748/12-08-16-December-political-release.pdf.

_____. 2017a. "Internet/broadband factsheet." January 12. http://www.pewinternet.org/fact-sheet/internet-broadband/.

_____. 2017b. "Support for same-sex marriage grows, even among groups that had been skeptical." http://www.people-press.org/2017/06/26/support-for-same-sex-marriage-grows-even-among-groups-that-had-been-skeptical/.

_____. 2018a. "Internet/broadband fact sheet." http://www.pewinternet.org/fact-sheet/internet-broadband/.

_____. 2018b. "Social media fact sheet." https://www.pewinternet.org/fact-sheet/social-media/.

_____. 2019. "A Closer Look at How Religious Restrictions Have Risen Around the World." https://www.pewforum.org/2019/07/15/a-closer-look-at-how-religious-restrictions-have-risen-around-the-world/.

Pew Research Social and Demographic Trends. 2010. "Interactive: The changing American family." http://www.pewsocialtrends.org/2010/11/18/five-decades-of-marriage-trends/.

Pfeffer, C. A. 2012. "Normative resistance and inventive pragmatism: Negotiating structure and agency in transgender families." *Gender & Society*, vol. 26, no. 4: 574–602.

_____. 2014. "'I don't like passing as a straight woman': Queer negotiations of identity and social group membership." *American Journal of Sociology*, vol. 120, no. 1: 1–44.

_____. 2017. *Queering Families: The Postmodern Partnerships of*

Cisgender Women and Transgender Men. New York: Oxford University Press.

Phillips, S. 2009. "Criminology: Legal disparities in the capital of capital punishment." *Journal of Criminal Law & Criminology,* vol. 99, no. 3: 717.

Picca, L. and Feagin, J. 2007. *Two-Faced Racism: Whites in the Backstage and Frontstage.* New York: Routledge.

Pierce, Fred. 2012. "Saudi Arabia takes a claim on the Nile." *National Geographic,* December. http://news .nationalgeographic.com/news/2012/12/121217-saudi-arabia -water-grabs ethiopia/.

Pilnick, Alison; Hindmarsh, Jon; and Teas Gill, Virginia. 2009. "Beyond 'doctor and patient': Developments in the study of healthcare interactions." *Sociology of Health & Illness,* vol. 31, no. 6: 787–802.

Pinto, Barbara. 2005. "Small town USA may offer solution to outsourcing: Company redeploys workers to rural towns instead of sending jobs overseas." *ABC World News Tonight,* August 25.

Plante, Thomas G.; and Boccaccini, Marcus. 1997. "The Santa Clara Strength of Religious Faith Questionnaire." *Pastoral Psychology,* vol. 45: 375–387.

Pleck, Elizabeth H. 2000. *Celebrating the Family: Ethnicity, Consumer Culture, and Family Ritual.* Cambridge, MA: Harvard University Press.

Plumer, Brad. 2013. "Poverty is growing twice as fast in the suburbs as in cities." *The Washington Post,* May 23. http://www .washingtonpost.com/blogs/wonkblog/wp/2013/05/23/poverty -is-now-growing-twice-as-fast-in-the-suburbs-as-in-the-city/.

Pollack, Andres. 1999. "Aerospace gets Japan's message: Without military largess, industry takes the lean path." *The New York Times,* March 9, p. C1.

Pollner, Melvin; and Stein, Jill. 1996. "Narrative mapping of social worlds: The voice of experience in Alcoholics Anonymous." *Journal of Symbolic Interaction,* vol. 19, no. 3: 203–223.

———. 2001. "Doubled-over in laughter: Humor and the construction of selves in Alcoholics Anonymous." In Jaber Gubrium and James Holstein, eds., *Institutional Selves: Personal Troubles in Organizational Context.* New York: Oxford University Press.

Pool, Robert. 1997. *Beyond Engineering: How Society Shapes Technology.* Oxford, UK: Oxford University Press.

Population Reference Bureau. 2010. "World population data sheet." http://www.prb.org/pdf10/10wpds_eng.pdf.

Port, Dina Roth. 2014. "Doulas: Not just for hippie moms." *Parents Magazine.* http://www.parents.com/pregnancy/giving-birth /doula/doulas-not-just-for-hippie-moms/.

Potok, M. 2017. "The year in hate and extremism intelligence report." Southern Poverty Law Center, Spring, no. 162.

———; Bolzendahl, Catherine; Geist, Claudia; and Carr Stellman, Lala. 2010. *Counted Out: Same-Sex Relations and Americans' Definition of Family.* New York: Russell Sage Foundation.

Powell, Brian; Bolzendahl, Catherine; Geist, Claudia; and Stellman, Lala Carr. 2010. *Counted Out: Same-Sex Relations and Americans' Definition of Family.* New York: Russell Sage Foundation.

Powell, L. M.; Slater, S.; Mirtcheva, D.; Bao, Y.; and Chaloupka, F. J. 2007. "Food store availability and neighborhood characteristics in the United States." *Preventive Medicine,* vol. 44, no. 3: 189–195.

Prince, Marcell; and Carols, Tovar. 2015. "How much U.S. oil and gas comes from fracking?" *Wall Street Journal.* April 1. http:// blogs.wsj.com/corporate-intelligence/2015/04/01/how-much -u-s-oil-and-gas-comes-from-fracking/.

Proctor, B. D.; Semega, J. L.; and Kollar, M. A. 2016. "Income and poverty in the United States: 2015." U.S. Census Bureau, September 16. https://www.census.gov/content/dam/Census /library/publications/2016/demo/p60-256.pdf.

Public Religion Research Institute. 2017. "America's changing religious identity: Findings from the 2016 American Values Atlas." https://www.prri.org/wp-content/uploads/2017/09 /PRRI-Religion-Report.pdf.

Pullum, Geoffrey K. 1991. *The Great Eskimo Vocabulary Hoax and Other Irreverent Essays on the Study of Language.* Chicago: University of Chicago Press.

Purnell, Jason; Camberos, Gabriela; and Fields, Robert. 2014. "For the sake of all." St. Louis, MO: Washington University in St. Louis, Saint Louis University. https://forthesakeofall.files .wordpress.com/2014/05/for-the-sake-of-all-report.pdf.

Putnam, Robert D. 1995. "Tuning in, tuning out: The strange disappearance of social capital in America." *Political Science & Politics,* vol. 28, no. 4: 664.

———. 2000. *Bowling Alone: The Collapse and Revival of American Community.* New York: Simon & Schuster.

Pyke, Karen D. 2010. "What is internalized racial oppression and why don't we study it? Acknowledging racism's hidden injuries." *Sociological Perspectives,* vol. 53, no. 4: 551–572.

Raanan, Raz; et al. 2015. "Autism Spectrum Disorder and particulate matter air pollution before, during, and after pregnancy: A nested case–control analysis within the Nurses' Health Study II Cohort." *Environmental Health Perspectives,* March. https://ehp.niehs.nih.gov/1408133/.

Rabin, Roni Caryn. 2008. "Severe heart attacks deadlier for women." *The New York Times,* December 8.

Rabow, Jerome; Stein, Jill; and Conley, Terri. 1999. "Teaching social justice and encountering society: The pink triangle experiment." *Youth and Society,* vol. 30, no. 4: 483–514.

Radway, A. Janice. 1991. *Reading the Romance: Women, Patriarchy, and Popular Literature.* Chapel Hill: University of North Carolina Press.

Rainee, L.; and Wellman, B. 2012. *Networked.* Cambridge, MA: MIT Press.

Rajaram, Shireen S. 2007. "An action research project: Community lead poisoning prevention." *Teaching Sociology,* vol. 35, no. 2: 138–150.

Randall, D. K. 2019. *Black Death at the Golden Gate.* New York: W. W. Norton.

Rasmussen, Terje. 2014. "Internet and the political public sphere." *Sociology Compass,* vol. 8, no. 12: 1315–1329. http://onlinelibrary .wiley.com/doi/10.1111/soc4.12228/full.

Ray, Brian. 1997. "Strengths of their own—home schoolers across America: Academic achievement, family characteristics, and longitudinal traits." Salem, OR: National Home Education Research Institute.

———. 2008. "Research facts on homeschooling." National Home Education Research Institute. http://www.nheri.org/Research -Facts-on-Homeschooling.html.

———. 2013. "Homeschooling associated with beneficial learner and societal outcomes but educators do not promote it." *Peabody Journal of Education: Issues of Leadership, Policy, and Organizations,* vol. 88, no. 3.

Ray, Rebecca; Sanes, Milla; and Schmitt, John. 2013. "No vacation nation revisited." Washington, DC, Center for Economic and Policy Research. http://cepr.net/documents/no-vacation -update-2014-04.pdf.

Reardon, Sean F. 2012. "The widening academic achievement gap between the rich and the poor." *Community Investments,* vol 24, (2): 19–39.

Reece, M.; Herbenick, D.; Schick, V.; Sanders, S.; Dodge, B.; and Fortenberry, J. 2010. "Condom use rates in a national probability sample of males and females, ages 14 to 94 in the United States." *Journal of Sexual Medicine*, vol. 7 (suppl. 5): 266–267.

Reeves, Aaron. 2015. "Neither class nor status: Arts participation and the social strata." *Sociology*, vol. 49, no. 4: 624–642.

Regnerus, Mark. 2012. "How different are the adult children of parents who have same-sex relationships? Findings from the New Family Structures Study." *Social Science Research*, vol. 41, no. 4: 752–770.

Reyes, Emily Alpert. 2013. "More married women in U.S. aren't having children." *Los Angeles Times*, December 8. http://articles.latimes.com/2013/dec/08/nation/la-na-childless-couples-20131208.

Reynolds, G. M.; and Shendruk, A. 2018. "Demographics of the U.S. military." Council on Foreign Relations. https://www.cfr.org/article/demographics-us-military.

Riesman, D. 1957. "The suburban dislocation." *Annals of the American Academy of Political and Social Science*, vol. 314: 123.

Rios, Victor. 2009. "The consequence of the criminal justice pipeline on Black and Latino Masculinity." *The Annals of the American Academy of Political and Social Science*. May: 150–162.

_____. 2017. *Human Targets: Schools, Police, and the Criminalization of Latino Youth*. Chicago: University of Chicago Press.

Ritzer, George. 1993. *The McDonaldization of Society: An Investigation into the Changing Character of Contemporary Social Life*. Thousand Oaks, CA: Pine Forge Press.

_____. 1996. *The McDonaldization of Society*. Thousand Oaks, CA: Pine Forge Press.

_____. 2013. *The McDonaldization of Society: 20th Anniversary Edition*. Thousand Oaks, CA: Sage.

_____; and Ryan, J. Michael. 2007. "Postmodern social theory and sociology: On symbolic exchange with a 'dead' theory." In Jason Powell and Tim Owen, eds., *Reconstructing Postmodernism: Critical Debates*. Hauppauge, NY: Nova Science Publishers.

Roberts, S.; Snee, H.; Hine, C.; Morey, Y.; and Watson, H., eds., 2016. *Digital Methods for Social Science: An Interdisciplinary Guide to Research Innovation*. Basingstoke, UK: Palgrave Macmillan.

Robertson, Joe. 2016. "Syrian families flee civil war, warily make new lives in Kansas City." *Kansas City Star*, September 24. http://www.kansascity.com/news/local/article103609747.html.

Robins, Douglas; Sanders, Clinton; and Cahill, Spencer. 1991. "Dogs and their people: Pet-facilitated interaction in a public setting." *Journal of Contemporary Ethnography*, vol. 20, no. 1: 3–25.

Robison, Jennifer. 2014. "Nevada again posts one of higher foreclosure rates in U.S." *Las Vegas Journal-Review*, February 12.

Robson, D. 2001. "Women and minorities in economics textbooks: Are they being adequately represented?" *Journal of Economic Education*, vol. 32, no. 2: 186–191.

Rojek, Chris. 1985. *Capitalism and Leisure Theory*. London: Tavistock.

_____. 1995. *Decentering Leisure: Rethinking Leisure Theory*. London: Sage.

_____. 2000. "Leisure and the rich today: Veblen's thesis after a century." *Leisure Studies*, vol. 19, no. 1: 1–15.

Roscoe, W. 2000. "How to become a berdache: Toward a unified analysis of gender." In G. Herdt, ed., *Third Sex, Third Gender: Beyond Sexual Dimorphism in Culture and History*. New York: Zone Books.

Rosen, Julia. 2019. "Is it our constitutional right to live in a world safe from climate change?" *Los Angeles Times*, June 3. https://www.latimes.com/science/la-sci-youth-climate-trial-juliana-20190603-story.html.

Rosenbaum, Emily. 2008. "Racial/ethnic differences in asthma prevalence: The role of housing and neighborhood environments." *Journal of Health and Social Behavior*, vol. 49, no. 2: 131–145.

Rosenberg, E. 2019. "The world's oldest person record stood for decades. Then came a Russian conspiracy theory." *The Washington Post*, January 12. https://www.washingtonpost.com/world/2019/01/12/how-madame-calment-worlds-oldest-person-became-fuel-russian-conspiracy-theory/.

Rosenfeld, Dana. 2003. *The Changing of the Guard: Lesbian and Gay Elders, Identity, and Social Change*. Philadelphia: Temple University Press.

Rosenhan, David. 1973. "On being sane in insane places." *Science*, vol. 179 (January): 250–258.

Rosenthal, A. M. 1964/2008. *Thirty-Eight Witnesses: The Kitty Genovese Case*. New York: Melville House.

Rosenthal, R.; and Jacobson, L. 1968. *Pygmalion in the Classroom: Teacher Expectation and Pupils' Intellectual Development*. New York: Rinehart and Winston.

Rosin, Hannah. 2012. *The End of Men: And the Rise of Women*. New York: Riverhead Books.

Ross, Andrew. 1997. "Introduction." In Andrew Ross, ed., *No Sweat: Fashion, Free Trade and the Rights of Garment Workers*. New York: Verso.

Rothblum, Esther. 1996. *Preventing Heterosexism and Homophobia*. Thousand Oaks, CA: Sage.

Rothkop, David. 1997. "In praise of cultural imperialism? Effects of globalization on culture." *Foreign Policy*, June 22.

Rothman, Lily. 2012. "A cultural history of mansplaining." *The Atlantic*, November 1. http://www.theatlantic.com/sexes/archive/2012/11/a-cultural-history-of-mansplaining/264380/.

Rothstein, Richard. 2017. *The Color of Law: A Forgotten History of How Our Government Segregated America*. New York: Liveright.

Roy, D. F. 1959. "Banana time: Job satisfaction and informal interaction." *Human Organization*, 18: 158–168.

Rubel, Paula; and Rosman, Abraham. 2001. "The collecting passion in America." *Zeitschrift fur Ethnologie* (English), vol. 126, no. 2: 313–330.

Rubin, Zick; and Peplau, Letitia Anne. 1975. "Who believes in a just world?" *Journal of Social Issues*, vol. 31, no. 3: 65–89.

Rupp, Leila; and Taylor, Verta. 2003. *Drag Queens at the 801 Cabaret*. Chicago: University of Chicago Press.

Russakoff, Rich; and Goodman, Mary. 2011. "Employee theft: Are you blind to it?" *CBS Money Watch*. July 14. http://www.cbsnews.com/8301-505143_162-48640192/employee-theft-are-you-blind-to-it/.

Russonello, Giovanni. 2016. "Race relations are at lowest point in Obama presidency, poll finds." *The New York Times*. July 13. https://www.nytimes.com/2016/07/14/us/most-americans-hold-grim-view-of-race-relations-poll-finds.html?_r=0.

Ryan, C.; Russell, S. T.; Huebner, D.; Diaz, R.; and Sanchez, J. 2010. "Family acceptance in adolescence and the health of LGBT young adults." *Journal of Child and Adolescent Psychiatric Nursing*, vol. 23, no. 4: 205–213.

Ryan, Caitlin; Huebner, David; Diaz, Rafael; and Sanchez, Jorge. 2009. "Family rejection as a predictor of negative health outcomes in white and Latino lesbian, gay, and bisexual young adults." *Pediatrics*, vol. 123, no. 1: 346–352.

Rymer, Russ, 1994. *Genie: A Scientific Tragedy.* New York: HarperCollins.

Sabin, Janice A.; and Greenwald, Anthony G. 2012. "The influence of implicit bias on treatment recommendations for 4 common pediatric conditions: Pain, urinary tract infection, attention deficit hyperactivity disorder, and asthma." *American Journal of Public Health,* vol. 102, no. 5: 988–995.

Sadker, Myra; and Sadker, David. 1995. *Failing at Fairness: How Our Schools Cheat Girls.* New York: Scribner.

Saez, E. 2019. "Striking it richer: The evolution of top incomes in the United States (updated with 2017 final estimates)." March 2. https://eml.berkeley.edu/~saez/saez-UStopincomes-2017.pdf.

———; and Zucman, G. 2016. "Wealth inequality in the United States since 1913: Evidence from capitalized income tax data." *Quarterly Journal of Economics,* vol. 131, no. 2: 519–578.

Sallie Mae. 2016. "Majoring in money: how college students manage their finances." http://news.salliemae.com/sites /salliemae.newshq.businesswire.com/files/doc_library/file /SallieMae_MajoringinMoney_2016.pdf.

Sampson, Robert J.; and Wilson, William Julius. 2005. "Toward a theory of race, crime and urban inequality." In Shaun L. Gabbidon and Helen Taylor Greene, eds., *Race, Crime and Justice: A Reader.* New York: Routledge.

Sampson, Robert J.; and Winter, Alix S. 2016. "The racial ecology of lead poisoning: Toxic inequality in Chicago neighborhoods, 1995–2013." *Du Bois Review,* 1–23. https://scholar.harvard.edu /files/alixwinter/files/sampson_winter_2016.pdf.

Santiago, Cassandra; and Criss, Doug. 2017. "An activist, a little girl and the heartbreaking origin of 'Me too.'" *CNN,* October 17. https://www.cnn.com/2017/10/17/us/me-too-tarana-burke -origin-trnd/index.html.

Sapir, Edward. 1949. *Selected Writings in Language, Culture, and Personality.* David G. Mandelbaum, ed. Berkeley: University of California Press.

Sassen, Saskia. 1991. *The Global City: New York, London, Tokyo.* Princeton, NJ: Princeton University Press.

Sawchuk, Stephen. 2017. "Even when states revise standards, the core of the Common Core remains." *Education Week,* November 13. https://www.edweek.org/ew/articles/2017/11/13/even-when -states-revise-standards-the-core.html.

Sayer, Andrew. 2016. *Why We Can't Afford the Rich.* Bristol, UK: Policy Press.

Sayer, Liana C. 2016. "Trends in women's and men's time use, 1965–2012: Back to the future?" In S. M. McHale, V. King, J. Van Hook, and A. Booth, eds., *Gender and Couple Relationships,* 43–77. New York: Springer.

Schegloff, Emanuel. 1986. "The routine as achievement." *Human Studies,* vol. 9, nos. 2–3: 111–151.

———. 1999. "What next? Language and social interaction study at the century's turn." *Research on Language and Social Interaction,* vol. 32, nos. 1–2: 141–148.

———. 2007. *Sequence Organization in Interaction: A Primer in Conversation Analysis,* vol. 1. Cambridge: Cambridge University Press.

Schein, Edgar H. 1997. *Organizational Culture and Leadership.* San Francisco: Jossey-Bass.

———. 2010. *Organizational Culture and Leadership,* 4th ed. Hoboken, NJ: Jossey-Bass.

Schell, Orville. 2002. "Gross national happiness." *Red Herring,* January 15. http://www.pbs.org/frontlineworld/stories/bhutan /gnh.html.

Scheyvens, Regina. 2000. "Promoting women's empowerment through involvement in ecotourism: Experiences from the Third World." *Journal of Sustainable Tourism,* vol. 8, no. 3: 232–249.

Schiller, Herbert I. 1976. *Communication and Cultural Domination.* White Plains, NY: International Arts and Sciences Press.

———. 1992. *Mass Communications and American Empire,* 2nd ed. Boulder, CO: Westview Press.

———. 1995. "The global information highway: Project for an ungovernable world." In J. Brook and I. A. Boal, eds., *Resisting the Virtual Life: The Culture and Politics of Information.* San Francisco: City Lights Books.

———. 1996. *Information Inequality.* New York: Routledge.

———; Schlenker, Jennifer A.; Caron, Sandra L.; and Halteman, William A. 1998. "A feminist analysis of *Seventeen* magazine: Content analysis from 1945 to 1995." *Sex Roles: A Journal of Research,* vol. 38, no. 1–2: 135.

Schlosser, Eric. 2002. *Fast Food Nation: The Dark Side of the All-American Meal.* New York: Perennial.

Schnaiberg, Allan. 1980. *The Environment: From Surplus to Scarcity.* New York: Oxford University Press.

———; Gould, Kenneth Allan. 1994. *Environment and Society: The Enduring Conflict.* New York: St. Martin's Press.

Schofield, Jack. 2004. "Social network software; software to help you network." *Computer Weekly,* March 16, p. 32.

Schor, Juliet B. 1999. *The Overspent American: Why We Want What We Don't Need.* New York: HarperCollins.

———; Fitzmaurice, Connor; Carfagna; Lindsey B.; and Attwood-Charles, Will. 2016. "Corrigendum to 'Paradoxes of openness and distinction in the sharing economy.'" [*Poetics,* vol. 54 (February): 66–81] *Poetics,* vol. 56 (June): 98.

Schutz, Alfred P. 1962. "The stranger: An essay in social psychology." In A. Brodersen, ed., *Collected Papers II: Studies in Social Theory.* Dordrecht, The Netherlands: Martinus Nijhoff.

Schwartz, M. S. 2019. "Disney officially owns 21st Century Fox." National Public Radio, March 20. https://www.npr.org/2019/03 /20/705009029/disney-officially-owns-21st-century-fox.

Schwellenbach, Nick. 2008. "A good time to be a white-collar criminal?" The Center for Public Integrity. https:// publicintegrity.org/accountability/a-good-time-to-be-a-white -collar-criminal/.

Schwimmer, B. 2001. "Figure 43. Hawaiian kin terms (actual usage)." http://www.umanitoba.ca/faculties/arts/anthropology /tutor/image_list/43.html.

Scott, Laura S. 2009. *Two Is Enough: A Couple's Guide to Living Childless by Choice.* Berkeley: Seal Press.

Scutt, J. A. 1983. *Even in the Best of Homes.* Ringwood, Victoria: Penguin Books.

Searing, Linda. 2010. "Study: Dying at home may be less traumatic for patients as well as caregivers." *The Washington Post,* September 27. http://www.washingtonpost.com/wp-dyn /content/article/2010/09/27/AR2010092705374.html.

Sedgwick, Eve Kosofsky. 1990. *Epistemology of the Closet.* Berkeley: University of California Press.

———. 1993. *Tendencies.* Durham, NC: Duke University Press.

———. 2014. "Writing the history of homophobia." In Jason Potts and Daniel Stout, eds., *Theory Aside.* Durham, NC: Duke University Press. https://www.dukeupress.edu/theory-aside.

Seekings, Jeremy; and Nattras, Nicoli. 2005. *Class, Race and Inequality in South Africa.* New Haven, CT: Yale University Press.

Segal, Lynne. 1990. *Slow Motion: Changing Masculinities, Changing Men.* New Brunswick, NJ: Rutgers University Press.

Seidman, Steven. 2003. *The Social Construction of Sexuality.* New York: W. W. Norton.

Seltzer, Judith A.; Schaeffer, Nora Cate; and Charng, Hong-Wen. 1989. "Family ties after divorce: The relationship between visiting and paying child support." *Journal of Marriage and the Family*, vol. 51, no. 4: 1013–1031.

Selyukh, Alina; Hollenhorst, Maria; and Park, Katie. 2017. "Big media companies and their many brands—in one chart." National Public Radio, December 22. https://www.npr.org/sections/alltechconsidered/2016/10/28/499495517/big-media-companies-and-their-many-brands-in-one-chart.

Semega, J. L. Fontenot, K. R., and Kollar, M. A. 2017. "Income and poverty in the United States: 2016." U.S. Census Bureau. https://www.census.gov/content/dam/Census/library/publications/2017/demo/P60-259.pdf.

Sennett, Richard. 1977. *The Fall of Public Man*. New York: W. W. Norton.

Severin, W. J.; and Tankard, J. W. 1997. *Communication Theories: Origins, Methods, and Uses in the Mass Media*, 4th ed. New York: Longman.

Sexton, Lori; Jenness, Valerie; and Sumner, Jennifer. 2009. "Where the margins meet: A demographic assessment of transgender inmates in men's prisons." Ucicorrections/seweb/uci.edu.

Shah, Anup. 2007. "Media conglomerates, mergers, concentration of ownership." *Global Issues*, April 29. http://www.globalissues.org/article/159/media-conglomerates-mergers-concentration-of-ownership.

Sharkey, Patrick. 2018. *Uneasy Peace: The Great Crime Decline, the Renewal of City Life, and the Next War on Violence*. New York: W. W. Norton.

Sharp, Shane. 2010. "How does prayer help manage emotions?" *Social Psychology Quarterly*, vol. 73: 417–437.

Sheff, Elisabeth. 2014. *The Polyamorists Next Door: Inside Multiple-Partner Relationships and Families*. Lanham, MD: Rowman and Littlefield.

Sherkat, Darren E. 2012. "The editorial process and politicized scholarship: Monday morning editorial quarterbacking and a call for scientific vigilance." *Social Science Research*, vol. 41, no. 6: 1346–1349.

Sherman, Alec. 2012. "SNAP (food stamps) and earned income tax credit had big antipoverty impact in 2011." Center on Budget and Policy Priorities. September 12. http://www.offthechartsblog.org/snap-food-stamps-and-earned-income-tax-credit-had-big-antipoverty-impact-in-2011.

Shiach, Morag. 1999. *Feminism and Cultural Studies*. New York: Oxford University Press.

Shin, R.; Daly, B.; and Vera, E. 2007. "The relationships of peer norms, ethnic identity, and peer support to school engagement in urban youth." *Professional School Counseling*, vol. 10: 379–388.

Shover, Neal; and Wright, John Paul. 2001. *Crimes of Privilege: Readings in White-Collar Crime*. New York: Oxford University Press.

Sianko, Natallia; and Small, Mark. 2017. "The future of GIS in the social sciences." *Kontakt*, vol. 19, no. 3: 169–170.

Simmel, Georg. 1950. *The Sociology of George Simmel*. Kurt Wolff, ed. New York: Free Press.

Simon, Julian. 1996. *The Ultimate Resource 2*. Princeton, NJ: Princeton University Press.

———. 2000. *The Great Breakthrough and Its Cause*. Ann Arbor: University of Michigan Press.

Singh, S.; and Durso, L. E. 2017. "Widespread discrimination continues to shape LGBT people's lives in both subtle and significant ways." Center for American Progress, May 2. https://www.americanprogress.org/issues/lgbt/news/2017/05/02/429529/widespread-discrimination-continues-shape-lgbt-peoples-lives-subtle-significant-ways/.

Skarzynska, Krystyna. 2004. "Politicians in television: The big five in impression formation." *Journal of Political Marketing*, vol. 3, no. 2: 31–45.

———. 2009. *Free Range Kids*. San Francisco: Jossey-Bass.

Slack, Kristin; et al. 2006. "Family economic well-being following the 1996 welfare reform: Trend data from five non-experimental panel studies." *Children and Youth Services Review*, vol. 29, no. 6: 698–720.

Smith, Aaron. 2015. "Searching for work in the digital era." Pew Research Center, November 19. http://www.pewinternet.org/2015/11/19/searching-for-work-in-the-digital-era/.

———. 2016a. "Gig work, online selling and home sharing." Pew Research Center. http://www.pewinternet.org/2016/11/17/gig-work-online-selling-and-home-sharing/.

———. 2016b. "Shared, collaborative and on demand: The new digital economy." Pew Research Center. http://www.pewinternet.org/2016/05/19/the-new-digital-economy/.

Smith, Dorothy. 1999. "Schooling for inequality." *Signs: Journal for Women in Culture and Society*, vol. 5, no. 4: 1147–1151.

Smith, Herbert L. 1990. "Specification problems in experimental and nonexperimental social research." *Sociological Methodology*, vol. 20: 59–91.

Smith, Kara. 2005. "Gender talk: A case study in prenatal socialization." *Women and Languages*, March 22.

Smith, Marc; and Kollock, Peter. 1998. *Communities in Cyberspace*. London: Routledge.

Smith, S. G.; Chen, J.; Basile, K. C.; Gilbert, L. K.; Merrick, M. T.; Patel, N.; Walling, M.; and Jain, A. 2017. The National Intimate Partner and Sexual Violence Survey (NISVS): 2010–2012 State Report. Atlanta, GA: National Center for Injury Prevention and Control, Centers for Disease Control and Prevention.

Solnit, Rebecca. 2008. "Men explain things to me: Facts didn't get in their way." *TomDispatch*. April 13. http://www.tomdispatch.com/post/174918.

Sonner, Scott. 2002. "Burning Man gives fodder for questing sociologists." *Associated Press*, August 28. http://www.religionnewsblog.com/641-Scientists_find_Burning_Man_a_research_bonanza.html.

Southern Education Foundation. 2015. "A new majority: Low income students now a majority in the nation's public schools." https://sefweb.wpengine.com/wp-content/uploads/2019/02/New-Majority-Update-Bulletin.pdf.

Southern Poverty Law Center. 2019. "Hate groups reach record high." https://www.splcenter.org/news/2019/02/19/hate-groups-reach-record-high.

Sparks, Sarah D. 2013. "Poor children are now a majority in 17 states' public schools." *Education Week*, October. http://www.edweek.org/ew/articles/2013/10/23/09poverty.h33.html.

———; and Adams, Caralee J. 2013. "High school poverty levels tied to college-going." *Education Week*. October. http://www.edweek.org/ew/articles/2013/10/23/09college.h33.html.

Spencer, Keith. 2017. "The gig economy goes to class." *Salon*. June 3. http://www.salon.com/2017/06/03/the-gig-economy-goes-to-class/.

Spencer, S. J.; Steele, C. M.; and Quinn, D. M. 1999. "Stereotype threat and women's math performance." *Journal of Experimental Social Psychology*, vol. 35: 4–28.

Springer, Kristen W.; and Mouzon, Dawne. 2011. "Masculinity and health care seeking among older men: Implications for men in different social classes." *Journal of Health and Social Behavior,* vol. 52, no. 2: 212–227.

Spurrell, M. 2019. "Airbnb and 23AndMe Will Help Plan a Trip to Your Homeland." *Conde Nast Traveler,* May 21. https://www.cntraveler.com/story/airbnb-and-23andme-will-help-plan-a-trip-to-your-homeland.

Srinivas, Lakshmi. 1998. "Active viewing: An ethnography of the Indian film audience." *Visual Anthropology,* vol. 11, no. 4: 323–353.

Stacey, J. 1998. *Brave New Families: Stories of Domestic Upheaval in Late-Twentieth-Century America.* Berkeley: University of California Press.

Stack, Carol. 1974. *All Our Kin.* New York: Harper & Row.

Stannard, David E. 1993. *American Holocaust: The Conquest of the New World.* New York: Oxford University Press.

Stanton, M. E. 1995. "Patterns of kinship and residence." In B. Ingoldsby and S. Smith, eds., *Families in Multicultural Perspective.* New York: Guilford Press.

Stapleton, Christine. 2002. "Donated blood sold off overseas after 9/11." *Atlanta Journal-Constitution,* September 8, p. 19A.

Stark, L. 2016. "Recognizing the role of emotional labor in the on-demand economy," *Harvard Business Review,* August 26. https://hbr.org/2016/08/recognizing-the-role-of-emotional-labor-in-the-on-demand-economy.

Stearns, Peter N. 2004. *Anxious Parents: A History of Modern Childrearing in America.* New York: New York University Press.

Steele, Claude M. 1997. "A threat in the air: How stereotypes shape intellectual identity and performance." *American Psychologist,* vol. 52, no. 6: 613–629.

———. 2010. *Whistling Vivaldi and Other Clues to How Stereotypes Affect Us.* New York: W. W. Norton.

Stein, Jill. 1997. "Rock musician careers: The culture of the long-term professional." Unpublished doctoral dissertation. University of California, Los Angeles.

Stein, Joel. 2016. "How trolls are ruining the Internet." *Time,* August 18. http://time.com/4457110/internet-trolls/.

Steiner, I. D. 1972. *Group Process and Productivity.* New York: Academic Press.

Steinmetz, Katy. 2014. "Clickbait, normcore, mansplain: Runners-up for Oxford's word of the year." *Time,* November 18. http://time.com/3590980/clickbait-normcore-mansplain-oxford-word-runners-up/.

Stepler, R. 2016. "World's centenarian population projected to grow eightfold by 2050." Pew Research Center, April 21. http://www.pewresearch.org/fact-tank/2016/04/21/worlds-centenarian-population-projected-to-grow-eightfold-by-2050/.

———. 2017. "Number of U.S. adults cohabiting with a partner continues to rise, especially among those 50 and older." Pew Research Center, April 6. http://www.pewresearch.org/fact-tank/2017/04/06/number-of-u-s-adults-cohabiting-with-a-partner-continues-to-rise-especially-among-those-50-and-older.

Stimson, Ida H. 1967. "Patterns of socialization into professions: The case of student nurses." *Sociological Inquiry,* vol. 37: 47–54.

Streib, J. 2015. "Marrying across class lines." *Contexts,* vol. 14, no. 2: 40–45.

Stroebaek, Pernille S. 2013. "Let's have a cup of coffee! Coffee and coping communities at work." *Symbolic Interaction,* vol. 36, no. 4: 381–397.

Stuart, Forrest. 2016. *Down, Out, and Under Arrest: Policing and Everyday Life in Skid Row.* Chicago: University of Chicago Press.

Substance Abuse and Mental Health Services Administration.

2015. *Behavioral Health Trends in the United States: Results from the 2014 National Survey on Drug Use and Health* (HHS Publication No. SMA 15-4927, NSDUH Series H-50). http://www.samhsa.gov/data/.

———. 2016. "Sexual orientation and estimates of adult substance use and mental health: Results from the 2015 National Survey on Drug Use and Health." https://www.samhsa.gov/data/sites/default/files/NSDUH-SexualOrientation-2015/NSDUH-SexualOrientation-2015/NSDUH-SexualOrientation-2015.htm.

Sudnow, David. 1972. "Temporal parameters of interpersonal observation." In D. Sudnow, ed., *Studies in Social Interaction.* New York: Free Press.

Sue, D. W. 2010. *Microaggressions in Everyday Life: Race, Gender, and Sexual Orientation.* Hoboken, NJ: John Wiley & Sons.

———; Capodilupo, Christina M.; Torino, Gina C.; Bucceri, Jennifer M.; Holder, Aisha M. B.; Nadal, Kevin L.; and Esquilin, Marta. 2007. "Racial microaggressions in everyday life: implications for clinical practice." *American Psychological Association,* vol. 62, no. 4: 271–86. https://world-trust.org/wp-content/uploads/2011/05/7-Racial-Microaggressions-in-Everyday-Life.pdf.

Sue, Valerie M.; and Ritter, Lois A. 2007. *Conducting Online Surveys.* Thousand Oaks, CA: Sage.

Sumner, William Graham. 1906. *Folkways: A Study of the Sociological Importance of Usages, Manners, Customs, Mores, and Morals.* Boston: Ginn and Co.

Sutherland, Edwin. 1939. *Principles of Criminology,* 3rd ed. Philadelphia: J. B. Lipincott.

———; Cressey, Donald R.; and Luckenbill, David F. 1992. *Principles of Criminology,* 11th ed. Dix Hills, NY: General Hall.

Swisher, Kara. 2017. "Google has fired the employee who penned a controversial memo on women and tech." *Recode,* August 7. https://www.recode.net/2017/8/7/16110696/firing-google-ceo-employee-penned-controversial-memo-on-women-has-violated-its-code-of-conduct.

Sycamore, Mattilda Bernstein. 2008. *That's Revolting! Queer Strategies for Resisting Assimilation.* New York: Soft Skull Press.

Syrluga, Susan; and Siddiqui, Faiz. 2016. "N.C. man told police he went to D.C. pizzeria with assault rifle to 'self-investigate' election-related conspiracy theory." *The Washington Post,* December 4.

Tassi, Paul. 2014. "'World of Warcraft' still a $1B powerhouse even as subscription MMOs decline." *Forbes,* July 19. http://www.forbes.com/sites/insertcoin/2014/07/19/world-of-warcraft-still-a-1b-powerhouse-even-as-subscription-mmos-decline/.

Telles, Edward. 2004. *Race in Another America: The Significance of Color in Brazil.* Princeton, NJ: Princeton University Press.

Theodorou, A. E. 2015. "Americans are in the middle of the pack globally when it comes to importance of religion." Pew Research Center, December 23. http://www.pewresearch.org/fact-tank/2015/12/23/americans-are-in-the-middle-of-the-pack-globally-when-it-comes-to-importance-of-religion.

Thomas, William I.; and Thomas, Dorothy. 1928. *The Child in America: Behavior Problems and Programs.* New York: Knopf.

Thompson, D. 2013. "How America's marriage crisis makes income inequality so much worse." *The Atlantic,* October 1. https://www.theatlantic.com/business/archive/2013/10/how-americas-marriage-crisis-makes-income-inequality-so-much-worse/280056/.

Thompson, John B. 2012. "The media and politics." In *The Wiley-Blackwell Companion to Political Sociology*. Chichester, West Sussex, UK: Wiley-Blackwell.

Thoreau, Henry David. 1854/1993. *Walden; or, a Life in the Woods*. Ticknor and Fields (1854); Everyman's Library (1993).

Thorne, Barrie. 1992. "Feminism and the family: Two decades of thought." In Barrie Thorne and Marilyn Yalom, eds., *Rethinking the Family: Some Feminist Questions*. Boston: Northeastern University Press.

_____. 1993. *Gender Play: Girls and Boys in School*. New Brunswick, NJ: Rutgers University Press.

Thornton, Stephen J. 2003. "Silence on gays and lesbians in social studies curriculum." *Social Education*, vol. 67, no. 4: 226.

Thun, Michael. 2013. "50-year trends in smoking-related mortality in the United States." *New England Journal of Medicine*. January 24.

Thye, Shane R.; and Lawler, Edward J., eds. 2002. *Advances in Group Processes: Group Cohesion, Trust and Solidarity*, vol. 19. Oxford, UK: Elsevier Science.

TICAS. 2018. "Student debt and the class of 2017." https://ticas.org/sites/default/files/pub_files/classof2017.pdf.

Tomlinson, John. 1991. *Cultural Imperialism*. Baltimore: John Hopkins University Press.

Travers, J.; and Milgram, S. 1969. "An experimental study of the small world problem." *Sociometry*, vol. 32, no. 4: 425–443.

Tremayne, M. 2014. "Anatomy of protest in the digital era: A network analysis of Twitter and Occupy Wall Street." *Social Movement Studies*, vol. 13, no. 1: 110–126.

Trexler, R. C. 2002. "Making the American berdache: Choice or constraint." *Journal of Social History*, vol. 35: 613–636.

Truman, J. L.; and Morgan, R. E. 2014. "Nonfatal domestic violence, 2003–2012." U.S. Bureau of Justice Statistics. https://www.bjs.gov/content/pub/pdf/ndv0312.pdf.

Tsugawa, Yusuke; Jena, Anupam B.; Figueroa, Jose F.; Orav, E. John; Blumenthal, Daniel M.; and Jha, Ashish K. 2016. "Physician gender and outcomes of hospitalized Medicare beneficiaries in the U.S." *JAMA Internal Medicine*, December 19. doi: 10.1001/jamainternmed.2016.7875.

Tugend, A. 2014. "It's clearly defined, but telecommuting is fast on the rise." *The New York Times*, March 7. http://www.nytimes.com/2014/03/08/your-money/when-working-in-your-pajamas-is-more-productive.html?_r=0.

Turkle, Sherry. 1997. *Life on the Screen: Identity in the Age of the Internet*. New York: Touchstone Books.

_____. 2005. *The Second Self: Computers and the Human Spirit*. Cambridge, MA: MIT Press.

_____. 2011. *Alone Together*. New York: Basic Books.

_____. 2015. *Reclaiming Conversation: The Power of Talk in a Digital Age*. New York: Penguin Press.

Turner, J. C.; and Reynolds, K. J. 2010. "The story of social identity." In T. Postmes and N. Branscombe, *Rediscovering Social Identity: Core Sources*. New York: Psychology Press.

Turner, Ralph. 1972. "Deviance avowal as neutralization of commitment." *Social Problems*, vol. 19, no. 3: 308–321.

_____. 1976. "The real self: From institution to impulse." *American Journal of Sociology*, vol. 81: 989–1016.

_____. 1978. "The role and the person." *American Journal of Sociology*, vol. 84, no. 1: 1–3.

_____; and Killian, Lewis M. 1987. *Collective Behavior*, 3rd ed. Englewood Cliffs, NJ: Prentice Hall.

Twine, France Winddance. 2011a. *Outsourcing the Womb: Race, Class and Gestational Surrogacy in a Global Market*. Florence, KY: Routledge.

_____. 2011b. *A White Side of Black Britain: Interracial Intimacy and Racial Literacy*. Durham, NC: Duke University Press.

Uggen, C.; and Manza, J. 2002. "Democratic contraction? Political consequences of felon disenfranchisement in the United States." *American Sociological Review*, vol. 67, no. 6: 777–803. http://www.jstor.org/stable/3088970.

Uggen, C.; Larson, R.; and Shannon, S. 2016. "6 million lost voters: State-level estimates of felony disenfranchisement, 2016." The Sentencing Project, October 6. https://www.sentencingproject.org/publications/6-million-lost-voters-state-level-estimates-felony-disenfranchisement-2016/.

Uggen, Christopher; Shannon, Sarah; and Manza, Jeff. 2012. "State-level estimates of felon disenfranchisement in the United States, 2010." The Sentencing Project, July. http://sentencingproject.org/doc/publications/fd_State_Level_Estimates_of_Felon_Disen_2010.pdf.

UNAIDS. 2018. "Fact sheet: World AIDS Day 2018." http://www.unaids.org/sites/default/files/media_asset/UNAIDS_FactSheet_en.pdf.

UNICEF. 2010. "Humanitarian Action Report 2010: Eastern and Southern Africa, feature story for Burundi." http://www.unicef.org/har2010/index_burundi_feature.html.

United Nations. 2000. "Ending violence against women and girls." State of the World Population 2000. https://www.unfpa.org/sites/default/files/pub-pdf/swp2000_eng.pdf.

_____. 2014a. "The human right to water and sanitation." May. http://www.un.org/waterforlifedecade/human_right_to_water.shtml.

_____. 2014b. "Transboundary waters." http://www.un.org/waterforlifedecade/transboundary_waters.shtml.

_____. 2019. "Nature's dangerous decline 'unprecedented'; species extinction rates 'accelerating.'" Intergovernmental Science-Policy Platform on Biodiversity and Ecosystem Services (IPBES). https://www.ipbes.net/news/Media-Release-Global-Assessment.

United Nations Conference on Trade and Development. 2014. "World Investment Report 2014: Annex Tables." http://unctad.org/en/pages/DIAE/World%20Investment%20Report/AnnexTables.aspx.

_____. 2017. "World Investment Report 2017: Annex Tables." http://unctad.org/en/Pages/DIAE/World%20Investment%20Report/Annex-Tables.aspx.

_____. 2018. "World investment report 2018." https://unctad.org/en/Pages/DIAE/World%20Investment%20Report/World_Investment_Report.aspx.

United Nations Department of Economic and Social Affairs (UN DESA). 2016. "The world's cities in 2016." http://www.un.org/en/development/desa/population/publications/pdf/urbanization/the_worlds_cities_in_2016_data_booklet.pdf.

_____. 2017. *World Population Prospects: The 2017 Revision*. New York: United Nations.

_____. 2018. "World urbanization prospects: The 2018 revision." May 16. https://population.un.org/wup/Publications/Files/WUP2018-KeyFacts.pdf.

United Nations High Commission on Refugees. 2016. "Syria conflict at 5 years: The biggest refugee and displacement crisis of our time demands a huge surge in solidarity." March 15. http://www.unhcr.org/afr/news/press/2016/3/56e6e3249/syria-conflict-5-years-biggest-refugee-displacement-crisis-time-demands.html.

United Nations Office of Drugs and Crime. 2019. *Global Report on*

Trafficking in Persons 2018. https://www.unodc.org/unodc/data
-and-analysis/glotip.html.

United Nations Water. 2013a. "Facts and Figures." http://
www.unwater.org/water-cooperation-2013/water cooperation/
facts-and-figures/en/.

———. 2013b. "Statistics: Graphs & Maps." www.unwater.org
/statistics_urb.html.

———. 2013c. "World Water Day 2013: International Year of Water
Cooperation." http://www.unwater.org/water-cooperation
-2013/water-cooperation/facts-and figures/en/.

United Nations World Commission on Environment and
Development. 1987. *Our Common Future.* Oxford, UK: Oxford
University Press.

Urry, John. 1990. *The Tourist Gaze.* London: Sage.

———. 1992. "The tourist gaze and the 'environment.'" *Theory,
Culture & Society,* vol. 9, no. 3: 1–26.

———. 2002. *The Tourist Gaze,* 2nd ed. London: Sage.

Urstadt, Bryant; and Frier, Sarah. 2016. "Welcome to Zuckerworld:
Facebook's really big plans for virtual reality." *Bloomberg
Businessweek.* July 27. https://www.bloomberg.com/features
/2016-facebook-virtual-reality/.

U.S. Bureau of Economic Analysis. 2016. "Activities of U.S.
multinational enterprises in the United States and abroad."
https://www.bea.gov/scb/pdf/2016/12%20December/1216
_activities_of_us_multinational_enterprises.pdf.

U.S. Bureau of Justice Statistics. 1982. "Prisoners 1925-81."
https://www.bjs.gov/content/pub/pdf/p2581.pdf.

———. 2014. "Prisoners in 2012." https://www.bjs.gov/content/pub
/pdf/p12tar9112.pdf.

———. 2015a. "Drug offenders in federal prison: Estimates of
characteristics based on linked data." https://www.bjs.gov
/content/pub/pdf/dofp12.pdf.

———. 2015b. "Investigation of the Ferguson Police Department."
https://www.justice.gov/sites/default/files/opa/press-releases
/attachments/2015/03/04/ferguson_police_department
_report.pdf.

U.S. Bureau of Labor Statistics. 2012a. "Employment outlook:
2010–2020 industry employment and output projections to
2020." https://www.bls.gov/opub/mlr/2012/01/art4full.pdf.

———. 2012b. "Unemployment rates for states." https://www.bls
.gov/web/laus/laumstrk.htm.

———. 2015a. "Economic news release: Table A-14. Unemployed
persons by industry and class of worker, not seasonally
adjusted." March 2. http://www.bls.gov/news.release/empsit
.t14.htm.

———. 2015b. "Industries at a glance." https://www.bls.gov/iag/tgs
/iag_index_naics.htm.

———. 2018a. "A profile of the working poor: 2016." https://www.bls
.gov/opub/reports/working-poor/2016/home.htm.

———. 2018b. "American time use survey—2017 results." https://
www.bls.gov/news.release/atus.nr0.htm.

———. 2018c. "Consumer expenditures—2017." https://www.bls
.gov/news.release/pdf/cesan.pdf.

———. 2018d. "Contingent and alternative employment
arrangements: May 2017." https://www.bls.gov/news.release
/conemp.nr0.htm.

———. 2018e. "Women in the labor force: A databook." https://www
.bls.gov/opub/reports/womens-databook/2018/home.htm.

———. 2019a. "Annual work stoppages involving 1,000 or more
workers, 1947–2017." https://www.bls.gov/news.release/wkstp
.t01.htm.

———. 2019b. "Industries at a glance: Leisure and hospitality."
https://www.bls.gov/iag/tgs/iag70.htm.

———. 2019c. "Labor force statistics from the current population
survey: Employed persons by detailed occupation, sex, race,
and Hispanic or Latino ethnicity." https://www.bls.gov/cps
/cpsaat11.htm.

———. 2019d. "Labor force statistics from the current population
survey: Employment status of the civilian noninstitutional
population 25 years and over by educational attainment, sex,
race, and Hispanic or Latino ethnicity." https://www.bls.gov
/cps/cpsaat07.htm.

———. 2019e. "Union members—2018." https://www.bls.gov/news
.release/union2.nr0.htm.

———. 2019f. "Work stoppages summary." https://www.bls.gov
/news.release/wkstp.nr0.htm.

U.S. Census Bureau. 2005. "Interim projections: Ranking of census
2000 and projected 2030 state population and change: 2000
to 2030." April. https://www.census.gov/Press-Release/www
/2005/stateproj7.xls.

———. 2012. "Shopping centers—number and gross leasable area:
1990–2010." https://www.census.gov/compendia/statab/2012
/tables/12s1061.pdf.

———. 2013. "Percent population residing in urban areas by county:
2010." https://www2.census.gov/geo/pdfs/maps-data/maps
/thematic/2010ua/UA2010_Urban_Pop_Map.pdf.

———. 2015a. "Fertility of women in the United States: 2014."
https://www.census.gov/hhes/fertility/data/cps/2014.html.

———. 2015b. "New Census Bureau report analyzes U.S. population
projections." March 3. https://www.census.gov/newsroom
/press-releases/2015/cb15-tps16.html.

———. 2015c. "Projections of the size and composition of the U.S.
population: 2014 to 2060." https://www.census.gov/content
/dam/Census/library/publications/2015/demo/p25-1143.pdf.

———. 2017. "Voting and registration in the election of November
2016." Table 10. https://www.census.gov/data/tables/time
-series/demo/voting-and-registration/p20-580.html.

———. 2018a. "America's families and living arrangements 2018."
Nov. 14. https://www.census.gov/data/tables/2018/demo
/families/cps-2018.html

———. 2018b. "Historical families tables." https://www.census.gov
/data/tables/time-series/demo/families/families.html.

———. 2018c. "Historical households tables." https://www.census
.gov/data/tables/time-series/demo/families/households.html.

———. 2018d. "Historical living arrangements of children," Nov.
14. https://www.census.gov/data/tables/time-series/demo
/families/children.html.

———. 2018e. "Historical marital status tables," Nov. 14. https://
www.census.gov/data/tables/time-series/demo/families
/marital.html.

———. 2018f. "Nevada and Idaho are the nation's fastest-growing
states." https://www.census.gov/newsroom/press-releases
/2018/estimates-national-state.html.

———. 2019a. "Educational attainment in the United States:
2018," Feb. 21. https://www.census.gov/data/tables/2018/demo
/education-attainment/cps-detailed-tables.html.

———. 2019b. "Fastest-growing cities primarily in the South and
West." https://www.census.gov/newsroom/press-releases/2019
/subcounty-population-estimates.html.

———. 2019c. "Irish-American Heritage Month and St. Patrick's
Day: March 2019." https://www.census.gov/newsroom/facts-for
-features/2019/irish-american-month.html.

———. 2019d. "National population by characteristics: 2010–2018."
https://www.census.gov/data/tables/time-series/demo/popest
/2010s-national-detail.html.

———. 2019e. "New Census Bureau estimates show counties in

South and West lead nation in population growth." https://www
.census.gov/newsroom/press-releases/2019/estimates-county
-metro.html.

———. 2019f. "Quick facts: California," June 20. https://www
.census.gov/quickfacts/CA.

———. 2019g. "Quick facts: Las Vegas city, Nevada." https://www
.census.gov/quickfacts/lasvegascitynevada.

U.S. Department of Agriculture (USDA). 2012. "Characteristics
and influential factors of food deserts." https://www.ers.usda
.gov/webdocs/publications/45014/30940_err140.pdf?v=41156.

———. 2015. "Food security in the U.S.: Key statistics and graphs."
https://www.ers.usda.gov/topics/food-nutrition-assistance
/food-security-in-the-us/key-statistics-graphics/.

———. 2018. "Household food security in the United States in 2017."
https://www.ers.usda.gov/publications/pub-details/?pubid
=90022.

U.S. Department of Commerce. 2012. "Summary estimates for
multinational companies: Employment, sales, and capital
expenditures for 2010." htpps://www.bea.gov/news releases
/international/mnc/mncnewsrelease.htm.

———. 2016a. "Fast facts: United States travel and tourism
industry: 2015." http://tinet.ita.doc.gov/outreachpages
/download_data_table/Fast_Facts_2015.pdf.

———. 2016b. "National population by characteristics tables:
2010–2015." https://www.census.gov/data/tables/2015/demo
/popest/nation-detail.html.

———. 2018. "Fast facts: United States travel and tourism industry:
2017." https://travel.trade.gov/outreachpages/download_data
_table/Fast_Facts_2017.pdf.

U.S. Department of Defense. 2014. *Report to the President of the
United States on Sexual Assault Prevention and Response.*
http://www.sapr.mil/public/docs/reports/FY14_POTUS/FY14
_DoD_Report_to_POTUS_Full_Report.pdf.

———. 2018. "Fiscal year 2017 annual report on sexual assault in
the military." https://www.sapr.mil/sites/default/files/FY17
_Annual_Report_Fact_Sheet.pdf.

U.S. Department of Education, National Center for Education
Statistics. 2013. "Number and percentage distribution of all
children ages 5–17 who were homeschooled and homeschooling
rate, by selected characteristics: 2011–12." http://nces.ed.gov
/pubs2013/2013028/tables/table_07.asp.

———. 2016a. "Digest of education statistics, Table 104.91:
Number and percentage distribution of spring 2002 high
school sophomores, by highest level of education completed,
and socioeconomic status and selected student characteristics
while in high school." https://nces.ed.gov/programs/digest/d16
/tables/dt16_104.91.asp.

———. 2016b. "Digest of education statistics, Table 302.30:
Percentage of recent high school completers enrolled in 2-year
and 4-year colleges, by income level: 1975 through 2015."
https://nces.ed.gov/programs/digest/d16/tables/dt16_302.30
.asp?current=yes.

———. 2016c. "Official cohort default rates for schools." Federal
Student Aid, September 28. https://www2.ed.gov/offices
/OSFAP/defaultmanagement/cdr.html.

———. 2017a. "The condition of education: 2016." https://nces.ed
.gov/programs/coe/.

———. 2017b. "Digest of education statistics: Degrees conferred
by postsecondary institutions, by level of degree and sex of
student: Selected years, 1869–70 through 2026–27." https://
nces.ed.gov/programs/digest/d16/tables/dt16_318.10.asp
?current=yes.

———. 2017c. "Digest of education statistics, Table 303.10: Total
fall enrollment in degree-granting postsecondary institutions."

https://nces.ed.gov/programs/digest/d16/tables/dt16_303.10
.asp?current=yes.

———. 2017d. "Digest of education statistics: Table 325.92, Degrees
in economics, history, political science and government, and
sociology conferred by postsecondary institutions, by level of
degree: Selected years, 1949–50 through 2014–15." https://nces
.ed.gov/programs/digest/current_tables.asp.

———. 2017e. "Homeschooling in the United States: 2012." https://
nces.ed.gov/pubs2016/2016096rev.pdf.

U.S. Department of Health and Human Services. 2016. "The
AFCARS report: Preliminary FY 2015 estimates as of June
2016 (23)." https://www.acf.hhs.gov/sites/default/files/cb
/afcarsreport23.pdf.

———. 2017. "Child maltreatment 2015." http://www.acf.hhs.gov
/programs/cb/research-data-technology/statistics-research
/child-maltreatment.

———. 2019. "Annual update of the HHS poverty guidelines."
Federal Register, vol. 84, no. 22. https://www.federalregister.gov
/documents/2019/02/01/2019-00621/annual-update-of-the
-hhs-poverty-guidelines.

U.S. Department of Housing and Urban Development. 2018. "The
2018 annual homeless assessment report (AHAR) to Congress."
https://www.hudexchange.info/resources/documents/2018
-AHAR-Part-1.pdf.

U.S. Department of Labor. 2012. "Extensive violations of federal,
state laws found among garment contractors at Los Angeles
Garment District location." http://www.dol.gov/opa/media
/press/whd/WHD20122378.htm.

U.S. Department of State. 2017. "Trafficking in Persons Report
2017." https://www.state.gov/documents/organization/271339
.pdf.

U.S. Elections Project. 2017. "Voter turnout demographics." http://
www.electproject.org/home/voter-turnout/demographics.

U.S. Energy Information Administration. 2013a. "Countries
overview." http://www.eia.gov/countries/index.cfm?topL
=conFjsdlkjfk.

———. 2013b. "World energy use to rise by 56 percent, driven by
growth in the developing world." http://www.eia.gov/pressroom
/releases/press395.cfm.

———. 2015. "Primary energy consumption by source." http://www
.eia.gov/totalenergy/data/monthly/pdf/sec1_7.pdf.

———. 2016. "Hydraulic fracturing accounts for about half
of current U.S. crude oil production." https://www.eia.gov
/todayinenergy/detail.php?id=25372.

———. 2017. "International energy outlook 2017." https://www.eia
.gov/outlooks/ieo/pdf/0484(2017).pdf.

———. 2018. "U.S. energy facts—explained." https://www.eia.gov
/energyexplained/.

———. 2019. "What countries are the top producers and consumers
of oil?" https://www.eia.gov/tools/faqs/faq.php?id=709&t=6.

U.S. Geological Survey. 2014. "How much water is there on, in, and
above the Earth?" https://water.usgs.gov/edu/earthhowmuch
.html.

U.S. Government Printing Office. 2011. "Budget of the U.S.
government." http://www.gpo.gov/fdsys/pkg/BUDGET-2011
-BUD/pdf/BUDGET-2011-BUD.pdf.

Useem, E. L. 1990. "You're good but you're not good enough:
Tracking students out of advanced mathematics." *American
Educator*, vol. 14, no. 3, 24–46.

Usher, Alexandra; and Kober, Nancy. 2011. "Keeping informed
about school vouchers: A review of major developments and
research." *Center on Education Policy*, July. http://www.cep
-dc.org/displayDocument.cfm?DocumentID=369#sthash
.WDWRI2p8.dpuf.

Valente, T. W. 2015. "Social networks and health behavior." In B. Rimer, K. Glanz, and V. Vishwanath, eds., *Health Behavior: Theory, Research & Practice*, 6th ed. New York: Wiley.

van den Berghe, P. L. 1979. *Human Family Systems: An Evolutionary View.* New York: Elsevier/North-Holland.

Vance, J. D. 2016. *Hillbilly Elegy: A Memoir of a Family and Culture in Crisis.* New York: Harper Collins.

Vandivere, Sharon; Malm, Karen; and Radel, Laura. 2009. "Adoption USA: A chartbook based on the 2007 National Survey of Adoptive Parents." U.S. Department of Health and Human Services, Office of the Assistant Secretary for Planning and Evaluation.

Vaughan, Diane. 1996. *The Challenger Launch Decisions: Risky Technology, Culture and Deviance at NASA.* Chicago: University of Chicago Press.

Vedantam, Shankar. 2010. "Why do Americans claim to be more religious than they are?" *Slate*, December 22. www.slate.com/id /2278923.

Velkoff, Victoria; and Lawson, Valerie. 1998. "Caregiving." *Gender and Aging*, December: 1–7.

Vespa, J. 2018. "The graying of America: More older adults than children by 2035." U.S. Census Bureau, September 6. https:// www.census.gov/library/stories/2018/03/graying-america .html.

———; Armstrong, D. M.; and Medina, L. 2018. "Demographic turning points for the United States: Population projections for 2020 to 2060." https://www.census.gov/content/dam/Census /library/publications/2018/demo/P25_1144.pdf.

Villarosa, Linda. 2018. "Why America's black mothers and babies are in a life-or-death crisis." *The New York Times*, April 11. https://www.nytimes.com/2018/04/11/magazine/black -mothers-babies-death-maternal-mortality.html.

Vilsack, Tom. 2016. "Rural America has already begun to rebound." *The New York Times,* September 19. https://www.nytimes.com /roomfordebate/2016/09/19/prosperity-is-up-but-not-for-rural -america/rural-america-has-already-begun-to-rebound.

Vincent, Danny. 2011. "China used prisoners in lucrative Internet gaming work." *The Guardian*, May 25. http://www.guardian .co.uk/world/2011/may/25/china-prisoners-internet-gaming -scam.

Vivarelli, Nick. 2017. "British TV rules Monte Carlo TV fest, with double wins for 'Victoria,' 'Fleabag.'" *Variety*, June 20. http:// variety.com/2017/tv/news/victoria-fleabag-score-multiple -prizes-at-monte-carlo-tv-fest-1202472767/.

Waber, B.; et al. 2010. "Productivity through coffee breaks: Changing social networks by changing break structure." *Massachusetts Institute of Technology.* January.

Wackernagel, Mathis; and Rees, William. 1996. *Our Ecological Footprint.* Gabriola Island, BC, Canada: New Society Press.

Wade, Lisa. 2017a. *American Hookup: The New Culture of Sex on Campus.* New York: W. W. Norton.

———. 2017b. "The modern marriage trap—and what to do about it." *Money Magazine.* January 10. http://time.com/money/4630251 /the-modern-marriage-trap-and-what-to-do-about-it/.

Waldron, T.; Roberts, B.; and Reamer, A. 2004. "Working hard, falling short: America's working families and the pursuit of economic security." A national report by the Working Poor Families Project. Baltimore: Annie E. Casey Foundation.

Waldron, Travis. 2016. "Nobody asked Rio's poor about the Olympics. So they yelled louder." *Huffington Post*, October 6. https://www.huffpost.com/entry/rio-favelas-olympics-protest -legacy_n_57e572d2e4b0e28b2b53cfc8.

Walker, Samuel. 1997. *Popular Justice: A History of American Criminal Justice.* New York: Oxford University Press.

Walsh, Declan. 2013. "Girl shot by Pakistani Taliban is discharged from hospital." *The New York Times*, January 4. http://www .nytimes.com/2013/01/05/world/asia/malala-yousafzai-shot -by-pakistani-taliban-is-discharged-from-hospital.html.

Wang, T. W.; Asman, K.; Gentzke, A. S.; et al. 2018. "Tobacco product use among adults—United States, 2017." *Morbidity and Mortality Weekly Report*, vol. 67: 1225–1232. http://dx.doi.org /10.15585/mmwr.mm6744a2.

Wang, Wendy. 2015. "The link between a college education and a lasting marriage." Pew Research Center, December 4. https:// www.pewresearch.org/fact-tank/2015/12/04/education-and -marriage/.

———. 2018. "Early marriage has fallen, especially among those without a college degree." Institute for Family Studies, March 16. https://ifstudies.org/blog/early-marriage-has-fallen -especially-among-those-without-a-college-degree.

Waters, Emily. 2016. "Lesbian, gay, bisexual, transgender, queer, and HIV-affected intimate partner violence in 2015." National Coalition of Anti-Violence Programs. http://www.avp.org /storage/documents/2015_ncavp_lgbtqipvreport.pdf.

Waters, Mary. 1990. *Ethnic Options: Choosing Identities in America.* Berkeley: University of California Press.

Wattel, Harold. 1958. "Levittown: A suburban community." In William M. Dobriner, ed., *The Suburban Community.* New York: Putnam.

Watts, Duncan. 2003. *Six Degrees: The Science of a Connected Age.* New York: W. W. Norton.

Wearing, Stephen; and Wearing, Michael. 1999. "Decommodifying ecotourism: Rethinking global–local interactions with host communities." *Loisir et Société/Society and Leisure*, vol. 22, no. 1: 39–70.

Weber, Max. 1930 (orig. 1905). *The Protestant Ethic and the Spirit of Capitalism.* Trans. Talcott Parsons. New York: Scribner's.

———. 1946 (orig. 1925). "Science as a vocation." In Hans Gerth and C. Wright Mills, ed. and trans., *From Max Weber: Essays in Sociology.* New York: Oxford University Press.

———. 1962 (orig. 1913). *Basic Concepts of Sociology.* Westport, CT: Greenwood Publishing.

———. 1968 (orig. 1921). *Economy and Society.* Ed. and trans. Guenther Roth and Claus Wittich. New York: Bedminster Press.

Weinberg, Adam; Bellows, Story; and Ekster, Dara. 2002. "Sustaining ecotourism: Insights and implications from two successful case studies." *Society and Natural Resources*, vol. 15, no. 4: 371–380.

Weinstein, Deena. 1991. *Heavy Metal: A Cultural Sociology.* New York: Macmillan/Lexington.

———. 2000. *Heavy Metal: The Music and Its Culture.* New York: DaCapo.

Weinstein, Henry. 2003. "Controversial ruling on pledge reaffirmed." *Los Angeles Times*, Metro Desk, March 1, 1:1.

Weir, Kirsten. 2016. "Policing in black and white." *Monitor on Psychology*, vol. 47, no. 11. https://www.apa.org/monitor/2016 /12/cover-policing.

Wellman, Barry. 2004. "Connecting community: On- and off-line." *Contexts*, vol. 3, no. 4: 22–28.

Werner, Carrie A. 2011. "The older population: 2010." U.S. Census Briefs. https://www.census.gov/prod/cen2010/briefs/c2010br -09.pdf

Weston, Kath. 1991. *Families We Choose.* New York: Columbia University Press.

Whalen, J.; Zimmerman, D.; and Whalen, M. 1988. "When words

fail: A single case analysis." *Social Problems*, vol. 35, no. 4: 335–362.

Wharton, Amy S.; and Blair-Loy, Mary. 2002. "Employees' use of work–family policies and the workplace social context." *Social Forces*, vol. 80, no. 3: 813–845.

Whitacre, Paula Tarnapol; Tsai, Peggy; and Mulligan, Janet. 2009. *The Public Health Effects of Food Deserts: Workshop Summary*. Washington, DC: The National Academies Press.

White, Glen. 1989. "Groupthink reconsidered." *Academy of Management Review*, vol. 14: 40–56.

Whorf, Benjamin. 1956. *Language, Thought and Reality: Selected Writings of Benjamin Lee Whorf*. John B. Carroll, ed. Cambridge, MA: MIT Press.

Whyte, W. H. 1956. *The Organization Man*. New York: Simon & Schuster.

Wicks-Lim, Jeannette; and Thompson, Jeffrey. 2010. "Combining minimum wage and earned income tax credit policies to guarantee a decent living standard to all U.S. workers." Political Economy Research Institute. October 18. http://www.peri.umass.edu/236/hash/9b8a787cfa16226190e4f96e582348cd/publication/428.

Wilkinson, Richard G. 2005. *The Impact of Inequality*. New York: New Press.

Williams, Christine L. 1992. "The glass escalator: Hidden advantages for men in the 'female' professions." *Social Problems*, vol. 39, no. 3: 253–267.

_____. 1995. *Still a Man's World: Men Who Do Women's Work*. Berkeley: University of California Press.

_____. 2013. "The glass escalator, revisited: Gender inequality in neoliberal times, SWS feminist lecturer." *Gender & Society*, vol. 27, no. 5: 609–629.

Williams, Patricia J. 1991. *The Alchemy of Race and Rights: Diary of a Law Professor*. Cambridge, MA: Harvard University Press.

_____. 1997. "Of race and risk." *The Nation*, December 29: 10.

Williams, Robin. 1965. *American Society: A Sociological Interpretation,* 2nd ed. New York: Knopf.

Wilson, Edward O. 1975/2000. *Sociobiology: The New Synthesis*. Cambridge, MA: The Belknap Press of Harvard University Press.

_____. 1978. *On Human Nature*. Cambridge, MA: Harvard University Press.

Wilson, Reid. 2014. "Watch the U.S. transition from a manufacturing economy to a service economy, in one gif." *The Washington Post*. September 3. https://www.washingtonpost.com/blogs/govbeat/wp/2014/09/03/watch-the-u-s-transition-from-a-manufacturing-economy-to-a-service-economy-in-one-gif/?utm_term=.5a7fb11a6e40.

Wilson, William Julius. 1980. *The Declining Significance of Race*. Chicago: University of Chicago Press.

_____. 1996. *When Work Disappears: The World of the New Urban Poor*. New York: Knopf.

_____. 2009. *More Than Just Race: Being Black and Poor in the Inner City*. New York: W. W. Norton.

Wing Sue, Derald. 2010. *Microaggressions in Everyday Life: Race, Gender, and Sexual Orientation*. Hoboken, NJ: Wiley.

_____; Capodilupo, C.; Torino, G.; Bucceri, J.; Holder, A.; Nadal, K.; and Esquilin, M. 2007. "Racial microaggressions in everyday life: Implications for clinical practice." *American Psychologist*, vol. 62, no. 4: 271–286.

Wirth, Louis. 1938. "Urbanism as a way of life." *American Journal of Sociology*, vol. 44: 3–24.

Wise, Tim. 2011. *White Like Me: Reflections on Race from a Privileged Son*. Berkeley, CA: Soft Skull Press.

_____. 2012. *Dear White America: A Letter to a New Minority*. San Francisco, CA: City Lights Books.

Wiseman, Rosalind. 2002. *Queen Bees and Wannabes*. New York: Three Rivers Press.

Wisenberg Brin, Dinah. 2013. "Telecommuting likely to grow despite high-profile defections." Society for Human Resource Management. July 24. http://www.shrm.org/hrdisciplines/technology/articles/pages/telecommuting-likely-to-grow-bans.aspx.

Wolf, Rosalie S. 2000. "The nature and scope of elder abuse." *Generations*, vol. 24 (summer): 6–12.

_____. 2004. "Changes in household wealth in the 1980s and 1990s in the U.S." Working paper no. 407. Levy Economics Institute of Bard College.

Wolff, E. N. 2017. "Household wealth trends in the United States, 1962 to 2016: Has middle class wealth recovered?" NBER Working Paper No. 24085. https://www.nber.org/papers/w24085.

Wolfinger, Nicholas H. 1999. "Trends in the intergenerational transmission of divorce." *Demography*, vol. 36, no. 3: 415–420.

_____. 2000. "Beyond the intergenerational transmission of divorce: Do people replicate the patterns of marital instability they grew up with?" *Journal of Family Issues*, vol. 21: 1061–1086.

_____. 2003. "Parental divorce and offspring marriage: Early or late?" *Social Forces*, vol. 82, no. 1: 337–353.

_____. 2005. *Understanding the Divorce Cycle: Children of Divorce and Their Own Marriages*. Cambridge, UK: Cambridge University Press.

_____. 2017. "New research on the intergenerational transmission of divorce." *Family Studies Blog*. January 24. https://ifstudies.org/blog/new-research-on-the-intergenerational-transmission-of-divorce.

Wolfson, Andrew. 2005. "A hoax most cruel." *Courier-Journal*. Louisville, KY. October 9. http://www.courier-journal.com/apps/pbcs.dll/article?AID=/20051009/NEWS01/510090392.

Wong, Julia Carrie. 2016. "Asian Americans decry 'whitewashed' Great Wall film starring Matt Damon." *The Guardian*. July 29. https://www.theguardian.com/film/2016/jul/29/the-great-wall-china-film-matt-damon-whitewashed.

Wood, Lisa J.; Giles-Corti, Billie; Bulsara, Max K.; and Bosch, Darcy. 2007. "More than a furry companion: The ripple effect of companion animals on neighborhood interactions and sense of community." *Society and Animals*, vol. 15: 43–56.

Wood, Megan Epler. 2002. *Ecotourism: Principles, Practices and Policies for Sustainability*. Burlington, VT: International Ecotourism Society.

World Bank. 2015. "CO_2 emissions (metric tons per capita)." http://data.worldbank.org/indicator/EN.ATM.CO2E.PC.

_____. 2017a. "Percent of employment in agriculture, U.S." http://data.worldbank.org/indicator/SL.AGR.EMPL.ZS?locations=US.

_____. 2017b. "World development indicators: Gross domestic product 2016." http://databank.worldbank.org/data/download/GDP.pdf.

_____. 2018. "Overcoming poverty and inequality in South Africa." http://documents.worldbank.org/curated/en/530481521735906534/pdf/124521-REV-OUO-South-Africa-Poverty-and-Inequality-Assessment-Report-2018-FINAL-WEB.pdf.

_____. 2019a. "World development indicators: Gross domestic product 2017." https://databank.worldbank.org/data/download/GDP.pdf.

_____. 2019b. "World development indicators." Table 2.14: Reproductive health. http://wdi.worldbank.org/table.

_____. 2019c. "World development indicators." Table 2.18: Mortality. http://wdi.worldbank.org/table.

World Health Organization (WHO). 1946. "Constitution of the World Health Organization." July 26. http://www.who.int /governance/eb/constitution/en/.

———. 2016. "Life expectancy at birth (years), 2000–2015: Life expectancy data by country." http://gamapserver.who.int/gho /interactive_charts/mbd/life_expectancy/atlas.html.

———. 2017. "The top 10 causes of death." http://www.who.int /mediacentre/factsheets/fs310/en/index1.html.

———. 2018a. "The top 10 causes of death." May 24. https://www .who.int/news-room/fact-sheets/detail/the-top-10-causes-of -death.

———. 2018b. "World health statistics: Life expectancy and healthy life expectancy data by country." http://apps.who.int/gho/data /node.main.688?lang=en.

Wray, M.; Miller, M.; Gurvey, J.; Carroll, J.; and Kawachi, I. 2008. "Leaving Las Vegas: Exposure to Las Vegas and risk of suicide." *Social Science and Medicine*, vol. 67, no. 11: 1882–1888.

Wright, Erik Olin. 1997. *Class Counts: Comparative Studies in Class Analysis.* Cambridge, UK: Cambridge University Press.

———; Costello, Cynthia; Hachen, David; and Spragues, Joey. 1982. "The American class structure." *American Sociological Review,* vol. 47, no. 6: 709–726.

Xu, J. Q.; Murphy, S. L.; Kochanek, K. D.; and Bastian, B. A. 2016. "Deaths: Final data for 2013." *National Vital Statistics Report,* vol. 64, no. 2. https://www.cdc.gov/nchs/data/nvsr/nvsr64 /nvsr64_02.pdf.

Yeung, King-To; and Martin, John Levi. 2003. "The looking glass self: An empirical test and elaboration." *Social Forces,* vol. 81, no. 3: 843–879.

Yin, Sandra. 2003. "The art of staying at home." *American Demographics*, vol. 25, no. 9 (November 1).

Yuan, Jada. 2007. "The White-Castle ceiling." *New York Magazine,* March 4.

Zellner, William W. 1995. *Countercultures: A Sociological Analysis.* New York: St. Martin's Press.

Zimbardo, Philip G. 1971. "The power and pathology of imprisonment." *Congressional Record* (Serial No. 15, October 25). Hearings before Subcommittee No. 3, of the Committee on the Judiciary, House of Representatives, 92nd Congress, First Session on Corrections, Part II, Prisons, Prison Reform and Prisoner's Rights: California. Washington, DC: U.S. Government Printing Office.

Zinn, Howard. 1995. *A People's History of America.* New York: HarperCollins.

Zirakzadeh, C. 1997. *Social Movements in Politics: A Comparative Study.* London: Longman.

Zraick, Karen. 2016. "In death, Qandeel Baloch, Pakistani social media star, is celebrated as a feminist hero." *The New York Times,* July 19. http://www.nytimes.com/2016/07/20/world /asia/qandeel-baloch-pakistan-murder-social-media.html ?_r=0.

Zukin, S. 1987. "Gentrification: Culture and capital in the urban core." *American Review of Sociology,* vol. 13: 139–147.

———. 1989. *Loft Living: Culture and Capital in Urban Change.* New Brunswick, NJ: Rutgers University Press.

———. 2004. *Point of Purchase: How Shopping Changed American Culture.* London: Routledge.

———. 2016. "Gentrification in three paradoxes." *City & Community,* vol. 15, no. 3. https://doi.org/10.1111/cico.12184.

Zurcher, Louis. 1977. *The Mutable Self.* Beverly Hills, CA: Sage.

Zweigenhaft, R. L.; and Domhoff, G. W. 2014. *The New CEOs: Women, African American, Latino, and Asian American Leaders of Fortune 500 Companies.* New York: Rowman and Littlefield.

Credits

About the Authors

Page v top: Gregory Wennerdahl, bottom: Doug Ellis Photography.

Part I

Page 4 left: John Keatley/Redux, center: courtesy of Victor Rios, right: Lillian Leung.

Chapter 1

Page 11: James Leynse/Corbis via Getty Images; **p. 13** top: Jeff Kravitz/FilmMagic/Getty Images, bottom: Fritz Goro/The LIFE Picture Collection/Getty Images; **p. 15**: Joe Raedle/Getty Images; **p. 16** left: McPHOTOs/ageFotostock, right: Demitrius Balevski/AP Photo; **p. 18** left: Bettmann/Corbis via Getty Images, top right: Hulton-Deutsch Collection/Corbis via Getty Images, bottom right: Herbert Spencer (1820-1903)(print)/London Library, St James's Square, London, UK/Bridgeman Images; **p. 19**: Bettmann/Corbis via Getty Images; **p. 20** top and bottom: American Sociological Association; **p. 21**: Bettmann/Corbis/via Getty Images; **p. 22**: Trip/Alamy; **p. 24** top: Librado Romero/The New York Times/Redux, bottom: Hulton Archive/Getty Images; **p. 26** left: Bettmann/Corbis/via Getty Images, center: Kristoffer Tripplaar/Alamy Stock Photo, right: Kris Connor/Getty Images, bottom: The Granger Collection, NY; **p. 28** top: Savitar, 1922. [Volume 28]. Courtesy of University Archives, University of Missouri at Columbia, bottom: Library of Congress; **p. 29** left: Library of Congress, right: From the Collections of the University of Pennsylvania Archives; **p. 31**: pictoKraft/Alamy Stock Photo; **p. 32** left: Steve Pyke/Getty Images, center: Bettmann/Corbis via Getty Images, right: Steve Pyke/Getty Images.

Chapter 2

Page 39: U.S. Census Bureau; **p. 41**: Bandura, Ross and Ross, from "Social Learning of Aggression through Imitation of Film-Mediated Aggressive Models," Journal of Abnormal and Social Psychology 66 (1963), 3-11.; **p. 42**: John Dominis/The LIFE Picture Collection/Getty Images; **p. 45**: Polly Thomas/Alamy Stock Photo; **p. 47**: Leila Cutler/Alamy Stock Photo; **p. 53**: Mick Stevens/Cartoon Stock; **p. 55** left and right: Michael Dunning/Getty Images; **p. 58**: Whitney Bush; **p. 59**: Luxy Images/Getty Images; **p. 61**: Corbis via Getty Images; **p. 62**: Curt Teich Postcard Archives Collection, Newberry Library.

Part II

Pages 66 and 67: Courtesy Verta Taylor and Leila Rupp.

Chapter 3

Page 72: Laura Doss/Corbis; **p. 73**: Eric Schwortz/Glasshouse Images/Alamy Stock Photo; **p. 74** clockwise from top left: William West/AFP/Getty Images, Elaine Thompson/AP Photo, Pascal Guyot/AFP/Getty Images, Carl De Souza/AFP/Getty Images, AarStudio/Getty Images; **p. 75**: Paramount Pictures/Courtesy of the Everett Collection; **p. 77**: Ted S. Warren/AP Photo; **p. 78** left: Alex Brandon/AP Photo, right: AP Photo/News Herald, Heather Leiphart; **p. 79**: Carolyn Cole/Los Angeles Times via Getty Images; **p. 81** left: John Amis/AFP/Getty Images, right: AP Photo/Marcio Jose Sanchez; **p. 82**: ©Androniki Christodoulou; **p. 84**: Alex Segre/Alamy; **p. 85**: Ashley Gilbertson/VII Photo/Redux; **p. 86**: Joshua Roberts/Reuters/Newscom; **p. 87**: Aflo/Shutterstock.

Chapter 4

Page 95: Carol and Mike Werner/Science Source; **p. 96**: ©Walt Disney Pictures/Courtesy: Everett Collection; **p. 97**: Smithsonian American Art Museum, Washington, DC/Art Resource, NY. © 2019 The Jacob and Gwendolyn Lawrence Foundation, Seattle/Artists Rights Society (ARS), New York.; **p. 99**: Blend Images/Alamy; **p. 103**: 20th Century Fox/Photofest; **p. 104**: Beth Dubber/Netflix/Kobal/REX/Shutterstock; **p. 105**: WENN Ltd/Alamy Stock Photo; **p. 107** left: Randy Stotler/AP Photo, right: Yun Jai-hyoung/AP Photo; **p. 108**: Al Hartmann/The Salt Lake Tribune; **p. 110**: Chip Somodevilla/Getty Images; **p. 111** top: Ross Setford/NZPA/AP Photo, center: Alan Chin, bottom: Madison J. Gray/AP Photo; **p. 112**: Hello Lovely/Blend Images/Getty Images; **p. 113**: Christian Beutler/Keystone/Redux.

Chapter 5

Page 120: Haraz N. Ghanbari/AP Photo; **p. 122** left: Bettmann/Corbis/via Getty Images, right: redsnapper/Alamy; **p. 123**: AP Photo/Tony Avelar; **p. 129** left: Jan Greune/LOOK-foto/Getty Images, Steve Skjold/Alamy; **p. 131**: David Paul Morris/Bloomberg via Getty Images; **p. 133**: From the film Obedience, © 1965 by Stanley Milgram and distributed by Alexander Street Press.; **p. 133**: Philip G. Zimbardo, Inc.; **p. 135**: AP Photo/Michel Euler; **p. 136**: Jon Hrusa/EPA/Shutterstock; **p. 137**: Scott Eisen/Getty Images; **p. 138**: ©2006 Scott Adams, Inc. Dist. by Andrews McMeel Syndication. Reprinted with permission. All rights reserved.; **p. 139**: Peter Noyce PLB/Alamy Stock Photo; **p. 141**: BLM Photo/Alamy.

Chapter 6

Page 147: Sebastien Micke/Paris Match/Contour by Getty Images; **p. 148** left: dpa picture alliance/Alamy Stock Photo, center: Thomas Cockrem/Alamy Stock Photo, right: (ca. 1899) [Woman wearing corset, brushing her hair, half-length portrait, standing, facing front]. , ca. 1899. [Photograph] Retrieved from the Library of Congress, https://www.loc.gov/item/90710046/.; **p. 149**: Glen Stubbe/Minneapolis Star Tribune/ZUMA Wire/Alamy Live News; **p. 151**: Marvel/Disney/Kobal/Shutterstock; **p. 153**: Tom Gannam/AP Photo; **p. 154**: Sony Pictures TV/Splash News/Newscom; **p. 157**: Allyson Riggs/Hulu/Kobal/Shutterstock; **p. 161**: Carlos Chavarria/The New York Times/Redux; **p. 162**: ©HBO/Courtesy: Everett Collection; **p. 163**: Knut Egil Wang/Moment/INSTITUTE; **p. 164** top: HBO/Kobal/Shutterstock, bottom: Jim Spellman/Getty Images.

Part III

Page 171 top and bottom: Sally Ryan/Zumapress/Newscom.

Chapter 7

Page 176: Florian Kopp/imageBROKER/Newscom; p. 177: AP Photo/Julio Cortez; p. 178: Mario Tama/Getty Images; p. 182 left: Gilles Mingasson/Getty Images, right: Tim Graham/Corbis via Getty Images; p. 184: E! Entertainment Television/Photofest; p. 185: BUILT Images/Alamy; p. 191: Kevin Mazur/WireImage/Getty Images; p. 192: Joseph Prezioso/AFP/Getty Images; p. 195: Michael Stravato/The New York Times/Redux Pictures; p. 197: Lucy Nicholson/Reuters/Newscom; p. 200: Anthony Hatley/Alamy Stock Photo; p. 201: Mario Tama/Getty Images; p. 202: Mario Anzuoni/Reuters/Newscom.

Chapter 8

Page 209 left: Jon Kopaloff/FilmMagic/Getty Images, right: Gary Roberts; p. 210: Library of Congress; p. 211 left: AP Photo/Craig Ruttle, right: Paul Warner/Getty Images; p. 215: AP Photo/David Goldman; p. 217: An Rong Xu/The New York Times/Redux; p. 218: Moviestore/REX/Shutterstock; p. 219: Ohio University Stars; p. 221: Slaven Vlasic/Getty Images for The New York Women's Foundation; p. 224: Francis Miller/The LIFE Picture Collection/Getty Images; p. 225: newsphoto/Alamy Stock Photo; p. 228: Michael Bryant/The Philadelphia Inquirer via AP; p. 231 left: Poppy Productions/AF Archive/Alamy Stock Photo, right: Guy D'Alema/©FX/courtesy Everett Collection; p. 233: Rodi Said/Reuters/Newscom; p. 234: MLB Photos via Getty Images.

Chapter 9

Page 241 left: Diptendu Dutta/AFP/Getty Images, right: ©Adam Ferguson; p. 242: Sarah Morris/Getty Images; p. 247 left: Jeff Neumann/©Showtime/courtesy Everett Collection, right: Paul Sarkis/©Showtime/courtesy Everett Collection; p. 250: Lynsey Addario/Getty Images Reportage; p. 253: Courtesy Everett Collection; p. 257: Planetpix/Alamy Stock Photo; p. 261: Don Smith/MCT/Newscom; p. 262: ©Jean-Pierre Laffont; p. 264: Joe Raedle/Getty Images.

Part IV

Page 268 left: Tannen Maury/Polaris Images, right: Phil Greer/KRT/Newscom.

Chapter 10

Page 268 left: Tannen Maury/Polaris Images, right: Phil Greer/KRT/Newscom; p. 274 left: Kyodo News/AP Photo, center: Olivier Hoslet/EPA-EFE/Shutterstock, right: SalamPix/ABACAPRESS.COM/Newscom; p. 276: Alasdair Rae, University of Sheffield; p. 277 Table 10.2: "Top 10 Spenders on Lobbying, 1998-2018," From the Center for Responsive Politics, OpenSecrets.org; p. 279 top left: John Tlumacki/The Boston Globe via Getty Images, top right: Laperruque/Alamy Stock Photo, bottom: Vincent Laforet/epa/Corbis via Getty Images; p. 281 left: HOME BOX OFFICE/Album/Newscom, right: TBS/Courtesy Everett Collection; p. 283: Ron Morgan via Cartoon Stock; p. 284: Jim Lo Scalzo/EPA-EFE/Shutterstock; p. 285: Gabriella Demczuk/Getty Images; p. 287: The Granger Collection, NY; p. 288 left: Thomas Trutschel/Photothek via Getty Images, right: Dhiraj Singh/Bloomberg via Getty Images; p. 291: Don Ryan/AP Photo; p. 293: Mario Anzuoni/Reuters/Newscom; p. 296 left: Leif Skoogfors/Corbis via Getty Images, right: J.L. Atlan/Corbis Sygma via Getty Images; p. 297 Figure 10.2: "Second Largest Religious Tradition in Each State, 2010," from the 2010 U.S. Religion Census, sponsored by the Association of Statisticians of American Religious Bodies. Reprinted with permission; p. 298: Leon Neal/Getty Images; p. 300: Hill Street Studios/Tetra Images, LLC/Alamy Stock Photo; p. 303: AP Photo/Sue Ogrocki.

Chapter 11

Page 313: Corbis via Getty Images; p. 314: Granger Collection, NY; p. 316: David Bacon/The Image Works; p. 317: 3 Arts Entertainment/Judgemental Films Inc/REX/Shutterstock; p. 319 left: Photo by FOX via Getty Images, right: 5th Year Prods/Avalon Tv/Gigapix/Mail Order Comedy/Kobal/Shutterstock; p. 320: AP Photo; p. 321: SeongJoon Cho/Bloomberg via Getty Images; p. 322: The Granger Collection. NY; p. 323: Ringo Chiu/ZUMA Wire/Alamy Live News; p. 325: AP Photo/Matt Rourke; p. 327: Bay Ismoyo/AFP/Getty Images; p. 329 left: Adam Berry/Getty Images, right: Mamunur Rashid/Alamy; p. 333: Ge Jin, copyright 2008; p. 334: Michael Routh/Alamy Stock Photo; p. 335: Hero Images/Corbis; p. 336 top: Gordon Chibroski/Portland Press Herald via Getty Images, Figure 11.1: "Paid Vacation and Paid Holidays, OECD Nations, in Working Days," from "No Vacation Nation Revisited" by Rebecca Ray, Milla Sanes and John Schmitt, 2013. Courtesy of the Center for Economic and Policy Research.

Chapter 12

Page 342 left: ©Hanna-Barbera Prod./Courtesy: Everett Collection, right: Twentieth Century Fox Television/Kobal/Shutterstock; p. 344: Frazer Harrison/Getty Images; p. 346: ©P. D. Eastman. Random House Books for Young Readers; 1 edition (June 12, 1960); p. 348: Peter "Hopper" Stone/ABC via Getty Images; p. 351: Gilles Mingasson/ABC Family via Getty Images; p. 352: Karl Merton Ferron/Baltimore Sun/MCT via Getty Images; p. 354: Ariel Skelley/Getty Images; p. 355: Essdras M Suarez/The Boston Globe via Getty Images; p. 356: Melissa Moseley/Skydance Prods/Kobal/Shutterstock; p. 357: Photo by TMZ.com/Splash News/Corbis. SI Cover: Sports Illustrated/Getty Images; p. 358 left: AF archive/Alamy Stock Photo, right: Lifestyle pictures/Alamy Stock Photo; p. 360: VCG/VCG via Getty Images.

Chapter 13

Page 366: Advertising Archives; p. 367: George Etheredge/The New York Times/Redux; p. 368: Gil Friesen Productions/Tremolo Productions/REX/Shutterstock; p. 372: Illustration by Rob Dobi; p. 374: Allstar Picture Library/AMAZON STUDIOS/AF Archive/Alamy Stock Photo; p. 376: Henny Ray Abrams/AFP/Getty Images; p. 377: Roland Schlager/EPA/Shutterstock; p. 378: Photo by John Paul Filo/CBS via Getty Images; p. 379: New York Daily News Archive/Getty Images; p. 381: Frank Micelotta/PictureGroup/Sipa USA/Newscom; p. 383: Kristin Callahan/REX/Shutterstock; p. 384: Andalou Agency/Getty Images; p. 385 left: Robert Voets/Showtime/Courtesy Everett Collection, right: Katie Yu/©The CW/Courtesy: Everett Collection; p. 387: Nicholson, Frank S., Artist, and Sponsor United States National Park Service. Wild life The national parks preserve all life. [Nyc: nyc art project, works projects administration, between 1936 and 1940] Photograph. Retrieved from the Library of Congress, https://www.loc.gov/item/92522682/.

Chapter 14

Page 393 left: Bartek Wrzesniowski/Alamy, right: AP Photo/Jae C. Hong; p. 394: Carlo Allegri/Reuters/Newscom; p. 395: Gabby Jones/Bloomberg via Getty Images; p. 397: Bettmann/Corbis via Getty Images; p. 399: Erica Yoon/The Roanoke Times; p. 400: Florian Plaucher/AFP/Getty Images; p. 402 left: AP Photo/David Goldman, right: Nikki Kahn/The Washington Post via Getty Images; p. 404: Xinhua/Daniel Castelo Branco/Agencia o Dia/AGENCIA ESTADO/eyevine/Redux; p. 405: Carlos Javier Ortiz/Redux; p. 407: Manny Crisostomo/Sacramento Bee/ZUMAPRESS.com/Alamy; p. 408: Erik S.

Lesser/The New York Times/Redux; **p. 409**: Ed Young/Design Pics Inc/ Alamy Stock Photo; **p. 410** left: 20th Century Fox/Kobal/Shutterstock, right: Liane Hentscher/ABC via Getty Images; **p. 414**: Jodi Cobb/NatGeoCreative.

Part V

Page 419 right: Lindsay Hebberd/Danita Delimont/Alamy, left: Gavin Hellier/robertharding/Alamy.

Chapter 15

Page 425: Eric Fougere/Sygma via Getty Images; **p. 431**: Emily Berl/Redux; **p. 433**: Marvel/©Walt Disney Studios Motion Pictures/Courtesy Everett Collection; **p. 435**: Photo by NY Daily News Archive via Getty Images; **p. 436**: Springfield News-Leader, Christina Dicken/AP Photo; **p. 438**: Dinodia/ age fotostock/Alamy; **p. 439** left: Eric De Castro/Reuters/Newscom, right:

NASA/Getty Images; **p. 440** left: Julio Etchart/Alamy, right: Rickey Rogers/ Reuters/Newscom; **p. 441**: Mohammed Seeneen/AP Photo; **p. 444:** Library of Congress; **p. 445**: Go Takayama/AFP/Getty Images; **p. 446**: Todd McInturf/ The Detroit News via AP; **p. 447**: Lukas Jackson/Reuters/Newscom.

Chapter 16

Page 453: Bettmann/Corbis via Getty Images; **p. 454** left: Guerilla/Alamy Stock Photo, right: Hero Images Inc./Corbis; **p. 455**: Carolyn Cole/Los Angeles Times via Getty Images; **p. 456** left: Mike Eliason/Santa Barbara County Fire Department, right: Andrew Burton/Getty Images; **p. 458**: Chuck Hodes/20th Century Fox TV/Imagine TV/Kobal/Shutterstock; **p. 459**: Ben Margot/AP Photo; **p. 460**: Andrew Burton/Getty Images; **p. 462**: Paul Marotta/Getty Images; **p. 464**: Cornelius Poppe, Scanpix/AP Photo; **p. 465**: Image courtesy of adbusters.org; **p. 467**: Dan Callister/Shutterstock; **p. 471**: Indranil Mukherjee/AFP/Getty Images; **p. 473**: David White.

Index

Note: Photos, captions, and material in figures or tables are indicated by *italicized* page numbers.

fast-food industry, 25, 85, 134, 139

favela housing, 199

FBI (Federal Bureau of Investigation), 160, 162, 164

Feagin, Joe, 216

Federal Communications Commission (FCC), 372–373, 374–375

Federal Housing Authority, 215

federal minimum wage, 193–194, 196–197, 463

federal poverty line, 193–194, *193*

Federal Reserve Board, 312

Feder-Alford, Elaine, 408

felon disenfranchisement, 275

female gender characteristics, 240–241

female sex characteristics, 239, *239*

Feminine Mystique, The (Friedan), 262, *262*

feminism, 14–15, 262–263, 278, 460

feminist theory, 24, *24*, 254, 343–344

feminization of poverty, 258, 259

fentanyl, 399

feral children, 95–96, *96*

Ferguson, Missouri, 215, *215*, 283

Fernandez, Ferdinand, 272

Ferris, Kerry, 384

fertility rate, 423

fertilizers, 444–445

feudal system, 182

fictive kin, 346

Fidelity Financial, 141

field notes, 43–46, 75–76, 96–97

Fields, James Alex, Jr., 86, 461

Fifteenth Amendment, 275, 463

"Fight for $15" campaign, 197

Fiji, 105

filter bubbles, 282–283

Final Exit, 414

Fine, Gary, 30, 39

Fingerman, Karen, 120

Finkenauer, Abby, 284

Finland, 163

Finley, Ron, 431, *431*

finstagram (fake Instagram), 92

firefighters (wildland), 333–334, *334*

First Amendment, 272, 278, 369–370

First Principles (Spencer), 18

first wave, of women's movement, 262, 263

Fischer, Claude, 124, 434

Fischer, Lisa, *368*

Fish, Stanley, 381

Fitzgerald, F. Scott, 200

527 groups, 277

Fletcher, Elliot, *247*

flight attendants, 113

Flint, Michigan, 390, 392, 402, 441, *446*, 447

Flintstones (TV show), *342*

Florida, 275, 285, 429, 462

Florida A&M University hazing, 116, 118

focus group, 46, 47

folkways, 77–78

Food and Drug Administration (FDA), 403

food deserts, 403–405, *405*

food production. *see* Agricultural Revolution; agriculture

food stamps, 195, 312

Forbes, on richest Americans, 202

Fordham University, 77

Forever 21, 458

Fortnite (online role-playing game), 124

foster care, 350–351

Fosters, The (TV show), *351*

Foucault, Michel, 32, *32*

Foursquare, 385, 386

Fourteenth Amendment, 264, 345

Fowler, James, 122

Fox News, 282

Fox Searchlight, 311

fracking (hydraulic fracturing), 439, 447

Francis (pope), *296*

Franken, Al, 280

Frankfurt School, 23

fraternities, *121*, 129–130, *129*, 148, 244–245

Free Application for Federal Student Aid (FAFSA), 286

free riders, 459

free will, 114

Freecycle (website), 465

freedom of expression, 278, 369–370, 374–375

freedom of the press, 278, 369–370

Freegans, 203, 465

freelancers, 324–325, 334

Freeman, Walter, *397*

French Polynesia, 404

French Revolution (1789), 274

Fresh Off the Boat (TV show), 230

Freud, Sigmund, 96–98, *97*

Freyre, Gilberto, 178–179

Friedan, Betty, 262, *262*

Friedenbach, Jennifer, 201

Friedman, Milton, 405–406

front (impression management tool), 101

frontstage (impression management tool), 101

Fukushima nuclear disaster, *445*

Full Frontal with Samantha Bee (TV show), *281*, 282

functionalism. *see* structural functionalism

fundamentalism, 299–300

funeral directors, 333

Furstenberg, Frank, 352

Fussell, Paul, 185

G

Gallup polls
    on discontentedness, 203
    on same-sex marriage, 255
    on telecommuting, 317

gambling, 419

Game of Thrones (TV show), 470

game stage (Mead), 98, 99

Gandhi, Indira, 298

Gans, Herbert, 21, 378, 430, 434

Gap, Inc., 197, 326, 327, 329, 330

garbage floats, *439*

Garber, Marjorie, 24

Garcia, Sylvia, 284

Garfield, Andrew, *383*

Garfinkel, Harold, 30, 254

Garner, Eric, 214, 283

Garza, Alicia, *221*

Gates, Bill, 325–326

Gates, Melinda, 325–326

Gates Foundation, 326

gay(s). *see* LGBTQ; sexuality and sexual orientation

Geertz, Clifford, 43–44, 46

Gen Xers, 225

gender. *see also* gender inequality and sexism; sexuality and sexual orientation
    conceptualizations of, 70, 241–242, 243
    conversational dynamics, 12–16
    crime and, 162, 164, 260–261, 264
    defined, 240–241
    doctor-patient relations and, 408–409
    domestic abuse and, 357
    in education, 245–246, 257–258

gender (continued)
in family life, 244–245, 255, 351–352, 357
gender identity, 98, 239, 240, 242, 243, 252. see also LGBTQ
gender role socialization, 54–55, 55, 103, 244–249
health and, 255–257, 403, 404, 408–409
intersectionality studies, 229–230, 261–262
life expectancy, 226, 255–256, 425
poverty and, 194, 351–352
remarriage patterns, 349
social movements and, 236, 238, 262–264
social networking and, 121
third-gender individuals, 240–241
volunteerism and, 335–336
in work and income, 121, 255, 257, 258–259, 258–259, 408–409
gender expression, 239, 242
gender inequality and sexism
defined, 249
education and, 287–288
family life and, 229–230, 259–260, 342–344, 353–355
forms of, 249–252
gendered language, 252
health and health care, 408
honor killings and, 140
religion and, 296, 297
research methodology and, 16, 53, 54–55, 59
second shift, 47, 48–50, 255, 259–260, 353–354, 354
social movements, 262–264
theoretical approaches to, 253–254, 253, 255, 342–344
work and, 113, 137, 228, 258–259, 258–259
gender role socialization
defined, 244
in families, 54–55, 55, 103, 244–245
media's influence on, 106–107, 246–249
in peer groups, 246
in schools, 245–246
genderfluid (genderqueer), 240, 242
gender-nonconforming, 242, 247, 247, 251, 254. see also LGBTQ
General Accounting Office (GAO), 329

General Electric, 327, 370
generalized other (Mead's other), 98, 99
genetics
CRISPR gene-editing technology, 360, 468
DNA tourism, 388
genetic screenings and testing, 360, 414
Human Genome Project, 414
nature vs. nurture debate, 93, 94–95
race and, 209–210
social change and, 468
Genie (social isolation case), 95–96
genocide, 221, 231–232
Genovese, Catherine "Kitty," 435, 435, 437
gentrification, 432
Geographic Information Systems (GIS), 49
Georgetown University, 77, 329
Georgia, 232
Gergen, Kenneth, 114
Germany, 132, 232, 337
Geronimus, Arline, 402–403
gerrymandering, 276, 276, 463–464
gestures and body language, 74–75, 74, 100–102
Get Out (film), 217
Ghana, 85, 85, 111, 111, 388
Ghost in the Shell (film), 218
Gibson, William, 82
gig economy, 324–325, 325
Gilbert, Jordan, 399
Gintis, Herbert, 288
GLAAD website, 252
Gladwell, Malcolm, 368
"glass ceiling" effect, 16
"glass escalator" effect, 16
Glenn, John, 280
global cities, 429–430
global climate change, 400–401, 440–441, 441–443, 446
global commodity chains, 330
global village, 470–471
global warming, 200, 441, 442, 443
globalization, 326–337
defined, 326, 470
global commodity chains, 330
international trade, 326–327
outsourcing, 331–332, 331
sweatshop labor, 327–330, 329, 332–333, 333

theoretical approaches to, 331
transnational corporations, 327, 327, 328
Weberian theory on, 25
world rankings, 328
Go Daddy, 86
godparents, 346
Goffman, Alice, 62
Goffman, Erving
on civil inattention, 436, 436
on dramaturgy, 30
on institutional medical contexts, 407–408
photograph, 29
on roles, 109
on self (theory of), 99–102, 100
on social class, 185
on stigmas, 155–157
on symbolic interactionism, 29–30
GoFundMe, 464
"gold farming," 332–333, 333
Goldrick-Rab, Sara, 174
Goldstein, Baruch, 298
Gonzaga University, 77
González, Emma, 462, 462
Good Doctor, The (TV show), 410
Good Samaritan laws, 437
Goodwin, Alfred, 272
Google
employee well-being at, 139, 141, 317–318
environmental practices of, 326
filter bubbles for searches on, 282–283
sexism at, 251
social change and, 374
Gore, Tipper, 375
Gottdiener, Mark, 418, 419
government. see also politics
communism and, 310
criminal justice system, 165–166
defined, 273
groupthink and, 130
population growth encouragement by, 427
separation of church and state, 272, 291, 299–300, 303, 303
socialism and, 310–312
types of, 273–276
Grace and Frankie (TV show), 356
Grand Canyon National Park, 444
Grande, Ariana, 87, 298
Grandi, Filippo, 233
Granovetter, Mark, 121

market research, 57, 58, *58*
Markle, Meghan, *225*
marriage
　break up of, 187, 255, 348–352, *356*
　defined, 341
　gender's impact on, 255
　interracial, *178*, 179, 344–345, *344*
　life expectancy and, 425
　mate-selection process, 344–345
　National Marriage Project, 50
　race and ethnicity, 190–191, 224–
　　226, 229–230, 234, 344–345
　racial assimilation through, 234
　same-sex marriage, 255, 264, *264*,
　　345, 349, 350, 354
　social mobility and, 202
　socioeconomic status and, 187,
　　190–191
　theoretical approaches to, 342,
　　343, *343*
　trends, 341, 344–345, *344*, 347–
　　349, *347–348*, 355
　two-career families, 47, 48–50
　work and income impacted by, 258
Married at First Sight (TV show), 4
Martin, Molly, 95
Martin, Trayvon, 220, 283, *460*, 461
Martineau, Harriet, 18, *18*
Martinez, Martha A., 121–122
Marvel, 370
Marvelous Mrs. Maisel, The (TV
　show), 374, *374*
Marx, Karl
　on alienation, 22, 315
　background, 21, *21*
　on capitalism, 21–22, 23, 324
　communism and, 21, 23
　conflict theory of, 21–23
　false consciousness, 23, 202
　on industrialism, 314–315
　on power, 314–315
　praxis principle of, 24
　on social class, 182–183
　survey use by, 49
　writings of, 21–23
Marxism, 21, 58. *see also* conflict
　theory
Maryland, 464
masculinity
　black masculinity, 223
　country masculinity, 334
　crime and, 260–261
　crisis of, 263
　passing, 223

stereotypes, 403
　toxic masculinity, 251–252
mash-ups, 33
mass behavior, 457–459
mass media and pop culture. *see also*
　media and media outlets
　advertising and the American
　　Dream, 203–204
　blockbuster hits and business of
　　movies, 371–372
　cities of tomorrow, 433–434
　deviance on television, 164–165
　family troubles in film, 358–359
　gender role socialization and,
　　248–249
　gossip websites, 30–31
　ideal *vs.* real culture portrayal in,
　　83–84
　media usage patterns, 52
　medicine on television, 410–411
　race realities on television,
　　230–231
　satirical news shows, 281–282
　social media networks, 124–125
　as socialization agent, 106–107
　unplugging from, 469–470
　work and workers as seen on TV,
　　317, 318–319, *319*
mass society theory, 461
Massachusetts, 286, 322, *322*
massenkultur, 376
massively multiplayer online
　role-playing games
　　(MMORPGs), 124, 332–
　　333, *333*
master status, 109, 157, 213, 222
mate selection, 342, 344–345. *see also*
　marriage
material culture, 23, 73, *73*, 150, 468
matriarchy, 249
Matza, David, 58, 159, 161, 167
Mauss, Armand, 466
Maynard, Brittany, 414–415
Mayo, Elton, 60
McCandless, Chris, 420, 422
McCarthy, Joseph, 272
McCarthyism, 29, 461
McCune, Jeffrey, 223
McDonaldization, 25, 85, 138–139,
　139, 461
McDonald's, 197, 320–322
McGrane, Bernard, 10, 11, 34, 469
McIntosh, Peggy, 217
McLoughlin, John, 437

McLuhan, Marshall, 470, 471
McVeigh, Timothy, 81
Mead, George Herbert, 26–27, *26*, 28,
　99, *99*
mealtime, observation of, 352–353
Mean Girls (film), 75, *75*
meanings
　conversation analysis and, 30
　media interpretive strategies for,
　　380–381
　symbolic interactionism and,
　　28, 29
means of production, 21–22
measles, 393–394
mechanical solidarity, 19
media and media outlets, 369–376.
　see also mass media and pop
　culture; television
　anti-marijuana propaganda, 146
　Bollywood experience, 363–364
　celebrity-fan relations, 382–383
　content analysis research, 53
　cultural change and, 85
　cultural diffusion and, 85–87
　cultural imperialism and, 470–471,
　　471, 472
　cultural leveling and, 87
　culture and, 376–378
　culture wars and, 83
　democracy and, 369–370
　effects of, 379–381
　gender role socialization and,
　　246–247
　groupthink issues, 130
　music and, 80
　politics and, *277*, 278–283, *279*
　polls and, 57
　regulation of, 372–373, 374–376
　as socialization agent, 105–106
　structure of media industries,
　　370–374, *373*
　theoretical approaches to, 379–381
Medicaid, 194–195, 312
Medical College Admissions Test
　　(MCAT), 407
medical ethics, 414
medical outsourcing, 331
medicalization, 396–398, 403,
　406–407
medically assisted suicide, 414
Medicare, 312, 412
medicine. *see* health and health care
Meetup.com, 367, 386
megacities, 429

power
    conflict theory on, 220–221
    in conversational dynamics, 14–16
    defined, 273
    deviance and, 159
    in doctor-patient relations,
        408–409
    gender inequality and, 14–16, 24
    government types and, 273–275
    leadership qualities and styles,
        136–137
    political power in United States,
        276–278
    in service work, 316–317
    of social institutions, *277*
    social network's influence and, 121
    theories on, 276–277, *277*
    types of, 136–137, 276–278
    Weberian theory on, 183–184
    in workplace, 16
power elite, 276–277, *277*
practical knowledge
    acquisition of, 30
    scientific knowledge *vs.*, 10, 12–13
pragmatism, 28
praxis, 24, 58
precarious labor, 189
prejudice, 214, 220, 225, 249–251
preparatory stage (Mead), 98, 99
preschool, 48, 104
prescriptions (sanctions), 131
*Presentation of Self in Everyday Life,
    The* (Goffman), 99
Pressley, Ayanna, 284
prestige, 182, 183–184, *183*
Preston, Samuel, 423
pretext traffic stops and searches,
    208, 229
Pretty Woman (film), 191
preventive medicine, 395
primary deviance, 154
primary groups, 119–120, *120*
primary sex characteristics, 239, *239*
Principles of Sociology, The (Spencer),
    18–19
Prison Pet Partnership Program, 108
prisons
    LGBTQ inmates in, 261
    open prisons, 163, *163*
    prison-industrial complex, 166
    race demographics, 229
    resocialization in, 108, 109
    school-to-prison pipeline, 165, 226
    as total institution, 109

privilege, 216–217, 249. *see also* white
    privilege
probability sampling, 50–51
productivity, teamwork and, 134–135
profane, as defined by religion, 19, 295
pro-feminist men's movement, 263
professional socialization, 332–
    334, *334*
profiling, 154, 283–285
progressive social change, 461
Prohibition, 468
proletariat, 21–22, 23, 315
Promises I Can Keep (Edin and
    Kefalas), 44
property crime, 160, *160*
propinquity, 344
proscriptions (sanctions), 131
prostitution, 261
*Protestant Ethic and the Spirit of
    Capitalism, The* (Weber), 25
Protestants
    politics and, 296, 303
    social values of, 210, 296
    trends, 299–300, *300*
    U.S. population, *297*, 299, *300*
    work ethic of, 24–25, 295
protests. *see also* social movement(s);
    specific protests
    collective behavior at, 455–
        459, *456*
    drag as, 67
    patriotism and, 283–285
    political, 283–285, *285*
psychoanalytic theory, 96–98, *100*
psychosexual stages of
    development, 97
public goods dilemma, 459
public housing, 170, 198
public life, 366–367
public sociology, 222
Puccini, Giacomo, 378
Puerto Rico, 404, 455
Pugh, M.D., 460
punishment. *see* sanctions
Putnam, Robert, 122–123, *122*, 385
Pygmalion in the Classroom
    (Rosenthal and
    Jacobson), 289

Q
Qatar, 423, 424
qualitative research, 39. *see also*
    ethnography
quantitative research, 39, 50, 55, 57

quasi-experimental methods, 55
Queen Bees and Wannabes
    (Wiseman), 75
queer, 243. *see also* LGBTQ
Queer as Folk (TV show), 247
Queer Eye for the Straight Guy (TV
    show), 247
queer theory, 24, 243, 341, 343–344
questions and questionnaires
    in interviews, 47–48
    in social network analysis, 56
    in surveys, 50
Quinn, Pauline (Kathy), 108
Quinney, Richard, 151

R
race and race relations. *see also* racism
    adoptions, 350–351
    crime and, 154–155, 162, 166,
        189–190, 229, *229*
    DNA tourism, 388
    education and, 187, 226
    emotion work and, 113
    family life and, 225–226
    genetics and, 94
    group dynamics and, 126–127,
        231–234
    health and health-care issues, 226,
        392, 402–403, *402*
    institutional racism, 23
    interracial marriages, *178*, 179,
        344–345, *344*
    intersectionality of, 178–179,
        221–222, 229–231
    marriage and, 190–191, 224–226,
        229–230, 234, 344–345
    methods for studying, 47, *47*, 55,
        59, 61
    minority groups and, 213
    passing and, 156–157, 222–223
    positive deviance, 166
    poverty and, 194
    race, defined, 209–210, 209–211
    racial identity, 34, 221–222, 234
    religion and, 296
    social change and, *453*
    social construction of, 209–
        211, 222
    social mobility and, 202
    social movements addressing, 463
    social stratification based on,
        176–177, 178–179
    theoretical approaches to, 28–29,
        219–224, *223*

industrialization and, 314
leisure and, 365, *366*
methods for studying, 47, *47*
models of, 180–181, *180*, 182
power elites and, 276–277
race and, 227
social mobility and, 182, 185–186,
     191–192, *192*, 202
as stratification system, 178–179
theories of, 182–186
in United States, 179–182, *180*
urbanization trends and, 430,
     432–433
work and income disparities, 227
social cohesion, 19, 20, 22, 78, 149–
     150, 384
social construction
defined, 101
of disabilities, 413
of emotions, 110–112
of gender, 242, 260–261
of health and illness, 393–394, *393*
of identity, 221–222
of masculinity, 44, 223, 251–252,
     260–261, 263
of mate selection, 345
of mental illness, 397–398
of race, 209–211, 223
of self, 101, 114
social contagion, 105, 122, 130–131
social control, 78–79, 147, 149, 156, 165
social control theory, 150, 151, *155*
social Darwinism, 18–19, 28
social demography, 49, 53
social dilemma(s), 458–459
social genomics (sociogenomics), 95
social groups. *see* group(s)
social identity theory, 136
social inequality. *see also* poverty;
     social class; social
     stratification systems;
     stratification
defined, 21, 175
deviance and, 148, 150–151, 161
in education, 172, 174, 287–290
global warming and, 200
in health and health care, 390, 392,
     401–405, 408
institutional failures and, 170–171,
     179, 268–269
intersectionality and, 178–179
technology and, 201
theoretical approaches to, 21–24,
     182–183, 184, *199*

social influence
in groups, 126–130, *126. see also*
     peer pressure
nature *vs.* nurture debate, 93,
     94–95
social institutions. *see also individual*
     social institutions
defined, 273
micro-macro link of, 285–286
power of, 272–273
separation of church and state, 272,
     291, 299–300, 303
theoretical approaches to, *277*
social isolation, 94–96, *96*
social justice
affirmative action and, 219
critical race theory and, 222
prison sentencing disparities
     and, 229
for racism, 214
religion and, 296–297
wealth gap and, 200
social learning, 244–245
social loafing, 134–136
social media. *see also individual sites*
activism on, 206
anomie levels and, 124
collectors and hobbyists on, 385
cyberbullying and, 152–153
Data Workshop on, 124–125
demographics for, 124
group connections via, 124–125
mobile technology growth and, 374
online radicalization, 86, *86*
otaku culture and, 82
politics and, 278–279, 282–283, 370
self-portrayal on, 90–92
social movements and, 462, 464
social network analysis of, 56, 124
socialization through, 112–114
terrorists' use of, 298
textual poaching on, 381
unplugging from, 469–470
social mobility, 182, 185–186, 191–192,
     192, 202
social movement(s), 459–468. *see also*
     specific movements
defined, 459–460
stages in, 466–468
theoretical approaches to, 461–
     466, *466*
trends, 460–461
social network analysis (SNA), 48–49,
     56–57, *56*, 124

social networking sites. *see also*
     individual sites
analysis of, 48–49, 56
anomie and, 124
business uses for, 130–131, *131*
personal uses for, 112, 114, 124–125
social networks
defined, 120
influences of, 120–122
online. *see* social networking sites
social network analysis (SNA),
     48–49, 56–57, *56*
theoretical approaches to, *121*
virtual, 112, 114
social reproduction, 184–185
social sciences, 9, *10*
Social Security, 195, 312, 356
social status, 106–107, 109–110
social stratification systems, 172–205.
     see also social class; social
     inequality; socioeconomic
     status
American Dream and, 202–204
caste system as, 176–178
and crime, 177–178, 189–191
defined, 175
education and, 180–181, *180*,
     187–188, *188*, 189
family and, 187, 188, 190–191
health and, 187
poverty and, 193–201, *193. see also*
     poverty
principles of, 175
slavery as, 175–176, 192
social mobility and, 182, 185–186,
     191–192, *192*, 202
social ties, 120
social welfare and welfare reform,
     194–197
social work, 29, 350–351
social workers, 454
socialism, 310–312
socialization
adult socialization, 107–109
agents of, 54–55, 103–107, *104*
conformity and, 130–134
defined, 93
emotions, social construction of,
     110–112
family life and, 354–356
gender role socialization, 54–55, *55*,
     103, 244–249
gender stereotypes and, 54–55, 103
human nature, 93

in education, 155, 214, 215, 226, 288–289
of gender, 12–13, 245–247
in the media, 246–247
of racial and ethnic groups, 224–225, 227, 229
self-fulfilling prophecy and, 154–155
status and, 109
stigma
of criminal record, 162, 177–178
defined, 155
of depression, 256
and deviance, 155–159
of interracial marriage, 225
passing and, 156–157, 222–223, 254
solo dads, 348
types of, 155–156
Stone, Emma, 218, *383*
Stone, Oliver, 437
Stonewall riots (New York City), 263
Straight Edge, 460
Strangers in Their Own Land (Hochschild), 216
stratification. *see* social stratification systems
Streetwise (Anderson), 154
Streib, Jessi, 187
"Strength of Weak Ties, The" (Granovetter), 121
strikes, 310, 322–323, *322–323*
structural functionalism
about, 19–21
on addiction, *401*
on college admissions, *33*
on deviance, 149–151, *155*
on education, 20, 289–299
on environmental issues, *432, 466*
on family life, 341, 342, *342–343*
on leisure, *375*
on poverty, *199*
on power, *277*
on race and racism, 220, *223*
on religion, *76*, 295–296
on sexism, 253, *253, 255*
on social change, *466*
on social classes, 184
on social institutions, *277*
on social networks, *121*
on society, *33, 76*
on sports, *375*
on urban sprawl, *432*
on values, 76, *76*
on work outsourcing, *331*

structural mobility, 192
structural racism, 220–221
structural strain theory, 150–151, *150, 155*
Stuart, Forrest, 190
Students for Sexual Health (organization), 77
Study of Sociology, The (Spencer), 18–19
subculture(s)
culture seen within, 79–80, *79*
defined, 80–81
of deviance, 157–158
gender and, 66–67
otaku, 82
peer groups as, 104
subjectivity, 59–60
suburban (urban) sprawl, 418–419, 430, *432*
suburbanization, 430
Sudan, 427
Sudnow, David, 185
suffrage movement, 262, 263, 275, 460, 463
suicide
anomie and, 122
Durkheim's view of, 19
family life and, 342
in Las Vegas, 392
LGBTQ youth and, 255, 258
media and, *104*, 105–106
medically assisted suicide, 414–415
Suicide (Durkheim), 19, 342
Sunnyside (television show), 27
Suomenlinna Island prison (Helsinki), 163
Super PACs, 278
superego, 97, *97*
Supermoms, 354, *354*
supersectors, of U.S. economy, 315
Supplemental Nutrition Assistance Program (SNAP), 195, 312
Suri, of Ethiopia, 148
surrogate mothers and births, 331–332, 360
Survey Monkey, 51
surveys, *39*, 42, 50–52, 127–129. *see also* U.S. Census Bureau
"survival of the fittest," 18
sustainability, 448
Sutherland, Edwin, 152, 161
Swaziland. *see* Eswatini
sweatshop labor, 327–330, *329*, 332–333, *333*

Sweden
monarchy of, 274
prisons in, 163
social stratification in, 178, 179
Swift, Taylor, *13*
symbolic (nonmaterial) culture, 73–76
symbolic ethnicity, 211, *211*
symbolic interactionism
about, 25–30
on addiction, *401*
on college admissions, *33*
on deviance, 152–155, *155*, 159
on education, 289
on environmental issues, *432, 466*
on family life, 341–342, *342–343, 343*
on leisure, *375*
on poverty, *199*
on power, *277*
on race and racism, 222–224, *223*
on religion, *76*, 297
on self (theory of), 99
on sexism, 254, *255*
on social change, *466*
on social classes, 185–186
on social institutions, *277*
on social networks, *121*
on society, *33, 76*
on sports, *375*
on urban sprawl, *432*
on values, *76*
on work outsourcing, *331*
synergy, 370, 371
syphilis study, 61
Syria, 233, *233*, 274, 298, 424
systemic (institutional) discrimination, 215, 220–221, 402–403

T
taboo(s), 78
Taft-Hartley Act (1947), 323
Taliban, 274, 464
TANF (Temporary Assistance for Needy Families), 194–195, 312
Target, 197, 326
target population, 46, 47
taste cultures, 378
taste publics, 378
tattoos, 148
Taylor, Verta, 66–67, 159
Tea Party movement, 83

environmental policy of, 326

fake news and, 370

gag orders issued by, 320

gender identity discrimination by, 70, 250

groupthink issues of, 130

hate crime statistics associated with, 164

inauguration of, 320, *320*

media outlets and, 130, 279–280, 370

political protests against, 285

racial references by, 214, 216

social media and, 282–283, 370

Trump, Ivanka, 329

Truth, Sojourner, 463

Tudors, of England, 274

Turkey, 231–232

Turkle, Sherry, 112, 124

Turner, Brock, 244

Turner, Ralph

on deviance avowal, 157–158

on group identification shift, 127, 128, 134

on status and roles, 109

Turpin family, 96

Tuskegee Syphilis Study, 61

20 Feet from Stardom (film), 368, *368*

Twenty Statements Test (TST), 127–129

21st Century Fox, 371, 372, *372*

24 (TV show), 27

twin studies, 95

Twine, France Winddance, 229–230, 331

Twitter

activism and, 206

as alternative media outlet, 373

demographics, 124

online radicalization with, 86

politics and, 282–228

rogue agency accounts on, 320

social movements' use of, 462

social network analysis of, 56

socialization through, 112

Trump and, 370

$2 a Day: Living on Almost Nothing in America (Edin and Shaefer), 195–196

two-career families, 47, 48–50, 255, 259–260, 353–354, *354*

"two-spirit" individuals, 240, 241

two-step flow model, 380

U

Uber, 324–325, *325*

Uganda, 404

Unbearable Weight (Bordo), 15

unchurched spirituality, 300

unconscious mind, 96–97

underclass, *180*, 181

underemployment, 188

unemployment, 15, 181, 188, 287, 398–399

Unification Church, *107*

Uniform Crime Report (UCR), 160, 162

union(s)

current trends, 310, 419

overview, 322–323, *322*

social movements and, 463, 468

Uniqlo, 458

Unitarian Universalist Association (UUA), 219

Unite the Right rally, 86, 216, 461

United Nations

on biodiversity, 440

on climate change, 442

on honor killing statistics, 140

on human trafficking, 256–257

on life span, 425

on sustainability, 448

on transnational corporations, 327

virtual reality film release by, 123

on water resources, 438, *438*

on world population growth, 426

United States. *see also specific races and ethnicities; specific states and cities*

American culture, 87–88

American Dream, 150, 181, 202–204, 430

anti-American sentiments, 88

body modification in, 148

capital punishment in, 165–166

city populations, 429–433, *429*

class mobility in, 182

complementary and alternative medicine (CAM) trends in, 412–414

corporal punishment in, 149

corporate America, 323–326

countercultures in, 81

crime in, *160*, 161–162, 166

criminal convictions as caste system in, 177–178

criminal justice system, 165

cultural diffusion from, 85–87

cultural diffusion to, 82, 87

cultural leveling and, 87

culture of poverty in, 197–198

culture wars in, 70, *81*, 83

domestic abuse trends, 357, 359

ecological footprint of citizens, 448

economy, 310, 312, 313, 314, 315. *see also* work and income

energy consumption, 439

environmentalism, 444–448

federal spending, 195, *195*

foreign policy, 88

hate crimes, 162, 164, 264

health trends, 393–395, *393–395*, 398–399

health-care reform, 226, 411–412

homelessness in, 201, *201*

human trafficking policy, 257

immigrant assimilation in, 232, 234

interracial marriages in, 224–225

leisure trends, 365, *367*, 387

life expectancy, 188, 226, 356

as majority-minority country, 213

marriage statistics, 224–226, 264

multiculturalism in, 234

Pledge of Allegiance, 270, 272

political system of, 275–278, *276–277*

population trends, 212–213, *213*, 423–428, 461

poverty in, 193–194, *193–194*, 195–196, 198–201

prestige of occupations in, 183, *183*

prison population, 163, 166

religion in, 297–304, *297, 299–300, 303*

separation of church and state, 272, 291, 299–300, 303

slavery and, 176, 313, *313*

social classes, 179–182, *180*

social mobility, 182, 191–192, 202–203

social welfare and welfare reform, 194–195, *195*

subcultures in, 66–67, 81

sweatshops in, 329

vacation mandate, lack of, 336–337, *336*

voting in, 275–276, *276*

water pollution in, 441

wealth distribution, 200, 310

World Trade Organization influence of, 121